GRE
SOLIC
PROFESSIONAL HANDBOOK
2008/2009

AUSTRALIA
Law Book Co.
Sydney

CANADA and USA
Carswell
Toronto

HONG KONG
Sweet & Maxwell Asia

NEW ZEALAND
Brookers
Wellington

SINGAPORE and MALAYSIA
Sweet & Maxwell Asia
Singapore and Kuala Lumpur

Reprinted from the *Parliament House Book*, published in looseleaf form and updated five times a year by W. Green, the Scottish Law Publisher

The following paperback titles are also available in the series:
Annotated Rules of the Court of Session 2008/2009
Sheriff Court Rules 2008/2009

Parliament House Book consists of the following Divisions:
A Fees and Stamps
B Courts, Upper
C Rules of the Court of Session (annotated)
D Courts, Lower
E Licensing
F Solicitors
G Legal Aid
H Bankruptcy and other Mercantile Statutes
I Companies
J Conveyancing, Land Tenure and Registration
K Family Law
L Landlord and Tenant
M Succession, Trusts, Liferents and Judicial Factors

GREENS SOLICITORS PROFESSIONAL HANDBOOK 2008/2009

Reprinted from
Division F (Solicitors)
of the *Parliament House Book*

Published in 2008 by W. Green & Son Ltd
21 Alva Street
Edinburgh EH2 4PS

Printed in the UK by CPI William Clowes Beccles NR34 7TL

No natural forests were destroyed to make this product;
only farmed timber was used and replanted

A CIP catalogue record for this book is available from the British Library

ISBN 9780414017269

DIVISION F

Solicitors

Alphabetical and chronological indexes of all statutes and regulations in Parliament House Book can be found at the beginning of this binder.

[1] Statutes

[1] Statutory Instruments

Practice Rules and Regulations

Law Society of Scotland

Codes etc

Practice Guidelines

Law Society Information

NOTE
[1] Any reference in any provision to government departments; or to, or to any part or officer of, any government department (however described in that provision) is to be read, so far as the effect of the Scotland Act 1998 (c. 46) makes it necessary or expedient to do so, as including or being a reference to, or to any corresponding part or member of the staff of, the Scottish Administration: effective July 1, 1999 by the Scotland Act 1998 (Consequential Modifications) (No.2) Order 1999 (S.I. 1999 No. 1820), art. 2.

[NEXT TEXT PAGE IS **F** 3]

Statutes

Solicitors (Scotland) Act 1980

(1980 c. 46)

An Act to consolidate certain enactments relating to solicitors and notaries public in Scotland. [1st August 1980]

Part I

Organisation

The Law Society of Scotland

Establishment and objects of Law Society of Scotland

[1] **1.**—(1) The Law Society of Scotland (referred to in this Act as "the Society") shall continue to exist and shall exercise the functions conferred upon it by this Act and sections 16 to 23 (which relate to the provision of conveyancing and executry services) of the 1990 Act.

(2) The object of the Society shall include the promotion of—

(*a*) the interests of the solicitors' profession in Scotland; and

(*b*) the interests of the public in relation to that profession.

(3) The Society may do anything that is incidental or conducive to the exercise of these functions or the attainment of those objects.

(4) Schedule 1 shall have effect in relation to the Society.

NOTE

[1] As amended by the Public Appointments and Public Bodies etc. (Scotland) Act 2003 (asp 4), s.12 (effective August 15, 2003).

Membership of Society

[1] **2.**—(1) Every solicitor having in force a practising certificate shall be a member of the Society.

(2) Notwithstanding any other provisions of this Act, the Council may admit as a member of the Society any solicitor not having in force a practising certificate on such terms and conditions (including the payment by him of a reduced annual subscription) as they may determine.

(3) Subject to subsection (2), a solicitor shall—

(*a*) be treated as if he were not a member of the Society while suspended from practice as a solicitor under any enactment;

(*b*) cease to be a member of the Society when his practising certificate ceases to have effect.

NOTE

[1] Read in conjunction with the European Communities (Lawyer's Practice) (Scotland) Regulations 2000 (SSI 2000/121), reg. 37(2) and Sched. 2 (effective May 22, 2000).

The Council of the Law Society

Establishment and functions of Council of Law Society

3.—(1) The business of the Society shall continue to be conducted by the Council of the Society (referred to in this Act as "the Council") the members of which shall be elected in accordance with the provisions of the scheme made under paragraph 2 of Schedule 1.

[1] (2) The Council shall have the functions conferred upon them by this Act and sections 16 to 23 of the 1990 Act.

NOTE

[1] As amended by the Public Appointments and Public Bodies etc. (Scotland) Act 2003 (asp 4), s.12 (effective August 15, 2003).

Discharge of functions of Council of the Law Society

[1] **3A.**—(1) The Council may arrange for any of their functions (other than excepted functions) to be discharged on their behalf by—

(a) a committee of the Council;

(b) a sub-committee of such a committee; or

(c) an individual (whether or not a member of the Society's staff).

(2) Where, under subsection (1)(a), the Council have arranged for any of their functions to be discharged by a committee, the committee may, with the approval of the Council, arrange for that function to be discharged on behalf of the Council by—

(a) a sub-committee of the committee; or

(b) an individual (whether or not a member of the Society's staff).

(3) Where, under subsection (1) or (2), the Council or a committee have arranged for any of the Council's functions to be discharged by a sub-committee, the sub-committee may, with the approval of the Council, arrange for that function to be discharged on behalf of the Council by a member of the Society's staff.

(4) A power given by subsection (1), (2) or (3) may be exercised so as to impose restrictions or conditions on the body or person by whom the function concerned is to be discharged.

(5) Any arrangement made under this section shall not arrange for any of the following functions of the Council to be discharged by an individual—

(a) under section 42A(1) or (2), or under section 33(1) of the 1990 Act, the functions of determining—

(i) whether to uphold or dismiss a conduct complaint (within the meaning of the said section 33(1)); and

(ii) what action to take in the matter; and

(b) under section 20(1) or (2) of the 1990 Act, the functions of determining—

(i) whether any of paragraphs (a) to (d) of the said section 20(1) apply to the practitioner; and

(ii) what action to take in the matter.

(6) An arrangement made under this section may identify an individual by name or by reference to an office or post which the individual holds.

(7) An arrangement under this section for the discharge of any of the functions of the Council may extend to any of the functions of the Society which is exercisable by the Council.

(8) Where any arrangement is made under this section for the discharge of any of the functions of the Council by a body or person, the function shall be exercised by that body or person in the name of the Council, except that, where the function in question is a function of the Society which is exercisable by the Council, it shall be exercised in the name of the Society.

(9) Any arrangement under this section for the discharge of any of the functions of the Council—

(a) does not affect the responsibility of the Council for the exercise of the function or any liability arising therefrom;

(b) does not prevent the Council from exercising the function; and

(c) may be revoked at any time by the Council and also, in the case of any arrangement made under subsection (2) or (3), by the committee or sub-committee which made that arrangement.

(10) In this section, "excepted functions" means—

(a) any function of the Council to make rules or regulations under this Act or any other enactment; and

(b) any function of the Council under paragraph 2 of Schedule 1 to prepare a scheme (scheme for the constitution of the Council etc.).

(11) This section is without prejudice to any other power which the Council may have to arrange for the discharge of their functions.

(12) During any period before—

(a) paragraph 14(6)(a) of Schedule 4 to the Public Appointments and Public Bodies etc. (Scotland) Act 2003 (asp 4) comes into force, subsection (5) applies as if paragraph (b) and the word "and" that precedes it were omitted;

(b) section 12(c) of that Act comes into force, subsection (5)(a) applies as if for the words "the 1990 Act" there were substituted "the Law Reform (Miscellaneous Provisions) (Scotland) Act 1990 (c.40) ("the 1990 Act")".

NOTE

[1] Inserted by the Council of the Law Society of Scotland Act 2003 (asp 14), s.1 (effective May 31, 2003).

Part II

Right to Practise as a Solicitor

Qualifications and Training

Qualifications for practising as solicitor

4. No person shall be qualified to practise as a solicitor unless—

(a) he has been admitted as a solicitor; and

(b) his name is on the roll; and

(c) subject to section 24, he has in force a certificate issued by the Council in accordance with the provisions of this Part authorising him to practise as a solicitor (referred to in this Act as a "practising certificate").

Training regulations

[1] **5.**—(1) The Council may, with the concurrence of the Lord President, make regulations for—

(a) practical training;

(b) attendance at a course of legal education;

(c) the passing of examinations.

(2) Regulations under this section—

(a) may make such incidental, consequential and supplemental provisions as the Council consider necessary or proper in relation to the matters specified in subsection (1);

(b) may include provision for the charging by the Council of fees and the application thereof; and

(c) may make different provisions for different circumstances.

NOTE

[1] Read in conjunction with the European Communities (Lawyer's Practice) (Scotland) Regulations 2000 (SSI 2000/121), reg.37(2) and Sch.2 (effective May 22, 2000).

Admission

Admission as solicitor

6.—(1) Subject to the provisions of this section, no person shall be admitted as a solicitor in Scotland unless—

(a) [*Repealed by the Employment Equality (Age) Regulations 2006 (SI 2006/1031) (effective October 1, 2006).*]

[1] (b) he has satisfied the Council—

(i) that he has complied with the provisions of any regulations made under section 5 that apply to him, and

(ii) that he is a fit and proper person to be a solicitor, and has obtained from the Council a certificate to that effect; and

(c) he has paid such sum in respect of his admission as has been fixed by the Council with the approval of the Lord President.

[1a] (2) Where—

(a) a person has complied with the requirements of subsection (1); but

(b) the Council have not lodged a petition for his admission as a solicitor within one month of his having so complied,

he may apply by petition to the court for admission as a solicitor; and if he produces the certificate mentioned in paragraph (b) of subsection (1) the court shall make an order admitting him as a solicitor.

(3) If any person has not obtained from the Council a certificate to the effect mentioned in paragraph (b) of subsection (1) but has otherwise satisfied the requirements of that subsection the court, on such an application being made by him and on being satisfied after such inquiry as it thinks fit, that—

(a) he is a fit and proper person to be admitted as a solicitor, and

[NEXT TEXT PAGE IS **F** 5]

(b) he is competent to be a solicitor,

may make an order admitting him as a solicitor.

[2] (3A) The Council may petition the court for the admission as a solicitor of an applicant who has complied with the requirements of subsection (1) above; and, where it does so it shall lodge the petition not later than one month after the applicant has first so complied.

[2] (3B) The Court shall, on a petition being made to it under subsection (3A) above, make an order admitting the applicant as a solicitor.

(4) Any order admitting a person as a solicitor under this section shall include a direction to the Council to enter the name of that person in the roll.

(5) Nothing in this section affects the operation of the Colonial Solicitors Act 1900 or any Order in Council made under that Act (admission as solicitors in Scotland of solicitors of certain overseas territories).

(6) Every person who has been enrolled as a law agent shall be deemed to be admitted as a solicitor.

NOTES

[1] As amended by the Law Reform (Miscellaneous Provisions) (Scotland) Act 1985 (c. 73), Sched. 1, Pt II, para. 2(a) and Sched. 4.

[1a] As substituted by the Law Reform (Miscellaneous Provisions) (Scotland) Act 1990 (c. 40), s.37(1) (effective 20th July 1992: S.I. 1992 No. 1599).

[2] Inserted by the Law Reform (Miscellaneous Provisions) (Scotland) Act 1985 (c. 73), Sched. 1, Pt II, para. 2(b).

The Roll

Keeping the roll

7.—(1) The Council shall continue to be the registrar of solicitors and shall keep at the office of their secretary a roll of solicitors (in this Act referred to as "the roll").

(2) The roll shall consist of the names in alphabetical order of all solicitors entered on it in accordance with section 8.

(3) Any person may inspect the roll during office hours without payment.

[1] (4) Schedule 2 (powers of Council in relation to roll of solicitors) shall have effect.

NOTE

[1] Added by the Solicitors (Scotland) Act 1988 (c. 42), Sched. 1, para. 2.

Entry in the roll

8.—(1) On production to the Council of an order under section 6 admitting a person as a solicitor and directing that his name be entered on the roll the Council shall enter the name of that person on the roll.

(2) Any solicitor whose name is entered on the roll (in this Act referred to as "an enrolled solicitor") shall, on such enrolment, inform the Council in writing of the address of his place of business, and shall on any change of that address, inform them in writing of his new address.

(3) The Council shall issue a certificate of enrolment to any enrolled solicitor who applies for it.

Removal of name from roll on request

[1] **9.** An enrolled solicitor who wishes his name, or any annotation made against his name under section 25A(3), to be removed from the roll of solicitors may make an application to the Council in that behalf, and the Council shall on the solicitor satisfying the Council that he has made adequate arrangements with respect to the business he has then in hand, remove the name of that solicitor or, as the case may be, the annotation against his name, from the roll.

NOTE

[1] As amended by the Solicitors (Scotland) Act 1988 (c. 42), Sched. 1, para. 3, and the Law Reform (Miscellaneous Provisions) (Scotland) Act 1990 (c. 40), Sched. 8, para. 29(2).

Restoration of name to roll on request

[1] **10.**—(1) A solicitor whose name has been struck off the roll other than by order of the court, shall only be entitled to have his name restored to the roll, if on an application in that behalf made by him to the Tribunal and after such inquiry as the Tribunal thinks proper, the Tribunal so orders.

(1A) On an application to the Council from a solicitor whose name, or any annotation against whose name, has been removed from the roll under section 9 the Council may, after such inquiry as they think proper, restore the name of that solicitor or, as the case may be, the annotation, to the roll.

(2) Rules made by the Tribunal under section 52 may—

(a) regulate the making, hearing and determining of applications under subsection (1);

(b) provide for payment by the applicant to the Council of such fee in respect of restoration to the roll as the rules may specify.

NOTE

[1] As amended by the Solicitors (Scotland) Act 1988 (c. 42), Sched. 1, para. 4, and the Law Reform (Miscellaneous Provisions) (Scotland) Act 1990 (c. 40), Sched. 8, para. 29(3).

Directions by Lord President

11.—(1) The Lord President may give directions to the Council in relation to the carrying out of their duties in connection with the keeping of the roll and they shall give effect to any such directions.

(2) [Repealed by the Solicitors (Scotland) Act 1988 (c. 42), Sched. 2.]

Power of court to prescribe fees

12. [Repealed by the Solicitors (Scotland) Act 1988 (c. 42), Sched. 2.]

Register of European lawyers

Keeping the register

[1] **12A.**—(1) The Council shall establish and maintain the register referred to in regulation 15 of the European Communities (Lawyer's Practice) (Scotland) Regulations 2000, and shall keep the register at the office of their secretary.

(2) The register shall consist of the names in alphabetical order of all European lawyers entered on it in accordance with regulation 17 of those regulations.

(3) Any person may inspect the register during office hours without payment.

(4) Schedule 2 (powers of Council in relation to roll of solicitors) shall apply to the register as it does to the roll and in its application to the register the words "section 7(3)" in paragraph 4 shall be read as if the words "section 12A" were substituted therefor.

NOTE

[1] Inserted by the European Communities (Lawyer's Practice) (Scotland) Regulations 2000 (S.S.I. 2000 No.121), reg. 37(1) and Sched. 1, para. 1(2) (effective May 22, 2000).

Information to be provided by registered European lawyers

[1] **12B.**—(1) Any registered European lawyer—

(a) shall, on registration, inform the Council in writing of the address of his place of business, his home professional title, and the name and address of the competent authority with which he is registered in his home state; and

(b) shall thereafter inform the Council of any change to the information required under paragraph (a) above.

(2) The Council shall issue a registration to any registered European lawyer who applies for it.

NOTE
[1] Inserted by the European Communities (Lawyer's Practice) (Scotland) Regulations 2000 (S.S.I. 2000 No.121), reg. 37(1) and Sched. 1, para.l(2) (effective May 22, 2000).

Removal of name from register on request

[1] **12C.** A registered European lawyer who wishes his name, or any annotation made against his name under section 25A(3), to be removed from the register may make an application to the Council in that behalf, and the Council shall, on the registered European lawyer satisfying the Council that he has made adequate arrangements with respect to the business he has then in hand, remove the name of that solicitor, or, as the case may be, the annotation against his name, from the register.

NOTE
[1] Inserted by the European Communities (Lawyer's Practice) (Scotland) Regulations 2000 (S.S.I. 2000 No.121), reg. 37(1) and Sched. 1, para. 1(2) (effective May 22, 2000).

Restoration of name to register on request

[1] **12D.**—(1) Subject to subsection (2), a registered European lawyer whose name has been removed from the register shall be entitled to have his name restored to the register only if, on an application in that behalf made by him to the Tribunaland after such enquiry as the Tribunal thinks proper, the Tribunal so orders.

(2) On an application to the Council by a registered European lawyer whose name, or any annotation against whose name, has been removed from the register under section 12C, the Council may, after such inquiry as they think proper, restore the name of the registered European lawyer or, as the case may be, the annotation, to the register.

(3) Rules made by the Tribunal under section 52 may—

(a) regulate the making, hearing and determining of applications under subsection (1);

(b) provide for payment by the applicant to the council of such fee in respect of restoration to the register as the rules may specify.

NOTE
[1] Inserted by the European Communities (Lawyer's Practice) (Scotland) Regulations 2000 (S.S.I. 2000 No.121), reg. 37(1) and Sched. 1, para. 1(2) (effective May 22, 2000).

Practising Certificates

Applications for practising certificates

13.—(1) Subject to this section and sections 14 to 24, the Council may make rules with respect to—

(a) applications for practising certificates;

(b) the issue of practising certificates;

(c) the keeping of a register of applications for and the issue of practising certificates.

(2) Any person may inspect the register during office hours without payment.

(3) The making of a false statement by a solicitor in an application for a practising certificate may be treated as professional misconduct by him for the purposes of Part IV, unless he proves the statement was made without intention to deceive.

Issue of practising certificate

14.—(1) The Council shall issue to an enrolled solicitor on application being duly made by him, a practising certificate in accordance with rules made by them under section 13.

(2) The Council shall not issue a practising certificate to a solicitor while he is suspended from practice.

Discretion of Council in special cases

15.—(1) In any case where this section has effect, the applicant shall, unless the Council otherwise order, give to the Council, not less than 6 weeks before he applies for a practising certificate, notice of his intention to do so; and the Council may in their discretion—

(a) grant or refuse the application, or

(b) decide to issue a certificate to the applicant subject to such conditions as the Council may think fit.

(2) Subject to subsections (3) and (4), this section shall have effect in any case where a solicitor applies for a practising certificate—

(a) [Repealed by the Law Reform (Miscellaneous Provisions) (Scotland) Act 1985 (c. 73), Sched. 1, Pt II, para. 3 and Sched. 4.]

(b) not having held a practising certificate in force within the period of 12 months following the date of his admission; or

(c) when a period of 12 months or more has elapsed since he held a practising certificate in force; or

(d) without having paid in full any fine imposed on him under Part IV; or

(e) without having paid in full any expenses for which he has been found liable under section 38 or Part IV; or

(f) when, having been suspended from practice, the period of suspension has expired; or

(g) when, having had his name struck off the roll, his name has been restored to the roll; or

(h) after his estate has been sequestrated or he has granted a trust deed for behoof of creditors, whether he has obtained his discharge or not; or

(i) when, after a complaint has been made—

(i) relating to his conduct of the business of a client his attention has been drawn by the Council to the matter, and he has not replied or has not furnished a reply which would enable the Council to dispose of the matter; or

(ii) of delay in the disposal of the business of a client he has not completed that business within such period as the Council may fix as being a reasonable period within which to do so,

and in either case has been notified in writing by the Council accordingly; or

[1] (j) while any thing required to be done by him by a direction of the Council under section 42A or of the Tribunal under section 53A (including any such direction as confirmed or varied on appeal) remains undone.

(3) Where a practising certificate free of conditions is issued by the Council under subsection (1) to a solicitor in relation to whom this section has effect by reason of any such circumstances as are mentioned in paragraphs (b), (c), (f), (g) or (h) of subsection (2), this section shall not thereafter have effect in relation to that solicitor by reason of those circumstances.

(4) Where the Council decide to issue a practising certificate subject to conditions, they may, if they think fit, postpone the issue of the certificate pending the hearing and determination of an appeal under section 16.

NOTE

[1] Inserted by the Solicitors (Scotland) Act 1988 (c. 42), Sched. 1, para. 5.

Appeals from decisions of Council

16.—[1] (1) Where

(a) an application for a practising certificate is duly made to the

Council otherwise than in a case where section 15 has effect and the Council refuse or neglect to issue a practising certificate, the applicant;

(b) the Council refuse to recognise a body corporate as being suitable in terms of section 34(1A)(b), the body corporate

may apply to the court, who may make such order in the matter as it thinks fit.

(2) Where the Council in exercise of the power conferred on them by section 15, refuse to issue a practising certificate, or issue a practising certificate subject to conditions, the applicant may appeal to the court against that decision within 14 days of being notified of it.

(3) On an appeal to the court under subsection (2) the court may—

(a) affirm the decision of the Council; or

(b) direct the Council to issue a practising certificate to the applicant subject to such conditions if any as the court may think fit; or

(c) make such other order as it thinks fit.

NOTE

[1] As amended by the Law Reform (Miscellaneous Provisions) (Scotland) Act 1985 (c.73), Sch.1, Pt.I, para.1.

Date and expiry of practising certificates

17.—(1) Every practising certificate issued in November of any year shall bear the date of 1st November in that year, and every other practising certificate shall bear the date of the day on which it was issued.

(2) Every practising certificate shall have effect from the date it bears under subsection (1).

(3) Subject to subsection (4), every practising certificate shall expire on 31st October next after it is issued.

(4) On the name of any solicitor being struck off the roll or on a solicitor being suspended from practice as a solicitor, any practising certificate for the time being in force of that solicitor shall cease to have effect, but in the case of suspension, if he ceases to be so suspended during the period for which the practising certificate would otherwise have continued in force, the certificate shall thereupon again have effect.

Suspension of practising certificates

[1] **18.**—[5] [4] (1) If—

(a) in pursuance of the Mental Health (Care and Treatment) (Scotland) Act 2003 a solicitor is, by reason of mental disorder, detained in hospital;

(b) a guardian is appointed to a solicitor under the Adults with Incapacity (Scotland) Act 2000 (asp 4);

(c) the estate of the solicitor is sequestrated;

(d) a solicitor grants a trust deed for behoof of creditors;

(e) a judicial factor is appointed on the estate of the solicitor under section 41;

any practising certificate for the time being in force of that solicitor shall cease to have effect, and he shall be suspended from practice as a solicitor.

[2] (1A) If—

(a) an administration or winding up order, or an appointment of a provisional liquidator, liquidator, receiver or judicial factor has been made in relation to the incorporated practice; or

(b) a resolution has been passed for the voluntary winding-up of an incorporated practice (other than a resolution passed solely for the purposes of reconstruction or amalgamation of the incorporated practice with another incorporated practice),

the recognition under section 34(1A) of the incorporated practice shall be thereby revoked.

[3] (2) On the occurrence of any of the circumstances mentioned in subsection (1), the solicitor in question shall intimate those circumstances to the Council in writing immediately.

(3) On the occurrence of the circumstances mentioned in paragraphs (d) or (e) of subsection (1) the trustee or as the case may be the judicial factor shall intimate his appointment to the Council in writing immediately.

[2] (3A) On the occurrence of the circumstances mentioned in—

(a) paragraph (a) of subsection (1A), the administrator, provisional liquidator, liquidator, receiver or, as the case may be, judicial factor appointed in relation to the incorporated practice;

(b) paragraph (b) of subsection (1A), the incorporated practice

shall immediately intimate that fact to the Council.

NOTES

[1] As amended by the Mental Health (Scotland) Act 1984 (c.36), Sch.3, para.46.

[2] Inserted by the Law Reform (Miscellaneous Provisions) (Scotland) Act 1985 (c.73), Sch.1, Pt.I, para.2.

[3] As amended by the Solicitors (Scotland) Act 1988 (c.42), Sch.2.

[4] As amended by the Adults with Incapacity (Scotland) Act 2000 (asp 4), s. 88 and Sch.5, para.15 (effective April 1, 2002).

[5] As amended by the Mental Health (Care and Treatment) (Scotland) Act 2003 (Modification of Enactments) Order (SSI 2005/465), art.2 and Sch.1 (effective September, 27 2005).

Further provisions relating to suspension of practising certificates

19.—(1) The provisions of this section have effect in relation to a practising certificate which has ceased to have effect by virtue of section 18 during the period when that certificate would, but for that section, have continued in force.

(2), (3) [Repealed by the Solicitors (Scotland) Act 1988 (c.42), Sch.2.]

(4) A practising certificate which has ceased to have effect by virtue of paragraphs (c) or (d) of section 18(1) shall again have effect on the solicitor being granted his discharge.

(5) A practising certificate which has ceased to have effect by virtue of paragraph (e) of section 18(1) shall again have effect on the judicial factor being granted his discharge.

[1,2] (5A) Where a solicitor is suspended from practice as a solicitor by virtue of paragraph (a) or (b) of section 18(1), the period of suspension shall, for the purposes of section 15(2)(f), expire on the solicitor ceasing to be detained in hospital or subject to guardianship or, as the case may be, on the *curator bonis* being discharged.

(6) Where a solicitor is suspended from practice as a solicitor by virtue of paragraphs (c), (d) or (e) of section 18(1), he may at any time apply to the Council to terminate the suspension.

(7) On an application under subsection (6), the Council may either—

(a) grant the application with or without conditions; or

(b) refuse the application.

(8) If on an application by a solicitor under subsection (6), the Council refuse the application or grant it subject to conditions, the solicitor may appeal against the decision to the court, who may—

(a) affirm the decision; or

(b) vary any conditions imposed by the Council; or

(c) terminate the suspension either with or without conditions.

NOTE

[1] Inserted by the Solicitors (Scotland) Act 1988 (c.42), Sch.1, para.6.

[2] As substituted by the Mental Health (Care and Treatment) (Scotland) Act 2003 (Modification of Enactments) Order (SSI 2005/465), art.2 and Sch.1 (effective September 27, 2005).

Council's duty to supply lists of solicitors holding practising certificates

[1,2] **20.**—(1) The Council shall send a list of all solicitors holding practising certificates for the practice year then current—

(a) to the Keeper of the Registers of Scotland;

(ab) to the Principal Clerk of Session;

(b) to each sheriff clerk;

as soon as practicable after 1st December in each year.

(2) The Council shall send a list of all solicitors who have rights of audience in—

(a) the Court of Session, to—

(i) the Principal Clerk of Session;

(ii) the Principal Clerk of the Judicial Office of the House of Lords; and

(iii) the Registrar to the Judicial Committee of the Privy Council; and

(b) the High Court of Justiciary, to the Principal Clerk of Justiciary,

as soon as practicable after 1st December in each year; and where, by virtue of an order under section 53(2)(ba), 53A(2)(ba) or 55(1)(ba), a solicitor's right of audience in any of those courts is suspended or revoked, the Council shall forthwith inform the persons mentioned in this subsection of that fact.

(3) The Council shall notify those persons to whom they have sent lists under this section of any changes in those lists.

NOTE

[1] As amended by the Law Reform (Miscellaneous Provisions) (Scotland) Act 1990 (c.40), Sch.8, para.29(4) and Sch.9.

[2] Read in conjunction with the European Communities (Lawyer's Practice) (Scotland) Regulations 2000 (SSI 2000/121), reg.37(2) and Sch.2 (effective May 22, 2000).

Consultants to hold practising certificates

[2] **21.**—(1) A consultant shall be treated for the purposes of this Act as a practising solicitor and the provisions relating to practising certificates and, subject to subsection (2), the Guarantee Fund shall apply to him.

(2) The Council may if they think fit exempt a consultant from any of the provisions of section 43 or Schedule 3 (the Guarantee Fund).

[1] (3) In this section "consultant" means any solicitor who

(a) not being in partnership with a solicitor or other solicitors causes or permits his name to be associated with the name of that solicitor or those solicitors or their firm's name,

(b) not being a director of an incorporated practice, causes or permits his name to be associated with that incorporated practice,

whether he is described as a consultant or adviser or in any other way.

NOTE

[1] As amended by the Law Reform (Miscellaneous Provisions) (Scotland) Act 1985 (c.73), Sch.1, Pt I, para.3.

[2] Read in conjunction with the European Communities (Lawyer's Practice) (Scotland) Regulations 2000 (SSI 2000/121), reg.37(2) and Sch.2 (effective May 22, 2000).

Evidence as to holding of practising certificates

22.—(1) Any list purporting to be issued by the Council and to contain the names of solicitors in Scotland who have before 1st December in any year obtained practising certificates for the period of 12 months from 1st November in that year shall, until the contrary is proved, be evidence that the persons named in that list are solicitors holding such certificates.

(2) The absence from any such list of the name of any person shall, until the contrary is proved, be evidence that the person is not qualified to practise as a solicitor under a certificate for the current year, but in the case of any such person an extract from the roll certified as correct by the Council shall be evidence of the facts appearing in the extract.

Offence to practise without practising certificate

23.—(1) Any person who practises as a solicitor or in any way holds himself out as entitled by law to practise as a solicitor without having in force a practising certificate shall be guilty of an offence under this Act unless he proves that he acted without receiving or without expectation of any fee, gain or reward, directly or indirectly.

(2) Without prejudice to any proceedings under subsection (1), failure on the part of a solicitor in practice to have in force a practising certificate may be treated as professional misconduct for the purposes of Part IV.

Professional misconduct for registered European lawyer to practise without a registration certificate

[1] **23A**. Failure on the part of a registered European lawyer in practice to have in force a current registration certificate may be treated as professional misconduct for the purposes of Part IV.

NOTE

[1]Inserted by the European Communities (Lawyer's Practice) (Scotland) Regulations 2000 (SSI 2000/121), reg.37(1) and Sch.1, para.1(4) (effective May 22, 2000).

[1]**23B.** Failure on the part of a registered foreign lawyer in practice to have in force a current registration certificate may be treated as professional misconduct for the purposes of Part IV.

NOTE

[1]Inserted by the Solicitors (Scotland) Act 1980 (Foreign Lawyers and Multi-national Practices) Regulations 2004 (SSI 2004/383), reg.3.

Saving of public officials

24. Nothing in this Act shall require a practising certificate to be taken out by a person who is by law authorised to act as a solicitor to a public department without admission, or by any assistant or officer appointed to act under the direction of any such solicitor.

Registration certficates for registered European Lawyers

Applications for registration certificates

[1] **24A.**—(1) Subject to sections 24B to 24G below, the Council may make rules with respect to—

(a) applications for;
(b) the issue of;
(c) the keeping of a register for and the issue of, registration certificates for registered European lawyers as it would make rules under section 13 with respect to practising certificates for enrolled solicitors.

(2) Any person may inspect the register referred to in subsection (1)(c) during office hours without payment.

(3) The making of a false statement by a registered European lawyer in an application for a registration certificate may be treated as professional misconduct by him for the purposes of Part IV, unless he proves the statement was made without intention to deceive.

NOTE

[1] Inserted by the European Communities (Lawyer's Practice) (Scotland) Regulations 2000 (SSI 2000/121), reg.37(1) and Sched.1, para.1(3) (effective May 22, 2000).

Issue of registration certificates

[1] **24B.**—(1) The Council shall issue to a registered European lawyer on application being made by him, a registration certificate in accordance with rules made by them under section 24A.

(2) The Council shall not issue a registration certificate to a registered European lawyer while his registration is suspended or withdrawn.

NOTE
[1] Inserted by the European Communities (Lawyer's Practice) (Scotland) Regulations 2000 (SSI 2000/121), reg.37(1) and Sch.1, para.1(3) (effective May 22, 2000).

Discretion of Council in special cases

[1] **24C.**—(1) In any case where this section has effect, the applicant shall, unless the Council otherwise order, give to the Council, not less than 6 weeks before he applies for a renewal of a registration certificate, notice of his intention to do so; and the Council may in their discretion—

(a) grant or refuse the application; or

(b) decide to issue a registration certificate to the applicant subject to such conditions as the Council may think fit.

(2) Subject to subsections (3) and (4) below, this section shall have effect in any case where a registered European lawyer applies for a renewal of a registration certificate—

(a) not having held a registration certificate in force within the period of 12 months following the date of his registration; or

(b) when a period of 12 months or more has elapsed since he held a registration certificate in force; or

(c) without having paid in full any fine imposed on him under Part IV; or

(d) without having paid in full any expenses for which he has been found liable under section 38 or Part IV; or

(e) when, having been suspended from practice, the period .of suspension has expired; or

(f) when, having had his registration withdrawn, he has been registered again; or

(g) after his estate has been sequestrated or he has granted a trust deed for behoof of creditors, whether he has obtained his discharge or not; or

(h) when, after a complaint has been made—

(i) relating to his conduct of the business of a client his attention has been drawn by the Council to the matter, and he has not replied or has not fumished a reply which would enable the Council to dispose of the matter; or

(ii) of delay in disposal of the business of a client he has not completed that business within such period as the Council may fix as being a reasonable period within which to do so,

and in either case has been notified in writing by the Council accordingly; or

(i) while any thing required to be done by him by a direction of the Council under section 42A or of the Tribunal under section 53A (including any such direction as confirmed or varied on appeal) remains undone.

(3) Where a registration certificate free of conditions is issued by the Council under subsection (1) to a registered European lawyer to whom that subsection has effect by reason of any such circumstances as are mentioned in paragraphs (a), (b), (e), (f) or (g) of subsection (2), this section shall not thereafter have effect in relation to that registered European lawyer by reason of those circumstances.

(4) Where the Council decide to issue a registration certificate subject to conditions, they may, if they think fit, postpone the issue of the registration certificate pending the hearing and determination of an appeal under section 24D.

NOTE
[1] Inserted by the European Communities (Lawyer's Practice) (Scotland) Regulations 2000 (SSI 2000/121), reg.37(1) and Sch.1, para.1(3) (effective May 22, 2000).

Appeals from decisions of Council

[1] **24D**—(1) Where—

(a) an application for a registration certificate is duly made to the Council otherwise than in a case where section 24C has effect and the Council refuse or neglect to issue a registration certificate, the applicant;

(b) the Council refuse to recognise a body corporate as being suitable in terms of section 34(1A) (b), the body corporate,

may apply to the court, who may make such order in the matter as it thinks fit.

(2) Where the Council in exercise of the power conferred on them by section 24C, refuse to issue a registration certificate, or issue a registration certificate subject to conditions, the applicant may appeal to the court against that decision within 14 days of being notified of it.

(3) On an appeal to the court under subsection (2) the court may—

(a) affirm the decision of the Council; or

(b) direct the Council to issue a registration certificate to the applicant subject to such conditions if any as the court thinks fit; or

(c) make such order as it thinks fit.

NOTE

[1] Inserted by the European Communities (Lawyer's Practice) (Scotland) Regulations 2000 (SSI 2000/121), reg.37(1) and Sch.1, para.1(3) (effective May 22, 2000).

Date and expiry of registration certificate

[1] **24E.**—(1) Every registration certificate issued in November of any year shall bear the date of 1st November in that year, and every other registration certificate shall bear the date on which it was issued.

(2) Every registration certificate shall have effect from the date it bears under subsection (1).

(3) Subject to subsection (4), every registration certificate shall expire on 31st October next after it is issued.

(4) On the name of a registered European lawyer being withdrawn from the register or on a registered European lawyer being suspended from practice as a registered European lawyer, any registration certificate for the time being in force of that registered European lawyer shall cease to have effect, but in the case of suspension, if he ceases to be so suspended during the period for which the registration would otherwise have continued in force, the registration certificate shall thereupon again have effect.

NOTE

[1] Inserted by the European Communities (Lawyer's Practice) (Scotland) Regulations 2000 (SSI 2000/121), reg.37(1) and Sch.1, para.1(3) (effective May 22, 2000).

Suspension of registration certificate

[1] **24F.**—[2](1) If—

(a) in pursuance of the Mental Health (Care and Treatment) (Scotland) Act 2003 a registered European lawyer is, by reason of mental disorder, detained in hospital;

(b) [*Repealed by the Adult Support and Protection (Scotland) Act 2007 (asp 10) Sch.2, para.1 (effective October 5, 2007).*]

(c) the estate of a registered European lawyer is sequestrated;

(d) a registered European lawyer grants a trust deed for behoof of creditors;

(e) a judicial factor is appointed on the estate of a registered European lawyer;

any registration certificate for the time being in force of that registered European lawyer shall cease to have effect, and he shall be suspended from practice as a registered European lawyer.

(2) On the occurrence of any of the circumstances mentioned in

subsection (1), the registered European lawyer in question shall intimate those circumstances to the Council in writing immediately.

(3) On the occurrence of the circumstances mentioned in paragraph (d) or (e) of subsection (1) the trustee or as the case may be the judicial factor shall intimate his appointment to the Council in writing immediately.

NOTE

[1] Inserted by the European Communities (Lawyer's Practice) (Scotland) Regulations 2000 (SSI 2000/121), reg.37(1) and Sch.1, para.1(3) (effective May 22, 2000).

[2] As amended by the Mental Health (Care and Treatment) (Scotland) Act 2003 (Modification of Enactments) Order 2005, art.2 and Sch.1 (effective September 27, 2005).

Further provisions relating to suspension of registration certificate

[1] **24G.**—(1) The provisions of this section shall have effect in relation to a registration certificate which has ceased to have effect by virtue of section 24F during the period when that registration certificate would, but for that section, have continued in force.

(2) A registration certificate which has ceased to have effect by virtue of paragraph (c) or (d) of section 24F(1) shall again have effect on the registered European lawyer being granted his discharge.

(3) A registration certificate which has ceased to have effect by virtue of paragraph (e) of section 24F(1) shall again have effect on the judicial factor being granted his discharge.

[2 3] (4) Where a registered European lawyer is suspended from practice as a registered European lawyer by virtue of paragraph (a) of section 24F(1), the period of suspension shall, for the purposes of section 24C(2)(e), expire on the registered European lawyer ceasing to be detained.

(5) Where a registered European lawyer is suspended from practice as a registered European lawyer by virtue of paragraph (c), (d) or (e) of section 24F(l), he may at any time apply to the Council to terminate the suspension.

(6) On an application under subsection (5), the Council may either—

(a) grant the application with or without conditions; or

(b) refuse the application.

(7) If on an application by a registered European lawyer under subsection (5) the Council refuse the application or grant it subject to conditions, the registered European lawyer may appeal against the decision to the court, who may—

(a) affirm the decision; or

(b) vary any conditions imposed by the Council; or

(c) terminate the suspension either with or without conditions.

NOTE

[1] Inserted by the European Communities (Lawyer's Practice) (Scotland) Regulations 2000 (SSI 2000/121), reg.37(1) and Sch.1, para.1(3) (effective May 22, 2000).

[2] As amended by the Mental Health (Care and Treatment) (Scotland) Act 2003 (Modification of Enactments) Order 2005, art.2 and Sch.1 (effective September 27, 2005).

[3] As amended by the Adult Support and Protection (Scotland) Act 2007 (asp 10) Sch.2, para.1 (effective October 5, 2007).

Rights of Solicitors

Rights of practising

25. Every person qualified to practise as a solicitor in accordance with section 4 may practise as a solicitor in any court in Scotland.

Rights of audience in the Court of Session, the House of Lords, the Judicial Committee of the Privy Council and the High Court of Justiciary

[1] **25A.**—[2,4] (1) Subject to regulations 6 and 11 of the European Communities (Lawyer's Practice) (Scotland) Regulations 2000 and without prejudice to section 103(8) of the Criminal Procedure (Scotland) Act 1995

(right of solicitor to appear before single judge) and section 48(2)(b) (extension of rights of audience by act of sederunt) of the Court of Session Act 1988, a solicitor who—

[3] (a) seeks a right of audience in, on the one hand, the Court of Session, the House of Lords and the Judicial Committee of the Privy Council or, on the other hand, the High Court of Justiciary and the Judicial Committee of the Privy Council; and

(b) has satisfied the Council as to the requirements provided for in this section,

shall have a right of audience in those courts or, as the case may be, that court.

(2) The requirements mentioned in subsection (1), in relation to the courts or, as the case may be, the court in which a solicitor seeks a right of audience, are that—

(a) he has completed, to the satisfaction of the Council, a course of training in evidence and pleading in relation to proceedings in those courts or that court;

(b) he has such knowledge as appears to the Council to be appropriate of—

(i) the practice and procedure of; and

(ii) professional conduct in regard to,

those courts or that court; and

(c) he has satisfied the Council that he is, having regard among other things to his experience in appropriate proceedings in the sheriff court, otherwise a fit and proper person to have a right of audience in those courts or that court.

(3) Where a solicitor has satisfied the Council as to the requirements of subsection (2) in relation to the courts or, as the case may be, the court in which he seeks a right of audience the Council shall make an appropriate annotation on the roll against his name.

(4) The Council shall make rules under this section as to—

(a) the matters to be included in, the methods of instruction to be employed in, and the qualifications of the person who will conduct, any course of training such as is mentioned in subsection (2)(a); and

[3] (b) the manner in which a solicitor's knowledge of the practice and procedure and professional conduct mentioned in subsection (2)(b) is to be demonstrated,

and separate rules shall be so made in relation to, on the one hand, the Court of Session, the House of Lords and the Judicial Committee of the Privy Council and, on the other hand, the High Court of Justiciary and the Judicial Committee of the Privy Council.

(5) The Council shall make rules of conduct in relation to the exercising of any right of audience held by virtue of this section.

(6) Where a solicitor having a right of audience in any of the courts mentioned in subsection (1) is instructed to appear in that court, those instructions shall take precedence before any of his other professional obligations, and the Council shall make rules—

(a) stating the order of precedence of those courts for the purposes of this subsection;

(b) stating general criteria to which solicitors should have regard in determining whether to accept instructions in particular circumstances; and

(c) securing, through such of their officers as they think appropriate, that, where reasonably practicable, any person wishing to be represented before any of those courts by a solicitor holding an appropriate right of audience is so represented,

and for the purposes of rules made under this subsection the Inner and Outer Houses of the Court of Session, and the High Court of Justiciary exercising its appellate jurisdiction, may be treated as separate courts.

(7) Subsection (6) does not apply to an employed solicitor whose contract of employment prevents him from acting for persons other than his employer.

(8) Subject to subsections (9) and (10), the provisions of section 34(2) and (3) apply to rules made under this section as they apply to rules made under that section and, in considering any rules made by the Council under subsection (5), the Lord President shall have regard to the desirability of there being common principles applying in relation to the exercising of rights of audience by all practitioners appearing before the Court of Session and the High Court of Justiciary.

(9) The Council shall, after any rules made under subsection (4) have been approved by the Lord President, submit such rules to the Secretary of State, and no such rules shall have effect unless the Secretary of State, after consulting the Director in accordance with section 64A, has approved them.

(10) The Council shall, after any rules made under subsection (5) have been approved by the Lord President, submit such rules to the Secretary of State.

(11) Where the Secretary of State considers that any rule submitted to him under section (10) would directly or indirectly inhibit the freedom of a solicitor to appear in court or undertake all the work preparatory thereto he shall consult the Director in accordance with section 64A.

(12) The Council may bring into force the rules submitted by them to the Secretary of State under subsection (10) with the exception of any such rule which he has, in accordance with section 64B, refused to approve.

(13) Nothing in this section affects the powers of any court in relation to any proceedings—

(a) to hear a person who would not otherwise have a right of audience before the court in relation to those proceedings; or

(b) to refuse to hear a person (for reasons which apply to him as an individual) who would otherwise have a right of audience before the court in relation to those proceedings, and where a court so refuses it shall give its reasons for that decision.

(14) Where a complaint has been made that a solicitor has been guilty of professional misconduct in the exercise of any right of audience held by him by virtue of this section, the Council may, or if so requested by the Lord President shall, suspend him from exercising that right pending determination of that complaint under Part IV.

(15) Where a function is conferred on any person or body by this section he or, as the case may be, they shall exercise that function as soon as is reasonably practicable.

NOTES

[1] Inserted by the Law Reform (Miscellaneous Provisions) (Scotland) Act 1990 (c.40), s. 24.

[2] As amended by the Criminal Procedure (Consequential Provisions) (Scotland) Act 1995 (c.40), Sch.4, para.31 (effective 1st April 1996: s. 7(2)).

[3] As amended by SI 1999/1042, Art. 4, Sch.2, para.7 (effective on commencement of s.44(1)(c) of the Scotland Act (c.44): May 20, 1999).

[4] As amended by the European Communities (Lawyer's Practice) (Scotland) Regulations 2000 (SSI 2000/121), reg.37(1) and Sch.1, para.1(5) (effective May 22, 2000).

Restriction on rights of practising

Offence for solicitors to act as agents for unqualified persons

26.—[1] (1) Any solicitor to whom this subsection applies who or incorporated practice which upon the account or for the profit of any unqualified person—

(a) acts as agent in any action or proceedings in any court, or

(b) permits or suffers his or, as the case may be, its name to be made use of in any way in any such action or proceedings; or

(c) draws or prepares any writ to which section 32 applies; or

(d) permits or suffers his or, as the case may be, its name to be made use of in the drawing or preparing of any such writ; or

(e) does any other act to enable that person to appear, act or practise in any respect as a solicitor or notary public,

knowing that person not to be a qualified solicitor or notary public, as the case may be, shall be guilty of an offence.

[2] (2) Subsection (1) applies to any solicitor, registered foreign lawyer or registered European lawyer pursuing professional activities within the meaning of the European Communities (Lawyer's Practice) (Scotland) Regulations 2000, not being a solicitor, registered foreign lawyer or registered European lawyer pursuing professional activities within the meaning of the European Communities (Lawyer's Practice) (Scotland) Regulations 2000 who is employed full-time on a fixed salary by a body corporate or employed by a law centre.

[1,2] (3) In this section "person" includes a body corporate but "unqualified person" does not include an incorporated practice, registered foreign lawyer, multi national practice or registered European lawyer pursuing professional activities within the meaning of the European Communities (Lawyer's Practice) (Scotland) Regulations 2000.

NOTE

[1] As amended by the Law Reform (Miscellaneous Provisions) (Scotland) Act 1985 (c.73), Sch.1, Pt I, para.4, and the Law Reform (Miscellaneous Provisions) (Scotland) Act 1990 (c.40), Sch.8, para.29(5)(c) (effective 17th March 1993: SI 1993/641). Prospective amendments in para.29(5)(a), (b) and (d), which states:

"(5) In section 26 of the 1980 Act (offence for solicitors to act as agents for unqualified persons)—

(a) in subsection (1)(c), at the beginning there shall be inserted 'subject to subsection (4),';

(b) in subsection (1)(d), at the beginning there shall be inserted 'subject to subsection (4),';

. . .

(d) after subsection (3) there shall be inserted—

'(4) Subsection (1)(c) and (d) shall not apply in relation to—

(a) writs relating to heritable or moveable property drawn or prepared upon the account of or for the profit of independent qualified conveyancers providing conveyancing services within the meaning of section 23 (interpretation of sections 16 to 22) of the Law Reform (Miscellaneous Provisions) (Scotland) Act 1990; or

(b) papers to found or oppose an application for a grant of confirmation in favour of executors drawn or prepared upon the account of or for the profit of an executry practitioner or recognised financial institution providing executry services within the meaning of the said section 23.' "

[2] As amended by the European Communities (Lawyer's Practice) (Scotland) Regulations 2000 (SSI 2000/121), reg.37(1) and Sch.1, para.1(6) and by the Solicitors (Scotland) Act 1980 (Foreign Lawyers and Multi-national Practices) Regulations 2004 (SSI 2004/383), reg.4.

Offence for solicitors to share fees with unqualified persons

27. [Repealed by the Law Reform (Miscellaneous Provisions) (Scotland) Act 1990 (c.40), Sch.9 (effective 17th March 1993: SI 1993/641.]

Offence for solicitors who are disqualified to seek employment without informing employer

[1] **28.** Any person who—

(a) has been struck off the roll; or

(b) suspended from practice as a solicitor; or

[2] (c) has had his registration as a registered European lawyer withdrawn; or

[2] (d) has been suspended from practice as a registered European lawyer,

and while so disqualified from practice seeks or accepts employment by a solicitor in connection with that solicitor's practice or by an incorporated practice or multi-national practice without previously informing him or, as the case may be, it that he is so disqualified shall be guilty of an offence; or

(e) has had his registration as a registered foreign lawyer withdrawn; or

(f) has been suspended from practice as a registered foreign lawyer.

NOTE

[1] As amended by the Law Reform (Miscellaneous Provisions) (Scotland) Act 1985 (c.73), Sch.1, Pt I, para.6.

[2] As amended by the European Communities (Lawyer's Practice) (Scotland) Regulations 2000 (SSI 2000/121), reg.37(1) and Sch.1, para.1(7) and by the Solicitors (Scotland) Act 1980 (Foreign Lawyers and Multi-national Practices) Regulations 2004 (SSI 2004/383), reg.5.

29. [Repealed by the Law Reform (Miscellaneous Provisions) (Scotland) Act 1990 (c.40), s. 39 and Sch.9.]

Liability for fees of other solicitor

[1,2] **30.** Where a solicitor, or an incorporated practice authorised by and acting for a client employs another solicitor or incorporated practice he or, as the case may be, it shall (whether or not he or, as the case may be, it discloses the client) be liable to the other solicitor or incorporated practice for that other solicitor's or incorporated practice's fees and outlays, unless at the time of the employment he or, as the case may be, it expressly disclaims any such liability.

NOTE

[1] As amended by the Law Reform (Miscellaneous Provisions) (Scotland) Act 1985 (c.73), Sch.1, Pt I, para.7.

[2] Read in conjunction with the European Communities (Lawyer's Practice) (Scotland) Regulations 2000 (SSI 2000/121), reg.37(2) and Sch.2 and the Solicitors (Scotland) Act 1980 (Foreign Lawyers and Multi-national Practices) Regulations 2004 (SSI 2004/383), reg.13.

Unqualified persons acting as solicitors

Offence for unqualified persons to pretend to be solicitor or notary public

[1] **31.**—[2] (1) Any person (including a body corporate) who, not having the relevant qualification, either by himself or together with others, wilfully and falsely—

(a) pretends to be a solicitor or notary public; or

[3] (aa) pretends to be a registered European lawyer; or

[4] (ab) pretends to be a registered foreign lawyer; or

[2] (b) takes or uses any name, title, addition or description implying that he is duly qualified to act as a solicitor or a notary public, registered European lawyer or registered foreign lawyer, as the case may be, or recognised by law as so qualified;

shall be guilty of an offence.

In this section, "unqualified person" does not include an incorporated practice.

(2) Any person (including a body corporate) who either by himself or together with others, wilfully and falsely—

(a) pretends to be an incorporated practice;

(b) takes or uses any name, title, addition or description implying that he is an incorporated practice,

shall be guilty of an offence.

(3) [Repealed by the Law Reform (Miscellaneous Provisions) (Scotland) Act 1990 (c.40), Sch.9.]

NOTES

[1] As amended by the Law Reform (Miscellaneous Provisions) (Scotland) Act 1985 (c.73), Sch.1, Pt I, para.8. Modified by the Copyright, Designs and Patents Act 1988 (c.48), s.278 (patent attorneys).

[2] As amended by the European Communities (Lawyer's Practice) (Scotland) Regulations 2000 (SSI 2000/121), reg.37(1) and Sch.1, para.1(8) and by the Solicitors (Scotland) Act 1980 (Foreign Lawyers and Multi-national Practices) Regulations 2004 (SSI 2004/383), reg.56.

[3] Inserted by the European Communities (Lawyer's Practice) (Scotland) Regulations 2000 (SSI 2000/121), reg.37(1) and Sch.1, para.1(7)(c) (effective May 22, 2000).

[4] Inserted by the Solicitors (Scotland) Act 1980 (Foreign Lawyers and Multi-national Practices) Regulations 2004 (SSI 2004/383), reg.6.

Offence for unqualified persons to prepare certain documents

[1,7] **32.**—[4] (1) Subject to the provisions of this section and regulations 6, 11, 12 and 13 of the European Communities (Lawyer's Practice) (Scotland) Regulations 2000, any unqualified person (including a body corporate) who draws or prepares—

(a) any writ relating to heritable or moveable estate; or

[2] (b) any writ relating to any action or proceedings in any court; or

(c) any papers on which to found or oppose an application for a grant of confirmation in favour of executors,

shall be guilty of an offence.

(2) Subsection (1) shall not apply—

(a) to an unqualified person if he proves that he drew or prepared the writ or papers in question without receiving, or without expecting to receive, either directly or indirectly, any fee, gain or reward (other than by remuneration paid under a contract of employment); or

(b) to an advocate; or

(c) to any public officer drawing or preparing writs in the course of his duty; or

(d) to any person employed merely to engross any writ; or

[3] (e) an incorporated practice; or

[7] (f) to a member of a body which has made a successful application under section 25 of the 1990 Act but only to the extent to which the member is exercising rights acquired by virtue of section 27 of that Act.

[5] (2A) Subsection (1)(a) shall not apply to a conveyancing practitioner providing conveyancing services within the meaning of section 23 of the Law Reform (Miscellaneous Provisions) (Scotland) Act 1990.

(2B) Subsection (1)(b) shall not apply to a person who is, by virtue of an act of sederunt made under section 32 (power of Court of Session to regulate procedure) of the Sheriff Courts (Scotland) Act 1971, permitted to represent [8][—

(a) a party to a summary cause;

(b) a debtor or hirer in proceedings for—

(i) a time order under section 129 of the Consumer Credit Act 1974 (time orders); or

(ii) variation or revocation, under section 130(6) of that Act (variation and revocation of time orders), of a time order made under section 129.]

(2C) Subsection (1)(c) shall not apply to an executry practitioner or a recognised financial institution providing executry services within the meaning of section 23 of the Law Reform (Miscellaneous Provisions) (Scotland) Act 1990.

(3) In this section "writ" does not include—

(a) a will or other testamentary writing;

(b) a document *in re mercatoria*, missive or mandate;

(c) a letter or power of attorney;

(d) a transfer of stock containing no trust or limitation thereof.

[6] (4) For the purposes of this section, "unqualified person" includes a registered foreign lawyer.

NOTES

[1] As amended by the Law Reform (Miscellaneous Provisions) (Scotland) Act 1990 (c.40), Sch.8, para.29(6).

[2] As amended by the Solicitors (Scotland) Act 1988 (c.42), Sch.1, para.7.

[3] Added by the Law Reform (Miscellaneous Provisions) (Scotland) Act 1985 (c.73), Sch.1, Pt I, para.9.

[4] As amended by the European Communities (Lawyer's Practice) (Scotland) Regulations 2000 (SSI 2000/121), reg.37(1) and Sch.1, para.1(9) (effective May 22, 2000).

[5] As amended by the Public Appointments and Public Bodies etc. (Scotland) Act 2003 (asp 4), Sch.4, para.7 (effective August 15, 2003).

[6] Added by the Solicitors (Scotland) Act 1980 (Foreign Lawyers and Multi-national Practices) Regulations 2004 (SSI 2004/383), reg.7 (effective October 1, 2004).

[7] As inserted by the Legal Profession and Legal Aid (Scotland) Act 2007 (asp 5) s.61 (effective March 19, 2007).

[8] Prospectively amended by the Consumer Credit Act 2006 (c.14) s.16(5) (effective October 1, 2008).

Unqualified persons not entitled to fees, etc.

[1] **33.** Subject to the provisions of regulations 12 and 13 of the European Communities (Lawyer's Practice) (Scotland) Regulations 2000, no fee, reward, outlay or expenses on account of or in relation to any act or proceeding done or taken by any person who—

(a) acts as a solicitor or as a notary public without being duly qualified so to act; or

(b) not being so qualified, frames or draws any writs to which section 32 applies,

shall be recoverable by any person in any action or matter.

This section does not apply to an incorporated practice or in relation to writs framed or drawn by a person who is, by virtue of an act of sederunt

 [NEXT TEXT PAGE IS F 21]

made under section 32 of the Sheriff Courts (Scotland) Act 1971, permitted to represent a party to a summary cause.

[2] (4) For the purposes of this section, "unqualified person" includes a registered foreign lawyer.

NOTE

[1] As amended by the Law Reform (Miscellaneous Provisions) (Scotland) Act 1985 (c.73), Sch.1, Pt 1, para.10, the Solicitors (Scotland) Act 1988 (c.42), Sch.1, para.8 and Sch.2, and the Law Reform (Miscellaneous Provisions) (Scotland) Act 1990 (c.40), Sch.8, para.29(7); further amended by the European Communities (Lawyer's Practice) (Scotland) Regulations 2000 (SSI 2000/121), reg.37(1) and Sch.1, para.1(10) (effective May 22, 2000).

[2] Inserted by the Solicitors (Scotland) Act 1980 (Foreign Lawyers and Multi-national Practices) Regulations 2004 (SSI 2004/383), reg.7.

Privilege of incorporated practices from disclosure etc.

[1,2] **33A.**—(1) Any communication made to or by an incorporated practice in the course of its acting as such for a client shall in any legal proceedings be privileged from disclosure in like manner as if the body had at all material times been a solicitor acting for the client.

(2) Any enactment or instrument making special provision in relation to a solicitor or other legal representative as to the disclosure of information, or as to the production, seizure or removal of documents, with respect to which a claim to professional privilege could be maintained, shall, with any necessary modifications, have effect in relation to an incorporated practice as it has effect in relation to a solicitor.

NOTE

[1] Inserted by the Law Reform (Miscellaneous Provisions) (Scotland) Act 1985 (c.73), Sch.1, Pt I, para.11.

[2] Read in conjunction with the European Communities (Lawyer's Practice) (Scotland) Regulations 2000 (SSI 2000/121), reg.37(2) and Sch.2 (effective May 22, 2000).

[3] **33B.** (1) Any communication made to or by a registered foreign lawyer in the course of his actings as such for a client shall in any legal proceedings be privileged from disclosure in like manner as if the registered foreign lawyer had at all material times been a solicitor acting for a client.

(2) Any enactment or instrument making special provision in relation to a solicitor or other legal representative as to the disclosure of information, or as to the production, seizure or removal of documents, with respect to which a claim to professional privilege could be maintained, shall, with any necessary modifications, have effect in relation to a registered foreign lawyer as it has effect in relation to a solicitor.

NOTE

[1] Inserted by the Solicitors (Scotland) Act 1980 (Foreign Lawyers and Multi-national Practices) Regulations 2004 (SSI 2004/383), reg.8.

PART III

PROFESSIONAL PRACTICE, CONDUCT AND DISCIPLINE OF SOLICITORS

Practice rules

Rules as to professional practice, conduct and discipline

[1,3,5] **34.**—(1) Subject to subsections (2) and (3), the Council may, if they think fit, make rules for regulating in respect of any matter the professional practice, conduct and discipline of solicitors and incorporated practices.

[2] (1A) Rules made under this section may—

(a) provide as to the management and control by—

(i) solicitors holding practising certificates or their executors;

(ii) other incorporated practices

of bodies corporate carrying on businesses consisting of the provision of professional services such as are provided by individuals and firms practising as solicitors being bodies the membership of which is restricted to such solicitors, executors and other incorporated practices;

(b) prescribe the circumstances in which such bodies may be recognised by the Council as being suitable to undertake the provision of any such services;

(c) prescribe the conditions which (subject to any exceptions provided by the rules) must at all times be satisfied by bodies corporate so recognised if they are to remain so recognised (which bodies, when and for so long as so recognised, are in this Act referred to as "incorporated practices");

(d) regulate the conduct of the affairs of incorporated practices; and

(e) provide—

(i) for the manner and form in which applications for recognition under this section are to be made, and for the payment of fees in connection with such applications;

(ii) for regulating the names that may be used by incorporated practices;

(iii) as to the period for which any recognition granted under this section shall (subject to the provisions of this Act) remain in force;

(iv) for the revocation of any such recognition on the grounds that it was granted as a result of any error or fraud;

(v) for the keeping by the Society of a list containing the names and places of business of all incorporated practices and for the information contained in any such list to be available for inspection;

(vi) for the rules made under any provision of this Act to have effect in relation to incorporated practices with such additions, omissions or other modifications as appear to the Council to be necessary or expedient;

(vii) for empowering the Council to take such steps as they consider necessary or expedient to ascertain whether or not any rules applicable to incorporated practices by virtue of this section are being complied with; and

(f) make such additional or different provision as the Council think fit in relation to solicitors who, or incorporated practices which, are partners in or directors of multi-disciplinary practices.

[6] (1B) Rules made under this section may—

(a) prevent a solicitor from entering a multi-national practice without the approval of the Council; and

(b) make different provision for the regulation of solicitors and registered foreign lawyers in a multi-national practice in the following different cases—

(i) where the principal place of business of the practice is outside Scotland and it has a place of business in Scotland;

(ii) where the principal place of business of the practice is in Scotland and it has a place of business outside Scotland;

(iii) where the principal place of business of the practice is in Scotland and it has no place of business outside Scotland.

[6] (1C) For the purposes of subsection (1B)(b), the principal place of business of a multi-national practice shall be determined by the Council who shall take into account factors set out in rules which may be made under this section.

(2) The Council shall, before making any rules under this section or section 35—

(a) send to each member of the Society a draft of the rules; and

(b) thereafter submit the draft rules to a meeting of the Society; and
(c) take into consideration any resolution passed at that meeting relating to amendments to the draft rules.

(3) Rules made under this section or section 35 shall not have effect unless the Lord President after considering any objections he thinks relevant has approved the rules so made.

(3A) Without prejudice to subsection (3), any rule made, whether before or after the coming into force of this subsection, by the Council under this section or section 35 which has the effect of prohibiting the formation of multi-disciplinary practices shall not have effect unless the Secretary of State, after consulting the Director in accordance with section 64A, has approved it.

(4) If any solicitor fails to comply with any rule made under this section that failure may be treated as professional misconduct for the purposes of Part IV.

[2] (4A) A certificate purporting to be signed by an officer of the Society and stating that any body corporate is or is not an incorporated practice shall, unless the contrary is proved, be sufficient evidence of that fact.

[2] (4B) Subject to the provisions of this Act, the Secretary of State may, by order made by statutory instrument subject to annulment in pursuance of a resolution of either House of Parliament, provide for any enactment or instrument passed or made before the commencement of [sub]section (1A) above and having effect in relation to solicitors to have effect in relation to incorporated practices with such additions, omissions, or other modifications as appear to him to be necessary or expedient.

NOTES

[1] As amended by the Law Reform (Miscellaneous Provisions) (Scotland) Act 1985 (c.73), Sch.1, Pt. I, para.12.

[2] Inserted by the Law Reform (Miscellaneous Provisions) (Scotland) Act 1985 (c.73), Sch.1, Pt. I, para.12(b) and (c).

[3] As amended by the Law Reform (Miscellaneous Provisions) (Scotland) Act 1990 (c.40), s.31(3) (effective March 17, 1993 by SI 1993/641).

[4] Inserted by the Law Reform (Miscellaneous Provisions) (Scotland) Act 1990 (c.40), s.31(3) (effective March 17, 1993 by SI 1993/641).

[5] Read in conjunction with the European Communities (Lawyer's Practice) (Scotland) Regulations 2000 (SSI 2000/121), reg.37(2) and Sch.2 and the Solicitors (Scotland) Act 1980 (Foreign Lawyers and Multi-national Practices) Regulations 2004 (SSI 2004/383), reg.14.

[6] Inserted by the Solicitors (Scotland) Act 1980 (Foreign Lawyers and Multi-national Practices) Regulations 2004 (SSI 2004/383), reg.9.

Accounts rules

Accounts rules

[1,5] **35.**—[2] (1) The Council shall, subject to section 34(2) and (3), make rules (in this Act referred to as "accounts rules")—

(a) as to the opening and keeping by solicitors and incorporated practices of accounts and deposits at the banks specified in subsection (2) or with a building society for moneys not belonging to them received by them in the course of their practice;
(b) as to the opening and keeping by solicitors and incorporated practices of—
  (i) a deposit or share account with a building society, or
  (ii) an account showing sums on loan to a local authority, being in either case for a client whose name is specified in the title of the account;
(c) as to the keeping by solicitors and incorporated practices of books and accounts containing particulars and information as to money not belonging to them received, held or paid by them in the course of their practice;

(d) as to the action which the Council may take to enable them to ascertain whether or not the rules are being complied with; and

(e) as to the recovery from solicitors of fees and other costs incurred by the Council in ascertaining whether or not a solicitor who has failed to comply with the accounts rules has remedied that failure and is complying with the rules.

[3] (2) The banks mentioned in paragraph (a) of subsection (1) are—

(a) the Bank of England;

(b) [Repealed by the Trustee Savings Banks Act 1985 (c.58), Sch.4.]

(c) the National Savings Bank;

(d) *[Repealed by the Postal Services Act 2000 (Consequential Modifications No.1) Order 2001, (SI 2001/1149), Art.3, Sched.2 (effective March 26, 2001).]*

[6](e) a person (other than a building society) who has permission under Part 4 of the Financial Services and Markets Act 2000 to accept deposits;

[6](ea) an EEA firm of the kind mentioned in paragraph 5(b) of Schedule 3 to the Financial Services and Markets Act 2000 which has permission under paragraph 15 of that Schedule (as a result of qualifying for authorisation under paragraph 12 of that Schedule) to accept deposits;

[6](2A) Paragraphs (e) and (ea) of subsection (2) must be read with—

(a) section 22 of the Financial Services and Markets Act 2000;

(b) any relevant order under that section; and

(c) Schedule 2 to that Act.

(3) If any solicitor fails to comply with any rule made under this section that failure may be treated as professional misconduct for the purposes of Part IV.

(4) Rules made under this section shall not apply to a solicitor—

(a) who is in employment as solicitor to a Minister of the Crown or a Government Department or as an assistant or officer appointed to act under the direction of such solicitor; or

[4] (b) who is in employment to which Part V of the Legal Aid (Scotland) Act 1986 applies; or

(c) who is in employment in an office connected with the administration of a local authority or a statutory undertaking or a designated body to which he has been appointed by the authority or the statutory undertakers or the persons responsible for the management of that body by reason of his being a solicitor,

so far as regards monies received, held or paid by him in the course of that employment.

In this subsection—

"local authority" means a local authority within the meaning of the Local Government (Scotland) Act 1973;

"statutory undertakers" means any persons (including a local authority) authorised by any enactment or statutory order or any scheme made under or confirmed by an enactment to construct, work or carry on any railway, light railway, tramway, road transport, water transport, canal, inland navigation, dock, harbour, pier or lighthouse undertaking or any undertaking for the supply of gas, electricity, hydraulic power or water;

"designated body" means any body whether corporate or unincorporate for the time being designated by the Council for the purposes of this section.

NOTES

[1] Extended by the Trustee Savings Banks Act 1985 (c.58), Sch.1, para.11(2)(*b*).

[2] As amended by the Law Reform (Miscellaneous Provisions) (Scotland) Act 1985 (c.73),

Sch.1, Pt. I, para.13, Pt. II, para.4 and Sch.4, and the Solicitors (Scotland) Act 1988 (c.42), Sch.1, para.9 and Sch.2.

[3] As amended by the Banking Act 1987 (c.22), Sch.6, para.9.

[4] As amended by the Legal Aid (Scotland) Act 1986 (c.47), Sch.3, para.7.

[5] Read in conjunction with the European Communities (Lawyer's Practice) (Scotland) Regulations 2000 (SSI 2000/121), reg.37(2) and Sch.2 and the Solicitors (Scotland) Act 1980 (Foreign Lawyers and Multi-national Practices) Regulations 2004 (SSI 2004/383), reg.14.

[6] Inserted by the Financial Services and Markets Act 2000 (Consequential Amendments and Repeals) Order 2001, (SI 2001/3649), art.222.

Interest on client's money

[1,3] **36.**—[2](1) Accounts rules shall make provision for requiring a solicitor or an incorporated practice, in such cases as may be prescribed by the rules—

(*a*) to keep in a separate deposit or savings account at a bank or with a building society, or on a separate deposit receipt at a bank, for the benefit of the client money received for or on account of a client; or

(*aa*) to keep in—

(i) a deposit or share account with a building society; or

(ii) an account showing sums on loan to a local authority,

being in either case an account kept by the solicitor in his or, as the case may be, by the incorporated practice in its own name for a specified client, money so received; or

(*b*) to make good to the client out of the solicitor's or, as the case may be, the incorporated practice's own money a sum equivalent to the interest which would have accrued if the money so received had been kept as mentioned in paragraph (*a*) or (*aa*).

(2) The cases in which a solicitor or incorporated practice may be required to act as mentioned in subsection (1) may be defined among other things by reference to the amount of any sum received or balance held or the period for which it is or is likely to be retained or held or both; and the rules may include provision for enabling a client (without prejudice to any other remedy) to require that any question arising under the rules in relation to the client's money be referred to and determined by the Society.

(3) Except as provided by the rules, a solicitor or incorporated practice shall not be liable by virtue of the relation between solicitor and client to account to any client for interest received by the solicitor or, as the case may be, the incorporated practice on monies lodged in an account at a bank or with a building society, or on deposit receipt, at a bank, being monies received or held for or on account of his or, as the case may be, its clients generally.

(4) Nothing in this section or in the rules shall affect any arrangement in writing whenever made between a solicitor and his client or an incorporated practice and its client as to the application of the client's money or interest on it.

NOTES

[1] As amended by the Law Reform (Miscellaneous Provisions) (Scotland) Act 1985 (c.73), Sched. 1, Pt. I, para.14, and the Solicitors (Scotland) Act 1988 (c.42), Sched. 1, para.10 and Sched. 2.

[2] As amended by the Law Reform (Miscellaneous Provisions) (Scotland) Act 1980 (c.55), s.25.

[3] Read in conjunction with the European Communities (Lawyer's Practice) (Scotland) Regulations 2000 (SSI 2000/121), reg.37(2) and Sch.2 and the Solicitors (Scotland) Act 1980 (Foreign Lawyers and Multi-national Practices) Regulations 2004 (SSI 2004/383), reg.14.

Accountant's certificates

[1,2] **37.**—(1) This section shall have effect for the purpose of securing satisfactory evidence of compliance with the accounts rules.

(2) Subject to the following provisions of this section, every solicitor and incorporated practice to whom the accounts rules apply shall, in accordance

with the rules made under subsection (3), deliver to the Council a certificate by an accountant (in this section referred to as an "accountant's certificate").

(3) The council shall make rules (in this Act referred to as "accountant's certificate rules") prescribing—

(*a*) the qualifications to be held by an accountant by whom an accountant's certificate may be given;

(*b*) the nature and extent of the examination to be made by an accountant of the books and accounts of a solicitor or his firm or of an incorporated practice and of any other relative documents with a view to the signing of an accountant's certificate;

(*c*) the intervals at which an accountant's certificate shall be delivered to the Council, not being more frequent than once in each practice year;

(*d*) the accounting period for which an accountant's certificate shall be delivered or the different accounting periods for which in different circumstances an accountant's certificate shall be delivered;

(e) the period within which an accountant's certificate shall be delivered; and

(f) the form and content of an accountant's certificate.

(4) The accountant's certificate rules may include such other provisions as the Council consider necessary or proper for the purpose of giving effect to the foregoing provisions of this section and for regulating any incidental, consequential or supplementary matters.

(5) The delivery of an accountant's certificate in pursuance of subsection (2) shall not be required in the case of—

(a) a solicitor who or incorporated practice which, in agreement with the Council, furnishes to the Council and keeps in force a fidelity bond by an insurance office or other institution accepted by the court as cautioners for a judicial factor appointed by the court for such amount as the Council may determine, guaranteeing the intromissions of the solicitor or his firm or, as the case may be, of the incorporated practice with money held by him or them or, as the case may be, it for or on behalf of clients; or

(b) a solicitor or incorporated practice who satisfies the Council that during the accounting period to which the accountant's certificate would ordinarily relate he has not in the course of his practice or, as the case may be, it has not held or received any money on behalf of clients.

(6) If the Council are of opinion that satisfactory evidence of compliance with the accounts rules for the time being in force will be secured by some method other than by delivery of an accountant's certificate under subsection (2), they may make rules—

(a) prescribing—

(i) that other method;

(ii) the terms and conditions to be observed in connection therewith; and

(iii) the procedure to be followed by solicitors or incorporated practices desiring to adopt that other method, and

(b) containing such incidental, consequential and supplementary provisions relative thereto as the Council may consider necessary or proper;

and a solicitor who satisfies the Council that he or, as the case may be, an incorporated practice which satisfies the Council that it is complying with rules made under this subsection shall not be required to deliver an accountant's certificate in pursuance of subsection (2).

(7) A certificate under the hand of the secretary of the Society certifying that a specified solicitor or incorporated practice has or has not, as the case may be, delivered to the Council an accountant's certificate, or supplied any evidence required from him or, as the case may be, it under this section or

under the accountant's certificate rules or, as the case may be, under any rules made under subsection (6), shall, unless the contrary is proved, be evidence of the fact so certified.

(8) Failure by a solicitor to comply with any provision of this section or of the accountant's certificate rules or of any rules made under subsection (6), so far as applicable to him, may be treated as professional misconduct for the purposes of Part IV.

NOTE

[1] As amended by the Law Reform (Miscellaneous Provisions) (Scotland) Act 1985 (c.73), Sched. 1, Pt. I, para.15 (reading the word "substituted" in para.15(c)(i) as "inserted").

[1] Read in conjunction with the European Communities (Lawyer's Practice) (Scotland) Regulations 2000 (SSI 2000/121), reg.37(2) and Sch.2 and the Solicitors (Scotland) Act 1980 (Foreign Lawyers and Multi-national Practices) Regulations 2004 (SSI 2004/383), reg.13 and 14.

Powers of Council to intervene

Powers where dishonesty alleged

[1,3] **38.**—(1) If the Council have reasonable cause to believe that a solicitor or an employee of his or an incorporated practice or any employee thereof has been guilty of any such dishonesty as is mentioned in section 43(2) they may—

(a) require the production or delivery to any person appointed by the Council at a time and place fixed by the Council of the documents to which this section applies;
(b) take possession of all such documents; and
(c) apply to the court for an order that no payment be made by any banker, building society or other body named in the order out of any banking account or any sum deposited in the name of such solicitor or his firm or, as the case may be, such incorporated practice without the leave of the court and the court may make such order.

(2) This section applies to the following documents—

(a) all books, accounts, deeds, securities, papers and other documents in the possession or control of such solicitor or his firm or, as the case may be, such incorporated practice;

[2] (b) all books, accounts, deeds, securities, papers and other documents relating to any trust of which he is a sole trustee or is a co-trustee only with one or more of his partners or employees or, as the case may be, of which the incorporated practice or one of its employees is a sole trustee or it is a co-trustee only with one or more of its employees.

(3) Part II of Schedule 3 shall have effect in relation to the powers of the Council under this section.

NOTES

[1] As amended by the Law Reform (Miscellaneous Provisions) (Scotland) Act 1985 (c.73), Sched. 1, Pt. I, para.16.

[2] As amended by the Solicitors (Scotland) Act 1988 (c.42), Sched. 1, para.11.

[3] Read in conjunction with the European Communities (Lawyer's Practice) (Scotland) Regulations 2000 (SSI 2000/121), reg.37(2) and Sch.2 and the Solicitors (Scotland) Act 1980 (Foreign Lawyers and Multi-national Practices) Regulations 2004 (SSI 2004/383), reg.13.

Powers where delay alleged

[1,2] **39.**—(1) If

(a) a complaint is made to the Society that there has been undue delay on the part of a solicitor or an incorporated practice in dealing with any matter in which he or his firm or, as the case may be, it is or has been concerned in a professional capacity, or any matter relating to a trust of which he is or was the sole trustee, or a co-trustee only with one or more of his partners or employees or, as the case may be, the incorporated practice or one of its employees was the sole trustee or it was a co-trustee only with one or more of its employees, and

(b) the Council are of opinion that the delay ought to be investigated,

the Council may by notice in writing at any time, and from time to time, require the solicitor or, as the case may be, incorporated practice to give an explanation of the delay.

(2) Any notice given by the Council under subsection (1) may specify a period, not being less than 21 days, within which they require an explanation to be furnished; and if within that period the solicitor or, as the case may be, incorporated practice does not reply or fails to furnish an explanation which the Council regard as sufficient and satisfactory, and he or, as the case may be, it is so informed in writing, section 38 shall apply in relation to that solicitor and his firm or, as the case may be, to that incorporated practice in so far as it relates to documents or payments connected with the matter complained of (but not otherwise) and shall so apply notwithstanding that the Council may not have reasonable cause to believe that the solicitor or, as the case may be, incorporated practice has been guilty of any such dishonesty as is mentioned in section 43(2).

NOTE

[1] As amended by the Law Reform (Miscellaneous Provisions) (Scotland) Act 1985 (c.23), Sched. 1, Pt. I, para.17.

[2] Read in conjunction with the European Communities (Lawyer's Practice) (Scotland) Regulations 2000 (SSI 2000/121), reg.37(2) and Sch.2 and the Solicitors (Scotland) Act 1980 (Foreign Lawyers and Multi-national Practices) Regulations 2004 (SSI 2004/383), reg.13.

Powers where excessive fees etc. charged

[1,2] **39A.**—(1) This section applies where the Council are satisfied, in the case of any solicitor or incorporated practice, after inquiry and after giving the solicitor or incorporated practice an opportunity of being heard, that the solicitor or incorporated practice has issued an account for professional fees and outlays of an amount which is grossly excessive (whether or not the account has been paid by or on behalf of the client or debited by the solicitor or incorporated practice to the account of any sums held on behalf of the client).

(2) Where this section applies the Council may—

(a) in the case of a solicitor, withdraw his practising certificate; or

(b) in the case of an incorporated practice, withdraw the practising certificates of all or any of the solicitors who are directors of the incorporated practice;

and a certificate so withdrawn shall cease to have effect and the solicitor shall be suspended from practice as a solicitor.

(3) On being satisfied by the solicitor or, as the case may be, incorporated practice that he or it has complied with the requirements of subsection (4) the Council, unless they are of the opinion that the solicitor or incorporated practice is liable to disciplinary proceedings under Part IV, shall terminate the suspension from practice of the solicitor or solicitors concerned and shall restore to him or them any practising certificates held by him or them for the practice year then current.

(4) The requirements referred to in subsection (3) are—

(a) to submit the account to the Auditor of the Court of Session for taxation together with all documents in the possession or control of the solicitor or incorporated practice which relate to the matters in respect of which the account was issued; and

(b) to refund to the client a sum not less than the relevant amount.

(5) The Council shall be entitled to be represented at a diet for taxation by

virtue of subsection (4)(a) and to make representations to the Auditor of Court.

(6) Where, on taxation of an account by virtue of subsection (4)(a), the amount due in respect of the account as taxed is the amount specified in the account as issued, the fee of the Auditor of Court shall be paid by the Council; but in any other case the fee shall be paid by the solicitor or, as the case may be, the incorporated practice.

(7) In subsection (4)(b) "the relevant amount" is the amount (if any) by which the sum received by the solicitor or incorporated practice in respect of the accouint exceeds the amount due in respect of the account as taxed.

(8) A solicitor may, within 21 days of receiving written notice of a decision of the Council under subsection (2) to withdraw his practising certificate, appeal to the Court against that decision; and on any such appeal the Court may give such directions in the matter, including directions as to the expenses of the proceedings before the Court, as it may think fit; and the order of the Court shall be final.

(9) The withdrawal of a solicitor's practising certificate under subsection (2) shall be without prejudice to the operation of section 35(3) or section 37(8).

NOTE

[1] Inserted by the Solicitors (Scotland) Act 1988 (c.42), s.4.

[2] Read in conjunction with the European Communities (Lawyer's Practice) (Scotland) Regulations 2000 (SSI 2000/121), reg.37(2) and Sch.2 and the Solicitors (Scotland) Act 1980 (Foreign Lawyers and Multi-national Practices) Regulations 2004 (SSI 2004/383), reg.13.

Powers where failure to comply with accounts rules, etc.

[1,3] **40.**—[2] (1) Where the Council are satisfied, in the case of any solicitor or incorporated practice, after enquiry and after giving the solicitor or, as the case may be, incorporated practice an opportunity of being heard, that the solicitor or, as the case may be, incorporated practice has failed or is failing to comply with any provisions of—

(a) section 35 or the accounts rules made under that section, or
(b) section 37 or the accountant's certificate rules or other rules made under that section,

so far as applicable in his or, as the case may be, its case (in this section referred to as "the applicable provisions"), the Council may, subject to the provisions of this section,

(a) withdraw the practising certificate held by the solicitor; or as the case may be—
(b) withdraw the practising certificate or certificates or any or all of the solicitors who are directors of the incorporated practice,

and a certificate so withdrawn shall thereupon cease to have effect and the solicitor shall be suspended from practice as a solicitor.

(2) On being satisfied by the solicitor that he or, as the case may be, by the incorporated practice that it is able and willing to comply with the applicable provisions, the Council, unless they are of opinion that the solicitor or, as the case may be, the incorporated practice is liable to disciplinary proceedings under Part IV, shall terminate the suspension from practice of the solicitor or solicitors concerned and shall restore to him or them any practising certificate or certificates held by him or them for the practice year then current.

(3) Within 21 days after receiving written notice of a decision of the Council under this section to withdraw his practising certificate, or to refuse to terminate his suspension from practice, a solicitor may appeal to the court against the decision; and on any such appeal the court may give such directions in the matter, including directions as to the expenses of the proceedings before the court, as it may think fit; and the order of the court shall be final.

(4) Any withdrawal of a solicitor's practising certificate by the Council in exercise of the power conferred by subsection (1) shall be without prejudice to the operation of section 35(3) or section 37(8).

NOTES

[1] As amended by the Law Reform (Miscellaneous Provisions) (Scotland) Act 1985 (c.73), Sched. 1, Pt. I, para.18.

[2] As amended by the Solicitors (Scotland) Act 1988 (c.42), Sch.1, para.12.

[3] Read in conjunction with the European Communities (Lawyer's Practice) (Scotland) Regulations 2000 (SSI 2000/121), reg.37(2) and Sch.2 and the Solicitors (Scotland) Act 1980 (Foreign Lawyers and Multi-national Practices) Regulations 2004 (SSI 2004/383), reg.13.

Appointment of judicial factor

[1,2] **41.** Where the Council, in exercise of any power conferred on them by the accounts rules, have caused an investigation to be made of the books, accounts and other documents of a solicitor or an incorporated practice, and, on consideration of the report of the investigation, the Council are satisfied—

(a) that the solicitor or, as the case may be the incorporated practice has failed to comply with the provisions of those rules, and

(b) that, in the case of a solicitor, in connection with his practice as such either—

(i) his liabilities exceed his assets in the business, or

(ii) his books, accounts and other documents are in such a condition that it is not reasonably practicable to ascertain definitely whether his liabilities exceed his assets, or

(iii) there is reasonable ground for apprehending that a claim on the Guarantee Fund may arise; or

(c) that, in the case of an incorporated practice, either—

(i) its liabilities exceed its assets, or

(ii) its books, accounts and other documents are in such a condition that it is not reasonably practicable to ascertain definitely whether its liabilities exceed its assets, or

(iii) there is reasonable ground for apprehending that a claim on the guarantee fund may arise,

the Council may apply to the court for the appointment of a judicial factor on the estate of the solicitor or as the case may be, of the incorporated practice; and the court, on consideration of the said report and after giving the solicitor or as the case may be, the incorporated practice an opportunity of being heard, may appoint a judicial factor on such estate, or do otherwise as seems proper to it.

NOTE

[1] As amended by the Law Reform (Miscellaneous Provisions) (Scotland) Act 1985 (c.73), Sched. 1, Pt. I, para.19, and the Solicitors (Scotland) Act 1988 (c.42), Sched. 1, para.13 and Sched. 2.

[2] Read in conjunction with the European Communities (Lawyer's Practice) (Scotland) Regulations 2000 (SSI 2000/121), reg.37(2) and Sch.2 and the Solicitors (Scotland) Act 1980 (Foreign Lawyers and Multi-national Practices) Regulations 2004 (SSI 2004/383), reg.13.

Distribution of sums in client bank account

[1,2] **42.**—(1) Subject to the provisions of this section, where, in any of the events mentioned in subsection (2) or (2A), the sum at the credit of any client account kept by a solicitor or an incorporated practice (or where several such accounts are kept by him or, as the case may be, by it the total of the sums at the credit of those accounts) is less than the total of the sums received by him in the course of his practice on behalf of his clients or, as the case may be, by it on behalf of its clients and remaining due by him or, as the case may be, by it to them, then, notwithstanding any rule of law to the contrary, the sum at the credit of the client account (or where several such

accounts are kept, the total of the sums at the credit of those accounts) shall be divisible proportionately among the clients of the solicitor or, as the case may be, the incorporated practice according to the respective sums received by him in the course of his practice on their behalf or, as the case may be, by it on their behalf and remaining due by him or as the case may be, by it to them.

(2) The events to which subsection (1) applies are in relation to any solicitor—

(a) the sequestration of his estate;

(b) the granting by him of a trust deed for behoof of creditors;

(c) the appointment of a judicial factor on his estate.

(2A) The events to which subsection (1) applies are in relation to any incorporated practice—

(a) the making of an administration or winding up order or the appointment of a provisional liquidator, liquidator, receiver or judicial factor; or

(b) the passing of a resolution for voluntary winding up (other than one passed solely for the purposes of reconstruction or amalgamation with another incorporated practice).

[2] (3) Where a solicitor or an incorporated practice keeps an account at a bank in his or, as the case may be, its own name for a specified client no regard shall be had for the purposes of this section to the sum at the credit of that account or to any sums received by the solicitor in the course of his practice on behalf of that client or, as the case may be, by the incorporated practice on that behalf and remaining due by him or, as the case may be, by it to that client, so far as these are represented by the sum at the credit of that bank account; nor shall any regard be had for such purposes to any—

(a) deposit or share account with a building society; or

(b) account showing sums on loan to a local authority,

being in either case an account kept by the solicitor in his own name or, as the case may be, by the incorporated practice in its own name for a specified client.

(4) For the purposes of this section any reference to an account at a bank includes a reference to a deposit receipt at a bank.

NOTES

[1] As amended by the Law Reform (Miscellaneous Provisions) (Scotland) Act 1985 (c.73), Sched. 1, Pt. I, para.20.

[2] As amended by the Law Reform (Miscellaneous Provisions) (Scotland) Act 1980 (c.55), s.25, and the Solicitors (Scotland) Act 1988 (c.42), Sch.2.

[3] Read in conjunction with the European Communities (Lawyer's Practice) (Scotland) Regulations 2000 (SSI 2000/121), reg.37(2) and Sch.2 and the Solicitors (Scotland) Act 1980 (Foreign Lawyers and Multi-national Practices) Regulations 2004 (SSI 2004/383), reg.13.

Powers where inadequate professional services alleged

[1,3] **42A.**—(1) Where—

(a) the Council receive, from any person having an interest, a complaint that professional services provided by a solicitor in connection with any matter in which he has been instructed by a client were inadequate; and

(b) the Council, after inquiry and after giving the solicitor an opportunity to make representations, uphold the complaint,

they may take such of the steps mentioned in subsection (2) as they think fit.

[2](2) The steps referred to in subsection (1) are—

(a) to determine that the amount of the fees and outlays to which the solicitor shall be entitled for the services shall be—

(i) nil; or

(ii) such amount as the Council may specify in the determination,

and to direct the solicitor to comply, or secure compliance, with such of the requirements set out in subsection (3) as appear to them to be necessary to give effect to the determination;

(b) to direct the solicitor to secure the rectification at his own expense of any such error, omission or other deficiency arising in connection with the services as the Council may specify;

(c) to direct the solicitor to take, at his own expense, such other action in the interests of the client as the Council may specify;

[4] (d) to direct the solicitor to pay to the client by way of compensation such sum, not exceeding £5,000, as the Council may specify.

(3) The requirements referred to in subsection (2)(a) are—

(a) to refund, whether wholly or to any specified extent, any amount already paid by or on behalf of the client in respect of the fees and outlays of the solicitor in connection with the services;

(b) to waive, whether wholly or to any specified extent, the right to recover those fees and outlays.

(4) Before making a determination in accordance with subsection (2)(a) the Council may submit the solicitor's account for the fees and outlays to the Auditor of the Court of Session for taxation.

(5) Where a solicitor in respect of whom a complaint of inadequate professional services is made was, at the time when the services were provided, an employee of another solicitor, a direction under this section shall specify and apply to that other solicitor as well as the solicitor in respect of whom the complaint is made.

(6) The Council shall intimate a determination or direction made under this section to every solicitor specified in it by sending a copy of the determination or direction to him.

(7) A solicitor in respect of whom a determination or direction has been made under this section may, within 21 days of the date on which the determination or direction is intimated to him, appeal to the Tribunal against the determination or direction.

(8) In the foregoing provisions of this section—

"client", in relation to any matter in which a solicitor has been instructed, includes any person on whose behalf the person who gave the instructions was acting;

"complaint" includes a complaint of provision of inadequate professional services remitted to the Council by the Tribunal under paragraph 8A of Schedule 4; and

"solicitor" includes—

(a) any solicitor, whether or not he had a practising certificate in force at the time of provision of the professional services which are alleged to be inadequate, and notwithstanding that subsequent to that time he has had his name removed from or struck off the roll, ceased to practise or been suspended from practice;

(b) a firm of solicitors, whether or not, since the provision of the professional services which are alleged to be inadequate—

(i) there has been any change in the firm by the addition of a new partner or the death or resignation of an existing partner; or

(ii) the firm has ceased to practise; and

(c) an incorporated practice, whether or not, since the provision of the professional services which are alleged to be inadequate—

(i) there has been any change in the persons exercising the management and control of the practice; or

(ii) the practice has ceased to be recognised by virtue of section 34(1A) or has been wound up.

NOTES

[1] Inserted by the Solicitors (Scotland) Act 1988 (c.42), s.1.

[2] As amended by the Law Reform (Miscellaneous Provisions) (Scotland) Act 1990 (c.40), Sch.8, para.29(8).

[3]Read in conjunction with the European Communities (Lawyer's Practice) (Scotland) Regulations 2000 (SSI 2000/121), reg.37(2) and Sch.2 and the Solicitors (Scotland) Act 1980 (Foreign Lawyers and Multi-national Practices) Regulations 2004 (SSI 2004/383), reg.13.

[4]As amended by the Solicitors (Scotland) Act 1980 (Compensation for Inadequate Professional Services) Order 2004 (SSI 2004/550) (effective April 1, 2005), art.2.

Inadequate professional services: Council's powers to monitor compliance with directions

[1,2] **42B.**—(1) The Council shall, by notice in writing, require every solicitor specified in—

(a) a direction made under section 42A; or

(b) such a direction as confirmed or varied on appeal by—

(i) the Tribunal; or

(ii) the Court,

to give, within such period being not less than 21 days as the notice may specify, an explanation of the steps which he has taken to comply with the direction.

(2) Where an appeal is made under subsection (7) of section 42A against a direction made under that section, any notice under subsection (1)(a) above relating to that direction shall cease to have effect.

(3) Where an appeal is made by virtue of subsection (2) of section 53B against a decision of the Tribunal under subsection (1) of that section, any notice under subsection (1)(b)(i) above relating to the direction confirmed or varied by that decision shall cease to have effect.

(4) In this section "solicitor" has the same meaning as in section 42A(8).

NOTE

[1] Inserted by the Solicitors (Scotland) Act 1988,(c.40), s.1.

[2]Read in conjunction with the European Communities (Lawyer's Practice) (Scotland) Regulations 2000 (SSI 2000/121), reg.37(2) and Sch.2 and the Solicitors (Scotland) Act 1980 (Foreign Lawyers and Multi-national Practices) Regulations 2004 (SSI 2004/383), reg.13.

Powers to examine documents and demand explanations in connection with complaints

[1,2] **42C.**—(1) Where the Council are satisfied that it is necessary for them to do so for the purpose of investigating a complaint made to them or remitted to them by the Tribunal alleging—

(a) professional misconduct by a solicitor;

(b) the failure of an incorporated practice to comply with any provision of this Act or of rules made under this Act applicable to that practice; or

(c) the provision by a solicitor or an incorporated practice of inadequate professional services,

the Council may give notice in writing in accordance with subsection (2) to the solicitor or his firm or to the incorporated practice or, where the solicitor is an employee of a firm or of an incorporated practice, to his employer.

(2) A notice under subsection (1) may require—

(a) the production or delivery to any person appointed by the Council, at a time and place specified in the notice, of all documents to which this section applies which are in the possession or control of the solicitor, firm or incorporated practice and relate to the matters to which the complaint relates (whether or not they relate also to other matters); and

(b) an explanation, within such period, not being less than 21 days, as the notice may specify, from the solicitor, firm or incorporated practice regarding the matters to which the complaint relates.

(3) This section applies to the documents specified in section 38(2).

(4) Part II of Schedule 3 shall have effect in relation to the powers conferred by subsection (1) to require the production or delivery of documents as it has effect in relation to the powers conferred by section 38, but with the following modifications—

(a) for the references in that Part to section 38 there shall be substituted references to this section; and

(b) for the reference in paragraph 5(1) in that Part to a person failing to produce or deliver documents immediately on being required by the Council to do so there shall be substituted a reference to a person failing to produce or deliver the documents within the time specified in the notice under subsection (1) of this section.

NOTE

[1] Inserted by the Solicitors (Scotland) Act 1988 (c.42), s.2.

[2] Read in conjunction with the European Communities (Lawyer's Practice) (Scotland) Regulations 2000 (SSI 2000/121), reg.37(2) and Sch.2 and the Solicitors (Scotland) Act 1980 (Foreign Lawyers and Multi-national Practices) Regulations 2004 (SSI 2004/383), reg.13.

Protection of clients

Guarantee Fund

[6] **43.**—(1) There shall be a fund to be called "The Scottish Solicitors Guarantee Fund" (in this Act referred to as "the Guarantee Fund"), which shall be vested in the Society and shall be under the control and management of the Council.

(2) Subject to the provisions of this section and of Schedule 3 the Guarantee Fund shall be held by the Society for the purpose of making grants in order to compensate persons who in the opinion of the Council suffer pecuniary loss by reason of dishonesty on the part of

[3] (a) any solicitor, registered foreign lawyer or registered European lawyer in practice in the United Kingdom, or any employee of such solicitor, registered foreign lawyer or registered European lawyer in connection with the practice of the solicitor, registered foreign lawyer or registered European lawyer, whether or not he had a practising certificate in force when the act of dishonesty was committed, and notwithstanding that subsequent to the commission of that act he may have died or had his name removed from or struck off the roll or may have ceased to practise or been suspended from practice; or

[3] (b) any incorporated practice or any director, manager, secretary or other employee of an incorporated practice, notwithstanding that subsequent to the commission of that act it may have ceased to be recognised under section 34(1A) or have been wound up.

(3) No grant may be made under this section—

(a) in respect of a loss made good otherwise;

(b) in respect of a loss which in the opinion of the Council has arisen while the solicitor was suspended from practice;

(c) to a solicitor or his representatives in respect of a loss suffered by him or them in connection with his practice as a solicitor by reason of dishonesty on the part of a partner or employee of his;

[1] (*cc*) to an incorporated practice or any director or member thereof in respect of a loss suffered by it or him by reason of dishonesty on the part of any director, manager, secretary or other employee of the incorporated practice in connection with the practice;

(d) unless an application for a grant is made to the Society in such manner, and within such period after the date on which the loss first came to the knowledge of the applicant, as may be prescribed by rules made under Schedule 3;

[4] (e) in respect of any default of a registered European lawyer, or any of his employees or partners, where such act or default takes place outside Scotland, unless the Council is satisfied that the act or default is closely connected with the registered European lawyer's practice in Scotland;

[5] (f) in respect of any act or default of a registered foreign lawyer, or any of his employees or partners, where such act or default takes place outside Scotland, unless the Council is satisfied that the act or default is closely connected with the registered foreign

lawyer's practice, or any of his partners' practice, in Scotland; or

[5] (g) in respect of any act or default of any member, director, manager, secretary or other employee of an incorporated practice which is a multi-national practice, where such act or default takes place outside Scotland, unless the Council is satisfied that the act or default is closely connected with the incorporated practice's practice in Scotland.

(4) The decision of the Council with respect to any application for a grant shall be final.

(5) The Council may refuse to make a grant, or may make a grant only to a limited extent, if they are of opinion that there has been negligence on the part of the applicant or of any person for whom he is responsible which has contributed to the loss in question.

(6) The Council or any committee appointed by them may administer oaths for the purpose of inquiry into any matters which affect the making or refusal of a grant from the Guarantee Fund.

(7) Part I of Schedule 3 shall have effect with respect to the Guarantee Fund, including the making of contributions thereto by solicitors and the administration and management of the Fund by the Council; but nothing in that Schedule shall apply to or in the case of a solicitor—

(a) who is not in practice as a solicitor; or

(b) who is suspended from practice as a solicitor during suspension; or

(c) who is in any such employment as is specified in section 35(4) or in the employment of an incorporated practice;

but where any solicitor in any such employment as is mentioned in paragraph (c) engages in private practice as a solicitor, the said Schedule and the other provisions of this Act relating to the Guarantee Fund shall apply to him and in his case so far as regards such private practice.

NOTES

[1] Inserted by the Law Reform (Miscellaneous Provisions) (Scotland) Act 1985 (c.73), s. 56 and Sched. 1, Pt. I, para.21.

[2] As amended by the Law Reform (Miscellaneous Provisions) (Scotland) Act 1985 (c.73), s.56 and Sched.1, Pt 1, para.21(c).

[3] As amended by the European Communities (Lawyer's Practice) (Scotland) Regulations 2000 (SSI 2000/121), reg.37(1) and Sch.1, para.1(11)(a) and by the Solicitors (Scotland) Act 1980 (Foreign Lawyers and Multi-national Practices) Regulations 2004 (SSI 2004/383), reg.10.

[4] Inserted by the European Communities (Lawyer's Practice) (Scotland) Regulations 2000 (SSI 2000/121), reg.37(1) and Sch.1, para.1(11)(b) (effective May 22, 2000).

[5] Inserted by the Solicitors (Scotland) Act 1980 (Foreign Lawyers and Multi-national Practices) Regulations 2004 (SSI 2004/383), reg.10.

[6] Read in conjunction with the Solicitors (Scotland) Act 1980 (Foreign Lawyers and Multi-national Practices) Regulations 2004 (SSI 2004/383), reg.13.

Professional indemnity

[1,2] **44.**—(1) The Council may make rules with the concurrence of the Lord President concerning indemnity for solicitors and incorporated practices and former solicitors against any class of professional liability, and the rules may for the purpose of providing such indemnity do all or any of the following things, namely—

(a) authorise or require the Society to establish and maintain a fund or funds;

(b) authorise or require the Society to take out and maintain insurance with an authorised insurer;

(c) require solicitors or any specified class of solicitors and incorporated practices or any specified class thereof to take out and maintain insurance with an authorised insurer.

(2) The Society shall have power, without prejudice to any of its other powers, to carry into effect any arrangements which it considers necessary or expedient for the purpose of the rules.

(3) Without prejudice to the generality of subsections (1) and (2) rules made under this section—

(a) may specify the terms and conditions on which indemnity is to be available, and any circumstances in which the right to it is to be excluded or modified;

(b) may provide for the management, administration and protection of any fund maintained by virtue of subsection (1)(a) and require solicitors or any class of solicitors and incorporated practices or any class of incorporated practices to make payments to any such fund;

(c) may require solicitors or any class of solicitors and incorporated practices or any class of incorporated practices to make payments by way of premium on any insurance policy maintained by the Society by virtue of subsection (1)(b);

(d) may prescribe the conditions which an insurance policy must satisfy for the purpose of subsection (1)(c);

(e) may authorise the Society to determine the amount of any payments required by the rules subject to such limits, or in accordance with such provisions, as may be prescribed by the rules;

(f) may specify circumstances in which, where a solicitor or incorporated practice for whom indemnity is provided has failed to comply with the rules, proceedings in respect of sums paid by way of indemnity in connection with a matter in relation to which he or, as the case may be, it has failed to comply may be taken against him or, as the case may be, it by the Society or by insurers;

(g) may specify circumstances in which solicitors and incorporated practices are exempt from the rules;

(h) may empower the Council to take such steps as they consider necessary or expedient to ascertain whether or not the rules are being complied with; and

(i) may contain incidental, procedural or supplementary provisions.

(4) Failure to comply with rules made under this section may be treated as professional misconduct for the purposes of Part IV, and any person may make a complaint in respect of that failure to the Discipline Tribunal.

[3] (5) In this section an "authorised insurer" is—

(a) a person who has permission under Part 4 of the Financial Services and Markets Act 2000 to effect or carry out contracts of general liability insurance;

(b) a person who has permission under Part 4 of that Act to effect or carry out contracts of insurance relating to accident, sickness, credit, suretyship, miscellaneous financial loss and legal expenses;

(c) an EEA firm of the kind mentioned in paragraph 5(d) of Schedule 3 to that Act, which has permission under paragraph 15 of that Schedule (as a result of qualifying for authorisation under paragraph 12 of that Schedule) to effect or carry out contracts of general liability insurance; or

(d) an EEA firm of the kind mentioned in paragraph 5(d) of Schedule 3 to that Act, which has permission under paragraph 15 of that Schedule (as a result of qualifying for authorisation under paragraph 12 of that Schedule) to effect or carry out contracts relating to accident, sickness, credit, suretyship, miscellaneous financial loss and legal expenses;

"professional liability" means any civil liability incurred by a solicitor or former solicitor in connection with his practice or in connection with any trust of which he is or formerly was a trustee and, as respects incorporated practices, means any liability incurred by it which if it had been incurred by a solicitor would constitute such civil liability.

[3] (6) The definition of "authorised insurer" in subsection (5) must be read with—

(a) section 22 of the Financial Services and Markets Act 2000;

(b) any relevant order under that section; and

(c) Schedule 2 to that Act.

NOTES

[1] As amended by the Law Reform (Miscellaneous Provisions) (Scotland) Act 1985 (c.73), Sched. 1, Pt. I, para.22, with effect from 30th December 1985.

[2] Read in conjunction with the European Communities (Lawyer's Practice) (Scotland) Regulations 2000 (SSI 2000/121), reg.37(2) and Sch.2 and the Solicitors (Scotland) Act 1980 (Foreign Lawyers and Multi-national Practices) Regulations 2004 (SSI 2004/383), reg.14.

[3] Inserted by the Financial Services and Markets Act 2000 (Consequential Amendments and Repeals) Order 2001, (SI 2001/3649), art.223.

Safeguarding interests of clients of solicitor struck off or suspended

[1,2] **45.**—(1) The following provisions of this section shall have effect in relation to the practice of a solicitor whose name is struck off the roll or who is suspended from practice as a solicitor under any provision of this Act and, in relation to any incorporated practice, the recognition under section 34(1A) of which is revoked.

(2) In the case of a solicitor, the solicitor shall within 21 days of the material date satisfy the Council that he has made suitable arrangements for making available to his clients or to some other solicitor or solicitors or incorporated practice instructed by his clients or by himself—

(a) all deeds, wills, securities, papers, books of accounts, records, vouchers and other documents in his or his firm's possession or control which are held on behalf of his clients or which relate to any trust of which he is sole trustee or co-trustee only with one or more of his partners or employees, and

(b) all sums of money due from him or his firm or held by him or his firm on behalf of his clients or subject to any such trust as aforesaid.

(2A) In the case of an incorporated practice, it shall within 21 days of the material date satisfy the Council that it has made suitable arrangements for making available to its clients or to some other solicitor or solicitors or incorporated practice instructed by its clients or itself—

(a) all deeds, wills, securities, papers, books of accounts, records, vouchers and other documents in its possession or control which are held on behalf of its clients or which relate to any trust of which it is sole trustee or co-trustee only with one or more of its employees; and

(b) all sums of money due from it or held by it on behalf of its clients or subject to any trust as aforesaid.

(3) If the solicitor or as the case may be, incorporated practice fails so to satisfy the Council the provisions of section 38 shall apply in relation to that solicitor or as the case may be, incorporated practice, notwithstanding that the Council may not have reasonable cause to believe that he or, as the case may be, any director, manager, secretary or other employee of the incorporated practice has been guilty of any such dishonesty as is mentioned in section 43(2).

(4) If the solicitor, immediately before the striking off or, as the case may be, the suspension, was a sole solicitor, the right to operate on, or otherwise deal with, any client account in the name of the solicitor or his firm shall on the occurrence of that event vest in the Society (notwithstanding any enactment or rule of law to the contrary) to the exclusion of any other person.

(5) In this section—

"material date" means whichever is the latest of—

(a) the date when the order of the Tribunal or court by or in pursuance of which the solicitor is struck off the roll or suspended from practice or, as the case may be, the recognition under section 34(1A) is revoked is to take effect;

(b) the last date on which

(i) an appeal against that order may be lodged or an application may be made to the court under section 54(2), or

(ii) an appeal against a decision of the Council under section 40 may be lodged;

(c) the date on which any such appeal is dismissed or abandoned; and

[3] "principal" means a solicitor who is a sole practitioner or is a partner in a firm of two or more solicitors or is a director of an incorporated practice which is a company or a solicitor who is a member of a multi-national practice having its principal place of business in Scotland;

"sole solicitor" means a solicitor practising under his own name or as a single solicitor under a firm name.

NOTES

[1] As amended by the Law Reform (Miscellaneous Provisions) (Scotland) Act 1985 (c.73), Sched. 1, Pt. I, para.23, with effect from 30th December 1985.

[2] Read in conjunction with the European Communities (Lawyer's Practice) (Scotland) Regulations 2000 (SSI 2000/121), reg.37(2) and Sch.2 and the Solicitors (Scotland) Act 1980 (Foreign Lawyers and Multi-national Practices) Regulations 2004 (SSI 2004/383), reg.13 (except with regard to s.45(4).

[3] As inserted by the Legal Profession and Legal Aid (Scotland) Act 2007 (asp 5) s.60(2)(b) (effective November 23, 2007).

Safeguarding interests of clients in certain other cases

[1] **46.**—(1) Where the Council are satisfied that a sole solicitor is incapacitated by illness or accident to such an extent as to be unable to operate on, or otherwise deal with, any client account in the name of the solicitor or his firm, and that no other arrangements acceptable to the Council have been made, the right to operate on, or otherwise deal with, that account shall vest in the Society (notwithstanding any enactment or rule of law to the contrary) to the exclusion of any other person so long, but only so long, as the Council are satisfied that such incapacity and absence of other acceptable arrangements continues.

(2) Where a sole solicitor ceases to practise for any reason other than that his name has been struck off the roll or that he has been suspended from practice, and the Council are not satisfied that suitable arrangements have been made for making available to his clients or to some other solicitor or solicitors instructed by his clients or on their behalf—

(a) all deeds, wills, securities, papers, books of accounts, records, vouchers and other documents in his or his firm's possession or control which are held on behalf of his clients or which relate to any trust of which he is the sole trustee, or a co-trustee only with one or more of his employees, and

(b) all sums of money due from him or his firm or held by him or his firm on behalf of his clients or subject to any such trust as aforesaid,

the provisions of section 38 shall apply in relation to that solicitor, notwithstanding that the Council may not have reasonable cause to believe that he has been guilty of any such dishonesty as is mentioned in section 43(2).

(3) Where a sole solicitor dies—

(a) the right to operate on or otherwise deal with any client account in the name of the solicitor or his firm shall vest in the Society (notwithstanding any enactment or rule of law to the contrary) to the exclusion of any personal representatives of the solicitor, and shall be exercisable as from the death of the solicitor; and

(b) if the Council are not satisfied that suitable arrangements have been made for making available to the solicitor's clients or to some other solicitor or solicitors instructed by his clients or on their behalf—

(i) all deeds, wills, securities, papers, books of accounts, records, vouchers and other documents which were in his or his firm's possession or control which were held on behalf of his clients or which relate to any trust of which he was the sole trustee, or a co-trustee only with one or more of his employees, and

(ii) all sums of money which were due from him or his firm or were held by him or his firm on behalf of his clients or subject to any such trust as aforesaid,

the provisions of section 38 shall apply in relation to that solicitor notwithstanding that the Council may not have reasonable cause to believe that he had been guilty of any such dishonesty as is mentioned in section 43(2).

(4) In a case where the Society have operated on or otherwise dealt with a client account by virtue of subsection (3) the Society shall be entitled to recover from the estate of the solicitor who has died such reasonable expenses as the Society have thereby incurred.

[2] (4A) Part II of Schedule 3 has effect in relation to the powers of the Council under subsection (2) or (3).

(5) In this section "sole solicitor" has the same meaning as in section 45.

NOTE

[1] Read in conjunction with the European Communities (Lawyer's Practice) (Scotland) Regulations 2000 (SSI 2000/121), reg.37(2) and Sch.2 (effective May 22, 2000).

[2] As inserted by the Legal Profession and Legal Aid (Scotland) Act 2007 (asp 5) Sch.5, para.1(16)(c) (effective November 23, 2007).

Restriction on employing solicitor struck off or suspended

[1,2] **47.**—(1) Unless he has the written permission of the Council to do so, a solicitor shall not, in connection with his practice as a solicitor and, unless it has such permission, an incorporated practice shall not, employ or remunerate any person who to his or, as the case may be, its knowledge is disqualified from practising as a solicitor by reason of the fact that his name has been struck off the roll or that he is suspended from practice as a solicitor.

(2) Any permission given by the Council for the purposes of subsection (1) may be given for such period and subject to such conditions as the Council think fit.

(3) A solicitor or, as the case may be, incorporated practice aggrieved by the refusal of the Council to grant any such permission as aforesaid, or by any conditions attached by the Council to the grant thereof, may appeal to the court; and on any such appeal the court may give such directions in the matter as it thinks fit.

(4) If any solicitor acts in contravention of this section or of any condition subject to which any permission has been given thereunder, his name shall be struck off the roll or he shall be suspended from practice as a solicitor for such period as the Tribunal, or, in the case of an appeal, the court, may think fit and if any incorporated practice so acts its recognition under section 34(1A) shall be revoked.

NOTES

[1] As amended by the Law Reform (Miscellaneous Provisions) (Scotland) Act 1985 (c.73), Sch.1, Pt I, para.24.

[2] Read in conjunction with the European Communities (Lawyer's Practice) (Scotland) Regulations 2000 (SSI 2000/121), reg.37(2) and Sch.2 and the Solicitors (Scotland) Act 1980 (Foreign Lawyers and Multi-national Practices) Regulations 2004 (SSI 2004/383), reg.13.

48. [*Repealed by the Law Reform (Miscellaneous Provisions) (Scotland) Act 1985, Sch.1, Pt II, para.5.*]

PART IV

COMPLAINTS AND DISCIPLINARY PROCEEDINGS

Lay Observer

49. [*Repealed by the Law Reform (Miscellaneous Provisions) (Scotland) Act 1990, Sch.9.*]

The Scottish Solicitors' Discipline Tribunal

The Tribunal

[1] **50.**—(1) For the purposes of this Part of this Act and sections 16 to 23 (which relate to the provision of conveyancing and executry services) of the 1990 Act there shall be a tribunal, which shall be known as the Scottish Solicitors' Discipline Tribunal and is in this Act referred to as "the Tribunal".

(2) Part I of Schedule 4 shall have effect in relation to the constitution of the Tribunal.

NOTE

[1] As amended by the Public Appointments and Public Bodies etc. (Scotland) Act 2003 (asp 4), s.13 (effective August 15, 2003).

Complaints to Tribunal

[1,4] **51.**—(1) A complaint may be made to the Tribunal by the Council; and, for the purpose of investigating and prosecuting complaints, the Council may appoint a solicitor to act as fiscal.

[5] (1A) In subsection (1) above, without prejudice to the generality of that subsection, the reference to a complaint includes a complaint in respect of conveyancing and executry practitioners and the provision by them of conveyancing and executry services (those expressions having the meanings given in section 23 of the 1990 Act).

(2) The persons mentioned in subsection (3) may report to the Tribunal any case where it appears that a solicitor may have been guilty of professional misconduct (including any case where it appears that a solicitor may have been seeking to make extraordinary and apparently unjustified claims against his client or against the Scottish Legal Aid Fund) or an incorporated practice may have failed to comply with any provision of this Act or of rules made under this Act applicable to it or a solicitor or an incorporated practice may have provided inadequate professional services, and any such report shall be treated by the Tribunal as a complaint under subsection (1).

[2] (3) The persons referred to in subsection (2) are—

(a) the Lord Advocate;

[3](aa) the Advocate General for Scotland;

(b) any judge;

(ba) the Dean of the Faculty of Advocates;

(c) the Auditor of the Court of Session;

(d) the Auditor of any sheriff court;

(e) the Scottish Legal Aid Board;

(f) the Scottish legal services ombudsman.

(4) Where a report is made to the Tribunal under subsection (2) the Tribunal may, if it thinks fit, appoint a solicitor to prosecute the complaint and the expenses of the solicitor, so far as not recoverable from the solicitor complained against, shall be paid out of the funds of the Tribunal.

NOTES

[1] As amended by the Law Reform (Miscellaneous Provisions) (Scotland) Act 1985, Sch.1,

Pt I, para.26, the Legal Aid (Scotland) Act 1986, Sched. 3, para.8, and the Solicitors (Scotland) Act 1988, Sched. 1, para.14.

[2] As amended by the Law Reform (Miscellaneous Provisions) (Scotland) Act 1990, Sched. 8, para.29(9).

[3] As amended by SI 1999/1042, Art. 4, Sch.2, para.7 (effective on commencement of s.44(1)(c) of the Scotland Act (c.44): May 20, 1999).

[4] Read in conjunction with the European Communities (Lawyer's Practice) (Scotland) Regulations 2000 (SSI 2000/121), reg.37(2) and Sch.2 and the Solicitors (Scotland) Act 1980 (Foreign Lawyers and Multi-national Practices) Regulations 2004 (SSI 2004/383), reg.13 (except the references to a solicitor appointed under subsections (1) and (4)).

[5] Inserted by the Public Appointments and Public Bodies etc. (Scotland) Act 2003 (asp 4), s.13 (effective August 15, 2003).

Procedure on complaints to Tribunal

[1,2] **52.**—[3] (1) Part II of Schedule 4 shall have effect in relation to the procedure and powers of the Tribunal in relation to any complaint concerning a solicitor or an incorporated practice.

[4] (2) Subject to the other provisions of this Part, the provisions of sections 16 to 23 of the 1990 Act, and of any rules of court made under this Act, the Tribunal, with the concurrence of the Lord President, may make rules—

(a) for regulating the making, hearing and determining of complaints made to it under this Act; and

(aa) for regulating the making, hearing and determining of appeals made to it under section 42A(7) or 53D(1);

(ab) for regulating the making, hearing and determining of—

(i) inquiries under subsection (2A) of section 20 of the 1990 Act; and

(ii) appeals under subsection (11)(b) of that section;

(b) generally as to the procedure of the Tribunal (including provision for hearings taking place in public or wholly or partly in private).

NOTES

[1] As amended by the Law Reform (Miscellaneous Provisions) (Scotland) Act 1985, Sched. 1, Pt I, para.27, the Solicitors (Scotland) Act 1988, Sched. 1, para.15 and the Public Appointments and Public Bodies etc. (Scotland) Act 2003 (asp 4), s.13 (effective August 15, 2003).

[2] Read in conjunction with the European Communities (Lawyer's Practice) (Scotland) Regulations 2000 (SSI 2000/121), reg.37(2) and Sch.2 (effective May 22, 2000).

[3] Read in conjunction with the Solicitors (Scotland) Act 1980 (Foreign Lawyers and Multi-national Practices) Regulations 2004 (SSI 2004/383), reg.13.

[4] Read in conjunction with the Solicitors (Scotland) Act 1980 (Foreign Lawyers and Multi-national Practices) Regulations 2004 (SSI 2004/383), reg.14.

Powers of Tribunal

[1,4] **53.**—(1) Subject to the other provisions of this Part, the powers exercisable by the Tribunal under subsection (2) shall be exercisable if—

(a) after holding an inquiry into a complaint against a solicitor the Tribunal is satisfied that he has been guilty of professional misconduct, or

(b) a solicitor has (whether before or after enrolment as a solicitor), been convicted by any court of an act involving dishonesty or has been sentenced to a term of imprisonment of not less than 2 years, or

(c) an incorporated practice has been convicted by any court of an offence, which conviction the Tribunal is satisfied renders it unsuitable to continue to be recognised under section 34(1A); or

(d) after holding an inquiry into a complaint, the Tribunal is satisfied that an incorporated practice has failed to comply with any provision of this Act or of rules made under this Act applicable to it.

[2] (2) Subject to subsection (1), the Tribunal may—

(a) order that the name of the solicitor be struck off the roll; or

(b) order that the solicitor be suspended from practice as a solicitor for such time as it may determine; or (ba) order that any right of audience held by the solicitor by virtue of section 25A be suspended or revoked;

(c) subject to subsection (3), impose on the solicitor or, as the case may be, the incorporated practice a fine not exceeding £10,000; or

(d) censure the solicitor or, as the case may be, the incorporated practice; or

(e) impose such fine and censure him or, as the case may be, it; or

(f) order that the recognition under section 34(1A) of the incorporated practice be revoked; or

(g) order that an investment business certificate issued to a solicitor, a firm of solicitors or an incorporated practice be—

(i) suspended for such time as they may determine; or

(ii) subject to such terms and conditions as it may direct; or

(iii) revoked.

(3) The Tribunal shall not impose a fine under subsection (2)(c) in any of the circumstances mentioned in subsection (1)(b).

(3A) The powers conferred by subsection (2)(c), (d) and (e) may be exercised by the Tribunal—

(a) in relation to a former solicitor, notwithstanding that his name has been struck off the roll or that he has, since the date of the misconduct, conviction or sentence referred to in subsection (1)(*a*) or (*b*), ceased to practise as a solicitor or been suspended from practice;

(*b*) in relation to a body corporate which was formerly an incorporated practice, notwithstanding that the body has, since the date of the conviction or failure referred to in subsection (1)(*c*) or (*d*), ceased to be recognised as an incorporated practice by virtue of section 34(1A).

(3B) The power conferred by subsection (2)(*ba*) may be exercised by the Tribunal either independently of, or in conjunction with, any other power conferred by that subsection.

(4) Any fine imposed by the Tribunal under subsection (2) shall be forfeit to Her Majesty.

(5) Where the Tribunal have exercised the power conferred by subsection (2) to censure, or impose a fine on, a solicitor, or both to censure and impose a fine, the Tribunal may order that the solicitor's practising certificate shall be subject to such terms and conditions as the Tribunal may direct; and the Council shall give effect to any such order of the Tribunal.

[1] (6) Where the Tribunal order that the name of a solicitor be struck off the roll, or that the solicitor be suspended from practice as a solicitor, or that any right of audience held by the solicitor by virtue of section 25A be suspended or revoked, the Tribunal may direct that the order shall take effect on the date on which it is intimated to the solicitor; and if any such direction is given the order shall take effect accordingly.

(6A) Where the Tribunal order that the recognition under section 34(1A) of an incorporated practice be revoked, the Tribunal shall direct that the order shall take effect on such date as the Tribunal specifies, being a date not earlier than 60 days after its order is intimated to the incorporated practice, and such an order shall take effect accordingly.

(6B) Where the Tribunal make an order under subsection (2)(*g*), they may direct that the order shall take effect on the date on which it is intimated to the solicitor, firm or incorporated practice; and if any such direction is given the order shall take effect accordingly.

(7) Where in relation to any such order as is mentioned in subsection (6) or (6A) the Tribunal give a direction under subsection (6) or, as the case may be, subsection (6A) and an appeal against the order is taken to the court under section 54, the order shall continue to have effect pending the determination or abandonment of the appeal unless, on an application under subsection (2) of section 54, the court otherwise directs.

[3] (8) The Secretary of State may, by order made by statutory instrument

subject to annulment in pursuance of a resolution of either House of Parliament, amend—

(*a*) paragraph (*c*) of subsection (2) by substituting for the amount for the time being specified in that paragraph such other amount as appears to him to be justified by a change in the value of money;

(*b*) the definition of "investment business certificate" in subsection (7A) by substituting for the reference to Rule 2.2 of the Solicitors (Scotland) (Conduct of Investment Business) Practice Rules 1988, or such reference replacing that reference as may for the time being be specified in that subsection, a reference to such Practice Rule as may from time to time replace Rule 2.2.

NOTES

[1] As amended by the Law Reform (Miscellaneous Provisions) (Scotland) Act 1985, Sch.1, Pt. I, para.28, the Solicitors (Scotland) Act 1988, Sch.1, para.16, and the Law Reform (Miscellaneous Provisions) (Scotland) Act 1990, Sch.8, para.29(10).

[2] As amended by the Law Reform (Miscellaneous Provisions) (Scotland) Act 1980, s.24, and SI 1987 No. 333.

[3] Inserted by the Law Reform (Miscellaneous Provisions) (Scotland) Act 1980, s.24 and as amended by the 1988 Act as noted above.

[4] Read in conjunction with the European Communities (Lawyer's Practice) (Scotland) Regulations 2000 (SSI 2000/121), reg.37(2) and Sch.2 and the Solicitors (Scotland) Act 1980 (Foreign Lawyers and Multi-national Practices) Regulations 2004 (SSI 2004/383), reg.13 (except with regard to subsections (2)(g), (6B) and (8)(b)).

Inadequate professional services: powers of Tribunal

[1,3] **53A.**—(1) Subject to the other provisions of this Part where—

(*a*) a complaint is made to the Tribunal that professional services provided by a solicitor in connection with any matter in which he has been instructed by a client were inadequate; and

(*b*) the Tribunal, after inquiry and after giving the solicitor an opportunity to make representations, upholds the complaint,

it may take such of the steps mentioned in subsection (2) as it thinks fit.

[2] (2) The steps referred to in subsection (1) are—

(*a*) to determine that the amount of the fees and outlays to which the solicitor shall be entitled for the services shall be—

(i) nil; or

(ii) such amount as the Tribunal may specify in the determination,

and by order direct the solicitor to comply, or secure compliance, with such of the requirements set out in subsection (3) as appear to it to be necessary to give effect to the determination;

(*b*) to direct the solicitor to secure the rectification at his own expense of any such error, omission or other deficiency arising in connection with the services as the Tribunal may specify;

(*ba*) to order that any right of audience held by the solicitor by virtue of section 25A be suspended or revoked;

(*c*) to direct the solicitor to take, at his own expense, such other action in the interests of the client as the Tribunal may specify;

[4] (*d*) to direct the solicitor to pay to the client by way of compensation such sum, not exceeding £5,000, as the Tribunal may specify.

(3) The requirements referred to in subsection (2)(*a*) are—

(*a*) to refund, whether wholly or to any specified extent, any amount already paid by or on behalf of the client in respect of the fees and outlays of the solicitor in connection with the services;

(*b*) to waive, whether wholly or to any specified extent, the right to recover those fees and outlays.

(4) Before making a determination in accordance with subsection (2)(*a*) the Tribunal may submit the solicitor's account for the fees and outlays to the Auditor of the Court of Session for taxation.

(5) Where a solicitor in respect of whom a complaint of inadequate

professional services is made was, at the time when the services were provided, an employee of another solicitor, a direction under this section shall specify and apply to that other solicitor as well as the solicitor in respect of whom the complaint is made.

(6) A direction of the Tribunal under this section shall be enforceable in like manner as an extract registered decree arbitral in favour of the Council bearing a warrant for execution issued by the sheriff court of any sheriffdom in Scotland.

(7) Section 54(1) shall apply to a direction of the Tribunal under this section (but not to a decision to submit an account for taxation under subsection (4)) as it applies to a decision of the Tribunal relating to discipline under this Act.

(8) In the foregoing provisions of this section "solicitor" and "client" have the same meanings as in section 42A(8).

NOTES

[1] Inserted by the Solicitors (Scotland) Act 1988, s.3.

[2] As amended by the Law Reform (Miscellaneous Provisions) (Scotland) Act 1990, Sch.8, para.29(11).

[3] Read in conjunction with the European Communities (Lawyer's Practice) (Scotland) Regulations 2000 (SSI 2000/121), reg.37(2) and Sch.2 and the Solicitors (Scotland) Act 1980 (Foreign Lawyers and Multi-national Practices) Regulations 2004 (SSI 2004/383), reg.13.

[4] As amended by the Solicitors (Scotland) Act 1980 (Compensation for Inadequate Professional Services) Order 2004 (SSI 2004/550) (effective April 1, 2005), art.2.

Inadequate professional services: appeal to Tribunal against Council determination or direction

[1,2] **53B.**—(1) On an appeal to the Tribunal under section 42A(7) the Tribunal may quash, confirm or vary the determination or direction being appealed against.

(2) Section 54(1) shall apply to a decision of the Tribunal under subsection (1) as it applies to a decision of the Tribunal relating to discipline under this Act.

NOTE

[1] Inserted by the Solicitors (Scotland) Act 1988, s.3.

[2] Read in conjunction with the European Communities (Lawyer's Practice) (Scotland) Regulations 2000 (SSI 2000/121), reg.37(2) and Sch.2 and the Solicitors (Scotland) Act 1980 (Foreign Lawyers and Multi-national Practices) Regulations 2004 (SSI 2004/383), reg.13.

Inadequate professional services: enforcement by Tribunal of Council direction

[1,2] **53C.**—(1) Where a solicitor fails to comply with a direction given by the Council under section 42A (including, as the case may be, such a direction as confirmed or varied on appeal by the Tribunal or the Court) within the period specified in the notice relating to that direction given to the solicitor under section 42B(1), or such longer period as the Council may allow, the Council shall make a complaint to the Tribunal and may appoint a solicitor to represent them in connection with the complaint.

(2) If after inquiry into a complaint made under subsection (1) the Tribunal is satisfied that the solicitor has failed to comply with the direction the Tribunal may order that the direction, or such part of it as the Tribunal thinks fit, shall be enforceable in like manner as an extract registered decree arbitral in favour of the Council bearing a warrant for execution issued by the sheriff court of any sheriffdom in Scotland.

(3) Paragraph 9 of Schedule 4 shall not apply to a complaint made under subsection (1).

NOTE

[1] Inserted by the Solicitors (Scotland) Act 1988, s.3.

[2] Read in conjunction with the European Communities (Lawyer's Practice) (Scotland) Regulations 2000 (SSI 2000/121), reg.37(2) and Sch.2 and the Solicitors (Scotland) Act 1980 (Foreign Lawyers and Multi-national Practices) Regulations 2004 (SSI 2004/383), reg.13.

[1,2] **53D.**—(1) Where, in accordance with rules made under this Act, the Council suspend or withdraw an investment business certificate or impose conditions or restrictions on it the solicitor, firm of solicitors or incorporated practice to whom it was issued may, within 21 days of the date of intimation of the decision of the Council, appeal to the Tribunal against that decision.

(2) On an appeal to the Tribunal under subsection (1) the Tribunal may quash, confirm or vary the decision being appealed against.

(3) Section 54(1) shall apply to a decision of the Tribunal under subsection (2) as it applies to a decision of the Tribunal relating to discipline under this Act.

NOTE

[1] Inserted by the Solicitors (Scotland) Act 1988 (c.42), Sched. 1, para.17.

[2] Read in conjunction with the European Communities (Lawyer's Practice) (Scotland) Regulations 2000 (SSI 2000/121), reg.37(2) and Sch.2 (effective May 22, 2000).

Appeals from decisions of Tribunal

[1,2] **54.**—(1) Any person aggrieved by a decision of the Tribunal relating to discipline under this Act may within 21 days of the date on which the decision of the Tribunal is intimated to that person, appeal against the decision to the court, and on any such appeal the court may give such directions in the matter as it thinks fit, including directions as to the expenses of the proceedings before the court and as to any order by the Tribunal relating to expenses; and the order of the court shall be final.

(2) Where

(*a*) the Tribunal has exercised the power conferred by section 53(6) to direct that its decision shall take effect on the date on which it is intimated to the solicitor concerned, the solicitor may, within 21 days of that date, apply to the court for an order varying or quashing the direction in so far as it relates to the date of taking effect;

(*b*) the Tribunal has ordered the revocation of the recognition under section 34(1A) of an incorporated practice, the incorporated practice may within 21 days of the date when the order is intimated to it apply to the court for an order varying (subject to the limit of 60 days referred to in subsection (6A) of section 53) the direction under that subsection; and on any such application the court may make the order applied for or such other order with respect to the matter as it thinks fit.

NOTE

[1] As amended by the Law Reform (Miscellaneous Provisions) (Scotland) Act 1985 (c.73), Sched. 1, Pt. I, para.29.

[2] Read in conjunction with the European Communities (Lawyer's Practice) (Scotland) Regulations 2000 (SSI 2000/121), reg.37(2) and Sch.2 and the Solicitors (Scotland) Act 1980 (Foreign Lawyers and Multi-national Practices) Regulations 2004 (SSI 2004/383), reg.13.

The Court

Powers of court

[3] **55.**—[1] (1) In the case of professional misconduct by any solicitor the court may—

(*a*) cause the name of that solicitor to be struck off the roll; or

(*b*) suspend the solicitor from practice as a solicitor for such period as the court may determine; or

(*ba*) suspend the solicitor from exercising any right of audience held by him by virtue of section 25A for such period as the court may determine; or

(*bb*) revoke any right of audience so acquired by him; or

(*c*) fine the solicitor; or

(*d*) censure him; and in any of those events,

(*e*) find him liable in any expenses which may be involved in the proceedings before the court.

(2) Subject to subsection (3), a decision of the court under this section shall be final.

(3) A solicitor whose name has been struck off the roll in pursuance of an order made by the court under subsection (1), may apply to the court for an order directing his name to be restored to the roll and the court may make such order.

[2] (3A) A solicitor whose rights of audience under section 25A have been revoked in pursuance of an order made by the court under subsection (1) may apply to the court for an order restoring those rights, and the court may make such order.

(4) An application under subsection (3) shall be by way of petition and intimation of any such petition shall be made to the Tribunal who shall be entitled to appear and to be heard in respect of the application.

NOTES

[1] As amended by the Law Reform (Miscellaneous Provisions) (Scotland) Act 1990 (c.40), Sched. 8, para.29(12).

[2] Inserted by the Law Reform (Miscellaneous Provisions) (Scotland) Act 1990 (c.40), Sch.8, para.29(12).

[3] Read in conjunction with the European Communities (Lawyer's Practice) (Scotland) Regulations 2000 (SSI 2000/121), reg.37(2) and Sch.2 and the Solicitors (Scotland) Act 1980 (Foreign Lawyers and Multi-national Practices) Regulations 2004 (SSI 2004/383), reg.13 (except with regard to subsections (1)(ba) and (bb) and (3A)).

Saving for jurisdiction of courts

[1] **56.** Except as otherwise expressly provided, nothing in this Part shall affect the jurisdiction exercisable by the court, or by any inferior court, over solicitors.

NOTE

[1] Read in conjunction with the European Communities (Lawyer's Practice) (Scotland) Regulations 2000 (SSI 2000/121), reg.37(2) and Sch.2 and the Solicitors (Scotland) Act 1980 (Foreign Lawyers and Multi-national Practices) Regulations 2004 (SSI 2004/383), reg.13.

Further provision as to compensation awards

[1,2] **56A.**—(1) The taking of any steps under section 42A(2) or 53A(2) shall not be founded upon in any proceedings for the purpose of showing that the solicitor in respect of whom the steps were taken was negligent.

(2) A direction under section 42A(2)(*d*) or 53A(2)(*d*) to a solicitor to pay compensation to a client shall not prejudice any right of that client to take proceedings against that solicitor for damages in respect of any loss which he alleges he has suffered as a result of that solicitor's negligence, and any sum directed to be paid to that client under either of those provisions may be taken into account in the computation of any award of damages made to him in any such proceedings.

(3) The Secretary of State may by order made by statutory instrument amend subsection (2)(d) of sections 42A and 53A by substituting for the sum for the time being specified in those provisions such other sum as he considers appropriate.

(4) Before making any such order the Secretary of State shall consult the Council.

(5) An order made under this section shall be subject to annulment in pursuance of a resolution of either House of Parliament.

NOTE

[1] Inserted by the Law Reform (Miscellaneous Provisions) (Scotland) Act 1990 (c.40), Sch.8, para.29(13).

[2] Read in conjunction with the European Communities (Lawyer's Practice) (Scotland) Regulations 2000 (SSI 2000/121), reg.37(2) and Sch.2 and the Solicitors (Scotland) Act 1980 (Foreign Lawyers and Multi-national Practices) Regulations 2004 (SSI 2004/383), reg.13.

PART V

NOTARIES PUBLIC

Admission and enrolment of solicitors as notaries public

[1] **57.**—(1) The offices and functions of—

(a) the clerk to the admission of notaries public; and

(b) the keeper of the register of notaries public,

are hereby transferred to the Council.

[3] (2) Any solicitor qualified to practise in accordance with section 4 may apply to the court to be admitted as a notary public; and on any such application the court may so admit the applicant and may direct the Council to register him in the register of notaries public.

(2A) A petition by the Council under section 6(3A) for the admission of a person as a solicitor may, if the person so requests, include an application for the person's admission as a notary public; and an order on any such petition admitting that person as a solicitor may admit him as a notary public and direct the Council to register him in the register of notaries public.

(2B) A petition by a person under section 6(2) for his admission as a solicitor may include an application for his admission as a notary public; and an order on any such petition admitting that person as a solicitor may admit him as a notary public and direct the Council to register him in the register of notaries public.

(3) It shall not be necessary for any person to find caution on his admission as a notary public.

[2] (4) The procedure to be followed on any application by a person to be admitted a notary public may be prescribed by rules of court.

(5) The Council may charge such reasonable fees as they consider appropriate in respect of the admission of any person as a notary public.

NOTES

[1] As amended by the Law Reform (Miscellaneous Provisions) (Scotland) Act 1990 (c.40), s.37(2) (effective 20th July 1992: SI 1992/1599).

[2] As amended by the Solicitors (Scotland) Act 1988 (c.42), Sch.1, para.18 and Sch.2.

[3] As amended by the Legal Profession and Legal Aid (Scotland) Act 2007 (asp 5) s.62(2) (effective November 23, 2007).

Removal from and restoration to register of names of notaries public

[1] **58.**—(1) In the case of any person who is both a solicitor and a notary public, if his name is struck off the roll of solicitors or is removed from that roll in pursuance of an order under any provision of this Act, the Council shall forthwith strike off or, as the case may be, remove his name from the register of notaries public.

(2) If the name of any such person, having been struck off or removed from the roll as aforesaid, is subsequently restored thereto in pursuance of an order under any provision of this Act, the Council shall forthwith restore the name to the register of notaries public.

(3) Where a person who is both a solicitor and a notary public is suspended from practising as a solicitor under this Act the Council shall forthwith remove the person's name from the register of notaries public.

(4) If the suspension of such a person as is mentioned in subsection (3) is terminated or otherwise comes to an end the Council shall restore the person's name to the register.

[2] (5) Where a person who is a solicitor and a notary public no longer has in force a practising certificate, the Council shall forthwith remove the person's name from the register of notaries public.

[2](6) If the person mentioned in subsection (5) becomes qualified to practise as a solicitor in accordance with section 4, the Council shall restore the person's name to the register of notaries public.

NOTE

[1] As amended by the Law Reform (Miscellaneous Provisions) (Scotland) Act 1990 (c.40), s.37(3) (effective 20th July 1992: SI 1992/1599).

[2] As inserted by the Legal Profession and Legal Aid (Scotland) Act 2007 (asp 5) s.62(3) (effective November 23, 2007).

Authority of notaries public to administer oaths, etc.

59.—(1) Subject to subsection (2), in any case where the administration of an oath, or the receipt of an affidavit or solemn affirmation, is authorised by or under any enactment, it shall be lawful for the oath to be administered, or, as the case may be, for the affidavit or affirmation to be received, by a notary public.

[1](2) Nothing in this section applies to an oath or affirmation relating to any matter or thing relating to the preservation of the peace or to the prosecution, trial or punishment of an offence, or to any proceedings before either House of Parliament or any committee thereof or before the Scottish Parliament or any committee thereof.

(3) This section is without prejudice to any other statutory provision relating to the administration of oaths by notaries public.

NOTE

[1] As amended by SI 1999/1042, art.3, Sch.1, Pt I, para.8 (effective May 6, 1999).

Rules regarding notaries public

[1] **59A.**—(1) Subject to subsections (2) and (3), the Council may, if they think fit, make rules for regulating in respect of any matter the admission, enrolment and professional practice of notaries public.

(2) The Council shall, before making any rules under this section—

(a) send to each notary public a draft of the rules; and

(b) take into consideration any representations made by any notary public on the draft.

(3) Rules made under this section shall not have effect unless the Lord President, after considering any representations the Lord President thinks relevant, has approved the rules so made.

(4) If a notary public fails to comply with any rule made under this section that failure may be treated as professional misconduct or unsatisfactory professional conduct on the part of the solicitor who is the notary public.

NOTE

[1] As inserted by the Legal Profession and Legal Aid (Scotland) Act 2007 (asp 5) s.63 (effective November 23, 2007).

Offence for notaries public to act for unqualified persons

60. [*Repealed by the Solicitors (Scotland) Act 1988 (c.42), Sch.2.*]

PART VI

MISCELLANEOUS AND GENERAL

Miscellaneous

Multi-national practices

[1,2,3] **60A.**—(1) Subject to the provisions of this section, solicitors and incorporated practices may enter into multi-national practices with registered foreign lawyers.

(2) The Council shall maintain a register of foreign lawyers, and may

make rules with regard to registration; and, without prejudice to the generality of the foregoing, such rules may include provision as to—

(a) the manner in which applications for registration are to be made;

[4] (aa) the information which shall accompany such applications;

(b) the fees payable in respect of such applications;

(c) conditions which may be imposed in respect of registration; and

(d) the period for which any such registration is to run.

(3) Section 34(2) and (3) apply to rules made under subsection (2) as they apply to rules made under that section.

(4) Any foreign lawyer may apply to the Council to be registered as such for the purposes of this section and the Council shall, if they are satisfied that the legal profession of which the applicant is a member is so regulated as to make it appropriate for him to be allowed to enter into a multi-national practice with solicitors or incorporated practices, enter his name on the register.

[4] (4A) Any person may inspect the register of foreign lawyers during office hours without payment.

[4] (4B) A registered foreign lawyer who wishes his name to be removed from the register of foreign lawyers may make an application to the Council in that behalf, and the Council shall, if the registered foreign lawyer satisfies the Council that he has made adequate arrangements with respect to the business that he has then in hand, remove the name of that foreign lawyer from the register of foreign lawyers.

[4] (4C) On an application to the Council by a foreign lawyer whose name has been removed from the register of foreign lawyers under subsection (4B), the Council may, after such inquiry as they think proper, restore the name of the foreign lawyer to the register of foreign lawyers.

[4] (4D) A foreign lawyer whose name has been removed (other than pursuant to an application made under subsection (4B)) from the register of foreign lawyers shall have his name restored to that register only if, on an application in that behalf made by him to the Tribunal and after such inquiry as the Tribunal thinks proper, the Tribunal so orders.

[4] (4E) Rules made by the Tribunal under section 52 (procedure on complaints to the Tribunal) may—

(a) regulate the making, hearing and determining of applications under subsection (4D); and

(b) provide for payment by the applicant to the Council of such fee in respect of restoration to the register of foreign lawyers as the rules may specify.

[4] (4F) Where, following an application under subsection (4), the Council decide not to enter the name of a foreign lawyer in the register of foreign lawyers the applicant may, within three months of the notification to him of the Council's decision (or later with the permission of the court), appeal to the court against the decision and, on such an appeal, the court may—

(a) order the Council to register the foreign lawyer;

(b) refuse the appeal; or

(c) remit the matter to the Council with such directions as it sees fit.

[4] (4G) Sections 24A to 24G (registration certificates for registered European lawyers) shall apply to registered foreign lawyers as they apply to registered European lawyers and any reference in those sections (as so applied) to a registration certificate shall be construed as a reference to a registration certificate for a registered foreign lawyer.

(5) Subject to subsection (6), the Secretary of State may by order made by statutory instrument provide that any enactment or instrument—

(a) [*Repealed by the Solicitors (Scotland) Act 1980 (Foreign Lawyers and Multi-national Practices) Regulations 2004 (SSI 2004/383), reg.11.*]

(b) having effect in relation to solicitors; and

(c) specified in the order,

shall have effect with respect to registered foreign lawyers as it has effect with respect to solicitors.

(6) Before making any order under subsection (5), the Secretary of State shall consult the Council.

(7) An order under subsection (5) may provide for an enactment or instrument to have effect with respect to registered foreign lawyers subject to such additions, omissions or other modifications as the Secretary of State specifies in the order.

(8) No order shall be made under subsection (5) unless a draft of the order has been approved by both Houses of Parliament.

NOTE

[1] Inserted by the Law Reform (Miscellaneous Provisions) (Scotland) Act 1990 (c.40), s.32 (in force March 17, 1993, only in respect of the provisions relating to the making of rules and orders in s.60A(2), (3) and (5)–(8): SI 1993/641).

[2] Read in conjunction with the European Communities (Lawyer's Practice) (Scotland) Regulations 2000 (SSI 2000/121), reg.37(2) and Sch.2 (effective May 22, 2000).

[3] Brought into force by SSI 2004/382 (effective October 1, 2004), in so far as not already in force.

[4] Inserted by the Solicitors (Scotland) Act 1980 (Foreign Lawyers and Multi-national Practices) Regulations 2004 (SSI 2004/383), reg.11.

Protection of banks

[1,2] **61.**—(1) Subject to the provisions of this section, no bank or building society shall, in connection with any transaction on any account of a solicitor or an incorporated practice kept with it or with any other bank or building society—

(*a*) incur any liability, or

(*b*) be under any obligation to make any inquiry, or

(*c*) be deemed to have any knowledge of any right of any person to any money paid or credited to the account,

which it would not incur, or be under, or be deemed to have (as the case may be) in the case of an account kept by a person entitled absolutely to all money paid or credited to it; but nothing in this subsection shall relieve the bank or building society from any liability or obligation under which it would be apart from this Act.

(2) In subsection (1) "account" does not include an account kept by a solicitor or an incorporated practice as trustee for a specified beneficiary.

(3) Notwithstanding anything in the preceding provisions of this section a bank or building society at which a solicitor or an incorporated practice keeps a special account for clients' money shall not, in respect of any liability of the solicitor or, as the case may be, the incorporated practice to the bank or building society (not being a liability in connection with that account) have or obtain any recourse or right, whether by way of set-off, counter-claim, charge or otherwise, against money standing to the credit of that account.

NOTE

[1] As amended by the Law Reform (Miscellaneous Provisions) (Scotland) Act 1985 (c.73), Sched. 1, Pt. I, para.31, and the Solicitors (Scotland) Act 1988 (c.42), Sch.1, para.19.

[2] Read in conjunction with the European Communities (Lawyer's Practice) (Scotland) Regulations 2000 (SSI 2000/121), reg.37(2) and Sch.2 and the Solicitors (Scotland) Act 1980 (Foreign Lawyers and Multi-national Practices) Regulations 2004 (SSI 2004/383), reg.13.

Solicitors' fees

[1,3] **61A.**—(1) Subject to the provisions of this section, and without prejudice to—

(*a*) section 32(1)(*i*) of the Sheriff Courts (Scotland) Act 1971; or

(*b*) section 5(*h*) of the Court of Session Act 1988,

where a solicitor and his client have reached an agreement in writing as to the solicitor's fees in respect of any work done or to be done by him for his client it shall not be competent, in any litigation arising out of any dispute as to the amount due to be paid under any such agreement, for the court to remit the solicitor's account for taxation.

(2) Subsection (1) is without prejudice to the court's power to remit a solicitor's account for taxation in a case where there has been no written agreement as to the fees to be charged.

(3) A solicitor and his client may agree, in relation to a litigation undertaken on a speculative basis, that, in the event of the litigation being successful, the solicitor's fee shall be increased by such a percentage as may, subject to subsection (4), be agreed.

[2] (4) The percentage increase which may be agreed under subsection (3) shall not exceed such limit as the court may, after consultation with the Council, prescribe by act of sederunt.

NOTE

[1] Inserted by the Law Reform (Miscellaneous Provisions) (Scotland) Act 1990 (c.40), s. 36(3) (effective 4th July 1992: SI 1992/1599).

[2] The court's power to enact an act of sederunt under subss. (3) and (4) was brought into force on July 4, 1992 by SI 1992/1599.

[3] Read in conjunction with the European Communities (Lawyer's Practice) (Scotland) Regulations 2000 (SSI 2000/121), reg.37(2) and Sch.2 and the Solicitors (Scotland) Act 1980 (Foreign Lawyers and Multi-national Practices) Regulations 2004 (SSI 2004/383), reg.13.

Charge for expenses out of property recovered

[1] **62.**—(1) Where a solicitor has been employed by a client to pursue or defend any action or proceeding, the court before which the action or proceeding has been heard or is depending may declare the solicitor entitled, in respect of the taxed expenses of or in reference to the action or proceeding, to a charge upon, and a right to payment out of, any property (of whatsoever nature, tenure or kind it may be) which has been recovered or preserved on behalf of the client by the solicitor in the action or proceeding; and the court may make such order for the taxation of, and for the raising and payment of, those expenses out of the said property as the court thinks just.

(2) Where a declaration has been made under subsection (1) any act done or deed granted by the client after the date of the declaration except an act or deed in favour of a *bona fide* purchaser or lender, shall be absolutely void as against the charge or right.

NOTE

[1] Read in conjunction with the European Communities (Lawyer's Practice) (Scotland) Regulations 2000 (SSI 2000/121), reg.37(2) and Sch.2 (effective May 22, 2000).

Council's power to recover expenses incurred under section 38, 45 or 46

[1,2] **62A.**—(1) Without prejudice to the Society's entitlement under section 46(4) to recover expenses, the Council shall be entitled to recover from a solicitor or incorporated practice in respect of whom it has taken action under section 38, 45, or 46, any expenditure reasonably incurred by it in so doing.

(2) Expenditure incurred in taking action under section 38 is recoverable under subsection (1) above only where notice has been served under paragraph 5(2) of Schedule 3 in connection with that action and—

(*a*) no application has been made in consequence under paragraph 5(4) of that Schedule; or

(*b*) the Court, on such an application, has made a direction under paragraph 5(5) of that Schedule.

NOTE

[1] Inserted by the Law Reform (Miscellaneous Provisions) (Scotland) Act 1985 (c.73), Sch.1, Pt. II, para.6.

[2] Read in conjunction with the European Communities (Lawyer's Practice) (Scotland)

Regulations 2000 (SSI 2000/121), reg.37(2) and Sch.2 and the Solicitors (Scotland) Act 1980 (Foreign Lawyers and Multi-national Practices) Regulations 2004 (SSI 2004/383), reg.13 (except with regard to references to s.46).

General

Penalties and time limit for prosecution of offences

[1,2] **63.**—(1) Any person guilty of an offence under this Act shall be liable on summary conviction to a fine not exceeding level 4 on the standard scale.

(2) Notwithstanding any provision of the Criminal Procedure (Scotland) Act 1975, the prosecution of any offence under this Act shall be commenced within 6 months of its first discovery by the prosecutor or in any event within 2 years after the commission of that offence.

(3) Where an offence under this Act is committed by a body corporate and is proved to have been committed with the consent or connivance of or to be attributable to any neglect on the part of—

(*a*) any director, secretary or other similar officer of the body corporate; or

(*b*) any person who was purporting to act in any such capacity,

he (as well as the body corporate) shall be guilty of the offence and shall be liable to be proceeded against and punished accordingly.

(4) Where an offence under this Act is committed by a partnership or by an unincorporated association (other than a partnership) and is proved to have been committed with the consent or connivance of a partner in the partnership or, as the case may be, a person concerned in the management or control of the association, he (as well as the partnership or association) shall be guilty of the offence and shall be liable to be proceeded against and punished accordingly.

NOTE

[1] As amended by virtue of the Criminal Procedure (Scotland) Act 1975 (c.21), ss. 289F and 289G, and by the Law Reform (Miscellaneous Provisions) (Scotland) Act 1990 (c.40), Sch.8, para.29(14) and Sch.9.

[2] Read in conjunction with the European Communities (Lawyer's Practice) (Scotland) Regulations 2000 (SSI 2000/121), reg.37(2) and Sch.2 and the Solicitors (Scotland) Act 1980 (Foreign Lawyers and Multi-national Practices) Regulations 2004 (SSI 2004/383), reg.13.

Service of notices, etc.

[1,2] **64.** Any notice or other document which is required or authorised under this Act to be given to, or served on, any person shall be taken to be duly given or served if it is delivered to him or left at, or sent by post to, his last-known place of business or residence or, in the case of an incorporated practice, if it is left at, or delivered or sent by post to, its registered office.

NOTE

[1] As amended by the Law Reform (Miscellaneous Provisions) (Scotland) Act 1985 (c.73), Sch.1, Pt. I, para.32.

[2] Read in conjunction with the European Communities (Lawyer's Practice) (Scotland) Regulations 2000 (SSI 2000/121), reg.37(2) and Sch.2 and the Solicitors (Scotland) Act 1980 (Foreign Lawyers and Multi-national Practices) Regulations 2004 (SSI 2004/383), reg.13.

Advisory and supervisory functions of the Director General of Fair Trading

[1] **64A.**—(1) Before considering any rule—

(*a*) made under section 25A(4) or (5); or

(*b*) such as is mentioned in section 34(3A),

the Secretary of State shall send a copy of the proposed rule in question to the Director.

(2) The Director shall consider whether the rule in question would have, or would be likely to have, the effect of restricting, distorting or preventing competition to any significant extent.

(3) When the Director has completed his consideration he shall give such advice to the Secretary of State as he thinks fit.

(4) The Director may publish any advice given by him under subsection (3).

(5) The Director shall, so far as practicable, exclude from anything

published under subsection (4) any matter—

(*a*) which relates to the affairs of a particular person; and

(*b*) the publication of which would, or might in the Director's opinion, seriously and prejudicially affect the interests of that person.

(6) For the purposes of the law of defamation, the publication of any advice or report by the Director under this section shall be absolutely privileged.

NOTE

[1] Inserted by the Law Reform (Miscellaneous Provisions) (Scotland) Act 1990 (c.40), s. 43.

Duty of Secretary of State

[1] **64B.** When he has received advice under section 64A(3) in relation to a rule made under section 25A(4) or (5) or such as is mentioned in section 34(3A), the Secretary of State may, having considered—

(*a*) that advice;

(*b*) whether the interests of justice require that there should be such a rule; and

(*c*) in relation to a rule made under section 25A(5), any relevant practice obtaining in the sheriff court,

approve or refuse to approve the rule.

NOTE

[1] Inserted by the Law Reform (Miscellaneous Provisions) (Scotland) Act 1990 (c.40), s.43.

Investigatory powers of the Director

[1] **64C.**—(1) For the purpose of investigating any matter under section 64A, the Director may by notice in writing—

(*a*) require any person to produce to him or to any person appointed by him for the purpose, at a time and place specified in the notice, any documents which are specified or described in the notice and which—

(i) are in that person's custody or under that person's control; and

(ii) relate to any matter relevant to the investigation; or

(*b*) require any person carrying on any business to furnish to him (within such time and in such manner and form as the notice may specify) such information as may be specified or described in the notice.

(2) A person shall not be required under this section to produce any document or disclose any information which he would be entitled to refuse to produce or disclose on the grounds of confidentiality between a client and his professional legal adviser in any civil proceedings.

(3) [*Repealed by the Enterprise Act 2002 (Consequential and Supplemental Provisions) Order 2003 (SI 2003/1398), Sch.1, para.2(2) (effective June 20, 2003).*]

NOTE

[1] Inserted by the Law Reform (Miscellaneous Provisions) (Scotland) Act 1990 (c.40), s.43.

Enforcement of notices under section 64C

[1] **64CA.**—(1) The court may, on an application by the Office of Fair Trading, enquire into whether any person ("the defaulter") has refused or otherwise failed, without reasonable excuse, to comply with a notice under section 64C(1).

(2) An application under subsection (1) shall include details of the possible failure which the Office of Fair Trading considers has occurred.

(3) In enquiring into a case under subsection (1), the court shall hear any witness who may be produced against or on behalf of the defaulter and any statement which may be offered in defence.

(4) Subsections (5) and (6) apply where the court is satisfied, after hearing any witnesses and statements as mentioned in subsection (3), that the

defaulter has refused or otherwise failed, without reasonable excuse, to comply with a notice under section 64C(1).

(5) The court may punish the defaulter as it would have been able to punish him had he been guilty of contempt of court.

(6) Where the defaulter is a body corporate or is a partnership constituted under the law of Scotland, the court may punish any director, officer or (as the case may be) partner of the defaulter as it would have been able to punish that director, officer or partner had he been guilty of contempt of court.

NOTE

[1] Inserted by the Enterprise Act 2002 (Consequential and Supplemental Provisions) Order 2003 (SI 2003/1398), art.2, Sch.1, para.2(3) (effective June 20, 2003).

Altering, etc. documents required to be produced under section 64C

[1] **64CB.**—(1) A person commits an offence if he intentionally alters, suppresses or destroys a document which he has been required to produce by a notice under section 64C(1).

(2) A person who commits an offence under subsection (1) shall be liable—

(a) on summary conviction, to a fine not exceeding the statutory maximum;

(b) on conviction on indictment, to imprisonment for a term not exceeding two years or to a fine or to both.

NOTE

[1] Inserted by the Enterprise Act 2002 (Consequential and Supplemental Provisions) Order 2003 (SI 2003/1398), art.2, Sch.1, para.2(3) (effective June 20, 2003).

Review of rules approved by the Secretary of State

[1] **64D.**—(1) Without prejudice to the power of the Council to review any rule made by them, where the Secretary of State has approved a rule under section 64B he may, and if so requested by the Lord President shall, require the Council to review its terms.

(2) When they have reviewed a rule following a requirement made under subsection (1), the Council may revise the rule in the light of that review, and shall then submit the rule as revised or, if they have not revised it, as previously approved to the Lord President and the Secretary of State.

(3) Where the Lord President and the Secretary of State are agreed that the terms of [any] rule as submitted to them are satisfactory, the Secretary of State shall approve the rule, and may direct the Council to bring it into force as soon as is practicable.

(4) Where either the Secretary of State or the Lord President is of the view that any rule, as submitted to them, is not satisfactory, but they do not agree as to what the terms of the rule should be, the rule shall continue to have effect as previously approved.

(5) Where the Secretary of State and the Lord President agree both that any rule submitted to them under subsection (2) is not satisfactory, and as to what the terms of the rule should be, the Secretary of State may direct the Council—

(*a*) to amend the rule in such manner as he and the Lord President consider appropriate; and

(*b*) to bring the rule, as so amended, into force as soon as is practicable.

(6) The provisions of sections 64A and 64B apply to rules submitted to the Secretary of State under this section as they apply to rules submitted to him under sections 25A(9) or (10) and 34(3A).

NOTE

[1] Inserted by the Law Reform (Miscellaneous Provisions) (Scotland) Act 1990 (c.40), s. 43.

Interpretation

65.—[1] (1) In this Act, except in so far as the context otherwise requires—

"accounts rules" has the meaning given by section 35;

"accountant's certificate rules" has the meaning given by section 37(3);

[4] "the 1990 Act" means the Law Reform (Miscellaneous Provisions) (Scotland) Act 1990 (c.40);

"advocate" means a member of the Faculty of Advocates;

"building society" means a building society within the meaning of the Building Societies Act 1986;

"client account" means a current or deposit or savings account at a bank or with a building society, or a deposit receipt, at a bank, being an account or, as the case may be, a deposit receipt in the title of which the word "client", "trustee", "trust" or other fiducial term appears, including—

(*a*) an account or deposit receipt for a client whose name is specified in the title of the account on deposit receipt, and

(*b*) an account such as is mentioned in paragraphs (*a*) and (*b*) of section 35(1);

"the Council" has the meaning given by section 3;

"the court" means the Court of Session;

"the Director" means the Director General of Fair Trading;

"foreign lawyer" means a person who is not a solicitor or an advocate but who is a member, and entitled to practise as such, of a legal profession regulated within a jurisdiction outwith Scotland;

"functions" includes powers and duties;

"inadequate professional services" means professional services which are in any respect not of the quality which could reasonably be expected of a competent solicitor, and cognate expressions shall be construed accordingly; and references to the provision of inadequate professional services shall be construed as including references to not providing professional services which such a solicitor ought to have provided;

"incorporated practice" has the meaning given by section 34(1A)(*c*);

"judge" includes sheriff;

"law centre" means a body—

(*a*) established for the purpose of providing legal services to the public generally as well as to individual members of the public; and

(*b*) which does not distribute any profits made either to its members or otherwise, but reinvests any such profits for the purposes of the law centre;

"Lord President" means the Lord President of the Court of Session;

"multi-disciplinary practice" means a body corporate or a partnership—

(*a*) having as one of its directors or, as the case may be, partners, a solicitor or an incorporated practice; and

(*b*) which offers services, including professional services such as are provided by individual solicitors, to the public; and

(*c*) where that solicitor or incorporated practice carries out, or supervises the carrying out of, any such professional services as may lawfully be carried out only by a solicitor;

"multi-national practice" means—

(*a*) a partnership whose members are solicitors or incorporated practices and registered foreign lawyers; or

(*b*) a body corporate whose members include registered foreign lawyers, and membership of which is restricted to solicitors, incorporated practices, registered foreign lawyers and other multi-national practices;

"notary public" means a notary public duly admitted in Scotland;

"practice year" means the year ending on 31st October;

"practising certificate" has the meaning given by section 4;

"property" includes property, whether heritable or moveable, and rights and interests in, to or over such property;

[2] "registered European lawyer" means a person registered with the Society in accordance with regulation 17 of the European Communities (Lawyer's Practice) (Scotland) Regulations 2000;

"registered foreign lawyer" means a foreign lawyer who is registered under section 60A;

"the roll" has the meaning given by section 7;

"the Society" has the meaning given by section 1;

"Scottish legal services ombudsman" means the ombudsman appointed under section 34 of the Law Reform (Miscellaneous Provisions) (Scotland) Act 1990;

"solicitor" means any person enrolled or deemed to have been enrolled as a solicitor in pursuance of this Act;

"the Tribunal" has the meaning given by section 50;

"unqualified person" means a person, other than a multi-disciplinary practice, who is not qualified under section 4 to act as a solicitor.

(2) Unless the context otherwise requires a reference—

[3] (*a*) in any enactment to law agents includes solicitors and registered European lawyers;

(*b*) in any enactment to the register of law agents kept in pursuance of the Law Agents (Scotland) Act 1873 includes the roll;

(*c*) in any enactment or instrument to the Solicitors Discipline (Scotland) Committee shall be construed as a reference to the Tribunal.

(*d*) in any enactment or instrument or other document to the General Council of Solicitors in Scotland shall be construed as a reference to the Council.

(*e*) in any enactment to a solicitor's or registered European lawyer's being entitled to practise in the court, or in any other court, or to act in any matter, by reason of his being enrolled in, or of his having subscribed, the list of solicitors practising in that court, shall be construed as a reference to his being entitled so to practise or act by reason of his name being included in the appropriate list provided under section 20.

(3) In this Act references to any enactment shall, except in so far as the context otherwise requires, be construed as references to that enactment as amended, extended or applied by or under any other enactment, including any enactment contained in this Act.

(4) In this Act, except in so far as the context otherwise requires—

(*a*) any reference to a numbered Part, section or Schedule is a reference to the Part or section of, or the Schedule to, this Act so numbered;

(*b*) a reference in a section to a numbered subsection is a reference to the subsection of that section so numbered;

(*c*) a reference in a section, subsection or Schedule to a numbered or lettered paragraph is a reference to the paragraph of that section, subsection or Schedule so numbered or lettered; and

(*d*) a reference to any provision of an Act (including this Act) includes a reference to any Schedule incorporated in the Act by that provision.

NOTES

[1] As amended by the Law Reform (Miscellaneous Provisions) (Scotland) Act 1985 (c.73), Sched., Pt. I, para.33, the Solicitors (Scotland) Act 1988 (c.42), s.5(1), Sched. 1, para.20 and Sched. 2, and the Law Reform (Miscellaneous Provisions) (Scotland) Act 1990 (c.40), Sched. 8, para.29(15) and Sched. 9 (all in force by 17th March 1993: S.I. 1993 No. 641).

[2] Inserted by the European Communities (Lawyer's Practice) (Scotland) Regulations 2000 (SSI 2000/121), reg. 37(2) and Sched. 1, para.1(12)(a) (effective May 22, 2000).

[3] As amended by the European Communities (Lawyer's Practice) (Scotland) Regulations 2000 (SSI 2000/121), reg. 37(1) and Sched. 1, para.1(8) (effective May 22, 2000).

[4] Inserted by the Public Appointments and Public Bodies etc. (Scotland) Act 2003 (asp 4), s.12 (effective August 15, 2003).

Transitional and savings provisions, and repeals

66.—(1) Schedule 6 (transitional and savings provisions) shall have effect, but the provisions of that Schedule shall not be taken as prejudicing the operation of section 16 of the Interpretation Act 1978 (general savings in respect of repeals).

(2) The enactments specified in Schedule 7 are hereby repealed to the extent shown in column 3 of that Schedule.

Citation, extent and commencement

67.—(1) This Act may be cited as the Solicitors (Scotland) Act 1980.

(2) This Act extends to Scotland only.

(3) This Act shall come into operation on the expiration of one month from the date on which it is passed.

SCHEDULES

Section 1 SCHEDULE 1

NOTE

[1]Read in conjunction with the European Communities (Lawyer's Practice) (Scotland) Regulations 2000 (SSI 2000/121), reg. 37(2) and Sched. 2 (effective May 22, 2000).

The Law Society of Scotland

Constitution and Proceedings

1. The Society shall be a body corporate with a common seal and may sue and be sued in its own name.

2. The Council shall prepare a scheme providing for—

(*a*) the constitution, election, and proceedings of the Council;

(*b*) the meetings of the Society;

(*c*) the appointment of a chairman, vice-chairman, secretary and other officers and employees of the Society;

[1] (*d*) the appointment and constitution of committees and sub-committees.

NOTE

[1]As amended by the Council of the Law Society of Scotland Act 2003 (asp 14), s.2(2) (effective May 31, 2003).

---

3. The scheme prepared under paragraph 2—

(*a*) may make provision enabling the Council to admit as honorary members of the Society persons who have ceased to be practising solicitors, no such honorary member being entitled to vote at meetings of the Society or liable to pay an annual subscription;

(*b*) shall make provision for the admission on application made in that behalf and on payment of the annual subscription as a member of the Society of any solicitor who by virtue of the provisions of section 24 is exempted from taking out a practising certificate;

[1] (*ba*) may make provision for persons other than solicitors to be members of a committee or sub-committee of the Council (including provision for such persons to constitute a majority of the members of the committee or sub-committee);

(*c*) may contain such other provisions with respect to the administration, management and proceedings of the Society as are considered necessary or proper and are consistent with the provisions of this Act.

NOTE

[1] Inserted by the Council of the Law Society of Scotland Act 2003 (asp 14), s.2(3) (effective May 31, 2003).

---

4. A scheme prepared under paragraph 2 shall have effect on being approved by a resolution passed by a majority of the members present in person or by proxy at a general meeting of the Society, or at an adjournment of such meeting.

5. The Society may by a resolution passed by a majority consisting of not less than two-thirds of the members of the Society present in person or by proxy at a meeting of the Society of which due notice specifying the intention to propose the resolution has been given, or at any adjournment of such meeting, rescind, add to or amend any of the provisions of the scheme so approved.

Revenue

[1] 6. Subject to paragraph 7, every member of the Society shall, for each year, pay to the Society such subscription as may be fixed from time to time by the Society in general meeting.

NOTE

[1] Substituted by the Law Reform (Miscellaneous Provisions) (Scotland) Act 1985, Sched. 1, Pt. II, para. 7.

---

[1] 6A. The subscription payable under paragraph 6 by a practising member (or the proportion of it so payable, calculated by reference to the number of months remaining in the practice year) shall be paid at the time of submission of his application for a practising certificate.

NOTE

[1] Inserted by the Law Reform (Miscellaneous Provisions) (Scotland) Act 1985, Sched. 1, Pt. II, para. 7.

---

[1] 7. The subscription payable by a solicitor in respect of the year or part thereof in which he is first included in the roll of solicitors and in respect of each of the two years immediately following shall be one half of the amount of the subscription fixed under paragraph 6 (reduced, in the case of a solicitor first included in the roll for only part of a year, in that year proportionately).

NOTE

[1] As amended by the Law Reform (Miscellaneous Provisions) (Scotland) Act 1985, Sched. 1, Pt. II, para. 7 and Sched. 4.

---

[1] 7A. The Society shall have power, subject to paragraphs 7B to 7D, to impose in respect of any year a special subscription on all members of the Society of such amount and payable at such time and for such specified purpose as it may determine.

[1] 7B. The Society may determine that an imposition under paragraph 7A shall not be payable by any category of member or shall be abated as respects any category of member.

[1] 7C. An imposition under paragraph 7A or a determination under that paragraph or paragraph 7B may be made only in general meeting.

[1] 7D. No imposition may be made under paragraph 7A above unless a majority of those members voting at the general meeting at which it is proposed has, whether by proxy or otherwise, voted in favour of its being made.

NOTE

[1] Paras. 7A to 7D inserted by the Law Reform (Miscellaneous Provisions) (Scotland) Act 1985, Sched. 1, Pt. II, para. 7. Para.7D amended by the Solicitors (Scotland) Act 1988, Sched. 1, para. 21.

---

8. Except as otherwise provided in this Act, the expenses of the Society shall be defrayed out of the subscriptions and other income received by the Society or the Council and out of other property belonging to the Society.

In this paragraph "expenses of the Society" includes the expenses of the Tribunal so far as not otherwise defrayed and any expenses incurred by the Council in exercise of their functions under this Act, and the reasonable travelling and maintenance expenses of members of the Council or committees of the Council incurred in attending meetings of the Council or committees, or otherwise incurred in the business of the Society.

9. Paragraph 8 does not affect any trust constituted for a special purpose.

Powers

10. The Society may—

(*a*) purchase or otherwise acquire land for any of the purposes of this Act;

(*b*) sell, lease or otherwise dispose of land so acquired;

(*c*) borrow for any of the purposes of this Act in such manner and on such security as they may determine;

(*d*) invest any monies not immediately required to meet expenses and other outlays of the Society in any investment in which trustees in Scotland are by law authorised to invest (but nothing in this sub-paragraph prevents the investment of any monies forming any part of any property held in trust for a special purpose in any class of investment authorised by the deed constituting the trust);

(*e*) accept any gift of property for the purposes of the Society;

(*f*) accept, hold and administer any gift of property or hold as trustees any property for any purpose which the Society consider to be for the benefit of solicitors in Scotland or their dependants or employees or any substantial body of such solicitors or dependants or employees; and

(*g*) subject to the provisions of this Act exercise the functions formerly exercised by the General Council of Solicitors in Scotland.

11. The Council may—

(*a*) act for and in the name of the Society in any matter other than a matter which in accordance with the provisions of this Schedule is to be determined by the Society in general meeting;

(*b*) without prejudice to any other powers they may have, take into consideration and make recommendations or representations with regard to any matters which are in their opinion of importance to solicitors in Scotland.

Exemption from liability for damages

[1] 11A. Neither the Society nor any of its officers or servants shall be liable in damages for anything done or omitted in the discharge or purported discharge of its functions unless the act or omission is shown to have been in bad faith.

NOTE

[1] Inserted by the Law Reform (Miscellaneous Provisions) (Scotland) Act 1990, Sch.8, para.29(16).

Attestation

12. [Repealed by the Requirements of Writing (Scotland) Act 1995 (c.7), Sch.5 (effective

1st August 1995: s. 15(2)). On 21 September 1995 the Council passed a resolution in the following terms:

"Any deed or document to which the Society is a party shall be held to be validly executed on behalf of the Society if it is subscribed on behalf of the Society by any two of the following:—
The President,
Vice-President,
Past President,
The Secretary."]

Section 11 [1] SCHEDULE 2

NOTE

[1] As amended by the Solicitors (Scotland) Act 1988 (c.42), Sched. 1, para. 22 and Sched. 2.

THE ROLL: POWERS OF THE COUNCIL AND ANCILLARY PROVISIONS

1. The Council (as registrar of solicitors) for the purpose of maintaining the roll as correctly as is reasonably practicable shall have power—

(*a*) to remove from the roll the name of any solicitor who has died;

(*b*) to send to any solicitor at his address as shown in the roll a letter enquiring whether he wishes to continue to have his name included in the roll and intimating that if no reply is made within the period of 6 months beginning with the date of the posting of the letter his name may be removed from the roll;

(c) to send any solicitor on the roll who has for at least 3 years been so enrolled in pursuance of regulations made by the Council under section 5 on an undertaking by him to serve a post qualifying year for practical training which the Council are not satisfied that he has implemented, a letter enquiring whether he intends to fulfil that undertaking and intimating that unless a reply which the Council regard as satisfactory is received within the period of 6 months beginning with the date of the posting of the letter his name may be removed from the roll; and

[NEXT TEXT PAGE IS **F** 55]

(d) if a reply indicating that he does not wish that his name shall continue to be included in the roll is returned by any solicitor to whom a letter has been so sent, or if no reply or in a case of a letter sent under subparagraph (c) a reply which the Council do not regard as satisfactory is returned within the period mentioned in subparagraph (b) or (c), as the case may be, by any such solicitor, to remove the name of that solicitor from the roll.

2. The Council may, on the application of a solicitor whose name has been removed from the roll in pursuance of paragraph 1(d), and on payment by him to the Council of such reasonable fee in respect of restoration as the Council may fix, order that his name shall be restored to the roll.

3. Any person aggrieved by a decision of the Council under paragraph 2 may appeal against the decision to the Court, and the provisions of section 40(3) shall, subject to any necessary modifications, apply to any such appeal.

4. Subject to section 7(3), the Council may charge such reasonable fees (including an annual fee payable by enrolled solicitors) as they may fix in connection with the keeping of the roll.

Section 43

SCHEDULE 3

PART I

THE SCOTTISH SOLICITORS GUARANTEE FUND

Contributions by Solicitors

[1] 1.—(1) Subject to the provisions of this Act, there shall be paid to the Society on behalf of the Guarantee Fund by every solicitor in respect of each year during which, or part of which, he is in practice as a solicitor, along with his application for a practising certificate, a contribution (hereafter referred to as an "annual contribution").

(2) The sum payable by a solicitor in respect of the year in which he first commences to practise after admission and in respect of each of the two years immediately following shall be one half of the annual contribution.

(2A) Sub-paragraphs (1) and (2) do not apply to solicitors who are directors of incorporated practices.

(2B) Subject to the provisions of this Act, there shall be paid to the Society on behalf of the Guarantee Fund by every incorporated practice in respect of each year during which, or part of which, it is recognised under section 34(1A) a contribution (hereafter referred to as an "annual corporate contribution") in accordance with the scale of such contributions referred to in sub-paragraph (3).

(3) The Council shall not later than 30th September in each year fix the amount, if any, of the annual contribution to be paid in respect of the following year and the scale of the annual corporate contributions to be so paid, which scale be fixed by reference to factors which shall include the number of solicitors who are directors or employees of each of the incorporated practices to which the scale relates.

[2] (4) No annual contribution shall be payable by a solicitor and no annual corporate contribution by an incorporated practice so long as the amount of the Guarantee Fund including the value of all investments forming part of the Fund and after providing for all outstanding liabilities, is in the opinion of the Council not less than £250,000 or such other sum as the Council may from time to time determine.

(5) If at any time the Council are of opinion that the liabilities of the Guarantee Fund render it expedient in order to secure the financial stability of the Fund, the Council may, by resolution of which not less than 10 days' previous notice in writing has been given to each member of the Council, impose upon every solicitor a contribution (hereafter referred to as a "special contribution") of the amount specified in the resolution, and upon every incorporated practice a contribution (hereafter referred to as a "special corporate contribution") in accordance with a scale of such contributions fixed by the Council as under sub-paragraph (3), and a special or special corporate contribution shall be payable to the Society in one sum or, if the Council so determine, by instalments on or before such date or dates as may be specified in the resolution.

(6) No special contribution shall be payable by a solicitor in the year in which he first commences to practice after admission nor in either of the 2 years immediately following.

(7) [Repealed by the Law Reform (Miscellaneous Provisions) (Scotland) Act 1985, Sch.1, Pt. II. para.8(c), with effect from 30th December 1985.]

(8) No annual contribution and no special contribution shall be payable by any solicitor who is in the employment of another solicitor or of a firm of solicitors or of an incorporated practice and who does not engage in practice as a solicitor on his own account.

(9) Without prejudice to any other method of recovering contributions payable to the Society

under this Schedule whether annual or special a practising certificate shall not be issued to a solicitor except on production of evidence of payment of the contributions (if any) due by him to the Fund on or before the issue of the certificate.

(10) In this Schedule the expression "year" means the period of 12 months commencing on 1st November or such other day as may be fixed by the Council.

NOTE

[1] As amended by the Law Reform (Miscellaneous Provisions) (Scotland) Act 1985 (c.73) s. 56 and, Sch.1, Pt. I, para.34, Pt. II, para.8, and Sch.4.

[2] At its meeting on July 26, 1996, the Council determined that the sum should be £2 million.

Contributions by registered European lawyers

[1] 1A.—(1) Subject to the provisions of this paragraph, paragraph (1) above shall apply to registered European lawyers as it applies to solicitors and references to a practising certificate shall include references to a registered European lawyer's registration certificate.

(2) Where a registered European lawyer can prove that—

(a) he is covered by a guarantee provided in accordance with the professional rules of his home State; and

(b the guarantee is equivalent in terms of the conditions and the extent of its cover to the Guarantee Fund, then to the extent that there is such equivalence that lawyer shall be exempt from the requirements of paragraph (1).

(3) Where the equivalence under sub paragraph (2) is only partial, the Society may specify the guarantee obligations a registered European lawyer is required to meet to comply with paragraph (1).

(4) Subparagraphs (2), (6) and (8) of paragraph (1) shall not apply.

(5) For the purposes of this paragraph the words "home State" have the same meaning as provided for in regulation 2 of the European Communities (Lawyer's Practice) (Scotland) Regulations 2000.

NOTE

[1]Inserted by the European Communities (Lawyer's Practice) (Scotland) Regulations 2000 (SSI 2000/121), reg.37(1) and Sch.1, para.1(13) (effective May 22, 2000).

Contributions by registered foreign lawyers

[1]1B.—(1) Subject to the provisions of this paragraph, paragraph 1 above shall apply to registered foreign lawyers as it applies to solicitors and in that paragraph as so applied references to a practising certificate shall be construed as references to a registered foreign lawyer's registration certificate.

(2) Where a registered foreign lawyer can prove that—

(a) he is covered by a guarantee provided in accordance with the rules of the legal profession of which he is a member; and

(b) the guarantee is equivalent in terms of the conditions and the extent of its cover to the Guarantee Fund,

then to the extent that there is such equivalence that lawyer shall be exempt from the requirements of paragraph 1.

(3) Where the equivalence referred to in sub paragraph (2) is only partial, the Society may specify the guarantee obligations a registered foreign lawyer is required to meet to comply with paragraph 1.

(4) The Council may, where it is satisfied that any acts or defaults on the part of a registered foreign lawyer would not result in a grant being made from the Guarantee Fund held under section 43, exempt that lawyer from the requirements of paragraph 1.

(5) Sub paragraphs (2), (6) and (8) of paragraph 1 shall not apply to registered foreign lawyers.

NOTE

[1] Inserted by the Solicitors (Scotland) Act 1980 (Foreign Lawyers and Multi-national Practices) Regulations 2004 (SSI 2004/383), reg.12.

Investment etc.

2.—(1) Monies not immediately required to meet sums payable out of the Guarantee Fund may be invested by the Society in any investments in which trustees in Scotland are by law authorised to invest.

(2) The Society may borrow money for the purposes of the Guarantee Fund in such manner and on such security as they may determine but the total sum due at any time in respect of any such loans shall not exceed [1] £1,250,000.

(3) The accounts of the Guarantee Fund shall be made up annually for the year ending 31st October or on such other day as may be fixed by the Council and shall be audited by an auditor appointed by the Society.

(4) As soon as the audit is completed the audited accounts and the auditor's report on the accounts shall be submitted to the Council and a copy of the audited accounts and the auditor's report shall be sent to the Lord Advocate and to every solicitor who is contributing to the Fund.

(5) All investments and other monies forming part of the Guarantee Fund and the books and accounts relating to that Fund shall be kept separate from the other investments and monies, books and accounts of the Society, and the investments and other monies forming part of the Guarantee Fund shall not be liable for any obligations, debts or liabilities incurred by the Society or the Council in relation to any business of the Society other than the business of the Guarantee Fund, nor shall the investments and other monies of the Society held for the purposes other than those relating to the Guarantee Fund be liable for any obligations, debts or liabilities incurred by the Society or the Council in relation to the Guarantee Fund.

NOTE

[1] Figure substituted by the Legal Profession and Legal Aid (Scotland) Act 2007 (asp 5) s.59 (effective November 23, 2007).

Insurance

3.—(1) The Society may enter into a contract of insurance with any person, body of persons or corporation authorised by law to carry on insurance business for guaranteeing the sufficiency of the Guarantee Fund or for any other purpose in relation to the Fund.

[1] (2) Any such contract of insurance may be entered into in relation to solicitors and incorporated practices generally or in relation to any solicitor or solicitors or incorporated practice or practices named therein.

(3) No person other than the Society shall have any right of action against a person, body or corporation with whom any such contract of insurance was entered into or have any right to any monies payable under that contract.

NOTE

[1] As amended by the Law Reform (Miscellaneous Provisions) (Scotland) Act 1985 (c.73), Sch.1, Pt. I, para.34.

Grants

[2] 4.—(1) Every application for a grant from the Guarantee Fund shall be in such form as may be prescribed by rules made under this Schedule and shall be accompanied, if so required by the Council, by a statutory declaration and the applicant shall produce to the Council such documents and other evidence as they demand.

[1] (2) The Council may, as a condition of making a grant out of the Guarantee Fund, require the person to whom the grant is made to assign to the Society at the expense of the Society any rights and remedies competent to him against the solicitor in question, his partner or employee or the incorporated practice in question or its employee or any other person in respect of the loss.

(3) A grant from the Guarantee Fund may at the discretion of the Council be paid in one sum or in such instalments as the Council may determine.

[2] (4) The Council may make rules with regard to the procedure to be followed in giving effect to the provisions of this Act relating to the Guarantee Fund, including matters to be prescribed

thereunder, and also with respect to any matters incidental, ancillary or supplemental to those provisions or concerning the administration, management or protection of the Guarantee Fund.

NOTE
[1] As amended by the Law Reform (Miscellaneous Provisions) (Scotland) Act 1985, Sched. 1, Pt. I, para. 34.
[2]Read in conjunction with the European Communities (Lawyer's Practice) (Scotland) Regulations 2000 (SSI 2000/121), reg.37(2) and Sch.2 of the Solicitors (Scotland) Act 1980 (Foreign Lawyers and Multi-national Practices) Regulations 2004 (SSI 2004/383), reg.14.

Section 38

PART II

Power of Council to investigate

[2] 5.—(1) If under section 38 any person (whether a solicitor or not) having possession or control of any documents mentioned in that section refuses or fails to produce or deliver them immediately on being required by the Council to do so or cause them to be so produced or delivered, the Council may apply to the court for an order requiring that person to produce or deliver the documents or to cause them to be produced or delivered to the person appointed at the place fixed by the Council within such time as the court may order.

[1] (2) Upon taking possession of any such documents which have been produced or delivered to the Council, the Council shall serve upon the solicitor or incorporated practice mentioned in section 38, and every such person, a notice giving particulars and the date on which they took possession.

(3) Every requirement made or notice given under section 38 or under this Part of this Schedule shall be in writing under the hand of such person as may be appointed by the Council for the purpose and may be served either personally or by registered letter or by a letter sent by recorded delivery service addressed to the last known place of business or residence of the person to whom the requirement is made or notice given.

(4) Within 14 days after service of a notice under sub-paragraph (2) the person upon whom such notice has been served may apply to the court for an order directing the Council to return such documents to the person from whom they were received by the Council or to such other person as the applicant may request and on the hearing of any such application the court may make the order applied for or such other order as they think fit.

(5) If no application is made to the court under sub-paragraph (4) or if the court on any such application directs that the documents in question remain in the custody or control of the Council, the Council may make enquiries to ascertain the person to whom they belong and may deal with the documents in accordance with the directions of that person.

NOTE
[1] As amended by the Law Reform (Miscellaneous Provisions) (Scotland) Act 1985, Sched. 1, Pt. I, para. 34.
[2]Read in conjunction with the European Communities (Lawyer's Practice) (Scotland) Regulations 2000 (SSI 2000/121), reg.37(2) and Sch.2 and the Solicitors (Scotland) Act 1980 (Foreign Lawyers and Multi-national Practices) Regulations 2004 (SSI 2004/383), reg.13.

Sections 50, 52

[1] SCHEDULE 4

NOTE
[1]Read in conjunction with the European Communities (Lawyer's Practice) (Scotland) Regulations 2000 (SSI 2000/121), reg.37(2) and Sch.2 and the Solicitors (Scotland) Act 1980 (Foreign Lawyers and Multi-national Practices) Regulations 2004 (SSI 2004/383), reg.13.

Constitution, Procedure and Powers of Tribunal

Part I

Constitution

[1] 1. The Tribunal shall consist of not more than 28 members.

NOTE

[1] As substituted by the Legal Profession and Legal Aid (Scotland) Act 2007 (asp 5) s.58(2) (effective November 23, 2007).

[1] **1A**. The Tribunal shall consist of equal numbers of—

(a) members (in this Part referred to as "solicitor members") appointed by the Lord President, who are solicitors recommended by the Council as representatives of the solicitors' profession throughout Scotland; and

(b) members (in this Part referred to as "non-lawyer members") appointed by the Lord President after consultation with the Scottish Ministers, who are not—

(i) solicitors;

(ii) advocates;

(iii) conveyancing practitioners or executry practitioners, within the meaning of section 23 of the Law Reform (Miscellaneous Provisions) (Scotland) Act 1990 (c.40) ("the 1990 Act");

(iv) persons exercising a right to conduct litigation or a right of audience acquired by virtue of section 27 of the 1990 Act.

NOTE

[1] As inserted by the Legal Profession and Legal Aid (Scotland) Act 2007 (asp 5) s.58(2) (effective November 23, 2007).

[1] **1B.** The validity of any proceedings of the Tribunal is not affected by a vacancy in membership of the Tribunal nor by any defect in the appointment of a member.

NOTE

[1] As inserted by the Legal Profession and Legal Aid (Scotland) Act 2007 (asp 5) s.58(2) (effective November 23, 2007).

[1] **1C.** The Scottish Ministers may by order made by statutory instrument amend paragraph 1 so as to vary the maximum number of members of the Tribunal.

NOTE

[1] As inserted by the Legal Profession and Legal Aid (Scotland) Act 2007 (asp 5) s.58(2) (effective November 23, 2007).

[1] **1D.** A statutory instrument containing an order made under paragraph 1C is subject to annulment in pursuance of a resolution of the Scottish Parliament.

NOTE

[1] As inserted by the Legal Profession and Legal Aid (Scotland) Act 2007 (asp 5) s.58(2) (effective November 23, 2007).

[1] 2. Each member of the Tribunal shall retire from office on the expiry of 5 years from the date of his appointment, but in the case

[2] (*a*) of a non-lawyer, may be re-appointed by the Lord President after consultation with the Secretary of State; and

(*b*) of a solicitor member, may be re-appointed by the Lord President on the recommendation of the Council.

NOTE

[1] As amended by the Law Reform (Miscellaneous Provisions) (Scotland) Act 1980, s. 24, and the Law Reform (Miscellaneous Provisions) (Scotland) Act 1990 (c. 40), Sch.8, para.29(17) (effective 20th July 1992: SI 1992/1599).

[2] As substituted by the Legal Profession and Legal Aid (Scotland) Act 2007 (asp 5) s.58(3) (effective November 23, 2007).

[1 2] 3. The Lord President may from time to time terminate the appointment of any member of the Tribunal, and may fill any vacancy therein by the appointment of a solicitor recommended by the Council or, as the case may be, after consultation with the Secretary of State, by the appointment of a non-lawyer member.

NOTE

[1] As amended by the Law Reform (Miscellaneous Provisions) (Scotland) Act 1990 (c. 40), Sch.8, para.29(17) (effective July 20, 1992: SI 1992/1599).

[2] As substituted by the Legal Profession and Legal Aid (Scotland) Act 2007 (asp 5) s.58(4) (effective November 23, 2007).

---

4. The Tribunal may appoint one of their number to be chairman, and may also appoint a clerk, who shall not be a member of the Tribunal, and, subject to the provisions of this Act, may regulate their procedure in such way as they may think fit.

5. The Tribunal shall be deemed to be properly constituted if—

(*a*) at least 4 members are present, and

(*b*) at least 1 lay member is present, and

(*c*) the number of solicitor members present exceeds the number of lay members present, and

(*d*) [*Repealed by the Legal Profession and Legal Aid (Scotland) Act 2007 (asp 5) s.58(5)(c) (effective November 23, 2007).*]

[1 2] 6. There shall be paid to the non-lawyer members of the Tribunal out of money provided by Parliament such fees and allowances as the Secretary of State may determine.

NOTE

[1] As amended by SI 1999/1820, Art. 4, Sch.2, para.65 (effective July 1, 1999).

[2] As substituted by the Legal Profession and Legal Aid (Scotland) Act 2007 (asp 5) s.58(6) (effective November 23, 2007).

[1] Part II

Procedure and Powers of Tribunal

NOTE

[1] Applied by the Legal Aid (Scotland) Act 1986, s.31(10).

Complaints

7. The making of a complaint to the Tribunal or the giving of any information in connection with a complaint shall confer qualified privilege.

8. A complaint made to the Tribunal shall not be withdrawn except with the Tribunal's leave and subject to such conditions with respect to expenses or otherwise as the Tribunal thinks fit.

[1] 8A. Where a complaint is made to the Tribunal by a person other than—

(a) the Council; or

(b) a person mentioned in section 51(3),

the Tribunal may remit the complaint to the Council.

NOTE

[1] Inserted by the Solicitors (Scotland) Act 1988, Sch.1, para.23.

[1] 9. Subject to Part IV, the Tribunal may dismiss a complaint against a solicitor or an incorporated practice—

(a) without requiring the solicitor or the incorporated practice to answer the allegations made against him or, as the case may be, it or without holding any inquiry if—

(i) they are of the opinion that the complaint discloses no *prima facie* case of professional misconduct on the part of the solicitor or, of failure on the part of the incorporated practice to comply with any provision of this Act or of rules made under this Act or, as the case may be, of provision of inadequate professional services; or

(ii) the complainer fails to comply with any rule made under section 52; or

(b) without hearing parties if they are of the opinion upon consideration of the complaint and other documents that they disclose no case of professional misconduct on the part of the solicitor or, of failure on the part of the incorporated practice to comply with any provision of this Act or of rules made under this Act or, as the case may be, of provision of inadequate professional services.

NOTE

[1] As amended by the Law Reform (Miscellaneous Provisions) (Scotland) Act 1985, Sch.1, Pt I, para.35, and the Solicitors (Scotland) Act 1988, Sch.1, para.23.

[1] 10. The Tribunal shall give notice of the complaint to the solicitor or incorporated practice against whom the complaint is made ("the respondent") and shall inquire into the complaint, giving him or, as the case may be, it reasonable opportunity of making his or, as the case may be, its defence.

NOTE

[1] As amended by the Law Reform (Miscellaneous Provisions) (Scotland) Act 1985, Sch.1, Pt I, para.35.

11. For the purpose of inquiring into the complaint the Tribunal may administer oaths and receive affirmations; and the complainer and respondent shall each be entitled—

(a) to require the evidence of parties, witnesses and others interested, and

(b) to call for and recover such evidence and documents, and examine such witnesses, as

they think proper, but no person shall be compelled to produce any document which he could not be compelled to produce in an action.

12. On a petition by the complainer or the respondent to the court, or to the sheriff having jurisdiction in any place in which the respondent carries on business, the court or, as the case may be, the sheriff, on production of copies (certified by the clerk of the Tribunal) of the complaint and answers, if lodged, together with a statement signed by the clerk specifying the place and date of the hearing of the complaint and certifying that notice to that effect has been given to the complainer and to the respondent, and on being satisfied that it would be proper to compel the giving of evidence by any witness or the production of documents by any haver, may—

(a) grant warrant for the citation of witnesses and havers to give evidence or to produce documents before the Tribunal, and for the issue of letters of second diligence against any witness or haver failing to appear after due citation;
(b) grant warrant for the recovery of documents; and
(c) appoint commissioners to take the evidence of witnesses, to examine havers, and to receive exhibits and productions.

Decisions

13. The Tribunal shall set out in their decision—

(a) in the case of a complaint, the facts proved, and
(b) in the case of a conviction, particulars of the conviction and sentence,

and shall in the case of a complaint add to their decision a note stating the grounds on which the decision has been arrived at.

[1] 14. Every decision of the Tribunal shall be signed by the chairman or other person presiding and shall, subject to paragraph 14A, be published in full.

NOTE

[1] As amended by the Law Reform (Miscellaneous Provisions) (Scotland) Act 1990 (c. 40), Sched. 8, para. 29(17) (effective 20th July 1992: S.I. 1992 No. 1599).

14A In carrying out their duty under paragraph 14, the Tribunal may refrain from publishing any names, places or other facts the publication of which would, in their opinion, damage, or be likely to damage, the interests of persons other than—

(a) the solicitor against whom the complaint was made; or
(b) his partners; or
(c) his or their families,

but where they so refrain they shall publish their reasons for so doing.

NOTE

[1] Inserted by the Law Reform (Miscellaneous Provisions) (Scotland) Act 1990 (c. 40), Sched. 8, para. 29(17) (effective 20th July 1992: S.I. 1992 No. 1599).

---

15. A copy of every decision by the Tribunal certified by the clerk shall be sent forthwith by the clerk to the respondent and to the complainer intimating the right of appeal available from that decision under this Act.

[1] 16. In the case of a decision by the Tribunal—

(a) ordering a solicitor to be struck off the roll; or
(*b*) ordering a solicitor to be suspended from practice; or
(*c*) censuring a solicitor or an incorporated practice; or
(*d*) fining a solicitor or an incorporated practice; or,
(*e*) ordering that the recognition under section 34(1A) of an incorporated practice be revoked; or,
(*f*) containing a direction under section 53A or an order under section 53C(2); or
(*g*) confirming or varying a determination or direction of the Council on an appeal under section 42A(7); or
(*h*) ordering that an investment business certificate issued to a solicitor, a firm of solicitors or an incorporated practice be—
    (i) suspended; or

(ii) subject to such terms and conditions as they may direct; or
(iii) revoked,

on the expiration of the days of appeal if any without an appeal being lodged or, where an appeal has been lodged, if and as soon as the appeal is withdrawn or a decision by the court is given in terms of subparagraphs (*a*) to (*h*) or in the case of a decision of the Tribunal under section 53(6) or (6B) which has not been varied or quashed by the court or under section 53(6A) which has not been varied by the court, the clerk of the Tribunal shall immediately send to the Council a copy of the decision of the Tribunal certified by him and a copy of the decision by the court in any appeal, and the Council shall forthwith give effect to any order as to striking the solicitor off the roll or as to revoking the recognition under section 34(1A) of an incorporated practice and to any terms and conditions directed by the Tribunal under section 53(5); and in any other case shall cause a note of the effect of the decision to be entered against the name of the solicitor in the roll.

NOTE
[1] As amended by the Law Reform (Miscellaneous Provisions) (Scotland) Act 1985, Sched. 1, Pt. I, para. 35, the Solicitors (Scotland) Act 1988, Sched. 1, para. 23, and the Law Reform (Miscellaneous Provisions) (Scotland) Act 1990, Sched. 8.

---

[1] 17. The Council shall forthwith intimate any order striking a solicitor off the roll or suspending a solicitor from practice to each sheriff clerk and to the Principal Clerk of Session, and shall, without prejudice to paragraph 14, cause a notice of the operative part of the order to be published in the *Edinburgh Gazette*.

NOTE
[1] As amended by the Law Reform (Miscellaneous Provisions) (Scotland) Act 1990 (c. 40), Sched. 8, para. 29(17), and 9.

---

18. The file of orders under this Act striking solicitors off the roll, suspending solicitors from practice, or restoring persons to the roll shall be open for inspection at the office of the Society at any reasonable hour by any person without payment of any fee.

[1] 18A. Without prejudice to paragraph 18, the Council shall ensure that a copy of every decision published under paragraph 14 is open for inspection at the office of the Society during office hours by any person without payment of any fee.

NOTE
[1] Inserted by the Law Reform (Miscellaneous Provisions) (Scotland) Act 1990 (c. 40), Sched. 8, para. 29(17) (effective 20th July 1992: S.I. 1992 No. 1599).

Expenses

19. Subject to the provisions of Part IV, the Tribunal may make in relation to any complaint against a solicitor such order as it thinks fit as to the payment by the complainer or by the respondent of the expenses incurred by the other party and by the Tribunal or a reasonable contribution towards those expenses.

20. On the application of the person in whose favour an order for expenses under paragraph 19 is made and on production of a certificate by the clerk of the Tribunal that the days of appeal against the order have expired without an appeal being lodged or, where such an appeal has been lodged, that the appeal has been dismissed or withdrawn, the court may grant warrant authorising that person to recover those expenses from the person against whom the order was made.

21. Such warrant shall have effect for execution and for all other purposes as if it were an extracted decree of court awarded against the person against whom the order of the Tribunal was made.

22. The expenses of the Tribunal so far as not otherwise defrayed shall be paid by the Society as part of the expenses of the Society.

[1] *Appeals*

NOTE

[1] Paras. 23–25 added by the Solicitors (Scotland) Act 1988, Sched.1, para. 23.

---

23. The foregoing provisions of Part II of this Schedule shall apply in relation to an appeal to the Tribunal under section 42A(7) or section 53D(1) as they apply in relation to a complaint, but with the following modifications—

(*a*) for references to a complaint there shall be substituted references to an appeal;
(*b*) for references to the respondent there shall be substituted references to the appellant;
(*c*) paragraphs 8A, 9 and 10 shall not apply; and
(*d*) in paragraph 19 the words "against a solicitor" shall be omitted.

24. Subject to Part IV, the Tribunal may dismiss an appeal without holding an inquiry if—

(*a*) they are of the opinion that the appeal is manifestly ill-founded; or
(*b*) the appellant fails to comply with any rule made under section 52.

25. The Tribunal shall give notice of the appeal to the person by whom the original complaint was made (referred to in this Schedule as "the complainer") and to the Council and shall enquire into the matter, giving the appellant and the complainer reasonable opportunity to make representations to the Tribunal.

SCHEDULE 5

[Repealed by the Law Reform (Miscellaneous Provisions) (Scotland) Act 1990, Sched. 9].

Section 66

SCHEDULE 6

Transitional and Savings Provisions

General

1.—(1) In so far as—

(*a*) any agreement, appointment, operation, authorisation, determination, scheme, instrument, order or regulation made by virtue of an enactment repealed by this Act, or
(*b*) any approval, consent, direction or notice given by virtue of such an enactment, or
(*c*) any complaint made or investigation begun by virtue of such enactment, or
(*d*) any other proceedings begun by virtue of such an enactment, or
(*e*) anything done or having effect as if done,

could, if a corresponding enactment in this Act were in force at the relevant time, have been made, given, begun or done by virtue of the corresponding enactment, it shall, if effective immediately before the corresponding enactment comes into force, continue to have effect thereafter as if made, given, begun or done by virtue of that corresponding enactment.

(2) Where—

(*a*) there is any reference in this Act (whether expressed or implied) to a thing done or required or authorised to be done, or a thing omitted, or to an event which has occurred, under or for the purposes of or by reference to or in contravention of this Act, then
(*b*) that reference shall be construed (subject to its context) as including a reference to the corresponding thing, done or required or authorised to be done, or omitted, or to the corresponding events which occurred, as the case may be, under

Powers of societies

or for the purposes of or by reference to or in contravention of any of the corresponding provisions of the repealed enactments.

2. Where any enactment passed before this Act or any instrument or document refers either

expressly or by implication to an enactment repealed by this Act, the reference shall (subject to its context) be construed as or as including a reference to the corresponding provision of this Act.

3. Where any period of time specified in an enactment repealed by this Act is current at the commencement of this Act, this Act has effect as if its corresponding provision has been in force when that period began to run.

Admission of enrolled law agent

4. Notwithstanding the repeal by this Act of section 15 of the Solicitors (Scotland) Act 1933, the court may grant an application to be admitted as a solicitor to any applicant who was on 28th June 1933 entitled to be admitted as an enrolled law agent according to the regulations for admission then in force under the Law Agents (Scotland) Act 1873.

Restriction of grant under Guarantee Fund

5. Notwithstanding the repeal by this Act of section 22(2)(*b*) of the Legal Aid and Solicitors (Scotland) Act 1949, no grant shall be made by the Council under section 43 in respect of a loss which in the opinion of the Council arose before 1st November 1951.

Rights of banks

6. Nothing in section 61(3) shall deprive a bank of any right existing on 1st November 1949.

Admission to societies

7. Notwithstanding the repeal by this Act of sections 44 and 45 of the Solicitors (Scotland) Act 1933 any society may—
(*a*) admit a solicitor as a member on such conditions as it thinks fit;
(*b*) accept as a qualification for admission an apprenticeship served under the provisions of this Act with a solicitor who is not a member.

8. The repeal of Section 35 of the Solicitors (Scotland) Act 1933 is without prejudice to powers of control exercisable by any society over its members, being powers the society were entitled to exercise immediately before 1st March 1934.

In this paragraph and in paragraph 7, "society" means a faculty or society of solicitors in Scotland, incorporated by Royal Charter or otherwise formed in accordance with law, other than the Law Society of Scotland.

Saving for non-qualified person to conduct certain proceedings

[1] 9. Nothing in this Act shall affect any enactment empowering any person, not being a person qualified to act as a solicitor, to conduct, defend or otherwise act in relation to any action or proceedings in any court.

NOTE
[1] As amended by the Solicitors (Scotland) Act 1988, Sched. 1, para. 24.

Register of law agents

10. Notwithstanding the repeal by this Act of section 18(1) of the Solicitors (Scotland) Act 1933, the Council shall continue to keep in their custody the Register of Law Agents kept under the Law Agents (Scotland) Act 1873 and any relative documents transferred to their custody by virtue of section 18(4) of the Solicitors (Scotland) Act 1949.

Certificate of admission

11. Notwithstanding the repeal by this Act of section 14 of the Solicitors (Scotland) Act 1933, the certificate of admission of a solicitor shall be in writing and signed by a judge of the court.

Law Reform (Miscellaneous Provisions) (Scotland) Act 1990

(1990 c. 40)

An Act, as respects Scotland, . . . to provide as to rights of audience in courts of law, legal services and judicial appointments, and for the establishment and functions of an ombudsman in relation to legal services; . . . and to make certain other miscellaneous reforms of the law. [November 1, 1990]

. . . . . .

Part I

Charities

1.–15. [*Not printed.*]

[1] Part II

Legal Services

NOTE

[1] Pt. II is to come into force on a day or days to be appointed: s.75(2): see notes to each section, *infra*.

Conveyancing and Executry Services

16.–19. [*Not printed.*]

Professional misconduct, inadequate professional services, etc.

[1] **20.**—(1) Where, after such inquiry as they consider appropriate (whether or not following a complaint to them) and after giving the practitioner concerned an opportunity to make representations, the Council are satisfied that a practitioner—

(a) is guilty of professional misconduct;

(b) has provided inadequate professional services;

(c) has failed to comply with rules made under section 17(11) or 18(10), or rules or regulations referred to in section 17(11B) or 18(10B), of this Act; or

(d) has been convicted of a criminal offence rendering him no longer a fit and proper person to provide conveyancing services as a conveyancing practitioner or, as the case may be, executry services as an executry practitioner,

they may take such of the steps out in subsection (2) below as they think fit and shall, without prejudice to subsection (6) below, intimate their decision to the practitioner by notice in writing.

(2) The steps referred to in subsection (1) above are—

(a) to determine that the amount of fees and outlays which the practitioner may charge in respect of such services as the Council may specify shall be—

(i) nil; or

(ii) such amount as the Council may specify in the determination,

and to direct the practitioner to comply, or secure compliance, with such of the requirements set out in subsection (5) below as appear to them to be necessary to give effect to the determination;

(b) to direct the practitioner to secure the rectification at his own expense of any such error, omission or other deficiency arising in connection with the services as the Council may specify;

(c) to attach conditions (or, as the case may be, further conditions) to the registration of the practitioner or to vary any condition so attached;

(d) . . .

(e) . . .

(f) in a case where the practitioner has provided inadequate professional services, to direct the practitioner to pay to the client by way of compensation such sum, not exceeding £1,000, as the Council may specify;

(g) . . .

(h) to make a report of the Council's findings to any other person exercising functions with respect to—

(i) the practitioner; or

(ii) any person employed by or acting on behalf of the practitioner in connection with the provision of the services.

(2A) Where—

(a) after holding an inquiry into a complaint against a practitioner, the Scottish Solicitors' Discipline Tribunal are satisfied that—

(i) he has been guilty of professional misconduct; or

(ii) he has provided inadequate professional services; or

(b) a practitioner has been convicted by any court of an act involving dishonesty or has been sentenced to a term of imprisonment of not less than 2 years,

the Tribunal may take such of the steps set out in subsection (2B) below as they think fit.

(2B) The steps referred to in subsection (2A) above are—

(a) to suspend or revoke the registration of the practitioner;

(b) subject to subsection (3) below, to impose on the practitioner a fine not exceeding £10,000;

(c) to censure the practitioner; and

(d) any of the steps which the Council may take in respect of a practitioner under subsection (2)(a) to (f) above.

(3) The Tribunal shall not impose a fine under subsection (2B)(b) above where, in relation to the subject matter of the Tribunal's inquiry, the practitioner has been convicted by any court of an offence involving dishonesty and sentenced to a term of imprisonment of not less than two years.

(4) Any fine imposed under subsection (2B)(b) above shall be treated for the purposes of section 203 of the Criminal Procedure (Scotland) Act 1975 (fines payable to HM Exchequer) as if it were a fine imposed in the High Court.

(5) The requirements referred to in subsection (2)(a) above are—

(a) to refund, whether in whole or to any specified extent, any amount already paid by or on behalf of the client in respect of the fees and outlays of the practitioner in connection with the services; and

(b) to waive, whether wholly or to any specified extent, the right to recover those fees and outlays.

(6) Where the Council make a direction under subsection (2)(a), (b) or (f) above, or the Scottish Solicitors' Discipline Tribunal, by virtue of subsection (2B)(d) above, make a similar direction, the Council or (as the case may be) the Tribunal shall, by notice in writing, require the practitioner to which the direction relates to give to the Council, within such period being not less than 21 days as the notice may specify, an explanation of the steps which he has taken to comply with the direction.

(7) Where a practitioner—

(a) fails to comply with a notice under subsection (6) above; or

(b) complies with such a notice but the Council are not satisfied as to the steps taken by the practitioner to comply with the direction to which the notice relates, the Council may apply to the Court of Session for an order requiring the practitioner to comply with the direction to which the notice relates within such time as the court may order.

(8) Where the Council take a step set out in subsection (2)(c) above or the Scottish Solicitors' Discipline Tribunal, by virtue of subsection (2B)(d) above, take a similar step or the Tribunal take a step set out in subsection (2B)(a) above and—

(a) any period specified in this section for applying for review or for the making of an appeal in respect of the matter has expired without such a review having been applied for or such an appeal having been made;

(b) where such an application or appeal is made, the matter is finally determined in favour of the Council's or, as the case may be, Tribunal's decision or the application or appeal is withdrawn,

the Council shall amend the register of executry practitioners or, as the case may be, the register of conveyancing practitioners accordingly.

(9)–(10) [*Repealed by the Public Appointments and Public Bodies etc. (Scotland) Act 2003 (asp 4), Sch.4, para.12(6)(j) (effective August 15, 2003).*]

(11) Where the Council take a step set out in subsection (2)(a) to (f) above, the practitioner concerned may—

(a) within 21 days of the date on which the Council's decision is intimated to him, apply to the Council to review their decision; and

(b) within 21 days of the date on which the outcome of such review is intimated to him, appeal to the Scottish Solicitors' Discipline Tribunal against the decision made in any such review; and the Tribunal may quash, confirm or vary that decision.

(11A) Within 21 days of the date on which—

(a) the outcome of any appeal under subsection (11)(b) above; or

(b) the taking of any step referred to in subsection (2B) above,

is intimated to the practitioner concerned, he may appeal to the Court of Session against the decision made by the Tribunal in the appeal or, as the case may be, to take such a step; and the Court may make such order in the matter as it thinks fit.

(12) [*Repealed by the Public Appointments and Public Bodies etc. (Scotland) Act 2003 (asp 4), Sch.4, para.12(6)(m) (effective August 15, 2003).*]

(13) The Secretary of State, after consulting the Council, may by order made by statutory instrument subject to annulment in pursuance of a resolution of either House of Parliament, amend subsection (2)(f) above by substituting for the sum for the time being specified in that provision such other sum as he considers appropriate.

(14) The taking of any steps under subsection (2) or (2B) above shall not be founded upon in any proceedings for the purpose of showing that the practitioner in respect of whom the steps were taken was negligent.

(15) A direction under subsection (2)(f) above to a practitioner to pay compensation to a client shall not prejudice any right of that client to take proceedings against that practitioner for damages in respect of any loss which he alleges he has suffered as a result of that practitioner's negligence, and any sum directed to be paid to that client under that provision may be taken into account in the computation of any award of damages made to him in any such proceedings.

(16) The Secretary of State may, by order made by statutory instrument subject to annulment in pursuance of a resolution of either House of Parliament, amend subsection (2B)(b) above by substituting for the amount for the time being specified in that provision such other amount as appears to him to be justified by a change in the value of money.

(17) In this section "executry practitioner" and "conveyancing practitioner" respectively include any executry practitioner or conveyancing

practitioner whether or not he was registered as such at the time when the subject matter of the Council's or, as the case may be, Tribunal's inquiry occurred and notwithstanding that subsequent to that time he has ceased to be so registered.

NOTE

[1] Brought into force on March 1, 1997 by SI 1996/2894; as amended by SI 1996/2966 and the Public Appointments and Public Bodies etc. (Scotland) Act 2003 (asp 4), Sch.4, para.12(6) (effective August 15, 2003).

Review of decisions

[1] **20A.**—(1) The Council shall establish a procedure under which they shall, on the application of any aggrieved person, review any relevant decision made by them.

(2) In subsection (1) above—

(a) "relevant decision" means—

(i) a refusal to grant an application for registration as a practitioner;

(ii) a decision to grant an application for registration as a practitioner subject to conditions; or

(iii) a decision to take any step set out in subsection (2)(a) to (f) of section 20 of this Act; and

(b) "aggrieved person" means the applicant or, as the case may be, the practitioner concerned.

NOTE

[1] Inserted by the Public Appointments and Public Bodies etc. (Scotland) Act 2003 (asp 4), Sch.4, para.12(7) (effective August 15, 2003).

Board's intervention powers

[1] **21.**—(1) The powers conferred on the Council by this section may be exercised if, after such inquiry (if any) as the Council consider appropriate, it appears to them to be desirable to do so for the purpose of protecting the interests of the clients, or prospective clients, of an independent conveyancing practitioner or an executry practitioner (each of which is in this section referred to as a "relevant practitioner").

(2) The Council may, in particular, exercise any such power where it appears to them that a relevant practitioner—

(a) is no longer a fit and proper person to provide conveyancing services or, as the case may be, executry services;

(b) has ceased, for whatever reason, to provide such services; or

(c) has failed, or is likely to fail, to comply with any rules or regulations referred to in section 20(1)(c) of this Act.

(3) The Council may direct the relevant practitioner not to dispose of, or otherwise deal with, except in accordance with the terms of the direction—

(a) any assets belonging to any client of the practitioner and held by or under the control of the practitioner in connection with his business as an independent conveyancing practitioner or, as the case may be, an executry practitioner; or

(b) any assets of the practitioner which are specified, or of a kind specified, in the direction.

(4) The Council may direct the relevant practitioner to transfer to the Council, or to such persons (in this section referred to as "the trustees") as may be specified in the direction—

(a) all assets belonging to any client of the practitioner and held by or under the control of the practitioner in connection with his business as an independent conveyancing practitioner or, as the case may be, an executry practitioner; or

(b) any assets of the practitioner which are specified, or of a kind specified, in the direction.

(5) A relevant practitioner to whom a direction is given may, within 21

days of the date on which the direction is received by him, apply to the Court of Session, which may make such order in the matter as it thinks fit.

(6) A relevant practitioner to whom a direction is given shall comply with it as soon as it takes effect (and whether or not he proposes to apply to the Court of Session under subsection (5) above).

(7) If, on an application to the Court of Session by the Council, the court is satisfied—

(a) that a relevant practitioner has failed, within a reasonable time, to comply with any direction given to him; or

(b) that there is a reasonable likelihood that a relevant practitioner will so fail,

the court may make an order requiring the practitioner, and any other person whom the court considers it appropriate to subject to its order, to take such steps as the court may direct with a view to securing compliance with the direction.

(8) Any assets which have been transferred as a result of a direction given under subsection (4) above shall be held by the Council, or by the trustees, on trust for the client or, as the case may be, the practitioner concerned.

(9) The trustees may deal with any assets which have been transferred to them only in accordance with directions given to them by the Council.

(10) If the Council have reasonable cause to believe that a relevant practitioner or an employee of a relevant practitioner has been guilty of dishonesty resulting in pecuniary loss to a client of the relevant practitioner, they may apply to the Court of Session for an order that no payment be made by any bank, building society or other body named in the order out of any bank, building society or other account or any sum deposited in the name of the relevant practitioner without the leave of the court and the court may make such an order.

(11) Any direction under this section—

(a) shall be given in writing;

(b) shall state the reason why it is being given;

(c) shall take effect on such date as may be specified in the direction (which may be the date on which it is served on the relevant practitioner); and

(d) may be varied or revoked by a further direction given by the Board.

(12) In this section—

"assets" includes any sum of money (in whatever form and whether or not in any bank, building society or other account) and any book, account, deed or other document held by the relevant practitioner on his own behalf in connection with his business as a relevant practitioner or on behalf of the client concerned; and

"independent conveyancing practitioner" and "executry practitioner" respectively include any independent conveyancing practitioner or executry practitioner whether or not he was registered as such at the time when the matter in relation to which the Council exercise or propose to exercise their powers under this section arose and notwithstanding that subsequent to that time he has ceased to be so registered.

NOTE

[1] Brought into force on March 1, 1997 by SI 1996/2894, as amended by SI 1996/2966 and the Public Appointments and Public Bodies etc. (Scotland) Act 2003 (asp 4), Sch.4, para.12(8) (effective August 15, 2003).

Powers of investigation

[1] **21A.**—(1) The Council may exercise the power conferred by subsection (3) below for any of the following purposes—

(a) an inquiry under subsection (1) of section 20 of this Act;

(b) a review under subsection (11)(a) of that section; and

(c) consideration by the Council whether to exercise the powers conferred on them by section 21 of this Act.

(2) The Scottish Solicitors' Discipline Tribunal may exercise the power conferred by subsection (3) below for any of the following purposes—

(a) an inquiry under subsection (2A) of section 20 of this Act; and

(b) an appeal under subsection (11)(b) of that section.

(3) The Council or, as the case may be, the Tribunal may give notice in writing to a practitioner specifying the subject matter of their investigation and requiring either or both of the following—

(a) the production or delivery to any person appointed by the Council or, as the case may be, the Tribunal, at a time and place specified in the notice, of such documents so specified as are in the possession or control of the practitioner and relate to the subject matter of the investigation;

(b) an explanation, within such period being not less than 21 days as the notice may specify, from the practitioner regarding the subject matter of the investigation.

(4) If a practitioner fails to comply with a notice under subsection (3)(a) above, the Council or, as the case may be, the Tribunal may apply to the Court of Session for an order requiring him to produce or deliver the documents to the person appointed at the place specified in the notice within such time as the court may order.

NOTE

[1] Inserted by the Public Appointments and Public Bodies etc. (Scotland) Act 2003 (asp 4), Sch.4, para.12(9) (effective August 15, 2003).

Procedures of the Scottish Solicitors' Discipline Tribunal etc.

[1] **21B.**—(1) Paragraphs 7 to 9, 11, 13 to 15 and 18A to 22 of Schedule 4 to the Solicitors (Scotland) Act 1980 (c.46) (which make provision as to certain powers and procedures of the Scottish Solicitors' Discipline Tribunal) apply in relation to complaints made against conveyancing and executry practitioners as they apply in relation to complaints against solicitors, but as if—

(a) in paragraph 8A, sub-paragraph (b) and the word "; or" immediately preceding it were omitted; and

(b) in paragraphs 9 and 19, the references to Part IV of that Act were references to sections 20 and 21A of this Act.

(2) Paragraphs 7, 8, 11, 13 to 15 and 18A to 22 of that Schedule to that Act apply in relation to any appeal under subsection (11)(b) of section 20 of this Act as they apply, by virtue of subsection (1) above, in relation to any complaint against conveyancing and executry practitioners, and—

(a) the modifications made to those paragraphs by paragraph 23(a), (b) and (d) of that Schedule apply for the purposes of that application of those paragraphs; and

(b) paragraphs 24 and 25 of that Schedule apply in relation to any such appeal as they apply in relation to an appeal to which those paragraphs apply, but as if the reference in paragraph 24 to Part IV of that Act were a reference to sections 20 and 21A of this Act.

(3) In the case of a decision by the Scottish Solicitors' Discipline Tribunal—

(a) to take any of the steps set out in subsection (2B) of section 20 of this Act; or

(b) in an appeal under subsection (11)(b) of that section,

subsection (4) below applies.

(4) Where this subsection applies and—

(a) no appeal has been made to the Court under subsection (11A) of section 20 of this Act against the decision; or

(b) such an appeal has been made but has—

(i) been withdrawn; or
(ii) resulted in the Tribunal's decision being upheld,

the clerk of the Tribunal shall send to the Council a copy of the decision of the Tribunal certified by him and the decision of the Court in any such appeal.

(5) If the decision of the Tribunal so certified is to suspend or revoke the registration of the practitioner under paragraph (a) of subsection (2B) of section 20 of this Act, the Council shall—

(a) give effect to the decision; and
(b) cause a note of the effect of the decision to be entered against the name of the practitioner in the register of conveyancing practitioners or, as the case may be, of executry practitioners.

NOTE
[1] Inserted by the Public Appointments and Public Bodies etc. (Scotland) Act 2003 (asp 4), Sch.4, para.12(9) (effective August 15, 2003).

Compensation fund

[1] **21C.**—(1) The Council shall establish and maintain a fund for the purpose of making grants to compensate persons who in the opinion of the Council have suffered pecuniary loss by reason of dishonesty in connection with the provision of—

(a) conveyancing services by or on behalf of an independent conveyancing practitioner; and
(b) executry services to the public for a fee, gain or reward by or on behalf of an executry practitioner.

(2) The Council may, for the purpose of guaranteeing the sufficiency of the fund mentioned in subsection (1) above, enter into a contract of insurance with any person authorised by law to carry out insurance business.

(3) The Scottish Ministers may—

(a) make contributions to the fund mentioned in subsection (1) above; and
(b) defray any premium, fee or other expense payable by the Council under or in relation to a contract entered into under subsection (2) above.

(4) The Council may, with the approval of the Scottish Ministers, make rules with regard to the operation of the fund mentioned in subsection (1) above and, without prejudice to the foregoing generality, such rules may make provision as to—

(a) contributions to be paid to the fund by independent conveyancing practitioners and by executry practitioners who provide executry services to the public for a fee, gain or reward;
(b) the procedure for making claims against the fund; and
(c) the administration, management and protection of the fund.

(5) The fund for the purpose of making grants to compensate persons by reason of dishonesty in connection with the provision of conveyancing and executry services maintained by the Scottish Conveyancing and Executry Services Board immediately before the coming into force of this subsection shall be transferred to and vested in the Council; and that fund shall be applied by the Council to the fund established under subsection (1) above.

(6) Any rules as to the fund transferred under subsection (5) above having effect immediately before the coming into force of this subsection shall have effect with respect to the fund established under subsection (1) above as if they were rules made under subsection (4) above; and the Council may amend or repeal any such rules.

NOTE
[1] Inserted by the Public Appointments and Public Bodies etc. (Scotland) Act 2003 (asp 4), Sch.4, para.12(9) (effective August 15, 2003).

Disclosure of documents etc.

[1] **22.**—(1) Any communication made to or by—

(a) an independent conveyancing practitioner or an executry practitioner in the course of his acting as such for a client;

shall in any action or proceedings in any court be protected from disclosure on the ground of confidentiality between client and professional legal adviser in like manner as if the practitioner had at all material times been a solicitor acting for the client.

(2) Any enactment or instrument making special provision in relation to a solicitor or other legal representative as to the disclosure of information, or as to the production, seizure or removal of documents, with respect to which a claim to confidentiality between client and professional legal adviser could be maintained, shall, with any necessary modifications, have effect in relation to—

(a) an independent conveyancing practitioner; and

(b) an executry practitioner;

as it has effect in relation to a solicitor.

NOTE

[1] Brought into force on March 1, 1997 by SI 1996/2894, as amended by SI 1996/2966 and the Public Appointments and Public Bodies etc. (Scotland) Act 2003 (asp 4), Sch.4, para.12(10) (effective August 15, 2003).

Interpretation of sections 16 to 22

[1] **23.** In sections 16 to 22 of this Act and this section, except where the context otherwise requires—

"conveyancing practitioner" means a person registered under section 17 in the register of conveyancing practitioners;

"conveyancing services" means the preparation of writs, contracts and other documents in connection with the transfer of heritable property and loans secured over such property, and services ancillary thereto, including (in the case of independent conveyancing practitioners) relevant notarial services, but does not include any services—

(a) relating to the arranging of loans; or

(b) falling within section 1(1)(a) of the Estate Agents Act 1979;

"the Council" means the Council of the Law Society of Scotland;

"executry practitioner" means a person registered under section 18 in the register of executry practitioners;

"executry services" means the drawing and preparation of papers on which to found or oppose an application for a grant of confirmation of executors and services in connection with the administration, ingathering, distribution and winding up of the estate of a deceased person by executors, but does not include anything which constitutes investment business within the meaning of the Financial Services Act 1986;

"inadequate professional services" means professional services which are in any respect not of the quality which could reasonably be expected of a competent practitioner; and references to the provision of inadequate professional services shall be construed as including references to not providing professional services which such a practitioner ought to have provided;

"independent conveyancing practitioner" means a conveyancing practitioner whose entry in the register of conveyancing practitioners has been annotated to that effect under section 17(1B);

"practitioner" means an executry practitioner or a conveyancing practitioner; and

"relevant notarial services" means the functions exercisable by independent conveyancing practitioners by virtue of section 14(1) and (2) of the Public Appointments and Public Bodies etc. (Scotland) Act 2003 (asp 4).

NOTE

[1] Brought into force on April 1, 1991 by SI 1991/822. As amended by the Public Appointments and Public Bodies etc. (Scotland) Act 2003 (asp 4), Sch.4, para.12(11) (effective August 15, 2003).

Rights of audience

Rights of audience in the Court of Session, the House of Lords, the Judicial Committee of the Privy Council and the High Court of Justiciary

24. [*Inserts s.25A in the Solicitors (Scotland) Act 1980 (c.46), supra.*]

Rights to conduct litigation and rights of audience

25.—(1) Any professional or other body may, for the purpose of enabling any of their members who is a natural person to acquire—

(a) rights to conduct litigation on behalf of members of the public; and

(b) rights of audience,

make an application in that regard to the Lord President and the Secretary of State.

(2) An application under subsection (1) above shall include a draft scheme—

(a) specifying—

(i) the courts;

(ii) the categories of proceedings;

(iii) the nature of the business; and

(iv) the rights to conduct litigation and the rights of audience,

in relation to which the application is made;

(b) describing—

(i) the training requirements which the body would impose upon any of their members who sought to acquire any right such as is mentioned in subsection (1) above; and

(ii) the code of practice which they would impose upon their members in relation to the exercise by those members of any rights acquired by them by virtue of this section,

in the event of the application being granted; and

(c) proposing arrangements for—

(i) the indemnification of members of the public against loss suffered by them through the actings of the body's members in the exercise by those members of any rights acquired by them by virtue of this section; and

(ii) the treatment by the body of complaints made to them by members of the public in relation to the actings of members of the body exercising rights acquired by virtue of this section,

and shall state that the body have complied with the provisions of Schedule 2 to this Act.

[1] (3) A code of practice such as is mentioned in subsection (2)(b)(ii) above shall include provision with regard to revoking, suspending or attaching conditions to the exercise of any right acquired by a member of the body by virtue of section 27 of this Act in consequence of a breach by that member of that code of practice; and shall in particular include provision enabling the body to comply with the provisions of section 27(4) of this Act.

(4) A draft scheme submitted under this section shall also include the proposals of the body in relation to such other matters as may be prescribed by the Secretary of State in regulations made under this section.

(5) Regulations under this section shall be made by statutory instrument subject to annulment in pursuance of a resolution of either House of Parliament.

(6) Schedule 2 shall have effect in relation to the publication of applications made under subsection (1) above.

NOTE

[1] As substituted by the Legal Profession and Legal Aid (Scotland) Act 2007 (asp 5) Sch.5, para.3(10)(d) (effective March 19, 2007).

Consideration of applications made under section 25

26.—(1) The Lord President shall consider the provision made in any draft scheme submitted to him under section 25(1) of this Act in relation to the matters mentioned in section 25(2); and the Secretary of State shall, subject to subsection (5) below and to section 40 of this Act, consider the provision so made in section 25(2)(b) and (c).

(2) In considering the code of practice included in the draft scheme by virtue of section 25(2)(b)(ii), the Lord President shall have regard to the desirability of there being common principles applying in relation to the exercising of rights to conduct litigation and rights of audience by all practitioners in relation to the court or, as the case may be, the courts, mentioned in the application.

(3) The Lord President and the Secretary of State shall—

(*a*) consult each other in considering a draft scheme submitted to them under section 25(1); and

(*b*) consider any written representations timeously made to them under Schedule 2 to this Act,

and may, either jointly or severally, make preliminary observations to the body concerned in relation to that draft; and the body may make such adjustments to the draft as appear to them to be appropriate, and the Lord President and the Secretary of State (who shall, in accordance with section 40, consult the Director in respect of any adjustments made in relation to the matters mentioned in section 25(2)(*b*) or (*c*)) shall thereafter consider the draft scheme as so adjusted.

(4) In considering a draft scheme under subsection (1) or (3) above, the Lord President and the Secretary of State shall have regard to whether the provisions of the draft scheme are such as—

(*a*) to achieve; and

(*b*) to ensure the maintenance of,

appropriate standards of conduct and practice by persons who may acquire rights to conduct litigation or rights of audience in the event of the draft scheme being approved.

(5) In relation to any code of practice such as is mentioned in section 25(2)(*b*)(ii), the duty of the Secretary of State under subsection (1) above is limited to a consideration of any provision of such a code as would, in his view, directly or indirectly inhibit the freedom of a member of the body concerned to undertake all the work necessary for the preparation of a case or for the presentation of a case before the court, other than such a provision which has that effect only by reason of the provision made in the draft scheme with respect to the matters mentioned in section 25(2)(*a*).

(6) After they have considered a draft scheme under subsections (1) and (3) above, if the Lord President and the Secretary of State—

(*a*) are satisfied with the draft scheme, the Lord President shall grant the application, and shall so inform the body;

(*b*) are not satisfied with the scheme, the Lord President shall refuse the application, and shall so inform the body, giving written reasons for the refusal,

and the Lord President shall send a copy of the letter granting or refusing the application to any person who has made representations in relation to the draft scheme under Schedule 2 to this Act.

(7) Where the Lord President has granted an application under subsection (6)(*a*) above, in relation to—

(*a*) civil proceedings, the Court of Session may by act of sederunt; and

(*b*) criminal proceedings, the High Court of Justiciary may by act of adjournal,

make such provision for giving effect to the scheme as appears to it to be appropriate.

Exercise of rights to conduct litigation and rights of audience

27.—(1) Where an application made under section 25 of this Act has been granted under section 26 of this Act, any member of the body concerned who has complied with the terms of the scheme in relation to the matters mentioned in section 25(2)(*b*)(i), and who appears to the body to be a fit and proper person, shall have the right to conduct litigation or rights of audience to which that compliance entitles him.

(2) Where a function is, whether expressly or by implication, conferred on any person or body by section 26 or this section he or, as the case may be, they shall exercise that function as soon as is reasonably practicable.

(3) Nothing in subsection (1) above affects the power of any court in relation to any proceedings—

(*a*) to hear a person who would not otherwise have a right of audience before that court in relation to those proceedings; or

(*b*) to refuse to hear a person (for reasons which apply to him as an individual) who would otherwise have a right of audience before that court in relation to those proceedings, and where a court so refuses it shall give its reasons for that decision.

(4) Where a complaint has been made that a person has been guilty of professional misconduct in the exercise of any right to conduct litigation or right of audience held by him by virtue of this section, the body of which he is a member may, or if so requested by the Lord President shall, suspend that person from exercising that right pending determination of that complaint by the body.

(5) Where a person holding a right of audience in any court by virtue of this section is instructed to appear in that court, those instructions shall take precedence before any of his other professional or business obligations, and the code of practice mentioned in section 25(2)(*b*)(ii) shall include rules—

(*a*) stating the order of precedence of courts for the purposes of this subsection;

(*b*) stating general criteria to which members of the body should have regard in determining whether to accept instructions in particular circumstances; and

(*c*) securing, through such of their officers as they think appropriate, that, where reasonably practicable, any person wishing to be represented before any court by one of their members holding an appropriate right of audience is so represented,

and, for the purposes of such rules, the Inner and Outer Houses of the Court of Session, and the High Court of Justiciary exercising its appellate jurisdiction, may be treated as separate courts.

(6) A person exercising any right of audience held by virtue of this section shall have the same immunity from liability for negligence in respect of his acts or omissions as if he were an advocate, and no act or omission on the part of any such person shall give rise to an action for breach of contract in relation to the exercise by him of such a right of audience.

(7) Any person who wilfully and falsely—

(*a*) pretends to have any right to conduct litigation or right of audience by virtue of this section; or

(*b*) where he has any such right, pretends to have any further such right which he does not have; or

(*c*) takes or uses any name, title, addition or description implying that he has any such right or, as the case may be, any further such right,

shall be guilty of an offence and liable on summary conviction to a fine not exceeding level 4 on the standard scale.

(8) For the purposes of section 25, section 26 and this section—

"right of audience" includes, in relation to any court, any such right exercisable by an advocate; and

"right to conduct litigation" means the right to exercise on behalf of a client all or any of the functions, other than any right of audience, which may be exercised by a solicitor in relation to litigation.

Surrender of rights to conduct litigation and rights of audience

28.—(1) Subject to the provisions of this section, where an application made under section 25 of this Act has been granted under section 26(6) of this Act, the body concerned may apply to the Lord President and the Secretary of State for permission to surrender any entitlement of their members to acquire rights to conduct litigation or rights of audience.

(2) The Lord President and the Secretary of State shall jointly issue directions as to the requirements with which any body wishing to surrender their members' entitlement will have to comply, and, without prejudice to the generality of the foregoing, any such directions may include provision—

(*a*) where members of a body have acquired rights to conduct litigation or rights of audience, as to the arrangements to be made for the completion of any work outstanding at the time the application is made; and

(*b*) relating to the particular circumstances of a particular body.

(3) An application under subsection (1) above shall describe the manner in which the body have complied, or will comply, with the directions issued under subsection (2) above.

(4) Where the Lord President and the Secretary of State are satisfied that the body concerned have complied, or will comply, with the directions issued under subsection (2) above, the Lord President shall grant the application, and shall so inform the body.

(5) With effect from the date on which an application under subsection (1) above is granted, any member of the body concerned who has acquired rights to conduct litigation or rights of audience by virtue of the scheme shall cease to hold those rights.

Revocation of rights granted under section 26

29.—(1) Where it appears to the Secretary of State that a body has failed to comply with a direction under section 42(6) of this Act, he may by order made by statutory instrument revoke the grant of the application made by that body under section 25 of this Act.

(2) No instrument shall be made under subsection (1) above unless a draft of the instrument has been laid before and approved by each House of Parliament.

(3) With effect from the date on which an order under subsection (1) above takes effect, any member of the body concerned who has acquired rights to conduct litigation or rights of audience by virtue of the scheme shall cease to hold those rights.

Regulation of right of English, Welsh and Northern Irish practitioners to practise in Scotland

[1] **30.**—(1) The Secretary of State, after consulting the Lord President, may by regulations prescribe circumstances in which, and conditions subject to which, practitioners who are qualified to practise in England and Wales or Northern Ireland may, in such capacity as may be prescribed, exercise in Scotland—

(a) prescribed rights of audience; or

(b) prescribed rights to conduct litigation,

without being entitled to do so apart from the regulations.

(2) The Secretary of State, after consulting the Lord President, may by regulations make provision for the purpose of enabling practitioners who are entitled to practise in England and Wales or Northern Ireland to become qualified to practise in Scotland on terms, and subject to conditions, corresponding or similar to those on which practitioners who are entitled to practise in member States may become qualified to practise in Scotland.

(3) Regulations made under subsection (1) above may, in particular—

(a) prescribe any right of audience which may not be exercised by a person in Scotland unless he is instructed to act together with a person who has that right of audience there;

(b) prescribe legal services which may not be provided by any person practising by virtue of the regulations;

(c) prescribe the title or description which must be used by any person practising by virtue of the regulations;

(d) provide for the body by whom and the means by which the qualification of any person claiming to be entitled to practise by virtue of the regulations is to be verified; and

(e) provide for such professional or other body as may be prescribed to have power to investigate and deal with any complaint made against a person practising by virtue of the regulations.

(4) Regulations made under subsection (1) or (2) above may modify any rule of law or practice which the Secretary of State considers should be modified in order to give effect to the regulations.

(5) Regulations under this section shall be made by statutory instrument subject to annulment in pursuance of a resolution of either House of Parliament.

(6) In this section "practitioner" means, in relation to England and Wales and Northern Ireland—

(a) a barrister or solicitor; and

(b) any person falling within such category as may be prescribed in regulations made by the Secretary of State after consultation with the Lord President.

NOTE

[1] In force June 3, 1991: SI 1991/1252.

Rules of Conduct

Rules of conduct etc.

[1] **31.**—(1) Any rule, whether made before or after the coming into force of this section, whereby an advocate is prohibited from forming a legal relationship with another advocate or with any other person for the purpose of their jointly offering professional services to the public shall have no effect unless it is approved by the Lord President and the Secretary of State; and before approving any such rule the Secretary of State shall consult the Director in accordance with section 40 of this Act.

(2) Where it appears to the Faculty of Advocates that any rule of conduct in relation to the exercise of an advocate's right of audience in the Court of Session is more restrictive than the equivalent rule in relation to the exercise of the equivalent right in the sheriff court, they may submit that rule to the Secretary of State for his approval, and the Secretary of State shall consult the Director in accordance with section 40 of this Act, and thereafter, having—

(a) considered any advice tendered to him by the Director;

(b) compared the rule applicable in the Court of Session with the equivalent rule applicable in the sheriff court; and

(c) considered whether the interests of justice require that there should be such a rule in the Court of Session,

he may approve or refuse to approve the rule.

(3) In section 34 of the 1980 Act (rules as to professional practice, conduct and discipline)—

(a) at the end of subsection (1A) there shall be inserted—

"and

(f) make such additional or different provision as the Council think fit in relation to solicitors who, or incorporated practices which, are partners in or directors of multi-disciplinary practices."; and

(b) after subsection (3) there shall be inserted—

"(3A) Without prejudice to subsection (3), any rule made, whether before or after the coming into force of this subsection, by the Council under this section or section 35 which has the effect of prohibiting the formation of multi-disciplinary practices shall not have effect unless the Secretary of State, after consulting the Director in accordance with section 64A, has approved it.".

NOTE
[1] In force March 17, 1993: SI 1993/641.

Multi-national practices

Multi-national practices

[1] **32.** [*Inserts s.60A in Solicitors (Scotland) Act 1980 (c.46), above.*]

NOTE
[1] In force October 1, 2004: SSI 2004/382.

Complaints in relation to legal services

Complaints in relation to legal services

[1] **33.**—(1) Where any person with an interest has made a complaint (a "conduct complaint") to a professional organisation that a practitioner has—

(a) been guilty of professional misconduct; or
(b) provided inadequate professional services,

the organisation shall investigate the matter, and shall thereafter make a written report to the complainer and the practitioner concerned of—

(i) the facts of the matter as found by the organisation; and
(ii) what action the organisation propose to take, or have taken, in the matter.

[2] (2) The organisation shall ensure that their procedures for dealing with conduct complaints do not conflict with the duty imposed by section 34A of this Act in relation to any report sent to them under that section.

(3)–(4) [*Repealed by the Scottish Legal Services Ombudsman and Commissioner for Local Administration in Scotland Act 1997 (c. 35), s.5(1)(b) and Sched.*][3]

[5] (5) For the purposes of this section and sections 34, 34A and 34B of this Act[4]—

"professional organisation" means—
(a) the Faculty of Advocates;
(b) the Council of the Law Society of Scotland;
(c) . . .
(d) a body which has made a successful application under section 25 of this Act; and

"practitioner" means, in relation to—
(a) the Faculty of Advocates, an advocate;
(b) the Council, a solicitor or a practitioner within the meaning of section 23 of this Act;
(c) . . .
(d) a body which has made a successful application under section 25 of this Act, any person exercising—
(i) a right to conduct litigation; or
(ii) a right of audience;
acquired by virtue of section 27 of this Act.

NOTES
[1] In force June 3, 1991: SI 1991/1252.
[2] As amended by 1997 (c.35), s.5(1)(a), effective July 22, 1997.
[3] Effective July 22, 1997.
[4] Inserted by 1997 (c.35), s.5(1)(c), effective July 22, 1997.
[5] As amended by the Public Appointments and Public Bodies etc. (Scotland) Act 2003 (asp 4), Sch.4, para.12(12) (effective August 15, 2003). Read in conjunction with the European Communities (Lawyer's Practice) (Scotland) Regulations 2000 (SSI 2000/121), reg.37(2) and Sch.2, para.6(2) (effective May 22, 2000) and SSI 2004/383, reg.16.

Scottish legal services ombudsman

Scottish legal services ombudsman

[1] **34.**—(1) The Secretary of State may, after consultation with the Lord President, and subject to subsection (9) below, appoint a person, to be

known as the Scottish legal services ombudsman, for the purpose of conducting investigations under this Act.[2]

[3] (1A) Subject to subsection (1E) below, the ombudsman may investigate any written complaint (a "handling complaint") made to him by or on behalf of any person which relates to the manner in which a conduct complaint made by or on behalf of that person has been dealt with by the professional organisation concerned.

[3] (1B) Subsection (1A) above applies whether or not the professional organisation concerned have treated the conduct complaint as a conduct complaint.

[3] (1C) The ombudsman may decide—

(a) not to investigate a handling complaint; or

(b) to discontinue his investigation of a handling complaint.

[3] (1D) If the ombudsman decides not to investigate a handling complaint or decides to discontinue his investigation of such a complaint he shall notify—

(a) the person who made the handling complaint; and

(b) the professional organisation concerned,

of his decision and the reason for it.

[3] (1E) The ombudsman shall not investigate a handling complaint where—

(a) the professional organisation concerned have not completed their investigation of the conduct complaint to which it relates; or

(b) it is made after the expiry of such period of time as may be specified for the purpose of this subsection in directions given by the Secretary of State by virtue of paragraph 2 of Schedule 3 to this Act.

[3] (1F) Paragraph (a) of subsection (1E) above does not apply if—

(a) the handling complaint is that the professional organisation concerned—

(i) have acted unreasonably in failing to start an investigation into the complaint; or

(ii) having started such an investigation, have failed to complete it within a reasonable time; or

(b) the ombudsman considers that, even though the complaint is being investigated by that organisation, an investigation by him is justified.

(2) The ombudsman shall make such investigation of any handling complaint as seems to him to be appropriate.[4]

[3] (2A) Where the ombudsman is conducting an investigation under this Act, he may require the professional organisation concerned—

(a) to provide him with such information, being information which is within the knowledge of the professional organisation, as he considers relevant to his investigation; or

(b) to produce to him such documents, being documents which are within the possession or control of the organisation, as he considers relevant to his investigation,

(including any information or, as the case may be, documents obtained by the organisation from the practitioner concerned while investigating the conduct complaint to which the handling complaint relates); and, notwithstanding any duty of confidentiality owed to any person by the professional organisation as respects any such information or, as the case may be, documents, the organisation shall comply with such a requirement.

[3] (2B) Where any information requested by the ombudsman under subsection (2A) above is not within the knowledge of the professional organisation concerned, or any documents so requested are not within their possession or control, the ombudsman may require the practitioner concerned in the conduct complaint to which the handling complaint relates—

(a) to provide him with that information, in so far as it is within the knowledge of the practitioner; or

(b) to produce to him those documents, if they are within the possession or control of the practitioner;

and, notwithstanding any duty of confidentiality owed to any person by the practitioner as respects any such information or, as the case may be, documents, the practitioner shall comply with such a requirement.

(3) [*Repealed by 1997 (c.35), s.1(6), effective July 22, 1997.*]

[2] (4) Where the ombudsman is conducting an investigation under this Act, he may at any time make a written interim report in relation to the investigation and shall send a copy of any such report to—

(a) the person who made the handling complaint; and
(b) the professional organisation concerned.

(5) The ombudsman may—

(a) if so requested by any person appointed to carry out equivalent functions in relation to the provision of legal services in England and Wales, investigate a complaint against a professional body in England and Wales on that person's behalf; and
(b) request any person appointed as mentioned in paragraph (a) above to investigate a complaint against an organisation in Scotland on his behalf.

(6)–(8) [*Repealed by the Public Appointments and Public Bodies etc. (Scotland) Act 2003 (asp 4), Sch.4, para.12(13)(a) (effective August 15, 2003).*]

[5] (9) The following shall not be eligible to be appointed as the ombudsman—

(a) advocates;
(b) solicitors;
(c) . . .
(d) executry practitioners within the meaning of section 23 of this Act;
(e), (f) . . .
(g) conveyancing practitioners within the meaning of section 23 of this Act; or
(h) any member or employee of a professional or other body any of whose members has acquired any right to conduct litigation or right of audience by virtue of section 27 of this Act.

(10) Schedule 3 to this Act shall have effect in relation to the ombudsman.

NOTES

[1] In force April 1, 1991 (subss. (1), (9)(a)–(c), (10) and Sch.3: SI 1991/822); June 3, 1991 (subss. (2)–(8): SI 1991/1252; March 1, 1997 (subs.(9)(d), (e) and (g): SI 1996/2894). Subsections (9)(f) and (h) remain prospective.

[2] Substituted by Scottish Legal Services Ombudsman and Commissioner for Local Administration in Scotland Act 1997 (c.35), s.1(2), effective two months following Royal Assent on May 21, *i.e.* July 22, 1997.

[3] Inserted by *ibid.*

[4] Part repealed by *ibid.*

[5] As amended by the Public Appointments and Public Bodies etc. (Scotland) Act 2003 (asp 4), Sch.4, para.12(13)(b) (effective August 15, 2003). Read in conjunction with the European Communities (Lawyer's Practice) (Scotland) Regulations 2000 (SSI 2000/121), reg.37(2) and Sch.2, para.6(3) (effective May 22, 2000) and SSI 2004/383, reg.16.

Ombudsman's final report and recommendations

34A.[1]—(1) Where the Scottish legal services ombudsman has completed an investigation under this Act he shall make a written report of his conclusions and shall send a copy of the report to—

(a) the person who made the handling complaint;
(b) the professional organisation concerned; and
(c) the practitioner concerned in the conduct complaint to which the handling complaint relates.

(2) If the ombudsman decides to make a complaint about the practitioner concerned to the appropriate disciplinary body he may include in the report under this section a statement to that effect.

(3) A report under this section may include one or more of the following recommendations—

(a) that the professional organisation concerned provide to the person making the handling complaint such information about the conduct complaint to which the handling complaint relates, and how it was dealt with, as the ombudsman considers appropriate;

(b) that the conduct complaint be investigated further by the professional organisation concerned;

(c) that the conduct complaint be reconsidered by the professional organisation concerned;

(d) that the professional organisation concerned consider exercising their powers in relation to the practitioner concerned;

(e) that the professional organisation concerned pay compensation of the stated amount to the person making the handling complaint for loss suffered by him, or inconvenience or distress caused to him, as a result of the way in which the conduct complaint was handled by that organisation;

(f) that the professional organisation to whom a recommendation under paragraph (e) above applies pay to the person making the handling complaint an amount specified by the ombudsman by way of reimbursement of the cost, or part of the cost, of making the handling complaint.

(4) Where a report under this section includes any recommendation, the report shall state the ombudsman's reasons for making the recommendation.

(5) For the purposes of the law of defamation the publication of any report of the ombudsman under this section and any publicity given under subsection (8) below shall be privileged unless the publication is proved to be made with malice.

(6) It shall be the duty of any professional organisation to whom a report is sent by the ombudsman under this section to have regard to the conclusions and recommendations set out in the report so far as relating to that organisation.

(7) Where a report sent to a professional organisation under this section includes a recommendation relating to them, the organisation shall, before the end of the period of three months beginning with the date on which the report was sent, notify the ombudsman, and the person who made the handling complaint, of—

(a) the action which they have taken to comply with the recommendation or in consequence of further consideration of the matter by them; or

(b) their decision not to comply wholly with a recommendation and any reason for that decision.

(8) Where, at the end of the period of three months mentioned in subsection (7) above, a professional organisation have not wholly complied with a recommendation relating to them in a report under this section, the ombudsman may take such steps as he considers reasonable to publicise that fact; but shall in so publicising it state any reason given to the ombudsman by the organisation for their not having so complied (or a summary by the ombudsman of any such reason).

(9) Any reasonable expenses incurred by the ombudsman under subsection (8) above may be recovered by him (as a civil debt) from the professional organisation concerned.

(10) In this section—

"the stated amount" means such amount as may be specified by the ombudsman, being an amount which does not exceed the prescribed amount; and

"the prescribed amount" means £1000 or such greater amount as may from time to time be specified by order made by the Secretary of

State by statutory instrument subject to annulment in pursuance of a resolution of either House of Parliament.

NOTE
[1] Inserted by Scottish Legal Services Ombudsman and Commissioner for Local Administration in Scotland Act 1997 (c.35), s.2, effective July 22, 1997.

Advisory functions of ombudsman

34B.[1]—(1) The Scottish legal services ombudsman may make recommendations to any professional organisation about their procedures for, and methods of, dealing with conduct complaints.

(2) It shall be the duty of a professional organisation to whom a recommendation is made under this section—

(a) to consider the recommendation; and

(b) to notify the ombudsman of the results of that consideration and any action which they have taken, or propose to take, in consequence of the recommendation.

NOTE
[1] Inserted by Scottish Legal Services Ombudsman and Commissioner for Local Administration in Scotland Act 1997 (c.35), s.3, effective July 22, 1997.

Judicial appointments

35. [*See Division B.*]

Solicitors' and counsel's fees

Solicitors' and counsel's fees

36. [*Inserts new section 61A into the Solicitors (Scotland) Act 1980 (c.46), above.*]

Miscellaneous and supplementary

Admission of solicitors and notaries public

[1] **37.**—(1) [*Amends s.6(2) of the Solicitors (Scotland) Act 1980 (c.46), above*].

(2) [*Amends s.57 of the Solicitors (Scotland) Act 1980 (c.46), above*].

(3) [*Amends s.58 of the Solicitors (Scotland) Act 1980 (c.46), above*].

NOTE
[1] In force July 20, 1992: SI 1992/1599.

Availability of legal aid in relation to services provided under this Act

38. [*Inserts new section 43A in the Legal Aid (Scotland) Act 1986 (c.47): Div. G below.*]

[1] **39.** [*Repeals s.29 of the Solicitors (Scotland) Act 1980 (c.46), above*].

NOTE
[1] In force September 30, 1991: SI 1991/2151.

Advisory and supervisory functions of the Director

[1] **40.**—(1) Before—

[2] (a) approving any rules made under section 17(11) or 18(10) of this Act; or

[2] (b) approving any rules—

(i) . . .

(ii) such as are mentioned in section 31(1) or (2),

of this Act; or

(c) considering any provisions of a draft scheme under section 26(1) or (3) of this Act,

the Secretary of State shall first send a copy of the proposed regulations, rules or provisions to the Director.

[2] (2) The Director shall consider whether any such rules or provisions as are mentioned in subsection (1) above would have, or would be likely to have, the effect of restricting, distorting or preventing competition to any significant extent.

(3) When the Director has completed his consideration he shall give such advice to the Secretary of State as he thinks fit.

(4) The Director may publish any advice given by him under subsection (3) above.

(5) The Director shall, so far as practicable, exclude from anything published under subsection (4) above any matter—

(a) which relates to the affairs of a particular person; and

(b) the publication of which would, or might in the Director's opinion, seriously and prejudicially affect the interests of that person.

(6) For the purposes of the law of defamation, the publication of any advice by the Director under this section shall be absolutely privileged.

NOTES

[1] In force September 30, 1991: SI 1991/2152.

[2] As amended by the Public Appointments and Public Bodies etc. (Scotland) Act 2003 (asp 4), Sch.4, para.12(14) (effective August 15, 2003).

Investigatory powers of the Director

[1] **41.**—(1) For the purpose of investigating any matter under section 40 of this Act, the Director may by notice in writing—

(a) require any person to produce to him or to any person appointed by him for the purpose, at a time and place specified in the notice, any documents which are specified or described in the notice and which—

(i) are in that person's custody or under that person's control; and

(ii) relate to any matter relevant to the investigation; or

(b) require any person carrying on any business to furnish to him (within such time and in such manner and form as the notice may specify) such information as may be specified or described in the notice.

(2) A person shall not be required under this section to produce any document or disclose any information which he would be entitled to refuse to produce or disclose on the grounds of confidentiality between a client and his professional legal adviser in any civil proceedings.

(3) [*Repealed by the Enterprise Act 2002 (Consequential and Supplemental Provisions) Order 2003 (SI 2003/1398), Sch.1, para.12(2) (effective June 20, 2003).*]

NOTE

[1] In force September 30, 1991: SI 1991/2152.

Enforcement of notices under section 41

[1] **41A.**—(1) The court may, on an application by the Office of Fair Trading, enquire into whether any person ("the defaulter") has refused or otherwise failed, without reasonable excuse, to comply with a notice under section 41(1).

(2) An application under subsection (1) shall include details of the possible failure which the Office of Fair Trading considers has occurred.

(3) In enquiring into a case under subsection (1), the court shall hear any witness who may be produced against or on behalf of the defaulter and any statement which may be offered in defence.

(4) Subsections (5) and (6) apply where the court is satisfied, after hearing any witnesses and statements as mentioned in subsection (3), that the defaulter has refused or otherwise failed, without reasonable excuse, to comply with a notice under section 41(1).

(5) The court may punish the defaulter as it would have been able to punish him had he been guilty of contempt of court.

(6) Where the defaulter is a body corporate or is a partnership constituted under the law of Scotland, the court may punish any director, officer or (as the case may be) partner of the defaulter as it would have been able to punish that director, officer or partner had he been guilty of contempt of court.

(7) In this section "the court" means the Court of Session.

NOTE

[1] Inserted by the Enterprise Act 2002 (Consequential and Supplemental Provisions) Order 2003 (SI 2003/1398), Sch.1, para.12(3) (effective June 20, 2003).

Altering, etc. documents required to be produced under section 41

[1] **41B.**—(1) A person commits an offence if he intentionally alters, suppresses or destroys a document which he has been required to produce by a notice under section 41(1).

(2) A person who commits an offence under subsection (1) shall be liable—

(a) on summary conviction, to a fine not exceeding the statutory maximum;

(b) on conviction on indictment, to imprisonment for a term not exceeding two years or to a fine or to both.

NOTE

[1] Inserted by the Enterprise Act 2002 (Consequential and Supplemental Provisions) Order 2003 (SI 2003/1398), Sch.1, para.12(3) (effective June 20, 2003).

Review of rules approved by the Secretary of State

[1] **42.**—(1) Where the Secretary of State has approved—

[2] (a) a rule under section 31(2) of this Act; or

(b) a draft scheme under section 26(6) of this Act,

he may and, where the Lord President, in the case of a draft scheme such as is mentioned in paragraph (b), so requests shall, require the body which made the rule or, as the case may be, the scheme to review its terms.

(2) When they have reviewed a rule or, as the case may be, a scheme, following a requirement made under subsection (1) above, the body concerned may revise the rule or scheme in the light of that review, and shall then submit the rule or scheme as revised or, if they have not revised it, as previously approved—

(a) in the case of a rule such as is mentioned in subsection (1)(a) above, to the Secretary of State; or

(b) in the case of a draft scheme such as is mentioned in subsection (1)(b) above, to the Secretary of State and the Lord President.

(3) Where a rule, whether revised or as previously approved, is submitted to the Secretary of State under subsection (2)(a) above, he may—

(a) approve the rule as submitted to him; or

(b) amend the rule in such manner as he considers appropriate,

and (except where the rule remains in the form previously approved) he may direct the body concerned to bring it into operation as soon as is practicable.

(4) Where the Lord President and the Secretary of State are agreed that the terms of a draft scheme submitted to them under subsection (2)(b) above are satisfactory, the Secretary of State may—

(a) approve the scheme; and

(b) (except where the scheme remains in the form previously approved) direct the body concerned to bring the scheme, as so amended, into force as soon as is practicable.

(5) Where either the Secretary of State or the Lord President is of the view that the terms of any such scheme so submitted to them are not satisfactory, but they do not agree as to what the terms of the scheme should be, the scheme shall continue to have effect as previously approved.

(6) Where the Secretary of State and the Lord President agree both that the terms of a scheme so submitted to them are not satisfactory, and as to what the terms of the scheme should be, the Secretary of State may amend the scheme in such manner as he and the Lord President consider appropriate; and may direct the body concerned to bring the scheme, as so amended, into force as soon as is practicable.

(7) The provisions of section 40(1)(b) and (c) of this Act shall apply to rules and schemes submitted under subsection (2) of this section as they apply to rules submitted under sections 17(15) and 31(2) and schemes submitted under section 25(1) of this Act.

NOTES

[1] In force September 30, 1991: SI 1991/2152.

[2] As amended by the Public Appointments and Public Bodies etc. (Scotland) Act 2003 (asp 4), Sch.4, para.12(15) (effective August 15, 2003).

Functions of Director in relation to certain rules made under the 1980 Act

43. [*New ss.64A–64D of the Solicitors (Scotland) Act 1980 (c.46) appear in the print of that Act, above.*]

Interpretation of Part II

[1] **44.** In this Part of this Act, unless the context otherwise requires—

"advocate" means a member of the Faculty of Advocates practising as such;

"the Director" means the Director General of Fair Trading;

"Lord President" means the Lord President of the Court of Session;

"solicitor" has the same meaning as in section 65(1) of the 1980 Act; and

"the 1980 Act" means the Solicitors (Scotland) Act 1980.

NOTE

[1] In force April 1, 1991: SI 1991/822.

PART III

THE LICENSING (SCOTLAND) ACT 1976

45.–55. [*See Division E.*]

PART IV

56.–72. [*See Divisions B, I and M.*]

PART V

GENERAL

Finance

73. [*Not printed.*]

Amendments and repeals

74.—(1) The enactments mentioned in Schedule 8 to this Act shall have effect subject to the amendments specified in that Schedule.

(2) The enactments mentioned in Schedule 9 to this Act are hereby repealed to the extent specified in the third column of that Schedule.

Citation, commencement and extent

75.—(1) This Act may be cited as the Law Reform (Miscellaneous Provisions) (Scotland) Act 1990.

(2) Subject to subsections (3) and (4) below, this Act shall come into force on such day as the Secretary of State may appoint by order made by statutory instrument and different days may be appointed for different provisions and for different purposes.

(3) The provisions of—

(a) Part III and section 66 of this Act and so much of section 74 as relates to those provisions; and

(b) sections 67, 70 and 71 of this Act and paragraphs 21 and 34 of Schedule 8 to this Act,

shall come into force at the end of the period of two months beginning with the day on which this Act is passed.

(4) Paragraph 27(3) of Schedule 8 to this Act shall come into force on the day on which this Act is passed.

(5) Subject to subsections (6) and (7) below, this Act extends to Scotland only.

(6) [*Repealed by the Requirements of Writing Scotland Act 1995, Sch.5*]

(7) Paragraph 17 of Schedule 1 to this Act, paragraph 11 of Schedule 3 to this Act and Schedule 9 to this Act so far as relating to the House of Commons Disqualification Act 1975 extend also to England and Wales and Northern Ireland.

SCHEDULES

SCHEDULE 1

[*Repealed*]

SCHEDULE 2

Publication of Applications Made Under Section 25

1. Any professional or other body making an application under section 25 of this Act shall, for a period of six weeks beginning with the date on which the application is submitted to the Lord President and the Secretary of State—

(a) make a copy of the draft scheme referred to in section 25(2) of this Act available for public inspection at a specified place; and

(b) on a request from any person—

(i) send him a copy of the draft scheme; or

(ii) make a copy of the draft scheme available for public inspection at a suitable place in his locality.

2. Any person may make written representations concerning any draft scheme submitted under section 25 of this Act, and such representations shall—

(a) be made to both the Lord President and the Secretary of State; and

(b) be delivered to both the Lord President and the Secretary of State before the expiry of the period of six weeks beginning with the date on which the application is made.

3. At the same time as an application under section 25 is submitted to the Lord President and the Secretary of State, the body making the application shall place an advertisement mentioning the matters referred to in paragraph 4 below in the *Edinburgh Gazette* and in a daily newspaper circulating throughout Scotland.

4. An advertisement such as referred to in paragraph 3 above shall state that—

(a) a copy of the draft scheme referred to in section 25(2) of this Act will be available for public inspection at a specified place for a period of six weeks beginning with the date on which the advertisement appears;

(b) a copy of the draft scheme will be—
   (i) sent, free of charge, to any person on request; or
   (ii) made available for public inspection at a suitable place in that person's locality;

(c) any person may make written representations concerning the draft scheme to the Lord President and the Secretary of State; and

(d) any such representations are to be delivered within the period of six weeks beginning with the date on which the application is made.

SCHEDULE 3

Scottish Legal Services Ombudsman

1.[1] The Scottish legal services ombudsman shall hold and vacate his office in accordance with the terms of his appointment and shall, on ceasing to hold office, be eligible for re-appointment.

2. The Secretary of State may give general directions to the ombudsman about the scope and discharge of his functions, and shall publish any such directions.

[3] 3.—(1) The Secretary of State may determine the terms and conditions of service, including remuneration, of the ombudsman.

(2) Where a person appointed to the office of ombudsman ceases to hold that office otherwise than on the expiry of the term of office specified in his appointment, and it appears to the Secretary of State that there are special circumstances which make it right for that person to receive compensation, the Secretary of State may, make a payment to that person of such amount as the Secretary of State may determine.

[3] 4. The Secretary of State may appoint staff for the ombudsman of such number, and on such terms and conditions of service, as he may determine; and such terms and conditions may include provision as to remuneration, and as to compensation for loss of employment (which may take the form of pensions, allowances or gratuities).

5. Neither the ombudsman nor his staff are, in such capacity, Crown servants.

6. The Secretary of State shall pay the expenses of the ombudsman and of his staff.

7.–8. [*Repealed by the Scottish Legal Services Ombudsman and Commissioner for Local Administration in Scotland Act 1997 (c.35), s.5(2), effective May 21, 1997.*]

9. The ombudsman shall make an annual report of the discharge of the functions conferred on him under this Act to the Secretary of State.

9A.[2] The ombudsman may, in addition to making a report under paragraph 9 above, report to the Secretary of State at any time on any matter relating to the discharge of the ombudsman's functions.

9B.[2] The ombudsman shall provide the Secretary of State with such information relating to the discharge of the ombudsman's functions as the Secretary of State may see fit to require.

10. The Secretary of State shall lay any report made to him under paragraph 9 above before each House of Parliament.

11. In Part III of Schedule 1 to the House of Commons Disqualification Act 1975 (offices disqualifying for membership) there shall be inserted at the appropriate place in alphabetical order the entry "Scottish legal services ombudsman appointed under section 34 of the Law Reform (Miscellaneous Provisions) (Scotland) Act 1990".

NOTES

[1] Amended by Scottish Legal Services Ombudsman and Commissioner for Local Administration in Scotland Act 1997 (c.35), s.5(2), effective July 22, 1997.

[2] Inserted by *ibid.*, s.4.

[3] As amended by SI 1999/1820, Art. 4, Sch.2, para.101(3) (effective July 1, 1999).

SCHEDULES 4–7

[*Not printed.*]

[NEXT TEXT PAGE IS **F** 85]

Property Misdescriptions Act 1991

(1991 c. 29)

ARRANGEMENT OF SECTIONS

An Act to prohibit the making of false or misleading statements about property matters in the course of estate agency business and property development business. [27th June 1991]

Offence of property misdescription

1.—(1) Where a false or misleading statement about a prescribed matter is made in the course of an estate agency business or a property development business, otherwise than in providing conveyancing services, the person by whom the business is carried on shall be guilty of an offence under this section.

(2) Where the making of the statement is due to the act or default of an employee the employee shall be guilty of an offence under this section; and the employee may be proceeded against and punished whether or not proceedings are also taken against his employer.

(3) A person guilty of an offence under this section shall be liable—

(a) on summary conviction, to a fine not exceeding the statutory maximum, and

(b) on conviction on indictment, to a fine.

(4) No contract shall be void or unenforceable, and no right of action in civil proceedings in respect of any loss shall arise, by reason only of the commission of an offence under this section.

(5) For the purposes of this section—

(a) "false" means false to a material degree,

(b) a statement is misleading if (though not false) what a reasonable person may be expected to infer from it, or from any omission from it, is false,

(c) a statement may be made by pictures or any other method of signifying meaning as well as by words and, if made by words, may be made orally or in writing,

(d) a prescribed matter is any matter relating to land which is specified in an order made by the Secretary of State,

(e) a statement is made in the course of an estate agency business if (but only if) the making of the statement is a thing done as mentioned in subsection (1) of section 1 of the Estate Agents Act 1979 and that Act either applies to it or would apply to it but for subsection (2)(a) of that section (exception for things done in course of profession by practising solicitor or employee),

(f) a statement is made in the course of a property development business if (but only if) it is made—

(i) in the course of a business (including a business in which the person making the statement is employed) concerned wholly or substantially with the development of land, and

(ii) for the purpose of, or with a view to, disposing of an interest in land consisting of or including a building, or a part of a building, constructed or renovated in the course of the business, and

(g) "conveyancing services" means the preparation of any transfer, conveyance, writ, contract or other document in connection with the disposal or acquisition of an interest in land, and services ancillary to that, but does not include anything done as mentioned in section 1(1)(a) of the Estate Agents Act 1979.

(6) For the purposes of this section any reference in this section or section 1 of the Estate Agents Act 1979 to disposing of or acquiring an interest in land—

(a) in England and Wales and Northern Ireland shall be construed in accordance with section 2 of that Act, and

(b) in Scotland is a reference to the transfer or creation of an "interest in land" as defined in section 28(1) of the Land Registration (Scotland) Act 1979.

(7) An order under this section may—

(a) make different provision for different cases, and

(b) include such supplemental, consequential and transitional provisions as the Secretary of State considers appropriate;

and the power to make such an order shall be exercisable by statutory instrument which shall be subject to annulment in pursuance of a resolution of either House of Parliament.

Due diligence defence

2.—(1) In proceedings against a person for an offence under section 1 above it shall be a defence for him to show that he took all reasonable steps and exercised all due diligence to avoid committing the offence.

(2) A person shall not be entitled to rely on the defence provided by subsection (1) above by reason of his reliance on information given by another unless he shows that it was reasonable in all the circumstances for him to have relied on the information, having regard in particular—

(*a*) to the steps which he took, and those which might reasonably have been taken, for the purpose of verifying the information, and

(*b*) to whether he had any reason to disbelieve the information.

(3) Where in any proceedings against a person for an offence under section 1 above the defence provided by subsection (1) above involves an allegation that the commission of the offence was due—

(*a*) to the act or default of another, or

(*b*) to reliance on information given by another,

the person shall not, without the leave of the court, be entitled to rely on the defence unless he has served a notice under subsection (4) below on the person bringing the proceedings not less than seven clear days before the hearing of the proceedings or, in Scotland, the diet of trial.

(4) A notice under this subsection shall give such information identifying or assisting in the identification of the person who committed the act or default, or gave the information, as is in the possession of the person serving the notice at the time he serves it.

Enforcement

3. The Schedule to this Act (which makes provision about the enforcement of this Act) shall have effect.

Bodies corporate and Scottish partnerships

4.—(1) Where an offence under this Act committed by a body corporate is proved to have been committed with the consent or connivance of, or to be attributable to neglect on the part of, a director, manager, secretary or other similar officer of the body corporate or a person who was purporting to act in such a capacity, he (as well as the body corporate) is guilty of the offence and liable to be proceeded against and punished accordingly.

(2) Where the affairs of a body corporate are managed by its members, subsection (1) above applies in relation to the acts and defaults of a member in connection with his functions of management as if he were a director of the body corporate.

(3) Where an offence under this Act committed in Scotland by a Scottish partnership is proved to have been committed with the consent or connivance of, or to be attributable to neglect on the part of, a partner, he (as well as the partnership) is guilty of the offence and liable to be proceeded against and punished accordingly.

Prosecution time limit

[1] **5.**—(1) No proceedings for an offence under section 1 above or paragraph 5(3), 6 of the Schedule to this Act shall be commenced after—

(*a*) the end of the period of three years beginning with the date of the commission of the offence, or

(*b*) the end of the period of one year beginning with the date of the discovery of the offence by the prosecutor,

whichever is the earlier.

(2) For the purposes of this section a certificate signed by or on behalf of the prosecutor and stating the date on which the offence was discovered by him shall be conclusive evidence of that fact; and a certificate stating that matter and purporting to be so signed shall be treated as so signed unless the contrary is proved.

NOTE

[1] As amended by the Enterprise Act 2002 (Part 9 Restrictions on Disclosure of Information) (Amendment and Specification) Order 2003 (SI 2003/1400), Sch.5 (effective June 20, 2003).

Financial provision

6. There shall be paid out of money provided by Parliament any increase attributable to this Act in the sums payable out of such money under any other Act.

Short title and extent

7.—(1) This Act may be cited as the Property Misdescriptions Act 1991.

(2) This Act extends to Northern Ireland.

Section 3

SCHEDULE

Enforcement

Enforcement authority

1.—(1) Every local weights and measures authority in Great Britain shall be an enforcement authority for the purposes of this Act, and it shall be the duty of each such authority to enforce the provisions of this Act within their area.

(2) The Department of Economic Development in Northern Ireland shall be an enforcement authority for the purposes of this Act, and it shall be the duty of the Department to enforce the provisions of this Act within Northern Ireland.

Prosecutions

2. [*Repealed by the Enterprise Act 2002 (c.40) Sch.26, para.1 (effective June 20, 2003).*]

Powers of officers of enforcement authority

3.—(1) If a duly authorised officer of an enforcement authority has reasonable grounds for suspecting that an offence under section 1 of this Act has been committed, he may—

(*a*) require a person carrying on or employed in a business to produce any book or document relating to the business, and take copies of it or any entry in it, or

[1] (*b*) require such a person to produce in a visible and legible documentary form any information so relating which is stored in any electronic form, and take copies of it,

for the purpose of ascertaining whether such an offence has been committed.

(2) Such an officer may inspect any goods for the purpose of ascertaining whether such an offence has been committed.

(3) If such an officer has reasonable grounds for believing that any documents or goods may be required as evidence in proceedings for such an offence, he may seize and detain them.

(4) An officer seizing any documents or goods in the exercise of his power under sub-paragraph (3) above shall inform the person from whom they are seized.

(5) The powers of an officer under this paragraph may be exercised by him only at a reasonable hour and on production (if required) of his credentials.

(6) Nothing in this paragraph—

(*a*) requires a person to produce a document if he would be entitled to refuse to produce it in proceedings in a court on the ground that it is the subject of legal professional privilege or, in Scotland, that it contains a confidential communication made by or to an advocate or a solicitor in that capacity, or

(*b*) authorises the taking possession of a document which is in the possession of a person who would be so entitled.

NOTE

[1] As substituted by the Criminal Justice and Police Act 2001 (c.16) Sch.2(2), para.20(b) (effective April 1, 2003).

4.—(1) A duly authorised officer of an enforcement authority may, at a reasonable hour and on production (if required) of his credentials, enter any premises for the purpose of ascertaining whether an offence under section 1 of this Act has been committed.

(2) If a justice of the peace, or in Scotland a justice of the peace or a sheriff, is satisfied—

(a) that any relevant books, documents or goods are on, or that any relevant information contained in a computer is available from, any premises, and that production or inspection is likely to disclose the commission of an offence under section 1 of this Act, or

(b) that such an offence has been, is being or is about to be committed on any premises,

and that any of the conditions specified in sub-paragraph (3) below is met, he may by warrant under his hand authorise an officer of an enforcement authority to enter the premises, if need be by force.

(3) The conditions referred to in sub-paragraph (2) above are—

(a) that admission to the premises has been or is likely to be refused and that notice of intention to apply for a warrant under that sub-paragraph has been given to the occupier,

(b) that an application for admission, or the giving of such a notice, would defeat the object of the entry,

(c) that the premises are unoccupied, and

(d) that the occupier is temporarily absent and it might defeat the object of the entry to await his return.

(4) In sub-paragraph (2) above "relevant", in relation to books, documents, goods or information, means books, documents, goods or information which, under paragraph 3 above, a duly authorised officer may require to be produced or may inspect.

(5) A warrant under sub-paragraph (2) above may be issued only if—

(a) in England and Wales, the justice of the peace is satisfied as required by that sub-paragraph by written information on oath,

(b) in Scotland, the justice of the peace or sheriff is so satisfied by evidence on oath, or

(c) in Northern Ireland, the justice of the peace is so satisfied by complaint on oath.

(6) A warrant under sub-paragraph (2) above shall continue in force for a period of one month.

(7) An officer entering any premises by virtue of this paragraph may take with him such other persons as may appear to him necessary.

(8) On leaving premises which he has entered by virtue of a warrant under sub-paragraph (2) above, an officer shall, if the premises are unoccupied or the occupier is temporarily absent, leave the premises as effectively secured against trespassers as he found them.

(9) In this paragraph "premises" includes any place (including any vehicle, ship or aircraft) except premises used only as a dwelling.

Obstruction of officers

5.—(1) A person who—
- (a) intentionally obstructs an officer of an enforcement authority acting in pursuance of this Schedule,
- (b) without reasonable excuse fails to comply with a requirement made of him by such an officer under paragraph 3(1) above, or
- (c) without reasonable excuse fails to give an officer of an enforcement authority acting in pursuance of this Schedule any other assistance or information which the officer may reasonably require of him for the purpose of the performance of the officer's functions under this Schedule,

shall be guilty of an offence.

(2) A person guilty of an offence under sub-paragraph (1) above shall be liable on summary conviction to a fine not exceeding level 5 on the standard scale.

(3) If a person, in giving any such information as is mentioned in sub-paragraph (1)(c) above,—
- (a) makes a statement which he knows is false in a material particular, or
- (b) recklessly makes a statement which is false in a material particular,

he shall be guilty of an offence.

(4) A person guilty of an offence under sub-paragraph (3) above shall be liable—
- (a) on summary conviction, to a fine not exceeding the statutory maximum, and
- (b) on conviction on indictment, to a fine.

Impersonation of officers

6.—(1) If a person who is not a duly authorised officer of an enforcement authority purports to act as such under this Schedule he shall be guilty of an offence.

(2) A person guilty of an offence under sub-paragraph (1) above shall be liable—
- (a) on summary conviction, to a fine not exceeding the statutory maximum, and
- (b) on conviction on indictment, to a fine.

Disclosure of information

7. [*Repealed by the Enterprise Act 2002 (c.40) Sch.26, para.1 (effective June 20, 2003).*]

Privilege against self-incrimination

8. Nothing in this Schedule requires a person to answer any question or give any information if to do so might incriminate him.

Proceeds of Crime Act 2002

(2002 c.29)

. . . . . .

PART 5

CIVIL RECOVERY OF THE RROCEEDS ETC OF UNLAWFUL CONDUCT

CHAPTER 1

INTRODUCTORY

General purpose of this Part

240.—(1) This Part has effect for the purposes of—

(a) enabling the enforcement authority to recover, in civil proceedings before the High Court or Court of Session, property which is, or represents, property obtained through unlawful conduct,

(b) enabling cash which is, or represents, property obtained through unlawful conduct, or which is intended to be used in unlawful conduct, to be forfeited in civil proceedings before a magistrates' court or (in Scotland) the sheriff.

(2) The powers conferred by this Part are exercisable in relation to any property (including cash) whether or not any proceedings have been brought for an offence in connection with the property.

"Unlawful conduct"

241.—(1) Conduct occurring in any part of the United Kingdom is unlawful conduct if it is unlawful under the criminal law of that part.

(2) Conduct which—

[1] (a) occurs in a country outside the United Kingdom and is unlawful under the criminal law applying in that country or territory, and

(b) if it occurred in a part of the United Kingdom, would be unlawful under the criminal law of that part,

is also unlawful conduct.

(3) The court or sheriff must decide on a balance of probabilities whether it is proved—

(a) that any matters alleged to constitute unlawful conduct have occurred, or

(b) that any person intended to use any cash in unlawful conduct.

NOTE

[1] As substituted by the Serious Organised Crime and Police Act 2005 (c.15), Sch.6, para.8(b) (effective January 1, 2006).

"Property obtained through unlawful conduct"

242. (1) A person obtains property through unlawful conduct (whether his own conduct or another's) if he obtains property by or in return for the conduct.

(2) In deciding whether any property was obtained through unlawful conduct—

(a) it is immaterial whether or not any money, goods or services were provided in order to put the person in question in a position to carry out the conduct,

(b) it is not necessary to show that the conduct was of a particular kind if it is shown that the property was obtained through conduct of one of a number of kinds, each of which would have been unlawful conduct.

CHAPTER 2

CIVIL RECOVERY IN THE HIGH COURT OR COURT OF SESSION

Proceedings for recovery orders

Proceedings for recovery orders in England and Wales or Northern Ireland

243.—(1) Proceedings for a recovery order may be taken by the enforcement authority in the High Court against any person who the authority thinks holds recoverable property.

(2) The enforcement authority must serve the claim form—

(a) on the respondent, and

(b) unless the court dispenses with service, on any other person who the authority thinks holds any associated property which the authority wishes to be subject to a recovery order,

wherever domiciled, resident or present.

(3) If any property which the enforcement authority wishes to be subject to a recovery order is not specified in the claim form it must be described in the form in general terms; and the form must state whether it is alleged to be recoverable property or associated property.

(4) The references above to the claim form include the particulars of claim, where they are served subsequently.

Proceedings for recovery orders in Scotland

244.—(1) Proceedings for a recovery order may be taken by the enforcement authority in the Court of Session against any person who the authority thinks holds recoverable property.

(2) The enforcement authority must serve the application—

(a) on the respondent, and

(b) unless the court dispenses with service, on any other person who the authority thinks holds any associated property which the authority wishes to be subject to a recovery order,

wherever domiciled, resident or present.

(3) If any property which the enforcement authority wishes to be subject to a recovery order is not specified in the application it must be described in the application in general terms; and the application must state whether it is alleged to be recoverable property or associated property.

"Associated property"

245.—(1) "Associated property" means property of any of the following descriptions (including property held by the respondent) which is not itself the recoverable property—

(a) any interest in the recoverable property,

(b) any other interest in the property in which the recoverable property subsists,

(c) if the recoverable property is a tenancy in common, the tenancy of the other tenant,

(d) if (in Scotland) the recoverable property is owned in common, the interest of the other owner,

(e) if the recoverable property is part of a larger property, but not a separate part, the remainder of that property.

(2) References to property being associated with recoverable property are to be read accordingly.

(3) No property is to be treated as associated with recoverable property consisting of rights under a pension scheme (within the meaning of sections 273 to 275).

Application for property freezing order

[1] **245A.**—(1) Where the enforcement authority may take proceedings for a

recovery order in the High Court, the authority may apply to the court for a property freezing order (whether before or after starting the proceedings).

(2) A property freezing order is an order that—

(a) specifies or describes the property to which it applies, and

(b) subject to any exclusions (see section 245C(1)(b) and (2)), prohibits any person to whose property the order applies from in any way dealing with the property.

(3) An application for a property freezing order may be made without notice if the circumstances are such that notice of the application would prejudice any right of the enforcement authority to obtain a recovery order in respect of any property.

(4) The court may make a property freezing order on an application if it is satisfied that the condition in subsection (5) is met and, where applicable, that the condition in subsection (6) is met.

(5) The first condition is that there is a good arguable case–

(a) that the property to which the application for the order relates is or includes recoverable property, and

(b) that, if any of it is not recoverable property, it is associated property.

(6) The second condition is that, if—

(a) the property to which the application for the order relates includes property alleged to be associated property, and

(b) the enforcement authority has not established the identity of the person who holds it,

the authority has taken all reasonable steps to do so.

NOTE

[1] As inserted by the Serious Organised Crime and Police Act 2005 (c.15), s.98(1) (effective January 1, 2006).

Variation and setting aside of order

[1] **245B.**—(1) The court may at any time vary or set aside a property freezing order.

(2) If the court makes an interim receiving order that applies to all of the property to which a property freezing order applies, it must set aside the property freezing order.

(3) If the court makes an interim receiving order that applies to some but not all of the property to which a property freezing order applies, it must vary the property freezing order so as to exclude any property to which the interim receiving order applies.

(4) If the court decides that any property to which a property freezing order applies is neither recoverable property nor associated property, it must vary the order so as to exclude the property.

(5) Before exercising power under this Chapter to vary or set aside a property freezing order, the court must (as well as giving the parties to the proceedings an opportunity to be heard) give such an opportunity to any person who may be affected by its decision.

(6) Subsection (5) does not apply where the court is acting as required by subsection (2) or (3).

NOTE

[1] As inserted by the Serious Organised Crime and Police Act 2005 (c.15), s.98(1) (effective January 1, 2006).

Exclusions

[1] **245C.**—(1) The power to vary a property freezing order includes (in particular) power to make exclusions as follows—

(a) power to exclude property from the order, and

(b) power, otherwise than by excluding property from the order, to make exclusions from the prohibition on dealing with the property to which the order applies.

(2) Exclusions from the prohibition on dealing with the property to which the order applies (other than exclusions of property from the order) may also be made when the order is made.

(3) An exclusion may, in particular, make provision for the purpose of enabling any person—

(a) to meet his reasonable living expenses, or

(b) to carry on any trade, business, profession or occupation.

(4) An exclusion may be made subject to conditions.

(5) Where the court exercises the power to make an exclusion for the purpose of enabling a person to meet legal expenses that he has incurred, or may incur, in respect of proceedings under this Part, it must ensure that the exclusion—

(a) is limited to reasonable legal expenses that the person has reasonably incurred or that he reasonably incurs,

(b) specifies the total amount that may be released for legal expenses in pursuance of the exclusion, and

(c) is made subject to the required conditions (see section 286A) in addition to any conditions imposed under subsection (4).

(6) The court, in deciding whether to make an exclusion for the purpose of enabling a person to meet legal expenses of his in respect of proceedings under this Part—

(a) must have regard (in particular) to the desirability of the person being represented in any proceedings under this Part in which he is a participant, and

(b) must, where the person is the respondent, disregard the possibility that legal representation of the person in any such proceedings might, were an exclusion not made, be funded by the Legal Services Commission or the Northern Ireland Legal Services Commission.

(7) If excluded property is not specified in the order it must be described in the order in general terms.

(8) The power to make exclusions must, subject to subsection (6), be exercised with a view to ensuring, so far as practicable, that the satisfaction of any right of the enforcement authority to recover the property obtained through unlawful conduct is not unduly prejudiced.

(9) Subsection (8) does not apply where the court is acting as required by section 245B(3) or (4).

NOTE

[1] As inserted by the Serious Organised Crime and Police Act 2005 (c.15), s.98(1) (effective January 1, 2006).

Restriction on proceedings and remedies

[1] **245D.**—(1) While a property freezing order has effect—

(a) the court may stay any action, execution or other legal process in respect of the property to which the order applies, and

(b) no distress may be levied against the property to which the order applies except with the leave of the court and subject to any terms the court may impose.

(2) If a court (whether the High Court or any other court) in which proceedings are pending in respect of any property is satisfied that a property freezing order has been applied for or made in respect of the property, it may either stay the proceedings or allow them to continue on any terms it thinks fit.

(3) If a property freezing order applies to a tenancy of any premises, no landlord or other person to whom rent is payable may exercise the right of forfeiture by peaceable re-entry in relation to the premises in respect of any failure by the tenant to comply with any term or condition of the tenancy, except with the leave of the court and subject to any terms the court may impose.

(4) Before exercising any power conferred by this section, the court must (as well as giving the parties to any of the proceedings concerned an opportunity to be heard) give such an opportunity to any person who may be affected by the court's decision.

NOTE
[1] As inserted by the Serious Organised Crime and Police Act 2005 (c.15), s.98(1) (effective January 1, 2006).

Interim receiving orders (England and Wales and Northern Ireland)

246.–255. [*Not reproduced.*]

Interim administration orders (Scotland)

Application for interim administration order

256.—(1) Where the enforcement authority may take proceedings for a recovery order in the Court of Session, the authority may apply to the court for an interim administration order (whether before or after starting the proceedings).

(2) An interim administration order is an order for—

(a) the detention, custody or preservation of property, and

(b) the appointment of an interim administrator.

(3) An application for an interim administration order may be made without notice if the circumstances are such that notice of the application would prejudice any right of the enforcement authority to obtain a recovery order in respect of any property.

(4) The court may make an interim administration order on the application if it is satisfied that the conditions in subsections (5) and, where applicable, (6) are met.

(5) The first condition is that there is a probabilis causa litigandi—

(a) that the property to which the application for the order relates is or includes recoverable property, and

(b) that, if any of it is not recoverable property, it is associated property.

(6) The second condition is that, if—

(a) the property to which the application for the order relates includes property alleged to be associated property, and

(b) the enforcement authority has not established the identity of the person who holds it,

the authority has taken all reasonable steps to do so.

(7) In its application for an interim administration order, the enforcement authority must nominate a suitably qualified person for appointment as interim administrator, but the nominee may not be a member of the staff of the Scottish Administration.

(8) The extent of the power to make an interim administration order is not limited by sections 257 to 264.

Functions of interim administrator

257.—(1) An interim administration order may authorise or require the interim administrator—

(a) to exercise any of the powers mentioned in Schedule 6,

(b) to take any other steps the court thinks appropriate,

for the purpose of securing the detention, custody or preservation of the property to which the order applies or of taking any steps under subsection (2).

(2) An interim administration order must require the interim administrator to take any steps which the court thinks necessary to establish—

(a) whether or not the property to which the order applies is recoverable property or associated property,

(b) whether or not any other property is recoverable property (in relation to the same unlawful conduct) and, if it is, who holds it.

(3) If—

(a) the interim administrator deals with any property which is not property to which the order applies, and

(b) at the time he deals with the property he believes on reasonable grounds that he is entitled to do so in pursuance of the order,

the interim administrator is not liable to any person in respect of any loss or damage resulting from his dealing with the property except so far as the loss or damage is caused by his negligence.

Inhibition of property affected by order

258.—(1) On the application of the enforcement authority, the Court of Session may, in relation to the property mentioned in subsection (2), grant warrant for inhibition against any person specified in an interim administration order.

(2) That property is heritable property situated in Scotland to which the interim administration order applies (whether generally or such of it as is specified in the application).

(3) The warrant for inhibition—

(a) has effect as if granted on the dependence of an action for debt by the enforcement authority against the person and may be executed, recalled, loosed or restricted accordingly, and

(b) has the effect of letters of inhibition and must forthwith be registered by the enforcement authority in the register of inhibitions and adjudications.

(4) Section 155 of the Titles to Land Consolidation (Scotland) Act 1868 (c. 101) (effective date of inhibition) applies in relation to an inhibition for which warrant is granted under subsection (1) as it applies to an inhibition by separate letters or contained in a summons.

(5) The execution of an inhibition under this section in respect of property does not prejudice the exercise of an interim administrator's powers under or for the purposes of this Part in respect of that property.

(6) An inhibition executed under this section ceases to have effect when, or in so far as, the interim administration order ceases to apply in respect of the property in relation to which the warrant for inhibition was granted.

(7) If an inhibition ceases to have effect to any extent by virtue of subsection (6) the enforcement authority must—

(a) apply for the recall or, as the case may be, the restriction of the inhibition, and

(b) ensure that the recall or restriction is reflected in the register of inhibitions and adjudications.

Duties of respondent etc.

259.—(1) An interim administration order may require any person to whose property the order applies—

(a) to bring the property to a place (in Scotland) specified by the interim administrator or place it in the custody of the interim administrator (if, in either case, he is able to do so),

(b) to do anything he is reasonably required to do by the interim administrator for the preservation of the property.

(2) An interim administration order may require any person to whose property the order applies to bring any documents relating to the property which are in his possession or control to a place (in Scotland) specified by the interim administrator or to place them in the custody of the interim administrator.

"Document" means anything in which information of any description is recorded.

Supervision of interim administrator and variation of order

260.—(1) The interim administrator, any party to the proceedings and any person affected by any action taken by the interim administrator, or who may be affected by any action proposed to be taken by him, may at any time apply to the court for directions as to the exercise of the interim administrator's functions.

(2) Before giving any directions under subsection (1), the court must (as well as giving the parties to the proceedings an opportunity to be heard) give such an opportunity to the interim administrator and to any person who may be interested in the application.

(3) The court may at any time vary or recall an interim administration order.

(4) Before exercising any power under this Chapter to vary or set aside an interim administration order, the court must (as well as giving the parties to the proceedings an opportunity to be heard) give such an opportunity to the interim administrator and to any person who may be affected by the court's decision.

Restrictions on dealing etc. with property

261.—(1) An interim administration order must, subject to any exclusions made in accordance with this section, prohibit any person to whose property the order applies from dealing with the property.

(2) Exclusions may be made when the interim administration order is made or on an application to vary the order.

(3) An exclusion may, in particular, make provision for the purpose of enabling any person—

(a) to meet his reasonable living expenses, or

(b) to carry on any trade, business, profession or occupation,

and may be made subject to conditions.

(4) But an exclusion may not be made for the purpose of enabling any person to meet any legal expenses in respect of proceedings under this Part.

(5) If the excluded property is not specified in the order it must be described in the order in general terms.

(6) The power to make exclusions must be exercised with a view to ensuring, so far as practicable, that the satisfaction of any right of the enforcement authority to recover the property obtained through unlawful conduct is not unduly prejudiced.

Restriction on proceedings and remedies

262.—(1) While an interim administration order has effect, the court may sist any action, execution or other legal process in respect of the property to which the order applies.

(2) If a court (whether the Court of Session or any other court) in which proceedings are pending in respect of any property is satisfied that an interim administration order has been applied for or made in respect of the property, the court may either sist the proceedings or allow them to continue on any terms it thinks fit.

(3) Before exercising any power conferred by this section, the court must (as well as giving the parties to any of the proceedings in question an opportunity to be heard) give such an opportunity to the interim administrator (if appointed) and any person who may be affected by the court's decision.

Exclusion of property which is not recoverable etc.

263.—(1) If the court decides that any property to which an interim administration order applies is neither recoverable property nor associated property, it must vary the order so as to exclude it.

(2) The court may vary an interim administration order so as to exclude from the property to which the order applies any property which is alleged

to be associated property if the court thinks that the satisfaction of any right of the enforcement authority to recover the property obtained through unlawful conduct will not be prejudiced.

(3) The court may exclude any property within subsection (2) on any terms or conditions, applying while the interim administration order has effect, which the court thinks necessary or expedient.

Reporting

264.—(1) An interim administration order must require the interim administrator to inform the enforcement authority and the court as soon as reasonably practicable if he thinks that—

(a) any property to which the order applies by virtue of a claim that it is recoverable property is not recoverable property,

(b) any property to which the order applies by virtue of a claim that it is associated property is not associated property,

(c) any property to which the order does not apply is recoverable property (in relation to the same unlawful conduct) or associated property, or

(d) any property to which the order applies is held by a person who is different from the person it is claimed holds it,

or if he thinks that there has been any other material change of circumstances.

(2) An interim administration order must require the interim administrator—

(a) to report his findings to the court,

(b) to serve copies of his report on the enforcement authority and on any person who holds any property to which the order applies or who may otherwise be affected by the report.

Arrestment of property affected by interim administration order

265.—(1) On the application of the enforcement authority or the interim administrator the Court of Session may, in relation to moveable recoverable property to which an interim administration order applies (whether generally or such of it as is specified in the application), grant warrant for arrestment.

(2) An application by the enforcement authority under subsection (1) may be made at the same time as the application for the interim administration order or at any time thereafter.

(3) Such a warrant for arrestment may be granted only if the property would be arrestable if the person entitled to it were a debtor.

(4) A warrant under subsection (1) has effect as if granted on the dependence of an action for debt at the instance of the enforcement authority or, as the case may be, the interim administrator against the person and may be executed, recalled, loosed or restricted accordingly.

(5) The execution of an arrestment under this section in respect of property does not prejudice the exercise of an interim administrator's powers under or for the purposes of this Part in respect of that property.

(6) An arrestment executed under this section ceases to have effect when, or in so far as, the interim administration order ceases to apply in respect of the property in relation to which the warrant for arrestment was granted.

(7) If an arrestment ceases to have effect to any extent by virtue of subsection (6) the enforcement authority or, as the case may be, the interim administrator must apply to the Court of Session for an order recalling or, as the case may be, restricting the arrestment.

Vesting and realisation of recoverable property

Recovery orders

266.—(1) If in proceedings under this Chapter the court is satisfied that any property is recoverable, the court must make a recovery order.

(2) The recovery order must vest the recoverable property in the trustee for civil recovery.

(3) But the court may not make in a recovery order—

(a) any provision in respect of any recoverable property if each of the conditions in subsection (4) or (as the case may be) (5) is met and it would not be just and equitable to do so, or

(b) any provision which is incompatible with any of the Convention rights (within the meaning of the Human Rights Act 1998 (c. 42)).

(4) In relation to a court in England and Wales or Northern Ireland, the conditions referred to in subsection (3)(a) are that—

(a) the respondent obtained the recoverable property in good faith,

(b) he took steps after obtaining the property which he would not have taken if he had not obtained it or he took steps before obtaining the property which he would not have taken if he had not believed he was going to obtain it,

(c) when he took the steps, he had no notice that the property was recoverable,

(d) if a recovery order were made in respect of the property, it would, by reason of the steps, be detrimental to him.

(5) In relation to a court in Scotland, the conditions referred to in subsection (3)(a) are that—

(a) the respondent obtained the recoverable property in good faith,

(b) he took steps after obtaining the property which he would not have taken if he had not obtained it or he took steps before obtaining the property which he would not have taken if he had not believed he was going to obtain it,

(c) when he took the steps, he had no reasonable grounds for believing that the property was recoverable,

(d) if a recovery order were made in respect of the property, it would, by reason of the steps, be detrimental to him.

(6) In deciding whether it would be just and equitable to make the provision in the recovery order where the conditions in subsection (4) or (as the case may be) (5) are met, the court must have regard to—

(a) the degree of detriment that would be suffered by the respondent if the provision were made,

(b) the enforcement authority's interest in receiving the realised proceeds of the recoverable property.

(7) A recovery order may sever any property.

(8) A recovery order may impose conditions as to the manner in which the trustee for civil recovery may deal with any property vested by the order for the purpose of realising it.

[1](8A) A recovery order made by a court in England and Wales or Northern Ireland may provide for payment under section 280 of reasonable legal expenses that a person has reasonably incurred, or may reasonably incur, in respect of—

(a) the proceedings under this Part in which the order is made, or

(b) any related proceedings under this Part.

[1] (8B) If regulations under section 286B apply to an item of expenditure, a sum in respect of the item is not payable under section 280 in pursuance of provision under subsection (8A) unless—

(a) the enforcement authority agrees to its payment, or

(b) the court has assessed the amount allowed by the regulations in respect of that item and the sum is paid in respect of the assessed amount.

(9) This section is subject to sections 270 to 278.

NOTE

[1] As inserted by the Serious Organised Crime and Police Act 2005 (c.15), Sch.6, para.15 (effective January 1, 2006).

Functions of the trustee for civil recovery

267.—(1) The trustee for civil recovery is a person appointed by the court to give effect to a recovery order.

(2) The enforcement authority must nominate a suitably qualified person for appointment as the trustee.

(3) The functions of the trustee are—

(a) to secure the detention, custody or preservation of any property vested in him by the recovery order,

(b) in the case of property other than money, to realise the value of the property for the benefit of the enforcement authority, and

(c) to perform any other functions conferred on him by virtue of this Chapter.

(4) In performing his functions, the trustee acts on behalf of the enforcement authority and must comply with any directions given by the authority.

(5) The trustee is to realise the value of property vested in him by the recovery order, so far as practicable, in the manner best calculated to maximise the amount payable to the enforcement authority.

(6) The trustee has the powers mentioned in Schedule 7.

(7) References in this section to a recovery order include an order under section 276 and references to property vested in the trustee by a recovery order include property vested in him in pursuance of an order under section 276.

Recording of recovery order (Scotland)

268.—(1) The clerk of the court must immediately after the making of a recovery order which relates to heritable property situated in Scotland send a certified copy of it to the keeper of the register of inhibitions and adjudications for recording in that register.

(2) Recording under subsection (1) is to have the effect, as from the date of the recovery order, of an inhibition at the instance of the trustee for civil recovery against the person in whom the heritable property was vest prior to that date.

Rights of pre-emption, etc.

269.—(1) A recovery order is to have effect in relation to any property despite any provision (of whatever nature) which would otherwise prevent, penalise or restrict the vesting of the property.

(2) A right of pre-emption, right of irritancy, right of return or other similar right does not operate or become exercisable as a result of the vesting of any property under a recovery order.

A right of return means any right under a provision for the return or reversion of property in specified circumstances.

(3) Where property is vested under a recovery order, any such right is to have effect as if the person in whom the property is vested were the same person in law as the person who held the property and as if no transfer of the property had taken place.

(4) References to rights in subsections (2) and (3) do not include any rights in respect of which the recovery order was made.

(5) This section applies in relation to the creation of interests, or the doing of anything else, by a recovery order as it applies in relation to the vesting of property.

Associated and joint property

270.—(1) Sections 271 and 272 apply if the court makes a recovery order in respect of any recoverable property in a case within subsection (2) or (3).

(2) A case is within this subsection if—

(a) the property to which the proceedings relate includes property which is associated with the recoverable property and is specified or described in the claim form or (in Scotland) application, and

(b) if the associated property is not the respondent's property, the claim form or application has been served on the person whose property it is or the court has dispensed with service.

(3) A case is within this subsection if—

(a) the recoverable property belongs to joint tenants, and

(b) one of the tenants is an excepted joint owner.

(4) An excepted joint owner is a person who obtained the property in circumstances in which it would not be recoverable as against him; and references to the excepted joint owner's share of the recoverable property are to so much of the recoverable property as would have been his if the joint tenancy had been severed.

(5) Subsections (3) and (4) do not extend to Scotland.

Agreements about associated and joint property

271.—(1) Where—

(a) this section applies, and

(b) the enforcement authority (on the one hand) and the person who holds the associated property or who is the excepted joint owner (on the other) agree,

the recovery order may, instead of vesting the recoverable property in the trustee for civil recovery, require the person who holds the associated property or who is the excepted joint owner to make a payment to the trustee.

(2) A recovery order which makes any requirement under subsection (1) may, so far as required for giving effect to the agreement, include provision for vesting, creating or extinguishing any interest in property.

(3) The amount of the payment is to be the amount which the enforcement authority and that person agree represents—

(a) in a case within section 270(2), the value of the recoverable property,

(b) in a case within section 270(3), the value of the recoverable property less the value of the excepted joint owner's share.

(4) But if—

(a) an interim receiving order or interim administration order applied at any time to the associated property or joint tenancy, and

[1] (b) the enforcement authority agrees that the person has suffered loss as a result of the order mentioned in paragraph (a),

the amount of the payment may be reduced by any amount the enforcement authority and that person agree is reasonable, having regard to that loss and to any other relevant circumstances.

(5) If there is more than one such item of associated property or excepted joint owner, the total amount to be paid to the trustee, and the part of that amount which is to be provided by each person who holds any such associated property or who is an excepted joint owner, is to be agreed between both (or all) of them and the enforcement authority.

(6) A recovery order which makes any requirement under subsection (1) must make provision for any recoverable property to cease to be recoverable.

NOTE

[1] As substituted by the Serious Organised Crime and Police Act 2005 (c.15), Sch.6, para.16(b) (effective January 1, 2006).

Associated and joint property: default of agreement

272.—(1) Where this section applies, the court may make the following provision if—

(a) there is no agreement under section 271, and

(b) the court thinks it just and equitable to do so.

(2) The recovery order may provide—

(a) for the associated property to vest in the trustee for civil recovery or (as the case may be) for the excepted joint owner's interest to be extinguished, or

(b) in the case of an excepted joint owner, for the severance of his interest.

(3) A recovery order making any provision by virtue of subsection (2)(a) may provide—

(a) for the trustee to pay an amount to the person who holds the associated property or who is an excepted joint owner, or

(b) for the creation of interests in favour of that person, or the imposition of liabilities or conditions, in relation to the property vested in the trustee,

or for both.

(4) In making any provision in a recovery order by virtue of subsection (2) or (3), the court must have regard to—

(a) the rights of any person who holds the associated property or who is an excepted joint owner and the value to him of that property or, as the case may be, of his share (including any value which cannot be assessed in terms of money),

(b) the enforcement authority's interest in receiving the realised proceeds of the recoverable property.

(5) If—

(a) an interim receiving order or interim administration order applied at any time to the associated property or joint tenancy, and

(b) the court is satisfied that the person who holds the associated property or who is an excepted joint owner has suffered loss as a result of the interim receiving order or interim administration order,

a recovery order making any provision by virtue of subsection (2) or (3) may require the enforcement authority to pay compensation to that person.

(6) The amount of compensation to be paid under subsection (5) is the amount the court thinks reasonable, having regard to the person's loss and to any other relevant circumstances.

[1](7) In subsection (5) the reference to the enforcement authority is, in the case of an enforcement authority in relation to England and Wales or Northern Ireland, a reference to the enforcement authority which obtained the property freezing order or interim receiving order concerned.

NOTE

[1] As inserted by the Serious Crime Act 2007 (c.27), Sch.8(2), para.87 (effective April 1, 2008).

Payments in respect of rights under pension schemes

273.—(1) This section applies to recoverable property consisting of rights under a pension scheme.

(2) A recovery order in respect of the property must, instead of vesting the property in the trustee for civil recovery, require the trustees or managers of the pension scheme—

(a) to pay to the trustee for civil recovery within a prescribed period the amount determined by the trustees or managers to be equal to the value of the rights, and

(b) to give effect to any other provision made by virtue of this section and the two following sections in respect of the scheme.

This subsection is subject to sections 276 to 278.

(3) A recovery order made by virtue of subsection (2) overrides the provisions of the pension scheme to the extent that they conflict with the provisions of the order.

(4) A recovery order made by virtue of subsection (2) may provide for the recovery by the trustees or managers of the scheme (whether by deduction from any amount which they are required to pay to the trustee for civil recovery or otherwise) of costs incurred by them in—

(a) complying with the recovery order, or

(b) providing information, before the order was made, to the enforcement authority, interim receiver or interim administrator.

(5) None of the following provisions applies to a court making a recovery order by virtue of subsection (2)—

(a) any provision of section 159 of the Pension Schemes Act 1993 (c. 48), section 155 of the Pension Schemes (Northern Ireland) Act 1993 (c. 49), section 91 of the Pensions Act 1995 (c. 26) or Article 89 of the Pensions (Northern Ireland) Order 1995 (S.I. 1995/3213 (N.I. 22)) (which prevent assignment and the making of orders that restrain a person from receiving anything which he is prevented from assigning),

(b) any provision of any enactment (whenever passed or made) corresponding to any of the provisions mentioned in paragraph (a),

(c) any provision of the pension scheme in question corresponding to any of those provisions.

Consequential adjustment of liabilities under pension schemes

274.—(1) A recovery order made by virtue of section 273(2) must require the trustees or managers of the pension scheme to make such reduction in the liabilities of the scheme as they think necessary in consequence of the payment made in pursuance of that subsection.

(2) Accordingly, the order must require the trustees or managers to provide for the liabilities of the pension scheme in respect of the respondent's recoverable property to which section 273 applies to cease.

(3) So far as the trustees or managers are required by the recovery order to provide for the liabilities of the pension scheme in respect of the respondent's recoverable property to which section 273 applies to cease, their powers include (in particular) power to reduce the amount of—

(a) any benefit or future benefit to which the respondent is or may be entitled under the scheme,

(b) any future benefit to which any other person may be entitled under the scheme in respect of that property.

Pension schemes: supplementary

275.—(1) Regulations may make provision as to the exercise by trustees or managers of their powers under sections 273 and 274, including provision about the calculation and verification of the value at any time of rights or liabilities.

(2) The power conferred by subsection (1) includes power to provide for any values to be calculated or verified—

(a) in a manner which, in the particular case, is approved by a prescribed person, or

(b) in accordance with guidance from time to time prepared by a prescribed person.

(3) Regulations means regulations made by the Secretary of State after consultation with the Scottish Ministers; and prescribed means prescribed by regulations.

(4) A pension scheme means an occupational pension scheme or a personal pension scheme; and those expressions have the same meaning as in the Pension Schemes Act 1993 (c. 48) or, in relation to Northern Ireland, the Pension Schemes (Northern Ireland) Act 1993 (c. 49).

(5) In relation to an occupational pension scheme or a personal pension scheme, the trustees or managers means—

(a) in the case of a scheme established under a trust, the trustees,

(b) in any other case, the managers.

(6) References to a pension scheme include—

(a) a retirement annuity contract (within the meaning of Part 3 of the Welfare Reform and Pensions Act 1999 (c. 30) or, in relation to Northern Ireland, Part 4 of the Welfare Reform and Pensions (Northern Ireland) Order 1999),

(b) an annuity or insurance policy purchased, or transferred, for the purpose of giving effect to rights under an occupational pension scheme or a personal pension scheme,

(c) an annuity purchased, or entered into, for the purpose of discharging any liability in respect of a pension credit under section 29(1)(b) of the Welfare Reform and Pensions Act 1999 (c. 30) or, in relation to Northern Ireland, Article 26(1)(b) of the Welfare Reform and Pensions (Northern Ireland) Order 1999.

(7) References to the trustees or managers—

(a) in relation to a retirement annuity contract or other annuity, are to the provider of the annuity,

(b) in relation to an insurance policy, are to the insurer.

(8) Subsections (3) to (7) have effect for the purposes of this group of sections (that is, sections 273 and 274 and this section).

Consent orders

276.—(1) The court may make an order staying (in Scotland, sisting) any proceedings for a recovery order on terms agreed by the parties for the disposal of the proceedings if each person to whose property the proceedings, or the agreement, relates is a party both to the proceedings and the agreement.

(2) An order under subsection (1) may, as well as staying (or sisting) the proceedings on terms—

(a) make provision for any property which may be recoverable property to cease to be recoverable,

(b) make any further provision which the court thinks appropriate.

(3) Section 280 applies to property vested in the trustee for civil recovery, or money paid to him, in pursuance of the agreement as it applies to property vested in him by a recovery order or money paid under section 271.

Consent orders: pensions

277.—(1) This section applies where recoverable property to which proceedings under this Chapter relate includes rights under a pension scheme.

(2) An order made under section 276—

(a) may not stay (in Scotland, sist) the proceedings on terms that the rights are vested in any other person, but

(b) may include provision imposing the following requirement, if the trustees or managers of the scheme are parties to the agreement by virtue of which the order is made.

(3) The requirement is that the trustees or managers of the pension scheme—

(a) make a payment in accordance with the agreement, and

(b) give effect to any other provision made by virtue of this section in respect of the scheme.

(4) The trustees or managers of the pension scheme have power to enter into an agreement in respect of the proceedings on any terms on which an order made under section 276 may stay (in Scotland, sist) the proceedings.

(5) The following provisions apply in respect of an order under section 276, so far as it includes the requirement mentioned in subsection (3).

(6) The order overrides the provisions of the pension scheme to the extent that they conflict with the requirement.

(7) The order may provide for the recovery by the trustees or managers of the scheme (whether by deduction from any amount which they are required to pay in pursuance of the agreement or otherwise) of costs incurred by them in—

(a) complying with the order, or

(b) providing information, before the order was made, to the enforcement authority, interim receiver or interim administrator.

(8) Sections 273(5) and 274 (read with section 275) apply as if the requirement were included in an order made by virtue of section 273(2).

(9) Section 275(4) to (7) has effect for the purposes of this section.

Limit on recovery

278.—(1) This section applies if the enforcement authority seeks a recovery order—

(a) in respect of both property which is or represents property obtained through unlawful conduct and related property, or

(b) in respect of property which is or represents property obtained through unlawful conduct where such an order, or an order under section 276, has previously been made in respect of related property.

(2) For the purposes of this section—

(a) the original property means the property obtained through unlawful conduct,

(b) the original property, and any items of property which represent the original property, are to be treated as related to each other.

(3) The court is not to make a recovery order if it thinks that the enforcement authority's right to recover the original property has been satisfied by a previous recovery order or order under section 276.

(4) Subject to subsection (3), the court may act under subsection (5) if it thinks that—

(a) a recovery order may be made in respect of two or more related items of recoverable property, but

(b) the making of a recovery order in respect of both or all of them is not required in order to satisfy the enforcement authority's right to recover the original property.

(5) The court may in order to satisfy that right to the extent required make a recovery order in respect of—

(a) only some of the related items of property, or

(b) only a part of any of the related items of property,

or both.

(6) Where the court may make a recovery order in respect of any property, this section does not prevent the recovery of any profits which have accrued in respect of the property.

(7) If—

(a) an order is made under section 298 for the forfeiture of recoverable property, and

(b) the enforcement authority subsequently seeks a recovery order in respect of related property,

the order under section 298 is to be treated for the purposes of this section as if it were a recovery order obtained by the enforcement authority in respect of the forfeited property.

(8) If—

(a) in pursuance of a judgment in civil proceedings (whether in the United Kingdom or elsewhere), the claimant has obtained property from the defendant ("the judgment property"),

(b) the claim was based on the defendant's having obtained the judgment property or related property through unlawful conduct, and

(c) the enforcement authority subsequently seeks a recovery order in respect of property which is related to the judgment property,

the judgment is to be treated for the purposes of this section as if it were a recovery order obtained by the enforcement authority in respect of the judgment property.

In relation to Scotland, "claimant" and "defendant" are to be read as "pursuer" and "defender".

(9) If—

(a) property has been taken into account in deciding the amount of a person's benefit from criminal conduct for the purpose of making a confiscation order, and

(b) the enforcement authority subsequently seeks a recovery order in respect of related property,

the confiscation order is to be treated for the purposes of this section as if it were a recovery order obtained by the enforcement authority in respect of the property referred to in paragraph (a).

(10) In subsection (9), a confiscation order means—

(a) an order under section 6, 92 or 156, or

(b) an order under a corresponding provision of an enactment mentioned in section 8(7)(a) to (g),

and, in relation to an order mentioned in paragraph (b), the reference to the amount of a person's benefit from criminal conduct is to be read as a reference to the corresponding amount under the enactment in question.

Section 278: supplementary

279.—(1) Subsections (2) and (3) give examples of the satisfaction of the enforcement authority's right to recover the original property.

(2) If—

(a) there is a disposal, other than a part disposal, of the original property, and

(b) other property (the representative property) is obtained in its place,

the enforcement authority's right to recover the original property is satisfied by the making of a recovery order in respect of either the original property or the representative property.

(3) If—

(a) there is a part disposal of the original property, and

(b) other property (the representative property) is obtained in place of the property disposed of,

the enforcement authority's right to recover the original property is satisfied by the making of a recovery order in respect of the remainder of the original property together with either the representative property or the property disposed of.

(4) In this section—

(a) a part disposal means a disposal to which section 314(1) applies,

(b) the original property has the same meaning as in section 278.

Applying realised proceeds

280.—(1) This section applies to—

(a) sums which represent the realised proceeds of property which was vested in the trustee for civil recovery by a recovery order or which he obtained in pursuance of a recovery order,

(b) sums vested in the trustee by a recovery order or obtained by him in pursuance of a recovery order.

(2) The trustee is to make out of the sums—

(a) first, any payment required to be made by him by virtue of section 272,

[1] (aa) next, any payment of legal expenses which, after giving effect to section 266(8B), are payable under this subsection in pursuance of provision under section 266(8A) contained in the recovery order,

[2] (b) then, any payment of expenses incurred by a person acting as an insolvency practitioner which are payable under this subsection by virtue of section 432(10),

and any sum which remains is to be paid to the enforcement authority.

[3] (3) The enforcement authority (unless it is the Scottish Ministers) may apply a sum received by him under subsection (2) in making payment of the remuneration and expenses of—

(a) the trustee; or

(b) any interim receiver appointed in, or in anticipation of, the proceedings for the recovery order.

[3] (4) Subsection (3)(a) does not apply in relation to remuneration of the trustee if the trustee is a member of the staff of the enforcement authority concerned.

NOTE

[1] As inserted by the Serious Organised Crime and Police Act 2005 (c.15), Sch.6, para.18 (effective January 1, 2006).

[2] As substituted by the Serious Organised Crime and Police Act 2005 (c.15), Sch.6, para.18 (effective January 1, 2006).

[3] As inserted by the Serious Organised Crime and Police Act 2005 (c.15), para.99 (effective July 1, 2005) and substituted by the Serious Crime Act 2007, Sch.8(2), para.88 (effective April 1, 2008).

Exemptions etc.

Victims of theft, etc.

281.—(1) In proceedings for a recovery order, a person who claims that any property alleged to be recoverable property, or any part of the property, belongs to him may apply for a declaration under this section.

(2) If the applicant appears to the court to meet the following condition, the court may make a declaration to that effect.

(3) The condition is that—

(a) the person was deprived of the property he claims, or of property which it represents, by unlawful conduct,

(b) the property he was deprived of was not recoverable property immediately before he was deprived of it, and

(c) the property he claims belongs to him.

(4) Property to which a declaration under this section applies is not recoverable property.

Other exemptions

282.—(1) Proceedings for a recovery order may not be taken against any person in circumstances of a prescribed description; and the circumstances may relate to the person himself or to the property or to any other matter.

In this subsection, prescribed means prescribed by an order made by the Secretary of State after consultation with the Scottish Ministers.

(2) Proceedings for a recovery order may not be taken in respect of cash found at any place in the United Kingdom unless the proceedings are also taken in respect of property other than cash which is property of the same person.

(3) Proceedings for a recovery order may not be taken against the Financial Services Authority in respect of any recoverable property held by the authority.

(4) Proceedings for a recovery order may not be taken in respect of any property which is subject to any of the following charges—

(a) a collateral security charge, within the meaning of the Financial Markets and Insolvency (Settlement Finality) Regulations 1999 (S.I. 1999/2979),

(b) a market charge, within the meaning of Part 7 of the Companies Act 1989 (c. 40),

(c) a money market charge, within the meaning of the Financial Markets and Insolvency (Money Market) Regulations 1995 (S.I. 1995/2049),

(d) a system charge, within the meaning of the Financial Markets and Insolvency Regulations 1996 (S.I. 1996/1469) or the Financial Markets and Insolvency Regulations (Northern Ireland) 1996 (S.R. 1996/252).

(5) Proceedings for a recovery order may not be taken against any person in respect of any recoverable property which he holds by reason of his acting, or having acted, as an insolvency practitioner.

Acting as an insolvency practitioner has the same meaning as in section 433.

Miscellaneous

Compensation

283.—(1) If, in the case of any property to which an interim receiving order or interim administration order has at any time applied, the court does not in the course of the proceedings decide that the property is recoverable property or associated property, the person whose property it is may make an application to the court for compensation.

(2) Subsection (1) does not apply if the court—

(a) has made a declaration in respect of the property by virtue of section 281, or

(b) makes an order under section 276.

(3) If the court has made a decision by reason of which no recovery order could be made in respect of the property, the application for compensation must be made within the period of three months beginning—

(a) in relation to a decision of the High Court in England and Wales, with the date of the decision or, if any application is made for leave to appeal, with the date on which the application is withdrawn or refused or (if the application is granted) on which any proceedings on appeal are finally concluded,

(b) in relation to a decision of the Court of Session or of the High Court in Northern Ireland, with the date of the decision or, if there is an appeal against the decision, with the date on which any proceedings on appeal are finally concluded.

(4) If, in England and Wales or Northern Ireland, the proceedings in respect of the property have been discontinued, the application for compensation must be made within the period of three months beginning with the discontinuance.

(5) If the court is satisfied that the applicant has suffered loss as a result of the interim receiving order or interim administration order, it may require the enforcement authority to pay compensation to him.

(6) If, but for section 269(2), any right mentioned there would have operated in favour of, or become exercisable by, any person, he may make an application to the court for compensation.

(7) The application for compensation under subsection (6) must be made within the period of three months beginning with the vesting referred to in section 269(2).

(8) If the court is satisfied that, in consequence of the operation of section 269, the right in question cannot subsequently operate in favour of the applicant or (as the case may be) become exercisable by him, it may require the enforcement authority to pay compensation to him.

(9) The amount of compensation to be paid under this section is the amount the court thinks reasonable, having regard to the loss suffered and any other relevant circumstances.

[1] (10) In the case of an enforcement authority in relation to England and Wales or Northern Ireland—

(a) the reference in subsection (5) to the enforcement authority is a reference to the enforcement authority which obtained the property freezing order or interim receiving order concerned, and

(b) the reference in subsection (8) to the enforcement authority is a reference to the enforcement authority which obtained the recovery order concerned.

NOTE

[1] As inserted by the Serious Crime Act 2007 (c.27) Sch.8(2), para.89 (effective April 1, 2008).

Payment of interim administrator or trustee (Scotland)

[1] **284.**—(1) Any fees or expenses incurred by an interim administrator, or a trustee for civil recovery appointed by the Court of Session, in the exercise of his functions are to be reimbursed by the Scottish Ministers as soon as is practicable after they have been incurred.

(2) The Scottish Ministers may apply a sum received by them under section 280(2) in making payment of such fees or expenses.

(3) Subsection (2) does not apply in relation to the fees of a trustee for civil recovery if the trustee is a member of their staff.

NOTE

[1] Existing s.284 renumbered as s.284(1) and s.284(2)–(3) inserted by the Serious Organised Crime and Police Act 2005 (c.15) s.99(3) (effective July 1, 2005).

Effect on diligence of recovery order (Scotland)

285.—(1) An arrestment or poinding of any recoverable property executed on or after the appointment of the trustee for civil recovery is ineffectual in a question with the trustee.

(2) Any recoverable property so arrested or poinded, or (if the property has been sold) the proceeds of sale, must be handed over to the trustee for civil recovery.

(3) A poinding of the ground in respect of recoverable property on or after such an appointment is ineffectual in a question with the trustee for civil recovery except for the interest mentioned in subsection (4).

(4) That interest is—

(a) interest on the debt of a secured creditor for the current half yearly term, and

(b) arrears of interest on that debt for one year immediately before the commencement of that term.

(5) On and after such appointment no other person may raise or insist in an adjudication against recoverable property or be confirmed as an executor-creditor on that property.

(6) An inhibition on recoverable property shall cease to have effect in relation to any heritable property comprised in the recoverable property on such appointment.

(7) [*Repealed by the Bankruptcy and Diligence etc. (Scotland) Act 2007 (asp.3) Sch.6(1), para.1 (effective April 1, 2008).*]

Scope of powers (Scotland)

286.—(1) Orders under this Chapter may be made by the Court of Session in respect of a person wherever domiciled, resident or present.

(2) Such an order may be made by the Court of Session in respect of moveable property wherever situated.

(3) But such an order in respect of a person's moveable property may not be made by the Court of Session where—

(a) the person is not domiciled, resident or present in Scotland, and

(b) the property is not situated in Scotland,

unless the unlawful conduct took place in Scotland.

Legal expenses excluded from freezing: required conditions

[1] **286A.**—(1) The Lord Chancellor may by regulations specify the required conditions for the purposes of section 245C(5) or 252(4).

(2) A required condition may (in particular)—

(a) restrict who may receive sums released in pursuance of the exclusion (by, for example, requiring released sums to be paid to professional legal advisers), or

(b) be made for the purpose of controlling the amount of any sum released in pursuance of the exclusion in respect of an item of expenditure.

(3) A required condition made for the purpose mentioned in subsection (2)(b) may (for example)—
- (a) provide for sums to be released only with the agreement of the enforcement authority;
- (b) provide for a sum to be released in respect of an item of expenditure only if the court has assessed the amount allowed by regulations under section 286B in respect of that item and the sum is released for payment of the assessed amount;
- (c) provide for a sum to be released in respect of an item of expenditure only if—
  - (i) the enforcement authority agrees to its release, or
  - (ii) the court has assessed the amount allowed by regulations under section 286B in respect of that item and the sum is released for payment of the assessed amount.

(4) Before making regulations under this section, the Lord Chancellor must consult such persons as he considers appropriate.

NOTE

[1] As inserted by the Serious Organised Crime and Police Act 2005 (c.15) Sch.6, para.20 (effective August 1, 2005).

Legal expenses: regulations for purposes of section 266(8B) or 286A(3)

[1] **286B.**—(1) The Lord Chancellor may by regulations—
- (a) make provision for the purposes of section 266(8B);
- (b) make provision for the purposes of required conditions that make provision of the kind mentioned in section 286A(3)(b) or (c).

(2) Regulations under this section may (in particular)—
- (a) limit the amount of remuneration allowable to representatives for a unit of time worked;
- (b) limit the total amount of remuneration allowable to representatives for work done in connection with proceedings or a step in proceedings;
- (c) limit the amount allowable in respect of an item of expense incurred by a representative or incurred, otherwise than in respect of the remuneration of a representative, by a party to proceedings.

(3) Before making regulations under this section, the Lord Chancellor must consult such persons as he considers appropriate.

NOTE

[1] As inserted by the Serious Organised Crime and Police Act 2005 (c.15) Sch.6, para.20 (effective August 1, 2005).

Financial threshold

287.—(1) At any time when an order specifying an amount for the purposes of this section has effect, the enforcement authority may not start proceedings for a recovery order unless the authority reasonably believes that the aggregate value of the recoverable property which the authority wishes to be subject to a recovery order is not less than the specified amount.

(2) The power to make an order under subsection (1) is exercisable by the Secretary of State after consultation with the Scottish Ministers.

[1] (3) If the authority applies for a property freezing order, an interim receiving order, a prohibitory property order or an interim administration order before starting the proceedings, subsection (1) applies to the application instead of to the start of the proceedings.

[1] (4) This section does not affect the continuation of proceedings for a recovery order which have been properly started or the making or continuing effect of a property freezing order, an interim receiving order, a prohibitory property order or an interim administration order which has been properly applied for.

NOTE
[1] As substituted by the Serious Organised Crime and Police Act 2005 (c.15) Sch.6, para.21 (effective January 1, 2006).

Limitation
288. [*Not reproduced.*]

Chapter 3

Recovery of Cash in Summary Proceedings

Searches

Searches
289.—(1) If a customs officer or constable who is lawfully on any premises has reasonable grounds for suspecting that there is on the premises cash—
(a) which is recoverable property or is intended by any person for use in unlawful conduct, and
(b) the amount of which is not less than the minimum amount,
he may search for the cash there.
(2) If a customs officer or constable has reasonable grounds for suspecting that a person (the suspect) is carrying cash—
(a) which is recoverable property or is intended by any person for use in unlawful conduct, and
(b) the amount of which is not less than the minimum amount,
he may exercise the following powers.
(3) The officer or constable may, so far as he thinks it necessary or expedient, require the suspect—
(a) to permit a search of any article he has with him,
(b) to permit a search of his person.
(4) An officer or constable exercising powers by virtue of subsection (3)(b) may detain the suspect for so long as is necessary for their exercise.
(5) The powers conferred by this section—
(a) are exercisable only so far as reasonably required for the purpose of finding cash,
(b) are exercisable by a customs officer only if he has reasonable grounds for suspecting that the unlawful conduct in question relates to an assigned matter (within the meaning of the Customs and Excise Management Act 1979 (c. 2)).
(6) Cash means—
(a) notes and coins in any currency,
(b) postal orders,
(c) cheques of any kind, including travellers' cheques,
(d) bankers' drafts,
(e) bearer bonds and bearer shares,
found at any place in the United Kingdom.
(7) Cash also includes any kind of monetary instrument which is found at any place in the United Kingdom, if the instrument is specified by the Secretary of State by an order made after consultation with the Scottish Ministers.
(8) This section does not require a person to submit to an intimate search or strip search (within the meaning of section 164 of the Customs and Excise Management Act 1979 (c. 2)).

Prior approval
290.—(1) The powers conferred by section 289 may be exercised only with the appropriate approval unless, in the circumstances, it is not practicable to obtain that approval before exercising the power.
(2) The appropriate approval means the approval of a judicial officer or (if that is not practicable in any case) the approval of a senior officer.

(3) A judicial officer means—
(a) in relation to England and Wales and Northern Ireland, a justice of the peace,
(b) in relation to Scotland, the sheriff.

(4) A senior officer means—
(a) in relation to the exercise of the power by a customs officer, a customs officer of a rank designated by the Commissioners of Customs and Excise as equivalent to that of a senior police officer,
(b) in relation to the exercise of the power by a constable, a senior police officer.

(5) A senior police officer means a police officer of at least the rank of inspector.

(6) If the powers are exercised without the approval of a judicial officer in a case where—
(a) no cash is seized by virtue of section 294, or
[1] (b) any cash so seized is not detained for more than 48 hours (calculated in accordance with section 295(1B))

the customs officer or constable who exercised the powers must give a written report to the appointed person.

(7) The report must give particulars of the circumstances which led him to believe that—
(a) the powers were exercisable, and
(b) it was not practicable to obtain the approval of a judicial officer.

(8) In this section and section 291, the appointed person means—
(a) in relation to England and Wales and Northern Ireland, a person appointed by the Secretary of State,
(b) in relation to Scotland, a person appointed by the Scottish Ministers.

(9) The appointed person must not be a person employed under or for the purposes of a government department or of the Scottish Administration; and the terms and conditions of his appointment, including any remuneration or expenses to be paid to him, are to be determined by the person appointing him.

NOTE
[1] As amended by the Serious Organised Crime and Police Act 2005 (c.15) s.100(3) (effective July 1, 2005).

Report on exercise of powers

291.—(1) As soon as possible after the end of each financial year, the appointed person must prepare a report for that year.

"Financial year" means—
(a) the period beginning with the day on which this section comes into force and ending with the next 31 March (which is the first financial year), and
(b) each subsequent period of twelve months beginning with 1 April.

(2) The report must give his opinion as to the circumstances and manner in which the powers conferred by section 289 are being exercised in cases where the customs officer or constable who exercised them is required to give a report under section 290(6).

(3) In the report, he may make any recommendations he considers appropriate.

(4) He must send a copy of his report to the Secretary of State or, as the case may be, the Scottish Ministers, who must arrange for it to be published.

(5) The Secretary of State must lay a copy of any report he receives under this section before Parliament; and the Scottish Ministers must lay a copy of any report they receive under this section before the Scottish Parliament.

Code of practice

292.—(1) The Secretary of State must make a code of practice in connection with the exercise by customs officers and (in relation to England and Wales and Northern Ireland) constables of the powers conferred by virtue of section 289.

(2) Where he proposes to issue a code of practice he must—

(a) publish a draft,

(b) consider any representations made to him about the draft by the Scottish Ministers or any other person,

(c) if he thinks it appropriate, modify the draft in the light of any such representations.

(3) He must lay a draft of the code before Parliament.

(4) When he has laid a draft of the code before Parliament he may bring it into operation by order.

(5) He may revise the whole or any part of the code issued by him and issue the code as revised; and subsections (2) to (4) apply to such a revised code as they apply to the original code.

(6) A failure by a customs officer or constable to comply with a provision of the code does not of itself make him liable to criminal or civil proceedings.

(7) The code is admissible in evidence in criminal or civil proceedings and is to be taken into account by a court or tribunal in any case in which it appears to the court or tribunal to be relevant.

Code of practice (Scotland)

293.—(1) The Scottish Ministers must make a code of practice in connection with the exercise by constables in relation to Scotland of the powers conferred by virtue of section 289.

(2) Where they propose to issue a code of practice they must—

(a) publish a draft,

(b) consider any representations made to them about the draft,

(c) if they think it appropriate, modify the draft in the light of any such representations.

(3) They must lay a draft of the code before the Scottish Parliament.

(4) When they have laid a draft of the code before the Scottish Parliament they may bring it into operation by order.

(5) They may revise the whole or any part of the code issued by them and issue the code as revised; and subsections (2) to (4) apply to such a revised code as they apply to the original code.

(6) A failure by a constable to comply with a provision of the code does not of itself make him liable to criminal or civil proceedings.

(7) The code is admissible in evidence in criminal or civil proceedings and is to be taken into account by a court or tribunal in any case in which it appears to the court or tribunal to be relevant.

Seizure and detention

Seizure of cash

294.—(1) A customs officer or constable may seize any cash if he has reasonable grounds for suspecting that it is—

(a) recoverable property, or

(b) intended by any person for use in unlawful conduct.

(2) A customs officer or constable may also seize cash part of which he has reasonable grounds for suspecting to be—

(a) recoverable property, or

(b) intended by any person for use in unlawful conduct,

if it is not reasonably practicable to seize only that part.

(3) This section does not authorise the seizure of an amount of cash if it or, as the case may be, the part to which his suspicion relates, is less than the minimum amount.

Detention of seized cash

295.—(1) While the customs officer or constable continues to have reasonable grounds for his suspicion, cash seized under section 294 may be detained initially for a period of 48 hours.

[1] (1A) The period of 48 hours mentioned in subsection (1) is to be calculated in accordance with subsection (1B).

[1] (1B) In calculating a period of 48 hours in accordance with this subsection, no account shall be taken of—

(a) any Saturday or Sunday,
(b) Christmas Day,
(c) Good Friday,
(d) any day that is a bank holiday under the Banking and Financial Dealings Act 1971 in the part of the United Kingdom within which the cash is seized, or
(e) any day prescribed under section 8(2) of the Criminal Procedure (Scotland) Act 1995 as a court holiday in a sheriff court in the sheriff court district within which the cash is seized.

(2) The period for which the cash or any part of it may be detained may be extended by an order made by a magistrates' court or (in Scotland) the sheriff; but the order may not authorise the detention of any of the cash—

(a) beyond the end of the period of three months beginning with the date of the order,
(b) in the case of any further order under this section, beyond the end of the period of two years beginning with the date of the first order.

(3) A justice of the peace may also exercise the power of a magistrates' court to make the first order under subsection (2) extending the period.

(4) An application for an order under subsection (2)—

(a) in relation to England and Wales and Northern Ireland, may be made by the Commissioners of Customs and Excise or a constable,
(b) in relation to Scotland, may be made by the Scottish Ministers in connection with their functions under section 298 or by a procurator fiscal,

and the court, sheriff or justice may make the order if satisfied, in relation to any cash to be further detained, that either of the following conditions is met.

(5) The first condition is that there are reasonable grounds for suspecting that the cash is recoverable property and that either—

(a) its continued detention is justified while its derivation is further investigated or consideration is given to bringing (in the United Kingdom or elsewhere) proceedings against any person for an offence with which the cash is connected, or
(b) proceedings against any person for an offence with which the cash is connected have been started and have not been concluded.

(6) The second condition is that there are reasonable grounds for suspecting that the cash is intended to be used in unlawful conduct and that either—

(a) its continued detention is justified while its intended use is further investigated or consideration is given to bringing (in the United Kingdom or elsewhere) proceedings against any person for an offence with which the cash is connected, or
(b) proceedings against any person for an offence with which the cash is connected have been started and have not been concluded.

(7) An application for an order under subsection (2) may also be made in respect of any cash seized under section 294(2), and the court, sheriff or justice may make the order if satisfied that—

(a) the condition in subsection (5) or (6) is met in respect of part of the cash, and
(b) it is not reasonably practicable to detain only that part.

(8) An order under subsection (2) must provide for notice to be given to persons affected by it.

NOTE
[1] As inserted by the Serious Organised Crime and Police Act 2005 (c.15) s.100(2) (effective July 1, 2005).

Interest

296.—[1] (1) If cash is detained under section 295 for more than 48 hours (calculated in accordance with section 295(1B)) it is at the first opportunity to be paid into an interest-bearing account and held there; and the interest accruing on it is to be added to it on its forfeiture or release.

(2) In the case of cash detained under section 295 which was seized under section 294(2), the customs officer or constable must, on paying it into the account, release the part of the cash to which the suspicion does not relate.

(3) Subsection (1) does not apply if the cash or, as the case may be, the part to which the suspicion relates is required as evidence of an offence or evidence in proceedings under this Chapter.

NOTE
[1] As amended by the Serious Organised Crime and Police Act 2005 (c.15) s.100(3) (effective July 1, 2005).

Release of detained cash

297.—(1) This section applies while any cash is detained under section 295.

(2) A magistrates' court or (in Scotland) the sheriff may direct the release of the whole or any part of the cash if the following condition is met.

(3) The condition is that the court or sheriff is satisfied, on an application by the person from whom the cash was seized, that the conditions in section 295 for the detention of the cash are no longer met in relation to the cash to be released.

(4) A customs officer, constable or (in Scotland) procurator fiscal may, after notifying the magistrates' court, sheriff or justice under whose order cash is being detained, release the whole or any part of it if satisfied that the detention of the cash to be released is no longer justified.

Forfeiture

Forfeiture

298.—(1) While cash is detained under section 295, an application for the forfeiture of the whole or any part of it may be made—

(a) to a magistrates' court by the Commissioners of Customs and Excise or a constable,

(b) (in Scotland) to the sheriff by the Scottish Ministers.

(2) The court or sheriff may order the forfeiture of the cash or any part of it if satisfied that the cash or part—

(a) is recoverable property, or

(b) is intended by any person for use in unlawful conduct.

(3) But in the case of recoverable property which belongs to joint tenants, one of whom is an excepted joint owner, the order may not apply to so much of it as the court thinks is attributable to the excepted joint owner's share.

(4) Where an application for the forfeiture of any cash is made under this section, the cash is to be detained (and may not be released under any power conferred by this Chapter) until any proceedings in pursuance of the application (including any proceedings on appeal) are concluded.

Appeal against decision under section 298

[1] **299.**—(1) Any party to proceedings for an order for the forfeiture of cash under section 298 who is aggrieved by an order under that section or by the decision of the court not to make such an order may appeal—

(a) in relation to England and Wales, to the Crown Court;

(b) in relation to Scotland, to the Sheriff Principal;

(c) in relation to Northern Ireland, to a county court.

(2) An appeal under subsection (1) must be made before the end of the period of 30 days starting with the day on which the court makes the order or decision.

(3) The court hearing the appeal may make any order it thinks appropriate.

(4) If the court upholds an appeal against an order forfeiting the cash, it may order the release of the cash.

NOTE

[1] As substituted by the Serious Organised Crime and Police Act 2005 (c.15) s.101(1) (effective July 1, 2005).

Application of forfeited cash

300.—(1) Cash forfeited under this Chapter, and any accrued interest on it—

(a) if forfeited by a magistrates' court in England and Wales or Northern Ireland, is to be paid into the Consolidated Fund,

(b) if forfeited by the sheriff, is to be paid into the Scottish Consolidated Fund.

(2) But it is not to be paid in—

(a) before the end of the period within which an appeal under section 299 may be made, or

(b) if a person appeals under that section, before the appeal is determined or otherwise disposed of.

Supplementary

Victims and other owners

301.—(1) A person who claims that any cash detained under this Chapter, or any part of it, belongs to him may apply to a magistrates' court or (in Scotland) the sheriff for the cash or part to be released to him.

(2) The application may be made in the course of proceedings under section 295 or 298 or at any other time.

(3) If it appears to the court or sheriff concerned that—

(a) the applicant was deprived of the cash to which the application relates, or of property which it represents, by unlawful conduct,

(b) the property he was deprived of was not, immediately before he was deprived of it, recoverable property, and

(c) that cash belongs to him,

the court or sheriff may order the cash to which the application relates to be released to the applicant.

(4) If—

(a) the applicant is not the person from whom the cash to which the application relates was seized,

(b) it appears to the court or sheriff that that cash belongs to the applicant,

(c) the court or sheriff is satisfied that the conditions in section 295 for the detention of that cash are no longer met or, if an application has been made under section 298, the court or sheriff decides not to make an order under that section in relation to that cash, and

(d) no objection to the making of an order under this subsection has been made by the person from whom that cash was seized,

the court or sheriff may order the cash to which the application relates to be released to the applicant or to the person from whom it was seized.

Compensation

302.—(1) If no forfeiture order is made in respect of any cash detained under this Chapter, the person to whom the cash belongs or from whom it was seized may make an application to the magistrates' court or (in Scotland) the sheriff for compensation.

[1] (2) If, for any period beginning with the first opportunity to place the cash in an interest-bearing account after the initial detention of the cash for 48 hours (calculated in accordance with section 295(1B), the cash was not held in an interest-bearing account while detained, the court or sheriff may order an amount of compensation to be paid to the applicant.

(3) The amount of compensation to be paid under subsection (2) is the amount the court or sheriff thinks would have been earned in interest in the period in question if the cash had been held in an interest-bearing account.

(4) If the court or sheriff is satisfied that, taking account of any interest to be paid under section 296 or any amount to be paid under subsection (2), the applicant has suffered loss as a result of the detention of the cash and that the circumstances are exceptional, the court or sheriff may order compensation (or additional compensation) to be paid to him.

(5) The amount of compensation to be paid under subsection (4) is the amount the court or sheriff thinks reasonable, having regard to the loss suffered and any other relevant circumstances.

(6) If the cash was seized by a customs officer, the compensation is to be paid by the Commissioners of Customs and Excise.

(7) If the cash was seized by a constable, the compensation is to be paid as follows—

(a) in the case of a constable of a police force in England and Wales, it is to be paid out of the police fund from which the expenses of the police force are met,

(b) in the case of a constable of a police force in Scotland, it is to be paid by the police authority or joint police board for the police area for which that force is maintained,

(c) in the case of a police officer within the meaning of the Police (Northern Ireland) Act 2000 (c. 32), it is to be paid out of money provided by the Chief Constable.

(8) If a forfeiture order is made in respect only of a part of any cash detained under this Chapter, this section has effect in relation to the other part.

NOTE

[1] As amended by the Serious Organised Crime and Police Act 2005 (c.15) s.100(3) (effective July 1, 2005).

"The minimum amount"

303.—(1) In this Chapter, the minimum amount is the amount in sterling specified in an order made by the Secretary of State after consultation with the Scottish Ministers.

(2) For that purpose the amount of any cash held in a currency other than sterling must be taken to be its sterling equivalent, calculated in accordance with the prevailing rate of exchange.

Chapter 4

General

Recoverable property

Property obtained through unlawful conduct

304.—(1) Property obtained through unlawful conduct is recoverable property.

(2) But if property obtained through unlawful conduct has been disposed of (since it was so obtained), it is recoverable property only if it is held by a person into whose hands it may be followed.

(3) Recoverable property obtained through unlawful conduct may be followed into the hands of a person obtaining it on a disposal by—

(a) the person who through the conduct obtained the property, or

(b) a person into whose hands it may (by virtue of this subsection) be followed.

Tracing property, etc.

305.—(1) Where property obtained through unlawful conduct ("the original property") is or has been recoverable, property which represents the original property is also recoverable property.

(2) If a person enters into a transaction by which—

(a) he disposes of recoverable property, whether the original property or property which (by virtue of this Chapter) represents the original property, and

(b) he obtains other property in place of it,

the other property represents the original property.

(3) If a person disposes of recoverable property which represents the original property, the property may be followed into the hands of the person who obtains it (and it continues to represent the original property).

Mixing property

306.—(1) Subsection (2) applies if a person's recoverable property is mixed with other property (whether his property or another's).

(2) The portion of the mixed property which is attributable to the recoverable property represents the property obtained through unlawful conduct.

(3) Recoverable property is mixed with other property if (for example) it is used—

(a) to increase funds held in a bank account,

(b) in part payment for the acquisition of an asset,

(c) for the restoration or improvement of land,

(d) by a person holding a leasehold interest in the property to acquire the freehold.

Recoverable property: accruing profits

307.—(1) This section applies where a person who has recoverable property obtains further property consisting of profits accruing in respect of the recoverable property.

(2) The further property is to be treated as representing the property obtained through unlawful conduct.

General exceptions

308.—(1) If—

(a) a person disposes of recoverable property, and

(b) the person who obtains it on the disposal does so in good faith, for value and without notice that it was recoverable property,

the property may not be followed into that person's hands and, accordingly, it ceases to be recoverable.

(2) If recoverable property is vested, forfeited or otherwise disposed of in pursuance of powers conferred by virtue of this Part, it ceases to be recoverable.

(3) If—

(a) in pursuance of a judgment in civil proceedings (whether in the United Kingdom or elsewhere), the defendant makes a payment to the claimant or the claimant otherwise obtains property from the defendant,

(b) the claimant's claim is based on the defendant's unlawful conduct, and

(c) apart from this subsection, the sum received, or the property obtained, by the claimant would be recoverable property, the property ceases to be recoverable.

In relation to Scotland, "claimant" and "defendant" are to be read as "pursuer" and "defender".

(4) If—

(a) a payment is made to a person in pursuance of a compensation order under Article 14 of the Criminal Justice (Northern Ireland) Order 1994 (S.I. 1994/2795 (N.I. 15)), section 249 of the Criminal Procedure (Scotland) Act 1995 (c. 46) or section 130 of the Powers of Criminal Courts (Sentencing) Act 2000 (c. 6), and

(b) apart from this subsection, the sum received would be recoverable property,

the property ceases to be recoverable.

(5) If—

(a) a payment is made to a person in pursuance of a restitution order under section 27 of the Theft Act (Northern Ireland) 1969 (c. 16 (N.I.)) or section 148(2) of the Powers of Criminal Courts (Sentencing) Act 2000 or a person otherwise obtains any property in pursuance of such an order, and

(b) apart from this subsection, the sum received, or the property obtained, would be recoverable property,

the property ceases to be recoverable.

(6) If—

(a) in pursuance of an order made by the court under section 382(3) or 383(5) of the Financial Services and Markets Act 2000 (c. 8) (restitution orders), an amount is paid to or distributed among any persons in accordance with the court's directions, and

(b) apart from this subsection, the sum received by them would be recoverable property,

the property ceases to be recoverable.

(7) If—

(a) in pursuance of a requirement of the Financial Services Authority under section 384(5) of the Financial Services and Markets Act 2000 (power of authority to require restitution), an amount is paid to or distributed among any persons, and

(b) apart from this subsection, the sum received by them would be recoverable property,

the property ceases to be recoverable.

(8) Property is not recoverable while a restraint order applies to it, that is—

(a) an order under section 41, 120 or 190, or

(b) an order under any corresponding provision of an enactment mentioned in section 8(7)(a) to (g).

(9) Property is not recoverable if it has been taken into account in deciding the amount of a person's benefit from criminal conduct for the purpose of making a confiscation order, that is—

(a) an order under section 6, 92 or 156, or

(b) an order under a corresponding provision of an enactment mentioned in section 8(7)(a) to (g),

and, in relation to an order mentioned in paragraph (b), the reference to the amount of a person's benefit from criminal conduct is to be read as a reference to the corresponding amount under the enactment in question.

(10) Where—

(a) a person enters into a transaction to which section 305(2) applies, and

(b) the disposal is one to which subsection (1) or (2) applies,

this section does not affect the recoverability (by virtue of section 305(2)) of any property obtained on the transaction in place of the property disposed of.

Other exemptions

309.—(1) An order may provide that property is not recoverable or (as the case may be) associated property if—

(a) it is prescribed property, or

(b) it is disposed of in pursuance of a prescribed enactment or an enactment of a prescribed description.

(2) An order may provide that if property is disposed of in pursuance of a prescribed enactment or an enactment of a prescribed description, it is to be treated for the purposes of section 278 as if it had been disposed of in pursuance of a recovery order.

(3) An order under this section may be made so as to apply to property, or a disposal of property, only in prescribed circumstances; and the circumstances may relate to the property or disposal itself or to a person who holds or has held the property or to any other matter.

(4) In this section, an order means an order made by the Secretary of State after consultation with the Scottish Ministers, and prescribed means prescribed by the order.

Granting interests

310.—(1) If a person grants an interest in his recoverable property, the question whether the interest is also recoverable is to be determined in the same manner as it is on any other disposal of recoverable property.

(2) Accordingly, on his granting an interest in the property ("the property in question")—

(a) where the property in question is property obtained through unlawful conduct, the interest is also to be treated as obtained through that conduct,

(b) where the property in question represents in his hands property obtained through unlawful conduct, the interest is also to be treated as representing in his hands the property so obtained.

Insolvency

Insolvency

311.—(1) Proceedings for a recovery order may not be taken or continued in respect of property to which subsection (3) applies unless the appropriate court gives leave and the proceedings are taken or (as the case may be) continued in accordance with any terms imposed by that court.

(2) An application for an order for the further detention of any cash to which subsection (3) applies may not be made under section 295 unless the appropriate court gives leave.

(3) This subsection applies to recoverable property, or property associated with it, if—

(a) it is an asset of a company being wound up in pursuance of a resolution for voluntary winding up,

(b) it is an asset of a company and a voluntary arrangement under Part 1 of the 1986 Act, or Part 2 of the 1989 Order, has effect in relation to the company,

(c) an order under section 2 of the 1985 Act, section 286 of the 1986 Act or Article 259 of the 1989 Order (appointment of interim trustee or interim receiver) has effect in relation to the property,

(d) it is an asset comprised in the estate of an individual who has been adjudged bankrupt or, in relation to Scotland, of a person whose estate has been sequestrated,

(e) it is an asset of an individual and a voluntary arrangement under Part 8 of the 1986 Act, or Part 8 of the 1989 Order, has effect in relation to him, or

(f) in relation to Scotland, it is property comprised in the estate of a person who has granted a trust deed within the meaning of the 1985 Act.

(4) An application under this section, or under any provision of the 1986 Act or the 1989 Order, for leave to take proceedings for a recovery order may be made without notice to any person.

(5) Subsection (4) does not affect any requirement for notice of an application to be given to any person acting as an insolvency practitioner or to the official receiver (whether or not acting as an insolvency practitioner).

(6) References to the provisions of the 1986 Act in sections 420 and 421 of that Act, or to the provisions of the 1989 Order in Articles 364 or 365 of that Order, (insolvent partnerships and estates of deceased persons) include subsections (1) to (3) above.

(7) In this section—

(a) the 1985 Act means the Bankruptcy (Scotland) Act 1985 (c. 66),

(b) the 1986 Act means the Insolvency Act 1986 (c. 45),

(c) the 1989 Order means the Insolvency (Northern Ireland) Order 1989 (S.I. 1989/2405 (N.I. 19)),

and in subsection (8) "the applicable enactment" means whichever enactment mentioned in paragraphs (a) to (c) is relevant to the resolution, arrangement, order or trust deed mentioned in subsection (3).

(8) In this section—

(a) an asset means any property within the meaning of the applicable enactment or, where the 1985 Act is the applicable enactment, any property comprised in an estate to which the 1985 Act applies,

(b) the appropriate court means the court which, in relation to the resolution, arrangement, order or trust deed mentioned in subsection (3), is the court for the purposes of the applicable enactment or, in relation to Northern Ireland, the High Court,

(c) acting as an insolvency practitioner has the same meaning as in section 433,

(d) other expressions used in this section and in the applicable enactment have the same meaning as in that enactment.

Delegation of enforcement functions

Performance of functions of Scottish Ministers by constables in Scotland

312.—(1) In Scotland, a constable engaged in temporary service with the Scottish Ministers in connection with their functions under this Part may perform functions, other than those specified in subsection (2), on behalf of the Scottish Ministers.

(2) The specified functions are the functions conferred on the Scottish Ministers by—

(a) sections 244(1) and (2) and 256(1) and (7) (proceedings in the Court of Session),

(b) section 267(2) (trustee for civil recovery),

(c) sections 271(3) and (4) and 272(5) (agreements about associated and joint property),

(d) section 275(3) (pension schemes),

(e) section 282(1) (exemptions),

(f) section 283(5) and (8) (compensation),

(g) section 287(2) (financial threshold),

(h) section 293(1) (code of practice),

(i) section 298(1) (forfeiture),

(j) section 303(1) (minimum amount).

Restriction on performance of Director's functions by police

313. [*Repealed subject to transitional and transitory provisions and savings as specified in SI 2008/755 arts 3–14 by the Serious Crime Act 2007 (c.27) Sch.14, para.1 (effective April 1, 2008)*.]

Obtaining and disposing of property

314.—(1) References to a person disposing of his property include a reference—

(a) to his disposing of a part of it, or

(b) to his granting an interest in it,

(or to both); and references to the property disposed of are to any property obtained on the disposal.

(2) A person who makes a payment to another is to be treated as making a disposal of his property to the other, whatever form the payment takes.

(3) Where a person's property passes to another under a will or intestacy or by operation of law, it is to be treated as disposed of by him to the other.

(4) A person is only to be treated as having obtained his property for value in a case where he gave unexecuted consideration if the consideration has become executed consideration.

Northern Ireland courts

315. In relation to the practice and procedure of courts in Northern Ireland, expressions used in this Part are to be read in accordance with rules of court.

General interpretation

316.—(1) In this Part—

"associated property" has the meaning given by section 245,

"cash" has the meaning given by section 289(6) or (7),

"constable", in relation to Northern Ireland, means a police officer within the meaning of the Police (Northern Ireland) Act 2000 (c. 32),

"country" includes territory,

"the court" (except in sections 253(2) and (3) and 262(2) and (3) and Chapter 3) means the High Court or (in relation to proceedings in Scotland) the Court of Session,

"dealing" with property includes disposing of it, taking possession of it or removing it from the United Kingdom,

"enforcement authority"—

(a) in relation to England and Wales and Northern Ireland, means the Director,

(b) in relation to Scotland, means the Scottish Ministers,

"excepted joint owner" has the meaning given by section 270(4),

"interest", in relation to land—

(a) in the case of land in England and Wales or Northern Ireland, means any legal estate and any equitable interest or power,

(b) in the case of land in Scotland, means any estate, interest, servitude or other heritable right in or over land, including a heritable security,

"interest", in relation to property other than land, includes any right (including a right to possession of the property),

"interim administration order" has the meaning given by section 256(2),

"interim receiving order" has the meaning given by section 246(2),

"the minimum amount" (in Chapter 3) has the meaning given by section 303,

"part", in relation to property, includes a portion,

"premises" has the same meaning as in the Police and Criminal Evidence Act 1984 (c. 60),

"property obtained through unlawful conduct" has the meaning given by section 242,

"recoverable property" is to be read in accordance with sections 304 to 310, "recovery order" means an order made under section 266,

"respondent" means—

(a) where proceedings are brought by the enforcement authority by virtue of Chapter 2, the person against whom the proceedings are brought,

(b) where no such proceedings have been brought but the enforcement authority has applied for an interim receiving order or interim administration order, the person against whom he intends to bring such proceedings,

"share", in relation to an excepted joint owner, has the meaning given by section 270(4),

"unlawful conduct" has the meaning given by section 241,

"value" means market value.

(2) The following provisions apply for the purposes of this Part.

(3) For the purpose of deciding whether or not property was recoverable at any time (including times before commencement), it is to be assumed that this Part was in force at that and any other relevant time.

(4) Property is all property wherever situated and includes—

(a) money,

(b) all forms of property, real or personal, heritable or moveable,

(c) things in action and other intangible or incorporeal property.

(5) Any reference to a person's property (whether expressed as a reference to the property he holds or otherwise) is to be read as follows.

(6) In relation to land, it is a reference to any interest which he holds in the land.

(7) In relation to property other than land, it is a reference—

(a) to the property (if it belongs to him), or

(b) to any other interest which he holds in the property.

(8) References to the satisfaction of the enforcement authority's right to recover property obtained through unlawful conduct are to be read in accordance with section 279.

[1] (8A) In relation to an order in England and Wales or Northern Ireland which is a recovery order, a property freezing order, an interim receiving order or an order under section 276, references to the enforcement authority are, unless the context otherwise requires, references to the enforcement authority which is seeking, or (as the case may be) has obtained, the order.

(9) Proceedings against any person for an offence are concluded when—

(a) the person is convicted or acquitted,

(b) the prosecution is discontinued or, in Scotland, the trial diet is deserted simpliciter, or

(c) the jury is discharged without a finding.

NOTE

[1] As inserted by the Serious Crime Act 2007 (c.27) Sch.8(2), para.91(3) (effective April 1, 2008).

. . . . . .

Part 7

Money Laundering

Offences

Concealing etc

[1] **327.**—(1) A person commits an offence if he—

(a) conceals criminal property;

(b) disguises criminal property;

(c) converts criminal property;

(d) transfers criminal property;
(e) removes criminal property from England and Wales or from Scotland or from Northern Ireland.

(2) But a person does not commit such an offence if—
(a) he makes an authorised disclosure under section 338 and (if the disclosure is made before he does the act mentioned in subsection (1)) he has the appropriate consent;
(b) he intended to make such a disclosure but had a reasonable excuse for not doing so;
(c) the act he does is done in carrying out a function he has relating to the enforcement of any provision of this Act or of any other enactment relating to criminal conduct or benefit from criminal conduct.

[2] (2A) Nor does a person commit an offence under subsection (1) if—
(a) he knows, or believes on reasonable grounds, that the relevant criminal conduct occurred in a particular country or territory outside the United Kingdom, and
(b) the relevant criminal conduct—
(i) was not, at the time it occurred, unlawful under the criminal law then applying in that country or territory, and
(ii) is not of a description prescribed by an order made by the Secretary of State.

[2] (2B) In subsection (2A) "the relevant criminal conduct" is the criminal conduct by reference to which the property concerned is criminal property.

[1] (2C) A deposit-taking body that does an act mentioned in paragraph (c) or (d) of subsection (1) does not commit an offence under that subsection if—
(a) it does the act in operating an account maintained with it, and
(b) the value of the criminal property concerned is less than the threshold amount determined under section 339A for the act.

(3) Concealing or disguising criminal property includes concealing or disguising its nature, source, location, disposition, movement or ownership or any rights with respect to it.

NOTE

[1] Inserted by the Serious Organised Crime and Police Act 2005, s.103, brought into force by SI 2005/1521 (effective July 1, 2005).

[2] Inserted by the Serious Organised Crime and Police Act 2005, s.102, brought into force by SI 2006/1085 (effective May 15, 2006).

Arrangements

328.—(1) A person commits an offence if he enters into or becomes concerned in an arrangement which he knows or suspects facilitates (by whatever means) the acquisition, retention, use or control of criminal property by or on behalf of another person.

(2) But a person does not commit such an offence if—
(a) he makes an authorised disclosure under section 338 and (if the disclosure is made before he does the act mentioned in subsection (1)) he has the appropriate consent;
(b) he intended to make such a disclosure but had a reasonable excuse for not doing so;
(c) the act he does is done in carrying out a function he has relating to the enforcement of any provision of this Act or of any other enactment relating to criminal conduct or benefit from criminal conduct.

[2] (3) Nor does a person commit an offence under subsection (1) if—
(a) he knows, or believes on reasonable grounds, that the relevant criminal conduct occurred in a particular country or territory outside the United Kingdom, and

(b) the relevant criminal conduct—
 (i) was not, at the time it occurred, unlawful under the criminal law then applying in that country or territory, and
 (ii) is not of a description prescribed by an order made by the Secretary of State.

[2] (4) In subsection (3) "the relevant criminal conduct" is the criminal conduct by reference to which the property concerned is criminal property.

[1] (5) A deposit-taking body that does an act mentioned in subsection (1) does not commit an offence under that subsection if—
(a) it does the act in operating an account maintained with it, and
(b) the arrangement facilitates the acquisition, retention, use or control of criminal property of a value that is less than the threshold amount determined under section 339A for the act.

NOTES

[1] Inserted by the Serious Organised Crime and Police Act 2005, s.103, brought into force by SI 2005/1521 (effective July 1, 2005).

[2] Inserted by the Serious Organised Crime and Police Act 2005, s.102, brought into force by SI 2006/1085 (effective May 15, 2006).

Acquisition, use and possession

329.—(1) A person commits an offence if he—
(a) acquires criminal property;
(b) uses criminal property;
(c) has possession of criminal property.

(2) But a person does not commit such an offence if—
(a) he makes an authorised disclosure under section 338 and (if the disclosure is made before he does the act mentioned in subsection (1)) he has the appropriate consent;
(b) he intended to make such a disclosure but had a reasonable excuse for not doing so;
(c) he acquired or used or had possession of the property for adequate consideration;
(d) the act he does is done in carrying out a function he has relating to the enforcement of any provision of this Act or of any other enactment relating to criminal conduct or benefit from criminal conduct.

[2] (2A) Nor does a person commit an offence under subsection (1) if—
(a) he knows, or believes on reasonable grounds, that the relevant criminal conduct occurred in a particular country or territory outside the United Kingdom, and
(b) the relevant criminal conduct—
 (i) was not, at the time it occurred, unlawful under the criminal law then applying in that country or territory, and
 (ii) is not of a description prescribed by an order made by the Secretary of State.

[2] (2B) In subsection (2A) "the relevant criminal conduct" is the criminal conduct by reference to which the property concerned is criminal property.

[1] (2C) A deposit-taking body that does an act mentioned in subsection (1) does not commit an offence under that subsection if—
(a) it does the act in operating an account maintained with it, and
(b) the value of the criminal property concerned is less than the threshold amount determined under section 339A for the act.

(3) For the purposes of this section—
(a) a person acquires property for inadequate consideration if the value of the consideration is significantly less than the value of the property;
(b) a person uses or has possession of property for inadequate consideration if the value of the consideration is significantly less than the value of the use or possession;

(c) the provision by a person of goods or services which he knows or suspects may help another to carry out criminal conduct is not consideration.

NOTES

[1] Inserted by the Serious Organised Crime and Police Act 2005, s.103, brought into force by SI 2005/1521 (effective July 1, 2005).

[2] Inserted by the Serious Organised Crime and Police Act 2005, s.102, brought into force by SI 2006/1085 (effective May 15, 2006).

Failure to disclose: regulated sector

[1] **330.**—(1) A person commits an offence if each of the conditions in subsections (2) to (4) are satisfied.

(2) The first condition is that he—

(a) knows or suspects, or

(b) has reasonable grounds for knowing or suspecting,

that another person is engaged in money laundering.

(3) The second condition is that the information or other matter—

(a) on which his knowledge or suspicion is based, or

(b) which gives reasonable grounds for such knowledge or suspicion,

came to him in the course of a business in the regulated sector.

[4] (3A) The third condition is—

(a) that he can identify the other person mentioned in subsection (2) or the whereabouts of any of the laundered property, or

(b) that he believes, or it is reasonable to expect him to believe, that the information or other matter mentioned in subsection (3) will or may assist in identifying that other person or the whereabouts of any of the laundered property.

[4] (4) The fourth condition is that he does not make the required disclosure to—

(a) a nominated officer, or

[8] (b) a person authorised for the purposes of this Part by the Director General of SOCA, as soon as is practicable after the information or other matter mentioned in subsection (3) comes to him.

[4] (5) The required disclosure is a disclosure of—

(a) the identity of the other person mentioned in subsection (2), if he knows it,

(b) the whereabouts of the laundered property, so far as he knows it, and

(c) the information or other matter mentioned in subsection (3).

[4] (5A) The laundered property is the property forming the subject-matter of the money laundering that he knows or suspects, or has reasonable grounds for knowing or suspecting, that other person to be engaged in.

[2] (6) But he does not commit an offence under this section if—

(a) he has a reasonable excuse for not making the required disclosure,

[6] (b) he is a professional legal adviser or other relevant professional adviser and—

(i) if he knows either of the things mentioned in subsection (5)(a) and (b), he knows the thing because of information or other matter that came to him in privileged circumstances, or

(ii) the information or other matter mentioned in subsection (3) came to him in privileged circumstances, or

[6] (c) subsection (7) or (7B) applies to him.

(7) This subsection applies to a person if—

(a) he does not know or suspect that another person is engaged in money laundering, and

(b) he has not been provided by his employer with such training as is specified by the Secretary of State by order for the purposes of this section.

[3] (7A) Nor does a person commit an offence under this section if—

(a) he knows, or believes on reasonable grounds, that the money laundering is occurring in a particular country or territory outside the United Kingdom, and

(b) the money laundering—

(i) is not unlawful under the criminal law applying in that country or territory, and

(ii) is not of a description prescribed in an order made by the Secretary of State.

[7] (7B) This subsection applies to a person if—

(a) he is employed by, or is in partnership with, a professional legal adviser or a relevant professional adviser to provide the adviser with assistance or support,

(b) the information or other matter mentioned in subsection (3) comes to the person in connection with the provision of such assistance or support, and

(c) the information or other matter came to the adviser in privileged circumstances.

(8) In deciding whether a person committed an offence under this section the court must consider whether he followed any relevant guidance which was at the time concerned—

(a) issued by a supervisory authority or any other appropriate body,

(b) approved by the Treasury, and

(c) published in a manner it approved as appropriate in its opinion to bring the guidance to the attention of persons likely to be affected by it.

(9) A disclosure to a nominated officer is a disclosure which—

(a) is made to a person nominated by the alleged offender's employer to receive disclosures under this section, and

[2] (b) is made in the course of the alleged offender's employment.

[5] (9A) But a disclosure which satisfies paragraphs (a) and (b) of subsection (9) is not to be taken as a disclosure to a nominated officer if the person making the disclosure—

[6] (a) is a professional legal adviser or other relevant professional

(b) makes it for the purpose of obtaining advice about making a disclosure under this section, and

(c) does not intend it to be a disclosure under this section.

[6] (10) Information or other matter comes to a professional legal adviser or other relevant professional adviser in privileged circumstances if it is communicated or given to him—

(a) by (or by a representative of) a client of his in connection with the giving by the adviser of legal advice to the client,

(b) by (or by a representative of) a person seeking legal advice from the adviser, or

(c) by a person in connection with legal proceedings or contemplated legal proceedings.

(11) But subsection (10) does not apply to information or other matter which is communicated or given with the intention of furthering a criminal purpose.

(12) Schedule 9 has effect for the purpose of determining what is—

(a) a business in the regulated sector;

(b) a supervisory authority.

(13) An appropriate body is any body which regulates or is representative of any trade, profession, business or employment carried on by the alleged offender.

[7] (14) A relevant professional adviser is an accountant, auditor or tax adviser who is a member of a professional body which is established for accountants, auditors or tax advisers (as the case may be) and which makes provision for—

(a) testing the competence of those seeking admission to membership of such a body as a condition for such admission; and

(b) imposing and maintaining professional and ethical standards for its members, as well as imposing sanctions for non-compliance with those standards.

NOTE

[1] s.330 of the Act shall not have effect in relation to a person who engages in any of the activities mentioned in paragraph 1(1)(f) to (n) of Sch.9 where the information or other matter on which knowledge or suspicion that another person is engaged in money laundering is based, or which gives reasonable grounds for such knowledge or suspicion, came to that person before March 1, 2004, the Proceeds of Crime Act 2002 (Business in the Regulated Sector and Supervisory Authorities) Order 2003, (SI 2003/3074), para.4.

[2] As amended by the Serious Organised Crime and Police Act 2005,s.105 and Sch.17, Pt.2, brought into force by SI 2005/1521 (effective July 1, 2005).

[3] Inserted by the Serious Organised Crime and Police Act 2005, s.102, brought into force by SI 2006/1085 (effective May 15, 2006).

[4] Substituted by the Serious Organised Crime and Police Act 2005, s.104, brought into force by SI 2005/1521 (effective July 1, 2005).

[5] Inserted by the Serious Organised Crime and Police Act 2005, s.104, brought into force by SI 2005/1521 (effective July 1, 2005).

[6] As amended by the Proceeds of Crime Act 2002 and Money Laundering Regulations 2003 (Amendment) Order 2006/308 art. 2 (effective February 21, 2006).

[7] Inserted by the Proceeds of Crime Act 2002 and Money Laundering Regulations 2003 (Amendment) Order 2006/308 art. 2 (effective February 21, 2006).

[8] As amended by the Serious Crime Act 2007 (c.27) Sch.8(6), para.126 (effective April 1, 2008).

Failure to disclose: nominated officers in the regulated sector

[1] **331.**—(1) A person nominated to receive disclosures under section 330 commits an offence if the conditions in subsections (2) to (4) are satisfied.

(2) The first condition is that he—

(a) knows or suspects, or

(b) has reasonable grounds for knowing or suspecting,

that another person is engaged in money laundering.

(3) The second condition is that the information or other matter—

(a) on which his knowledge or suspicion is based, or

(b) which gives reasonable grounds for such knowledge or suspicion,

came to him in consequence of a disclosure made under section 330.

[3] (3A) The third condition is—

(a) that he knows the identity of the other person mentioned in subsection (2), or the whereabouts of any of the laundered property, in consequence of a disclosure made under section 330,

(b) that that other person, or the whereabouts of any of the laundered property, can be identified from the information or other matter mentioned in subsection (3), or

(c) that he believes, or it is reasonable to expect him to believe, that the information or other matter will or may assist in identifying that other person or the whereabouts of any of the laundered property.

[3,4] (4) The fourth condition is that he does not make the required disclosure to a person authorised for the purposes of this Part by the Director General of SOCA as soon as is practicable after the information or other matter mentioned in subsection (3) comes to him.

[3] (5) The required disclosure is a disclosure of—

(a) the identity of the other person mentioned in subsection (2), if disclosed to him under section 330,

(b) the whereabouts of the laundered property, so far as disclosed to him under section 330, and

(c) the information or other matter mentioned in subsection (3).

[3] (5A) The laundered property is the property forming the subject-matter of the money laundering that he knows or suspects, or has reasonable grounds for knowing or suspecting, that other person to be engaged in.

[3] (6) But he does not commit an offence under this section if he has a reasonable excuse for not making the required disclosure.

[2] (6A) Nor does a person commit an offence under this section if—

(a) he knows, or believes on reasonable grounds, that the money laundering is occurring in a particular country or territory outside the United Kingdom, and

(b) the money laundering—

(i) is not unlawful under the criminal law applying in that country or territory, and

(ii) is not of a description prescribed in an order made by the Secretary of State.

(7) In deciding whether a person committed an offence under this section the court must consider whether he followed any relevant guidance which was at the time concerned—

(a) issued by a supervisory authority or any other appropriate body,

(b) approved by the Treasury, and

(c) published in a manner it approved as appropriate in its opinion to bring the guidance to the attention of persons likely to be affected by it.

(8) Schedule 9 has effect for the purpose of determining what is a supervisory authority.

(9) An appropriate body is a body which regulates or is representative of a trade, profession, business or employment.

NOTE

[1] s.330 of the Act shall not have effect in relation to a person who engages in any of the activities mentioned in paragraph 1(1)(f) to (n) of Sch.9 where the information or other matter on which knowledge or suspicion that another person is engaged in money laundering is based, or which gives reasonable grounds for such knowledge or suspicion, came to that person before March 1, 2004, the Proceeds of Crime Act 2002 (Business in the Regulated Sector and Supervisory Authorities) Order 2003, (SI 2003/3074), para.4.

[2] Inserted by the Serious Organised Crime and Police Act 2005, s.102, brought into force by SI 2006/1085 (effective May 15, 2006).

[3] Substituted by the Serious Organised Crime and Police Act 2005, s.104, brought into force by SI 2005/1521 (effective July 1, 2005).

[4] As amended by the Serious Crime Act 2007 (c.27) Sch.8(6), para.127 (effective April 1, 2008).

Failure to disclose: other nominated officers

332.—(1) A person nominated to receive disclosures under section 337 or 338 commits an offence if the conditions in subsections (2) to (4) are satisfied.

(2) The first condition is that he knows or suspects that another person is engaged in money laundering.

[2] (3) The second condition is that the information or other matter on which his knowledge or suspicion is based came to him in consequence of a disclosure made under the applicable section.

[3] (3A) The third condition is—

(a) that he knows the identity of the other person mentioned in subsection (2), or the whereabouts of any of the laundered property, in consequence of a disclosure made under the applicable section,

(b) that that other person, or the whereabouts of any of the laundered property, can be identified from the information or other matter mentioned in subsection (3), or

(c) that he believes, or it is reasonable to expect him to believe, that the information or other matter will or may assist in identifying that other person or the whereabouts of any of the laundered property.

[3,4] (4) The fourth condition is that he does not make the required disclosure to a person authorised for the purposes of this Part by the Director General of SOCA as soon as is practicable after the information or other matter mentioned in subsection (3) comes to him.

[3] (5) The required disclosure is a disclosure of—

(a) the identity of the other person mentioned in subsection (2), if disclosed to him under the applicable section,

(b) the whereabouts of the laundered property, so far as disclosed to him under the applicable section, and
(c) the information or other matter mentioned in subsection (3).

[3] (5A) The laundered property is the property forming the subject-matter of the money laundering that he knows or suspects that other person to be engaged in.

[3] (5B) The applicable section is section 337 or, as the case may be, section 338.

[3] (6) But he does not commit an offence under this section if he has a reasonable excuse for not making the required disclosure.

[1] (7) Nor does a person commit an offence under this section if—
(a) he knows, or believes on reasonable grounds, that the money laundering is occurring in a particular country or territory outside the United Kingdom, and
(b) the money laundering—
  (i) is not unlawful under the criminal law applying in that country or territory, and
  (ii) is not of a description prescribed in an order made by the Secretary of State.

NOTES

[1] Inserted by the Serious Organised Crime and Police Act 2005, s.102, brought into force by SI 2006/1085 (effective May 15, 2006).

[2] As amended by the Serious Organised Crime and Police Act 2005, s.104, brought into force by SI 2005/1521 (effective July 1, 2005).

[3] Substitutedby the Serious Organised Crime and Police Act 2005, s.104, brought into force by SI 2005/1521 (effective July 1, 2005).

[4] As amended by the Serious Crime Act 2007 (c.27) Sch.8(6), para.128 (effective April 1, 2008).

Tipping off

333. [*Repealed by the Terrorism Act 2000 and Proceeds of Crime Act 2002 (Amendment) Regulations (SI 2007/3398) Sch.2, para.3 (effective December 26, 2007)*.]

Tipping off: regulated sector

[1] **333A.**—(1) A person commits an offence if—
(a) the person discloses any matter within subsection (2);
(b) the disclosure is likely to prejudice any investigation that might be conducted following the disclosure referred to in that subsection; and
(c) the information on which the disclosure is based came to the person in the course of a business in the regulated sector.

(2) The matters are that the person or another person has made a disclosure under this Part—
(a) to a constable,
(b) to an officer of Revenue and Customs,
(c) to a nominated officer, or
(d) to a member of staff of the Serious Organised Crime Agency authorised for the purposes of this Part by the Director General of that Agency,

of information that came to that person in the course of a business in the regulated sector.

(3) A person commits an offence if—
(a) the person discloses that an investigation into allegations that an offence under this Part has been committed is being contemplated or is being carried out;
(b) the disclosure is likely to prejudice that investigation; and
(c) the information on which the disclosure is based came to the person in the course of a business in the regulated sector.

(4) A person guilty of an offence under this section is liable—

(a) on summary conviction to imprisonment for a term not exceeding three months, or to a fine not exceeding level 5 on the standard scale, or to both;
(b) on conviction on indictment to imprisonment for a term not exceeding two years, or to a fine, or to both.

(5) This section is subject to–
(a) section 333B (disclosures within an undertaking or group etc),
(b) section 333C (other permitted disclosures between institutions etc), and
(c) section 333D (other permitted disclosures etc).

NOTE
[1] As inserted by the Terrorism Act 2000 and Proceeds of Crime Act 2002 (Amendment) Regulations (SI 2007/3398) Sch.2, para.4 (effective December 26, 2007).

Disclosures within an undertaking or group etc

[1] **333B.**—(1) An employee, officer or partner of an undertaking does not commit an offence under section 333A if the disclosure is to an employee, officer or partner of the same undertaking.

(2) A person does not commit an offence under section 333A in respect of a disclosure by a credit institution or a financial institution if—
(a) the disclosure is to a credit institution or a financial institution,
(b) the institution to whom the disclosure is made is situated in an EEA State or in a country or territory imposing equivalent money laundering requirements, and
(c) both the institution making the disclosure and the institution to whom it is made belong to the same group.

(3) In subsection (2) "group" has the same meaning as in Directive 2002/87/EC of the European Parliament and of the Council of 16th December 2002 on the supplementary supervision of credit institutions, insurance undertakings and investment firms in a financial conglomerate.

(4) A professional legal adviser or a relevant professional adviser does not commit an offence under section 333A if—
(a) the disclosure is to professional legal adviser or a relevant professional adviser,
(b) both the person making the disclosure and the person to whom it is made carry on business in an EEA State or in a country or territory imposing equivalent money laundering requirements, and
(c) those persons perform their professional activities within different undertakings that share common ownership, management or control.

NOTE
[1] As inserted by the Terrorism Act 2000 and Proceeds of Crime Act 2002 (Amendment) Regulations (SI 2007/3398) Sch.2, para.4 (effective December 26, 2007).

Other permitted disclosures between institutions etc

[1] **333C.**—(1) This section applies to a disclosure—
(a) by a credit institution to another credit institution,
(b) by a financial institution to another financial institution,
(c) by a professional legal adviser to another professional legal adviser, or
(d) by a relevant professional adviser of a particular kind to another relevant professional adviser of the same kind.

(2) A person does not commit an offence under section 333A in respect of a disclosure to which this section applies if—
(a) the disclosure relates to—
(i) a client or former client of the institution or adviser making the disclosure and the institution or adviser to whom it is made,

(ii) a transaction involving them both, or
(iii) the provision of a service involving them both;
(b) the disclosure is for the purpose only of preventing an offence under this Part of this Act;
(c) the institution or adviser to whom the disclosure is made is situated in an EEA State or in a country or territory imposing equivalent money laundering requirements; and
(d) the institution or adviser making the disclosure and the institution or adviser to whom it is made are subject to equivalent duties of professional confidentiality and the protection of personal data (within the meaning of section 1 of the Data Protection Act 1998).

NOTE
[1] As inserted by the Terrorism Act 2000 and Proceeds of Crime Act 2002 (Amendment) Regulations (SI 2007/3398) Sch.2, para.4 (effective December 26, 2007).

Other permitted disclosures etc

[1] **333D.**—(1) A person does not commit an offence under section 333A if the disclosure is—
(a) to the authority that is the supervisory authority for that person by virtue of the Money Laundering Regulations 2007 (S.I. 2007/2157); or
(b) for the purpose of—
(i) the detection, investigation or prosecution of a criminal offence (whether in the United Kingdom or elsewhere),
(ii) an investigation under this Act, or
(iii) the enforcement of any order of a court under this Act.

(2) A professional legal adviser or a relevant professional adviser does not commit an offence under section 333A if the disclosure—
(a) is to the adviser's client, and
(b) is made for the purpose of dissuading the client from engaging in conduct amounting to an offence.

(3) A person does not commit an offence under section 333A(1) if the person does not know or suspect that the disclosure is likely to have the effect mentioned in section 333A(1)(b).

(4) A person does not commit an offence under section 333A(3) if the person does not know or suspect that the disclosure is likely to have the effect mentioned in section 333A(3)(b).

NOTE
[1] As inserted by the Terrorism Act 2000 and Proceeds of Crime Act 2002 (Amendment) Regulations (SI 2007/3398) Sch.2, para.4 (effective December 26, 2007).

Interpretation of sections 333A to 333D

[1] **333E.**—(1) For the purposes of sections 333A to 333D, Schedule 9 has effect for determining—
(a) what is a business in the regulated sector, and
(b) what is a supervisory authority.

(2) In those sections—
"credit institution" has the same meaning as in Schedule 9;
"financial institution" means an undertaking that carries on a business in the regulated sector by virtue of any of paragraphs (b) to (i) of paragraph 1(1) of that Schedule.

(3) References in those sections to a disclosure by or to a credit institution or a financial institution include disclosure by or to an employee, officer or partner of the institution acting on its behalf.

(4) For the purposes of those sections a country or territory imposes "equivalent money laundering requirements" if it imposes requirements equivalent to those laid down in Directive 2005/60/EC of the European Parliament and of the Council of 26th October 2005 on the prevention of the

use of the financial system for the purpose of money laundering and terrorist financing.

(5) In those sections "relevant professional adviser" means an accountant, auditor or tax adviser who is a member of a professional body which is established for accountants, auditors or tax advisers (as the case may be) and which makes provision for—

(a) testing the competence of those seeking admission to membership of such a body as a condition for such admission; and

(b) imposing and maintaining professional and ethical standards for its members, as well as imposing sanctions for non-compliance with those standards.

NOTE

[1] As inserted by the Terrorism Act 2000 and Proceeds of Crime Act 2002 (Amendment) Regulations (SI 2007/3398) Sch.2, para.4 (effective December 26, 2007).

Penalties

334.—(1) A person guilty of an offence under section 327, 328 or 329 is liable—

(a) on summary conviction, to imprisonment for a term not exceeding six months or to a fine not exceeding the statutory maximum or to both, or

(b) on conviction on indictment, to imprisonment for a term not exceeding 14 years or to a fine or to both.

(2) A person guilty of an offence under section 330, 331, 332 or 333 is liable—

(a) on summary conviction, to imprisonment for a term not exceeding six months or to a fine not exceeding the statutory maximum or to both, or

(b) on conviction on indictment, to imprisonment for a term not exceeding five years or to a fine or to both.

[3] (3) A person guilty of an offence under section 339(1A) is liable on summary conviction to a fine not exceeding level 5 on the standard scale.

NOTE

[3] Inserted by the Serious Organised Crime and Police Act 2005, s.105, brought into force by SI 2005/1521 (effective July 1, 2005).

Consent

Appropriate consent

335.—(1) The apropriate consent is—

(a) the consent of a nominated officer to do a prohibited act if an authorised disclosure is made to the nominated officer;

(b) the consent of a constable to do a prohibited act if an authorised disclosure is made to a constable;

(c) the consent of a customs officer to do a prohibited act if an authorised disclosure is made to a customs officer.

(2) A person must be treated as having the appropriate consent if—

(a) he makes an authorised disclosure to a constable or a customs officer, and

(b) the condition in subsection (3) or the condition in subsection (4) is satisfied.

(3) The condition is that before the end of the notice period he does not receive notice from a constable or customs officer that consent to the doing of the act is refused.

(4) The condition is that—

(a) before the end of the notice period he receives notice from a constable or customs officer that consent to the doing of the act is refused, and

(b) the moratorium period has expired.

(5) The notice period is the period of seven working days starting with the first working day after the person makes the disclosure.

(6) The moratorium period is the period of 31 days starting with the day on which the person receives notice that consent to the doing of the act is refused.

(7) A working day is a day other than a Saturday, a Sunday, Christmas Day, Good Friday or a day which is a bank holiday under the Banking and Financial Dealings Act 1971 (c.80) in the part of the United Kingdom in which the person is when he makes the disclosure.

(8) References to a prohibited act are to an act mentioned in section 327(1), 328(1) or 329(1) (as the case may be).

(9) A nominated officer is a person nominated to receive disclosures under section 338.

(10) Subsections (1) to (4) apply for the purposes of this Part.

Nominated officer: consent

336.—(1) A nominated officer must not give the appropriate consent to the doing of a prohibited act unless the condition in subsection (2), the condition in subsection (3) or the condition in subsection (4) is satisfied.

(2) The condition is that—

[1] (a) he makes a disclosure that property is criminal property to a person authorised for the purposes of this Part by the Director General of the Serious Organised Crime Agency, and

(b) such a person gives consent to the doing of the act.

(3) The condition is that—

[1] (a) he makes a disclosure that property is criminal property to a person authorised for the purposes of this Part by the Director General of the Serious Organised Crime Agency, and

(b) before the end of the notice period he does not receive notice from such a person that consent to the doing of the act is refused.

(4) The condition is that—

[1] (a) he makes a disclosure that property is criminal property to a person authorised for the purposes of this Part by the Director General of the Serious Organised Crime Agency,

(b) before the end of the notice period he receives notice from such a person that consent to the doing of the act is refused, and

(c) the moratorium period has expired.

(5) A person who is a nominated officer commits an offence if—

(a) he gives consent to a prohibited act in circumstances where none of the conditions in subsections (2), (3) and (4) is satisfied, and

(b) he knows or suspects that the act is a prohibited act.

(6) A person guilty of such an offence is liable—

(a) on summary conviction, to imprisonment for a term not exceeding six months or to a fine not exceeding the statutory maximum or to both, or

(b) on conviction on indictment, to imprisonment for a term not exceeding five years or to a fine or to both.

(7) The notice period is the period of seven working days starting with the first working day after the nominated officer makes the disclosure.

(8) The moratorium period is the period of 31 days starting with the day on which the nominated officer is given notice that consent to the doing of the act is refused.

(9) A working day is a day other than a Saturday, a Sunday, Christmas Day, Good Friday or a day which is a bank holiday under the Banking and Financial Dealings Act 1971 (c.80) in the part of the United Kingdom in which the nominated officer is when he gives the appropriate consent.

(10) References to a prohibited act are to an act mentioned in section 327(1), 328(1) or 329(1) (as the case may be).

(11) A nominated officer is a person nominated to receive disclosures under section 338.

NOTE
[1] As amended by the Serious Organised Crime and Police Act 2005, Sch.4, para.173, brought into force by SI 2006/378 (effective April 1, 2006).

Disclosures

Protected disclosures

337.—(1) A disclosure which satisfies the following three conditions is not to be taken to breach any restriction on the disclosure of information (however imposed).

(2) The first condition is that the information or other matter disclosed came to the person making the disclosure (the discloser) in the course of his trade, profession, business or employment.

(3) The second condition is that the information or other matter—

(a) causes the discloser to know or suspect, or

(b) gives him reasonable grounds for knowing or suspecting,

that another person is engaged in money laundering.

(4) The third condition is that the disclosure is made to a constable, a customs officer or a nominated officer as soon as is practicable after the information or other matter comes to the discloser.

[2] (4A) Where a disclosure consists of a disclosure protected under subsection (1) and a disclosure of either or both of—

(a) the identity of the other person mentioned in subsection (3), and

(b) the whereabouts of property forming the subject-matter of the money laundering that the discloser knows or suspects, or has reasonable grounds for knowing or suspecting, that other person to be engaged in,

the disclosure of the thing mentioned in paragraph (a) or (b) (as well as the disclosure protected under subsection (1)) is not to be taken to breach any restriction on the disclosure of information (however imposed).

(5) A disclosure to a nominated officer is a disclosure which—

[3] (a) is made to a person nominated by the discloser's employer to receive disclosures under section 330 or this section, and

[1] (b) is made in the course of the discloser's employment.

NOTES
[1] As amended by the Serious Organised Crime and Police Act 2005,s.105 and Sch.17, Pt.2, brought into force by SI 2005/1521 (effective July 1, 2005).
[2] Inserted by the Serious Organised Crime and Police Act 2005, s.104, brought into force by SI 2005/1521 (effective July 1, 2005).
[3] As amended by the Serious Organised Crime and Police Act 2005, s.106, brought into force by SI 2005/1521 (effective July 1, 2005).

Authorised disclosures

338.—[1] (1) For the purposes of this Part a disclosure is authorised if—

(a) it is a disclosure to a constable, a customs officer or a nominated officer by the alleged offender that property is criminal property, and

[2] (c) the first, second or third condition set out below is satisfied.

(2) The first condition is that the disclosure is made before the alleged offender does the prohibited act.

[4] (2A) The second condition is that—

(a) the disclosure is made while the alleged offender is doing the prohibited act,

(b) he began to do the act at a time when, because he did not then know or suspect that the property constituted or represented a person's benefit from criminal conduct, the act was not a prohibited act, and

(c) the disclosure is made on his own initiative and as soon as is practicable after he first knows or suspects that the property constitutes or represents a person's benefit from criminal conduct.

[3] (3) The third condition is that—

(a) the disclosure is made after the alleged offender does the prohibited act,

[5] (b) he has a reasonable excuse for his failure to make the disclosure before he did the act, and

(c) the disclosure is made on his own initiative and as soon as it is practicable for him to make it.

(4) An authorised disclosure is not to be taken to breach any restriction on the disclosure of information (however imposed).

(5) A disclosure to a nominated officer is a disclosure which—

(a) is made to a person nominated by the alleged offender's employer to receive authorised disclosures, and

[2] (b) is made in the course of the alleged offender's employment.

(6) References to the prohibited act are to an act mentioned in section 327(1), 328(1) or 329(1) (as the case may be).

NOTE

[1] Subsection (1)(b) (except the word "and" at the end) repealed by the Serious Organised Crime and Police Act 2005, s.105 and Sch.17, Pt.2, brought into force by SI 2005/1521 (effective July 1, 2005).

[2] As amended by the Serious Organised Crime and Police Act 2005, s. 105 and Sch.17, Pt.2, brought into force by SI 2005/1521 (effective July 1, 2005).

[3] As amended by the Serious Organised Crime and Police Act 2005, s. 106, brought into force by SI 2005/1521 (effective July 1, 2005).

[4] Inserted by the Serious Organised Crime and Police Act 2005, s. 106, brought into force by SI 2005/1521 (effective July 1, 2005).

[5] As substituted by the Terrorism Act 2000 and Proceeds of Crime Act 2002 (Amendment) Regulations (SI 2007/3398) Sch.2, para.6 (effective December 26, 2007).

Form and manner of disclosures

339.—(1) The Secretary of State may by order prescribe the form and manner in which a disclosure under section 330, 331, 332 or 338 must be made.

[1] (1A) A person commits an offence if he makes a disclosure under section 330, 331, 332 or 338 otherwise than in the form prescribed under subsection (1) or otherwise than in the manner so prescribed.

[1] (1B) But a person does not commit an offence under subsection (1A) if he has a reasonable excuse for making the disclosure otherwise than in the form prescribed under subsection (1) or (as the case may be) otherwise than in the manner so prescribed.

[1] (2) The power under subsection (1) to prescribe the form in which a disclosure must be made includes power to provide for the form to include a request to a person making a disclosure that the person provide information specified or described in the form if he has not provided it in making the disclosure.

[1] (3) Where under subsection (2) a request is included in a form prescribed under subsection (1), the form must—

(a) state that there is no obligation to comply with the request, and

(b) explain the protection conferred by subsection (4) on a person who complies with the request.

(4) A disclosure made in pursuance of a request under subsection (2) is not to be taken to breach any restriction on the disclosure of information (however imposed).

(5) [*Repealed by the Serious Organised Crime and Police Act 2005, Sch.17, Pt.2, brought into force by SI 2005/1521 (effective July 1, 2005)*]

(6) [*Repealed by the Serious Organised Crime and Police Act 2005, Sch.17, Pt.2, brought into force by SI 2005/1521 (effective July 1, 2005)*]

(7) Subsection (2) does not apply to a disclosure made to a nominated officer.

NOTE
[1] Substituted by the Serious Organised Crime and Police Act 2005, s. 105, brought into force by SI 2005/1521 (effective July 1, 2005).

[1] **Disclosures to SOCA**

339ZA. Where a disclosure is made under this Part to a constable or an officer of Revenue and Customs, the constable or officer of Revenue and Customs must disclose it in full to a person authorised for the purposes of this Part by the Director General of the Serious Organised Crime Agency as soon as practicable after it has been made.

NOTE
[1] As inserted by the Terrorism Act 2000 and Proceeds of Crime Act 2002 (Amendment) Regulations (SI 2007/3398) Sch.2, para.7 (effective December 26, 2007).

Threshold amounts

Threshold amounts

[1] **339A**—(1) This section applies for the purposes of sections 327(2C), 328(5) and 329(2C).

(2) The threshold amount for acts done by a deposit-taking body in operating an account is £250 unless a higher amount is specified under the following provisions of this section (in which event it is that higher amount).

(3) An officer of Revenue and Customs, or a constable, may specify the threshold amount for acts done by a deposit-taking body in operating an account—

(a) when he gives consent, or gives notice refusing consent, to the deposit-taking body's doing of an act mentioned in section 327(1), 328(1) or 329(1) in opening, or operating, the account or a related account, or

(b) on a request from the deposit-taking body.

(4) Where the threshold amount for acts done in operating an account is specified under subsection (3) or this subsection, an officer of Revenue and Customs, or a constable, may vary the amount (whether on a request from the deposit-taking body or otherwise) by specifying a different amount.

(5) Different threshold amounts may be specified under subsections (3) and (4) for different acts done in operating the same account.

(6) The amount specified under subsection (3) or (4) as the threshold amount for acts done in operating an account must, when specified, not be less than the amount specified in subsection (2).

(7) The Secretary of State may by order vary the amount for the time being specified in subsection (2).

(8) For the purposes of this section, an account is related to another if each is maintained with the same deposit-taking body and there is a person who, in relation to each account, is the person or one of the persons entitled to instruct the body as respects the operation of the account.

NOTE
[1] Inserted by the Serious Organised Crime and Police Act 2005, s. 103, brought into force by SI 2005/1521 (effective July 1, 2005).

Interpretation

Interpretation

340.—(1) This section applies for the purposes of this Part.

(2) Criminal conduct is conduct which—

(a) constitutes an offence in any part of the United Kingdom, or

(b) would constitute an offence in any part of the United Kingdom if it occurred there.

(3) Property is criminal property if—

(a) it constitutes a person's benefit from criminal conduct or it represents such a benefit (in whole or part and whether directly or indirectly), and
(b) the alleged offender knows or suspects that it constitutes or represents such a benefit.

(4) It is immaterial—
(a) who carried out the conduct;
(b) who benefited from it;
(c) whether the conduct occurred before or after the passing of this Act.

(5) A person benefits from conduct if he obtains property as a result of or in connection with the conduct.

(6) If a person obtains a pecuniary advantage as a result of or in connection with conduct, he is to be taken to obtain as a result of or in connection with the conduct a sum of money equal to the value of the pecuniary advantage.

(7) References to property or a pecuniary advantage obtained in connection with conduct include references to property or a pecuniary advantage obtained in both that connection and some other.

(8) If a person benefits from conduct his benefit is the property obtained as a result of or in connection with the conduct.

(9) Property is all property wherever situated and includes—
(a) money;
(b) all forms of property, real or personal, heritable or moveable;
(c) things in action and other intangible or incorporeal property.

(10) The following rules apply in relation to property—
(a) property is obtained by a person if he obtains an interest in it;
(b) references to an interest, in relation to land in England and Wales or Northern Ireland, are to any legal estate or equitable interest or power;
(c) references to an interest, in relation to land in Scotland, are to any estate, interest, servitude or other heritable right in or over land, including a heritable security;
(d) references to an interest, in relation to property other than land, include references to a right (including a right to possession).

(11) Money laundering is an act which—
(a) constitutes an offence under section 327, 328 or 329,
(b) constitutes an attempt, conspiracy or incitement to commit an offence specified in paragraph (a),
(c) constitutes aiding, abetting, counselling or procuring the commission of an offence specified in paragraph (a), or
(d) would constitute an offence specified in paragraph (a), (b) or (c) if done in the United Kingdom.

(12) For the purposes of a disclosure to a nominated officer—
(a) references to a person's employer include any body, association or organisation (including a voluntary organisation) in connection with whose activities the person exercises a function (whether or not for gain or reward), and
(b) references to employment must be construed accordingly.

[1] (13) References to a constable include references to a person authorised for the purposes of this Part by the Director General of SOCA.

[2] (14) "Deposit-taking body" means—
(a) a business which engages in the activity of accepting deposits, or
(b) the National Savings Bank.

NOTES

[1] As amended by the Serious Organised Crime and Police Act 2005, Sch.4, para.173, brought into force by SI 2006/378 (effective April 1, 2006) and the Serious Crime Act 2007 (c.27) Sch.8(6), para.130 (effective April 1, 2008).

[2] Inserted by the Serious Organised Crime and Police Act 2005, s. 103, brought into force by SI 2005/1521 (effective July 1, 2005).

PART 8

INVESTIGATIONS

CHAPTER 1

INTRODUCTION

Investigations

341.—(1) For the purposes of this Part a confiscation investigation is an investigation into—

(a) whether a person has benefited from his criminal conduct, or
(b) the extent or whereabouts of his benefit from his criminal conduct.

(2) For the purposes of this Part a civil recovery investigation is an investigation into—

(a) whether property is recoverable property or associated property,
(b) who holds the property, or
(c) its extent or whereabouts.

(3) But an investigation is not a civil recovery investigation if—

(a) proceedings for a recovery order have been started in respect of the property in question,
(b) an interim receiving order applies to the property in question,
(c) an interim administration order applies to the property in question, or
(d) the property in question is detained under section 295.

(4) For the purposes of this Part a money laundering investigation is an investigation into whether a person has committed a money laundering offence.

Offences of prejudicing investigation

342.—(1) This section applies if a person knows or suspects that an appropriate officer or (in Scotland) a proper person is acting (or proposing to act) in connection with a confiscation investigation, a civil recovery investigation or a money laundering investigation which is being or is about to be conducted.

(2) The person commits an offence if—

(a) he makes a disclosure which is likely to prejudice the investigation, or
(b) he falsifies, conceals, destroys or otherwise disposes of, or causes or permits the falsification, concealment, destruction or disposal of, documents which are relevant to the investigation.

(3) A person does not commit an offence under subsection (2)(a) if—

(a) he does not know or suspect that the disclosure is likely to prejudice the investigation,
(b) the disclosure is made in the exercise of a function under this Act or any other enactment relating to criminal conduct or benefit from criminal conduct or in compliance with a requirement imposed under or by virtue of this Act, or
(c) he is a professional legal adviser and the disclosure falls within subsection (4).

(4) A disclosure falls within this subsection if it is a disclosure—

(a) to (or to a representative of) a client of the professional legal adviser in connection with the giving by the adviser of legal advice to the client, or
(b) to any person in connection with legal proceedings or contemplated legal proceedings.

(5) But a disclosure does not fall within subsection (4) if it is made with the intention of furthering a criminal purpose.

(6) A person does not commit an offence under subsection (2)(b) if—

(a) he does not know or suspect that the documents are relevant to the investigation, or

(b) he does not intend to conceal any facts disclosed by the documents from any appropriate officer or (in Scotland) proper person carrying out the investigation.

(7) A person guilty of an offence under subsection (2) is liable—

(a) on summary conviction, to imprisonment for a term not exceeding six months or to a fine not exceeding the statutory maximum or to both, or

(b) on conviction on indictment, to imprisonment for a term not exceeding five years or to a fine or to both.

(8) For the purposes of this section—

(a) "appropriate officer" must be construed in accordance with section 378;

(b) "proper person" must be construed in accordance with section 412;

[1] (c) Schedule 9 has effect for determining what is a business in the regulated sector.

NOTE

[1] As inserted by the Terrorism Act 2000 and Proceeds of Crime Act 2002 (Amendment) Regulations (SI 2007/3398) Sch.2, para.8(3) (effective December 26, 2007).

CHAPTER 2

ENGLAND AND WALES AND NORTHERN IRELAND

[*Not reproduced.*]

CHAPTER 3

SCOTLAND

Production orders

Production orders

380.—(1) The sheriff may, on an application made to him by the appropriate person, make a production order if he is satisfied that each of the requirements for the making of the order is fulfilled.

(2) In making a production order in relation to property subject to a civil recovery investigation, the sheriff shall act in the exercise of his civil jurisdiction.

(3) The application for a production order must state that—

(a) a person specified in the application is subject to a confiscation investigation or a money laundering investigation, or

(b) property specified in the application is subject to a civil recovery investigation.

(4) The application must also state that—

(a) the order is sought for the purposes of the investigation;

(b) the order is sought in relation to material, or material of a description, specified in the application;

(c) a person specified in the application appears to be in possession or control of the material.

(5) A production order is an order either—

(a) requiring the person the application for the order specifies as appearing to be in possession or control of material to produce it to a proper person for him to take away, or

(b) requiring that person to give a proper person access to the material,

within the period stated in the order.

(6) The period stated in a production order must be a period of seven days beginning with the day on which the order is made, unless it appears to the sheriff that a longer or shorter period would be appropriate in the particular circumstances.

Requirements for making of production order

381.—(1) These are the requirements for the making of a production order.

(2) There must be reasonable grounds for suspecting that—

(a) in the case of a confiscation investigation, the person the application for the order specifies as being subject to the investigation has benefited from his criminal conduct;

(b) in the case of a civil recovery investigation, the property the application for the order specifies as being subject to the investigation is recoverable property or associated property;

(c) in the case of a money laundering investigation, the person the application for the order specifies as being subject to the investigation has committed a money laundering offence.

(3) There must be reasonable grounds for believing that the person the application specifies as appearing to be in possession or control of the material so specified is in possession or control of it.

(4) There must be reasonable grounds for believing that the material is likely to be of substantial value (whether or not by itself) to the investigation for the purposes of which the order is sought.

(5) There must be reasonable grounds for believing that it is in the public interest for the material to be produced or for access to it to be given, having regard to—

(a) the benefit likely to accrue to the investigation if the material is obtained,

(b) the circumstances under which the person the application specifies as appearing to be in possession or control of the material holds it.

Order to grant entry

382.—(1) This section applies if a sheriff makes a production order requiring a person to give a proper person access to material on any premises.

(2) The sheriff may, on an application made to him by the appropriate person and specifying the premises, make an order to grant entry in relation to the premises.

(3) An order to grant entry is an order requiring any person who appears to the appropriate person to be entitled to grant entry to the premises to allow a proper person to enter the premises to obtain access to the material.

Further provisions

383.—(1) A production order does not require a person to produce, or give access to, any items subject to legal privilege.

(2) A production order has effect in spite of any restriction on the disclosure of information (however imposed).

(3) A proper person may take copies of any material which is produced, or to which access is given, in compliance with a production order.

(4) Material produced in compliance with a production order may be retained for so long as it is necessary to retain it (as opposed to copies of it) in connection with the investigation for the purposes of which the order was made.

(5) But if a proper person has reasonable grounds for believing that—

(a) the material may need to be produced for the purposes of any legal proceedings, and

(b) it might otherwise be unavailable for those purposes,

it may be retained until the proceedings are concluded.

Computer information

384.—(1) This section applies if any of the material specified in an application for a production order consists of information contained in a computer.

(2) If the order is an order requiring a person to produce the material to a proper person for him to take away, it has effect as an order to produce the material in a form in which it can be taken away by him and in which it is visible and legible.

(3) If the order is an order requiring a person to give a proper person access to the material, it has effect as an order to give him access to the material in a form in which it is visible and legible.

Government departments

385.—(1) A production order may be made in relation to material in the possession or control of an authorised government department.

(2) An order so made may require any officer of the department (whether named in the order or not) who may for the time being be in possession or control of the material to comply with it.

(3) If an order contains such a requirement—

(a) the person on whom it is served must take all reasonable steps to bring it to the attention of the officer concerned;

(b) any other officer of the department who is in receipt of the order must also take all reasonable steps to bring it to the attention of the officer concerned.

(4) If the order is not brought to the attention of the officer concerned within the period stated in the order (in pursuance of section 380(5)) the person on whom it is served must report the reasons for the failure to—

(a) the sheriff in the case of an order made for the purposes of a confiscation investigation or a money laundering investigation;

(b) the sheriff exercising a civil jurisdiction in the case of an order made for the purposes of a civil recovery investigation.

(5) In this section, "authorised government department" includes a government department which is an authorised department for the purposes of the Crown Proceedings Act 1947 (c. 44) and the Scottish Administration.

Supplementary

386.—(1) An application for a production order or an order to grant entry may be made ex parte to a sheriff in chambers.

(2) Provision may be made by rules of court as to the discharge and variation of production orders and orders to grant entry.

(3) Rules of court under subsection (2) relating to production orders and orders to grant entry—

(a) made in a confiscation investigation or a money laundering investigation shall, without prejudice to section 305 of the Criminal Procedure (Scotland) Act 1995 (c. 46) be made by act of adjournal;

(b) made in a civil recovery investigation shall, without prejudice to section 32 of the Sheriff Courts (Scotland) Act 1971 (c. 58) be made by act of sederunt.

(4) An application to discharge or vary a production order or an order to grant entry may be made to the sheriff by—

(a) the person who applied for the order;

(b) any person affected by the order.

(5) The sheriff may—

(a) discharge the order;

(b) vary the order.

Search warrants

Search warrants

387.—(1) The sheriff may, on an application made to him by the appropriate person, issue a search warrant if he is satisfied that either of the requirements for the issuing of the warrant is fulfilled.

(2) In issuing a search warrant in relation to property subject to a civil

recovery investigation, the sheriff shall act in the exercise of his civil jurisdiction.

(3) The application for a search warrant must state that—

(a) a person specified in the application is subject to a confiscation investigation or a money laundering investigation, or

(b) property specified in the application is subject to a civil recovery investigation.

(4) A search warrant is a warrant authorising a proper person—

(a) to enter and search the premises specified in the application for the warrant, and

(b) to seize and retain any material specified in the warrant which is found there and which is likely to be of substantial value (whether or not by itself) to the investigation for the purposes of which the application is made.

(5) The requirements for the issue of a search warrant are—

(a) that a production order made in relation to material has not been complied with and there are reasonable grounds for believing that the material is on the premises specified in the application for the warrant, or

(b) that section 388 is satisfied in relation to the warrant.

(6) An application for a search warrant may be made ex parte to a sheriff in chambers.

Requirements where production order not available

388.—(1) This section is satisfied in relation to a search warrant if—

(a) subsection (2) applies, and

(b) either the first or the second set of conditions is complied with.

(2) This subsection applies if there are reasonable grounds for suspecting that—

(a) in the case of a confiscation investigation, the person specified in the application for the warrant has benefited from his criminal conduct;

(b) in the case of a civil recovery investigation, the property specified in the application for the warrant is recoverable property or associated property;

(c) in the case of a money laundering investigation, the person specified in the application for the warrant has committed a money laundering offence.

(3) The first set of conditions is that there are reasonable grounds for believing that—

(a) any material on the premises specified in the application for the warrant is likely to be of substantial value (whether or not by itself) to the investigation for the purposes of which the warrant is sought,

(b) it is in the public interest for the material to be obtained, having regard to the benefit likely to accrue to the investigation if the material is obtained, and

(c) it would not be appropriate to make a production order for any one or more of the reasons in subsection (4).

(4) The reasons are—

(a) that it is not practicable to communicate with any person against whom the production order could be made;

(b) that it is not practicable to communicate with any person who would be required to comply with an order to grant access to the material or to grant entry to the premises on which the material is situated;

(c) that the investigation might be seriously prejudiced unless a proper person is able to secure immediate access to the material.

(5) The second set of conditions is that—

(a) there are reasonable grounds for believing that there is material on the premises specified in the application for the warrant and that the material falls within subsection (6), (7) or (8),

(b) there are reasonable grounds for believing that it is in the public interest for the material to be obtained, having regard to the benefit likely to accrue to the investigation if the material is obtained, and

(c) any one or more of the requirements in subsection (9) is met.

(6) In the case of a confiscation investigation, material falls within this subsection if it cannot be identified at the time of the application but it—

(a) relates to the person specified in the application, the question whether he has benefited from his criminal conduct or any question as to the extent or whereabouts of his benefit from his criminal conduct, and

(b) is likely to be of substantial value (whether or not by itself) to the investigation for the purposes of which the warrant is sought.

(7) In the case of a civil recovery investigation, material falls within this subsection if it cannot be identified at the time of the application but it—

(a) relates to the property specified in the application, the question whether it is recoverable property or associated property, the question as to who holds any such property, any question as to whether the person who appears to hold any such property holds other property which is recoverable property, or any question as to the extent or whereabouts of any property mentioned in this paragraph, and

(b) is likely to be of substantial value (whether or not by itself) to the investigation for the purposes of which the warrant is sought.

(8) In the case of a money laundering investigation, material falls within this subsection if it cannot be identified at the time of the application but it—

(a) relates to the person specified in the application or the question whether he has committed a money laundering offence, and

(b) is likely to be of substantial value (whether or not by itself) to the investigation for the purposes of which the warrant is sought.

(9) The requirements are—

(a) that it is not practicable to communicate with any person entitled to grant entry to the premises;

(b) that entry to the premises will not be granted unless a warrant is produced;

(c) that the investigation might be seriously prejudiced unless a proper person arriving at the premises is able to secure immediate entry to them.

Further provisions: general

389. A search warrant does not confer the right to seize any items subject to legal privilege.

Further provisions: confiscation, civil recovery and money laundering

390.—(1) This section applies to search warrants sought for the purposes of confiscation investigations, civil recovery investigations or money laundering investigations.

(2) A warrant continues in force until the end of the period of one month starting with the day on which it is issued.

(3) A warrant authorises the person executing it to require any information which is held in a computer and is accessible from the premises specified in the application for the warrant, and which the proper person believes relates to any matter relevant to the investigation, to be produced in a form—

(a) in which it can be taken away, and

(b) in which it is visible and legible.

(4) Copies may be taken of any material seized under a warrant.

(5) A warrant issued in relation to a civil recovery investigation may be issued subject to conditions.

(6) A warrant issued in relation to a civil recovery investigation may include provision authorising the person executing it to do other things which—

(a) are specified in the warrant, and

(b) need to be done in order to give effect to it.

(7) Material seized under a warrant issued in relation to a civil recovery investigation may be retained for so long as it is necessary to retain it (as opposed to copies of it) in connection with the investigation for the purposes of which the warrant was issued.

(8) But if the Scottish Ministers have reasonable grounds for believing that—

(a) the material may need to be produced for the purposes of any legal proceedings, and

(b) it might otherwise be unavailable for those purposes,

it may be retained until the proceedings are concluded.

Disclosure orders

Disclosure orders

391.—(1) The High Court of Justiciary, on an application made to it by the Lord Advocate in relation to confiscation investigations, or the Court of Session, on an application made to it by the Scottish Ministers in relation to civil recovery investigations, may make a disclosure order if it is satisfied that each of the requirements for the making of the order is fulfilled.

(2) No application for a disclosure order may be made in relation to a money laundering investigation.

(3) The application for a disclosure order must state that—

(a) a person specified in the application is subject to a confiscation investigation and the order is sought for the purposes of the investigation, or

(b) property specified in the application is subject to a civil recovery investigation and the order is sought for the purposes of the investigation.

(4) A disclosure order is an order authorising the Lord Advocate or the Scottish Ministers to give to any person the Lord Advocate considers or the Scottish Ministers consider has relevant information, notice in writing requiring him to do, with respect to any matter relevant to the investigation for the purposes of which the order is sought, any or all of the following—

(a) answer questions, either at a time specified in the notice or at once, at a place so specified;

(b) provide information specified in the notice, by a time and in a manner so specified;

(c) produce documents, or documents of a description, specified in the notice, either at or by a time so specified or at once, and in a manner so specified.

(5) Relevant information is information (whether or not contained in a document) which the Lord Advocate considers or the Scottish Ministers consider to be relevant to the investigation.

(6) A person is not bound to comply with a requirement imposed by a notice given under a disclosure order unless evidence of authority to give the notice is produced to him.

Requirements for making of disclosure order

392.—(1) These are the requirements for the making of a disclosure order.

(2) There must be reasonable grounds for suspecting that—

(a) in the case of a confiscation investigation, the person specified in the application for the order has benefited from his criminal conduct;

(b) in the case of a civil recovery investigation, the property specified in the application for the order is recoverable property or associated property.

(3) There must be reasonable grounds for believing that information which may be provided in compliance with a requirement imposed under the order is likely to be of substantial value (whether or not by itself) to the investigation for the purposes of which the order is sought.

(4) There must be reasonable grounds for believing that it is in the public interest for the information to be provided, having regard to the benefit likely to accrue to the investigation if the information is obtained.

Offences

393.—(1) A person commits an offence if without reasonable excuse he fails to comply with a requirement imposed on him under a disclosure order.

(2) A person guilty of an offence under subsection (1) is liable on summary conviction to—

(a) imprisonment for a term not exceeding six months,

(b) a fine not exceeding level 5 on the standard scale, or

(c) both.

(3) A person commits an offence if, in purported compliance with a requirement imposed on him under a disclosure order, he—

(a) makes a statement which he knows to be false or misleading in a material particular, or

(b) recklessly makes a statement which is false or misleading in a material particular.

(4) A person guilty of an offence under subsection (3) is liable—

(a) on summary conviction, to imprisonment for a term not exceeding six months or to a fine not exceeding the statutory maximum or to both, or

(b) on conviction on indictment, to imprisonment for a term not exceeding two years or to a fine or to both.

Statements

394.—(1) A statement made by a person in response to a requirement imposed on him under a disclosure order may not be used in evidence against him in criminal proceedings.

(2) But subsection (1) does not apply—

(a) in the case of proceedings under Part 3,

(b) on a prosecution for an offence under section 393(1) or (3),

(c) on a prosecution for perjury, or

(d) on a prosecution for some other offence where, in giving evidence, the person makes a statement inconsistent with the statement mentioned in subsection (1).

(3) A statement may not be used by virtue of subsection (2)(d) against a person unless—

(a) evidence relating to it is adduced, or

(b) a question relating to it is asked,

by him or on his behalf in the proceedings arising out of the prosecution.

Further provisions

395.—(1) A disclosure order does not confer the right to require a person to answer any question, provide any information or produce any document which he would be entitled to refuse to answer, provide or produce on grounds of legal privilege.

(2) A disclosure order has effect in spite of any restriction on the disclosure of information (however imposed).

(3) The Lord Advocate and the Scottish Ministers may take copies of any documents produced in compliance with a requirement to produce them which is imposed under a disclosure order.

(4) Documents so produced may be retained for so long as it is necessary to retain them (as opposed to a copy of them) in connection with the investigation for the purposes of which the order was made.

(5) But if the Lord Advocate has, or the Scottish Ministers have, reasonable grounds for believing that—

(a) the documents may need to be produced for the purposes of any legal proceedings, and

(b) they might otherwise be unavailable for those purposes,

they may be retained until the proceedings are concluded.

Supplementary

396.—(1) An application for a disclosure order may be made ex parte to—

(a) in the case of an order made in a confiscation investigation, a judge of the High Court of Justiciary;

(b) in the case of an order made in a civil recovery investigation, a judge of the Court of Session,

in chambers.

(2) Provision may be made by rules of court as to the discharge and variation of disclosure orders.

(3) Rules of court under subsection (2) relating to disclosure orders—

(a) made in a confiscation investigation shall, without prejudice to section 305 of the Criminal Procedure (Scotland) Act 1995 (c. 46) be made by act of adjournal;

(b) made in a civil recovery investigation shall, without prejudice to section 5 of the Court of Session Act 1988 (c. 36), be made by act of sederunt.

(4) An application to discharge or vary a disclosure order may be made to a judge of the court which made the order by—

(a) the Lord Advocate or the Scottish Ministers;

(b) any person affected by the order.

(5) The court may—

(a) discharge the order;

(b) vary the order.

Customer information orders

Customer information orders

397.—(1) The sheriff may, on an application made to him by the appropriate person, make a customer information order if he is satisfied that each of the requirements for the making of the order is fulfilled.

(2) In making a customer information order in relation to property subject to a civil recovery investigation the sheriff shall act in the exercise of his civil jurisdiction.

(3) The application for a customer information order must state that—

(a) a person specified in the application is subject to a confiscation investigation or a money laundering investigation, or

(b) property specified in the application is subject to a civil recovery investigation and a person specified in the application appears to hold the property.

(4) The application must also state that—

(a) the order is sought for the purposes of the investigation;

(b) the order is sought against the financial institution or financial institutions specified in the application.

(5) An application for a customer information order may specify—

(a) all financial institutions,

(b) a particular description, or particular descriptions, of financial institutions, or

(c) a particular financial institution or particular financial institutions.

(6) A customer information order is an order that a financial institution covered by the application for the order must, on being required to do so by notice in writing given by the appropriate person, provide any such customer information as it has relating to the person specified in the application.

(7) A financial institution which is required to provide information under a customer information order must provide the information to a proper person in such manner, and at or by such time, as that person requires.

(8) If a financial institution on which a requirement is imposed by a notice given under a customer information order requires the production of evidence of authority to give the notice, it is not bound to comply with the requirement unless evidence of the authority has been produced to it.

Meaning of customer information

398.—(1) "Customer information", in relation to a person and a financial institution, is information whether the person holds, or has held, an account or accounts at the financial institution (whether solely or jointly with another) and (if so) information as to—

(a) the matters specified in subsection (2) if the person is an individual;

(b) the matters specified in subsection (3) if the person is a company or limited liability partnership or a similar body incorporated or otherwise established outside the United Kingdom.

(2) The matters referred to in subsection (1)(a) are—

(a) the account number or numbers;

(b) the person's full name;

(c) his date of birth;

(d) his most recent address and any previous addresses;

(e) the date or dates on which he began to hold the account or accounts and, if he has ceased to hold the account or any of the accounts, the date or dates on which he did so;

(f) such evidence of his identity as was obtained by the financial institution under or for the purposes of any legislation relating to money laundering;

(g) the full name, date of birth and most recent address, and any previous addresses, of any person who holds, or has held, an account at the financial institution jointly with him;

(h) the account number or numbers of any other account or accounts held at the financial institution to which he is a signatory and details of the person holding the other account or accounts.

(3) The matters referred to in subsection (1)(b) are—

(a) the account number or numbers;

(b) the person's full name;

(c) a description of any business which the person carries on;

(d) the country or territory in which it is incorporated or otherwise established and any number allocated to it under the Companies Act 1985 (c. 6) or the Companies (Northern Ireland) Order 1986 (S.I. 1986/ 1032 (N.I. 6)) or corresponding legislation of any country or territory outside the United Kingdom;

(e) any number assigned to it for the purposes of value added tax in the United Kingdom;

(f) its registered office, and any previous registered offices, under the Companies Act 1985 or the Companies (Northern Ireland) Order 1986 (S.I. 1986/1032 (N.I. 6)) or anything similar under corresponding legislation of any country or territory outside the United Kingdom;

(g) its registered office, and any previous registered offices, under the Limited Liability Partnerships Act 2000 (c. 12) or anything similar under corresponding legislation of any country or territory outside Great Britain;

(h) the date or dates on which it began to hold the account or accounts and, if it has ceased to hold the account or any of the accounts, the date or dates on which it did so;

(i) such evidence of its identity as was obtained by the financial institution under or for the purposes of any legislation relating to money laundering;

(j) the full name, date of birth and most recent address and any previous addresses of any person who is a signatory to the account or any of the accounts.

(4) The Scottish Ministers may by order provide for information of a description specified in the order—

(a) to be customer information, or

(b) no longer to be customer information.

[1] (5) Money laundering is an act which—

(a) constitutes an offence under section 327, 328 or 329 of this Act or section 18 of the Terrorism Act 2000 (c. 11), or

(aa) constitutes an offence specified in section 415(1A) of this Act,

(b) would constitute an offence specified in paragraph (a) or (aa) if done in the United Kingdom.

NOTE

[1] As amended by the Serious Organised Crime and Police Act 2005 (c.15) s.107(3)(b) (effective July 1, 2005).

Requirements for making of customer information order

399.—(1) These are the requirements for the making of a customer information order.

(2) In the case of a confiscation investigation, there must be reasonable grounds for suspecting that the person specified in the application for the order has benefited from his criminal conduct.

(3) In the case of a civil recovery investigation, there must be reasonable grounds for suspecting that—

(a) the property specified in the application for the order is recoverable property or associated property;

(b) the person specified in the application holds all or some of the property.

(4) In the case of a money laundering investigation, there must be reasonable grounds for suspecting that the person specified in the application for the order has committed a money laundering offence.

(5) In the case of any investigation, there must be reasonable grounds for believing that customer information which may be provided in compliance with the order is likely to be of substantial value (whether or not by itself) to the investigation for the purposes of which the order is sought.

(6) In the case of any investigation there must be reasonable grounds for believing that it is in the public interest for the customer information to be provided, having regard to the benefit likely to accrue to the investigation if the information is obtained.

Offences

400.—(1) A financial institution commits an offence if without reasonable excuse it fails to comply with a requirement imposed on it under a customer information order.

(2) A financial institution guilty of an offence under subsection (1) is liable on summary conviction to a fine not exceeding level 5 on the standard scale.

(3) A financial institution commits an offence if, in purported compliance with a customer information order, it—

(a) makes a statement which it knows to be false or misleading in a material particular, or

(b) recklessly makes a statement which is false or misleading in a material particular.

(4) A financial institution guilty of an offence under subsection (3) is liable—

(a) on summary conviction, to a fine not exceeding the statutory maximum, or

(b) on conviction on indictment, to a fine.

Statements

401.—(1) A statement made by a financial institution in response to a customer information order may not be used in evidence against it in criminal proceedings.

(2) But subsection (1) does not apply—

(a) in the case of proceedings under Part 3,

(b) on a prosecution for an offence under section 400(1) or (3), or

(c) on a prosecution for some other offence where, in giving evidence, the financial institution makes a statement inconsistent with the statement mentioned in subsection (1).

(3) A statement may not be used by virtue of subsection (2)(c) against a financial institution unless—

(a) evidence relating to it is adduced, or

(b) a question relating to it is asked,

by or on behalf of the financial institution in the proceedings arising out of the prosecution.

Further provisions

402. A customer information order has effect in spite of any restriction on the disclosure of information (however imposed).

Supplementary

403.—(1) An application for a customer information order may be made ex parte to a sheriff in chambers.

(2) Provision may be made by rules of court as to the discharge and variation of customer information orders.

(3) Rules of court under subsection (2) relating to customer information orders—

(a) made in a confiscation investigation or a money laundering investigation shall, without prejudice to section 305 of the Criminal Procedure (Scotland) Act 1995 (c. 46), be made by act of adjournal;

(b) made in a civil recovery investigation shall, without prejudice to section 32 of the Sheriff Courts (Scotland) Act 1971 (c. 58), be made by act of sederunt.

(4) An application to discharge or vary a customer information order may be made to the sheriff by—

(a) the person who applied for the order;

(b) any person affected by the order.

(5) The sheriff may—

(a) discharge the order;

(b) vary the order.

Account monitoring orders

Account monitoring orders

404.—(1) The sheriff may, on an application made to him by the appropriate person, make an account monitoring order if he is satisfied that each of the requirements for the making of the order is fulfilled.

(2) In making an account monitoring order in relation to property subject to a civil recovery investigation, the sheriff shall act in the exercise of his civil jurisdiction.

(3) The application for an account monitoring order must state that—

(a) a person specified in the application is subject to a confiscation investigation or a money laundering investigation, or

(b) property specified in the application is subject to a civil recovery investigation and a person specified in the application appears to hold the property.

(4) The application must also state that—

(a) the order is sought for the purposes of the investigation;

(b) the order is sought against the financial institution specified in the application in relation to account information of the description so specified.

(5) Account information is information relating to an account or accounts held at the financial institution specified in the application by the person so specified (whether solely or jointly with another).

(6) The application for an account monitoring order may specify information relating to—

(a) all accounts held by the person specified in the application for the order at the financial institution so specified,

(b) a particular description, or particular descriptions, of accounts so held, or

(c) a particular account, or particular accounts, so held.

(7) An account monitoring order is an order that the financial institution specified in the application for the order must, for the period stated in the order, provide account information of the description specified in the order to the proper person in the manner, and at or by the time or times, stated in the order.

(8) The period stated in an account monitoring order must not exceed the period of 90 days beginning with the day on which the order is made.

Requirements for making of account monitoring order

405.—(1) These are the requirements for the making of an account monitoring order.

(2) In the case of a confiscation investigation, there must be reasonable grounds for suspecting that the person specified in the application for the order has benefited from his criminal conduct.

(3) In the case of a civil recovery investigation, there must be reasonable grounds for suspecting that—

(a) the property specified in the application for the order is recoverable property or associated property;

(b) the person specified in the application holds all or some of the property.

(4) In the case of a money laundering investigation, there must be reasonable grounds for suspecting that the person specified in the application for the order has committed a money laundering offence.

(5) In the case of any investigation, there must be reasonable grounds for believing that account information which may be provided in compliance with the order is likely to be of substantial value (whether or not by itself) to the investigation for the purposes of which the order is sought.

(6) In the case of any investigation, there must be reasonable grounds for believing that it is in the public interest for the account information to be provided, having regard to the benefit likely to accrue to the investigation if the information is obtained.

Statements

406.—(1) A statement made by a financial institution in response to an account monitoring order may not be used in evidence against it in criminal proceedings.

(2) But subsection (1) does not apply—

(a) in the case of proceedings under Part 3;

(b) in the case of proceedings for contempt of court, or

(c) on a prosecution for an offence where, in giving evidence, the financial institution makes a statement inconsistent with the statement mentioned in subsection (1).

(3) A statement may not be used by virtue of subsection (2)(c) against a financial institution unless—

(a) evidence relating to it is adduced, or

(b) a question relating to it is asked,

by or on behalf of the financial institution in the proceedings arising out of the prosecution.

Further provisions

407. An account monitoring order has effect in spite of any restriction on the disclosure of information (however imposed).

Supplementary

408.—(1) An application for an account monitoring order may be made ex parte to a sheriff in chambers.

(2) Provision may be made by rules of court as to the discharge and variation of account monitoring orders.

(3) Rules of court under subsection (2) relating to account monitoring orders—

(a) made in a confiscation investigation or a money laundering investigation shall, without prejudice to section 305 of the Criminal Procedure (Scotland) Act 1995 (c. 46), be made by act of adjournal;

(b) made in a civil recovery investigation shall, without prejudice to section 32 of the Sheriff Courts (Scotland) Act 1971 (c. 58), be made by act of sederunt.

(4) An application to discharge or vary an account monitoring order may be made to the sheriff by—

(a) the person who applied for the order;

(b) any person affected by the order.

(5) The sheriff may—

(a) discharge the order;

(b) vary the order.

General

Jurisdiction of sheriff

409.—(1) A sheriff may grant a production order, search warrant, customer information order or account monitoring order under this Act in relation to property situated in any area of Scotland notwithstanding that it is outside the area of that sheriff.

(2) Any such order or warrant may, without being backed or endorsed by another sheriff, be executed throughout Scotland in the same way as it may be executed within the sheriffdom of the sheriff who granted it.

(3) This section is without prejudice to any existing rule of law or to any other provision of this Act.

Code of practice

410.—(1) The Scottish Ministers must prepare a code of practice as to the exercise by proper persons of functions they have under this Chapter.

(2) After preparing a draft of the code the Scottish Ministers—

(a) must publish the draft;

(b) must consider any representations made to them about the draft;

(c) may amend the draft accordingly.

(3) After the Scottish Ministers have proceeded under subsection (2) they must lay the code before the Scottish Parliament.

(4) When they have done so, the Scottish Ministers may bring the code into operation on such day as they may appoint by order.

(5) A proper person must compy with a code of practice which is in operation under this section in the exercise of any function he has under this Chapter.

(6) If a proper person fails to comply with any provision of a code of practice issued under this section he is not by reason only of that failure liable in any criminal or civil proceedings.

(7) But the code of practice is admissible in evidence in such proceedings and a court may take account of any failure to comply with its provisions in determining any questions in the proceedings.

(8) The Scottish Ministers may from time to time revise a code previously brought into operation under this section; and the preceding provisions of

this section apply to a revised code as they apply to the code as first prepared.

Performance of functions of Scottish Ministers by constables in Scotland

411.—(1) In Scotland, a constable engaged in temporary service with the Scottish Ministers in connection with their functions under this Part may perform functions, other than those specified in subsection (2), on behalf of the Scottish Ministers.

(2) The specified functions are the functions conferred on the Scottish Ministers by—

(a) section 380(1) (production orders),
(b) section 382(2) (entry orders),
(c) section 386(4) (supplementary to production and entry orders),
(d) section 387(1) (search warrants),
(e) section 391(1) (disclosure orders),
(f) section 396(4) (supplementary to disclosure orders),
(g) section 397(1) (customer information orders),
(h) section 403(4) (supplementary to customer information orders),
(i) section 404(1) (account monitoring orders),
(j) section 408(4) (supplementary to account monitoring orders).

Interpretation

412. In this Chapter, unless the context otherwise requires—

"appropriate person" means—

(a) the procurator fiscal, in relation to a confiscation investigation or a money laundering investigation,

(b) the Scottish Ministers, in relation to a civil recovery investigation;

references to a "constable" include references to a customs and excise officer;

"legal privilege" means protection in legal proceedings from disclosure, by virtue of any rule of law relating to the confidentiality of communications; and "items subject to legal privilege" are—

(a) communications between a professional legal adviser and his client, or

(b) communications made in connection with or in contemplation of legal proceedings and for the purposes of those proceedings,

which would be so protected.

"premises" include any place and, in particular, include—

(a) any vehicle, vessel, aircraft or hovercraft;

(b) any offshore installation within the meaning of section 1 of the Mineral Workings (Offshore Installations) Act 1971 (c. 61) and any tent or movable structure;

"proper person" means—

(a) a constable, in relation to a confiscation investigation or a money laundering investigation;

(b) the Scottish Ministers or a person named by them, in relation to a civil recovery investigation.

Chapter 4

Interpretation

Criminal conduct

413.—(1) Criminal conduct is conduct which—

(a) constitutes an offence in any part of the United Kingdom, or
(b) would constitute an offence in any part of the United Kingdom if it occurred there.

(2) A person benefits from conduct if he obtains property or a pecuniary advantage as a result of or in connection with the conduct.

(3) References to property or a pecuniary advantage obtained in connection with conduct include references to property or a pecuniary advantage obtained in both that connection and some other.

(4) If a person benefits from conduct his benefit is the property or pecuniary advantage obtained as a result of or in connection with the conduct.

(5) It is immaterial—

(a) whether conduct occurred before or after the passing of this Act, and

(b) whether property or a pecuniary advantage constituting a benefit from conduct was obtained before or after the passing of this Act.

Property

414.—(1) Property is all property wherever situated and includes—

(a) money;

(b) all forms of property, real or personal, heritable or moveable;

(c) things in action and other intangible or incorporeal property.

(2) "Recoverable property" and "associated property" have the same meanings as in Part 5.

(3) The following rules apply in relation to property—

(a) property is obtained by a person if he obtains an interest in it;

(b) references to an interest, in relation to land in England and Wales or Northern Ireland, are to any legal estate or equitable interest or power;

(c) references to an interest, in relation to land in Scotland, are to any estate, interest, servitude or other heritable right in or over land, including a heritable security;

(d) references to an interest, in relation to property other than land, include references to a right (including a right to possession).

Money laundering offences

415.—(1) An offence under section 327, 328 or 329 is a money laundering offence.

[1] (1A) Each of the following is a money laundering offence—

(a) an offence under section 93A, 93B or 93C of the Criminal Justice Act 1988;

(b) an offence under section 49, 50 or 51 of the Drug Trafficking Act 1994;

(c) an offence under section 37 or 38 of the Criminal Law (Consolidation) (Scotland) Act 1995;

(d) an offence under article 45, 46 or 47 of the Proceeds of Crime (Northern Ireland) Order 1996.

(2) Each of the following is a money laundering offence—

(a) an attempt, conspiracy or incitement to commit an offence specified in subsection (1);

(b) aiding, abetting, counselling or procuring the commission of an offence specified in subsection (1).

NOTE

[1] As inserted by the Serious Organised Crime and Police Act 2005 (c.15) s.107(4) (effective July 1, 2005).

Other interpretative provisions

416.—(1) These expressions are to be construed in accordance with these provisions of this Part—

civil recovery investigation: section 341(2) and (3)
confiscation investigation: section 341(1)
money laundering investigation: section 341(4)

(2) In the application of this Part to England and Wales and Northern Ireland, these expressions are to be construed in accordance with these provisions of this Part—

account information: section 370(4)
account monitoring order: section 370(6)
appropriate officer: section 378
customer information: section 364
customer information order: section 363(5)
disclosure order: section 357(4)
document: section 379
order to grant entry: section 347(3)
production order: section 345(4)
search and seizure warrant: section 352(4)
senior appropriate officer: section 378
[1] senior member of SOCA's staff: section 378(8).

(3) In the application of this Part to Scotland, these expressions are to be construed in accordance with these provisions of this Part—

account information: section 404(5)
account monitoring order: section 404(7)
customer information: section 398
customer information order: section 397(6)
disclosure order: section 391(4)
production order: section 380(5)
proper person: section 412
search warrant: section 387(4).

(4) "Financial institution" means a person carrying on a business in the regulated sector.

(5) But a person who ceases to carry on a business in the regulated sector (whether by virtue of paragraph 5 of Schedule 9 or otherwise) is to continue to be treated as a financial institution for the purposes of any requirement under—

(a) a customer information order, or
(b) an account monitoring order,

to provide information which relates to a time when the person was a financial institution.

(6) References to a business in the regulated sector must be construed in accordance with Schedule 9.

(7) "Recovery order", "interim receiving order" and "interim administration order" have the same meanings as in Part 5.

(8) References to notice in writing include references to notice given by electronic means.

(9) This section and sections 413 to 415 apply for the purposes of this Part.

NOTE

[1] As inserted by the Serious Crime Act 2007 (c.27) Sch.8(4), para.117(b) (effective April 1, 2008).

. . . . . .

Section 330

SCHEDULE 9

Regulated Sector and Supervisory Authorities

[1] Part 1

Regulated Sector

Business in the regulated sector

1.—(1) A business is in the regulated sector to the extent that it consists of—

(a) the acceptance by a credit institution of deposits or other repayable funds from the public, or the granting by a credit institution of credits for its own account;

(b) the carrying on of one or more of the activities listed in points 2 to 12 and 14 of Annex 1 to the Banking Consolidation Directive by an undertaking other than—
 (i) a credit institution; or
 (ii) an undertaking whose only listed activity is trading for own account in one or more of the products listed in point 7 of Annex 1 to the Banking Consolidation Directive and which does not act on behalf of a customer (that is, a third party which is not a member of the same group as the undertaking);

(c) the carrying on of activities covered by the Life Assurance Consolidation Directive by an insurance company authorised in accordance with that Directive;

(d) the provision of investment services or the performance of investment activities by a person (other than a person falling within Article 2 of the Markets in Financial Instruments Directive) whose regular occupation or business is the provision to other persons of an investment service or the performance of an investment activity on a professional basis;

(e) the marketing or other offering of units or shares by a collective investment undertaking;

(f) the activities of an insurance intermediary as defined in Article 2(5) of the Insurance Mediation Directive, other than a tied insurance intermediary as mentioned in Article 2(7) of that Directive, in respect of contracts of long-term insurance within the meaning given by article 3(1) of, and Part II of Schedule 1 to, the Financial Services and Markets Act 2000 (Regulated Activities) Order 2001;

(g) the carrying on of any of the activities mentioned in paragraphs (b) to (f) by a branch located in an EEA State of a person referred to in those paragraphs (or of an equivalent person in any other State), wherever its head office is located;

(h) the activities of the National Savings Bank;

(i) any activity carried on for the purpose of raising money authorised to be raised under the National Loans Act 1968 under the auspices of the Director of Savings;

(j) the carrying on of statutory audit work within the meaning of section 1210 of the Companies Act 2006 (meaning of "statutory auditor" etc) by any firm or individual who is a statutory auditor within the meaning of Part 42 of that Act (statutory auditors);

(k) the activities of a person appointed to act as an insolvency practitioner within the meaning of section 388 of the Insolvency Act 1986 (meaning of "act as insolvency practitioner") or article 3 of the Insolvency (Northern Ireland) Order 1989;

(l) the provision to other persons of accountancy services by a firm or sole practitioner who by way of business provides such services to other persons;

(m) the provision of advice about the tax affairs of other persons by a firm or sole practitioner who by way of business provides advice about the tax affairs of other persons;

(n) the participation in financial or real property transactions concerning—
 (i) the buying and selling of real property (or, in Scotland, heritable property) or business entities;
 (ii) the managing of client money, securities or other assets;
 (iii) the opening or management of bank, savings or securities accounts;
 (iv) the organisation of contributions necessary for the creation, operation or management of companies; or
 (v) the creation, operation or management of trusts, companies or similar structures,

by a firm or sole practitioner who by way of business provides legal or notarial services to other persons;

(o) the provision to other persons by way of business by a firm or sole practitioner of any of the services mentioned in sub-paragraph (4);

(p) the carrying on of estate agency work (within the meaning given by section 1 of the Estate Agents Act 1979 (estate agency work)) by a firm or a sole practitioner who carries on, or whose employees carry on, such work;

(q) the trading in goods (including dealing as an auctioneer) whenever a transaction involves the receipt of a payment or payments in cash of at least 15,000 euros in total, whether the transaction is executed in a single operation or in several operations which appear to be linked, by a firm or sole trader who by way of business trades in goods;

(r) operating a casino under a casino operating licence (within the meaning given by section 65(2) of the Gambling Act 2005 (nature of licence)).

(2) For the purposes of sub-paragraph (1)(a) and (b) "credit institution" means—

(a) a credit institution as defined in Article 4(1)(a) of the Banking Consolidation Directive; or

(b) a branch (within the meaning of Article 4(3) of that Directive) located in an EEA state of an institution falling within paragraph (a) (or of an equivalent institution in any other State) wherever its head office is located.

(3) For the purposes of sub-paragraph (1)(n) a person participates in a transaction by assisting in the planning or execution of the transaction or otherwise acting for or on behalf of a client in the transaction.

(4) The services referred to in sub-paragraph (1)(o) are—

(a) forming companies or other legal persons;

(b) acting, or arranging for another person to act—

(i) as a director or secretary of a company;

(ii) as a partner of a partnership; or

(iii) in a similar position in relation to other legal persons;

(c) providing a registered office, business address, correspondence or administrative address or other related services for a company, partnership or any other legal person or arrangement;

(d) acting, or arranging for another person to act, as—

(i) a trustee of an express trust or similar legal arrangement; or

(ii) a nominee shareholder for a person other than a company whose securities are listed on a regulated market.

(5) For the purposes of sub-paragraph (4)(d) "regulated market"—

(a) in relation to any EEA State, has the meaning given by point 14 of Article 4(1) of the Markets in Financial Instruments Directive; and

(b) in relation to any other State, means a regulated financial market which subjects companies whose securities are admitted to trading to disclosure obligations which are contained in international standards and are equivalent to the specified disclosure obligations.

(6) For the purposes of sub-paragraph (5) "the specified disclosure obligations" means disclosure requirements consistent with—

(a) Article 6(1) to (4) of Directive 2003/6/EC of the European Parliament and of the Council of 28th January 2003 on insider dealing and market manipulation;

(b) Articles 3, 5, 7, 8, 10, 14 and 16 of Directive 2003/71/EC of the European Parliament and of the Council of 4th November 2003 on the prospectuses to be published when securities are offered to the public or admitted to trading;

(c) Articles 4 to 6, 14, 16 to 19 and 30 of Directive 2004/109/EC of the European Parliament and of the Council of 15th December 2004 relating to the harmonisation of transparency requirements in relation to information about issuers whose securities are admitted to trading on a regulated market; or

(d) Community legislation made under the provisions mentioned in paragraphs (a) to (c).

(7) For the purposes of sub-paragraph (1)(j) and (l) to (q) "firm" means any entity, whether or not a legal person, that is not an individual and includes a body corporate and a partnership or other unincorporated association.

(8) For the purposes of sub-paragraph (1)(q) "cash" means notes, coins or travellers' cheques in any currency.

NOTES

[1] Substituted by the Proceeds of Crime Act 2002 (Business in the Regulated Sector and Supervisory Authorities) Order 2003, (SI 2003/3074), Sch.1 and substituted subject to transitional provisions specified in SI 2007/3287 art.3 by the Proceeds of Crime Act 2002 (Business in the Regulated Sector and Supervisory Authorities) Order (SI 2007/3287) art.2 (effective December 15, 2007).

[2] As amended by the Proceeds of Crime act 2002 (Business in the Regulated Sector) Order 2006 (SI 2006/2385) reg.2 (effective April 6, 2007).

[3] As substituted by the Capital Requirements Regulations 2006 (SI 2006/3221) Sch.4, para.7 (effective January 1, 2007).

[3] PART 2

SUPERVISORY AUTHORITIES

4.—(1) The following bodies are supervisory authorities—

(a) the Commissioners for Her Majesty's Revenue and Customs;

(b) the Department of Enterprise, Trade and Investment in Northern Ireland;

(c) the Financial Services Authority;

(d) the Gambling Commission;

(e) the Office of Fair Trading;

[1] (f) the Secretary of State; and

[1, 2] (g) the professional bodies listed in sub-paragraph (2).

(2) The professional bodies referred to in sub-paragraph (1)(g) are—

(a) the Association of Accounting Technicians;

(b) the Association of Chartered Certified Accountants;

(c) the Association of International Accountants;

(d) the Association of Taxation Technicians;

(e) the Chartered Institute of Management Accountants;

(f) the Chartered Institute of Public Finance and Accountancy;

(g) the Chartered Institute of Taxation;

(h) the Council for Licensed Conveyancers;

(i) the Faculty of Advocates;

(j) the Faculty Office of the Archbishop of Canterbury;

(k) the General Council of the Bar;

(l) the General Council of the Bar of Northern Ireland;

(m) the Insolvency Practitioners Association;

(n) the Institute of Certified Bookkeepers;

(o) the Institute of Chartered Accountants in England and Wales;

(p) the Institute of Chartered Accountants in Ireland;

(q) the Institute of Chartered Accountants of Scotland;

(r) the Institute of Financial Accountants;

(s) the International Association of Book-keepers;

(t) the Law Society;

(u) the Law Society for Northern Ireland; and

(v) the Law Society of Scotland.

NOTES

[1] Inserted by the Proceeds of Crime Act 2002 (Business in the Regulated Sector and Supervisory Authorities) Order 2003, (SI 2003/3074), para.3, and substituted by the Pensions Act 2004 (c.35), Sch.12, para.80 (effective April 6, 2005, SI 2005/695).

[2] Substituted by the Gambling Act 2005, Sch.16, para.19, brought into force by SI 2005/2455 (effective October 1, 2005).

[3] As substituted subject to transitional provisions specified in SI 2007/3287 art.3 by the Proceeds of Crime Act 2002 (Business in the Regulated Sector and Supervisory Authorities) Order (SI 2007/3287) art.2 (effective December 15, 2007).

Part 3

Power to Amend

5. The Treasury may by order amend Part 1 or 2 of this Schedule.

[1]Legal Profession and Legal Aid (Scotland) Act 2007

NOTE

[1] This Act is not yet in force but for the sections brought into force by the Commencement Orders printed following this Act.

2007 asp 5

CONTENTS

PART 1

THE SCOTTISH LEGAL COMPLAINTS COMMISSION

Establishment

Conduct or services complaints against practitioners

Appeals

Handling by relevant professional organisations of conduct complaints

Finance

Rules as to Commission's practice and procedure

Part 5
General

The Bill for this Act of the Scottish Parliament was passed by the Parliament on 14th December 2006 and received Royal Assent on 19th January 2007.

An Act of the Scottish Parliament to establish the Scottish Legal Complaints Commission; to make provision as regards complaints against members of the legal profession in Scotland and other matters concerning the regulation of that profession; to make provision in connection with the administration of the Scottish Legal Aid Fund, including a register of advice organisations in connection with advice and assistance; and for connected purposes.

PART I

THE SCOTTISH LEGAL COMPLAINTS COMMISSION

Establishment

The Scottish Legal Complaints Commission

1.—(1) There is established a body to be known as the Scottish Legal Complaints Commission (referred to in this Act as "the Commission").

(2) Schedule 1 makes further provision about the status, constitution, proceedings etc. of the Commission.

Conduct or services complaints against practitioners

Receipt of complaints: preliminary steps

2.—(1) Where the Commission receives a complaint by or on behalf of any of the persons mentioned in subsection (2)—

(a) suggesting—

(i) professional misconduct or unsatisfactory professional conduct by a practitioner other than a firm of solicitors or an incorporated practice;

(ii) that a conveyancing practitioner or an executry practitioner has been convicted of a criminal offence rendering the practitioner no longer a fit and proper person to provide conveyancing services as a conveyancing practitioner or, as the case may be, executry services as an executry practitioner,

(a complaint suggesting any such matter being referred to in this Part as a "conduct complaint");

(b) suggesting that professional services provided by a practitioner in connection with any matter in which the practitioner has been instructed by a client were inadequate (referred to in this Part as a "services complaint"),

it must, subject to subsection (3) and sections 3 and 4 and any provision in rules made under section 32(1) as to eligibility for making complaints, take the preliminary steps mentioned in subsection (4).

(2) The persons are—

(a) as respects a conduct complaint, any person;

(b) as respects a services complaint—

(i) any person who appears to the Commission to have been directly affected by the suggested inadequate professional services;
(ii) the Lord Advocate;
(iii) the Advocate General for Scotland;
(iv) any judge (including a sheriff);
(v) the Auditor of the Court of Session;
(vi) the Auditor of any sheriff court;
(vii) the Scottish Legal Aid Board;
(viii) any relevant professional organisation.

(3) The Commission is not to take the preliminary steps mentioned in subsection (4), and is not to take any further action under any other provision of this Part, in relation to any element of a conduct complaint which is about a practitioner acting in a judicial capacity in a court or tribunal specified by order by the Scottish Ministers.

(4) The preliminary steps are—
(a) to determine whether or not the complaint is frivolous, vexatious or totally without merit;
(b) where the Commission determines that the complaint is any or all of these things, to—
(i) reject the complaint;
(ii) give notice in writing to the complainer and the practitioner that it has rejected the complaint as frivolous, vexatious or totally without merit (or two or all of these things).

Existence of specified regulatory scheme

3.—(1) Where any element of a complaint referred to in section 2(1) is capable of being dealt with under a specified regulatory scheme, the Commission is prevented from dealing with the element but only to the extent that the element is capable of being dealt with under the specified regulatory scheme.

(2) Where the circumstances referred to in subsection (1) apply, the Commission must give notice in writing to that effect to—
(a) the complainer and the practitioner;
(b) such other persons as may be specified by the Scottish Ministers by order.

(3) Notice under subsection (2) must specify under which specified regulatory scheme the Commission considers the element is capable of being dealt with.

(4) Where the circumstances referred to in subsection (1) apply, notice under subsection (2) must in addition specify that the fact that the Commission is prevented by subsection (1) from dealing with the complaint to the extent that the complaint is capable of being dealt with under the specified regulatory scheme does not prevent the Commission taking the preliminary steps referred to in section 2(4) and dealing with the complaint under any provision of this Part to the extent that it is able.

(5) In this section "specified regulatory scheme" means a scheme specified as such by the Scottish Ministers by order.

Complaint not made timeously or made prematurely

4.—(1) Where a complaint referred to in section 2(1) is not made timeously, the Commission is not to take the preliminary steps referred to in section 2(4) in relation to it, and is not to take any further action under any other provision of this Part (except this section), in relation to it.

(2) Where a complaint referred to in section 2(1) is made prematurely, the Commission need not take the preliminary steps referred to in section 2(4) in relation to it, and need not take any further action under any other provision of this Part (except this section), in relation to it.

(3) For the purposes of subsection (1), a complaint is not made timeously where—

(a) rules made under section 32(1) fix time limits for the making of complaints;
(b) the complaint is made after the expiry of the time limit applicable to it;
(c) the Commission does not extend the time limit in accordance with the rules.

(4) For the purposes of subsection (2), a complaint is made prematurely where—

(a) the complainer has not previously communicated the substance of it to the practitioner, the practitioner's firm or, as the case may be, where the practitioner is an employee of another practitioner that other practitioner (referred to in this Part as the "employing practitioner") and given the practitioner, the firm or the employing practitioner what the Commission considers is a reasonable opportunity to deal with it;
(b) rules made under section 32(1) either—
  (i) do not provide for circumstances in which the Commission will take the steps and further action referred to in that subsection; or
  (ii) do provide for such circumstances but none is applicable in relation to the complaint.

(5) Where the circumstances referred to in subsection (1) or (2) apply, the Commission must give notice in writing to the complainer and practitioner to that effect.

(6) Where the circumstances referred to in subsection (2) apply, notice under subsection (5) must specify whether or not the Commission is proceeding to take the preliminary steps referred to in section 2(4).

Determining nature of complaint

5.—(1) Where the Commission proceeds to determine under section 2(4) whether a complaint is frivolous, vexatious or totally without merit and determines that it is none of these things, it must determine whether the complaint constitutes—

(a) a conduct complaint;
(b) a services complaint,

including whether (and if so to what extent) the complaint constitutes separate complaints falling within more than one of these categories and if so which of the categories.

(2) Where it appears to the Commission that the complaint may constitute both—

(a) a conduct complaint; and
(b) a separate services complaint,

it must consult, co-operate and liaise with the relevant professional organisation and have regard to any views expressed by the organisation on the matter before making a determination under subsection (1) as respects the complaint.

(3) A relevant professional organisation must co-operate and liaise with the Commission in relation to subsection (2).

Complaint determined to be conduct complaint

6. Where, or to the extent that, the Commission determines under section 5(1) that a complaint is a conduct complaint, it must—

(a) remit the complaint to the relevant professional organisation to deal with (and give to the organisation any material which accompanies the conduct complaint);
(b) give notice in writing to the complainer and the practitioner by sending to each of them a copy of the determination and specifying—
  (i) the reasons for the determination;
  (ii) that the conduct complaint is being remitted under this section for investigation and determination by the relevant professional organisation;

(iii) the relevant professional organisation to which it is being remitted;

(iv) that the relevant professional organisation is under a duty under this Act to deal with the conduct complaint.

Services complaint: notice

7. Where, or to the extent that, the Commission determines under section 5(1) that a complaint is a services complaint, it must give notice in writing to the complainer and the practitioner by sending to each of them a copy of the determination and specifying the reasons for the determination.

Services complaint: local resolution or mediation

8.—(1) This section applies where the Commission determines under section 5(1) that a complaint by or on behalf of a person referred to in section 2(2)(b)(i) is a services complaint.

(2) Where the Commission considers that either—

(a) the complaint has been made prematurely (within the meaning of section 4(4)); or

(b) the practitioner, the practitioner's firm or the employing practitioner has made no attempt, or an insufficient attempt, to achieve a negotiated settlement with the complainer,

the Commission may, by notice in writing to the complainer and the practitioner refer the complaint back to the practitioner, the practitioner's firm or, as the case may be, the employing practitioner requesting that the practitioner, the firm or the employing practitioner attempt to achieve such a settlement.

(3) Where the Commission refers a complaint back to the practitioner, the practitioner's firm or the employing practitioner under subsection (2), it may, by notice in writing, require the practitioner, the firm or the employing practitioner to give, before the end of such period being not less than 21 days as the notice specifies, an account and explanation of the steps which the practitioner, firm or employing practitioner has taken to attempt to achieve a negotiated settlement.

(4) Where the Commission considers it appropriate to do so, it may, by notice in writing to the complainer and the practitioner, offer to mediate in relation to the complaint.

(5) The Commission may enter into mediation in relation to a complaint only if both the complainer and the practitioner accept the offer made under subsection (4).

(6) The Commission must discontinue mediation in relation to a complaint if either the complainer or the practitioner withdraws consent to the mediation and may do so in any other circumstances; and, if mediation is discontinued, the Commission must give notice in writing to the complainer and the practitioner of its decision.

Services complaint: Commission's duty to investigate and determine

9.—(1) Where—

(a) the Commission does not refer a services complaint back to the practitioner, the practitioner's firm or the employing practitioner under section 8(2) (because it considers that the practitioner, firm or employing practitioner has made a sufficient attempt to achieve a negotiated settlement);

(b) the Commission refers a services complaint back to the practitioner, the practitioner's firm or the employing practitioner under that section but—

(i) no attempt to achieve a negotiated settlement takes place;

(ii) such an attempt takes place but is discontinued or a negotiated settlement is not accepted by both the practitioner and the complainer;

(c) mediation by virtue of section 8(5) in relation to the complaint—
(i) does not take place;
(ii) takes place but is discontinued or the outcome of the mediation is not accepted by both the complainer and the practitioner;
(d) the Commission determines under section 5(1) that a complaint by or on behalf of any person referred to in sub-paragraphs (ii) to (viii) of section 2(2)(b) is a services complaint,

the Commission must, subject to section 15(2) and (5), investigate the complaint and after giving the complainer and the practitioner an opportunity to make representations, subject to subsections (2) to (4), determine it by reference to what the Commission considers is fair and reasonable in the circumstances.

(2) Where the complainer is a person referred to in section 2(2)(b)(i) the Commission must, subject to subsection (3), propose to the practitioner and the complainer a settlement as respects the complaint which it considers is fair and reasonable in the circumstances.

(3) Where the practitioner was, at the time the services were provided, an employee of an employing practitioner, a proposal under subsection (2) to the practitioner and the complainer must also be made to the employing practitioner.

(4) Where the practitioner and the complainer, and where subsection (3) applies the employing practitioner, accept a settlement proposed by the Commission under subsection (2) as respects the complaint, the Commission is not to determine the complaint under subsection (1).

Commission upholds services complaint

10.—(1) Where the Commission makes a determination under section 9(1) upholding a services complaint, it may take such of the steps mentioned in subsection (2) as it considers fair and reasonable in the circumstances.

(2) The steps are, subject to subsection (3)—
(a) to determine that the amount of the fees and outlays to which the practitioner is entitled for the services provided to the client and to which the complaint relates, is to be—
(i) nil; or
(ii) such amount as the Commission may specify in the determination,

and to direct the practitioner to comply or secure compliance with such of the requirements set out in subsection (5) as appear to the Commission to be necessary to give effect to the determination;
(b) to direct the practitioner to secure the rectification at the practitioner's own expense of any such error, omission or other deficiency arising in connection with the services as the Commission may specify;
(c) to direct the practitioner to take, at the practitioner's own expense, such other action in the interests of the complainer as the Commission may specify;
(d) where the Commission considers that the complainer has been directly affected by the inadequate professional services, to direct the practitioner to pay compensation of such amount, not exceeding £20,000, as the Commission may specify to the complainer for loss, inconvenience or distress resulting from the inadequate professional services;
(e) where the Commission considers that the practitioner may not have sufficient competence in relation to any aspect of the law or legal practice, to report the matter to the relevant professional organisation.

(3) Where the practitioner was, at the time when the services were provided, an employee (referred to in this section as an "employee practitioner") of an employing practitioner—

(a) a direction under subsection (2)(a), (b) or (c) must be to the employing practitioner instead of the employee practitioner;

(b) a direction under subsection (2)(d)—

(i) may be to and direct either the employing practitioner or, if the Commission considers it appropriate, the employee practitioner to pay all of the compensation directed to be paid under that subsection in relation to the complaint concerned;

(ii) may be to and direct the employee practitioner to pay such part of the total amount of compensation directed to be paid under that subsection in relation to the complaint concerned as the Commission considers appropriate and if it does so, must be to and direct the employing practitioner to pay the remainder of the total amount;

(c) a copy of any report under subsection (2)(e) must be sent to the employing practitioner.

(4) The Commission must, in considering what steps to take under subsection (2), take into account any—

(a) prior direction by it under subsection (2)(d) that the employee practitioner concerned or, where subsection (3) applies, the employing practitioner, pay to the complainer an amount by way of compensation;

(b) award of damages by the court to the complainer;

(c) other compensation ordered (whether by determination, direction or otherwise) by a tribunal or other professional body to be paid to the complainer,

in relation to the subject matter of the complaint.

(5) The requirements referred to in subsection (2)(a) are to—

(a) refund, whether wholly or to any specified extent any amount already paid by or on behalf of the client in respect of fees and outlays of the practitioner in connection with the services;

(b) waive, whether wholly or to any specified extent, the right to recover the fees and outlays.

(6) Before making a determination in accordance with subsection (2)(a), the Commission may submit the practitioner's accounts for the fees and outlays to the Auditor of the Court of Session for taxation.

(7) The Scottish Ministers may by order, after consulting—

(a) the relevant professional organisations;

(b) such groups of persons representing consumer interests as they consider appropriate,

amend subsection (2)(d) by substituting for the amount for the time being specified in that subsection such other amount as they consider appropriate.

Fair and reasonable: matters to be taken into account by Commission

11. In considering what is fair and reasonable in the circumstances, the Commission is to take into account the relevant law (including levels of damages awarded by courts in similar circumstances) and relevant codes of practice, professional rules, standards and guidance.

Services complaint: notice where not upheld or upheld

12.—(1) The Commission must give notice in writing of a—

(a) determination by it under section 9(1) not to uphold a services complaint;

(b) determination by it under that section upholding any such complaint;

(c) determination, direction or report by it under section 10(2),

to the complainer and every practitioner specified in it and, where section 10(3) applies, to the employing practitioner by sending to each of them a copy of the determination, the direction or, as the case may be, the report.

(2) Where the determination is made by a determination committee by virtue of paragraph 13(2)(d)(i) or, as the case may be, (ii) of schedule

1, notice under subsection (1) must specify the reasons for the determination.

Services complaint: reports

13.—(1) The Commission may, if it considers it appropriate to do so in any particular case, publish a report of—

(a) any mediation which has taken place by virtue of section 8(5) in relation to a services complaint, the outcome of which is accepted by both the complainer and the practitioner;

(b) an investigation of a services complaint under section 9 and—

(i) any settlement proposed under subsection (2) of that section as respects the complaint, which is accepted as mentioned in subsection (4) of that section;

(ii) any determination of the complaint under subsection (1) of that section;

(c) a determination, direction or report under section 10(2).

(2) A report under subsection (1) must not (unless the complainer consents)—

(a) mention the name of the complainer;

(b) include any particulars which, in the opinion of the Commission, are likely to identify the complainer.

(3) A report under subsection (1) may only—

(a) mention the name of the practitioner complained of; or

(b) include any particulars which, in the opinion of the Commission, are likely to identify the practitioner,

if the practitioner consents or the condition in subsection (4) is met.

(4) The condition is that—

(a) the case is exceptional;

(b) in the opinion of the Commission, it is in the public interest for the identity of the practitioner concerned to be included in the report; and

(c) the Commission has given not less than 4 weeks notice in writing to the practitioner that it intends to identify the practitioner in the report, specifying the reasons for its decision.

Determination under section 9(1) or taking of steps under section 10(2): effect in relation to proceedings

14.—(1) Neither the making of a determination under section 9(1) upholding a complaint, nor the taking of any steps under section 10(2) may be founded upon in any proceedings.

(2) A direction under section 10(2)(d) to a practitioner to pay compensation to a complainer does not prejudice any right of the complainer to take proceedings against the practitioner for damages in respect of any loss which the complainer claims to have suffered; and any amount directed to be paid to the complainer under that section may be taken into account in the computation of any award of damages made to the complainer in any such proceedings.

Complaint appears during mediation or investigation to fall within different category

15.—(1) Where a relevant professional organisation at any time during any mediation by it, or its investigation, of a conduct complaint remitted to it under section 6(a) considers that it is reasonably likely that the complaint (or any element of it) may instead constitute a services complaint, it must—

(a) suspend the mediation or, as the case may be, the investigation;

(b) consult, co-operate and liaise with the Commission as respects the matter;

(c) send the complaint and any material which relates to it and which is in the organisation's possession to the Commission;

(d) give notice in writing to the complainer and the practitioner that it so considers and is so doing.

(2) Where the Commission at any time during its mediation by virtue of section 8(5) in relation to, or investigation by virtue of section 9(1) of, a services complaint considers that it is reasonably likely that the complaint (or any element of it) may instead constitute a conduct complaint, it must—

(a) suspend the mediation or investigation;

(b) send a copy of the complaint and any material which relates to it and which is in the Commission's possession to the relevant professional organisation;

(c) consult, co-operate and liaise with the relevant professional organisation as respects the matter;

(d) give notice in writing to the complainer, the practitioner and the relevant professional organisation that it so considers and is so doing.

(3) Where, in the circumstances referred to in subsection (1) or (2) the Commission, having regard to the views expressed by the relevant professional organisation as respects the matter, considers that—

(a) its determination under section 5(1) as respects the complaint should be confirmed (to any extent), it must so determine; and the determination under this paragraph must specify the extent to which the determination under that section is confirmed;

(b) a complaint (or any element of a complaint) which was determined by it under section 5(1) to constitute—

(i) a conduct complaint constitutes instead a services complaint;

(ii) a services complaint constitutes instead a conduct complaint,

it must determine accordingly.

(4) Where, or to the extent that, the Commission determines under subsection (3)(a) to confirm to any extent its determination under section 5(1)—

(a) it must give notice in writing to the complainer, the practitioner and the relevant professional organisation by sending to each of them a copy of the determination and specifying the reasons for the determination;

(b) any suspension under subsection (1)(a) or (2)(a) ceases.

(5) Where the Commission determines under subsection (3)(b) that a complaint (or any element of a complaint) which was determined by it under section 5(1) to constitute a services complaint constitutes instead a conduct complaint, it must—

(a) remit the conduct complaint to the relevant professional organisation to deal with (and give to the organisation any material referred to in section 6(a));

(b) give notice in writing to the complainer, the practitioner and the relevant professional organisation by sending to each of them a copy of the determination and specifying—

(i) the reasons for the determination;

(ii) that the conduct complaint is being remitted under paragraph (a);

(iii) the relevant professional organisation to which it is being remitted;

(iv) that the relevant professional organisation is under a duty under this Act to deal with the conduct complaint.

(6) Where the Commission determines under subsection (3)(b) that a complaint (or any element of a complaint) which was determined by it under section 5(1) to constitute a conduct complaint constitutes instead a services complaint—

(a) it must give notice in writing to the complainer, the practitioner and the relevant professional organisation by sending to each of them a copy of the determination and specifying the reasons for the determination;

(b) sections 8 to 12 apply to the services complaint as they apply where a determination is made under section 5(1) that a complaint constitutes a services complaint.

Power to monitor compliance with directions under section 10(2)

16.—(1) The Commission must, by notice in writing, require every practitioner specified in any direction under section 10(2) to give, before the end of such period being not less than 21 days as the notice specifies, an account and explanation of the steps which the practitioner has taken to comply with the direction.

(2) Where an appeal against any such direction is made under section 21(1), any notice under subsection (1) relating to the direction ceases to have effect pending the outcome of the appeal.

Power to examine documents and demand explanations in connection with conduct or services complaints

17.—(1) Where the Commission is satisfied that it is necessary for it to do so for the purposes of section 2, 4, 5, 8, 9, 10, 15 or 16, it may give notice in writing in accordance with subsection (2) to the practitioner, the practitioner's firm or, as the case may be, the employing practitioner.

(2) Notice under subsection (1) may require—

(a) the production or delivery to any person appointed by the Commission, at a time and place specified in the notice, of all documents mentioned in subsection (3) which are in the possession or control of the practitioner, the firm or, as the case may be, the employing practitioner and which relate to the matters to which the complaint relates (whether or not they relate also to other matters);

(b) an explanation, within such period being not less than 21 days as the notice specifies, from the practitioner, the firm or, as the case may be, the employing practitioner regarding the matters to which the complaint relates.

(3) The documents are—

(a) all books, accounts, deeds, securities, papers and other documents in the possession or control of the practitioner, the firm or, as the case may be, the employing practitioner;

(b) all books, accounts, deeds, securities, papers and other documents relating to any trust of which the practitioner is the sole trustee or a co-trustee only with one or more of the practitioner's partners or employees or, as the case may be, where the practitioner is an incorporated practice of which the practice or one of its employees is a sole trustee or it is a co-trustee only with one or more of its employees.

(4) Where the Commission is satisfied that it is necessary for it to do so for the purposes of section 2, 4, 5, 8, 9, 10 or 15, it may give notice in writing in accordance with subsection (5) to the complainer.

(5) Notice under subsection (4) may require—

(a) the production or delivery to any person appointed by the Commission at a time and place specified in the notice, of all documents mentioned in subsection (6) which are in the possession or control of the complainer and which relate to the matters to which the complaint relates (whether or not they relate to other matters);

(b) an explanation, within such period being not less than 21 days as the notice specifies, from the complainer regarding the matters to which the complaint relates.

(6) The documents are all books, accounts, deeds, securities, papers and other documents in the possession or control of the complainer.

(7) Schedule 2 makes further provision about the powers of the Commission under this section.

Power of Commission to recover certain expenses

18.—(1) The Commission is, subject to subsection (2), entitled to recover from a practitioner, the practitioner's firm or, as the case may be, the employing practitioner, in respect of whom it has taken any action by virtue of section 17, any expenditure reasonably incurred by it in so doing.

(2) Expenditure incurred in taking action by virtue of section 17 is recoverable under subsection (1) only where notice has been served under paragraph 2(a) of schedule 2 in connection with that action and either—

(a) no application has been made in consequence under paragraph 3 of that schedule; or

(b) the court, on such an application, has made a direction under paragraph 4 of that schedule.

Documents and information from third parties

19.—(1) Where the Commission has requested that documents or information in the possession or control of a person be produced for the purposes of an investigation by it under this Act and the person refuses or fails to produce the documents or information, the Commission may apply to the court for an order under subsection (2).

(2) An order by the court under this subsection may require a person to produce or deliver the documents or information or to cause them or it to be produced or delivered to the person appointed at the place fixed by the Commission within such time as the court may order.

(3) The court may make an order under subsection (2) only if—

(a) it appears—

(i) the documents sought are; or

(ii) the information sought is,

relevant to the investigation; and

(b) it is in the public interest for the documents or information to be produced.

(4) Where the Commission receives possession of any such documents or information which have been produced or delivered to it, it must without delay serve on the person from whom the documents or information were received, a notice giving particulars and the date on which it took possession.

(5) Before the expiry of the period of 14 days after service of a notice under subsection (4) the person on whom the notice has been served may apply to the court for an order directing return of the documents or information to the person from whom they were received by the Commission or to such other person as the applicant may request; and on the hearing of any such application the court may make the order applied for or such other order as it thinks fit.

(6) If no application is made to the court under subsection (5), or if the court on any such application directs that the documents or information in question remain in the custody or control of the Commission, the Commission may make enquiries to ascertain the person to whom they belong and may deal with the documents or information in accordance with the directions of that person.

(7) This section does not apply to documents or information in the possession or control of—

(a) the person who made the complaint from which the investigation arises;

(b) the practitioner concerned;

(c) a relevant professional organisation.

Enforcement of Commission direction under section 10(2)

20. A direction by the Commission under section 10(2) is enforceable in like manner as an extract registered decree arbitral in its favour bearing a warrant for execution issued by the sheriff court of any sheriffdom in Scotland.

Appeals

Appeal against Commission decisions

21.—(1) Any person mentioned in subsection (2) may, with the leave of the court, appeal against any decision of the Commission under the preceding sections of this Part as respects a complaint on any ground set out in subsection (4).

(2) Those persons are—

(a) the complainer;

(b) the practitioner to whom the complaint relates;

(c) the practitioner's firm;

(d) the employing practitioner;

(e) the relevant professional organisation.

(3) An appeal under subsection (1) must be made before the expiry of the period of 28 days beginning with the day on which notice of the decision was given to the complainer and the practitioner; but the court may, on cause shown, consider an appeal made after the expiry of that period.

(4) The grounds referred to in subsection (1) are—

(a) that the Commission's decision was based on an error of law;

(b) that there has been a procedural impropriety in the conduct of any hearing by the Commission on the complaint;

(c) that the Commission has acted irrationally in the exercise of its discretion;

(d) that the Commission's decision was not supported by the facts found to be established by the Commission.

(5) The Commission is to be a party in any proceedings on an appeal under subsection (1).

(6) In this section and in section 22, "decision" includes any determination, direction or other decision and also includes the making of any report under section 10(2)(e).

Appeal: supplementary provision

22.—(1) On any appeal under section 21(1), the court may make such order as it thinks fit (including an order substituting its own decision for the decision appealed against).

(2) Where such an order upholds a services complaint or confirms a decision of the Commission to uphold a services complaint, the court may direct that such of the steps mentioned in 10(2) as it considers fair and reasonable in the circumstances be taken.

(3) On any appeal under section 21(1) the court may make such ancillary order (including an order as to the expenses of the appeal) as it thinks fit.

(4) A decision of the court under this section is final.

Handling by relevant professional organisations of conduct complaints

Handling by relevant professional organisations of conduct complaints: investigation by Commission

23.—(1) The Commission may, subject to subsection (4), carry out such investigation as appears to it to be appropriate of any complaint made to it by or on behalf of any person which relates to the manner in which a conduct complaint made by or on behalf of that person and remitted to a relevant professional organisation under section 6(a) or 15(5)(a) has been dealt with by the organisation (such a complaint being referred to in this Act as a "handling complaint").

(2) The Commission may decide—

(a) not to investigate a handling complaint;

(b) to discontinue the investigation of a handling complaint.

(3) If the Commission decides not to investigate, or to discontinue the investigation of, a handling complaint it must give notice in writing to—

(a) the person who made the handling complaint;
(b) the relevant professional organisation;
(c) the practitioner concerned in the conduct complaint to which the handling complaint relates,

by sending to each of them a copy of the decision and specifying the reasons for the decision.

(4) The Commission must not investigate a handling complaint where either—

(a) the relevant professional organisation has not completed its investigation of the conduct complaint to which the handling complaint relates; or
(b) the handling complaint is made after the expiry of the period of 6 months after such date as the Scottish Ministers may specify by order,

but paragraph (a) does not apply in any of the circumstances mentioned in subsection (5).

(5) The circumstances are that—

(a) the handling complaint is that the relevant professional organisation—
  (i) has acted unreasonably in failing to start an investigation into the complaint; or
  (ii) having started such an investigation, has failed to complete it within a reasonable time; or
(b) the Commission considers that, even though the complaint is being investigated by the organisation, an investigation by the Commission is justified.

(6) Where the Commission decides that subsection (4)(a) does not prevent it investigating a handling complaint because any of the circumstances referred to in subsection (5) apply, it must give notice in writing to—

(a) the person who made the handling complaint;
(b) the relevant professional organisation;
(c) the practitioner concerned in the conduct complaint to which the handling complaint relates,

by sending to each of them a copy of the decision and specifying the reasons for the decision.

(7) An order under subsection (4)(b) may specify different dates for different purposes.

(8) Where the Commission is conducting an investigation under this section, it may at any time make a written interim report in relation to the investigation and must send a copy of any such report to—

(a) the person who made the handling complaint;
(b) the relevant professional organisation;
(c) the practitioner concerned in the conduct complaint to which the handling complaint relates.

(9) The Scottish Ministers may by order amend the period of time referred to in subsection (4)(b).

Investigation under section 23: final report and recommendations

24.—(1) Where the Commission has completed an investigation under section 23 it must—

(a) make a written report of its conclusions;
(b) send a copy of the report to—
  (i) the person who made the handling complaint;
  (ii) the relevant professional organisation;
  (iii) the practitioner concerned in the conduct complaint to which the handling complaint relates.

(2) A report under this section may include one or more of the following recommendations—

(a) that the relevant professional organisation provide to the person making the handling complaint such information about the conduct complaint to which the handling complaint relates, and how it was dealt with, as the Commission considers appropriate;

(b) that the conduct complaint be investigated further by the relevant professional organisation;

(c) that the conduct complaint be reconsidered by the relevant professional organisation;

(d) that the relevant professional organisation consider exercising its powers in relation to the practitioner concerned;

(e) that the relevant professional organisation pay compensation of such amount, not exceeding £5000, as the Commission may specify to the person making the handling complaint for loss, inconvenience or distress resulting from the way in which the conduct complaint was handled by the organisation;

(f) that the relevant professional organisation pay to the person making the handling complaint an amount specified by the Commission by way of reimbursement of the cost, or part of the cost, of making the handling complaint.

(3) Where a report under this section includes any recommendation, the report must state the reasons for making the recommendation.

(4) A relevant professional organisation to whom a report is sent by the Commission under this section must have regard to the conclusions and recommendations set out in the report so far as relating to the organisation.

(5) Where a report sent to a relevant professional organisation under this section includes a recommendation relating to it, the organisation must, before the end of the period of 3 months beginning with the date on which the report was sent, notify the Commission, the person who made the handling complaint and the practitioner concerned, in writing, of—

(a) the action which it has taken to comply with the recommendations or in consequence of further consideration of the matter by it;

(b) its decision not to comply wholly with a recommendation and any reason for that decision.

(6) Where the Commission is either—

(a) notified under subsection (5)(b) that the relevant professional organisation has decided not to comply wholly with a recommendation; or

(b) of the opinion that the relevant professional organisation has not complied wholly with a recommendation before the end of the period of 3 months beginning with the date on which the report was sent to the organisation under this section,

the Commission may direct the professional organisation to comply with that recommendation if the Commission thinks fit; and the organisation must comply with the direction.

(7) For the purposes of subsection (6), a "recommendation" means any recommendation referred to in paragraphs (a) to (c), (e) or (f) of subsection (2).

(8) The Scottish Ministers may by order, after consulting—

(a) the relevant professional organisations;

(b) such groups of persons representing consumer interests as they consider appropriate,

amend subsection (2)(e) by substituting for the amount for the time being specified in that subsection such other amount as they consider appropriate.

Failure to comply with recommendation

25.—(1) If the Commission considers that a relevant professional organisation has failed to comply with a direction under section 24(6), the Commission may apply by petition to the court for the organisation to be dealt with in accordance with subsection (2).

(2) Where such a petition is presented, the court may inquire into the matter and after hearing—

(a) any witnesses who may be produced against or on behalf of the professional organisation; and

(b) any statement that may be offered in defence,

may order the organisation to comply with the recommendation with which the direction under section 24(6) is concerned.

Abolition of Scottish legal services ombudsman

26.—(1) The office of the Scottish legal services ombudsman ("the ombudsman") is abolished on such date as the Scottish Ministers may by order specify.

(2) The Scottish Ministers may not make an order under subsection (1) unless the ombudsman has no exercisable functions.

(3) The functions of the ombudsman cease to be exercisable except in relation to the advice, services and activities mentioned in section 77(2).

Finance

Annual general levy

27.—(1) Each—

(a) advocate practising as such;

(b) conveyancing practitioner or executry practitioner;

(c) person exercising a right to conduct litigation or a right of audience acquired by virtue of section 27 of the 1990 Act;

(d) solicitor who has in force a practising certificate,

must, subject to subsection (2) and section 29(2), pay to the Commission in respect of each financial year a contribution (referred to in this Part as "the annual general levy").

(2) Each relevant professional organisation—

(a) must secure the collection by it, from all of the persons falling within the categories referred to in paragraphs (a) to (d) of subsection (1) as respects whom it is the relevant professional organisation, of the annual general levy due by them;

(b) must pay to the Commission a sum representing the total amount which falls to be collected by it under paragraph (a) in respect of each financial year.

(3) Any—

(a) sum due to the Commission under subsection (2)(b);

(b) interest due on any such sum at such rate as may be specified by the Scottish Ministers by order from the date the sum is due under rules made under section 32(1) until it is paid,

may be recovered by it (as a debt) from the relevant professional organisation which is liable under that subsection to pay the sum.

(4) A relevant professional organisation may recover (as a debt), from any person falling within the categories referred to in paragraphs (a) to (d) of subsection (1) as respects whom it is the relevant professional organisation—

(a) any sum due by the person to the Commission under that subsection;

(b) any interest due on any such sum at such rate as may be specified by the Scottish Ministers by order from the date the sum is due under rules made under section 32(1) until it is paid.

(5) If any person who is liable under subsection (1) to pay the annual general levy fails to pay any amount of the levy, or pays any such amount late, the failure or late payment may be treated as professional misconduct or unsatisfactory professional conduct.

Complaints levy

28.—(1) A practitioner against whom a services complaint is made must pay to the Commission, in the circumstances mentioned in subsection (2), a contribution in relation to the complaint (referred to in this Part as "the complaints levy").

(2) The circumstances are where—

(a) any of the following applies—

(i) mediation by virtue of section 8(5) takes place in relation to the complaint and the outcome of the mediation is accepted by both the complainer and the practitioner;

(ii) a settlement proposed as respects the complaint by the Commission under section 9(2) is accepted as mentioned in section 9(4);

(iii) the Commission makes a determination under section 9(1) upholding the complaint; and

(b) the amount of the levy has not been determined as nil and the Commission does not in accordance with rules made under section 32(1) waive the requirement to pay the levy.

(3) Any—

(a) sum due by a practitioner to the Commission under subsection (1);

(b) interest due on any such sum at such rate as may be specified by the Scottish Ministers by order from the date the sum is due under rules made under section 32(1) until it is paid,

may be recovered by it (as a debt) from the practitioner.

(4) If any person who is liable under subsection (1) to pay the complaints levy fails to pay any amount of the levy, or pays any such amount late, the failure or late payment may be treated as professional misconduct or unsatisfactory professional conduct.

Amount of levies and consultation

29.—(1) The amount of the—

(a) annual general levy;

(b) complaints levy,

in respect of each financial year is such amount as may be determined by the Commission, having had regard to any views expressed in its consultation under subsection (4) in respect of the financial year in question.

(2) The amount of the annual general levy must be the same amount for each of the individuals who are liable under section 27(1) to pay it; but rules made under section 32(1) may provide for circumstances in which the Commission may waive a portion of the amount which would otherwise require to be paid.

(3) The Commission may determine different amounts (including an amount of nil) for the complaints levy in different circumstances.

(4) The Commission must, in January each year, consult each relevant professional organisation and its members on the Commission's proposed budget for the next financial year.

(5) The proposed budget must—

(a) include—

(i) an estimate as respects resource requirements;

(ii) the proposed amount of the annual general levy and the complaints levy;

(b) be accompanied by information as to the Commission's projected work plan for the next financial year.

(6) Each relevant professional organisation must, for the purpose of informing the Commission in relation to—

(a) the inclusion in the Commission's proposed budget for each financial year of the proposed amount of the annual general levy;

(b) the Commission's determination under subsection (1) of the amount of the annual general levy in respect of each financial year,

provide the Commission with an estimate of the number of persons as respects whom it is the relevant professional organisation and who it anticipates should be liable under section 27(1) to pay the annual general levy for the financial year concerned.

(7) The Commission must secure so far as is reasonably practicable that,

taking one financial year with another, the amount of the annual general levy and the complaints levy is reasonably sufficient to meet its expenditure.

(8) The Commission must, no later than 31 March in each year, publish the responses it has received in the consultation carried out by it under subsection (4) in the immediately preceding January.

(9) Subsection (1) does not apply to responses which are subject to an express request in writing for confidentiality.

(10) The Commission must lay a copy of the finalised budget before the Parliament no later than 30 April in each year.

Grants or loans by the Scottish Ministers

30.—(1) The Scottish Ministers may make grants to the Commission of such amounts as they consider appropriate.

(2) Any grant under this section may be made on such terms and subject to such conditions (including conditions as to repayment) as the Scottish Ministers consider appropriate; and the Scottish Ministers may from time to time after the grant is made vary such terms and conditions.

(3) For the purpose of the exercise of any of its duties or powers under this Part—

(a) the Commission may, subject to such conditions as the Scottish Ministers think fit, borrow from them;

(b) the Scottish Ministers may lend to the Commission,

sums of such amounts as the Ministers may determine.

(4) Any loan made in pursuance of subsection (3) is to be repaid to the Scottish Ministers at such times and by such methods, and interest on the loan is to be paid to them at such times and at such rates, as they may from time to time direct.

Guarantees

31.—(1) The Scottish Ministers may guarantee, in such manner and on such conditions as they think fit, the discharge of any financial obligation in connection with any sums borrowed by the Commission.

(2) Immediately after any guarantee is given under this section, the Scottish Ministers must lay a statement of the guarantee before the Parliament.

(3) Where any sum is paid out in fulfilment of a guarantee under this section, the Commission must make to the Scottish Ministers, at such times and in such manner as they may from time to time direct—

(a) payments of such amount as they may so direct in or towards repayment of the sums so paid out;

(b) payments of interest, at such rate as they may so direct, on the amount outstanding for the time being in respect of sums so paid out.

Rules as to Commission's practice and procedure

Duty of Commission to make rules as to practice and procedure

32.—(1) The Commission must make rules as to its practice and procedure and, as soon as practicable after making or varying those rules, publish them and make them available to the public in a form which is readily accessible.

(2) Schedule 3 makes further provision as respects provision which—

(a) must be included;

(b) may in particular be included,

in the rules.

(3) The rules may make different provision for different categories of complaint.

(4) The Commission must keep the rules under review and must vary the provisions of the rules whenever it considers it appropriate to do so.

(5) The Commission must, before making rules or varying the rules, consult with—

(a) the Lord President of the Court of Session;

(b) the Scottish Ministers;

(c) the relevant professional organisations;

(d) such groups of persons representing consumer interests as it considers appropriate,

as to the proposed content of the rules to be made or varied.

Forwarding complaints, advice, monitoring etc.

Duty of relevant professional organisations to forward complaints to Commission

33. Where a relevant professional organisation receives a complaint from a person other than the Commission about—

(a) the conduct of, or any services provided by, a practitioner;

(b) its handling of a conduct complaint remitted to it under section 6(a) or 15(5)(a),

it must without delay send the complaint and any material which accompanies it to the Commission.

Commission's duty to provide advice

34.—(1) The Commission must, so far as is reasonably practicable, provide advice to any person who requests it as respects the process of making a services complaint or a handling complaint to it.

(2) Where the Commission receives a complaint suggesting what purports to be professional misconduct or unsatisfactory professional conduct by a practitioner who is a firm of solicitors or an incorporated practice—

(a) it must inform the person that a complaint to it suggesting such misconduct or such conduct may be made only against a named practitioner who is an individual;

(b) where the complaint received is not about a named practitioner who is an individual, it must so far as is reasonably practicable offer advice to the person with a view to assisting the person to reformulate the complaint so that it is about such a named practitioner.

(3) Where a person in requesting or being offered such advice expresses a preference for receiving it by a particular means (as, for example, in writing, by telephone, by means of a recording or an explanation in person), the Commission must, so far as is reasonably practicable, give effect to the preference.

Services complaints: monitoring, reports, protocols and information sharing

35.—(1) The Commission must monitor practice and identify any trends in practice as respects the way in which practitioners have dealt with matters that result in services complaints being dealt with by the Commission under sections 8 to 12.

(2) The Commission must prepare and publish reports on any trends in practice which it identifies under subsection (1) at such intervals as it considers appropriate.

(3) The Commission must—

(a) enter into protocols with the relevant professional organisations as respects the sharing of information by it with them in relation to—

(i) numbers of services complaints dealt with by it;

(ii) such trends as it may identify in relation to such complaints;

(iii) settlements proposed by it under section 9(2), which are accepted as mentioned in subsection (4) of that section;

(iv) the substance of any services complaints which might be relevant to section 31(3) of the 1986 Act;

(v) determinations by it under section 9(1) upholding services complaints;

(vi) failure by practitioners to comply with directions by it under section 10(2), notice by it under section 16 or 17(1) or requirements by it under section 37(3);

(b) share information with the relevant professional organisations in accordance with the protocols.

(4) The relevant professional organisations must enter into protocols with the Commission for the purposes of subsection (3)(a).

Conduct complaints: monitoring, reports, guidance and recommendations

36.—(1) The Commission must monitor practice and identify any trends in practice as respects the way in which—

(a) practitioners have dealt with matters that result in conduct complaints being remitted to the relevant professional organisations under section 6(a) or 15(5)(a);

(b) the relevant professional organisations have dealt with conduct complaints so remitted.

(2) The Commission must prepare and publish reports on any trends in practice which it identifies under subsection (1) at such intervals as it considers appropriate.

(3) The Commission may—

(a) give guidance to the relevant professional organisations as to the timescales within which they should aim to complete their investigation of or, as the case may be, determine conduct complaints remitted to them under section 6(a) or 15(5)(a);

(b) make recommendations to any relevant professional organisation about the organisation's procedures for, and methods of dealing with, conduct complaints so remitted to it.

(4) Each relevant professional organisation to which the Commission makes a recommendation under subsection (3)(b) must—

(a) consider the recommendation;

(b) notify the Commission in writing of—

(i) the results of the consideration;

(ii) any action the organisation has taken or proposes to take in consequence of the recommendation.

(5) The Commission may carry out, for any of the purposes of this section, audits of the records held by the relevant professional organisations relating to conduct complaints remitted to them under section 6(a) or 15(5)(a).

Obtaining of information from relevant professional organisations

37.—(1) The Commission may require any relevant professional organisation to—

(a) provide it with such information, being information which is within the knowledge of the organisation, as the Commission considers relevant for any of the purposes of section 23, 24 or 36;

(b) to produce to it such documents, being documents which are within the possession or control of the organisation, as the Commission considers relevant for any of those purposes.

(2) The information required to be provided or the documents required to be produced under subsection (1) may include information or, as the case may be, documents obtained by the relevant professional organisation from a practitioner while investigating a conduct complaint against the practitioner remitted to it under section 6(a) or 15(5)(a); and the organisation must comply with such a requirement.

(3) Where any information required by the Commission under subsection (1) is not within the knowledge of the relevant professional organisation, or

any documents required to be produced under that subsection are not within the possession or control of the organisation, the Commission may require the practitioner concerned—

(a) to provide it with that information in so far as it is within the knowledge of the practitioner;

(b) to produce to it those documents if they are within the practitioner's possession or control.

(4) Schedule 2 makes further provision about the powers of the Commission under this section.

Efficient and effective working

38.—(1) In relation to any investigation or report undertaken by it under this Act, the Commission must liaise with the relevant professional organisation with a view to minimising any unnecessary duplication in relation to any investigation or report undertaken, or to be undertaken, by the relevant professional organisation.

(2) In relation to any investigation or report undertaken by it under this Act, each relevant professional organisation must liaise with the Commission with a view to minimising any unnecessary duplication in relation to any investigation or report undertaken, or to be undertaken, by the Commission.

Monitoring effectiveness of guarantee funds etc.

39.—(1) The Commission may monitor the effectiveness of—

(a) the Scottish Solicitors Guarantee Fund vested in the Society and controlled and managed by the Council under section 43(1) of the 1980 Act ("the Guarantee Fund");

(b) arrangements carried into effect by the Society under section 44(2) of that Act ("the professional indemnity arrangements");

(c) any funds or arrangements maintained by any relevant professional organisation which are for purposes analogous to those of the Guarantee Fund or the professional indemnity arrangements as respects its members.

(2) The Commission may make recommendations to the relevant professional organisation concerned about the effectiveness (including improvement) of the Guarantee Fund, the professional indemnity arrangements or any such funds or arrangements as are referred to in subsection (1)(c).

(3) The Commission may request from the relevant professional organisation such information as the Commission considers relevant to its functions under subsections (1) and (2).

(4) Where a relevant professional organisation fails to provide information requested under subsection (3), it must give reasons to the Commission in respect of that failure.

How practitioners deal with complaints: best practice notes

40.—The Commission may issue guidance to the relevant professional organisations or to practitioners as respects how practitioners deal with complaints made to them about—

(a) their professional conduct or the professional services provided by them;

(b) the professional conduct of, or professional services provided by, any of their employees who are practitioners,

and any such guidance may recommend or include recommendations as respects standards for systems by practitioners for dealing with such complaints.

Miscellaneous

Power by regulations to amend duties and powers of Commission

41.—(1) The Scottish Ministers may, after consulting—

(a) the Commission;

(b) the relevant professional organisations;

(c) such other persons or groups of persons as they consider appropriate,

by regulations modify the provisions of this Part for the purposes of adjusting the duties imposed, or the powers conferred, by it on the Commission (including imposing new duties or conferring new powers).

(2) Regulations under subsection (1) may contain such incidental, supplemental, consequential, transitional, transitory or saving provision as the Scottish Ministers consider necessary or expedient for the purposes of that subsection (including modification of any enactment, instrument or document).

Reports: privilege

42. For the purposes of the law of defamation, the publication of any report under section 13(1), 23(8), 24, 35(2), 36(2) or paragraph 16 of schedule 1 is privileged unless the publication is proved to be made with malice.

Restriction upon disclosure of information: Commission

43.—(1) Except as permitted by subsection (3), no information mentioned in subsection (2) may be disclosed.

(2) The information is information—

(a) contained in a conduct complaint, services complaint or handling complaint;

(b) which is given to or obtained by the Commission or any person acting on its behalf in the course of, or for the purposes of—

(i) any consideration of such a complaint;

(ii) an investigation (including any report of such an investigation) into a services complaint or a handling complaint.

(3) Such information may be disclosed—

(a) for the purpose of enabling or assisting the Commission to exercise any of its functions;

(b) where the disclosure is required by or by virtue of any provision made by or under this Act or by any other enactment or other rule of law.

(4) Any person who, in contravention of subsection (1), knowingly discloses any information obtained when employed by, or acting on behalf of, the Commission is guilty of an offence and liable, on summary conviction, to a fine not exceeding level 4 on the standard scale.

Exemption from liability in damages

44.—(1) Neither the Commission nor any person who is, or is acting as, a member of the Commission or an employee of the Commission is to be liable in damages for anything done or omitted in the discharge, or purported discharge, of the Commission's functions.

(2) Subsection (1) does not apply—

(a) if the act or omission is shown to have been in bad faith;

(b) so as to prevent an award of damages made in respect of an act or omission on the ground that the act or omission was unlawful as a result of section 6(1) of the Human Rights Act 1998 (c.42).

Giving of notices etc. under Part 1

45.—(1) Any notice which is required under this Part to be given in writing is to be treated as being in writing if it is received in a form which is legible and capable of being used for subsequent reference.

(2) Any notice which is required under this Part to be given to any person—

(a) is duly given—

(i) where the person is not an incorporated practice, if it is left at, or delivered or sent by post to, the person's last known place of business or residence;

(ii) where the person is an incorporated practice, if it is left at or delivered or sent by post to the practice's registered office;

(iii) where the person is a practitioner who is a firm of solicitors or an incorporated practice, if it is sent to the person by electronic means but only if the practitioner agrees to that means of sending;

(iv) where the person is an individual, if it is sent to the person by electronic means but only if the individual agrees to that means of sending;

(v) to any person, if it is given in such other manner as may be prescribed by regulations by the Scottish Ministers;

(b) if permitted by paragraph (a) to be sent, and sent, by electronic means is, unless the contrary is proved, deemed to be delivered on the next working day which follows the day on which the notice is sent.

(3) Regulations under subsection (2)(a)(v) may—

(a) in particular provide that notice required to be given to a person who is not an individual may be given by addressing or sending it to such person appointed by the person for that purpose or to such person falling within such other categories prescribed in the regulations as appear to the Scottish Ministers to be appropriate;

(b) make different provision for different purposes.

(4) In subsection (2)(b), "working day" means any day other than a Saturday, a Sunday or a day which, under the Banking and Financial Dealings Act 1971 (c. 80), is a bank holiday in Scotland.

Interpretation of Part 1

46.—(1) In this Part, unless the context otherwise requires—

"advocate" means a member of the Faculty of Advocates;

"annual general levy" has the meaning given by section 27(1);

"client"—

(a) (in relation to any matter in which the practitioner has been instructed) includes any person on whose behalf the person who gave the instructions was acting;

(b) where the practitioner is an employee of a person who is not a practitioner, includes (in relation to any matter in which the practitioner has been instructed by the employer) the employer;

"complainer" means the person who makes the complaint and, where the complaint is made by the person on behalf of another person, includes that other person;

"complaint" includes any expression of dissatisfaction;

"complaints levy" has the meaning given by section 28(1);

"the Commission" means the Scottish Legal Complaints Commission;

"conduct complaint" has the meaning given by section 2(1)(a);

"conveyancing practitioner" means a person registered under section 17 of the 1990 Act in the register of conveyancing practitioners;

"the Council" means the Council of the Law Society of Scotland;

"the court" means the Court of Session;

"employing practitioner" has the meaning given by section 4(4)(a);

"executry practitioner" means a person registered under section 18 of the 1990 Act in the register of executry practitioners;

"handling complaint" has the meaning given by section 23(1);

"inadequate professional services"—

(a) means, as respects a practitioner who is—

(i) an advocate, professional services which are in any respect not of the quality which could reasonably be expected of a competent advocate;

(ii) a conveyancing practitioner or an executry practitioner, professional services which are in any respect not of the quality which could reasonably be expected of a competent conveyancing practitioner or, as the case may be, a competent executry practitioner;

(iii) a firm of solicitors or an incorporated practice, professional services which are in any respect not of the quality which could reasonably be expected of a competent firm of solicitors or, as the case may be, a competent incorporated practice;

(iv) a person exercising a right to conduct litigation or a right of audience acquired by virtue of section 27 of the 1990 Act, professional services which are in any respect not of the quality which could reasonably be expected of a competent person exercising such a right;

(v) a solicitor, professional services which are in any respect not of the quality which could reasonably be expected of a competent solicitor;

(b) includes any element of negligence in respect of or in connection with the services,

and cognate expressions are to be construed accordingly;

"incorporated practice" has the meaning given by section 34(1A)(c) of the 1980 Act;

"practising certificate" has the meaning given by section 4 of the 1980 Act;

"practitioner" means—

(a) an advocate and includes any advocate whether or not a member of the Faculty of Advocates at the time when it is suggested the conduct complained of occurred or the services complained of were provided and notwithstanding that subsequent to that time the advocate has ceased to be such a member;

(b) a conveyancing practitioner and includes any such practitioner, whether or not registered at that time and notwithstanding that subsequent to that time the practitioner has ceased to be so registered;

(c) an executry practitioner and includes any such practitioner, whether or not registered at that time and notwithstanding that subsequent to that time the practitioner has ceased to be so registered;

(d) a firm of solicitors, whether or not since that time there has been any change in the firm by the addition of a new partner or the death or resignation of an existing partner or the firm has ceased to practise;

(e) an incorporated practice, whether or not since that time there has been any change in the persons exercising the management and control of the practice or the practice has ceased to be recognised by virtue of section 34(1A) of the 1980 Act or has been wound up;

(f) a person exercising a right to conduct litigation or a right of audience acquired by virtue of section 27 of the 1990 Act and includes any such person, whether or not the person had acquired the right at that time and notwithstanding that subsequent to that time the person no longer has the right;

(g) a solicitor, whether or not the solicitor had a practising certificate in force at that time and notwithstanding that subsequent to that time the name of the solicitor has been removed from or struck off the roll or the solicitor has ceased to practise or has been suspended from practice;

"relevant professional organisation" means, in relation to a complaint as respects a practitioner who is—

(a) an advocate, the Faculty of Advocates;

(b) a conveyancing practitioner, an executry practitioner, a firm of solicitors or an incorporated practice, the Council;

(c) a person exercising a right to conduct litigation or a right of audience acquired by virtue of section 27 of the 1990 Act, the body which made a successful application under section 25 of that Act and of which the person is a member;

(d) a solicitor, the Council;

"the roll" means the roll of solicitors kept by the Council by virtue of section 7(1) of the 1980 Act;

"services complaint" has the meaning given by section 2(1)(b);

"the Society" means the Law Society of Scotland;

"solicitor" means any person enrolled or deemed to have been enrolled as a solicitor in pursuance of the 1980 Act;

"unsatisfactory professional conduct" means, as respects a practitioner who is—

(a) an advocate, professional conduct which is not of the standard which could reasonably be expected of a competent and reputable advocate;

(b) a conveyancing practitioner or an executry practitioner, professional conduct which is not of the standard which could reasonably be expected of a competent and reputable conveyancing practitioner or, as the case may be, a competent and reputable executry practitioner;

(c) a person exercising a right to conduct litigation or a right of audience acquired by virtue of section 27 of this Act, professional conduct which is not of the standard which could reasonably be expected of a competent and reputable person exercising such a right;

(d) a solicitor, professional conduct which is not of the standard which could reasonably be expected of a competent and reputable solicitor,

but which does not amount to professional misconduct and which does not comprise merely inadequate professional services; and cognate expressions are to be construed accordingly.

(2) For the avoidance of doubt, anything done by any Crown Counsel or procurator fiscal in relation to the prosecution of crime or investigation of deaths is not done in relation to any matter in which the Crown Counsel or procurator fiscal has been instructed by a client.

(3) For the avoidance of doubt, the exercise of discretion by any Crown Counsel or procurator fiscal in relation to the prosecution of crime or investigation of deaths is not in itself capable of constituting professional misconduct or unsatisfactory professional conduct.

(4) In subsections (2) and (3), "procurator fiscal" has the same meaning as in section 307 of the Criminal Procedure (Scotland) Act 1995 (c.46).

PART 2

CONDUCT AND SERVICES COMPLAINTS ETC.: OTHER MATTERS

Conduct complaints: duty of relevant professional organisations to investigate etc.

47.—(1) Where a conduct complaint is remitted to a relevant professional organisation under section 6(a) or 15(5)(a), the organisation must, subject to section 15(1) and (6), investigate it.

(2) After investigating a conduct complaint, the relevant professional organisation must make a written report to the complainer and the practitioner of—

(a) the facts of the matter as found by the organisation;

(b) what action the organisation proposes to take, or has taken, in the matter.

(3) Each relevant professional organisation must ensure that its procedures for dealing with conduct complaints do not conflict with the duty imposed on it by section 24(4) or (5) in relation to any report sent to it under that section or any direction by the Commission under section 24(6).

(4) In this section and sections 48 to 52, words and expressions have the same meanings as in section 46.

Conduct complaints and reviews: power of relevant professional organisations to examine documents and demand explanations

48.—(1) Where a relevant professional organisation is satisfied that it is necessary for it to do so for the purposes of an investigation by it into a conduct complaint under section 47 or a review by it of a decision in relation to a conduct complaint, it may—

(a) give notice in writing in accordance with subsection (2) to the practitioner, the practitioner's firm or, as the case may be, the employing practitioner;

(b) give notice in writing in accordance with subsection (4) to the complainer.

(2) Notice under subsection (1)(a) may require—

(a) the production or delivery to any person appointed by the relevant professional organisation, at a time and place specified in the notice, of all documents mentioned in subsection (3) which are in the possession or control of the practitioner, the firm or, as the case may be, the employing practitioner and which relate to the matters to which the complaint relates (whether or not they relate also to other matters);

(b) an explanation, within such period being not less than 21 days as the notice specifies, from the practitioner, the firm or, as the case may be, the employing practitioner regarding the matters to which the complaint relates.

(3) The documents are—

(a) all books, accounts, deeds, securities, papers and other documents in the possession or control of the practitioner, the firm or, as the case may be, the employing practitioner;

(b) all books, accounts, deeds, securities, papers and other documents relating to any trust of which the practitioner is the sole trustee or a co-trustee only with one or more of the practitioner's partners or employees or, as the case may be, where the practitioner is an incorporated practice of which the practice or one of its employees is a sole trustee or it is a co-trustee only with one or more of its employees.

(4) Notice under subsection (1)(b) may require—

(a) the production or delivery to any person appointed by the relevant professional organisation at a time and place specified in the notice, of all documents mentioned in subsection (5) which relate to the matters to which the complaint relates (whether or not they relate to other matters);

(b) an explanation, within such period being not less than 21 days as the notice specifies, from the complainer regarding the matters to which the complaint relates.

(5) The documents are all books, accounts, deeds, securities, papers and other documents in the possession or control of the complainer.

(6) Schedule 4 makes further provision about the powers of a relevant professional organisation under this section.

Conduct complaints: financial impropriety

49.—(1) If, in the course of an investigation into a conduct complaint under section 47, a relevant professional organisation has reasonable cause to believe that the practitioner, the practitioner's firm (or any employee thereof) or, as the case may be, the employing practitioner, has been guilty of any financial impropriety it may apply to the court for an order under subsection (2).

(2) An order under this subsection is that no payment be made by any banker, building society or other body named in the order out of—

(a) any banking account in the name of such practitioner or firm; or

(b) any sum deposited in the name of such practitioner or firm,

without the leave of the court.

Power of relevant professional organisations to recover certain expenses

50.—(1) A relevant professional organisation is, subject to subsection (2), entitled to recover from a practitioner, the practitioner's firm or, as the case may be, the employing practitioner, in respect of whom it has taken any action by virtue of section 48(1)(a) or 49, any expenditure reasonably incurred by it in so doing.

(2) Expenditure incurred in taking action by virtue of section 48(1)(a) is recoverable under subsection (1) only where notice has been served under paragraph 2(a) of schedule 4 in connection with that action and—

(a) no application has been made in consequence under paragraph 3 of that schedule; or

(b) the court, on such an application, has made a direction under paragraph 4 of that schedule.

Powers in relation to documents and information from third parties

51.—(1) Where a relevant professional organisation has requested that documents or information in the possession or control of a person be produced for the purposes of an investigation by it into a conduct complaint under section 47 or a review by it of a decision in relation to a conduct complaint, and the person refuses or fails to produce the documents or information, the organisation may apply to the court for an order under subsection (2).

(2) An order by the court under this subsection may require a person to produce or deliver the documents or information or to cause them or it to be produced or delivered to the person appointed at the place fixed by the relevant professional organisation within such time as the court may order.

(3) Subsections (3) to (7) of section 19 apply for the purposes of this section as they apply for the purposes of that section but subject to the modification that for the references in subsections (4) to (6) to "the Commission" substitute "the relevant professional organisation".

Restriction upon disclosure of information: relevant professional organisations

52.—(1) Except as permitted by subsection (3), no information mentioned in subsection (2) may be disclosed.

(2) The information is information—

(a) contained in a conduct complaint;

(b) which is given to or obtained by a relevant professional organisation or any person acting on its behalf in the course of, or for the purposes of—

(i) any consideration of such a complaint;

(ii) an investigation (including any report of such an investigation) into such a complaint.

(3) Such information may be disclosed—

(a) for the purpose of enabling or assisting the relevant professional organisation to exercise any of its functions in relation to such a complaint;

(b) where the disclosure is required by or by virtue of any provision made by or under this Act or by any other enactment or other rule of law.

(4) Any person who, in contravention of subsection (1), knowingly discloses any information obtained when employed by, or acting on behalf of, a relevant professional organisation is guilty of an offence and liable, on summary conviction, to a fine not exceeding level 4 on the standard scale.

Unsatisfactory professional conduct: solicitors

53.—(1) The 1980 Act is amended as follows.

(2) After section 42, insert—

"Unsatisfactory professional conduct: Council's powers

42ZA.—(1) Where a conduct complaint suggesting unsatisfactory professional conduct by a practitioner who is a solicitor is remitted to the Council under section 6(a) or 15(5)(a) of the 2007 Act, the Council must having—

(a) investigated the complaint under section 47(1) of that Act and made a written report under section 47(2) of that Act;

(b) given the solicitor an opportunity to make representations,

determine the complaint.

(2) Where a complaint is remitted to the Council under section 53ZA, the Council—

(a) must—

(i) notify the solicitor specified in it and the complainer of that fact and that the Council are required to investigate the complaint as a complaint of unsatisfactory professional conduct;

(ii) so investigate the complaint;

(iii) having so investigated the complaint and given the solicitor an opportunity to make representations, determine the complaint;

(b) may rely, in their investigation, on any findings in fact which the Tribunal makes available to them under section 53ZA(2) as respects the complaint.

(3) Where the Council make a determination under subsection (1) or (2) upholding the complaint, they—

(a) shall censure the solicitor;

(b) may take any of the steps mentioned in subsection (4) which they consider appropriate.

(4) The steps are—

(a) where the Council consider that the solicitor does not have sufficient competence in relation to any aspect of the law or legal practice, to direct the solicitor to undertake such education or training as regards the law or legal practice as the Council consider appropriate in that respect;

(b) subject to subsection (6), to direct the solicitor to pay a fine not exceeding £2,000;

(c) where the Council consider that the complainer has been directly affected by the conduct, to direct the solicitor to pay compensation of such amount, not exceeding £5,000, as they may specify to the complainer for loss, inconvenience or distress resulting from the conduct.

(5) The Council may, in considering the complaint, take account of any previous determination by them, the Tribunal or the Court upholding a complaint against the solicitor of unsatisfactory professional conduct or professional misconduct (but not a complaint in respect of which an appeal is pending or which has been quashed ultimately on appeal).

(6) The Council shall not direct the solicitor to pay a fine under subsection (4)(b) where, in relation to the subject matter of the complaint, the solicitor has been convicted by any court of an act involving dishonesty and sentenced to a term of imprisonment of not less than 2 years.

(7) Any fine directed to be paid under subsection (4)(b) above shall be treated for the purposes of section 211(5) of the Criminal Procedure (Scotland) Act 1995 (fines payable to HM Exchequer) as if it were a fine imposed in the High Court.

(8) The Council shall intimate—

(a) a determination under subsection (1) or (2);

(b) any censure under subsection (3)(a);

(c) any direction under subsection (4),

to the complainer and the solicitor specified in it by sending to each of them a copy of the determination, censure or, as the case may be, the direction and by specifying the reasons for the determination.

(9) A solicitor in respect of whom a determination upholding a conduct complaint has been made under subsection (1) or (2), or a direction has been made under subsection (4) may, before the expiry of the period of 21 days beginning with the day on which the determination or, as the case may be, the direction is intimated to him, appeal to the Tribunal against the—

(a) determination;

(b) direction (whether or not he is appealing against the determination).

(10) A complainer may, before the expiry of the period of 21 days beginning with the day on which a determination under subsection (1) or (2) not upholding the conduct complaint is intimated to him, appeal to the Tribunal against the determination.

(11) Where the Council have upheld the conduct complaint but have not directed the solicitor under subsection (4)(c) to pay compensation, the complainer may, before the expiry of the period of 21 days beginning with the day on which the determination upholding the complaint is intimated to him, appeal to the Tribunal against the Council's decision not to make a direction under that subsection.

(12) A complainer to whom the Council have directed a solicitor under subsection (4)(c) to pay compensation may, before the expiry of the period of 21 days beginning with the day on which the direction under that subsection is intimated to him, appeal to the Tribunal against the amount of the compensation directed to be paid.

(13) The Scottish Ministers may by order made by statutory instrument—

(a) amend subsection (4)(b) by substituting for the amount for the time being specified in that subsection such other amount as appears to them to be justified by a change in the value of money;

(b) after consulting the Council and such groups of persons representing consumer interests as they consider appropriate, amend subsection (4)(c) by substituting for the amount for the time being specified in that subsection such other amount as they consider appropriate.

(14) A statutory instrument containing an order under—

(a) subsection (13)(a) is subject to annulment in pursuance of a resolution of the Scottish Parliament;

(b) subsection (13)(b) is not to be made unless a draft of the instrument has been laid before, and approved by resolution of, the Scottish Parliament.

(15) In this section, "complainer" means the person who made the complaint and, where the complaint was made by the person on behalf of another person, includes that other person.

Unsatisfactory professional conduct: Council's powers to monitor compliance with direction under section 42ZA(4)

42ZB.—(1) The Council shall, by notice in writing, require every solicitor who is specified in—

(a) a direction made under section 42ZA(4); or
(b) such a direction as confirmed or varied on appeal by—
 (i) the Tribunal; or
 (ii) the Court,

to give, before the expiry of such period being not less than 21 days as the notice specifies, an explanation of the steps which he has taken to comply with the direction.

(2) Where an appeal is made under section 42ZA(9) or (12) or 54A(1) or (2) against a direction made under section 42ZA(4), any notice under subsection (1)(a) above relating to the direction shall cease to have effect pending the outcome of the appeal.".

(3) After section 53 (powers of Tribunal), insert—

"Remission of complaint by Tribunal to Council

53ZA.—(1) Where, after holding an inquiry under section 53(1) into a complaint of professional misconduct against a solicitor, the Tribunal—

(a) is not satisfied that he has been guilty of professional misconduct;
(b) considers that he may be guilty of unsatisfactory professional conduct,

it must remit the complaint to the Council.

(2) Where the Tribunal remits a complaint to the Council under subsection (1), it may make available to the Council any of its findings in fact in its inquiry into the complaint under section 53(1).

Powers of Tribunal on appeal: unsatisfactory professional conduct

53ZB.—(1) On an appeal to the Tribunal under section 42ZA(9) the Tribunal—

(a) may quash or confirm the determination being appealed against;
(b) if it quashes the determination, shall quash the censure accompanying the determination;
(c) may quash, confirm or vary the direction being appealed against;
(d) may, where it considers that the solicitor does not have sufficient competence in relation to any aspect of the law or legal practice, direct the solicitor to undertake such education or training as regards the law or legal practice as the Tribunal considers appropriate in that respect;
(e) may, subject to subsection (5), fine the solicitor an amount not exceeding £2000;
(f) may, where it considers that the complainer has been directly affected by the conduct, direct the solicitor to pay compensation of such amount, not exceeding £5,000, as it may specify to the complainer for loss, inconvenience or distress resulting from the conduct.

(2) On an appeal to the Tribunal under section 42ZA(10) the Tribunal—

(a) may quash the determination being appealed against and make a determination upholding the complaint;
(b) if it does so, may, where it considers that the complainer has been directly affected by the conduct, direct the solicitor to pay compensation of such amount, not exceeding £5,000, as it may specify to the complainer for loss, inconvenience or distress resulting from the conduct;
(c) may confirm the determination.

(3) On an appeal to the Tribunal under section 42ZA(11) the Tribunal may, where it considers that the complainer has been directly affected by

the conduct, direct the solicitor to pay compensation of such amount, not exceeding £5,000, as it may specify to the complainer for loss, inconvenience or distress resulting from the conduct.

(4) On an appeal under section 42ZA(12) the Tribunal may quash, confirm or vary the direction being appealed against.

(5) The Tribunal shall not direct the solicitor to pay a fine under subsection (1)(e) where, in relation to the subject matter of the complaint, the solicitor has been convicted by any court of an act involving dishonesty and sentenced to a term of imprisonment of not less than 2 years.

(6) Any fine directed to be paid under subsection (1)(e) above shall be treated for the purposes of section 211(5) of the Criminal Procedure (Scotland) Act 1995 (fines payable to HM Exchequer) as if it were a fine imposed in the High Court.

(7) A direction of the Tribunal under this section is enforceable in like manner as an extract registered decree arbitral in favour of the Council bearing a warrant for execution issued by the sheriff court of any sheriffdom in Scotland.

(8) The Scottish Ministers may by order made by statutory instrument—

(a) amend subsection (1)(e) by substituting for the amount for the time being specified in that subsection such other amount as appears to them to be justified by a change in the value of money;

(b) after consulting the Council and such groups of persons representing consumer interests as they consider appropriate, amend subsection (1)(f) by substituting for the amount for the time being specified in that subsection such other amount as they consider appropriate.

(9) A statutory instrument containing an order under—

(a) subsection (8)(a) is subject to annulment in pursuance of a resolution of the Scottish Parliament;

(b) subsection (8)(b) is not to be made unless a draft of the instrument has been laid before, and approved by resolution of, the Scottish Parliament.

(10) In this section, "complainer" has the same meaning as in section 42ZA.

Enforcement of Council direction: unsatisfactory professional conduct

53ZC. Where a solicitor fails to comply with a direction given by the Council under section 42ZA(4) (including such a direction as confirmed or varied on appeal by the Tribunal or, as the case may be, the Court) before the expiry of the period specified in the notice relating to that direction given to him under section 42ZB(1), or such longer period as the Council may allow, the direction shall be enforceable in like manner as an extract registered decree arbitral in favour of the Council bearing a warrant for execution issued by the sheriff court of any sheriffdom in Scotland.".

(4) After section 54 (appeals from decisions of Tribunal), insert—

"Appeals from decisions of Tribunal: unsatisfactory professional conduct

54A.—(1) A solicitor in respect of whom a decision has been made by the Tribunal under section 53ZB(1), (2), (3) or (4) may, before the expiry of the period of 21 days beginning with the day on which the decision is intimated to him, appeal to the Court against the decision.

(2) A complainer may, before the expiry of the period of 21 days beginning with the day on which a decision by the Tribunal under section 53ZB to which this subsection applies is intimated to him, appeal to the Court against the decision.

(3) Subsection (2) applies to the following decisions of the Tribunal under section 53ZB—

(a) a decision under subsection (1)(a) quashing the Council's determination upholding the complaint;

(b) a decision under subsection (1)(c) quashing or varying a direction by the Council that the solicitor pay compensation;

(c) a decision under subsection (1)(f) directing the solicitor to pay compensation;

(d) a decision under subsection (2)(b) not to direct the solicitor to pay compensation;

(e) a decision under subsection (2)(c) confirming the Council's decision not to uphold the complaint;

(f) a decision under subsection (3) confirming the Council's decision not to direct the solicitor to pay compensation;

(g) a decision under subsection (4) quashing the Council's direction that the solicitor pay compensation or varying the amount of compensation directed to be paid.

(4) On an appeal under subsection (1) or (2), the Court may give such directions in the matter as it thinks fit, including directions as to the expenses of the proceedings before the Court and as to any order by the Tribunal relating to expenses.

(5) A decision of the Court under subsection (4) shall be final.

(6) In this section, "complainer" has the same meaning as in section 42ZA.".

(5) After section 55 (powers of Court), insert—

"Powers of Court: unsatisfactory professional conduct

55A.—(1) In the case of unsatisfactory professional conduct by a solicitor the Court may—

(a) fine the solicitor an amount not exceeding £2000;

(b) where it considers that the complainer has been directly affected by the conduct, direct the solicitor to pay compensation of such amount, not exceeding £5,000, as it may specify to the complainer for loss, inconvenience or distress resulting from the conduct;

(c) find the solicitor liable in any expenses which may be involved in the proceedings before it.

(2) A decision of the Court under subsection (1) shall be final.

(3) The Scottish Ministers may by order made by statutory instrument—

(a) amend subsection (1)(a) by substituting for the amount for the time being specified in that subsection such other amount as appears to them to be justified by a change in the value of money;

(b) after consulting the Council and such groups of persons representing consumer interests as they consider appropriate, amend subsection (1)(b) by substituting for the amount for the time being specified in that subsection such other amount as they consider appropriate.

(4) A statutory instrument containing an order under—

(a) subsection (3)(a) is subject to annulment in pursuance of a resolution of the Scottish Parliament;

(b) subsection (3)(b) is not to be made unless a draft of the instrument has been laid before, and approved by resolution of, the Scottish Parliament.

(5) In this section, "complainer" has the same meaning as in section 42ZA.".

(6) In section 65(1) (interpretation), after the definition of "unqualified person" insert ";

"unsatisfactory professional conduct" as respects a solicitor has the meaning given (as respects a practitioner who is a solicitor) by section 46 of the 2007 Act".

Unsatisfactory professional conduct: conveyancing or executry practitioners

54.—(1) The 1990 Act is amended as follows.

(2) After section 20 (professional misconduct etc. by conveyancing or executry practitioners), insert—

"Remission of complaint by Tribunal to Council

20ZA.—(1) Where, after holding an inquiry under section 20(2A) into a complaint of professional misconduct against a practitioner, the Tribunal—

(a) are not satisfied that he has been guilty of professional misconduct;

(b) consider that he may be guilty of unsatisfactory professional conduct,

they must remit the complaint to the Council.

(2) Where the Tribunal remit a complaint to the Council under subsection (1), they may make available to the Council any of their findings in fact in their inquiry into the complaint under section 20(2A).

Unsatisfactory professional conduct

20ZB.—(1) Where a conduct complaint suggesting unsatisfactory professional conduct by a practitioner is remitted to the Council under section 6(a) or 15(5)(a) of the 2007 Act, the Council must having—

(a) investigated the complaint under section 47(1) of that Act and made a written report under section 47(2) of that Act;

(b) given the practitioner an opportunity to make representations,

determine the complaint.

(2) Where a complaint is remitted to the Council under section 20ZA, the Council—

(a) must—

(i) notify the practitioner specified in it and the complainer of that fact and that the Council are required to investigate the complaint as a complaint of unsatisfactory professional conduct;

(ii) so investigate the complaint;

(iii) having so investigated the complaint and given the practitioner an opportunity to make representations, determine the complaint;

(b) may rely, in their investigation, on any findings in fact which the Tribunal make available to them under section 20ZA(2) as respects the complaint.

(3) Where the Council make a determination under subsection (1) or (2) upholding the complaint, they—

(a) shall censure the practitioner;

(b) may take any of the steps mentioned in subsection (4) which they consider appropriate.

(4) The steps are—

(a) where the Council consider that the practitioner does not have sufficient competence in relation to any aspect of conveyancing law or legal practice or, as the case may be, executry law or legal practice, to direct him to undertake such education or training as regards the law or legal practice concerned as the Council consider appropriate in that respect;

(b) subject to subsection (6) below, to direct the practitioner to pay a fine not exceeding £2,000;

(c) where the Council consider that the complainer has been directly affected by the conduct, to direct the practitioner to pay compensation of such amount, not exceeding £5,000, as they may specify to the complainer for loss, inconvenience or distress resulting from the conduct.

(5) The Council may, in considering the complaint, take account of any previous determination by them, the Tribunal or the court upholding a complaint against the practitioner of unsatisfactory professional conduct or professional misconduct (but not a complaint in respect of which an appeal is pending or which has been quashed ultimately on appeal).

(6) The Council shall not direct the practitioner to pay a fine under subsection (4)(b) above where, in relation to the subject matter of the complaint, he has been convicted by any court of an offence involving dishonesty and sentenced to a term of imprisonment of not less than 2 years.

(7) Any fine directed to be paid under subsection (4)(b) above shall be treated for the purposes of section 211(5) of the Criminal Procedure (Scotland) Act 1995 (fines payable to HM Exchequer) as if it were a fine imposed in the High Court.

(8) The Council shall intimate—

(a) a determination under subsection (1) or (2);

(b) any censure under subsection (3)(a);

(c) any direction under subsection (4),

to the complainer and the practitioner by sending to each of them a copy of the determination, the censure or, as the case may be, the direction and by specifying the reasons for the determination.

(9) A practitioner in respect of whom a determination upholding a conduct complaint has been made under subsection (1) or (2), or a direction has been made under subsection (4) may, before the expiry of the period of 21 days beginning with the day on which the determination or, as the case may be, the direction is intimated to him, appeal to the Tribunal against the—

(a) determination;

(b) direction (whether or not he is appealing against the determination).

(10) A complainer may, before the expiry of the period of 21 days beginning with the day on which a determination under subsection (1) or (2) not upholding the conduct complaint is intimated to him, appeal to the Tribunal against the determination.

(11) Where the Council have upheld the conduct complaint but have not directed the practitioner under subsection (4)(c) to pay compensation, the complainer may, before the expiry of the period of 21 days beginning with the day on which the determination upholding the complaint is intimated to him, appeal to the Tribunal against the Council's decision not to make a direction under that subsection.

(12) A complainer to whom the Council have directed a practitioner under subsection (4)(c) to pay compensation may, before the expiry of the period of 21 days beginning with the day on which the direction under that subsection is intimated to him, appeal to the Tribunal against the amount of the compensation directed to be paid.

(13) The Scottish Ministers may by order made by statutory instrument—

(a) amend subsection (4)(b) by substituting for the amount for the time being specified in that subsection such other amount as appears to them to be justified by a change in the value of money;

(b) after consulting the Council and such groups of persons representing consumer interests as they consider appropriate, amend subsection (4)(c) by substituting for the amount for the time being specified in that subsection such other amount as they consider appropriate.

(14) A statutory instrument containing an order under—

(a) subsection (13)(a) is subject to annulment in pursuance of a resolution of the Scottish Parliament;

(b) subsection (13)(b) is not to be made unless a draft of the instrument has been laid before, and approved by resolution of, the Scottish Parliament.

Unsatisfactory professional conduct: Council's powers to monitor compliance with direction under section 20ZB(4)

20ZC.—(1) The Council shall, by notice in writing, require every practitioner who is specified in—

(a) a direction made under section 20ZB(4); or

(b) such a direction as confirmed or varied on appeal by—

(i) the Tribunal; or

(ii) the court,

to give, before the expiry of such period being not less than 21 days as the notice specifies, an explanation of the steps which he has taken to comply with the direction.

(2) Where an appeal is made under section 20ZB(9) or (12) or 20D(1) or (2) against a direction made under section 20ZB(4), any notice under subsection (1) above relating to the direction shall cease to have effect pending the outcome of the appeal.".

(3) After section 20A (review by Council of certain of their decisions), insert—

"Unsatisfactory professional conduct: powers of Tribunal on appeal

20B.—(1) On an appeal to the Tribunal under section 20ZB(9) the Tribunal—

(a) may quash or confirm the determination being appealed against;

(b) if they quash the determination, shall quash the censure accompanying the determination;

(c) may quash, confirm or vary the direction being appealed against;

(d) may, where they consider that the practitioner does not have sufficient competence in relation to any aspect of conveyancing law or legal practice or, as the case may be, executry law or legal practice, direct him to undertake such education or training as regards the law or legal practice concerned as the Tribunal consider appropriate in that respect;

(e) may, subject to subsection (5), fine the practitioner an amount not exceeding £2000;

(f) may, where they consider that the complainer has been directly affected by the conduct, direct the practitioner to pay compensation of such amount, not exceeding £5,000, as they may specify to the complainer for loss, inconvenience or distress resulting from the conduct.

(2) On an appeal to the Tribunal under section 20ZB(10) the Tribunal—

(a) may quash the determination being appealed against and make a determination upholding the complaint;

(b) if they do so, may, where they consider that the complainer has been directly affected by the conduct, direct the practitioner to pay compensation of such amount, not exceeding £5,000, as they may specify to the complainer for loss, inconvenience or distress resulting from the conduct;

(c) may confirm the determination.

(3) On an appeal to the Tribunal under section 20ZB(11) the Tribunal may, where they consider that the complainer has been directly affected by the conduct, direct the practitioner to pay compensation of such amount, not exceeding £5,000, as they may specify to the complainer for loss, inconvenience or distress resulting from the conduct.

(4) On an appeal under section 20ZB(12) the Tribunal may quash, confirm or vary the direction being appealed against.

(5) The Tribunal shall not direct the practitioner to pay a fine under subsection (1)(e) where, in relation to the subject matter of the complaint, he has been convicted by any court of an offence involving dishonesty and sentenced to a term of imprisonment of not less than 2 years.

(6) Any fine directed to be paid under subsection (1)(e) shall be treated for the purposes of section 211(5) of the Criminal Procedure (Scotland) Act 1995 (fines payable to HM Exchequer) as if it were a fine imposed in the High Court.

(7) A direction of the Tribunal under this section is enforceable in like manner as an extract registered decree arbitral in favour of the Council bearing a warrant for execution issued by the sheriff court of any sheriffdom in Scotland.

(8) The Scottish Ministers may by order made by statutory instrument—

(a) amend subsection (1)(e) by substituting for the amount for the time being specified in that subsection such other amount as appears to them to be justified by a change in the value of money;

(b) after consulting the Council and such groups of persons representing consumer interests as they consider appropriate, amend subsection (1)(f) by substituting for the amount for the time being specified in that subsection such other amount as they consider appropriate.

(9) A statutory instrument containing an order under—

(a) subsection (8)(a) is subject to annulment in pursuance of a resolution of the Scottish Parliament;

(b) subsection (8)(b) is not to be made unless a draft of the instrument has been laid before, and approved by resolution of, the Scottish Parliament.

Unsatisfactory professional conduct: enforcement of Council direction

20C. Where a practitioner fails to comply with a direction given by the Council under section 20ZB(4) (including such a direction as confirmed or varied on appeal by the Tribunal or, as the case may be, the court) before the expiry of the period specified in the notice relating to that direction given to the practitioner under section 20ZC(1), or such longer period as the Council may allow, the direction shall be enforceable in like manner as an extract registered decree arbitral in favour of the Council bearing a warrant for execution issued by the sheriff court of any sheriffdom in Scotland.

Unsatisfactory professional conduct: appeal from decisions of Tribunal

20D.—(1) A practitioner in respect of whom a decision has been made by the Tribunal under section 20B(1), (2), (3) or (4) may, before the expiry of the period of 21 days beginning with the day on which the decision is intimated to him, appeal to the court against the decision.

(2) A complainer may, before the expiry of the period of 21 days beginning with the day on which a decision by the Tribunal under section 20B to which this subsection applies is intimated to him, appeal to the court against the decision.

(3) Subsection (2) applies to the following decisions of the Tribunal under section 20B—

(a) a decision under subsection (1)(a) quashing the Council's determination upholding the complaint;

(b) a decision under subsection (1)(c) quashing or varying a direction by the Council that the practitioner pay compensation;

(c) a decision under subsection (1)(f) directing the practitioner to pay compensation;

(d) a decision under subsection (2)(b) not to direct the practitioner to pay compensation;

(e) a decision under subsection (2)(c) confirming the Council's decision not to uphold the complaint;

(f) a decision under subsection (3) confirming the Council's decision not to direct the practitioner to pay compensation;

(g) a decision under subsection (4) quashing the Council's direction that the practitioner pay compensation or varying the amount of compensation directed to be paid.

(4) On an appeal under subsection (1) or (2), the court may give such directions in the matter as it thinks fit, including directions as to the expenses of the proceedings before the court and as to any order by the Tribunal relating to expenses.

(5) A decision of the court under subsection (4) shall be final.

Unsatisfactory professional conduct: powers of court on appeal

20E.—(1) On an appeal under section 20D, the court may—

(a) fine the practitioner an amount not exceeding £2000;

(b) where it considers that the complainer has been directly affected by the conduct, direct the practitioner to pay compensation of such amount, not exceeding £5,000, as it may specify to the complainer for loss, inconvenience or distress resulting from the conduct;

(c) find the practitioner liable in any expenses which may be involved in the proceedings before it.

(2) A decision of the court under subsection (1) shall be final.

(3) The Scottish Ministers may by order made by statutory instrument—

(a) amend subsection (1)(a) by substituting for the amount for the time being specified in that subsection such other amount as appears to them to be justified by a change in the value of money;

(b) after consulting the Council and such groups of persons representing consumer interests as they consider appropriate, amend subsection (1)(b) by substituting for the amount for the time being specified in that subsection such other amount as they consider appropriate.

(4) A statutory instrument containing an order under—

(a) subsection (3)(a) is subject to annulment in pursuance of a resolution of the Scottish Parliament;

(b) subsection (3)(b) is not to be made unless a draft of the instrument has been laid before, and approved by resolution of, the Scottish Parliament.".

Report by Commission to Council under section 10(2)(e)

55.—(1) After section 42ZB of the 1980 Act (as inserted by section 53(2) of this Act), insert—

"Report by Commission to Council under section 10(2)(e) of the 2007 Act: Council's powers

42ZC.—(1) Where the Council receive a report from the Commission under section 10(2)(e) of the 2007 Act as respects a practitioner who is a solicitor, they may direct him to undertake such education or training as regards the law or legal practice as the Council consider appropriate in the circumstances.

(2) The Council shall by notice in writing—

(a) intimate a direction under subsection (1) to the solicitor;

(b) require the solicitor to give, before the expiry of such period being not less than 21 days as the notice specifies, an explanation of the steps which he has taken to comply with the direction.

(3) Where an appeal is made under section 42ZD(1) or (3) against a direction under subsection (1), any notice under subsection (2)(b) relating to the direction shall cease to have effect pending the outcome of the appeal.

Direction under section 42ZC(2): appeal by practitioner

42ZD.—(1) A solicitor in respect of whom a direction has been made under section 42ZC(1) may, before the expiry of the period of 21 days beginning with the day on which it is intimated to him, appeal to the Tribunal against the direction.

(2) On an appeal to the Tribunal under subsection (1), the Tribunal may quash, confirm or vary the direction being appealed against.

(3) The solicitor may, before the expiry of the period of 21 days beginning with the day on which the Tribunal's decision under subsection (2) is intimated to him, appeal to the Court against the decision.

(4) On an appeal to the Court under subsection (3), the Court may give such directions in the matter as it thinks fit, including directions as to the expenses of the proceedings before the Court and as to any order by the Tribunal relating to expenses.

(5) A decision of the Court on an appeal under subsection (3) shall be final.".

(2) After section 20ZC of the 1990 Act (as inserted by section 54(2) of this Act), insert—

"Report by Commission to Council under section 10(2)(e) of the 2007 Act: Council's powers

20ZD.—(1) Where the Council receive a report from the Commission under section 10(2)(e) of the 2007 Act as respects a practitioner, they may direct him to undertake such education or training as regards conveyancing law or legal practice or, as the case may be, executry law or legal practice as they consider appropriate in the circumstances.

(2) The Council shall by notice in writing—

(a) intimate a direction under subsection (1) to the practitioner;

(b) require the practitioner to give, before the expiry of such period being not less than 21 days as the notice specifies, an explanation of the steps which he has taken to comply with the direction.

(3) Where an appeal is made under section 20ZE(1) or (3) against a direction under subsection (1), any notice under subsection (2)(b) relating to the direction shall cease to have effect pending the outcome of the appeal.

Direction under section 20ZD(1): appeal by practitioner

20ZE.—(1) A practitioner in respect of whom a direction has been made under section 20ZD(1) may, before the expiry of the period of 21 days beginning with the day on which it is intimated to him, appeal to the Tribunal against the direction.

(2) On an appeal to the Tribunal under subsection (1), the Tribunal may quash, confirm or vary the direction being appealed against.

(3) The practitioner may, before the expiry of the period of 21 days beginning with the day on which the Tribunal's decision under subsection (2) is intimated to him, appeal to the court against the decision.

(4) On an appeal to the court under subsection (3), the court may give such directions in the matter as it thinks fit, including directions as to the expenses of the proceedings before the court and as to any order by the Tribunal relating to expenses.

(5) A decision of the court on an appeal under subsection (3) shall be final.".

Powers to fine and award compensation for professional misconduct etc.

56.—(1) In section 53 of the 1980 Act (powers of Tribunal)—

(a) in subsection (2), after paragraph (ba) insert—

"(bb) where the solicitor has been guilty of professional misconduct, and where the Tribunal consider that the complainer has been directly affected by the misconduct, direct the solicitor to pay compensation of such amount, not exceeding £5,000, as the Tribunal may specify to the complainer for loss, inconvenience or distress resulting from the misconduct;";

(b) after subsection (7B) (as inserted by paragraph 1(19)(b) of schedule 5 to this Act), insert—

"(7C) The Scottish Ministers may by order made by statutory instrument, after consulting the Council and such groups of persons representing consumer interests as they consider appropriate, amend paragraph (bb) of subsection (2) by substituting for the amount for the time being specified in that paragraph such other amount as they consider appropriate.

(7D) A statutory instrument containing an order under subsection (7C) is not to be made unless a draft of the instrument has been laid before, and approved by resolution of, the Scottish Parliament.";

(c) after subsection (8), insert—

"(9) In subsection (2)(bb), "complainer" has the same meaning as in section 42ZA.".

(2) In section 55 of the 1980 Act (powers of Court)—

(a) in subsection (1)—

(i) after paragraph (bb), insert—

"(bc) where the Court considers that the complainer has been directly affected by the misconduct, direct the solicitor to pay compensation of such amount, not exceeding £5,000, as it may specify to the complainer for loss, inconvenience or distress resulting from the misconduct; or";

(ii) in paragraph (c), after "solicitor" insert "an amount not exceeding £10,000";

(b) after subsection (4) insert—

"(5) The Scottish Ministers may by order made by statutory instrument—

(a) after consulting the Council and such groups of persons representing consumer interests as they consider appropriate, amend paragraph (bc) of subsection (1) by substituting for the amount for the time being specified in that paragraph such other amount as they consider appropriate;

(b) amend paragraph (c) of subsection (1) by substituting for the amount for the time being specified in that subsection such other amount as appears to them to be justified by a change in the value of money.

(6) A statutory instrument containing an order under—

(a) subsection (5)(a) is not to be made unless a draft of the instrument has been laid before, and approved by resolution of, the Scottish Parliament;

(b) subsection (5)(b) is subject to annulment in pursuance of a resolution of the Scottish Parliament.

(7) In this section, "complainer" has the same meaning as in section 42ZA."

(3) In section 20 of the 1990 Act (professional misconduct, etc.)—

(a) in subsection (2), after paragraph (c) insert—

"(ca) where the Council consider that the complainer has been directly affected by the professional misconduct or, as the case may be, the matter referred to in paragraph (d) of subsection (1), to direct the practitioner to pay compensation of such amount, not exceeding £5,000, as the Council may specify to the complainer for loss, inconvenience or distress resulting from the misconduct or, as the case may be, the matter;

(cb) subject to subsection (2ZA) below, to impose on the practitioner a fine not exceeding £2,000;";

(b) after that subsection, insert—

"(2ZA) The Council shall not impose a fine under subsection (2)(cb) above where, in relation to the subject matter of the complaint, the practitioner has been convicted by any court of an offence involving dishonesty and sentenced to a term of imprisonment of not less than 2 years.

(2ZB) Any fine imposed under subsection (2)(cb) above shall be treated for the purposes of section 211(5) of the Criminal Procedure (Scotland) Act 1995 (fines payable to HM Exchequer) as if it were a fine imposed in the High Court.";

(c) in subsection (2B), after paragraph (a) insert—

"(aa) where the practitioner has been guilty of professional misconduct, and where the Tribunal consider that the complainer has been directly affected by the misconduct, to direct the practitioner to pay compensation of such amount, not exceeding £5,000, as the Tribunal may specify to the complainer for loss, inconvenience or distress resulting from the misconduct;";

(d) after subsection (11F) (as inserted by paragraph 3(4)(k) of schedule 5 to this Act), insert—

"(11G) The Scottish Ministers may by order made by statutory instrument, after consulting the Council and such groups of persons representing consumer interests as they consider appropriate, amend subsection (2)(ca) or (2B)(aa) by substituting for the amount for the time being specified in that provision such other amount as they consider appropriate.

(11H) A statutory instrument containing an order under subsection (11G) is not to be made unless a draft of the instrument has been laid before, and approved by resolution of, the Scottish Parliament.".

Review of and appeal against decisions on remitted conduct complaints: cases other than unsatisfactory professional conduct

57.—(1) In section 54 of the 1980 Act (appeals from decisions of Tribunal in cases other than unsatisfactory professional conduct)—

(a) after subsection (1), insert—

"(1A) A solicitor or an incorporated practice may, before the expiry of the period of 21 days beginning with the day on which any decision by the Tribunal mentioned in subsection (1B) is intimated to him or, as the case may be, it appeal to the Court against the decision.

(1B) The decision is—

(a) where the Tribunal was satisfied as mentioned in section 53(1)(a), the finding that the solicitor has been guilty of professional misconduct;

(b) where the Tribunal was satisfied as mentioned in section 53(1)(d), the finding that the incorporated practice has failed to comply with any provision of this Act or of any rule made under this Act applicable to the practice;

(c) in any case falling within paragraph (a) or (b), or where the decision was made because of the circumstances mentioned in section 53(1)(b) or (c), any decision under section 53(2) or (5).

(1C) The Council may, before the expiry of the period of 21 days beginning with the day on which a decision by the Tribunal under section 53(2) or (5) is intimated to them, appeal to the Court against the decision; but the Council may not appeal to the Court against a decision of the Tribunal under section 53(2)(bb).

(1D) Where the Tribunal has found that a solicitor has been guilty of professional misconduct but has not directed him under section 53(2)(bb) to pay compensation, the complainer may, before the expiry of the period of 21 days beginning with the day on which the Tribunal's finding is intimated to him, appeal to the Court against the decision of the Tribunal not to make a direction under that subsection.

(1E) A complainer to whom the Tribunal has directed a solicitor under section 53(2)(bb) to pay compensation may, before the expiry of the period of 21 days beginning with the day on which the direction under that subsection is intimated to him, appeal to the Court against the amount of the compensation directed to be paid.

(1F) On an appeal under any of subsections (1A) to (1E), the Court may give such directions in the matter as it thinks fit, including directions as to the expenses of the proceedings before the Court and as to any order by the Tribunal relating to expenses.

(1G) A decision of the Court under subsection (1A), (1B), (1C), (1D), (1E) or (1F) shall be final.";

(b) in subsection (2), after paragraph (b) insert ";

(c) the Tribunal has exercised the power conferred by section 53(6B) to direct that its order shall take effect on the day on which it is intimated to the solicitor, firm of solicitors or incorporated practice concerned, the solicitor, firm of solicitors or incorporated practice may, before the expiry of the period of 21 days beginning with that day, apply to the court for an order varying or quashing the direction in so far as it relates to the day on which the order takes effect";

(c) after that subsection, insert—

"(2A) In subsections (1D) and (1E), "complainer" has the same meaning as in section 42ZA.

(2B) Subsection (1) does not apply to any element of a decision of the Tribunal to which subsections (1A) to (1G) and paragraph (c) of subsection (2) apply.

(2C) Subsections (1A) to (1G), and paragraph (c) of subsection (2), apply to any element of a decision of the Tribunal which does not relate to the provision of advice, services or activities referred to in section 77(2) of the 2007 Act.".

(2) In section 20 of the 1990 Act (professional misconduct etc. by conveyancing or executry practitioners)—

(a) after subsection (8), insert—

"(8A) Where the Council are satisfied that a practitioner is guilty of professional misconduct or that the circumstances referred to in subsection (1)(d) apply as respects a practitioner, the practitioner may—

(a) before the expiry of the period of 21 days beginning with the day on which the finding by the Council to that effect is intimated to him, apply to the Council for a review by them of the finding;

(b) before the expiry of the period of 21 days beginning with the day on which the outcome of the review is intimated to him, appeal to the Tribunal against the decision of the Council in the review; and the Tribunal may quash or confirm the decision.";

(b) after subsection (11), insert—

"(11ZA) Where the Council find that a practitioner is guilty of professional misconduct or that the circumstances referred to in subsection (1)(d) apply as respects a practitioner but do not direct him under subsection (2)(ca) to pay compensation, the complainer may, before the expiry of the period of 21 days beginning with the day on which the Council's finding is intimated to him, apply to the Council for a review by them of their decision not to direct the practitioner under subsection (2)(ca) to pay compensation.

(11ZB) A complainer to whom the Council have directed a practitioner under subsection (2)(ca) to pay compensation may, before the expiry of the period of 21 days beginning with the day on which the direction under that subsection is intimated to him, apply to the Council for a review by them of the direction.

(11ZC) The complainer may, before the expiry of the period of 21 days beginning with the day on which the outcome of the review under subsection (11ZA) or (11ZB) is intimated to him, appeal to the Tribunal against the decision of the Council in the review; and the Tribunal may quash, confirm or vary the decision.";

(c) in subsection (11A)—
   (i) in paragraph (a), after "subsection" insert "(8A)(b) or";
   (ii) after that paragraph, insert—
      "(aa) a finding by the Tribunal that a practitioner is guilty of professional misconduct or that the circumstances mentioned in subsection (1)(d) apply as respects the practitioner; or";
   (iii) for the words "or, as the case may be," substitute "the finding referred to in paragraph (aa) or, as the case may be, the decision";

(d) after that subsection, insert—

"(11B) The complainer may, before the expiry of the period of 21 days beginning with the day on which the outcome of any appeal under subsection (11ZC) is intimated to him, appeal to the court against the Tribunal's decision in the appeal.

(11C) Where after holding an inquiry into a complaint against a practitioner, the Tribunal find that he has been guilty of professional misconduct or that the circumstances referred to in subsection (2A)(b) apply as respects him, but do not direct the practitioner under subsection (2B)(aa) to pay compensation, the complainer may, before the expiry of the period of 21 days beginning with the day on which the Tribunal's finding is intimated to him, appeal to the court against the decision of the Tribunal not to make a direction under that subsection.

(11D) A complainer to whom the Tribunal have directed a practitioner under subsection (2B)(aa) to pay compensation may, before the expiry of the period of 21 days beginning with the day on which the direction under that subsection is intimated to him, appeal to the court against the amount of the compensation directed to be paid.

(11E) In an appeal under subsection (11C) or (11D), the court may make such order in the matter as it thinks fit.".

PART 3

LEGAL PROFESSION: OTHER MATTERS

Constitution of Scottish Solicitors' Discipline Tribunal

58.—(1) Schedule 4 to the 1980 Act is amended as follows.

(2) For paragraph 1 substitute—

"**1.** The Tribunal shall consist of not more than 28 members.

1A. The Tribunal shall consist of equal numbers of—

(a) members (in this Part referred to as "solicitor members") appointed by the Lord President, who are solicitors recommended by the Council as representatives of the solicitors' profession throughout Scotland; and

(b) members (in this Part referred to as "non-lawyer members") appointed by the Lord President after consultation with the Scottish Ministers, who are not—
   (i) solicitors;
   (ii) advocates;
   (iii) conveyancing practitioners or executry practitioners, within the meaning of section 23 of the Law Reform (Miscellaneous Provisions) (Scotland) Act 1990 (c.40) ("the 1990 Act");
   (iv) persons exercising a right to conduct litigation or a right of audience acquired by virtue of section 27 of the 1990 Act.

1B. The validity of any proceedings of the Tribunal is not affected by a vacancy in membership of the Tribunal nor by any defect in the appointment of a member.

1C. The Scottish Ministers may by order made by statutory instrument amend paragraph 1 so as to vary the maximum number of members of the Tribunal.

1D. A statutory instrument containing an order made under paragraph 1C is subject to annulment in pursuance of a resolution of the Scottish Parliament.".

(3) In paragraph 2(a), for "lay" substitute "non-lawyer".

(4) In paragraph 3, for "lay" substitute "non-lawyer".

(5) In paragraph 5—

(a) in sub-paragraph (b), for "1 lay member is" substitute "2 solicitor members are";

(b) for sub-paragraph (c) substitute—

"(c) at least 2 non-lawyer members are present.";

(c) sub-paragraph (d) is repealed.

(6) In paragraph 6, for "lay" substitute "non-lawyer".

Scottish Solicitors Guarantee Fund: borrowing limit

59. In paragraph 2(2) of Schedule 3 (Scottish Solicitors Guarantee Fund) to the 1980 Act, for "£20,000" substitute "£1,250,000".

Safeguarding interests of clients

60.—(1) The 1980 Act is amended as follows.

(2) In section 45 (safeguarding interests of clients of solicitors struck off or suspended)—

(a) after subsection (4), insert—

"(4A) Where—

(a) a solicitor is restricted from acting as a principal; and

(b) immediately before the restriction the solicitor was a sole solicitor,

the right to operate on, or otherwise deal with, any client account in the name of the solicitor or the solicitor's firm shall on the occurrence of those circumstances vest in the Society (notwithstanding any enactment or rule of law to the contrary) to the exclusion of any other person until such time as the Council have approved acceptable other arrangements in respect of the client account.";

(b) in subsection (5), after the definition of "material date", insert—

" "principal" means a solicitor who is a sole practitioner or is a partner in a firm of two or more solicitors or is a director of an incorporated practice which is a company or a solicitor who is a member of a multi-national practice having its principal place of business in Scotland;".

Offence for unqualified persons to prepare certain documents

61. In section 32(2) of the 1980 Act (offence for unqualified persons to prepare certain documents), after paragraph (e) add "; or

(f) to a member of a body which has made a successful application under section 25 of the 1990 Act but only to the extent to which the member is exercising rights acquired by virtue of section 27 of that Act".

Notaries public to be practising solicitors

62.—(1) The 1980 Act is amended as follows.

(2) In section 57(2), after "solicitor" insert "qualified to practise in accordance with section 4".

(3) In section 58, after subsection (4) insert—

"(5) Where a person who is a solicitor and a notary public no longer has in force a practising certificate, the Council shall forthwith remove the person's name from the register of notaries public.

(6) If the person mentioned in subsection (5) becomes qualified to practise as a solicitor in accordance with section 4, the Council shall restore the person's name to the register of notaries public.".

Regulation of notaries public

63. After section 59 of the 1980 Act, insert—

"59A Rules regarding notaries public

(1) Subject to subsections (2) and (3), the Council may, if they think fit, make rules for regulating in respect of any matter the admission, enrolment and professional practice of notaries public.

(2) The Council shall, before making any rules under this section—

(a) send to each notary public a draft of the rules; and

(b) take into consideration any representations made by any notary public on the draft.

(3) Rules made under this section shall not have effect unless the Lord President, after considering any representations the Lord President thinks relevant, has approved the rules so made.

(4) If a notary public fails to comply with any rule made under this section that failure may be treated as professional misconduct or unsatisfactory professional conduct on the part of the solicitor who is the notary public.".

PART 4

LEGAL AID

Criminal legal aid in solemn proceedings

64.—(1) The 1986 Act is amended as follows.

(2) In section 22(1)(b)(i) (automatic availability of criminal legal aid), for "23(1)(a)" substitute "23A(1)".

(3) In section 23 (power of the court to grant legal aid)—

(a) paragraph (a) of subsection (1); and

(b) paragraph (a) of subsection (2),

are repealed.

(4) After that section, insert—

"Legal aid in solemn proceedings

23A.—(1) Criminal legal aid shall be available on an application made to the Board, where a person is being prosecuted under solemn procedure, if the Board is satisfied after consideration of the person's financial circumstances that the expenses of the case cannot be met without undue hardship to the person or the person's dependants.

(2) Legal aid made available to a person under subsection (1) may be subject to such conditions as the Board considers expedient; and such conditions may be imposed at any time.

(3) The Board may require a person receiving legal aid under subsection (1) to comply with such conditions as it considers expedient to enable it to satisfy itself from time to time that it is reasonable for him to continue to receive criminal legal aid.

(4) The Board shall establish a procedure under which any person whose application for legal aid under subsection (1) has been refused may apply to the Board for a review of the application.

(5) The Board shall establish a procedure under which any person receiving criminal legal aid under subsection (1) which is subject to conditions by virtue of subsection (2) may apply to the Board for a review of any such condition.".

(5) In section 25(4) (legal aid in appeals), after "23" insert ", 23A".

(6) In section 25AB(4) (legal aid in references, appeals or applications for special leave to appeal to the Judicial Committee or the Privy Council), after "23" insert ", 23A".

(7) In section 30(3)(a) (legal aid in contempt proceedings), after "23" insert ", 23A".

Criminal legal aid: conditions and reviews

65.—(1) Section 24 (legal aid in summary proceedings) of the 1986 Act is amended in accordance with subsections (2) to (6) of this section.

(2) In subsection (1), for "subsection" substitute "subsections (1A), (2) and".

(3) After subsection (1) insert—

"(1A) Legal aid made available to a person under subsection (1) may be subject to such conditions as the Board considers expedient; and such conditions may be imposed at any time.".

(4) In subsection (2), after "that" insert

"—

(a) after consideration of the financial circumstances of the person, the expenses of the case cannot be met without undue hardship to him or his dependants;

(b) ".

(5) After subsection (5) insert—

"(5A) The Board shall establish a procedure under which any person receiving criminal legal aid under this section which is subject to conditions by virtue of subsection (1A) may apply to the Board for a review of any such condition.".

(6) In subsection (6)—

(a) the word "has either" is repealed;

(b) at the beginning of paragraph (a) insert "has";

(c) at the end of paragraph (a) "or" is repealed;

(d) at the beginning of paragraph (b) insert "has";

(e) at the end of paragraph (b) insert "; or

(c) is no longer receiving criminal legal aid in connection with proceedings because the Board is no longer satisfied as to the matters mentioned in paragraphs (a) and (b) of subsection (1)".

(7) Section 25 (legal aid in appeals) of the 1986 Act is amended in accordance with subsections (8) and (9) of this section.

(8) After subsection (2A) insert—

"(2B) Where a person is no longer receiving criminal legal aid because the Board is no longer satisfied as mentioned in subsection (2)(c) above the High Court may, at any time prior to the disposal of the appeal, whether or not on application made to it, notwithstanding the Board no longer being so satisfied, determine that it is in the interests of justice that the person should receive criminal legal aid in connection with the appeal, and the Board shall forthwith make such legal aid available to him.

(2C) Legal aid made available to a person under subsection (2) may be subject to such conditions as the Board considers expedient; and such conditions may be imposed at any time.".

(9) After subsection (3) insert—

"(3A) The Board shall establish a procedure under which any person whose application for criminal legal aid under subsection (2) has been refused may apply to the Board for a review of his application.

(3B) The Board shall establish a procedure under which any person receiving criminal legal aid under subsection (2) which is subject to conditions by virtue of subsection (2C) may apply to the Board for a review of any such condition.".

(10) Section 25AB (legal aid in references, appeals or applications for special leave to appeal to the Judicial Committee of the Privy Council) is amended in accordance with subsections (11) and (12) of this section.

(11) After subsection (2) insert—

"(2A) Legal aid made available to a person under subsection (2) may be subject to such conditions as the Board considers expedient; and such conditions may be imposed at any time.".

(12) After subsection (3) insert—

"(3A) The Board shall establish a procedure under which any person whose application for criminal legal aid under subsection (2) has been refused may apply to the Board for a review of his application.

(3B) The Board shall establish a procedure under which any person receiving criminal legal aid under this section which is subject to conditions by virtue of subsection (2A) may apply to the Board for a review of any such condition.".

Criminal Legal Assistance Register: removal of name following failure to comply with code

66.—(1) Section 25D (removal of name from Register following failure to comply with code) of the 1986 Act is amended as follows.

(2) In subsection (1), after "be" insert ", or may not have been,".

(3) After subsection (4), insert—

"(4A) Where, after carrying out the procedures mentioned in subsection (1) above and, where a time limit has been set under subsection (3) above, after the expiry of that time limit, the Board is satisfied that, regardless of whether or not there is current compliance with the code—

(a) the firm have not complied with the code in a material regard, it may remove the names of the firm and, subject to subsection (5) below, of any registered solicitors connected with the firm from the Register;

(b) the solicitor has not complied with the code in a material regard, it may remove his name from the Register.".

(4) In subsection (5), after "(4)(a)" insert "or (4A)(a)".

(5) In subsection (8), after "(4)" insert "or (4A)".

Register of advice organisations: advice and assistance

67.—(1) The 1986 Act is amended as follows.

(2) In section 4(2)(a) (Scottish Legal Aid Fund), after "counsel" insert "or registered organisation".

(3) In section 6 (definitions)—

(a) in subsection (1)—

(i) in the definition of "advice and assistance" after paragraph (a) insert—

"(aa) oral or written advice provided by an adviser—

(i) on the application of Scots law to any specified categories of circumstances which have arisen in relation to the person seeking advice;

(ii) as to any steps which that person might appropriately take having regard to the application of Scots law to those circumstances;";

(ii) in that definition, after paragraph (b) insert—

"(c) assistance provided to a person by an adviser in taking any steps mentioned in paragraph (aa)(ii) above, by taking such steps on his behalf or by assisting him in so taking them;";

(iii) in the definition of "assistance by way of representation", after the word "means" insert ", subject to section 12B(3) of this Act,";

(b) in subsection (2), before the definition of "client" insert—

" "adviser" means a person who is approved by a registered organisation for the purposes of providing advice and assistance on behalf of the organisation and who is the person by whom advice and assistance is provided;".

(4) In section 10 (financial limit)—

(a) in subsection (1)—

(i) after the word "solicitor" where it first occurs insert "or, as the case may be, adviser";

(ii) in paragraph (a), after the word "solicitor" insert "or adviser";

(b) in subsection (3)—

(i) after paragraph (a) insert—

"(aa) any outlays which may be incurred by the registered organisation (which approved the adviser) in, or in connection with, the providing of the advice and assistance;";

(ii) after paragraph (b) insert—

"(ba) any fees (not being charges for outlays) which, apart from section 11 of this Act, would be properly chargeable by the registered organisation (which approved the adviser) in respect of the advice and assistance;".

(5) In section 12 (payments of fees or outlays otherwise than through clients' contributions)—

(a) in subsection (3), after the word "solicitor" where it first occurs insert "or, as the case may be, the registered organisation,";

(b) in paragraph (d) of that subsection, after "solicitor" insert "or the registered organisation".

(6) After section 12, insert—

"Register of advice organisations

Register of advice organisations

12A.—(1) The Board shall establish and maintain a register of advice organisations ("the register of advice organisations") of organisations approved by the Board as registered organisations in relation to the provision of advice and assistance by persons approved by such organisations as advisers.

(2) A person who—

(a) is a solicitor;

(b) is an advocate;

(c) is a conveyancing practitioner or an executry practitioner, within the meaning of section 23 of the Law Reform (Miscellaneous Provisions) (Scotland) Act 1990 (c.40);

(d) has acquired any right to conduct litigation or right of audience by virtue of section 27 of that Act,

may not be an adviser.

(3) Schedule 1A makes further provision about advisers and registered organisations, the register of advice organisations, code of practice for advisers etc.

Advice and assistance

12B.—(1) The Scottish Ministers may by regulations specify categories of circumstances for the purposes of paragraph (aa) of the definition of "advice and assistance" in section 6(1) of this Act.

(2) The power under subsection (1) may specify different categories for different purposes.

(3) In this Act—

(a) "advice and assistance" as defined in section 6(1)(c) is limited to the extent to which it is competent for the adviser to perform any steps on behalf of the person or by assisting him in so taking them;

(b) "assistance by way of representation" as defined in section 6(1) includes advice and assistance provided by an adviser but only to the extent to which it is competent for the adviser to perform such steps referred to in that definition.".

(7) In section 33 (fees and outlays of solicitors and counsel)—

(a) after subsection (1) insert—

"(1A) A registered organisation shall be paid out of the Fund in accordance with section 4(2)(a) of this Act in respect of any fees or outlays properly incurred by it in respect of the advisers it approves providing advice and assistance under this Act.";

(b) in subsection (2), after "counsel" insert "and, in respect of advice and assistance as mentioned in paragraph (b) of this subsection, advisers".

(8) In section 41 (interpretation)—

(a) after the definition of "advice and assistance" insert—

""adviser" has the meaning given to it in section 6(2) of this Act;

"adviser code" means the code of practice in relation to the register of advice organisations for the time being in force under Schedule 1A to this Act;";

(b) after the definition of "the Register" insert—

""the register of advice organisations" means the register established and maintained under section 12A of this Act;";

(c) after the definition of "registered firm" insert—

""registered organisation" means an organisation whose name appears on the register of advice organisations;".

(9) After Schedule 1 (Scottish Legal Aid Board) to the 1986 Act, insert—

"SCHEDULE 1A

FURTHER PROVISION IN RELATION TO THE REGISTER OF ADVICE ORGANISATIONS

(INTRODUCED BY SECTION 12A(3))

Register of advice organisations

1.—(1) An organisation which satisfies the Board that it complies with the relevant provisions of the adviser code shall be approved by the Board as an organisation that may approve a person to provide advice and assistance on behalf of the organisation; and the Board shall make an appropriate entry on the register of advice organisations.

(2) An individual may apply for entry on the register of advice organisations as an organisation; and if the Board is satisfied that the individual complies with the relevant provisions of the adviser code in relation to an organisation, the Board shall approve the individual and treat the individual as an organisation for the purposes of this Schedule.

(3) The Board must make the register of advice organisations available for public inspection, without charge, at all reasonable times.

(4) In this Schedule an "organisation" includes—

(a) a firm of solicitors;

(b) an incorporated practice within the meaning of section 34(1A)(c) of the Solicitors (Scotland) Act 1980 (c. 46).

Applications

2.—(1) An application for entry on the register of advice organisations shall be made in such form as the Board may determine, and shall be accompanied by such documents as the Board may specify.

(2) On receipt of an application the Board shall make such enquiries as it thinks appropriate for the purposes of determining whether the applicant complies with the relevant provisions of the adviser code.

(3) The Board may determine an application to be entered on the register of advice organisations by—

(a) granting the application; or

(b) refusing the application.

(4) Where the Board decides to refuse an application it shall as soon as practicable thereafter send the applicant, by recorded delivery, a written note of its reasons.

Further provision on applications

3.—(1) In determining any application for entry on the register of advice organisations, the Board may limit the grant of the application to any of the particular categories of circumstances as specified by virtue of section 12B(1).

(2) Where the Board limits the grant of an application as mentioned in sub-paragraph (1), the entry made on the register under paragraph 1(1) must state the categories in relation to which the organisation is registered; and any adviser approved by the organisation may provide advice and assistance under this Act only in relation to those categories.

Adviser code

4.—(1) The Board shall prepare a code of practice (an "adviser code") in relation to advisers and registered organisations.

(2) The adviser code prepared under sub-paragraph (1) must include—

(a) the conditions to be complied with in order to qualify for registration;

(b) the types of organisations eligible for registration;

(c) the conditions to be complied with in order for a person to be approved by a registered organisation as an adviser;

(d) the laying down of standards, conduct, practice and training expected in relation to—

(i) the provision of advice and assistance by advisers;

(ii) the supervision of such activity by registered organisations;

(e) arrangements for dealing with complaints about the activities of advisers and registered organisations;

(f) arrangements for monitoring the activities of advisers and registered organisations.

(3) The adviser code prepared under sub-paragraph (1) has effect on such date as the Board may confirm.

(4) But the adviser code may not have effect unless and until it has been—

(a) approved by the Scottish Ministers; and

(b) the Board has laid a copy of the prepared code before the Scottish Parliament.

(5) The Board is to publish the adviser code in such way as, in its opinion, is likely to bring it to the attention of those interested in it.

(6) The Board is to—

(a) keep the adviser code under review; and

(b) revise it where appropriate.

(7) The provisions of this paragraph apply in relation to any revision of the adviser code as they apply in relation to the version originally prepared.

(8) Registered organisations shall comply with the relevant requirements of the adviser code.

Monitoring

5. The Board is to monitor—

(a) the provision of advice and assistance and related activities by advisers;

(b) compliance with the adviser code by registered organisations.

Removal of name from the register of advice organisations

6.—(1) Where it appears to the Board (whether or not following a complaint made to it) that a registered organisation may not be, or may not have been, complying with the adviser code, it shall investigate the matter in such manner as it thinks fit.

(2) Where the Board conducts an investigation under sub-paragraph (1) it must allow the registered organisation concerned the opportunity to make representations.

(3) Following an investigation under sub-paragraph (1), the Board may give the registered organisation concerned an opportunity, within such time as it may specify, to remedy any defect in the compliance with the adviser code.

(4) Where, after carrying out the procedures mentioned in sub-paragraph (1) and, where a time limit has been set under sub-paragraph (3), after the expiry of that time limit, the Board is satisfied that the registered organisation is not complying with the adviser code, it shall remove from the register of advice organisations the name of the organisation.

(5) Where, after carrying out the procedures mentioned in sub-paragraph (1) and, where a time limit has been set under sub-paragraph (3), after the expiry of that time limit, the Board is satisfied that, regardless of whether or not there is current compliance with the code, the registered organisation has not complied with the code in a material regard, it may remove the name of the organisation from the register of advice organisations.

(6) Where the Board decides to remove the name of an organisation from the register of advice organisations in accordance with sub-paragraph (4) it shall as soon as practicable thereafter send the organisation, by recorded delivery, a written note of its reasons.

Appeals

7.—(1) A decision by the Board to refuse an application under paragraph 2(3)(b) may be appealed by the applicant to the Court of Session within 21 days of the receipt of the notification of the Board's reasons under paragraph 2(4).

(2) A decision by the Board under paragraph 6(4) or (5) to remove from the register of advice organisations the name of a registered organisation may be appealed to the Court of Session within 21 days of the receipt of the notification of the Board's reasons under paragraph 6(6); but the making of an appeal shall not have the effect of restoring the name to the register of advice organisations.

(3) An appeal under sub-paragraph (1) or (2) may be on questions of both fact and law and the court, after hearing such evidence and representations as it considers appropriate, may make such order as it thinks fit.".

Scottish Legal Aid Board: grants for certain purposes

68.—(1) The 1986 Act is amended as follows.

(2) In section 4 (Scottish Legal Aid Fund)—

(a) at the beginning of subsection (2)(a) insert "subject to section 4A(13),";

(b) after subsection (2)(ab) insert—

"(ac) such sums as are, by virtue of section 4A, due out of the Fund to any person;";

(c) after subsection (3)(ac) insert—

"(ad) any sums recovered from a person in connection with a grant made by the Board in accordance with section 4A;".

(3) After that section insert—

"Power of Board to make grants for certain purposes

4A.—(1) The Board may, on an application made to it by any person, make grants of such amount and subject to such conditions (including conditions as to repayment) as it may determine to the person in respect of—

(a) any of the matters mentioned in subsection (2);

(b) any of the purposes mentioned in subsection (3).

(2) The matters are—

(a) any civil legal aid or advice and assistance in relation to civil matters provided, or to be provided, by any solicitor or counsel;

(b) any advice and assistance in relation to civil matters provided, or to be provided, by any adviser;

(c) any advice, assistance or representation (not falling within paragraphs (a) or (b)) provided, or to be provided, by any person, which is connected to civil matters.

(3) The purposes are facilitating, supporting and developing the provision of any of the matters referred to in subsection (2).

(4) The Scottish Ministers must specify a limit to the total amount that may be paid out of the Fund by virtue of subsection (1).

(5) In specifying any limit under subsection (4) the Scottish Ministers must specify the period in relation to which that limit applies.

(6) Any grant made under subsection (1) must be made in accordance with an approved plan.

(7) The Board must prepare and publish a plan as to the criteria which the Board will apply in considering whether or not to make such a grant; and the Board must submit the plan to the Scottish Ministers for approval.

(8) The Scottish Ministers may approve a plan submitted to them under subsection (7) with or without modification.

(9) The Scottish Ministers may at any time—

(a) approve a modification of an approved plan proposed by the Board or withdraw approval of such a plan or modification;

(b) require the Board to prepare and publish a plan under subsection (7).

(10) An application under subsection (1) must include such information as the Board may reasonably require.

(11) In preparing and publishing the plan under subsection (7) the Board must do so in accordance with such directions as the Scottish Ministers may give.

(12) Any money due to a person by virtue of this section shall be paid to the person by the Board out of the Fund.

(13) Any money paid to a person under subsection (1) as provided in subsection (12), in respect of—

(a) any civil legal aid or advice and assistance provided by any solicitor or counsel;

(b) any advice and assistance provided by an adviser,

shall be taken to be a payment in accordance with this Act; and no other payment may be made out of the Fund in respect of that civil legal aid or, as the case may be, advice and assistance.

(14) In this section, "approved plan" means a plan approved, for the time being, by the Scottish Ministers under subsection (8); and includes any part or modification of the plan so approved.

(15) For the purposes of this section, "person" includes a body corporate or unincorporate.".

Financial limit: advice and assistance

69.—(1) Section 10 (financial limit) of the 1986 Act is amended as follows.

(2) In subsection (1)(b)—

(a) after "except" insert ", subject to subsection (4),";

(b) at the end insert "or in the circumstances set out in subsection (1A)".

(3) After subsection (1) insert—

"(1A) The circumstances are that—

(a) the advice and assistance requires to be given urgently; and

(b) it is not possible to seek the approval of the Board before the advice and assistance requires to be given,

and following which an application may be made under subsection (1B) for the Board's approval.

(1B) If the Board is satisfied that the circumstances set out in subsection (1A) were present it may, on application by the solicitor or adviser concerned, give its approval to the limit having been exceeded.".

(4) After subsection (3) insert—

"(4) In the circumstances set out in subsection (5), no application may be made for the Board's approval for the cost of giving the advice and assistance—

(a) to exceed the limit applicable under this section; or

(b) to that limit having been exceeded.

(5) The circumstances are that the matter with which the advice and assistance is concerned is not—

(a) specified as a distinct matter for the purposes of advice and assistance by virtue of regulations made under this Act; or

(b) being treated as if it were a distinct matter by virtue of such regulations.".

Further provision in relation to the Fund: advice and assistance

70.—(1) In section 4 of the 1986 Act (Scottish Legal Aid Fund) in subsection (2), after paragraph (b) insert—

"(ba) any sums as are, by virtue of section 12C of this Act, due out of the Fund;".

(2) After section 12B of that Act (inserted by section 67 of this Act) insert—

"Advice and assistance: further provision in relation to the Fund

Further provision in relation to the Fund: advice and assistance

12C.—(1) This section applies where, in respect of any matter in connection with which advice and assistance has been provided, the sums mentioned in section 4(3)(aa), (ca) and (cb) which are payable into the Fund have been so paid.

(2) There shall be paid out of the Fund any sum which, in the opinion of the Board the party concerned would have been likely to receive, after the operation of section 12(3), if the advice and assistance provided had not been provided—

(a) by virtue of a grant made under section 4A; or

(b) by a solicitor in the course of employment to which Part V of this Act applies.".

Availability of civil legal aid for defamation or verbal injury

71.—(1) The 1986 Act is amended as follows.

(2) In section 14 (availability of civil legal aid), after subsection (1B) insert—

"(1C) In the case of proceedings described in paragraph 1 of Part II of Schedule 2 to this Act, civil legal aid shall be available to a person only if, in addition to the requirements which have to be met under subsection (1) and section 15 of this Act and subject to paragraph 2 of Part II of Schedule 2, such criteria as may be set out by the Scottish Ministers in directions given to the Board are met.

(1D) A direction given under subsection (1C) may—

(a) include criteria in respect of which the Board may require to satisfy itself;

(b) make different provision for different purposes;

(c) be varied or revoked at any time.

(1E) Where the Scottish Ministers give a direction under subsection (1C)—

(a) the Board must comply with it;

(b) the Scottish Ministers must arrange for the direction to be published in such manner as they consider appropriate.".

(3) In Part II of Schedule 2 (excepted proceedings)—

(a) in paragraph 1, after "to" insert "section 14(1C) and";

(b) in paragraph 2, the words ", and legal" to the end are repealed.

Civil legal aid: conditions and reviews

72.—(1) Section 14 (availability of civil legal aid) of the 1986 Act is amended in accordance with subsections (2) and (3) of this section.

(2) In subsection (1), for "subsection" substitute "subsections (1F) and".

(3) After subsection (1E) (inserted by section 71(2) of this Act), insert—

"(1F) Legal aid made available to a person under subsection (1) may be subject to such conditions as the Board considers expedient; and such conditions may be imposed at any time.

(1G) The Board shall establish a procedure under which any person receiving civil legal aid under this section which is subject to conditions by virtue of subsection (1F) may apply to the Board for a review of any such condition.".

(4) Section 29 (legal aid in certain proceedings relating to children) of the 1986 Act is amended in accordance with subsections (5) and (6) of this section.

(5) After subsection (5) insert—

"(5A) Legal aid made available to a person under subsection (2)(d) above or subsection (9) below may be subject to such conditions as the Board considers expedient; and such conditions may be imposed at any time.".

(6) After subsection (6) insert—

"(6A) The Board shall establish a procedure under which any person whose application for legal aid under subsection (2)(d) above or subsection (9) below has been refused may apply to the Board for a review of his application.

(6B) The Board shall establish a procedure under which any person receiving legal aid under subsection (2)(d) above or subsection (9) below which is subject to conditions by virtue of subsection (5A) may apply to the Board for a review of any such condition.".

Availability of legal aid: Judicial Committee of the Privy Council

73.—(1) In section 25AB (legal aid in references, appeals or applications for special leave to appeal to the Judicial Committee of the Privy Council) of the 1986 Act—

(a) in subsection (1), for "or 13(a)" substitute ", 13(a) or 33";

(b) in subsection (4), after "11" insert "or 33".

(2) In paragraph 1 of Part 1 of Schedule 2 to that Act, for "and 13(b)" substitute ", 13(b), 32 and 33".

Solicitors employed by the Scottish Legal Aid Board

74.—(1) In section 4 (Scottish Legal Aid Fund) of the 1986 Act, after subsection (2)(a) insert—

"(aza) any expenses incurred by the Board in connection with the provision by solicitors employed by it by virtue of section 27(1) of this Act of—

(i) advice and assistance in relation to civil matters;

(ii) civil legal aid;

(iii) any services as are mentioned in section 26(2) of this Act;".

(2) In section 26 (employment to which Part V applies)—

(a) in subsection (2)—

(i) the word "local" is repealed;

(ii) in paragraph (a), for "its function" substitute "any function it has";

(b) in subsection (3)(a)—

(i) the word "local" is repealed;

(ii) after "concerned" insert "(whether wholly or partly)".

(3) In section 27 (arrangements for employment to which Part V applies) of that Act—

(a) after subsection (1), insert—

"(1A) The provisions of paragraph 8 of Schedule 1 to this Act shall apply to solicitors employed by the Board by virtue of subsection (1) as they apply to employees appointed by the Board under that paragraph.";

(b) subsections (2) and (3) are repealed.

Contributions, and payments out of property recovered

75.—(1) The 1986 Act is amended as follows.

(2) In section 4 (Scottish Legal Aid Fund) in subsection (2), after paragraph (ab) insert—

"(aba) any sums repayable to a person in accordance with section 17(2C) of this Act;

(abb) any sums payable to a person in accordance with section 17(2D) of this Act;".

(3) In that section, after subsection (3)(c) insert—

"(ca) any sum recovered as to expenses under an award of a court or an agreement or otherwise in favour of any person in respect of any matter in connection with which advice and assistance has been provided to the person—

(i) by virtue of a grant made under section 4A; or

(ii) by a solicitor in the course of employment to which Part V of this Act applies;

(cb) any sum which is to be paid out of property (of whatever nature and wherever situated) recovered or preserved for any person in respect of any matter in connection with which advice and assistance has been provided to the person (including his rights under any settlement arrived at in connection with that matter in order to avoid or bring to an end any proceedings)—

(i) by virtue of a grant made under section 4A; or

(ii) by a solicitor in the course of employment to which Part V of this Act applies;".

(4) In section 17 (contributions, and payments out of property recovered), after subsection (2B) insert—

"(2C) If the total contribution to the Fund made by a person in respect of any proceedings exceeds the net liability of the Fund on the person's account, the excess shall be repaid to the person.

(2D) Any sums paid to the Board under subsection (2B) which are no longer required to meet the net liability of the Fund on a person's account, having taken into account any relevant sums paid to the Board under subsection (2A), shall be paid to the person.

(2E) Nothing in subsection (2B) shall prejudice the power of the court to allow any damages or expenses to be set off.

(2F) In this section, the reference to a "net liability of the Fund" on a legally assisted person's account is a reference to the aggregate amount of—

(a) the sums paid or payable to a solicitor or counsel out of the Fund on the person's account, in respect of the proceedings in question; and

(b) any sums paid or payable to a solicitor, counsel or registered organisation (in respect of the advisers it approves) out of the Fund on the person's account, for advice and assistance in connection with the proceedings in question or any matter to which those proceedings relate,

being sums not recouped by the Fund out of expenses in respect of those proceedings, or as a result of any right which the person may have to be indemnified against such expenses.

(2G) Where the solicitor for a legally assisted person is employed by the Board for the purposes of Part V of this Act, references in subsection (2F) to sums payable out of the Fund include references to sums which would have been so payable had the legal aid and, as the case may be, advice and assistance been provided in circumstances other than those specified in subsection (2I).

(2H) Where—

(a) civil legal aid is or has been provided in respect of the proceedings in question by virtue of a grant made under section 4A; and

(b) advice and assistance is or has been provided in connection with the proceedings by virtue of a grant made under section 4A,

references in subsection (2F) to sums payable out of the Fund include references to sums which would have been so payable had the legal aid and, as the case may be, advice and assistance been provided in circumstances other than those specified in subsection (2I).

(2I) The circumstances are that the legal aid and, as the case may be, advice and assistance has been provided—

(a) by virtue of a grant made under section 4A; or

(b) by a solicitor in the course of employment to which Part V of this Act applies.".

Regulations under section 36 of the 1986 Act

76.—(1) Section 36 (regulations) of the 1986 Act is amended as follows.

(2) After paragraph (c) of subsection (2) insert—

"(ca) make provision allowing the Board to determine—

(i) the matters which, subject to subsection (2A), are or are not to be treated as distinct matters for the purposes of advice and assistance;

(ii) on a case by case basis, matters which may be treated as if they were distinct matters for the purposes of advice and assistance;".

(3) After subsection (2) insert—

"(2A) Regulations made under this section which include provision as mentioned in subsection (2)(ca)(i) must include provision to the effect that—

(a) any determination by the Board as to the matters which are or are not to be so treated as distinct matters may only be made after consultation with the Law Society;

(b) where a matter has been determined by the Board to be so treated as a distinct matter, the Board may not determine that the matter is no longer to be so treated unless the Scottish Ministers consent.".

Part 5

General

Advice, services or activities to which Act does not apply

77.—(1) Nothing in this Act applies to—

(a) any element of a complaint relating to;

(b) the provision by a practitioner of,

the advice, services or activities mentioned in subsection (2).

(2) The advice, services or activities are—

(a) activities carried out by virtue of a group licence issued under section 22(1)(b) of the Consumer Credit Act 1974 (c. 39);

(b) activities of an insolvency practitioner within the meaning of Part 13 of the Insolvency Act 1986 (c. 45);

(c) activities mentioned in paragraph (a) of paragraph 5(1) of Schedule 3 to the Financial Services Act 1986 (c. 60);

(d) immigration advice or immigration services, both within the meaning of section 82(1) of the Immigration and Asylum Act 1999 (c.33);

(e) regulated activity within the meaning of section 22 of the Financial Services and Markets Act 2000 (c.8), other than activity falling within paragraph (f) below, in respect of which the Financial Services Authority has by virtue of Part 20 of that Act arranged for its regulatory role to be carried out by the Law Society of Scotland;

(f) exempt regulated activities within the meaning of section 325(2) of the Financial Services and Markets Act 2000 (c.8).

(3) In subsection (1), "complaint" and "practitioner" have the same meanings as in section 46.

Ancillary provision

78.—(1) The Scottish Ministers may by order make such incidental, supplemental, consequential, transitional, transitory or saving provision as they consider necessary or expedient for the purposes, or in consequence, of, or for giving full effect to, this Act or any provision of it.

(2) An order under this section may—

(a) make different provision for different purposes;

(b) modify any enactment, instrument or document.

Regulations or orders

79.—(1) Any power conferred by this Act on the Scottish Ministers to make orders or regulations—

(a) must be exercised by statutory instrument;

(b) may be exercised so as to make different provision for different purposes.

(2) A statutory instrument containing an order or regulations made under this Act (except an order made under section 26(1) or 82(2)) is, subject to subsection (3), subject to annulment in pursuance of a resolution of the Parliament.

(3) A statutory instrument containing—

(a) an order under section 10(7) or 24(8);

(b) regulations under section 41(1);

(c) an order under—

(i) section 78(1) containing provisions which add to, replace or omit any part of the text of an Act;

(ii) paragraph 2(7) of schedule 1,

is not to be made unless a draft of the instrument has been laid before, and approved by resolution of, the Parliament.

Interpretation

80. In this Act—

"the 1980 Act" means the Solicitors (Scotland) Act 1980 (c. 46);
"the 1986 Act" means the Legal Aid (Scotland) Act 1986 (c. 47);
"the 1990 Act" means the Law Reform (Miscellaneous Provisions) (Scotland) Act 1990 (c.40).

Minor and consequential modifications

81. Schedule 5 makes—

(a) minor modifications;

(b) modifications consequential on the provisions of this Act.

Short title and commencement

82.—(1) This Act may be cited as the Legal Profession and Legal Aid (Scotland) Act 2007.

(2) The provisions of this Act, except this section and sections 46, 79 and 80 come into force on such day as the Scottish Ministers may by order appoint.

(3) Different days may be appointed under subsection (2) for different purposes.

SCHEDULE 1

THE SCOTTISH LEGAL COMPLAINTS COMMISSION

(introduced by section 1(2))

1. *Status*

(1) The Commission is a body corporate.

(2) The Commission is not to be regarded as a servant or agent of the Crown, or having any status, immunity or privilege of the Crown, nor are its members or its employees to be regarded as civil servants, nor its property as property of, or held on behalf of, the Crown.

2. *Membership of the Commission*

(1) The Commission is to consist of the following members—

(a) a person to chair the Commission ("the chairing member"); and

(b) 8 other members.

(2) Members are appointed by the Scottish Ministers, having consulted the Lord President of the Court of Session ("the Lord President").

(3) The chairing member and 4 other members of the Commission must be members (in this schedule referred to as "non-lawyer members") who are not within any of the categories mentioned in sub-paragraph (6).

(4) There must be 4 members of the Commission (in this schedule referred to as "lawyer members") who are within any of the categories mentioned in sub-paragraph (6).

(5) Of the lawyer members 3 must have practised within any, or any combination, of the categories mentioned in sub-paragraph (6) for at least 10 years.

(6) The categories are—

(a) solicitors;

(b) advocates;

(c) conveyancing practitioners or executry practitioners;

(d) persons exercising a right to conduct litigation or a right of audience acquired by virtue of section 27 of the 1990 Act.

(7) The Scottish Ministers may, subject to sub-paragraphs (8) and (9), by order amend—

(a) sub-paragraph (1)(b) to alter the number of other members referred to there;

(b) sub-paragraph (3) to alter the number of other members referred to there;

(c) sub-paragraph (4) to alter the number of members referred to there;

(d) sub-paragraph (5) to alter the number of lawyer members referred to there.

(8) The number of non-lawyer members must be greater than the number of lawyer members.

(9) The number of—

(a) non-lawyer members must be no fewer than 4 and no greater than 8;

(b) lawyer members must be no fewer than 3 and no greater than 7.

3. *Terms of appointment etc.*

(1) Subject to sub-paragraph (2), each member is to be appointed for a period of 5 years.

(2) Appointments that constitute the Commission for the first time are to be in accordance with sub-paragraph (3).

(3) Each member is to be appointed for a period of not less than 4 years and not exceeding 6 years.

(4) A member—

(a) may by giving notice in writing to the Scottish Ministers resign office as a member of the Commission;

(b) otherwise, holds and vacates office in accordance with the terms and conditions of appointment.

(5) A person is, on ceasing to be a member, eligible for reappointment for a single further period; but not before a period of 3 years has elapsed.

4. *In appointing members, the Scottish Ministers are to have regard to the desirability of including*—

(a) persons who have experience of, and have shown capacity in—

(i) consumer affairs or complaints handling;

(ii) the provision of advice to members of the public on or in relation to such matters;

(b) persons who have experience of, and shown capacity in, the practice and provision of legal education and training;

(c) persons who have experience of, and shown capacity in—

(i) civil or criminal proceedings;

(ii) court procedures and practice generally;

(iii) the practice and provision of other legal services;

(iv) the monitoring of legal services;

(d) persons who have such other skills, knowledge or experience as the Scottish Ministers consider to be relevant in relation to the exercise of the Commission's functions.

5. *Removal of members*

(1) Subject to sub-paragraph (2), the chairing member may, by written notice, remove a member from office if the chairing member is satisfied as regards any of the following matters—

(a) that the member becomes insolvent;

(b) that the member—

(i) has been absent from meetings of the Commission for a period longer than 6 consecutive months without the permission of the Commission;

(ii) has been convicted of a criminal offence;

(iii) is otherwise unable or unfit to discharge the functions of a member or is unsuitable to continue as a member.

(2) The chairing member may not remove a member from office without the agreement of the Lord President of the Court of Session.

(3) The Lord President may, by written notice, remove the chairing member from office if the Lord President is satisfied as regards any of the matters mentioned in sub-paragraph (1)(a) or (b).

(4) For the purpose of sub-paragraph (1)(a) a member becomes insolvent on—

(a) the approval of a voluntary arrangement proposed by the member;

(b) being adjudged bankrupt;

(c) the member's estate being sequestrated;

(d) entering into a debt arrangement programme under Part 1 of the Debt Arrangement and Attachment (Scotland) Act 2002 (asp 17) as the debtor;

(e) granting a trust deed for creditors.

6. *Disqualification from membership*

(1) A person is disqualified from appointment, and from holding office, as a member of the Commission if that person is—

(a) a member of the House of Commons;

(b) a member of the Scottish Parliament;

(c) a member of the European Parliament.

(2) A person who has held any of the offices set out in sub-paragraph (1)(a) to (c) is also disqualified from appointment as a member of the Commission for a period of one year starting from the day on which the person last held any of those offices.

7. *Remuneration, allowances and pensions for members*

(1) The Commission is to pay to its members such remuneration as the Scottish Ministers may in each case determine.

(2) The Commission is to pay to its members such allowances as the Scottish Ministers may in each case determine.

(3) The Commission may, with the approval of the Scottish Ministers—

(a) pay or make arrangements for the payment;

(b) make payments towards the provision;

(c) provide and maintain schemes (whether contributory or not) for the payment,
of such pensions, allowances or gratuities to or in respect of any person who is or has ceased to be a member of the Commission, as the Commission may determine.

(4) The reference in sub-paragraph (3) to pensions, allowances and gratuities includes a reference to pensions, allowances and gratuities by way of compensation for loss of office.

8. *Chief executive and other employees*

(1) The Commission is to employ a chief executive.

(2) The chief executive is, with the approval of the Scottish Ministers, to be appointed by the Commission on such terms and conditions as the Commission may, with such approval, determine.

(3) The Commission may (subject to any directions given under sub-paragraph (4)) appoint such other employees on such terms and conditions as the Commission may determine.

(4) The Scottish Ministers may give directions to the Commission as regards the appointment of employees under sub-paragraph (3) (including the number of appointments) and as regards terms and conditions of their employment.

(5) The Commission must comply with directions given to it under sub-paragraph (4).

(6) The Commission may, with the approval of the Scottish Ministers—

(a) pay or make arrangements for the payment;

(b) make payments towards the provision;

(c) provide and maintain schemes (whether contributory or not) for the payment,
of such pensions, allowances or gratuities to or in respect of any person who is or has ceased to be an employee of it, as the Commission may determine.

(7) The reference in sub-paragraph (6) to pensions, allowances and gratuities includes a reference to pensions, allowances and gratuities by way of compensation for loss of employment.

9. *Accountable officer*

(1) The chief executive is the accountable officer for the purposes of this paragraph.

(2) The functions of the accountable officer are—

(a) signing the accounts of the expenditure and receipts of the Commission;

(b) ensuring the propriety and regularity of the finances of the Commission;

(c) ensuring that the resources of the Commission are used economically, efficiently and effectively;

(d) the duty mentioned in sub-paragraph (3).

(3) The duty is, where the accountable officer is required by the Commission to act in some way but considers that to do so would be inconsistent with the proper performance of the functions specified in sub-paragraph (2)(a) to (c), to—

(a) obtain written authority from the Commission before taking the action;

(b) send a copy of the authority as soon as possible to the Auditor General for Scotland.

10. *Procedure*

(1) Subject to sub-paragraph (2)—

(a) any quorum of the Commission as contained in rules made under section 32(1) must consist of a greater number of non-lawyer members than lawyer members;

(b) the chairing member must, if present, chair meetings of the Commission or any committee of the Commission;

(c) if the chairing member is not available to be present at a meeting of the Commission or any committee of the Commission, the chairing member is to appoint another non-lawyer member to chair the meeting or committee;

(d) the chairing member has a casting vote; and any person appointed by that member under sub-sub-paragraph (c) has a casting vote for the purposes of that appointment;

(e) the validity of any proceedings of the Commission, or any of its committees, is not affected by a vacancy in membership nor by any defect in the appointment of a member.

(2) Sub-paragraph (1) does not apply to a determination committee established under paragraph 11(1)(a).

11. *Committees*

(1) The Commission—

(a) must establish one or more determination committees in accordance with rules made under section 32(1) for the purpose of exercising any functions mentioned in paragraph 13(2) which a determination committee is authorised by the Commission to exercise;

(b) may establish other committees for any other purposes relating to its functions.

(2) Subject to sub-paragraph (3)—

(a) the Commission is to determine the composition of its committees;

(b) any quorum of a committee as contained in rules made by virtue of section 32 must consist of a greater number of non-lawyer members than lawyer members;

(c) a committee of the Commission is to comply with any directions given to it by the Commission.

(3) Sub-paragraph (2) does not apply to a determination committee established under sub-paragraph (1)(a).

12. *General powers*

(1) The Commission may do anything which appears to it to be necessary or expedient for the purpose of, or in connection with, or appears to it to be conducive to, the exercise of the Commission's functions.

(2) In particular the Commission may—

(a) enter into contracts;

(b) with the consent of the Scottish Ministers, borrow money;

(c) with the consent of the Scottish Ministers, acquire and dispose of land;

(d) obtain advice or assistance from any person who, in the Commission's opinion, is qualified to give it.

(3) The Commission may pay to any person from whom advice or assistance is obtained such fees, remuneration and allowances as the Commission may, with the approval of the Scottish Ministers, determine.

13. *Delegation of functions*

(1) The Commission may, subject to sub-paragraphs (2), (3) and (4), authorise—

(a) the chief executive;

(b) any of its committees;

(c) any of its members;

(d) any of its other members of staff,

to exercise such of its functions (to such extent) as it may determine.

(2) The Commission may authorise—

(a) the function of deciding under section 2(4)(a) whether a complaint is frivolous, vexatious or totally without merit to be exercised only by any of its committees or by one of the Commission's members;

(b) the function of deciding under section 3(1) whether—

(i) any element of a complaint is capable of being dealt with under a specified regulatory scheme;

(ii) the extent (if any) to which the Commission is able to take the preliminary steps referred to in section 2(4) in relation to the complaint and to deal with it under Part 1,

to be exercised only by one of the Commission's members;

(c) the function of deciding whether any element of a complaint is about the exercise of discretion by any Crown Counsel or procurator fiscal in relation to the prosecution of crime or investigation of deaths to be exercised only by one of the Commission's members;

(d) the following functions to be exercised only by a determination committee—

(i) the making of a determination under section 9(1);

(ii) the making of a determination or direction under section 10(2);

(iii) the making of any decision or the publication of a report under section 13;

(iv) the making of a decision under section 23(2);

(v) the making of a direction under section 24(6).

(3) The Commission may not authorise the exercise of any of the following functions under sub-paragraph (1)—

(a) the approval of annual reports and accounts;

(b) making of rules under section 32(1);

(c) determining the amount of the annual general levy and the complaints levy under section 29(1);

(d) the approval of any budget or other financial plan.

(4) Sub-paragraph (1) does not affect the responsibility of the Commission for the exercise of its functions.

14. *Location of office*

(1) Subject to sub-paragraph (2), the Commission's determination of the location of the Commission's office premises is subject to the approval of the Scottish Ministers.

(2) The Scottish Ministers may direct the Commission as to the location of the Commission's office premises; and the Commission must comply with any such direction.

15. *Accounts*

(1) The Commission must—

(a) keep proper accounts and accounting records;

(b) prepare in respect of each financial year a statement of accounts; and

(c) send the statement of accounts to the Scottish Ministers,

in accordance with such directions as the Scottish Ministers may give.

(2) The Scottish Ministers must as soon as practicable—

(a) send the statement of accounts to the Auditor General for Scotland for auditing;

(b) lay the audited statement before the Parliament.

(3) If requested by any person, the Commission is to make available at any reasonable time, without charge, in printed or electronic form, their audited accounts, so that they may be inspected by that person.

16. *Reports*

(1) As soon as practicable after the end of each financial year, the Commission must prepare a report on—

(a) the discharge of the Commission's functions during that year; and

(b) such action the Commission proposes to take in the following year in pursuance of its functions.

(2) The Commission must—

(a) send a copy of the report to the Scottish Ministers; and

(b) publish the report.

(3) In preparing and publishing the report the Commission must do so in accordance with such directions as the Scottish Ministers may give.

(4) The Scottish Ministers must as soon as practicable lay a copy of the report before the Parliament.

(5) The Commission may publish such other reports on matters relevant to the functions of the Commission as it considers appropriate.

SCHEDULE 2

Further powers of Commission under section 17 or 37

(introduced by sections 17(7) and 37(4))

1. Where the Commission—

(a) gives notice under subsection (1) of section 17 to any person having possession or control of any documents mentioned in subsection (3) of that section;

(b) gives notice under section 17(4) to any person having possession or control of any documents mentioned in subsection (6) of that section;

(c) requires any person under section 37(1) or (3) to provide it with information or documents referred to in that section,

and the person refuses or fails to produce or deliver any of the documents or the information within the time specified in the notice or requirement or to cause them to be so produced or delivered, the Commission may apply to the court for an order requiring the person to produce or deliver the documents or information or to cause them or it to be produced or delivered to the person appointed at the place fixed by the Commission within such time as the court may order.

2. Where the Commission takes possession of any such documents or information which have or has been produced or delivered to it, it must—

(a) in the case mentioned in paragraph 1(a) or (c), without delay serve on the practitioner against whom the complaint is made, and any other person to whom the notice was given or requirement made;

(b) in the case mentioned in paragraph 1(b), without delay serve on the complainer,

a notice giving particulars and the date on which it took possession.

3. Before the expiry of the period of 14 days after service of a notice under paragraph 2 the person on whom the notice has been served may apply to the court for an order directing the Commission to return such documents or information to the person from whom they were received by the Commission or to such other person as the applicant may request; and on the hearing of any such application the court may make the order applied for or such other order as it thinks fit.

4. If no application is made to the court under paragraph 3, or if the court on any such application directs that the documents or information in question remain in the custody or control of the Commission, the Commission may make enquiries to ascertain the person to whom they belong and may deal with the documents or information in accordance with the directions of the person.

SCHEDULE 3

Rules as to Commission's practice and procedure

(introduced by section 32(2))

Provision which must be included

1. The rules as to the Commission's practice and procedure made under section 32(1) must include provision—

(a) regulating the making to the Commission of complaints under Part 1, including—

(i) when a complaint is to be regarded as made for the purposes of the Part;

(ii) the eligibility of persons to make such complaints on behalf of other persons (whether living or not);

(b) requiring the Commission not to—

(i) investigate a services complaint by virtue of section 9;

(ii) remit a conduct complaint to a relevant professional body under section 6(a) or 15(5)(a);

(iii) investigate a handling complaint by virtue of section 23,

unless the complainer has, for the purposes of Parts 1 and 2 of this Act, waived any right of confidentiality in relation to the matters to which the complaint relates;

(c) regulating the handling by it of complaints under Part 1;

(d) regulating the proposal by the Commission under section 9(2) of a settlement of a complaint and how an accepted settlement is to be constituted;

(e) requiring the Commission—

(i) where it considers it appropriate, to hold a hearing in relation to a complaint being dealt with by it under Part 1;

(ii) to decide whether such a hearing should be in public or private;

(f) as to—

(i) the evidence which may be required or admitted;

(ii) the extent to which it may be oral or written;

(iii) the consequences of a person's failure to produce any information or document which the person has been required to produce;

(g) as to when reasons are to be given (in circumstances where they are not required by this Act to be given)—

(i) for the Commission's determinations, directions, decisions or recommendations under Part 1;

(ii) in respect of what matters relating to the determinations, directions, decisions or recommendations;

(h) as to the membership of a determination committee, including in particular provision requiring—

(i) that any such committee has at least 3 members, of which the majority are non-lawyer members of the Commission;

(ii) that any such committee is chaired by a lawyer member of the Commission;

(iii) where the Commission has under section 9(2) proposed a settlement as respects a complaint and the settlement has not been accepted as mentioned in section 9(4), that the members of the committee determining the complaint under section 9(1) or making a determination or direction under section 10(2), by virtue of paragraph 13(2) of schedule 1, must not have been involved in any aspect of the investigation of the complaint (including deciding under section 2(4)(a) whether the complaint was frivolous, vexatious or totally without merit) or the formulation or making by the Commission of the proposed settlement;

(i) requiring, where the Commission itself (and not one of its determination committees) determines a complaint under section 9(1) or makes a determination or direction under section 10(2) in relation to a complaint, that any member of the Commission involved in doing so must not have been involved in any aspect of the investigation of the complaint (including any matter referred to in paragraph 13(2)(a) to (c) of schedule 1) or the formulation or making by the Commission under section 9(2) of a proposed settlement as respects the complaint;

(j) as to the charging of interest at such rate as may be specified by the Scottish Ministers by order under section 27(3)(b) on any amount of the annual general levy due to be paid to the Commission by a relevant professional organisation under section 27(2)(b) from the date the amount is due under the rules until it is paid;

(k) as to the charging of interest at such rate as may be specified by the Scottish Ministers by order under section 28(3)(b) on any amount of the complaints levy due to the Commission from the date the amount is due under the rules until it is paid;

(l) subject to schedule 1, regulating its own meetings (including any quorum) and that of its committees.

Provision which may in particular be included

2. The rules as to the Commission's practice and procedure made under section 32(1) may in particular include provision—

(a) fixing time limits for the making of complaints against practitioners or relevant professional organisations or the stages of its investigation under Part 1;
(b) as to—
   (i) extension of any time limit fixed by it under the rules;
   (ii) the circumstances in which such extension may be made;
(c) as to the circumstances in which the Commission is not prevented by section 4(2) from taking the steps and further action referred to in that section in relation to a complaint which is made prematurely (within the meaning of section 4(4));
(d) as to the circumstances in which the Commission may rely on—
   (i) with the agreement of the body concerned, findings in fact of a relevant professional organisation, the Scottish Solicitors' Discipline Tribunal or such other body as the Scottish Ministers may by order specify which has disciplinary functions;
   (ii) previous findings in fact of the Commission;
(e) securing that a procedural defect in relation to—
   (i) the making of;
   (ii) the Commission dealing with,

a complaint under Part 1 is not to have an effect under the Part where the Commission considers that appropriate in the interests of fairness;

(f) as to the collection of the amount of the annual general levy to be paid to it by the relevant professional organisations and of any complaints levy due to it by practitioners;
(g) as to the recovery by it from the relevant professional organisations of the annual general levy due to be paid to it by them and from practitioners of any complaints levy due by them;
(h) as to the circumstances in which the Commission may—
   (i) waive a portion of the annual general levy which would otherwise be payable under section 27(1);
   (ii) refund any portion of an amount paid under that section;
(i) as to the circumstances in which the Commission may waive the requirement under section 28(1) to pay the complaints levy in any case;
(j) as to the calculation of the total amount of the annual general levy each relevant professional organisation is due to collect under section 27(2)(a) in respect of each financial year and notification of each such organisation of the amount so calculated by the Commission.

3. In this schedule—

"lawyer member" has the meaning given by paragraph 2(4) of schedule 1;

"non-lawyer member" has the meaning given by paragraph 2(3) of that schedule.

SCHEDULE 4

Further powers of relevant professional organisations under section 48

(introduced by section 48)

1. Where a relevant professional organisation gives notice—

(a) under section 48(1)(a) to any person having possession or control of any documents mentioned in subsection (3) of that section;
(b) under section 48(1)(b) to any person having possession or control of any documents mentioned in subsection (5) of that section,

and the person refuses or fails to produce or deliver any of the documents within the time specified in the notice or to cause them to be so produced or delivered, the relevant professional organisation may apply to the court for an order requiring the person to produce or deliver the documents or to cause them to be produced or delivered to the person appointed at the place fixed by the relevant professional organisation within such time as the court may order.

2. Where a relevant professional organisation takes possession of any such documents which have been produced or delivered to it, it must—

(a) in the case mentioned in paragraph 1(a), without delay serve on the practitioner against whom the complaint is made, and any other person to whom the notice was given;

(b) in the case mentioned in paragraph 1(b), without delay serve on the complainer,

a notice giving particulars and the date on which it took possession.

3. Before the expiry of the period of 14 days after service of a notice under paragraph 2 the person on whom the notice has been served may apply to the court for an order directing the relevant professional organisation to return such documents to the person from whom they were received by the relevant professional organisation or to such other person as the applicant may request; and on the hearing of any such application the court may make the order applied for or such other order as it thinks fit.

4. If no application is made to the court under paragraph 3, or if the court on any such application directs that the documents in question remain in the custody or control of the relevant professional organisation, the relevant professional organisation may make enquiries to ascertain the person to whom they belong and may deal with the documents in accordance with the directions of that person.

SCHEDULE 5

Minor and consequential modifications

(introduced by section 81)

Solicitors (Scotland) Act 1980 (c. 46)

1.—(1) The 1980 Act is amended as follows.

(2) In section 3A(5) (discharge of functions of Council of Law Society)—

(a) in paragraph (a)—

(i) at the beginning, insert "that";

(ii) for the word ", or", where it first occurs, substitute ";

(aa) that under section 47(2) of the 2007 Act of determining what action to propose, or take, as respects a conduct complaint remitted to them under section 6(a) or 15(5)(a) of that Act;

(ab) that under—

(i) section 42ZA(1) or (2) of this Act or section 20ZB(1) or (2) of the 1990 Act of determining whether or not to uphold a conduct complaint so remitted which suggests unsatisfactory professional conduct;

(ii) section 42ZA(3)(b) of this Act or section 20ZB(3)(b) of the 1990 Act of determining what steps to take when upholding such a conduct complaint;

(ac) that under section 51(1) of this Act of determining whether or not to make a complaint to the Tribunal as respects a conduct complaint so remitted which suggests professional misconduct;

(ad) that";

(iii) the words "the functions" are repealed;

(b) in paragraph (b)—

(i) before "under" insert "that";

(ii) the words ", the functions" are repealed.

(3) In section 15(2) (discretion of Council in special cases as respects application for practising certificate)—

(a) in paragraph (d), after the word "under" insert "section 42ZA(4)(b) or";

(b) in paragraph (i)—

(i) the words ", after a complaint has been made" are repealed;

(ii) in sub-paragraph (i), for the words "relating to his conduct of the business of a client" substitute "the Council are investigating a conduct complaint remitted to them under section 6(a) or 15(5)(a) of the 2007 Act,";

(iii) in sub-paragraph (ii), at the beginning insert "after a complaint has been made".

(4) In section 20(2) (Council's duty to supply lists of solicitors holding practising certificates), after the words "55(1)(ba)" insert "or (bb)".

(5) In section 25A (rights of audience of solicitors in Court of Session etc.), after subsection (14), insert—

"(14A) Where the Commission makes a determination under section 9(1) of the 2007 Act upholding a services complaint against a solicitor, the Council may, if they consider that the complaint has a bearing on his fitness to exercise any right of audience held by him by virtue of this section and that it is appropriate to do so, suspend or revoke the right.".

(6) In section 34 (rules as to professional practice, conduct and discipline)—

(a) after subsection (4) insert—

"(4ZA) If any solicitor fails to comply with any rule made under this section, that failure may be treated as professional misconduct or unsatisfactory professional conduct.";

(b) after subsection (4B), insert—

"(4C) Subsection (4) does not apply to any failure to which subsection (4ZA) applies.

(4D) Subsection (4ZA) applies to any element of failure which does not involve the provision of advice, services or activities referred to in section 77(2) of the 2007 Act.".

(7) In section 35(3) (failure by solicitor to comply with rule made under section 35 may be treated as professional misconduct for certain purposes), for the words "for the purposes of Part IV" substitute "or as unsatisfactory professional conduct.".

(8) In section 37(8) (failure by solicitor to comply with section 37, accountant's certificates rules etc. may be treated as professional misconduct for certain purposes), for the words "for the purposes of Part IV" substitute "or as unsatisfactory professional conduct.".

(9) In section 38 (powers where dishonesty alleged), after subsection (3) insert—

"(4) This section does not apply to any element of dishonesty other than that involving the provision of advice, services or activities referred to in section 77(2) of the 2007 Act.".

(10) In section 39 (powers where undue delay alleged), after subsection (2), insert—

"(3) This section does not apply to any element of undue delay other than that involving the provision of advice, services or activities referred to in section 77(2) of the 2007 Act.".

(11) In section 39A (powers where excessive fees etc. charged), after subsection (9) insert—

"(10) The Council shall notify the Commission of any case—

(a) where any of the following things occur—

(i) they withdraw a practising certificate under subsection (2);

(ii) they terminate a suspension from practice and restore a practising certificate under subsection (3);

(iii) the Court makes an order under subsection (8); and

(b) which does not involve a complaint remitted to the Council under section 6(a) or 15(5)(a) of the 2007 Act.".

(12) In section 40 (powers where failure to comply with accounts rules, etc.), after subsection (4), insert—

"(5) The Council shall notify the Commission of any case—

(a) where any of the following things occur—

(i) they withdraw a practising certificate under subsection (1);

(ii) they terminate a suspension from practice and restore a practising certificate under subsection (2);

(iii) the Court makes an order under subsection (3); and

(b) which does not involve a complaint remitted to the Council under section 6(a) or 15(5)(a) of the 2007 Act.".

(13) In section 42C (powers to examine documents and demand explanations in connection with complaints)—

(a) in subsection (3), for the words "documents specified in section 38(2)" substitute "following documents—

(a) all books, accounts, deeds, securities, papers and other documents in the possession or control of the solicitor or his firm or, as the case may be, the incorporated practice;

(b) all books, accounts, deeds, securities, papers and other documents relating to any trust of which the solicitor is a sole trustee or is a co-trustee only with one or more of his partners or employees or, as the case may be, of which the incorporated practice or one of its employees is a sole trustee or of which the practice is a co-trustee only with one or more of its employees.";

(b) in subsection (4), for the words "section 38" in each place where they occur substitute "sections 38, 45 and 46";

(c) after that subsection, insert—

"(5) This section does not apply to any element of professional misconduct other than that involving the provision of advice, services or activities referred to in section 77(2) of the 2007 Act.".

(14) In section 44(4) (failure to comply with rules made under section may be treated as professional misconduct for certain purposes), for the words from "for" to the end substitute "or unsatisfactory professional conduct.".

(15) In section 45 (safeguarding interests of clients of solicitors struck off or suspended)—

(a) in subsection (1), after "section", where it first occurs, insert "(except subsection (4A))";

(b) for subsection (3), substitute—

"(3A) If the solicitor or, as the case may be, the incorporated practice fails so to satisfy the Council, the Council may—

(a) require the production or delivery to any person appointed by them at a time and place fixed by them of the documents mentioned in subsection (3B);

(b) take possession of all such documents; and

(c) apply to the Court for an order that no payment be made by any banker, building society or other body named in the order out of any banking account or any sum deposited in the name of the solicitor or his firm or, as the case may be, the incorporated practice without the leave of the Court and the Court may make such order.

(3B) The documents are—

(a) all books, accounts, deeds, securities, papers and other documents in the possession or control of the solicitor or his firm or, as the case may be, the incorporated practice;

(b) all books, accounts, deeds, securities, papers and other documents relating to any trust of which the solicitor is a sole trustee or is a co-trustee only with one or more of his partners or employees or, as the case may be, of which the incorporated practice or one of its employees is a sole trustee or of which the practice is a co-trustee only with one or more of its employees.";

(c) after subsection (4A) (as inserted by section 60(2)(a) of this Act), insert—

"(4B) Part II of Schedule 3 has effect in relation to the powers of the Council under subsection (3A).";

(d) in subsection (5), the word "and" following the definition of "material date" is repealed.

(16) In section 46 (safeguarding interests of clients in certain other cases)—

(a) in each of subsections (2) and (3) for the words from "the provisions of section 38" to the end, substitute—

"the Council may do any of the things mentioned in subsection (3A)";

(b) after subsection (3), insert—

"(3A) The things are to—

(a) require the production or delivery to any person appointed by the Council at a time and a place fixed by them of the documents mentioned in subsection (3B);

(b) take possession of all such documents; and

(c) apply to the Court for an order that no payment be made by any banker, building society or other body named in the order out of any banking account or any sum deposited in the name of the solicitor or his firm without the leave of the Court and the Court may make such order.

(3B) The documents are—

(a) all books, accounts, deeds, securities, papers and other documents in the possession or control of the solicitor or his firm;

(b) all books, accounts, deeds, securities, papers and other documents relating to any trust of which he is a sole trustee or is a co-trustee only with one or more of his employees.";

(c) after subsection (4), insert—

"(4A) Part II of Schedule 3 has effect in relation to the powers of the Council under subsection (2) or (3).".

(17) In section 51 (complaints by Council and public office holders to Tribunal), after subsection (2) insert—

"(2A) The power in subsection (2) to report to the Tribunal any case where it appears that a solicitor may have been guilty of professional misconduct does not apply to any element of professional misconduct other than that involving the provision of advice, services or activities referred to in section 77(2) of the 2007 Act.".

(18) In section 52 (procedure on certain complaints and appeals to Tribunal)—

(a) in the section title, after the word "complaints" insert "and appeals";

(b) in subsection (1), after the word "complaint" insert "or appeal";

(c) in subsection (2)—

(i) in paragraph (aa), after the words "42A(7)" insert ", 42ZA(9), (10), (11) or (12), 42ZD(1)";

(ii) in sub-paragraph (ii) of paragraph (ab), for the words "(11)(b)" substitute "(8A)(b), (11)(b) or (11ZC)";

(iii) after that sub-paragraph insert—

"(iii) appeals under section 20ZB(9), (10), (11) or (12) or 20ZE(1) of that Act;";

(d) after that subsection, insert—

"(3) Rules made by the Tribunal under subsection (2) for regulating the making, hearing or determining of appeals referred to in paragraph (aa) or (ab)(ii) of that subsection may include provision as to persons being entitled, or required by the Tribunal, to appear or be represented at the appeal.".

(19) In section 53 (power of Tribunal to fine for professional misconduct etc.)—

(a) after subsection (3), insert—

"(3ZA) The Tribunal shall not impose a fine under subsection (2)(c)—

(a) where the Tribunal is proceeding on the ground referred to in subsection (1)(a) and the solicitor, in relation to the subject matter of the Tribunal's inquiry, has been convicted by any court of an act involving dishonesty and sentenced to a term of imprisonment of not less than 2 years;

(b) where the Tribunal is proceeding on the ground referred to in subsection (1)(b).";

(b) after subsection (7A), insert—

"(7B) A direction of the Tribunal under this section is enforceable in like manner as an extract registered decree arbitral in its favour bearing a warrant for execution issued by the sheriff court of any sheriffdom in Scotland.";

(c) after subsection (9) (as inserted by section 56(1)(c) of this Act), insert—

"(10) The powers of the Tribunal under paragraph (bb) of subsection (2), and subsection (3ZA), apply to any element of a decision of the Tribunal which does not relate to the provision of advice, services or activities referred to in section 77(2) of the 2007 Act.

(11) Subsection (3) does not apply to any element of a decision of the Tribunal to which subsection (3ZA) applies.".

(20) In section 53D (suspension etc. of investment business certificates: appeal to Tribunal), for subsection (3) substitute—

"(2A) The solicitor, firm of solicitors or, as the case may be, the incorporated practice may, before the expiry of the period of 21 days beginning with the day on which the decision of the Tribunal under subsection (2) is intimated to him or, as the case may be, it, appeal to the Court against the decision.

(2B) The Council may, before the expiry of the period of 21 days beginning with the day on which the decision of the Tribunal under subsection (2) is intimated to them, appeal to the Court against the decision.

(2C) On an appeal under subsection (2A), the Court may give such directions in the matter as it thinks fit, including directions as to the expenses of the proceedings before the Court and as to any order by the Tribunal relating to expenses.

(2D) A decision of the Court under subsection (2C) shall be final.".

(21) In section 55 (powers of Court), after subsection (7) (as inserted by section 56(2)(b) of this Act), insert—

"(8) The power under paragraph (bc) of subsection (1) applies to any element of a decision of the Court which does not relate to the provision of advice, services or activities referred to in section 77(2) of the 2007 Act.".

(22) In section 62A(2) (Council's power to recover expenses under section 38, 45 or 46), after the words "38" insert ", 45 or 46".

(23) In section 65(1) (interpretation)—

(a) after the definition of "the 1990 Act", insert—

""the 2007 Act" means the Legal Profession and Legal Aid (Scotland) Act 2007 (asp 5);";

(b) after the definition of "client account", insert—

""the Commission" means the Scottish Legal Complaints Commission;".

(24) In section 65, after subsection (4) insert—

"(5) In this Act, references to "inadequate professional services" do not include any professional services other than the advice, services or activities referred to in section 77(2) of the 2007 Act.".

(25) In Schedule 3, Part II (power of Council to investigate), in paragraph 5(1), (2) and (3), after the words "section 38" in each place where they occur insert ", 45 or 46".

(26) In Schedule 4 (Constitution, Procedure and Powers of Tribunal)—

(a) paragraph 8A is repealed;

(b) in paragraph 15, for the words "and to the complainer" substitute ", the complainer and, as the case may be, the person who made the complaint as respects which the appeal was made to the Tribunal";

(c) in paragraph 23—

(i) after first "section", insert "42ZA(9), (10), (11) or (12), section 42ZD(1),";

(ii) in sub-paragraph (a), after the word "complaint" insert "(except in paragraph 14A)";

(iii) sub-paragraph (b) is repealed;

(iv) in sub-paragraph (c), the words "8A" are repealed;

(v) after paragraph (c), insert—

"(ca) in paragraph 11, for the words "complainer and respondent" there shall be substituted "parties to the appeal";

(cb) in paragraph 12—

(i) for the words "the complainer or the respondent" there shall be substituted "any party to the appeal";

(ii) for the word "respondent" where it second appears there shall be substituted "solicitor, the firm of solicitors or, as the case may be, the incorporated practice";

(iii) for the words "complainer and to the respondent" there shall be substituted "parties to the appeal";

(cc) in paragraph 14A(a), after the word "complaint" there shall be inserted "(as respects which the appeal was made)";

(cd) in paragraph 15, for the words "respondent, the complainer and, as the case may be, the person who made the complaint as respects which the appeal was made to the Tribunal" there shall be substituted "parties to the appeal and, if the person who made the complaint as respects which the appeal was made was not a party to the appeal, to that person";

(ce) in paragraph 16, after paragraph (e) there shall be inserted—

"(ea) under section 42ZD(2); or

(eb) under section 53ZB(1), (2), (3) or (4); or";";

(vi) for paragraph (d), there shall be substituted—

"(d) in paragraph 19, for the words from the beginning to "respondent" there shall be substituted "The Tribunal may make such order as it thinks fit as to the payment by any party to the appeal";";

(d) in paragraph 25, for the words from "person" to first "and" substitute "solicitor, the firm of solicitors or, as the case may be, the incorporated practice, to the person who made the complaint in respect of which the appeal was made and, as the case may be,".

Legal Aid (Scotland) Act 1986 (c. 47)

2.—(1) The 1986 Act is amended as follows.

(2) In section 12 (payment of fees or outlays otherwise than through clients' contributions), subsection (1) is repealed.

(3) In section 19(3)(b) (expenses out of the Fund), the word "severe" is repealed.

(4) In section 25D(6)(a) (removal of name from Register following failure to comply with code)—

(a) at the beginning insert "within such period of time as the Board shall direct (in the case concerned) and";

(b) the word "forthwith," is repealed.

(5) In section 34(2) (confidentiality of information)—

(a) after paragraph (a), insert—

"(aa) for the purpose of any determination or investigation by the Scottish Legal Complaints Commission under the Legal Profession and Legal Aid (Scotland) Act 2007 (asp 5) ("the 2007 Act");";

(b) in paragraph (b) for "complaint of professional misconduct" substitute "conduct complaint, remitted by the Scottish Legal Complaints Commission under section 6(a) or 15(5)(a) of the 2007 Act";

(c) at the end, insert

";

(f) for the purposes of, or required by virtue of, section 50 of the Freedom of Information (Scotland) Act 2002 (asp 13)".

Law Reform (Miscellaneous Provisions) (Scotland) Act 1990 (c.40).

3.—(1) The 1990 Act is amended as follows.

(2) In section 17 (conveyancing practitioners), after subsection (11B) insert—

"(11C) Failure by a practitioner to comply with any rule made under subsection (11) or any rule or regulation referred to in subsection (11B) may be treated as professional misconduct or unsatisfactory professional conduct.".

(3) In section 18 (executry practitioners), after subsection (10B) insert—

"(10C) Failure by a practitioner to comply with any rule made under subsection (10) or any rule or regulation referred to in subsection (10B) may be treated as professional misconduct or unsatisfactory professional conduct.".

(4) In section 20 (professional misconduct, inadequate professional services, etc. by conveyancing or executry practitioners)—

(a) in the section title, the words "inadequate professional services," are repealed;

(b) in subsection (1)—

(i) for the words "(whether or not following a complaint to them)" substitute "into a conduct complaint remitted to them under section 6(a) or 15(5)(a) of the 2007 Act suggesting professional misconduct by a practitioner or that the circumstances referred to in paragraph (a)(ii) of section 2(1) of the 2007 Act apply as respects a practitioner";

(ii) paragraphs (b) and (c) are repealed;

(c) in subsection (2), paragraphs (a), (b) and (f) are repealed;

(d) in subsection (2A)(a)—
(i) for the word "complaint" substitute "conduct complaint";
(ii) for the words "the Scottish Solicitor's Discipline Tribunal" substitute "the Tribunal";
(iii) sub-paragraph (ii), and the word "or" following it, are repealed;
(e) in subsection (2B)(d), for the word "(f)" substitute "(c)";
(f) in subsection (6)—
(i) for the words "(a), (b) or (f)" substitute "(a) or (b)";
(ii) for the words "the Scottish Solicitors' Discipline Tribunal" substitute "the Tribunal";
(iii) after the words "similar direction,", insert "or where the Council make a direction under subsection (2)(ca) or the Tribunal make a direction under subsection (2B)(aa),";
(g) in subsection (7), for the words "Court of Session" substitute "court";
(h) in subsection (8), for the words "the Scottish Solicitors' Discipline Tribunal" substitute "the Tribunal";
(i) in subsection (11)—
(i) for the word "(f)" substitute "(cb)";
(ii) in paragraph (b), for the words "the Scottish Solicitors' Discipline Tribunal" substitute "the Tribunal";
(j) in subsection (11A)—
(i) for the words "Court of Session" substitute "court";
(ii) for the word "Court", where it second occurs, substitute "court";
(k) after subsection (11E) (as inserted by section 57(2)(d) of this Act), insert—
"(11F) A direction of the Tribunal under this section is enforceable in like manner as an extract registered decree arbitral in its favour bearing a warrant for execution issued by the sheriff court of any sheriffdom in Scotland.";
(l) subsections (13), (14) and (15) are repealed;
(m) in subsection (16), after the word "subsection" insert "(2)(cb) or".

(5) In section 20A (review by Council of decisions), in subsection (2)(a)(iii) for the word "(f)" substitute "(cb)".

(6) In section 21 (intervention powers)—
(a) in the section title, for the word "Board's" substitute "Council's";
(b) in subsection (2)—
(i) after paragraph (a), insert "or";
(ii) paragraph (c), and the preceding "or", are repealed;
(c) in each of subsections (5), (6), (7) and (10), for the words "Court of Session" substitute "court";
(d) after subsection (11), insert—
"(11A) Where the Council make a direction under subsection (3) or (4) or apply to the court for an order under subsection (10), the Council shall notify the Commission to that effect and provide it with details of their findings in any inquiry held by virtue of subsection (1) as respects the practitioner concerned.".

(7) In section 21A (powers of investigation in relation to conveyancing or executry practitioners)—
(a) in subsection (1)—
(i) for the words "any of the following purposes—" substitute "the purpose of";
(ii) paragraphs (a) and (b), and the word "and" following paragraph (b), are repealed;
(iii) in paragraph (c), for the words "the Council", where it second occurs, substitute "them";
(b) in subsection (2)—
(i) for the words "the Scottish Solicitors' Discipline Tribunal" substitute "the Tribunal";
(ii) in paragraph (b), for the words "(11)(b)" substitute "(8A)(b), (11)(b) or (11ZC)".

(8) In section 21B (procedures of Tribunal etc. in relation to conveyancing or executry practitioners)—
(a) in the section title, for the words "the Scottish Solicitors' Discipline Tribunal" substitute "the Tribunal";
(b) in subsection (1)—
(i) for the words "the Scottish Solicitors' Discipline Tribunal" substitute "the Tribunal";
(ii) for paragraph (a), substitute—
"(a) in paragraph 9(a)(i) and (b), the words "or, as the case may be, of provision of inadequate professional services" were omitted;";

(c) in subsection (2)—

(i) for the words "(11)(b)" substitute "(8A)(b), (11)(b) or (11ZC)";

(ii) after the words "section 20", insert ", 20ZB(9), (10), (11) or (12) or 20ZE(1);

(iii) in paragraph (a), for the word "(b)" substitute "(ca), (cc), (cd)";

(iv) in paragraph (b), after the words "this Act" insert "and as regards paragraph 25 also as if for the words "the solicitor, the firm of solicitors or, as the case may be, the incorporated practice" there were substituted "the practitioner";

(d) in subsection (3)—

(i) for the words "the Scottish Solicitors' Discipline Tribunal" substitute "the Tribunal";

(ii) in paragraph (b), for the words "(11)(b)" substitute "(8A)(b), (11)(b) or (11ZC)";

(e) in subsection (4)—

(i) for the word "Court", in both places where it occurs, substitute "court";

(ii) in paragraph (a), after the word "(11A)" insert "(11B), (11C) or (11D)".

(9) In section 23 (interpretation of sections 16 to 22)—

(a) before the definition of "conveyancing practitioner", insert—

" "complainer" means the person who made the complaint and, where the complaint was made by the person on behalf of another person, includes that other person;";

(b) after the definition of "the Council", insert—

" "the court" means the Court of Session;";

(c) the definition of "inadequate professional services" is repealed;

(d) after the definition of "relevant notarial services", insert

";

"the Tribunal" means the Scottish Solicitors' Discipline Tribunal;

"unsatisfactory professional conduct" has the meaning given (as respects a conveyancing practitioner or, as the case may be, an executry practitioner) by section 46 of the 2007 Act".

(10) In section 25 (rights to conduct litigation and rights of audience)—

(a) in subsection (2)(b)(ii), for the words "this section" substitute "section 27 of this Act";

(b) in subsection (2)(c)(i), for the words "this section" substitute "section 27 of this Act in the event of the application being granted";

(c) in subsection (2)(c)(ii)—

(i) for the words from "made" to "public" substitute "remitted to the body under section 6(a) or 15(5)(a) of the 2007 Act";

(ii) the words "the actings of" are repealed;

(iii) for the words "this section" substitute "section 27 of this Act in the event of the application being granted";

(d) in subsection (3), for the words "this section" substitute "section 27 of this Act".

(11) In section 33 (complaints in relation to legal services) after subsection (5) insert—

"(6) This section does not apply to any element of a conduct complaint other than that involving the provision of advice, services or activities referred to in section 77(2) of the 2007 Act.".

(12) In section 44, after the definition of "the 1980 Act" insert—

" "the 2007 Act" means the Legal Profession and Legal Aid (Scotland) Act 2007 (asp 5).".

Ethical Standards in Public Life etc. (Scotland) Act 2000 (asp 7)

4. In the Ethical Standards in Public Life etc. (Scotland) Act 2000, in schedule 3 (devolved public bodies) after the entry relating to the Scottish Legal Aid Board insert—

"The Scottish Legal Complaints Commission".

Freedom of Information (Scotland) Act 2002 (asp 13)

5. In the Freedom of Information (Scotland) Act 2002, in schedule 1 (Scottish public authorities) after paragraph 92 insert—

"92A. The Scottish Legal Complaints Commission.".

Public Appointments and Public Bodies etc. (Scotland) Act 2003 (asp 4)

6. In the Public Appointments and Public Bodies etc. (Scotland) Act 2003, in schedule 2 (specified authorities) after the entry relating to the Scottish Legal Aid Board insert—

"Scottish Legal Complaints Commission".

The Legal Profession and Legal Aid (Scotland) Act 2007 (Commencement No. 1) Order 2007

(SSI 2007/57)

[February 8, 2007]

The Scottish Ministers, in exercise of the powers conferred by section 82(2) of the Legal Profession and Legal Aid (Scotland) Act 2007, hereby make the following Order:

Citation and interpretation

1.—(1) This Order may be cited as the Legal Profession and Legal Aid (Scotland) Act 2007 (Commencement No. 1) Order 2007.

(2) In this Order "the Act" means the Legal Profession and Legal Aid (Scotland) Act 2007.

Appointed day

2. 8th February 2007 is the appointed day for the coming into force of the following provisions of the Act—

(a) section 69(1), (2)(a) and (4);
(b) section 71;
(c) section 73; and
(d) section 76.

The Legal Profession and Legal Aid (Scotland) Act 2007 (Commencement No. 2) Order 2007

(SSI 2007/140)

[March 19, 2007]

The Scottish Ministers, in exercise of the powers conferred by section 82(2) of the Legal Profession and Legal Aid (Scotland) Act 2007, hereby make the following Order:

Citation

1. This Order may be cited as the Legal Profession and Legal Aid (Scotland) Act 2007 (Commencement No.2) Order 2007.

Appointed day

2. 19th March 2007 is the appointed day for the coming into force of the following provisions of the Legal Profession and Legal Aid (Scotland) Act 2007—

(a) section 1 so far as relating to paragraphs 1 to 7, 12 and 14 of schedule 1;
(b) section 44;
(c) section 61;
(d) section 81 so far as relating to paragraph 3(10) of schedule 5;
(e) paragraphs 1 to 7, 12 and 14 of schedule 1; and
(f) paragraph 3(10) of schedule 5.

The Legal Profession and Legal Aid (Scotland) Act 2007 (Commencement No. 3) Order 2007

(SSI 2007/335)

[July 30, 2007]

The Scottish Ministers make the following Order in exercise of the powers conferred by section 82(2) of the Legal Profession and Legal Aid (Scotland) Act 2007.

Citation

1. This Order may be cited as the Legal Profession and Legal Aid (Scotland) Act 2007 (Commencement No. 3) Order 2007.

Appointed day

2. 30th July 2007 is the appointed day for the coming into force of the following provisions of the Legal Profession and Legal Aid (Scotland) Act 2007—

(a) section 67;
(b) section 68; and
(c) section 74.

The Legal Profession and Legal Aid (Scotland) Act 2007 (Commencement No. 4) Order 2007

(SSI 2007/497)

[November 23, 2007]

The Scottish Ministers make the following Order in exercise of the powers conferred by section 82(2) of the Legal Profession and Legal Aid (Scotland) Act 2007.

Citation

1. This Order may be cited as the Legal Profession and Legal Aid (Scotland) Act 2007 (Commencement No. 4) Order 2007.

Appointed day

2. 23rd November 2007 is the appointed day for the coming into force of the following provisions of the Legal Profession and Legal Aid (Scotland) Act 2007:–

(a) section 1, in so far as not already commenced;
(b) sections 27, 29, 30, 31, 32, 34, 39, 41, 58, 59, 60, 62, 63 and 78;
(c) section 81, so far as relating to paragraph 1(15) and (16) and paragraph 6 of schedule 5;
(d) paragraphs 8 to 11, 13, 15 and 16 of schedule 1;
(e) schedule 3; and
(f) paragraph 1(15) and (16) and paragraph 6 of schedule 5.

 [NEXT TEXT PAGE IS **F** 101]

Statutory Instruments

Property Misdescriptions (Specified Matters) Order 1992

(SI 1992 No. 2834)

[11th November 1992]

The Secretary of State, in exercise of the powers conferred upon him by section 1 of the Property Misdescriptions Act 1991, hereby makes the following Order:

1. This Order may be cited as the Property Misdescriptions (Specified Matters) Order 1992 and shall come into force on 4th April 1993.

2. The matters contained in the Schedule to this Order are hereby specified to the extent described in that Schedule for the purposes of section 1(1) of the Property Misdescriptions Act 1991.

Article 2

SCHEDULE

SPECIFIED MATTERS

1. Location or address.

2. Aspect, view, outlook or environment.

3. Availability and nature of services, facilities or amenities.

4. Proximity to any services, places, facilities or amenities.

5. Accommodation, measurements or sizes.

6. Fixtures and fittings.

7. Physical or structural characteristics, form of construction or condition.

8. Fitness for any purpose or strength of any buildings or other structures on land or of land itself.

9. Treatments, processes, repairs or improvements or the effects thereof.

10. Conformity or compliance with any scheme, standard, test or regulations or the existence of any guarantee.

11. Survey, inspection, investigation, valuation or appraisal by any person or the results thereof.

12. The grant or giving of any award or prize for design or construction.

13. History, including the age, ownership or use of land or any building or fixture and the date of any alterations thereto.

14. Person by whom any building, (or part of any building), fixture or component was designed, constructed, built, produced, treated, processed, repaired, reconditioned or tested.

15. The length of time during which land has been available for sale either generally or by or through a particular person.

16. Price (other than the price at which accommodation or facilities are available and are to be provided by means of the creation or disposal of an interest in land in the circumstances specified in section 23(1)(a) and (b) of the Consumer Protection Act 1987 or Article 16(1)(a) and (b) of the Consumer Protection (NI) Order 1987 (which relate to the creation or disposal of certain interests in new dwellings)) and previous price.

17. Tenure or estate.

18. Length of any lease or of the unexpired term of any lease and the terms and conditions of a lease (and, in relation to land in Northern Ireland, any fee farm grant creating the relation of landlord and tenant shall be treated as a lease).

19. Amount of any ground-rent, rent or premium and frequency of any review.

20. Amount of any rent-charge.

21. Where all or any part of any land is let to a tenant or is subject to a licence, particulars of the tenancy or licence, including any rent, premium or other payment due and frequency of any review.

22. Amount of any service or maintenance charge or liability for common repairs.

23. Council tax payable in respect of a dwelling within the meaning of section 3, or in Scotland section 72, of the Local Government Finance Act 1992 or the basis or any part of the basis on which that tax is calculated.

24. Rates payable in respect of a non-domestic hereditament within the meaning of section 64 of the Local Government Finance Act 1988 or, in Scotland, in respect of lands and heritages shown on a valuation roll or the basis or any part of the basis on which those rates are calculated.

25. Rates payable in respect of a hereditament within the meaning of the Rates (Northern Ireland) Order 1977 or the basis or any part of the basis on which those rates are calculated.

26. Existence or nature of any planning permission or proposals for development, construction or change of use.

27. In relation to land in England and Wales, the passing or rejection of any plans of proposed building work in accordance with section 16 of the Building Act 1984 and the giving of any completion certificate in accordance with regulation 15 of the Building Regulations 1991.

28. In relation to land in Scotland, the granting of a warrant under section 6 of the Building (Scotland) Act 1959 or the granting of a certificate of completion under section 9 of that Act.

29. In relation to land in Northern Ireland, the passing or rejection of any plans of proposed building work in accordance with Article 13 of the Building Regulations (Northern Ireland) Order 1979 and the giving of any completion certificate in accordance with building regulations made under that Order.

30. Application of any statutory provision which restricts the use of land or which requires it to be preserved or maintained in a specified manner.

31. Existence or nature of any restrictive covenants, or of any restrictions on resale, restrictions on use, or pre-emption rights and, in relation to land in Scotland, (in addition to the matters mentioned previously in this paragraph) the existence or nature of any reservations or real conditions.

32. Easements, servitudes or wayleaves.

33. Existence and extent of any public or private right of way.

[NEXT TEXT PAGE IS **F** 116/1]

Money Laundering Regulations 1993

(S.I. 1993 No. 1933)

ARRANGEMENT OF REGULATIONS

The Treasury being a government department designated for the purposes of section 2(2) of the European Communities Act 1972 in relation to measures relating to preventing the use of the financial system for the purpose of money laundering, in exercise of the powers conferred by that section hereby make the following regulations:—

General

Citation and commencement

1.—(1) These Regulations may be cited as the Money Laundering Regulations 1993.

(2) These Regulations shall come into force on 1st April 1994.

Interpretation

2.—[1] (1) In these Regulations—

"applicant for business" means a person seeking to form a business relationship, or carry out a one-off transaction, with a person who is carrying out relevant financial business in the United Kingdom;

"the Banking Consolidation Directive" means Directive 2000/12/EC of the European Parliament and of the Council of 20 March 2000 relating to the taking up and pursuit of the business of credit institutions;

"business relationship" has the meaning given by regulation 3 below;

"Case 1", "Case 2", "Case 3" and "Case 4" have the meanings given in regulation 7 below;

"constable" includes a person commissioned by the Commissioners of Customs and Excise;

"European institution" has the same meaning as in Banking Coordination (Second Council Directive) Regulations 1992;

"insurance business" means long term business within the meaning of the Insurance Companies Act 1982;

"the Money Laundering Directive" means the Council Directive on prevention of the use of the financial system for the purpose of money laundering (No. 91/308/EEC);

"one-off transaction" means any transaction other than a transaction carried out in the course of an established business relationship formed by a person acting in the course of relevant financial business;

"relevant financial business" has the meaning given by regulation 4 below; and

"supervisory authority" has the meaning given by regulation 15 below.

(2) In these Regulations "ecu" means the european currency unit as defined in article 1 of Council Regulation No. 3180/78/EEC; and the exchange rates as between the ecu and the currencies of the member States to be applied for each year beginning on 31st December shall be the rates applicable on the last day of the preceding October for which rates for the currencies of all the member States were published in the Official Journal of the Communities.

(3) In these Regulations, except in so far as the context otherwise requires, "money laundering" means doing any act which constitutes an offence under—

(a) section 23A or 24 of the Drug Trafficking Offences Act 1986 (which relate to the handling etc. of proceeds of drug trafficking);

(b) section 42A or 43 of the Criminal Justice (Scotland) Act 1987 (which relate to the handling etc. of proceeds of drug trafficking);

(c) section 93A, 93B or 93C of the Criminal Justice Act 1988 (which relate to the handling etc. of proceeds of certain other criminal conduct);

(d) section 11 of the Prevention of Terrorism (Temporary Provisions) Act 1989 (which relates to financial assistance for terrorism);

(e) section 14 of the Criminal Justice (International Co-operation) Act 1990 (concealing or transferring proceeds of drug trafficking);

(f) Article 29 or 30 of the Criminal Justice (Confiscation) (Northern Ireland) Order 1990 (which relate to the handling etc. of proceeds of drug trafficking);

(g) section 53 or 54 of the Northern Ireland (Emergency Provisions) Act 1991 (which relate to the handling etc. of proceeds of terrorist-related activities); or

(h) any provision, whenever made, which has effect in Northern Ireland and corresponds to any of the provisions mentioned in sub-paragraph (a) or (c) above;

or, in the case of an act done otherwise than in England and Wales, Scotland or, as the case may be, Northern Ireland would constitute such an offence if done in England and Wales, Scotland or Northern Ireland.

(4) The reference in paragraph (3) above to doing any act which would constitute an offence under the provisions mentioned in sub-paragraph (c) of that paragraph shall, for the purposes of these Regulations, be construed as a reference to doing any act which would constitute an offence under those provisions if, for the definition of "criminal conduct" in section 93A(7) of the Criminal Justice Act 1988, there were substituted—

"(7) In this Part of this Act "criminal conduct" means—

(a) conduct which constitutes an offence to which this Part of this Act applies; or

(b) conduct which—

(i) would constitute such an offence if it had occurred in England and Wales or (as the case may be) Scotland; and

(ii) contravenes the law of the country in which it occurred."

(5) For the purposes of these Regulations, any provision having effect in Northern Ireland which corresponds to the provisions referred to in paragraph 3(c) above shall be construed as if it had been amended by a provision which corresponds to paragraph (4) above, with appropriate modifications.

(6) For the purposes of this regulation, a business relationship formed by any person acting in the course of relevant financial business is an established business relationship where that person has obtained, under procedures maintained by him in accordance with regulation 7 below, satisfactory evidence of the identity of the person who, in relation to the formation of that business relationship, was the applicant for business.

NOTE

[1] Inserted by the Banking Consolidation Directive (Consequential Amendments) Regulations 2000 (S.I. 2000 No. 2952) Reg. 11.

Business relationships

3.—(1) Any reference in this regulation to an arrangement between two or more persons is a reference to an arrangement in which at least one person is acting in the course of a business.

(2) For the purposes of these Regulations, "business relationship" means any arrangement between two or more persons where—

(a) the purpose of the arrangement is to facilitate the carrying out of transactions between the persons concerned on a frequent, habitual or regular basis; and

(b) the total amount of any payment or payments to be made by any person to any other in the course of that arrangement is not known or capable of being ascertained at the time the arrangement is made.

Relevant financial business

4.—(1) For the purposes of these Regulations, "relevant financial business" means, subject to paragraph (2) below, the business of engaging in one or more of the following—

(a) deposit-taking business carried on by a person who is for the time being authorised under the Banking Act 1987;

(b) acceptance by a building society of deposits made by any person (including the raising of money from members of the society by the issue of shares);

(c) business of the National Savings Bank;

(d) business carried on by a credit union within the meaning of the Credit Unions Act 1979 or the Credit Unions (Northern Ireland) Order 1985;

(e) any home regulated activity carried on by a European institution in respect of which the requirements of paragraph 1 of Schedule 2 to the Banking Coordination (Second Council Directive) Regulations 1992 have been complied with;

(f) investment business within the meaning of the Financial Services Act 1986;

(g) any activity carried on for the purpose of raising money authorised to be raised under the National Loans Act 1968 under the auspices of the Director of National Savings;

[1] (h) any of the activities in points 1 to 12, or 14, of Annex 1 to the Banking Consolidation Directive (the text of which is, for convenience of reference, set out in the Schedule to these Regulations), other than an activity falling within sub-paragraphs (a) to (g) above;

(i) insurance business carried on by a person who has received official authorisation pursuant to Article 6 or 27 of the First Life Directive.

(2) A business is not relevant financial business in so far as it consists of—

(a) any of the following activities carried on by a society registered under the Industrial and Provident Societies Act 1965—

(i) the issue of withdrawable share capital within the limit set by section 6 of that Act; or

(ii) the acceptance of deposits from the public within the limit set by section 7(3) of that Act;

(b) the issue of withdrawable share capital within the limit set by section 6 of the Industrial and Provident Societies Act (Northern Ireland) 1969 by a society registered under that Act;

(c) activities carried on by the Bank of England;

(d) in relation to any person who is an exempted person for the purposes of section 45 of the Financial Services Act 1986 (miscellaneous exemptions for holders of certain judicial and other offices), such of the activities as are specified in that section in relation to that person; or

(e) in relation to any person who is an exempted person for the purposes of any order made under section 46 of the Financial Services Act 1986 which was made before the date on which these Regulations come into force, any activities carried on by him or, as the case may be, such of the activities as are specified in such an order in relation to him.

(3) For the purposes of paragraph (1)(f) above, any reference in these Regulations to the carrying on of relevant financial business in the United Kingdom shall be construed in accordance with section 1(3) of the Financial Services Act 1986.

(4) In this regulation—

"building society" has the same meaning as in the Building Societies Act 1986;

"deposit-taking business" has the same meaning as in the Banking Act 1987;

"the First Life Directive" means the First Council Directive on the coordination of laws, regulations and administrative provisions relating to the taking up and pursuit of the business of direct life assurance (No. 79/267/EEC).

NOTE

[1] Inserted by the Banking Consolidation Directive (Consequential Amendments) Regulations 2000 (S.I. 2000 No. 2952) Reg. 11.

Systems and training to prevent money laundering

Systems and training to prevent money laundering

5.—(1) No person shall, in the course of relevant financial business carried on by him in the United Kingdom, form a business relationship, or carry out a one-off transaction, with or for another unless that person—

(a) maintains the following procedures established in relation to that business—
   (i) identification procedures in accordance with regulations 7 and 9 below;
   (ii) record-keeping procedure in accordance with regulation 12 below;
   (iii) except where the person concerned is an individual who in the course of relevant financial business does not employ or act in association with any other person, internal reporting procedures in accordance with regulation 14 below; and
   (iv) such other procedures of internal control and communication as may be appropriate for the purposes of forestalling and preventing money laundering;

(b) takes appropriate measures from time to time for the purposes of making employees whose duties include the handling of relevant financial business aware of—
   (i) the procedures under sub-paragraph (a) above which are maintained by him and which relate to the relevant financial business in question, and
   (ii) the enactments relating to money laundering; and

(c) provides such employees from time to time with training in the recognition and handling of transactions carried out by, or on behalf of, any person who is, or appears to be, engaged in money laundering.

(2) Any person who contravenes this regulation shall be guilty of an offence and liable—

(a) on conviction on indictment, to imprisonment not exceeding a term of two years or a fine or both,

(b) on summary conviction, to a fine not exceeding the statutory maximum.

(3) In determining whether a person has complied with any of the requirements of paragraph (1) above, a court may take account of—

(a) any relevant supervisory or regulatory guidance which applies to that person;

(b) in a case where no guidance falling within sub-paragraph (a) above applies, any other relevant guidance issued by a body that regulates, or is representative of, any trade, profession, business or employment carried on by that person.

(4) In proceedings against any person for an offence under this regulation, it shall be a defence for that person to show that he took all reasonable steps and exercised all due diligence to avoid committing the offence.

(5) In this regulation—

"enactments relating to money laundering" means the enactments referred to in regulation 2(3) above and the provisions of these Regulations; and

"supervisory or regulatory guidance" means guidance issued, adopted or approved by a supervisory authority.

Offences by bodies corporate, partnerships and unincorporated associations

6.—(1) Where an offence under regulation 5 above committed by a body corporate is proved to have been committed with the consent or connivance of, or to be attributable to any neglect on the part of, any director, manager, secretary or other similar officer of the body corporate or any person who was purporting to act in any such capacity he, as well as the body corporate, shall be guilty of that offence and shall be liable to be proceeded against and punished accordingly.

(2) Where the affairs of a body corporate are managed by the members, paragraph (1) above shall apply in relation to the acts and defaults of a

member in connection with his functions of management as if he were a director of a body corporate.

(3) Where an offence under regulation 5 above committed by a partnership, or by an unincorporated association other than a partnership, is proved to have been committed with the consent or connivance of, or is attributable to any neglect on the part of, a partner in the partnership or (as the case may be) a person concerned in the management or control of the association, he, as well as the partnership or association, shall be guilty of that offence and shall be liable to be proceeded against and punished accordingly.

Identification procedures

Identification procedures; business relationships and transactions

7.—(1) Subject to regulations 8 and 10 below, identification procedures maintained by a person are in accordance with this regulation if in Cases 1 to 4 set out below they require, as soon as is reasonably practicable after contact is first made between that person and an applicant for business concerning any particular business relationship or one-off transaction—

(a) the production by the applicant for business of satisfactory evidence of his identity; or

(b) the taking of such measures specified in the procedures as will produce satisfactory evidence of his identity;

and the procedures are, subject to paragraph (6) below, in accordance with this regulation if they require that where that evidence is not obtained the business relationship or one-off transaction in question shall not proceed any further.

(2) Case 1 is any case where the parties form or resolve to form a business relationship between them.

(3) Case 2 is any case where, in respect of any one-off transaction, any person handling the transaction knows or suspects that the applicant for business is engaged in money laundering, or that the transaction is carried out on behalf of another person engaged in money laundering.

(4) Case 3 is any case where, in respect of any one-off transaction, payment is to be made by or to the applicant for business of the amount of ecu 15,000 or more.

(5) Case 4 is any case where, in respect of two or more one-off transactions—

(a) appears at the outset to a person handling any of the transactions—

(i) that the transactions are linked, and

(ii) that the total amount, in respect of all of the transactions, which is payable by or to the applicant for business is ecu15,000 or more; or

(b) at any later stage, it comes to the attention of such a person that paragraphs (i) and (ii) of sub-paragraph (a) above are satisfied.

(6) The procedures referred to in paragraph (1) above are in accordance with this regulation if, when a report is made in circumstances falling within Case 2 (whether in accordance with regulation 14 or directly to a constable), they provided for steps to be taken in relation to the one-off transaction in question in accordance with any directions that may be given by a constable.

(7) In these Regulations references to satisfactory evidence of a person's identity shall be construed in accordance with regulation 11(1) below.

Payment by post etc.

8.—(1) Where satisfactory evidence of the identity of an applicant for business would, apart from this paragraph, be required under identification procedures in accordance with regulation 7 above but—

(a) the circumstances are such that a payment is to be made by the applicant for business; and

(b) it is reasonable in all the circumstances—

(i) for the payment to be sent by post or by any electronic means which is effective to transfer funds; or

(ii) for the details of the payment to be sent by post, to be given on the telephone or to be given by any other electronic means;

then, subject to paragraph (2) below, the fact that the payment is debited from an account held in the applicant's name at an institution mentioned in paragraph (4) below (whether the account is held by the applicant alone or jointly with one or more other persons) shall be capable of constituting the required evidence of identity.

(2) Paragraph (1) above shall not have effect to the extent that—

(a) the circumstances of the payment fall within Case 2; or

(b) the payment is made by any person for the purpose of opening a relevant account with an institution falling within paragraph (4)(a) or (b) below.

(3) For the purposes of paragraph (1)(b) above, it shall be immaterial whether the payment or its details are sent or given to a person who is bound by regulation 5(1) above or to some other person acting in his behalf.

(4) The institutions referred to in paragraph (1) above are—

[1] (a) an institution which is for the time being authorised by the Financial Services Authority under the Banking Act 1987 or by the Building Societies Commission under the Building Societies Act 1986;

(b) a European authorised institution within the meaning of the Banking Coordination (Second Council Directive) Regulations 1992; or

(c) any other institution which is an authorised credit institution.

[2] (5) For the purposes of this regulation—

"authorised credit institution" means a credit institution, as defined in Article 1 of the Banking Consolidation Directive, which is authorised to carry on the business of a credit institution by a competent authority of a member State; and

"relevant account" means an account from which a payment may be made by any means to a person other than the applicant for business, whether such a payment—

(a) may be made directly to such a person from the account by or on behalf of the applicant for business; or

(b) may be made to such a person indirectly as a result of—

(i) a direct transfer of funds from an account from which no such direct payment may be made to another account, or

(ii) a change in any of the characteristics of the account.

NOTE

[1] As amended by the Bank of England Act 1998 (Consequential Amendments of Subordinate Legislation Order 1998 (S.I. 1998 No. 1129), Art. 2, Sched. 1, para. 15.

[2] Inserted by the Banking Consolidation Directive (Consequential Amendments) Regulations 2000 (S.I. 2000 No. 2952) Reg. 11.

Identification procedures; transactions on behalf of another

9.—(1) This regulation applies where, in relation to a person who is bound by regulation 5(1) above, an applicant for business is or appears to be acting otherwise than as principal.

(2) Subject to regulation 10 below, identification procedures maintained by a person are in accordance with this regulation if, in a case to which this regulation applies, they require reasonable measures to be taken for the purpose of establishing the identity of any person on whose behalf the applicant for business is acting.

(3) In determining, for the purposes of paragraph (2) above, what constitutes reasonable measures in any particular case regard shall be had to all the circumstances of the case and, in particular, to best practice which,

for the time being, is followed in the relevant field of business and which is applicable to those circumstances.

(4) Without prejudice to the generality of paragraph (3) above, if the conditions mentioned in paragraph (5) below are fulfilled in relation to an applicant for business who is, or appears to be, acting as an agent for a principal (whether undisclosed or disclosed for reference purposes only) it shall be reasonable for a person bound by regulation 5(1) above to accept a written assurance from the applicant for business to the effect that evidence of the identity of any principal on whose behalf the applicant for business may act in relation to that person will have been obtained and recorded under procedures maintained by the applicant for business.

(5) The conditions referred to in paragraph (4) above are that, in relation to the business relationship or transaction in question, there are reasonable grounds for believing that the applicant for business—

(a) acts in the course of a business in relation to which an overseas regulatory authority exercises regulatory functions; and

(b) is based or incorporated in, or formed under the law of, a country other than a member State in which there are in force provisions at least equivalent to those required by the Money Laundering Directive.

(6) In paragraph (5) above, "overseas regulatory authority" and "regulatory functions" have the same meaning as in section 82 of the Companies Act 1989.

Identification procedures; exemptions

10.—(1) Subject to paragraph (2) below, identification procedures under regulations 7 and 9 above shall not require any steps to be taken to obtain evidence of any person's identity—

(a) where there are reasonable grounds for believing that the applicant for business is a person who is bound by the provisions of regulation 5(1) above;

(b) where there are reasonable grounds for believing that the applicant for business is otherwise a person who is covered by the Money Laundering Directive;

(c) where any one-off transaction is carried out with or for a third party pursuant to an introduction effected by a person who has provided an assurance that evidence of the identity of all third parties introduced by him will have been obtained and recorded under procedures maintained by him, where that person identifies the third party and where—

(i) that person falls within sub-paragraph (a) or (b) above; or

(ii) there are reasonable grounds for believing that the conditions mentioned in regulation 9(5)(a) and (b) above are fulfilled in relation to him;

(d) where the person who would otherwise be required to be identified, in relation to a one-off transaction, is the person to whom the proceeds of that transaction are payable but to whom no payment is made because all of those proceeds are directly reinvested on this behalf in another transaction—

(i) of which a record is kept, and

(ii) which can result only in another reinvestment made on that person's behalf or in a payment made directly to that person;

(e) in relation to insurance business consisting of a policy of insurance in connection with a pension scheme taken out by virtue of a person's contract of employment or occupation where the policy—

(i) contains no surrender clause, and

(ii) may not be used as collateral for a loan;

(f) in relation to insurance business in respect of which a premium is payable in one instalment of an amount not exceeding ecu 2,500; or

(g) in relation to insurance business in respect of which a periodic premium is payable and where the total payable in respect of any calendar year does not exceed ecu 1,000.

(2) Nothing in this regulation shall apply in circumstances falling within Case 2.

(3) In this regulation "calendar year" means a period of twelve months beginning on 31st December.

Identification procedures; supplementary provisions

11.—(1) For the purposes of these regulations, evidence of identity is satisfactory if—

(a) it is reasonably capable of establishing that the applicant is the person he claims to be; and

(b) the person who obtains the evidence is satisfied, in accordance with the procedures maintained under these Regulations in relation to the relevant financial business concerned, that it does establish that fact.

(2) In determining for the purposes of regulation 7(1) above the time span in which satisfactory evidence of a person's identity has to be obtained, in relation to any particular business relationship or one-off transaction, all the circumstances shall be taken into account including, in particular—

(a) the nature of the business relationship or one-off transaction concerned;

(b) the geographical locations of the parties;

(c) whether it is practical to obtain the evidence before commitments are entered into between the parties or before money passes;

(d) in relation to Case 3 or 4, the earliest stage at which there are reasonable grounds for believing that the total amount payable by an applicant for business is ecu 15,000 or more.

Record-keeping procedures

Record-keeping procedures

12.—(1) Record-keeping procedures maintained by a person are in accordance with this regulation if they require the keeping, for the prescribed period, of the following records—

(a) in any case where, in relation to any business relationship that is formed or one-off transaction that is carried out, evidence of a person's identity is obtained under procedures maintained in accordance with regulation 7 or 9 above, a record that indicates the nature of the evidence and—

(i) comprises a copy of the evidence;

(ii) provides such information as would enable a copy of it to be obtained; or

(iii) in a case where it is not reasonably practicable to comply with paragraph (i) or (ii) above, provides sufficient information to enable the details as to a person's identity contained in the relevant evidence to be re-obtained; and

(b) a record containing details relating to all transactions carried out by that person in the course of relevant financial business.

(2) For the purposes of paragraph (1) above, the prescribed period is, subject to paragraph (3) below, the period of at least five years commencing with—

(a) in relation to such records as are described in sub-paragraph (a), the date on which the relevant business was completed within the meaning of paragraph (4) below; and

(b) in relation to such records as are described in sub-paragraph (b), the date on which all activities taking place in the course of the transaction in question were completed.

(3) Where a person who is bound by the provisions of regulation 5(1) above—

(a) forms a business relationship or carries out a one-off transaction with another person;

(b) has reasonable grounds for believing that that person has become insolvent; and

(c) after forming that belief, takes any step for the purpose of recovering all or part of the amount of any debt payable to him by that person which has fallen due;

the prescribed period for the purposes of paragraph (1) above is the period of at least five years commencing with the date on which the first such step is taken.

(4) For the purposes of paragraph (2)(a) above, the date on which relevant business is completed is, as the case may be—

(a) in circumstances falling within Case 1, the date of the ending of the business relationship in respect of whose formation the record under paragraph (1)(a) above was compiled;

(b) in circumstances falling within Case 2 or 3, the date of the completion of all activities taking place in the course of the one-off transaction in respect of which the record under paragraph (1)(a) above was compiled;

(c) in circumstances falling within Case 4, the date of the completion of all activities taking place in the course of the last one-off transaction in respect of which the record under paragraph (1)(a) above was compiled:

and where the formalities necessary to end a business relationship have not been observed, but a period of five years has elapsed since the date on which the last transaction was carried out in the course of that relationship, then the date of the completion of all activities taking place in the course of that last transaction shall be treated as the date on which the relevant business was completed.

Record-keeping procedures; supplementary provisions

13.—(1) For the purposes of regulation 12(3)(b) above, a person shall be taken to be insolvent if, but only if, in England and Wales—

(a) he has been adjudged bankrupt or has made a composition or arrangement with his creditors;

(b) an order has been made with respect to him under section 112, 112A or 112B of the County Courts Act 1984 (administration orders, orders restricting enforcement and administration orders with composition provisions);

(c) he has died and his estate falls to be administered in accordance with an order under section 421 of the Insolvency Act 1986 (insolvent estates of deceased persons); or

[2](d) where that person is a company, a winding up order has been made or a resolution for voluntary winding up has been passed with respect to it, or it has entered administration, or a receiver or manager of its undertaking has been duly appointed, or possession has been taken, by or on behalf of the holders of any debentures secured by a floating charge, of any property of the company comprised in or subject to the charge, or a voluntary arrangement proposed for the purpose of Part I of the Insolvency Act 1986 has been approved under that Part, or a compromise or arrangement in accordance with section 425 of the Companies Act 1985 has taken effect.

(2) For the purposes of regulation 12(3)(b) above, a person shall be taken to be insolvent if, but only if, in Scotland—

(a) his estate has been sequestrated, he has granted a trust deed for the benefit of his creditors or he has made a composition or arrangement for the benefit of his creditors; or

[2] (b) where that person is a company, a winding up order has been made or a resolution for voluntary winding up has been passed with respect to it, or it has entered administration, or a receiver has been appointed under a floating charge over any property of the company, or a voluntary arrangement proposed for the purpose of Part I of the Insolvency Act 1986 has been approved under that Part, or a compromise or arrangement in accordance with section 425 of the Companies Act 1985 has taken effect.

(3) For the purposes of regulation 12(3)(b) above, a person shall be taken to be insolvent if, but only if, in Northern Ireland—

(a) he has been adjudged bankrupt or has made a composition or arrangement with his creditors;

(b) an administration order has been made with respect to him under Article 80 of the Judgements Enforcement (Northern Ireland) Order 1981 (power to make administration order on application of debtor);

(c) he has died and his estate falls to be administered in accordance with an order under Article 365 of the Insolvency (Northern Ireland) Order 1989 (insolvent estates of deceased persons); or

(d) where that person is a company, a winding up order or an administration order has been made or a resolution for voluntary winding up has been passed with respect to it, or a receiver or manager of its undertaking has been duly appointed, or possession has been taken, by or on behalf of the holders of any debentures secured by a floating charge, of any property of the company comprised in or subject to the charge, or a voluntary arrangement proposed for the purpose of Part II of the Insolvency (Northern Ireland) Order 1988 has been approved under that Part, or a compromise or arrangement in accordance with Article 418 of the Companies (Northern Ireland) Order 1986 has taken effect.

[1] (4) Where a person bound by regulation 5(1) above—

(a) is an appointed representative; and

(b) is not—

(i) an authorised person within the meaning of the Financial Services Act 1986,

(ii) authorised under the Building Societies Act 1986 or the Banking Act 1987, or

(iii) a European institution;

it shall be the responsibility of the appointed representative's principal to ensure that record-keeping procedures in accordance with regulation 12 above are maintained in respect of any relevant financial business carried out by the appointed representative for which the principal has accepted responsibility in writing under section 44 of the Financial Services Act 1986.

(5) Where record-keeping procedures in accordance with regulation 12 above are not maintained in respect of business relationships formed, and one-off transactions carried out, in the course of such relevant financial business as is referred to in paragraph (4) above, an appointed representative's principal shall be regarded as having contravened regulation 5 in respect of those procedures and he, as well as the appointed representative, shall be guilty of an offence and shall be liable to be proceeded against and punished accordingly.

(6) Section 44(2) of the Financial Services Act 1986 (construction of references to appointed representative, his principal and investment business carried out by an appointed representative) shall for the purposes of paragraphs (4) and (5) above as it applies for the purposes of that Act.

NOTES

[1] As amended by the Financial Services and Markets Act 2000 (Consequential Amendments) Order 2002 (SI 2002/1555), art.35, effective July 3, 2002.

[2] As amended by The Enterprise Act 2002 (Insolvency) Order 2003 (SI 2003/2096), Sch., para.53.

Internal reporting procedures

14. Internal reporting procedures maintained by a person are in accordance with this regulation if they include provision—

(a) identifying a person ("the appropriate person") to whom a report is to be made of any information or other matter which comes to the attention of a person handling relevant financial business and which, in the opinion of the person handling that business, gives rise to a knowledge or suspicion that another person is engaged in money laundering;

(b) requiring that any such report be considered in the light of all other relevant information by the appropriate person, or by another designated person, for the purpose of determining whether or not the information or other matter contained in the report does give rise to such a knowledge or suspicion;

(c) for any person charged with considering a report in accordance with sub-paragraph (b) above to have reasonable access to other information which may be of assistance to him and which is available to the person responsible for maintaining the internal reporting procedures concerned; and

(d) for securing that the information or other matter contained in a report is disclosed to a constable where the person who has considered the report under the procedures maintained in accordance with the preceding provisions of this regulation knows or suspects that another person is engaged in money laundering.

Duty of supervisory authorities to report evidence of money laundering

Supervisory authorities

15.—(1) References in these Regulations to supervisory authorities shall be construed in accordance with the following provisions.

(2) For the purposes of these Regulations, each of the following is a supervisory authority—

(a) the Bank of England;

[1] (aa) the Financial Services Authority;

(b) the Building Societies Commission;

(c) a designated agency within the meaning of the Financial Services Act 1986;

(d) a recognised self-regulating organisation within the meaning of the Financial Services Act 1986;

(e) a recognised professional body within the meaning of the Financial Services Act 1986;

(f) a transferee body within the meaning of the Financial Services Act 1986;

(g) a recognised self-regulating organisation for friendly societies within the meaning of the Financial Services Act 1986;

(h) the Secretary of State;

(i) the Treasury;

(j) the Council of Lloyd's;

(k) the Director General of Fair Trading;

(l) the Friendly Societies Commission;

(m) the Chief Registrar of Friendly Societies;

(n) the Central Office of the Registry of Friendly Societies;

(o) the Registrar of Friendly Societies for Northern Ireland;

(p) the Assistant Registrar of Friendly Societies for Scotland.

(3) These Regulations apply to the Secretary of State in the exercise, in relation to any person carrying on relevant financial business, of his

functions under the enactments relating to insurance companies, companies or insolvency or under the Financial Services Act 1986.

NOTE

[1] Inserted by the Bank of England Act 1998 (Consequential Amendments of Subordinate Legislation Order 1998 (S.I. 1998 No. 1129), Art. 2, Sched. 1, para. 13.

Supervisors etc. to report evidence of money laundering

16.—(1) Subject to paragraph (2) below, where a supervisory authority—

(a) obtains any information; and

(b) is of the opinion that the information indicates that any person has or may have been engaged in money laundering,

the authority shall, as soon as is reasonably practicable, disclose that information to a constable.

(2) Where any person is a secondary recipient of information obtained by a supervisory authority, and that person forms such an opinion as is mentioned in paragraph (1)(b) above, that person may disclose the information to a constable.

(3) Where any person within paragraph (6) below—

(a) obtains any information whilst acting in the course of any investigation, or discharging any functions, to which his appointment or authorisation relates; and

(b) is of the opinion that the information indicates that any person has or may have been engaged in money laundering,

that person shall, as soon as is reasonably practicable, either disclose that information to a constable or disclose that information to the supervisory authority by whom he was appointed or authorised.

(4) Any disclosure made by virtue of the preceding provisions of this regulation shall not be treated as a breach of any restriction imposed by statute or otherwise.

(5) Any information—

(a) which has been disclosed to a constable by virtue of the preceding provisions of this regulation; and

(b) which would, apart from the provisions of paragraph (4) above, be subject to such a restriction as is mentioned in that paragraph;

may be disclosed by the constable, or any person obtaining the information directly or indirectly from him, in connection with the investigation of any criminal offence or for the purposes of any criminal proceedings, but not otherwise.

(6) Persons falling within this paragraph are—

(a) a person or inspector appointed under section 17 of the Industrial Assurance Act 1923 or section 65 or 66 of the Friendly Societies Act 1992;

(b) an inspector appointed under section 49 of the Industrial and Provident Societies Act 1965 or section 18 of the Credit Unions Act 1979;

(c) an inspector appointed under section 431, 432, 442 or 446 of the Companies Act 1985 or under Article 424, 425, 435 or 439 of the Companies (Northern Ireland) Order 1986;

(d) a person or inspector appointed under section 55 or 56 of the Building Societies Act 1986;

(e) an inspector appointed under section 94 or 177 of the Financial Services Act 1986;

(f) a person appointed under section 41 of the Banking Act 1987; and

(g) a person authorised to

require the production of documents under section 44 of the Insurance Companies Act 1982, section 447 of the Companies Act 1985, section 106 of the Financial Services Act 1986, Article 440 of the Companies (Northern Ireland) Order 1986 or section 84 of the Companies Act 1989.

(7) In this regulation "secondary recipient", in relation to information obtained by a supervisory authority, means any person to whom that information has been passed by the authority.

Transitional provisions

Transitional provisions

17.—(1) Nothing in these Regulations shall require a person who is bound by regulation 5(1) above to maintain procedures in accordance with regulations 7 and 9 which require evidence to be obtained, in respect of any business relationship formed by him before the date on which these Regulations come into force, as to the identity of the person with whom that relationship has been formed.

(2) For the purposes of regulation 2(6) above, any business relationship referred to in paragraph (1) above shall be treated as if it were an established business relationship. (12)(3) In regulation 10(1)(g), the reference to the total payable in respect of any calendar year not exceeding ecu 1,000 shall, for the period commencing with the coming into force of these regulations and ending with 30th December 1994, be construed as a reference to the total payable in respect of that period not exceeding ecu 750.

Regulation 4(1)

SCHEDULE

"ANNEX

List of Activities Subject to Mutual Recognition

1. Acceptance of deposits and other repayable funds from the public.
2. Lending.
3. Financial leasing.
4. Money transmission services.
5. Issuing and administering means of payment (*e.g.* credit cards, travellers; cheques and bankers' drafts).
6. Guarantees and commitments.
7. Trading for own account or for account of customers in:
   (a) money market instruments (cheques, bills, CDs, etc.);
   (b) foreign exchange;
   (c) financial futures and options;
   (d) exchange and interest rate instruments;
   (e) transferable securities.
8. Participation in securities issues and the provision of services related to such issues.
9. Advice to undertakings on capital structure, industrial strategy and related questions and advice and services relating to mergers and the purchase of undertakings.
10. Money broking.
11. Portfolio management and advice.
12. Safekeeping and administration of securities.
13. Credit reference services.
14. Safe custody services."

The Money Laundering Regulations 2003

(SI 2003/3075)

[*Repealed by the Money Laundering Regulations 2007 (SI 2007/2157) reg.1(3) (effective December 15, 2007).*]

The Money Laundering Regulations 2007

(SI 2007/2157)

[December 15, 2007]

Contents

Part 1

General

Part 2

Customer Due Diligence

Part 3

Record-keeping, Procedures and Training

Part 4

Supervision and Registration

Interpretation

Supervision

Registration of high value dealers, money service businesses and trust or company service providers

25. Duty to maintain registers
26. Requirement to be registered
27. Applications for registration in a register maintained under regulation 25
28. Fit and proper test
29. Determination of applications under regulation 27
30. Cancellation of registration in a register maintained under regulation 25

Requirement to inform the Authority

31. Requirement on authorised person to inform the Authority

Registration of Annex I financial institutions, estate agents etc.

32. Power to maintain registers
33. Requirement to be registered
34. Applications for and cancellation of registration in a register maintained under regulation 32

Financial provisions

35. Costs of supervision

PART 5

ENFORCEMENT

Powers of designated authorities

36. Interpretation
37. Power to require information from, and attendance of, relevant and connected persons
38. Entry, inspection without a warrant etc.
39. Entry to premises under warrant
40. Failure to comply with information requirement
41. Powers of relevant officers

Civil penalties, review and appeals

42. Power to impose civil penalties
43. Review procedure
44. Appeals

Criminal offences

45. Offences
46. Prosecution of offences
47. Offences by bodies corporate etc.

PART 6

MISCELLANEOUS

48. Recovery of charges and penalties through the court
49. Obligations on public authorities
50. Transitional provisions: requirement to be registered
51. Minor and consequential amendments

SCHEDULE 1—ACTIVITIES LISTED IN POINTS 2 TO 12 AND 14 OF ANNEX I TO THE BANKING CONSOLIDATION DIRECTIVE
SCHEDULE 2—FINANCIAL ACTIVITY, SIMPLIFIED DUE DILIGENCE AND POLITICALLY EXPOSED PERSONS
SCHEDULE 3—PROFESSIONAL BODIES
SCHEDULE 4—CONNECTED PERSONS
SCHEDULE 5—6 [*NOT REPRODUCED.*]

The Treasury are a government department designated for the purposes of section 2(2) of the European Communities Act 1972 in relation to measures relating to preventing the use of the financial system for the purpose of money laundering;

The Treasury, in exercise of the powers conferred on them by section 2(2) of the European Communities Act 1972 and by sections 168(4)(b), 402(1)(b), 417(1) and 428(3) of the Financial Services and Markets Act 2000, make the following Regulations:

PART 1

GENERAL

Citation, commencement etc.

1.—(1) These Regulations may be cited as the Money Laundering Regulations 2007 and come into force on 15th December 2007.

(2) These Regulations are prescribed for the purposes of sections 168(4)(b) (appointment of persons to carry out investigations in particular cases) and 402(1)(b) (power of the Authority to institute proceedings for certain other offences) of the 2000 Act.

(3) The Money Laundering Regulations 2003 are revoked.

Interpretation

2.—(1) In these Regulations—

"the 2000 Act" means the Financial Services and Markets Act 2000;

"Annex I financial institution" has the meaning given by regulation 22(1);

"auditor", except in regulation 17(2)(c) and (d), has the meaning given by regulation 3(4) and (5);

"authorised person" means a person who is authorised for the purposes "the Authority" means the Financial Services Authority;

"the banking consolidation directive" means Directive 2006/48/EC of the European Parliament and of the Council of 14th June 2006 relating to the taking up and pursuit of the business of credit institutions;

"beneficial owner" has the meaning given by regulation 6;

"business relationship" means a business, professional or commercial relationship between a relevant person and a customer, which is expected by the relevant person, at the time when contact is established, to have an element of duration;

"cash" means notes, coins or travellers' cheques in any currency;

"casino" has the meaning given by regulation 3(13);

"the Commissioners" means the Commissioners for Her Majesty's Revenue and Customs;

"consumer credit financial institution" has the meaning given by regulation 22(1);

"credit institution" has the meaning given by regulation 3(2);

"customer due diligence measures" has the meaning given by regulation 5;

"DETI" means the Department of Enterprise, Trade and Investment in Northern Ireland;

"the electronic money directive" means Directive 2000/46/EC of the European Parliament and of the Council of 18th September 2000 on the taking up, pursuit and prudential supervision of the business of electronic money institutions;

"estate agent" has the meaning given by regulation 3(11);

"external accountant" has the meaning given by regulation 3(7);

"financial institution" has the meaning given by regulation 3(3);

"firm" means any entity, whether or not a legal person, that is not an individual and includes a body corporate and a partnership or other unincorporated association;

"high value dealer" has the meaning given by regulation 3(12);

"the implementing measures directive" means Commission Directive 2006/70/EC of 1st August 2006 laying down implementing measures for the money laundering directive;

"independent legal professional" has the meaning given by regulation 3(9);

"insolvency practitioner", except in regulation 17(2)(c) and (d), has the meaning given by regulation 3(6);

"the life assurance consolidation directive" means Directive 2002/83/EC of the European Parliament and of the Council of 5th November 2002 concerning life assurance;

"local weights and measures authority" has the meaning given by section 69 of the Weights and Measures Act 1985(local weights and measures authorities);

"the markets in financial instruments directive" means Directive 2004/39/EC of the European Parliament and of the Council of 12th April 2004 on markets in financial instruments;

"money laundering" means an act which falls within section 340(11) of the Proceeds of Crime Act 2002;

"the money laundering directive" means Directive 2005/60/EC of the European Parliament and of the Council of 26th October 2005 on the prevention of the use of the financial system for the purpose of money laundering and terrorist financing;

"money service business" means an undertaking which by way of business operates a currency exchange office, transmits money (or any representations of monetary value) by any means or cashes cheques which are made payable to customers;

"nominated officer" means a person who is nominated to receive disclosures under Part 7 of the Proceeds of Crime Act 2002 (money laundering) or Part 3 of the Terrorism Act 2000 (terrorist property);

"non-EEA state" means a state that is not an EEA state;

"notice" means a notice in writing;

"occasional transaction" means a transaction (carried out other than as part of a business relationship) amounting to 15,000 euro or more, whether the transaction is carried out in a single operation or several operations which appear to be linked;

"the OFT" means the Office of Fair Trading;

"ongoing monitoring" has the meaning given by regulation 8(2);

"regulated market"—

(a) within the EEA, has the meaning given by point 14 of Article 4(1) of the markets in financial instruments directive; and

(b) outside the EEA, means a regulated financial market which subjects companies whose securities are admitted to trading to disclosure obligations which are contained in international standards and are equivalent to the specified disclosure obligations;

"relevant person" means a person to whom, in accordance with regulations 3 and 4, these Regulations apply;

"the specified disclosure obligations" means disclosure requirements consistent with—

(a) Article 6(1) to (4) of Directive 2003/6/EC of the European Parliament and of the Council of 28th January 2003 on insider dealing and market manipulation;

(b) Articles 3, 5, 7, 8, 10, 14 and 16 of Directive 2003/71/EC of the European Parliament and of the Council of 4th November 2003 on the prospectuses to be published when securities are offered to the public or admitted to trading;

(c) Articles 4 to 6, 14, 16 to 19 and 30 of Directive 2004/109/EC of the European Parliament and of the Council of 15th December 2004 relating to the harmonisation of transparency requirements in relation to information about issuers whose securities are admitted to trading on a regulated market; or

(d) Community legislation made under the provisions mentioned in sub-paragraphs (a) to (c);

"supervisory authority" in relation to any relevant person means the supervisory authority specified for such a person by regulation 23;

"tax adviser" (except in regulation 11(3)) has the meaning given by regulation 3(8);

"terrorist financing" means an offence under—

(a) section 15 (fund-raising), 16 (use and possession), 17 (funding arrangements), 18 (money laundering) or 63 (terrorist finance: jurisdiction) of the Terrorism Act 2000;

(b) paragraph 7(2) or (3) of Schedule 3 to the Anti-Terrorism, Crime and Security Act 2001 (freezing orders);

(c) article 7, 8 or 10 of the Terrorism (United Nations Measures) Order 2006; or

(d) article 7, 8 or 10 of the Al-Qaida and Taliban (United Nations Measures) Order 2006;

"trust or company service provider" has the meaning given by regulation 3(10).

(2) In these Regulations, references to amounts in euro include references to equivalent amounts in another currency.

(3) Unless otherwise defined, expressions used in these Regulations and the money laundering directive have the same meaning as in the money laundering directive and expressions used in these Regulations and in the implementing measures directive have the same meaning as in the implementing measures directive.

Application of the Regulations

3.—(1) Subject to regulation 4, these Regulations apply to the following persons acting in the course of business carried on by them in the United Kingdom ("relevant persons")—

(a) credit institutions;

(b) financial institutions;

(c) auditors, insolvency practitioners, external accountants and tax advisers;

(d) independent legal professionals;

(e) trust or company service providers;

(f) estate agents;

(g) high value dealers;

(h) casinos.

(2) "Credit institution" means—

(a) a credit institution as defined in Article 4(1)(a) of the banking consolidation directive; or

(b) a branch (within the meaning of Article 4(3) of that directive) located in an EEA state of an institution falling within sub-paragraph (a) (or an equivalent institution whose head office is located in a non-EEA state) wherever its head office is located,

when it accepts deposits or other repayable funds from the public or grants credits for its own account (within the meaning of the banking consolidation directive).

(3) "Financial institution" means—

(a) an undertaking, including a money service business, when it carries out one or more of the activities listed in points 2 to 12 and 14 of Annex 1 to the banking consolidation directive (the relevant text of which is set out in Schedule 1 to these Regulations), other than—

(i) a credit institution;
(ii) an undertaking whose only listed activity is trading for own account in one or more of the products listed in point 7 of Annex 1 to the banking consolidation directive where the undertaking does not have a customer,

and, for this purpose, "customer" means a third party which is not a member of the same group as the undertaking;

(b) an insurance company duly authorised in accordance with the life assurance consolidation directive, when it carries out activities covered by that directive;

(c) a person whose regular occupation or business is the provision to other persons of an investment service or the performance of an investment activity on a professional basis, when providing or performing investment services or activities (within the meaning of the markets in financial instruments directive), other than a person falling within Article 2 of that directive;

(d) a collective investment undertaking, when marketing or otherwise offering its units or shares;

(e) an insurance intermediary as defined in Article 2(5) of Directive 2002/92/EC of the European Parliament and of the Council of 9th December 2002 on insurance mediation, with the exception of a tied insurance intermediary as mentioned in Article 2(7) of that Directive, when it acts in respect of contracts of long-term insurance within the meaning given by article 3(1) of, and Part II of Schedule 1 to, the Financial Services and Markets Act 2000 (Regulated Activities) Order 2001;

(f) a branch located in an EEA state of a person referred to in sub-paragraphs (a) to (e) (or an equivalent person whose head office is located in a non-EEA state), wherever its head office is located, when carrying out any activity mentioned in sub-paragraphs (a) to (e);

(g) the National Savings Bank;

(h) the Director of Savings, when money is raised under the auspices of the Director under the National Loans Act 1968.

(4) "Auditor" means any firm or individual who is a statutory auditor within the meaning of Part 42 of the Companies Act 2006 (statutory auditors), when carrying out statutory audit work within the meaning of section 1210 of that Act.

(5) Before the entry into force of Part 42 of the Companies Act 2006 the reference in paragraph (4) to—

(a) a person who is a statutory auditor shall be treated as a reference to a person who is eligible for appointment as a company auditor under section 25 of the Companies Act 1989 (eligibility for appointment) or article 28 of the Companies (Northern Ireland) Order 1990; and

(b) the carrying out of statutory audit work shall be treated as a reference to the provision of audit services.

(6) "Insolvency practitioner" means any person who acts as an insolvency practitioner within the meaning of section 388 of the Insolvency Act 1986 (meaning of "act as insolvency practitioner") or article 3 of the Insolvency (Northern Ireland) Order 1989.

(7) "External accountant" means a firm or sole practitioner who by way of business provides accountancy services to other persons, when providing such services.

(8) "Tax adviser" means a firm or sole practitioner who by way of business provides advice about the tax affairs of other persons, when providing such services.

(9) "Independent legal professional" means a firm or sole practitioner who by way of business provides legal or notarial services to other persons, when participating in financial or real property transactions concerning—

(a) the buying and selling of real property or business entities;

(b) the managing of client money, securities or other assets;
(c) the opening or management of bank, savings or securities accounts;
(d) the organisation of contributions necessary for the creation, operation or management of companies; or
(e) the creation, operation or management of trusts, companies or similar structures,

and, for this purpose, a person participates in a transaction by assisting in the planning or execution of the transaction or otherwise acting for or on behalf of a client in the transaction.

(10) "Trust or company service provider" means a firm or sole practitioner who by way of business provides any of the following services to other persons—

(a) forming companies or other legal persons;
(b) acting, or arranging for another person to act—
 (i) as a director or secretary of a company;
 (ii) as a partner of a partnership; or
 (iii) in a similar position in relation to other legal persons;
(c) providing a registered office, business address, correspondence or administrative address or other related services for a company, partnership or any other legal person or arrangement;
(d) acting, or arranging for another person to act, as—
 (i) a trustee of an express trust or similar legal arrangement; or
 (ii) a nominee shareholder for a person other than a company whose securities are listed on a regulated market,

when providing such services.

(11) "Estate agent" means—

(a) a firm; or
(b) sole practitioner,

who, or whose employees, carry out estate agency work (within the meaning given by section 1 of the Estate Agents Act 1979 (estate agency work)), when in the course of carrying out such work.

(12) "High value dealer" means a firm or sole trader who by way of business trades in goods (including an auctioneer dealing in goods), when he receives, in respect of any transaction, a payment or payments in cash of at least 15,000 euros in total, whether the transaction is executed in a single operation or in several operations which appear to be linked.

(13) "Casino" means the holder of a casino operating licence and, for this purpose, a "casino operating licence" has the meaning given by section 65(2) of the Gambling Act 2005 nature of licence).

(14) In the application of this regulation to Scotland, for "real property" in paragraph (9) substitute "heritable property".

Exclusions

4.—(1) These Regulations do not apply to the following persons when carrying out any of the following activities—

(a) a society registered under the Industrial and Provident Societies Act 1965 when it—
 (i) issues withdrawable share capital within the limit set by section 6 of that Act (maximum shareholding in society); or
 (ii) accepts deposits from the public within the limit set by section 7(3) of that Act (carrying on of banking by societies);
(b) a society registered under the Industrial and Provident Societies Act (Northern Ireland) 1969, when it—
 (i) issues withdrawable share capital within the limit set by section 6 of that Act (maximum shareholding in society); or
 (ii) accepts deposits from the public within the limit set by section 7(3) of that Act (carrying on of banking by societies);
(c) a person who is (or falls within a class of persons) specified in any of paragraphs 2 to 23, 25 to 38 or 40 to 49 of the Schedule to the

Financial Services and Markets Act 2000 (Exemption) Order 2001, when carrying out any activity in respect of which he is exempt;

(d) a person who was an exempted person for the purposes of section 45 of the Financial Services Act 1986 (miscellaneous exemptions) immediately before its repeal, when exercising the functions specified in that section;

(e) a person whose main activity is that of a high value dealer, when he engages in financial activity on an occasional or very limited basis as set out in paragraph 1 of Schedule 2 to these Regulations; or

(f) a person, when he prepares a home information pack or a document or information for inclusion in a home information pack.

(2) These Regulations do not apply to a person who falls within regulation 3 solely as a result of his engaging in financial activity on an occasional or very limited basis as set out in paragraph 1 of Schedule 2 to these Regulations.

(3) Parts 2 to 5 of these Regulations do not apply to—

(a) the Auditor General for Scotland;

(b) the Auditor General for Wales;

(c) the Bank of England;

(d) the Comptroller and Auditor General;

(e) the Comptroller and Auditor General for Northern Ireland;

(f) the Official Solicitor to the Supreme Court, when acting as trustee in his official capacity;

(g) the Treasury Solicitor.

(4) In paragraph (1)(f), "home information pack" has the same meaning as in Part 5 of the Housing Act 2004 (home information packs).

Part 2

Customer Due Diligence

Meaning of customer due diligence measures

5. "Customer due diligence measures" means—

(a) identifying the customer and verifying the customer's identity on the basis of documents, data or information obtained from a reliable and independent source;

(b) identifying, where there is a beneficial owner who is not the customer, the beneficial owner and taking adequate measures, on a risk-sensitive basis, to verify his identity so that the relevant person is satisfied that he knows who the beneficial owner is, including, in the case of a legal person, trust or similar legal arrangement, measures to understand the ownership and control structure of the person, trust or arrangement; and

(c) obtaining information on the purpose and intended nature of the business relationship.

Meaning of beneficial owner

6.—(1) In the case of a body corporate, "beneficial owner" means any individual who—

(a) as respects any body other than a company whose securities are listed on a regulated market, ultimately owns or controls (whether through direct or indirect ownership or control, including through bearer share holdings) more than 25% of the shares or voting rights in the body; or

(b) as respects any body corporate, otherwise exercises control over the management of the body.

(2) In the case of a partnership (other than a limited liability partnership), "beneficial owner" means any individual who—

(a) ultimately is entitled to or controls (whether the entitlement or control is direct or indirect) more than a 25% share of the capital or profits of the partnership or more than 25% of the voting rights in the partnership; or

(b) otherwise exercises control over the management of the partnership.

(3) In the case of a trust, "beneficial owner" means—

(a) any individual who is entitled to a specified interest in at least 25% of the capital of the trust property;

(b) as respects any trust other than one which is set up or operates entirely for the benefit of individuals falling within sub-paragraph (a), the class of persons in whose main interest the trust is set up or operates;

(c) any individual who has control over the trust.

(4) In paragraph (3)—

"specified interest" means a vested interest which is—

(a) in possession or in remainder or reversion (or, in Scotland, in fee); and

(b) defeasible or indefeasible;

"control" means a power (whether exercisable alone, jointly with another person or with the consent of another person) under the trust instrument or by law to—

(a) dispose of, advance, lend, invest, pay or apply trust property;

(b) vary the trust;

(c) add or remove a person as a beneficiary or to or from a class of beneficiaries;

(d) appoint or remove trustees;

(e) direct, withhold consent to or veto the exercise of a power such as is mentioned in sub-paragraph (a), (b), (c) or (d).

(5) For the purposes of paragraph (3)—

(a) where an individual is the beneficial owner of a body corporate which is entitled to a specified interest in the capital of the trust property or which has control over the trust, the individual is to be regarded as entitled to the interest or having control over the trust; and

(b) an individual does not have control solely as a result of—

(i) his consent being required in accordance with section 32(1)(c) of the Trustee Act 1925 (power of advancement);

(ii) any discretion delegated to him under section 34 of the Pensions Act 1995 (power of investment and delegation);

(iii) the power to give a direction conferred on him by section 19(2) of the Trusts of Land and Appointment of Trustees Act 1996 (appointment and retirement of trustee at instance of beneficiaries); or

(iv) the power exercisable collectively at common law to vary or extinguish a trust where the beneficiaries under the trust are of full age and capacity and (taken together) absolutely entitled to the property subject to the trust (or, in Scotland, have a full and unqualified right to the fee).

(6) In the case of a legal entity or legal arrangement which does not fall within paragraph (1), (2) or (3), "beneficial owner" means—

(a) where the individuals who benefit from the entity or arrangement have been determined, any individual who benefits from at least 25% of the property of the entity or arrangement;

(b) where the individuals who benefit from the entity or arrangement have yet to be determined, the class of persons in whose main interest the entity or arrangement is set up or operates;

(c) any individual who exercises control over at least 25% of the property of the entity or arrangement.

(7) For the purposes of paragraph (6), where an individual is the beneficial owner of a body corporate which benefits from or exercises control over the property of the entity or arrangement, the individual is to be regarded as

benefiting from or exercising control over the property of the entity or arrangement.

(8) In the case of an estate of a deceased person in the course of administration, "beneficial owner" means—

(a) in England and Wales and Northern Ireland, the executor, original or by representation, or administrator for the time being of a deceased person;

(b) in Scotland, the executor for the purposes of the Executors (Scotland) Act 1900.

(9) In any other case, "beneficial owner" means the individual who ultimately owns or controls the customer or on whose behalf a transaction is being conducted.

(10) In this regulation—

"arrangement", "entity" and "trust" means an arrangement, entity or trust which administers and distributes funds;

"limited liability partnership" has the meaning given by the Limited Liability Partnerships Act 2000.

Application of customer due diligence measures

7.—(1) Subject to regulations 9, 10, 12, 13, 14, 16(4) and 17, a relevant person must apply customer due diligence measures when he—

(a) establishes a business relationship;

(b) carries out an occasional transaction;

(c) suspects money laundering or terrorist financing;

(d) doubts the veracity or adequacy of documents, data or information previously obtained for the purposes of identification or verification.

(2) Subject to regulation 16(4), a relevant person must also apply customer due diligence measures at other appropriate times to existing customers on a risk-sensitive basis.

(3) A relevant person must—

(a) determine the extent of customer due diligence measures on a risk-sensitive basis depending on the type of customer, business relationship, product or transaction; and

(b) be able to demonstrate to his supervisory authority that the extent of the measures is appropriate in view of the risks of money laundering and terrorist financing.

(4) Where—

(a) a relevant person is required to apply customer due diligence measures in the case of a trust, legal entity (other than a body corporate) or a legal arrangement (other than a trust); and

(b) the class of persons in whose main interest the trust, entity or arrangement is set up or operates is identified as a beneficial owner,

the relevant person is not required to identify all the members of the class.

(5) Paragraph (3)(b) does not apply to the National Savings Bank or the Director of Savings.

Ongoing monitoring

8.—(1) A relevant person must conduct ongoing monitoring of a business relationship.

(2) "Ongoing monitoring" of a business relationship means—

(a) scrutiny of transactions undertaken throughout the course of the relationship (including, where necessary, the source of funds) to ensure that the transactions are consistent with the relevant person's knowledge of the customer, his business and risk profile; and

(b) keeping the documents, data or information obtained for the purpose of applying customer due diligence measures up-to-date.

(3) Regulation 7(3) applies to the duty to conduct ongoing monitoring under paragraph (1) as it applies to customer due diligence measures.

Timing of verification

9.—(1) This regulation applies in respect of the duty under regulation 7(1)(a) and (b) to apply the customer due diligence measures referred to in regulation 5(a) and (b).

(2) Subject to paragraphs (3) to (5) and regulation 10, a relevant person must verify the identity of the customer (and any beneficial owner) before the establishment of a business relationship or the carrying out of an occasional transaction.

(3) Such verification may be completed during the establishment of a business relationship if—

(a) this is necessary not to interrupt the normal conduct of business; and

(b) there is little risk of money laundering or terrorist financing occurring,

provided that the verification is completed as soon as practicable after contact is first established.

(4) The verification of the identity of the beneficiary under a life insurance policy may take place after the business relationship has been established provided that it takes place at or before the time of payout or at or before the time the beneficiary exercises a right vested under the policy.

(5) The verification of the identity of a bank account holder may take place after the bank account has been opened provided that there are adequate safeguards in place to ensure that—

(a) the account is not closed; and

(b) transactions are not carried out by or on behalf of the account holder (including any payment from the account to the account holder),

before verification has been completed.

Casinos

10.—(1) A casino must establish and verify the identity of—

(a) all customers to whom the casino makes facilities for gaming available—

(i) before entry to any premises where such facilities are provided; or

(ii) where the facilities are for remote gaming, before access is given to such facilities; or

(b) if the specified conditions are met, all customers who, in the course of any period of 24 hours—

(i) purchase from, or exchange with, the casino chips with a total value of 2,000 euro or more;

[1](ii) pay the casino 2,000 euro or more for the use of gaming machines; or

(iii) pay to, or stake with, the casino 2,000 euro or more in connection with facilities for remote gaming.

(2) The specified conditions are—

(a) the casino verifies the identity of each customer before or immediately after such purchase, exchange, payment or stake takes place, and

(b) the Gambling Commission is satisfied that the casino has appropriate procedures in place to monitor and record—

(i) the total value of chips purchased from or exchanged with the casino;

(ii) the total money paid for the use of gaming machines; or

(iii) the total money paid or staked in connection with facilities for remote gaming,

by each customer.

(3) In this regulation—

"gaming", "gaming machine", "remote operating licence" and "stake" have the meanings given by, respectively, sections 6(1) (gaming & game of chance), 235 (gaming machine), 67 (remote gambling) and 353(1) (interpretation) of the Gambling Act 2005;

"premises" means premises subject to—

(a) a casino premises licence within the meaning of section 150(1)(a) of the Gambling Act 2005 (nature of licence); or

(b) a converted casino premises licence within the meaning of paragraph 65 of Part 7 of Schedule 4 to the Gambling Act 2005 (Commencement No. 6 and Transitional Provisions) Order 2006;

"remote gaming" means gaming provided pursuant to a remote operating licence.

NOTE

[1] As amended by the Money Laundering (Amendment) Regulations (SI 2007/3299) reg.2(a) (effective December 15, 2007).

Requirement to cease transactions etc.

11.—(1) Where, in relation to any customer, a relevant person is unable to apply customer due diligence measures in accordance with the provisions of this Part, he—

(a) must not carry out a transaction with or for the customer through a bank account;

(b) must not establish a business relationship or carry out an occasional transaction with the customer;

(c) must terminate any existing business relationship with the customer;

(d) must consider whether he is required to make a disclosure by Part 7 of the Proceeds of Crime Act 2002 or Part 3 of the Terrorism Act 2000.

(2) Paragraph (1) does not apply where a lawyer or other professional adviser is in the course of ascertaining the legal position for his client or performing his task of defending or representing that client in, or concerning, legal proceedings, including advice on the institution or avoidance of proceedings.

(3) In paragraph (2), "other professional adviser" means an auditor, accountant or tax adviser who is a member of a professional body which is established for any such persons and which makes provision for—

(a) testing the competence of those seeking admission to membership of such a body as a condition for such admission; and

(b) imposing and maintaining professional and ethical standards for its members, as well as imposing sanctions for non-compliance with those standards.

Exception for trustees of debt issues

12.—(1) A relevant person—

(a) who is appointed by the issuer of instruments or securities specified in paragraph (2) as trustee of an issue of such instruments or securities; or

(b) whose customer is a trustee of an issue of such instruments or securities,

is not required to apply the customer due diligence measure referred to in regulation 5(b) in respect of the holders of such instruments or securities.

(2) The specified instruments and securities are—

(a) instruments which fall within article 77 of the Financial Services and Markets Act 2000 (Regulated Activities) Order 2001; and

(b) securities which fall within article 78 of that Order.

Simplified due diligence

13. —(1) A relevant person is not required to apply customer due diligence measures in the circumstances mentioned in regulation 7(1)(a), (b) or (d) where he has reasonable grounds for believing that the customer, transaction or product related to such transaction, falls within any of the following paragraphs.

(2) The customer is—

(a) a credit or financial institution which is subject to the requirements of the money laundering directive; or

(b) a credit or financial institution (or equivalent institution) which—

(i) is situated in a non-EEA state which imposes requirements equivalent to those laid down in the money laundering directive; and

(ii) is supervised for compliance with those requirements.

(3) The customer is a company whose securities are listed on a regulated market subject to specified disclosure obligations.

(4) The customer is an independent legal professional and the product is an account into which monies are pooled, provided that—

(a) where the pooled account is held in a non-EEA state—

(i) that state imposes requirements to combat money laundering and terrorist financing which are consistent with international standards; and

(ii) the independent legal professional is supervised in that state for compliance with those requirements; and

(b) information on the identity of the persons on whose behalf monies are held in the pooled account is available, on request, to the institution which acts as a depository institution for the account.

(5) The customer is a public authority in the United Kingdom.

(6) The customer is a public authority which fulfils all the conditions set out in paragraph 2 of Schedule 2 to these Regulations.

(7) The product is—

(a) a life insurance contract where the annual premium is no more than 1,000 euro or where a single premium of no more than 2,500 euro is paid;

(b) an insurance contract for the purposes of a pension scheme where the contract contains no surrender clause and cannot be used as collateral;

(c) a pension, superannuation or similar scheme which provides retirement benefits to employees, where contributions are made by an employer or by way of deduction from an employee's wages and the scheme rules do not permit the assignment of a member's interest under the scheme (other than an assignment permitted by section 44 of the Welfare Reform and Pensions Act 1999 (disapplication of restrictions on alienation) or section 91(5)(a) of the Pensions Act 1995 (inalienability of occupational pension)); or

(d) electronic money, within the meaning of Article 1(3)(b) of the electronic money directive, where—

(i) if the device cannot be recharged, the maximum amount stored in the device is no more than 150 euro; or

(ii) if the device can be recharged, a limit of 2,500 euro is imposed on the total amount transacted in a calendar year, except when an amount of 1,000 euro or more is redeemed in the same calendar year by the bearer (within the meaning of Article 3 of the electronic money directive).

(8) The product and any transaction related to such product fulfils all the conditions set out in paragraph 3 of Schedule 2 to these Regulations.

(9) The product is a child trust fund within the meaning given by section 1(2) of the Child Trust Funds Act 2004.

Enhanced customer due diligence and ongoing monitoring

14.—(1) A relevant person must apply on a risk-sensitive basis enhanced customer due diligence measures and enhanced ongoing monitoring—

(a) in accordance with paragraphs (2) to (4);

(b) in any other situation which by its nature can present a higher risk of money laundering or terrorist financing.

(2) Where the customer has not been physically present for identification purposes, a relevant person must take specific and adequate measures to compensate for the higher risk, for example, by applying one or more of the following measures—

(a) ensuring that the customer's identity is established by additional documents, data or information;

(b) supplementary measures to verify or certify the documents supplied, or requiring confirmatory certification by a credit or financial institution which is subject to the money laundering directive;

(c) ensuring that the first payment is carried out through an account opened in the customer's name with a credit institution.

(3) A credit institution ("the correspondent") which has or proposes to have a correspondent banking relationship with a respondent institution ("the respondent") from a non-EEA state must—

(a) gather sufficient information about the respondent to understand fully the nature of its business;

(b) determine from publicly-available information the reputation of the respondent and the quality of its supervision;

(c) assess the respondent's anti-money laundering and anti-terrorist financing controls;

(d) obtain approval from senior management before establishing a new correspondent banking relationship;

(e) document the respective responsibilities of the respondent and correspondent; and

(f) be satisfied that, in respect of those of the respondent's customers who have direct access to accounts of the correspondent, the respondent—

(i) has verified the identity of, and conducts ongoing monitoring in respect of, such customers; and

(ii) is able to provide to the correspondent, upon request, the documents, data or information obtained when applying customer due diligence measures and ongoing monitoring.

(4) A relevant person who proposes to have a business relationship or carry out an occasional transaction with a politically exposed person must—

(a) have approval from senior management for establishing the business relationship with that person;

(b) take adequate measures to establish the source of wealth and source of funds which are involved in the proposed business relationship or occasional transaction; and

(c) where the business relationship is entered into, conduct enhanced ongoing monitoring of the relationship.

(5) In paragraph (4), "a politically exposed person" means a person who is—

(a) an individual who is or has, at any time in the preceding year, been entrusted with a prominent public function by—

(i) a state other than the United Kingdom;

(ii) a Community institution; or

(iii) an international body,

including a person who falls in any of the categories listed in paragraph 4(1)(a) of Schedule 2;

(b) an immediate family member of a person referred to in sub-paragraph (a), including a person who falls in any of the categories listed in paragraph 4(1)(c) of Schedule 2; or

(c) a known close associate of a person referred to in sub-paragraph (a), including a person who falls in either of the categories listed in paragraph 4(1)(d) of Schedule 2.

(6) For the purpose of deciding whether a person is a known close associate of a person referred to in paragraph (5)(a), a relevant person need only have regard to information which is in his possession or is publicly known.

Branches and subsidiaries

15.—(1) A credit or financial institution must require its branches and subsidiary undertakings which are located in a non-EEA state to apply, to the extent permitted by the law of that state, measures at least equivalent to those set out in these Regulations with regard to customer due diligence measures, ongoing monitoring and record-keeping.

(2) Where the law of a non-EEA state does not permit the application of such equivalent measures by the branch or subsidiary undertaking located in that state, the credit or financial institution must—

(a) inform its supervisory authority accordingly; and

(b) take additional measures to handle effectively the risk of money laundering and terrorist financing.

(3) In this regulation "subsidiary undertaking"—

(a) except in relation to an incorporated friendly society, has the meaning given by section 1162 of the Companies Act 2006 (parent and subsidiary undertakings) and, in relation to a body corporate in or formed under the law of an EEA state other than the United Kingdom, includes an undertaking which is a subsidiary undertaking within the meaning of any rule of law in force in that state for purposes connected with implementation of the European Council Seventh Company Law Directive 83/349/EEC of 13th June 1983 on consolidated accounts;

(b) in relation to an incorporated friendly society, means a body corporate of which the society has control within the meaning of section 13(9)(a) or (aa) of the Friendly Societies Act 1992 (control of subsidiaries and other bodies corporate).

(4) Before the entry into force of section 1162 of the Companies Act 2006 the reference to that section in paragraph (3)(a) shall be treated as a reference to section 258 of the Companies Act 1985 (parent and subsidiary undertakings).

Shell banks, anonymous accounts etc.

16.—(1) A credit institution must not enter into, or continue, a correspondent banking relationship with a shell bank.

(2) A credit institution must take appropriate measures to ensure that it does not enter into, or continue, a corresponding banking relationship with a bank which is known to permit its accounts to be used by a shell bank.

(3) A credit or financial institution carrying on business in the United Kingdom must not set up an anonymous account or an anonymous passbook for any new or existing customer.

(4) As soon as reasonably practicable on or after 15th December 2007 all credit and financial institutions carrying on business in the United Kingdom must apply customer due diligence measures to, and conduct ongoing monitoring of, all anonymous accounts and passbooks in existence on that date and in any event before such accounts or passbooks are used.

(5) A "shell bank" means a credit institution, or an institution engaged in equivalent activities, incorporated in a jurisdiction in which it has no physical presence involving meaningful decision-making and management, and which is not part of a financial conglomerate or third-country financial conglomerate.

(6) In this regulation, "financial conglomerate" and "third-country financial conglomerate" have the meanings given by regulations 1(2) and 7(1) respectively of the Financial Conglomerates and Other Financial Groups Regulations 2004.

Reliance

17.—(1) A relevant person may rely on a person who falls within paragraph (2) (or who the relevant person has reasonable grounds to believe falls within paragraph (2)) to apply any customer due diligence measures provided that—

(a) the other person consents to being relied on; and

(b) notwithstanding the relevant person's reliance on the other person, the relevant person remains liable for any failure to apply such measures.

(2) The persons are—

(a) a credit or financial institution which is an authorised person;

(b) a relevant person who is—

(i) an auditor, insolvency practitioner, external accountant, tax adviser or independent legal professional; and

(ii) supervised for the purposes of these Regulations by one of the bodies listed in Part 1 of Schedule 3;

(c) a person who carries on business in another EEA state who is—

(i) a credit or financial institution, auditor, insolvency practitioner, external accountant, tax adviser or independent legal professional;

(ii) subject to mandatory professional registration recognised by law; and

(iii) supervised for compliance with the requirements laid down in the money laundering directive in accordance with section 2 of Chapter V of that directive; or

(d) a person who carries on business in a non-EEA state who is—

(i) a credit or financial institution (or equivalent institution), auditor, insolvency practitioner, external accountant, tax adviser or independent legal professional;

(ii) subject to mandatory professional registration recognised by law;

(iii) subject to requirements equivalent to those laid down in the money laundering directive; and

(iv) supervised for compliance with those requirements in a manner equivalent to section 2 of Chapter V of the money laundering directive.

(3) In paragraph (2)(c)(i) and (d)(i), "auditor" and "insolvency practitioner" includes a person situated in another EEA state or a non-EEA state who provides services equivalent to the services provided by an auditor or insolvency practitioner.

(4) Nothing in this regulation prevents a relevant person applying customer due diligence measures by means of an outsourcing service provider or agent provided that the relevant person remains liable for any failure to apply such measures.

(5) In this regulation, "financial institution" excludes money service businesses.

Directions where Financial Action Task Force applies counter-measures

18. The Treasury may direct any relevant person—

(a) not to enter into a business relationship;

(b) not to carry out an occasional transaction; or

(c) not to proceed any further with a business relationship or occasional transaction,

with a person who is situated or incorporated in a non-EEA state to which the Financial Action Task Force has decided to apply counter-measures.

PART 3

RECORD-KEEPING, PROCEDURES AND TRAINING

Record-keeping

19.—(1) Subject to paragraph (4), a relevant person must keep the records specified in paragraph (2) for at least the period specified in paragraph (3).

(2) The records are—

(a) a copy of, or the references to, the evidence of the customer's identity obtained pursuant to regulation 7, 8, 10, 14 or 16(4);

(b) the supporting records (consisting of the original documents or copies) in respect of a business relationship or occasional transaction which is the subject of customer due diligence measures or ongoing monitoring.

(3) The period is five years beginning on—

(a) in the case of the records specified in paragraph (2)(a), the date on which—

(i) the occasional transaction is completed; or

(ii) the business relationship ends; or

(b) in the case of the records specified in paragraph (2)(b)—

(i) where the records relate to a particular transaction, the date on which the transaction is completed;

(ii) for all other records, the date on which the business relationship ends.

(4) A relevant person who is relied on by another person must keep the records specified in paragraph (2)(a) for five years beginning on the date on which he is relied on for the purposes of regulation 7, 10, 14 or 16(4) in relation to any business relationship or occasional transaction.

(5) A person referred to in regulation 17(2)(a) or (b) who is relied on by a relevant person must, if requested by the person relying on him within the period referred to in paragraph (4)—

(a) as soon as reasonably practicable make available to the person who is relying on him any information about the customer (and any beneficial owner) which he obtained when applying customer due diligence measures; and

(b) as soon as reasonably practicable forward to the person who is relying on him copies of any identification and verification data and other relevant documents on the identity of the customer (and any beneficial owner) which he obtained when applying those measures.

(6) A relevant person who relies on a person referred to in regulation 17(2)(c) or (d) (a "third party") to apply customer due diligence measures must take steps to ensure that the third party will, if requested by the relevant person within the period referred to in paragraph (4)—

(a) as soon as reasonably practicable make available to him any information about the customer (and any beneficial owner) which the third party obtained when applying customer due diligence measures; and

(b) as soon as reasonably practicable forward to him copies of any identification and verification data and other relevant documents on the identity of the customer (and any beneficial owner) which the third party obtained when applying those measures.

(7) Paragraphs (5) and (6) do not apply where a relevant person applies customer due diligence measures by means of an outsourcing service provider or agent.

(8) For the purposes of this regulation, a person relies on another person where he does so in accordance with regulation 17(1).

Policies and procedures

20.—(1) A relevant person must establish and maintain appropriate and risk-sensitive policies and procedures relating to—

(a) customer due diligence measures and ongoing monitoring;

(b) reporting;

(c) record-keeping;

(d) internal control;

(e) risk assessment and management;

(f) the monitoring and management of compliance with, and the internal communication of, such policies and procedures, in order to prevent activities related to money laundering and terrorist financing.

(2) The policies and procedures referred to in paragraph (1) include policies and procedures—

(a) which provide for the identification and scrutiny of—

(i) complex or unusually large transactions;

(ii) unusual patterns of transactions which have no apparent economic or visible lawful purpose; and

(iii) any other activity which the relevant person regards as particularly likely by its nature to be related to money laundering or terrorist financing;

(b) which specify the taking of additional measures, where appropriate, to prevent the use for money laundering or terrorist financing of products and transactions which might favour anonymity;

(c) to determine whether a customer is a politically exposed person;

(d) under which—

(i) an individual in the relevant person's organisation is a nominated officer under Part 7 of the Proceeds of Crime Act 2002 and Part 3 of the Terrorism Act 2000;

(ii) anyone in the organisation to whom information or other matter comes in the course of the business as a result of which he knows or suspects or has reasonable grounds for knowing or suspecting that a person is engaged in money laundering or terrorist financing is required to comply with Part 7 of the Proceeds of Crime Act 2002 or, as the case may be, Part 3 of the Terrorism Act 2000; and

(iii) where a disclosure is made to the nominated officer, he must consider it in the light of any relevant information which is available to the relevant person and determine whether it gives rise to knowledge or suspicion or reasonable grounds for knowledge or suspicion that a person is engaged in money laundering or terrorist financing.

(3) Paragraph (2)(d) does not apply where the relevant person is an individual who neither employs nor acts in association with any other person.

(4) A credit or financial institution must establish and maintain systems which enable it to respond fully and rapidly to enquiries from financial investigators accredited under section 3 of the Proceeds of Crime Act 2002 (accreditation and training), persons acting on behalf of the Scottish Ministers in their capacity as an enforcement authority under that Act, officers of Revenue and Customs or constables as to—

(a) whether it maintains, or has maintained during the previous five years, a business relationship with any person; and

(b) the nature of that relationship.

(5) A credit or financial institution must communicate where relevant the policies and procedures which it establishes and maintains in accordance with this regulation to its branches and subsidiary undertakings which are located outside the United Kingdom.

(6) In this regulation—

"politically exposed person" has the same meaning as in regulation 14(4);

"subsidiary undertaking" has the same meaning as in regulation 15.

Training

21. A relevant person must take appropriate measures so that all relevant employees of his are—

(a) made aware of the law relating to money laundering and terrorist financing; and

(b) regularly given training in how to recognise and deal with transactions and other activities which may be related to money laundering or terrorist financing.

Part 4

Supervision and Registration

Interpretation

Interpretation

22.—(1) In this Part—

"Annex I financial institution" means any undertaking which falls within regulation 3(3)(a) other than—

(a) a consumer credit financial institution;

(b) a money service business; or

(c) an authorised person;

"consumer credit financial institution" means any undertaking which falls within regulation 3(3)(a) and which requires, under section 21 of the Consumer Credit Act 1974 (businesses needing a licence), a licence to carry on a consumer credit business, other than—

(a) a person covered by a group licence issued by the OFT under section 22 of that Act (standard and group licences);

(b) a money service business; or

(c) an authorised person.

(2) In paragraph (1), "consumer credit business" has the meaning given by section 189(1) of the Consumer Credit Act 1974 (definitions) and, on the entry into force of section 23(a) of the Consumer Credit Act 2006 (definitions of "consumer credit business" and "consumer hire business"), has the meaning given by section 189(1) of the Consumer Credit Act 1974 as amended by section 23(a) of the Consumer Credit Act 2006.

Supervision

Supervisory authorities

23.—(1) Subject to paragraph (2), the following bodies are supervisory authorities—

(a) the Authority is the supervisory authority for—

(i) credit and financial institutions which are authorised persons;

(ii) trust or company service providers which are authorised persons;

(iii) Annex I financial institutions;

(b) the OFT is the supervisory authority for—

(i) consumer credit financial institutions;

(ii) estate agents;

(c) each of the professional bodies listed in Schedule 3 is the supervisory authority for relevant persons who are regulated by it;

(d) the Commissioners are the supervisory authority for—

(i) high value dealers;

(ii) money service businesses which are not supervised by the Authority;

(iii) trust or company service providers which are not supervised by the Authority or one of the bodies listed in Schedule 3;

(iv) auditors, external accountants and tax advisers who are not supervised by one of the bodies listed in Schedule 3.

(e) the Gambling Commission is the supervisory authority for casinos;

(f) DETI is the supervisory authority for—

(i) credit unions in Northern Ireland;

(ii) insolvency practitioners authorised by it under article 351 of the Insolvency (Northern Ireland) Order 1989;

(g) the Secretary of State is the supervisory authority for insolvency practitioners authorised by him under section 393 of the Insolvency Act 1986 (grant, refusal and withdrawal of authorisation).

(2) Where under paragraph (1) there is more than one supervisory authority for a relevant person, the supervisory authorities may agree that one of them will act as the supervisory authority for that person.

(3) Where an agreement has been made under paragraph (2), the authority which has agreed to act as the supervisory authority must notify the relevant person or publish the agreement in such manner as it considers appropriate.

(4) Where no agreement has been made under paragraph (2), the supervisory authorities for a relevant person must cooperate in the performance of their functions under these Regulations.

Duties of supervisory authorities

24.—(1) A supervisory authority must effectively monitor the relevant persons for whom it is the supervisory authority and take necessary measures for the purpose of securing compliance by such persons with the requirements of these Regulations.

(2) A supervisory authority which, in the course of carrying out any of its functions under these Regulations, knows or suspects that a person is or has engaged in money laundering or terrorist financing must promptly inform the Serious Organised Crime Agency.

(3) A disclosure made under paragraph (2) is not to be taken to breach any restriction, however imposed, on the disclosure of information.

(4) The functions of the Authority under these Regulations shall be treated for the purposes of Parts 1, 2 and 4 of Schedule 1 to the 2000 Act (the Financial Services Authority) as functions conferred on the Authority under that Act.

Registration of high value dealers, money service businesses and trust or company service providers

Duty to maintain registers

25.—(1) The Commissioners must maintain registers of—

(a) high value dealers;

(b) money service businesses for which they are the supervisory authority; and

(c) trust or company service providers for which they are the supervisory authority.

(2) The Commissioners may keep the registers in any form they think fit.

(3) The Commissioners may publish or make available for public inspection all or part of a register maintained under this regulation.

Requirement to be registered

26.—(1) A person in respect of whom the Commissioners are required to maintain a register under regulation 25 must not act as a—

(a) high value dealer;

(b) money service business; or

(c) trust or company service provider,

unless he is included in the register.

(2) Paragraph (1) and regulation 29 are subject to the transitional provisions set out in regulation 50.

Applications for registration in a register maintained under regulation 25

27.—(1) An applicant for registration in a register maintained under regulation 25 must make an application in such manner and provide such information as the Commissioners may specify.

(2) The information which the Commissioners may specify includes—

(a) the applicant's name and (if different) the name of the business;

(b) the nature of the business;
(c) the name of the nominated officer (if any);
(d) in relation to a money service business or trust or company service provider—
   (i) the name of any person who effectively directs or will direct the business and any beneficial owner of the business; and
   (ii) information needed by the Commissioners to decide whether they must refuse the application pursuant to regulation 28.

(3) At any time after receiving an application and before determining it, the Commissioners may require the applicant to provide, within 21 days beginning with the date of being requested to do so, such further information as they reasonably consider necessary to enable them to determine the application.

(4) If at any time after the applicant has provided the Commissioners with any information under paragraph (1) or (3)—
(a) there is a material change affecting any matter contained in that information; or
(b) it becomes apparent to that person that the information contains a significant inaccuracy,

he must provide the Commissioners with details of the change or, as the case may be, a correction of the inaccuracy within 30 days beginning with the date of the occurrence of the change (or the discovery of the inaccuracy) or within such later time as may be agreed with the Commissioners.

(5) The obligation in paragraph (4) applies also to material changes or significant inaccuracies affecting any matter contained in any supplementary information provided pursuant to that paragraph.

(6) Any information to be provided to the Commissioners under this regulation must be in such form or verified in such manner as they may specify.

Fit and proper test

28.—(1) The Commissioners must refuse to register an applicant as a money service business or trust or company service provider if they are satisfied that—
(a) the applicant;
(b) a person who effectively directs, or will effectively direct, the business or service provider;
(c) a beneficial owner of the business or service provider; or
(d) the nominated officer of the business or service provider,

is not a fit and proper person.

(2) For the purposes of paragraph (1), a person is not a fit and proper person if he—
(a) has been convicted of—
   (i) an offence under the Terrorism Act 2000;
   (ii) an offence under paragraph 7(2) or (3) of Schedule 3 to the Anti-Terrorism, Crime and Security Act 2001 (offences);
   (iii) an offence under the Terrorism Act 2006;
   (iv) an offence under Part 7 (money laundering) of, or listed in Schedule 2 (lifestyle offences: England and Wales), 4 (lifestyle offences: Scotland) or 5 (lifestyle offences: Northern Ireland) to, the Proceeds of Crime Act 2002;
   (v) an offence under the Fraud Act 2006 or, in Scotland, the common law offence of fraud;
   (vi) an offence under section 72(1), (3) or (8) of the Value Added Tax Act 1994 (offences); or
   (vii) the common law offence of cheating the public revenue;
(b) has been adjudged bankrupt or sequestration of his estate has been awarded and (in either case) he has not been discharged;
(c) is subject to a disqualification order under the Company Directors Disqualification Act 1986;

(d) is or has been subject to a confiscation order under the Proceeds of Crime Act 2002;
(e) has consistently failed to comply with the requirements of these Regulations, the Money Laundering Regulations 2003 or the Money Laundering Regulations 2001;
(f) has consistently failed to comply with the requirements of regulation 2006/1781/EC of the European Parliament and of the Council of 15th November 2006 on information on the payer accompanying the transfer of funds;
(g) has effectively directed a business which falls within sub-paragraph (e) or (f);
(h) is otherwise not a fit and proper person with regard to the risk of money laundering or terrorist financing.

(3) For the purposes of this regulation, a conviction for an offence listed in paragraph (2)(a) is to be disregarded if it is spent for the purposes of the Rehabilitation of Offenders Act 1974.

Determination of applications under regulation 27

29.—(1) Subject to regulation 28, the Commissioners may refuse to register an applicant for registration in a register maintained under regulation 25 only if—
(a) any requirement of, or imposed under, regulation 27 has not been complied with;
(b) it appears to the Commissioners that any information provided pursuant to regulation 27 is false or misleading in a material particular; or
(c) the applicant has failed to pay a charge imposed by them under regulation 35(1).

(2) The Commissioners must within 45 days beginning either with the date on which they receive the application or, where applicable, with the date on which they receive any further information required under regulation 27(3), give the applicant notice of—
(a) their decision to register the applicant; or
(b) the following matters—
(i) their decision not to register the applicant;
(ii) the reasons for their decision;
(iii) the right to require a review under regulation 43; and
(iv) the right to appeal under regulation 44(1)(a).

(3) The Commissioners must, as soon as practicable after deciding to register a person, include him in the relevant register.

Cancellation of registration in a register maintained under regulation 25

30.—(1) The Commissioners must cancel the registration of a money service business or trust or company service provider in a register maintained under regulation 25(1) if, at any time after registration, they are satisfied that he or any person mentioned in regulation 28(1)(b), (c) or (d) is not a fit and proper person within the meaning of regulation 28(2).

(2) The Commissioners may cancel a person's registration in a register maintained by them under regulation 25 if, at any time after registration, it appears to them that they would have had grounds to refuse registration under regulation 29(1).

(3) Where the Commissioners decide to cancel a person's registration they must give him notice of—
(a) their decision and, subject to paragraph (4), the date from which the cancellation takes effect;
(b) the reasons for their decision;
(c) the right to require a review under regulation 43; and
(d) the right to appeal under regulation 44(1)(a).

(4) If the Commissioners—

(a) consider that the interests of the public require the cancellation of a person's registration to have immediate effect; and

(b) include a statement to that effect and the reasons for it in the notice given under paragraph (3),

the cancellation takes effect when the notice is given to the person.

Requirement to inform the Authority

Requirement on authorised person to inform the Authority

31.—(1) An authorised person whose supervisory authority is the Authority must, before acting as a money service business or a trust or company service provider or within 28 days of so doing, inform the Authority that he intends, or has begun, to act as such.

(2) Paragraph (1) does not apply to an authorised person who—

(a) immediately before 15th December 2007 was acting as a money service business or a trust or company service provider and continues to act as such after that date; and

(b) before 15th January 2008 informs the Authority that he is or was acting as such.

(3) Where an authorised person whose supervisory authority is the Authority ceases to act as a money service business or a trust or company service provider, he must immediately inform the Authority.

(4) Any requirement imposed by this regulation is to be treated as if it were a requirement imposed by or under the 2000 Act.

(5) Any information to be provided to the Authority under this regulation must be in such form or verified in such manner as it may specify.

Registration of Annex I financial institutions, estate agents etc.

Power to maintain registers

32.—(1) The supervisory authorities mentioned in paragraph (2), (3) or (4) may, in order to fulfil their duties under regulation 24, maintain a register under this regulation.

(2) The Authority may maintain a register of Annex I financial institutions.

(3) The OFT may maintain registers of—

(a) consumer credit financial institutions; and

(b) estate agents.

(4) The Commissioners may maintain registers of—

(a) auditors;

(b) external accountants; and

(c) tax advisers,

who are not supervised by the Secretary of State, DETI or any of the professional bodies listed in Schedule 3.

(5) Where a supervisory authority decides to maintain a register under this regulation, it must take reasonable steps to bring its decision to the attention of those relevant persons in respect of whom the register is to be established.

(6) A supervisory authority may keep a register under this regulation in any form it thinks fit.

(7) A supervisory authority may publish or make available to public inspection all or part of a register maintained by it under this regulation.

Requirement to be registered

33. Where a supervisory authority decides to maintain a register under regulation 32 in respect of any description of relevant persons and establishes a register for that purpose, a relevant person of that description may not carry on the business or profession in question for a period of more than six months beginning on the date on which the supervisory authority establishes the register unless he is included in the register.

Applications for and cancellation of registration in a register maintained under regulation 32

34.—(1) Regulations 27, 29 (with the omission of the words "Subject to regulation 28" in regulation 29(1)) and 30(2), (3) and (4) apply to registration in a register maintained by the Commissioners under regulation 32 as they apply to registration in a register maintained under regulation 25.

(2) Regulation 27 applies to registration in a register maintained by the Authority or the OFT under regulation 32 as it applies to registration in a register maintained under regulation 25 and, for this purpose, references to the Commissioners are to be treated as references to the Authority or the OFT, as the case may be.

(3) The Authority and the OFT may refuse to register an applicant for registration in a register maintained under regulation 32 only if—

- (a) any requirement of, or imposed under, regulation 27 has not been complied with;
- (b) it appears to the Authority or the OFT, as the case may be, that any information provided pursuant to regulation 27 is false or misleading in a material particular; or
- (c) the applicant has failed to pay a charge imposed by the Authority or the OFT, as the case may be, under regulation 35(1).

(4) The Authority or the OFT, as the case may be, must, within 45 days beginning either with the date on which it receives an application or, where applicable, with the date on which it receives any further information required under regulation 27(3), give the applicant notice of—

- (a) its decision to register the applicant; or
- (b) the following matters—
  - (i) that it is minded not to register the applicant;
  - (ii) the reasons for being minded not to register him; and
  - (iii) the right to make representations to it within a specified period (which may not be less than 28 days).

(5) The Authority or the OFT, as the case may be, must then decide, within a reasonable period, whether to register the applicant and it must give the applicant notice of—

- (a) its decision to register the applicant; or
- (b) the following matters—
  - (i) its decision not to register the applicant;
  - (ii) the reasons for its decision; and
  - (iii) the right to appeal under regulation 44(1)(b).

(6) The Authority or the OFT, as the case may be, must, as soon as reasonably practicable after deciding to register a person, include him in the relevant register.

(7) The Authority or the OFT may cancel a person's registration in a register maintained by them under regulation 32 if, at any time after registration, it appears to them that they would have had grounds to refuse registration under paragraph (3).

(8) Where the Authority or the OFT proposes to cancel a person's registration, it must give him notice of—

- (a) its proposal to cancel his registration;
- (b) the reasons for the proposed cancellation; and
- (c) the right to make representations to it within a specified period (which may not be less than 28 days).

(9) The Authority or the OFT, as the case may be, must then decide, within a reasonable period, whether to cancel the person's registration and it must give him notice of—

- (a) its decision not to cancel his registration; or
- (b) the following matters—
  - (i) its decision to cancel his registration and, subject to paragraph (10), the date from which cancellation takes effect;
  - (ii) the reasons for its decision; and

(iii) the right to appeal under regulation 44(1)(b).

(10) If the Authority or the OFT, as the case may be—

(a) considers that the interests of the public require the cancellation of a person's registration to have immediate effect; and

(b) includes a statement to that effect and the reasons for it in the notice given under paragraph (9)(b),

the cancellation takes effect when the notice is given to the person.

(11) In paragraphs (3) and (4), references to regulation 27 are to be treated as references to that paragraph as applied by paragraph (2) of this regulation.

Financial provisions

Costs of supervision

35.—(1) The Authority, the OFT and the Commissioners may impose charges—

(a) on applicants for registration;

(b) on relevant persons supervised by them.

(2) Charges levied under paragraph (1) must not exceed such amount as the Authority, the OFT or the Commissioners (as the case may be) consider will enable them to meet any expenses reasonably incurred by them in carrying out their functions under these Regulations or for any incidental purpose.

(3) Without prejudice to the generality of paragraph (2), a charge may be levied in respect of each of the premises at which a person carries on (or proposes to carry on) business.

(4) The Authority must apply amounts paid to it by way of penalties imposed under regulation 42 towards expenses incurred in carrying out its functions under these Regulations or for any incidental purpose.

(5) In paragraph (2), "expenses" in relation to the OFT includes expenses incurred by a local weights and measures authority or DETI pursuant to arrangements made for the purposes of these Regulations with the OFT—

(a) by or on behalf of the authority; or

(b) by DETI.

PART 5

ENFORCEMENT

Powers of designated authorities

Interpretation

36. In this Part—

"designated authority" means—

(a) the Authority;

(b) the Commissioners;

(c) the OFT; and

(d) in relation to credit unions in Northern Ireland, DETI;

"officer", except in regulations 40(3), 41 and 47 means—

(a) an officer of the Authority, including a member of the Authority's staff or an agent of the Authority;

(b) an officer of Revenue and Customs;

(c) an officer of the OFT;

(d) a relevant officer; or

(e) an officer of DETI acting for the purposes of its functions under these Regulations in relation to credit unions in Northern Ireland;

"recorded information" includes information recorded in any form and any document of any nature;

"relevant officer" means—

(a) in Great Britain, an officer of a local weights and measures authority;

(b) in Northern Ireland, an officer of DETI acting pursuant to arrangements made with the OFT for the purposes of these Regulations.

Power to require information from, and attendance of, relevant and connected persons

37.—(1) An officer may, by notice to a relevant person or to a person connected with a relevant person, require the relevant person or the connected person, as the case may be—

(a) to provide such information as may be specified in the notice;

(b) to produce such recorded information as may be so specified; or

(c) to attend before an officer at a time and place specified in the notice and answer questions.

(2) For the purposes of paragraph (1), a person is connected with a relevant person if he is, or has at any time been, in relation to the relevant person, a person listed in Schedule 4 to these Regulations.

(3) An officer may exercise powers under this regulation only if the information sought to be obtained as a result is reasonably required in connection with the exercise by the designated authority for whom he acts of its functions under these Regulations.

(4) Where an officer requires information to be provided or produced pursuant to paragraph (1)(a) or (b)—

(a) the notice must set out the reasons why the officer requires the information to be provided or produced; and

(b) such information must be provided or produced—

(i) before the end of such reasonable period as may be specified in the notice; and

(ii) at such place as may be so specified.

(5) In relation to information recorded otherwise than in legible form, the power to require production of it includes a power to require the production of a copy of it in legible form or in a form from which it can readily be produced in visible and legible form.

(6) The production of a document does not affect any lien which a person has on the document.

(7) A person may not be required under this regulation to provide or produce information or to answer questions which he would be entitled to refuse to provide, produce or answer on grounds of legal professional privilege in proceedings in the High Court, except that a lawyer may be required to provide the name and address of his client.

(8) Subject to paragraphs (9) and (10), a statement made by a person in compliance with a requirement imposed on him under paragraph (1)(c) is admissible in evidence in any proceedings, so long as it also complies with any requirements governing the admissibility of evidence in the circumstances in question.

(9) In criminal proceedings in which a person is charged with an offence to which this paragraph applies—

(a) no evidence relating to the statement may be adduced; and

(b) no question relating to it may be asked,

by or on behalf of the prosecution unless evidence relating to it is adduced, or a question relating to it is asked, in the proceedings by or on behalf of that person.

(10) Paragraph (9) applies to any offence other than one under—

(a) section 5 of the Perjury Act 1911 (false statements without oath);

(b) section 44(2) of the Criminal Law (Consolidation)(Scotland) Act 1995 (false statements and declarations); or

(c) Article 10 of the Perjury (Northern Ireland) Order 1979 (false unsworn statements).

(11) In the application of this regulation to Scotland, the reference in paragraph (7) to—

(a) proceedings in the High Court is to be read as a reference to legal proceedings generally; and

[1](b) an entitlement on grounds of legal professional privilege is to be read as a reference to an entitlement on the grounds of confidentiality of communications—

(i) between a professional legal adviser and his client; or

(ii) made in connection with or in contemplation of legal proceedings and for the purposes of those proceedings.

NOTE

[1] As amended by the Money Laundering (Amendment) Regulations (SI 2007/3299) reg.2(b) (effective December 15, 2007).

Entry, inspection without a warrant etc.

38.—(1) Where an officer has reasonable cause to believe that any premises are being used by a relevant person in connection with his business or professional activities, he may on producing evidence of his authority at any reasonable time—

(a) enter the premises;

(b) inspect the premises;

(c) observe the carrying on of business or professional activities by the relevant person;

(d) inspect any recorded information found on the premises;

(e) require any person on the premises to provide an explanation of any recorded information or to state where it may be found;

(f) in the case of a money service business or a high value dealer, inspect any cash found on the premises.

(2) An officer may take copies of, or make extracts from, any recorded information found under paragraph (1).

(3) Paragraphs (1)(d) and (e) and (2) do not apply to recorded information which the relevant person would be entitled to refuse to disclose on grounds of legal professional privilege in proceedings in the High Court, except that a lawyer may be required to provide the name and address of his client and, for this purpose, regulation 37(11) applies to this paragraph as it applies to regulation 37(7).

(4) An officer may exercise powers under this regulation only if the information sought to be obtained as a result is reasonably required in connection with the exercise by the designated authority for whom he acts of its functions under these Regulations.

(5) In this regulation, "premises" means any premises other than premises used only as a dwelling.

Entry to premises under warrant

39.—(1) A justice may issue a warrant under this paragraph if satisfied on information on oath given by an officer that there are reasonable grounds for believing that the first, second or third set of conditions is satisfied.

(2) The first set of conditions is—

(a) that there is on the premises specified in the warrant recorded information in relation to which a requirement could be imposed under regulation 37(1)(b); and

(b) that if such a requirement were to be imposed—

(i) it would not be complied with; or

(ii) the recorded information to which it relates would be removed, tampered with or destroyed.

(3) The second set of conditions is—

(a) that a person on whom a requirement has been imposed under regulation 37(1)(b) has failed (wholly or in part) to comply with it; and

(b) that there is on the premises specified in the warrant recorded information which has been required to be produced.

(4) The third set of conditions is—

(a) that an officer has been obstructed in the exercise of a power under regulation 38; and

(b) that there is on the premises specified in the warrant recorded information or cash which could be inspected under regulation 38(1)(d) or (f).

(5) A justice may issue a warrant under this paragraph if satisfied on information on oath given by an officer that there are reasonable grounds for suspecting that—

(a) an offence under these Regulations has been, is being or is about to be committed by a relevant person; and

(b) there is on the premises specified in the warrant recorded information relevant to whether that offence has been, or is being or is about to be committed.

(6) A warrant issued under this regulation shall authorise an officer—

(a) to enter the premises specified in the warrant;

(b) to search the premises and take possession of any recorded information or anything appearing to be recorded information specified in the warrant or to take, in relation to any such recorded information, any other steps which may appear to be necessary for preserving it or preventing interference with it;

(c) to take copies of, or extracts from, any recorded information specified in the warrant;

(d) to require any person on the premises to provide an explanation of any recorded information appearing to be of the kind specified in the warrant or to state where it may be found;

(e) to use such force as may reasonably be necessary.

[1](7) Where a warrant is issued by a justice under paragraph (1) or (5) on the basis of information on oath given by an officer of the Authority, for "an officer" in paragraph (6) substitute "a constable".

(8) In paragraphs (1), (5) and (7), "justice" means—

(a) in relation to England and Wales, a justice of the peace;

(b) in relation to Scotland, a justice within the meaning of section 307 of the Criminal Procedure (Scotland) Act 1995 (interpretation);

(c) in relation to Northern Ireland, a lay magistrate.

[1](9) In the application of this regulation to Scotland, the references in paragraphs (1), (5) and (7) to information on oath are to be read as references to evidence on oath.

NOTE

[1] As amended by the Money Laundering (Amendment) Regulations (SI 2007/3299) reg.2(c) (effective December 15, 2007).

Failure to comply with information requirement

40.—(1) If, on an application made by—

(a) a designated authority; or

(b) a local weights and measures authority or DETI pursuant to arrangements made with the OFT—

 (i) by or on behalf of the authority; or

 (ii) by DETI,

it appears to the court that a person (the "information defaulter") has failed to do something that he was required to do under regulation 37(1), the court may make an order under this regulation.

(2) An order under this regulation may require the information defaulter—

(a) to do the thing that he failed to do within such period as may be specified in the order;

(b) otherwise to take such steps to remedy the consequences of the failure as may be so specified.

(3) If the information defaulter is a body corporate, a partnership or an unincorporated body of persons which is not a partnership, the order may require any officer of the body corporate, partnership or body, who is (wholly or partly) responsible for the failure to meet such costs of the application as are specified in the order.

(4) In this regulation, "court" means—

(a) in England and Wales and Northern Ireland, the High Court or the county court;

[1](b) in Scotland, the Court of Session or the sheriff court.

NOTE

[1] As amended by the Money Laundering (Amendment) Regulations (SI 2007/3299) reg.2(d) (effective December 15, 2007).

Powers of relevant officers

41.—(1) A relevant officer may only exercise powers under regulations 37 to 39 pursuant to arrangements made with the OFT—

(a) by or on behalf of the local weights and measures authority of which he is an officer ("his authority"); or

(b) by DETI.

(2) Anything done or omitted to be done by, or in relation to, a relevant officer in the exercise or purported exercise of a power in this Part shall be treated for all purposes as having been done or omitted to be done by, or in relation to, an officer of the OFT.

(3) Paragraph (2) does not apply for the purposes of any criminal proceedings brought against the relevant officer, his authority, DETI or the OFT, in respect of anything done or omitted to be done by the officer.

(4) A relevant officer shall not disclose to any person other than the OFT and his authority or, as the case may be, DETI information obtained by him in the exercise of such powers unless—

(a) he has the approval of the OFT to do so; or

(b) he is under a duty to make the disclosure.

Civil penalties, review and appeals

Power to impose civil penalties

42.—(1) A designated authority may impose a penalty of such amount as it considers appropriate on a relevant person who fails to comply with any requirement in regulation 7(1), (2) or (3), 8(1) or (3), 9(2), 10(1), 11(1), 14(1), 15(1) or (2), 16(1), (2), (3) or (4), 19(1), (4), (5) or (6), 20(1), (4) or (5), 21, 26, 27(4) or 33 or a direction made under regulation 18 and, for this purpose, "appropriate" means effective, proportionate and dissuasive.

(2) The designated authority must not impose a penalty on a person under paragraph (1) where there are reasonable grounds for it to be satisfied that the person took all reasonable steps and exercised all due diligence to ensure that the requirement would be complied with.

(3) In deciding whether a person has failed to comply with a requirement of these Regulations, the designated authority must consider whether he followed any relevant guidance which was at the time—

(a) issued by a supervisory authority or any other appropriate body;

(b) approved by the Treasury; and

(c) published in a manner approved by the Treasury as suitable in their opinion to bring the guidance to the attention of persons likely to be affected by it.

[1](4) In paragraph (3), an "appropriate body" means any body which

regulates or is representative of any trade, profession, business or employment carried on by the person.

(5) Where the Commissioners decide to impose a penalty under this regulation, they must give the person notice of—

(a) their decision to impose the penalty and its amount;
(b) the reasons for imposing the penalty;
(c) the right to a review under regulation 43; and
(d) the right to appeal under regulation 44(1)(a).

(6) Where the Authority, the OFT or DETI proposes to impose a penalty under this regulation, it must give the person notice of—

(a) its proposal to impose the penalty and the proposed amount;
(b) the reasons for imposing the penalty; and
(c) the right to make representations to it within a specified period (which may not be less than 28 days).

(7) The Authority, the OFT or DETI, as the case may be, must then decide, within a reasonable period, whether to impose a penalty under this regulation and it must give the person notice of—

(a) its decision not to impose a penalty; or
(b) the following matters—
   (i) its decision to impose a penalty and the amount;
   (ii) the reasons for its decision; and
   (iii) the right to appeal under regulation 44(1)(b).

(8) A penalty imposed under this regulation is payable to the designated authority which imposes it.

NOTE

[1] As substituted by the Money Laundering (Amendment) Regulations (SI 2007/3299) reg.2(e) (effective December 15, 2007).

Review procedure

43.—(1) This regulation applies to decisions of the Commissioners made under—

(a) regulation 29, to refuse to register an applicant;
(b) regulation 30, to cancel the registration of a registered person; and
(c) regulation 42, to impose a penalty.

(2) Any person who is the subject of a decision to which this regulation applies may by notice to the Commissioners require them to review that decision.

(3) The Commissioners need not review any decision unless the notice requiring the review is given within 45 days beginning with the date on which they first gave notice of the decision to the person requiring the review.

(4) Where the Commissioners are required under this regulation to review any decision they must either—

(a) confirm the decision; or
(b) withdraw or vary the decision and take such further steps (if any) in consequence of the withdrawal or variation as they consider appropriate.

(5) Where the Commissioners do not, within 45 days beginning with the date on which the review was required by a person, give notice to that person of their determination of the review, they are to be taken for the purposes of these Regulations to have confirmed the decision.

Appeals

44.—(1) A person may appeal from a decision by—

(a) the Commissioners on a review under regulation 43; and
(b) the Authority, the OFT or DETI under regulation 34 or 42.

(2) An appeal from a decision by—

(a) the Commissioners is to a VAT and duties tribunal;

(b) the Authority is to the Financial Services and Markets Tribunal;
(c) the OFT is to the Consumer Credit Appeals Tribunal; and
(d) DETI is to the High Court.

(3) The provisions of Part 5 of the Value Added Tax Act 1994 (appeals), subject to the modifications set out in paragraph 1 of Schedule 5, apply in respect of appeals to a VAT and duties tribunal made under this regulation as they apply in respect of appeals made to such a tribunal under section 83 (appeals) of that Act.

(4) The provisions of Part 9 of the 2000 Act (hearings and appeals), subject to the modifications set out in paragraph 2 of Schedule 5, apply in respect of appeals to the Financial Services and Markets Tribunal made under this regulation as they apply in respect of references made to that Tribunal under that Act.

(5) Sections 40A (the Consumer Credit Appeals Tribunal), 41 (appeals to the Secretary of State under Part 3) and 41A (appeals from the Consumer Credit Appeals Tribunal) of the Consumer Credit Act 1974 apply in respect of appeals to the Consumer Credit Appeal Tribunal made under this regulation as they apply in respect of appeals made to that Tribunal under section 41 of that Act.

(6) A VAT and duties tribunal hearing an appeal under paragraph (2) has the power to—

(a) quash or vary any decision of the supervisory authority, including the power to reduce any penalty to such amount (including nil) as they think proper; and
(b) substitute their own decision for any decision quashed on appeal.

(7) Notwithstanding paragraph (2)(c), until the coming into force of section 55 of the Consumer Credit Act 2006 (the Consumer Credit Appeals Tribunal), an appeal from a decision by the OFT is to the Financial Services and Markets Tribunal and, for these purposes, the coming into force of that section shall not affect—

(a) the hearing and determination by the Financial Service and Markets Tribunal of an appeal commenced before the coming into force of that section ("the original appeal"); or
(b) any appeal against the decision of the Financial Services and Markets Tribunal with respect to the original appeal.

(8) The modifications in Schedule 5 have effect for the purposes of appeals made under this regulation.

Criminal offences

Offences

45.—(1) A person who fails to comply with any requirement in regulation 7(1), (2) or (3), 8(1) or (3), 9(2), 10(1), 11(1)(a), (b) or (c), 14(1), 15(1) or (2), 16(1), (2), (3) or (4), 19(1), (4), (5) or (6), 20(1), (4) or (5), 21, 26, 27(4) or 33, or a direction made under regulation 18, is guilty of an offence and liable—

(a) on summary conviction, to a fine not exceeding the statutory maximum;
(b) on conviction on indictment, to imprisonment for a term not exceeding two years, to a fine or to both.

(2) In deciding whether a person has committed an offence under paragraph (1), the court must consider whether he followed any relevant guidance which was at the time—

(a) issued by a supervisory authority or any other appropriate body;
(b) approved by the Treasury; and
(c) published in a manner approved by the Treasury as suitable in their opinion to bring the guidance to the attention of persons likely to be affected by it.

(3) In paragraph (2), an "appropriate body" means any body which regulates or is representative of any trade, profession, business or employment carried on by the alleged offender.

(4) A person is not guilty of an offence under this regulation if he took all reasonable steps and exercised all due diligence to avoid committing the offence.

(5) Where a person is convicted of an offence under this regulation, he shall not also be liable to a penalty under regulation 42.

Prosecution of offences

46.—(1) Proceedings for an offence under regulation 45 may be instituted by—

(a) the Director of Revenue and Customs Prosecutions or by order of the Commissioners;
(b) the OFT;
(c) a local weights and measures authority;
(d) DETI;
(e) the Director of Public Prosecutions; or
(f) the Director of Public Prosecutions for Northern Ireland.

(2) Proceedings for an offence under regulation 45 may be instituted only against a relevant person or, where such a person is a body corporate, a partnership or an unincorporated association, against any person who is liable to be proceeded against under regulation 47.

(3) Where proceedings under paragraph (1) are instituted by order of the Commissioners, the proceedings must be brought in the name of an officer of Revenue and Customs.

(4) Where a local weights and measures authority in England or Wales proposes to institute proceedings for an offence under regulation 45 it must give the OFT notice of the intended proceedings, together with a summary of the facts on which the charges are to be founded.

(5) A local weights and measures authority must also notify the OFT of the outcome of the proceedings after they are finally determined.

(6) A local weights and measures authority must, whenever the OFT requires, report in such form and with such particulars as the OFT requires on the exercise of its functions under these Regulations.

(7) Where the Commissioners investigate, or propose to investigate, any matter with a view to determining—

(a) whether there are grounds for believing that an offence under regulation 45 has been committed by any person; or
(b) whether such a person should be prosecuted for such an offence,

that matter is to be treated as an assigned matter within the meaning of section 1(1) of the Customs and Excise Management Act 1979.

(8) Paragraphs (1) and (3) to (6) do not extend to Scotland.

[1](9) In its application to the Commissioners acting in Scotland, paragraph (7)(b) shall be read as referring to the Commissioners determining whether to refer the matter to the Crown Office and Procurator Fiscal Service with a view to the Procurator Fiscal determining whether a person should be prosecuted for such an offence.

NOTE

[1] As inserted by the Money Laundering (Amendment) Regulations (SI 2007/3299) reg.2(f) (effective December 15, 2007).

Offences by bodies corporate etc.

47.—(1) If an offence under regulation 45 committed by a body corporate is shown—

(a) to have been committed with the consent or the connivance of an officer of the body corporate; or
(b) to be attributable to any neglect on his part,

the officer as well as the body corporate is guilty of an offence and liable to be proceeded against and punished accordingly.

(2) If an offence under regulation 45 committed by a partnership is shown—

(a) to have been committed with the consent or the connivance of a partner; or

(b) to be attributable to any neglect on his part,

the partner as well as the partnership is guilty of an offence and liable to be proceeded against and punished accordingly.

(3) If an offence under regulation 45 committed by an unincorporated association (other than a partnership) is shown—

(a) to have been committed with the consent or the connivance of an officer of the association; or

(b) to be attributable to any neglect on his part,

that officer as well as the association is guilty of an offence and liable to be proceeded against and punished accordingly.

(4) If the affairs of a body corporate are managed by its members, paragraph (1) applies in relation to the acts and defaults of a member in connection with his functions of management as if he were a director of the body.

(5) Proceedings for an offence alleged to have been committed by a partnership or an unincorporated association must be brought in the name of the partnership or association (and not in that of its members).

(6) A fine imposed on the partnership or association on its conviction of an offence is to be paid out of the funds of the partnership or association.

(7) Rules of court relating to the service of documents are to have effect as if the partnership or association were a body corporate.

(8) In proceedings for an offence brought against the partnership or association—

(a) section 33 of the Criminal Justice Act 1925 (procedure on charge of offence against corporation) and Schedule 3 to the Magistrates' Courts Act 1980 (corporations) apply as they do in relation to a body corporate;

(b) section 70 (proceedings against bodies corporate) of the Criminal Procedure (Scotland) Act 1995 applies as it does in relation to a body corporate;

(c) section 18 of the Criminal Justice (Northern Ireland) Act 1945 (procedure on charge) and Schedule 4 to the Magistrates' Courts (Northern Ireland) Order 1981 (corporations) apply as they do in relation to a body corporate.

(9) In this regulation—

"officer"—

(a) in relation to a body corporate, means a director, manager, secretary, chief executive, member of the committee of management, or a person purporting to act in such a capacity; and

(b) in relation to an unincorporated association, means any officer of the association or any member of its governing body, or a person purporting to act in such capacity; and

"partner" includes a person purporting to act as a partner.

PART 6

MISCELLANEOUS

Recovery of charges and penalties through the court

48. Any charge or penalty imposed on a person by a supervisory authority under regulation 35(1) or 42(1) is a debt due from that person to the authority, and is recoverable accordingly.

Obligations on public authorities

49.—(1) The following bodies and persons must, if they know or suspect or have reasonable grounds for knowing or suspecting that a person is or has engaged in money laundering or terrorist financing, as soon as reasonably practicable inform the Serious Organised Crime Agency—

(a) the Auditor General for Scotland;
(b) the Auditor General for Wales;
(c) the Authority;
(d) the Bank of England;
(e) the Comptroller and Auditor General;
(f) the Comptroller and Auditor General for Northern Ireland;
(g) the Gambling Commission;
(h) the OFT;
(i) the Official Solicitor to the Supreme Court;
(j) the Pensions Regulator;
(k) the Public Trustee;
(l) the Secretary of State, in the exercise of his functions under enactments relating to companies and insolvency;
(m) the Treasury, in the exercise of their functions under the 2000 Act;
(n) the Treasury Solicitor;
(o) a designated professional body for the purposes of Part 20 of the 2000 Act (provision of financial services by members of the professions);
(p) a person or inspector appointed under section 65 (investigations on behalf of Authority) or 66 (inspections and special meetings) of the Friendly Societies Act 1992;
(q) an inspector appointed under section 49 of the Industrial and Provident Societies Act 1965 (appointment of inspectors) or section 18 of the Credit Unions Act 1979 (power to appoint inspector);
(r) an inspector appointed under section 431 (investigation of a company on its own application), 432 (other company investigations), 442 (power to investigate company ownership) or 446 (investigation of share dealing) of the Companies Act 1985 or under Article 424, 425, 435 or 439 of the Companies (Northern Ireland) Order 1986;
(s) a person or inspector appointed under section 55 (investigations on behalf of Authority) or 56 (inspections and special meetings) of the Building Societies Act 1986;
(t) a person appointed under section 167 (appointment of persons to carry out investigations), 168(3) or (5) (appointment of persons to carry out investigations in particular cases), 169(1)(b) (investigations to support overseas regulator) or 284 (power to investigate affairs of a scheme) of the 2000 Act, or under regulations made under section 262(2)(k) (open-ended investment companies) of that Act, to conduct an investigation; and
(u) a person authorised to require the production of documents under section 447 of the Companies Act 1985 (Secretary of State's power to require production of documents), Article 440 of the Companies (Northern Ireland) Order 1986 or section 84 of the Companies Act 1989 (exercise of powers by officer).

(2) A disclosure made under paragraph (1) is not to be taken to breach any restriction on the disclosure of information however imposed.

Transitional provisions: requirement to be registered

50.—(1) Regulation 26 does not apply to an existing money service business, an existing trust or company service provider or an existing high value dealer until—

(a) where it has applied in accordance with regulation 27 before the specified date for registration in a register maintained under regulation 25(1) (a "new register")—
 (i) the date it is included in a new register following the determination of its application by the Commissioners; or
 (ii) where the Commissioners give it notice under regulation 29(2)(b) of their decision not to register it, the date on which the

Commissioners state that the decision takes effect or, where a statement is included in accordance with paragraph (3)(b), the time at which the Commissioners give it such notice;

(b) in any other case, the specified date.

(2) The specified date is—

(a) in the case of an existing money service business, 1st February 2008;

(b) in the case of an existing trust or company service provider, 1st April 2008;

(c) in the case of an existing high value dealer, the first anniversary which falls on or after 1st January 2008 of the date of its registration in a register maintained under regulation 10 of the Money Laundering Regulations 2003.

(3) In the case of an application for registration in a new register made before the specified date by an existing money service business, an existing trust or company service provider or an existing high value dealer, the Commissioners must include in a notice given to it under regulation 29(2)(b)—

(a) the date on which their decision is to take effect; or

(b) if the Commissioners consider that the interests of the public require their decision to have immediate effect, a statement to that effect and the reasons for it.

(4) In the case of an application for registration in a new register made before the specified date by an existing money services business or an existing trust or company service provider, the Commissioners must give it a notice under regulation 29(2) by—

(a) in the case of an existing money service business, 1st June 2008;

(b) in the case of an existing trust or company service provider, 1st July 2008; or

(c) where applicable, 45 days beginning with the date on which they receive any further information required under regulation 27(3).

(5) In this regulation—

"existing money service business" and an "existing high value dealer" mean a money service business or a high value dealer which, immediately before 15th December 2007, was included in a register maintained under regulation 10 of the Money Laundering Regulations 2003;

"existing trust or company service provider" means a trust or company service provider carrying on business in the United Kingdom immediately before 15th December 2007.

Minor and consequential amendments

51. Schedule 6, which contains minor and consequential amendments to primary and secondary legislation, has effect.

Regulation 3(3)(a)

SCHEDULE 1

ACTIVITIES LISTED IN POINTS 2 TO 12 AND 14 OF ANNEX I TO THE BANKING CONSOLIDATION DIRECTIVE

2. Lending including, inter alia: consumer credit, mortgage credit, factoring, with or without recourse, financing of commercial transactions (including forfeiting).

3. Financial leasing.

4. Money transmission services.

5. Issuing and administering means of payment (e.g. credit cards, travellers' cheques and bankers' drafts).

6. Guarantees and commitments.

7. Trading for own account or for account of customers in:

(a) money market instruments (cheques, bills, certificates of deposit, etc.);

(b) foreign exchange;

(c) financial futures and options;
(d) exchange and interest-rate instruments; or
(e) transferable securities.

8. Participation in securities issues and the provision of services related to such issues.
9. Advice to undertakings on capital structure, industrial strategy and related questions and advice as well as services relating to mergers and the purchase of undertakings.
10. Money broking.
11. Portfolio management and advice.
12. Safekeeping and administration of securities.
14. Safe custody services

Regulations 4(1)(e) and (2), 13(6) and (8) and 14(5).

SCHEDULE 2

Financial Activity, Simplified Due Diligence and Politically Exposed Persons

Financial activity on an occasional or very limited basis

1. For the purposes of regulation 4(1)(e) and (2), a person is to be considered as engaging in financial activity on an occasional or very limited basis if all the following conditions are fulfilled—

(a) the person's total annual turnover in respect of the financial activity does not exceed £64,000;
(b) the financial activity is limited in relation to any customer to no more than one transaction exceeding 1,000 euro, whether the transaction is carried out in a single operation, or a series of operations which appear to be linked;
(c) the financial activity does not exceed 5% of the person's total annual turnover;
(d) the financial activity is ancillary and directly related to the person's main activity;
(e) the financial activity is not the transmission or remittance of money (or any representation of monetary value) by any means;
(f) the person's main activity is not that of a person falling within regulation 3(1)(a) to (f) or (h);
(g) the financial activity is provided only to customers of the person's main activity and is not offered to the public.

Simplified due diligence

2. For the purposes of regulation 13(6), the conditions are—

(a) the authority has been entrusted with public functions pursuant to the Treaty on the European Union, the Treaties on the European Communities or Community secondary legislation;
(b) the authority's identity is publicly available, transparent and certain;
(c) the activities of the authority and its accounting practices are transparent;
(d) either the authority is accountable to a Community institution or to the authorities of an EEA state, or otherwise appropriate check and balance procedures exist ensuring control of the authority's activity.

3. For the purposes of regulation 13(8), the conditions are—

(a) the product has a written contractual base;
(b) any related transaction is carried out through an account of the customer with a credit institution which is subject to the money laundering directive or with a credit institution situated in a non-EEA state which imposes requirements equivalent to those laid down in that directive;
(c) the product or related transaction is not anonymous and its nature is such that it allows for the timely application of customer due diligence measures where there is a suspicion of money laundering or terrorist financing;
(d) the product is within the following maximum threshold—
  (i) in the case of insurance policies or savings products of a similar nature, the annual premium is no more than 1,000 euro or there is a single premium of no more than 2,500 euro;
  (ii) in the case of products which are related to the financing of physical assets where the legal and beneficial title of the assets is not transferred to the customer until the termination of the contractual relationship (whether the transaction is carried out in a single operation or in several operations which appear to be linked), the annual payments do not exceed 15,000 euro;
  (iii) in all other cases, the maximum threshold is 15,000 euro;
(e) the benefits of the product or related transaction cannot be realised for the benefit of

third parties, except in the case of death, disablement, survival to a predetermined advanced age, or similar events;

(f) in the case of products or related transactions allowing for the investment of funds in financial assets or claims, including insurance or other kinds of contingent claims—

(i) the benefits of the product or related transaction are only realisable in the long term;

(ii) the product or related transaction cannot be used as collateral; and

(iii) during the contractual relationship, no accelerated payments are made, surrender clauses used or early termination takes place.

Politically exposed persons

4.—(1) For the purposes of regulation 14(5)—

(a) individuals who are or have been entrusted with prominent public functions include the following—

(i) heads of state, heads of government, ministers and deputy or assistant ministers;

(ii) members of parliaments;

(iii) members of supreme courts, of constitutional courts or of other high-level judicial bodies whose decisions are not generally subject to further appeal, other than in exceptional circumstances;

(iv) members of courts of auditors or of the boards of central banks;

(v) ambassadors, chargés d'affaires and high-ranking officers in the armed forces; and

(vi) members of the administrative, management or supervisory bodies of state-owned enterprises;

(b) the categories set out in paragraphs (i) to (vi) of sub-paragraph (a) do not include middle-ranking or more junior officials;

(c) immediate family members include the following—

(i) a spouse;

(ii) a partner;

(iii) children and their spouses or partners; and

(iv) parents;

(d) persons known to be close associates include the following—

(i) any individual who is known to have joint beneficial ownership of a legal entity or legal arrangement, or any other close business relations, with a person referred to in regulation 14(5)(a); and

(ii) any individual who has sole beneficial ownership of a legal entity or legal arrangement which is known to have been set up for the benefit of a person referred to in regulation 14(5)(a).

(2) In paragraph (1)(c), "partner" means a person who is considered by his national law as equivalent to a spouse.

Regulations 17(2)(b), 23(1)(c) and 32(4)

SCHEDULE 3

Professional Bodies

Part 1

1. Association of Chartered Certified Accountants
2. Council for Licensed Conveyancers
3. Faculty of Advocates
4. General Council of the Bar
5. General Council of the Bar of Northern Ireland
6. Institute of Chartered Accountants in England and Wales
7. Institute of Chartered Accountants in Ireland
8. Institute of Chartered Accountants of Scotland
9. Law Society
10. Law Society of Scotland
11. Law Society of Northern Ireland

Part 2

12. Association of Accounting Technicians

13. Association of International Accountants
14. Association of Taxation Technicians
15. Chartered Institute of Management Accountants
16. Chartered Institute of Public Finance and Accountancy
17. Chartered Institute of Taxation
18. Faculty Office of the Archbishop of Canterbury
19. Insolvency Practitioners Association
20. Institute of Certified Bookkeepers
21. Institute of Financial Accountants
[1]**22.** International Association of Book-keepers

NOTE
[1] As inserted by the Money Laundering (Amendment) Regulations (SI 2007/3299) reg.2(g) (effective December 15, 2007).

Regulation 37(2)

SCHEDULE 4

Connected persons

Corporate bodies

1. If the relevant person is a body corporate ("BC"), a person who is or has been—
(a) an officer or manager of BC or of a parent undertaking of BC;
(b) an employee of BC;
(c) an agent of BC or of a parent undertaking of BC.

Partnerships

2. If the relevant person is a partnership, a person who is or has been a member, manager, employee or agent of the partnership.

Unincorporated associations

3. If the relevant person is an unincorporated association of persons which is not a partnership, a person who is or has been an officer, manager, employee or agent of the association.

Individuals

4. If the relevant person is an individual, a person who is or has been an employee or agent of that individual.

Regulation 44(8)

SCHEDULE 5

Modifications in Relation to Appeals

[*Not reproduced.*]

Regulation 51

SCHEDULE 6

Minor and Consequential Amendments

[*Not reproduced.*]

[NEXT TEXT PAGE IS **F** 117]

The European Communities (Lawyer's Practice) (Scotland) Regulations 2000

(SSI 2000/121)

[April 27, 2000]

Arrangement of Sections

Part I

Introductory

Part II

Practice of Professional Activities by a Registered European Lawyer

Part III

Registration

Part IV

Regulation and Discipline

Part V

Entry into the Profession of Solicitor or Advocate

The Scottish Ministers, in exercise of the powers conferred upon them by section 2(2) of the European Communities Act 1972 and all other powers enabling them in that behalf, hereby make the following Regulations:

PART I

INTRODUCTORY

Citation, commencement, transitional and extent

1.—(1) These Regulations may be cited as the European Communities (Lawyer's Practice) (Scotland) Regulations 2000 and shall come into force on 22nd May 2000, except for regulations 21 and 22, which shall come into force on 22nd November 2000.

[1] (2) Where, on 22nd May 2000, a European lawyer is practising professional activities under his home professional title on a permanent basis in Scotland or commences such practice by 21st November 2000, he shall apply to be registered in accordance with regulation 16 by 21st November 2000 where he intends to practise those activities on a permanent basis after that date.

[1] (3) On or after 22nd November 2000, a European lawyer shall not practise as referred to in paragraph (2) without being registered in accordance with regulation 16, unless he was already practising before that date and has made an application for registration which has not been determined.

[1] (4) In paragraphs (3) and (5), an application for registration shall, as at a particular date, be taken not to have been determined if as at that date the applicant—

(a) has not received a rejection of his application and the period for such a rejection or a deemed rejection has not yet expired; or

(b) is appealing against a rejection of the application(including a deemed rejection) and the appeal has not been determined.

[1] (5) Regulations 21(1)(b) and 22 shall not apply to a European lawyer whilst that lawyer satisfies all the following conditions—

(a) immediately before 22nd November 2000 he was practising on a permanent basis in any part of the United Kingdom;

(b) before 22nd November 2000 he applied for registration to any of the barristers' professional bodies or England and Wales or Northern Ireland solicitors' professional bodies, or to the Faculty of Advocates or the Law Society of Scotland; and

(c) his application for registration has not yet been determined.

(6) These Regulations extend to Scotland and insofar as they extend beyond Scotland they do so only as a matter of Scots law.

NOTE
[1] With regard to "relevant lawyers" (SSI 2004/302, reg.2(2)) for "22nd May 2000", where it occurs substitute "16th September 2004"; for "21st November 2000", wherever it occurs, substitute "15th March 2005"; and for "22nd November 2000", wherever it occurs, substitute "16th March 2005" (The European Communities (Lawyer's Practice) (Scotland) Amendment Regulations 2004, SSI 2004/302, reg.2(4)).

Interpretation

2.—(1) In these Regulations, unless the context otherwise requires—

"advocate" means a member of the Faculty of Advocates;

"barrister" means a person who is a barrister of England and Wales or, as the case may be, Northern Ireland, and practising as such;

"barristers' professional bodies" means the Inns of Court and the General Council of the Bar of England and Wales and the Executive Council of the Inn of Court of Northern Ireland;

"competent authority", in relation to Scotland, means either of the bodies designated as a competent authority by regulation 4 to undertake the activities required by the Directive set out in that regulation;

"the Directive" means of the European Communities Parliament and Council Directive No.98/5/EC to facilitate practice of the profession of lawyer on a permanent basis in certain states other than the State in which the professional qualification was obtained;

"England and Wales or Northern Ireland registered European lawyer" means a European lawyer who is registered with one of the barristers' professional bodies or England and Wales or Northern Ireland solicitors' professional bodies and whose registration has not been withdrawn or suspended;

"England and Wales or Northern Ireland solicitors' professional bodies" means the Law Society and the Law Society of Northern Ireland respectively;

"European lawyer" has the meaning given in paragraphs (2) and (3);

"home State" means the State in paragraph (4) in which a European lawyer acquired his authorisation to pursue professional activities and, if he is authorised in more than one of those States, it shall mean any of those States;

"home professional title" means, in relation to a European lawyer, the professional title or any of the professional titles specified in relation to his home State in paragraph (4) under which he is authorised in his home State to pursue professional activities;

"Irish barrister" means a European lawyer who is authorised in the Republic of Ireland to pursue professional activities under the professional title of barrister and whose home State is the Republic of Ireland;

"Irish solicitor" means a European lawyer who is authorised in the Republic of Ireland to pursue professional activities under the professional title of solicitor and whose home State is the Republic of Ireland;

"member of the professional body" means a practising solicitor or advocate, as the case may be;

"professional body" means the Law Society of Scotland or the Faculty of Advocates;

"Qualification Regulations" means the European Communities (Recognition of Professional Qualifications) Regulations 1991;

"registered European lawyer" means a European lawyer who is registered with a professional body in accordance with regulation 17 and whose registration has not been withdrawn or suspended;

"solicitor" shall have the same meaning as in section 65(1) of the Solicitors (Scotland) Act 1980;

"supreme court" means the Court of Session, the High Court of Justiciary, the Lands Valuation Appeal Court, the House of Lords (hearing an appeal from the Court of Session) or the Judicial Committee of the Privy Council (hearing a reference or an appeal under the Scotland Act 1998).

(2) In these Regulations, "European lawyer" means a person who is—

(a) a national of the United Kingdom or of a State listed in paragraph (4);

(b) authorised in any of the States listed in paragraph (4) to pursue professional activities under any of the professional titles appearing in that paragraph; and

(c) subject to paragraph (3), not a solicitor or advocate, or under the law of England and Wales or Northern Ireland, a solicitor or barrister.

(3) Where a person is a European lawyer registered with more than one of the following—

(a) the Law Society of Scotland or the Faculty of Advocates; or

(b) the England and Wales or Northern Ireland solicitors' professional bodies or the barristers' professional bodies, and subsequently acquires the title used by members of one of the bodies referred to in sub paragraph (b) then notwithstanding paragraph (2)(c), that person shall continue to fall within the definition of a European lawyer in relation to the relevant professional body referred to in sub paragraph (a) for the period that he remains registered with that other professional body.

(4) The States and professional titles referred to in the definition of European lawyer in paragraph (1) are as follows—

State	*Professional titles*
Belgium	Avocat/Advocaat/Rechtsanwalt
Denmark	Advokat
Germany	Rechtsanwalt
Greece	Dikegoros
Spain	Abogado/Advocat/Avogado/Abokatu
France	Avocat
Republic of Ireland	Barrister/Solicitor
Italy	Avvocato
Luxembourg	Avocat
Netherlands	Advocaat
Austria	Rechtsanwalt
Portugal	Advogado
Finland	Asianajaja/Advokat
Sweden	Advokat
[1] Switzerland	Avocat/Advokat/Rechtsanwalt/Anwalt/ Fürsprecher/Fürsprech/Avvocato
[1] Iceland	Lögmaður
[1] Liechtenstein	Rechtsanwalt
[1] Norway	Advokat
[1] Czech Republic	Advokát
[1] Estonia	Vandeadvokaat
[1] Cyprus	Δικηγόρος (Dikegoros)
[1] Latvia	Zvērināts advokāts
[1] Lithuania	Advokatas
[1] Hungary	Ügyvéd
[1] Malta	Avukat/Prokuratur legali
[1] Poland	Adwokat/Radca prawny
[1] Slovenia	Odvetnik/Odvetnica
[1] Slovakia	Advokát/Komerčný právnik"
[2] Bulgaria	
[2] Romania	Avocat

(5) For the purposes of regulations 4(2)(d), 5(3) and 24(1) registration with the Faculty of Advocates shall be construed as membership of it.

(6) Unless the context otherwise requires, any reference in these Regulations to a numbered regulation, Part or Schedule is a reference to a regulation or Part of, or a Schedule to, these Regulations and any reference in a regulation to a numbered paragraph is a reference to the paragraph bearing that number in that regulation.

NOTE

[1] As inserted by the European Communities (Lawyer's Practice) (Scotland) Amendment Regulations (SSI 2004/302) reg.3 (effective September 16, 2004).

[2] As inserted subject to transitional provisions as specified in SSI 2007/358 reg.2(1) and (2) by the European Communities (Lawyer's Practice) (Scotland) Amendment Regulations (SI 2007/358) reg.3(2) (effective September 25, 2007).

Purpose of Regulations

3.—(1) The purpose of these Regulations is to implement the Directive in or as regards Scotland.

(2) The provisions of these Regulations shall have effect for the purpose of facilitating the practice of the profession of lawyer on a permanent basis by a European lawyer registered or registering in Scotland.

(3) References in these regulations to practice or professional activities shall not include the provision of services by lawyers within the meaning of the European Communities (Services of Lawyers) Order 1978.

Competent authorities

4.—(1) The Law Society of Scotland is designated as the competent authority for the purposes of-

(a) receiving applications for registration by European lawyers under Part III of these Regulations;
(b) receiving applications from registered European lawyers for entry into the profession of solicitor;
(c) the regulation of registered European lawyers registered with it; and
(d) the provision of certificates attesting to registration of solicitors with it.

(2) The Faculty of Advocates is designated as the competent authority for the purposes of—

(a) receiving applications for registration by European lawyers under Part III of these Regulations;
(b) receiving applications from registered European lawyers for entry into the profession of advocate;
(c) the regulation of registered European lawyers registered with it; and
(d) the provision of certificates attesting to registration of advocates with it.

Exchange of information

5.—(1) In order to facilitate the application of the Directive and to prevent its provisions from being misapplied, a professional body may supply to or receive from-

(a) another professional body;
(b) the England and Wales or Northern Ireland solicitors' professional bodies or barristers' professional bodies; or
(c) an authority in any of the States listed in regulation 2(4) which has been designated by that State under the Directive as a competent authority in that State,

any information relating to a European lawyer or to any person with whom he jointly practises.

(2) Subject to paragraph (1) or as otherwise required by law in the interests of justice, a professional body shall preserve the confidentiality of

any information received in accordance with paragraph (1) relating to a European lawyer or to any person with whom he jointly practises.

(3) A competent authority in Scotland shall provide a certificate attesting to the registration of a solicitor or advocate registered with it and his authorisation to practise when requested to do so by that solicitor or advocate or by a competent authority in a State listed in regulation 2(4).

Part II

Practice of Professional Activities by a Registered European Lawyer

Practice of professional activities

6.—(1) Subject to the provisions of these Regulations, a registered European lawyer shall be entitled to carry out under his home professional title any professional activities whether in Scotland or elsewhere that may lawfully be carried out by a member of the professional body with which he is registered and any enactment or rule of law or practice with regard to the carrying out of professional activities by members of that professional body shall be interpreted and applied accordingly.

(2) A registered European lawyer who is in salaried employment may carry out professional activities whether in Scotland or elsewhere under his home professional title to the same extent that an employed member of the professional body with which he is registered may do so.

Title and description to be used by a registered European lawyer

7.—(1) Where a registered European lawyer is engaged in any professional activities in pursuance of regulation 6(1) he shall comply with the requirements set out in paragraph (2).

(2) The requirements referred to in paragraph (1) are that a registered European lawyer shall—

(a) use his home professional title expressed in an officiallanguage of his home State in a manner which avoids confusion with the title of solicitor or advocate;

(b) indicate the professional organisation by which he is authorised to practise or the court of law before which he is entitled to practise in that State;

(c) indicate the professional body with which he is registered in Scotland and that he is a registered European lawyer with that body; and

(d) if applicable indicate any England and Wales or Northern Ireland solicitors' professional bodies or barristers' professional bodies with which he may be registered and that he is an England and Wales or Northern Ireland registered European lawyer with that body or those bodies.

Joint practice

8. Where a registered European lawyer carries out professional activities in pursuance of regulation 6(1) under his home professional title as part of a joint practice he shall do so to the same extent and in the same manner as a member of the professional body with which he is registered may do so, with—

(a) a member of the professional body with which he is registered;

(b) a registered European lawyer who is registered with the same professional body; or

(c) any other person permitted by the professional body with which he is registered.

Name of joint practice

9.—(1) Subject to paragraph (2), where a registered European lawyer is a member of a joint practice in his home State, he may use the name of that practice with his home professional title when practising as a registered European lawyer.

(2) Rules of conduct of the professional body with which a registered European lawyer is registered may prohibit the use by him of the name of the joint practice of which he is a member in the home State to the extent that—

(a) that name is also used by persons who are not European lawyers or solicitors of any part of the United Kingdom; and
(b) those rules prohibit members of that professional body (whether or not practising as such) from using that name.

Notification of joint practice

10.—(1) Where a European lawyer is a member of a joint practice in his home State, he shall inform the professional body with which he intends to register and provide it with the following information:-

(a) the name of the joint practice;
(b) his place of business;
(c) the name and place of business of any member of his joint practice;
(d) any other relevant information about the joint practice requested by the professional body.

(2) A European lawyer shall notify that professional body of any changes in the information whether before or after registration.

Representation in legal proceedings

11.—(1) Subject to paragraphs (2) and (4), no enactment or rule of law or practice shall prevent a registered European lawyer from pursuing professional activities relating to the representation of a client in any proceedings before any court, tribunal or public authority (including addressing the court, tribunal or public authority) only because he is not a solicitor or advocate.

(2) In proceedings referred to in paragraph (1), where the professional activities in question may (but for these Regulations) be lawfully provided only by a solicitor or advocate, a registered European lawyer shall act in conjunction with a solicitor or advocate who is entitled to practise before the court, tribunal or public authority concerned and who could lawfully provide those professional activities.

(3) The solicitor or advocate referred to in paragraph (2) shall, where necessary, be answerable to the court, tribunal or public authority concerned in relation to the proceedings.

(4) A registered European lawyer shall not have a right of audience in a supreme court unless he has completed the course of training in evidence, pleading and practice in relation to that court which must be completed by any member of the professional body with which he is registered who seeks a right of audience in that court.

Property transactions

[1] **12.** A registered European lawyer is not entitled, by virtue of regulation 6(1), to prepare for remuneration any deed creating or transferring an interest in land unless he has a home professional title obtained in Denmark, the Republic of Ireland, Finland, Sweden, Cyprus, the Czech Republic, Hungary, Iceland, Liechtenstein, Norway or Slovakia.

NOTE

[1] As substituted by the European Communities (Lawyer's Practice) (Scotland) Amendment Regulations (SSI 2004/302) reg.4 (effective September 16, 2004).

Executries

[1] **13.** A registered European lawyer is not entitled, by virtue of regulation 6(1), to prepare for remuneration any deed for obtaining title to administer

the estate of a deceased person unless he has a home professional title obtained in Denmark, Germany, the Republic of Ireland, Austria, Finland, Sweden, Cyprus, the Czech Republic, Hungary, Iceland, Liechtenstein, Norway or Slovakia.

NOTE

[1] As substituted by the European Communities (Lawyer's Practice) (Scotland) Amendment Regulations (SSI 2004/302) reg.5 (effective September 16, 2004).

Legal aid

14. A registered European lawyer may provide professional activities by way of legal advice and assistance or legal aid under the Legal Aid (Scotland) Act 1986 and references to a solicitor, counsel or legal representative in that and any other enactment relating to legal advice and assistance or legal aid shall be interpreted accordingly.

Part III

Registration

Establishment and maintenance of registers of registered European lawyers

15. Each of the professional bodies shall establish and maintain a register of registered European lawyers.

Application to be entered on a register

16.—(1) Subject to paragraph (6) and regulation 18, a European lawyer who wishes to pursue professional activities under his home professional title on a permanent basis in Scotland or any other part of the United Kingdom shall apply to be entered on the register maintained by a professional body under regulation 15.

(2) A European lawyer who wishes to register with a professional body in accordance with paragraph (1) shall provide the professional body with certificates confirming his registration with the competent authority in each home State under whose home professional title he intends to practise.

(3) A professional body may require that the certificate referred to in paragraph (2) shall not have been issued more than three months before the date of the application under this regulation.

(4) An application for registration under this regulation shall comply with any applicable rules or regulations made by the relevant professional body and shall be accompanied by the appropriate fee.

(5) Subject to regulation 18, an application for registration under this regulation shall not be affected by any other application or registration with the barristers' professional bodies or the England and Wales or Northern Ireland solicitors' professional bodies.

(6) Paragraph (1) shall not apply to a European lawyer who wishes to pursue professional activities under his home professional title on a permanent basis in Scotland or any other part of the United Kingdom where that lawyer is an England and Wales or Northern Ireland registered European lawyer.

Registration by professional body

17.—(1) Subject to regulation 18, a professional body shall enter on its register the name of a European lawyer who applies to it in accordance with regulation 16.

(2) Where a professional body registers a European lawyer in accordance with paragraph (1), it shall inform the competent authority in the home state of the registration.

Restrictions on registration

18.—(1) A European lawyer shall not be registered at the same time both with the Law Society of Scotland and the Faculty of Advocates.

(2) An Irish solicitor shall not be entered on a register maintained under regulation 15 by the Faculty of Advocates.

(3) An Irish barrister shall not be entered on a register maintained under regulation 15 by the Law Society of Scotland.

(4) A European lawyer registered with any of the barristers' professional bodies shall not be entered on a register maintained under regulation 15 by the Law Society of Scotland.

(5) A European lawyer registered with any of the England and Wales and Northern Ireland solicitors' professional bodies shall not be entered on a register maintained under regulation 15 by the Faculty of Advocates.

Time limit for decision and notification by professional body

19.—(1) A professional body shall consider an application for registration under regulation 16 as soon as is reasonably practicable, and shall notify the

European lawyer of its decision, and if the application is rejected, or granted subject to conditions, the reasons upon which the rejection or the imposition of conditions is based, within four months of receipt of an application complying with regulation 16(2) and (4).

(2) Where the professional body fails to take a decision and notify the European lawyer within four months in accordance with paragraph (1), it shall be deemed to have taken a decision to reject his application and to have notified it to him on the last day of that period.

(3) Where the professional body withdraws or suspends a registration, it shall notify the European lawyer of its decision and the reasons upon which the withdrawal or suspension is based.

Appeal by European lawyer

20.—(1) Within three months of the notification to him of the professional body's decision, or later with the permission of the Court of Session, the European lawyer may appeal against the decision by appeal in Form 41.19 to the Court of Session.

(2) The Court of Session may, for the purpose of determining any appeal under this Part—

(a) order the professional body to register the European lawyer;

(b) refuse the appeal; or

(c) remit the matter to the professional body with such directions as it sees fit.

(3) The Court of Session shall give reasons for its decision.

Offence of pretending to be a registered European lawyer

[1] **21.**—(1) A person who without being a registered European lawyer,

(a) wilfully pretends to be a registered European lawyer or takes or uses any name, title, designation or description implying that he is a registered European lawyer whether in Scotland or elsewhere; or

(b) subject to paragraph (2), carries on professional activities in Scotland under one of the professional titles listed in regulation 2(4) or under any name, designation or description implying that he is entitled to pursue those activities under one of those professional titles;

shall be guilty of an offence and liable on summary conviction to a fine not exceeding level 4 on the standard scale.

(2) Paragraph (1)(b) shall not apply to a person who satisfies any of the following conditions—

(a) he is not a national of the United Kingdom or of any of the States listed in regulation 2(4);

(b) he is a solicitor or advocate under the law of Scotland or a solicitor or barrister under the law of England and Wales or Northern Ireland;

(c) he is an England and Wales or Northern Ireland registered European lawyer; or

(d) he is providing services within the meaning of the European Communities (Services of Lawyers) Order 1978.

NOTE

[1] Applies to "relevant lawyers" (SSI 2004/302, reg.2(2)) only as from March 16, 2005 (The European Communities (Lawyer's Practice) (Scotland) Amendment Regulations 2004, SSI 2004/302, reg.2(3)).

Fees, rewards, outlays and expenses of an unregistered European lawyer.

[1] **22.** Where a European lawyer is carrying on professional activities under his home professionaltitle in Scotland any fees, rewards, outlays or expenses in respect of those activities shall not be recoverable by him or any other person unless that European lawyer is a registered European lawyer, or an England and Wales or Northern Ireland registered European lawyer.

NOTE

[1] Applies to "relevant lawyers" (SSI 2004/302, reg.2(2)) only as from March 16, 2005 (The European Communities (Lawyer's Practice) (Scotland) Amendment Regulations 2004, SSI 2004/302, reg.2(3)).

Evidence of registration

23. Any certificate purporting to be signed by an officer of a professional body and stating that a person—

(a) is, or is not, registered as a European lawyer with that professional body; or

(b) was, or was not, registered with that professional body during a period specified in the certificate,

shall, unless the contrary is proved, be evidence of that fact and be taken to have been so signed.

Publication of names of registered European lawyers

24.—(1) Where a professional body publishes the names of solicitors or advocates registered with it, it shall also publish the names of any European lawyers registered with it.

(2) In this regulation, "publishes" or "publish" includes the provision of information to a legal publisher.

PART IV

REGULATION AND DISCIPLINE

Rules of professional conduct applicable

25. Where a registered European lawyer is practising under his home professional title whether in Scotland or elsewhere, he shall be subject to the same rules of professional conduct as a member of the professional body with which he is registered.

Disciplinary proceedings applicable

26.—(1) Where it is alleged that a registered European lawyer has failed to comply with the rules of professional conduct to which he is subject under regulation 25, he shall be subject to the same rules of procedure, penalties and remedies as a member of the professional body with which he is registered and shall, if appropriate, be subject to disciplinary proceedings brought by an appropriate authority.

(2) Any sanction against a registered European lawyer in relation to disciplinary proceedings may include withdrawal or suspension of his registration.

(3) The appropriate authority shall give reasons for its decision.

(4) In this regulation, an appropriate authority means—

(a) where the registered European lawyer is registered with the Law Society of Scotland, the Scottish Solicitors' Discipline Tribunal;

(b) where the registered European lawyer is registered with the Faculty of Advocates, that body.

Disciplinary proceedings against a registered European lawyer

27.—(1) Where a professional body intends to begin disciplinary proceedings against a registered European lawyer, it shall–

(a) inform the competent authority in his home State as soon as possible of the intention to begin those proceedings and furnish it with all the relevant details;

(b) co-operate with that authority throughout those proceedings; and

(c) inform that authority of the decision reached in those proceedings including the decision in any appeal, as soon as practicable after the decision is given.

(2) Subject to paragraph (3), where the competent authority in the registered European lawyer's home State withdraws his authorisation to practise under the home professional title either temporarily or permanently, his registration with the professional body shall be automatically withdrawn to the same extent.

(3) Where a registered European lawyer is authorised to practise under a home professional title in two or more home States, his registration shall be withdrawn in accordance with paragraph (2) if his authorisation to practise under a home professional title has been withdrawn in one or more of those home States.

(4) Where there is an appeal against a decision in disciplinary proceedings against a registered European lawyer, the body responsible for hearing the appeal shall afford the competent authority in the registered European lawyer's home State an opportunity to make representations in relation to that appeal.

Disciplinary proceedings against a solicitor or advocate

28. Where a professional body intends to begin disciplinary proceedings against a solicitor or advocate practising in a State listed in regulation 2(4), it shall inform the competent authority in that State of-

(a) the intention to begin those proceedings and furnish it with all of the relevant details; and

(b) the decision reached in those proceedings, including the decision in any appeal, as soon as practicable after the decision is given.

PART V

ENTRY INTO THE PROFESSION OF SOLICITOR OR ADVOCATE

Application by registered European lawyer

29.—(1) Where a registered European lawyer applies to the professional body with which he has been registered to become a solicitor or advocate, as the case may be, and that professional body requires him to pass an aptitude test under regulation 6(1)(b)(ii) of the Qualification Regulations, he may apply to the professional body for an exemption from that requirement on the grounds that he falls within paragraph (2) or (3) of this regulation.

(2) A person falls within this paragraph if—

(a) he is a European lawyer and has been registered with that professional body for at least three years; and

(b) he has for a period of at least three years effectively and regularly pursued in Scotland professional activities, in accordance with regulation 6, under his home professional title in the law of Scotland including Community law.

(3) A person falls within this paragraph if—

(a) he is a European lawyer and has been registered with that professional body for at least three years;

(b) he has for a period of at least three years effectively and regularly pursued in Scotland professional activities, in accordance with regulation 6, under his home professional title; and

(c) he has for a period of less than three years effectively and regularly pursued in Scotland, professional activities, in accordance with regulation 6, under his home professional title in the law of Scotland.

Decision by professional body

30.—(1) Subject to paragraph (3), the professional body shall grant an exemption applied for under regulation 29 if it considers that the requirements under paragraph (2) or (3) of regulation 29 have been met.

(2) The registration of a registered European lawyer shall cease from the date he is granted entry into the profession of solicitor or advocate.

(3) The professional body may refuse to grant an exemption if it considers that the registered European lawyer would be unfit to practise as a solicitor or advocate.

Evidence in support of application for exemption under regulation 29(2)

31.—(1) Where a registered European lawyer makes an application under paragraph (2) of regulation 29, he shall provide the professional body with any relevant information and documentation which it may reasonably require.

(2) The professional body may verify the effective and regular nature of the professional activity pursued and may, if necessary, request the registered European lawyer to provide, orally or in writing, clarification of, or further details on, the information and documentation referred to in paragraph (1)

Evidence in support of application for exemption under regulation 29(3)

32.—(1) Where a registered European lawyer makes an application under paragraph (3) of regulation 29, he shall provide the professional body with any relevant information and documentation it may reasonably require.

(2) In deciding whether to grant an application under paragraph (3) of regulation 29, the professional body shall take into account the professional activities the registered European lawyer has pursued during the period he has been registered and any knowledge and professional experience he has gained of, and any training he has received in, the law of Scotland, and the rules of professional conduct of the profession concerned.

(3) Subject to paragraph (4), in the case of an application under paragraph (3) of regulation 29, the professional body shall, by means of an interview, assess and verify the registered European lawyer's effective and regular professional activity and his capacity to continue that activity.

(4) Where a professional body believes that an interview is unnecessary and intends to grant an application under paragraph (3) of regulation 29, it may dispense with that requirement.

Meaning of "effectively and regularly pursued"

33. For the purposes of regulations 29 to 32 activities shall be regarded as effectively and regularly pursued if they are actually exercised without any interruption other than that resulting from the events of everyday life.

Time limit for decision and notification by professional body

34.—(1) A professional body shall consider an application under regulation 29 as soon as is reasonably practicable, and shall notify the applicant of its decision and, if the application is rejected, the reasons for the rejection, within four months of receipt of all the relevant information and documentation required under regulations 31 and 32.

(2) Where the professional body fails to take a decision and notify the registered European lawyer within four months in accordance with paragraph (1), it shall be deemed to have taken a decision to reject his application and to have notified it to him on the last day of that period.

Appeal by registered European lawyer

35.—(1) Within three months of the notification to him of the professional body's decision, or later with the permission of the Court of Session, the registered European lawyer may appeal against the decision by appeal in Form 41.19 to the Court of Session.

(2) The Court of Session may, for the purpose of determining any appeal under this Part—

(a) grant the exemption applied for;
(b) refuse the appeal; or

(c) remit the matter to the professional body with such directions as the appeal body sees fit.

(3) The Court of Session shall give reasons for its decision.

Practice under the title of solicitor or advocate

36.—(1) This regulation applies where a registered European lawyer ("the lawyer") is granted entry into the profession of solicitor or advocate.

(2) Subject to paragraph (3), the lawyer shall be entitled to continue to practise in Scotland or elsewhere under his home professional title, and to use his home professional title, expressed in an official language of his home State, alongside the title of solicitor or advocate as the case may be, provided that he continues to be authorised in his home State to pursue professional activities under that title.

(3) For the purposes of rules of professional conduct, including those relating to disciplinary and complaints procedures, the lawyer's continuing practice in Scotland or elsewhere under his home professional title insofar as it relates to that lawyer's practice as a solicitor or advocate shall be deemed to form part of his practice as a solicitor or advocate, and those rules shall apply to his practice under his home professional title as they do to his practice as a solicitor or advocate.

(4) Where this regulation applies, a lawyer's registration in accordance with regulation 17 with the professional body whose title he has acquired shall cease from the date he is entitled to use that title.

PART VI

SUPPLEMENTARY PROVISIONS

Modification and extension of enactments

37.—(1) Schedule 1, which makes amendments to the Solicitors (Scotland) Act 1980, shall have effect.

(2) Schedule 2, which applies enactments, with modifications and extensions shall have effect in relation to registered European lawyers.

SCHEDULES

Regulation 37(1)

SCHEDULE 1

AMENDMENTS TO THE SOLICITORS (SCOTLAND) ACT 1980

1.—(1) The Solicitors (Scotland) Act 1980 is amended as follows.

(2) After section 12, there shall be inserted—

Register of European lawyers

Keeping the register

12A.—(1) The Council shall establish and maintain the register referred to in regulation 15 of the European Communities (Lawyer's Practice) (Scotland) Regulations 2000, and shall keep the register at the office of their secretary.

(2) The register shall consist of the names in alphabetical order of all European lawyers entered on it in accordance with regulation 17 of those regulations.

(3) Any person may inspect the register during office hours without payment.

(4) Schedule 2 (powers of Council in relation to roll of solicitors) shall apply to the register as it does to the roll and in its application to the register the words "section 7(3)" in paragraph 4 shall be read as if the words "section 12A" were substituted therefor.

Information to be provided by registered European lawyers

12B.—(1) Any registered European lawyer-

(a) shall, on registration, inform the Council in writing of the address of his place of business, his home professional title, and the name and address of the competent authority with which he is registered in his home state; and

(b) shall thereafter inform the Council of any change to the information required under paragraph (a) above.

(2) The Council shall issue a registration to any registered European lawyer who applies for it.

Removal of name from register on request

12C. A registered European lawyer who wishes his name, or any annotation made against his name under section 25A(3), to be removed from the register may make an application to the Council in that behalf, and the Council shall, on the registered European lawyer satisfying the Council that he has made adequate arrangements with respect to the business he has then in hand, remove the name of that solicitor, or, as the case may be, the annotation against his name, from the register.

Restoration of name to register on request

12D.—(1) Subject to subsection (2), a registered European lawyer whose name has been removed from the register shall be entitled to have his name restored to the register only if, on an application in that behalf made by him to the Tribunaland after such enquiry as the Tribunal thinks proper, the Tribunal so orders.

(2) On an application to the Council by a registered European lawyer whose name, or any annotation against whose name, has been removed from the register under section 12C, the Council may, after such inquiry as they think proper, restore the name of the registered European lawyer or, as the case may be, the annotation, to the register.

(3) Rules made by the Tribunal under section 52 may—

(a) regulate the making, hearing and determining of applications under subsection (1);

(b) provide for payment by the applicant to the council of such fee in respect of restoration to the register as the rules may specify.

(3) After section 24 there shall be inserted—

Registration certificates for registered European Lawyers

Applications for registration certificates

24A.—(1) Subject to sections 24B to 24G below, the Council may make rules with respect to—

(a) applications for;

(b) the issue of;

(c) the keeping of a register for and the issue of,

registration certificates for registered European lawyers as it would make rules under section 13 with respect to practising certificates for enrolled solicitors.

(2) Any person may inspect the register referred to in subsection (1)(c) during office hours without payment.

(3) The making of a false statement by a registered European lawyer in an application for a registration certificate may be treated as professional misconduct by him for the purposes of Part IV, unless he proves the statement was made without intention to deceive.

Issue of registration certificates

24B.—(1) The Council shall issue to a registered European lawyer on application being made by him, a registration certificate in accordance with rules made by them under section 24A.

(2) The Council shall not issue a registration certificate to a registered European lawyer while his registration is suspended or withdrawn.

Discretion of Council in special cases

24C.—(1) In any case where this section has effect, the applicant shall, unless the Council otherwise order, give to the Council, not less than 6 weeks before he applies for a renewal of a registration certificate, notice of his intention to do so; and the Council may in their discretion—

(a) grant or refuse the application; or

(b) decide to issue a registration certificate to the applicant subject to such conditions as the Council may think fit.

(2) Subject to subsections (3) and (4) below, this section shall have effect in any case where a registered European lawyer applies for a renewal of a registration certificate—

(a) not having held a registration certificate in force within the period of 12 months following the date of his registration; or

(b) when a period of 12 months or more has elapsed since he held a registration certificate in force; or

(c) without having paid in full any fine imposed on him under Part IV; or

(d) without having paid in full any expenses for which he has been found liable under section 38 or Part IV; or

(e) when, having been suspended from practice, the period of suspension has expired; or

(f) when, having had his registration withdrawn, he has been registered again; or

(g) after his estate has been sequestrated or he has granted a trust deed for behoof of creditors, whether he has obtained his discharge or not; or

(h) when, after a complaint has been made—

(i) relating to his conduct of the business of a client his attention has been drawn by the Council to the matter, and he has not replied or has not furnished a reply which would enable the Council to dispose of the matter; or

(ii) of delay in disposal of the business of a client he has not completed that business within such period as the Council may fix as being a reasonable period within which to do so,

and in either case has been notified in writing by the Council accordingly; or

(i) while any thing required to be done by him by a direction of the Council under section 42A or of the Tribunal under section 53A (including any such direction as confirmed or varied on appeal) remains undone.

(3) Where a registration certificate free of conditions is issued by the Council under subsection (1) to a registered European lawyer to whom that subsection has effect by reason of any such circumstances as are mentioned in paragraphs (a), (b), (e), (f) or (g) of subsection (2), this section shall not thereafter have effect in relation to that registered European lawyer by reason of those circumstances.

(4) Where the Council decide to issue a registration certificate subject to conditions, they may, if they think fit, postpone the issue of the registration certificate pending the hearing and determination of an appealunder section 24D.

Appeals from decisions of Council

24D.—(1) Where—

(a) an application for a registration certificate is duly made to the Council otherwise than in a case where section 24C has effect and the Council refuse or neglect to issue a registration certificate, the applicant;

(b) the Council refuse to recognise a body corporate as being suitable in terms of section 34(1A) (b), the body corporate,

may apply to the court, who may make such order in the matter as it thinks fit.

(2) Where the Council in exercise of the power conferred on them by section 24C, refuse to issue a registration certificate, or issue a registration certificate subject to conditions, the applicant may appeal to the court against that decision within 14 days of being notified of it.

(3) On an appeal to the court under subsection (2) the court may-

(a) affirm the decision of the Council; or

(b) direct the Council to issue a registration certificate to the applicant subject to such conditions if any as the court thinks fit; or

(c) make such order as it thinks fit.

Date and expiry of registration certificate

24E.—(1) Every registration certificate issued in November of any year shall bear the date of 1st November in that year, and every other registration certificate shall bear the date on which it was issued.

(2) Every registration certificate shall have effect from the date it bears under subsection (1).

(3) Subject to subsection (4), every registration certificate shall expire on 31st October next after it is issued.

(4) On the name of a registered European lawyer being withdrawn from the register or on a registered European lawyer being suspended from practice as a registered European lawyer, any registration certificate for the time being in force of that registered European lawyer shall cease to have effect, but in the case of suspension, if he ceases to be so suspended during the period for which the registration would otherwise have continued in force, the registration certificate shall thereupon again have effect.

Suspension of registration certificate

24F.—(1) If—

(a) in pursuance of the Mental Health (Scotland) Act 1984 a registered European lawyer is, by reason of mental disorder, admitted to a hospital and becomes liable to be detained there or becomes subject to guardianship;

(b) a curator bonis is appointed on the estate of a registered European lawyer;

(c) the estate of a registered European lawyer is sequestrated;

(d) a registered European lawyer grants a trust deed for behoof of creditors;

(e) a judicial factor is appointed on the estate of a registered European lawyer;

any registration certificate for the time being in force of that registered European lawyer shall cease to have effect, and he shall be suspended from practice as a registered European lawyer.

(2) On the occurrence of any of the circumstances mentioned in subsection (1), the registered European lawyer in question shall intimate those circumstances to the Council in writing immediately.

(3) On the occurrence of the circumstances mentioned in paragraph (d) or (e) of subsection (1) the trustee or as the case may be the judicial factor shall intimate his appointment to the Council in writing immediately.

Further provisions relating to suspension of registration certificate

24G.—(1) The provisions of this section shall have effect in relation to a registration certificate which has ceased to have effect by virtue of section 24F during the period when that registration certificate would, but for that section, have continued in force.

(2) A registration certificate which has ceased to have effect by virtue of paragraph (c) or (d) of section 24F(1) shall again have effect on the registered European lawyer being granted his discharge.

(3) A registration certificate which has ceased to have effect by virtue of paragraph (e) of section 24F(1) shall again have effect on the judicial factor being granted his discharge.

(4) Where a registered European lawyer is suspended from practice as a registered European lawyer by virtue of paragraph (a) or (b) of section 24F(1), the period of suspension shall, for the purposes of section 24C(2)(e), expire on the registered European lawyer ceasing to be liable to be detained or subject to guardianship or, as the case may be, on the curator bonis being discharged.

(5) Where a registered European lawyer is suspended from practice as a registered European lawyer by virtue of paragraph (c), (d) or (e) of section 24F(1), he may at any time apply to the Council to terminate the suspension.

(6) On an application under subsection (5), the Council may either-

(a) grant the application with or without conditions; or

(b) refuse the application.

(7) If on an application by a registered European lawyer under subsection (5) the Council refuse the application or grant it subject to conditions, the registered European lawyer may appeal against the decision to the court, who may-

(a) affirm the decision; or

(b) vary any conditions imposed by the Council; or

(c) terminate the suspension either with or without conditions.

(4) After section 23 there shall be inserted—

Professional misconduct for registered European lawyer to practise without a registration certificate

23A. Failure on the part of a registered European lawyer in practice to have in force a current registration certificate may be treated as professional misconduct for the purposes of Part IV.".

(5) At the beginning of section 25A, there shall be inserted the words "Subject to regulations 6 and 11 of the European Communities (Lawyer's Practice) (Scotland) Regulations 2000 and".

(6) In section 26—

(a) in subsection (2), after the word "solicitor", in each place where it occurs, there shall be inserted the words "or registered European lawyer pursuing professional activities within the meaning of the European Communities (Lawyer's Practice) (Scotland) Regulations 2000";

(b) at the end of subsection (3) there shall be inserted the words "or a registered European lawyer pursuing professional activities within the meaning of the European Communities (Lawyer's Practice) (Scotland) Regulations 2000".

(7) In section 28, after the word "solicitor" where it first occurs, there shall be inserted—

" ; or

(c) has had his registration as a registered European lawyer withdrawn; or

(d) has been suspended from practice as a registered European lawyer,".

(8) In section 31(1)—

(a) the word "unqualified", in each place where it occurs, is repealed.

(b) after the word "who" there shall be inserted the words ", not having the relevant qualification,".

(c) after paragraph (a) there shall be inserted—

"(aa) pretends to be a registered European lawyer; or"; and

(d) in paragraph (b), after the word "public", there shall be inserted "or registered European lawyer, as the case may be,".

(9) In section 32(1), after the word "section", there shall be inserted the words "and regulations 6, 11, 12 and 13 of the European Communities (Lawyer's Practice) (Scotland) Regulations 2000".

(10) At the beginning of section 33 there shall be inserted the words "Subject to the provisions of regulations 12 and 13 of the European Communities (Lawyer's Practice) (Scotland) Regulations 2000,".

(11) In section 43-

(a) in subsection (2) after the word "solicitor" in each place where it occurs there shall be inserted the words "or registered European lawyer".

(b) in subsection (3)—

(i) after sub-paragraph (cc), the word "or" is repealed;

(ii) at the end of paragraph (d) there shall be inserted—

" ; or

(e) in respect of any default of a registered European lawyer, or any of his employees or partners, where such act or default takes place outside Scotland, unless the Council is satisfied that the act or default is closely connected with the registered European lawyer's practice in Scotland.".

(12) In section 65—

(a) in subsection (1), after the definition of "property" there is inserted—

" "registered European lawyer" means a person registered with the Society in accordance with regulation 17 of the European Communities (Lawyer's Practice) (Scotland) Regulations 2000;";

(b) at the end of subsection (2)(a) there shall be added the words "and registered European lawyers"; and

(c) in subsection (2)(e), after the word "solicitor's" there shall be inserted the words "or registered European lawyer's".

(13) After paragraph 1 of Part 1 of Schedule 3 there shall be inserted—

Contributions by registered European lawyers

1A.—(1) Subject to the provisions of this paragraph, paragraph (1) above shall apply to registered European lawyers as it applies to solicitors and references to a practising certificate shall include references to a registered European lawyer's registration certificate.

(2) Where a registered European lawyer can prove that-

(a) he is covered by a guarantee provided in accordance with the professional rules of his home State; and

(b) the guarantee is equivalent in terms of the conditions and the extent of its cover to the Guarantee Fund,

then to the extent that there is such equivalence that lawyer shall be exempt from the requirements of paragraph (1).

(3) Where the equivalence under sub paragraph (2) is only partial, the Society may specify the guarantee obligations a registered European lawyer is required to meet to comply with paragraph (1).

(4) Subparagraphs (2), (6) and (8) of paragraph (1) shall not apply.

(5) For the purposes of this paragraph the words "home State" have the same meaning as provided for in regulation 2 of the European Communities (Lawyer's Practice) (Scotland) Regulations 2000.

Regulation 37(2)

SCHEDULE 2

Application, Extension and Modification of Enactments to Registered European Lawyers

Part I

Solicitors (Scotland) Act 1980

1.—(1) The provisions of the Solicitors (Scotland) Act 1980 shall have effect in relation to registered European lawyers as modified or extended by the provisions mentioned in these subparagraphs.

(2) Subsections (1) and (3) of section 2 shall apply to registered European lawyers as they apply to solicitors and any reference to a solicitor's practising certificate shall include reference to a registered European lawyer's registration certificate.

(3) The power to make regulations under section 5 shall also be exercisable in relation to registered European lawyers.

(4) The power to make rules under the following provisions:-

(a) section 34 (rules as to professional practice, conduct and discipline);
(b) section 35 (accounts rules);
(c) section 36 (interest on client's money);
(d) section 37 (accountant's certificates);
(e) section 44 (professional indemnity);
(f) section 52(2) (procedure on complaints to Tribunal);
(g) paragraph 4(1) and (4) of Part I of Schedule 3;

shall also be exercisable in relation to registered European lawyers and a reference in any of these provisions to a solicitor shall include a reference to a registered European lawyer and any references to a solicitor's practising certificate shall include references to a registered European lawyer's registration certificate.

(5) Any of the powers referred to in subparagraph (4) may be exercised so as to make different provision with respect to different categories of registered European lawyers and in different circumstances.

(6) Sections 20, 21, 30, 33A, 38 to 42, 42B, 42C, 51, 52(1), 53A to 54, 56, 56A, 60A to 64, Schedule 1 and paragraph 5 of Part II of Schedule 3 shall apply to registered European lawyers as they apply to solicitors and any references to a solicitor's practising certificate shall include references to a registered European lawyer's registration certificate.

(7) Sections 42A, 45, 46, 47 and 55 shall apply to registered European lawyers as they apply to solicitors and references in those sections to—

(a) the roll shall for this purpose include references to the register of European lawyers; and
(b) being struck off the roll shall for this purpose include references to being removed from the register of European lawyers.

(8) Section 43 shall apply to registered European lawyers as it applies to solicitors and references to a practising certificate shall include references to a registered European lawyer's registration certificate and references to the roll shall include references to the register of European lawyers and references to being struck off the roll shall include being removed from that register.

(9) Sections 53 and 55 and Schedule 4 shall apply to registered European lawyers as they apply to solicitors and any references in those sections and that Schedule to—

(a) solicitors shall include registered European lawyers;
(b) a solicitor's practising certificate shall include reference to a registered European lawyer's registration certificate;
(c) the roll shall include the register of European lawyers;
(d) enrolment shall include registration on the register of European lawyers; and
(e) being struck off the roll shall include being removed from that register.

PART II

OTHER ENACTMENTS AND PROVISIONS

1. In the Rehabilitation of Offenders Act 1974 (Exceptions Order) 1975 the reference to "solicitor" and "advocate" in Part 1 of Schedule 1 to the Order shall include reference to a registered European lawyer.

2. In the Estate Agents Act 1979[11] the reference to a practising solicitor in section 1(2)(a) (which exempts solicitors from that Act) shall include a reference to a registered European lawyer, and the partner of a registered European lawyer providing professional services in accordance with rules made under section 34 of the Solicitors (Scotland) Act 1980.

[1]3. For the purposes of Part 20 of the Financial Services and Markets Act 2000 (provision of financial services by members of the professions), a registered European lawyer and any partner shall be treated as—

(a) a member of the profession in relation to which the Law Society of Scotland is established; and
(b) as subject to the rules of the Law Society of Scotland.

4. For the purposes of section 391 of the Insolvency Act 1986 (recognised professional bodies for insolvency practitioners) registered European lawyers and their partners shall be deemed to be—

(a) part of the solicitors' profession; and
(b) subject to the Law Society of Scotland's rules on the practice of their profession.

5. [*Repealed by the Financial Services and Markets Act 2000 (Consequential Amendments and Repeals) Order (SI 2001/3649) Pt 7(II), art.263(3) (effective December 1, 2001).*]

6.—(1) The Law Reform (Miscellaneous Provisions) (Scotland) Act 1990 shall be modified as follows.

(2) In section 33(5) in the definition of "practitioner" the references to "an advocate" and "a solicitor" shall be interpreted as including references to a registered European lawyer;

(3) In section 34(9) the references to "advocates" and "solicitors" shall be interpreted as including references to a registered European lawyer.

NOTE

[1] As substituted by the Financial Services and Markets Act 2000 (Consequential Amendments and Repeals) Order (SI 2001/3649) Pt 7(II), art.263(2) (effective December 1, 2001).

The European Communities (Lawyer's Practice) (Scotland) Amendment Regulations 2004

(SSI 2004/302)

[September 16, 2004]

The Scottish Ministers, in exercise of the powers conferred by section 2(2) of the European Communities Act 1972 and of all other powers enabling them in that behalf, hereby make the following Regulations:

Citation, commencement and interpretation

1.—(1) These Regulations may be cited as the European Communities (Lawyer's Practice) (Scotland) Amendment Regulations 2004 and shall come into force on 16th September 2004.

(2) In these Regulations, any reference to a regulation by number alone means the regulation so numbered in the European Communities (Lawyer's Practice) (Scotland) Regulations 2000.

Transitional provisions

2.—(1) In this regulation "relevant lawyer" means a European lawyer, as defined by the European Communities (Lawyer's Practice) (Scotland) Regulations 2000 as they are amended by these Regulations, who satisfies either or both of the conditions set out in paragraph (2) of this regulation.

(2) Those conditions are that—

(a) that person is a national of Switzerland, Iceland, Liechtenstein, Norway, the Czech Republic, Estonia, Cyprus, Latvia, Lithuania, Hungary, Malta, Poland, Slovenia or Slovakia; or
(b) that person is authorised in any of those States to pursue professional activities under any of the professional titles appearing in regulation 2(4) as it is amended by these Regulations, opposite the name of that State.

(3) Regulations 21 and 22 shall apply to a relevant lawyer only as from 16th March 2005.

(4) Regulation 1(2) to (5) shall apply to a relevant lawyer with the following modifications—

(a) for "22nd May 2000", where it occurs in paragraph (2), there shall be substituted "16th September 2004";
(b) for "21st November 2000", wherever it occurs, there shall be substituted "15th March 2005"; and
(c) for "22nd November 2000", wherever it occurs, there shall be substituted "16th March 2005".

Amendments to European Communities (Lawyer's Practice) (Scotland) Regulations 2000

3. In the table in regulation 2(4) (definition of European lawyer), after the entry relating to Sweden, there shall be inserted—

Switzerland	Avocat/Advokat/Rechtsanwalt/Anwalt/ Fürsprecher/Fürsprech/Avvocato
Iceland	Lögmaður
Liechtenstein	Rechtsanwalt
Norway	Advokat
Czech Republic	Advokát
Estonia	Vandeadvokaat
Cyprus	Δικηγόρος (Dikegoros)
Latvia	Zvērināts advokāts
Lithuania	Advokatas
Hungary	Ügyvéd
Malta	Avukat/Prokuratur legali
Poland	Adwokat/Radca prawny
Slovenia	Odvetnik/Odvetnica
Slovakia	Advokát/Komerčný právnik".

4. In regulation 12 (property transactions), for "or Sweden" there shall be substituted ", Sweden, Cyprus, the Czech Republic, Hungary, Iceland, Liechtenstein, Norway or Slovakia".

5. In regulation 13 (executries), for "or Sweden" there shall be substituted ", Sweden, Cyprus, Iceland, Liechtenstein, Norway or Slovakia".

The Solicitors (Scotland) Act 1980 (Foreign Lawyers and Multi-national Practices) Regulations 2004

(SSI 2004/383)

[October 1, 2004]

The Scottish Ministers, in exercise of the powers conferred by section 2(2) of the European Communities Act 1972 and all other powers enabling them in that behalf, hereby make the following Regulations:

Citation, commencement, extent and interpretation

1.—(1) These Regulations may be cited as the Solicitors (Scotland) Act 1980 (Foreign Lawyers and Multi national Practices) Regulations 2004 and shall come into force on 1st October 2004.

(2) These Regulations extend to Scotland and insofar as they extend beyond Scotland they do so only as a matter of Scots law.

(3) Expressions used in these Regulations have the same meanings as they have in the Solicitors (Scotland) Act 1980.

Amendment and modification of the 1980 Act

2. The Solicitors (Scotland) Act 1980 is amended and applied in accordance with these Regulations.

New section 23B

3. After section 23A insert—

" **23B.** Failure on the part of a registered foreign lawyer in practice to have in force a current registration certificate may be treated as professional misconduct for the purposes of Part IV.".

Amendment of section 26

4. In section 26 (offence for solicitors to act as agents for unqualified persons)—

(a) in subsection (2), after "solicitor" in both places where it appears, insert ", registered foreign lawyer";

(b) in subsection (3), after "incorporated practice" insert ", registered foreign lawyer, multi national practice".

Amendment of section 28

5. In section 28 (offence for solicitors who are disqualified to seek employment without informing employer)—

(a) after paragraph (d) insert—

"; or

(e) has had his registration as a registered foreign lawyer withdrawn; or

(f) has been suspended from practice as a registered foreign lawyer,";

(b) after "incorporated practice" insert "or multi-national practice".

Amendment of section 31

6. In section 31(1) (offence for unqualified persons to pretend to be solicitor or notary public)—

(a) after paragraph (aa) insert—

"(ab) pretends to be a registered foreign lawyer; or"; and

(b) in paragraph (b), for "or registered European lawyer" substitute ", registered European lawyer or registered foreign lawyer".

Amendment of section 32

7. After section 32(3) (offence for unqualified person to prepare certain documents) insert—

"(4) For the purposes of this section, "unqualified person" includes a registered foreign lawyer.".

New section 33B

8. After section 33A (privilege of incorporated practice from disclosure etc.) insert—

"**33B.**—(1) Any communication made to or by a registered foreign lawyer in the course of his actings as such for a client shall in any legal proceedings be privileged from disclosure in like manner as if the registered foreign lawyer had at all material times been a solicitor acting for a client.

(2) Any enactment or instrument making special provision in relation to a solicitor or other legal representative as to the disclosure of information, or as to the production, seizure or removal of documents, with respect to which a claim to professional privilege could be maintained, shall, with any necessary modifications, have effect in relation to a registered foreign lawyer as it has effect in relation to a solicitor.".

Amendment of section 34

9. After section 34(1A) (rules as to professional practice, conduct and discipline) insert—

"(1B) Rules made under this section may—

(a) prevent a solicitor from entering a multi-national practice without the approval of the Council; and

(b) make different provision for the regulation of solicitors and registered foreign lawyers in a multi-national practice in the following different cases—

(i) where the principal place of business of the practice is

outside Scotland and it has a place of business in Scotland;
(ii) where the principal place of business of the practice is in Scotland and it has a place of business outside Scotland;
(iii) where the principal place of business of the practice is in Scotland and it has no place of business outside Scotland.

(1C) For the purposes of subsection (1B)(b), the principal place of business of a multi-national practice shall be determined by the Council who shall take into account factors set out in rules which may be made under this section.".

Amendment of section 43

10. In section 43 (Guarantee Fund)—

(a) in subsection (2)(a), after "solicitor" in each place where it appears insert ", registered foreign lawyer"; and
(b) in subsection (3)—
  (i) at the end of paragraph (d) omit "or"; and
  (ii) after paragraph (e) insert—
  " ;
  (f) in respect of any act or default of a registered foreign lawyer, or any of his employees or partners, where such act or default takes place outside Scotland, unless the Council is satisfied that the act or default is closely connected with the registered foreign lawyer's practice, or any of his partners' practice, in Scotland; or
  (g) in respect of any act or default of any member, director, manager, secretary or other employee of an incorporated practice which is a multi-national practice, where such act or default takes place outside Scotland, unless the Council is satisfied that the act or default is closely connected with the incorporated practice's practice in Scotland.".

Amendment of section 60A

11. In section 60A (multi national practices)—

(a) in subsection (2), after paragraph (a) insert—
"(aa) the information which shall accompany such applications;";
(b) after subsection (4) insert—

"(4A) Any person may inspect the register of foreign lawyers during office hours without payment.

(4B) A registered foreign lawyer who wishes his name to be removed from the register of foreign lawyers may make an application to the Council in that behalf, and the Council shall, if the registered foreign lawyer satisfies the Council that he has made adequate arrangements with respect to the business that he has then in hand, remove the name of that foreign lawyer from the register of foreign lawyers.

(4C) On an application to the Council by a foreign lawyer whose name has been removed from the register of foreign lawyers under subsection (4B), the Council may, after such inquiry as they think proper, restore the name of the foreign lawyer to the register of foreign lawyers.

(4D) A foreign lawyer whose name has been removed (other than pursuant to an application made under subsection (4B)) from the register of foreign lawyers shall have his name restored to that register only if, on an application in that behalf made by him to the Tribunal and after such inquiry as the Tribunal thinks proper, the Tribunal so orders.

(4E) Rules made by the Tribunal under section 52 (procedure on complaints to the Tribunal) may—

(a) regulate the making, hearing and determining of applications under subsection (4D); and

(b) provide for payment by the applicant to the Council of such fee in respect of restoration to the register of foreign lawyers as the rules may specify.

(4F) Where, following an application under subsection (4), the Council decide not to enter the name of a foreign lawyer in the register of foreign lawyers the applicant may, within three months of the notification to him of the Council's decision (or later with the permission of the court), appeal to the court against the decision and, on such an appeal, the court may—

(a) order the Council to register the foreign lawyer;

(b) refuse the appeal; or

(c) remit the matter to the Council with such directions as it sees fit.

(4G) Sections 24A to 24G (registration certificates for registered European lawyers) shall apply to registered foreign lawyers as they apply to registered European lawyers and any reference in those sections (as so applied) to a registration certificate shall be construed as a reference to a registration certificate for a registered foreign lawyer."; and

(c) in subsection (5), omit paragraph (a).

Amendment of Schedule 3

12. After paragraph 1A of Schedule 3, insert—

"Contributions by registered foreign lawyers

1B.—(1) Subject to the provisions of this paragraph, paragraph 1 above shall apply to registered foreign lawyers as it applies to solicitors and in that paragraph as so applied references to a practising certificate shall be construed as references to a registered foreign lawyer's registration certificate.

(2) Where a registered foreign lawyer can prove that—

(a) he is covered by a guarantee provided in accordance with the rules of the legal profession of which he is a member; and

(b) the guarantee is equivalent in terms of the conditions and the extent of its cover to the Guarantee Fund,

then to the extent that there is such equivalence that lawyer shall be exempt from the requirements of paragraph 1.

(3) Where the equivalence referred to in sub paragraph (2) is only partial, the Society may specify the guarantee obligations a registered foreign lawyer is required to meet to comply with paragraph 1.

(4) The Council may, where it is satisfied that any acts or defaults on the part of a registered foreign lawyer would not result in a grant being made from the Guarantee Fund held under section 43, exempt that lawyer from the requirements of paragraph 1.

(5) Sub paragraphs (2), (6) and (8) of paragraph 1 shall not apply to registered foreign lawyers.".

Modification of provisions of the 1980 Act

13. Sections 30, 37, 38, 39, 39A, 40, 41, 42, 42A, 42B, 42C, 43, 45 (except subsection (4)), 47, 51 (except the references to a solicitor appointed under subsections (1) and (4)), 52(1), 53 (except subsections (2)(g), (6B) and (8)(b)), 53A, 53B, 53C, 54, 55 (except subsections (1)(ba) and (bb) and (3A)), 56, 56A, 61, 61A, 62A (except the references in that section to section 46), 63 and 64, paragraph 5 of Schedule 3 and Schedule 4 shall apply to registered foreign lawyers as they apply to solicitors and any reference in those sections as so applied—

(a) to a solicitor's practising certificate shall be construed as a reference to a registered foreign lawyer's registration certificate;

(b) to the roll shall be construed as a reference to the register of foreign lawyers;
(c) to enrolment shall be construed as a reference to registration on the register of foreign lawyers; and
(d) to being struck off the roll shall be construed as a reference to being removed from the register of foreign lawyers.

Rule-making powers

14.—(1) The power to make rules under—
(a) section 34 (rules as to professional practice, conduct and discipline);
(b) section 35 (accounts rules);
(c) section 36 (interest on client's money);
(d) section 37 (accountant's certificates);
(e) section 44 (professional indemnity);
(f) section 52(2) (procedure on complaints to the Tribunal) of; and
(g) paragraph 4(1) and (4) of Schedule 3 (Guarantee Fund—grants) to,
the 1980 Act shall also be exercisable in relation to registered foreign lawyers and a reference in any of those provisions—
(i) to a solicitor shall include a reference to a registered foreign lawyer; and
(ii) to a solicitor's practising certificate shall include a reference to a registered foreign lawyer's registration certificate.

(2) Any of the powers referred to in paragraph (1) may be exercised so as to make different provision with respect to—
(a) different categories of registered foreign lawyer;
(b) different categories of incorporated practice; and
(c) different circumstances.

Modification of the Rehabilitation of Offenders Act 1974 (Exceptions) Order 1975

15. In the Rehabilitation of Offenders Act 1974 (Exceptions) Order 1975 the reference to "solicitor" in Part 1 of Schedule 1 shall include a reference to a registered foreign lawyer.

Modification of the Law Reform (Miscellaneous Provisions) (Scotland) Act 1990

16. Sections 33(5) and 34(9) of the Law Reform (Miscellaneous Provisions) (Scotland) Act 1990 shall apply to registered foreign lawyers as they apply to solicitors.

Proceeds of Crime Act 2002 (Money Laundering: Exceptions to Overseas Conduct Defence) Order 2006

(SI 2006/1070)

[May 15, 2006]

The Secretary of State, in exercise of the powers conferred upon him by sections 327(2A)(b)(ii), 328(3)(b)(ii) and 329(2A)(b)(ii) of the Proceeds of Crime Act 2002, makes the following Order:

1. This Order may be cited as the Proceeds of Crime Act 2002 (Money Laundering: Exceptions to Overseas Conduct Defence) Order 2006 and shall come into force on 15th May 2006.

2.—(1) Relevant criminal conduct of a description falling within paragraph (2) is prescribed for the purposes of sections 327(2A)(b)(ii), 328(3)(b)(ii) and 329(2A)(b)(ii) of the Proceeds of Crime Act 2002 (exceptions to defence where overseas conduct is legal under local law).

(2) Such relevant criminal conduct is conduct which would constitute an offence punishable by imprisonment for a maximum term in excess of 12 months in any part of the United Kingdom if it occurred there other than—

(a) an offence under the Gaming Act 1968;

(b) an offence under the Lotteries and Amusements Act 1976, or

(c) an offence under section 23 or 25 of the Financial Services and Markets Act 2000

Practice Rules and Regulations

Admission as Solicitor (Scotland) Regulations 1991

Rules dated 20th November 1991, made by the Council of The Law Society of Scotland with the concurrence of the Lord President of the Court of Session under section 5 of the Solicitors (Scotland) Act 1980.

ARRANGEMENT OF REGULATIONS

PART I—INTRODUCTORY

Title and commencement

1. These Regulations may be cited as the Admission as Solicitor (Scotland) Regulations 1991 and shall come into operation on 1st January 1992.

Interpretation

2.—(1) In these Regulations, unless the context otherwise requires—

"the Act" means the Solicitors (Scotland) Act 1980 (as amended);

"Certificate of Fitness" means a certificate issued by the Council under the hand of the Secretary that the person to whom the certificate applies has fulfilled the applicable conditions and requirements prescribed in these Regulations and in any enactment for admission as a solicitor in Scotland;

"the Council" means the Council of the Society or, where the Council has delegated powers for the consideration of applications under the Regulations, a Committee of the Council or such other body or individual to whom such powers have been delegated;

"degree" means a degree, other than an honorary degree, granted by a University;

"Degree in Law" means the degree of Bachelor of Laws (LL.B.) granted by one of the Universities of Aberdeen, Dundee, Edinburgh, Glasgow and Strathclyde;

"Diploma" means a Diploma in Legal Practice granted by one of the Universities of Aberdeen, Dundee, Edinburgh, Glasgow and Strathclyde;

"employer" means an employing solicitor who is a party to a pre-Diploma, post-Diploma or non-Diploma training contract;

"employing solicitor" means a solicitor who holds a practising certificate issued under section 14 of the Act and who—

(i) is engaged as a principal in private practice in Scotland, or

(ii) is employed as a solicitor by a regional council, islands area council or district council in Scotland, or

(iii) is in such other employment as a solicitor in Scotland as the Council may approve,

and the expression "employing solicitor" shall include a firm or an incorporated practice of solicitors as defined in the Act;

"Entrance Certificate" means a certificate issued by the Council under the hand of the Secretary to the effect that the person to whom the certificate applies has fulfilled the applicable conditions and requirements prescribed in these Regulations and in any enactment for admission as a solicitor in Scotland to entitle him to enter into a post-Diploma or a non-Diploma training contract;

"Examiner" means an examiner appointed under regulation 18 of these Regulations;

"intrant" means a person seeking to become a solicitor in Scotland;

"non-Diploma training contract" has the meaning assigned by regulation 12 of these Regulations;

"post-Diploma training contract" means a contract under regulation 9 of these Regulations which is entered into between an employing solicitor and an intrant who holds an Entrance Certificate;

"pre-Diploma training contract" means a contract which is entered into between an employing solicitor and an intrant who is qualified under the provisions of regulation 6 of and the Schedule to these Regulations;

"Preliminary Entrance Certificate" means a certificate issued by the Council under the hand of the Secretary to the effect that the person to whom the certificate applies has fulfilled all the conditions and requirements prescribed in these Regulations and in any enactment for admission as a solicitor in Scotland to entitle him to enter into a pre-Diploma training contract;

"the 1986 Regulations" means the Admission as Solicitor (Scotland) Regulations 1986;

"the Secretary" means the Secretary of the Society and includes any person authorised by the Council to act on behalf of the Secretary for the purpose of these Regulations;

"the Society" means the Law Society of Scotland;

"the Society's examinations" means examinations set under regulation 20(1) of these Regulations;

"trainee" means an intrant who is a party to a pre-Diploma, post-Diploma or non-Diploma training contract;

"University" means—

(i) any University in Great Britain, or

(ii) the Council for National Academic Awards, or

(iii) any other University or Institute recognised by the Council for the purposes of these Regulations.

(2) The provisions of the Interpretation Act 1978 shall apply for the interpretation of these Regulations as they apply to the interpretation of an Act of Parliament.

Conditions precedent to admission

3. Subject to the provisions of section 6 of the Act and of these Regulations, every intrant shall, as a condition precedent to his admission as a solicitor, comply with these Regulations so far as applicable to him and the Council may require any intrant to satisfy it by such means as it considers necessary as to such compliance.

Application of these Regulations

4. These Regulations shall apply to all intrants other than

(*a*) intrants (hereinafter referred to as "1986 intrants") who have presented themselves for any of the Society's Examinations, obtained a Preliminary Entrance Certificate or obtained an Entrance Certificate under the 1986 Regulations and

(*b*) intrants eligible under the EC Qualified Lawyers Transfer (Scotland) Regulations 1990. Any 1986 intrants who wish to do so may, by notice in writing to the Council, elect to proceed to admission under these Regulations but such election, once made, shall be irrevocable.

Part II—Entrance Qualifications

(A) *Pre-Diploma training contracts*

Service under a pre-Diploma training contract

5.—(1) Any intrant who for the purpose of qualifying for an Entrance Certificate proposes to meet the requirements of regulation 7(2)(ii)(b) of these Regulations without obtaining a Degree in Law shall be required to enter into a pre-Diploma training contract with an employing solicitor.

(2) The period of training under a pre-Diploma training contract shall comprise three years of full-time training, provided always that any intrant may, with the written consent of the Council, undergo training on a part-time basis provided that the Council is satisfied that the total time spent working under such a training contract shall equate to three years of full-time training.

(3) Every pre-Diploma training contract shall be in or as nearly as may be in such form as the Council may from time to time prescribe and shall, subject to the provisions of regulation 17(1) of these Regulations, contain an obligation on the employing solicitor to provide training for the intrant in—

(a) conveyancing;

(b) litigation; and

(c) either

(i) trusts and executries, or

(ii) the legal work of a public authority.

(4) Subject to the consent of the employer, an intrant who is a party to a pre-Diploma training contract may be permitted to attend, during office hours, classes in law at a University or elsewhere.

Preliminary Entrance Certificate

6.—(1) An intrant may not enter into a pre-Diploma training contract unless he holds a Preliminary Entrance Certificate issued by the Council.

(2) An intrant shall be entitled to a Preliminary Entrance Certificate if he satisfies the Council that—

(a) he is a fit and proper person to be a solicitor; and

[1] (b) he is qualified under the provisions of the First Schedule to these Regulations or such other requirement as may be approved by the Council from time to time.

(3) The Council shall have power, in the case of an intrant who, being at least 23 years of age, satisfies the Council both that he is a fit and proper person to be a solicitor and, having regard to evidence of academic attainment and to any experience of legal work, as to his fitness to enter into a pre-Diploma training contract, to grant to such an intrant a Preliminary Entrance Certificate without requiring compliance with sub-paragraph (2)(b) of this regulation.

NOTE

[1] As amended by the Admission as a Solicitor (Scotland) (Amendment) Regulations 1996 (effective August 1, 1996).

(B) *Entrance Certificates*

Issue of Entrance Certificate

7.—(1) An intrant may not enter into either a post-Diploma or a non-Diploma training contract unless he holds an Entrance Certificate.

(2) An intrant shall be entitled to an Entrance Certificate if he satisfies the Council that—

(i) he is a fit and proper person to be a solicitor; and

(ii) either (a) he holds a Degree in Law or a certificate that he is entitled to graduate in such a Degree notwithstanding that he has not so graduated; or (b) he has served for a period of three years under a pre-Diploma training contract and has passed or obtained exemption from the Society's examinations; or (c) he is an intrant to whom the provisions of any of regulations 28, 30, 31 or 32 of these Regulations apply; and

(iii) unless exempt in terms of regulation 27 or Part V of these Regulations, he has obtained a Diploma.

Withdrawal of Entrance Certificate

8. An intrant's Entrance Certificate may be withdrawn by the Council in such exceptional circumstances as the Council may in its sole discretion determine and, in any event, an intrant's Entrance Certificate shall automatically lapse if a trainee does not enter into a training contract within two years of the date of said Entrance Certificate or such extended period as the Council may in its discretion determine.

(C) *Post-Diploma training contracts*

Service under a post-Diploma training contract

9.—(1) Subject to regulation 27 or Part V of these Regulations, it shall be a requirement for admission as a solicitor in Scotland that an intrant shall serve under a post-Diploma training contract entered into with an employing solicitor.

(2) The period of training under a post-Diploma training contract shall comprise two years of full-time training, provided always that any intrant may, with the written consent of the Council, undergo training on a part-time basis provided that the Council is satisfied that the total time spent working under such a training contract shall equate to two years of full-time training.

(3) Every post-Diploma training contract shall be in or as nearly as may be in such a form as the Council may from time to time prescribe.

Commencement of post-Diploma training contract

10. In the case of an intrant who is required to hold a Diploma, the commencement of his post-Diploma training contract shall be within a period of two years of the date of 1st January first occurring after the date when the intrant became eligible for the award of the Diploma provided that the Council may in its discretion extend such period but may, in granting such extension, impose such conditions as it thinks fit.

Service elsewhere in Scotland, UK and EC

11. Subject to the prior approval of the employer and the Council in each case, a trainee under a post-Diploma training contract may be permitted in order to extend the range of his training—

(a) to undertake legal work under appropriate supervision within Scotland on secondment to one or more solicitors, or

(b) to undertake legal work for a period or periods not exceeding in the aggregate six months in any other part of the United Kingdom or any country which is a member of the European Community, and such period or periods of legal work shall be reckoned as part of the trainee's period of service under his post-Diploma training contract.

(D) *Non-Diploma training contracts*

Service under a non-Diploma training contract

12.—(1) An intrant who is exempt from holding a Diploma under regulation 27 or Part V of these Regulations shall serve under a non-Diploma training contract entered into with an employing solicitor.

(2) The non-Diploma training contract shall be in similar terms to a post-Diploma training contract and shall be subject to the same conditions and requirements as are specified in these Regulations in relation to post-Diploma training contracts; provided that the minimum period of time which an intrant is required to serve under a non-Diploma training contract shall be the appropriate period specified in these Regulations or such other period as the Council may in its discretion determine.

(E) *General provisions affecting training contracts*

Provisions as to employing solicitors and intrants

13.—(1) An employing solicitor shall not, without consent in writing of the Council, employ any trainee, unless he is in practice as a solicitor in Scotland at the time and has been in continuous practice for a period of at least three years immediately prior to his employing the trainee or where the employing solicitor is a firm or incorporated practice, at least one of the partners or directors thereof, as the case may be, has been in such continuous practice.

[1] (2)(a) An employing solicitor who—

(i) is engaged in practice as a sole principal, or

(ii) is a firm or an incorporated practice with two or three partners or directors, shall not employ any trainee related to the employing solicitor or any of the partners, directors or members of the employing solicitor within any of the categories of relationship specified in the Second Schedule to these Regulations.

(b) An employing solicitor who is a firm or an incorporated practice with no less than four partners or directors shall not employ any trainee related to any of the partners, directors or members of the employing solicitor within any of the categories of relationship specified in the Third Schedule to these Regulations.

(c) A pre-Diploma or non-Diploma training contract entered into between an employing solicitor and a trainee in breach of paragraphs (a) or (b) of this Regulation shall be of no effect for the purposes of the compliance with these Regulations.

(d) Notwithstanding the provisions of Regulation 40, the Council shall have power, in what it deems to be exceptional circumstances and taking into account the merits of a particular case, to waive the provisions of paragraphs (a) and (b) of this Regulation, subject to the imposition of such conditions as it may reasonably require, and a decision to grant such a waiver shall be taken by a simple majority of the members voting thereon.

(3) If the Council after due inquiry decides that an employing solicitor would be unable to fulfil or is not fulfilling the proper obligations of an employer under a training contract either in relation to a particular application to employ a trainee or in relation to a particular contract or generally, it shall intimate its decision to the solicitor and the solicitor, notwithstanding that he satisfies the provisions of paragraph (1) of this regulation, shall not thereafter engage or retain the services of any trainee without the consent in writing of the Council.

(4) Any person aggrieved by a decision of the Council under paragraph (3) of this regulation may, within 21 days of the date of written intimation of the decision, appeal to the Court of Session.

(5) The total number of intrants employed at any time under pre-Diploma, post-Diploma and non-Diploma training contracts shall not, except with the consent of the Council, exceed:—

- (i) in the case of a solicitor practising on his own under his own name or as a sole solicitor under a firm name, one;
- (ii) in the case of a firm or an incorporated practice of solicitors, twice the number of partners in the firm, or twice the number of directors of the incorporated practice, as the case may be;
- (iii) in the case of a firm or an incorporated practice of solicitors having more than one office, within each such office, twice the number of solicitors having their principal place of business within that office;
- (iv) in the case of a solicitor employed by a regional council, islands area council or district council in Scotland, the number of solicitors employed by the said regional, islands area or district council in each case, or such larger number as the Council may in special circumstances allow; and
- (v) in the case of any other solicitor practising in Scotland, such number as the Council may in each case determine.

NOTE

[1] As amended by the Admission as a Solicitor (Scotland) (Amendment) Regulations 1996 (effective August 1, 1996).

Registration of training contracts

14.—(1) For the purposes of these Regulations, the Council shall establish and maintain a register of pre-Diploma training contracts, a register of post-Diploma training contracts and a register of non-Diploma training contracts.

(2) Every such contract shall be produced by the intrant to the Council for registration within three months from its commencement and thereafter shall be presented for registration in the Books of Council and Session by the Society at the expense of the intrant.

(3) When an intrant produces his contract to the Council, he shall pay such registration fee as the Council may from time to time prescribe.

(4) If an intrant's contract and the prescribed registration fee are not presented to the Council within three months from the date of the commencement of the contract, the period of service under the contract shall for the purposes of these Regulations be reckoned, if the Council so directs, as commencing only from the date of production of the contract to the Council or such earlier date as the Council may determine.

Service under training contracts

15. For the purposes of these Regulations and subject to regulations 5, 9 and 11 hereof,

(1) a trainee during the term of his training contract shall not during office hours engage in any other gainful employment or otherwise absent himself from his employer's business without the prior consent of his employer and of the Council;

(2) service by a trainee under any type of training contract shall be continuous, provided however that in exceptional circumstances, the Council may, in considering whether or not such service has been continuous and provided that the employer is prepared to certify the trainee's fitness to become a solicitor in due course or to continue as a solicitor as the case may be, disregard short periods of absence by the trainee from employment, not exceeding an aggregate of six months;

(3) if

(a) during the term of any training contract either the trainee or the employer has been continuously absent from the employer's place of business for an aggregate period of at least three months within any period of six months without reasonable cause, or

(b) the Council, after due and diligent enquiry and after affording the parties the opportunity to make representations, is of the reasonable opinion that the training contract ought to be terminated, assigned or extended,

it may by notice in writing to the parties terminate the training contract with effect from such date as may be specified in the notice or may require an assignation of the training contract or an extension to it as the case may be or may take such other action as it thinks fit.

Further training contracts or extension of training contracts

16.—(1) Where, before the expiration of the period of service under a pre-Diploma, post-Diploma or non-Diploma training contract, such contract is terminated for any reason, an intrant shall be entitled and may be required, subject to such conditions as the Council may impose, to enter into a further pre-Diploma, post-Diploma or non-Diploma training contract as the case may be with another employing solicitor.

(2) Where there is a dispute between the parties to a pre-Diploma, post-Diploma or non-Diploma training contract, the Council may require an assignation of the training contract or an extension to it as the case may be or may take such other action as it thinks fit.

Consent to transfer of training contracts

17.—(1) Subject to the provisions of regulation 5(3) of these Regulations, an employer under a pre-Diploma training contract shall, if requested by his trainee or if called upon to do so by the Council, assign such pre-Diploma training contract to another employing solicitor approved by the Council, to enable the trainee either to complete his training in the three prescribed areas of practice or to extend the range of his training generally, or for any other reason which the Council shall consider reasonable.

(2) A post-Diploma or non-Diploma training contract shall not be assigned by the employer without the consent in writing of the Council; and an employer shall be obliged to assign a post-Diploma or non-Diploma training contract if called upon to do so by the Council.

(3) Every such assignation shall, together with the relevant supporting documents, be produced to the Council within six weeks from the date of assignation for registration in the relevant Register of Training Contracts kept in accordance with the provisions of regulation 14 of these Regulations and, where the assignation has not been registered within said period, service prior to its registration shall be reckoned as part of the trainee's service under the training contract only to such extent as the Council may in its discretion determine.

(4) Any person seeking registration of an assignation of a training contract shall pay to the Council such fee as it may from time to time determine.

Part III—Qualifications and Examinations

Appointment of examiners

18.—(1) In order to test the suitability and qualifications of intrants, the Council shall from time to time nominate and appoint fit and proper persons to be Examiners and hold examinations in accordance with this part of these Regulations, which examinations shall be under the management and control of the Council.

(2) The Examiners shall comply with all directions that may be given by

the Council with respect to the number of papers to be set on any subject, the number of questions to be set and to be answered and the percentage mark to be attained to qualify for a pass and any other matters in connection with the examinations.

(3) The Examiners shall be appointed for such period of time and be paid such remuneration as the Council may from time to time determine.

Eligibility of intrants

19. An intrant shall not be entitled, except with the consent of the Council, to present himself for any of the Society's examinations unless he—

(i) holds a Preliminary Entrance Certificate and is serving under a pre-Diploma training contract or, that contract having terminated, has already presented himself for one or more of the Society's examinations; or

(ii) holds, or is entitled to graduate with, a Degree in Law which does not include passes in all the subjects prescribed by Regulation 20(1) of these Regulations.

Examinations

20.—(1) The Society's examinations shall consist of examinations in the laws of Scotland in accordance with the syllabus prescribed by the Council from time to time.

(2) An intrant shall not be permitted to sit any one examination on more than four occasions or later than four years from the date of the first of the Society's examinations for which he presented himself except with the consent of the Council following on a recommendation by the Society's Examiners, which consent may be given subject to such conditions as are deemed appropriate.

Award of distinction

21. A certificate of distinction in any subject may be awarded to an intrant at the discretion of the Examiners.

Conduct, dates and places of examinations

22.—(1) Diets for the Society's examinations shall be held in Edinburgh not less than twice each year and additional diets may be held as considered necessary by the Examiners.

(2) Intrants intending to present themselves as candidates at any of the Society's examinations shall give three weeks' notice in writing of their intention to the Secretary, provided that the Examiners may at their discretion allow an intrant who has not given such notice to present himself for any examination.

(3) Every candidate shall be examined in writing and may be required by the Examiners to present himself for oral examination.

(4) Every candidate shall be required to advise the Society of any permanent change of address.

Fees

23. A candidate shall tender with his application to sit any examination such fee as may be prescribed by the Council from time to time.

Part IV—Exemptions from Examinations and Diploma

Faculty of Advocates' examinees

24. The Council may exempt from any of the Society's examinations an intrant who has obtained a pass in the corresponding examination in the examinations for admission to the Faculty of Advocates.

Equivalent passes

25. Where an intrant seeks exemption from any of the Society's examinations, the Examiner in the appropriate subject shall be consulted and, provided such Examiner is satisfied that the intrant has passed an equivalent examination in the laws of Scotland to a standard approved by the Council, then the Council may grant such exemption.

Further exemptions for intrants from elsewhere in UK

26. Where the terms of regulation 29 or 30 of these Regulations do not apply, the Council may, on application by an intrant who has passed the examinations required for admission as a solicitor or barrister in England and Wales or Northern Ireland, in any such case within a reasonable time prior to such application, determine which of the Society's examinations, if any, such intrant shall be required to pass for the purposes of regulation 7 of these Regulations, and grant consent in terms of regulation 19 hereof accordingly, subject always to such conditions as the Council may impose, including conditions as to the period of time during which the examinations must be passed.

Exemptions from Diploma

27. An intrant who seeks to obtain a Certificate of Fitness under these Regulations and who satisfies the Council that there are exceptional circumstances which justify his being exempted from obtaining a Diploma may be granted a Certificate of Fitness on such conditions, including the passing of examinations, as the Council may in its discretion prescribe; provided that an intrant who receives such exemption shall be required to serve for a period of not less than three years under a non-Diploma training contract with an employing solicitor, in terms similar to those of a post-Diploma training contract.

PART V—REQUIREMENTS FOR SPECIAL INTRANTS

Scottish advocates

28. Notwithstanding any other provisions herein contained and unless the Council otherwise determines, an intrant who is a member of the Faculty of Advocates shall be exempt from

(a) pre-Diploma training,
(b) the Society's examinations and
(c) the Diploma, but he shall be required to undergo six months of non-Diploma training prior to applying for admission in terms of regulation 33 of these Regulations.

English/Welsh and Northern Irish solicitors

29. Notwithstanding any other provisions herein contained and unless the Council otherwise determines, an intrant who has been admitted as a solicitor in England and Wales or Northern Ireland and who provides such evidence as the Council may require that he is a fit and proper person to be admitted as a solicitor in Scotland shall be exempt from (a) the Society's examinations, (b) the Diploma and (c) any period of training, but he shall be required to pass in such manner as the Council may require an intra-UK transfer test comprising examinations in conveyancing, trusts and succession, Scots criminal law, with civil and criminal evidence and procedure and (unless admitted as aforesaid prior to 1st January 1992) European Community law and institutions or such other examinations as may be prescribed by the Council from time to time prior to applying for admission in terms of regulation 33 of these Regulations.

English/Welsh and Northern Irish barristers

30. Notwithstanding any other provisions herein contained, an intrant who is a member of the Bar in England and Wales or Northern Ireland who (i) provides such evidence as the Council may require that he is a fit and proper person to be admitted as a solicitor in Scotland and (ii) can demonstrate that he has had five years of recent active practice since his call to the Bar shall be exempt from (a) pre-Diploma training, (b) the Society's examinations and (c) the Diploma, but he shall be required to pass in such manner as the Council may require an intra-UK transfer test comprising examinations in conveyancing, trusts and succession, Scots criminal law, with civil and criminal evidence and procedure and (unless called as aforesaid prior to 1st January 1992) European Community law and institutions and such other examinations and undergo a period of six months of non-Diploma training or such longer period as the Council may in its discretion determine prior to applying for admission in terms of regulation 33 of these Regulations.

Colonial solicitors

31. Notwithstanding any other provisions herein contained, an intrant to whom the Colonial Solicitors Act 1900 and any Order in Council made thereunder apply shall be required to pass the Society's examinations and undergo one year of non-Diploma training prior to applying for admission in terms of regulation 33 of these Regulations but such intrant shall be exempt from pre-Diploma training and the Diploma.

Other overseas lawyers

32. Notwithstanding any other provisions herein contained and unless the Council otherwise determines, a practising lawyer from outwith the United Kingdom to whom the Colonial Solicitors Act 1900 and the E.C. Qualified Lawyers Transfer (Scotland) Regulations 1990 do not apply shall require (i) to satisfy the Council that he is qualified to undertake within the jurisdiction in which he qualified or practises, professional work equivalent in its nature to that of a solicitor or advocate in Scotland, (ii) to provide such evidence as the Council may require that he is a fit and proper person to be admitted as a solicitor in Scotland and (iii) to pass the Society's examinations, gain the Diploma and complete one year of post-Diploma training prior to applying for admission in terms of regulation 33 of these Regulations but such intrant shall be exempt from pre-Diploma training.

Part VI—Procedure for Admission as Solicitor

Eligibility for Certificate of Fitness

33. Subject to the provisions of section 6 of the Act and of these Regulations, an intrant shall be entitled to apply for a Certificate of Fitness for the purposes of section 6 of the Act if—

(1) (a) he has passed or obtained exemption from any or all of the required examinations, or

(b) he has obtained or is entitled to obtain a Degree in Law which includes passes in subjects corresponding to all the subjects prescribed in the syllabus referred to in regulation 20(1) of these Regulations, unless otherwise exempt, or, where such Degree does not include passes in all such subjects, he obtains passes therein in the Society's examinations, or otherwise passes corresponding subjects at the standard required for a Degree in Law; and

(2) he holds a Diploma, unless he is exempted from doing so in terms of these Regulations; and

(3) (a) he has completed not less than one year of his two-year period of service under a post-Diploma training contract and has submitted to the Council

(i) a declaration in conformity with regulation 34(1)(a) of these Regulations and

(ii) an undertaking in such form as the Council may prescribe that he will complete the remaining period of service under such contract in fulfilment of his obligation under that contract, or

(b) he has completed the full period of service under a post-Diploma training contract and has submitted to the Council a declaration in conformity with regulation 35 of these Regulations, or

(c) he has completed the full period of service under a non-Diploma training contract as is prescribed for him by the Council and has submitted to the Council a declaration in conformity with regulation 35 of these Regulations, and

(d) in the event that any such declaration is dated more than 12 months prior to its submission to the Council or if, for any other reason the Council so requires, he has submitted to the Council such further evidence as it may require that he continues to be a fit and proper person to be admitted as a solicitor in Scotland; and

(4) being an intrant to whom regulation 29 of these Regulations applies, he has submitted to the Council such further evidence as it may require that he continues to be a fit and proper person to be admitted as a solicitor in Scotland.

Applicants admitted after one year of post-Diploma training—employer's declaration

34.—(1) In the case of an intrant to whom regulation 33(3)(a) of these Regulations applies, he shall (a) submit to the Council a declaration by his employer in such form as the Council may prescribe certifying that, during the first year of his post-Diploma training contract, he has fulfilled his obligations under such contract and is, in the opinion of his employer, a fit and proper person to be admitted as a solicitor in Scotland and (b) on completion of his full period of service under his post-Diploma training contract, submit to the Council a declaration by his employer in such form as the Council may prescribe certifying that in his opinion the intrant continues to be a fit and proper person to be a solicitor in Scotland, provided always that, in any case where the employer of an intrant has declined to provide any such declaration, the Council may, after due enquiry and where it appears reasonable to do so, waive the requirement for such declaration from the employer, subject to such conditions as it may in its discretion determine.

(2) In determining whether the intrant is a fit and proper person to be admitted as a solicitor, the employer shall have regard not only to the moral character of the intrant but also to his aptitude for and application to his duties and his conduct generally.

Applicants admitted after two years of post-Diploma training—employer's declaration

35.—(1) In the case of an intrant to whom regulation 33(3)(b) or (c) of these Regulations applies, the Council shall not grant a Certificate of Fitness to him unless he submits to the Council a declaration by his employer in such form as the Council may prescribe certifying that in his opinion the intrant has fulfilled his obligations under the training contract and is a fit and proper person to be admitted as a solicitor in Scotland, provided always that, in any case where the employer of an intrant has declined to provide any such declaration, the Council may, after due inquiry and where it appears reasonable to do so, waive the requirement for such declaration from the employer.

(2) In determining whether the intrant is a fit and proper person to be admitted as a solicitor, the employer shall have regard not only to the moral

character of the intrant but also to his aptitude for and application to his duties and his conduct generally.

Qualified Practising Certificates

36. Where an intrant is admitted as a solicitor by virtue of regulation 33(3)(a) of these Regulations or otherwise while still undergoing post-Diploma training and applies for a Practising Certificate, the Council may in its discretion issue such Certificate subject to such qualifications as it may see fit, provided that such qualifications shall apply only until the grant of an employer's declaration pursuant to regulation 34(1)(b) of these Regulations or until the requirement for such a declaration is waived by the Council in terms of regulation 34(1)(b) of these Regulations.

Applicants for admission after five years

37. Where an application for a Certificate of Fitness is made by an intrant under these Regulations more than five years after the date on which he became entitled to apply therefor, the Council may, after due enquiry and where it appears reasonable to do so, refuse the application or grant the application subject to such conditions as it may reasonably require.

Part VII—General

Revocations

38. The Admission as Solicitor (Scotland) Regulations 1976 are hereby revoked.

Breaches of the Regulations

39. Contravention of any of the foregoing Regulations may be treated as professional misconduct for the purposes of Part IV of the Act (Complaints and Disciplinary Proceedings).

General Council discretion

[1] **40.** Subject to Regulation 13(2)(d), the Council may, in what it deems to be exceptional circumstances and taking into account the merits of a particular case, vary, waive, modify or otherwise alter any provision of these Regulations, provided that a motion to do so is supported by two-thirds of the members voting thereon.

NOTE

[1] As amended by the Admission as a Solicitor (Scotland) (Amendment) Regulations 1996 (effective November 1, 1996).

FIRST SCHEDULE

An intrant will be deemed to be duly qualified for the purposes of regulation 6(2)(b) of these Regulations if he complies with any of paragraphs (a) to (f) below—

Scottish Certificate of Education

(a) (1) passes in at least five of the Approved Subjects in the Scottish Certificate of Education, as provided from time to time by the Universities Central Council on Admissions, at no more than two sittings, said passes to include:—

- (i) a pass at Higher grade in English at not less than "B",
- (ii) a pass at Higher grade in a subject chosen from one of the following groups—
  - (a) a group comprising mathematics or an approved science, or
  - (b) a group comprising an approved language other than English, and
- (iii) a pass at Higher, Ordinary or Standard grade in a subject chosen from the group not chosen under sub-paragraph (ii) above, provided that if at Ordinary or Standard grade, such pass is at not less than grade 3 and

(2) a total of such points as the Council may from time to time determine in respect of the subjects passed, calculated as follows:—

a pass at Higher grade at—

"A" being valued at three points,
"B" being valued at two points, and
"C" being valued at one point.
Provided that if he has insufficient points or subject passes, he may add to these equivalent passes and points under (b)(1) and (2) below.

General Certificate of Education

(b) (1) passes in at least five of the Approved Subjects in the General Certificate of Education, as provided from time to time by the Universities Central Council on Admissions, at no more than two sittings, said passes to include:—

(i) a pass at the Advanced level in English, at not less than "C" standard,
(ii) a pass at the Advanced level in a subject chosen from one of the following groups—
 (a) a group comprising mathematics or an approved science, or
 (b) a group comprising an approved language other than English, and
(iii) a pass at the Advanced or Ordinary level or GCSE in a subject chosen from the group not chosen under sub-paragraph (ii) above; and

(2) a total of such points as the Council may from time to time determine in respect of the subjects passed, calculated as follows:—
a pass at the Advanced level at—
"A" being valued at four points,
"B" being valued at three points,
"C" being valued at two points, and
"D" being valued at one point.
Provided that if he has insufficient points or subject passes, he may add to these equivalent passes and points under (a)(1) and (2) above.

HND in Legal Studies

(c) a Scottish Higher National Diploma in Legal Studies from any College of Further Education approved by the Council offering such Diploma and also a pass in English at Higher grade in the Scottish Certificate of Education at not less than "B" or its equivalent.

University Degree

(d) a degree of any University, other than an honorary degree or a Degree in Law, or is entitled to graduate in such a degree notwithstanding that he has not so graduated.

Chartered Accountant

(e) membership of the Institute of Chartered Accountants of Scotland or of the Institute of Chartered Accountants in England and Wales or of the Association of Certified and Corporate Accountants.

Commissioned Officer

(f) a commission as a commissioned officer in one of the British armed services, where his commission has been obtained following study at a Royal Naval, Army or Royal Air Force college.

[1] SECOND SCHEDULE

son/daughter	husband/wife
grandson/granddaughter	son-in-law/daughter-in-law
father/mother	father-in-law/mother-in-law
brother/sister	brother-in-law/sister-in-law
nephew/niece	stepson/stepdaughter
uncle/aunt	stepfather/stepmother
first cousins	stepbrother/stepsister

[1] THIRD SCHEDULE

son/daughter	husband/wife
grandson/granddaughter	stepson/stepdaughter
father/mother	stepfather/stepmother
brother/sister	stepbrother/stepsister

NOTE
[1] As inserted by the Admission as a Solicitor (Scotland) (Amendment) Regulations 1996 (effective August 1, 1996).

EC Qualified Lawyers Transfer (Scotland) Regulations 1994

EC Qualified Lawyers Transfer (Scotland) Regulations 1994 made by the Council of the Law Society of Scotland in June 1994 with the concurrence of the Lord President of the Court of Session under section 5 of the Solicitors (Scotland) Act 1980.

Title and commencement

1. These regulations may be cited as the EC Qualified Lawyers Transfer (Scotland) Regulations 1994 and shall come into operation on 1st July 1994.

Definitions and interpretation

2.—(1) In these Regulations, unless the context otherwise requires—

"the Act" means the Solicitors (Scotland) Act 1980;

"the Society" means The Law Society of Scotland;

"the Council" means the Council of the Society;

"the Directive" means the Directive of the Council of the European Communities for recognition of Higher Education Diplomas dated 21st December 1988 and numbered 89/48/EEC;

"applicant" means a person seeking admission as a solicitor in Scotland under these Regulations;

"the Test" means the qualified lawyers transfer test being the aptitude test defined in Article 1(*g*) of the Directive and being an assessment of competence in the subjects specified in these Regulations;

"the court" means the Court of Session.

(2) The provisions of the Interpretation Act 1978 shall apply to the interpretation of these Regulations as they apply to the interpretation of an Act of Parliament.

(3) The headings to these Regulations do not form part of these Regulations.

Scope of regulations

3. These Regulations shall apply to any lawyer making application for admission as a solicitor in Scotland pursuant to the Directive or legislation implementing the Directive in the United Kingdom.

Eligibility

4.—(1) An applicant shall submit his application in writing to the Society and shall—

(i) make payment of such fee for assessment of his application by the Society as the Council shall from time to time prescribe; and

(ii) provide such evidence as the Society may require that he

(*a*) is a person to whom the Directive and in consequence these Regulations may apply; and

(*b*) is a fit and proper person to be a solicitor.

(2) The Council shall within a period of four months after presentation by the applicant of all relevant documentation, issue a written statement giving its decision as to whether or not the applicant is eligible to seek admission as a solicitor in Scotland.

(3) Where it is established that an applicant is eligible to seek admission in terms of regulation 4(2), the Council shall specify those subjects (if any) in the Test which the applicant shall be required to pass and any other conditions which the applicant must satisfy, having regard to the nature and extent of the applicant's experience (if any) of legal practice in Scotland and any academic or other qualification in the law of Scotland.

The Test

5.—(1) An applicant who has established his eligibility conform to regulation 4 shall be required to pass the Test in such subjects as are specified in the written statement referred to in regulation 4(2).

(2) The Test shall be an assessment by written and oral examination of an applicant's competence in the following subjects—

(*a*) the Scottish law of Property including for this purpose the law of trusts and succession and family law;

(*b*) the Scottish Legal System including for this purpose the law of evidence and civil and criminal procedure;

(*c*) European Community Law and Institutions;

(*d*) Professional Conduct including for this purpose a knowledge of the Solicitors' (Scotland) Accounts Rules in force from time to time; and

(*e*) such other subjects as the Council may from time to time reasonably prescribe.

(3) The Council may delegate to appropriately qualified persons the examination of applicants taking the Test and the Test will be held at such times as the Council may determine.

(4) An applicant shall be required to give such notice of his intention to sit the Test and pay to the Society such fee for the Test as the Council shall from time to time prescribe.

(5) An applicant who has failed to pass the Test on four separate occasions shall not be again entitled to present himself for the Test.

(6) Unless the Council in exceptional circumstances otherwise determines, an applicant shall require to pass the Test at a single diet.

(7) The Council may at its sole discretion and subject to such reasonable conditions as it may impose, in what it deems to be appropriate circumstances, and taking into account the particular merits of an applicant, exempt him from all or any part of the Test or from the provisions of regulation 5(5).

Certificate of fitness

6. Where an applicant has

(*a*) passed or gained exemption from the Test or any part thereof; and

(*b*) complied with any conditions imposed upon him by the Council in terms of these Regulations; and

(*c*) satisfied the Council that he remains a fit and proper person to be a solicitor

he shall be entitled to obtain from the Council a certificate in terms of section 6(1)(*b*)(ii) of the Act and thereafter to call upon the Council to apply to the court on his behalf for admission as a solicitor in terms of section 6(3A) of the Act.

Application of these regulations

7. These Regulations shall have effect in relation to applications for admission as a solicitor in Scotland received by the Society from applicants on or after 1st January 1994.

Revocation of 1990 regulations

8. The EC Qualified Lawyers Transfer (Scotland) Regulations 1990 are hereby revoked.

Admission as Solicitor (Scotland) Regulations 2001

Rules dated 25th April 2001, made by the Council of The Law Society of Scotland with the concurrence of the Lord President of the Court of Session under section 5 of the Solicitors (Scotland) Act 1980.

ARRANGEMENT OF REGULATIONS

PART I

INTRODUCTORY

Title and commencement

1. These Regulations may be cited as the Admission as Solicitor (Scotland) Regulations 2001 and shall come into operation on 1st May 2001.

Interpretation

2.—(1) In these Regulations, unless the context otherwise requires:—

"Accreditation Procedure" means the procedure whereby the Council approves the courses offered by Universities in Scotland for the Degree of Bachelor of Laws and the courses offered by Universities, and other institutions, in Scotland for the Diploma;

"the Act" means the Solicitors (Scotland) Act 1980 (as amended);

"Certificate of Fitness" means a certificate issued by the Council under the hand of the Secretary that the person to whom the certificate applies has fulfilled the applicable conditions and requirements prescribed in these Regulations and in any enactment for admission as a solicitor in Scotland;

"the Council" means the Council of the Society or, where the Council has delegated powers for the consideration of applications under these Regulations, a Committee of the Council or such other body or individual to whom such powers have been delegated;

"degree" means a degree, other than an honorary degree, granted by a University;

"Degree in Law" means, until such date as the Accreditation Procedure first comes into effect, the degree of Bachelor of Laws (LL.B.) granted by one of the Universities of Aberdeen, Dundee, Edinburgh, Glasgow or Strathclyde and, after such date, the degree of Bachelor of Laws granted by any University in Scotland that is from time to time accredited by the Council in respect of the degree of Bachelor of Laws;

"Diploma" means, until such date as the Accreditation Procedure first comes into effect, the Diploma in Legal Practice granted by one of the Universities of Aberdeen, Dundee or Edinburgh or jointly by the Universities of Glasgow and Strathclyde and, after such date, the Diploma in Legal Practice granted by any University, or other institution, in Scotland that is from time to time accredited by the Council in respect of the Diploma in Legal Practice or granted jointly by any such University or other institution with any other such University or institution;

"the Directive" means Directive No. 98/5/EC of the European Parliament and Council and legislation and regulations (including regulations or rules of the Council) implementing that Directive in Scotland;

"employer" means a training solicitor who is a party to a training contract and references to "employ" and similar words include otherwise taking on a trainee under a training contract;

"Entrance Certificate" means a certificate issued by the Council under the hand of the Secretary to the effect that the person to whom the certificate applies has fulfilled the applicable conditions and requirements prescribed in these Regulations and in any enactment for admission as a solicitor in Scotland to entitle him to enter into a post-Diploma training contract or a non-Diploma training contract;

"Examiner" means an examiner appointed under regulation 19 of these Regulations;

"intrant" means a person seeking to become a solicitor in Scotland;

"non-Diploma training contract" means a training contract entered into between a training solicitor and an intrant who is exempt from holding a Diploma under these Regulations;

"post-Diploma training contract" means a training contract under regulation 7 of these Regulations which is entered into between a training solicitor and an intrant who holds an Entrance Certificate;

"practising certificate" has the meaning given by section 4 of the Act;

"pre-Diploma training contract" means a training contract which is entered into between a training solicitor and an intrant who is qualified under the provisions of regulation 11 of, and the Schedule to, these Regulations;

"Preliminary Entrance Certificate" means a certificate issued by the Council under the hand of the Secretary to the effect that the person to whom the certificate applies has fulfilled the applicable conditions and requirements prescribed in these Regulations and in any enactment for admission as a solicitor in Scotland to entitle him to enter into a pre-Diploma training contract;

"Professional Competence Course" means the professional competence course approved by the Council and offered by any University, or other institution, in Scotland that is from time to time approved by the Council in respect of that course or offered jointly by any such University or other institution with any other such University or institution;

"the 1986 Regulations" means the Admission as Solicitor (Scotland) Regulations 1986;

"the 1991 Regulations" means the Admission as Solicitor (Scotland) Regulations 1991;

"the 1994 Regulations" means the EC Qualified Lawyers Transfer (Scotland) Regulations 1994 and any other regulations from time to time applicable to an intrant making an application pursuant to the Directive referred to in regulation 3 of those regulations;

"the Secretary" means the Secretary of the Society and includes any person authorised by the Council to act on behalf of the Secretary for the purpose of these Regulations;

"the Society" means the Law Society of Scotland;

"the Society's examinations" means examinations set under regulation 21(1) of these Regulations;

"solicitor" means any person enrolled or deemed to have been enrolled as a solicitor in pursuance of the Act;

"Test of Professional Competence" means the test of professional competence set by, or on behalf of, the Society;

"trainee" means an intrant who is a party to a training contract;

"training contract" means a non-Diploma training contract, a post-Diploma training contract or a pre-Diploma training contract;

"training solicitor" means a solicitor who holds a practising certificate issued under section 14 of the Act and who:—

(a) is engaged as a principal in private practice; or
(b) is in employment as a solicitor,

and the expression "training solicitor" shall include a firm or an incorporated practice of solicitors as defined in the Act or a multi-national practice (as defined in the Act); and

"University" means:—

(a) any university in the United Kingdom; or
(b) the former Council for National Academic Awards; or
(c) any other University or institute recognised by the Council for the purposes of these Regulations.

(2) The provisions of the Interpretation Act 1978 shall apply for the interpretation of these Regulations as they apply to the interpretation of an Act of Parliament.

NOTE

[1] As amended by the Solicitors (Scotland) (Registered Foreign Lawyers) etc. Practice Rules 2005, Sch.5 (effective May 1, 2005).

Conditions precedent to admission

3. Subject to the provisions of section 6 of the Act and these Regulations, every intrant shall, as a condition precedent to his admission as a solicitor, comply with these Regulations so far as applicable to him and the Council may require any intrant to satisfy it by such means as it considers necessary as to such compliance.

Application of these Regulations

4.—(1) These Regulations shall apply to all intrants other than:—

(a) intrants (hereinafter referred to as "1986 intrants") who have presented themselves for any of the Society's examinations, obtained a Preliminary Entrance Certificate or obtained an Entrance Certificate under the 1986 Regulations;

(b) intrants (hereinafter referred to as "1991 intrants") who have presented themselves for any of the Society's examinations, obtained a Preliminary Entrance Certificate or obtained an Entrance Certificate under the 1991 Regulations;

(c) intrants eligible under the 1994 Regulations; and

(d) intrants eligible under the Directive.

(2) Any 1986 intrants or 1991 intrants who wish to do so may, by notice in writing to the Council, elect to proceed to admission under these Regulations but such election, once made, shall be irrevocable. In the absence of such an election, 1986 intrants shall proceed to admission under the 1986 Regulations and 1991 intrants shall proceed to admission under the 1991 Regulations.

(3) Notwithstanding regulation 4(1) of these Regulations, any person who is the subject of a decision by the Council made after the date these Regulations come into operation under the 1986 Regulations, the 1991 Regulations or the 1994 Regulations and who is aggrieved by that decision may, within 21 days of written intimation of the decision, appeal to the Court of Session.

Part II

Entrance Qualifications

(A) Entrance Certificate

Issue of Entrance Certificate

5.—(1) An intrant may not enter into either a post-Diploma training contract or a non-Diploma training contract unless he holds an Entrance Certificate.

(2) An intrant shall be entitled to an Entrance Certificate if he satisfies the Council that:—

(a) he is a fit and proper person to be a solicitor;

(b) (i) he holds a Degree in Law or a certificate that he is entitled to graduate in such a Degree notwithstanding that he has not so graduated; or (ii) he has served for a period of three years under a pre-Diploma training contract and has passed or obtained exemption from the Society's examinations; or (iii) he is an intrant to whom the provisions of any of regulations 29, 31, 32 or 33 of these Regulations apply; and

(c) unless exempt in terms of regulation 28(1) or Part V of these Regulations, he has obtained a Diploma.

Lapse of Entrance Certificate

6. An intrant's Entrance Certificate shall automatically lapse if he does not enter into either a post-Diploma training contract or a non-Diploma training contract within one year of the date of said Entrance Certificate or such extended period as may be permitted by the Council in any particular case.

(B) Post-Diploma training contract

Service under a post-Diploma training contract

7.—(1) Subject to regulation 28(1) and Part V of these Regulations, it shall be a requirement for admission as a solicitor in Scotland that an intrant shall serve under a post-Diploma training contract entered into with a training solicitor.

(2) The period of training under a post-Diploma training contract shall comprise two years of full-time training, provided always that any intrant may, with the written consent of the Council, undergo training on a part-time basis provided that the Council is satisfied that the total time spent working under such a post-Diploma training contract shall equate to two years of full-time training.

(3) Every post-Diploma training contract shall be in, or as nearly as may be in, such a form as the Council may from time to time prescribe.

Commencement of post-Diploma training contract

8.—(1) In the case of an intrant who is required to hold a Diploma, the commencement of his post-Diploma training contract shall be within a period of two years of the date of 1st January first occurring after the date when the intrant became entitled to the award of the Diploma provided that the Council may in its discretion extend such period but may, in granting such extension, impose such conditions as it thinks fit.

(2) In exercising its discretion under regulation 8(1) of these Regulations the Council shall have regard to the appropriateness of any work, paid or voluntary, and courses undertaken by the intrant since the intrant became entitled to the award of the Diploma and also the endeavours of the intrant to obtain a post-Diploma training contract.

Service elsewhere in Scotland and in other jurisdictions

9.—(1) Subject to the prior approval of the employer and the Council in each case, a trainee under a post-Diploma training contract may be permitted in order to extend the range of his training:—

(a) to undertake legal work under appropriate supervision within Scotland on secondment; and/or

(b) to undertake legal work under appropriate supervision for a period or periods not exceeding in the aggregate six months in any other part of the United Kingdom or any country which is a member of the European Union.

The period of any such secondment and such other period or periods of legal work shall be reckoned as part of the trainee's period of service under his post-Diploma training contract.

(2) A trainee may serve under a post-Diploma training contract at his employer's place of business outwith Scotland, but such a trainee shall not, without the prior approval of the Council, during the period of his post-Diploma training contract spend a period or periods exceeding in the aggregate six months at any such place of business outwith Scotland.

(C) Pre-Diploma training contract

Service under a pre-Diploma training contract

10.—(1) Any intrant who for the purpose of qualifying for an Entrance Certificate proposes to meet the requirements of regulation 5(2)(b)(ii) of these Regulations without obtaining a Degree in Law shall be required to enter into a pre-Diploma training contract with a training solicitor.

(2) The period of training under a pre-Diploma training contract shall comprise three years of full-time training, provided always that any intrant may, with the written consent of the Council, undergo training on a part-time basis provided that the Council is satisfied that the total time spent working under such a pre-Diploma training contract shall equate to three years of full-time training.

(3) Every pre-Diploma training contract shall be in, or as nearly as may be in, such form as the Council may from time to time prescribe and shall, subject to the provisions of regulation 17(1) of these Regulations, contain an obligation on the training solicitor to provide training for the intrant in:—

(a) conveyancing;

(b) litigation; and
(c) either
  (i) trusts and executries; or
  (ii) where the training solicitor is not engaged in private practice, the legal work of the training solicitor.

(4) Subject to the consent of the employer, an intrant who is a party to a pre-Diploma training contract may be permitted to attend, during office hours, classes in law at a University or other institution.

(D) Preliminary Entrance Certificate

Issue of Preliminary Entrance Certificate

11.—(1) An intrant may not enter into a pre-Diploma training contract unless he holds a Preliminary Entrance Certificate.

(2) An intrant shall be entitled to a Preliminary Entrance Certificate if he satisfies the Council that:—
(a) he is a fit and proper person to be a solicitor; and
(b) he is qualified under the provisions of the Schedule to these Regulations.

(3) The Council shall have power, in the case of an intrant who, being at least 21 years of age, satisfies the Council both that he is a fit and proper person to be a solicitor and, having regard to evidence of academic attainment and to any experience of legal work, as to his fitness to enter into a pre-Diploma training contract, to grant to such an intrant a Preliminary Entrance Certificate without requiring compliance with regulation (2)(b) of this regulation.

(4) In the event that any of the certificates referred to in paragraphs (a), (b) or (c) of the Schedule are no longer generally available, the Council may specify such alternative qualifications and/or levels of attainment for the purpose of those paragraphs as seem to it to be the nearest equivalent to those certificates and level of pass referred to in the Schedule.

(E) Non-Diploma training contract

Service under a non-Diploma training contract

12.—(1) Subject to regulation 30 of these Regulations, an intrant who is exempt from holding a Diploma under regulation 28(1) or Part V of these Regulations shall serve under a non-Diploma training contract entered into with a training solicitor.

(2) The non-Diploma training contract shall be in similar terms to a post-Diploma training contract and shall be subject to the same conditions and requirements as are specified in these Regulations in relation to post-Diploma training contracts; provided that the minimum period of time which an intrant is required to serve under a non-Diploma training contract shall be either three years or, where applicable, the appropriate period specified in regulations 29, 31 or 32 of these Regulations.

(F) General provisions affecting training contract

Provisions as to training solicitors and intrants

[1] **13.**—(1) A training solicitor shall not, without the consent in writing of the Council, employ any trainee, unless he is in practice as a solicitor at the time and has been in continuous practice for a period of at least three years immediately prior to his employing the trainee or, where the training solicitor is a firm or incorporated practice, at least one of the partners or directors (in the case of an incorporated practice which is a company) or members (in the case of an incorporated practice which is a limited liability partnership) thereof, as the case may be, has been in such continuous practice or, where the training solicitor is a multi-national practice, at least

one of the solicitors who is a member thereof has been in such continuous practice.

(2) The total number of intrants employed at any time under training contracts shall not, except with the consent of the Council, exceed:—

(a) in the case of a solicitor practising on his own under his own name or as a sole solicitor under a firm name, one;

(b) in the case of a firm or an incorporated practice of solicitors, twice the number of partners in the firm, or twice the number of directors (being individuals) of an incorporated practice which is a company, or twice the number of members (being individuals) of an incorporated practice which is a limited liability partnership, as the case may be;

[2] (ba) in the case of a multi-national practice, twice the number of solicitors who are members of the multi-national practice;

(c) in the case of a firm or an incorporated practice of solicitors having more than one office, within each such office, twice the number of solicitors having their principal place of business within that office but subject always, in respect of the firm or incorporated practice of solicitors as a whole, to the maximum specified by paragraph (b) above;

[2] (ca) in the case of a multi-national practice having more than one office, within each office, twice the number of solicitors having their principal place of business within that office, but subject always, in respect of the multi-national practice as a whole, to the maximum specified by paragraph (ba) above;

(d) in the case of a solicitor in employment, twice the number of solicitors employed by the solicitor's employer who are entitled, in terms of regulation 13(1) of these Regulations, to employ a trainee without the consent in writing of the Council but subject always, in respect of the solicitor's employer as a whole, (i) where the solicitor's employer falls within paragraph (a) or (b) above, to the maximum specified by, as the case may be, paragraph (a) or (b) above, and (ii) in any other case, to a maximum of twice the number of solicitors employed by the solicitor's employer who are so entitled;

(e) in the case of a solicitor in employment where the solicitor's employer has more than one office, within each such office, twice the number of solicitors having their principal place of business in that office but subject always, in respect of the solicitor's employer as a whole, to the maxima specified by paragraph (d) above; and

(f) in the case of any other solicitor, such number as the Council may in each case determine.

NOTES

[1] As amended by the Solicitors (Scotland) (Registered Foreign Lawyers) etc. Practice Rules 2005, Sch.5 (effective May 1, 2005).

[2] Inserted by the Solicitors (Scotland) (Registered Foreign Lawyers) etc. Practice Rules 2005, Sch.5 (effective May 1, 2005).

Registration of training contracts

14.—(1) For the purposes of these Regulations, the Council shall establish and maintain a register of pre-Diploma training contracts, a register of post-Diploma training contracts and a register of non-Diploma training contracts.

(2) Every training contract shall be produced by the intrant to the Council for registration within three months from its commencement and thereafter shall be presented for registration in the Books of Council and Session by the Society at the expense of the intrant.

(3) When an intrant produces his training contract to the Council, he shall pay such registration fee as the Council may from time to time prescribe.

(4) If an intrant's training contract and the prescribed registration fee are not presented to the Council within three months from the date of the commencement of the training contract, the period of service under the training contract shall for the purposes of these Regulations be reckoned, if the Council so directs, as commencing only from the date of presentation of the training contract to the Council or such earlier date as the Council may determine.

(5) Every assignation of a training contract shall, together with the relevant supporting documents, be produced by the trainee to the Council within six weeks from the date of assignation for registration in the relevant register of training contracts and, where the assignation has not been registered within said period, service after the assignation, but prior to its registration, shall be reckoned as part of the trainee's service under the training contract only to such extent as the Council may determine.

(6) Any person seeking registration of an assignation of a training contract shall pay to the Council such fee as it may from time to time determine.

Service under training contracts

15.—(1) The employer and the trainee shall each comply with their respective obligations under any training contract.

(2) For the purposes of these Regulations and subject to regulations 7, 9, 10 and 12 of these Regulations:—

- (a) a trainee during the term of his training contract shall not during office hours engage in any other gainful employment or otherwise absent himself from his employer's business without the prior consent of his employer and of the Council;
- (b) service by a trainee under a training contract shall be continuous, provided however that in exceptional circumstances, the Council may, in considering whether or not such service has been continuous and provided that the employer is prepared to certify the trainee's fitness to become a solicitor in due course or to continue as a solicitor, as the case may be, disregard short periods of absence by the trainee from employment, not exceeding an aggregate of six months; and
- (c) service by a trainee under a training contract shall be in Scotland.

Intervention in training contracts

16.—(1) The Council may make enquiries concerning any aspect of a training contract and the conduct of the parties to that contract and the Council shall be entitled to require the evidence of the employer, the trainee, any solicitor and any intrant and to call for and recover such evidence and documents from any such person as the Council thinks proper.

(2) If the Council, after enquiry and after affording the parties to the training contract the opportunity to make representations, is of the opinion that a party to a training contract is not, as a result of the acts or omissions of the other party to the training contract, receiving the benefits it should receive from that training contract, the Council may require that other party to take such steps as the Council may request to ensure that those benefits are so received.

(3) Without prejudice to the generality of regulation 16(2) of these Regulations, if:—

- (a) during the term of any training contract either the trainee or the employer has been continuously absent from the employer's place of business for an aggregate period of at least three months within any period of six months without reasonable cause; or
- (b) the Council, after enquiry and after affording the parties to the training contract the opportunity to make representations, is of the opinion that a training contract ought to be terminated, assigned or extended; or

(c) there is a dispute between the parties to a training contract

the Council may be notice in writing to the parties to the training contract require the termination of the training contract with effect from such date as may be specified in the notice or may require an assignation of the training contract or an extension to it, as the case may be, or may take such other action as it thinks fit. Where the Council has by notice required the termination of a training contract any service by the trainee under that training contract after the date specified in the notice shall not be reckoned as part of his period of service for the purpose of regulation 34 of these Regulations.

(4) Where, before the expiration of the period of service under a training contract, such training contract is terminated for any reason, an intrant shall be entitled and may be required, subject to such conditions as the Council may impose, to enter into a further training contract with another training solicitor.

(5) An employer shall be obliged to assign a post-Diploma training contract or non-Diploma training contract if called upon to do so by the Council.

(6) An intrant's Entrance Certificate may be withdrawn by the Council in such exceptional circumstances as the Council may in its sole discretion determine.

(7) If the Council after enquiry decides that a training solicitor would be unable to fulfil or is not fulfilling the proper obligations of an employer under a training contract either in relation to a particular application to employ a trainee or in relation to a particular training contract or generally, it shall intimate its decision to the solicitor and the solicitor, notwithstanding that he satisfies the provisions of regulation 13(1) of these Regulations, shall not thereafter engage or retain the services of any trainee without the consent in writing of the Council.

Consent to transfer of training contract

17.—(1) An employer under a pre-Diploma training contract shall, if requested by his trainee or if called upon to do so by the Council, assign such pre-Diploma training contract to another training solicitor, approved by the Council, to enable the trainee either to complete his training in the three areas of practice described in (a), (b) and (c)(i) of regulation 10(3) of these Regulations or to extend the range of his training generally, or for any other reason which the Council shall consider reasonable.

(2) A training contract shall not be assigned by the employer without the consent in writing of the Council.

(G) Professional Competence Course and Test of Professional Competence

Requirement

18. For an intrant to whom these Regulations apply it shall, subject to regulation 28(2) and (3) and Part V of these Regulations, be a requirement for admission as a solicitor in Scotland that he shall have:—

(a) completed the Professional Competence Course or given the undertaking referred to in regulation 38(2)(b) of these Regulations; and

(b) passed the Test of Professional Competence or given the undertaking referred to in regulation 38(2)(b) of these Regulations.

Part III

Qualifications and Examinations

Appointment of Examiners

19.—(1) In order to test the suitability and qualifications of intrants, the Council shall from time to time nominate and appoint fit and proper persons to be Examiners and hold examinations in accordance with this part of these Regulations, which examinations shall be under the management and control of the Council.

(2) The Examiners shall comply with all directions that may be given by the Council with respect to the number of papers to be set on any subject, the number of questions to be set and to be answered and the percentage mark to be attained to qualify for a pass and any other matters in connection with the examinations.

(3) The Examiners shall be appointed for such period of time and be paid such remuneration as the Council may from time to time determine.

Eligibility of intrants

20. An intrant shall not be entitled to present himself for any of the Society's examinations unless he:—

(a) holds a Preliminary Entrance Certificate and is serving under a pre-Diploma training contract or, that contract having terminated, had, prior to such termination, already presented himself for one or more of the Society's examinations; or

(b) holds, or is entitled to graduate with, a Degree in Law which does not include passes in all the subjects in the syllabus prescribed by regulation 21(1) of these Regulations.

Examinations

21.—(1) The Society's examinations shall consist of examinations in the laws of Scotland in accordance with the syllabus prescribed by the Council from time to time.

(2) An intrant shall not be permitted to sit any one examination on more than four occasions or later than four years from the date of the first of the Society's examinations for which he presented himself except with the consent of the Council following on a recommendation by the Examiners, which consent may be given subject to such conditions as are deemed appropriate.

Award of distinction

22. A certificate of distinction in any subject may be awarded to an intrant at the discretion of the Examiners.

Conduct, dates and places of examinations

23.—(1) Diets for the Society's examinations shall be held in Edinburgh not less than twice each year and additional diets may be held in such circumstances as the Examiners, with the approval of the Council, may determine.

(2) Intrants intending to present themselves as candidates at any of the Society's examinations shall give three weeks' notice in writing of their intention to the Secretary, provided that the Examiners may at their discretion allow an intrant who has not given such notice to present himself for any examination.

(3) Every candidate shall be examined in writing and may be required by the Examiners to present himself for oral examination.

(4) Every candidate shall be required to advise the Society of any permanent change of address.

Fees

24. A candidate shall tender with his application to sit any examination such fee as may be prescribed by the Council from time to time.

PART IV

EXEMPTIONS

Faculty of Advocates' examinees

25. The Council may exempt from any of the Society's examinations an intrant who has obtained a pass in the corresponding examination in the examinations for admission to the Faculty of Advocates.

Corresponding passes

26. Where an intrant seeks exemption from any of the Society's examinations, provided the Council is satisfied that the intrant has passed a corresponding examination in the laws of Scotland to a standard approved by the Council, then the Council may grant such exemption.

Further exemptions for intrants from elsewhere in the UK

27. Where the terms of regulation 30 or 31 of these Regulations do not apply, the Council may, on application by an intrant who has passed the examinations required for admission as a solicitor or barrister in England and Wales or Northern Ireland within a reasonable time prior to such application, determine which of the Society's examinations, if any, such intrant shall be required to pass for the purposes of regulation 5(2)(b) of these Regulations and, notwithstanding regulation 20 of these Regulations, and subject always to such conditions as the Council may impose, including conditions as to the period of time during which the examinations must be passed, such an intrant shall be entitled to present himself for the Society's examinations.

Exemptions from Diploma, Professional Competence Course and Test of Professional Competence

28.—(1) An intrant who seeks to obtain a Certificate of Fitness under these Regulations and who satisfies the Council that there are exceptional circumstances which justify his being exempted from obtaining a Diploma may be granted a Certificate of Fitness on such conditions, including the passing of examinations, as the Council may in its discretion prescribe; provided that an intrant who receives such exemption shall be required to serve for a period of not less than three years under a non-Diploma training contract with a training solicitor, in terms similar to those of a post-Diploma training contract.

(2) An intrant who seeks to obtain a Certificate of Fitness under these Regulations and who satisfies the Council that there are exceptional circumstances which justify his being exempted from completing a Professional Competence Course may be granted a Certificate of Fitness on such conditions as the Council may in its discretion prescribe.

(3) An intrant who has become entitled to the award of the Diploma prior to 1st October 2000 shall be exempt from both passing the Test of Professional Competence and completing the Professional Competence Course.

PART V

REQUIREMENTS FOR SPECIAL INTRANTS

Scottish advocates

29. Notwithstanding any other provisions herein contained, but always without prejudice to regulation 41 of these Regulations, an intrant who is a member of the Faculty of Advocates, has had two years of recent active practice of Scots law since being called and who provides such evidence as the Council may require that he is a fit and proper to be admitted as a solicitor in Scotland shall be exempt from:—

(a) pre-Diploma training,
(b) the Society's examinations, and
(c) the Diploma

but he shall be required to complete the Professional Competence Course, pass the Test of Professional Competence and undergo six months of non-Diploma training prior to applying for admission in terms of regulation 34 of these Regulations.

English/Welsh and Northern Irish solicitors

30. Notwithstanding any other provisions herein contained, but always without prejudice to regulation 41 of these Regulations, an intrant who has been admitted as a solicitor in England and Wales or Northern Ireland and who provides such evidence as the Council may require that he is a fit and proper person to be admitted as a solicitor in Scotland shall be exempt from:—

(a) the Society's examinations,
(b) the Diploma,
(c) any period of training, and
(d) completing the Professional Competence Course and passing the Test of Professional Competence

but he shall be required to pass in such manner as the Council may require an intra-UK transfer test comprising examinations in conveyancing, trusts and succession, Scots criminal law, with civil and criminal evidence and procedure and (unless admitted as aforesaid prior to 1st January 1992) European Community law and institutions or such other examinations as may be prescribed by the Council from time to time prior to applying for admission in terms of regulation 34 of these Regulations.

English/Welsh and Northern Irish barristers

31. Notwithstanding any other provisions herein contained, but always without prejudice to regulation 41 of these Regulations, an intrant who is a member of the Bar in England and Wales or Northern Ireland, who provides such evidence as the Council may require that he is a fit and proper person to be admitted as a solicitor in Scotland and can demonstrate that he has had five years of recent active practice of law in the United Kingdom since his call to the Bar shall be exempt from:—

(a) pre-Diploma training,
(b) the Society's examinations, and
(c) the Diploma

but he shall be required to complete the Professional Competence Course, pass the Test of Professional Competence, pass in such manner as the Council may require an intra-UK transfer test comprising examinations in conveyancing, trusts and succession, Scots criminal law, with civil and criminal evidence and procedure and (unless called as aforesaid prior to 1st January 1992) European Community law and institutions or such other examinations as may be prescribed by the Council from time to time and undergo a period of six months of non-Diploma training, or such longer period as the Council may in its discretion determine, prior to applying for admission in terms of regulation 34 of these Regulations.

Colonial solicitors

32. Notwithstanding any other provisions herein contained, but always without prejudice to regulation 41 of these Regulations, an intrant to whom the Colonial Solicitors Act 1900, and any Order in Council made thereunder, apply and who provides such evidence as the Council may require that he is a fit and proper person to be admitted as a solicitor in Scotland shall be exempt from

(a) pre-Diploma training, and
(b) the Diploma

but he shall be required to complete the Professional Competence Course, pass the Test of Professional Competence, pass the Society's examinations and undergo one year of non-Diploma training prior to applying for admission in terms of regulation 34 of these Regulations.

Other overseas lawyers

33. Notwithstanding any other provisions herein contained, but always without prejudice to regulation 41 of these Regulations, a practising lawyer from outwith the United Kingdom to whom the Colonial Solicitors Act 1900, and any Order in Council made thereunder, the 1994 Regulations or the Directive do not apply shall be exempt from pre-Diploma training but he shall be required to satisfy the Council that he is qualified to undertake within the jurisdiction in which he qualified or practises professional work equivalent in its nature to that of a solicitor or advocate in Scotland, to provide such evidence as the Council may require that he is a fit and proper person to be admitted as a solicitor in Scotland and to pass the Society's examinations, gain the Diploma, complete the Professional Competence Course, pass the Test of Professional Competence and complete one year of post-Diploma training prior to applying for admission in terms of regulation 34 of these Regulations.

PART VI

PROCEDURE FOR ADMISSION AS SOLICITOR

Eligibility for Certificate of Fitness

34. Subject to the provisions of section 6 of the Act and these Regulations, an intrant shall be entitled to apply for a Certificate of Fitness for the purposes of section 6 of the Act if:—

(1)(a) he has passed or obtained exemption from all of the required Society's examinations; or

(b) he has obtained or is entitled to obtain a Degree in Law which includes passes in subjects which the Council is satisfied correspond to all the subjects prescribed in the syllabus referred to in regulation 21(1) of these Regulations or, where such Degree does not include passes in subjects which correspond to all the subjects prescribed, he obtains passes in the remaining prescribed subjects in the Society's examinations, or otherwise passes corresponding subjects at the standard required for a Degree in Law; and

(2) he holds a Diploma, unless he is exempted from the requirement to hold a Diploma in terms of these Regulations; and

(3)(a) he has completed the Professional Competence Course, or is exempt therefrom, and has passed the Test of Professional Competence, or is exempt therefrom; or

(b) he has complied with regulation 34(4)(a) or (c) of these Regulations; and

(4)(a) he has completed not less than one year of his two-year period of service under a post-Diploma training contract and has submitted to the Council:—

(i) a declaration in conformity with regulation 36(1) of these Regulations;

(ii) an undertaking in such form as the Council may prescribe that he will complete the remaining period of service under such training contract in fulfilment of his obligation under that training contract;

(iii) an undertaking in conformity with regulation 38(1) of these Regulations; and

(iv) undertakings in conformity with regulation 38(2) of these Regulations; or

(b) he has completed the full period of service under a post-Diploma training contract and has submitted to the Council a declaration in conformity with regulation 37 of these Regulations; or

(c) he has completed not less than two years of the full period of service under a non-Diploma training contract and he has submitted to the Council a declaration in conformity with regulation 36(2) of these Regulations and the undertakings referred to in regulation 34(4)(a) of these Regulations; or

(d) he has completed the full period of service under a non-Diploma training contract as is prescribed for him under these Regulations and has submitted to the Council a declaration in conformity with regulation 37 of these Regulations; or

(e) he is an intrant to whom regulation 33 of these Regulations applies and he has completed not less than one year of service under a post-Diploma training contract and has submitted to the Council a declaration in conformity with regulation 37 of these Regulations; and

(5) he has submitted to the Council such further evidence as it may require that he continues to be a fit and proper person to be admitted as a solicitor in Scotland.

Enquiries by Council

35. Without prejudice to any obligation in these Regulations on an intrant, including any intrant who is admitted as a solicitor by virtue of regulation 34(4)(a) or (c) of these Regulations while still a party to a post-Diploma training contract or a non-Diploma training contract, to satisfy the Council he is a fit and proper person to be admitted as, or be, a solicitor in Scotland, the Council may make enquiries concerning the intrant, both as regards those matters mentioned in regulation 36(3) of these Regulations and otherwise. For these purposes the Council shall be entitled to require the evidence of the intrant, his employer, any solicitor and any other intrant and to call for and recover such evidence and documents from any such person as the Council thinks proper.

Applicants admitted after one year of post-Diploma training or two years of non-Diploma training—employer's declaration

36.—(1) In the case of an intrant to whom regulation 34(4)(a) of these Regulations applies, the Council shall not grant a Certificate of Fitness to him unless he submits to the Council a declaration by his employer in such form as the Council may prescribe certifying that, during the first year of his post-Diploma training contract, he has fulfilled his obligations under such contract and is, in the opinion of his employer, a fit and proper person to be admitted as a solicitor in Scotland and, on completion of his full period of service under his post-Diploma training contract, such an intrant shall submit to the Council a declaration by his employer in such form as the Council may prescribe certifying that in his opinion the intrant continues to be a fit and proper person to be a solicitor in Scotland, provided always that, in any case where the employer of an intrant has declined to provide any such declaration, the Council may, after due enquiry and where it appears reasonable to do so, waive the requirement for such declaration from the employer, subject to such conditions as it may in its discretion determine.

(2) In the case of an intrant to whom regulation 34(4)(c) of these Regulations applies, the Council shall not grant a Certificate of Fitness to him unless he submits to the Council a declaration by his employer in such form as the Council may prescribe certifying that, during the first two years of his non-Diploma training contract, he has fulfilled his obligations under such contract and is, in the opinion of his employer, a fit and proper person to be admitted as a solicitor in Scotland and, on completion of his full period of service under his non-Diploma training contract, such an intrant

shall submit to the Council a declaration by his employer in such form as the Council may prescribe certifying that in his opinion the intrant continues to be a fit and proper person to be a solicitor in Scotland, provided always that, in any case where the employer of an intrant has declined to provide any such declaration, the Council may, after due enquiry and where it appears reasonable to do so, waive the requirement for such declaration from the employer, subject to such conditions as it may in its discretion determine.

(3) In forming an opinion whether the intrant is a fit and proper person to be admitted as a solicitor, the employer shall have regard not only to the moral character of the intrant but also to his aptitude for, and application to, his duties and his conduct generally.

Applicants admitted after two years of post-Diploma training or to whom regulation 33 applies—employer's declaration

37.—(1) In the case of an intrant to whom regulation 34(4)(b), (d) or (e) of these Regulations applies, the Council shall not grant a Certificate of Fitness to him unless he submits to the Council a declaration by his employer in such form as the Council may prescribe certifying that in his opinion the intrant has fulfilled his obligations under the training contract and is a fit and proper person to be admitted as a solicitor in Scotland, provided always that, in any case where the employer of an intrant has declined to provide any such declaration, the Council may, after due enquiry and where it appears reasonable to do so, waive the requirement for such declaration from the employer.

(2) In forming an opinion whether the intrant is a fit and proper person to be admitted as a solicitor, the employer shall have regard not only to the moral character of the intrant but also to his aptitude for and application to his duties and his conduct generally.

Undertaking by certain intrants

[1] **38.**—(1) In the case of an intrant to whom regulation 34(4)(a) or (c) of these Regulations applies, the intrant shall, before applying for a Certificate of Fitness, give an undertaking in such form as the Council may prescribe that he will not engage in professional practice on his own account and will only act as a professional assistant to a practising solicitor or a firm of practising solicitors or an incorporated practice (as defined in the Act) or a multi-national practice (as defined in the Act) in each case in Scotland. Such undertaking shall only bind the intrant until the date of grant of an employer's declaration that the intrant continues to be a fit and proper person to be a solicitor in Scotland pursuant to regulation 36(1) or (2) of these Regulations or the date the requirement for such a declaration is waived by the Council in terms of those regulations.

(2) Subject to regulation 38(4) of these Regulations, in the case of an intrant to whom regulation 34(4)(a) or (c) of these Regulations applies, the intrant shall, before applying for a Certificate of Fitness:—

(a) give an undertaking in such form as the Council may prescribe that, if he has not on or before the last day of his service under his training contract completed the Professional Competence Course, he will not practise as a solicitor after that last day; and

(b) give an undertaking in such form as the Council may prescribe that, if he has not on or before the last day of his service under his training contract passed the Test of Professional Competence, he will not practice as a solicitor after that last day.

(3) Undertakings given for the purpose of regulation 38(2) of these Regulations shall only bind the intrant until the later to occur of the date the intrant completes the Professional Competence Course and the date the intrant passes the Test of Professional Competence.

(4) An intrant who is exempt from completing the Professional Competence Course or who has, at the date he applies for a Certificate of

Fitness, completed the Professional Competence Course shall not be required to give the undertaking referred to in regulation 38(2)(a) of these Regulations and an intrant who is exempt from passing the Test of Professional Competence or who has, at the date he applies for a Certificate of Fitness, passed the Test of Professional Competence shall not be required to give the undertaking referred to in regulation 38(2)(b) of these Regulations.

NOTE

[1] As amended by the Solicitors (Scotland) (Registered Foreign Lawyers) etc. Practice Rules 2005, Sch.5 (effective May 1, 2005).

Applicants for admission after five years

39. Where an application for a Certificate of Fitness is made by an intrant under these Regulations more than five years after the date on which he became entitled to apply therefor, the Council may, after due enquiry and where it appears reasonable to do so, refuse the application or grant the application subject to such conditions as it may require.

PART VII

GENERAL

Right of appeal

40. Any person who is the subject of a decision by the Council under any of these Regulations and who is aggrieved by that decision may, within 21 days of written intimation of the decision, appeal to the Court of Session.

Council's discretion

41.—(1) The Council may in its discretion relieve any person from the consequences of any failure to comply with these Regulations where it is satisfied that such failure to comply is due to mistake, oversight or excusable cause, such not being wilful non-observance of these Regulations.

(2) The Council may, where the circumstances of a particular intrant are exceptional waive any provision of these Regulations applying to such intrant, provided that any such waiver may be subject to such conditions as the Council may in its discretion determine.

(3) The Council may, where the circumstances of a particular intrant are exceptional, determine that any of the exemptions provided by regulations 29, 30, 31, 32 and 33 of these Regulations shall not apply to such intrant.

(4) The Council may, where the circumstances of a particular intrant are exceptional, permit such intrant to depart from the terms of any undertaking given by him pursuant to regulation 38 of these Regulations.

Photograph

42. The Council may require any intrant to supply the Council with a recent photograph of the intrant for the purpose of verifying the identity of the intrant or otherwise and the Council may retain any photograph so supplied.

SCHEDULE

An intrant will be deemed to be duly qualified for the purposes of regulation 11(2)(b) of these Regulations if he complies with any of paragraphs (a) to (f) below:—

Scottish Certificate of Education

(a) (1) passes in at least five of the subjects in the Scottish Certificate of Education, as approved from time to time by the Universities Central Council on Admissions, at no more than two sittings, said passes to include:—

(i) a pass at Higher grade in English at not less than "B",
(ii) a pass at Higher grade in a subject chosen from one of the following groups:—
(a) a group comprising mathematics or an approved science, or
(b) a group comprising an approved language other than English, and
(iii) a pass at Higher, Ordinary or Standard grade in a subject chosen from the group not chosen under sub-paragraph (ii) above, provided that if at Ordinary or Standard grade, such pass is at not less than grade 3 and

(2) a total of such points as the Council may from time to time determine in respect of the subjects passed, calculated as follows:—
a pass at Higher grade at:—
"A" being valued at three points,
"B" being valued at two points, and
"C" being valued at one point.
Provided that if he has insufficient points or subject passes, he may add to these equivalent passes and points under (b)(1) and (2) below.

General Certificate of Education

(b) (1) passes in at least five of the subjects in the General Certificate of Education, as approved from time to time by the Universities Central Council on Admissions, at no more than two sittings, said passes to include:—
(i) a pass at the Advanced level in English, at not less than "C" standard,
(ii) a pass at the Advanced level in a subject chosen from one of the following groups:—
(a) a group comprising mathematics or an approved science, or
(b) a group comprising an approved language other than English, and
(iii) a pass at the Advanced or Ordinary level or GCSE in a subject chosen from the group not chosen under subparagraph (ii) above; and

(2) a total of such points as the Council may from time to time determine in respect of the subjects passed, calculated as follows:—
a pass at the Advanced level at:—
"A" being valued at four points,
"B" being valued at three points,
"C" being valued at two points, and
"D" being valued at one point.
Provided that if he has insufficient points or subject passes, he may add to these equivalent passes and points under (a)(1) and (2) above.

HND in Legal Studies

(c) a Scottish Higher National Diploma in Legal Studies from any College of Further Education approved by the Council offering such Diploma and also a pass in English at Higher grade in the Scottish Certificate of Education at not less than "B" or its equivalent.

University Degree

(d) a degree of any University, other than a Degree in Law, or an entitlement to graduate in such a degree notwithstanding that he has not so graduated.

Chartered Accountant

(e) membership of the Institute of Chartered Accountants of Scotland or of the Institute of Chartered Accountants in England and Wales or of the Association of Certified and Corporate Accountants.

Commissioned Officer

(f) a commission as a commissioned officer in one of the British armed services, where his commission has been obtained following study at a Royal Naval, Army or Royal Air Force college.

In this Schedule references to the Scottish Certificate of Education shall be construed as including the Scottish Qualifications Certificate.

Solicitors (Scotland) (Advertising and Promotion) Practice Rules 2006

[June 2006]

Rules dated 24th March 2006 made by the Council of the Law Society of Scotland under section 34(1) of the Solicitors (Scotland) Act 1980 and approved by the Lord President of the Court of Session in terms of section 34(3) of the said Act.

Citation and commencement

1.—(1) These Rules may be cited as the Solicitors (Scotland) (Advertising and Promotion) Practice Rules 2006.

(2) These Rules shall come into operation on 1st June 2006.

Definitions and interpretation

2.—(1) In these Rules, unless the context otherwise requires:

the "2005 Rules" means the Solicitors (Scotland) (Registered Foreign Lawyers) etc Practice Rules 2005;

the "Act" means the Solicitors (Scotland) Act 1980;

the "Council" means the Council of the Society;

"established client" means a person for whom a solicitor has acted on at least one previous occasion, but does not include a person:

(a) whom the solicitor knows or ought reasonably to know to be exclusively a client of another solicitor; or

(b) for whom the solicitor has acted only on the instructions of another solicitor;

"general circulation" means circulation to a group of persons (including bodies corporate) who can be categorised by a common description;

"practice" means professional practice of the solicitor and includes any area of practice;

"the Secretary" means the Secretary of the Society and includes any person authorized by the Council to act on behalf of the Secretary;

"services" means services provided by a solicitor and includes any part of such services;

"the Society" means the Law Society of Scotland;

"solicitor" means a solicitor holding a practising certificate under the Act and includes a firm of solicitors, an incorporated practice and any association of solicitors and shall include a registered foreign lawyer to whom these rules apply in terms of rule 4(2) or (3) of the 2005 Rules and a Scottish multi-national practice and a Scottish branch of a multi-national practice (in each case as defined in rule 7 of the 2005 Rules);

"specialist" means an individual solicitor who possesses knowledge of and expertise in a particular branch or area of law or legal practice significantly greater than that which might reasonably be expected to be possessed by a solicitor who is not a specialist in that branch or area of law or legal practice.

(2) The Interpretation Act 1978 applies to the interpretation of these Rules as it applies to the interpretation of an Act of Parliament.

(3) The headings to these Rules do not form part of these Rules.

Advertising and promotion of services

3. Subject to rules 4 and 7, a solicitor shall be entitled to advertise and promote his services in any way he thinks fit.

4. A solicitor shall not make a direct or indirect approach whether verbal or written to any person whom he knows or ought reasonably to know to be the client of another solicitor with the intention to solicit business from that person.

5. Rule 4 shall not preclude the general circulation by a solicitor of material promoting that solicitor's services whether or not the persons to whom it is directed are established clients.

6. A solicitor shall not be in breach of these Rules by reason only of his claim to be a specialist in any particular field of law or legal practice, provided that:

(a) the onus of proof that any such claim is justified shall be on the solicitor making it; and

(b) an advertisement of or by a solicitor or other material issued by or on behalf of a solicitor making any such claim shall conform otherwise to the requirements of rule 7.

7. An advertisement of or by a solicitor or promotional material issued by or on behalf of a solicitor or any promotional activity by or on behalf of a solicitor shall be decent and shall not:

(a) contain any inaccuracy or misleading statement;

(b) be of such nature or character or be issued or done by such means as may reasonably be regarded as bringing the profession into disrepute;

(c) identify any client or item of his business without the prior written consent of the client; or

(d) be defamatory or illegal.

8. Any advertisement, promotional material or promotional activity of or by a solicitor (whether or not the solicitor be named or referred to therein) and any advertisement, promotional material or promotional activity of or by a third party which relates to the services of a solicitor shall be presumed to have been issued or promoted with the authority of the solicitor.

Contravention of these rules

9.—(1) Where an advertisement or promotional material or activity by a solicitor, or by a third party which relates to the services of a solicitor, is deemed by the Council to contravene any of these Rules, the Council may by way of written notice duly given to the solicitor require him forthwith, or from such date as the notice may stipulate, to withdraw, terminate or cancel the advertisement or promotional material or activity as the case may require and not to repeat the same during the currency of the notice.

(2) A notice given by the Council to a solicitor under paragraph 1 shall be signed by the Secretary and shall be deemed to have been duly given if it is delivered to the solicitor or left or sent by recorded delivery post to his last known place of business.

(3) It shall be the duty of a solicitor to obtemper any notice duly given to him under this rule. A solicitor aggrieved by the terms of any such notice may, within 14 days of the date thereof, make written representations concerning that notice to the Council, which shall, within two months of the receipt of such representations, either confirm or withdraw such notice; provided that should the Council neither confirm nor withdraw such notice within the two month period, that notice shall be deemed to have been withdrawn at the expiry of that period.

10. Breach of any of these Rules may be treated as professional misconduct for the purposes of Part IV of the Act (Complaints and Disciplinary Proceedings).

Waiver

11. The Council shall have power to waive any of the provisions of these Rules in any particular case.

Revocation of previous rules

12.—(1) The Solicitors (Scotland) (Advertising and Promotion) Practice Rules 1995 are hereby revoked.

(2) For the purposes of rule 4 of the 2005 Rules, these rules constitute re-making of the Solicitors (Scotland) (Advertsing & Promotion) Practice Rules 1995.

PROFESSIONAL PRACTICE GUIDELINE

In addition to the foregoing Rules the Council have also approved the following guideline on the advertising of solicitors' fees, whether that is done by the solicitor or by another party such as an estate agent.

Guideline on Advertising Fees

Where a solicitor's fees for his services are advertised either by the solicitor or by a third party whether or not the solicitor is named in such an advertisement the advertisement must include mention of outlays and VAT with no less prominence than the fees. Failure to mention outlays and VAT with no less prominence than the fees may be regarded as misleading and inaccurate and therefore in breach of rule 7(a) of the Solicitors (Scotland) (Advertising and Promotion) Practice Rules 1995. In terms of rule 10 of those rules, breach of any of the rules may be treated as professional misconduct.

Solicitors (Scotland) (ARTL Mandates) Rules 2006

Rules dated 27th October 2006, made by the Council of the Law Society of Scotland under section 34 of the Solicitors (Scotland) Act 1980 and approved by the Lord President of the Court of Session under section 34(3) of that Act.

Citation and Commencement

1.—(1) These Rules may be cited as the Solicitors (Scotland) (ARTL Mandates) Rules 2006.

(2) These Rules shall come into effect on 1st January 2007.

Definitions and Interpretation

2.—(1) In these Rules, unless the context otherwise requires:—

"the Act means the Solicitors (Scotland) Act 1980;

"ARTL System" has the same meaning as in section 28(1) of the Land Registration (Scotland) Act 1979 as that section is amended by the Automated Registration of Title to Land (Electronic Communications) (Scotland) Order 2006;

"the Council" means the Council of the Society;

"electronic communication" has the same meaning as in the Electronic Communications Act 2000;

"the Keeper" means the Keeper of the Registers of Scotland;

"the Land Register" means the Land Register of Scotland;

"mandate" means a mandate in the form prescribed from time to time by the Council;

"the Society" means the Law Society of Scotland; and

"solicitor" means a solicitor holding a practising certificate under the Act and includes a firm of solicitors, an incorporated practice and a multi-national practice.

(2) The Interpretation Act 1978 applies to the interpretation of these Rules as it applies to the interpretation of an Act of Parliament.

(3) The headings to these Rules do not form part of these Rules.

ARTL Mandates

3. No solicitor shall authenticate, or apply for registration in the Land Register of, a document created as an electronic communication within the ARTL System on behalf of any person unless that solicitor has obtained a mandate in his favour subscribed by that person authorising the authentication and registration of that document.

Archiving and Retention of Mandates

4.—(1) A solicitor shall, within 14 days of applying for registration in the Land Register within the ARTL System, send the principal of each mandate obtained in terms of rule 3 hereof to the Keeper for archiving and return to that solicitor.

(2) A solicitor shall retain the principal of each mandate obtained in his favour in terms of rule 3 in accordance with practice guidelines issued from time to time by the Council.

Waiver

5. The Council shall have power to waive any of the provisions of these rules in any particular circumstance or case.

Professional Misconduct

6. If a solicitor fails to comply with these Rules that failure may be treated as professional misconduct for the purposes of Part IV of the Act.

Solicitors (Scotland) (Associates, Consultants and Employees) Practice Rules 2001

Rules dated 28th September 2001, made by the Council of the Law Society of Scotland under section 34(1) of the Solicitors (Scotland) Act 1980 and approved by the Lord President of the Court of Session in terms of section 34(3) of the said Act.

Citation and Commencement

1.—(1) These rules may be cited as the Solicitors (Scotland) (Associates, Consultants and Employees) Practice Rules 2001.

(2) These rules shall come into operation on 30th November 2001.

Definitions and Interpretation

2.—(1) In these rules, unless the context otherwise requires—

[1] "2005 Rules" means the Solicitors (Scotland) (Registered Foreign Lawyers) etc Practice Rules 2005;

"Act" means the Solicitors (Scotland) Act 1980;

[2] "solicitor" means a solicitor holding a practising certificate under the Act and includes a firm of solicitors and an incorporated practice and shall include a registered foreign lawyer to whom these rules apply in terms of rule 4(2) or (3) of the 2005 Rules and a Scottish multi-national practice (as defined in rule 7(1) of the 2005 Rules);

"Council" means the Council of the Society;

"the Society" means the Law Society of Scotland, established under the Act;

"consultant" means a solicitor whose practising certificate is held by him free of conditions imposed in terms of sections 15, 24C or other relevant sections of the Act or by any Regulations made thereunder or by the Scottish Solicitors' Discipline Tribunal or by the Court of Session and who, not being in partnership with a solicitor, or a director of an incorporated practice which is a company, or a member of an incorporated practice which is a limited liability partnership makes his services and advice available to that solicitor or incorporated practice.

"private practice" means practice by a solicitor acting on his own account (whether as an individual or as a partner or as an incorporated practice);

"associate" means a solicitor, whose practising certificate is held by him free of conditions imposed in terms of sections 15, 24C or other relevant sections of the Act or by any Regulations made thereunder or by the Scottish Solicitors' Discipline Tribunal or by the Court of Session who is in the employment of another solicitor whether fulltime or part-time and who has been afforded the status of "associate" of that other solicitor;

"employee" means a bona fide employee of a solicitor, whether full-time or part-time, and includes a solicitor in the employment of that other solicitor who has been afforded the status of consultant to or associate of that other solicitor; and

"the Secretary" means the Secretary of the Society and includes any person authorised by the Council to act on behalf of the Secretary.

(2) The Interpretation Act 1978 applies to the interpretation of these rules as it applies to the interpretation of an Act of Parliament.

(3) The headings to these rules do not form part of these rules.

NOTES

[1] Inserted by the Solicitors (Scotland) (Registered Foreign Lawyers) etc. Practice Rules 2005, Sch.5 (effective May 1, 2005).

[2] As amended by the Solicitors (Scotland) (Registered Foreign Lawyers) etc. Practice Rules 2005, Sch.5 (effective May 1, 2005).

Nameplate and Professional Stationery

3. No solicitor engaged in private practice shall cause or permit the name of any person to appear on his nameplate or professional stationery unless that person is:

(a) a partner of that solicitor,
(b) if the solicitor is an incorporated practice which is a company, a director of that incorporated practice,
(c) if the solicitor is an incorporated practice which is a limited liability partnership, a member of that limited liability partnership,
[1](ca) if the solicitor is a multi-national practice, a member of that multi-national practice".
(d) a consultant to that solicitor,
(e) an associate of that solicitor, or
(f) an employee of that solicitor.

NOTE

[1] Inserted by the Solicitors (Scotland) (Registered Foreign Lawyers) etc. Practice Rules 2005, Sch.5 (effective May 1, 2005).

Statement as to Status

4. Where a solicitor in terms of rule 3 hereof causes or permits the name of a consultant, associate or employee to appear on his nameplate or professional stationery, the status and designation of such consultant, associate or employee shall be unambiguously stated in such a manner as to distinguish clearly such consultant, associate or employee from a principal solicitor, the partners of a firm of solicitors, the directors of an incorporated practice which is a company, or the members of an incorporated practice which is a limited liability partnership, as the case may be.

Contravention of these Rules

5.—(1) In the event that the Council shall determine that a solicitor has contravened these rules, the Council may, by written notice duly given to him, require that solicitor from such date as the notice may stipulate, to amend that solicitor's nameplate or professional stationery in such a manner as shall comply with these rules.

(2) A notice given by the Council to a solicitor under paragraph (1) hereof shall be signed by the Secretary and shall be deemed to have been duly given if it is delivered to him or left at or sent by recorded delivery post to his last known place of business.

Waiver

6. The Council shall have power to waive any of the provisions of these rules in any particular case.

Revocation of Previous Rules

7. The Solicitors (Scotland) (Associates, Consultants and Employees) Practice Rules 1996 are hereby revoked.

Solicitors (Scotland) (Civil Legal Aid and Advice and Assistance) Practice Rules 2003

Made on 29th August 2003 and amended on 25th June 2004 with the approval of the Lord President all in terms of section 34 of the Solicitors (Scotland) Act 1980.

Citation and commencement

1.—(1) These rules may be cited as the Solicitors (Scotland) (Civil Legal Aid and Advice and Assistance) Practice Rules 2003.

(2) These rules shall come into operation on 1st October 2003, save for rule 3(3) which shall come into operation on 1st October 2004.

Interpretation

2.—[1] (1) In these rules, unless the context otherwise requires:

"the Act" means the Solicitors (Scotland) Act 1980;

"the 1986 Act" means the Legal Aid (Scotland) Act 1986;

"advice and assistance" means either or both of (i) advice and assistance on a civil matter or on a matter arising out of Part II of the Children (Scotland) Act 1995 and (ii) assistance by way of representation on a civil matter, within the meaning of section 6 of the 1986 Act, and to which Part II of the 1986 Act applies;

"associated solicitor" means, in relation to a practice unit, a solicitor who:

(a) is that practice unit,

(b) is a partner of that practice unit, where it is a firm,

(c) is a director or a member of that practice unit, where it is an incorporated practice,

[3](ca) is a member of a practice unit where that practice unit is a multi-national practice,

(d) is an employee of that practice unit, or

(e) is a consultant to that practice unit;

"the Board" means the Scottish Legal Aid Board, established by the 1986 Act;

[2] "children's legal aid" means legal aid to which section 29 of the 1986 Act applies;

"civil legal aid" has the meaning given to it in Part III of the 1986 Act;

"compliance" means compliance in all material respects, and "comply" shall be construed accordingly;

"compliance certificate" means a certificate awarded by the Council in terms of rule 6;

"the Council" means the Council of the Society;

"employee" includes an associate;

"the Fund" has the meaning given to it in section 4(1) of the 1986 Act;

"incorporated practice" has the meaning given to it in section 34(1A) of the Act;

"legal aid" means (i) advice and assistance, (ii) civil legal aid and (iii) children's legal aid;

"legal aid files" means, in relation to a practice unit:

(a) any files, papers or documents or copies thereof,

(b) copies in printed format of any data held in any way, and

(c) copies other than in printed format of any data held in any way

relating to the provision (whether current or past) of legal aid by that practice unit or the procedures followed, or to be followed in doing so;

[4] "practice unit" means (i) a solicitor who is a sole practitioner, (ii) a firm of solicitors or (iii) an incorporated practice and also includes a multi-national practice;

"registered practice unit" means a practice unit that is registered;

"registration" means registration with the Board as a practice unit for the purpose of providing legal aid, and "registered" shall be construed accordingly;

"relevant date" means the relevant date as defined in rule 7;

"reviewer" means a person appointed by the Council in terms of rule 15;

"the Society" means the Law Society of Scotland; and

"solicitor" means a solicitor holding a practising certificate under the Act.

(2) The Interpretation Act 1978 applies to the interpretation of these rules as it applies to the interpretation of an Act of Parliament.

NOTE

[1] As amended by the Solicitors (Scotland) (Civil Legal Aid and Advice and Assistance) (Amendment) Rules 2004, Sch.1 (effective July 2004).

[2] Inserted by the Solicitors (Scotland) (Civil Legal Aid and Advice and Assistance) (Amendment) Rules 2004, Sch.1 (effective July 2004).

[3] Inserted by the Solicitors (Scotland) (Registered Foreign Lawyers) etc. Practice Rules 2005, Sch.5 (effective May 1, 2005).

[4] As amended by the Solicitors (Scotland) (Registered Foreign Lawyers) etc. Practice Rules 2005, Sch.5 (effective May 1, 2005).

Provision of legal aid

3.—(1) No solicitor shall:

(a) grant any application for advice and assistance,

(b) sign any application for civil legal aid as a solicitor nominated by the applicant, or

[1] (c) sign any application for children's legal aid as a solicitor nominated by the applicant

unless he satisfies a condition set out in paragraph (2), and provided that rule 9 does not apply to him.

(2) A solicitor satisfies a condition set out in this paragraph if he is acting:

(a) as a registered practice unit, or

(b) as a partner of a registered practice unit which is a firm or a director or member of a registered practice unit which is an incorporated practice, or

(c) as an employee of a registered practice unit, or

(d) as a consultant to a registered practice unit, or

(e) in the course of his employment by the Board, or

(f) pursuant to the terms of an exemption granted to him by the Council in terms of rule 16(1).

[2] (3) No solicitor, firm of solicitors, incorporated practice or multinational practice shall apply to the Board for the registration of a practice unit which does not hold a compliance certificate.

NOTE

[1] Inserted by the Solicitors (Scotland) (Civil Legal Aid and Advice and Assistance) (Amendment) Rules 2004, Sch.1 (effective July 2004).

[2] As amended by the Solicitors (Scotland) (Registered Foreign Lawyers) etc. Practice Rules 2005, Sch.5 (effective May 1, 2005).

Quality assurance scheme

[1] **4.** The Council shall publish, and may from time to time amend, guidelines in relation to the provision of legal aid which shall set out the standards expected of solicitors and practice units in relation to the carrying out of such work. The Council may publish separate guidelines in relation to the provision of different types of legal aid. In providing legal aid, solicitors shall comply with those guidelines.

NOTE
[1] As amended by the Solicitors (Scotland) (Civil Legal Aid and Advice and Assistance) (Amendment) Rules 2004, Sch.1 (effective July 2004).

Obligation on practice units to ensure compliance with guidelines

5. A practice unit shall ensure compliance with the guidelines published in terms of rule 4 by any person undertaking any activity pursuant to the provision of legal aid by that practice unit.

Applications

6.—(1) The Council shall, subject to paragraph (3), on application for a compliance certificate being made by a practice unit, make such enquiry as to the ability of that practice unit to comply with the guidelines published in terms of rule 4 as the Council thinks fit, which may include interviewing any solicitor who is, or is to be, an associated solicitor of that practice unit, and a review of that practice unit pursuant to rules 14(1) and (2). That enquiry may be made on behalf of the Council by a reviewer. If that enquiry and review, if any, demonstrate that the practice unit complies, or will when it begins to provide legal aid comply, with the guidelines published pursuant to rule 4, the Council shall award a certificate to that effect to that practice unit, stating the date the practice unit was reviewed pursuant to rules 14 (1) and (2), or, if it has not been so reviewed, stating that fact. If that enquiry and review, if any, do not demonstrate that the practice unit complies, or will when it begins to provide legal aid comply with the guidelines published pursuant to rule 4, the Council shall, subject to rule 10, reject the application.

(2) A practice unit may within six months of the relevant date apply for a review pursuant to rule 14(3), and provided that no previous review of that practice unit has been made pursuant to rule 14(3) since that date, the Council shall, subject to rule 14(4), instruct a review of that practice unit pursuant to rule 14(3) to be carried out not more than 12 months after the relevant date.

(3) No application made pursuant to paragraph (1) shall be considered by the Council if it is made by a practice unit:

- (a) having a compliance certificate on which a note has been made pursuant to rule 7, or
- (b) within six months of
  - (i) renunciation of the compliance certificate of that practice unit pursuant to rule 8(2), or
  - (ii) rejection of any application by that practice unit in terms of paragraph (1), or
- (c) within 12 months of withdrawal of the compliance certificate of that practice unit pursuant to rule 7 or 8(1).

(4) Applications made pursuant to paragraphs (1) and (2) shall be in the form determined by the Council from time to time.

Requirement for further review and withdrawal of compliance certificate on failure to apply or pay for further review

[1] **7.** If, having regard to the results of a review carried out pursuant to rule 14(2), together with other relevant information, the Council decides that a practice unit should be further reviewed pursuant to rule 14(3), then it shall make a note to that effect on the compliance certificate of that practice unit. If that practice unit has not:

- (a) made any application in terms of rule 6(2) within six months of the date on which the decision is made to make such a note (the date of such decision being the "relevant date"), or
- (b) in a case where the instruction of a review pursuant to rule 14(3) is made conditional by the Council on payment of the sum as provided for in rule 14(4), paid that sum to the Council by the date required by the Council,

the Council may withdraw the compliance certificate of that practice unit and if it does so, that compliance certificate shall cease to have effect from the date on which notification of that withdrawal is received by that practice unit.

NOTE

[1] Substituted by the Solicitors (Scotland) (Civil Legal Aid and Advice and Assistance) (Amendment) Rules 2004, Sch.1 (effective July 2004).

Withdrawal and renunciation of compliance certificate

8.—(1) If, having regard to the results of a review carried out pursuant to rule 14(3), the Council decides that a practice unit does not comply with the guidelines published pursuant to rule 4, then it shall withdraw the compliance certificate of that practice unit, and that compliance certificate shall cease to have effect from the date on which notification of that withdrawal is received by that practice unit, and the provisions of rule 9 shall apply.

(2) A practice unit may renounce its compliance certificate at any time by giving written notice to that effect to the Council. A notice of renunciation shall take effect from the date on which it is received by the Council, and the compliance certificate of that practice unit shall be withdrawn and cease to have effect from that date, and the provisions of rule 9 shall apply.

Effect of withdrawal or renunciation of compliance certificate

[1] **9.**—(1) If the compliance certificate of a practice unit has been withdrawn pursuant to rule 7 or 8(1) or renounced pursuant to rule 8(2), then with effect from the date specified in rule 7,8(1) or 8(2), as the case may be, on which that compliance certificate ceases to have effect, no associated solicitor shall:

(a) grant any application for advice and assistance,

(b) sign any application for civil legal aid as a solicitor nominated by the applicant, or

(c) sign any application for children's legal aid.

(2) No later than 28 days from the date specified in paragraph (1) each associated solicitor in a practice unit to which paragraph (1) applies who has granted any application for advice and assistance or has signed any application for civil legal aid as a solicitor nominated by the applicant or any application for children's legal aid or is otherwise providing legal aid shall:

(a) cease the provision of legal aid,

(b) in each case involving advice and assistance, notify the client in receipt of advice and assistance in writing that he and his practice unit must cease to act for that client, and

(c) in each case involving civil legal aid or children's legal aid, notify the applicant and the Board in writing that he and his practice unit must cease to act for the applicant, and supply to the Board a statement of his reasons for ceasing to act.

(3) Each associated solicitor referred to in paragraph (2) shall, in each case involving civil legal aid or children's legal aid, co-operate with the applicant and the Board in the transfer of civil legal aid or children's legal aid files to another solicitor nominated by the applicant in terms of an application made by the applicant to the Board and granted by the Board.

(4) No practice unit to which paragraph (1) applies and no associated solicitor shall apply to the Board for payment out of the Fund of any fees or outlays incurred in respect of any legal aid which is provided by that associated solicitor after the expiry of the 28 day period referred to in paragraph (2).

NOTE

[1] As amended by the Solicitors (Scotland) (Civil Legal Aid and Advice and Assistance) (Amendment) Rules 2004, Sch.1 (effective July 2004).

Giving of reasons

10. Where the Council is minded to:

(a) reject an application in terms of rule 6(1), or

(b) make a note on a compliance certificate pursuant to rule 7, or

(c) withdraw a compliance certificate pursuant to rule 8(1)

then it shall give written notice of that fact to the relevant practice unit and supply that practice unit with copies of any information it proposes to rely on in coming to any such decision (with any deletions necessary to protect the identity of any person as appropriate), including any report made in terms of rule 14(7), and shall have regard to written representations made to it by or on behalf of that practice unit, any associated solicitor and any other interested person.

Appeals

11.—(1) Where the Council has:

(a) rejected an application in terms of rule 6(1),

(b) made a note on a compliance certificate pursuant to rule 7, or

(c) withdrawn a compliance certificate pursuant to rule 8(1),

a practice unit which is the subject of any such decision and which is aggrieved by it may, within 21 days of written intimation of that decision, appeal to the Outer House of the Court of Session. The decision of the Outer House in relation to such an appeal shall be final.

(2) For the avoidance of doubt, in circumstances where a compliance certificate has been withdrawn in terms of rule 8(1) and an appeal against that decision is made in terms of paragraph (1), the provisions of rule 9 shall, subject to rule 16(2), continue to apply.

Updating of certificate

12. Where, as a result of a review of a practice unit having a compliance certificate carried out pursuant to rule 14, the Council is satisfied that such a practice unit complies with the guidelines published pursuant to rule 4, the Council shall update the compliance certificate of that practice unit to show the date of that review.

Register of practice units holding compliance certificate

13.—(1) The Council shall maintain a register of practice units in relation to which a compliance certificate is in effect.

(2) The Council may supply copies of entries in the register in paragraph (1) to such persons as it thinks fit.

Reviews

[1] **14.**—(1) To enable it to ascertain whether a practice unit which holds, or has applied for, a compliance certificate complies, or will comply, with the guidelines published pursuant to rule 4, the Council may instruct a review of that practice unit by a reviewer specified by the Council. Where that practice unit has any legal aid files the Council may by written notice require any associated solicitor to deliver to the reviewer, or so far as he is able, to procure that any other person so delivers, by a date and to an address to be specified by that reviewer, the legal aid files specified by him. The reviewer shall review any such legal aid files, and carry out such other enquiry as he sees fit, with the object of ascertaining whether that practice unit complies or will comply with the guidelines published pursuant to rule 4. Where that practice unit does not have any legal aid files, the reviewer shall carry out such enquiry as he thinks fit with the object of ascertaining whether that practice unit complies or will comply with the guidelines published pursuant to rule 4.

(2) Where, following a review in terms of paragraph (1) or on the basis of information received by it, it appears to the Council that a review at the premises of any practice unit is necessary or desirable to determine whether that practice unit complies or will comply with the guidelines published pursuant to rule 4, or where the Council reaches agreement to do so with a practice unit that would otherwise be subject to a review in terms of paragraph (1), the Council may by written notice require any associated solicitor to allow, or so far as he is able, to procure that any other person allows, access for that purpose by a reviewer on a date or dates to be specified by the Council to any premises, legal aid files or person. Where that practice unit has any legal aid files, the reviewer shall visit the premises, may review all or any such files and may carry out such other enquiry as he thinks fit with a view to ascertaining whether that practice unit complies or will comply with the guidelines published pursuant to rule 4. Where that practice unit has no legal aid files, the reviewer shall visit the premises and carry out such enquiry as he thinks fit with a view to ascertaining whether that practice unit complies or will comply with the guidelines published pursuant to rule 4.

(3) A review in terms of this paragraph, which shall only be instructed pursuant to rule 6(2) subject to paragraph (4), is a review of a practice unit by a reviewer specified by the Council. The Council may by written notice require any associated solicitor to allow, or so far as he is able, to procure that any other person allows, access by a reviewer to any premises, legal aid files or person. Where that practice unit has any legal aid files, the reviewer shall visit the premises, may review all or any such files and may carry out such other enquiry as he thinks fit with a view to ascertaining whether that practice unit complies or will comply with the guidelines published pursuant to rule 4. Where that practice unit has no legal aid files, the reviewer shall visit the premises and carry out such enquiry as he thinks fit with a view to ascertaining whether that practice unit complies or will comply with the guidelines published pursuant to rule 4.

(4) The Council may make the instruction pursuant to rule 6(2) of a review of a practice unit in terms of paragraph(3) conditional upon that practice unit paying or agreeing to pay to the Council such sum as may be required to meet the fees and costs incurred in connection with that review. The amount of such sum shall be fixed by the Council.

[2] (4A)Where a practice unit that would otherwise be subject to a review in terms of paragraph (1) reaches agreement with the Council that it is instead reviewed in terms of paragraph (2) pursuant to a request by that practice unit, the agreement of the Council to do so may be made conditional upon that practice unit paying or agreeing to pay to the Council such sum as may be required to meet the fees and costs incurred in connection with that review. The amount of such sum shall be fixed by the Council.

(5) A solicitor who is a partner, director or member of a practice unit or who is a sole practitioner shall ensure that any sum required to be paid by him or that practice unit in terms of paragraphs (4) or 4(A) is paid.

(6) A solicitor shall comply with all requirements placed on him in terms of paragraphs (1) to (3) above, and shall give reasonable co-operation to any reviewer acting in the course of any review or enquiry in terms of these rules.

(7) Where:

(a) in relation to a practice unit

(i) a reviewer has completed his review of that practice unit in terms of paragraph (1), or

(ii) a reviewer has completed his review of that practice unit in terms of paragraph (2) or (3), or.

(iii) any matter arises which in the opinion of a reviewer requires to be brought to the attention of the Council, or

(b) the Council requests it,

that reviewer shall make a written report to the Council on that review or matter or pursuant to that request.

NOTES

[1] As amended by the Solicitors (Scotland) (Civil Legal Aid and Advice and Assistance) (Amendment) Rules 2004, Sch.1 (effective July 2004).

[2] Inserted by the Solicitors (Scotland) (Civil Legal Aid and Advice and Assistance) (Amendment) Rules 2004, Sch.1 (effective July 2004).

Reviewers

15.—(1) In order to carry out reviews in terms of rule 14 and any other enquiry permitted or required in terms of these rules, the Council may appoint any person who consents to such appointment as a reviewer. Such a person shall be a solicitor.

(2) A reviewer shall comply with any directions that may be given by the Council in respect of matters connected with reviews in terms of rule 14 or any other enquiry permitted or required in terms of these rules.

(3) A reviewer shall be appointed for such term and be paid such remuneration as the Council may from time to time determine.

Exemption and waiver

16.—(1) The Council may exempt any solicitor from the requirement to satisfy the conditions contained in paragraphs (a) to (e) of rule 3(2), subject to such conditions, if any, as it considers appropriate.

(2) The Council may waive any provision of these rules, either generally or in relation to any particular case, subject to such conditions, if any, as it considers appropriate.

(3) The Council may, where the circumstances of any practice unit are exceptional, consider any application made by such practice unit pursuant to rule 6(1) notwithstanding the provisions of rule 6(3), subject to such conditions, if any, as it considers appropriate.

[NEXT TEXT PAGE IS F 253]

Solicitors (Scotland) Accounts, Accounts Certificate, Professional Practice and Guarantee Fund Rules 2001

Rules dated 28th September 2001, made by the Council of the Law Society of Scotland under sections 34(1), 35(1), 37(6) and 43 of, and paragraph 4(4) of Part I of Schedule 3 to, the Solicitors (Scotland) Act 1980 and approved by the Lord President of the Court of Session under section 34(3) of the said Act.

Part I—General

Citation, Commencement, Revocation and Saving Provisions

1.—(1) These Rules may be cited as the Solicitors (Scotland) Accounts etc Rules 2001.

(2) These Rules shall come into operation on 1st February 2002.

(3) The Scottish Solicitors' Guarantee Fund Rules 1995, the Solicitors (Scotland) Accounts Rules 1997 and the Solicitors (Scotland) Accounts Certificate Rules 1997 are hereby revoked, provided that such revocation—

(a) shall not affect the validity of any application made or other thing done under the Scottish Solicitors' Guarantee Fund Rules 1995, and

(b) shall not cause the interruption of the time periods specified in rules 13 and 14 of the Solicitors (Scotland) Accounts Rules 1997 or rule 3 of the Solicitors (Scotland) Accounts Certificate Rules 1997 nor affect any obligation to deliver a Certificate (whether (i) outstanding at the date of revocation or (ii) in respect of the accounting period (under the Solicitors (Scotland) Accounts Certificate Rules 1997) which ends after the date of revocation) in terms of the Solicitors (Scotland) Accounts Certificate Rules 1997 nor the rights of the Society against any solicitor in respect of his failure to deliver such a Certificate.

Interpretation

2.—(1) In these Rules, unless the context otherwise requires

"accounting period" shall mean—

(a) a period not exceeding six months in duration, the first period commencing on the expiry of the immediately preceding accounting period (under the Solicitors (Scotland) Accounts Certificate Rules 1997) after the commencement of these Rules and each period thereafter commencing on the expiry of the immediately preceding period; or

(b) where there is no such immediately preceding accounting period a period not exceeding six months in duration, the first period commencing on the date on which Part II of these Rules applies to the solicitor or, having ceased to apply, applies again to that solicitor and each period thereafter commencing on the expiry of the immediately preceding period;

"the Act" means the Solicitors (Scotland) Act 1980;

"balance his books" means to prepare and bring to a balance a trial balance being a schedule or list of balances both debit and credit extracted from the accounts in both firm and client ledgers and including the cash and bank balances from the cash book;

"bank" means the Bank of England, the National Savings Bank, the Post Office in the exercise of its powers to provide banking services and an institution authorised under the Banking Act 1987 and which operates within the bankers' automated clearing system provided however that an authorised bank not operating within the bankers' automated clearing system may be approved by the Council for the purposes of this sub-paragraph;

"Certificate" shall mean a certificate in the form set out in Schedule 1, 2a or 2b (as the case may be) to these Rules, or in such other form as the Council may from time to time approve;

"client account" means a current, deposit, or savings account or other form of account or a deposit receipt at a branch of a bank in the United Kingdom in the name of the solicitor in the title of which the word "client", "trustee", "trust", or other fiduciary term appears and includes an account or a deposit receipt with a bank, a deposit, share or other account with a building society authorised under the Building Societies Act 1986, a current or general account with a building society operating such an account within the bankers automated clearing system or an account showing sums on loan to a local authority being in such cases in name of the solicitor for a client whose name is specified in the title of the account or receipt;

"clients' money" means money (not belonging to him) received by a solicitor whether as a solicitor or as a trustee in the course of his practice;

"the Council" means the Council of the Society;

"incorporated practice" shall have the meaning given in section 34(1)(A) of the Act;

"local authority" means a council within the meaning of the Local Government etc. (Scotland) Act 1994;

[1] "Money Laundering Regulations" means the Money Laundering Regulations 2007 (S.I. 2007 No. 2157);

[1] "relevant person" has the meaning given by Regulation 2(1) of the Money Laundering Regulations;

"partner" means a partner of a firm of solicitors or a director or member of an incorporated practice which is a company or a member of an incorporated practice which is a limited liability partnership;

"print-out" means a printed or typewritten copy of any account or other information stored in a computer;

"the Society" means the Law Society of Scotland;

[2] "solicitor" means a solicitor holding a practising certificate under the Act and includes a firm of solicitors and an incorporated practice and also includes a registered foreign lawyer and a multi-national practice; and

"practice year" shall have the meaning given in section 65(1) of the Act.

(2) The Interpretation Act 1978 applies to the interpretation of these Rules as it applies to the interpretation of an Act of Parliament.

NOTES

[1] As amended by Solicitors (Scotland) Accounts, Accounts Certificate, Professional Practice and Guarantee Fund (Amendment) Rules 2004, Sch.1 (effective September 1, 2004) and by the Solicitors (Scotland) Accounts etc. (Amendment No.2) Rules 2007, r.3 (effective December 15, 2007).

[2] As amended by the Solicitors (Scotland) (Registered Foreign Lawyers) etc. Practice Rules 2005, Sch.5 (effective May 1, 2005).

Rules not to apply to solicitors in certain employments

3.—(1) Parts II and III of these Rules shall not apply to a solicitor who is in any of the employments mentioned in sub-sections (4)(a), (b) and (c) of section 35 of the Act so far as regards movies received, held or paid by him in the course of that employment.

(2) Parts IV, V and VI of these Rules shall not apply to such a solicitor as is referred to in paragraph (1) of this Rule so far as regards anything done or omitted to be done by him in the course of that employment.

Part II—Accounts rules

Clients' money to be paid into client account

4.—(1) Subject to the provisions of Rule 7 every solicitor shall—

(a) ensure that at all times the sum at the credit of the client account, or where there are more such accounts than one, the total of the sums at the credit of those accounts, shall not be less than the total of the clients' money held by the solicitor; and

(b) pay into a client account without delay any sum of money exceeding £50 held for or received from or on behalf of a client.

(2) Where money is held by the solicitor in a client account in which the name of the client is specified and where no money is due to that client by the solicitor or the amount due is less than the amount in the specified client account, the sum in that account or, as the case may be, the excess, shall not be treated as clients' money for the purposes of paragraph (1)(a) of this Rule.

(3) Nothing herein contained shall—

(a) empower a solicitor, without the express written authority of the client, to deposit any money held by the solicitor for that client with a bank or on share, deposit or other account with a building society or on loan account with a local authority in name of the solicitor for that client, except on such terms as will enable the amount of the share or deposit or loan or any part thereof to be uplifted or withdrawn on notice not exceeding one calendar month;

(b) relieve a solicitor of his responsibilities to the client to ensure that all sums belonging to that client and held in a client account in terms of these Rules are available when required for that client or for that client's purpose; and

(c) preclude the overdrawing by a solicitor of a client account in which the name of the client for whom it is held is specified where that client has given written authority to overdraw, and an overdraft on such account shall not be taken into account to ensure compliance with paragraph (1)(a) of this Rule.

Other payments to client accounts

5. There may be paid into a client account—

(a) such money belonging to the solicitor as may be necessary for the purpose of opening the account or required to ensure compliance with Rule 4(1)(a); and

(b) money to replace any sum which may by mistake or accident have been withdrawn from the account.

Drawings from client account

6.—(1) So long as money belonging to one client is not withdrawn without his written authority for the purpose of meeting a payment to or on behalf of another client, there may be drawn from a client account—

(a) money required for payment to or on behalf of a client;

(b) money required for or to account of payment of a debt due to the solicitor by a client or in or to account of repayment of money expended by the solicitor on behalf of a client;

(c) money drawn on a client's authority;

(d) money properly required for or to account of payment of the solicitor's professional account against a client which has been debited to the ledger account of the client in the solicitor's books and where a copy of said account has been rendered;

(e) money for transfer to a separate client account kept or to be kept for the client only;

(f) money which may have been paid into the account under paragraph (a) of Rule 5 and which is no longer required to ensure compliance with Rule 4(1)(a); and

(g) money which may by mistake or accident have been paid into the account.

[1] (2) Where money drawn from a client account by cheque is payable to a person's account with any bank or building society, the cash book and ledger entries relating thereto and said cheque shall include the name of the person whose account is to be credited with the payment.

NOTE

[1] As amended by Solicitors (Scotland) Accounts, Accounts Certificate, Professional Practice and Guarantee Fund (Amendment) Rules 2004, Sch.1 (effective September 1, 2004).

Exceptions from Rule 4

7. Notwithstanding any of the provisions of this Part of these Rules, a solicitor shall not be obliged to pay into a client account, but shall be required to record in his books, clients' money held or received by him—

(a) in the form of cash which is without delay paid in cash to the client or a third party on the client's behalf;
(b) in the form of a cheque or draft or other bill of exchange which is endorsed over to the client or to a third party on the client's behalf and which is not passed by the solicitor through a bank account;
(c) which he pays without delay into a separate bank, building society or local authority deposit account opened or to be opened in name of the client or of some person named by the client;
(d) which the client for his own convenience has requested the solicitor in writing to withhold from such account;
(e) for or to account of payment of a debt due to the solicitor from the client or in repayment in whole or in part of money expended by the solicitor on behalf of the client; or
(f) expressly on account of a professional account incurred to the solicitor by the client, or as an agreed fee or to account of an agreed fee for business done by the solicitor for the client where a copy of said account has been rendered.

Accounts required to be kept in books of solicitor

8.—(1) A solicitor shall at all times keep properly written up such books and accounts as are necessary—

(a) to show all his dealing with—
  (i) clients' money held or received or paid or in any way intromitted with by him;
  (ii) any other money dealt with by him through a client account;
  (iii) any bank overdrafts or loans procured by him in his own name for behoof of a client or clients; and
  (iv) any other money held by the solicitor in a separate account in the title of which the client's name is specified; and
(b) (i) to show separately in respect of each client all money of the categories specified in sub-paragraph (a) of this paragraph which is received, held or paid by him on account of that client; and
  (ii) to distinguish all money of the said categories received, held or paid by him from any other money received, held or paid by him.

(2) Without prejudice to paragraph (1) above, this Rule shall apply to money received or payments made by a solicitor by virtue of any power of attorney in his favour.

(3) All dealings referred to in paragraph (1) of this Rule shall be recorded—

(a) in a clients' cash book, or a clients' column of a cash book, or
(b) in a record of sums transferred from the ledger account of one client to that of another, as may be appropriate, and in addition in a clients' ledger or a clients' column of a ledger.

(4) Every solicitor shall—

(a) at all times keep properly written up such books and accounts as are necessary to show the true financial position of his practice; and

(b) balance his books monthly and on the last day of each accounting period.

(5) The "books", "accounts", "ledger" and "records" referred to in these Rules shall be deemed to include loose-leaf books and such cards or other permanent records as are necessary for the operation of any system of book-keeping, mechanical or computerised.

(6) Where a solicitor maintains the accounts required by these Rules on a computerised system which does not rely on a visible ledger card for its operation such system must be such that—

(a) an immediate print-out can be obtained of any account notwithstanding that immediate visual access is available; and

(b) all accounts which for any reason may require to be removed from the working store of the system must before removal be copied on to a storage medium which will enable a visual record of the detailed entries therein to be produced and be filed in alphabetical or other suitable order, indexed and retained for the period set out in paragraph (7) of this Rule.

(7) A solicitor shall preserve for at least ten years from the date of the last entry therein all books and accounts kept by him under this Rule or a copy thereof in a form which will enable a visible record of the detailed entries therein to be produced from such a copy.

Client bank statements to be regularly reconciled

9.—(1) Every solicitor shall within one month of the coming into force of these Rules or of his commencing practice on his own account (either alone or in partnership or as an incorporated practice), and thereafter at intervals not exceeding one month, cause the balance between the client bank lodged and drawn columns of his cash book or the balance of his client bank ledger account as the case may be to be agreed with his client bank statements and shall retain such reconciliation statements showing this agreement for a period of three years from the dates they were respectively carried out.

(2) On the same date or dates specified in paragraph (1) of this Rule every solicitor shall extract from his clients' ledger a list of balances due by him to clients and prepare a statement comparing the total of the said balances with the reconciled balance in the client bank account and retain such lists of balances and statements for a period of three years from the dates they were respectively carried out.

Client funds invested in specified accounts

[1]**10.**—(1) Every solicitor shall within three months of the coming into force of these Rules or of his commencing practice on his own account (either alone or in partnership or as an incorporated practice or as a member of a multi-national practice), and thereafter at intervals not exceeding three months and coinciding with the date of a reconciliation in terms of Rule 9 hereof, cause the balance between the client deposited and withdrawn columns of his cash book or the balance on his client invested funds ledger account as the case may be to be agreed with his client passbooks, building society printouts, special deposit accounts, local authority deposits, joint deposits or other statements or certificates and shall retain such reconciliation statements showing this agreement for a period of three years from the dates they were respectively carried out.

(2) On the same date or dates specified in paragraph (1) of this Rule every solicitor shall extract from his client ledger a list of funds invested by him in his name for specified clients and prepare a statement comparing the total of the said balances with the reconciled investment funds and retain such lists of balances and statements for a period of three years from the dates they were respectively carried out.

NOTE
[1] As amended by the Solicitors (Scotland) (Registered Foreign Lawyers) etc. Practice Rules 2005, Sch.5 (effective May 1, 2005).

Interest to be earned for a client

11.—(1) Where a solicitor holds money for or on account of a client and, having regard to the amount of such money and the length of time for which it or any part of it is likely to be held, it is reasonable that interest should be earned for the client, the solicitor shall so soon as practicable place money or, as the case may be, such part thereof, in a separate interest bearing client account in the title of which the client's name is specified and shall account to the client for any interest earned thereon, failing which the solicitor shall pay to the client out of his own money a sum equivalent to the interest which would have accrued for the benefit of the client if the sum he ought to have placed in such an interest bearing client account under this Rule had been so placed.

(2) Without prejudice to the generality of paragraph (1) of this Rule it shall be deemed reasonable that interest should be earned for a client from the date on which a solicitor receives for or on account of the client a sum of money not less than £500 which at the time of its receipt is unlikely within two months thereafter to be either wholly disbursed or reduced by payments to a sum less than £500.

(3) Without prejudice to any other remedy which may be available, any client who feels aggrieved that interest has not been paid under this Rule shall be entitled to require the solicitor to obtain a certificate from the Society as to whether or not interest ought to have been earned and, if so, the amount of such interest, and upon the issue of such certificate any interest certified to be due shall be payable by the solicitor to the client.

(4) Nothing in this Rule shall affect any arrangement in writing, whenever made, between a solicitor and his client as to the application of a client's money or interest thereon provided such arrangement was made prior to the said application.

(5) For the purposes of this Rule only, money held by a solicitor for or on account of a client—

(a) for the purpose of paying stamp duty, recording dues or other outlays on behalf of the client; or

(b) for or to account of the solicitor's professional account where said account has been rendered,

shall not be regarded as clients' money.

Application of Rules in case of firm of solicitors or incorporated practice

[1] **12.**—(1) Each partner of a firm of solicitors or member of an incorporated practice or a multi-national practice shall be responsible for securing compliance by the firm or incorporated practice or a multi-national practice with the provisions of these Rules.

(2) Without prejudice to paragraph (1) of this Rule within one month of the coming into force of these Rules or of its commencing practice on its own account every firm of solicitors or incorporated practice or a multi-national practice shall designate one or more of the partners of the firm or the directors or members of the incorporated practice or a multi-national practice as Designated Cashroom Partner or Partners who will be responsible for the supervision of the staff and systems employed by the firm or incorporated practice or a multi-national practice to carry out the provisions of these Rules and for securing compliance by the firm or incorporated practice or a multi-national practice with the provisions of these Rules.

(3) Every firm of solicitors or incorporated practice shall deliver to the Council a Certificate listing the name or names of the Designated Cashroom Partner or Partners and the period or periods in respect of which he was, or

they were, designated during the accounting period in respect of which the Certificate is delivered.

NOTES

[1] As amended by the Solicitors (Scotland) (Registered Foreign Lawyers) etc. Practice Rules 2005, Sch.5 (effective May 1, 2005).

Savings of right of solicitor against client

13. Nothing in these Rules shall deprive a solicitor of or prejudice him with reference to any recourse or right in law, whether by way of lien, set-off, counter-claim, charge or otherwise, against monies standing to the credit of a client account or against monies due to a client by a third party.

Part III—Accounts certificate

Obligation to deliver a Certificate

14.—(1) A solicitor shall deliver to the Council within one calendar month of the completion of each accounting period a Certificate in respect of that period. In respect of an accounting period for which no client monies have been held the Certificate shall be in the form set out in Schedule 2a or 2b to these Rules and in all other cases shall be in the form set out in Schedule 1 to these Rules.

(2) The Council may, in any case on cause satisfactory to it being shown, extend the period of one calendar month within which a Certificate is required following a balancing of books, but such extension shall in no case exceed three months from the date on which the Certificate should have been delivered.

Who may sign a Certificate

15. The Certificate under these Rules must be signed by two partners, one of whom must be the current Designated Cashroom Partner, unless the solicitor is a sole practitioner.

Where solicitor practises in two or more places

16. In the case of a solicitor who has two or more places of business and where separate books and accounts are maintained for each office a separate Certificate shall be submitted in respect of each such place of business. In any such case the client account balance shall be struck on the same date in respect of each place of business.

Notice to a solicitor under this Part and Part II of these Rules

[2 1] **17.** Every notice to be given by the Council under this Part or Part II of these Rules to a solicitor shall be in writing and signed by the Secretary of the Society or a Director of the Society and shall be sent by recorded delivery post to the solicitor at his place of business as defined in the Constitution of the Society or in the case of a solicitor who has ceased to hold a practising certificate at his last known address, and shall be deemed to have been received by the solicitor within forty-eight hours of the time of posting. In the case of a firm or incorporated practice or multi-national practice the written notice shall be given to each person who is known to the Council to be a partner of the firm, or a director of the incorporated practice (where that incorporated practice is a company), or a member of the incorporated practice (where that incorporated practice is a limited liability partnership) or a member of the multi-national practice and it shall not be necessary to give notice to the firm or incorporated practice or multi-national practice also.

NOTE

[1] As amended by the Solicitors (Scotland) (Registered Foreign Lawyers) etc. Practice Rules 2005, Sch.5 (effective May 1, 2005).

[2] As amended by the Solicitors (Scotland) Accounts, etc (Amendment) Rules 2006, s.3(1), (effective December 1, 2006).

Reservation of power of Council to require an inspection or authorise an investigation

18. The delivery of a Certificate to the Council in terms of these Rules shall not prejudice the power of the Council to require an inspection or to authorise an investigation as provided for in Rule 19 of these Rules.

Part IV—Inspections and Investigations

Inspections and investigations on behalf of Council

19.—(1) To enable the Council to ascertain—

(a) whether or not these Rules are being complied with, and

(b) whether or not the practice of the solicitor is being conducted in such a manner as may put at risk the interests of the public or the interests of the profession,

the Council may, by written notice, require any solicitor to produce at a time to be fixed by the Council and at a place to be fixed by the Council, or in the option of the solicitor at his place of business, documents, records and other information concerning the conduct of his practice (in this Rule referred to as "documents, records and other information") including, without prejudice to the foregoing generality, his books of account, bank passbooks, loose leaf bank statements, deposit receipts, documents of joint deposit, building society pass books, local authority deposits, separate statements of bank overdrafts or loans procured by him in his own name or for a client or clients, statements of account, vouchers, magnetic storage disks, print-outs, microfilm records, relative correspondence and any powers of attorney in his favour for the inspection of a person or persons authorised by the Council.

(2) If at any time there is a reasonable apprehension on the part of the Council

(a) that a solicitor has not complied with, is not complying with or may not comply with these Rules, or

(b) that the practice of the solicitor has been, is being or may be being conducted in such a manner as may put at risk the interests of the public or the interests of the profession,

the Council may authorise a person or persons to conduct such investigation into the conduct of the solicitor and his practice as the Council may consider appropriate. The Council shall, subject to paragraph (5) of this Rule, give written notice of its authorisation of such a person or persons to conduct such investigation to the solicitor concerned.

(3) It shall be the duty of a solicitor to provide a person or persons authorised by the Council under paragraph (1) or (2) of this Rule reasonable co-operation in the conduct of that person's or persons' inspection or investigation (as the case may be) including, without prejudice to the foregoing generality, the production of documents, records and other information as such person or persons may reasonably require.

(4) Any person or persons authorised by the Council under paragraph (1) or (2) of this Rule shall report to the Council upon the result of his inspection or investigation (as the case may be).

[2,1](5) A written notice given by the Council to a solicitor under paragraph (1) or (2) and, where appropriate, paragraph (6) of this Rule shall be signed by the Secretary of the Society or a Director of the Society and shall be sent by recorded delivery post to the solicitor at his place of business as defined in the Constitution of the Society or in the case of a solicitor who has ceased to hold a practising certificate at his last known address, and shall be deemed to have been received by the solicitor within forty-eight hours of the time of posting. In the case of a firm or incorporated practice or multi-national practice the written notice shall be given to each person who is known to the Council to be a partner of the firm, or a director of the incorporated practice

(where that incorporated practice is a company), or a member of the incorporated practice (where that incorporated practice is a limited liability partnership) or a member of the multi-national practice and it shall not be necessary to give notice to the firm or incorporated practice or multi-national practice also. Notwithstanding the provisions of this paragraph, if, in a case falling within paragraph (2) of this Rule, the Council shall reasonably consider that urgent action is required to protect the interests of the public or the interests of the profession, the Council may dispense with the notice required in terms of this paragraph and make such other order as to notification as it considers appropriate.

[4] (6) Where, following an inspection of the documents, records and other information of a solicitor in terms of paragraph (1) of this Rule or an investigation in terms of paragraph (2) of this Rule, or following any further inspection or investigation in terms of this paragraph, it appears to the Council that the solicitor has not complied with these Rules or that the practice of the solicitor has been or is being conducted in such a manner as may put at risk the interests of the public or the interests of the profession, the Council may instruct a further inspection of the documents, records and other information of the solicitor or a further investigation. If it so instructs, the Council may by written notice require the solicitor to pay, or agree with the solicitor that he will pay, to the Council the reasonable costs of any such further inspection or investigation, provided always that such written notice is given to the solicitor, or such agreement is reached with the solicitor, not more than twelve months after the date of the immediately preceding inspection or investigation.

[3] (7) The costs referred to in paragraph (6) of this Rule shall be determined by reference to a daily rate which shall be fixed by the Council from time to time. The amount of any such costs shall be intimated by a Director of the Society to the solicitor following such further inspection or investigation.

[5] (8) It shall be the duty of a solicitor upon whom a notice in terms of paragraph (6) of this Rule has been served or with whom an agreement in terms of paragraph (6) of this Rule has been reached to make payment forthwith of the amount of costs intimated in terms of paragraph (7) of this Rule.

(9) Any sum paid to the Council in terms of paragraph (8) of this Rule shall accrue to the Guarantee Fund.

NOTES

[1] As amended by the Solicitors (Scotland) (Registered Foreign Lawyers) etc. Practice Rules 2005, Sch.5 (effective May 1, 2005).

[2] As amended by the Solicitors (Scotland) Accounts, etc (Amendment) Rules 2006, s.3(2), (effective December 1, 2006).

[3] As amended by the Solicitors (Scotland) Accounts, etc (Amendment) Rules 2006, s.3(3), (effective December 1, 2006).

[4] As amended by the Solicitors (Scotland) Accounts, etc (Amendment) Rules 2007, s.3(1) (effective May 1, 2007).

[5] As amended by the Solicitors (Scotland) Accounts, etc (Amendment) Rules 2007, s.3(2) (effective May 1, 2007).

PART V—PROFESSIONAL PRACTICE

Bridging loans

20. A solicitor shall not enter into or maintain any contract or arrangement with a bank or other lender in terms of which the solicitor may draw down loan or overdraft facilities in his name on behalf of clients unless—

(1) the solicitor shall, in every case before drawing down any sums in terms of such contract or arrangement, have intimated in writing to the bank or other lender—

(a) the name and present address of the client for whom the loan or overdraft facilities are required; and

(b) the arrangements for repayment of the loan or overdraft facilities; and

(2) the contract or arrangement does not impose personal liability for repayment of any such loan or overdraft facilities on the solicitor.

Borrowing from clients

21. A solicitor shall not borrow money from his client unless his client is in the business of lending money or his client has been independently advised in regard to the making of the loan.

Prohibition on solicitor acting for lender to the solicitor or connected persons

22.—[1,2,3] (1) No solicitor shall, and nor shall that solicitor's firm or incorporated practice or multi-national practice, act for or pursuant to the written requirements of a lender in the constitution, variation, assignation or discharge of a standard security securing a loan which has been advanced or is to be advanced to or has been guaranteed or is to be guaranteed by—

(a) the solicitor, where he is a sole practitioner or a partner of a firm or a member of an incorporated practice or multi-national practice,

(b) the solicitor's spouse or civil partner, where the solicitor is a sole practitioner or a partner of a firm or a member of an incorporated practice or multi-national practice,

(c) any partner of the solicitor,

(d) the spouse or civil partner of any such partner,

(e) any sole practitioner who, or partner of a firm or member of an incorporated practice or multi-national practice which, employs the solicitor, or the spouse or civil partner of any such sole practitioner, partner or member,

(f) any firm or incorporated practice or multi-national practice which employs the solicitor,

(g) any incorporated practice or multi-national practice of which the solicitor or his spouse or civil partner is a member,

(h) any partnership or limited partnership of which any of the persons specified in sub-paragraphs (a) to (g) inclusive of this paragraph is a partner or member, or

(i) any company in which any person specified in sub-paragraphs (a) to (h) inclusive of this paragraph holds shares, whether directly or indirectly, other than a holding amounting to not more than 5% of the issued shares in a public company quoted on a recognised stock exchange.

(2) For the avoidance of doubt, rule 5(1)(f) of the Solicitors (Scotland) Practice Rules 1986 shall not apply to any such loan as is referred to in paragraph (1).

(3) For the purposes of this Rule "loan" shall include an obligation ad factum praestandum or any obligation to pay money and "lender" shall include any person to whom said obligation is owed.

(4) This Rule shall not apply if—

(a) the lender to any of the persons specified in paragraph (1) is the solicitor, or

[1] (b) the borrower's obligations under the standard security have been fully implemented before the solicitor accepts instructions or in any way begins to act in relation to the discharge of such standard security.

(5) The Council shall have power to waive any of the provisions of this Rule in any particular circumstances or case. Any waiver may be granted subject to such conditions as the Council shall think fit.

NOTES

[1] As amended by Solicitors (Scotland) Accounts, Accounts Certificate, Professional Practice and Guarantee Fund (Amendment) Rules 2004, Sch.1 (effective September 1, 2004).

[2] As amended by the Solicitors (Scotland) (Registered Foreign Lawyers) etc. Practice Rules 2005, Sch.5 (effective May 1, 2005).

[3] As amended by the Solicitors (Scotland) (Miscellaneous Amendments) Rules 2006, Rule 3 Sch.1(4).

Powers of Attorney

23.—(1) This Rule shall, subject to paragraph (2) below, apply to movies received or payments made by a solicitor by virtue of any power of attorney in his favour.

(2) In the event of any power of attorney granted in favour of a solicitor continuing to have effect by virtue of sections 15 or 88 of the Adults with Incapacity (Scotland) Act 2000 any money of the granter held or received by the solicitor shall be clients' money.

(3) Every solicitor shall deliver to the Council a list of any powers of attorney in the solicitor's favour held or granted during an accounting period, the list to be as set out in the Certificate.

Money laundering

[1] **24.**—[2](1) Every solicitor shall, in respect of all business carried on by the solicitor in relation to which the solicitor is not a relevant person, comply with the provisions of the Money Laundering Regulations as if the solicitor were a relevant person.

[2](2) For the avoidance of doubt, paragraph (1) is without prejudice to the application of the Money Laundering Regulations to all business carried on by a solicitor in respect of which the solicitor is a relevant person.

(3) Every solicitor shall comply with the provisions of Part 7 of the Proceeds of Crime Act 2002.

NOTE

[1] As amended by Solicitors (Scotland) Accounts, Accounts Certificate, Professional Practice and Guarantee Fund (Amendment) Rules 2004, Sch.1 (effective September 1, 2004).

[2] As amended by the Solicitors (Scotland) Accounts etc. (Amendment No.2) Rules 2007, r.4 (effective December 15, 2007).

Part VI Guarantee Fund

Interpretation for Part VI

25. In this Part of these Rules, unless the context otherwise requires—

(a) "the Fund" means the Scottish Solicitors Guarantee Fund;

[2] (b) "the Secretary" means the Secretary of the Society;

(c) "loss" means pecuniary loss by reason of dishonesty on the part of

(i) any solicitor in practice in the United Kingdom, or any employee of such solicitor in connection with the practice of the solicitor, and whether or not he had a practising certificate in force when the act of dishonesty was committed, and notwithstanding that subsequent to the commission of that act he may have died or had his name removed from or struck off the Roll of Solicitors or may have ceased to practise or been suspended from practice; or

[1] (ii) any incorporated practice or multi-national practice or any director, manager, secretary or other employee of an incorporated practice or member or other employee of a multi-national practice, notwithstanding that subsequent to the commission of that act it may have ceased to be recognised under section 34(1)(A) of the Act or to be a multi-national practice or have been wound up.

NOTE

[1] As amended by the Solicitors (Scotland) (Registered Foreign Lawyers) etc. Practice Rules 2005, Sch.5 (effective May 1, 2005).

[2] As amended by the Solicitors (Scotland) Accounts, etc (Amendment) Rules 2006, s.3(4), (effective December 1, 2006).

Payments into and out of the Fund

26.—(1) There shall be carried to the credit of the Fund—

(a) All contributions paid by solicitors under section 43 of, and Schedule 3 to, the Act;

(b) All interest, dividends and other income, and accretions of capital arising from investments of the Fund;

(c) All moneys borrowed for the purposes of the Fund;

(d) All sums received by the Society in respect of contracts of insurance entered into under paragraph 3 of Schedule 3 to the Act;

(e) All sums recovered by the Society in consequence of the provisions of sub-paragraph (2) of paragraph 4 of Schedule 3 to the Act; and

(f) Any other moneys which may belong or accrue to the Fund or be received by the Society in respect of the Fund.

(2) There shall from time to time be paid out of the Fund

(a) The expenses of constituting and administering the Fund, including the remuneration of officers and employees of, and other expenses incurred by, the Society in relation to the Fund under or in the exercise of powers conferred by the Act;

(b) All grants made by the Society under section 43 of the Act;

(c) All premiums payable by the Society under contracts of insurance entered into under paragraph 3 of Schedule 3 to the Act;

(d) All interest and other sums payable in respect of sums borrowed by the Society for the purposes of the Fund; and

(e) Any other moneys payable out of the Fund in accordance with the Act or any Rules relating to the Fund made thereunder.

27. (1) Any person who wishes to apply to the Society for a grant from the Fund in respect of a loss shall, as soon as is reasonably practicable after the date on which the loss first came to his or her knowledge and in any event within 12 months of that date, make an application in or substantially in the form set out in Schedule 3 to these Rules and shall deliver the same to the Secretary.

(2) The Council shall be entitled to treat an application as having been abandoned if such documents and other evidence as the Council may demand in terms of paragraph 4(1) of Schedule 3 to the Act are not produced to it within three months of any such demand.

Council may require institution of proceedings

28. The Council before deciding whether or not to make a grant out of the Fund may require in respect of any application the pursuit by the applicant of any civil remedy which may be available in respect of the loss or the taking by him or her of steps with a view to the institution of criminal proceedings in respect of the dishonesty leading to the loss or the making of a complaint to the Scottish Solicitors' Discipline Tribunal.

Council may waive requirements

29. The Council may, in any case on cause satisfactory to it being shown, waive any of the provisions of this Part of these Rules as regards the time limits within which an application may be made or oral evidence may be tendered or documents or information produced.

Notice by Council

30. Any requirement of the Council under this Part of these Rules may be communicated by a notice in writing which may be delivered personally or sent by recorded delivery post to the addressee at his or her last known address. Any such notice sent by post shall be deemed to have been received by the addressee within forty-eight hours of the time of posting.

[1] SCHEDULE I

NOTE
[1] As amended April 2007.

FORM OF CERTIFICATE

(IN RESPECT OF AN ACCOUNTING PERIOD ENDING ON OR AFTER 1 AUGUST 2006).

The Secretary
The Law Society of Scotland
26 Drumsheugh Gardens
Edinburgh EH3 7YR

Dear Sir

I/We confirm that, within the premises at (Note(a)), ...
....
being the address at which I/we carry on practice as solicitor(s) that I/we have maintained the necessary books of account, bank passbooks, bank statements, deposit receipts including building society or local authority deposits, statements, deposit receipts and other accounting records required by the Solicitors (Scotland) Accounts etc. Rules 2001 for the accounting period from .... to ....and I/we certify subject to the points referred to under item 4 of additional matters noted overleaf:

Note (b)
1) That the accounting records are up to date and balanced as at the last day of the accounting period, and
2) That the accounting records, to the best of my/our knowledge and belief, are in accordance with the terms of the Solicitors (Scotland) Accounts etc. Rules 2001, and
3) That all outstanding reconciling entries noted as at the balance dates disclosed overleaf under Rules 9 and 10 have been entered in the records or confirmed as correct, and
4) That the following Powers of Attorney were held by the undernoted or granted in favour of the undernoted during the accounting period:

GRANTER ATTORNEY DATE GRANTED

and

5) That during the said accounting period the Designated Cashroom Partner(s) in terms of Rule 12 of the Solicitors (Scotland) Accounts etc. Rules 2001 was/were as follows:

NAME DATE DESIGNATED DATE DESIGNATION CEASED

6) That during that time the Money Laundering Reporting Officer(s) in terms of Rule 24 of the Solicitors (Scotland) Accounts etc. Rules 2001 was/were as follows:

NAME DATE APPOINTED DATE APPOINTMENT CEASED

I solemnly and sincerely declare that the information given by me in this Certificate is true to the best of my knowledge and belief.

CURRENT DESIGNATED CASHROOM PARTNER

(FULL NAME) ....

SIGNATURE .... DATE ....

SECOND SIGNATORY

(FULL NAME) ....

SIGNATURE .... DATE ....

ADDITIONAL MATTERS

1.	Client account reconciliations as at	....	....
	Note (c)		
	(i) (a) Monies held on general client account	£	£ ....
	(b) Monies due to clients	£	£ ....
	(c) Surplus or deficit	£	£ ....
	(ii) (a) Funds held for named clients	£	£ ....
	(b) Monies due to named clients	£	£ ....
	(iii) (a) Loans for named clients	£	£ ....
	(b) Balances due by named clients	£	£ ....
	Note (d)		
2.	Firm's account balances		
	Due to the firm	£	£ ....
	Due by the firm	£	£ ....

[1] 3. If the assistance of an external accountant was needed to prepare this Certificate, please indicate the scope of the assistance here. (If none, state NONE):

Note (e)

4. Other matters which require to be reported:
(If no other matters, state NONE)

NOTES

(a) State addresses of all places of business of the solicitor or firm of solicitors in respect of whom the Certificate is granted.

(b) This balance is to be a balance of the whole books covering client and non-client accounts.

(c) These dates are those quarterly dates required to be reconciled under the terms of Rule 10.

(d) These balances should disclose bridging loans taken on behalf of named clients under Rule 20.

[1](e) It is anticipated that many solicitors will instruct an external accountant to assist them in the checking of the accounting records and/or the preparation of the Certificate in respect of investment business. If the services of an external accountant are required you should indicate the extent of the help offered. The following tasks are examples of the assistance which may be obtained from the accountant:

1) The preparation of day books, ledgers and other records for client's or firm's accounting records; or
2) Reconciling the funds' position under Rules 9 and 10; or
3) Testing for compliance with aspects of the Accounts Rules as agreed per a letter of engagement; or
4) Balancing the client's or firm's accounting records; or
5) Conducting a review of compliance with all aspects of the Accounts Rules in support of the solicitor's certification of compliance with the Rules.

NOTES

[1] As amended or inserted by the Solicitors (Scotland) Accounts, Accounts Certificate, Professional Practice and Guarantee Fund (Amendment) Rules 2004, Sch.1 (effective September 1, 2004).

[1] SCHEDULE 2a

NOTE
[1] As amended February 2005 and April 2007.

FORM OF CERTIFICATE

Solicitors (Scotland) Accounts etc Rules 2001

(In respect of an Accounting Period for which **no client monies have been held**)

NAME: ....

BUSINESS ADDRESS:

....

....

Tel No: .... Fax No: ....

I hereby confirm to the Council of the Law Society of Scotland that:

(Note 1) (a) I/We have contributed to the Guarantee Fund in respect of the practice year;
(b) I/We submit accounts to the Scottish Legal Aid Board for payment to my/our own account;
(c) I/We make any payments due to third parties from my/our bank account in advance or not later than the date on which the matching remittance is lodged in the firm bank account.
(Note 2) (d) I/We have not handled client monies during the accounting period
from: ....
to: ....
(e) If circumstances change with the result that I/we require to hold or intromit with client monies, I/we shall immediately advise the Council.

I solemnly and sincerely declare that the information given by me in this Certificate is true to the best of my knowledge and belief.

CURRENT DESIGNATED CASHROOM PARTNER

(FULL NAME) ....

SIGNATURE .... DATE ....

SECOND SIGNATORY

(FULL NAME) ....

SIGNATURE .... DATE ....

Note 1. The current practice year for this figure commences on 1st November within the accounting year which includes the six-month period shown at item (d);
Note 2. The accounting period must be six months or less and follow immediately on from the previous accounting period without a gap or overlap in the dates concerned.

[1] SCHEDULE 2b

NOTE
[1] As amended April 2007.

FORM OF CERTIFICATE

Solicitors (Scotland) Accounts etc Rules 2001

(In respect of an Accounting Period ending on or after 1 August 2006 for which **no client monies have been held**)

Name: ....

Address:
....

....

Tel No: ....

Fax No: ....

E-mail: ....

I hereby confirm to the Council of the Law Society of Scotland:

(a) I have contributed to the Guarantee Fund in respect of the practice year; (*Note 1)
(b) I act solely as an agent for other solicitors, or I render fee notes directly to private clients before being paid a fee for work done.
(c) I do not submit accounts to the Scottish Legal Aid Board and have not received any fee directly from them.
(d) I have not handled client monies during the accounting period and have not operated a client bank account.
(e) If circumstances change with the result that I require to hold or intromit with client monies, I shall immediately advise the Council.
(f) Accounting Period: (*Note 2)
From..To..

I solemnly and sincerely declare that the information given by me in this Certificate is true to the best of my knowledge and belief.

FULL NAME ....

SIGNATURE ....

DATE ....

*Note 1. The current practice year for this figure commences on 1st November within the accounting year which includes the six-month period shown at item (e).
*Note 2. The accounting period must be six months or less and follow immediately on from the previous accounting period without a gap or overlap in the dates concerned.

SCHEDULE 3

THE LAW SOCIETY OF SCOTLAND
THE SCOTTISH SOLICITORS' GUARANTEE FUND

Application Form for a Grant out of the Scottish Solicitors' Guarantee Fund

To: The Law Society of Scotland
The Law Society's Hall
26 Drumsheugh Gardens
Edinburgh EH3 7YR

I, (Full name of applicant) ....
Designation ....
Address ....
....
Post Code .... Telephone Number ....

hereby apply to the Council of The Law Society of Scotland that in the exercise of the absolute discretion conferred upon them by the Solicitors (Scotland) Act 1980, they make to me a grant of £.......................... or such other sum as they may think proper out of the Scottish Solicitors' Guarantee Fund by way of compensation for a pecuniary loss sustained by me by reason of the dishonesty of

Name ....
Designation ....
Address ....
Firm ....
Status in firm if known ....
Date the original notice of claim was sent to the Secretary ....

Schedule of Particulars

Please state as clearly and concisely as you can the answers to the following questions:—

1. Please give details of the loss which you have sustained
....
....
....
....

2. If the money or other property in respect of which your loss has been sustained came into the possession of the solicitor, or his or her employee, please give the date or dates when this happened.
....
....
....
....

3. Please also give full particulars of any such money or property.
....
....
....
....

4. Please explain why you allege dishonesty.
....
....
....
....

5. State the date on which your loss first came to your attention ....

6. Explain briefly how this happened.

....
....
....
....

7. If you have any documents which you think would help your claim, please list them here and enclose a copy of each.

....
....
....
....

8. Are you aware of any other application that may be made in respect of this loss? Yes/no* *Please delete as appropriate.

If yes, please give name and address of other applicant.

....
....
....
....

9. Are you aware of any civil, criminal or disciplinary hearings arising out of this matter? Yes/no* *Please delete as appropriate.

If yes, please give details including the result if known.

....
....
....
....

10. Have you taken court or other proceedings in respect of your loss? Yes/no* *Please delete as appropriate.
(a) If yes, please give brief details.

....
....
....
....

(b) If no, are you considering taking court or other proceedings in respect of your loss? Yes/no* *Please delete as appropriate.

11. Do you have a solicitor acting on your behalf?
Yes/no* *Please delete as appropriate.
If yes, please give his name, firm, address and telephone number

Name ....
Firm ....
Address ....
....
Post Code .... Telephone Number ....

12. Is there **any other relevant information** which you think would be of assistance to the Guarantee Fund Committee in considering your application?
If so, please detail.

....
....
....
....

I solemnly and sincerely declare that the information given by me in this application is true to the best of my knowledge and belief, and I make this solemn declaration conscientiously believing the same to be true, and by virtue of the Statutory Declarations Act 1835.

.... Claimant

Declared at ....
on (date) ....
before me ....

(This application should be signed in the presence of a Notary Public, Commissioner for Oaths, Justice of the Peace or other person authorised to administer oaths.)

INDEX FOR THE SOLICITORS (SCOTLAND) ACCOUNTS, ACCOUNTS CERTIFICATE, PROFESSIONAL PRACTICE AND GUARANTEE FUND RULES 2001

Solicitors (Scotland) Practice Rules 1986

Rules made by the Council of the Law Society of Scotland and approved by the Lord President of the Court of Session pursuant to section 34 of the Solicitors (Scotland) Act 1980.

1.—(1) These rules may be cited as the Solicitors (Scotland) Practice Rules 1986.

(2) These rules shall come into operation with respect to transactions commenced on or after 1st January 1987.

2.—(1) In these rules, unless the context otherwise requires:—

[1] "2005 Rules" means the Solicitors (Scotland) (Registered Foreign Lawyers) etc Practice Rules 2005;

"the Act" means the Solicitors (Scotland) Act 1980;

"client" includes prospective client;

"Council" means the Council of the Society;

"established client" means a person for whom a solicitor or his firm has acted on at least one previous occasion;

"employed solicitor" means a solicitor employed by his employer for the purpose, wholly or partly, of offering legal services to the public whether or not for a fee;

"firm" includes any office at which that firm carries on practice and any firm in which that firm has a direct interest through one or more of its partners, or members;

"the Society" means the Law Society of Scotland established under the Act;

[2] "solicitor" means a solicitor holding a practising certificate under the Act, or an incorporated practice or a firm of solicitors and shall include a registered foreign lawyer to whom these rules apply in terms of rule 4(2) or (3) of the 2005 Rules and a Scottish multinational practice (as defined in rule 7(1) of the 2005 Rules);

"transaction" includes a contract and any negotiations leading thereto.

(2) The Interpretation Act 1978 applies to the interpretation of these rules as it applies to the interpretation of an Act of Parliament.

NOTES

[1] Inserted by the Solicitors (Scotland) (Registered Foreign Lawyers) etc. Practice Rules 2005, Sch.5 (effective May 1, 2005).

[2] As amended by the Solicitors (Scotland) (Registered Foreign Lawyers) etc. Practice Rules 2005, Sch.5 (effective May 1, 2005).

3. A solicitor shall not act for two or more parties whose interests conflict.

4. Without prejudice to the generality of rule 3 hereof an employed solicitor whose only or principal employer is one of the parties to a transaction shall not act for any other party to that transaction; provided always that such solicitor may, where no dispute arises or appears likely to arise between the parties to that transaction, act for more than one party thereto, if and only if:—

(a) the parties are associated companies, public authorities, public bodies, or government departments or agencies;

(b) the parties are connected one with the other within the meaning of section 533 Income and Corporation Taxes Act 1970.

5.—(1) Without prejudice to the generality of rule 3 hereof, a solicitor, or two or more solicitors practising either as principal or employee in the same firm or in the employment of the same employer, shall not at any stage, act for both seller and purchaser in the sale or purchase or conveyance of heritable property, or for both landlord and tenant, or assignor and assignee in a lease of heritable property for value or for lender and borrower in a loan to be secured over heritable property; provided, however, that where no dispute arises or might reasonably be expected to arise between the parties and that, other than in the case of exception (a) hereto, the seller or landlord of residential property is not a builder or developer, this rule shall not apply if:—

(a) the parties are associated companies, public authorities, public bodies, or government departments or agencies;

[1] (b) the parties are connected one with the other within the meaning of section 839 Income and Corporation Taxes Act 1988;

[2] (c) the parties are related by blood, adoption, marriage or civil partnership, one to the other, or the purchaser, tenant, assignee or borrower is so related to an established client; or

(d) both parties are established clients or the prospective purchaser, tenant, assignee or borrower is an established client; or

(e) there is no other solicitor in the vicinity whom the client could reasonably be expected to consult; or

(f) in the case of a loan to be secured over heritable property, the terms of the loan have been agreed between the parties before the solicitor has been instructed to act for the lender, and the granting of the security is only to give effect to such agreement.

(2) In all cases falling within exceptions (c), (d) and (e) both parties shall be advised by the solicitor at the earliest practicable opportunity that the solicitor, or his firm, has been requested to act for both parties, and that if a dispute arises, they or one of them will require to consult an independent solicitor or solicitors, which advice shall be confirmed by the solicitor in writing as soon as may be practicable thereafter.

NOTE

[1] As amended by the Solicitors (Scotland) (Miscellaneous Amendments) Rules 2006, r.3 Sch.(1).

[2] As amended by the Solicitors (Scotland) (Miscellaneous Amendments) Rules 2006, r.3 Sch.(2).

6. A solicitor shall unless the contrary be proved be presumed for the purposes of rules 4 and 5 hereof to be acting for a party for whom he prepares an offer whether complete or not, in connection with a transaction of any kind specified in these rules, for execution by that party.

7. A solicitor acting on behalf of a party or prospective party to a transaction of any kind specified in rule 5 hereof shall not issue any deed, writ, missive or other document requiring the signature of another party or prospective party to him without informing that party in writing that:—

(a) such signature may have certain legal consequences, and

(b) he should seek independent legal advice before signature.

8. Where a solicitor, or two or more solicitors practising as principal or employee in the same firm or in the employment of the same employer, knowingly intends or intend to act on behalf of two or more prospective purchasers or tenants (other than prospective joint purchasers or tenants) of heritable property (in this rule referred to as "the clients"), the clients shall be informed of such intention, and a single solicitor shall not, where he has given any advice to one of the clients with respect to the price or rent to be offered, or with respect to any other material condition of the prospective bargain, give advice to another of the clients in respect of such matters.

9. The Council shall have power to waive any of the provisions of these rules in any particular circumstances or case.

10. Breach of any of these rules may be treated as professional misconduct for the purposes of Part IV of the Act (complaints and disciplinary proceedings).

Solicitors (Scotland) (Continuing Professional Development) Regulations 1993

Regulations dated 29th July 1993 made by the Council of the Law Society of Scotland with the concurrence of the Lord President of the Court of Session under section 5 of the Solicitors (Scotland) Act 1980.

1.—(1) These Regulations may be cited as the Solicitors (Scotland) (Continuing Professional Development) Regulations 1993.

(2) These Regulations shall come into operation on 1st November 1993.

2.—(1) In these Regulations unless the context otherwise requires:—

"the Act" means the Solicitors (Scotland) Act 1980;

"the Council" means the Council of the Law Society of Scotland;

"solicitor" means a solicitor holding a practising certificate under the Act;

"continuing professional development" means relevant education and study by a solicitor to develop his or her professional knowledge, skills and abilities.

(2) The Interpretation Act 1978 applies to the interpretation of these Regulations as it applies to the interpretation of an Act of Parliament.

3. From 1st November 1993 every solicitor shall undertake continuing professional development the nature and timing of which shall be prescribed by the Council from time to time.

4. Every solicitor shall keep a record of continuing professional development undertaken to comply with these Regulations and produce that record to the Council on demand.

5. The Council shall have power to waive any of the provisions of these Regulations in any particular circumstances or case and to revoke such a waiver.

6. Breach of any of these Regulations may be treated as professional misconduct for the purposes of Part IV of the Act (Complaints and Disciplinary Proceedings).

[NEXT TEXT PAGE IS **F** 272/1]

The Scottish Solicitors' Discipline Tribunal Procedure Rules 2005

with the concurrence of the Lord President of the Court of Session under section 52 of the Solicitors (Scotland) Act 1980

Part I—Introductory

1.—(1) These Rules may be cited as the Scottish Solicitors' Discipline Tribunal Procedure Rules 2005 and shall come into force on 1st April 2005.

(2)The Interpretation Act 1978, shall apply to the interpretation of these Rules as it applies to the interpretation of an Act of Parliament.

Part II—Complaints against Solicitors

2. Save as hereinafter provided, any complaint against a solicitor or a former solicitor for professional misconduct or in respect of inadequate professional services or any complaint against an incorporated practice or multi-national practice of failure to comply with any relevant statutory provisions or rules, shall be in writing under the hand of the complainer in the Form No I set out in the Schedule annexed to these Rules, and shall be sent to or lodged with the Clerk to the Tribunal. Along with the complaint the complainer shall also send to or lodge with the Clerk an affidavit by the complainer stating in concise numbered paragraphs the matters of fact on which he bases his complaint, and the specific charge(s) of professional misconduct and/or inadequate professional services and that the same to the best of his knowledge and belief are true, which affidavit shall be in the Form No II set out in the said Schedule to these Rules.

Where the complainer is the Council of the Law Society of Scotland (hereinafter referred to as "the Society") it shall not be necessary that the complaint be supported by an affidavit, but the complaint shall contain a statement setting forth in concise numbered paragraphs the matters of fact on which the Society bases its complaint and the specific charge(s) of professional misconduct and/or inadequate professional services.

Where a solicitor or former solicitor in respect of whom a complaint of inadequate professional services is made was, at the time when the services were provided, an employee of another solicitor or solicitors, the instance of the complaint shall contain the name of that other solicitor or those other solicitors.

Where a complaint may result in an order affecting the Investment Business Certificate of a firm, the instance of the complaint shall contain the names of all the solicitors who are partners in that firm.

Where the respondent is an incorporated practice or multi-national practice, the instance of the complaint shall contain the names of all the solicitors who are or at the time when the services were provided were members of that incorporated practice or multi-national practice and any associated incorporated practice or multi-national practice.

If a report is made to the Tribunal under section 51 of the Solicitors (Scotland) Act 1980 as amended ("the 1980 Act") by any of the parties referred to in that section, it shall not be necessary that such report be supported by an affidavit, and the report shall be dealt with as if it were a complaint and affidavit.

3. Where a complaint is made to the Tribunal by a person other than the Society or a person mentioned in section 51(3) of the 1980 Act, the Tribunal may remit the complaint to the Society whether or not the complaint is made in accordance with rule 2.

4. On receiving a complaint made, in the opinion of the Tribunal, in accordance with rule 2 the Tribunal shall consider the same, and it may from time to time and either before or after fixing a day for the hearing require the complainer to supply such further information and documents in support of the complaint as it thinks fit. In any case where, in the opinion of the Tribunal, no *prima facie* case against the solicitor, or former solicitor, or the incorporated practice or multi-national practice and all solicitors whose names appear in the instance of the complaint is disclosed the Tribunal shall give notice to the complainer and provide him with an opportunity to make representation in writing within seven days of such notice before making any order in writing dismissing the complaint.

5. If, in the opinion of the Tribunal, any complaint as originally lodged with the Clerk to the Tribunal or as supplemented in accordance with the procedure in rule 4 discloses a *prima facie* case the Tribunal shall serve a full copy of the complaint and affidavit as lodged or of the complaint as made by the Society and (in the appropriate case) as supplemented and shall allow answers to be lodged within such time as the Tribunal may appoint. If answers are lodged, a full copy thereof shall be sent by the party lodging said answers to the complainer, and a certificate that this has been done shall be sent to the Clerk of the Tribunal. On the expiry of the date appointed for lodging answers and whether answers have been lodged or not, the Tribunal, if on considering the documents lodged is of the opinion that no further action by it is called for, shall give notice to the complainer and provide him with an opportunity to make representation in writing within seven days of such notice before making any order dismissing the complaint; but otherwise the Tribunal shall fix a day for hearing the complaint and shall serve a notice thereof on the complainer and on the solicitor, or former solicitor, or the incorporated practice or multi-national practice and all solicitors whose names appear in the instance of the complaint. The day, time and place to be fixed for the hearing shall be in the discretion of the Tribunal, but parties concerned shall receive at least twenty-one days' notice thereof, unless all parties and the Tribunal agree to proceed on shorter notice.

6. The notice to be given to the parties under rule 5 may be in the Forms Nos III, IV, V set out in the Schedule to these Rules, and shall be sent by recorded delivery post or intimated by sheriff officer to the solicitor or former solicitor or the incorporated practice or multi-national practice and all solicitors whose names appear in the instance of the complaint and to the complainer at the respective addresses given in the complaint; said notice shall require the complainer and the respondents respectively to furnish to the Clerk to the Tribunal and also to each other a list of all documents on which they respectively propose to rely, and also a list of all witnesses whom they respectively propose to examine. Such lists shall, unless otherwise ordered by the Tribunal, be furnished by the complainer and by the respondents respectively in the case of lists of documents at least fourteen days, and in the case of lists of witnesses at least four days, before the day fixed for the hearing and so far as practicable each list of documents sent to the other party shall be accompanied by a copy of the documents referred to therein provided that if such lists are not furnished as aforesaid, the Tribunal at the hearing may have regard to any prejudice which may have been occasioned to the party not receiving the list or lists timeously.

7. Any party may inspect the documents contained in the list to be furnished by another party in terms of rule 6; the said documents shall be lodged with the Clerk to the Tribunal at least ten days before the date fixed for the hearing. If any party desires production of any documents, he may not later than seven days before the date fixed for the hearing send a list of such documents to the other party with a request that the same shall be lodged forthwith. In the event of the other party declining or failing to comply with the said request, the party requiring production shall be entitled to apply for and to obtain from the Tribunal an order on the other party to produce the said documents, if after considering the written submissions of the parties the Tribunal is of opinion that it is necessary for the proper consideration of the complaint that production should be made.

8. Each of the parties shall be in attendance and any incorporated practice or multi-national practice shall be represented on the day and at the time and place fixed for the hearing and shall then be prepared to lead all competent evidence. If any party fails to appear or any incorporated practice or multi-national practice fails to be represented at the hearing the Tribunal may, upon formal proof that the notice of the day fixed for the hearing has been duly posted or intimated to that party or incorporated practice or multi-national practice as the case may be in terms of rule 5, proceed to hear and determine the complaint in the absence of the party who failed to appear or incorporated practice or multi-national practice which has failed to be represented.

9. In any case in which the solicitor or former solicitor does not appear or any incorporated practice or multi-national practice is not represented and the Tribunal under rule 8 determines to proceed in the absence of such solicitor or former solicitor or representative of an incorporated practice or multi-national practice, as the case may be, the Tribunal may, either as to the whole case or as to any particular fact or facts, proceed and act upon evidence given by affidavit.

10. The Tribunal shall announce its decision as soon as reasonably practicable after the complaint has been considered by it. If the decision of the Tribunal is not pronounced on the day of the hearing it shall not be necessary to hold a hearing for the purpose of announcing the decision, but whether such a hearing be held or not, a copy of the decision certified by the Clerk to the Tribunal shall in accordance with the provisions of paragraph 15 of the Fourth Schedule to the 1980 Act be sent forthwith to each party with an intimation of the right of appeal competent under the provisions of section 54 of the 1980 Act. Where the decision of the Tribunal is pronounced outwith a hearing, the Tribunal shall arrange to hear parties on the matter of expenses.

11. Where any report is made to the Tribunal in pursuance of section 51 of the 1980 Act, the Tribunal, if it thinks fit, may appoint a solicitor to act as prosecutor in the complaint, and the expenses of such a solicitor, so far as not recoverable from the solicitor or former solicitor or any incorporated practice or complained against, shall be paid out of the funds of the Tribunal.

12. No complaint shall be withdrawn after it has been received by the Clerk to the Tribunal, except by the special leave of the Tribunal. Application for leave to withdraw shall be made not later than the day fixed for the hearing, unless the Tribunal otherwise directs. In granting leave to withdraw the Tribunal may attach such terms as to expenses or otherwise as it thinks fit.

13. The procedures in rules 2-12 shall apply equally to complaints in respect of conveyancing and executry practitioners in respect of the regulation, making, hearing and determining of inquiries under subsection (2A) of section 20 of the Law Reform (Miscellaneous Provisions) Scotland Act 1990 and to registered foreign lawyers, subject to the amendment of Forms Nos I, II, III, IV and V as appropriate.

PART III—CONVICTIONS

14. Where information is received by the Society from which it appears that a solicitor or former solicitor has, whether before or after enrolment, been convicted by any court of an act involving dishonesty, or sentenced to a term of imprisonment of not less than two years or an incorporated practice or multi-national practice has been convicted by any court of an offence which may render it unsuitable to continue to be recognised under section 34(1A) of the 1980 Act, the Society shall, as soon as may be, submit the information in the form of a complaint to the Tribunal so that the Tribunal may take such action, if any, as it thinks proper under section 53(1)(b) of the 1980 Act.

15. The Tribunal shall cause to be sent to the solicitor, former solicitor or incorporated practice or multi-national practice concerned particulars of the information submitted by the Society and shall invite the respondent to submit in writing to the Tribunal within such period as it may determine any explanations or observations which the respondent may wish to offer.

16. After the expiration of that period, whether such explanations or observations have been lodged or not, the Tribunal shall fix a date for the hearing of the case, and shall give not less than twenty-one days' notice thereof in writing to the respondent. The day, time and place of the hearing shall be in the discretion of the Tribunal.

17. The Tribunal shall announce its decision as soon as reasonably practicable after the hearing. It shall not be necessary to hold a hearing for the purpose of announcing the decision. A copy of the decision certified by the Clerk to the Tribunal shall in accordance with the provision of paragraph 15 of the Fourth Schedule to the 1980 Act be sent forthwith to the respondent with an intimation of the right to appeal competent under the provisions of section 54 of the 1980 Act. Where the decision of the Tribunal is pronounced outwith a hearing, the Tribunal shall arrange to hear parties on the matter of expenses.

18. The procedures in rules 14-17 shall apply equally in respect of convictions of conveyancing and executry practitioners in respect of regulating the making, hearing and determining of inquiries under subsection (2A) of section 20 of the Law Reform (Miscellaneous Provisions) Scotland Act 1990 and in relation to registered foreign lawyers.

Part IV—Appeals By Solicitors

19. Every appeal to the Tribunal shall be in writing in the Form No VI set out in the Schedule annexed to these Rules and shall be accompanied by a copy of the determination or direction appealed against, and any relative schedule or report and shall be sent to or lodged with the Clerk to the Tribunal within twenty-one days of the date on which the decision of the Society was sent to the appellant.

20. The respondents to an appeal shall be the Society and such other party, if any, who may have complained to the Society under section 42A(1)(a) of the 1980 Act.

21. On receiving a notice of appeal made, in the opinion of the Tribunal, in accordance with rule 19 the Tribunal shall consider the same, and it may from time to time and either before or after fixing a date for the hearing require the appellant to supply such further information and documents in support of the appeal as it thinks fit. In any case where in the opinion of the Tribunal the appeal is manifestly ill-founded or if the appellant fails to comply with any of these Rules, the Tribunal shall give notice to the appellant and provide him with the opportunity to make representation within seven days of such notice in writing before making any order in writing dismissing the appeal.

22. If in the opinion of the Tribunal, any appeal as originally lodged with the Clerk to the Tribunal or as supplemented does not fall to be dismissed under rule 21, the Tribunal shall serve upon each of the respondents a full copy of the statement of appeal and (in the appropriate case) as supplemented and shall allow answers to be lodged within such time as the Tribunal may appoint. If answers are lodged, a full copy shall be sent by each respondent lodging answers to the appellant, and a certificate that this has been done shall be sent by such respondents to the Clerk to the Tribunal. On the expiry of the date appointed for lodging answers and whether answers have been lodged or not, the Tribunal if on considering the documents lodged is of the opinion that no further action by it is called for, shall give notice to the appellant and provide him with the opportunity to make representation in writing within seven days of such notice before making any order dismissing the appeal; but otherwise the Tribunal shall fix a date for hearing the appeal and shall serve a notice thereof on the appellant and on each respondent. The day, time and place to be fixed for the hearing shall be in the discretion of the Tribunal, but the parties concerned shall receive at least twenty-one days' notice thereof, unless all parties and the Tribunal agree to proceed on shorter notice.

23. The notices to be given to parties under rule 22 may be in the Forms Nos VII, VIII and IX set out in the Schedule to these Rules and shall be sent by recorded delivery post to the appellant and to each of the respondents.

24. The Tribunal may on the application of a party *ex proprio motu* require any party to produce any document within such period as the Tribunal may determine.

25. Each of the parties shall be in attendance on the day and at the time and place fixed for the hearing. If any party fails to appear at the hearing the Tribunal may, upon formal proof that the notice of the day fixed for the hearing has been duly posted or intimated to that party in terms of rule 22, proceed to hear and determine the appeal in the absence of that party.

26. The Tribunal shall announce its decision as soon as reasonably practicable after the appeal has been considered by it. If the decision of the Tribunal is not pronounced on the day of the hearing it shall not be necessary to hold a hearing for the purpose of announcing the decision but whether such a hearing be held or not, a copy of the decision certified by the Clerk to the Tribunal shall, in accordance with the provisions of paragraph 15 of the Fourth Schedule to the 1980 Act be sent forthwith to the appellant and each respondent with an intimation of the right of appeal competent under the provisions of section 54 of the 1980 Act. Where the decision of the Tribunal is pronounced outwith a hearing, the Tribunal shall arrange to hear parties on the matter of expenses.

27. No appeal shall be withdrawn after it has been received by the Clerk to the Tribunal except by the special leave of the Tribunal. In granting leave to withdraw, the Tribunal may attach such terms as to expenses or otherwise as it shall think fit.

28. The procedures in rules 19-27 shall apply equally to appeals by conveyancing and executry practitioners in respect of regulating the making, hearing and determining of appeals under subsection (11)(b) of section 20 of the Law Reform (Miscellaneous Provisions) Scotland Act 1990 and in respect of registered foreign lawyers, subject to the amendment of Forms Nos VI, VII, VIII and IX as appropriate.

PART V—RESTORATION TO THE ROLL OF SOLICITORS

29. An application to the Tribunal for restoration to the Roll of Solicitors under section 10 of the 1980 Act by a person who has been struck off the Roll by order of the Tribunal shall be in writing in the Form No X set out in the Schedule to these Rules and shall be verified by affidavit in the Form No XI set out in the said Schedule. The application shall set forth the occupation or occupations of the applicant since his name was struck off the Roll. The application and affidavit shall be sent to or lodged with the Clerk to the Tribunal and shall be supported by letters from two solicitors who at the date of application are in practice and who declare that they know the applicant.

30. The Tribunal may if it thinks fit, require the applicant to give notice by advertisement or otherwise as it may direct that an application for restoration to the Roll has been made by the applicant and that the same will be disposed of by the Tribunal on a date appointed for the hearing. If any person desires to object to the application he shall give notice in writing to the solicitor and to the Clerk to the Tribunal at least ten days before the day fixed for the hearing, specifying the grounds of his objection. Styles of notice for such objection are in Form No XII Nos 1 and 2, set out in the Schedule to these Rules.

31. The Tribunal shall afford to the applicant an opportunity of being heard by the Tribunal and of adducing evidence. The Tribunal may require such evidence as it thinks necessary concerning the identity and character of the applicant, his conduct since his name was struck off the Roll and his suitability for restoration to the Roll and for this purpose may receive written or oral evidence.

32. If the objector appears on the day fixed for the hearing and if the Tribunal is of the opinion, after considering the notice of objection and after hearing the solicitor (if it thinks fit to do so) that the notice discloses a *prima facie* case for inquiry, the Tribunal shall afford to the objector an opportunity of being heard by the Tribunal and of adducing evidence.

33. Subject to the foregoing provisions, the procedure of the Tribunal in connection with applications for restoration to the Roll shall be such as the Tribunal may determine.

34. A copy of the decision of the Tribunal in the application, certified by the Clerk to the Tribunal shall, in accordance with the provision of paragraph 15 of the Fourth Schedule to the 1980 Act, be sent forthwith to the applicant with an intimation of the right of appeal competent under the provisions of section 54 of that Act.

35. In all cases in which the final decision whether by the Tribunal or by the court is to order restoration to the Roll, such decision shall be intimated to the Registrar of Solicitors who shall forthwith give effect thereto.

36. An applicant shall as a condition of having his name restored to the Roll of Solicitors pay to the Registrar of Solicitors, where the name of the applicant was struck off the Roll by order of the Discipline Tribunal, a fee of £500 or such other sum as may be fixed from time to time by the Tribunal.

37. The procedures in rules 29-36 shall apply equally to registered foreign lawyers seeking to make application for restoration to the Register of Foreign Lawyers.

Part VI—General

38. The Tribunal may appoint from its number a Chairman and Vice Chairmen, any one of whom may preside at hearings of the Tribunal. In the event of the Tribunal being unable to reach a majority decision the Chairman shall have a casting vote.

39. The Tribunal may hear all proceedings in public or in private as it thinks fit and may pronounce its decision in public or in private as it thinks fit. Where any party wishes any proceedings to be heard in private, a motion shall be submitted to the Tribunal in writing, not less than fourteen days prior to the date of the hearing.

40. The Tribunal may on its own motion, or on the application of the parties, or one of them, at any time and from time to time, postpone or adjourn a hearing upon such terms as to expenses or otherwise as, to the Tribunal, shall appear just. It shall not do so at the request of one party only unless, having regard to the grounds upon which, and the time at which, such request is made and to the convenience of the parties, it deems it reasonable to do so. The Chairman may, in regard to the foregoing, exercise the functions of the Tribunal who shall give to the parties such notice of any postponed or adjourned hearing as it deems to be reasonable in the circumstances.

41. If it shall appear to the Tribunal that the allegation contained in a complaint, affidavit, statement or report should be amended or added to, the Tribunal may permit such amendment or addition, and it may also require the same to be embodied in a further complaint, affidavit, statement or report, if in the judgment of the Tribunal such amendment or addition is not within the scope of the original complaint, affidavit, statement or report, provided always that if, in consequence of such amendment or addition, any party applies for an adjournment, the Tribunal may at its discretion grant an adjournment of the hearing, upon such terms as to the Tribunal shall appear just. Upon a hearing, the Tribunal may permit an appellant to amend his statement of appeal or a respondent to amend or withdraw his answers, provided always that if in consequence of such amendment or withdrawal any party applies for an adjournment the Tribunal may at its discretion grant an adjournment of the hearing, upon such terms as to the Tribunal shall appear just.

42. Shorthand notes of proceedings before the Tribunal may be taken by a shorthand writer appointed by the Tribunal or if no shorthand writer be available for any date appointed for a hearing the proceedings may be recorded electronically; the notes may be transcribed if the Tribunal thinks fit, and if transcribed any party to the proceedings shall be entitled to inspect the transcript thereof. The shorthand writer or transcriber of the recorded proceedings shall, if required, supply to the Tribunal and to any person entitled to be heard upon an appeal against a decision of the Tribunal, but to no other person, a copy of the transcript if made, on payment of his charges.

43. The Tribunal may from time to time dispense with any requirements of these Rules respecting notices, affidavits, documents, service or time, where it appears to the Tribunal to be just to do so.

44. The Tribunal may extend, and with consent of parties may at their discretion reduce, the time for doing anything under these Rules.

45. All complaints, reports, affidavits and statements of appeal shall be filed by the Clerk to the Tribunal. The Tribunal may order that any books, papers or other exhibits produced or used at a hearing before it shall be retained by the Clerk to the Tribunal until the time for appealing has expired, or if notice of appeal is given, until the appeal is heard or otherwise disposed of.

46. All orders, determinations, directions and decisions of the Tribunal shall be signed on behalf of the Tribunal by its Chairman or other member presiding or in the event of indisposition of such person by another member present and a copy of such orders or decisions purporting to be signed by the Chairman or other member shall be *prima facie* evidence of the due making thereof. Prior to any appeal being lodged or intimation being made to the Council of the Law Society in terms of paragraph 16 of the Fourth Schedule to the 1980 Act the Chairman or other member presiding may correct any clerical error contained in an order or decision and the order or decision so amended shall of new be intimated to the parties.

47. The Clerk to the Tribunal includes any depute clerk authorised by the Tribunal to act on its behalf.

48. The Tribunal may direct that any question of fact or law which appears to be in issue may be decided at a preliminary hearing. If in the opinion of the Tribunal, a decision on that question substantially disposes of the whole case, the Tribunal may treat the preliminary hearing as a hearing of the case and may give such direction as it thinks fit to dispose of the case. The decision of the Tribunal relating to any preliminary issue may be given orally at the end of the hearing or reserved and, in any event, whether there has been a hearing or not, must be recorded as soon as possible in a document which, save in the case of a decision by consent, must also contain a statement of reasons for the decision and must be signed by the Chairman or other member presiding.

49. If any direction given to a party under these Rules is not complied with by that party, the Tribunal may before or at the hearing dismiss the whole or part of the complaint/submission/appeal/application, strike out the whole or part of the written submission of the party who has not complied and, where appropriate, direct that such party shall be barred from contesting the complaint/submission/appeal/application altogether; but the Tribunal must not dismiss, strike out or give such a direction as aforesaid unless it has sent notice to the party who has not complied, giving that party an opportunity to comply within the period specified in the notice or to establish why the Tribunal should not dismiss, strike out or give such a direction as aforesaid.

50. Where two or more complaints have been lodged in respect of the same respondent the Tribunal may, on the application of a party to the proceedings or on its own initiative, direct that the complaints be conjoined and heard together.

51. If after commencement of any hearing, a member is absent, the proceedings may, with the consent of the parties be heard by the remaining members present, provided that the Tribunal is still properly constituted as provided in paragraph 5 of Schedule 4 to the 1980 Act and the Tribunal shall be deemed to be properly constituted.

52. Without prejudice to any other powers it may have, the Tribunal may exclude from any hearing, or part of it, any person (including a party to the proceedings or the party's representative) whose conduct has disrupted the hearing or whose conduct has otherwise interfered with the administration of justice. It the Tribunal decides to exclude a party it must allow the party's representative sufficient time to consult with the party.

53. If the Chairman is satisfied that any party is unable through physical or mental sickness or impairment to attend the Tribunal and that the party's inability is likely to continue for a long time, the Chairman may make such arrangements as may appear best suited, in all the circumstances of the case, for disposing fairly of the complaint/submission/appeal/application.

54. The Scottish Solicitors' Discipline Tribunal Rules 2002 are hereby revoked without prejudice to any order, reference or appointment made or instruction given or finding pronounced or other thing done thereunder and such order, reference, appointment, instruction, finding or other thing so far as the same could have been made, given, pronounced or done under these

Rules shall have effect as if made, given, pronounced or done under these Rules.

SCHEDULE

FORM I

FORM OF COMPLAINT

To the Scottish Solicitors' Discipline Tribunal, constituted under the Solicitors (Scotland) Act 1980.

COMPLAINT by A.B. against C.D.

I, the undersigned A.B. hereby request that C.D. of be required to answer the allegations contained in the affidavit which accompanies this application, and that the Tribunal issues such Order under section 53 of the Solicitors (Scotland) Act 1980, in the matter as it may think right.

Dated ....

....Signature

....Address

....Designation

FORM II

FORM OF AFFIDAVIT BY COMPLAINER

At the day of in presence of , one of Her Majesty's Justices of the Peace for , compeared A.B. of , who being solemnly sworn and interrogated, depones as follows, viz.:—

1. C.D. has been employed by him in a professional capacity for the last ten years (or as the case may be).

2. (*Here state the facts concisely in numbered paragraphs, and show the deponent's means of knowledge.)*

All which is truth as the deponent shall answer to God.

FORM III

THE SCOTTISH SOLICITORS' DISCIPLINE TRIBUNAL

(Notice of Complaint)

Complaint by A.B.

against

C.D.

To: C.D. of

TAKE NOTICE that a complaint has been made by A.B. of to the Scottish Solicitors' Discipline Tribunal, constituted under the Solicitors (Scotland) Act 1980, requesting that you be required to answer the allegations contained in the complaint whereof a copy accompanies this notice, and that the Tribunal may issue such Order under section 53 of the Solicitors (Scotland) Act 1980, in the matter as it thinks right.

The Tribunal has appointed that answers to the complaint shall be lodged with the Clerk at within fourteen days from the date hereof, and that a copy of such answers shall, at the same time, be intimated to

Dated this day of 20 .

....

Clerk to the Tribunal

(*N.B.*—A print of the Rules made under the said Act is sent herewith for your information and guidance.)

FORM IV

THE SCOTTISH SOLICITORS' DISCIPLINE TRIBUNAL

(Notice to respondent of date fixed for the hearing)

Complaint by A.B.

against

C.D.

To: C.D. of

TAKE NOTICE that the Scottish Solicitors' Discipline Tribunal has fixed the day of at within for the hearing of this complaint, and if you fail then to appear the Tribunal may in accordance with the Rules made under the Solicitors (Scotland) Act 1980, proceed in your absence.

You are required by the said Rules to furnish to the said A.B. and to the Clerk to the Tribunal at at least fourteen days before the said day of , a list of all the documents on which you propose to rely. Under the said Rules the said A.B. is also required to furnish you with a list of documents on which he proposes to rely. The said documents must be lodged with the Clerk to the Tribunal at least ten days before the date fixed for the hearing.

Either party may inspect the documents included in the list furnished by the other. A copy of any document mentioned in the list of either party must, on application and at the expense of the party requiring it, be furnished to that party by the other within three days after receipt of the application.

If either party desires production of any documents not included in the other party's list he may, not later than seven days before the date fixed for the hearing, send a list of such documents to the other party with a request that the same shall be lodged forthwith, and not later than four days before the date fixed for the hearing. In the event of the other party declining or failing to comply with the said request, the party requiring production shall be entitled to apply for and to obtain from the Tribunal an order on the other party to produce the said documents, if after considering the written submissions of the parties the Tribunal is of the opinion that it is necessary for the proper consideration of the complaint that production should be made.

Dated this day of 20 .

....

Clerk to the Tribunal

FORM V

THE SCOTTISH SOLICITORS' DISCIPLINE TRIBUNAL

(Notice to the complainer of the date fixed for the hearing)

To: A.B. of

TAKE NOTICE that answers to your complaint have/have not been lodged and that the day of 20 has been fixed by the Scottish Solicitors' Discipline Tribunal for the hearing of your complaint against C.D., Solicitor of . The Tribunal will sit at within .

You are required by the Rules made under the Solicitors (Scotland) Act 1980, to furnish to the said C.D. and to the Clerk to the Tribunal at at least fourteen days before the said day of a list of all the documents on which you propose to rely, and at least fourteen days before the said date a list of the witnesses whom you propose to examine. So far as practicable said list of documents sent to C.D. shall be accompanied by a copy of the documents referred to therein. The said documents must be lodged with the Clerk to the Tribunal at least ten days before the date fixed for the hearing. Under the Rules of the Tribunal the said C.D. is also required to furnish, within the said respective periods, a list of the documents (if any) on which he proposes to rely, and a list of the witnesses (if any) whom he proposes to examine. The said documents must be lodged with the Clerk to the Tribunal at least ten days before the date fixed for the hearing. Under the Rules of the Tribunal the said C.D. is also required to furnish, within the said respective period, a list of documents (if any) on which he proposes to rely, and a list of witnesses (if any) whom he proposes to examine.

Either party may inspect the documents included in the list furnished by the other. A copy of any document mentioned in the list of either party must, on the application and at the expense of the party requiring it, be furnished to that party by the other within three days after receipt of a written request therefore. If either party desires production of any documents he may, not later than seven days before the date fixed for the hearing, send a list of such documents to the other party with a request that the same shall be lodged forthwith, and not later than four days before the date fixed for the hearing. In the event of the other party declining or failing to comply with the said request, the party requiring production shall be entitled to apply for and to obtain from the Tribunal an order on the other party to produce the said documents, if after considering the written submissions of the parties the Tribunal is of the opinion that it is necessary for the proper consideration of the complaint that production should be made.

In the event of a party complained of not appearing, and of the Tribunal being asked to proceed in his absence, you must be prepared to prove that any notice on which you rely was duly served on the solicitor in accordance with the Rules issued under the said Act.

Dated this day of 20

....

Clerk to the Tribunal

FORM VI

THE SCOTTISH SOLICITORS' DISCIPLINE TRIBUNAL

FORM OF APPEAL TO THE TRIBUNAL

To the Scottish Solicitors' Discipline Tribunal constituted under the Solicitors (Scotland) Act 1980

APPEAL by A.B. against a determination/direction/order of the Council of the Law Society of Scotland dated

I, the undersigned A.B., hereby appeal against the determination/direction/order of the Council of the Law Society of Scotland dated and intimated to me on a copy of which is produced herewith.

The grounds of my appeal are as follows *(here state concisely in numbered paragraphs, the grounds of the appeal)*.

I hereby request the Tribunal *(here state the Order which you wish the Tribunal to pronounce in your favour)*.

In the consideration of the matter by the Council of the Law Society, the complainer was *(name and address of the party or parties whose complaint to the Law Society resulted in the decision appealed against)*.

Dated ....

.... Signature

[Address and

.... [place or places

[of business

FORM VII

FORM OF INTIMATION OF APPEAL

APPEAL by A.B. against a determination/direction/order of the Council of the Law Society of Scotland dated

To: The Secretary
The Law Society of Scotland
or
C.D. of

TAKE NOTICE that an appeal has been lodged with the Scottish Solicitors' Discipline Tribunal by A.B. against a determination/direction/order of the Council of the Law Society of Scotland dated . A copy of the statement of appeal accompanies this notice.

The Tribunal has appointed that answers to the statement of appeal shall be lodged with the Clerk at within days from the date hereof, and that a copy of such answers shall, at the same time, be intimated to .

Dated this day of 20

....

Clerk to the Tribunal

FORM VIII

FORM OF NOTICE TO AN APPELLANT OF DATE FIXED FOR THE HEARING OF AN APPEAL

To A.B. of

TAKE NOTICE that answers to your statement of appeal have been lodged by and and that the day of has been fixed for the hearing of your appeal. The Tribunal will sit at at and if you fail then to appear the Tribunal may in accordance with the Rules made under the Solicitors (Scotland) Act 1980 proceed in your absence.

You are required by the said Rules to furnish to and to and to the Clerk to the Tribunal at at least fourteen days before the said day of a list of all the documents on which you propose to rely. The said documents must be lodged with the Clerk to the Tribunal at least seven days before the date fixed for the hearing.

Dated this day of 20

....
Clerk to the Tribunal

FORM IX

FORM OF NOTICE TO THE RESPONDENT OF DATE FIXED FOR THE HEARING OF AN APPEAL

APPEAL by against a determination/direction/orde of the Council of the Law Society of Scotland dated

TAKE NOTICE that the Scottish Solicitors' Discipline Tribunal has fixed the day of at within for the hearing of this appeal, and if you fail then to appear, the Tribunal may in accordance with the Rules made under the Solicitors (Scotland) Act 1980 proceed in your absence.

You are required by the said Rules to furnish to and to and to the Clerk to the Tribunal at at least fourteen days before the said day of a list of all the documents on which you propose to rely. The said documents must be lodged with the Clerk to the Tribunal at least seven days before the date fixed for the hearing.

Dated this day of 20

....
Clerk to the Tribunal

FORM X

FORM OF APPLICATION BY A SOLICITOR FOR RESTORATION TO ROLL OF SOLICITORS

To the Scottish Solicitors' Discipline Tribunal constituted under the Solicitors (Scotland) Act 1980

1. I, the undersigned A.B. hereby apply to the Discipline Tribunal under section 10 of the Solicitors (Scotland) Act, 1980, for an order restoring my name to the Roll of Solicitors.

2. I was admitted a Solicitor on the day of in the year .

3. On in the year , I was struck off the Roll of Solicitors by order of the Discipline Committee/Tribunal.

4. Since then my occupations have been as follows:—

(Here specify in the case of each employment the name and address of the employer, the nature of the work on which the applicant was employed and the period of employment.)

5. The following persons are prepared on request to testify to the Discipline Tribunal concerning my identity and character, my conduct since my name was struck off from the Roll and my suitability for restoration to the Roll.

(Here state the names and addresses of the persons prepared to testify.)

.... *Signature*

.... *Address*

FORM XI

FORM OF AFFIDAVIT BY APPLICANT FOR RESTORATION TO ROLL OF SOLICITORS

At on the day of in presence of , one of Her Majesty's Justices of the Peace for compeared A.B. of who being solemnly sworn and interrogated, depones as follows, viz.:—

1. The deponent, was admitted as a Solicitor on the day of in the year , and on the day of in the year , was struck off the Roll of Solicitors by order of the Solicitors' Discipline (Scotland) Committee/the Scottish Solicitors' Discipline Tribunal.

2. The particulars of his occupations since then as set forth in the application for restoration to the Roll now produced, and marked "A", are true.

3. The deponent is not aware and does not know of any cause of complaint or proceedings which might have arisen out of his conduct since his name was struck off the Roll.

All which is truth as the deponent shall answer to God.

FORM XII

FORMS OF NOTICE OF OBJECTION TO AN APPLICATION BY A SOLICITOR FOR THE RESTORATION OF HIS NAME TO THE ROLL OF SOLICITORS

No. 1

FORM OF NOTICE TO BE GIVEN TO THE SOLICITOR

To C.D. of , Solicitor.

TAKE NOTICE that I object to the application made by you to the Scottish Solicitors' Discipline Tribunal for restoration of your name to the Roll of Solicitors, on the following grounds, viz.:—

(The grounds of objection to be stated in articulate numbered paragraphs.)

Dated ....

....*Signature*

.... *Address*

.... *Designation*

No. 2

FORM OF NOTICE TO BE GIVEN TO THE TRIBUNAL

To the Scottish Solicitors' Discipline Tribunal.

TAKE NOTICE that I object to the application made by C.D. of to the Scottish Solicitors' Discipline Tribunal for restoration of his name to the Roll of Solicitors, on the following grounds, viz.:—

(The grounds of objection to be stated in articulate numbered paragraphs.)

Dated ....

.... *Signature*

.... *Address*

.... *Designation*

Solicitors (Scotland) (Restriction on Association) Practice Rules 2004

Rules dated 28th May 2004, made by the Council of the Law Society of Scotland and approved by the Lord President of the Court of Session in terms of section 34 of the Solicitors (Scotland) Act 1980.

Citation

1.—(1) These Rules maybe cited as the Solicitors (Scotland) (Restriction on Association) Practice Rules 2004.

(2) These Rules shall come into operation on 1st September 2004.

Definitions and Interpretation

2.—(1) In these Rules, unless the context otherwise requires:

"the Act" means the Solicitors (Scotland) Act 1980;

"the Council" means the Council of the Society;

"the Society" means the Law Society of Scotland; and

[1] "solicitor" means any person enrolled as a solicitor in pursuance of the Act and includes a firm of solicitors, an incorporated practice and any association of solicitors and also includes a registered foreign lawyer and a multi-national practice.

(2) The Interpretation Act 1978 applies to the interpretation of these Rules as it applies to the interpretation of an Act of Parliament.

NOTE

[1] As amended by the Solicitors (Scotland) (Registered Foreign Lawyers) etc. Practice Rules 2005, Sch.5 (effective May 1, 2005).

Restriction on Association etc

[1] **3.** Notwithstanding the restrictions contained in section 47 of the Act (restrictions on employing solicitor struck off or suspended), no solicitor shall, in connection with his practice as a solicitor, without the prior written permission of the Council, which may be given for such period and subject to such conditions as the Council thinks fit, associate in business with or provide facilities for any person who to his knowledge is disqualified from practising as a solicitor or whose name has been removed from the register of foreign lawyers by the Scottish Solicitors' Discipline Tribunal or whose certificate of registration as a registered foreign lawyer has been suspended in accordance with section 24F of the Solicitors (Scotland) Act 1980 by reason of the fact that his name has been struck off the roll of solicitors or that he is suspended from practising as a solicitor.

NOTE

[1] As amended by the Solicitors (Scotland) (Registered Foreign Lawyers) etc. Practice Rules 2005, Sch.5 (effective May 1, 2005).

Revocation

4. The Solicitors (Scotland) Practice Rules 1975 are hereby revoked.

Solicitors (Scotland) (Cross-Border Code of Conduct) Practice Rules 2003

Rules dated 29th August 2003, made by the Council of the Law Society of Scotland under section 34(1) of the Solicitors (Scotland) Act 1980 and approved by the Lord President of the Court of Session under section 34(3) of that Act.

Citation, commencement and revocation

1.—(1) These rules may be cited as the Solicitors (Scotland) (Cross-Border Code of Conduct) Practice Rules 2003 and shall come into force on 1st October 2003.

(2) The Solicitors (Scotland) (Cross-Border Code of Conduct) Practice Rules 1989 are hereby revoked.

Interpretation

2.—(1) In these rules, unless the context otherwise requires:—

"the Act" means the Solicitors (Scotland) Act 1980 as amended;

"the Code" means the Code of Conduct for lawyers in the European Union adopted by the Council of the Bars and Law Societies of the European Union on 28th October 1988 as amended on 28th November 1998 and 6th December 2002, and as the same may be varied, supplemented, amended, consolidated or replaced from time to time;

"Council" means the Council of the Society;

"cross-border practice" means—

(a) all professional contacts with lawyers of Member States other than the United Kingdom; and

(b) the professional activities of a solicitor in a Member State other than the United Kingdom whether or not the solicitor is physically present in that Member State;

"Member State" means a member state of the European Union or of the European Economic Area;

"the Society" means the Law Society of Scotland;

[1] "solicitor" means a solicitor holding a practising certificate under the Act and includes a firm of solicitors and an incorporated practice and also includes a registered foreign lawyer and a multi-national practice;

(2) The Interpretation Act 1978 applies to the interpretation of these rules as it applies to the interpretation of an Act of Parliament.

NOTE

[1] As amended by the Solicitors (Scotland) (Registered Foreign Lawyers) etc. Practice Rules 2005, Sch.5 (effective May 1, 2005).

Conduct of cross-border practice

3. A solicitor conducting cross-border practice shall observe and be bound by the terms of the Code at all times.

Waiver and modification

4. The Council may waive or modify any of the provisions of these rules as they apply to a solicitor in any particular case.

Code of Conduct for Lawyers in the European Union

This Code of Conduct for Lawyers in the European Union was originally adopted at the CCBE Plenary Session held on 28 October 1988, and subsequently amended during the CCBE Plenary Sessions on 28 November 1998 and 6 December 2002.

CONTENTS

1. Preamble

1.1. The Function of the Lawyer in Society

In a society founded on respect for the rule of law the lawyer fulfils a special role. His duties do not begin and end with the faithful performance of what he is instructed to do so far as the law permits. A lawyer must serve the interests of justice as well as those whose rights and liberties he is trusted to assert and defend and it is his duty not only to plead his client's cause but to be his adviser.

A lawyer's function therefore lays on him a variety of legal and moral obligations (sometimes appearing to be in conflict with each other) towards:

- the client;
- the courts and other authorities before whom the lawyer pleads his client's cause or acts on his behalf;
- the legal profession in general and each fellow member of it in particular;
- the public for whom the existence of a free and independent profession, bound together by respect for rules made by the profession itself, is an essential means of safeguarding human rights in face of the power of the state and other interests in society.

1.2. The Nature of Rules of Professional Conduct

1.2.1. Rules of professional conduct are designed through their willing acceptance by those to whom they apply to ensure the proper performance by the lawyer of a function which is recognised as essential in all civilized societies. The failure of the lawyer to observe these rules must in the last resort result in a disciplinary sanction.

1.2.2. The particular rules of each Bar or law Society arise from its own traditions. They are adapted to the organisation and sphere of activity of the profession in the Member State concerned and to its judicial and administrative procedures and to its national legislation. It is neither possible nor desirable that they should be taken out of their context nor that an attempt should be made to give general application to rules which are inherently incapable of such application.

The particular rules of each Bar and Law Society nevertheless are based on the same values and in most cases demonstrate a common foundation.

1.3. The Purpose of the Code

1.3.1. The continued integration of the European Union and European Economic Area and the increasing frequency of the cross-border activities of lawyers within the European Economic Area have made necessary in the public interest the statement of common rules which apply to all lawyers from the European Economic Area whatever Bar or Law Society they belong to in relation to their cross-border practice. A particular purpose of the statement of those rules is to mitigate the difficulties which result from the application of "double deontology" as set out in Article 4 of the E.C. Directive 77/249 of 22nd March 1977.

1.3.2. The organisations representing the legal profession through the CCBE propose that the rules codified in the following articles:

- be recognised at the present time as the expression of a consensus of all the Bars and Law Societies of the European Union and European Economic Area;
- be adopted as enforceable rules as soon as possible in accordance with national or EEA procedures in relation to the cross-border activities of the lawyer in the European Union and European Economic Area;
- be taken into account in all revisions of national rules of deontology or professional practice with a view to their progressive harmonisation.

They further express the wish that the national rules of deontology or professional practice be interpreted and applied whenever possible in a way consistent with the rules in this Code.

After the rules in this Code have been adopted as enforceable rules in relation to his cross-border activities the lawyer will remain bound to observe the rules of the Bar or Law Society to which he belongs to the extent that they are consistent with the rules in this Code.

1.4. Field of Application Ratione Personae

The following rules shall apply to lawyers of the European Union and the European Economic Area as they are defined by the Directive 77/249 of 22nd March 1977.

1.5. Field of Application Ratione Materiae

Without prejudice to the pursuit of a progressive harmonisation of rules of deontology or professional practice which apply only internally within a Member State, the following rules shall apply to the cross-border activities of the lawyer within the European Union and the European Economic Area. Cross-border activities shall mean:

(a) all professional contacts with lawyers of Member States other than his own;
(b) the professional activities of the lawyer in a Member State other than his own, whether or not the lawyer is physically present in that Member State.

1.6. Definitions

In these rules:

"Home Member State" means the Member State of the Bar or Law Society to which the lawyer belongs.

"Host Member State" means any other Member State where the lawyer carries on cross-border activities.

"Competent authority" means the professional organisation(s) or authority(ies) of the Member State concerned responsible for the laying down of rules of professional conduct and the administration of discipline of lawyers.

2. General Principles

2.1. Independence

2.1.1. The many duties to which a lawyer is subject require his absolute independence, free from all other influence, especially such as may arise from his personal interests or external pressure. Such independence is as necessary to trust in the process of justice as the impartiality of the judge. A lawyer must therefore avoid any impairment of his independence and be careful not to compromise his professional standards in order to please his client, the court or third parties.

2.1.2. This independence is necessary in non-contentious matters as well as in litigation. Advice given by a lawyer to his client has no value if it is given only to ingratiate himself, to serve his personal interests or in response to outside pressure.

2.2. Trust and Personal Integrity

Relationships of trust can only exist if a lawyer's personal honour, honesty and integrity are beyond doubt. For the lawyer these traditional virtues are professional obligations.

2.3. Confidentiality

2.3.1. It is of the essence of a lawyer's function that he should be told by his client things which the client would not tell to others, and that he should be the recipient of other information on a basis of confidence. Without the certainty of confidentiality there cannot be trust. Confidentiality is therefore a primary and fundamental right and duty of the lawyer.

The lawyer's obligation of confidentiality serves the interest of the administration of justice as well as the interest of the client. It is therefore entitled to special protection by the State.

2.3.2. A lawyer shall respect the confidentiality of all information that becomes known to him in the course of his professional activity.

2.3.3. The obligation of confidentiality is not limited in time.

2.3.4. A lawyer shall require his associates and staff and anyone engaged by him in the course of providing professional services to observe the same obligation of confidentiality.

2.4. Respect for the Rules of Other Bars and Law Societies

Under the laws of the European Union and the European Economic Area a lawyer from another Member State may be bound to comply with the rules of the Bar or Law Society of the Host Member State. Lawyers have a duty to inform themselves as to the rules which will affect them in the performance of any particular activity.

Member organisations of CCBE are obliged to deposit their codes of conduct at the Secretariat of CCBE so that any lawyer can get hold of the copy of the current code from the Secretariat.

2.5. Incompatible Occupations

2.5.1. In order to perform his functions with due independence and in a manner which is consistent with his duty to participate in the administration of justice a lawyer is excluded from some occupations.

2.5.2. A lawyer who acts in the representation or the defence of a client in legal proceedings or before any public authorities in a Host Member State shall there observe the rules regarding incompatible occupations as they are applied to lawyers of the Host Member State.

2.5.3. A lawyer established in a Host Member State in which he wished to participate directly in commercial or other activities not connected with the practice of the law shall respect the rules regarding forbidden or incompatible occupations as they are applied to lawyers of that Member State.

2.6. Personal Publicity

2.6.1. A lawyer is entitled to inform the public about his services provided that the information is accurate and not misleading, and respectful of the obligation of confidentiality and other core values of the profession.

2.6.2.1 Personal publicity by a lawyer in any form of media such as by press, radio, television, by electronic commercial communications or otherwise is permitted to the extent it complies with the requirements of 2.6.1.

2.7. The Client's Interest

Subject to due observance of all rules of law and professional conduct, a lawyer must always act in the best interests of his client and must put those interests before his own interests or those of fellow members of the legal profession.

2.8. Limitation of Lawyer's Liability towards his Client

To the extent permitted by the law of the Home Member State and the Host Member State, the lawyer may limit his liabilities towards his client in accordance with rules of the Code of Conduct to which he is subject.

3. Relations with Clients

3.1. Acceptance and Termination of Instructions

3.1.1. A lawyer shall not handle a case for a party except on his instructions. He may, however, act in a case in which he has been instructed by another lawyer who himself acts for the party or where the case has been assigned to him by a competent body.

The lawyer should make reasonable efforts to ascertain the identity, competence and authority of the person or body who instructs him when the specific circumstances show that the identity, competence and authority are uncertain.

3.1.2. A lawyer shall advise and represent his client promptly, conscientiously and diligently. He shall undertake personal responsibility for the discharge of the instructions given to him. He shall keep his client informed as to the progress of the matter entrusted to him.

3.1.3. A lawyer shall not handle a matter which he knows or ought to know he is not competent to handle, without co-operating with a lawyer who is competent to handle it.

A lawyer shall not accept instructions unless he can discharge those instructions promptly having regard to the pressure of other work.

3.1.4. A lawyer shall not be entitled to exercise his right to withdraw from a case in such a way or in such circumstances that the client may be unable to find other legal assistance in time to prevent prejudice being suffered by the client.

3.2. Conflict of Interest

3.2.1. A lawyer may not advise, represent or act on behalf of two or more clients in the same matter if there is a conflict, or a significant risk of a conflict, between the interests of those clients.

3.2.2. A lawyer must cease to act for both client when a conflict of interests arises between those clients and also whenever there is a risk of a breach of confidence or where his independence may be impaired.

3.2.3. A lawyer must also refrain from acting for a new client if there is a risk of a breach of confidence entrusted to the lawyer by a former client or if the knowledge which the lawyer possesses of the affairs of the former client would give an undue advantage to the new client.

3.2.4. Where lawyers are practising in association, paragraphs 3.2.1 to 3.2.3 above shall apply to the association and all its members.

3.3. Pactum de Quota Litis

3.3.1. A lawyer shall not be entitled to make a pactum de quota litis.

3.3.2. By "pactum de quota litis" is meant an agreement between a lawyer and his client entered into prior to final conclusion of a matter to which the client is a party, by virtue of which the client undertakes to pay the lawyer a share of the result regardless of whether this is represented by a sum of money or by any other benefit achieved by the client upon the conclusion of the matter.

3.3.3. The pactum de quota litis does not include an agreement that fees be charged in proportion to the value of a matter handled by the lawyer if this is in accordance with an officially approved fee scale or under the control of competent authority having jurisdiction over the lawyer.

3.4. Regulation of Fees

3.4.1. A fee charged by a lawyer shall be fully disclosed to his client and shall be fair and reasonable.

3.4.2. Subject to any proper agreement to the contrary between a lawyer and his client fees charged by a lawyer shall be subject to regulation in accordance with the rules applied to members of the Bar or Law Society to which he belongs. If he belongs to more than one Bar or Law Society the rules applied shall be those with the closest connection to the contract between the lawyer and his client.

3.5. Payment on Account

If a lawyer requires a payment on account of his fees and/or disbursements such payment should not exceed a reasonable estimate of the fees and probable disbursements involved.

Failing such payment, a lawyer may withdraw from the case or refuse to handle it, but subject always to paragraph 3.1.4 above.

3.6. Fee Sharing with Non-Lawyers

3.6.1. Subject as after-mentioned a lawyer may not share his fees with a person who is not a lawyer except where an association between the lawyer and the other person is permitted by the laws of the Member State to which the lawyer belongs.

3.6.2. The provisions of 3.6.1 above shall not preclude a lawyer from paying a fee, commission or other compensation to a deceased lawyer's heirs or to a retired lawyer in respect of taking over the deceased or retired lawyer's practice.

3.7. Cost Effective Resolution and Availability of Legal Aid

3.7.1. The lawyer should at all times strive to achieve the most cost effective resolution of the client's dispute and should advise the client at appropriate stages as to the desirability of attempting a settlement and/or a reference to alternative dispute resolution.

3.7.2. A lawyer shall inform his client of the availability of legal aid where applicable.

3.8. Clients funds

3.8.1. When lawyers at any time in the course of their practice come into possession of funds on behalf of their clients or third parties (hereinafter called "client's funds") it shall be obligatory:

3.8.1.1. That client's funds shall always be held in an account of a bank or similar institution subject to supervision of Public Authority and that all clients' funds received by a lawyer should be paid into such an account unless the client explicitly or by implication agrees that the funds should be dealt with otherwise.

3.8.1.2. That any account in which the client's funds are held in the name of the lawyer should indicate in the title or designation that the funds are held on behalf of the client or clients of the lawyer.

3.8.1.3. That any account or accounts in which client's funds are held in the name of the lawyer should at all times contain a sum which is not less than the total of the client's funds held by the lawyer.

3.8.1.4. That all funds shall be paid to clients immediately or upon such conditions as the client may authorise.

3.8.1.5. That payments made from client's funds on behalf of a client to any other person including:

(a) payments made to or for one client from funds held for another client;

(b) payment of the lawyer's fees,

be prohibited except to the extent that they are permitted by law or are ordered by the court and have the express or implied authority of the client for whom the payment is being made.

3.8.1.6. That the lawyer shall maintain full and accurate records, available to each client on request, showing all his dealings with his client's funds and distinguishing client's funds from other funds held by him.

3.8.1.7. That the competent authorities in all Member States should have powers to allow them to examine and investigate on a confidential basis the financial records of lawyer's client's funds to ascertain whether or not the rules which they make are being complied with and to impose sanctions upon lawyers who fail to comply with those rules.

3.8.2. Subject as aftermentioned, and without prejudice to the rules set out in 3.8.1 above, a lawyer who holds client's funds in the course of carrying on practice in any Member State must comply with the rules relating to holding and accounting for client's funds which are applied by the competent authorities of the Home Member State.

3.8.3. A lawyer who carries on practice or provides services in a Host Member State may with the agreement of the competent authorities of the Home and Host Member State concerned comply with the requirements of the Host Member State to the exclusion of the requirements of the Home Member State. In that event he shall take reasonable steps to inform his clients that he complies with the requirements in force in the Host Member State.

3.9. Professional Indemnity Insurance

3.9.1. Lawyers shall be insured at all times against claims based on professional negligence of an extent which is reasonable having regard to the nature and extent of the risks which each lawyer may incur in his practice.

3.9.2. When a lawyer provides services or carries out practice in a Host Member State the following shall apply:

3.9.2.1. The lawyer must comply with any Rules relating to his obligation to insure against his professional liability as a lawyer which are in force in his Home Member State.

3.9.2.2. A lawyer who is obliged so to insure in his Home Member State and who provides services or carries out practice in any Host Member State shall use his best endeavours to obtain insurance cover on the basis required in his Home Member State extended to services which he provides or practice which he carries out in a Host Member State.

3.9.2.3. A lawyer who fails to obtain the extended insurance cover referred to in paragraph 3.9.2.2 above or who is not obliged so to insure in his Home Member State and who provides services or carries out practice in a Host Member State shall in so far as possible obtain insurance cover against his professional liability as a lawyer whilst acting for clients in that Host Member State on at least a basis equivalent to that required of lawyers in the Host Member State.

3.9.2.4. To the extent that a lawyer is unable to obtain the insurance cover required by the foregoing rules, he shall inform such of his clients as might be effected.

3.9.2.5. A lawyer who carries out practice or provides services in a Host Member State may with the agreement of the competent authorities of the Home and Host Member States concerned comply with such insurance requirements as are in force in the Host Member State to the exclusion of the insurance requirements of the Home Member State. In this event he shall take reasonable steps to inform his clients that he is insured according to the requirements in force in the Host Member State.

4. Relations with the Courts

4.1 Applicable Rules of Conduct in Court

A lawyer who appears, or takes part in a case before a court or tribunal in a Member State, must comply with the rules of conduct applied before that court or tribunal.

4.2. Fair Conduct of Proceedings

A lawyer must always have due regard for the fair conduct of proceedings. He must not, for example, make contact with the judge without first informing the lawyer acting for the opposing party or submit exhibits, notes or documents to the judge without communicating them in good time to the lawyer on the other side unless such steps are permitted under the relevant rules of procedure. To the extent not prohibited by law a lawyer must not divulge or submit to the court any proposals for settlement of the case made by the other party or its lawyer without the express consent by the other party's lawyer.

4.3. Demeanour in Court

A lawyer shall while maintaining due respect and courtesy towards the court defend the interests of his client honourably and fearlessly without regard to his own interests or to any consequences to himself or to any other person.

4.4. False or Misleading Information

A lawyer shall never knowingly give false or misleading information to the court.

4.5. Extension to Arbitrators Etc.

The rules governing a lawyer's relations with the courts apply also to his relations with arbitrators and any other persons exercising judicial or quasi-judicial functions, even on an occasional basis.

5. Relations between Lawyers

5.1. Corporate Spirit of the Profession

5.1.1. The corporate spirit of the profession requires a relationship of trust and co-operation between lawyers for the benefit of their clients and in order to avoid unnecessary litigation and other behaviour harmful to the reputation of the profession. It can, however, never justify setting the interests of the profession against those of the client.

5.1.2. A lawyer should recognise all other lawyers of Member States as professional colleagues and act fairly and courteously towards them.

5.2. Co-operation Among Lawyers of Different Member States

5.2.1. It is the duty of a lawyer who is approached by a colleague from another Member State not to accept instructions in a matter which he is not competent to undertake. He should in such case be prepared to help his colleague to obtain the information necessary to enable him to instruct a lawyer who is capable of providing the service asked for.

5.2.2. Where a lawyer of a Member State co-operates with a lawyer from another Member State, both have a general duty to take into account the differences which may exist between their respective legal systems and the professional organisations, competences and obligations of lawyers in the Member States concerned.

5.3. Correspondence Between Lawyers

5.3.1. If a lawyer sending a communication to a lawyer in another Member State wishes it remain confidential or without prejudice he should clearly express this intention when communicating the document.

5.3.2. If the recipient of the communication is unable to ensure its status as confidential or without prejudice he should return it to the sender without revealing the contents to others.

5.4. Referral Fees

5.4.1. A lawyer may not demand or accept from another lawyer or any other person a fee, commission or any other compensation for referring or recommending the lawyer to a client.

5.4.2. A lawyer may not pay anyone a fee, commission or any other compensation as a consideration for referring a client to himself.

5.5. Communication with Opposing Parties

A lawyer shall not communicate about a particular case or matter directly with any person whom he knows to be represented or advised in the case or matter by another lawyer, without the consent of that other lawyer (and shall keep the other lawyer informed of any such communications).

5.6. (Deleted by decision of the CCBE Plenary Session in Dublin on December 6th, 2002)

5.7. Responsibility for Fees

In professional relations between members of Bars of different Member States, where a lawyer does not confine himself to recommending another lawyer or introducing him to the client but himself entrusts a correspondent with a particular matter or seeks his advice, he is personally bound, even if the client is insolvent, to pay the fees, costs and outlays which are due to the foreign correspondent. The lawyers concerned may, however, at the outset of the relationship between them make special arrangements on this matter. Further, the instructing lawyer may at any time limit his personal responsibility to the amount of the fees, costs and outlays incurred before intimation to the foreign lawyer of his disclaimer of responsibility for the future.

5.8. Training Young Lawyers

In order to improve trust and co-operation amongst lawyers of different Member States for the clients' benefit there is a need to encourage a better knowledge of the laws and procedures in different Member States. Therefore, when considering the need for the profession to give good training to young lawyers, lawyers should take into account the need to give training to young lawyers from other Member States.

5.9. Disputes amongst Lawyers in Different Member States

5.9.1. If a lawyer considers that a colleague in another Member State has acted in breach of a rule of professional conduct he shall draw the matter to the attention of his colleague.

5.9.2. If any personal dispute of a professional nature arises amongst lawyers in different Member States they should if possible first try to settle it in a friendly way.

5.9.3. A lawyer shall not commence any form of proceedings against a colleague in another Member State on matters referred to in 5.9.1 or 5.9.2 above without first informing the Bars or Law Societies to which they both belong for the purpose of allowing both Bars or Law Societies concerned an opportunity to assist in reaching a settlement.

[NEXT TEXT PAGE IS **F** 289]

Registered European Lawyers (Rules of Professional Conduct) (Scotland) Rules 2001

Rules dated 25 May 2001 made by the Council of the Law Society of Scotland under sections 5, 34(1), 35(1), 37(6) and 43 of, and Schedule 3 to, the Solicitors (Scotland) Act 1980 and approved by the Lord President of the Court of Session under section 34(3) of the said Act and with his concurrence under section 5(1) of the said Act.

Title and Commencement

1. These rules may be cited as the Registered European Lawyers (Rules of Professional Conduct) (Scotland) Rules 2001 and shall come into operation on 1 July 2001.

Definitions and Interpretation

2.—(1) In these rules, unless the context otherwise requires:—

"the Act" means the Solicitors (Scotland) Act 1980 as amended;

"the Council" means the Council of the Society;

"the Directive" means Directive No. 98/5/EC of the European Parliament and Council to facilitate practice of the profession of lawyer on a permanent basis in certain states other than the state in which the professional qualification was obtained;

"European lawyer" shall have the meaning given in paragraphs (2) and (3) of the Principal Regulations;

"the European Lawyers Regulations" means the European Lawyers (Registration) (Scotland) Regulations 2001 made by the Council and dated 25 May 2001;

"the PI Insurance Rules" means the Solicitors (Scotland) Professional Indemnity Insurance Rules 1995 made by the Council and dated 31 March 1995;

"the Practising Certificate Rules" means the Solicitors (Scotland) Practising Certificate Rules 1988 made by the Council and dated 29 July 1988;

"the Principal Regulations" means the European Communities (Lawyer's Practice) (Scotland) Regulations 2000 (SSI 2000 No. 121);

"registered European lawyer" shall have the meaning given in section 65(1) of the Act;

"rules of professional conduct" means rules, regulations, codes of conduct and practice guidelines made or to be made, issued or to be issued, or adopted or to be adopted by the Council or the Society under any rule-making power contained in the Act or delegated legislation or otherwise available to the Council or the Society and as such rules, regulations, codes of conduct and practice guidelines are in force from time to time and shall include, without limiting the foregoing generality, rules, regulations, codes of conduct and practice guidelines relating to professional practice, conduct and discipline, accounts, accounts certificates, the Scottish Solicitors Guarantee Fund, training or admission; and

"the Society" means the Law Society of Scotland.

(2) The provisions of the Interpretation Act 1978 shall apply to the interpretation of these rules as they apply to the interpretation of an Act of Parliament.

(3) The headings to these rules do not form part of these rules.

Purpose of Rules

3. The purpose of these rules is to give further effect to Article 6(1) of the Directive and to regulation 25 of the Principal Regulations.

Applicability of Rules of Professional Conduct

4.—(1) A registered European lawyer shall be subject to the same rules of professional conduct as a solicitor in Scotland.

(2) In particular, but without limiting the generality of paragraph (1) above, a registered European lawyer shall be subject to the rules of professional conduct as set out in the Schedule to these rules.

(3) Notwithstanding paragraph (1) above, a registered European lawyer shall not be subject to the PI Insurance Rules or the Practising Certificate Rules but shall instead be subject to the European Lawyers Regulations.

Construction of Rules of Professional Conduct

5.—(1) Subject to paragraph (2) below, and unless the contrary intention is expressed in any such rule, references in any rule of professional conduct to—

(a) "solicitors" shall include references to registered European lawyers;
(b) "a practising certificate" shall include references to a registered European lawyer's certificate of registration; and
(c) "the roll" shall include references to the register of European lawyers.

(2) In their application to registered European lawyers, the rules of professional conduct shall be construed subject to any contrary provision contained in the Directive, the Principal Regulations or the European Lawyers Regulations.

SCHEDULE

Rule 4(2)

Rules of Professional Conduct

Rules and Regulations

1975: Solicitors (Scotland) Practice Rules ....
1981: Solicitors (Scotland) Practice Rules ....
1986: Solicitors (Scotland) Practice Rules ....
1989: Solicitors (Scotland) (Cross-border Code of Conduct) Practice Rules
1991: Solicitors (Scotland) Practice Rules ....
Solicitors (Scotland) (Multi-Disciplinary Practices) Practice Rules .
1992: Solicitors (Scotland) Order of Precedence, Instructions and Representation Rules ....
Solicitors (Scotland) (Admission with Extended Rights of Audience) Rules ....
Code of Conduct (Scotland) Rules ....
1993: Solicitors (Scotland) (Continuing Professional Development) Regulations ....
Solicitors (Scotland) (Written Fee Charging Agreements) Practice Rules ....
1994: Solicitors (Scotland) Investment Business Training Regulations .....
EC Qualified Lawyers Transfer (Scotland) Regulations ....
1995: Solicitors (Scotland) (Advertising and Promotion) Practice Rules ..
Scottish Solicitors' Guarantee Fund Rules ....
1996: Solicitors (Scotland) (Restriction on Practice as a Principal) Practice Rules ....
Solicitors (Scotland) (Associates, Consultants and Employees) Practice Rules ....
1997: Solicitors (Scotland) Accounts Rules ....
Solicitors (Scotland) Accounts Certificate Rules ....
Solicitors (Scotland) Investment Business Compliance Certificate Rules ....

Solicitors (Scotland) (Practice Management Course) Practice Rules
Solicitors (Scotland) (Conduct of Investment Business) Practice Rules ....
2001: Admission as Solicitor (Scotland) Regulations ....
Solicitors (Scotland) (Incorporated Practices) Practice Rules ....

Codes of Conduct

1996: Code of Conduct for Criminal Work ....
1999: Code of Conduct for Scottish Solicitors ....

Practice Guidelines

1992: Law Society Guidelines for the Recruitment of Staff to Undertake Investment Business ....
1994: Conflict of Interest in Commercial Security Transactions ....
1995: Guide to Professional Conduct and Ethics in Insolvency ....
1996: Law Society Guidance Notes on Exhibition of Title Deeds ....
1997: Law Society Guidance Notes to the Investment Business Rules and Regulations ....
Law Society Guidance Notes on Capital Adequacy ....
Simple Guide to the Solicitors (Scotland) Accounts Rules 1997, Solicitors (Scotland) Accounts Certificate Rules 1997, Money Laundering Regulations 1993 ....
Suggested List of Items that should be Special Areas of Concern to Designated Cashroom Partners ....
Guidance on Retention/Destruction of Files and Records ....
1998: Law Society Guidelines on Retention of Funds ....
and Law Society Guidelines on Faxed and E-Mail Documents ....
1999 Law Society Guidelines on Property Schedules and Mortgage Advice Service ....
Law Society Guidelines for Compliance with Continuing Professional
Development Regulations ....
Law Society Guidelines on Conflict of Interest ....
Law Society Guidelines on Confidentiality ....
Law Society Guidelines on Mandates in Executries ....
Law Society Guidelines on Conflict of Interest and Ranking Agreements ....
Law Society Guidelines on Closing of Files ....
Law Society Guidelines on Terms of Business ....
Law Society Guidelines on Mandates ....
Law Society Guidelines on Avoidance of Delay in Concluding Missives ....
Law Society Guidelines on Fixed Price Offers ....
Law Society Guidelines on Powers of Attorney ....
Law Society Guidelines on Acting for Separated Spouses ....
Law Society Guidelines on Comments to the Media by Solicitors ..
Law Society Guidelines on Sending Document to Unrepresented Party for Signature ....
Law Society Guidelines on Settlement Cheques Sent to be Held as Undelivered ....
Law Society Revised Guidelines on Closing Dates and Notes of Interest ....
Law Society Guidelines on Duty to Lodge a Joint Minute and move for decree ....
Law Society Guidelines on Conflict of Interest between Borrower and Spouse ....
Law Society's Risk Management Flowchart and Procedures ....

European Lawyers (Registration) (Scotland) Regulations 2001

The European Lawyers (Registration) (Scotland) Regulations 2001 dated 25 May 2001 made by the Council of the Law Society of Scotland under regulation 16 of the European Communities (Lawyer's Practice) (Scotland) Regulations 2000 and section 24A of the Solicitors (Scotland) Act 1980.

Title and Commencement

1. These regulations may be cited as the European Lawyers (Registration) (Scotland) Regulations 2001 and shall come into operation on 1 July 2001.

Definitions and Interpretation

2.—(1) In these regulations, unless the context otherwise requires:—

"the Act" means the Solicitors (Scotland) Act 1980 as amended;

"applicant" means a European lawyer who wishes to pursue professional activities under his home professional title on a permanent basis in Scotland and who wishes to apply pursuant to regulation 16 of the Principal Regulations to be entered on the register established and maintained by the Society pursuant to regulation 15 of the Principal Regulations and section 12A of the Act;

"certificate of registration" means a certificate of registration in respect of a registered European lawyer issued in accordance with the provisions of the Act in, or substantially in, the form set out in Schedule 1 to these regulations;

"the Council" means the Council of the Society;

"the Directive" means Directive No. 98/5/EC of the European Parliament and Council to facilitate practice of the profession of lawyer on a permanent basis in certain states other than the state in which the professional qualification was obtained;

"European lawyer" shall have the meaning given in paragraphs (2) and (3) of regulation 2 of the Principal Regulations;

"the Guarantee Fund" means The Scottish Solicitors Guarantee Fund as referred to in section 43 of the Act;

"grouping" means any entity, whether or not having legal personality, formed under the law of a Member State of the European Community, within which lawyers pursue their professional activities jointly under a joint name;

"home State" shall have the meaning given in paragraph (1) of regulation 2 of the Principal Regulations;

"home professional title" shall have the meaning given in paragraph (1) of regulation 2 of the Principal Regulations;

"lawyer" means a person who is a national of a Member State of the European Community and who is authorised to pursue his professional activities under one of the professional titles referred to in paragraph (4) of regulation 2 of the Principal Regulations;

"principal" means a European lawyer or a registered European lawyer who is a sole practitioner or a partner in a firm of lawyers or a member of an incorporated practice of lawyers or of a grouping of lawyers;

"the Principal Regulations" means the European Communities (Lawyer's Practice) (Scotland) Regulations 2000 (SSI 2000 No 121);

"registered European lawyer" shall have the meaning given in section 65(1) of the Act;

"the Society" means the Law Society of Scotland; and

"year" means the period of twelve months ending on 31 October.

(2) The provisions of the Interpretation Act 1978 shall apply to the

interpretation of these regulations as they apply to the interpretation of an Act of Parliament.

(3) The headings to these regulations do not form part of these regulations.

Purpose of Regulations

3. The purpose of the Principal Regulations is to implement the Directive in Scotland. These regulations make provision in respect of applications for registration with the Society by European lawyers pursuant to regulation 16 of the Principal Regulations and in respect of applications for, and the issue of, certificates of registration for registered European lawyers pursuant to section 24A of the Act.

Application for Registration

4. An applicant shall apply in writing to the Society for registration by completing (so far as applicable to him) and signing a form in, or substantially in, the form set out in Schedule 2 to these regulations, and by making payment of such fee(s) as the Council shall from time to time prescribe.

Determination of Application

5. The Council shall determine an application pursuant to regulation 4 in accordance with the Principal Regulations.

Entry on Register and Issue of Certificate of Registration to Applicant

6. If the Council grants an application pursuant to regulation 4 it shall-

(a) cause the name of the applicant to be entered on the register of European lawyers established and maintained by the Society pursuant to regulation 15 of the Principal Regulations and section 12A of the Act; and

(b) subject always to the provisions of regulations 9 and 10, cause a certificate of registration to be issued to the applicant.

Application for Certificate of Registration by Registered European Lawyer

7. A registered European lawyer who wishes to obtain a certificate of registration shall apply for the same by completing (so far as applicable to him) and signing a form in, or substantially in, the form set out in Schedule 2 to these regulations and by making payment of such fee(s) as the Council shall from time to time prescribe.

Issue of Certificate of Registration to Registered European Lawyer

8. Subject always to the provisions of regulations 9 and 10 and to the provisions of the Act and the Principal Regulations in respect of withdrawal or suspension of registration the Council shall, on receipt of an application pursuant to regulation 7 which has been duly completed and signed, cause a certificate of registration to be issued to the registered European lawyer without delay. Any such certificate may, in accordance with the provisions of the Act, and in particular section 24C thereof, be issued subject to conditions.

Professional Indemnity Insurance

9. The Council shall not issue a certificate of registration to any applicant making application pursuant to regulation 4 or to any registered European lawyer making application pursuant to regulation 7 unless he provides, along with his application—

(a) evidence that a certificate of professional indemnity insurance has been issued to him or to the practice unit in or for which he practises being insurance which is equivalent in terms of the conditions and extent of its cover to the professional indemnity insurance which is

required of solicitors in Scotland by the Council; or
(b) evidence that he is covered by professional indemnity insurance taken out in accordance with the professional rules of his home State and that such insurance is equivalent in terms of the conditions and the extent of its cover to the insurance referred to in paragraph (a) above; or
(c) where the insurance referred to in paragraph (b) above is less than equivalent in terms of the conditions and the extent of its cover to the insurance referred to in paragraph (a) above, evidence of the conditions and extent of cover of professional indemnity insurance taken out in accordance with the professional rules of his home State and, to the extent of the lack of equivalence, evidence that a certificate of insurance has been issued as specified in paragraph (a) above.

Guarantee Fund

10. The Council shall not issue a certificate of registration to any applicant making application pursuant to regulation 4 or to any registered European lawyer making application pursuant to regulation 7 unless he provides, along with his application-
(a) a contribution by him or by the practice unit in or for which he practises to the Society on behalf of the Guarantee Fund in terms of section 43 of, and Schedule 3 to, the Act; or
(b) evidence that he is covered by a guarantee taken out in accordance with the professional rules of his home State and that such guarantee is equivalent in terms of the conditions and the extent of its cover to the Guarantee Fund; or
(c) where the guarantee referred to in paragraph (b) above is less than equivalent in terms of the conditions and the extent of its cover to the Guarantee Fund, evidence of the conditions and extent of cover of the guarantee taken out in accordance with the professional rules of his home State and, to the extent of the lack of equivalence:
(i) a contribution as specified in paragraph (a) above; or
(ii) evidence that a guarantee (other than such as is specified in paragraph (a) above) has been issued to him or the practice unit in or for which he practises.

Register of Applications and Certificates of Registration Issued

11.—(1) The Council shall cause to be kept in respect of each year a register of applications for certificates of registration and of certificates issued.

(2) The register shall be in such form as the Council may determine.

SCHEDULE 1

Regulation 2(1)

Form of Certificate of Registration

PURSUANT to regulation 16 of the European Communities (Lawyer's Practice) (Scotland) Regulations 2000 and section 24B of the Solicitors (Scotland) Act 1980

THE COUNCIL OF THE LAW SOCIETY OF SCOTLAND HEREBY CERTIFIES that

has lodged with the Council an application in writing pursuant to the said Regulations and Act, is entitled, subject to the provisions of the said

Regulations and Act, to carry out under his/her home professional title any professional activities whether in Scotland or elsewhere that may lawfully be carried out by a member of The Law Society of Scotland *until the thirty first day of October two thousand and* and is a registered European lawyer with The Law Society of Scotland.

[This certificate is subject to the following conditions:]*

GIVEN under the hand of the Secretary of
THE LAW SOCIETY OF SCOTLAND
this day
of 20

Secretary

Entered

* Delete if inapplicable. Conditions may be imposed in the circumstances specified in section 24C of the Solicitors (Scotland) Act 1980.

SCHEDULE 2

Regulations 4 and 7

Form of Application for a Certificate of Registration

FORM OF APPLICATION FOR REGISTRATION AS A EUROPEAN LAWYER AND FOR A CERTIFICATE OF REGISTRATION
FORM OF APPLICATION FOR A CERTIFICATE OF REGISTRATION FOR A REGISTERED EUROPEAN LAWYER

If this is the first time that you have applied to be registered as a European Lawyer with the Law Society of Scotland please complete the entire form and complete, sign and date the declaration at Part 1. If you are already registered with the Law Society of Scotland as a European lawyer please check that the information printed below is correct and amend or complete it to the extent that it is not correct or is incomplete, and complete, sign and date the declaration at Part 2.

APPLICATION FOR REGISTRATION

1. Your Full Name and Personal Details

Surname ....

First name(s) ....

Title (ie Mr/Mrs/Miss/Ms/Dr/Prof) ....

Sex: Male/Female ....

Address ....

Town ....

Region ....

Country ....

Post Code ....

Telephone ....

Fax ....

E-mail ....

Date of Birth ....

Place of Birth ....

Nationality ....

2. Name and address of your place or places of business in Scotland

Name ....

Address ....

Town ....

Region ....

Country ....

Post Code ....

Telephone ....

Fax ....

E-mail ....

3. Any business name and address of yours elsewhere in the United Kingdom and in any Member State of the European Community

Name ....
Address ....
Town ....
Region ....
Country ....
Post Code ....
Telephone ....
Fax ....
E-mail ....

4. Please confirm your current status

Partner ....
Sole Principal ....
Assistant ....
Consultant ....
Director ....
Other (please specify) ....

5. Are you a partner, director or member of any firm or grouping?

Yes/No ....

6. Name and address of the principal place of business of any firm or grouping of which you are a partner, director or member

Name ....
Address ....
Town ....
Region ....
Country ....
Post Code ....
Telephone ....
Fax ....
E-mail ....

7. Are any partners of that firm or members or directors of that grouping not lawyers?

Yes/No ....

8. Is the capital of that firm or grouping held entirely or partly by persons who are not lawyers?

Yes/No ....

9. Is the name under which that firm or grouping practises used by persons who are not lawyers?

Yes/No ....

10. Is the decision making power in that firm or grouping exercised de facto or de jure by persons who are not lawyers?

Yes/No ....

11. Your home professional title(s) expressed in an official language of each of your home States under whose home professional title you intend to practise in Scotland and also expressed in English

Title in official language of home state ....
Title in English ....
Title in official language of home state ....
Title in English ....
Title in official language of home state ....
Title in English ....

12. Name and address of the competent authority (i.e. Bar, Chamber, Law Society and/or Court) with which you are registered in each home State under whose home professional title you intend to practise in Scotland

Name ....
Address ....
Town ....
Region ....
Country ....
Post Code ....
Telephone ....
Fax ....
E-Mail ....

13. Have you completed your training?

Yes/No ....

14. Are you currently authorised to practise by the competent authority or authorities whose details you have provided in answer to question 12?

Yes/No ....

15. Have you previously made an application for registration under the Establishment Directive?

In the Scottish jurisdiction (Yes/No) ....

In another jurisdiction (Yes/No) ....

If yes, which one(s) ....

....

16. Full details of professional indemnity insurance as is required of you (or of your firm or grouping) in accordance with the rules which your home State(s) lays down for professional activities pursued in its territory, together with full details of the conditions and extent of cover actually taken out by you (or by your firm or grouping) in respect of professional indemnity insurance.

17. Full details of membership of any professional guarantee fund as is required of you (or of your firm or grouping) in accordance with the rules which your home State(s) lays down for professional activities pursued in its territory, together with full details of the conditions and extent of cover actually taken out by you (or by your firm or grouping) in respect of any professional guarantee fund.

18. Material events

Have formal proceedings alleging professional misconduct by you been started before a court or disciplinary tribunal in any jurisdiction? If yes in any case, please give details.

Yes/No ....

Have you ever been struck off or suspended from practice as a result of disciplinary proceedings in any jurisdiction?

Yes/No ....

Have you been subject to any other disciplinary sanctions in any jurisdiction?

Yes/No ....

Are there any material events which have occurred relating to your fitness to practise since your last application (if any) for registration (e.g. bankruptcy)?

Yes/No ....

Part 1 — APPLICATION FOR FIRST REGISTRATION

I enclose herewith:—

(a) proof that I am a national of a Member State of the European Community,
(b) a recent photograph of myself, which I have signed on the reverse and which I agree that the Council of the Law Society of Scotland may retain,
(c) a certificate or certificates, dated not more than three months before the date of this application, confirming my registration with the competent authority in each home State under whose home professional title I intend to practise in Scotland and, where that certificate is not in English, a certified translation of it into English, and
(d) payment of the registration fee of £ .

I hereby declare that I am not registered as a European Lawyer pursuant to the European Communities (Lawyers Practice) (Scotland) Regulations 2000 with the Faculty of Advocates in Scotland or with the Inns of Court and the General Council of the Bar of England and Wales or with the Executive Council of the Inn of Court of Northern Ireland and that I am not a barrister in the Republic of Ireland.

I hereby declare that I am authorised to practise under the professional title(s) specified in my response to question 11 above.

I hereby declare that the information supplied in this application is complete and accurate and that I shall advise the Law Society of Scotland immediately of any significant changes to the information provided in this form which may occur before the decision on my application is finalised.

I hereby agree to abide by the rules of professional conduct of the Law Society of Scotland during the period of my registration and I also agree that my home Bar, Chamber, Law Society and/or Court and any other Bar, Chamber, Law Society and/or Court with which I am registered from time to time and the Law Society of Scotland can freely exchange all relevant information about my professional activities.

I hereby apply for registration as a European Lawyer and for a certificate of registration for the year ending 31 October 20

Dated this day of 20

.... (Signature)

Part 2 — APPLICATION FOR SUBSEQUENT CERTIFICATE OF REGISTRATION

I enclose herewith:—

(a) a certificate or certificates, dated not more than three months before the date of this application, confirming my registration with the competent authority in each home State under whose home professional title I intend to continue to practise in Scotland and, where that certificate is not in English, a certified translation of it into English, and

(b) payment of the registration fee of £ .

I hereby declare that I am not registered as a European Lawyer pursuant to the European Communities (Lawyers Practice) (Scotland) Regulations 2000 with the Faculty of Advocates in Scotland or with the Inns of Court and the General Council of the Bar of England and Wales or with the Executive Council of the Inn of Court of Northern Ireland and that I am not a barrister in the Republic of Ireland.

I hereby declare that I am authorised to practise under the professional title(s) specified at question 11 above.

I hereby declare that the information set out in this application is complete and accurate and that I shall advise the Law Society of Scotland immediately of any significant changes to the information provided in this form which may occur before the decision on my application is finalised.

Declaration in regard to the Solicitors (Scotland) Accounts Rules :

1. I hereby declare that I have complied with the Solicitors (Scotland) Accounts Rules in so far as they are applicable to me.
2. I hereby declare that I have not held or received clients' money during the practice year ended 31 October 20 .

(Delete 1 or 2 above, whichever is inapplicable).

I hereby agree to abide by the rules of professional conduct of the Law Society of Scotland during the period of my registration and I also agree that my home Bar, Chamber, Law Society and/or Court and any other Bar, Chamber, Law Society and/or Court with which I am registered from time to time and the Law Society of Scotland can freely exchange all relevant information about my professional activities.

I hereby apply for a certificate of registration for the year ending 31 October 20

Dated this day of 20

.... (Signature)

NOTES

1. Where there is insufficient space for a full answer to any of the questions on this form, please provide the additional information on a continuation sheet under reference to the relevant numbered question.

2. For the purpose of question 5, a "firm" means a partnership and a "grouping" means any other entity, whether or not having legal personality, formed under the law of a Member State of the European Community, within which lawyers pursue their professional activities jointly under a joint name.

3. If you have answered no to question 5, then you need not answer questions 6 to 10.

4. Please note, in relation to questions 11 and 12, that you should supply the required information in respect of each home State under whose professional title you intend to practise in Scotland.

5. Please provide full information in answering questions 16 and 17. This information is required in order that the Law Society can assess whether the cover which is taken out either by you or by your firm or grouping is equivalent to the cover required of solicitors in Scotland in respect of professional indemnity insurance and membership of a guarantee fund. All applicants are required to provide this information. It will assist the processing of your application if you are able to supply copies of relevant certificates of insurance together with policy schedules specifying the conditions and extent of the cover.

6. If you have answered yes to any part of question 18, please give full details.

7. Documents such as a photocopy of your passport will generally be acceptable proof of your nationality.

8. It is essential that the certificate or certificates confirming your registration with the competent authority in each home State under whose home professional title you intend to practise in Scotland is/are dated not more than three months before the date on which you sign this application form. It is also essential that the certificate or certificates confirm your date of admission, that you are entitled to practise under the relevant home professional title, specify any limitations on your entitlement to practise under the relevant home professional title, and confirm that there are either no completed or pending disciplinary proceedings against you, or give full details if there are or have been such proceedings.

9. The registration fee is £[ ]. It must be enclosed with this application form and cheques should be made payable to "The Law Society of Scotland" and crossed "& Co".

Solicitors (Scotland) (Written Fee Charging Agreements) Practice Rules 1993

Rules dated 29th July 1993 made by the Council of the Law Society of Scotland and approved by the Lord President of the Court of Session in terms of section 34 of the Solicitors (Scotland) Act 1980.

1. These Rules may be cited as the Solicitors (Scotland) (Written Fee Charging Agreements) Practice Rules 1993.

2. These Rules shall come into operation on 1st August 1993.

3. In these Rules unless the context otherwise requires:—

[1] "2005 Rules" means the Solicitors (Scotland) (Registered Foreign Lawyers) etc Practice Rules 2005;

"the Act" means the Solicitors (Scotland) Act 1980;

"the Council" means the Council of the Law Society of Scotland;

[2] "solicitor" means a solicitor holding a practising certificate under the Act and includes a firm of solicitors and an incorporated practice and shall include a registered foreign lawyer to whom these rules apply in terms of rule 4(2) or (3) of the 2005 Rules and a Scottish multi-national practice and a Scottish branch of a multi-national practice (in each case as defined in rule 7 of the 2005 Rules);

"written fee charging agreement" means an agreement in writing between a solicitor and his client as to the solicitor's fees in respect of any work done or to be done by the solicitor for his client entered into in terms of section 61(A)(1) of the Act.

NOTES

[1] Inserted by the Solicitors (Scotland) (Registered Foreign Lawyers) etc. Practice Rules 2005, Sch.5 (effective May 1, 2005).

[2] As amended by the Solicitors (Scotland) (Registered Foreign Lawyers) etc. Practice Rules 2005, Sch.5 (effective May 1, 2005).

4. A written fee charging agreement shall not contain a consent to registration for preservation and execution.

5. The Council shall have power on cause shown to waive the provisions of these Rules in any particular case, and to revoke such a waiver.

6. Breach of any of these Rules may be treated as professional misconduct for the purposes of Part IV of the Act (Complaints and Disciplinary Proceedings).

Solicitors (Scotland) (Industrial Action by Solicitors) Practice Rules 2003

Rules dated 27th June 2003, made by the Council of The Law Society of Scotland and approved by the Lord President of the Court of Session under section 34 of the Solicitors (Scotland) Act 1980.

1.—(1) These rules may be cited as the Solicitors (Scotland) Practice Rules 2003.

(2) These rules shall come into operation on 1st September 2003.

2.—(1) In these rules, unless the content otherwise requires:—

"Courts" means the civil and criminal courts in Scotland, the House of Lords, the Judicial Committee of the Privy Council, the Court of Justice of the European Communities and the European Court of Human Rights.

"dispute" means a "trade dispute" as defined in section 29 of the Trade Union and Labour Relations Act 1974.

"Industrial action" means an act done or taken by a solicitor in contemplation or furtherance of a dispute.

(2) Words and expressions defined in the Solicitors (Scotland) Act 1980 shall, unless the content otherwise requires, have the same meanings in these rules.

(3) The Interpretation Act 1978 applies to these rules as it applies to an Act of Parliament.

3. Subject to rule 4 hereof, a solicitor may take industrial action.

4.—(1) Notwithstanding that a solicitor is taking or has taken industrial action, he will (a) fulfil his professional duties to the courts or to the Scottish Parliament and to the Parliament of the United Kingdom of Great Britain and Northern Ireland, and (b) fulfil any personal obligation undertaken by him other than an obligation which is imposed upon him under the terms and conditions of his employment.

(2) Notwithstanding that a solicitor is about to take, is taking or has taken industrial action, he will take all reasonable steps open to him to secure the consent of the appropriate body organising such industrial action to his acting as a solicitor (a) where a failure to do so could result in danger to any member or members of the public and (b) where a failure to do so would cause serious damage to a party other than his employer.

Solicitors (Scotland) Professional Indemnity Insurance Rules 2005

[June 2005]

Rules dated 29 April 2005 made by the Council of the Law Society of Scotland with the concurrence of the Lord President of the Court of Session under section 44 of the Solicitors (Scotland) Act 1980

Citation, commencement, revocation and transitional provisions

1.—(1) These Rules may be cited as the Solicitors (Scotland) Professional Indemnity Insurance Rules 2005.

(2) These Rules shall come into operation on 1 June 2005.

(3) The Solicitors (Scotland) Professional Indemnity Insurance Rules 1995 (the "1995 Rules") are hereby revoked.

(4) All acts done under or pursuant to the 1995 Rules shall be treated as having been done under or pursuant to these Rules, except insofar as they are inconsistent with these Rules.

Definitions and interpretation

2.—(1) In these Rules, unless the context otherwise requires—

"the Act" means the Solicitors (Scotland) Act 1980;

"acceptable alternative insurer" means a person so designated by the Council in terms of rule 8;

"authorised insurer" means any person permitted under the Financial Services and Markets Act 2000 to carry on liability insurance business or pecuniary loss insurance business;

"brokers" means the brokers from time to time appointed by the Council to act on behalf of the Society and its members in relation to any master policy entered into by the Society in terms of these Rules;

"the Council" means the Council of the Society;

"principal place of business" means the principal place of business of a multi-national practice determined in accordance with the Solicitors (Scotland) (Principal Place of Business) Practice Rules 2005;

"the Society" means the Law Society of Scotland; and

"solicitor" means a solicitor holding a practising certificate under the Act and includes a firm of solicitors and an incorporated practice, and also includes registered foreign lawyers and multi-national practices.

(2) The Interpretation Act 1978 applies to the interpretation of these Rules as it applies to the interpretation of an Act of Parliament.

Application

3. These Rules apply to every solicitor who is, or is held out to the public as, a principal in private practice in Scotland.

Principals in private practice

4.—(1) For the purposes of these Rules, a solicitor who is a sole practitioner, a partner of a firm of solicitors, a member or director of an incorporated practice or a member of a multi-national practice having its principal place of business in Scotland is a principal in private practice in Scotland.

(2) A solicitor shall not be deemed to be a principal in private practice or to be held out as such by reason only—

(a) that he is a member of a multi-national practice having its principal place of business outwith Scotland; or

(b) that he practises only as consultant or associate to another solicitor provided that if his name appears on the name-plate or letter paper of such other solicitor it is accompanied by the designation "Consultant" or "Associate"; or

(c) in the case of a solicitor employed by another solicitor that the former in carrying out work for his employer uses his own name.

Master policy

5.—(1) The Society shall take out and maintain with authorised insurers to be determined from time to time by the Council a master policy in terms to be approved by the Council to provide indemnity against such classes of professional liability as the Council may decide. The Council at its discretion may amend the terms of the master policy from time to time.

(2) Subject to rule 7, the master policy shall provide indemnity for all solicitors to whom these Rules apply and for such former solicitors and other parties as may be mentioned in the master policy.

(3) The limits of indemnity and the self-insured amounts under the master policy shall be as may be determined from time to time by the Council.

(4) Nothing in these Rules shall prohibit any solicitor from arranging with the insurers to extend the cover provided by the master policy if and on such terms as the insurers may agree.

Obligation to be insured under master policy

6. Subject to rule 7, every solicitor to whom these Rules apply shall be obliged to be insured under the master policy and—

(a) to comply with the terms of the master policy and of any certificate of insurance issued to him thereunder; and

(b) to produce along with each application for a practising certificate a certificate from the brokers certifying that the solicitor in question is insured under the master policy for the practice year then commencing or the part thereof still to run as the case may be, or such other evidence of such insurance as may be acceptable to the Council.

Exceptions

7.—(1) The master policy need not provide indemnity for any solicitor to whom these Rules apply who is a member of a multi-national practice.

(2) Where in terms of paragraph (1) no indemnity is provided by the master policy in respect of a solicitor to whom these Rules apply:—

(a) that solicitor shall not be obliged to comply with rule 6, and

(b) that solicitor shall be obliged to be insured with an acceptable alternative insurer, in terms equivalent to the terms of the master policy or acceptable to the Council and:—

(i) shall comply with the terms of that insurance policy and of any certificate of insurance issued to him thereunder; and

(ii) shall produce along with each application for a practising certificate (or, if he is a registered foreign lawyer, registration certificate) a certificate certifying that he is insured for the practice year in question or the part thereof still to run as the case may be, or such other evidence of such insurance as may be acceptable to the Council.

Acceptable alternative insurer

8. The Council shall designate an authorised insurer or authorised insurers as an acceptable alternative insurer or as acceptable alternative insurers for the purposes of rule 7.

Waiver

9. The Council shall have power in any case or class of case to waive any of the provisions of these Rules and to revoke any such waiver.

Additional powers

10. The Council is hereby empowered to take such steps as it may consider expedient in order to—

(a) ascertain whether or not these Rules are being complied with; or

(b) satisfy itself with regard to any matters arising out of the master policy or any insurance policy taken out in accordance with rule 7(2)(b).

Professional practice

11. Failure to comply with these Rules may be treated as professional misconduct for the purposes of Part IV of the Act.

Solicitors (Scotland) Professional Indemnity Insurance Contingency Fund Rules 2007

Rules dated 29th June 2007 made by the Council of the Law Society of Scotland with the concurrence of the Lord President of the Court of Session under section 44 of the Solicitors (Scotland) Act 1980.

Citation and Commencement

1.—(1) These Rules may be cited as the Solicitors (Scotland) Professional Indemnity Insurance Contingency Fund Rules 2007.

(2) These Rules shall come into operation on 1st September 2007.

Definitions and Interpretation

2.—(1) In these Rules—

"the Act" means the Solicitors (Scotland) Act 1980;

"contingency fund" means the fund which was established in terms of Rule 6(2) of the Solicitors (Scotland) Professional Indemnity Insurance Rules 1995 for the purpose of refunding to practice units such portion of the premiums paid by them as was attributable to circumstances intimated in accordance with the master policy if and when the brokers were satisfied that no claim would result from such circumstances;

"contingency fund monies" means the monies which remain in the contingency fund as at the date specified in Rule 1(2);

"professional indemnity purpose" means any purpose concerning indemnity for solicitors and former solicitors of the Society against any class of professional liability which is not otherwise funded—

(a) in terms of rules made under section 44 of the Act, or

(b) by the Society in terms of arrangements for such indemnity in respect of its activities;

"the Society" means the Law Society of Scotland; and

"solicitors" means solicitors holding practising certificates under the Act and includes firms of solicitors and incorporated practices, and also includes registered foreign lawyers and multi-national practices; and "former solicitors" shall be construed accordingly.

(2) The Interpretation Act 1978 applies to the interpretation of these Rules as it applies to the interpretation of an Act of Parliament.

Contingency Fund Monies

3.—(1) The Society shall manage and administer the contingency fund monies.

(2) The Society may use the contingency fund monies for any professional indemnity purpose.

(3) The Society may use the contingency fund monies to pay costs and expenses reasonably incurred in connection with the management and administration of those monies or with their use for any professional indemnity purpose.

Solicitors (Scotland) (Incorporated Practices) Practice Rules 2001

Rules dated 25th May 2001, made by the Council of the Law Society of Scotland under section 34(1) of the Solicitors (Scotland) Act 1980 and approved by the Lord President of the Court of Session in terms of section 34(3) of the said Act.

Citation and Commencement

1.—(1) These rules may be cited as the Solicitors (Scotland) (Incorporated Practices) Practice Rules 2001.

(2) These rules shall come into operation on 1st July 2001.

Definitions

2.—(1) In these rules, unless the context otherwise requires:—

"the Act" means the Solicitors (Scotland) Act 1980;

[1] "the 1986 Act" means the Company Directors Disqualification Act 1986 and shall include that Act as applied to limited liability partnerships and any legislation in any other jurisdiction having equivalent effect;

"company" shall have the meaning given in section 735 of the Companies Act 1985;

"the Council" means the Council of the Society;

"incorporated practice" means a body corporate recognised by the Council in terms of section 34(1A) of the Act and these rules as being suitable to undertake the provision of professional services such as are provided by solicitors;

"limited liability partnership" means a body corporate incorporated under the Limited Liability Partnerships Act 2000;

"registrar of companies" means the registrar or other officer performing under the Companies Act 1985 the duty of registration of companies or of registration of limited liability partnerships, as the case may be;

"the Secretary" means the Secretary of the Society and includes any person authorised by the Council to act on his behalf;

"the Society" means the Law Society of Scotland established under the Act; and

[1] "solicitor" means any person enrolled as a solicitor in pursuance of the Act and who holds a practising certificate under the Act free of conditions imposed in terms of section 15, section 24C or other sections of the Act, or any regulations made thereunder or by the Scottish Solicitors Discipline Tribunal; and shall include a firm of solicitors and an association of solicitors and also includes a registered foreign lawyer.

(2) The Interpretation Act 1978 applies to the interpretation of these rules as it applies to the interpretation of an Act of Parliament.

(3) The headings to these rules do not form part of these rules.

NOTE

[1] As amended by the Solicitors (Scotland) (Registered Foreign Lawyers) etc. Practice Rules 2005, Sch.5 (effective May 1, 2005).

Permission

3. Subject to the provisions of these rules, a solicitor or an incorporated practice may trade as a body corporate in terms of section 34(1A) of the Act provided:—

(a) any such body corporate has been recognised by the Council as an incorporated practice;

(b) the control of any such body corporate is exclusively by solicitors or other incorporated practices;

(c) the membership of any such body corporate is restricted to solicitors or other incorporated practices; and
(d) the registered office of any such body corporate is situated in Scotland.

Application

4. Any person wishing to form an incorporated practice shall, at least three months prior to the anticipated date of commencement of business as such incorporated practice, submit to the Council:—

(a) in all cases—
  (i) the names, designations and business addresses of all solicitors who will be members of the incorporated practice;
  (ii) the names, and addresses of the registered offices, of all incorporated practices which will be members of the incorporated practice;
  (iii) the proposed name, and address of the registered office, of the incorporated practice;
  (iv) a completed form of application for recognition as an incorporated practice in terms of the schedule to these rules; and
  (v) the fee to be prescribed from time to time by the Council in connection with such application;
(b) in the case of an incorporated practice which is to be a company-
  (i) the names, designations and business addresses of all solicitors or incorporated practices who will be directors of the incorporated practice; and
  (ii) a draft of the memorandum and articles of association of the incorporated practice;
(c) in the case of an incorporated practice which is to be a limited liability partnership, a draft of the incorporation document of the incorporated practice; and
(d) in the case of an incorporated practice to be incorporated with limited liability, an irrevocable undertaking to the Council by each of the solicitors and incorporated practices who will be members of the incorporated practice that he or it or they will jointly and severally along with the other members of the incorporated practice reimburse to the Society grants paid out of the Scottish Solicitors' Guarantee Fund in terms of section 43 of the Act to a person who has suffered pecuniary loss by reason of dishonesty on the part of the incorporated practice or any member, director, manager, secretary or other employee thereof and that to any extent to which the Society shall have been unable to recover the amount of said grants from the incorporated practice or any liquidator or administrator thereof.

Memorandum and Articles of Association

5.—(1) The memorandum and articles of association of an incorporated practice which is a company shall contain provisions which show that it complies and will continue to comply with these rules (as in force from time to time) including, without prejudice to the foregoing generality, provisions to the following effect:—

(a) that no person shall be appointed or re-appointed or act as a director unless he is a member of the incorporated practice duly qualified within the meaning of sub-paragraph (d) hereof;
(b) that no person other than a person duly qualified to act as a director may be appointed as an alternate director;
(c) that a director or alternate director shall vacate office if he ceases to be a member of the company or to be qualified to act as a director;
(d) that no person shall be capable of being a member of the incorporated practice or (subject to sub-paragraph (f) hereof) enjoy any of the rights of members unless he or it is a solicitor or an incorporated practice;

(e) that (subject to sub-paragraph (f) hereof) any member who ceases to be a solicitor or incorporated practice shall forthwith transfer his or its shares or other interest in the incorporated practice to another solicitor or incorporated practice, or otherwise cease to be a member of the incorporated practice;

(f) that, in the case of an incorporated practice which has a share capital, the executor of a deceased member of the incorporated practice shall have no voting rights in respect of his membership of the incorporated practice; and

(g) that, in the case of an incorporated practice limited by guarantee, membership shall cease on death.

(2) The memorandum and articles of association of an incorporated practice which is a company shall contain provisions to anticipate and to deal with the situation where for whatever reason there is no longer a solicitor, or other validly constituted incorporated practice, exercising the day to day management and control of the incorporated practice. Without prejudice to the foregoing, the memorandum and articles shall contain specific provisions for:—

(a) the operation in the situation aforesaid of all client accounts in the name of the incorporated practice; and

(b) suitable arrangements in the situation aforesaid for making available to its clients or to some other solicitor or incorporated practice instructed by its clients or itself:—

(i) all deeds, wills, securities, papers, books of account, records, vouchers and other documents in its possession or control which are held on behalf of its clients or which relate to any trust of which it is sole trustee or co-trustee only with one or more of its employees; and

(ii) all sums of money due from it or held by it on behalf of its clients or subject to any trust as aforesaid.

(3) The memorandum and articles of association of an incorporated practice which is a company shall be only in terms previously approved by the Council, following submission of a draft thereof in terms of rule 4(b)(ii), and thereafter no such incorporated practice shall alter its memorandum and articles without the prior consent of the Council.

(4) The Council may charge a fee in respect of its examination and, if thought fit, its approval of the memorandum and articles of association of an incorporated practice which is a company or any alteration thereof and such fee shall be in addition to the fee referred to in rule 4(a)(v).

Undertaking to Council

6. Every solicitor who and every incorporated practice which becomes a member of an incorporated practice which is incorporated with limited liability shall grant an undertaking to the Council on the same terms as the undertaking described in rule 4(d).

Ongoing Provisions

7.—(1) The members and directors of an incorporated practice which is a company shall ensure that the conditions of its memorandum and articles of association are given effect to at all times and without delay.

(2) The Council may at any time require an incorporated practice which is a company to demonstrate that the requirements of rule 5 are being complied with.

(3) Incorporated practices shall notify the Council within fourteen days of such change of:—

(a) any change in the address of the registered office of the incorporated practice; and

(b) any change in the members or directors of an incorporated practice.

(4) Incorporated practices shall send to the Secretary a copy of all

documents which require to be filed with the registrar of companies or the Accountant in Bankruptcy contemporaneously with the despatch of such documents to the registrar of companies or the Accountant in Bankruptcy.

(5) Incorporated practices shall send to the Secretary a copy of all certificates issued by the registrar of companies forthwith upon receipt thereof by the incorporated practice.

(6) No person shall be a member of an incorporated practice unless he is a solicitor or an incorporated practice.

(7) No person who is not a member of an incorporated practice shall enjoy any of the rights of membership except (subject to rule 5(1)(f)) an executor of a deceased member of the incorporated practice *qua executor of that member*.

(8) Where a member of an incorporated practice dies or for any other reason ceases to hold a current practising certificate or, as the case may be, has its certificate of recognition revoked under rule 10 hereof the incorporated practice shall immediately take the necessary steps, whether in terms of its memorandum or articles of association or otherwise, to ensure compliance with paragraphs (6) and (7) of this rule.

(9) No person shall be appointed or shall act as a director of an incorporated practice which is a company unless he is a member thereof.

(10) Every incorporated practice to which these rules apply shall require to be insured against such classes of professional liability as are indemnified by the Master Policy (as referred to in the Solicitors (Scotland) Professional Indemnity Insurance Rules 1995) and the Council shall prescribe from time to time the limits of indemnity and self-insured amounts applicable to incorporated practices and may prescribe different limits for different incorporated practices or classes of incorporated practices.

(11) The Council shall maintain a list containing the names and places of business of all incorporated practices, which list shall be open for inspection at the office of the Society during the office hours by any person without payment of any fee.

Company Directors Disqualification Act 1986

8.—(1) In the event that a disqualification order under the 1986 Act is made against a person who is a member or a director of an incorporated practice, whether in respect of his conduct in relation to any incorporated practice of which he is a member or director, or otherwise, that person shall, forthwith upon such order being made, notify the Council and shall supply a copy of the order to the Council.

(2) Subject to paragraph (3) of this rule, the consent of the Council shall be required:—

(a) for any such person as is referred to in paragraph (1) of this rule to become or remain a member or director of an incorporated practice; and

(b) for any other person against whom a disqualification order under the 1986 Act has been made to become a member or director of an incorporated practice.

(3) The consent of the Council shall not be required pursuant to paragraph (2) of this rule if, and to the extent that, the court has given its consent to any such person as is specified in paragraph (2) of this rule becoming or remaining a director of an incorporated practice which is a company or a member of an incorporated practice which is a limited liability partnership.

(4) Any person who requires the consent of the Council pursuant to paragraph (2) of this rule shall provide all reasonable co-operation with any request from the Council for information and documentation regarding the circumstances of the relevant disqualification order.

(5) In giving or refusing its consent pursuant to paragraph (2) of this rule, the Council shall have regard to the facts and circumstances surrounding the

making of the relevant disqualification order and to the terms thereof, to the interests of the public in relation to the profession of solicitor and to the effect of any refusal of consent on the person concerned and on any incorporated practice of which he may be a member or director. Any consent may be given subject to such conditions as the Council considers it appropriate to impose.

(6) In the event, and to the extent, that the Council shall refuse a consent pursuant to paragraph (2)(a) of this rule or shall give such a consent subject to conditions which require the person to whom it is given to cease to be a member and/or a director of an incorporated practice which is a company and/or a member of an incorporated practice which is a limited liability partnership, the person affected shall immediately cease to be such a member and/or director and/or member of such incorporated practice.

(7) For the avoidance of doubt, any person against whom a disqualification order under the 1986 Act is made which prohibits that person from being a director of an incorporated practice which is a company or from being a member of an incorporated practice which is a limited liability partnership shall immediately cease to be such a director or member and shall not seek to apply for the consent of the Council in respect of that particular disqualification pursuant to paragraph (2) of this rule.

(8) In paragraphs (1), (2) and (5) of this rule, references to the term "member" in connection with an incorporated practice shall include reference both to membership of an incorporated practice which is a company and to membership of an incorporated practice which is a limited liability partnership.

Recognition

9.—(1) The Council shall consider every application made to it in terms of these rules, and, if the Council is satisfied by the applicant(s) that a body corporate has complied in all respects with the requirements of these rules, the Council shall issue to the applicant(s) a certificate recognising the proposed body corporate as an incorporated practice which certificate shall state:—

(a) the name and registered number of the incorporated practice;
(b) whether the incorporated practice will carry on business with liability which is unlimited or limited by guarantee or limited by share capital or as a limited liability partnership; and
(c) the date of the certificate of recognition.

(2) The certificate of recognition or a true copy of it shall at all times be displayed at every place of business of the incorporated practice.

(3) An incorporated practice which proposes to re-register as unlimited under section 49 or as limited under section 51 of the Companies Act 1985 shall, before applying for re-registration under section 49 or passing a resolution under section 51, submit to the Council an application to be allowed to re-register accordingly. Such application shall be in the form *mutatis mutandis* required by rule 4 for the recognition of an incorporated practice in the form proposed after re-registration. If the Council is satisfied by the applying incorporated practice that it has complied in all respects with the requirements of these rules, the Council shall issue to the applying incorporated practice a certificate entitling it to apply for or to resolve to be re-registered as aforesaid and containing the information specified in paragraph (1) of this rule. The incorporated practice shall not apply for or resolve to be re-registered as aforesaid until such certificate has been issued and shall so apply or resolve within one month of the date of such certificate. The certificate of authorisation for re-registration or a true copy of it shall at all times be displayed at every place of business of the incorporated practice along with the certificate of recognition.

Revocation of Certificate of Recognition

10. A certificate of recognition of an incorporated practice may be revoked by the Council if:—

(a) recognition of the incorporated practice was granted by the Council by reason of error or fraud; or

(b) an incorporated practice goes into liquidation (other than members' voluntary liquidation approved by the Council for the purpose of amalgamation or reconstruction) or if a provisional liquidator, receiver or judicial factor is appointed to such incorporated practice or if an administrator within the meaning of the Insolvency Act 1986 is appointed to such incorporated practice or if such incorporated practice enters into a voluntary arrangement under Part I of the Insolvency Act 1986, or if such incorporated practice is struck off the register of companies or the register of limited liability partnerships; or

(c) control of an incorporated practice ceases for any reason, however temporarily, to be exclusively by solicitors or other incorporated practices; or

(d) any solicitor who is a director or member of the incorporated practice has been excluded in terms of section 31 of the Legal Aid (Scotland) Act 1986 or any statutory re-enactment thereof; or

(e) such incorporated practice has failed to comply with any of the provisions of these rules.

Other Practice Rules

[1] **11.** All rules made under the Act in respect of solicitors as defined in the Act shall apply in all respects *mutatis mutandis* to incorporated practices.

NOTE

[1] As amended by the Solicitors (Scotland) (Registered Foreign Lawyers) etc. Practice Rules 2005, Sch.5 (effective May 1, 2005).

Power of Waiver

12. The Council shall have power to waive any of the provisions of these rules in any particular circumstances or case.

Revocation of previous Rules and Saving Provision

13. The Solicitors (Scotland) (Incorporated Practices) Practice Rules 1997 are hereby revoked, but such revocation shall not affect the validity of any application made, certificate granted or other thing done under the said rules and such application, certificate or thing shall have effect as if it were made, granted or done under these rules.

SCHEDULE

FORM OF APPLICATION FOR RECOGNITION AS AN INCORPORATED PRACTICE

No. 20

We the undernoted hereby apply for a certificate of recognition by the Council as an incorporated practice

Name etc. of the Proposed Incorporated Practice

....

name of body corporate (a)

....

registered office of body corporate (a)

....
registered number of body corporate (a)

....
date of incorporation of body corporate (a)

SOLICITORS WHO WILL BE MEMBERS OF THE INCORPORATED PRACTICE (B)

Name	Designation (c)	Places of business (d)	Place of business as at date of last practising certificate (if applicable) (e)	Date and number of last practising certificate (if applicable)
1.	....	(1)	....	....
		....	....	
		....	....	
		(2)		
		....		
		....		
2.	....	(1)	....	....
		....	....	
		....	....	
		(2)		
		....		
		....		

etc.

INCORPORATED PRACTICES WHICH WILL BE MEMBERS OF THE INCORPORATED PRACTICE (B)

Name	Address of Registered Office	Date and Number of Certificate of Recognition
1.	....	....
	....	
	....	
2.	....	....
	....	
	....	

etc.

IN THE CASE OF AN INCORPORATED PRACTICE WHICH IS A COMPANY, SOLICITORS WHO WILL BE DIRECTORS OF THE INCORPORATED PRACTICE (F)

Name	Designation (c)	Places of business (d)	Place of business as at date of last practising certificate (if applicable) (e)	Date and number of last practising certificate (if applicable)
1.	....	(1)	....	....
		....	....	
		....	....	
		(2)		
		....		
		....		
2.	....	(1)	....	....
		....	....	
		....	....	
		(2)		
		....		
		....		

etc.

Dated this day of 20

(g)

Signatures

....

....

....

FORM OF INCORPORATION

To assist the Council in its duties under these rules state here:—

(a) Whether the incorporated practice will carry on business with unlimited unliability; or

(b) Whether the incorporated practice will carry on business limited by guarantee; or

(c) Whether the incorporated practice will carry on business limited by share capital; or

(d) Whether the incorporated practice will carry on business as a limited liability partnership; or

(e) whether any member or director of the incorporated practice is subject to a disqualification order under the Company Directors Disqualification Act 1986—if so, please provide full details

Notes:

(a) If the body corporate has not yet been incorporated or registered insert the proposed name and the address of the proposed registered office and explain the circumstances in a covering letter.

(b) Details of **all** proposed members of the incorporated practice must be given.

(c) *i.e.* WS, SSC, Advocate in Aberdeen, or solicitor.

(d) All places of business if more than one should be stated. The principal place of business should be given first.

(e) If the applicant's place of business has changed since his last practising certificate was issued, the address which appeared on his practising certificate should be stated.

(f) In the case of an incorporated practice which is a company, all proposed directors must be members of the incorporated practice.

(g) All proposed solicitor members of the incorporated practice must sign. In the case of proposed incorporated practice members, a director, or in the case of a limited liability partnership, a member, of the incorporated practice must sign.

Further Notes

1. This form when completed and signed should be forwarded along with, in the case of an incorporated practice which is or is to be a company, its proposed memorandum and articles of association and, in all cases, a remittance for the appropriate fee. Remittances should be made payable to "The Law Society of Scotland" and should be crossed "account payee only".

2. To permit the Council adequate time to carry out its duties in terms of these rules, any person wishing to form an incorporated practice should, at least three months prior to the anticipated date of commencement of business as such incorporated practice, submit to the Council the documentation required under these rules.

Solicitors (Scotland) (Incidental Financial Business) Practice Rules 2004

Rules dated 28th May 2004, made by the Council of the Law Society of Scotland (a) under section 34(1) of the Solicitors (Scotland) Act 1980 and approved by the Lord President of the Court of Session under section 34(3) of that Act and (b) (the Law Society of Scotland being a designated professional body for the purposes of the Financial Services and Markets Act 2000 under section 332(3) of that Act) approved by the Financial Services Authority under section 332(5) of that Act.

Part I

General

Citation, Commencement, Revocation and Savings

1.—(1)These Rules may be cited as the Solicitors (Scotland) (Incidental Financial Business) Practice Rules 2004 and shall come into operation on 31st October 2004, subject to paragraphs (2) to (4).

(2) Rules 24(f) and 25(b) and Part IV shall come into operation, so far as they relate to long-term care insurance mediation activity, on 31st October 2004, and shall come into operation generally on 14th January 2005.

(3) Rules 6, 7 and 11 shall come into operation, so far as they relate to applications for incidental financial business licences for the practice year commencing on 1st November 2004, on 1st August 2004.

(4) Rules 26 and 27 shall come into operation on 9th October 2004.

(5) The Solicitors (Scotland) (Incidental Investment Business) Practice Rules 2001 are revoked with effect from 31st October 2004.

(6) Notwithstanding the revocation of the Solicitors (Scotland) (Incidental Investment Business) Practice Rules 2001:

(a) the obligation upon a licensed person (as defined in those Rules) to deliver to the Council within one calendar month of the completion of each accounting period (as defined in those Rules) an Incidental Investment Business Compliance Certificate (as defined in those Rules) in respect of that period shall remain in force but only to the extent that one further Incidental Investment Business Compliance Certificate shall be delivered to the Council in respect of the accounting period current on 31st October 2004 which Certificate shall be delivered within one calendar month of the completion of that accounting period; and

(b) the provisions of rules 10 (notification of changes to personnel/ section 328 directions and section 329 orders), 14 (inspections by Council) and 18 (record-keeping requirements) of those Rules shall continue in force in respect of incidental investment business (as defined in those Rules) carried on prior to 31st October 2004.

Definitions and Interpretation

2.—(1) In these Rules, unless the context otherwise requires:

[1]"2005 Rules" means the Solicitors (Scotland) (Registered Foreign Lawyers) etc Practice Rules 2005;

"accounting period" means, in respect of a licensed person, a period not exceeding six months immediately following the previous accounting period, the first such accounting period commencing on the later of:

(a) save as provided by rule 18(2), 31st October 2004 and

(b) the date on which an incidental financial business licence has been granted to that licensed person or, having been withdrawn, suspended or not renewed, is granted again to that licensed person or is reinstated following suspension;

"the Act" means the Financial Services and Markets Act 2000;

"the 1980 Act" means the Solicitors (Scotland) Act 1980;

"the Amendment (No 1) Order" means the Financial Services and Markets Act 2000 (Regulated Activities) (Amendment) (No 1) Order 2003;

"the Amendment (No 2) Order" means the Financial Services and Markets Act 2000 (Regulated Activities) (Amendment) (No 2) Order 2003;

"bankruptcy proceedings" means an award of sequestration, bankruptcy order or equivalent in any other jurisdiction;

"consultant" has the meaning given by section 21 of the 1980 Act;

"contract of insurance" has the meaning given by article 3(1) of the Order;

"contract of long-term care insurance" has the meaning given by article 1 (4) of the Amendment (No 2) Order;

"contract of long-term insurance" has the meaning given by article 3(1) of the Order; "the Council" means the Council of the Society;

"the Directive" means Directive 2002/92/EC of the European Parliament and of the Council of the European Union on insurance mediation;

"exempt person" means a person who is exempt from the general prohibition as a result of an exemption order made under section 38(1) of the Act or as a result of section 39(1) or 285(2) or (3) of the Act;

[2] "firm" means a solicitor who is a sole practitioner or a partnership or association of solicitors or an incorporated practice and also includes a Scottish multi-national practice (as defined in rule 7(1) of the 2005 Rules);

"the FSA" means the Financial Services Authority;

"the general prohibition" has the meaning given by section 19(2) of the Act;

"incidental financial business" means regulated activities which may, as a result of Part XX of the Act and these Rules, be carried on by a firm without breaching the general prohibition and includes: > without limitation, insurance mediation activity, long-term care insurance mediation activity and mortgage mediation activity;

"Incidental Financial Business Compliance Certificate" means a certificate in the form set out in Schedule 3 or in such other form as the Council may from time to time prescribe;

"incidental financial business licence" means a licence granted by the Council in terms of Part III;

"incorporated practice" has the meaning given by section 34(1A) of the 1980 Act;

"insurance intermediary" means a person who carries on insurance mediation activity;

"insurance mediation activity" means any of the following regulated activities carried on in relation to a contract of insurance or rights to or interests in a life policy:

(i) dealing in investments as agent (Article 21 of the Order);

(ii) arranging (bringing about) deals in investments (Article 25(1) of the Order);

(iii) making arrangements with a view to transactions in investments (Article 25(2) of the Order);

(iv) assisting in the administration and performance of a contract of insurance (Article 39A of the Order);

(v) advising on investments (Article 53 of the Order);

(vi) agreeing to carryon a regulated activity in (i) to (v) (Article 64 of the Order).

"licensed person" means a firm which is licensed by the Society to carryon incidental financial business in terms of these Rules;

"long-term care insurance mediation activity" has the meaning given by article 22 of the Amendment (No 2) Order;

"member state" means a state which is a member state of the European Union;

"mortgage mediation activity", in relation to regulated mortgage contracts, has the meaning given by article 26 of the Amendment (No 1) Order;

[2] "officer" means, in the case of a firm which is a partnership, a partner of that firm, in the case of a sole practitioner, that sole practitioner, in the case of an incorporated practice which is a company, a director of that incorporated practice, and in the case of an incorporated practice which is a limited liability partnership, a member of that limited liability partnership or a member of a multi-national practice;

"the Order" means the Financial Services and Markets Act 2000 (Regulated Activities) Order 2001;

"personal recommendation" means a recommendation given to a specific person, and "personally recommending" shall be interpreted accordingly;

"practice year" means the year commencing on 1st November and ending on the subsequent 31 st October;

"registered European lawyer" has the meaning given by section 65(1) of the 1980 Act;

"regulated activity" has the meaning given by section 22 of the Act;

"regulated mortgage contract" has the meaning given by article 61 (3) of the Order;

"retail client" means a client who is a natural person who is acting for purposes which are outside his trade, business or profession;

"the Secretary" means the Secretary of the Society;

"the Society" means the Law Society of Scotland; and

[2] "solicitor" means a solicitor holding a practising certificate under the 1980 Act and shall include a registered foreign lawyer to whom these rules apply in terms of rule 4(2) or (3) of the 2005 Rules.

(2) The Interpretation Act 1978 applies to the interpretation of these Rules as it applies to the interpretation of an Act of Parliament.

(3) The headings to these Rules do not form part of these Rules.

(4) References in these Rules to incidental financial business or regulated activities carried on by a firm shall include such business or activities carried on by an individual as an officer or an employee of the firm and employees shall include solicitor and non-solicitor employees and consultants.

NOTES

[1] Inserted by the Solicitors (Scotland) (Registered Foreign Lawyers) etc. Practice Rules 2005, Sch.5 (effective May 1, 2005).

[2] As amended by the Solicitors (Scotland) (Registered Foreign Lawyers) etc. Practice Rules 2005, Sch.5 (effective May 1, 2005).

Purpose and Scope of Rules

3.—(1) These Rules make provision for the carrying on by firms of incidental financial business.

(2) These Rules apply in respect of firms where the activities constituting incidental financial business are the only regulated activities carried on by the firm (other than regulated activities in relation to which it is an exempt person).

(3) These Rules apply in respect of incidental financial business carried on in, into or from the United Kingdom, and (with effect from the commencement of Part IV) to firms carrying on incidental financial business which is insurance mediation activity in or into another member state.

Part II

Incidental Financial Business

Prohibition on Carrying on Incidental Financial Business

4. No firm shall carryon incidental financial business unless it has been licensed by the Society to do so in terms of these Rules.

Criteria for Carrying on Incidental Financial Business

5. Subject to rules 3(2) and 4, a firm may carryon incidental financial business—

(a) to the extent that there is not in force a direction of the FSA under section 328(1) of the Act or an order of the FSA under section 329(1) of the Act preventing the firm from carrying on a regulated activity or regulated activities;

(b) to the extent that the regulated activities are not of a description, nor do they relate to an investment of a description, specified in any order made by the Treasury under section 327(6) of the Act;

(c) provided that the firm must not receive from a person other than its client any pecuniary reward or other advantage, for which it does not account to its client, arising out of its carrying on any regulated activity;

(d) provided that the manner of the provision by the firm of any service in the course of carrying on a regulated activity must be incidental to the provision by it of professional services;

(e) provided that the firm carries on only regulated activities which arise out of, or are complementary to, the provision by it of a particular professional service to a particular client; and

(f) provided that the firm is controlled or managed by officers who are solicitors.

Part III

Licences

Application for Licence

6.— (1) An application for an incidental financial business licence may be made by a firm by submitting to the Secretary:

(a) a completed form of application in the form set out in Schedule I or in such other form as the Council may from time to time prescribe; and

(b) the fee to be prescribed from time to time by the Council in connection with such application, which fee shall be submitted at the same time as the completed form of application.

(2) At any time after receiving an application and before determining it, the Council may require the applicant to furnish additional information and such additional information shall be in such form or verified in such manner as the Council may specify.

(3) An application for an incidental financial business licence for the practice year commencing on 1st November 2004 shall be made by a firm not later than 31st August 2004. Paragraph 1 (b) shall not apply to such an application.

Grant and Refusal

7.—(1) Subject to paragraph (2), the Council may, on an application duly made in accordance with rule 6, grant or refuse to grant an incidental financial business licence or may grant such licence subject to such conditions or restrictions as it considers appropriate.

(2) The Council shall refuse to grant an incidental financial business licence unless it is satisfied that:

(a) the applicant is a firm; and
(b) the main business of the applicant is the practice of professional services which are subject to supervision and regulation by the Society.

(3) The Council shall advise an applicant for an incidental financial business licence, in writing, whether it has been granted an incidental financial business licence, in which case the date of grant shall be specified, as shall any conditions or restrictions which the Council considers appropriate in respect of that licence, or whether it has been refused an incidental financial business licence, in which case the reasons for refusal shall be given.

(4) In the event that the Council shall have granted an incidental financial business licence to an applicant, it shall, at the same time as so advising the applicant in terms of paragraph (3), issue to the applicant a certificate confirming that the applicant is licensed to carry on incidental financial business. Any certificate issued to an applicant in terms of rule 7(4) of the Solicitors (Scotland) (Incidental Investment Business) Practice Rules 2001 and remaining in force immediately prior to 31st October 2004 shall be deemed to have been issued in terms of this rule.

(5) The Council shall cause to be kept in respect of each practice year a register of applications for incidental financial business licences and of licences granted. The register shall be in such form as the Council may determine.

Duration, Renewal and Annual Fee

8.—(1) An incidental financial business licence shall expire at the end of each practice year and shall require to be renewed annually. The fee for the renewal of an incidental financial business licence shall be payable annually on or before 1 st November. For the avoidance of doubt, the certificate referred to in rule 7 (4) shall not require to be reissued upon the renewal of an incidental financial business licence.

(2) The amount of the fee referred to in paragraph (1) shall be such as the Council may from time to time prescribe.

Withdrawal, Suspension and Lapse

9.—(1) An incidental financial business licence shall lapse automatically upon the licensed person ceasing to practise as a solicitor or solicitors or ceasing to be a firm.

(2) An incidental financial business licence shall lapse automatically upon the licensed person becoming authorised by the FSA to carryon regulated activities.

(3) An incidental financial business licence shall lapse automatically upon a direction under section 328(1) or an order under section 329(1) of the Act being made in relation to the licensed person, such lapse to be to the extent necessary to secure compliance with the direction or order.

(4) An incidental financial business licence granted to an incorporated practice shall lapse automatically on the revocation of the recognition of that incorporated practice.

(5) An incidental financial business licence granted to a sole practitioner shall be suspended automatically on the occurrence in relation to that solicitor of any of the circumstances mentioned in section 18(1) of the 1980 Act and an incidental financial business licence granted to a firm comprising two or more solicitors shall be suspended automatically on the occurrence in relation to that firm of any of the circumstances mentioned in section 18(1)(c), (d) and (e) of the 1980 Act; provided that, in either case, such suspension shall cease to have effect on the occurrence of the events specified in section 19(4), (5) or (5A) of the 1980 Act.

(6) An incidental financial business licence granted to a registered European lawyer shall be suspended automatically on the occurrence in relation to that lawyer of any of the circumstances mentioned in section 24F(I) of the 1980 Act and an incidental financial business licence granted to

a firm comprising two or more registered European lawyers shall be suspended automatically on the occurrence in relation to that firm of any of the circumstances mentioned in section 24F(1)(c), (d) and (e) of the 1980 Act; provided that, in either case, such suspension shall cease to have effect on the occurrence of the events specified in section 24G(2), (3) or (4) of the 1980 Act.

(7) An incidental financial business licence granted to an incorporated practice shall be suspended automatically on the occurrence in relation to that incorporated practice of any of the circumstances mentioned in section 18(1A) of the 1980 Act.

[1] (7A) An incidental financial business licence granted to a multi-national practice which is a body corporate shall be suspended automatically on the occurrence in relation to that multi-national practice of any of the events specified in relation to incorporated practices in section 18(1A) of the 1980 Act.

(8) An incidental financial business licence may be suspended by the Council if, within 30 days of the due date for payment of any fee required under rule 8(1), payment has not been made, provided that such suspension shall cease to have effect on payment being made.

(9) An incidental financial business licence may be suspended by the Council if the licensed person has not, within one month (or within such extended period as the Council may have authorised in terms of rule 20) of the completion of its accounting period, delivered to the Council an Incidental Financial Business Compliance Certificate in accordance with Part V of these Rules, provided that such suspension shall cease to have effect on the date of the production to the Council of an Incidental Financial Business Compliance Certificate.

(10) An incidental financial business licence may be suspended or withdrawn by the Council if the licensed person has failed to comply with any provision of these Rules other than those provisions failure to comply with which may result in suspension pursuant to paragraph (8) or (9), provided that an incidental financial business licence may be withdrawn by the Council if the licensed person has had its incidental financial business licence suspended pursuant to paragraph (8) on two or more occasions or pursuant to paragraph (9) on two or more occasions. In exercising its discretion to suspend or withdraw in such circumstances, the Council shall have regard to the materiality of any such failure to comply and to any previous failures to comply.

(11) The Council shall advise the licensed person of any suspension or withdrawal pursuant to paragraphs (8), (9) or (10) by notice in writing, which notice shall specify the date upon which the suspension or withdrawal shall take effect. In the case of a suspension, the licensed person may represent either orally *or* in writing to the Council that such suspension should be terminated and, in considering any such representation, the Council shall have regard to the efforts made by the licensed person to remedy the failure to comply which gave rise to the suspension.

(12) Where an incidental financial business licence has lapsed or has been or is to be withdrawn or suspended, whether automatically or otherwise, the Council may direct the licensed person whose incidental financial business licence has lapsed or has been or is to be withdrawn or suspended, to take such action and make such arrangements as are necessary, in the view of the Council, to ensure the speedy and satisfactory completion and/or transfer to another licensed person of clients' outstanding incidental financial business.

(13) Any licensed person whose incidental financial business licence has lapsed or is withdrawn or suspended in terms of this rule 9 may, in a case of automatic lapse or suspension, within 21 days of the occurrence of the event which has given rise to such lapse or suspension and, in a case of withdrawal or suspension by the Council, within 21 days of being notified by the Council of such withdrawal or suspension, appeal to the Court of Session.

NOTE
[1] Inserted by the Solicitors (Scotland) (Registered Foreign Lawyers) etc. Practice Rules 2005, Sch.5 (effective May 1, 2005).

Notification of Changes to Information, Section 328 Directions and Section 329 Orders

10.—(1) A licensed person shall notify the Secretary in writing of any change to the information provided to the Society on the form of application submitted in terms of rule 6(1) orto the additional information (if any) provided in terms of rule 6(2).

(2) The notification referred to in paragraph (1) shall be given by the licensed person within one month of any change referred to in paragraph (1).

(3) A licensed person shall notify the Secretary in writing in the event that a direction of the FSA under section 328(1) or an order under section 329(1) of the Act is made in relation to the licensed person.

(4) The notification referred to in paragraph (3) shall be given by the licensed person within one month of the direction or order referred to in paragraph (3) being made, and shall be accompanied by a copy of the direction or order.

(5) A licensed person shall notify the Secretary in writing in the event that the licensed person becomes authorised by the FSA to carryon regulated activities.

(6) The notification referred to in paragraph (5) shall be given by the licensed person within one month of the authorisation referred to in paragraph (5) coming into effect, and shall be accompanied by a copy of the certificate of authorisation.

Part IV

Insurance Mediation Activity

Registration for the Purposes of Insurance Mediation Activity

11.—(1) Every firm which carries on incidental financial business which is insurance mediation activity shall give the Council the details required by the Council of the officer responsible for the conduct of that business.

(2) The Council shall notify the FSA of any details disclosed to it pursuant to paragraph (1).

(3) Every firm which carries on any incidental financial business which is insurance mediation activity shall give the Council the details required by the Council of those persons involved in that business, which may include details of any criminal record and of any bankruptcy proceedings in relation to those persons.

(4) The details required to be given to the Council in terms of this rule may form part of the information required by the form of application referred to in rule 6, and changes in those details shall be notified to the Council in terms of rule 10(2).

Requirement of Good Repute

12.—(1) No person having a criminal record disclosing a serious criminal offence involving any crime against property or related to financial activities shall be involved in insurance mediation activity on behalf of any firm, whether as an officer, employee, consultant or otherwise.

(2) No person who is subject to bankruptcy proceedings shall be involved in insurance mediation activity on behalf of any firm, whether as an officer, employee, consultant or otherwise.

Prohibition on Carrying on Business

13. No licensed person shall carryon incidental financial business which is insurance mediation activity if it is not registered with the FSA for that purpose.

Provision of Information

14.—(1) Subject to paragraph (2), where a contract of insurance is to be concluded with a client in relation to which a licensed person has conducted insurance mediation activity, the information set out in Schedule 2 must be provided to the client:

(a) on paper or other durable medium available and accessible to the client;

(b) in a clear and accurate manner, comprehensible to the client; and

(c) in an official language of the member state of the commitment or in any other language agreed by the licensed person and the client.

(2) The information to be provided pursuant to paragraph (1):

(a) may be provided orally if:

(i) the client requests this; or

(ii) the client requires immediate cover; and

(b) need not be provided before the conclusion of the contract if the contract is concluded by telephone at the client's request and the client gives his explicit consent to receiving limited information after the conclusion of the contract.

(3) Where paragraph (2) applies, the client must be provided with the information set out in Schedule 2, in a manner which complies with sub-paragraphs (a) to (c) of paragraph (1), immediately after the conclusion of the contract.

(4) If the contract is concluded by a licensed person acting as an insurance intermediary by telephone with a retail client, the retail client must be informed on initial contact of:

(a) the name of the licensed person and, if the call is initiated by the insurance intermediary, the commercial purpose of the call; and

(b) where relevant, the identity of the person in contact with the retail client and his
link with the licensed person.

(5) Where the contact of a licensed person with a client is limited to introducing that client to another insurance intermediary, the client must be given the information specified in paragraph 1 to 5, 8 and 9 of Schedule 2 on initial contact. The information may be provided orally or in writing.

(6) Where the information required to be supplied pursuant to paragraph (5) is given orally, the information must also be provided by the licensed person, in a manner which complies with sub-paragraphs (a) to (c) of paragraph 0); immediately after the initial contact with the client.

(7) Where a licensed person acts as an insurance intermediary in relation to a contract of insurance, and selects contracts from a limited number of insurance undertakings or from a single insurance undertaking then it must maintain, and keep up to date, for each type of contract of insurance that it deals with, a list of insurance undertakings that it selects from or deals with and the relevant list must be made available to any client, in writing, on request.

Scope of Services

15. Where a licensed person acts as an insurance intermediary and holds itself out as providing advice to clients on particular types of contracts of insurance on the basis of a fair analysis of the market, it must not provide such advice unless it has analysed a sufficiently large number of contracts available in the relevant sector or sectors of the market to be able to give advice on a contract of insurance which is adequate to meet the client's needs.

Statement of Demands and Needs

16.—(1) Where a licensed person makes a personal recommendation to a client of a specific contract of insurance, or arranges for a client to enter into a specific contract of insurance, it must, before the conclusion of that contract, provide the client with a statement of his demands and needs in respect of that insurance contract. In addition to stating the demands and needs of the client, the statement must:

(a) confirm whether the licensed person has personally recommended that contract; and

(b) explain the reasons for personally recommending that contract.

(2) The statement referred to in paragraph (1) must reflect the complexity of the contract of insurance proposed.

(3) Unless paragraph (4) applies, the statement referred to in paragraph (1) must be provided in writing.

(4) A licensed person may provide the statement referred to in paragraph (1) orally if:

(a) the client requests it; or

(b) immediate cover is necessary;

but in both cases the licensed person must provide that statement in writing immediately after the conclusion of the contract.

Notification of Establishment and Services in other Member States

17.—(1) Any licensed person intending to exercise its right under article 6(1) of the Directive to carryon business for the first time in or into a member state (other than the United Kingdom) shall notify the FSA of that intention and whether such business will be conducted through a branch or on a services basis.

(2) A licensed person who has complied with paragraph (1) may commence business one month after the date on which it is notified by the FSA that the FSA has informed the competent authorities of the member state in or into which that licensed person intends to carryon business of that licensed person's intention. If those competent authorities do not wish to be informed of that licensed person's intention, that licensed person may commence business immediately upon notification by the FSA of that fact to that licensed person.

Part V

Compliance and Monitoring

Obligation to Deliver Incidental Financial Business Compliance Certificate

18.—(1) Every licensed person shall deliver to the Secretary, within one calendar month of the completion of each accounting period, an Incidental Financial Business Compliance Certificate in respect of that period.

(2) A licensed person may deliver an Incidental Financial Business Compliance Certificate in respect of the accounting period as defined in the Solicitors (Scotland) (Incidental Investment Business) Practice Rules 200I which includes the date referred to in rule 1(1).

(3) An Incidental Financial Business Compliance Certificate shall be signed by an officer of the licensed person.

Where a Licensed Person Practises in Two or More Places

19. In the case of a licensed person which has two or more places of business and where separate financial business records are maintained by the licensed person for each place of business, a separate Incidental Financial Business Compliance Certificate shall be delivered in respect of each place of business.

Power of Council to Extend Period of Time Referred to in Rule 18(1)

20. The Council may, in any case on satisfactory cause shown, extend the period of one calendar month within which an Incidental Financial Business

Compliance Certificate requires to be delivered provided that such extension shall in no case exceed three months from the date of completion of the relevant accounting period.

Inspections by Council

21.—(1) To enable the Council to ascertain whether or not a licensed person is complying with these Rules, the Council may, by written notice, require that licensed person to produce at a time to be fixed by the Council and at a place to be fixed by the Council, or at the option of the licensed person at its place of business, documents, records and other information concerning the conduct of its practice in relation to these Rules including, without prejudice to the foregoing generality, files and relative correspondence (in this Rule referred to as "documents, records and other information"), for inspection by a person or persons appointed by the Council.

(2) If at any time there is a reasonable apprehension on the part of the Council that a firm has not complied with, is not complying with or may not comply with these Rules, including, but without prejudice to the foregoing generality, by carrying on incidental financial business in contravention of rule 4 or 13, the Council may, by written notice, require that firm to produce at a time to be fixed by the Council and at a place to be fixed by the Council, or at the option of the firm at its place of business, documents, records and other information for inspection by a person or persons appointed by the Council.

(3) It shall be the duty of a licensed person or a firm or solicitor to provide a person or persons appointed by the Council under paragraph (1) or (2) reasonable co-operation in the conduct of that person's or persons' inspection including, without prejudice to the foregoing generality, the production of documents, records and other information as such person or persons may reasonably require.

(4) Any person or persons appointed by the Council under paragraph (I) or (2) shall report to the Council upon the result of his inspection.

(5) A written notice given by the Council to a licensed person or to a firm under paragraph (1) or (2) and, where appropriate, paragraph (6), shall be signed by the Secretary, the Chief Accountant of the Society or a Director of the Society and shall be sent by recorded delivery post to the licensed person or firm at its place of business as defined in the Constitution of the Society or in the case of a sole practitioner who has ceased to hold a practising certificate to his last known address, and shall be deemed to have been received by the licensed person or firm within forty-eight hours of the time of posting. In the case of a partnership the written notice shall be given to each person who is known to the Council to be a partner thereof, and in the case of an incorporated practice to each person known to the Council to be a director thereof (where that incorporated practice is a company), or to each person known to the Council to be a member thereof (where that incorporated practice is a limited liability partnership); and it shall not be necessary to give notice to the partnership or incorporated practice.

(6) Where, following an inspection of the documents, records and other information of a licensed person or firm in terms of paragraph (1) or (2), it appears to the Council that the licensed person or firm has not complied with these Rules, the Council may instruct a further inspection of the documents, records and other information of the licensed person or firm and, if it so instructs, the Council may by written notice require the licensed person or firm to pay to the Council the reasonable costs of such further inspection, provided always that such written notice is given to the licensed person or firm not more than one year after the date of the inspection first referred to in this paragraph. The amount of such sum shall be fixed by the Council and intimated to the licensed person or firm following such further inspection.

(7) It shall be the duty of a licensed person or firm upon whom a notice in terms of paragraph (6) has been served to make payment forthwith of the amount so intimated.

PART VI

MISCONDUCT DISCLOSURE TRAINING AND RECORDS

Terms of Business

22. Whenever it intends or expects to carry out incidental financial business for a client, a licensed person shall so advise its client by sending to that client terms of business which contain, in a manner that is clear, fair and not misleading, the statements and the information specified in Schedule 4 and/or such other statements or information as the Council may from time to time prescribe.

Disclosure

23.—(1) For the avoidance of doubt, but with the exception of the terms of business referred to in rule 22, a firm shall not be required to make any disclosure to the effect that it is a licensed person or otherwise on its stationery or any other material which it may publish.

(2) A licensed person shall display at each of its places of business its certificate (or a copy thereof) issued pursuant to rule 7 (4), confirming that the licensed person is licensed to carryon incidental financial business.

Training

24. In respect of the carrying on of incidental financial business by it, a licensed person shall:

(a) advance and maintain the competence of all officers and employees carrying on incidental financial business;

(b) ensure that all officers and employees carrying on incidental financial business remain competent for the functions they carry out;

(c) ensure that all officers and employees carrying on incidental financial business are adequately supervised in relation to the attainment and maintenance of competence;

(d) ensure that the training for and the competence of all officers and employees carrying
on incidental financial business are regularly reviewed;

(e) in dealing with the commitments set out in paragraphs (a) to (d), take account of the level of competence that is necessary having regard to the nature of its business and the role of all officers and employees carrying on incidental financial business; and

(f) ensure that a reasonable proportion of the officers of the firm who are responsible *for* insurance mediation activity and all other persons directly involved in insurance mediation activity demonstrate the knowledge and ability necessary *for* the performance of their duties, having regard to the nature of the business and the roles of those persons.

Record Keeping Requirements

25. In respect of the carrying on of incidental financial business by it, a licensed person shall:

(a) ensure that all instructions from clients to carry out specific incidental financial business are performed as soon as possible unless it would be contrary to the best interests of the client to do so;

(b) retain records of all statements of demands and needs made in accordance with rule 16 in connection with personal recommendations made to clients in the course of insurance mediation activity for at least three years from the date on which the personal recommendation was made;

(c) retain records of all instructions from clients to carry out specific incidental financial business on their behalf and all instructions from the licensed person to any third party to effect such incidental financial business for at least 10 years from the date of the instruction;
(d) retain records of any pecuniary award or other advantage received by the licensed person as a result of carrying on incidental financial business on behalf of a client and records of the accounting by the licensed person to its client in respect of such pecuniary award or other advantage for at least 10 years from the date of the accounting;
(e) take appropriate technical and organisational measures to ensure the safe keeping of assets held by the licensed person on behalf of its clients or third parties; and
(f) ensure that, where the licensed person takes the advice of a third party authorised by the FSA to carry on regulated activities, that such third party provides independent advice.

Distance Marketing of Financial Services

26. Licensed persons shall comply with the terms of the Financial Services (Distance Marketing) Regulations 2004 so far as applicable to them.

Professional Misconduct

27. If any solicitor fails to comply with these Rules that failure may be treated as professional misconduct by that solicitor *for* the purposes of Part IV of the 1980 Act.

SCHEDULE 1

Rule 6

Form of Application for an Incidental Financial Business Licence

(All information to be completed in BLOCK CAPITALS)

1 Name of Firm ....

Address of Principal Place of Business ....

....

Town ....

Post Code ....

2 For the officer who will be responsible for the conduct of any incidental financial business of the firm which is insurance mediation activity (including long-term care insurance mediation activity) please complete the following information:

Officer Responsible for the Conduct of Insurance Mediation

(i) Forename ....
(ii) Surname ....
(iii) Date of Birth ....
[2] (iv) Criminal record ....
[3] (v) Bankruptcy ....

3 For each solicitor who will be carrying on incidental financial business (whether in the principal office or in a branch office) please complete the following information:

Solicitor Information

A
(i) Forename ....
(ii) Surname ....
(iii) Date of Birth ....
[1] (iv) Type(s) of Incidental Financial Business carried on (please tick appropriate box)
MMA ☐
LTC ☐

B
(i) Forename ....
(ii) Surname ....
(iii) Date of Birth ....
[1] (iv) Type(s) of Incidental Financial Business carried on (please tick appropriate box
MMA ☐
LTC ☐

1M ☐
IB ☐
[2] (v) Criminal record ....
[3] (vi) Bankruptcy ....

1M ☐
IB ☐
[2] (v) Criminal record ....
[3] (vi) Bankruptcy ....

C (i) Forename ....
(ii) Surname ....
(iii) Date of Birth ....
[1] (iv) Type(s) of Incidental Financial Business carried on (please tick appropriate box)
MMA ☐
LTC ☐
1M ☐
IB ☐
[2] (v) Criminal record ....
[3] (vi) Bankruptcy ....

D (i) Forename ....
(ii) Surname ....
(iii) Date of Birth ....
[1] (iv) Type(s) of Incidental Financial Business carried on (please tick appropriate box
MMA ☐
LTC ☐
1M ☐
IB ☐
[2] (v) Criminal record ....
[3] (vi) Bankruptcy ....

E (i) Forename ....
(ii) Surname ....
(iii) Date of Birth ....
[1] (iv) Type(s) of Incidental Financial Business carried on (please tick appropriate box)
MMA ☐
LTC ☐
1M ☐
IB ☐
[2] (v) Criminal record ....
[3] (vi) Bankruptcy ....

F (i) Forename ....
(ii) Surname ....
(iii) Date of Birth ....
[1] (iv) Type(s) of Incidental Financial Business carried on (please tick appropriate box
MMA ☐
LTC ☐
1M ☐
IB ☐
[2] (v) Criminal record ....
[3] (vi) Bankruptcy ....

Please add any additional names with details on a separate sheet of paper.

For **each** non-solicitor who will be carrying on incidental financial business (whether in the principal office or in a branch office) please complete the following information:

Non-Solicitor Information

A (i) Forename ....
(ii) Surname ....
(iii) Date of Birth ....
[1] (iv) Type(s) of Incidental Financial Business carried on (please tick appropriate box)
MMA ☐
LTC ☐
1M ☐
IB ☐
[2] (v) Criminal record ....
[3] (vi) Bankruptcy ....

B (i) Forename ....
(ii) Surname ....
(iii) Date of Birth ....
[1] (iv) Type(s) of Incidental Financial Business carried on (please tick appropriate box
MMA ☐
LTC ☐
1M ☐
IB ☐
[2] (v) Criminal record ....
[3] (vi) Bankruptcy ....

C (i) Forename ....
(ii) Surname ....
(iii) Date of Birth ....
[1] (iv) Type(s) of Incidental Financial Business carried on (please tick appropriate box)
MMA ☐
LTC ☐
1M ☐
IB ☐
[2] (v) Criminal record ....
[3] (vi) Bankruptcy ....

D (i) Forename ....
(ii) Surname ....
(iii) Date of Birth ....
[1] (iv) Type(s) of Incidental Financial Business carried on (please tick appropriate box
MMA ☐
LTC ☐
1M ☐
IB ☐
[2] (v) Criminal record ....
[3] (vi) Bankruptcy ....

E

(i) Forename ....
(ii) Surname ....
(iii) Date of Birth ....
[1] (iv) Type(s) of Incidental Financial Business carried on (please tick appropriate box)

MMA ☐
LTC ☐
1M ☐
IB ☐

[2] (v) Criminal record ....
[3] (vi) Bankruptcy ....

F

(i) Forename ....
(ii) Surname ....
(iii) Date of Birth ....
[1] (iv) Type(s) of Incidental Financial Business carried on (please tick appropriate box

MMA ☐
LTC ☐
1M ☐
IB ☐

[2] (v) Criminal record ....
[3] (vi) Bankruptcy ....

Please add any additional names with details on a separate sheet of paper.

4 Date from which an incidental financial business licence required ....

5 I/we confirm that I am/we are not authorised to carryon regulated activities by the Financial Services Authority under the Financial Services and Markets Act 2000.

6 I/We undertake that I/we shall carry out no regulated activities (other than regulated activities in relation to which I am/we are an exempt person) except incidental financial business.

7 I/We undertake that I/we shall not receive from a person other than my/our client any pecuniary reward or other advantage for which I/we shall not account to my/our client, arising out of my/our carrying on regulated activity.

8 I/We undertake that I/we shall not carry out regulated activities which are of a description, or relate to an investment of a description, specified in any order made by the Treasury for the purposes of section 327(6) of the Financial Services and Markets Act 2000.

9 I/We undertake that I/we shall comply with any directions given by the Financial Services Authority under section 328(1) of the Financial Services and Markets Act 2000.

10 I/We hereby apply for an incidental financial business licence pursuant to rule 6 of the Solicitors (Scotland) (Incidental Financial Business) Practice Rules 2004.

Dated this day of 20

....(Signature)

....(Print Name)

[1] Please give details of the type(s) of incidental financial business in which the relevant person is involved. This should be detailed as mortgage mediation activity (MMA), long-term care insurance mediation activity (LTC), insurance mediation activity (other than long-term care insurance mediation activity) (1M) and/or investment business (IB) as appropriate.
[2] This information need only be given in respect of persons involved in long-term care insurance mediation activity or insurance mediation activity. Only details of convictions relevant in terms of rule 12(1) need be given.
[3] This information need only be given in respect of persons involved in long-term care insurance mediation activity or insurance mediation activity. Only details relevant in terms of rule 12 (2) need be given. "Bankruptcy proceedings" are defined in rule 2(1) as meaning an award of sequestration, bankruptcy order or equivalent in any other jurisdiction.

General Notes:

(a) The terms "regulated activity", "exempt person", "incidental financial business", "insurance mediation activity", "long-term care insurance mediation activity" and "mortgage mediation activity" are defined in the Solicitors (Scotland) (Incidental Financial Business) Practice Rules 2004 and are further explained in the Society's Guidance Notes on the Rules. "Investment business" means all incidental financial business which is not insurance mediation activity, long-term care insurance mediation activity or mortgage mediation activity.
(b) In responding to question 2, please set out the names of *the* person who will be responsible for the conduct of incidental financial business which is insurance mediation activity.

(c) In responding to question 3, please set out the names of *all* persons who you expect will be carrying on incidental financial business—an incidental financial business licence granted by the Society will only permit the persons specified in the application form (and changes to that list subsequently notified in terms of the Rules) to carryon such business.

SCHEDULE 2

Rule 14

Information to be Disclosed Before or Immediately after Conclusion of a Contract of Insurance

1 The name and address of the licensed person.

2 The licensed person's statutory status as a person licensed by the Society to conduct incidental financial business, including insurance mediation activity. This must be done by using the standard statement contained in PROF 4.1.3 R (2) of the FSA's Professional Firms Sourcebook relating to insurance mediation and mortgage activities.

3 The fact that items 1 and 2 may be checked on the FSA's register by visiting the FSA's website http://www.fsa.gov.uk/register or by contacting the FSA on 0845 606 1234.

4 Whether the licensed person has any holding, direct or indirect, representing more than 10 per cent of the voting rights of or the capital in an insurance undertaking.

5 Whether an insurance undertaking or parent of an insurance undertaking has a holding, direct or indirect, representing more than 10 per cent of the voting rights of or capital in the licensed person.

6 In relation to the contract of insurance provided, whether the licensed person has selected or dealt with the contract:

(a) on the basis of a fair analysis of the market; or
(b) from a limited number of insurance undertakings; or
(c) from a single insurance undertaking.

If sub-paragraph (b) or (c) applies, the licensed person must also disclose whether it is contractually obliged to conduct insurance mediation activity in this way.

7 If the contract of insurance provided has not been selected on the basis of a fair analysis of the market, the client can request a copy of the list of the insurance undertakings the licensed person selects from or deals with in relation to that contract.

8 The details referred to in paragraph (d) of Schedule 4.

9 The details referred to in paragraph (e) of Schedule 4.

SCHEDULE 3

Rule 18

Incidental Financial Business Compliance Certificate

To be printed on the licensed person's headed paper

To: The Secretary
The Law Society of Scotland
26 Drumsheugh Gardens
Edinburgh EH3 7YR

Dear Sir/Madam

INCIDENTAL FINANCIAL BUSINESS COMPLIANCE CERTIFICATE

The accounting period to which the undernoted declarations relate ("the relevant period") is

From .... to ....

1. **Incidental Financial Business**
I/We certify that, during the relevant period, I/we carried out no regulated activities (other than regulated activities in relation to which I was/we were an exempt person) except incidental financial business.

2. **No pecuniary reward or other advantage**
I/We certify that, during the relevant period, I/we did not receive from a person other than my/our client any pecuniary reward or other advantage for which I/we did not account to my/our client, arising out of my/our carrying on any regulated activity.

3. **Orders made under section 327(6) of the Financial Services and Markets Act 2000**
I/We certify that, during the relevant period, I/we have not carried out regulated activities which are of a description, or relate to an investment of a description, specified in any order made by the Treasury for the purposes of section 327(6) of the Financial Services and Markets Act 2000.

4. **Directions made under section 328 of the Financial Services and Markets Act 2000**
I/We certify that, during the relevant period, I/we complied with any directions given by the Financial Services Authority under section 328(1) of the Financial Services and Markets Act 2000.

5. **Orders made under section 329 ofthe Financial Services and Markets Act 2000**
I/We certify that, during the relevant period, I was/we were not the subject of an order made by the Financial Services Authority under section 329(1) of the Financial Services and Markets Act 2000.

6. **Compliance**
I/We certify that I/we have, during the relevant period, complied with the requirements of the Solicitors (Scotland) (Incidental Financial Business) Practice Rules 2004 and in particular with:

(a) Part VI of those Rules; and

(b) my/our obligation in terms of rules 10 and 11 (4) of those Rules.

Dated this day of 20

Officer .... (Signature)

....(Print Name)

Name of Licensed Person (in block capitals) ....

Address ....

....

SCHEDULE 4

Rule 22

Terms of Business

The terms of business referred to in rule 22 shall contain the following statements and disclosures:

(a) a statement as to the nature of the specific incidental financial business activities carried on by the licensed person for the client-and the fact that these are limited in scope;
(b) a statement that the licensed person is licensed by the Law Society of Scotland to carry on incidental financial business;
(c) a statement that the licensed person is not authorised by the Financial Services Authority under the Financial Services and Markets Act 2000;
(d) disclosure of the compensation arrangements in respect of the carrying on of incidental financial business by that licensed person, making reference to the licensed person's professional indemnity insurance under the Law Society of Scotland's Master Policy (or the equivalent cover in respect of a registered European lawyer) and to the Scottish Solicitors Guarantee Fund (or the equivalent cover in respect of a registered European lawyer); and
(e) disclosure of the complaints procedure which is operated by the licensed person, which shall include details of the licensed person's internal complaints procedure, details of the right of a client to complain to the Law Society of Scotland and details of the right of a client to complain against any finding of the Law Society of Scotland to the Scottish legal services ombudsman.

Solicitors (Scotland) (Multi-Disciplinary Practices) Practice Rules 1991

Rules dated 3rd May 1991, made by the Council of The Law Society of Scotland and approved by the Lord President of the Court of Session in terms of section 34 of the Solicitors (Scotland) Act 1980.

1.—(1) These rules may be cited as the Solicitors (Scotland) (Multi-Disciplinary Practices) Practice Rules 1991.

(2) These rules shall come into operation on 3rd May 1991.

2.—(1) In these rules unless the context otherwise requires:—

"the Act" means the Solicitors (Scotland) Act 1980;

"the Council" means the Council of the Society;

"legal relationship" means membership of a partnership or a joint venture which is not a partnership, or membership or directorship of a corporate body;

"multi-disciplinary practice" means a body corporate or partnership:—

(a) having as one of its directors, or as the case may be, partners, a solicitor or an incorporated practice; and

(b) which offers services, including professional services, such as are provided by individual solicitors, to the public; and

(c) where a solicitor or incorporated practice carries out, or supervises the carrying out, or makes provision of legal services;

"the Society" means the Law Society of Scotland;

[1] "solicitor" means any person enrolled as a solicitor in pursuance of the Act, and includes a firm of solicitors or incorporated practice and any association of solicitors and also includes a registered foreign lawyer and a multi-national practice.

(2) The Interpretation Act 1978 applies to these rules as it applies to an Act of Parliament.

NOTE

[1] As amended by the Solicitors (Scotland) (Registered Foreign Lawyers) etc. Practice Rules 2005, Sch.5 (effective May 1, 2005).

3. Rule 3 of the Solicitors (Scotland) Practice Rules 1964 is hereby repealed.

4. A solicitor shall not form a legal relationship with a person or body who is not a solicitor with a view to their jointly offering professional services as a multi-disciplinary practice to any person or body.

5. The Council shall have power to waive any of the provisions of these rules in any particular case or cases.

6. Breach of these rules may be treated as professional misconduct for the purposes of Part IV of the Act (Complaints and Disciplinary Proceedings).

Solicitors' (Scotland) Practising Certificate Rules 2007

Rules dated 31 August 2007 made by the Council of the Law Society of Scotland under section 13 of the Solicitors (Scotland) Act 1980.

Citation and Commencement

1.—(1) These Rules may be cited as the Solicitors (Scotland) Practising Certificate Rules 2007.

(2) These Rules shall come into operation on 1 September 2007.

Interpretation

2.—(1) In these Rules, unless the context otherwise requires—

"the 2005 Rules" means the Solicitors (Scotland) Professional Indemnity Insurance Rules 2005;

"the Act" means the Solicitors (Scotland) Act 1980;

"application" means an application for a practising certificate;

"the Council" means the Council of the Society;

"multi-national practice" has the meaning given by section 65(1) of the Act;

"practice year" means a period of twelve months ending on 31 October;

"practising certificate" means a certificate issued by the Council in accordance with the provisions of Part II of the Act authorising a person to practise as a solicitor;

"principal" means a solicitor who is a sole practitioner or a partner in a firm of solicitors or a member of an incorporated practice or a member of a multi-national practice;

"Society" means the Law Society of Scotland.

(2) The Interpretation Act 1978 applies to these Rules as it applies to an Act of Parliament.

Application for practising certificate

3. A solicitor who wishes to obtain a practising certificate for a practice year shall complete and sign a form in or substantially in the form set out in Part I of the Schedule to these Rules.

Issue of practising certificate

4.—(1) Subject to sections 14(2) and 15 of the Act and to Rule 5, on receipt of an application which has been duly completed and signed, the Council shall issue a practising certificate to the applicant without delay.

(2) A practising certificate shall be in or substantially in the form set out in Part II of the Schedule to these Rules.

Professional indemnity insurance

5. The Council shall not issue a practising certificate to any solicitor making an application unless he provides, with his application—

(a) evidence that a certificate of insurance has been issued to the practice unit of which he is a principal for the practice year for which the application is made, in terms of the master policy taken out and maintained by the Society pursuant to Rule 5 of the 2005 Rules; or

(b) where Rule 7 of the 2005 Rules applies, evidence that a certificate of insurance satisfying the requirements of Rule 7(2)(b) of the 2005 Rules has been issued to him or to the multi-national practice of which he is a member for the practice year for which the application is made; or

(c) a declaration that he is not a principal.

Register of applications and practising certificates issued

6.—(1) The Council shall keep, in respect of each practice year, a register of applications and of practising certificates issued.

(2) The register shall be in or substantially in the form set out in Part III of the Schedule to these Rules and may be divided into parts according to the districts in which solicitors practise as the Council may determine.

(3) The register shall be open for inspection by any person during office hours without payment.

Revocation and saving

7. The Solicitors (Scotland) Practising Certificate Rules 1988 are revoked, but such revocation shall not affect the validity of any application made, certificate granted or other thing done under the said Rules and any such application, certificate or thing shall have effect as if it were made, granted or done under these Rules.

SCHEDULE

PART I

Form of application for a Practising Certificate

Principal Contact Address: Roll Number

Tel No:

Email:

Principal ☐

Associate ☐

Consultant ☐

Employee ☐

Notary ☐

Other firms / trading names where you work (if any):

Firm name

Firm name

Firm name

Other jurisdictions in which you hold a Practising Certificate (if any):

Country

Regulator

Country

Regulator

Country

Regulator

Regulatory Posts held (if any):

ARTL Practice Manager ☐

ARTL Local Registration Authority ☐

Client Relations Partner ☐

Designated Cashroom Partner ☐

Money Laundering Reporting Officer ☐

Risk Management Contact ☐

I declare the above information correct at today's date subject to any changes I have made in ink. ☐

1.1 Fee Payable

Annual Membership Fee	£
Guarantee Fund Contribution	£
Fee for Retention on Roll	£
Incidental Financial Business Fee	£
Total Payable	£

1(a) I am liable to contribute to the Scottish Solicitors' Guarantee Fund. ☐

OR:

1(b) I am exempt from payment of a contribution to the Scottish Solicitors' Guarantee Fund as I am not a principal engaged in private practice in Scotland. ☐

2(a) I herewith provide evidence of Insurance in terms of the Solicitors (Scotland) Professional Indemnity Insurance Rules 2005. ☐

OR:

2(b) I am exempt from providing evidence of insurance as I am not a Principal in private practice in Scotland. ☐

3 In regard to the year ended 31 October 200?

3(a) I have complied with the Society's CPD Rules. ☐

3(b) And: I have complied with the Solicitors (Scotland) Accounts etc Rules 2001, any exceptions having been advised to the Society. ☐

OR:

3(c) I have not held or received clients' money at any time during the practice year. ☐

4 I declare I am not aware of any reason why I may not be granted a Practising Certificate and hereby apply for a Practising Certificate for the year to 31 October 200? ☐

5 I understand that the making of a false statement by a solicitor in an application for a Practising Certificate may be treated as professional misconduct for the purposes of the Solicitors (Scotland) Act 1980. (See Section 13(3)) ☐

Signature ☐ Date ☐

I would like the Society to keep me informed about developments in the following areas of law and practice: (please tick as appropriate)

Agricultural	☐	Child & Family	☐	Commercial Law	☐
Conveyancing	☐	Civil Court Work	☐	Criminal Court Work	☐
Discrimination	☐	Employment	☐	Human Rights	☐

Immigration ☐ Intellectual Property ☐ Legal Aid ☐

Trusts & Estates ☐ Public Law ☐

I do not wish to be kept informed on anything other than Regulatory matters. ☐

I do not wish my information to be passed to third parties as defined in the Guidance Notes ☐

Data Protection Act. See Guidance Notes on www.lawscot.org.uk.

PART II

Form of Practising Certificate

No.

PURSUANT to the Solicitors (Scotland) Act 1980

THE COUNCIL OF THE LAW SOCIETY OF SCOTLAND HEREBY CERTIFIES, that

having lodged with the Council an application pursuant to the said Act, is entitled to practise as a solicitor until the thirty-first day of October Two thousand and
and is a member of the Law Society of Scotland.

GIVEN under the hand of the
Secretary of THE LAW SOCIETY OF
SCOTLAND
this day
of 20

Secretary

Entered

PART III

Form of Register of Application for and of Issue of Practising Certificates for year to 31st October 20

Name		Designation	Place(s) of business	Date of admission	No. of Certificate	Certificate Issued	Remarks
Surname	Forename						

Solicitors (Scotland) (Practice Management Course) Practice Rules 2004

Rules dated 28th May 2004 made by the Council of the Law Society of Scotland under section 34(1) of the Solicitors (Scotland) Act 1980 and approved by the Lord President of the Court of Session in terms of section 34(3) of the said Act.

Citation and Commencement

1—(1) These Rules may be cited as the Solicitors (Scotland) (Practice Management Course) Practice Rules 2004.

(2) These Rules shall come into operation on 1st September 2004.

Definitions and Interpretation

2.—(1) In these Rules, unless the context otherwise requires:

[1] "2005 Rules" means the Solicitors (Scotland) (Registered Foreign Lawyers) etc Practice Rules 2005;

"the Act" means the Solicitors (Scotland) Act 1980;

"the Council" means the Council of the Society;

"Practice Management Course" means a course of practical training in the management of solicitors' practices, the duration, form and content of which shall be prescribed by the Council from time to time;

[2] "practice unit" means the business of a sole practitioner, a firm of two or more solicitors or an incorporated practice or a Scottish multinational practice (as defined in rule 7(1) of the 2005 Rules); and

[2] "principal" means a solicitor who is a sole practitioner or is a partner in a firm of two or more solicitors or is a director of an incorporated practice which is a company or is a member of an incorporated practice which is a limited liability partnership or a member of a multi-national practice;

"the Society" means the Law Society of Scotland, established under the Act.

[2] "solicitor" means any person enrolled as a solicitor in pursuance of the Act and who holds a practising certificate free of conditions imposed in terms of sections 15, 24C or other relevant sections of the Act, or by any Regulations made thereunder or by the Scottish Solicitors' Discipline Tribunal or by the Court of Session and shall include a registered foreign lawyer to whom these rules apply in terms of rule 4(2) or (3) of the 2005 Rules;

(2) The Interpretation Act 1978 applies to the interpretation of these Rules as it applies to the interpretation of an Act of Parliament.

(3) The headings to these Rules do not form part of these Rules.

NOTES

[1] Inserted by the Solicitors (Scotland) (Registered Foreign Lawyers) etc. Practice Rules 2005, Sch.5 (effective May 1, 2005).

[2] As amended by the Solicitors (Scotland) (Registered Foreign Lawyers) etc. Practice Rules 2005, Sch.5 (effective May 1, 2005).

Attendance at Practice Management Course

3. Subject to rule 4 hereof a solicitor who becomes a principal of a practice unit shall be obliged to attend a Practice Management Course within a period not exceeding twelve months after the date on which he becomes such a principal, or such other period as may be determined by the Council in any particular case.

Exemption

4. Rule 3 shall not apply to a solicitor who—

(a) has attended a Practice Management Course within twelve months preceding the date on which he becomes a principal, or
(b) has been a principal within three years preceding the date.

Waiver

5. The Council shall have power to waive any of the provisions of these Rules in any particular circumstances or case.

Revocation of Previous Rules

6. The Solicitors (Scotland) (Practice Management Course) Practice Rules 2001 are hereby revoked.

Solicitors (Scotland) (Client Communication) Practice Rules 2005

Rules dated 24th March 2005, made by the Council of the Law Society of Scotland under section 34(1) of the Solicitors (Scotland) Act 1980 and approved by the Lord President of the Court of Session in terms of section 34(3) of the said Act.

Citation and Commencement

1.—(1) These Rules may be cited as the Solicitors (Scotland) (Client Communication) Practice Rules 2005.

(2) These Rules shall come into operation on 1st August 2005.

Definitions and Interpretation

2.—(1) In these Rules, unless the context otherwise requires:—

"the 1986 Act" means the Legal Aid (Scotland) Act 1986;

"the Act" means the Solicitors (Scotland) Act 1980;

"advice and assistance" means advice and assistance as defined in section 6(1) of the 1986 Act to which Part II of the 1986 Act applies;

"civil legal aid" has the meaning given to it in section 13(2) of the 1986 Act;

"client" means a person who instructs a solicitor or to whom a solicitor tenders for business;

"the Council" means the Council of the Society;

"legal aid" has the meaning given to it in section 41 of the 1986 Act;

"the Society" means the Law Society of Scotland;

"solicitor" means a solicitor holding a practising certificate under the Act and includes a firm of solicitors and an incorporated practice; and

"special urgency work" has the meaning given to it in Regulation 18 of the Civil Legal Aid (Scotland) Regulations 2002.

(2) The Interpretation Act 1978 applies to the interpretation of these Rules as it applies to the interpretation of an Act of Parliament.

(3) The headings to these Rules do not form part of these Rules.

Provision of Information

3. A solicitor shall when tendering for business or at the earliest practical opportunity upon receiving instructions to undertake any work on behalf of a client, provide the following information to the client in writing:

(a) details of the work to be carried out on behalf of the client;

(b) save where the client is being provided with legal aid or advice and assistance, details of either—

  (i) an estimate of the total fee to be charged for the work, including VAT and outlays which may be incurred in the course of the work; or

  (ii) the basis upon which a fee will be charged for the work, including VAT and outlays which may be incurred in the course of the work;

(c) if the client is being provided with advice and assistance or legal aid—

  (i) where advice and assistance is being provided, details of the level of contribution required from the client, and

  (ii) where civil legal aid, special urgency work or advice and assistance is being provided,

  an indication of the factors which may affect any contribution which may be required from the client or any payment which may be required from property recovered or preserved;

(d) the identity of the person or persons who will principally carry out the work on behalf of the client; and

(e) the identity of the person whom the client should contact if the client becomes concerned in any way with the manner in which the work is being carried out.

Exceptions

4.—(1) Where a client regularly instructs a solicitor in the same type of work, he need not be provided with the information set out in rule 3 in relation to a new instruction to do that type of work, provided that he has previously been supplied with that information in relation to a previous instruction to do that type of work and is informed of any differences between that information and the information which, if this paragraph (1) did not apply, would have been required to be provided to him in terms of rule 3.

(2) Where there is no practical opportunity for a solicitor to provide the information set out in rule 3 to a client before the conclusion of the relevant work for that client then that information need not be provided to that client.

(3) Where a client is a child under the age of 12 years then the information set out in rule 3 need not be provided to that client.

Waiver

5. The Council shall have the power to waive any of the provisions of these Rules either generally or in any particular circumstances or case, provided that such waiver may be made subject to such conditions as the Council may in its discretion determine.

Professional Misconduct

6. Breach of these Rules may be treated as professional misconduct for the purposes of Part IV of the Act (Complaints and Disciplinary Proceedings).

Repeals

7. The Solicitors (Scotland) (Client Communication) (Residential Conveyancing) Practice Rules 2003 are hereby revoked.

[NEXT TEXT PAGE IS **F** 337]

Solicitors (Scotland) (Restriction on Practice) Practice Rules 2001

Rules dated 28th September 2001, made by the Council of the Law Society of Scotland and approved by the Lord President of the Court of Session in terms of sections 1(3) and 34 of the Solicitors (Scotland) Act 1980.

1.—(1) These Rules may be cited as the Solicitors (Scotland) (Restriction on Practice) Practice Rules 2001.

(2) These Rules shall come into force into operation on 30th November 2001.

2.—(1) In these Rules, unless the context otherwise requires:

[1] "2005 Rules" means the Solicitors (Scotland) (Registered Foreign Lawyers) etc Practice Rules 2005;

"the Act" means the Solicitors (Scotland) Act 1980;

"the Council" means the Council of the Society;

[2] "solicitor" means any person enrolled as a solicitor in pursuance of the Act and shall include a registered foreign lawyer to whom these rules apply in terms of rule 4(2) or (3) of the 2005 Rules;

[2] "principal" means a solicitor who is a sole practitioner or is a partner in a firm of two or more solicitors or is a director of an incorporated practice which is a company or a member of an incorporated practice which is a limited liability partnership or a solicitor who is a member of a Scottish multi-national practice (as defined by rule 7(1) of the 2005 Rules);

"2001 Regulations" means the Admission as Solicitor (Scotland) Regulations 2001;

"2001 intrant" means a solicitor who has complied with the 2001 Regulations before being admitted;

"the Society" means the Law Society of Scotland established under the Act; and

"unrestricted practising certificate" means practising certificate held by a solicitor free of conditions imposed in terms of section 15 or other relevant sections of the Act or any Regulations made thereunder, or by the Scottish Solicitors' Discipline Tribunal or by the Court of Session.

(2) Words and expressions defined in the 2001 Regulations shall, unless the context otherwise requires, have the same meaning in these Rules.

(3) The Interpretation Act 1978 applies to these Rules as it applies to an Act of Parliament.

NOTES

[1] Inserted by the Solicitors (Scotland) (Registered Foreign Lawyers) etc. Practice Rules 2005, Sch.5 (effective May 1, 2005).

[2] As amended by the Solicitors (Scotland) (Registered Foreign Lawyers) etc. Practice Rules 2005, Sch.5 (effective May 1, 2005).

3.—(1) Subject as aforementioned, a solicitor shall not practise as a principal unless he has been employed as a solicitor for a cumulative period of three years, one year of which shall immediately precede his commencing practice as a principal.

(2) Rule 3(1) shall not apply if the solicitor, who commences practice as a principal:

(a) is assumed into and remains in partnership with at least one other solicitor who has practised as a principal for a period of not less that three years prior to the assumption into partnership of the solicitor;

(b) is appointed and remains a director of an incorporated practice which is a company having as one of its directors a solicitor who has practised as a principal for a period of not less than three years prior to the appointment of the solicitor as such director;

(c) becomes and remains a member of an incorporated practice which is a limited liability partnership having as one of its members a solicitor who has practised as a principal for a period of not less than three years prior to the solicitor becoming such a member.

(3) Subject to Rule 3(4), employment shall only be counted for the purpose of Rule 3(1) of at the time the solicitor held an unrestricted practising certificate.

(4) Employment that would otherwise have counted for the purpose of Rule 3(1) shall not be so counted if at the time—

(a) the solicitor was bound by an undertaking given pursuant to Regulation 38(1) of the 2001 Regulations; or

(b) the solicitor was bound by any undertaking given pursuant to Regulation 38(2) of the 2001 Regulations.

(5) Notwithstanding any other provision in this Rule 3, a 2001 intrant shall not practise as a principal unless he has completed the Professional Competence Course, or is exempt therefrom, and passed the Test of Professional Competence, or is exempt therefrom.

(6) The provision of Rules 3(1) and (2) shall not apply to any solicitor who commenced practice as a principal before the coming into operation of these Rules.

4. Notwithstanding that he may hold a practising certificate, a 2001 intrant who has given any undertaking pursuant to Regulation 38(2) of the 2001 Regulations shall not after the last day of his service under his training contract practise as a solicitor or in any way hold himself out as entitled by law to practise as a solicitor while he is bound by any such undertaking.

5. The Council shall have power to waive any of the provisions of these Rules in any particular case or cases on cause shown and subject to such conditions as they may impose.

6. The Solicitors (Scotland) (Restriction on Practice as a Principal) Practice Rules 1996 are hereby revoked.

7. Breach of these rules may be treated as professional misconduct for the purposes of Part IV of the Act (Complaints and Disciplinary Proceedings).

Solicitors (Scotland) Practice Rules 1991

Rules dated 3rd May 1991, made by the Council of The Law Society of Scotland and approved by the Lord President of the Court of Session under section 34 of the Solicitors (Scotland) Act 1980 as amended.

1.—(1) These rules may be cited as the Solicitors (Scotland) Practice Rules 1991.

(2) These rules shall come into operation on 3rd May 1991.

2.—(1) In these rules unless the context otherwise requires:

[1] "2005 Rules" means the Solicitors (Scotland) (Registered Foreign Lawyers) etc Practice Rules 2005;

"the Act" means the Solicitors (Scotland) Act 1980 as amended;

"the Council" means the Council of the Law Society of Scotland established under the Act;

"lawyer" means a member of the Faculty of Advocates in Scotland or a legal practitioner offering legal services to the public, who is qualified and licensed to practise in accordance with the law of a legal jurisdiction other than that of Scotland, and includes a firm of lawyers, a law centre, a European Economic Interest Group the membership of which is exclusively lawyers, an incorporated practice of lawyers and any association (whether corporate or unincorporate) consisting exclusively of lawyers or exclusively of lawyers and solicitors;

[2] "solicitor" means any person enrolled as a solicitor in pursuance of the Act and includes a firm of solicitors, an incorporated practice and any association of solicitors and shall include a registered foreign lawyer to whom these rules apply in terms of rule 4(2) or (3) of the 2005 Rules and a Scottish multi-national practice and a Scottish branch of a multi-national practice (in each case as defined in rule 7 of the 2005 Rules);

(2) The Interpretation Act 1978 applies to these rules as it applies to an Act of Parliament.

NOTES

[1] Inserted by the Solicitors (Scotland) (Registered Foreign Lawyers) etc. Practice Rules 2005, Sch.5 (effective May 1, 2005).

[2] As amended by the Solicitors (Scotland) (Registered Foreign Lawyers) etc. Practice Rules 2005, Sch.5 (effective May 1, 2005).

3. Rules 2, 4, 5 and 6 of the Solicitors (Scotland) Practice Rules 1964 are hereby repealed.

4. A solicitor shall not share with any unqualified person any profits or fees or fee derived from any business transacted by the solicitor of a kind which is commonly carried on by solicitors in Scotland in the course of or in connection with their practice; provided always that the provisions of this rule shall not apply to the sharing of profits or fees where:—

(i) a person who has ceased to practise as a solicitor shall receive from any solicitor a share of the profits or fees of the latter, as a price or value of the business which he has transferred to the latter or shall receive a share of such profits as a voluntary or other allowance out of the profits or fees of a business in which he had been a partner; or

[1] (ii) the widow, civil partner, heirs, executors, representatives, next of kin or dependants of any deceased solicitor receive from any solicitor who has purchased or succeeded to the business of such deceased solicitor or from any firm of solicitors of which such

deceased solicitor was a partner at his death any share of the profits of such business; or

(iii) the salary of any clerk or assistant of a solicitor who is wholly employed by such solicitor is partly or wholly paid in the form of a percentage on the profits of such solicitor's business or any part thereof; or

(iv) such profits or fees are received by any public officer in respect of work done in the course of his duty; or

(v) an agreement for sharing such profits or fees is made between a solicitor and a lawyer;

(vi) such profits or fees are received by an officer of a public body who is a solicitor or by the public body and are dealt with in accordance with Statutory Provisions.

NOTE

[1] As amended by the Solicitors (Scotland) (Miscellaneous Amendments) Rules 2006, r.3 Sch.(3).

5. The Council shall have power to waive any of the provisions of these rules in any particular case or cases.

6. Breach of these rules may be treated as professional misconduct for the purposes of Part IV of the Act (Complaints and Disciplinary Proceedings).

"Fee sharing: making the rules work" (2004) 49 (2) J.L.S.S., 42.

The Solicitors (Scotland) Practice Rules 1991 prohibit solicitors from sharing "with any unqualified person any profits or fees or fee derived from any business transacted by the solicitor of a kind which is commonly carried on by solicitors in Scotland in the course of or in connection with their practice"; with certain limited exceptions. Those exceptions are, broadly, retired partners and their executors, heirs or representatives; clerks or assistants who are wholly employed in the solicitors firm; public officers in respect of work done in the course of their duty; and other lawyers —including lawyers in other jurisdictions—and law centres. The Professional Practice Committee has recently undertaken a review of the practice rules particularly in the light of developments in England and Wales which were briefly referred to in last month's Journal (page 40).

The Law Society (of England and Wales) have proposed changes to their similar rules which would allow solicitors to enter into fee sharing arrangements which (a) facilitate the introduction of capital; (b) facilitate the provision of services to the practice; (c) pay for referral of business except for Criminal Court work. The provisions are not unfettered and multi discipline partnerships will continue to be prohibited. Solicitors will require to supply details of all such arrangements and the percentage of the annual gross fees of the practice which has been paid to each fee sharer to the Law Society; solicitors will require to disclose to the client any referral arrangement involving payment by the solicitor to a third party; and such an arrangement should not compromise the solicitors independence or impose any constraints or conditions which affect the client.

In its review the Society's Professional Practice Committee came to the conclusion that the Scottish practice rules should not be amended but that this article should be published to advise the profession in Scotland of how the Committee interpret the practice rules with particular regard to arrangements which would be regarded as breaching the rules and arrangements which would not.

The Committee take the view that the principle type of arrangement which the practice rules prohibit is an arrangement to pay commission for the introduction of business on a case by case basis. Solicitors are entitled to pay for the cost of marketing or promoting the practice. They are entitled to pay a fee to be included on a panel to whom referrals will be made provided that that fee is not expressed as a specific sum per referral or as a percentage of the fees chargeable for referred business. A flat fee is not in breach of the rules and that may be a fee which is reviewed periodically.

Solicitors in Scotland are entitled to pay for the provision of services to the practice. To that extent the rules are not interpreted literally, as on one view the rules would prohibit the payment of rates and utility charges out of the firm's fee income. That is not how the rules are interpreted. Even if the service is provided by the person who introduces the client, solicitors are entitled to pay for the service. However the service must be a real service and not merely the introduction of the client. The Committee have also decided that the carrying out of a money laundering check by the introducer would not be a service for which payment could be made as that is an obligation on solicitors themselves in terms of the Accounts Rules. Services which have been accepted as not breaching the rules have included carrying out hearing tests; taking statements of witnesses; obtaining photographs of a locus; and completing a detailed client questionnaire relating to the particular matter in which the solicitor is instructed. The introduction of capital in return for a percentage of the solicitors fees would be regarded as breaching the practice rules, but the provision of loan funds with a variable rate of interest expressed as a percentage of the funds advanced would not.

The inclusion of a commission paid to an introducer as an outlay in a solicitors fee note—and not a hidden part of the fee—would not be in breach of the rules.

Finally solicitors are of course entitled to receive commission from third parties for the introduction of business, but the existence of such arrangements should be disclosed to the client although the actual amount of commission does not need to be disclosed unless the client specifically seeks that information. Such commission received must relate to any work undertaken by the solicitors in connection with the business referred. If no work has been undertaken, unless the commission is of a nominal amount it should be accounted for to the client.

Bruce Ritchie, Director of Professional Practice

Solicitors (Scotland) (Rights of Audience in the High Court of Justiciary and Judicial Committee of the Privy Council) Rules 2002

The Council of the Law Society of Scotland in exercise of the powers conferred on it by section 25A(4) of the Solicitors (Scotland) Act 1980, hereby makes the following Rules:

Citation and coming into effect

1.—(1) These Rules may be cited as the Solicitors (Scotland) (Rights of Audience in the High Court of Justiciary and Judicial Committee of the Privy Council) Rules 2002.

(2) These Rules shall have effect from 1st March 2003 having been approved by the Lord President and Scottish Ministers, following consultation with the Director General of Fair Trading in accordance with section 25A of the Solicitors (Scotland) Act 1980.

Interpretation

2. In these Rules, unless the context otherwise requires:

"applicant" means a solicitor who seeks a right of audience in the Court;

"Council" means the Council of the Law Society of Scotland;

"course of training" means a course of training in evidence, procedure and pleadings in relation to proceedings in the Court;

"Court" means the High Court of Justiciary and the Judicial Committee of the Privy Council;

"knowledge" means knowledge of the practice and procedures of and professional conduct in the Court;

"relevant date" means the date on which the applicant informs the Council that he seeks a right of audience in the Court;

"right of audience" means a right of audience in the Court.

Course of training in evidence and pleading

3.—(1) The matters to be included in the course of training are those matters specified in the Schedule hereto.

(2) The methods of instruction to be employed in the course of training are:

(*a*) lectures, the provision of written instructional material and audio-visual or other practical demonstration by the persons conducting the course upon the matters specified;

(*b*) discussion of the applicant's performance by the persons conducting the course based on observation and assessment of the applicant's presentation of oral advocacy.

(3) The persons who conduct the course of training shall be:

(*a*) solicitors or advocates of at least 5 years' standing; or

(*b*) persons who have been employed at a university in Scotland for at least 5 years full-time during the 10 years prior to the coming into force of these Rules;

and who have experience in the matters specified in paragraph (1) of this rule.

Demonstration of knowledge

4.—(1) An applicant's knowledge of the practice, procedure and professional conduct in the Court shall be demonstrated by evidence that he has:

(*a*) passed in not more than 2 attempts a written examination set by examiners appointed by the Council within 30 months of the relevant date; or

(*b*) passed examinations for admission to the Faculty of Advocates which are considered by the Council to be equivalent to the written examination referred to above.

(2) The examiners appointed by the Council for the purposes of rule 4(1) shall be solicitors with a right of audience in the Court or advocates or Professors of Law in a Scottish university, in each case of at least 10 years' standing.

SCHEDULE

Matters to be included in the Course of Training (rule 3(1))

1. The practical applications of the law of evidence in connection with the presentation of cases in the Court.

2. The procedure employed in the Court.

3. The presentation by applicants to the persons conducting the course of examples of oral advocacy in the manner required by the Court.

Solicitors (Scotland) (Rights of Audience in the Court of Session, the House of Lords and the Judicial Committee of the Privy Council) Rules 2002

The Council of the Law Society of Scotland in exercise of the powers conferred on it by section 25A(4) of the Solicitors (Scotland) Act 1980, hereby makes the following Rules:

Citation and coming into effect

1.—(1) These Rules may be cited as the Solicitors (Scotland) (Rights of Audience in the Court of Session, the House of Lords and the Judicial Committee of the Privy Council) Rules 2003.

(2) These Rules shall have effect from 1st March 2003 having been approved by the Lord President and Scottish Ministers, following consultation with the Director General of Fair Trading in accordance with section 25A of the Solicitors (Scotland) Act 1980.

Interpretation

2. In these Rules, unless the context otherwise requires:

"applicant" means a solicitor who seeks a right of audience in the Court;

"Council" means the Council of the Law Society of Scotland;

"course of training" means a course of training in evidence, procedure and pleadings in relation to proceedings in the Court;

"Court" means the Court of Session, the House of Lords and the Judicial Committee of the Privy Council;

"knowledge" means knowledge of the practice and procedures of and professional conduct in the Court;

"relevant date" means the date on which the applicant informs the Council that he seeks a right of audience in the Court;

"right of audience" means a right of audience in the Court.

Course of training in evidence, pleading and procedure

3.—(1) The matters to be included in the course of training are those matters specified in Part 1 of the Schedule hereto.

(2) The methods of instruction to be employed in the course of training are those specified in Part 2 of the Schedule hereto.

(3) The persons who conduct the course of training, including the course convener, shall be:

(*a*) solicitors or advocates of at least 5 years' standing; or

(*b*) persons who have been employed at a university in Scotland for at least 5 years full-time during the 10 years prior to the coming into force of these Rules;

and who have experience in the matters specified in paragraph (1) of this rule.

Demonstration of knowledge

4.—(1) An applicant's knowledge of the practice, procedure and professional conduct in the Court shall be demonstrated by evidence that he has:

(*a*) passed in not more than 2 attempts a written examination on such matters set by examiners appointed by the Council within 30 months of the relevant date; or

(*b*) passed examinations for admission to the Faculty of Advocates which arc considered by the Council to be equivalent to the written examination referred to in rule 4(1)(a).

(2) The examiners appointed by the Council for the purposes of rule 4(1) shall be solicitors with a right of audience in the Court, or advocates, or

professors of law in a Scottish university, in each case of at least 10 years' standing.

Revocation

5. The Admission as a Solicitor with Extended Rights (Scotland) Rules 1992 and Solicitors (Scotland) (Admission with Extended Rights of Audience) Rules 1995 are revoked with effect from 28th February 2003.

SCHEDULE

Part 1

Matters to be Included in the Course of Training (rule 3(1))

1. The preparation and submission to the persons conducting the course of examples of the forms and style of written pleadings used in the presentation of cases in the Court of Session.

2. The practical applications of the law of evidence in connection with the presentation of cases in the Court of Session.

3. The procedure employed in the Court.

4. The presentation by applicants to the persons conducting the course of examples of oral advocacy in the manner required by the Court.

Part 2

The Methods of Instruction to be used in the Course of Training (rule 3(2))

1. Lectures, the provision of written instructional material, and audio-visual or other practical demonstration by the persons conducting the course of training in relation to any of the matters specified in Part 1 of this Schedule.

2. Attendance for a period, to be specified by the course convener, of up to 6 days sitting in on proceedings in the Court of Session, not being proceedings involving the applicant or any member or employee of the applicant's firm unless the convener shall direct otherwise, in both or either of the Outer House (including the Commercial Court) and the Inner House, observing, with or without the supervision of the persons conducting the course of training, the manner in which cases are conducted in that Court.

3. Discussion of the applicant's performance by those conducting the course, and the provision of comment and criticism by them upon the applicant's presentation of oral advocacy.

4. Consideration by those conducting the course of the applicant's written work and the provision of criticism and comment thereon.

Solicitors (Scotland) Order of Precedence, Instructions and Representation Rules 1992

Rules made by the Council of the Law Society of Scotland and approved by the Lord President of the Court of Session pursuant to section 25A of the Solicitors (Scotland) Act 1980.

Title and commencement

1. These Rules may be cited as the Solicitors (Scotland) Order of Precedence, Instructions and Representation Rules 1992 and shall come into force on 31st October 1992.

Interpretation

2.—(1) In these Rules, unless the context otherwise requires—

"the Society" means the Law Society of Scotland;

"the Council" means the Council of the Society;

"the Secretary" means the Secretary of the Society and includes any person authorised by the Council to act on behalf of the Secretary for the purposes of these Rules;

"Courts" means the Court of Session, the House of Lords, the Judicial Committee of the Privy Council and the High Court of Justiciary and the expression "court" shall be construed accordingly;

"extended rights" means a right of audience in the Court of Session, the House of Lords and the Judicial Committee of the Privy Council or, as the case may be, the High Court of Justiciary;

"instructions" means for the purpose of rule 5—

(a) where a solicitor has on behalf of his firm arranged with another firm for the representation of his client before a court by a solicitor-advocate, the agreement for representation between the two firms; and

(b) where a client has arranged on his own behalf with a firm of solicitors his representation before a court by a solicitor-advocate, the agreement for representation between him and the firm;

"a solicitor-advocate" means a solicitor who has been granted extended rights.

(2) Any reference in these Rules to a firm of solicitors shall be deemed to include a solicitor practising solely on his own account.

(3) The provisions of the Interpretation Act 1978 shall apply to these Rules as they apply to an Act of Parliament.

Order of precedence of court

3. Where a solicitor-advocate accepts instructions to appear in a court, those instructions shall:—

(i) take precedence before any other professional obligation;

(ii) themselves be in the following order of precedence—

(a) where the solicitor-advocate has extended rights in the civil courts only—
House of Lords
Inner House of the Court of Session
Outer House of the Court of Session;

(*b*) where the solicitor-advocate has extended rights in the High Court of Justiciary only—
High Court of Justiciary exercising its appellate jurisdiction
High Court of Justiciary;

(*c*) where the solicitor-advocate has extended rights in all courts—
House of Lords
High Court of Justiciary exercising its appellate jurisdiction

High Court of Justiciary
Inner House of the Court of Session
Outer House of the Court of Session.

Subject to the above order of precedence instructions shall take priority according to the date, or, if on the same date, the time when they are delivered, or, if orally transmitted, when they have been accepted by the solicitor-advocate.

Priority of instructions

4. Notwithstanding the general rule stated in rule 3 the solicitor-advocate shall have regard to the following considerations in determining which instructions are to be accepted:—

(*a*) the seriousness, importance or value of the case;
(*b*) in the case of an appeal, that the solicitor-advocate has appeared for the client in the lower court;
(*c*) in the case of an adjourned diet or continued hearing, that the solicitor-advocate appeared at the previous diet or hearing;
(*d*) in the case of a debate on the pleadings, that the solicitor-advocate was responsible for drafting or revising the pleadings, particularly where a difficult or delicate point of law is involved to which the solicitor-advocate has already devoted a substantial amount of time and research;
(*e*) in the case of a proof or trial, that the solicitor-advocate was involved to a substantial extent in drafting the pleadings, debating the pleadings, consulting with the client or advising on the pre-trial or pre-proof preparations;
(*f*) that the client has, for the purposes of the case, come to rely on the advice and guidance of the solicitor-advocate to an unusual extent;
(*g*) that because of the nature or circumstances of the case, or because of the limited time available, it would be unusually difficult for either counsel or another solicitor-advocate adequately to prepare for appearance;
(*h*) that a suitable fee has been tendered with instructions or conversely that the instructions were given on the basis of an agreement with the client that no fee or only a modified fee will be paid.

If in doubt as to what his decision should be, the solicitor-advocate should consult the Secretary.

Cancellation of instructions

5.—(1) Acceptance of instructions involves a professional commitment on which the client and the court are entitled to rely. A solicitor-advocate is not entitled without good cause to cancel instructions once accepted so as to relieve himself of that professional commitment.

(2) In considering whether, and if so when, to cancel instructions after having accepted them, a solicitor-advocate should have in mind the following considerations—

(*a*) so long as instructions to do so have been accepted and not cancelled a solicitor-advocate owes a duty to the client and the court to attend in court when the case is called;
(*b*) a solicitor-advocate owes a duty to the client and the court to ensure, as far as he can, that the case is properly prepared and properly presented;
(*c*) a solicitor-advocate owes a duty to the client and the court to remain in attendance until the trial or hearing has been completed;
(*d*) a solicitor-advocate owes a duty to his fellow solicitor-advocates to avoid placing them unnecessarily in a position where they have to take over his cases at short notice and face the client and the court without adequate time for preparation.

It may also be appropriate to take into account the considerations mentioned in rule 4 above.

(3) Where a solicitor-advocate has been instructed by a solicitor and has:—

(*a*) an actual clash of commitments he shall, subject to rule 6(1), without delay intimate the cancellation of the instructions with which he cannot comply and return the relevant papers; or

(*b*) a foreseeable clash of commitments he shall, subject to rule 6(1), immediately inform the instructing solicitor of the situation and comply with any subsequent instructions as to alternative arrangements in the event of his being unable to appear.

(4) Where a solicitor-advocate has been instructed directly by a client and has:—

(*a*) an actual clash of commitments; or

(*b*) a foreseeable clash of commitments;

he shall, subject to rule 6(1) immediately inform the client of the situation, and comply with any subsequent instructions as to alternative arrangements in the event of his being unable to appear.

(5) In the case of proceedings before the High Court of Justiciary on appeal, there is a particular obligation on the solicitor-advocate who represented the appellant at the trial and has recommended an appeal to present that appeal.

Securing representation

6.—(1) Where a solicitor or a solicitor-advocate is unable, in a difficult or urgent situation, to secure representation for a person wishing to be represented by a solicitor-advocate before any court he shall inform the Secretary of the situation.

(2) Where the Secretary is informed under paragraph (1) he shall:—

(*a*) nominate and appoint an appropriate solicitor-advocate to represent the client; or if this is not reasonably practicable,

(*b*) consult the Dean of the Faculty of Advocates.

7. These Rules do not apply to an employed solicitor-advocate whose contract of employment prevents him from acting for persons other than his employer.

FORM OF UNDERTAKING

Rule

1. Name and address of instructed firm: ....

....

2. Name and address of instructing party (if solicitor, insert firm name and reference)

....

....

3. Case name and number: ....

4. Name of solicitor-advocate: ....

5. I/We* the instructing party have arranged my/our client's* representation in the above case with the instructed firm by the above solicitor-advocate. It has been explained that the above solicitor-advocate may cancel the arrangement to appear if he receives other instructions which have priority. If he receives such instructions in a difficult or urgent situation, he may not be able to consult me/us* as to an alternative representative.

6. I/We*, the instructing party, authorise the instructed firm, in the above situation, to contact the Law Society of Scotland in order that they may on my/our* behalf make alternative arrangements for representation by any other solicitor-advocate or if there is no such person

who can appear, by counsel; and I/We* undertake to pay the charges due for such representation.

.... (Signature of instructing party)

.... (Date)

.... (Signature of witness)	.... (Signature of witness)
.... (Occupation)	.... (Occupation)
.... (Address)	.... (Address)
....	....
....	....

**delete as appropriate*

Solicitors (Scotland) Rules of Conduct for Solicitor Advocates 2002

The Council of the Law Society of Scotland in exercise of the powers conferred on it by section 25A(4) of the Solicitors (Scotland) Act 1980, hereby makes the following Rules:

Citation and coming into effect

1.—(1) These Rules may be cited as the Solicitors (Scotland) Rules of Conduct for Solicitor Advocates 2002 and shall come into force on 1st March 2003 having been approved by the Lord President and Scottish Ministers in accordance with section 25A of the Solicitors (Scotland) Act 1980.

(2) The Code of Conduct (Scotland) Rules 1992 are revoked with effect from the date of commencement of these Rules.

Interpretation

2.—(1) In these Rules, unless the context otherwise requires:

"a solicitor" means a solicitor enrolled with the Society and who holds a full practising certificate;

"a solicitor advocate" means a solicitor who has been granted Rights of Audience.

"Court" means the Court of Session, the House of Lords, the Judicial Committee of the Privy Council and the High Court of Justiciary;

"Rights of Audience" means a right of audience in the Court of Session, the House of Lords and the Judicial Committee of the Privy Councilor, as the case may be, the High Court of Justiciary and the Judicial Committee of the Privy Council;

"rules of conduct" means the Rules of Conduct for Solicitors exercising Rights of Audience set out in the Schedule to these Rules;

"the Council" means the Council of the Society;

"the Secretary" means the Secretary of the Society and includes any person authorised by the Council to act on behalf of the Secretary for the purposes of these Rules;

"the Society" means the Law Society of Scotland;

(2) The provisions of the Interpretation Act 1978 shall apply to these Rules as they apply to an Act of Parliament.

3. A solicitor advocate shall observe and comply with the rules of conduct when exercising Rights of Audience.

4. Where a solicitor advocate is in any doubt as to the propriety of any course of conduct he should:

(*a*) seek the advice of the Secretary;

(*b*) explain the position to the Secretary including anything which may be relevant to the advice sought.

5. The Council may, at its discretion, waive compliance with any of these Rules.

6. Breach of any of these Rules may be treated as professional misconduct for the purposes of Part IV of the Solicitors (Scotland) Act 1980 (Complaints and Disciplinary Proceedings).

SCHEDULE

Rules of Conduct for Solicitors exercising Rights of Audience

1. The acceptance of instructions by a solicitor advocate

(1) A solicitor advocate accepts that it is the responsibility of the Council of the Society to make rules to secure, through the Secretary whom failing

such of its officers as it thinks appropriate, that, where reasonably practicable, any person wishing to be represented before a court by a solicitor advocate is so represented.

(2) A solicitor advocate shall not accept instructions as a solicitor advocate (as opposed to a solicitor) without satisfying himself that it is proper for him to accept them. A solicitor advocate shall be entitled at all stages of the case at his sole discretion to decide whether he requires the assistance of a solicitor or other representative of his firm or of the instructing firm in connection with the preparation of the case and also at consultations with the client and at the presentation of the case in court.

(3) There are circumstances in which a solicitor advocate is entitled and indeed bound to refuse instructions.

(4) A solicitor advocate may not allow his personal interests to affect the performance of his professional duty. Accordingly, he should not accept instructions to act in his professional capacity in circumstances where he has a direct personal interest in the outcome. Where he has, or may have, an indirect personal interest in the outcome (e.g. where he is asked to act for a company in which he is a major shareholder or for an organisation in which he holds office although unremunerated), he should consult the Secretary before accepting instructions. Where a conflict of personal interest arises later, he should inform the instructing solicitor or client and cancel instructions.

(5) A solicitor advocate may not accept instructions on any basis which would deprive him of the responsibility for the conduct of the case or fetter his discretion to act in consultation with the client in accordance with his professional judgment and public duty.

(6) A solicitor advocate must not accept instructions to act in circumstances where, in his professional opinion, the case is unstatable in law or where the case is only statable if facts known to him are misrepresented to, or concealed from, the court. If such circumstances arise after he has accepted instructions, he should decline to act further. There may, however, be exceptional circumstances in which it is proper for a solicitor advocate, in order to assist the court, to present a case which he believes to be unstatable in law. In such circumstances, the solicitor advocate must explain to the client that he cannot do more than explain the client's position to the court, and that he will be bound to draw the court's attention to such statutory provisions or binding precedents as have led him to the conclusion that the case is unstatable.

2. Duty in relation to other members of the legal profession

(1) A solicitor advocate has a duty of loyalty to professional colleagues.

(2) The efficient conduct of litigation under the adversarial system depends on mutual trust between those acting for different parties. Discussion and negotiation between professional colleagues may achieve settlement of a case or at least dispose of incidental points which would otherwise take up time and cause unnecessary expense. It is therefore essential that counsel and solicitor advocates should be able to discuss cases with each other on the basis that confidence will be respected and that agreements and undertakings will be honoured.

(3) It must, however, also be remembered that all have a duty to act in the best interests of the respective clients. Solicitor advocates cannot assume that everything said to opposing professional colleagues will be treated in confidence and not disclosed to the solicitor advocate or the client. It is therefore desirable, at the outset of such discussions that the basis of the discussion be clarified. If it is intended to disclose information on a basis of confidence, this should be stated.

Correspondingly, if one party to the discussion is not prepared to treat information as confidential he should say so before the information is disclosed.

(4) There an agreement is reached following such discussions or an undertaking is given by counsel or solicitor advocate to another it is binding in honour between them and should be reported as soon as possible so that it can, if necessary, be incorporated in a formal exchange of letters. Alternatively, a joint minute should be drafted and initialled by counsel or solicitor advocate who should also bear in mind that once recorded in writing the written agreement supersedes the verbal agreement.

3. Duties in relation to an instructing solicitor

(1) A solicitor advocate when instructed by a solicitor must respect the fact that the solicitor's relationship is different from, and likely to be more continuing than, his own. He should do nothing, beyond what his professional duty requires, to upset the solicitor-client relationship or destroy the trust which the client has in the solicitor.

(2) When a solicitor advocate has reason to believe that a solicitor has been guilty of professional misconduct (as opposed to professional negligence) he has a duty to the client, the court and the profession to take appropriate action.

If the matter comes to his knowledge in the course of proceedings in court, it may be necessary to take immediate action, and if an adjournment is necessary for this purpose, it should be asked for. If the matter does not call for immediate action, the solicitor advocate should consult the Secretary before making any formal complaint or report.

(3) If a solicitor advocate feels compelled to criticise the conduct of a solicitor in respect of something falling short of professional misconduct, he should avoid doing so in the presence of the client and should in any event ask the solicitor to explain what he has done and why before criticising his conduct.

(4) A solicitor advocate where instructed by a solicitor or directly by a client should consider carefully whether he should attend a consultation without his instructing solicitor or another representative of his firm or of the instructing firm being present. The presence of the solicitor or representative will protect both the solicitor-advocate and the solicitor should a dispute arise later as to what advice the solicitor-advocate gave or what instructions he was given by the client.

(5) In exceptional circumstances, it may be unavoidable that a solicitor advocate instructed by a solicitor has to speak to the client without the solicitor being present. Such an occasion will however be rare, and when it arises the solicitor should be told as soon as possible what transpired.

4. Duties in relation to the client

(1) *Confidentiality*. It is a fundamental duty of the solicitor advocate not to disclose or use any information communicated to him in his professional capacity other than for the purpose for which it was communicated to him, so long as it remains in confidence and has not otherwise been made public. Any conversations relating to a 'Case which take place between a solicitor advocate and those representing the other side, including Crown counsel, are confidential and should not be revealed to anyone other than the client or those who are professionally concerned with the case. If he wishes to discuss a case with a colleague, for example, for the purpose of seeking his advice about law, he should do so only in terms which do not disclose, or risk disclosure of, the identity of the client or other parties involved.

This applies equally where a solicitor advocate is asked to give a written opinion or to advise in consultation. There may be good reasons, unknown to him, why the client or instructing solicitor would not even wish it to be known that his advice has been sought. Idle gossip about cases and clients, even if the facts are publicly known, is damaging to the reputation of the solicitor advocate and the profession.

(2) *Duty to uphold the interests of the client.* A solicitor advocate should remember that the client relies on him to exercise his professional skill and judgment in the client's best interests. He must at all times do, and be seen to do, his best for the client and he must be fearless in defending his client's interests, regardless of the consequences to himself (including, if necessary, incurring the displeasure of the bench). But he must also remember that his client's best interests require him to give honest advice however unwelcome that advice may be to the client and that duty to the client is only one of several duties which he must strive to reconcile.

(3) *Conflict between client and instructing solicitor (e.g. where the client may have a claim for professional negligence against his solicitor).* Where it appears to a solicitor advocate who is instructed by a solicitor that a conflict of interest has arisen or may arise between the client and the instructing solicitor, it is his duty to take steps to ensure that the client is so advised in order that he can get the advice of another solicitor. It will depend on the circumstances how this can be done. The great majority of instructing solicitors can be relied upon, when the conflict has been pointed out, to take the necessary steps themselves. It will therefore normally be inappropriate to mention the matter in the presence of the client. But it may be necessary to record the solicitor advocate's advice as to the existence of a conflict in a formal note and to ask the instructing solicitor to send it to the client, or to deal with the matter at consultation with the client. In extreme cases, it may be the duty of the solicitor advocate to refuse to act further on the instructions of the solicitor concerned, but before doing so he should where practicable intimate in writing to the instructing solicitor that it is his intention to refuse to act further.

(4) *Cancellation of instructions.* In any case where the solicitor-advocate feels obliged to cancel instructions, he must do so without delay and take such steps as are necessary to ensure that the client, and where appropriate the instructing solicitor, knows why he has withdrawn. Where he feels obliged to cancel in the course of a trial or other hearing, he must formally intimate to the court that he has cancelled instructions and is withdrawing from acting and must protect the interests of the client by moving for an adjournment so that the client can get other advice. He is under no obligation to explain in detail to the court or tribunal his reasons for cancellation, since to do so may prejudice his client, and he should not yield to pressure to do so. If in doubt as to whether he is entitled or bound to cancel he should seek the advice of the Secretary, and if necessary obtain an adjournment to do so.

5. Special duties in criminal cases

(1) *Pleas.* Where the Crown offers to accept a reduced or restricted plea, the defending solicitor advocate has a duty to advise the accused of that offer and to obtain his instructions about it. Likewise, where any limited offer to plead is made by an accused, it should (if considered in law to be appropriate) be conveyed to the Crown for consideration, without delay. For avoidance of doubt, it is prudent to obtain written instructions from the accused, for the tendering of a plea. In no circumstances should the solicitor advocate tender any plea on behalf of the accused unless instructions to do so have been obtained.

(2) In advising as to the possible consequences of a plea of guilty, a solicitor advocate should refrain from making any positive forecast of the possible sentence beyond drawing the attention of the accused to the normally anticipated range of sentences in the circumstances of that particular case.

(3) *Confessions.* Where an accused person makes a confession to a solicitor advocate and the solicitor advocate is satisfied in law that such confession amounts to guilt, the solicitor advocate must explain to the accused (if he is not pleading guilty) that the conduct of his defence will be

limited by that confession. It must be emphasised to the accused that no substantive defence involving an assertion or a suggestion of innocence will be put forward on his behalf and that, if he is not satisfied with this, he should seek other advice. A solicitor advocate should consider whether it is advisable to obtain confirmation in writing from the accused that he has been so advised and that he accepts such an approach to the conduct of his defence.

(4) So long as an accused maintains his innocence, the solicitor advocate's duty lies in advising him on the law appropriate to his case and the conduct thereof. The solicitor advocate may not put pressure on him to tender a plea of guilty, whether to a restricted charge or not, so long as he maintains his innocence. Nor should the solicitor advocate accept instructions to tender a plea in mitigation on a basis inconsistent with the plea of guilty. The solicitor advocate should always consider very carefully whether it is proper, in the interests of justice, to accept instructions to tender a plea of guilty. He should ensure that the accused is fully aware of the consequences and should insist that the instructions to plead guilty are recorded in writing.

(5) *Acting for co-accused.* Save in the most exceptional circumstances, a solicitor advocate should not accept instructions to act for more than one accused or appellant.

6. The duty to the court

(1) *Duties in relation to matters of law.* Where a solicitor advocate is aware of a previous decision binding on the court, or of a statutory provision relevant to a point of law in issue, it is his duty to draw that decision or provision to the attention of the court whether or not it supports his argument and whether or not it has been referred to by his opponent.

(2) Where there is no contradictor, a solicitor advocate should inform the court of authorities relevant to that case, even when such authority may be against his interest.

(3) In proceedings before the House of Lords, a solicitor advocate should have in mind the observations of Lord Chancellor Birkenhead in *Glebe Sugar Refining Co v Greenock Harbour Trustees* 1921 SC (HL) 72,73-74.

7. Duties in relation to matters of fact

(1) In relation to matters of fact, a solicitor advocate should have two principles in mind:

(*a*) It is for the court, not for a solicitor advocate, to assess the credibility of witnesses; and

(*b*) a solicitor advocate must not, directly or indirectly, deceive or mislead the court.

(2) *In court.* When conducting a case in court, a solicitor advocate should base his questions upon his instructions, the precognitions and the productions supplemented by information obtained at consultation and, after evidence has been led, upon the evidence.

(3) A solicitor advocate should not state his personal opinion on matters of fact. It is particularly important to observe this rule when addressing a jury. A solicitor advocate must not make observations on matters of fact which are not based on, or justified by, the evidence. In a criminal trial, he should not under any circumstances express either directly or indirectly a personal belief in the innocence of the accused.

(4) A solicitor advocate may not be a party to the giving of evidence which he knows to be perjured evidence, or to any other course that would enable a case to be put forward on behalf of a client which the client has informed him is unfounded in fact.

(5) A solicitor advocate may not put to a witness any question suggesting that the witness has been guilty of a crime, fraud or other illegal or improper conduct unless he has personally satisfied himself that there is evidence which could, if necessary, be led in support of the suggestion.

(6) *Interviewing witnesses.* There is no general rule that a solicitor advocate may not discuss the case with a potential witness, but a solicitor advocate when instructed by a solicitor, is entitled to insist that he accepts instructions on the basis that he, the solicitor advocate, will not do so.

(7) In cases where a solicitor advocate has not accepted instructions on such a basis he must avoid doing or saying anything which could have the effect of, or could be construed as, inducing the client or skilled witness to "tailor" his evidence to suit the case.

(8) Once a proof or trial has begun, a solicitor advocate must not interview any potential witness in relation to what has been said in court in the absence of that witness.

(9) Some cases cannot be properly prepared or conducted if the foregoing rules against interviewing potential witnesses are followed strictly according to the letter. The client may be accompanied at consultation by a relative or friend who is also a potential witness. Where the client is a corporate persona, those who can speak for the corporation may also be potential witnesses, although in that case it is usually better to discuss the case with someone who is not personally involved and can take a more objective view of it. Some witnesses may be witnesses to fact as to part of their evidence and expert witnesses giving opinion evidence as to another part. It may be essential in a case raising technical issues to discuss points arising from the evidence with a skilled witness who has not yet given evidence. In such cases, a solicitor advocate must use his discretion. But he should always act according to the spirit of the rule—namely, that a solicitor advocate should not under any circumstances do or say anything which might suggest to the witness that he should give evidence otherwise than in accordance with his honest recollection or opinion.

(10) A solicitor advocate may not, except with the consent of his opponent and of the court, communicate with any witness, including his client, once that witness has begun to give evidence until that evidence is concluded.

(11) As to interviewing the client or witnesses in the absence of an instructing solicitor, see paragraphs 3(4) and 3(5) above.

(12) *Confessions to a solicitor advocate by accused persons.* It follows from the rules stated in paragraphs 5(3) and 5(4) that, where an accused person has admitted that he committed the act with which he is charged (whether or not the admission is an explicit admission of guilt in law), a solicitor advocate may not conduct the defence on a basis inconsistent with that admission. Thus, he may not put to a witness any question suggesting, or tending to suggest, that the accused did not commit the act. *A fortiori*, he may not seek to set up a special defence of alibi or incrimination.

(13) Subject to the rule stated in the previous paragraph, a solicitor advocate may

- (*a*) take any proper objection to the jurisdiction of the court, to the competency or relevancy of the indictment, or to the admissibility of evidence;
- (*b*) test the evidence for the prosecution by cross-examination;
- (*c*) cross-examine or lead evidence in support of a special defence of insanity or (depending on the tenor of the accused's admission) self-defence;
- (*d*) cross-examine or lead evidence for the purpose of explaining the actings of the accused or supporting a plea in mitigation;
- (*e*) make submissions as to the sufficiency in law of the evidence to support a verdict of guilty.

(14) *Ex parte statements of fact by a solicitor advocate at the bar.* The court frequently must rely on statements as to matters of fact made at the bar, for example, in the Motion Roll and certain types of Petition procedure. Such statements are made on the responsibility of the solicitor advocate as an officer of the court and a solicitor advocate must therefore be scrupulously

careful that anything stated as fact is justified by the information in his possession. If the court asks a question which a solicitor advocate cannot answer on the information in his possession, he must say that he cannot answer it and, if necessary, ask leave to take instructions on the matter. This rule applies whether or not the opposing party is represented in court.

(15) *Pleadings.* A solicitor advocate must have a proper basis on precognition or in the light of consultation with the client for stating a fact in any pleadings.

8. The duty of courtesy

(1) Discourtesy is as offensive in court as it is outside, and is detrimental to the reputation of a solicitor advocate and of the bench, to the interests of the client and to public confidence in the administration of justice.

(2) In the examination of witnesses, and particularly in the cross-examination of hostile witnesses, a solicitor advocate must remember that the law places him in a privileged position which he should not abuse, for example, by bullying or insulting behaviour or by making offensive or personal remarks.

(3) A solicitor advocate should seek to uphold a relationship of mutual trust and courtesy with the bench.

(4) A failure to appear in court on time should always, as a matter of courtesy, be the subject of an apology. If the court is still sitting, and has not yet passed on to other business, the proper time to make the apology is at once on arrival in court.

The apology should always be in open court to the bench. It is not sufficient to offer an apology through the Macer or Clerk of Court.

9. The duty to attend court

(1) It is the duty of the solicitor advocate to arrange his affairs so as to avoid a reasonably foreseeable clash of commitments.

(2) Having accepted instructions to appear, it is the solicitor advocate's responsibility to ensure, unless (in a civil case only) other arrangements have been made with an instructing solicitor, that he is present in court on the day and at the time appointed and thereafter until the trial or hearing is concluded. Where unforeseen circumstances make it impossible for him to be present and he is unable to contact the Secretary, he must ensure that someone else is present at or before the time appointed to explain his absence and, if necessary, to move for an adjournment.

(3) Since instructions to appear in the High Court of Justiciary and the Inner House take precedence over instructions to appear in the Outer House, it follows that if a solicitor advocate has accepted instructions to appear in the High Court or the Inner House, including instructions for the Single Bills, it is his duty to ensure that he is present there at the appointed time, even though he also has instructions to appear in the Outer House. If a clash of commitments appears likely, and he is unable to contact the Secretary, he should ensure that someone else is present to appear in the Outer House in his place and, if necessary, to move for an adjournment until he is free to appear there. If a conflict arises due to unforeseen circumstances and he finds himself still detained in the Outer House when he must appear in the High Court or the Inner House, he should inform the Lord Ordinary that he requires to go to the High Court or the Inner House as the case may be and ask for an adjournment so that he can do so.

(4) If a solicitor advocate engaged in a proof or other hearing in the Outer House expects to be in difficulty because he is required to attend elsewhere in the Outer House to deal with an important matter on the Motion Roll on the same day, he or a representative from his firm should inform the Clerk of Court as soon as possible so that the judge concerned may be alerted to the problem and take such action as is appropriate. It has been accepted that

in such circumstances the start of the proof might reasonably be delayed until the solicitor advocate's business in the other court has been completed.

(5) Where a senior solicitor advocate appears with a junior solicitor advocate he should only be absent from court if he is satisfied that his junior will be present and will be able to deal properly with any matter which may arise.

10. Responsibility for pleadings and presentation in civil actions

(1) A solicitor advocate who signs any pleadings accepts personal responsibility to the court for their contents. He has a professional responsibility for any other pleadings drafted by him, except where his draft has been altered without his knowledge and consent. Where a solicitor advocate finds that pleadings drafted by him have been altered without his knowledge and consent, it is his professional duty to consider whether he can support the case on the basis of the pleadings so altered.

(2) Since a solicitor advocate accepts responsibility for pleadings or documents he has signed, he should not sign in his own name pleadings drafted by someone else save in exceptional circumstances. Papers may be signed in that way provided the solicitor advocate concerned is satisfied that the solicitor advocate for whom he signs cannot reasonably be found and he is also satisfied that the paper is in proper form for submission to the court.

(3) The presentation of a case in court is a matter for the sole professional responsibility and discretion of the solicitor advocate.

11. Speculative actions

In speculative actions, a solicitor advocate has a particular responsibility to the court both with regard to his own assessment of the merits of the case and with regard to the advice which he gives. The nature of the responsibility undertaken by counsel and solicitor was stated thus by Lord President Normand (*X Insurance Co v A & B* 1936 SC 225, 239):

> "It has long been recognised by the Courts that this is a perfectly legitimate basis on which to carryon litigation and a reasonable indulgence to people who while they are not qualified for admission to [Legal Aid] are nevertheless unable to finance a costly litigation.
>
> But it is equally recognised that there is involved in such business a grave risk of abuse unless it is carried out with strict regard to honour by all who are professionally concerned in it. Before acting in business of this kind it is the imperative duty of the solicitor and of the counsel to consider whether the party for whom they are to act has a reasonable prospect of success.
>
> The reasons for this are obvious, and need no discussion. If a solicitor, when asked to conduct the case on a speculative footing, is, after consideration, unable to advise that there is a reasonable prospect of success, he should refuse to conduct the case. But, if he has reasonable doubts about the prospects of success, he is justified in consulting counsel. If counsel advises that the action may properly be raised, the solicitor is entitled to follow his advice, and in the future conduct of the action he is bound to act in accordance with counsel's instructions. If he does this after having fairly disclosed to counsel all the information at his disposal, he will not be exposed to a charge of professional misconduct. In order that the prospects of success may be fairly estimated by the solicitor and by counsel in their turn, it is in most cases, where questions of fact are involved, a necessary precaution that fair and honest precognitions of the chief witnesses who will be relied on should be taken at the outset." (See also the opinion of Lord Fleming at 250–251.)

12. Criminal appeals

(1) In advising on criminal appeals, a solicitor advocate has a duty, first, to consider whether there are grounds for an appeal which he is prepared to state to the court and, second, if in his opinion there are none, to refuse to act further in the case: *Scott v HM Advocate* 1946 JC 68 per Lord President Normand at 69.

(2) Having advised that an appeal is statable, a solicitor advocate may later come to the view that it is not. If so, he must promptly inform his client that he can no longer act in the case.

13. Opposing a party litigant

Where a solicitor advocate appears against a party litigant, he must avoid taking unfair advantage of the party litigant and must, consistently with his duty to the client, co-operate with the court in enabling the party litigant's case to be fairly stated and justice to be done. But he must not sacrifice the interests of the client to those of the party litigant.

Solicitors (Scotland) (Supreme Courts) Practice Rules 2003

Rules dated 31st January 2003 made by the Council of the Law Society of Scotland under section 34(1) of the Solicitors (Scotland) Act 1980.

Citation and commencement

1.—(1) These Rules may be cited as the Solicitors (Scotland) (Supreme Courts) Practice Rules 2003.

(2) These Rules shall come into operation on 1st March 2003.

Definitions and interpretation

2.—(1) In these Rules unless the context otherwise requires:

"advocate" means a member of the Faculty of Advocates;

"Court" means the Court of Session, the House of Lords, the Judicial Committee of the Privy Council and the High Court of Justiciary;

"Rights of Audience" means a right of audience in the Court or any of them;

"solicitor" means any person enrolled as a solicitor in pursuance of the Act and holding a Practising Certificate;

"solicitor advocate" means a solicitor who has been granted Rights of Audience;

"the Act" means the Solicitors (Scotland) Act 1980;

"the Council" means the Council of the Law Society of Scotland established under the Act;

(2) The Interpretation Act 1978 applies to these Rules as it applies to an Act of Parliament;

(3) The headings to these Rules do not form part of these Rules.

Appearance in a court

3. Where in the course of advising a client a solicitor identifies a situation which may require appearance in a Court, he shall advise his client:

(1) that appearance before a particular Court is restricted to a solicitor advocate or an advocate;

(2) of the advantages and disadvantages of instructing appearance by a solicitor advocate and by an advocate respectively, which advice, subject to the foregoing generality, shall cover

(*a*) the gravity and complexity of the case;

(*b*) the nature of practice, including specialisation, and experience of the solicitor advocate;

(*c*) the likely cost of instructing a solicitor advocate and of instructing an advocate;

(3) that the decision whether a solicitor advocate or an advocate should be instructed is entirely that of the client.

Waiver

4. The Council may, at its discretion, waive compliance with any of these Rules.

Breach

5. Breach of any of these Rules may be treated as professional misconduct for the purposes of Part IV of the Act (complaints and disciplinary proceedings).

Explanatory Note on the Multi-National Practices (MNPs) Rules

Introduction

1. Section 60A of the Solicitors (Scotland) Act 1980 ("the 1980 Act") makes provision for multi-national practices. It was inserted by section 32 of the Law Reform (Miscellaneous Provisions) (Scotland) Act 1990 but was not, as originally enacted, sufficient to enable proper regulation of such practices. In light of the inadequacies of section 60A, it was never fully brought into force. Over the last year, the Society has been working with the Scottish Executive in order to cure the deficiencies of section 60A.

As a result of those discussions, the Scottish Parliament has passed the Solicitors (Scotland) Act 1980 (Foreign Lawyers and Multi-National Practices) Regulations 2004 (SSI 2004 No 383), which came into force on 1 October 2004. These regulations supplement the provisions contained in section 60A of the 1980 Act so as to create a workable framework for the regulation by the Society of multi-national practices.

The Scottish Parliament also passed the Law Reform (Miscellaneous Provisions) (Scotland) Act 1990 (Commencement No 15) Order 2004 (SSI 2004 No 382). This brought fully into force section 60A of the 1980 Act with effect from 1 October 2004, and the coming into force of these two sets of Regulations has enabled the Society to draft further rules in order to regulate MNPs and the registered foreign lawyers in them. There will be four sets of rules, as explained below.

Solicitors (Scotland) (Foreign Lawyers) (Registration) Rules 2004

2. These rules came into force on 1st February 2005. These are the rules which provide for the registration of foreign lawyers, *i.e.* lawyers from jurisdictions outwith Scotland (including England and Wales). It is a requirement of the 1980 Act that foreign lawyers must be registered with the Society before they can enter into MNPs with Scottish solicitors or incorporated practices.

Solicitors (Scotland) (Multi-National Practices) Practice Rules 2005

3. In summary, these Rules govern the entering into of MNPs by solicitors, firms of solicitors and incorporated practices. The Rules require solicitors, firms of solicitors and incorporated practices to seek the approval of the Council prior to entering into an MNP. In order to be able to give that approval, the Council requires to be satisfied that the applicant solicitor (or firm or incorporated practice) will become a member of an MNP as that term is defined in section 65 of the 1980 Act. The Council also has to be satisfied that the MNP of which that solicitor (or firm or incorporated practice) will be a member is or will be so regulated as to make it appropriate for solicitors to be allowed to enter it.

In order to qualify as an MNP in terms of section 65 of the 1980 Act, all of the foreign lawyers within the practice must be registered by the Society, and hence these Rules should be read along with the Solicitors (Scotland) (Foreign Lawyers) (Registration) Rules 2004. As mentioned, these provide for the registration of foreign lawyers and contain two important safeguards for the profession. The first is that anyone who wishes to become a registered foreign lawyer must satisfy the Council that he is a fit and proper person. Secondly, he must also satisfy the Council that the legal profession of which he is a member is so regulated as to make it appropriate for him to be allowed to enter into MNPs with Scottish solicitors. The registration rules also contain provisions in respect of professional indemnity insurance and guarantee fund matters.

Solicitors (Scotland) (MNP Principal Place of Business) Practice Rules 2005

4. The model of regulation which was proposed by the Society's Working Party on MNPs in January 2004 depended on the location of the principal place of business of an MNP. The Working Party's intention had been that if the principal place of business of the MNP was located outwith Scotland, but with a branch in Scotland, the Society would adopt a secondary regulator role. If, however, the principal place of business was located within Scotland, but there were branches outwith Scotland, then the Society would adopt a lead regulatory role.

This remains the general intention, although in respect of Scottish/English MNPs, discussions have taken place with the Law Society of England and Wales and it is likely that there will be a degree of shared regulation in this situation. The principal area which this affects is the Accounts Rules. However, as a result of discussions with LSEW, it is expected that it will be possible to issue guidance to Scottish/English MNPs as to how compliance with both the Scottish and the English Accounts Rules can be achieved without requiring separate cashrooms or separate procedures.

In any event, the Principal Place of Business Rules are relevant in that they are the means of determining how many of the Society's rules are applied to registered foreign lawyers. Generally, a higher degree of regulation is imposed on registered foreign lawyers in an MNP whose principal place of business is located in Scotland.

Solicitors (Scotland) (Registered Foreign Lawyers) etc Practice Rules 2005

5. The purpose of the Rules is to set out which of the rules of the Society are to apply to registered foreign lawyers and in which circumstances. Certain rules apply to all registered foreign lawyers, while other rules apply to none. Additionally, further rules are applied to registered foreign lawyers who are members of MNPs having their principal place of business in Scotland. Similarly, certain rules are applied to the Scottish practice of any registered foreign lawyer—this is designed to deal with branches of MNPs, where the principal place of business is located outwith Scotland.

These branches will be subject to a higher degree of regulation than the part of the MNP which is located outwith Scotland. The relevant rules are listed in the Schedules to the draft. As a result of the application of specific rules of the Society to foreign lawyers, it is also necessary to amend a variety of rules of the Society and these amendments are also set out in a Schedule to the Rules.

Finally, in addition to specific amendments to the Admission Regulations of the Society, certain of the provisions of those Regulations are specifically applied to registered foreign lawyers. The effect of the amendments made to the Admission Regulations and the specific application of certain provisions to registered foreign lawyers is designed to ensure that there will be no problem with MNPs taking on trainee solicitors. Specific provision is necessary to apply these Regulations to registered foreign lawyers as a matter of professional practice, conduct and discipline (*i.e.* in terms of section 34 of the 1980 Act) since regulations made under section 5 of the 1980 Act (as the Admission Regulations are) are not applicable to registered foreign lawyers.

Solicitors (Scotland) (Foreign Lawyers) (Registration) Rules 2004

The Solicitors (Scotland) (Foreign Lawyers) (Registration) Rules 2004 dated 24th September 2004 made by the Council of the Law Society of Scotland under section 60A(2) of the Solicitors (Scotland) Act 1980 and approved by the Lord President of the Court of Session under section 34(3) of that Act.

Title and Commencement

1.—(1) These rules may be cited as the Solicitors (Scotland) (Foreign Lawyers) (Registration) Rules 2004.

(2) These rules shall come into operation on 1st February 2005.

Definitions and Interpretation

2.—(1) In these rules, unless the context otherwise requires:

"the Act" means the Solicitors (Scotland) Act 1980;

"applicant" means a person who wishes to become a registered foreign lawyer or a registered foreign lawyer who wishes to renew his registration;

"the Council" means the Council of the Society;

"European Lawyer" shall have the meaning given in regulation 2(2) and (3) of the European Communities (Lawyer's Practice) (Scotland) Regulations 2000;

"foreign lawyer" shall have the meaning given in section 65(1) of the Act;

"Guarantee Fund" means The Scottish Solicitors Guarantee Fund as referred to in section 43 of the Act;

"grouping" means any entity, whether or not having legal personality, within which lawyers pursue their professional activities jointly under a joint name;

"home jurisdiction" shall mean a jurisdiction in which a foreign lawyer is a member of a legal profession;

"home professional title" means a professional title used by a foreign lawyer as a member of a legal profession in his home jurisdiction;

"incorporated practice" shall have the meaning given in section 34(1A) of the Act;

"multi-national practice" shall have the meaning given in section 65(1) of the Act;

"principal" means a registered foreign lawyer who is a partner in a firm of lawyers or

a member or director of an incorporated practice or a member of a multi-national practice;

"register" shall mean the register of foreign lawyers established and maintained by

the Council pursuant to section 60(A)(2) of the Act, and "registered" and

"registration" shall be construed accordingly;

"the Society" means the Law Society of Scotland; and

"year" means the period ending on the next 31 October.

(2) The provisions of the Interpretation Act 1978 shall apply to the interpretation of these rules as they apply to the interpretation of an Act of Parliament.

(3) The headings to these rules do not form part of these rules.

Application for registration

3. An applicant shall apply in writing to the Society for registration by completing (so far as applicable to him) and signing a form in, or substantially in, the form set out in the Schedule to these rules, and by making payment of such application fee(s) as the Council shall from time to time prescribe.

Requirements for registration

4.—(1) No applicant shall be registered unless—

(a) he has completed an application form in terms of rule 3;

(b) he has paid such application fee(s) as the Council has prescribed in accordance with rule 3;

(c) he is a foreign lawyer;

(d) he has satisfied the Council—

(i) that he is a fit and proper person to be a registered foreign lawyer;

(ii) that the legal profession of which he is a member is so regulated as to make it appropriate for the applicant to be allowed to enter into multi-national practices with solicitors or incorporated practices; and

(iii) that he is, or will on registration become, a principal of a multi-national practice;

(e) he provides—

(i) evidence that he is covered (or will on registration be covered) by a certificate of professional indemnity insurance issued to him, or to the multi-national practice of which he is a principal or of which he will on registration become a principal, which is equivalent in terms of the conditions and extent of its cover to the professional indemnity insurance which is required of solicitors in Scotland by the Council; or

(ii) evidence that he is covered by professional indemnity insurance taken out in accordance with the professional rules of his home jurisdiction and that such insurance is equivalent in terms of the conditions and extent of its cover to the professional indemnity insurance which is required of solicitors in Scotland by the Council; or

(iii) where the insurance referred to in sub-paragraph (e)(ii) is less than equivalent in terms of the conditions and extent of its cover to the insurance referred to at sub-paragraph (e)(i), evidence of professional indemnity insurance taken out in accordance with the professional rules of his home jurisdiction and, to the extent of the lack of equivalence, evidence of insurance cover as specified in sub-paragraph (e)(i); or

(iv) such evidence as may be required by the Council that he has satisfied its requirements as to the professional indemnity insurance cover required of registered foreign lawyers as they apply to him;

(f) he provides—

(i) a contribution by him, or the multi-national practice of which he is a principal or of which he will on registration become a principal, to the Society on behalf of the Guarantee Fund as required by the Council; or

(ii) evidence that he is covered by a guarantee taken out in accordance with the professional rules of his home jurisdiction and that such guarantee is equivalent in terms of the conditions and extent of its cover to the Guarantee Fund; or

(iii) where the guarantee referred to in sub-paragraph (f)(ii) is less than equivalent to the Guarantee Fund, evidence of the terms of the conditions and extent of the guarantee taken out in accordance with the professional rules of his home jurisdiction and, to the extent of the lack of equivalence, a contribution as specified in paragraph (f)(i); or

(iv) such evidence as may be required by the Council that he has satisfied its requirements as to the guarantee fund cover required of registered foreign lawyers as they apply to him;

(g) he is not an advocate or a barrister in England and Wales or

Northern Ireland, or the Republic of Ireland, and has made a declaration to that effect; and

(h) he is not a European Lawyer registered with the Society or the Faculty of Advocates or with the barristers' professional bodies in England and Wales, Northern Ireland or the Republic of Ireland, and has made a declaration to that effect.

(2) The Council shall, where satisfied that an applicant complies with paragraph (1), register that applicant.

Entry on register

5.—(1) If the Council grants an application pursuant to rule 4, it shall cause the name of the applicant to be entered on the register.

(2) The duration of registration shall be one year.

Removal from register

6. A person shall be removed from the register if he ceases to comply with any requirement set out in rule 4(1).

Waiver

7. The Council may waive or modify any provision of these rules either generally or in respect of any particular case, subject to such conditions, if any, as it considers appropriate.

SCHEDULE **Rule 3**

Form of Application for Registration as a Foreign Lawyer

If this is the first time that you have applied to be registered as a foreign lawyer with the Law Society of Scotland please complete the entire form and complete, sign and date the declaration at Part 1. If you are already registered with the Law Society of Scotland as a foreign lawyer please check that the information printed below is correct and amend or complete it to the extent that it is not correct or is incomplete, and complete, sign and date the declaration at Part 2.

Notes on the completion of this Form of Application appear below.

APPLICATION FOR REGISTRATION

1. Your full name and personal details

Surname ....

First name(s) ....

Title (e.g. Mr/Mrs/Miss/Ms/Dr/Prof) ....

Sex: Male/Female

Address ....

Town ....

Region ....

Country ....

Post Code ....

Telephone ....

Fax ....

E-mail ....

Date of Birth ....

Place of Birth ....

Nationality ....

2. Name and address of the multi-national practice of which you wish to become/are a principal

Name ....
Address ....
Town ....
Region ....
Country ....
Post Code ....
Telephone ....
Fax ....
E-mail ....

3. Any business name(s) and address(es) of yours used in your practice as a foreign lawyer

Name ....
Address ....
Town ....
Region ....
Country ....
Post Code ....
Telephone ....
Fax ....
E-mail ....

4. Please confirm your current status

Partner ....
Sole Principal ....
Assistant ....
Consultant ....
Director ....
Other (Please specify) ....

5. Are you a partner, director or member of any firm(s) or grouping(s)?

Yes/No ....

6. Names and address of the principal place of business of any firm(s) or grouping(s) of which you are a partner, director or member

Name ....
Address ....
Town ....
Region ....
Country ....
Post Code ....
Telephone ....

Fax ....

E-mail ....

7. Are any partners of that firm or members or directors of that grouping not lawyers?

Yes/No ....

8. Is the capital of that firm or grouping held entirely or partly by persons who are not lawyers?

Yes/No ....

9. Is the name under which that firm or grouping practises used by persons who are not lawyers?

Yes/No ....

10. Is the decision-making power in that firm or grouping exercised in fact or in law by persons who are not lawyers?

Yes/No ....

11. Your home professional title(s) in an official language of the relevant home jurisdiction(s) and (where that language is not English) also expressed in English

Title in official language of home state ....

Title in English ....

Title in official language of home state ....

Title in English ....

Title in official language of home state ....

Title in English ....

12. Name and address of the competent authority (e.g. Bar, Chamber, Law Society and/or Court) with which you are registered in each home jurisdiction

Name ....

Address ....

Town ....

Region ....

Country ....

Post Code ....

Telephone ....

Fax ....

E-mail ....

13. Have you completed your training?

Yes/No ....

14. Are you currently authorised to practise by the competent authority or authorities whose details you have provided in answer to question 12?

Yes/No ....

15. Have you previously made an application for registration under the Solicitors (Scotland) (Foreign Lawyers) (Registration) Rules 2004 or the European Lawyers (Registration) (Scotland) Regulations 2001 or the equivalent procedure of any other jurisdiction?

In the Scottish jurisdiction (Yes/No) ....
In another jurisdiction (Yes/No) ....
If yes, which one(s) ....

16. Full details of professional indemnity insurance as is required of you (or of your firm or grouping) in accordance with the rules which your home jurisdiction(s) lays down for professional activities pursued in its territory, together with full details of the conditions and extent of cover actually taken out by you (or by your firm or grouping) in respect of professional indemnity insurance

17. Full details of membership of any professional guarantee fund as is required of you (or of your firm or grouping) in accordance with the rules which your home jurisdiction(s) lays down for professional activities pursued in its territory, together with full details of the conditions and extent of cover actually taken out by you (or by your firm or grouping) in respect of any professional guarantee fund

18. Material events

18.1. Have formal proceedings alleging professional misconduct by you been started before a court or disciplinary tribunal in any jurisdiction? If yes in any case, please give details.

Yes/No ....

18.2. Have you ever been struck off or suspended from practice as a result of disciplinary proceedings in any jurisdiction?

Yes/No ....

18.3. Have you been subject to any other disciplinary sanctions in any jurisdiction?

Yes/No ....

18.4. Are there any material events which have occurred relating to your fitness to practise since your last application (if any) for registration (e.g. bankruptcy, criminal conviction, and breach of any of the professional rules of any of the bodies named in question 12 or any of the rules of the Law Society of Scotland as they apply to you)?

Yes/No ....

Part 1

Application for First Registration

I enclose herewith—

1. documentary evidence which is a sufficient means of establishing my nationality and identity, incorporating a good photographic likeness of myself;
2. a recent photograph of myself, which I have signed on the reverse and which I agree that the Council of the Law Society of Scotland may retain;
3. a certificate or certificates, dated not more than three months before the date of my application, confirming my registration with the competent authority in my home jurisdiction in which I am a member (entitled to practise as such) of a legal profession and confirming my good standing with that competent authority and, where any such certificate is not in English, a certified translation of it into English;
4. payment of the application fee of £350.00;
5. evidence in respect of professional indemnity insurance cover as required by rule 4(1)(e);
6. payment of the contribution required by rule 4(1)(f) or the evidence required thereby; and
7. written confirmation from the practice named in my response to question 2 that I will on registration be or continue to be a principal of that practice.

I hereby declare that I am not a solicitor or an advocate in Scotland or a barrister in England or Wales, that I am not registered as a European Lawyer pursuant to the European Communities (Lawyers Practice) (Scotland) Regulations 2000 with the Faculty of Advocates in Scotland or with the Inns of Court and the General Council of the Bar of England and Wales or with the Executive Council of the Inn of Court of Northern Ireland and that I am not a barrister in the Republic of Ireland.

I hereby declare that I am authorised to practise under the professional title(s) specified in my response to question 11.

I hereby declare that I will on registration be or continue to be a principal of the practice named in my response to question 2.

I hereby declare that I do not practise in Scotland, that I do not intend to practise in Scotland and that I do not consider that any act or default of mine will be so closely connected with the practice of any other member of the multi-national practice named in my response to question 2 in Scotland that such act or default could give rise to any claim on the Guarantee Fund. (Delete if inapplicable.) I hereby declare that the information supplied in this application is complete and accurate and that I shall advise the Law Society of Scotland immediately of any material changes to that information or if any declaration made by me ceases to be true, whether prior to or during the period of my registration.

I hereby agree to abide by the rules of professional conduct of the Law Society of Scotland as they apply to me during the period of my registration and I also agree that my home Bar, Chamber, Law Society and/or Court and any other Bar, Chamber, Law Society and/or Court with which I am registered from time to time and the Law Society of Scotland can freely exchange all relevant information about my professional activities.

I hereby apply for registration as a foreign lawyer and for a certificate of registration for the year ending 31 October 20

Dated this day of 20

....(Signature)

Part 2

Application for Subsequent Registration

I enclose herewith—

1. a certificate or certificates, dated not more than three months before the date of my application, confirming my registration with the competent authority in my home jurisdiction in which I am a member (entitled to practise as such) of a legal profession and confirming my good standing with that competent authority and, where any such certificate is not in English, a certified translation of it into English;
2. payment of the application fee of £350.00;
3. evidence in respect of professional indemnity insurance cover as required by rule 4(1)(e);
4. payment of the contribution required by rule 4(1)(f) or the evidence required thereby; and
5. written confirmation from the practice named in my response to question 2 that I am a principal of that practice.

I hereby declare that I am not a solicitor or an advocate in Scotland or a barrister in England or Wales, that I am not registered as a European Lawyer pursuant to the European Communities (Lawyers Practice) (Scotland) Regulations 2000 with the Faculty of Advocates in Scotland or with the Inns of Court and the General Council of the Bar of England and Wales or with the Executive Council of the Inn of Court of Northern Ireland and that I am not a barrister in the Republic of Ireland.

I hereby declare that I am authorised to practise under the professional title(s) specified in my response to question 11.

I hereby declare that I am a principal of the practice named in my response to question 2.

I hereby declare that I do not practise in Scotland, that I do not intend to practise in Scotland and that I do not consider that any act or default of mine will be so closely connected with the practice of any other member of the multi-national practice named in my response to question 2 in Scotland that such act or default could give rise to any claim on the Guarantee Fund. (Delete if inapplicable.)

I hereby declare that the information supplied in this application is complete and accurate and that I shall advise the Law Society of Scotland immediately of any material changes to that information or if any declaration made by me ceases to be true, whether prior to or during the period of my registration.

Declaration in regard to the Solicitors (Scotland) Accounts etc. Rules:

1. I hereby declare that I have complied with the Solicitors (Scotland) Accounts etc. Rules in so far as they are applicable to me.
2. I hereby declare that I have not held or received clients' money during the practice year ended 31 October 20 .

(Delete 1 or 2 above, whichever is inapplicable.)

I hereby agree to abide by the rules of professional conduct of the Law Society of Scotland as they apply to me during the period of my registration and I also agree that my home Bar, Chamber, Law Society and/or Court and any other Bar, Chamber, Law Society and/or Court with which I am registered from time to time and the Law Society of Scotland can freely exchange all relevant information about my professional activities.

I hereby apply for a certificate of registration for the year ending 31 October 20

Dated this day of 20

....(Signature)

Notes

1. Where there is insufficient space for a full answer to any of the questions on this form, please provide the additional information on a continuation sheet under reference to the relevant numbered question.
2. For the purpose of question 2, the practice referred to may be one which is not currently a multi-national practice but will become one on your joining it as a principal.
3. For the purpose of question 5, a "firm" means a partnership and a "grouping" means any entity whether or not having legal personality within which lawyers pursue their professional activities jointly under a joint name.
4. If you have answered no to question 5, then you need not answer questions 6 to 10.
5. Please note, in relation to questions 11 and 12, that you should supply the required information in respect of each home State under whose professional title you intend to practise in Scotland.
6. Please provide full information in answering questions 16 and 17. This information is required in order that the Law Society can assess whether the cover which is taken out either by you or by your firm or grouping is equivalent to the cover required of solicitors in Scotland in respect of professional indemnity insurance and membership of a guarantee fund. All applicants are required to provide this information. It will assist the processing of your application if you are able to supply copies of relevant certificates of insurance together with policy schedules specifying the conditions and extent of the cover.
7. If you have answered yes to any part of question 18, please give full details.
8. Documents such as a photocopy of your passport will generally be acceptable proof of your nationality and identity, where a sufficiently good reproduction of your photographic likeness is produced and where that copy is certified as true and accurate by a state official or other trustworthy person, whose name and address are provided.
9. It is essential that the certificate or certificates confirming your registration with the competent authority in your home jurisdiction and your good standing with that authority are dated not more than three months before the date on which you sign this application form. It is also essential that the certificate or certificates confirm your date of admission, that you are entitled to practise under the relevant home professional title, specify any limitations on your entitlement to practise under the relevant home professional title, and confirm that there are either no completed or pending disciplinary proceedings against you, or give full details if there are or have been such proceedings.
10. The registration fee is £350.00. It must be enclosed with this application form and cheques should be made payable to "The Law Society of Scotland" and crossed "& Co".

Solicitors (Scotland) (Multi-National Practices) Practice Rules 2005

Rules dated 24th March 2005, made by the Council of the Law Society of Scotland under section 34 of the Solicitors (Scotland) Act 1980 and approved by the Lord President of the Court of Session in terms of section 34(3) of that Act.

Citation and commencement

1.—(1) These Rules may be cited as the Solicitors (Scotland) (Multi-National Practices) Practice Rules 2005.

(2) These Rules shall come into effect on 1st May 2005.

Definitions and interpretation

2.—(1) In these Rules, unless the context otherwise requires—

"the Act" means the Solicitors (Scotland) Act 1980;

"the Council" means the Council of the Society;

"enter a multi-national practice" means to become a member of a multi-national practice whether by joining a multi-national practice or by being a member of a practice which becomes a multi-national practice;

"member" means, in relation to a practice, a principal of that practice;

"multi-national practice" has the meaning given in section 65 of the Act;

"principal place of business" means the principal place of business of a multi-national practice as determined by the Council in terms of the Solicitors (Scotland) (MNP Principal Place of Business) Rules 2005;

"the Society" means the Law Society of Scotland;

"solicitor" means a solicitor holding a practising certificate under the Act and includes a firm of solicitors and an incorporated practice and also includes a multi-national practice.

(2) The Interpretation Act 1978 applies to the interpretation of these Rules as it applies to the interpretation of an Act of Parliament.

(3) The headings to these Rules do not form part of these Rules.

Restriction

3. No solicitor may enter a multi-national practice having any place of business in Scotland unless he obtains the approval of the Council in terms of rule 5.

Application

4.—(1) Any solicitor seeking the approval of the Council in terms of rule 5 shall, at least three months prior to the anticipated date of his entering the multi-national practice, submit to the Council an application in the form set out in the Schedule to these Rules, accompanied by the additional information set out in that Schedule.

(2) Where more than one solicitor is seeking the approval of the Council in terms of rule 5 then those solicitors may jointly submit an application in terms of paragraph (1).

Giving of approval

5.—(1) Where the Council is satisfied, on receiving any application in terms of rule 4 from a solicitor to enter a practice—

(a) that he will on its approval being given be a member of a multi-national practice, and

(b) that the multi-national practice of which he will be a member is or will be so regulated as to make it appropriate for solicitors to be allowed to enter it, the Council may approve that solicitor entering that practice.

(2) Where any solicitor has been given approval to enter into a practice in terms of paragraph (1), the Council may withdraw that approval if at any time it ceases to be satisfied that either of the conditions set out in that paragraph remains true.

Charging of fees

6. The Council may charge a fee in respect of its examination of an application submitted in terms of these Rules.

Provision of information

7.—(1) While a solicitor remains a member of a multi-national practice, he shall inform the Council of any changes to the information which was supplied by him in any application made to the Council to enter into that multi-national practice in terms of rule 4.

(2) If a solicitor ceases to be a member of a multi-national practice he shall inform the Council of that fact.

Approved multi-national practices

8. The Council may maintain a list of multi-national practices which solicitors may enter without seeking its approval notwithstanding rule 3, and may require the members of any multinational practice wishing to be added to or to remain on any such list to supply such information as it may require.

Waiver

9. The Council may waive any provision of these Rules, either generally or in relation to any particular case, subject to such conditions, if any, as it considers appropriate.

Applicability to registered foreign lawyers

10. These Rules are only applicable to registered foreign lawyers so far as they apply to any multi-national practice of which that registered foreign lawyer is a member.

SCHEDULE

Rule 4

Form Of Application To Enter Into A Multi-National Practice

[I/We] [*delete as appropriate*] the undernoted hereby seek the approval of the Council to enter a multi-national practice

1. Details of applicant(s)

Name ....Name ....
Firm/Practice ....Firm/Practice ....
Business Address ....Business Address ....

[*Please give details of any other applicants on a separate sheet of paper.*]

2. Details of multi-national practice to be entered

Name ....
Address ....
....

[*Please provide details of any other places of business on a separate sheet of paper.*]

Date of incorporation (if appropriate) ....
Place of incorporation (if appropriate) ....

3. Is the practice referred to at question 2 currently—
a firm of solicitors regulated by the Society ....
an incorporated practice regulated by the Society ....

a multi-national practice ....
a firm or body corporate whose membership is restricted to foreign lawyers ....
not yet in existence ....

4. Please attach written confirmation from the practice named in response to question 2 that you will on the Council's approval being given be a member of that practice, or (where the practice is not yet in existence) other written evidence to that effect.

5. If the practice referred to at question 2 is not a firm of solicitors or an incorporated practice regulated by the Society, please explain the circumstances of the practice in a covering letter.

6. What is the principal place of business of the practice referred to at question 2 (as determined by the Council)?

....

If the principal place of business of the practice referred to at question 2 has not been determined by the Council, then this application should be accompanied by an application for the principal place of business of that practice to be determined in accordance with the Solicitors (Scotland) (Principal Place of Business) Rules 2005.

7. In relation to each of the members of the practice referred to at question 2 who will be members of that practice at the date when the applicant(s) wish to enter it, please supply the following information—

Name ....
Address ....
....

Is this person currently a solicitor or registered foreign lawyer? Yes / No

8. If any of the persons referred to in question 7 is not currently a solicitor or registered foreign lawyer, please attach a copy of his application for registration as a foreign lawyer in terms of the Solicitors (Scotland) (Foreign Lawyers) (Registration) Rules 2004.

[I/we] declare that the practice referred to in question 2 is or will on [my/our] entering it become [a partnership whose members are solicitors or incorporated practices and registered foreign lawyers, and membership of which is restricted to solicitors, incorporated practices and registered foreign lawyers] [a body corporate whose members include registered foreign lawyers, and membership of which is restricted to solicitors, incorporated practices, registered foreign lawyers and other multi-national practices] [*Delete as appropriate*].

Dated this day of 20

Signatures

....

....

[*Please continue on a separate sheet of paper if required.*]

Notes

1. If the practice referred to in question 2 does not yet exist, please give details of the proposed name and address, and details of the proposed place and date of incorporation (if appropriate).

2. This form should be accompanied by a remittance for the appropriate fee. Remittances should be made payable to "The Law Society of Scotland" and should be crossed "account payee only".

Solicitors (Scotland) (MNP Principal Place Of Business) Practice Rules 2005

Rules dated 24th March 2005, made by the Council of the Law Society of Scotland under section 34(1) of the Solicitors (Scotland) Act 1980 and approved by the Lord President of the Court of Session in terms of section 34(3) of that Act.

Citation and commencement

1.—(1) These Rules may be cited as the Solicitors (Scotland) (MNP Principal Place of Business) Practice Rules 2005.

(2) These Rules shall come into effect on 1st May 2005.

Definitions and interpretation

2.—(1) In these Rules, unless the context otherwise requires—

"the Act" means the Solicitors (Scotland) Act 1980;

"the Council" means the Council of the Society;

"foreign lawyer" has the meaning given in section 65 of the Act;

"location" means, in relation to a person, the place of business at which that person primarily practises or, if there is no such place of business, the place of business at which he is based or from which he is managed;

"member" means, in relation to a multi-national practice, a principal of that practice;

"MNP" means multi-national practice;

"multi-national practice" has the meaning given in section 65 of the Act;

"new determination" means a determination that the principal place of business of a multi-national practice is a place of business other than that provisionally determined in accordance with rule 4(1);

"the Society" means the Law Society of Scotland;

"solicitor" means a solicitor holding a practising certificate under the Act and includes a firm of solicitors and an incorporated practice and also includes a registered foreign lawyer and a multi-national practice.

(2) A person is "associated with" a multi-national practice if—

(a) he is a partner of that multi-national practice;

(b) he is a member or director of that multi-national practice;

(c) he is an employee of that multi-national practice; or

(d) he is a consultant to that multi-national practice.

(3) The Interpretation Act 1978 applies to the interpretation of these Rules as it applies to the interpretation of an Act of Parliament.

(4) The headings to these Rules do not form part of these Rules.

Determinations

3.—(1) The Council may, on application made in terms of rule 6(1), determine the principal place of business of a multi-national practice.

(2) The Council may determine the principal place of business of a multi-national practice whose principal place of business has not been determined in accordance with an application made in terms of rule 6(1).

(3) Subject to rule 9, the Council may change its determination of the principal place of business of a multi-national practice.

Provisional determinations

4.—(1) The Council may, on application made in terms of rule 6(2), provisionally determine the principal place of business of a proposed multi-national practice.

(2) Where the principal place of business of a multi-national practice has been provisionally determined that place of business shall be treated as the principal place of business of that multi-national practice.

(3) The Council may change or revoke any provisional determination made in accordance with paragraph (1).

(4) Following the constitution of a multi-national practice whose principal place of business has been provisionally determined in accordance with paragraph (1)—

(a) the provisional determination may not be revoked, and
(b) the Council shall confirm the provisional determination or make a new determination; and such confirmation or new determination shall be treated as a determination made in accordance with rule 3(1).

Relevant factors

5.—(1) In determining the principal place of business of a multi-national practice in terms of rule 3(1) or (2) or in changing any such determination in terms of rule 3(3) or in confirming a provisional determination or making a new determination in terms of rule 4(4), the Council shall have regard to the following—

(a) any election made by or on behalf of the multi-national practice;
(b) the locations of the place or places of business of the multi-national practice;
(c) the number of solicitors holding a practising certificate under the Act who are associated with the multi-national practice both as an absolute number and as a proportion of the total number of solicitors and foreign lawyers associated with that multi-national practice;
(d) the number of solicitors holding a practising certificate under the Act who are members of the multi-national practice both as an absolute number and as a proportion of the total number of members of that multi-national practice;
(e) the locations of the solicitors and foreign lawyers associated with the multinational practice and the identity of the legal professions of which those foreign lawyers are members;
(f) the locations of the members of the multi-national practice;
(g) the identity of the persons exercising management control over the multinational practice, the number of them who are solicitors holding a practising certificate in terms of the Act and each of their locations;
(h) the law applicable to the constitutive documents or arrangements of the multinational practice; and
(i) the law practised by the multi-national practice. (2) In determining the principal place of business of a multi-national practice, the Council may have regard to any other factor which it considers relevant.

(3) In provisionally determining the principal place of business of a proposed multi-national practice in terms of rule 4(1) or in changing or revoking that provisional determination in terms of rule 4(3), the Council shall have regard to the factors set out at paragraphs (1) and (2) as they may be ascertained in relation to the proposed multi-national practice from the information supplied to it in or in connection with an application in terms of rule 6(2) and other information available to it.

Application

6.—(1) A solicitor who is a member of a multi-national practice may seek a determination of the principal place of business of that multi-national practice by the Council in terms of rule 3(1).

(2) A solicitor who proposes to be a member of a proposed multi-national practice may seek a provisional determination of the principal place of business of that proposed multi-national practice by the Council in terms of rule 4(1).

(3) Any solicitor seeking a determination by the Council in terms of rule

3(1) or 4(1) shall submit to the Council an application in the form set out in the Schedule to these Rules, accompanied by the additional information set out in that Schedule, and shall, upon request by the Council, supply any other information required by the Council in connection with that application.

Charging of fees

7. The Council may charge a fee in respect of its examination of an application submitted in terms of these Rules.

Provision of information

8. The Council may require any solicitor who is a member of or associated with a multinational practice or who proposes to be a member of or associated with a proposed multinational practice to supply it with any information it considers necessary in connection with—

(a) any determination in terms of rule 3(1) or (2); or
(b) any possible change in determination in terms of rule 3(3); or
(c) any provisional determination in terms of rule 4(1); or
(d) any possible change or revocation of a provisional determination in terms of rule 4(3); or
(e) the confirmation of a provisional determination or the making of a new determination in accordance with rule 4(4).

Notice

9. Where the Council is minded to change its determination of the principal place of business of a multi-national practice in terms of rule 3(3) it shall give written notice of that fact to the relevant multi-national practice, together with copies of any information it proposes to rely on in making that change (with any deletions necessary to protect the identity of any person as appropriate). In making its decision as to whether to change its determination of the principal place of business of that multi-national practice, the Council shall have regard to any written representations made to it by or on behalf of that practice.

Waiver

10. The Council may waive any provision of these Rules, either generally or in relation to any particular case, subject to such conditions, if any, as it considers appropriate.

Application to registered foreign lawyers

11. These Rules shall apply to registered foreign lawyers.

SCHEDULE **Rule 6(1)**

FORM OF APPLICATION FOR A DETERMINATION OF THE PRINCIPAL PLACE OF BUSINESS OF A MULTI-NATIONAL PRACTICE

[I/We] [*delete as appropriate*] the undernoted hereby seek a determination by the Council of the principal place of business of a multi-national practice

1. Details of applicant
Name ....
Firm/Practice ....
Business Address ....
....

2. Details of multi-national practice whose principal place of business is to be determined
Name ....
Address ....
....

[*Please provide details of any other places of business on a separate sheet of paper.*]

3. Has the multi-national practice made any election of a place of business which it wishes to be determined to be its principal place of business? If yes, please provide details.

   ....

4. Please give the number of solicitors holding a practising certificate under the Act who are associated with the multi-national practice.

   ....

5. Please give the number of foreign lawyers associated with the multi-national practice.

   ....

6. Please give the number of solicitors holding a practising certificate under the Act who are members of the multi-national practice.

   ....

7. Please provide details of the total number of the other members of the multi-national practice.

Registered foreign lawyers ....
Registered European lawyers ....
Firms of solicitors ....
Incorporated practices ....
Multi-national practices ....
Other (please provide details) ....

Solicitors (Scotland) (Registered Foreign Lawyers) Etc Practice Rules 2005

Rules dated 24th March 2005, made (i) by the Council of the Law Society of Scotland under section 34, section 35 and section 36 of the Solicitors (Scotland) Act 1980 and approved by the Lord President of the Court of Session in terms of section 34(3) of that Act; (ii) by the Council with the concurrence of the Lord President in terms of section 5 and section 44 of that Act; and (iii) by the Council under section 37 of and paragraph 4(1) and (4) of Schedule 3 to that Act.

Citation and commencement

1.—(1) These Rules may be cited as the Solicitors (Scotland) (Registered Foreign Lawyers) etc Practice Rules 2005.

(2) These Rules shall come into effect on 1st May 2005.

Definitions and interpretation

2.—(1) In these Rules, unless the context otherwise requires—

"the Act" means the Solicitors (Scotland) Act 1980;

"Admission Regulations" means the Admission as Solicitor (Scotland) Regulations 2001;

"the Council" means the Council of the Society;

"member body" means, in relation to a multi-national practice, any firm of solicitors, incorporated practice or multi-national practice which is a member of that multi-national practice or of any member body of that multi-national practice;

"multi-national practice" has the meaning given in section 65 of the Act;

"principal place of business" means the principal place of business of a multi-national practice as determined by the Council in terms of the Solicitors (Scotland) (MNP Principal Place of Business) Rules 2005;

"registered foreign lawyer" has the meaning given in section 65 of the Act;

"rules of the Society" means the rules from time to time made under section 34 (rules as to professional practice, conduct and discipline), section 35 (accounts rules), section 36 (interest on client's money), section 37 (accountant's certificates) and section 44 (professional indemnity) of, and paragraph 4(1) and (4) of Schedule 3 (Guarantee Fund—grants) to, the Act;

"Scottish practice" means practice in or from Scotland, and practice in Scotland includes practice outwith Scotland where the practice relates to a Scottish matter;

"the Society" means the Law Society of Scotland;

"solicitor" has the meaning given in section 65 of the Act;

(2) The Interpretation Act 1978 applies to the interpretation of these Rules as it applies to the interpretation of an Act of Parliament.

(3) The headings to these Rules do not form part of these Rules.

General application

3.—(1) The rules of the Society listed in Schedule 1 shall apply to registered foreign lawyers.

(2) Except where otherwise provided by these Rules or by other rules of the Society, any future rules of the Society shall apply to registered foreign lawyers as they apply to solicitors.

(3) For the purpose of its application to a registered foreign lawyer reference in any rule of the Society applied to that registered foreign lawyer by paragraph (2)—

(a) to a solicitor (howsoever defined) shall include reference to that registered foreign lawyer; and

(b) to a solicitor's practising certificate shall include reference to that registered foreign lawyer's registration certificate.

(4) Reference in any rule or regulation made by the Society, in terms of the Act or otherwise, to a multi-national practice shall not of itself apply that rule or regulation to any registered foreign lawyer who is a member of that multi-national practice where that rule would not otherwise apply to him.

Specific application

4.—(1) No rule of the Society listed in Schedule 2, or any modification or re-making of any such rule unless such modification or re-making otherwise provides, shall apply to any registered foreign lawyer.

(2) The rules of the Society listed in Schedule 3, and any modification or re-making of any such rule unless such modification or re-making otherwise provides, shall apply to any registered foreign lawyer who is a member of a multi-national practice having its principal place of business in Scotland.

(3) The rules of the Society listed in Schedule 4, and any modification or re-making of any such rule unless such modification or re-making otherwise provides, shall apply to the Scottish practice of any registered foreign lawyer.

Amendments

5. The rules of the Society and other rules and regulations set out in Schedule 5 shall be amended as set out in that Schedule.

Admission Regulations

6. As a matter of professional practice, conduct and discipline, the provisions of the Admission Regulations set out in Schedule 6 shall apply to registered foreign lawyers as set out in that Schedule.

References to multi-national practices

7.—(1) Where any rule of the Society refers to a "Scottish multi-national practice", that term shall mean a multi-national practice having its principal place of business in Scotland.

(2) Where any rule of the Society refers to a "Scottish branch of a multi-national practice", that term shall mean a multi-national practice, but only so far as that multi-national practice is acting in pursuance of the Scottish practice of (i) any solicitor who is a member of that multi-national practice, or

(ii) a member body of that multi-national practice, or

(iii) any registered foreign lawyer who is such a member.

Breaches of rules and regulations by multi-national practices

8. Where any rule or regulation made by the Society, in terms of the Act or otherwise, applies to a multi-national practice, no registered foreign lawyer or solicitor who, or member body which, is a member of that multi-national practice or of a member body of that multinational practice shall cause or knowingly permit that multi-national practice not to comply with that rule or regulation so far as it is applicable to that multi-national practice, even where that rule or regulation does not apply to him.

Waivers

9. The Council may waive any provision of these Rules, either generally or in relation to any particular case, subject to such conditions, if any, as it considers appropriate.

Rule 3(1) SCHEDULE 1

RULES OF THE SOCIETY WHICH APPLY TO ALL REGISTERED FOREIGN LAWYERS

Solicitors (Scotland) (Multi-Disciplinary Practices) Practice Rules 1991 Solicitors (Scotland) Professional Indemnity Insurance Rules 1995 Solicitors (Scotland) Accounts etc Rules 2001 Solicitors (Scotland) (Cross-Border Code of Conduct) Practice Rules 2003 Solicitors (Scotland) (Restriction on Association) Practice Rules 2004

Rule 4(1) SCHEDULE 2

RULES OF THE SOCIETY WHICH DO NOT APPLY TO ANY REGISTERED FOREIGN LAWYER

Registered European Lawyers (Rules of Professional Conduct) (Scotland) Rules 2001 Solicitors (Scotland) (Civil Legal Aid and Advice and Assistance) Practice Rules 2003

Note: There are other rules and regulations made under the Solicitors (Scotland) Act 1980 and otherwise which are not made under section 34 (rules as to professional practice, conduct and discipline), section 35 (accounts rules), section 36 (interest on client's money), section 37 (accountant's certificates) or section 44 (professional indemnity) of, or paragraph 4(1) or (4) of Schedule 3 to, the Act. These are not "rules of the Society" as defined in these Rules and are therefore not applied to registered foreign lawyers. For the avoidance of doubt, the following rules are in that category:
Solicitors (Scotland) Practising Certificate Rules 1988
Admission as Solicitor (Scotland) Regulations 1991
Solicitors (Scotland) Order of Precedence, Instructions and Representation Rules 1992
Solicitors (Scotland) (Continuing Professional Development) Regulations 1993
EC Qualified Lawyers Transfer (Scotland) Regulations 1994
Admission as Solicitor (Scotland) Regulations 2001 (though see rule 6 and Schedule 6)
European Lawyers (Registration) (Scotland) Regulations 2001
Solicitors (Scotland) (Rights of Audience in the Court of Session, the House of Lords and the Judicial Committee of the Privy Council) Rules 2002
Solicitors (Scotland) (Rights of Audience in the High Court of Justiciary and Judicial Committee of the Privy Council) Rules 2002
Solicitors (Scotland) Rules of Conduct for Solicitor Advocates 2002

Rule 4(2) SCHEDULE 3

RULES OF THE SOCIETY WHICH APPLY TO REGISTERED FOREIGN LAWYERS WHO ARE MEMBERS OF MULTI-NATIONAL PRACTICES HAVING THEIR PRINCIPAL PLACE OF BUSINESS IN SCOTLAND

Solicitors (Scotland) Practice Rules 1986
Solicitors (Scotland) Practice Rules 1991
Solicitors (Scotland) (Written Fee Charging Agreements) Practice Rules 1993
Solicitors (Scotland) (Advertising and Promotion) Practice Rules 1995
Solicitors (Scotland) (Associates, Consultants and Employees) Practice Rules 2001
Solicitors (Scotland) (Incorporated Practices) Practice Rules 2001
Solicitors (Scotland) (Practice Management Course) Practice Rules 2001
Solicitors (Scotland) (Restriction on Practice) Practice Rules 2001
Solicitors (Scotland) (Industrial Action by Solicitors) Practice Rules 2003
Solicitors (Scotland) (Supreme Courts) Practice Rules 2003
Solicitors (Scotland) (Incidental Financial Business) Practice Rules 2004
Solicitors (Scotland) (Client Communication) Practice Rules 2005
Solicitors (Scotland) (Client Relations Partner) Practice Rules 2005

Rule 4(3) SCHEDULE 4

RULES OF THE SOCIETY WHICH APPLY TO THE SCOTTISH PRACTICE OF REGISTERED FOREIGN LAWYERS

Solicitors (Scotland) Practice Rules 1986
Solicitors (Scotland) Practice Rules 1991

Rule 5 SCHEDULE 5

AMENDMENTS

Solicitors (Scotland) Practice Rules 1986

1. In rule 2(1) insert after "requires"—
""2005 Rules" means the Solicitors (Scotland) (Registered Foreign Lawyers) etc Practice Rules 2005;".
2. In rule 2(1) in the definition of "solicitor" insert after "practice"—
"or a firm of solicitors and shall include a registered foreign lawyer to whom these rules apply in terms of rule 4(2) or (3) of the 2005 Rules and a Scottish multi-national practice (as defined in rule 7(1) of the 2005 Rules)".

Solicitors (Scotland) (Multi-Disciplinary Practices) Practice Rules 1991

3. In rule 2(1) in the definition of "solicitor" insert after "association of solicitors"—
"and also includes a registered foreign lawyer and a multi-national practice".

Solicitors (Scotland) Practice Rules 1991

4. In rule 2(1) insert after "requires"—
""2005 Rules" means the Solicitors (Scotland) (Registered Foreign Lawyers) etc Practice Rules 2005;".
5. In rule 2(1) in the definition of "solicitor" insert after "association of solicitors"—
"and shall include a registered foreign lawyer to whom these rules apply in terms of rule 4(2) or (3) of the 2005 Rules and a Scottish multi-national practice and a Scottish branch of a multi-national practice (in each case as defined in rule 7 of the 2005 Rules)".

Solicitors (Scotland) (Written Fee Charging Agreements) Practice Rules 1993

6. In rule 3 insert after "requires"—
""2005 Rules" means the Solicitors (Scotland) (Registered Foreign Lawyers) etc Practice Rules 2005;".
7. In rule 3 in the definition of "solicitor" insert after "practice"—
"and shall include a registered foreign lawyer to whom these rules apply in terms of rule 4(2) or (3) of the 2005 Rules and a Scottish multi-national practice and a Scottish branch of a multi-national practice (in each case as defined in rule 7 of the 2005 Rules)".

Solicitors (Scotland) (Advertising and Promotion) Practice Rules 1995

8. In rule 2(1) insert after "requires"—
""2005 Rules" means the Solicitors (Scotland) (Registered Foreign Lawyers) etc Practice Rules 2005;".
9. In rule 2(1) in the definition of "solicitor" insert after "association of solicitors"—
"and shall include a registered foreign lawyer to whom these rules apply in terms of rule 4(2) or (3) of the 2005 Rules and a Scottish multi-national practice and a Scottish branch of a multi-national practice (in each case as defined in rule 7 of the 2005 Rules)".

Solicitors (Scotland) Professional Indemnity Insurance Rules 1995

10. In rule 2(1) in the definition of "solicitor" insert after "practice"—
"and also includes a registered foreign lawyer and a multi-national practice".

Admission as Solicitor (Scotland) Regulations 2001

11. In regulation 2(1) in the definition of "training solicitor" insert after "Act" the second time it appears—
"or a multi-national practice (as defined in the Act)".
12. In regulation 13(1) insert after "practice" the sixth time it appears—

"or, where the training solicitor is a multi-national practice, at least one of the solicitors who is a member thereof has been in such continuous practice".

13. In regulation 13(2) insert after paragraph (b)—

"(ba) in the case of a multi-national practice, twice the number of solicitors who are members of the multi-national practice;".

14. In regulation 13(2) insert after paragraph (c)—

"(ca) in the case of a multi-national practice having more than one office, within each office, twice the number of solicitors having their principal place of business within that office, but subject always, in respect of the multi-national practice as a whole, to the maximum specified by paragraph (ba) above;".

15. In regulation 38(1) insert after "(as defined in the Act)"—

"or a multi-national practice (as defined in the Act)".

Solicitors (Scotland) Accounts etc Rules 2001

16. In rule 2(1) in the definition of "solicitor" insert after "practice"—

"and also includes a registered foreign lawyer and a multi-national practice.".

17. In rule 10(1) insert after "incorporated practice"—

"or as a member of a multi-national practice".

18. In rule 12 insert after "incorporated practice" each time it appears—

"or a multi-national practice".

19. In rule 17 insert after "incorporated practice" the first and sixth time it appears—

"or multi-national practice".

20. In rule 17 insert after "(where that incorporated practice is a limited liability partnership)"—

"or a member of the multi-national practice".

21. In rule 19(5) insert after "incorporated practice" the first and sixth time it appears—

"or multi-national practice".

22. In rule 19(5) insert after "(where that incorporated practice is a limited liability partnership)"—

"or a member of the multi-national practice".

23. In rule 22 insert after "incorporated practice" each time it appears—

"or multi-national practice".

24. In rule 25(c)(ii) insert after "incorporated practice" the first time it appears—

"or multi-national practice".

25. In rule 25(c)(ii) insert after "incorporated practice" the second time it appears—

"or member or other employee of a multi-national practice".

26. In rule 25(c)(ii) insert after "Act"—

"or to be a multi-national practice".

Solicitors (Scotland) (Associates, Consultants and Employees) Practice Rules 2001

27. In rule 2(1) insert after "requires"—

""2005 Rules" means the Solicitors (Scotland) (Registered Foreign Lawyers) etc Practice Rules 2005;".

28. In rule 2(1) in the definition of "solicitor" insert after "practice"—

"and shall include a registered foreign lawyer to whom these rules apply in terms of rule 4(2) or (3) of the 2005 Rules and a Scottish multi-national practice (as defined in rule 7(1) of the 2005 Rules)".

29. In rule 3 insert after paragraph (c)—

"(ca) if the solicitor is a multi-national practice, a member of that multi-national practice".

Solicitors (Scotland) (Incorporated Practices) Practice Rules 2001

30. In rule 2(1) in the definition of "the 1986 Act" insert after "partnerships"—

"and any legislation in any other jurisdiction having equivalent effect".

31. In rule 2(1) in the definition of "solicitor" insert after "association of solicitors"—

"and also includes a registered foreign lawyer."

32. In rule 11 insert after "Act"—

"in respect of solicitors as defined in the Act".

Solicitors (Scotland) (Practice Management Course) Practice Rules 2004

33. In rule 2(1) insert after "requires"—
""2005 Rules" means the Solicitors (Scotland) (Registered Foreign Lawyers) etc Practice Rules 2005;".

34. In rule 2(1) in the definition of "solicitor" insert after "Session"—
"and shall include a registered foreign lawyer to whom these rules apply in terms of rule 4(2) or (3) of the 2005 Rules".

35. In rule 2(1) in the definition of "principal" insert after "partnership"—
"or a member of a multi-national practice".

36. In rule 2(1) in the definition of "practice unit" insert after "practice"—
"or a Scottish multi-national practice (as defined in rule 7(1) of the 2005 Rules)".

Solicitors (Scotland) (Restriction on Practice) Practice Rules 2001

37. In rule 2(1) insert after "requires"—
""2005 Rules" means the Solicitors (Scotland) (Registered Foreign Lawyers) etc Practice Rules 2005;".

38. In rule 2(1) in the definition of "solicitor" insert after "Act"—
"and shall include a registered foreign lawyer to whom these rules apply in terms of rule 4(2) or (3) of the 2005 Rules".

39. In rule 2(1) in the definition of "principal" insert after "partnership"—
"or a solicitor who is a member of a Scottish multi-national practice (as defined by rule 7(1) of the 2005 Rules)".

Solicitors (Scotland) (Civil Legal Aid and Advice and Assistance) Practice Rules 2003

40. In rule 2(1) in the definition of "associated solicitor" insert after paragraph (c)—
"(ca) is a member of a practice unit where that practice unit is a multi-national practice,".

41. In rule 2(1) in the definition of "practice unit" insert after "practice" where it appears the second time—
"and also includes a multi-national practice".

42. In rule 3(3) delete "or incorporated practice" and insert—
", incorporated practice or multi-national practice".

Solicitors (Scotland) (Cross-Border Code of Conduct) Practice Rules 2003

43. In rule 2(1) in the definition of "solicitor" insert after "practice"—
"and also includes a registered foreign lawyer and a multi-national practice."

Solicitors (Scotland) (Incidental Financial Business) Practice Rules 2004

44. In rule 2(1) insert after "requires"—
""2005 Rules" means the Solicitors (Scotland) (Registered Foreign Lawyers) etc Practice Rules 2005;".

45. In rule 2(1) in the definition of "firm" insert after "practice"—
"and also includes a Scottish multi-national practice (as defined in rule 7(1) of the 2005 Rules)".

46. In rule 2(1) in the definition of "officer" insert after "partnership" the third time it appears—
"or a member of a multi-national practice".

47. In rule 2(1) in the definition of "solicitor" insert after "Act"—
"and shall include a registered foreign lawyer to whom these rules apply in terms of rule 4(2) or (3) of the 2005 Rules".

48. In rule 9 insert after paragraph (7)—
"(7A) An incidental financial business licence granted to a multi-national practice which is a body corporate shall be suspended automatically on the occurrence in relation to that multinational practice of any of the events specified in relation to incorporated practices in section 18(1A) of the 1980 Act."

Solicitors (Scotland) (Restriction on Association) Practice Rules 2004

49. In rule 2(1) in the definition of "solicitor" insert after "association of solicitors"—
"and also includes a registered foreign lawyer and a multi-national practice".

50. In rule 3 insert after "solicitor" the fourth time it appears—

"or whose name has been removed from the register of foreign lawyers by the Scottish Solicitors' Discipline Tribunal or whose certificate of registration as a registered foreign lawyer has been suspended in accordance with section 24F of the Solicitors (Scotland) Act 1980".

Solicitors (Scotland) (Client Relations Partner) Practice Rules 2005

51. In rule 2(1) insert after "requires"—

" "2005 Rules" means the Solicitors (Scotland) (Registered Foreign Lawyers) etc Practice Rules 2005;".

52. In rule 2(1) in the definition of "practice unit" insert after "practice" the second time it appears—

"and shall include a Scottish multi-national practice (as defined in rule 7(1) of the 2005 Rules)".

Solicitors (Scotland) (Client Communication) Practice Rules 2005

53. In rule 2(1) insert after "requires"—

" "2005 Rules" means the Solicitors (Scotland) (Registered Foreign Lawyers) etc Practice Rules 2005;".

54. In rule 2(1) in the definition of "solicitor" insert after "practice"—

"and shall include a registered foreign lawyer to whom these rules apply in terms of rule 4(2) or (3) of the 2005 Rules and a Scottish multi-national practice (as defined in rule 7(1) of the 2005 Rules)".

Rule 6

SCHEDULE 6

PROVISIONS OF ADMISSION REGULATIONS APPLICABLE TO REGISTERED FOREIGN LAWYERS IN TERMS OF RULE 6

1. The Council shall be entitled to require the evidence of a registered foreign lawyer in terms of regulations 16(1) and 35 of the Admission Regulations as if he were a solicitor (as defined in the Admission Regulations).

2. A registered foreign lawyer shall be responsible, as a member of a multi-national practice, for the compliance of that multi-national practice with any obligation placed upon it by the Admission Regulations as a training solicitor, including without limitation the obligations placed upon it by regulations 13(1), 13(2), 16(1), 16(3), 16(5), 16(7), 17, 35, 36(3) and 37(2).

Solicitors (Scotland) (Client Relations Partner) Practice Rules 2005

Rules dated 24th March 2005, made by the Council of the Law Society of Scotland under section 34(1) of the Solicitors (Scotland) Act 1980 and approved by the Lord President of the Court of Session in terms of section 34(3) of the said Act.

Citation and Commencement

1.—(1) These Rules may be cited as the Solicitors (Scotland) (Client Relations Partner) Practice Rules 2005.

(2) These Rules shall come into force on 1st June 2005.

Interpretation

2.—(1) In these Rules, unless the context otherwise requires—

[1]"2005 Rules" means the Solicitors (Scotland) (Registered Foreign Lawyers) etc Practice Rules 2005;

"the Act" means the Solicitors (Scotland) Act 1980;

"Client Relations Partner" means a principal of a practice unit so designated by that practice unit in terms of these Rules;

"complaint" means a written complaint made to the Client Relations Partner of a practice unit, in relation to that practice unit, which, if it were made to the Society, would have to be investigated in terms of section 33(1) of the Law Reform (Miscellaneous Provisions) (Scotland) Act 1990;

"the Council" means the Council of the Society;

[2]"practice unit" means (i) a solicitor who is a sole practitioner, (ii) a firm of solicitors or (iii) an incorporated practice and shall include a Scottish multi-national practice (as defined in rule 7(1) of the 2005 Rules) [[3] and shall include, for the purposes of rules 3(4), 3(5), 3(6), 5(2), 6 and 7, a practice unit which is dissolved or ceases to carry on business];

"principal" means a solicitor who is a sole practitioner or is a partner in a firm of two or more solicitors or is a director of an incorporated practice which is a company or is a member of an incorporated practice which is a limited liability partnership [[3] and shall include, for the purposes of rules 3(4), 3(5), 3(6) and 5(2), any person who was such a practitioner, partner, director or member in a practice unit which is dissolved or ceases to carry on business]; and

"the Society" means the Law Society of Scotland.

(2) The Interpretation Act 1978 applies to the interpretation of these Rules as it applies to the interpretation of an Act of Parliament.

NOTES

[1] Inserted by the Solicitors (Scotland) (Registered Foreign Lawyers) etc. Practice Rules 2005, Sch.5 (effective May 1, 2005).

[2] As amended by the Solicitors (Scotland) (Registered Foreign Lawyers) etc. Practice Rules 2005, Sch.5 (effective May 1, 2005).

[3] Prospectively inserted by the Solicitors (Scotland) (Client Relations Partner) Practice (Amendment) Rules 2007, r.3 (effective January 15, 2008).

Appointment of a Client Relations Partner

3.—(1) By each date set out in paragraph (2) a practice unit shall designate one of its principals as its Client Relations Partner, who shall be responsible for dealing with complaints made to that practice unit.

(2) A practice unit shall designate a person in terms of paragraph (1) within 28 days of—

(a) the date of commencement of these Rules,

(b) the date of its commencing practice on its own account; and

(c) every subsequent date when the office of Client Relations Partner in the practice unit becomes vacant.

(3) A practice unit which is a solicitor who is a sole practitioner at any date referred to in paragraph (2) shall be deemed to have designated that solicitor as its Client Relations Partner at that date.

[[1](4) In the event of the dissolution or cessation of the business of a practice unit, that practice unit shall, within 28 days after the date of dissolution or cessation (whichever is the earlier), designate one of its principals as its Client Relations Partner and notify the Council in writing of the information set out in the Schedule in, or substantially in, the form set out in the Schedule.]

[[1](5) Until a practice unit designates a Client Relations Partner and notifies the Council in accordance with paragraph (4), or if it does not so designate and notify, the Client Relations Partner designated by that practice unit in terms of paragraph (1) shall, notwithstanding the dissolution or cessation of business, continue to be responsible for dealing with complaints made against that practice unit, whether they have been made before or after the dissolution or cessation.]

[1](6) A Client Relations Partner responsible in terms of paragraphs (4) or (5) for dealing with complaints made against a practice unit shall continue to be responsible for—

(a) complaints made in the period of two years after the date of dissolution or cessation of that practice unit; and

(b) complaints made before that date,
until such date as those complaints are concluded.]

NOTE

[1] Prospectively inserted by the Solicitors (Scotland) (Client Relations Partner) Practice (Amendment) Rules 2007, r.3(3) (effective January 15, 2008).

Additional Client Relations Partners

4.—(1) Where a practice unit has more than one place of business, it may designate a Client Relations Partner in respect of each place of business. Each Client Relations Partner shall be responsible for dealing with complaints in relation to a specified place or places of business.

(2) No practice unit may designate more than one Client Relations Partner in respect of any place of business.

(3) Where a practice unit has two or more Client Relations Partners, it shall designate one Client Relations Partner as the lead Client Relations Partner. The lead Client Relations Partner shall be responsible for dealing with complaints in any case of doubt as to which Client Relations Partner is responsible.

Registration

5.—(1) A practice unit shall [[1]except as provided in rule 3(4),], within 28 days of the designation of a Client Relations Partner, notify the Council in writing of the information set out in the Schedule in, or substantially in, the form set out in the Schedule.

(2) A practice unit shall, within 28 days of any change in any of the information provided to the Council in accordance with this rule [[2]or rule 3(4)], notify the Council in writing of such change in, or substantially in, the form set out in the Schedule.

NOTES

[1] Prospectively inserted by the Solicitors (Scotland) (Client Relations Partner) Practice (Amendment) Rules 2007, r.4 (effective January 15, 2008).

[2] Prospectively inserted by the Solicitors (Scotland) (Client Relations Partner) Practice (Amendment) Rules 2007, r.5 (effective January 15, 2008).

Records to be Kept

6. A practice unit shall ensure that its Client Relations Partner or Partners maintains a central record of each written complaint and the way it is dealt with.

Written Procedure

7.—(1) A practice unit shall ensure that the procedure to be followed by it when handling complaints is set out in writing.

(2) Any client or former client of a practice unit who requests a copy of the procedure referred to in paragraph (1) from that practice unit shall be supplied with a copy of it within 28 days of such request.

Waiver

8. The Council shall have the power to waive any of the provisions of these Rules either generally or in any particular circumstances or case, provided that such waiver may be made subject to such conditions as the Council may determine.

Professional Practice

9. Failure to comply with these Rules may be treated as professional misconduct for the purposes of Part IV of the Solicitors (Scotland) Act 1980.

SCHEDULE **Rule 5**

NOTIFICATION OF CLIENT RELATIONS PARTNER OR OF CHANGE IN DETAILS

Details of Practice Unit
Name ....
Address ....
....

Details of Client Relations Partner
Name ....
Address ....
....
Tel. No. ....
E-mail ....
Address of place(s) of business for which Client Relations Partner is responsible
....
....
....
....
.... (continue on separate sheet if necessary)

Have any other Client Relations Partners been appointed in respect of the practice unit? Yes/ No

Has the Client Relations Partner named above been designated as lead Client Relations Partner for the practice unit? Yes/ No

Constitution of the Law Society of Scotland

Scheme under the Solicitors (Scotland) Act 1980, approved at a General Meeting of the Society held on 23rd September 1988 and having, by virtue of section 1 of, and Schedule 1 to, the said Act, effect as if enacted in that Act.

Title and Interpretation

Title

1.—(1) This Scheme may be cited as the Constitution of the Law Society of Scotland.

(2) This constitution shall come into operation on 1st November 1988.

Interpretation

[1] **2.**—(1) In this Constitution unless the context otherwise requires:—

"the Act" means the Solicitors (Scotland) Act 1980;

"the Council" means the Council of the Society;

"financial year" means the period of twelve months ending on 31st October.

"a member of the Society" means a solicitor who in terms of Section 2(1) of the Act has in force a practising certificate, and any other solicitor who has paid the current annual membership subscription to the Society and whose name appears upon the Roll of Solicitors kept by the Council;

"place of business", in relation to a member of the Society means the member's place of business, or if the member has more than one place of business, the member's principal place of business, as specified in the member's practising certificate, if the member has one, or in a notice of change of place of business given by the member to the Society after the issue of the member's practising certificate, if the member has given such a notice, or if the member does not have a place of business, his residence, and references to the constituency in which a member practises shall be construed as a reference to the constituency in which such member has his place of business;

[2] "the President" means the chairman of the Society provided for in terms of paragraph 2(c) of Schedule 1 to the Act and includes, in the case of the absence of the President or his inability to act as President, the Vice-President;

"the Secretary" means the Secretary of the Society and includes any person authorised by the President to act on behalf of the Secretary;

"the Society" means The Law Society of Scotland established by the Solicitors (Scotland) Act 1949;

[2] "the Vice-President" means the vice-chairman of the Society provided for in terms of paragraph 2(c) of Schedule 1 to the Act;

(2) The Interpretation Act 1978 applies to the interpretation of this Constitution as it applies to the interpretation of an Act of Parliament.

NOTES

[1] As amended by a Resolution of the members of the Law Society of Scotland to amend the Constitution of the Law Society of Scotland (effective May 2004).

[2] Inserted by a Resolution of the members of the Law Society of Scotland to amend the Constitution of the Law Society of Scotland (effective May 2004).

Constitution and Election of Members of Council

Constitution of the Council

[1] **3.** The Council shall consist of 44 members of the Society elected in accordance with the provisions in this Constitution, together with such *ex officiis* members as there may be from time to time in terms hereof and such number of members, not exceeding nine, as may be co-opted by the Council in terms of Article 4 hereof.

NOTE

[1] As amended, 27th September 1991.

Election of members of Council by constituencies

4.—[1] (1) For the purpose of the election of members of Council, there shall be the several geographical constituencies listed in the first column of Part 1 of the First Schedule to this Constitution, and there shall be a separate election in each constituency. For the purposes of this Article and of the First and Second Schedules to this Constitution, a member of the Society having a place of business which is not in any such constituency shall be treated as having a place of business within such constituency as such member may select.

(2) A member of the Society shall be entitled to vote in the constituency in which such member's place of business is situated and in that constituency only.

(3) The members of the Society in each of the several constituencies shall elect the number of members of Council as set out in the second column of the said Part of the said Schedule opposite to the constituency.

(4) Constituencies shall be arranged in three groups as set out in Part II of the said Schedule and the Council shall arrange that in each year there will be an annual election in one of such groups taken in rotation.

(5) The Council may co-opt as full members of Council such number of members of the Society not exceeding nine in all as the Council may determine. Such persons shall hold office for such term not exceeding three years as the Council may fix and different terms may be fixed for different persons. There shall be no limitation upon the number of terms for which such a person may be co-opted.

(6) Only a member of the Society may be elected or co-opted or continue to be a member of Council.

NOTE

[1] Substituted by a Resolution of the members of the Law Society of Scotland to amend the Constitution of the Law Society of Scotland (effective May 2004).

Term of office of members of Council

5. A member of Council shall retire from office on the day immediately before the day fixed by the Council for the annual election of members of the Council in the third year after such member's election. A retiring member shall be eligible for re-election.

Date of election of members of Council

6. The annual election of members of Council in terms of Article 4(4) hereof shall be held in the month of May in each year on a date to be fixed by the Council.

Returning officer

7. The Secretary shall act as returning officer for the election in each constituency.

Conduct of election

8.—(1) Subject to the provisions of this Constitution the election of members of Council for a constituency shall be conducted in accordance with the provisions of the Second Schedule hereto and of any regulations made thereunder.

(2) No election held under this Constitution shall be invalidated by reason of any misdescription or non-compliance with the provisions thereof or of any regulations thereunder or by reason of any miscount or of the non-delivery, loss or miscarriage of any document required to be sent under this Constitution or regulations thereunder, if it appears to the Returning Officer that the election was conducted substantially in accordance with this Constitution and the regulations and that the result of such misdescription, non-compliance, miscount, non-delivery, loss or miscarriage does not affect the return of any candidate at the election.

Expenses of election

9. All expenses properly incurred by the returning officer or by the Society in relation to the holding of an election of members of Council shall be paid by the Society.

Failure of constituency to elect members of Council

[1] **10.** If the members of the Society in a constituency fail to elect the number of members of Council for the constituency as herein prescribed, the Council may fill the vacancy by appointing a member of the Society to be a member of Council representing the constituency. Such member of the Society shall have his place of business within such constituency or as close thereto as may be reasonably practicable.

NOTE

[1] As amended by a Resolution by the members of the Law Society of Scotland to amend the Constitution of the Law Society of Scotland (effective May 2004).

Casual vacancies in Council

11.—(1) A member of Council may at any time resign from office by a notice in writing signed by such member and delivered to the Secretary. The resignation shall take effect upon the delivery of the notice or on a date not later than such member's date of retiral from office in terms of Article 5 hereof specified by such member in such notice, whichever is the later.

(2) The office of a member of Council shall be vacated if such member is absent, without leave of the President, from three consecutive meetings of the Council, with effect from the conclusion of that third meeting of Council. Such leave may be given retrospectively.

(3) Council may by a majority of three-quarters of members present and voting, suspend a member of Council from attendance at meetings of Council and its committees.

(4) If the office of a member of Council becomes vacant before the expiration of such member's term of office whether by death, resignation or otherwise, an election by the electors in the constituency shall be held as soon as practicable in order to fill the vacancy on a date to be fixed by the Council and shall be conducted in the same manner as an election in ordinary course; and the provisions of this Constitution including the Second Schedule hereto relating to elections shall apply subject to any necessary modifications: provided that if the vacancy arises within three months before the date on which the vacating member would have retired in ordinary course the vacancy shall not be filled until the next election in the constituency. A person elected to fill a casual vacancy under this provision shall hold office only for the unexpired period of office of the member in whose place such person is elected and shall be eligible for re-election.

MEETINGS OF SOCIETY

Meetings of Society

12.—(1) General Meetings of the Society shall comprise the Annual General Meeting and Special General Meetings.

(2) An Annual General Meeting shall be held each year at such time on such date and at such place as the Council may appoint but not more than 15 months after the last preceding Annual General Meeting.

(3) Special General Meetings of the Society shall be convened by the Secretary on the instructions of the President or of the Council or on a requisition signed by not less than 20 members of the Society. The requisition must state the objects of the meeting. It must be deposited with the Secretary and may consist of several documents in like form each signed by one or more requisitionists. A Special General Meeting required by requisition shall be held within 28 days of receipt of the requisition at such time on such date and at such place as the President, whom failing the Vice-President, may appoint.

(4) Fourteen days' notice at least (exclusive of the day on which the notice is sent but inclusive of the day for which the notice is given), specifying the place, day, and hour of any General Meeting and the business to be considered shall be given to each member of the Society. A notice of a General Meeting shall be deemed to have been effected at the expiration of 24 hours after the letter containing the notice is sent. The accidental omission to give notice of a meeting to, or the non-receipt of notice of a meeting by any member shall not invalidate the proceedings at the meeting.

Proceedings at General Meetings of the Society

13.—(1) The President, whom failing the Vice-President, shall preside at a General Meeting, and if at any meeting neither the President nor the Vice-President is present, the members present shall choose one of their number who is a member of Council to preside.

(2) The business of the Annual General Meeting shall be to consider the Report of the Council, the statement of accounts of the Society and the report of the auditors thereon, to elect auditors, and any other business specified in the notice of the meeting. A copy of the Report of the Council shall be made available to the members of the Society on the Society's website from the date the notice of the Annual General Meeting is sent to the members of the Society. If, after the notice of Annual General Meeting has been sent to the members of the Society, a member requests a copy of the Report, the Council shall promptly send a copy to the member. At the option of the member that copy shall be sent either in paper or electronic form to the member at his place of business.

(3) The Council shall include in the notice of the Annual General Meeting any item relating to the business of the Society specified in a requisition made by not less than 10 members of the Society and received by the Secretary not less than 42 days before the meeting. The business of any Special General Meeting shall be to consider only the business specified in the notice of meeting.

(4) No business shall be transacted at any General Meeting unless a quorum of members of the Society is present within half an hour after the time appointed for the meeting. Twenty members personally present shall be a quorum. A meeting at which a quorum is not present, if not convened on a requisition shall stand adjourned to a day and hour to be fixed by the majority of the members present, and if convened on a requisition shall fail and not be held.

(5) Subject to the provisions of this Constitution and to any directions given by the Society in General Meeting, the Council may make standing orders with regard to the conduct of the business at meetings of the Society, including the adjournment of meetings.

(6) Subject to the provisions of paragraph 5 of Schedule 1 to the Act, no resolution passed at a General Meeting shall be binding on the Society until it has been adopted by the Council or has been confirmed at the next General Meeting, and it shall be the duty of the Council, if it does not adopt the resolution, to bring the same before the next General Meeting accordingly, but this provision shall not apply to a resolution proposed by the Council and passed at the meeting at which it has been proposed.

Voting at General Meetings

14.—(1) At any General Meeting a resolution put to the vote of the meeting shall be decided by a show of hands unless a poll is (before or on the declaration of the result of the show of hands) demanded by at least three members present in person and unless a poll is so demanded a declaration by the chairman of the meeting that a resolution has, on a show of hands, been carried or carried unanimously or by a particular majority or lost, and an entry to that effect in the minutes of the proceedings of the Society shall be conclusive evidence of the fact, without proof of the number or proportion of the votes recorded in favour of, or against, that resolution: always provided that a poll may not be demanded in the case of a resolution with regard to the appointment of a chairman of the meeting or the adjournment of the meeting or in the case of a motion that the question be now put or that the meeting move to the next business.

(2) If a poll is demanded, it shall be taken at once in such manner as the chairman directs, and the result of the poll shall be deemed to be the resolution of the meeting at which the poll was demanded.

(3) In the case of an equality of votes, whether on a show of hands or on a poll, the chairman of the meeting at which the show of hands takes place or at which the poll is taken shall be entitled to a second or casting vote.

(4) On a show of hands every member present in person shall have one vote.

(5) On a poll, votes may be given either personally or by proxy.

(6) The instrument appointing a proxy shall be deposited with the Secretary at any time after the notice is sent calling the General Meeting and not less than 48 hours before the time for holding the meeting or adjourned meeting at which the person named in the instrument proposes to vote, and in default the instrument of proxy shall not be treated as valid. A proxy must be a member of the Society.

President, Vice-President, Past President and Honorary Vice-President of the Society

President, Vice-President, Past President and Honorary Vice-President

15.—(1) The Council shall at its first meeting after the 1st day of November in each year, receive nominations for the office of President and Vice-President and shall thereafter elect at its first meeting after the 1st day of December in each year one of its number who has been a member of Council for at least three years to be President of the Society, and another of its number who has also been a member of Council for at least three years to be Vice-President of the Society, to hold office as from the date of the first meeting of the Council held after the next annual election of members of the Council; provided always that if at or prior to the latter date the President elect or Vice-President elect ceases to be a member of Council, his election as President or Vice-President shall be void as at the date of such cessation, and the Council shall at its first meeting held not less than four weeks after the date of such cessation, proceed to a new election of President or Vice-President as the case may be. Provided that if there are two or more nominations for either office the resulting competition shall be decided by postal ballot. If there are three or more nominations for either office the election shall be conducted by the single transferable vote method.

(2) Notwithstanding Article 5 hereof, the President and Vice-President shall hold office until the date from which their respective successors take office. A President or Vice-President shall cease to hold office if he ceases to be a member of the Society. The President shall be eligible for re-election to that office for each of the two succeeding years, but shall not again be eligible to be President until a period of at least two years has elapsed since he last held that office.

(3) The Vice-President shall not again be eligible to be Vice-President until at least one year has elapsed since he last held that office.

(4) The President or Vice-President may resign at any time from office as such by a signed notice in writing delivered to the Secretary, and the resignation shall take effect upon the delivery of the notice or on a date not later than the date on which he would otherwise have demitted office specified in the said notice, whichever is the later.

(5) (*a*) On a casual vacancy occurring in the office of President or Vice-President at a time when there is a President elect or Vice-President elect as the case may be appointed to take up office in the ensuing month of May, the President elect or Vice-President elect shall immediately assume office as President or Vice-President as the case may be; and the resulting additional period of office, which will terminate at the first meeting of the Council held after the next annual election of members of the Council, shall be disregarded in applying the provisions of Articles 15(2) and 15(3) hereof.

(*b*) On a casual vacancy occurring in the office of President at a time when there is no President elect, the Vice-President shall assume the additional office of Interim President until the next meeting of the Council held less than four weeks after the date of the occurrence of the said vacancy, when the Council shall elect a new President.

(*c*) On a casual vacancy occurring in the office of Vice-President at a time when there is no Vice-President elect, the Council shall as soon as practicable appoint one of its number to fill the vacancy until the date of the first meeting of the Council held after the next annual election of members of the Council.

(6) From the date upon which the President ceases to hold office as such except when he has resigned in terms of Article 15(4) hereof he shall serve as Past President of the Society for a period of one year. If the Past President is not or if during his period of office he should cease to be a member of Council, he shall *ex officio* be a member of Council until the expiry of his period of office. The Past President may resign as provided in Article 15(4) hereof and shall cease to hold office if he ceases to be a member of the Society.

(7) The Council may at any meeting elect one of its number or a former one of its number to be Honorary Vice-President of the Society to hold office until the next annual election of members of Council and to carry out such duties as may from time to time be prescribed by the Council. If the Honorary Vice-President is not a member of Council or if during his period of office he should cease to be a member of Council, he shall *ex officio* be a member of Council until the expiry of his period of office. An Honorary Vice-President shall not be eligible for re-election as such. An Honorary Vice-President may resign as provided in Article 15(4) hereof and shall cease to hold office if he ceases to be a member of the Society.

Admission of Honorary and Other Members of Society

Honorary members of Society

16.—(1) The Council may admit as an honorary member of the Society any person of distinction in the legal profession whether or not such person is or has been a member of the Society.

(2) Unless he is a member of the Society an honorary member shall have no right to vote at meetings of the Society or in elections of members of

Council and shall not be liable in payment of any annual subscription to the Society.

Admission as members of solicitors exempt from holding practising certificates

17. The Council shall, on application and on payment of the annual subscription, admit as a member of the Society any solicitor who is exempt from taking out a practising certificate.

Honorary Presidents of Society

Honorary Presidents

18. *[Deleted by a Resolution of the members of the Law Society of Scotland to amend the Constitution of the Law Society of Scotland (effective May 2004).]*

Secretary and Staff

Secretary and staff

19.—(1) The Council shall appoint a Secretary of the Society who shall be chief executive officer of the Council and it shall pay a suitable remuneration for his services and may make such provision for pension or other rights for his benefit as it thinks proper. The Secretary shall perform such duties as the Council may from time to time determine.

(2) The Council shall appoint such other staff as it thinks necessary for the efficient discharge of the functions of the Society and of the Council, and shall pay to every member of staff appointed under this Article suitable remuneration and may make such provision for pension or other rights for his benefit as it thinks proper.

Accounts

Accounts

20.—(1) The Council shall keep proper books of accounts with regard to all sums of money received and expended by the Society, the Council and staff of the Society, and the matters in respect of which the receipt and expenditure take place.

(2) The Council shall keep such bank accounts in name of the Society as the Council may determine, and, save as otherwise directed by the Council, there shall be paid into the said bank accounts all sums received by the Society or the Council or staff of the Society or otherwise all payments due to be met by the Society or the Council or otherwise payable out of the funds of the Society. The Council may give directions with respect to keeping, paying money into, and operating on the several bank accounts.

Accounts to be made up yearly and submitted for audit

21.—(1) Immediately after the end of each financial year the Council shall cause the accounts of the Society for that year to be brought to a balance and a balance sheet prepared.

(2) The Council shall cause the accounts for the financial year to be audited as soon as practicable after the end of the year by the auditors appointed by the Society at the Annual General Meeting. A copy of the accounts, or an abstract thereof, and of the auditors' certificate thereon shall be made available to the members of the Society on the Society's website from the date the notice of the Annual General Meeting at which the statement of accounts of the Society and the report of the auditors thereon are to be considered is sent to the members of the Society. If, after the notice of the Annual General Meeting has been sent to the members of the Society, a member requests a copy of the accounts, or an abstract thereof, and of the auditor's certificate thereon to the member. At the option of the member

that copy shall be sent either in paper or electronic form to the member at his place of business.

(3) If a vacancy arises in the office of auditor of the accounts of the Society between Annual General Meetings, the Council may appoint an auditor to fill the vacancy until the next Annual General Meeting and fix the remuneration.

MISCELLANEOUS

Committees and Sub-Committees of the Council

[1] **22.**—(1) The Council may constitute committees and sub-committees and shall specify their remit and duties and may specify any restriction or condition on the committee or sub-committee which it considers appropriate.

(2) A committee may constitute sub-committees and shall specify their remit and duties and may specify any restriction or condition on the sub-committee which it considers appropriate.

(3) A sub-committee constituted by a committee shall not have any remit or duty beyond those of that committee, and shall obey any restriction or condition placed upon that committee.

(4) The Council may appoint or remove any member of a committee or sub-committee. A committee may appoint or remove a member of any sub-committee constituted by it.

(5) A committee, or the Convener thereof, shall (if so authorised by the Council in the remit of the committee) have the power to co-opt any person as a member of that committee.

(6) A member of a committee or sub-committee need not be a member of the Council or of the Society and a committee or sub-committee may have a majority of members who are not members of the Council or of the Society.

NOTE

[1] As substituted, September 1, 2003.

Notice to members of Society

23. Any notice or other document required by or under this Constitution to be sent to a member of the Society shall be sent to such member at his place of business.

Council may hold referendum of members of the Society

24. The Council may if it thinks fit and shall on a requisition signed by not fewer than 50 members of the Society and deposited with the Secretary ascertain the views of the members of the Society at any time on any question affecting the Society or the members thereof by holding a referendum of its members and the Council shall make such arrangements as it considers proper for that purpose, including issuing to every member of the Society a voting paper and arranging for the scrutiny of voting papers. The Council shall include in its annual report a report of any referendum taken during the year.

Standing orders

[1] **25.**—(1) Subject to the provisions of this Constitution, the Council may by standing orders make provision with respect to—

(a) keeping minutes of General Meetings of the Society; and

(b) any other matters which the Council considers would facilitate the conduct of business of meetings of the Society, or of the Council, or of any committee or sub-committee of the Council.

(2) Standing orders made under this Article or under any other provision of this Constitution may be varied or revoked at any time by the Council.

NOTE
[1] As substituted, September 1, 2003.

Validity of acts of Council

26. The acts and proceedings of the Council shall not be invalidated by any vacancy among its members or by any defect in the election or qualification of any member.

Expenses of members of Council and committees

27. There shall be paid to the members of the Council and of committees thereof such travelling and other expenses in respect of attendance at meetings as may be approved by the Council.

Common Seal of Society

Common seal of Society

28. The Secretary shall be responsible for the custody of the common seal of the Society. The seal shall not be affixed to any instrument except by order of the Council or of a committee of the Council specifically authorised for the purpose.

FIRST SCHEDULE

[1] *PART I*

NOTE
[1] As amended, March 22, 1996 and March 18, 2005.

Constituencies for election of members of Council of the Law Society of Scotland.

Constituencies	Number of members of Council to be elected by constituency
Sheriff Court District of Aberdeen	2
Sheriff Court Districts of Stonehaven, Peterhead and Banff	1
Sheriff Court Districts of Airdrie	1
Sheriff Court District of Hamilton and Lanark	1
Sheriff Court Districts of Arbroath and Forfar	1
Sheriff Court District of Ayr	1
Sheriff Court District of Kilmarnock	1
Sheriff Court Districts of Campbeltown, Dunoon, Oban, Rothesay and Fort William	1
Sheriff Court District of Greenock	1
Sheriff Court District of Paisley	1
Sheriff Court Districts of Dumfries, Kirkcudbright and Stranraer	2
Sheriff Court District of Dundee	2
Sheriff Court District of Dunfermline	1
Sheriff Court District of Kirkcaldy	1
Sheriff Court District of Cupar	1
Sheriff Court District of Edinburgh	7
Sheriff Court Districts of Elgin and Nairn	1
Sheriff Court Districts of Haddington, Peebles, Jedburgh, Duns and Selkirk	2
Sheriffdom of Glasgow and Strathkelvin	7
Sheriff Court District of Perth	1
Sheriff Court District of Stirling, Falkirk and Alloa	2
Sheriff Court Districts of Kirkwall, Lerwick, Portree, Lochmaddy and Stornoway	1

Constituencies	Number of members of Council to be elected by constituency
Sheriff Court District of Dumbarton	1
Sheriff Court District of Linlithgow	1
Sheriff Court Districts of Inverness, Dingwall, Tain, Dornoch and Wick	1
England and Wales	1
	43

PART II

Grouping of constituencies for purposes of Article 4 so as to determine the rotation of the retiral of members of Council and of elections.

[1] *First Group*

Sheriffdom of Glasgow and Strathkelvin	7
Sheriff Court Districts of Campbeltown, Dunoon, Oban, Rothesay and Fort William	1
Sheriff Court District of Greenock	1
Sheriff Court District of Paisley	1
Sheriff Court District of Dunfermline	1
Sheriff Court District of Kirkcaldy	1
Sheriff Court District of Cupar	1
Sheriff Court District of Perth	1
Sheriff Court Districts of Arbroath and Forfar	1
England and Wales	1
	16

NOTE
[1] As amended, March 22, 1996.

[1] *Second Group*

Sheriff Court District of Edinburgh	7
Sheriff Court District of Aberdeen	2
Sheriff Court Districts of Stonehaven, Peterhead and Banff	1
Sheriff Court Districts of Dumfries, Kirkcudbright and Stranraer	2
Sheriff Court Districts of Airdrie	1
Sheriff Court District of Hamilton and Lanark	1
	14

NOTE
[1] As amended, March 18, 2005.

[1] *Third Group*

Sheriff Court District of Dundee	2
Sheriff Court District of Ayr	1
Sheriff Court District of Kilmarnock	1
Sheriff Court Districts of Stirling, Falkirk and Alloa	2
Sheriff Court Districts of Haddington, Peebles, Jedburgh, Duns and Selkirk	2
Sheriff Court Districts of Elgin and Nairn	1
Sheriff Court Districts of Kirkwall, Lerwick, Portree, Lochmaddy and Stornoway	1
Sheriff Court District of Dumbarton	1
Sheriff Court District of Linlithgow	1
Sheriff Court Districts of Inverness, Dingwall, Tain, Dornoch and Wick	1
	13

NOTE
[1] As amended, March 18, 2005.

SECOND SCHEDULE

PART I

Rules with Regard to the Election of Members of Council

Roll of electors

[1] 1. The Secretary shall cause to be prepared, for each election, a roll of electors showing the names and places of business of every member of the Society who, on the date six weeks before the date of the election, had his place of business in the constituency for which the election is to be held.

Notice of election

2. The returning officer shall on or before a date not later than five weeks before the day of the elections in the various constituencies concerned cause a notice of election of the members of Council for the various constituencies to be published in the Journal issued by the Society or in such other manner as the Council may determine. The notice of election shall be in the appropriate form set out in Part II of this Schedule or in a form substantially to the like effect.

Nominations

[2] 3. No person may be elected a member of Council unless a nomination paper in respect of such person is lodged with the returning officer at the place stated in the notice of election on or before a date specified in the notice of election, not less than three weeks before the day of election. No person may be nominated as a candidate for election by a constituency unless he is a member of the Society having a place of business in the constituency for which the election is to be held. A nomination paper in respect of a candidate shall be signed by two proposers being electors within the constituency, and shall contain a signed statement by the candidate that he consents to be nominated and that, if elected, he will act as a member of Council. The nomination paper shall be in the appropriate form set out in Part II of this Schedule or in a form substantially to the like effect. No person may sign more nomination papers in respect of candidates than there are members of Council to be elected by the constituency; and if he signs more than is permitted, his signature shall be inoperative in all but those papers up to the permitted number which are first delivered. The returning officer shall treat as null and void any nomination paper which does not comply with any of the foregoing provisions.

A nomination may be withdrawn at any time before the latest date for lodging nomination papers.

Uncontested elections

4. If on the latest date for lodging nomination papers the number of persons remaining validly nominated for a constituency does not exceed the number of persons to be elected by the constituency, the returning officer shall cause a notice to be published in the Journal of the Society or in such other manner as the Council may determine intimating the election of the persons nominated as members of Council and that no voting will take place in the constituency.

Voting in contested elections

5.—(1) If the number of persons remaining validly nominated for a constituency exceeds the number of members to be elected by the constituency, the members of Council shall be elected in accordance with the following provision of this Schedule and with the provisions of any regulations made thereunder.

(2) The returning officer shall immediately after the latest date for lodging nomination papers cause voting papers and identification envelopes to be prepared in respect of each constituency in which the election is taking place. Voting papers prepared by the returning officer shall contain the names, places of business, date of birth, professional degrees, diplomas or qualifications, date of admission as a solicitor, date of joining practice or employer, date of assumption as a partner or position now held with employer, and (where appropriate) service to local Faculty or the Society and service on Council and committees of the Society, of the persons nominated for the constituency and state the place to which voting papers are to be returned and the latest date (being the date of election) and time by which they may be received, and the identification envelope shall bear a declaration of identity. Each voting paper and identification envelope shall be in the appropriate form set out in Part II of this Schedule or in a form substantially to the like effect.

(3) The returning officer shall on or before a date to be fixed by the Council, being not less than 10 days before the day of election, send a voting paper to each elector in the various constituencies concerned at such elector's place of business together with an identification

envelope and a covering envelope. Each elector shall be entitled to receive one voting paper, an identification envelope, and a covering envelope and no more; and votes may not be given except upon the voting paper provided by the returning officer.

(4) An elector in recording his vote (a) shall place a cross (thus X) on the right-hand side of the voting paper opposite the name of each candidate for whom he votes; and (b) shall sign the declaration upon the identification envelope. Each elector shall have as many votes as there are members to be elected from the constituency.

(5) The returning officer shall in the case of each constituency immediately after the last day fixed for the return of voting papers cause the validity of the votes to be ascertained by an examination of the identification envelopes and by such other relevant evidence (if any) as there may be, and shall cause the identification envelopes found to be valid to be opened and the voting papers withdrawn, kept folded face inwards, and placed apart. An identification envelope which has not been signed by the voter shall, together with the voting paper therein contained, be treated as invalid.

(6) The returning officer shall then examine the voting papers for each constituency and shall reject as invalid any voting paper (a) on which votes are given for more candidates than the elector is entitled to vote for, or (b) on which anything is written or marked by which the elector can be identified, except the number on the back, or (c) which is unmarked or void for uncertainty, or (d) which is defaced.

Any voting paper which the returning officer has rejected shall be marked with the word "Rejected".

(7) The returning officer shall, in the case of each constituency, cause the votes found to be valid to be counted in his presence and shall declare the result of the election. The returning officer shall forthwith give to every person elected on a vote notice of his election, and shall furnish to the Society and also publish in the journal of the Society, or in such other manner as the Council may determine, a list of the persons certified by him to have been duly elected, whether as a result of an uncontested election or a contested election.

Power to returning officer to cancel election

6. Notwithstanding anything in this Schedule, if after the latest date for lodging nomination papers a candidate withdraws with the result that the number of the remaining candidates does not exceed the number of persons to be elected by the constituency, the returning officer may cancel the election and declare the remaining candidates to be the elected members for the constituency.

Provisions in case of death of candidate

7. If a candidate remaining validly nominated dies before the last day fixed for lodging nomination papers his nomination shall be treated as having been withdrawn, but if such a candidate dies after that day, but before the day of election, the returning officer shall order a fresh election to be held.

Power to make regulations varying for certain purposes provisions of schedule

8. Notwithstanding anything in this Schedule, the Council may make regulations varying the provisions of this Schedule by prescribing a method of voting otherwise than by means of the combination of the voting paper and the identification envelope as herein before provided, and by prescribing another form of voting paper and making such other consequential amendments of the provisions of this Schedule as appear to the Council to be necessary.

Decision of returning officer final

9. Any question arising with regard to the validity of a nomination paper, a voting paper, or otherwise in connection with an election held under this Constitution shall be determined by the returning officer, whose decision shall be final.

NOTES

[1] Substituted by a Resolution by the members of the Law Society of Scotland to amend the Constitution of the Law Society of Scotland (effective May 2004).

[2] As amended by a Resolution by the members of the Law Society of Scotland to amend the Constitution of the Law Society of Scotland (effective May 2004).

PART II

[1] NOTICE OF ELECTION

THE LAW SOCIETY OF SCOTLAND

Election of Members of Council

NOTICE IS HEREBY GIVEN that, pursuant to the Solicitors (Scotland) Act 1980 and the Constitution of the Law Society of Scotland, an election of members of Council representing the solicitors having places of business in the several constituencies undernoted is about to be held. Every member of the Society having a place of business as defined in Article 2 of the Constitution of the Society in a constituency at 1st November, 19 is entitled to one vote for each candidate up to the number of members of Council to be elected by that constituency. A member of the Society cannot vote in more than one constituency.

Constituencies	Number of members of Council to be elected by constituency

The returning officer for the purposes of this election is (*Name and Address*).
No person may be elected a member of Council unless he or she is a member of the Society and unless a nomination paper in respect of such person is sent or delivered by hand so as to reach the office of the returning officer at or before noon on the day of 19

Forms of nomination papers may be obtained from the returning officer on application. Every person proposed for election for a constituency must be nominated by a separate nomination paper in the appropriate form contained in Part II of the Second Schedule to the said Constitution, and every nomination paper must be subscribed by two proposers, being electors in the constituency, and shall contain a statement subscribed by the candidate that he or she consents to be nominated and that, if elected, he or she accepts office as a member of the Council.

No person may sign more nomination papers than the number of members to be elected by the constituency.

Dated 19 *Returning Officer*

NOTE

[1] As amended by members of the Law Society of Scotland, July 1995.

FORM OF NOMINATION PAPER

THE LAW SOCIETY OF SCOTLAND

Election of Members of Council

Constituency

We, A.B. and C.D. (*here insert names of proposers and places of business*), being electors in this constituency, hereby nominate E.F. (*here insert name and place of business of candidate*), being a member of the Society, for election as a member of the Council of the Society at the next ensuing election.

Given under our hand this (*insert date*) 19
A.B.
C.D.

I, the nominee for election, consent to be nominated as a candidate, and if elected agree to accept office as a member of the Council of the Society. I am a member of the Society.

E.F.

To the Returning Officer
(*Name and Address*).

[1] FORM OF VOTING PAPER

THE LAW SOCIETY OF SCOTLAND

Election of Members of Council

CONSTITUENCY

Election of members of Council by the constituency.

Names and Places of business of candidates	

DIRECTIONS FOR THE GUIDANCE OF ELECTORS

The elector may vote for candidates.

If the elector votes for more than the number of candidates referred to in the previous line his voting paper will be treated as invalid.

The elector will place a cross on the right-hand side of the voting paper opposite the name of each candidate for whom the elector votes, thus X, and will not sign or otherwise mark this voting paper.

If the elector inadvertently spoils a voting paper the elector may return it to the returning officer, who will, if satisfied of such inadvertence, if time permits, forward another paper.

This paper must be folded *face inwards* and placed in the "Identification Envelope", which must be securely fastened and signed and then placed in the covering envelope, which must be sent or delivered by hand to the returning officer (*Name and Address*), and must be received there before noon on the day of 19

(Back of voting paper)

Official
Stamp and
Number

Note: The number on the voting paper should be the same as that on the identification envelope issued with it.

(Form of Declaration of Identification Envelope)

To

Place of business

I, the undersigned, hereby declare that I am the person to whom the enclosed voting paper was addressed as above and that I have not marked any other voting paper in this election.

Signature

NOTE
[1] As amended by members of the Law Society of Scotland, July 1995.

Standing Orders of The Law Society of Scotland

Standing Orders made by the Council of the Law Society of Scotland in terms of Article 25 of the Constitution of the Society.

Interpretation

1.—(1) "the Act" means the Solicitors (Scotland) Act 1980; and other expressions used in these Orders shall have the same respective meanings as in the Constitution of the Society.

(2) The Interpretation Act 1978 applies to the interpretation of these Standing Orders as it applied to the interpretation of an Act of Parliament.

(3) In these Orders, references to "the Secretary" include, in the event of the Secretary's absence or incapacity, the Registrar or any other person authorised by the President to act on behalf of the Secretary.

(4) These Orders may be cited as the Law Society of Scotland Standing Orders, 2004, and have effect to regulate all proceedings of the Society on and after 1 April 2004.

Conduct of Business at General Meetings of Society

Authority of the Chair

2. The decision of the Chairman of a General Meeting of the Society on any question relating to procedure or order at the meeting shall be final and conclusive.

Motions and Amendments at Meetings of Society

3.—(a) Every motion submitted to a General Meeting, except those relating to routine matters or the conduct or procedure of the meeting, shall be in writing and signed by the mover, who shall be a member, and shall relate to business specified in the notice calling the meeting.

(b) In the case of any motion, any member may propose—

(i) an amendment of the motion by substitution, deletion and/or addition.

(ii) the direct negative.
(iii) that the debate be adjourned, or
(iv) that the question be now put or that the meeting move to the next business.

(c) All proposals under 3(b)(i), (iii) and (iv) but not (ii) shall require a seconder.

(d) Movers of motions and of proposals under 3(b)(i),(ii) or (iii) shall be allowed five minutes to speak and other speakers shall be allowed three minutes. The Chairman may, at his discretion, allow a specific extension of time to any speaker.

(e) Without the permission of the Chairman, no member shall be entitled to speak more than once on any motion or on any proposal under 3(b)(i), (ii) or (iii) (unless on a point of order or information) except that movers of motions and of proposals under 3(b)(i), (ii) or (iii) may reply, and shall be allowed three minutes therefor. In replying, members shall confine themselves to answering previous speakers and shall not introduce new matter. Movers of motions shall have the opportunity of closing the debate.

(f) Proposers and seconders of a proposal, under 3(b)(iv) shall not be permitted initially to speak in support of the proposal. When the proposal has been proposed and seconded, the Chairman will ask the meeting whether any member wishes to move the direct negative and, if he does, whether he has the support of one other member. If no member and supporting member wishes so to do, the proposal will be stated by the Chairman to have been carried unanimously. If the direct negative is moved and supported as aforesaid the proposer of the proposal will be allowed three minutes to speak to the proposal and the seconder two minutes to speak to it. The mover of the direct negative will be allowed three minutes to speak in support of the negative and the said supporting member two minutes to speak to it. No other member will be allowed to speak and, at the conclusion of the four speeches herein referred to, the proposal will forthwith be put to the meeting.

(g) Points of order shall be confined strictly to the conduct or procedure of the meeting.

(h) No motion or proposal may be withdrawn except with the concurrence of its seconder and, in the case of a motion, by permission of the meeting.

(i) No member shall unless with the permission of the Chairman move more than once that any one motion be amended.

Adjournment of General Meetings of the Society and suspension of Standing Orders

4.—(a) The Chairman may with the consent of any General Meeting of the Society at which a quorum is present, and shall, if so instructed by the meeting, adjourn the meeting from time to time and from place to place, but no business shall be transacted at any adjourned meeting other than the business left unfinished at the meeting at which the adjournment took place. When a meeting is adjourned for more than 14 days, seven days' notice of the adjourned meeting shall be given to each member but, save as aforesaid, it shall not be necessary to give any notice of an adjournment. It shall not be necessary in any case to give notice of the business to be transacted at an adjourned meeting.

(b) At any General Meeting of the Society a motion to suspend Standing Orders may be made and may be spoken to only by the mover who shall be allowed five minutes for that purpose. Such a motion if seconded shall be put forthwith to the meeting and shall not be passed unless it be supported by two-thirds of the members voting thereon. Any such suspension shall relate to one item of business only, or shall be for a fixed period of time not extending beyond the conclusion of that General Meeting.

Minutes of General Meetings of the Society

5.—(1) Minutes shall be kept by or on behalf of the Secretary recording—

(a) the names and places of business of the members present at each meeting; and

(b) all resolutions and proceedings at such meetings of the Society.

(2) The minutes of each General Meeting of the Society shall be submitted to the following Annual General Meeting of the Society and if approved as a true record shall be signed by the Chairman of the meeting to which it relates or the Chairman of the meeting at which the minute is approved.

Meetings of the Council

Ordinary Meetings of the Council

6.—(1) Subject to the other provisions of these Orders, ordinary meetings of the Council shall be held at the office of the Society, or at such other place as the Council may from time to time determine, and the Council shall hold not less than 7 meetings in each year for the transaction of Council business.

(2) The Secretary shall call a meeting of the Council—

(a) on being required so to do by the President (or, in the event of the absence or incapacity of the President, the Vice-President), such meeting to be held at a date and time directed by the President or Vice-President, or

(b) on receiving a requisition in writing for that purpose, specifying the business proposed to be transacted at the meeting, signed by not less than nine members of the Council, which meeting shall be held within 14 days of receipt of the requisition at a date and time directed by the President or (in the event of the absence or incapacity of the President) the Vice-President.

(3) A member of Council who wishes an item of business to be considered at an ordinary meeting of the Council shall give notice thereof in writing to the Secretary and such item shall (if the notice is received at least two days before the date when, in the ordinary course of events, notice of the meeting would be issued) be included in the agenda in the next notice issued under paragraph (4) of this Order.

(4) The Secretary shall give to every member of the Council written notice of the time and place of every ordinary meeting of Council, and—

(a) such notice shall be deemed to have been duly given if it is sent by ordinary mail (or a document exchange in which the addressee has provided an address to be used for the purpose) to the place of business of the member so that it would arrive, in the ordinary course of events, at least seven days before the date of the meeting.

(b) the notice shall specify the business proposed to be transacted at the meeting, but the President (or person actually presiding at the meeting of the Council) may, if it appears to him that any additional item of business should receive consideration, allow that matter to be dealt with although not mentioned in the notice.

Special Meetings of the Council

7.—(1) Notwithstanding anything in Order 6—

(a) if the President (or, in the event of the absence or incapacity of the President, the Vice-President) considers that any item of business is of such urgency that the giving of notice in accordance with paragraph 6(4) would be prejudicial to the interests of the public or of the solicitors' profession, he may require the Secretary to call a meeting of the Council to be held on giving not less than three days' notice.

(b) a meeting called under this paragraph shall conduct only the item of business for which it was called.

(2) Notwithstanding any of the other provisions of these Orders—

(a) in the event that a matter arises which, in the opinion of the President or the Vice-President or the immediate Past President, or in their absence the Secretary, requires powers of discretion to be exercised by the Council in terms of Section 38, 39A, 40, 41, 45 or 46 of the Solicitors (Scotland)Act 1980 more urgently than is allowed for by the foregoing provisions of this Order, the Secretary shall call a meeting of the Council for the purpose of dealing with such matter and the following provisions of this paragraph shall apply to that meeting.

(b) such a meeting may be held on giving not less than 24 hours notice, and shall conduct only the item of business for which it was called.

Notice may be given by facsimile or email

8.—(1) This Order applies to all meetings of the Council.

(2) Notwithstanding any other provision of these Orders as to the form of a notice of a meeting or as to the manner and time of its delivery—

(a) any notice calling a meeting [to which this Order applies] [of the Council] shall be in writing but may be given by facsimile transmission or by e-mail to the facsimile number or e-mail address given to the Society by a member of Council for this purpose;

(b) any notice sent by facsimile or by email shall be deemed to have been received by the addressee immediately on sending whether or not it is actually received;

Attendance by Audio Conference

9.—(1) This Order applies to all meetings of the Council.

(2) A meeting to which this Order applies may consist of a conference between members of Council who are not all in one place, but each of whom is able to speak to each of the others and to be heard by all of the others simultaneously and a member of Council taking part in such a meeting shall be deemed to be present in person at the meeting and accordingly shall be entitled to vote and to be counted in the quorum.

Proceedings at meetings of the Council

10.—(1) The President (or, in the event of the absence or incapacity of the President, the Vice-President) shall preside at each meeting of the Council, but if both be not present the members present shall choose one of their number to preside; in the following provisions of this Order, "the Chairman" means the person in fact presiding over a meeting in accordance with this paragraph.

(2) No business shall be transacted at a meeting of the Council unless at least nine members are present.

(3) The decision of the Chairman on any question relating to procedure or order at the meeting shall be final.

(4) Except where different provision is expressly made, or the context otherwise requires, the procedures for the conduct of business of the Council shall be those applicable to the conduct of business at General Meetings of the Society.

(5) Questions coming and arising before the Council shall, except in so far as may be otherwise expressly provided, be decided by a majority of the members voting on the question. In the event of an equality of votes, the Chairman shall be entitled to a second or casting vote.

(6) The Council may adjourn a meeting of the Council to any other day, hour and place.

(7) A motion the purport of which, in the opinion of the Chairman, is to alter or rescind a decision of the Council, shall not be competent within three months from the date of the passing of that decision.

(8) The Secretary shall keep (or cause to be kept) Minutes of all meetings of the Council, and—

(a) the Minutes of each meeting shall record the names of members attending, and all resolutions and proceedings at, that meeting.

(b) subject to sub-paragraph (c) below, the Minutes of each meeting shall be submitted to the following meeting for confirmation (either as written or with such amendments as the Council shall direct) of their factual accuracy, but draft minutes approved by the Chairman shall be sufficient evidence of the proceedings pending such confirmation.

(c) a meeting called in terms of Order 7(1) or 7(2) shall not consider the Minutes of any earlier meeting; any Minutes which, apart from this sub-paragraph, would be submitted to such a meeting shall be submitted to the next meeting called in terms of Order 6(4).

Elections of President and Vice-President

11.—(1) Subject to the following provisions of this Order, the provisions of the Second Schedule to the Constitution shall apply (with such amendments as may be necessary) to a postal ballot held under Article 15(1) of the Constitution as they apply to an election of members of the Council.

(2) Each member of the Council shall be entitled to receive, for each election, a ballot paper, a plain envelope, and an identification envelope.

(3) The marked ballot paper shall be placed in the plain envelope, which the voter shall then seal and (without making any mark thereon) place inside the identification envelope.

(4) After verifying the validity of the votes in terms of paragraph 5(5) of Part 1 of the Second Schedule, the returning officer shall—

(i) cause the valid identification envelopes to be opened and the plain envelopes removed therefrom and (still sealed) placed apart, then

(ii) cause the plain envelopes to be shuffled, then

(iii) cause the ballot papers to be removed from the plain envelopes and counted.

Appointment of Council Committees

Constitution of Committees and Sub-Committees

12.—(1) The Council may, in terms of Article 22(1) of the Society's Constitution, constitute such committees and sub-committees as are necessary or convenient to carry out the work of the Council, and shall specify (and may from time to time amend) the remit of each committee and sub-committee that it constitutes.

(2) A committee may, unless its remit provides otherwise, constitute such sub-committees as are necessary or convenient to carry out the work of the committee, and shall specify (and may from time to time amend) the remit of each sub-committee that it constitutes.

(3) A sub-committee constituted by a committee shall not have any remit beyond that of the committee which constituted it.

(4) In this Order, "remit" means a written statement setting out the functions, powers, duties and responsibilities of a committee or sub-committee and regulating its membership and procedures.

Membership of Committees and Sub-Committees

13.—(1) Each committee and sub-committee constituted by the Council shall have such members as the Council, on the nomination of the President, shall from time to time appoint; the Council shall appoint one of the members to be Convener of the Committee and may appoint a member to be Vice-Convener of the Committee.

(2) Each sub-committee constituted by a committee shall have a Convener appointed by the committee from among its own members and such other

members (subject to the terms of its remit) as may from time to time be appointed by the Convener of the Committee.

(4) A committee or sub-committee (or the Convener thereof) shall, if its remit so provides, have the power to co-opt any person as a member for a specified purpose or for a specified period of time not exceeding one year.

(5) A member of a committee or sub-committee need not be a member of the Council or of the Society, and a committee or sub-committee may have a majority of members who are not members of the Council or of the Society.

(6) The President and Vice-President shall, by virtue of their respective offices, be members of all committees and sub-committees.

(7) Conveners and Vice-Conveners shall hold office from the dates specified in their respective appointments until (unless a different date is specified in the appointment) 31 May next following their appointment, or (in either case) until the earlier occurrence of one of the following events—

(a) resignation;
(b) death or mental incapacity;
(c) removal by a resolution of the Council supported by two-thirds of the Council members voting thereon;
(d) in the case of a member who is a solicitor, striking off or suspension from practice;

but a Convener or Vice-Convener retiring by reason of the expiry of his period of appointment shall be eligible to be re-appointed.

(8) Subject to paragraph (7) above, members of committees shall hold office for three years (or such shorter period, if any, as is specified in their appointments) or until the earlier occurrence of one of the following events—

(a) resignation;
(b) death or mental incapacity;
(c) removal by a resolution of the Council supported by two-thirds of the Council members voting thereon;
(d) in the case of a member who is a solicitor, striking off or suspension from practice;

but a member retiring by reason of the expiry of his period of appointment shall be eligible to be re-appointed.

(9) Notwithstanding any other provision of this Order, a member of a Committee shall be deemed to have resigned if he is absent from three successive meetings of the Committee; but this paragraph shall not apply if such absence was with the approval (which may be given retrospectively)—

(a) in the case of a Convener, of the President;
(b) in any other case, of the Convener of the Committee.

Committee Secretaries

14. Each committee and sub-committee shall have a committee secretary, being a member of the Society's staff assigned for that purpose by or on behalf of the Secretary of the Society.

Savings for Existing Committees

15. Nothing in Orders 12 and 13 affects the constitution or membership of committees and sub-committees which were in existence on 31 March 2004, save that the members of such committees and sub-committees shall remain in office until 31 May 2004 or until the earlier occurrence of one of the following events—

(a) resignation;
(b) death or mental incapacity;
(c) removal by a resolution of the Council supported by two-thirds of the Council members voting thereon;
(d) in the case of a member who is a solicitor, striking off or suspension from practice;

but a member retiring by reason of the passage of time shall be eligible to be re-appointed.

Conduct of Committee Business

Meetings of Committees

16.—(1) In this Order, and in Order 17, unless the context requires otherwise—

(a) references to the Convener include (if the Convener is absent or unable to act) the Vice-Convener or, if the relevant committee has no Vice-Convener, the Committee Secretary;

(b) references to a committee include (unless the context requires otherwise) a sub-committee

(2) Subject to the following provisions of this Order, each committee shall meet as often as is necessary for the effective performance of its remit.

(3) The dates, times and places of meetings shall be such as the committee may determine or otherwise as directed by the Convener.

(4) The Committee Secretary shall call a meeting of a committee—

(a) upon being required to do so by the President or by the Convener of that committee, such meeting to be held at a date, time and place specified by the President or the Convener, or

(b) on receiving a request in writing for that purpose, specifying the business proposed to be transacted at the meeting, signed by not less than one quarter of the members of the committee, such meeting to be held within ten days of the receipt of the request, at a date, time and place specified by the Convener.

(5) The Committee Secretary shall give to every member of the committee written notice of the time and place of every meeting of the committee, and—

(a) such notice shall be deemed to have been duly given if it is sent by ordinary mail (or a document exchange in which the addressee has provided an address to be used for the purpose) to the address provided by the member for that purpose so that it would arrive, in the ordinary course of events, at least seven days before the date of the meeting.

(b) the business proposed to be transacted at the meeting shall be specified in the notice or in a separate notice sent (in similar manner) so as to arrive, in the ordinary course of events, at least three days before the meeting; but the Convener (or person actually presiding at the meeting) may, if it appears to him that any additional item of business should receive consideration, allow that matter to be dealt with although not mentioned in the notice.

(6) Notwithstanding anything in paragraph (4) of this Order—

(a) if the Convener considers that any item of business is of such urgency that the giving of notice in accordance with paragraph (5) would be prejudicial to the interests of the public or of the solicitors' profession, he may require the Committee Secretary to call a meeting of the committee to be held on giving not less than three days' notice.

(b) a meeting called under this paragraph shall conduct only the item of business for which it was called.

(7) Order 8, paragraph 2 applies to all committee meetings.

(8) Order 9, paragraph 2 applies to all committee meetings.

Procedure at Meetings

17.—(1) The Convener (or, in the event of the absence or incapacity of the Convener, the Vice-Convener, if there is one) shall preside at each meeting of the committee, but if both be not present the members present shall choose one of their number to preside (in which event, references in this Order to "the Convener" include the person so chosen).

(2) Except where different provision is expressly made, or the context otherwise requires, the procedures for the conduct of the business of a committee shall be those applicable to the conduct of the business of the Council.

(3) No business shall be transacted at a meeting of a committee unless at least three members are present.

(4) The Committee Secretary shall keep, or cause to be kept, Minutes of all meetings of the committees, and—

(a) the Minutes of each meeting shall record the names of members attending, and all resolutions and proceedings at, that meeting.

(b) the Minutes of each meeting shall be submitted to the following meeting for confirmation (either as written or with such amendments as the Committee shall direct) of their factual accuracy, but draft minutes approved by the Convener shall be sufficient evidence of the proceedings pending such confirmation.

(5) Subject to paragraph (3) of this Order, a Committee may meet and conduct business notwithstanding any vacancy in its membership.

(6) The provisions of this Order have effect subject to any contrary or inconsistent provisions made by the Council in the remit of any committee.

Repeal of Standing Orders

The Standing Orders approved by the Council on 23rd September, 1988 are hereby repealed.

NOTE:

Procedure for consideration of draft Rules submitted in terms of section 34 or section 35 of the Act to a General Meeting of the Society

Draft Rules to be submitted to a General Meeting of the Society in terms of sections 34 or 35 of the Act shall be sent, wherever practicable, at least 28 days before the date of the General Meeting. Any member who wishes to submit proposals for amendments to such Rules to be considered at the General Meeting shall submit such amendments supported by six members of the Society to the Secretary not later than 14 days before said General Meeting and the Secretary shall send notice of such duly submitted and supported amendments to each member of the Society not later than 72 hours before the said General Meeting.

Codes, etc.

Code of Conduct for Scottish Solicitors 2002

INTRODUCTION

In common with lawyers in most parts of the world, solicitors in Scotland have always been expected, by the general public and by their professional colleagues and others, to observe certain standards of professional conduct. The standards are required in order to establish the essential relationship of trust between lawyer and client, between lawyer and court, and between lawyer and other members of the legal profession.

All solicitors in Scotland require to be members of the Law Society of Scotland and for many years specific practice rules have been promulgated by the Society as a self-regulatory organisation for solicitors. Some of these rules have been included in Acts of Parliament and the Society's authority for promulgating additional practice rules comes from Parliament itself and the rules are subject to the consent of the Lord President of the Court of Session. These rules are binding upon solicitors. They stem from and have the force of statutory authority.

The Law of Scotland was and is founded upon principles which have the same validity and authority as Acts of Parliament. In the same way, in addition to the written rules governing solicitors in Scotland, there are other commonly accepted standards of conduct which solicitors are expected to meet.

The CCBE (Conseil des Barreaux de la Communaute Europeenne), comprising representatives of all the governing bodies of lawyers in the European Community, adopted in 1988 a Code of Conduct for lawyers within the community which governs conduct of lawyers in relation to activities crossing over from one country to another.

In addition, the CCBE Code is to be taken into account in all revisions of national rules with a view to the progressive harmonisation of codes and regulations governing lawyers within the European Community.

All the standards of professional conduct, whether contained in Acts of Parliament or in practice rules (written or unwritten) which are binding upon solicitors in Scotland are based upon certain values and principles which form the foundation of the profession and reflect the legal, moral and professional obligations of the solicitor to:

(a) the clients;
(b) the courts and other authorities before whom a lawyer pleads his client's cause or acts on his behalf;
(c) the public; and
(d) the legal profession in general and each fellow member of it in particular.

Should any solicitor transgress any of these rules, then such transgression may give rise to disciplinary proceedings and amount to professional misconduct or some lesser finding.

The following Code contains a statement of the basic values and principles which form the foundation of the solicitor profession. It is not intended to be an exhaustive list of all the detailed practice rules and detailed obligations of solicitors, but it is the foundation for those rules and may be referred to for guidance in assessing whether or not a solicitor's conduct meets the standard required of a member of the profession.

Code of Conduct for Scottish Solicitors 2002

Preamble

I. The function of the lawyer in society

In a society founded on respect for the rule of law lawyers fulfil a special role. Their duties do not begin and end with the faithful performance of what they are instructed to do so far as the law permits. Lawyers must serve the interests of justice as well as those whose rights and liberties they are trusted to assert and defend and it is their duty not only to plead their clients' cause but also to be their adviser.

The function of lawyers therefore imposes on them a variety of legal and moral obligations (sometimes appearing to be in conflict with each other) towards:—

(a) the clients;
(b) the courts and other authorities before whom the lawyers plead their clients' cause or act on their behalf;
(c) the public for whom the existence of a free and independent profession, bound together by respect for rules made by the profession itself, is an essential means of safeguarding human rights in face of the power of the state and other interests in society.
(d) the legal profession in general and each fellow member of it in particular.

II. The nature of rules of professional conduct

Rules of professional conduct are designed to ensure the proper performance by the lawyer of a function which is recognised as essential in all civilised societies. The failure of the lawyer to observe these rules must in the last resort result in a disciplinary sanction. The willing acceptance of those rules and of the need for disciplinary sanction ensures the highest possible standards.

The particular rules of all the Bar Associations and Law Societies in the European Community are based on identical values and in most cases demonstrate a common foundation which is also reflected in Bar Associations and Law Societies throughout the world.

The Code

1. Independence

Independence is essential to the function of solicitors in their relationships with all parties and it is the duty of all solicitors that they do not allow their independence to be impaired irrespective of whether or not the matter in which they are acting involves litigation

Independence means that solicitors must not allow themselves to be restricted in their actings on behalf of or in giving advice to their clients, nor must they allow themselves to be influenced by motives inconsistent with the principles of this Code. For example, solicitors must not compromise their professional standards in order to promote their own interests or the interests of parties other than their clients. Advice must not be given simply to ingratiate solicitors with their clients, courts or third parties. Non-independent advice may be worse than useless in that it may actively encourage someone to undertake a course of action which is not in his or her best interests.

When representing clients in court solicitors appear as agents and speak for their clients, but this does not mean that they are permitted to put forward statements or arguments which they know to be untruthful or misleading. Similarly, in relation to other services solicitors, although acting as agents, must remain independent for their advice and actings to be of value.

[1] 2. The interests of the client

Solicitors must always act in the best interests of their clients subject to preserving their independence as solicitors and to the due observance of the law, professional practice rules and the principles of good professional conduct. Solicitors must not permit their own personal interests or those of the legal profession in general to influence their actings on behalf of clients; further, their actings must be free of all political considerations

Solicitors in advising clients must not allow their advice to be influenced by the fact that a particular course of action would result in the solicitor being able to charge a higher fee. Solicitors are not permitted to "buy" or pay for business introductions, although commission may be paid to a fellow lawyer.

Solicitors should not allow themselves to be persuaded by clients to pursue matters or courses of action which the solicitors consider not to be in the clients' interests. It may be appropriate for solicitors to refuse to act where clients are not prepared to follow the advice given.

Where solicitors are consulted about matters in which they have a personal or a financial interest the position should be made clear to the clients and where appropriate solicitors should insist that the clients consult other solicitors. The Discipline Tribunal has made it clear that a solicitor must not accept instructions to draft a will containing a legacy in his favour or in favour of a business partner or an immediate family member (including a civil partner). The Tribunal recognises only two exceptions to this general rule, namely a token legacy (which must not be a share of the residue) and a will by a close member of the solicitor's family. A solicitor may make a will for his spouse or civil partner in which the solicitor is the sole or main beneficiary. A will containing a share of residue may also be made for a parent, grandparent, child, collateral, aunt or uncle (and equivalent in-laws) provided that the solicitor his spouse civil partner or child as the case may be, does not benefit more than their expectation on intestacy.

Solicitors are the agents of their clients and as such are not permitted to conceal any profit deriving from their actings for clients and must make known to their clients the source of any commission so arising.

NOTE

[1] As amended by the Professional Pracctice Committee and approved by the Council (effective February 2006).

3. Conflict

Solicitors (including firms of solicitors) shall not act for two or more clients in matters where there is a conflict of interest between the clients or for any client where there is a conflict between the interest of the client and that of the solicitor or the solicitor's firm

In considering whether or not to accept instructions from more than one party and where there is potential for a conflict arising at a later date, solicitors must have regard to any possible risk of breaches of confidentiality and impairment of independence. If, having decided to proceed, a conflict should later arise solicitors must not continue to act for all the parties and in most cases they will require to withdraw from acting for all of the parties. There may, however, be certain circumstances which would result in a significant disadvantage to one party were the solicitor not to continue to act for that party and there is no danger of any breach of confidentiality in relation to the other party. In these very special cases, the solicitor may continue to act for one party.

Solicitors must accept instructions only from clients or recognised agents authorised to give instructions on behalf of the clients; for example, persons authorised by a power of attorney or another lawyer. Where a solicitor is requested to act for more than one party in respect of the same matter, the solicitor must be reasonably satisfied that there is no apparent conflict among the interests of all the parties and that each party is indeed authorising the solicitor to act.

[1] 4. Confidentiality

The observance of client confidentiality is a fundamental duty of solicitors

This duty applies not only to the solicitors but also to their partners and staff, and the obligation is not terminated by the passage of time. This principle is so important that it is recognised by the courts as being essential to the administration of justice and to the relationship of trust which must exist between solicitor and client. However some legislation and, in special circumstances, the court may require a solicitor to break the obligation of confidentiality particularly if the client is using the solicitor to further a criminal purpose.

NOTE

[1] As amended by the Professional Practice Committee and approved by the Council (effective June 2004).

5. Provision of a professional service

Solicitors must provide adequate professional services

Solicitors are under a professional obligation to provide adequate professional services to their clients. An adequate professional service requires the legal knowledge, skill, thoroughness and preparation necessary to the matter in hand. Solicitors should not accept instructions unless they can adequately discharge these. This means that as well as being liable for damages assessable by a court of law for any act of negligence in dealing with a client's affairs, a solicitor may face disciplinary action by the Law Society in respect of a service to a client which is held to be an inadequate professional service.

[1] (a) *Solicitors must act on the basis of their clients' proper instructions or on the instructions of another solicitor who acts for the client*

Solicitors act as the agents of the clients and must have the authority of the clients for their actions.

A client may withdraw authority at any time by giving due notification to the solicitor. However, such withdrawal cannot act retrospectively.

Solicitors require to discuss with and advise their clients on the objectives of the work carried out on behalf of the clients and the means by which the objectives are to be pursued. Acceptance of instructions from clients does not constitute an endorsement or approval of the clients' political, social or moral views, activities or motivations. With the agreement of the client a solicitor may restrict the objectives and the steps to be taken consistent with the provision of an adequate professional service. A solicitor may not accept an improper instruction; for example, to assist a client in a matter which the solicitor knows to be criminal or fraudulent, but, subject to any relevant legislation, a solicitor may advise on the legal consequences of any proposed course of conduct or assist a client in determining the validity, scope or application of the law.

Solicitors are free to refuse to undertake instructions, but once acting should withdraw from a case or transaction only for good cause and where possible in such a manner that the clients' interests are not adversely affected. This obligation will not, however, prevent solicitors from exercising their rights at law to recover their justified fees and outlays incurred on behalf of their clients.

NOTE
[1] As amended by the Professional Practice Committee and approved by the Council (effective June 2004).

(b) *A solicitor shall act only in those matters where the solicitor is competent to do so*

Where a solicitor considers that the service to a client would be inadequate owing to the solicitor's lack of knowledge or experience it would be improper for the solicitor to accept instructions and agree to act.

(c) *Solicitors shall accept instructions only where the matter can be carried out with due expedition and solicitors shall maintain appropriate systems in order to ensure that the matter is dealt with effectively*

Where a solicitor considers, for example, that the service to a client would be inadequate, owing to pressure of work or the like so that the matter would not be dealt with within a reasonable period of time, it would be

 [NEXT TEXT PAGE IS F 1005]

improper for the solicitor to accept instructions and agree to act.

(d) *Solicitors are required to exercise the level of skill appropriate to the matter*

In deciding whether or not to accept instructions from a client, and in the carrying out of those instructions, a solicitor must have regard to the nature and complexity of the matter in hand and apply to the work the appropriate level of professional skills.

[1] (e) *Solicitors shall communicate effectively with their clients and others*

Solicitors shall provide to their clients in writing at the earliest practical opportunity information in relation to:

1 The work to be carried out by the solicitor
2 The fees and outgoings to be charged by the solicitor or basis upon which such fees and outgoings are to be charged, such as the hourly rate to be charged. If the basis is Legal Advice and Assistance or Legal Aid, the contribution payable (if any) and the consequences of preserving or recovering property should be referred to as should a legally aided client's liability for the expenses of his/her opponent.
3 The identity of the person or persons by whom the work will be carried out.
4 The identity of the person to whom the client should refer in the event of there being any dissatisfaction in relation to the work;

unless in exceptional circumstances it is considered inappropriate to do so.

Clients who provide a regular flow of instruction of the same type of business and subject matter should receive such a communication whenever the terms previously communicated are amended.

Solicitors are required to try to ensure that their communications with their clients and others on behalf of their clients are effective. This includes providing clients with relevant information regarding the matter in hand and the actions taken on their behalf.

Solicitors should advise their clients of any significant development in relation to their case or transaction and explain matters to the extent reasonably necessary to permit informed decisions by clients regarding the instructions which require to be given by them. Information should be clear and comprehensive and where necessary or appropriate confirmed in writing. In particular solicitors should advise clients in writing when it becomes known that the cost of work will materially exceed any estimate that has been given and should also advise the client when the limit of the original estimate is being approached.

The duty to communicate effectively extends to include the obligation on solicitors to account to their clients in respect of all relevant monies passing through the solicitor's hands

NOTE

[1] The Council approved these amendments to the Code of Conduct, with effect from February 1999.

(f) *Solicitors shall not act, nor shall they cease to act for clients summarily or without just cause, in a manner which would prejudice the course of justice*

Where the matter in issue involves the courts or otherwise involves the administration of justice, a solicitor must have regard to the course of justice in considering whether or not to cease acting on behalf of a client. The solicitor may not simply and suddenly decide that it would no longer be appropriate to act for the client.

(g) *Solicitors shall comply with the specific rules issued from time to time by the Law Society of Scotland*

Subject to the consent of the Lord President of the Court of Session the Law Society is empowered to issue specific practice rules regarding the conduct of solicitors and other matters affecting the affairs of clients. All solicitors must comply with these rules. A list of the titles of such rules currently in force is annexed to this Code.

6. Professional fees

The fees charged by solicitors shall be fair and reasonable in all the circumstances

Factors to be considered in relation to the reasonableness of the fee include:—

(a) the importance of the matter to the client;
(b) the amount or value of any money, property or transaction involved;
(c) the complexity of the matter or the difficulty or novelty of the question raised;
(d) the skill, labour, specialised knowledge and responsibility involved on the part of the solicitor;
(e) the time expended;
(f) the length, number and importance of any documents or other papers prepared or perused; and
(g) the place where and the circumstances in which the services or any part thereof are rendered and the degree of urgency involved.

7. Trust and personal integrity

Solicitors must act honestly at all times and in such a way as to put their personal integrity beyond question

Solicitors' actions and personal behaviour must be consistent with the need for mutual trust and confidence among clients, the courts, the public and fellow lawyers. For example, solicitors must observe the Accounts Rules which govern the manner in which clients' funds may be held by solicitors and which are designed to ensure that clients' monies are safeguarded. Solicitors who are dishonest in a matter not directly affecting their clients are nonetheless guilty of professional misconduct.

8. Relations with the courts

Solicitors must never knowingly give false or misleading information to the court and must maintain due respect and courtesy towards the court while honourably pursuing the interests of their clients

For example, it would be improper for a solicitor to put forward on behalf of a client a statement of events or a legal argument which the solicitor knew to be false or misleading. Accordingly, if a client requests a solicitor to put forward a false story the solicitor must refuse to do so.

In the course of investigation a solicitor must not do or say anything which could affect evidence or induce a witness, a party to an action, or an accused person to do otherwise than give in evidence a truthful and honest statement of that person's recollections.

9. Relations between lawyers

Solicitors shall not knowingly mislead colleagues or where they have given their word go back on it

A solicitor must act with fellow solicitors in a manner consistent with persons having mutual trust and confidence in each other.

It is in the public interest and for the benefit of clients and the administration of justice that there be a corporate professional spirit based upon relationships of trust and co-operation between solicitors. For example, the settlement of property transactions in Scotland is facilitated by the underlying trust between solicitors. A specific example of this is the payment of the price by a cheque drawn by the purchaser's solicitor on a joint stock bank in favour of the seller's solicitor. Were the purchaser's solicitor to instruct the bank to stop payment of the cheque such action could amount to professional misconduct.

It is not permissible for a solicitor to communicate about any item of business with a person whom the solicitor knows to be represented by another solicitor. A solicitor in such circumstances must always communicate with the solicitor acting for that person and not go behind the solicitor's back.

The rules governing the advertising of solicitors' services take into account the need to maintain mutual trust and confidence, while permitting solicitors to market their services effectively and to compete with one another.

10. Civic professionalism

Solicitors have a duty not only to act as guardians of national liberties, but also to seek improvements in the law and the legal system

It is the striving by solicitors for improvement both in general terms and in relation to the individual needs of a particular client that prevents the law and legal services "from degenerating into a trade or mere mechanical act" (Lord Cooper, *Selected Papers*, Edinburgh 1957, p. 77). Many solicitors fulfil this obligation through working on the many committees of the Law Society of Scotland, including those not only commenting and advising on proposed legislative changes and areas of law reform but also recommending and promoting new ideas for reform. Others are involved at the highest level with other reforming bodies and many seek public appointment, both locally and at a national level.

This duty extends beyond the issues of freedom and liberty, through the entire system of law, to the day-to-day legal services provided by solicitors.

11. Discrimination

Solicitors must not discriminate on grounds of race, sex, sexual orientation, religion or disability in their professional dealings with clients, employees or other lawyers

Legislation already provides that it is unlawful to discriminate against individuals either directly or indirectly in respect of their race, sex or marital status. However, solicitors should be prepared to observe not only the letter but also the spirit of the anti-discrimination legislation in dealings with clients, employees and others. In particular, solicitors should ensure that within their own firms, there is no discrimination in employment policy and that opportunities for promotion and advancement are open on an equal basis to all employees. In addition, solicitors should give active consideration to opportunities for the disabled.

[1] Code of Conduct for Criminal Work

NOTE

[1] Reproduced with kind permission of the Law Society of Scotland.

The following Code contains a statement of good practice for those solicitors conducting criminal work. It does not have the status of a Practice Rule but may be referred to for guidance in assessing whether a solicitor's conduct meets the standard required of a member of the profession.

Article 1—Seeking Business

(1) A solicitor shall seek or accept only those instructions which emanate from the client properly given and should not accept instructions given as a result of an inducement or subject to any improper constraint or condition.

GUIDANCE NOTE

This statement of good practice is a reminder that a solicitor is an officer of the court and as such has obligations and duties to the Court. It is a reminder that a solicitor should always act properly when dealing with criminal law work.

It is essential that a solicitor should at all times remain independent of the client and that the solicitor should be free to give appropriate legal advice. Accordingly no instructions should be accepted in circumstances where it could be alleged that inducements have been offered in exchange for instructions. No instructions should be accepted in circumstances where those instructions are subject for whatever reason to restrictions or constraints which compromise the solicitors freedom to give appropriate independent legal advice. It follows that a client should not be considered as a "friend" and that the solicitor must always remain "at arms length" from the client. This will ensure that both the client and the court can be confident that the advice tendered by the solicitor is impartial and independent.

A solicitor should accept instructions only from the client directly and not from a third party on behalf of the client. There may be circumstances in which a solicitor is asked by the family or a friend of the accused person to visit the accused in custody. It is the duty of every solicitor to check with the police station to ascertain if the person in custody has requested another solicitor or the duty solicitor. If the person in custody has indeed requested the services of another solicitor or the duty solicitor, then the solicitor contacted by the family or friend may not visit the police station.

Moreover, instructions must come directly from the person detained and not by virtue of the police arranging for a specific solicitor to be contacted who is unknown to and has not been requested by the accused.

Any instructions given as a result of an inducement by a third party on the solicitor's behalf must not be accepted. A solicitor will be deemed to be strictly liable for the actions of third parties who contact potential clients and any third party who contacts potential clients shall be deemed to have acted on the instructions of the solicitor whether or not the solicitor is instructed as a result of the third party's approach. If the client's co-accused is instructing a solicitor contact must be made through that solicitor. All reasonable steps must be taken to ascertain the identity of the co-accused's solicitor.

Solicitors are reminded of the terms of Section 31 of The Legal Aid (Scotland) Act 1986. Any contract of agency between a solicitor and a client which is based upon any inducement may be illegal and may be subject to action in the criminal or civil courts. Such contracts may also form the basis of a complaint of professional misconduct and may lead to disqualification in terms of Section 31.

Article 2—Conflict of Interest

(2) A solicitor should not accept instructions from more than one accused in the same matter.

GUIDANCE NOTE

This statement reflects the awareness which solicitors have always had of the obvious potential conflict of interest that will arise when instructions are accepted from more than one accused person in the same case, even though that conflict may not arise and the defence is common to all accused. Nevertheless, solicitors should not place themselves in the position whereby they may obtain information confidential to the defence of one accused which at the same time may be detrimental to the defence of another.

Accordingly when it becomes apparent to the solicitor that he has received instructions from two or more parties in the same case a solicitor may accept instructions from one of the accused and any others must be told immediately that separate representation must be sought.

Solicitors are also reminded that great care must be taken in situations where one of the solicitor's clients gives evidence against another client of that solicitor. The client, who is acting as a witness, is entitled to have his confidentiality respected as against the interests of the accused. In some situations, such as where the accused is incriminating or attacking the character of the client, who is a witness, there will be a conflict of interest and the solicitor should not act.

A solicitor should not apply for a Legal Aid Certificate for more than one accused person in any matter. However, a duty solicitor should responsibly carry out his duties under the Legal Aid scheme and be aware of the terms of this statement.

A solicitor may suggest that an accused seeks representation from a particular solicitor but that alternative solicitor must be based within the same jurisdiction as the accused. However the choice of a solicitor always lies with the accused person and a solicitor must always ask an accused if he wishes a particular solicitor to be instructed before a recommendation can be made.

Article 3—Preparation and Conduct of Criminal Cases

(3) A solicitor is under a duty to prepare and conduct criminal cases by carrying out work which is actually and reasonably necessary and having due regard to economy.

GUIDANCE NOTE

It is essential at each stage of the conduct of a criminal case that the necessary preparation is undertaken timeously. It is essential that a solicitor should use his best endeavours to discover all relevant information and evidence relating both to the Crown case and any substantive case for the defence.

The solicitor must remember that his primary duties are to the client and the court and ensure that the case is properly prepared and there is no prejudice to the client.

Every solicitor should carry out these duties in a responsible and professional manner. With these duties uppermost in mind, the solicitor must not view criminal cases only as a means of financial enrichment.

For the purposes of cases which are legally aided, this statement is declaratory of Regulation 7(1) of the Criminal Legal Aid (Scotland) (Fees) Regulations 1989. Regulation 7(1) states that "subject to the provisions of Regulations 4, 5, 6 and 9 and paragraph (2) of this Regulation, a solicitor shall be allowed such amount of fees as shall be determined to be reasonable remuneration for work actually and reasonably done, and travel and waiting time actually and reasonably undertaken or incurred, due regard being had to economy".

When requested, files and information should be provided to the Scottish Legal Aid Board.

Abuse of the Legal Aid system may be fraudulent and may be considered as professional misconduct and may lead to disqualification under Section 31 of the Legal Aid (Scotland) Act 1986.

Any complaints can be dealt with in terms of Section 31 of the Legal Aid (Scotland) Act 1986.

Article 4—Identification of Solicitors

(4) A solicitor who seeks access to any party who is in custody should have in his possession a form of identification provided by the Law Society of Scotland and should exhibit this upon request.

GUIDANCE NOTE

This statement is designed to prohibit unqualified employees or individuals from attending meetings with persons in custody. It will ensure not only that impersonation of solicitors or trainees is made more difficult but also that only those persons qualified to provide independent legal advice are granted access. Acceptable forms of confirmation of identity include the production of a valid identification card issued by the Law Society of Scotland; of a valid CCBE card provided by the Law Society of Scotland or of a valid and current practising certificate together with a form of visual identification.

Article 5—Custody Visits

(5) Only a solicitor or trainee solicitor who has been instructed to do so may visit the client in custody.

GUIDANCE NOTE

This Statement restricts access to a person in custody in a police office, prison and cell area.

There are occasions when a solicitor has taken instructions from the family or friend of an accused and has then visited a person in custody. It is the duty of every solicitor to check with the police station to ascertain if the person in custody has requested another solicitor or duty solicitor. If the person in custody has indeed requested the services of another solicitor or the duty solicitor, then the solicitor contacted by the family or friend may not visit the police station.

Moreover, instructions must come directly from the person detained and not by virtue of the police arranging for a specific solicitor to be contacted who is unknown to and has not been requested by the accused.

Article 6—Property to Persons in Custody

(6) A business card and legal documents should be the only items given by a solicitor to a person in custody.

GUIDANCE NOTE

It has become apparent that certain solicitors have attended to the so called "needs" of their clients in custody by providing them with cigarettes, newspapers, meals, access to the solicitor's mobile phone and money. Actings of this sort may be a contravention of Section 41(1) of the Prisons (Scotland) Act 1989 which forbids certain forms of donation. In addition, this statement shall include the giving to family or friends of the person in custody any items for onward transmission.

Article 7—Legal Aid Mandates

(7) All legal aid mandates requesting the transfer of papers and legal aid relating to a criminal matter shall be completed and executed by the assisted person in the form agreed by the Scottish Legal Aid Board and the Law

Society of Scotland.

GUIDANCE NOTE

The matter is governed by the Criminal Legal Aid (Scotland) Regulations 1996, paragraph 17(3), which states "where an assisted person desires that a solicitor, other than the solicitor presently nominated by him shall act for him, he shall apply to the Board for authority to nominate another specified solicitor to act for him and shall inform the Board of the reason for his application; and the Board, if it is satisfied that there is good reason for the application, may grant the application".

It seems clear from a plain construction of this Regulation that changes of agency where the client is legally aided in a criminal case can only take place if the Board gives the client authority to nominate another specified solicitor. Until the Board gives its authority the client cannot instruct another solicitor unless he wishes to do so without the benefit of legal aid, which fact should be notified to the Board.

Therefore the chronology of transfers of agency in criminal cases should be (1) the client approaches his proposed new solicitor to ascertain if he is willing to act; (2) client applies to Board for authority to transfer the agency; (3) Board grants authority; (4) client instructs new solicitor; (5) new solicitor serves mandate on previous solicitor.

The Board's authority to transfer must ante-date any mandate.

The Statement would solve many issues including inducements to transfer agency and "mandate wars". Adoption of this interpretation would of course mean that legally aided clients and fee paying clients will not be treated precisely equally. However, that objection has to be seen in the light of the need to comply with the Regulations which effectively impose a statutory suspensive condition on any mandate and the requirement that solicitors will require to inform a transferring client that instructions cannot be accepted until the Regulations are complied with.

Any complaints about conduct under this section can be dealt with in terms of section 31 of the Legal Aid (Scotland) Act 1986.

Article 8—Consultation with clients at liberty

(8) A solicitor should not consult with a client, who is at liberty unless the consultation takes place in (1) the solicitor's office; (2) a court; (3) a hospital; or (4) the locus; a solicitor may exceptionally attend the house of a client who is unable to attend the solicitor's office due to illness.

GUIDANCE NOTE

The solicitor should not visit a client within his home unless it is impossible for the client to attend the offices of the solicitor through ill health.

A solicitor leaves himself open to various allegations and indeed risks if he should attend at the home of a client. All solicitors should be aware that there is a risk. For example a solicitor could be within a house which contains drugs or stolen goods.

It will not always be possible to consult with an accused within a solicitor's own office. However, such consultations should take place within a similar office environment, such as the interview rooms within a Court building. However, it is accepted that there will be occasions when it is not possible or appropriate to interview a client within an office environment, for example when the client is in hospital. The onus is on a solicitor to justify an interview at any other place if called upon to do so. The geography and rural nature of Scotland will be taken into account.

Article 9—Expenses

(9) No payments in money or kind should be made to an accused person, a member of the accused person's family or potential witnesses.

GUIDANCE NOTE

The only payments which a solicitor is entitled to make to an accused person, to members of his family or to witnesses are the legitimate expenses paid to witnesses who were cited to appear at Court on behalf of the defence. It is appropriate for a solicitor to advance travel vouchers to a witness who shall be travelling a significant distance.

Any payment of expenses made by a solicitor should be properly recorded and vouched.

Article 10—Defence Witnesses

(10) Only those witnesses relevant to a case should be cited to attend court.

GUIDANCE NOTE

Ideally, a witness should be interviewed before citation. A solicitor must take all reasonable steps to obtain directly from a witness the potential evidence in a case. It is accepted that this is not always possible and indeed a solicitor could leave himself open to criticism and complaint if he should not cite a witness when he has been specifically instructed to do so by an accused person. Nevertheless, a solicitor must at all times be in a position to justify the citation of all witnesses in a case.

Defence witnesses should be cited sufficiently far in advance of the Trial Diet to give them adequate warning of the requirement to attend court. Where possible, witnesses should be cited prior to the Intermediate Diet in order to ascertain at that stage whether there is any difficulty about the defence witnesses attendance at court for the Trial Diet. Common courtesy demands that defence witnesses should be given adequate notice of their requirement to attend court as witnesses.

In providing a citation, a solicitor should advise the witness of their right to claim legitimate expenses. These include travelling to and from Court. Neither witnesses nor indeed an accused person should be transported to Court by a solicitor.

In recent times it has been suggested that some persons with no involvement in a case have been cited to attend court only to provide these persons with expenses. Additionally, it has been asserted that parties have been brought to Court from custody, who have no relevance whatsoever to the case but who are cited simply to allow them to meet other prisoners at Court. Such actions cannot be tolerated.

Solicitors should make a point of speaking to defence witnesses at court in order, as a matter of courtesy, to advise them of the court procedure and the likely timetabling for the case in respect of which they have been cited.

Solicitors should advise their clients that they as professional persons ultimately take the decision as to which defence witnesses require to be cited. Solicitors are the judges of whether or not a particular witness's evidence is relevant. In addition, solicitors should ensure that legitimate expenses claimed by defence witnesses are paid promptly. Witnesses of course require to be advised that any claim for expenses require to be properly vouched.

A solicitor should keep a contemporaneous record of his actings and financial dealings in terms of this Code and provide this if so requested by the Law Society of Scotland.

Article 11—Sensitive material and the client

(11.1) A solicitor should not show a client sensitive material related to his case at all, other than in circumstances where the solicitor is present and it is possible to exercise adequate supervision to prevent the client retaining possession of the material or making a copy of it.

(11.2) A solicitor should not give a client for retention by him, even on a temporary basis, copies of witness precognitions; witness statements; productions or like documents relating to his case, unless there are exceptional circumstances justifying such a course in a particular case. If the solicitor

believes that such exceptional circumstances exist he should, when giving the items to the client, explain that the items must be retained securely by the client; must be kept confidential; must not be shown to others, let alone released to others; must not be copied and must be returned to the solicitor by a fixed date, which must be as soon as possible having regard to the circumstances justifying giving the items to the client in the first place.

(11.3) "Sensitive material" for the purposes of Article 11.1 above includes—

- *(a) a precognition or statement of a victim of a sexual offence;*
- *(b) a photograph or pseudo photograph of any such victim or a deceased victim;*
- *(c) a medical or other report or statement relating to the physical condition of any such victim or a deceased victim;*
- *(d) any document, other than a document served on the client by the Crown or by a co-accused, containing the addresses or telephone numbers of witnesses or their relative/friends or information from which their addresses and telephone numbers could be deduced.*

GUIDANCE NOTE

From time to time the Society has been asked to give its views of the practice of giving to accused persons copies of the precognitions or statements of witnesses and of other documents associated with the accused's case.

In the vast majority of criminal cases the accused is in receipt of Legal Aid and it has been judicially declared that the accused has no proprietorial claim on the case papers. These belong to the solicitor. Where solicitors have sought to justify the practice of giving copies of precognitions and other documents to an accused, they have usually done so by seeking to rely on the duty which a solicitor has to communicate information to a client and thereafter to take instructions in respect of that information.

The view of the Society is that a solicitor should not give copies of precognitions/statements or documents to an accused, unless there are exceptional circumstances justifying a departure from this general practice. Exceptional circumstances might include a case of particular length or complexity, necessitating giving the accused copies of documents to allow the formulation of a response. Even in this situation, the solicitor should only allow the client limited controlled access on the clear understanding that the client must keep the documents confidential and as to how long they may be kept.

In the view of the Society, under no circumstances should a client ever be given possession of sensitive documents such as precognitions and statements of victims in sexual cases, medical or post mortem reports, explicit photographs, or any documents which might disclose the private address or telephone numbers of witnesses.

There are unfortunate and worrying examples of problems which can arise if the guidelines are not observed: e.g. copies of witness statements could be circulated in the public domain, leading to witnesses being intimidated; the statements of victims of sexual crimes could be used as a form of pornography within prison; an extract from a firearms register complete with addresses and types of weapon has been circulated in a prison.

In addition, those solicitors who observe best practice find themselves coming under pressure from clients who indicate that instructions will be withdrawn if they are not provided with copy precognitions.

Article 12—Retention of Papers

(12.1) In general terms, the solicitor should be aware of the general guidelines on retention and destruction of papers as issued from time to time by the Law Society of Scotland.

(12.2) In murder cases and other cases involving life imprisonment, the papers should be retained indefinitely.

(12.3) In other Solemn and in any Summary case, the papers should be retained for 3 years.

As a general rule, a solicitor might regard it as good practice in every case to retain indefinitely a copy of the Complaint or Indictment and a copy of the Legal Aid Certificate.

GUIDANCE NOTE

Another issue associated with case papers is the question of the length of time such papers should be retained once a case has been concluded and how such papers should ultimately be destroyed if at all.

The options for retention are—

(1) indefinitely;
(2) destruction after a fixed period;
(3) destruction at the discretion of the solicitor; or
(4) a combination of the above, depending on the nature of the case and the likelihood or risk that reference to the original case papers will be necessary.

The Society is conscious of the consequences of recommending retention of too many papers for too long, having regard to the difficulties of office storage and the expense of "off-site" storage. On the other hand, certain types of cases involve offences of such gravity, complexity or high public profile, that the possibility of issues arising in future years is a real one. Solicitors should be aware of the existence of the Scottish Criminal Cases Review Commission and for the need to retain files where solicitors believe that there is a possibility that it will be of future importance to the client. Other offences may have sentence implications in the short to mid-term: e.g. petitions for restoration of a driving licence after disqualification; reimposing the unexpired portion of a sentence after re-offending. Solemn cases might be expected to throw up more difficulties than Summary. In legally aided cases, solicitors are reminded that in terms of the Code of Practice in relation to Criminal Legal Assistance, issued by the Scottish Legal Aid Board, records shall be maintained and accessible for a period 3 years from the date of payment of the relevant account by the Board.

Destruction of case papers

Solicitors should note that when case papers are being destroyed, it is vital that this is done in a comprehensive, secure and confidential way. If the solicitor does not destroy the papers personally, then they should be destroyed by a suitably qualified commercial firm.

Article 13—Precognition of Witnesses

(13) When carrying out precognition of witnesses, whether personally, through directly employed staff, or through external precognition agents, the nominated solicitor or instructing solicitor has responsibility for the manner in which contact is made with the witnesses and the manner in which the witnesses are actually precognosced. In particular, it is the duty of the solicitor to ensure that any matters associated with the witness of which he is aware which would affect the taking of the precognition or the mode of contact, such as age, disability or other vulnerable status, are taken into account by him and communicated to any precognition agent.

GUIDANCE NOTE

When precognoscing witnesses, a solicitor has responsibility to ensure that this is done in a way which is as sympathetic as possible to the needs of the witness. A solicitor does not discharge this responsibility simply by passing to a precognition agent a copy of the list of witnesses and asking the precognition agent to commence precognoscing them. Where a solicitor is aware of information about witnesses which would affect the way in which they ought to be contacted or the way in which they should be precognosced, such as that they are children, that they are disabled in some way or anything else, the solicitor has a duty to ensure that the precognition agent is equipped with enough information about the case to carry out the precognition work properly. A solicitor who fails to ensure that the precognition agent is aware of such sensitive information which is known to the solicitor does not thereafter avoid responsibility for distress or inconvenience etc. which is caused to the witness by a failure to observe the particular characteristics of the witness.

Every witness should be contacted in writing by the solicitor in advance with effective information about the process of precognition. This should include information about to whom to complain, if things are perceived to go wrong. There should be no "cold calling".

Notice should be given as to who will take the precognition and due regard should be had to the venue and timing for the convenience of the witness.

It should be pointed out that the witness may have a friend or supporter present, provided that person is not also a witness in the case under investigation.

Care should be taken with vulnerable witnesses or witnesses who might be subjected to intimidation. The nature of the charge should be considered and it might be appropriate to precognosce the reporting officer with a view to obtaining information about witnesses prior to precognoscing them.

It may be that in certain cases the gender of the precognition taker should be considered. Crimes of indecency may, at least as far as victims are concerned, be better precognosced by precognoscers of the same sex.

Prior to the taking of the precognition, the witness should be able to satisfy himself that the precognition taker is who he says he is. Those instructed by solicitors to obtain precognitions should carry identification and a letter of authority from the instructing solicitor.

In cases involving more than one accused, there will obviously be separate and different interests but liaison between solicitors can very often result in a witness only having to undergo one session rather than a number of separate sessions. Where possible, multiple precognitions of civilian witnesses by each accused should be avoided unless this is absolutely essential in the interests of justice and of the accused.

The witness should be given a copy of these guidelines.

Other Rules of Professional Conduct

A solicitor should at all times comply with good professional practice and the ethics of the solicitors' profession as set out in practice rules, other codes of conduct and textbooks on professional ethics.

GUIDANCE NOTE

The essence of professional ethics is such that it cannot be codified. Many texts provide guidance on the professional behaviour expected of solicitors. Solicitors have a duty to inform themselves of these texts and to approach their work in a manner consistent with the principles of good ethical practice. A solicitor acting outwith the terms of this Code may be called upon to justify his conduct.

Code of Conduct for European Lawyers

This Code of Conduct for European Lawyers was originally adopted at the CCBE Plenary Session held on 28 October 1988, and subsequently amended during the CCBE Plenary Sessions on 28 November 1998, 6 December 2002 and 19 May 2006. The Code includes an Explanatory Memorandum which was updated during the CCBE Plenary Session on 19 May 2006.

CONTENTS

1. Preamble

1.1. The Function of the Lawyer in Society

In a society founded on respect for the rule of law the lawyer fulfils a special role. The lawyer's duties do not begin and end with the faithful performance of what he or she is instructed to do so far as the law permits. A lawyer must serve the interests of justice as well as those whose rights and liberties he or she is trusted to assert and defend and it is the lawyer's duty not only to plead the client's cause but to be the client's adviser. Respect for the lawyer's professional function is an essential condition for the rule of law and democracy in society.

A lawyer's function therefore lays on him or her a variety of legal and moral obligations (sometimes appearing to be in conflict with each other) towards:

— the client;
— the courts and other authorities before whom the lawyer pleads the client's cause or acts on the client's behalf;
— the legal profession in general and each fellow member of it in particular;
— the public for whom the existence of a free and independent profession, bound together by respect for rules made by the profession itself, is an essential means of safeguarding human rights in face of the power of the state and other interests in society.

1.2. The Nature of Rules of Professional Conduct

1.2.1. Rules of professional conduct are designed through their willing acceptance by those to whom they apply to ensure the proper performance by the lawyer of a function which is recognised as essential in all civilised societies. The failure of the lawyer to observe these rules may result in disciplinary sanctions.

1.2.2. The particular rules of each Bar or Law Society arise from its own traditions. They are adapted to the organisation and sphere of activity of the profession in the Member State concerned and to its judicial and administrative procedures and to its national legislation. It is neither possible nor desirable that they should be taken out of their context nor that an attempt should be made to give general application to rules which are inherently incapable of such application.

The particular rules of each Bar and Law Society nevertheless are based on the same values and in most cases demonstrate a common foundation.

1.3. The Purpose of the Code

1.3.1. The continued integration of the European Union and European Economic Area and the increasing frequency of the cross-border activities of lawyers within the European Economic Area have made necessary in the public interest the statement of common rules which apply to all lawyers from the European Economic Area whatever Bar or Law Society they belong to in relation to their cross-border practice. A particular purpose of the statement of those rules is to mitigate the difficulties which result from the application of "double deontology", notably as set out in Articles 4 and 7.2 of Directive 77/249/EEC and Articles 6 and 7 of Directive 98/5/EC.

1.3.2. The organisations representing the legal profession through the CCBE propose that the rules codified in the following articles:

— be recognised at the present time as the expression of a consensus of all the Bars and Law Societies of the European Union and European Economic Area;
— be adopted as enforceable rules as soon as possible in accordance with national or EEA procedures in relation to the cross-border

activities of the lawyer in the European Union and European Economic Area;

— be taken into account in all revisions of national rules of deontology or professional practice with a view to their progressive harmonisation.

They further express the wish that the national rules of deontology or professional practice be interpreted and applied whenever possible in a way consistent with the rules in this Code.

After the rules in this Code have been adopted as enforceable rules in relation to a lawyer's cross-border activities the lawyer will remain bound to observe the rules of the Bar or Law Society to which he or she belongs to the extent that they are consistent with the rules in this Code.

1.4. Field of Application *Ratione Personae*

This Code shall apply to lawyers as they are defined by Directive 77/249/EEC and by Directive 98/5/EC and to lawyers of the Observer Members of the CCBE.

1.5. Field of Application *Ratione Materiae*

Without prejudice to the pursuit of a progressive harmonisation of rules of deontology or professional practice which apply only internally within a Member State, the following rules shall apply to the cross-border activities of the lawyer within the European Union and the European Economic Area. Cross-border activities shall mean:

(a) all professional contacts with lawyers of Member States other than the lawyer's own;

(b) the professional activities of the lawyer in a Member State other than his or her own, whether or not the lawyer is physically present in that Member State.

1.6. Definitions

In this Code:

"Member State" means a member state of the European Union or any other state whose legal profession is included in Article 1.4.

"Home Member State" means the Member State where the lawyer acquired the right to bear his or her professional title.

"Host Member State" means any other Member State where the lawyer carries on cross-border activities.

"Competent Authority" means the professional organisation(s) or authority(ies) of the Member State concerned responsible for the laying down of rules of professional conduct and the administration of discipline of lawyers.

"Directive 77/249/EEC" means Council Directive 77/249/EEC of 22 March 1977 to facilitate the effective exercise by lawyers of freedom to provide services.

"Directive 98/5/EC" means Directive 98/5/EC of the European Parliament and of the Council of 16 February 1998 to facilitate practice of the profession of lawyer on a permanent basis in a Member State other than that in which the qualification was obtained.

2. General Principles

2.1. Independence

2.1.1. The many duties to which a lawyer is subject require the lawyer's absolute independence, free from all other influence, especially such as may arise from his or her personal interests or external pressure. Such independence is as necessary to trust in the process of justice as the impartiality of the judge. A lawyer must therefore avoid any impairment of his or her independence and be careful not to compromise his or her professional standards in order to please the client, the court or third parties.

2.1.2. This independence is necessary in non-contentious matters as well as in litigation. Advice given by a lawyer to the client has no value if the lawyer gives it only to ingratiate him- or herself, to serve his or her personal interests or in response to outside pressure.

2.2. Trust and Personal Integrity

Relationships of trust can only exist if a lawyer's personal honour, honesty and integrity are beyond doubt. For the lawyer these traditional virtues are professional obligations.

2.3. Confidentiality

2.3.1. It is of the essence of a lawyer's function that the lawyer should be told by his or her client things which the client would not tell to others, and that the lawyer should be the recipient of other information on a basis of confidence. Without the certainty of confidentiality there cannot be trust. Confidentiality is therefore a primary and fundamental right and duty of the lawyer.

The lawyer's obligation of confidentiality serves the interest of the administration of justice as well as the interest of the client. It is therefore entitled to special protection by the State.

2.3.2. A lawyer shall respect the confidentiality of all information that becomes known to the lawyer in the course of his or her professional activity.

2.3.3. The obligation of confidentiality is not limited in time.

2.3.4. A lawyer shall require his or her associates and staff and anyone engaged by him or her in the course of providing professional services to observe the same obligation of confidentiality.

2.4. Respect for the Rules of Other Bars and Law Societies

When practising cross-border, a lawyer from another Member State may be bound to comply with the professional rules of the Host Member State. Lawyers have a duty to inform themselves as to the rules which will affect them in the performance of any particular activity.

Member organisations of the CCBE are obliged to deposit their codes of conduct at the Secretariat of the CCBE so that any lawyer can get hold of the copy of the current code from the Secretariat.

2.5. Incompatible Occupations

2.5.1. In order to perform his or her functions with due independence and in a manner which is consistent with his or her duty to participate in the administration of justice a lawyer may be prohibited from undertaking certain occupations.

2.5.2. A lawyer who acts in the representation or the defence of a client in legal proceedings or before any public authorities in a Host Member State shall there observe the rules regarding incompatible occupations as they are applied to lawyers of the Host Member State.

2.5.3. A lawyer established in a Host Member State in which he or she wishes to participate directly in commercial or other activities not connected with the practice of the law shall respect the rules regarding forbidden or incompatible occupations as they are applied to lawyers of that Member State.

2.6. Personal Publicity

2.6.1. A lawyer is entitled to inform the public about his or her services provided that the information is accurate and not misleading, and respectful of the obligation of confidentiality and other core values of the profession.

2.6.2. Personal publicity by a lawyer in any form of media such as by press, radio, television, by electronic commercial communications or otherwise is permitted to the extent it complies with the requirements of 2.6.1.

2.7. The Client's Interest

Subject to due observance of all rules of law and professional conduct, a lawyer must always act in the best interests of the client and must put those interests before the lawyer's own interests or those of fellow members of the legal profession.

2.8. Limitation of Lawyer's Liability towards the Client

To the extent permitted by the law of the Home Member State and the Host Member State, the lawyer may limit his or her liabilities towards the client in accordance with the professional rules to which the lawyer is subject.

3. Relations with Clients

3.1. Acceptance and Termination of Instructions

3.1.1. A lawyer shall not handle a case for a party except on that party's instructions. The lawyer may, however, act in a case in which he or she has been instructed by another lawyer acting for the party or where the case has been assigned to him or her by a competent body.

The lawyer should make reasonable efforts to ascertain the identity, competence and authority of the person or body who instructs him or her when the specific circumstances show that the identity, competence and authority are uncertain.

3.1.2. A lawyer shall advise and represent the client promptly, conscientiously and diligently. The lawyer shall undertake personal responsibility for the discharge of the client's instructions and shall keep the client informed as to the progress of the matter with which the lawyer has been entrusted.

3.1.3. A lawyer shall not handle a matter which the lawyer knows or ought to know he or she is not competent to handle, without co-operating with a lawyer who is competent to handle it.

A lawyer shall not accept instructions unless he or she can discharge those instructions promptly having regard to the pressure of other work.

3.1.4. A lawyer shall not be entitled to exercise his or her right to withdraw from a case in such a way or in such circumstances that the client may be unable to find other legal assistance in time to prevent prejudice being suffered by the client.

3.2. Conflict of Interest

3.2.1. A lawyer may not advise, represent or act on behalf of two or more clients in the same matter if there is a conflict, or a significant risk of a conflict, between the interests of those clients.

3.2.2. A lawyer must cease to act for both or all of the clients concerned when a conflict of interests arises between those clients and also whenever there is a risk of a breach of confidence or where the lawyer's independence may be impaired.

3.2.3. A lawyer must also refrain from acting for a new client if there is a risk of breach of a confidence entrusted to the lawyer by a former client or if the knowledge which the lawyer possesses of the affairs of the former client would give an undue advantage to the new client.

3.2.4. Where lawyers are practising in association, paragraphs 3.2.1 to 3.2.3 above shall apply to the association and all its members.

3.3. *Pactum de Quota Litis*

3.3.1. A lawyer shall not be entitled to make a *pactum de quota litis*.

3.3.2. By "*pactum de quota litis*" is meant an agreement between a lawyer and the client entered into prior to final conclusion of a matter to which the client is a party, by virtue of which the client undertakes to pay the lawyer a share of the result regardless of whether this is represented by a sum of money or by any other benefit achieved by the client upon the conclusion of the matter.

3.3.3. "*Pactum de quota litis*" does not include an agreement that fees be charged in proportion to the value of a matter handled by the lawyer if this is in accordance with an officially approved fee scale or under the control of the Competent Authority having jurisdiction over the lawyer.

3.4. Regulation of Fees

A fee charged by a lawyer shall be fully disclosed to the client, shall be fair and reasonable, and shall comply with the law and professional rules to which the lawyer is subject.

3.5. Payment on Account

If a lawyer requires a payment on account of his or her fees and/or disbursements such payment should not exceed a reasonable estimate of the fees and probable disbursements involved.

Failing such payment, a lawyer may withdraw from the case or refuse to handle it, but subject always to paragraph 3.1.4 above.

3.6. Fee Sharing with Non-Lawyers

3.6.1. A lawyer may not share his or her fees with a person who is not a lawyer except where an association between the lawyer and the other person is permitted by the laws and the professional rules to which the lawyer is subject.

3.6.2. The provisions of 3.6.1 above shall not preclude a lawyer from paying a fee, commission or other compensation to a deceased lawyer's heirs or to a retired lawyer in respect of taking over the deceased or retired lawyer's practice.

3.7. Cost of Litigation and Availability of Legal Aid

3.7.1. The lawyer should at all times strive to achieve the most cost effective resolution of the client's dispute and should advise the client at appropriate stages as to the desirability of attempting a settlement and/or a reference to alternative dispute resolution.

3.7.2. A lawyer shall inform the client of the availability of legal aid where applicable.

3.8. Client Funds

3.8.1. Lawyers who come into possession of funds on behalf of their clients or third parties (hereinafter called "client funds") have to deposit such money into an account of a bank or similar institution subject to supervision by a public authority (hereinafter called a "client account"). A client account shall be separate from any other account of the lawyer. All client funds received by a lawyer should be deposited into such an account unless the owner of such funds agrees that the funds should be dealt with otherwise.

3.8.2. The lawyer shall maintain full and accurate records showing all the lawyer's dealings with client funds and distinguishing client funds from other funds held by the lawyer. Records may have to be kept for a certain period of time according to national rules.

3.8.3. A client account cannot be in debit except in exceptional circumstances as expressly permitted in national rules or due to bank charges, which cannot be influenced by the lawyer. Such an account cannot be given as a guarantee or be used as a security for any reason. There shall not be any set-off or merger between a client account and any other bank account, nor shall the client funds in a client account be available to defray money owed by the lawyer to the bank.

3.8.4. Client funds shall be transferred to the owners of such funds in the shortest period of time or under such conditions as are authorised by them.

3.8.5. The lawyer cannot transfer funds from a client account into the lawyer's own account for payment of fees without informing the client in writing.

3.8.6. The Competent Authorities in Member States shall have the power to verify and examine any document regarding client funds, whilst respecting the confidentiality or legal professional privilege to which it may be subject.

3.9. Professional Indemnity Insurance

3.9.1. Lawyers shall be insured against civil legal liability arising out of their legal practice to an extent which is reasonable having regard to the nature and extent of the risks incurred by their professional activities.

3.9.2. Should this prove impossible, the lawyer must inform the client of this situation and its consequences.

4. Relations with the Courts

4.1. Rules of Conduct in Court

A lawyer who appears, or takes part in a case, before a court or tribunal must comply with the rules of conduct applied before that court or tribunal.

4.2. Fair Conduct of Proceedings

A lawyer must always have due regard for the fair conduct of proceedings.

4.3. Demeanour in Court

A lawyer shall while maintaining due respect and courtesy towards the court defend the interests of the client honourably and fearlessly without regard to the lawyer's own interests or to any consequences to him- or herself or to any other person.

4.4. False or Misleading Information

A lawyer shall never knowingly give false or misleading information to the court.

4.5. Extension to Arbitrators etc.

The rules governing a lawyer's relations with the courts apply also to the lawyer's relations with arbitrators and any other persons exercising judicial or quasi-judicial functions, even on an occasional basis.

5. Relations between Lawyers

5.1. Corporate Spirit of the Profession

5.1.1. The corporate spirit of the profession requires a relationship of trust and co-operation between lawyers for the benefit of their clients and in order to avoid unnecessary litigation and other behaviour harmful to the reputation of the profession. It can, however, never justify setting the interests of the profession against those of the client.

5.1.2. A lawyer should recognise all other lawyers of Member States as professional colleagues and act fairly and courteously towards them.

5.2. Co-operation among Lawyers of Different Member States

5.2.1. It is the duty of a lawyer who is approached by a colleague from another Member State not to accept instructions in a matter which the lawyer is not competent to undertake. The lawyer should in such case be prepared to help that colleague to obtain the information necessary to enable him or her to instruct a lawyer who is capable of providing the service asked for.

5.2.2. Where a lawyer of a Member State co-operates with a lawyer from another Member State, both have a general duty to take into account the differences which may exist between their respective legal systems and the professional organisations, competences and obligations of lawyers in the Member States concerned.

5.3. Correspondence between Lawyers

5.3.1. If a lawyer intends to send communications to a lawyer in another Member State, which the sender wishes to remain confidential or without prejudice he or she should clearly express this intention prior to communicating the documents.

5.3.2. If the prospective recipient of the communications is unable to ensure their status as confidential or without prejudice he or she should inform the sender accordingly without delay.

5.4. Referral Fees

5.4.1. A lawyer may not demand or accept from another lawyer or any other person a fee, commission or any other compensation for referring or recommending the lawyer to a client.

5.4.2. A lawyer may not pay anyone a fee, commission or any other compensation as a consideration for referring a client to him- or herself.

5.5. Communication with Opposing Parties

A lawyer shall not communicate about a particular case or matter directly with any person whom he or she knows to be represented or advised in the case or matter by another lawyer, without the consent of that other lawyer (and shall keep the other lawyer informed of any such communications).

5.6. (Deleted by decision of the Plenary Session in Dublin on 6 December 2002)

5.7. Responsibility for Fees

In professional relations between members of Bars of different Member

States, where a lawyer does not confine him- or herself to recommending another lawyer or introducing that other lawyer to the client but instead him- or herself entrusts a correspondent with a particular matter or seeks the correspondent's advice, the instructing lawyer is personally bound, even if the client is insolvent, to pay the fees, costs and outlays which are due to the foreign correspondent. The lawyers concerned may, however, at the outset of the relationship between them make special arrangements on this matter. Further, the instructing lawyer may at any time limit his or her personal responsibility to the amount of the fees, costs and outlays incurred before intimation to the foreign lawyer of the instructing lawyer's disclaimer of responsibility for the future.

5.8. Continuing Professional Development

Lawyers should maintain and develop their professional knowledge and skills taking proper account of the European dimension of their profession.

5.9. Disputes amongst Lawyers in Different Member States

5.9.1. If a lawyer considers that a colleague in another Member State has acted in breach of a rule of professional conduct the lawyer shall draw the matter to the attention of that colleague.

5.9.2. If any personal dispute of a professional nature arises amongst lawyers in different Member States they should if possible first try to settle it in a friendly way.

5.9.3. A lawyer shall not commence any form of proceedings against a colleague in another Member State on matters referred to in 5.9.1 or 5.9.2 above without first informing the Bars or Law Societies to which they both belong for the purpose of allowing both Bars or Law Societies concerned an opportunity to assist in reaching a settlement.

EXPLANATORY MEMORANDUM

This Explanatory Memorandum was prepared at the request of the CCBE Standing Committee by the CCBE's deontology working party, who were responsible for drafting the first version of the Code of Conduct itself. It seeks to explain the origin of the provisions of the Code, to illustrate the problems which they are designed to resolve, particularly in relation to cross-border activities, and to provide assistance to the Competent Authorities in the Member States in the application of the Code. It is not intended to have any binding force in the interpretation of the Code. The Explanatory Memorandum was updated on the occasion of the CCBE Plenary Session on 19 May 2006.

The original versions of the Code are in the French and English languages. Translations into other Community languages are prepared under the authority of the national delegations.

Commentary on Article 1.1—The Function of the Lawyer in Society

The Declaration of Perugia, adopted by the CCBE in 1977, laid down the fundamental principles of professional conduct applicable to lawyers throughout the EC. The provisions of Article 1.1 reaffirm the statement in the Declaration of Perugia of the function of the lawyer in society which forms the basis for the rules governing the performance of that function.

Commentary on Article 1.2—The Nature of Rules of Professional Conduct

These provisions substantially restate the explanation in the Declaration of Perugia of the nature of rules of professional conduct and how particular rules depend on particular local circumstances but are nevertheless based on common values.

Commentary on Article 1.3—The Purpose of the Code

These provisions introduce the development of the principles in the Declaration of Perugia into a specific Code of Conduct for lawyers throughout the EU and the EEA, and lawyers of the Observer Members of the CCBE, with particular reference to their cross-border activities (defined in Article 1.5). The provisions of Article 1.3.2 lay down the specific intentions of the CCBE with regard to the substantive provisions in the Code.

***Commentary on Article 1.4—Field of Application* Ratione Personae**

The rules are stated to apply to all lawyers as defined in the Lawyers Services Directive of 1977 and the Lawyers Establishment Directive of 1998, and lawyers of the Observer Members of the CCBE. This includes lawyers of the states which subsequently acceded to the Directives, whose names have been added by amendment to the Directives. The Code accordingly applies to all the lawyers represented on the CCBE, whether as full Members or as Observer Members, namely:

Austria	Rechtsanwalt;
Belgium	avocat / advocaat / Rechtsanwalt;
Bulgaria	advokat;
Croatia	odvjetnik;
Cyprus	dikegóros;
Czech Republic	advokát;
Denmark	advokat;
Estonia	vandeadvokaat;
Finland	asianajaja / advokat;
FYROMacedonia	advokat;
France	avocat;
Germany	Rechtsanwalt;
Greece	dikegóros;
Hungary	ügyvéd;
Iceland	lögmaður;
Ireland	barrister, solicitor;
Italy	avvocato;
Latvia	zvērināts advokāts;
Liechtenstein	Rechtsanwalt;
Lithuania	advokatas;
Luxembourg	avocat / Rechtsanwalt;
Malta	avukat, prokuratur legali;
Netherlands	advocaat;
Norway	advokat;
Poland	adwokat, radca prawny;
Portugal	advogado;
Romania	avocat;
Slovakia	advokát / advokátka;
Slovenia	odvetnik / odvetnica;
Spain	abogado / advocat / abokatu / avogado;
Sweden	advokat;
Switzerland	Rechtsanwalt / Anwalt / Fürsprech / Fürsprecher / avocat / avvocato /advokat;
Turkey	avukat;
Ukraine	advocate;
United Kingdom	advocate, barrister, solicitor.

It is also hoped that the Code will be acceptable to the legal professions of other non-member states in Europe and elsewhere so that it could also be applied by appropriate conventions between them and the Member States.

Commentary on Article 1.5—Field of Application Ratione Materiae

The rules are here given direct application only to "cross-border activities", as defined, of lawyers within the EU and the EEA and lawyers of the Observer Members of the CCBE - see above on Article 1.4, and the definition of "Member State" in Article 1.6. (See also above as to possible extensions in the future to lawyers of other states.) The definition of cross-border activities would, for example, include contacts in state A even on a matter of law internal to state A between a lawyer of state A and a lawyer of state B; it would exclude contacts between lawyers of state A in state A of a matter arising in state B, provided that none of their professional activities takes place in state B; it would include any activities of lawyers of state A in state B, even if only in the form of communications sent from state A to state B.

Commentary on Article 1.6—Definitions

This provision defines a number of terms used in the Code, "Member State", "Home Member State", "Host Member State", "Competent Authority", "Directive 77/249/EEC" and "Directive 98/5/EC".The reference to "where the lawyer carries on cross-border activities" should be interpreted in the light of the definition of "cross-border activities" in Article 1.5.

Commentary on Article 2.1—Independence

This provision substantially reaffirms the general statement of principle in the Declaration of Perugia.

Commentary on Article 2.2—Trust and Personal Integrity

This provision also restates a general principle contained in the Declaration of Perugia.

Commentary on Article 2.3—Confidentiality

This provision first restates, in Article 2.3.1, general principles laid down in the Declaration of Perugia and recognised by the ECJ in the *AM&S* case (157/79). It then, in Articles 2.3.2 to 4, develops them into a specific rule relating to the protection of confidentiality. Article 2.3.2 contains the basic rule requiring respect for confidentiality. Article 2.3.3 confirms that the obligation remains binding on the lawyer even if he or she ceases to act for the client in question. Article 2.3.4 confirms that the lawyer must not only respect the obligation of confidentiality him- or herself but must require all members and employees of his or her firm to do likewise.

Commentary on Article 2.4—Respect for the Rules of Other Bars and Law Societies

Article 4 of the Lawyers Services Directive contains the provisions with regard to the rules to be observed by a lawyer from one Member State providing services on an occasional or temporary basis in another Member State by virtue of Article 49 of the consolidated EC treaty, as follows:

(a) activities relating to the representation of a client in legal proceedings or before public authorities shall be pursued in each Host Member State under the conditions laid down for lawyers established in that state, with the exception of any conditions requiring residence, or registration with a professional organisation, in that state;

(b) a lawyer pursuing these activities shall observe the rules of professional conduct of the Host Member State, without prejudice to the lawyer's obligations in the Member State from which he or she comes;

(c) when these activities are pursued in the UK, "rules of professional conduct of the Host Member State" means the rules of professional conduct applicable to solicitors, where such activities are not reserved for barristers and advocates. Otherwise the rules of professional conduct applicable to the latter shall apply. However, barristers from Ireland shall always be subject to the rules of professional conduct applicable in the UK to barristers and advocates. When these activities are pursued in Ireland "rules of professional conduct of the Host Member State" means, in so far as they govern the oral presentation of a case in court, the rules of professional conduct applicable to barristers. In all other cases the rules of professional conduct applicable to solicitors shall apply. However, barristers and advocates from the UK shall always be subject to the rules of professional conduct applicable in Ireland to barristers; and

(d) a lawyer pursuing activities other than those referred to in (a) above shall remain subject to the conditions and rules of professional conduct of the Member State from which he or she comes without prejudice to respect for the rules, whatever their source, which govern the profession in the Host Member State, especially those concerning the incompatibility of the exercise of the activities of a lawyer with the exercise of other activities in that state, professional secrecy, relations with other lawyers, the prohibition on the same lawyer acting for parties with mutually conflicting interests, and publicity. The latter rules are applicable only if they are capable of being observed by a lawyer who is not established in the Host Member State and to the extent to which their observance is objectively justified to ensure, in that state, the proper exercise of a lawyer's activities, the standing of the profession and respect for the rules concerning incompatibility.

The Lawyers Establishment Directive contains the provisions with regard to the rules to be observed by a lawyer from one Member State practising on a permanent basis in another Member State by virtue of Article 43 of the consolidated EC treaty, as follows:

(a) irrespective of the rules of professional conduct to which he or she is subject in his or her Home Member State, a lawyer practising under his home-country professional title shall be subject to the same rules of professional conduct as lawyers practising under the relevant professional title of the Host Member State in respect of all the activities the lawyer pursues in its territory (Article 6.1);

(b) the Host Member State may require a lawyer practising under his or her home-country professional title either to take out professional indemnity insurance or to become a member of a professional guarantee fund in accordance with the rules which that state lays down for professional activities pursued in its territory. Nevertheless, a lawyer practising under his or her home-country professional title shall be exempted from that requirement if the lawyer can prove that he or she is covered by insurance taken out or a guarantee provided in accordance with the rules of the Home Member State, insofar as such insurance or guarantee is equivalent in terms of the conditions and extent of cover. Where the equivalence is only partial, the Competent Authority in the Host Member State may require that additional insurance or an additional guarantee be contracted to cover the elements which are not already covered by the insurance or guarantee contracted in accordance with the rules of the Home Member State (Article 6.3); and

(c) a lawyer registered in a Host Member State under his or her home-country professional title may practise as a salaried lawyer in the employ of another lawyer, an association or firm of lawyers, or a public or private enterprise to the extent that the Host Member State so permits for lawyers registered under the professional title used in that state (Article 8).

In cases not covered by either of these Directives, or over and above the requirements of these Directives, the obligations of a lawyer under Community law to observe the rules of other Bars and Law Societies are a matter of interpretation of any relevant provision, such as the Directive on Electronic Commerce (2000/31/EC). A major purpose of the Code is to minimise, and if possible eliminate altogether, the problems which may arise from "double deontology", that is the application of more than one set of potentially conflicting national rules to a particular situation (see Article 1.3.1).

Commentary on Article 2.5—Incompatible Occupations

There are differences both between and within Member States on the extent to which lawyers are permitted to engage in other occupations, for example in commercial activities. The general purpose of rules excluding a lawyer from other occupations is to protect the lawyer from influences which might impair the lawyer's independence or his or her role in the administration of justice. The variations in these rules reflect different local conditions, different perceptions of the proper function of lawyers and different techniques of rule-making. For instance in some cases there is a complete prohibition of engagement in certain named occupations, whereas in other cases engagement in other occupations is generally permitted, subject to observance of specific safeguards for the lawyer's independence.

Articles 2.5.2 and 3 make provision for different circumstances in which a lawyer of one Member State is engaging in cross-border activities (as defined in Article 1.5) in a Host Member State when he or she is not a member of the Host State legal profession.Article 2.5.2 imposes full observation of Host State rules regarding incompatible occupations on the lawyer acting in national legal proceedings or before national public authorities in the Host State. This applies whether the lawyer is established in the Host State or not.

Article 2.5.3, on the other hand, imposes "respect" for the rules of the Host State regarding forbidden or incompatible occupations in other cases, but only where the lawyer who is established in the Host Member State wishes to participate directly in commercial or other activities not connected with the practice of the law.

Commentary on Article 2.6—Personal Publicity

The term "personal publicity" covers publicity by firms of lawyers, as well as individual lawyers, as opposed to corporate publicity organised by Bars and Law Societies for their members as a whole. The rules governing personal publicity by lawyers vary considerably in the Member States. Article 2.6 makes it clear that there is no overriding objection to personal publicity in cross-border practice. However, lawyers are nevertheless subject to prohibitions or restrictions laid down by their home professional rules, and a lawyer will still be subject to prohibitions or restrictions laid down by Host State rules when these are binding on the lawyer by virtue of the Lawyers Services Directive or the Lawyers Establishment Directive.

Commentary on Article 2.7—The Client's Interest

This provision emphasises the general principle that the lawyer must always place the client's interests before the lawyer's own interests or those of fellow members of the legal profession.

Commentary on Article 2.8—Limitation of Lawyer's Liability towards the Client

This provision makes clear that there is no overriding objection to limiting a lawyer's liability towards his or her client in cross-border practice, whether by contract or by use of a limited company, limited partnership or limited liability partnership. However it points out that this can only be contemplated where the relevant law and the relevant rules of conduct permit—and in a number of jurisdictions the law or the professional rules prohibit or restrict such limitation of liability.

Commentary on Article 3.1—Acceptance and Termination of Instructions

The provisions of Article 3.1.1 are designed to ensure that a relationship is maintained between lawyer and client and that the lawyer in fact receives instructions from the client, even though these may be transmitted through a duly authorised intermediary. It is the responsibility of the lawyer to satisfy him- or herself as to the authority of the intermediary and the wishes of the client.

Article 3.1.2 deals with the manner in which the lawyer should carry out his or her duties. The provision that the lawyer shall undertake personal responsibility for the discharge of the instructions given to him or her means that the lawyer cannot avoid responsibility by delegation to others. It does not prevent the lawyer from seeking to limit his or her legal liability to the extent that this is permitted by the relevant law or professional rules—see Article 2.8.

Article 3.1.3 states a principle which is of particular relevance in cross-border activities, for example when a lawyer is asked to handle a matter on behalf of a lawyer or client from another state who may be unfamiliar with the relevant law and practice, or when a lawyer is asked to handle a matter relating to the law of another state with which he or she is unfamiliar.

A lawyer generally has the right to refuse to accept instructions in the first place, but Article 3.1.4 states that, having once accepted them, the lawyer has an obligation not to withdraw without ensuring that the client's interests are safeguarded.

Commentary on Article 3.2—Conflict of Interest

The provisions of Article 3.2.1 do not prevent a lawyer acting for two or more clients in the same matter provided that their interests are not in fact in conflict and that there is no significant risk of such a conflict arising. Where a lawyer is already acting for two or more clients in this way and subsequently there arises a conflict of interests between those clients or a risk of a breach of confidence or other circumstances where the lawyer's independence may be impaired, then the lawyer must cease to act for both or all of them.

There may, however, be circumstances in which differences arise between two or more clients for whom the same lawyer is acting where it may be appropriate for the lawyer to attempt to act as a mediator. It is for the lawyer in such cases to use his or her own judgement on whether or not there is such a conflict of interest between them as to require the lawyer to cease to act. If not, the lawyer may consider whether it would be appropriate to explain the position to the clients, obtain their agreement and attempt to act as mediator to resolve the difference between them, and only if this attempt to mediate should fail, to cease to act for them.

Article 3.2.4 applies the foregoing provisions of Article 3 to lawyers practising in association. For example a firm of lawyers should cease to act when there is a conflict of interest between two clients of the firm, even if different lawyers in the firm are acting for each client. On the other hand, exceptionally, in the "chambers" form of association used by English barristers, where each lawyer acts for clients individually, it is possible for different lawyers in the association to act for clients with opposing interests.

Commentary on Article 3.3—**Pactum de Quota Litis**

These provisions reflect the common position in all Member States that an unregulated agreement for contingency fees (*pactum de quota litis*) is contrary to the proper administration of justice because it encourages speculative litigation and is liable to be abused. The provisions are not, however, intended to prevent the maintenance or introduction of arrangements under which lawyers are paid according to results or only if the action or matter is successful, provided that these arrangements are under sufficient regulation and control for the protection of the client and the proper administration of justice.

Commentary on Article 3.4—Regulation of Fees

Article 3.4 lays down three requirements: a general standard of disclosure of a lawyer's fees to the client, a requirement that they should be fair and reasonable in amount, and a requirement to comply with the applicable law and professional rules. In many Member States machinery exists for regulating lawyers' fees under national law or rules of conduct, whether by reference to a power of adjudication by the Bar authorities or otherwise. In situations governed by the Lawyers Establishment Directive, where the lawyer is subject to Host State rules as well as the rules of the Home State, the basis of charging may have to comply with both sets of rules.

Commentary on Article 3.5—Payment on Account

Article 3.5 assumes that a lawyer may require a payment on account of the lawyer's fees and/or disbursements, but sets a limit by reference to a reasonable estimate of them. See also on Article 3.1.4 regarding the right to withdraw.

Commentary on Article 3.6—Fee Sharing with Non-Lawyers

In some Member States lawyers are permitted to practise in association with members of certain other approved professions, whether legal professions or not. The provisions of Article 3.6.1 are not designed to prevent fee sharing within such an approved form of association. Nor are the provisions designed to prevent fee sharing by the lawyers to whom the Code applies (see on Article 1.4 above) with other "lawyers", for example lawyers from non-Member States or members of other legal professions in the Member States such as notaries.

Commentary on Article 3.7—Cost of Litigation and Availability of Legal Aid

Article 3.7.1 stresses the importance of attempting to resolve disputes in a way which is cost-effective for the client, including advising on whether to attempt to negotiate a settlement, and whether to propose referring the dispute to some form of alternative dispute resolution.

Article 3.7.2 requires a lawyer to inform the client of the availability of legal aid where applicable. There are widely differing provisions in the Member States on the availability of legal aid. In cross-border activities a lawyer should have in mind the possibility that the legal aid provisions of a national law with which the lawyer is unfamiliar may be applicable.

Commentary on Article 3.8—Client Funds

The provisions of Article 3.8 reflect the recommendation adopted by the CCBE in Brussels in November 1985 on the need for minimum regulations to be made and enforced governing the proper control and disposal of clients' funds held by lawyers within the Community. Article 3.8 lays down minimum standards to be observed, while not interfering with the details of national systems which provide fuller or more stringent protection for clients' funds.

The lawyer who holds clients' funds, even in the course of a cross-border activity, has to observe the rules of his or her home Bar. The lawyer needs to be aware of questions which arise where the rules of more than one Member State may be applicable, especially where the lawyer is established in a Host State under the Lawyers Establishment Directive.

Commentary on Article 3.9—Professional Indemnity Insurance

Article 3.9.1 reflects a recommendation, also adopted by the CCBE in Brussels in November 1985, on the need for all lawyers in the Community to be insured against the risks arising from professional negligence claims against them.Article 3.9.2 deals with the situation where insurance cannot be obtained on the basis set out in Article 3.9.1.

Commentary on Article 4.1—Rules of Conduct in Court

This provision applies the principle that a lawyer is bound to comply with the rules of the court or tribunal before which the lawyer practises or appears.

Commentary on Article 4.2—Fair Conduct of Proceedings

This provision applies the general principle that in adversarial proceedings a lawyer must not attempt to take unfair advantage of his or her opponent. The lawyer must not, for example, make contact with the judge without first informing the lawyer acting for the opposing party or submit exhibits, notes or documents to the judge without communicating them in good time to the lawyer on the other side unless such steps are permitted under the relevant rules of procedure. To the extent not prohibited by law a lawyer must not divulge or submit to the court any proposals for settlement of the case made by the other party or its lawyer without the express consent of the other party's lawyer. See also on Article 4.5 below.

Commentary on Article 4.3—Demeanour in Court

This provision reflects the necessary balance between respect for the court and for the law on the one hand and the pursuit of the client's best interest on the other.

Commentary on Article 4.4—False or Misleading Information

This provision applies the principle that the lawyer must never knowingly mislead the court. This is necessary if there is to be trust between the courts and the legal profession.

Commentary on Article 4.5—Extension to Arbitrators etc.

This provision extends the preceding provisions relating to courts and other bodies exercising judicial or quasi-judicial functions.

Commentary on Article 5.1—Corporate Spirit of the Profession

These provisions, which are based on statements in the Declaration of

Perugia, emphasise that it is in the public interest for the legal profession to maintain a relationship of trust and cooperation between its members. However, this cannot be used to justify setting the interests of the profession against those of justice or of clients (see also on Article 2.7).

Commentary on Article 5.2—Co-operation among Lawyers of Different Member States

This provision also develops a principle stated in the Declaration of Perugia with a view to avoiding misunderstandings in dealings between lawyers of different Member States.

Commentary on Article 5.3—Correspondence between Lawyers

In certain Member States communications between lawyers (written or by word of mouth) are normally regarded as to be kept confidential as between the lawyers. This means that the content of these communications cannot be disclosed to others, cannot normally be passed to the lawyers' clients, and at any event cannot be produced in court. In other Member States, such consequences will not follow unless the correspondence is marked as "confidential".

In yet other Member States, the lawyer has to keep the client fully informed of all relevant communications from a professional colleague acting for another party, and marking a letter as "confidential" only means that it is a legal matter intended for the recipient lawyer and his or her client, and not to be misused by third parties.

In some states, if a lawyer wishes to indicate that a letter is sent in an attempt to settle a dispute, and is not to be produced in a court, the lawyer should mark the letter as "without prejudice".

These important national differences give rise to many misunderstandings. That is why lawyers must be very careful in conducting cross-border correspondence.

Whenever a lawyer wants to send a letter to a professional colleague in another Member State on the basis that it is to be kept confidential as between the lawyers, or that it is "without prejudice", the lawyer should ask in advance whether the letter can be accepted on that basis. A lawyer wishing that a communication should be accepted on such a basis must express that clearly at the head of the communication or in a covering letter.

A lawyer who is the intended recipient of such a communication, but who is not in a position to respect, or to ensure respect for, the basis on which it is to be sent, must inform the sender immediately so that the communication is not sent. If the communication has already been received, the recipient must return it to the sender without revealing its contents or referring to it in any way; if the recipient's national law or rules prevent the recipient from complying with this requirement, he or she must inform the sender immediately.

Commentary on Article 5.4—Referral Fees

This provision reflects the principle that a lawyer should not pay or receive payment purely for the reference of a client, which would risk impairing the client's free choice of lawyer or the client's interest in being referred to the best available service. It does not prevent fee-sharing arrangements between lawyers on a proper basis (see also on Article 3.6 above).

In some Member States lawyers are permitted to accept and retain commissions in certain cases provided the client's best interests are served, there is full disclosure to the client and the client has consented to the retention of the commission. In such cases the retention of the commission by the lawyer represents part of the lawyer's remuneration for the service provided to the client and is not within the scope of the prohibition on referral fees which is designed to prevent lawyers making a secret profit.

Commentary on Article 5.5—Communication with Opposing Parties

This provision reflects a generally accepted principle, and is designed both to promote the smooth conduct of business between lawyers and to prevent any attempt to take advantage of the client of another lawyer.

Commentary on Article 5.6—Change of Lawyer

Article 5.6 dealt with change of lawyer. It was deleted from the Code on 6 December 2002.

Commentary on Article 5.7—Responsibility for Fees

These provisions substantially reaffirm provisions contained in the Declaration of Perugia. Since misunderstandings about responsibility for unpaid fees are a common cause of difference between lawyers of different Member States, it is important that a lawyer who wishes to exclude or limit his or her personal obligation to be responsible for the fees of a foreign colleague should reach a clear agreement on this at the outset of the transaction.

Commentary on Article 5.8—Continuing Professional Development

Keeping abreast of developments in the law is a professional obligation. In particular it is essential that lawyers are aware of the growing impact of European law on their field of practice.

Commentary on Article 5.9—Disputes amongst Lawyers in Different Member States

A lawyer has the right to pursue any legal or other remedy to which he or she is entitled against a colleague in another Member State. Nevertheless it is desirable that, where a breach of a rule of professional conduct or a dispute of a professional nature is involved, the possibilities of friendly settlement should be exhausted, if necessary with the assistance of the Bars or Law Societies concerned, before such remedies are exercised.

Practice Guidelines

Conflict of Interest in Commercial Security Transactions

[March 1994]

The Scottish banks have confirmed that they all now intend to introduce policies in the very near future whereby in commercial security transactions they will instruct separate solicitors to represent them. Their solicitors will, as has been the custom recover their fees and outlays from the borrower. It is the intention of the Scottish banks that they will use solicitors throughout Scotland and will not centralise their commercial security work. Furthermore the banks have indicated that they will expect those solicitors whom they instruct to charge reasonable fees.

[The President] understands that while this agreement has been reached with the Scottish banks, other banks operating in Scotland and members of the British Bankers Association will adopt similar policies.

Notwithstanding this general policy, the Scottish banks wish to reserve the right to instruct the borrower's solicitor to act for them, in what they described as *de minimis* cases. Each bank may adopt a different view on what constitutes a *de minimis* case, but the Council expects that the banks will act responsibly when deciding on their individual policies.

The Council believes it would be helpful if a definition is provided of a commercial security transaction. It is:

"A commercial security transaction relates to the secured lending to a customer of a bank or other lending institution where the purpose of the loan is clearly for the customer's business purposes."

However we must remind you, that should you receive instructions to act for a lender and a borrower in *any* type of transaction, but particularly a commercial security transaction you must exercise your judgment standing the provisions of the Solicitors (Scotland) Practice Rules 1986 (the Conflict of Interest Rules) as to whether you can properly act for both parties. It is appropriate that in exercising that judgment you take account of the circumstances which might arise. There follow certain examples which you may find helpful when you exercise your professional judgment. You should not forget, that should you decide to act for both lender and borrower (even in what purports to be a *de minimis* case) and ultimately a claim arises, you may have exposed yourself and your firm to the risk of bearing a double excess/deductible and the possibility of a loading on your master policy premium.

Finally, please do not hesitate to contact the Society if you feel you require further advice or guidance in this type of transaction.

Examples of conflicts of interest in commercial security transactions

The following illustrate some of the instances where lenders and borrowers have separate interests in commercial security transactions.

Disclosure of all relevant circumstances

1. Either:

(*a*) the solicitor may know more of the borrower's position than has been communicated to the lender or *vice versa*; or

(*b*) there may have been a reluctance by the borrower or lender fully to disclose their respective positions because of dual representation.

This clearly affects the extent to which impartial "best advice" can be given.

Ongoing negotiations

2. Negotiations between the borrower and lender may have only reached the "Outline Terms' stage—requiring further detailed consideration or negotiation of covenants/undertakings/events of default. In such negotiations the borrower and lender may have different negotiating strengths—and thus there may be competing pressures on the solicitor as to whose interests are to be promoted.

Defects in title

3. While a borrower may be prepared to "live with" a minor defect in title or some lack of planning or building consent the lender may take an entirely different stance.

Security by companies

4. Apart from the complexities and time restraints for registration of security, companies may well be subject to negative or restrictive covenants or powers affecting the security on which the borrower but not necessarily the lender, may be prepared to take a commercial view. This may merit separate consideration and advice.

Competing creditors ranking agreements

5. The circumstances as to the inter-relationship/enforcement of security between lenders may merit separate consideration and advice. Banks may not have "standard forms" of ranking agreements and this clearly may involve a solicitor in preparing a document and negotiating its terms on points which have a bearing on the borrower's position.

Security over commercial property

6. The permitted use, associated licences/quotas and specific standard conditions may merit separate consideration and advice as they may not be covered by pre-printed "standard" bank forms. Particular risks arise on the transfer of a licence where the lender's interests will sometimes conflict with the borrower's commercial ambitions.

Leased property as security

7. The circumstances in which a lender requires protection in the event of irritancy may merit separate consideration and advice. Invariably the borrower is trying to strike the best deal while he is in occupancy while the lender needs protection in the event of the borrower's failure through insolvency or otherwise.

Enforcement of security

8. The solicitor acting for both borrower and lender may be placed in difficulty in the event of subsequent enforcement of a security. For whom does the solicitor act in such circumstances? Do both clients know and understand their respective positions?

Powerful clients

9. A major business client may bring subtle or even open pressures on a solicitor to follow a particular course or to turn a blind eye to a matter which could prejudice a lender's position, *e.g.* discrepancies between a valuation and purchase price.

All sums due: securities

10. Solicitors should be mindful to advise fully, joint obligants (husbands and wives) of the nature of an "all sums due" security. In particular it should be drawn to their attention that additional loans for example in respect of one obligant's business, may give rise to further secured borrowings without the other obligant requiring to sign the documentation.

Companies—*ultra vires*

11. Following changes to the *ultra vires* doctrine lenders may be able to rely on the provisions of what is now section 35 of the 1985 Companies Act.

If the solicitors involved act solely for the lender they would, as a generality, be entitled to rely on these same provisions if asked to do so by the instructing lender. On the other hand if the solicitors act also for the borrowing company it is quite clear that the solicitors would require to carry out a full examination of the company's memorandum and articles of association, since section 35 only provides protection for third parties—it does not for example excuse the directors from any liability arising from acting *ultra vires*. In such circumstances the solicitors, as agents for the lender, would become aware of any *ultra vires* aspect of the arrangements and the lender could be similarly tainted with this knowledge.

[1] Law Society Guidelines on Conflict of Interest

NOTE
[1] As amended in May 1999.

Conflict of interest

It is a well established principle that solicitors should not act for clients where there is a conflict of interest between them. This was codified in the 1986 Practice Rules (*Parliament House Book*, Volume 3, Page F 328) in which Rule 3 states, "a solicitor shall not act for two or more parties whose interests conflict". That statement is entirely unqualified and is the guiding principle which governs the rest of those Practice Rules. Conflict of interest was amplified in the Code of Conduct published in October 1989 (*Parliament House Book*, Volume 3, Page F 1001). Article 3 of the Code of Conduct states, "Solicitors (including firms of solicitors) shall not act for two or more clients in matters where there is a conflict of interest between the clients or for any client where there is a conflict between the interests of the client and that of the solicitor or the solicitor's firm."

Neither the Rules nor the Code of Conduct contains a definition of conflict of interest. As somebody said it is hard to define but you know it when you see it. Unfortunately many solicitors only seem to see it long after it has appeared and when it is too late. There is a straightforward way of looking at this. If you would give different advice to different clients about the same matter there is a conflict of interest between them. It does not matter that the clients may be agreed about what they wish to do.

Conflict of interest is not a matter for the judgment of the client—it is a matter for the judgment of the solicitor. Only the solicitor has the breadth of experience, training and knowledge to fully advise a client where his interest lies. Jane Ryder in her book Professional Conduct for Scottish Solicitors states, "Where facts are disclosed to a solicitor on behalf of one client which may be prejudicial if disclosed to another client without the authority of the first, there is almost certainly a conflict of interest . . . the critical test is whether the solicitor can adequately discharge all duties to his or her respective clients equally." (Pages 61 and 62).

The Discipline Tribunal have expressed concern in their Annual Reports about continuing failure to recognise a conflict of interest and follow the Practice Rules.

Conflict of interest in court matters:

1. Matrimonial

It is trite to say that you should not sue your own client, but the question of conflict in court matters goes further than that. In matrimonial cases the same firm of solicitors should not act for both husband and wife in negotiating a separation agreement—or even in preparing a document that reflects the parties' own agreement. The parties have separate interests and the same firm should not act for both of them. If one of them refuses to get separate independent advice, they cannot be forced to do so but you should ensure that you only act for one.

You would be entitled to deal with the other as an unrepresented party—in which case you *must* (in terms of Rule 7 of the 1986 Rules) advise the unrepresented party in writing when sending a document for signature that such signature would have legal consequences and they should seek independent legal advice before signing. You should not spell out what the consequences might be as that would be giving advice. If the unrepresented party does not obtain separate advice and signs and returns the document to you, you would be entitled to treat it as delivered on behalf of your client and to deal with it accordingly. In 1998 the Discipline Tribunal found a solicitor guilty of professional misconduct for failing to comply with Rule 7 and said that whatever pressures might be put upon the solicitor . . . "Where professional obligations arise it is not sufficient for a solicitor merely to follow the instructions of his client."

In many separations the matrimonial home will require to be sold. The Professional Practice Committee issued a Guideline about this in July 1998 (page F 1220). Unless the parties have agreed in writing how the sale proceeds will be distributed (either as part of a wider agreement or as a separate stand alone agreement) neither of the solicitors' firms acting for the individuals should act in the sale. A separate firm should be instructed. This was emphasised in a recent reported case (*Dawson v. R. Gordon Marshall & Co.*, 1996 G.W.D. 1243 issue of 21st June) where Lord Osborne held that by not accounting to the husband for his share of the proceeds in accordance with the title, the solicitors had acted improperly. In that case the solicitors in fact had retained the balance of the proceeds and were in a position to implement the court's decree but they required to meet the expenses of a defended proof in the Court of Session.

If the parties *have* reached an agreement dealing with the free proceeds, and that means an agreement signed by the parties themselves, the solicitors acting for one of the spouses in the matrimonial affairs may act in the sale but must account to both parties in accordance with the signed agreement. They cannot accept unilateral instructions from one of them to alter that. That would be a conflict situation requiring them to immediately withdraw from acting. The mirror image is that if you are consulted by a married couple in connection with the sale of their property and at that time or subsequently you discover that they are separated you would be entitled to accept the instructions to act in the sale but you would require to advise each of them to seek separate independent advice in relation to their matrimonial position. Unless and until a written agreement dealing with the free proceeds is intimated to you, you would require to account to the spouses in accordance with the title.

2. Criminal matters—acting for co-accused

The Code of Conduct for Criminal Work (F 1008) states in Article 2, "A solicitor should not accept instructions from more than one accused in the same matter." The Code was drawn up by the Criminal Law Committee who were of the view that there is always a potential for conflict between co-accused. For example if one pleads guilty he becomes a compellable witness against the other. Witnesses do not always come up to precognition. A solicitor who accepts instructions and subsequently has to abandon one of the clients is placed in a compromised position not only by virtue of having potentially breached the Conflict of Interest Rules but also by virtue of being likely to possess confidential information relating to the client for whom he has had to cease acting. The Rules of Conduct for Solicitor Advocates prohibit them from acting for more than one accused person "save in the most exceptional circumstances".

Conflict of interest in conveyancing

Conflict in conveyancing transactions is dealt with in Rules 5, 6, 7 and 8 of the 1986 Practice Rules. Rule 5 is without prejudice to the generality of Rule 3 (above) and states—reading short—that the same firm of solicitors shall not *at any stage* act for both seller and purchaser, landlord and tenant, or assignor and assignee in a lease of heritable property for value provided that, where no dispute arises *or might reasonably be expected to arise,* and the seller of residential property is not a builder or developer, the rule shall not apply in certain particular situations. It is worth bearing in mind that when something goes wrong and a complaint is made to the Society or a claim is made under the Master Policy, the circumstances will be looked at with the benefit of hindsight. With hindsight it is clear that the disputes that regularly arise in conveyancing transactions are all disputes which could reasonably have been foreseen such as difficulties with the title; unauthorised alterations; or problems with the purchaser's funding. If a dispute does arise in the middle of a transaction where the same firm are acting for both sides, the solicitors must take immediate steps to cease acting for at least one of the parties and advise them that they should consult an independent solicitor. It is almost always a mistake to attempt to resolve matters and solicitors are generally digging a deeper hole for themselves if they try and do so. It must always be remembered that the Rules are there not only for the protection of clients but also for the protection of solicitors.

The exceptions to the general prohibition are—again reading short—(a) associated companies or public bodies; (b) connected parties within the meaning of a now repealed section of the Income and Corporation Taxes Act (since replaced by Section 839 of the ICTA 1988); (c) parties related by blood, adoption or marriage; (d) established clients; and (e) where there is no other solicitor in the vicinity whom the client could reasonably be expected to consult.

In category (a) associated companies means in the same group of companies and not just having directions and/or shareholders in common. Category (c)—parties related by blood etc—is not restricted to any particular degree of relationship but it is unwise to stray beyond the forbidden degrees of marriage.

The most commonly used exemption is the established client—category (d). An established client is defined as "a person for whom a solicitor or his firm has acted on at least one previous occasion". The Professional Practice Committee are of the view that this does not mean that the solicitor requires to have ceased acting in the previous matter—it can be a continuing matter. It must however be a matter in respect of which the solicitor has opened a file with something that the client could be charged for even if he has not in fact been charged for it or may never be charged for it.

Category (e)—no other solicitor in the vicinity—has been interpreted by the Committee as restricted to isolated rural and island communities. It is not applicable anywhere in central Scotland. The matter was raised in connection with a small Highland town which had one full time and one part time solicitor's practice. The Committee decided that this exemption was not available even in that situation, where the nearest other town with a firm of solicitors was nine miles away.

In every case where the solicitors are acting for both parties by virtue of categories (c), (d) or (e) the second part of Rule 5 requires that both parties be advised by the solicitor at the earliest practicable opportunity that the firm have been requested to act for them and that if a dispute arises they or one of them will require to consult an independent solicitor. This advice must be confirmed by the solicitor in writing "as soon as may be practicable thereafter". This does not mean when the offer has been submitted or is about to be submitted. It means when you are first instructed by the purchaser in respect of a property you are selling or in which you know you are to be instructed by the seller if the sale is being dealt with by an external estate agent.

These letters—known as Rule 5 (2) letters—are mandatory and even if you are entitled to act and there is no conflict of interest, failure to send out such a letter is a breach of the Rule. Although you may think that that will not matter if there is no actual difficulty, when the Society's accountants carry out a routine inspection of your firm they will ask for files where the firm has acted for both buyer and seller and report back to the Society where no Rule 5 (2) letters appear in the file. That may lead by itself to a complaint of professional misconduct. Indeed in its Annual Report for 1998 the Discipline Tribunal highlighted a case where they found a solicitor guilty of misconduct for not complying with this Rule. The Tribunal said "it does not mitigate the gravity of any breach that none of the clients involved had been prejudiced or were dissatisfied with the solicitor's conduct of the transaction".

"At any stage"

Rule 5 prohibits the same firm from acting "at any stage". This is interpreted strictly by the Professional Practice Committee. For example:

(1) acting as an estate agent only is acting at a stage for the seller even if all offers are to be submitted to a different firm of solicitors. You would not be entitled to act or give any advice to a prospective purchaser who does not fall within one of the exemptions.

(2) Giving advice about a mortgage or finance for a property is acting at a stage. Again you would only be able to give such advice to a prospective purchaser who is an established client or in respect of whom one of the other exemptions is available. This means you have to be careful about what you say in your property particulars if you are selling the property. The Committee published a Guideline (see page F 1217) that if you market your mortgage advice service in your property particulars you must include a notice that you may not be able to act for the recipient. You would be entitled to say that you will arrange for the prospective client to see another solicitor—so that he stays within the Profession for such advice rather than going off to a mortgage broker.

Builders and Developers

Of course you cannot give any advice to a purchaser at all if you are acting for a seller who is a builder or developer. "Developer" has been considered by the Professional Practice Committee. Firstly, a Housing Association is a developer. Secondly, a person who is by trade a builder or developer selling in the course of his business houses or plots which are part of a larger development is clearly a developer but such a person selling a site or house as a single unit and not part of a larger development has also been treated by the Discipline Tribunal as a developer. For example a builder selling a house which has been bought as a trade-in would still be a builder for the purposes of Rule 5.

Thirdly, a person who is not by trade a builder or developer but is selling individual plots or houses which are part of a larger development has the temporary status of a developer (*e.g.* a farmer selling residential plots in a field).

However, a person who is not by trade a builder or developer but is selling a single plot or site is no longer regarded as a developer. A solicitor acting for such a seller who is consulted by the purchaser would be entitled to act for the purchaser if he falls within one of the exemptions to the rule. That is again always provided there is no actual conflict of interest between the parties and no dispute is reasonably likely to arise—which will remain a matter for the judgment of the solicitor. In such transactions there could well be conflicting interests *e.g.* rights of access; other servitudes; maintenance of private roadway; etc. The safest way to avoid such difficulties is to decline to accept instructions from both parties in the first place.

Conflict of interest in relation to loans

1. General:

Rule 5 also deals with acting for lender and borrower. In terms of Rule 5(1)(f) the terms of the loan must have been agreed between the parties before the solicitor has been instructed by the lender and the granting of the security is only to give effect to such agreement. You must always remember that the lender is also a client. The lender/borrower rule is still subject to the question of an actual conflict of interest or a dispute which may reasonably be likely to arise. Difficulties have arisen in a number of cases which have been reported—mainly in relation to commercial securities—but the lessons are also relevant to domestic security transactions. There are some extremely valuable articles by Professor Robert Rennie in the Journal of April 1994 (the lender's need to know); February 1995 (the expanding duty of care) and October 1995 (certificates of title). There was also a useful item in the caveat column in the Journal of February 1995 at Page 71.

2. Commercial securities:

In relation to commercial securities there was a Presidential circular in March 1994 advising that banks would normally instruct their own solicitors except in what they regarded as *de minimis* cases. The letter—which is printed in the *Parliament House Book*, Volume 3 at Page F 1201—contained a number of examples where there is a greater scope for conflict of interest in commercial transactions. It is worth noting that about 25 per cent of all claims on the Master Policy arise out of defective security work.

As stated above if it goes wrong it will all be looked at with the benefit of hindsight. A breach of the conflict of interest rules will lead to a double deductible (excess) as well as a potential finding of professional misconduct. The current excess is £2,000 per partner up to a maximum of ten partners. Double that at £4,000 and the firm could be uninsured for £40,000 as well as having to face a loading of up to 250 per cent of the premium over a period of five years. Remember there are only about 1,200 firms of solicitors in Scotland and there is therefore a very small insurance pool to fund the Master Policy. Because of the discount/loading position, unless you have a very substantial claim you will find that the policy is really an instalment payment plan.

3. Home secured for business loan—Guarantors:

There is a clear conflict of interest between a borrower and a guarantor; for example where the jointly owned home is to be put up as security for a business loan to only one of the owners. The same firm of solicitors should not act for both of them. Not only must you make it clear that you are not acting for the owner who is not getting the benefit of the loan—when sending the standard security for signature by that person you must accompany it with a letter in terms of Rule 7 of the 1986 Rules as stated earlier (see Matrimonial). In the case of *Smith v. Bank of Scotland* (1997 S.L.T. 1061) the House of Lords decided that the lender has a duty to advise such a joint owner to seek independent advice. However, in *Forsythe v. Royal Bank of Scotland*, 2000 S.L.T. 1295, Lord Macfadyen held that the lenders' security was valid even though the same firm acted for lenders, borrower and guarantor. That may help the lenders but it does focus attention on the solicitors conduct in acting for parties with conflicting interest.

The matter was further considered by the English Courts in *Royal Bank of Scotland v. Etridge and Zwebner v. Mortgage Corporation Ltd* in relation to the duties owed to a spouse who is asked to put up her share of the matrimonial home as security. (See Article by Alistair Sim in Journal of March 1999 at Page 40: Reproduced at **F** 1211 *infra*.)

4. House purchase funded by relative:

A further specific area in relation to loans to be wary of is the house purchase which is being funded by other members of the family *e.g.* a council house with an elderly entitled tenant. There are clearly different interests to be protected in these situations. The entitled tenant is entitled to the discount as a statutory right. He or she may also be entitled to security of tenure. The person putting up the money is entitled to have that investment protected or at least to get advice about that. Should this be by

Standard Security? What about interest and terms of repayment? It is essential to recognise that these interests may not have been addressed by the parties themselves, and you need to make sure that these matters are fully understood by the parties and that there is no dispute between them about what is to happen before you can act. Although in these situations the clients will want it all done as cheaply as possible, that is their problem.

The golden rule in this as in all other professional practice matters is never to convert your client's problem into your own professional problem. If you are faced with a finding of professional misconduct and/or an expensive insurance claim, it could be the most costly fee you have ever earned.

5. *Your own security:*

Finally, in relation to loans—and not strictly speaking conflict of interest—the Society receives a considerable number of enquiries from solicitors about their own purchase and sale. The matter is governed by Rule 22 of the Accounts Rules. That Rule means that the firm cannot act for the lender in the creation, variation or discharge of a Standard Security where the borrower is a partner, the spouse of a partner, or a company or a partnership in which either of them have an interest. The definition of loan is wide enough to include a guarantee of a loan to children, parents or others. In relation to discharges there is an exception where the borrowers' obligations under the Standard Security have been fully implemented no later than two months before a discharge is obtained from the lender. For further guidance see the Guide to the Accounts Rules (F1235).

Law Society Guidelines on Conflict of Interest and Ranking Agreements

The Professional Practice Committee have agreed that a Guideline should be published on conflict of interest in relation to a Ranking Agreement. The Committee are of the view that there is a conflict of interest between lenders in relation to a Ranking Agreement and that the same firm should not act for more than one lender even in *de minimis* cases.

Consideration should also be given to whether there is a conflict of interest between lender and borrower in relation to a Ranking Agreement. Whether there is will depend on the particular circumstances of each case.

Law Society Guidelines on Conflict of Interest between Borrower and Spouse

[(March 1999)]

ALISTAIR SIM considers the lessons that can be learned from two English cases involving issues of enforceability of securities

Claims regularly arise out of problems over enforceability of securities. Some of these problems arise out of alleged deficiencies in advice tendered to the parties or information reported to the lender. The duties of solicitors in relation to the latter have been the subject of a great deal of litigation in recent times. A certain amount of this litigation has gone on south of the border, however it has a potential impact here.

Two cases raise issues of interest and concern. The decisions in these cases do not necessarily represent the law in Scotland, but it is well worth considering the cases to establish whatever lessons can be learned.

The case of *Royal Bank of Scotland plc v. Etridge* (*No. 2*), *The Times*, August 17, 1998 (CA) involved spouses who were contesting proceedings for repossession of matrimonial homes on the basis that their signature of mortgages were procured by misrepresentation or undue influence on the part of the borrower.

How could solicitors be at risk in this situation? A lending institution will inevitably consider alternative remedies in the event of its inability to enforce a security. If the security relates to matrimonial property and the difficulty in enforcing the security arises because the spouse alleges that the security was procured by misrepresentation or undue influence on the part of the borrower or lender, the lender may well consider possible remedies against the solicitor instructed to advise the spouse and procure the spouses signature.

Zwebner v. Mortgage Corporation Limited [1997] P.N.L.R. 504, Lloyd, J., Ch D involved a loan to be secured over a property belonging to the borrower and another party. The solicitor instructed to act for the lender issued a report on title in which there was an undertaking that all appropriate documents would be properly executed on completion. The solicitor sent the security deed to the borrower for execution by both the borrower and his co-proprietor. On the borrower's insolvency, the co-proprietor alleged that she was not bound by the security deed as her signature on the security deed had been forged. The lender was successful in recovering from the solicitor on the basis that, whether or not the solicitor had been at fault, the report on title amounted to a warranty that the security deed had been properly executed.

The terms of the judgment suggest that in England and Wales at least, the solicitor's duty of care to the lender may require the solicitor to be satisfied that the signatures of all signatories to a security deed are genuine.

It is beyond the scope of this note to consider the implications of these decisions in legalistic terms. While readers are encouraged to consider the full implications of the decisions the comments here are limited to managing risk.

The objective as always must be to do as much as reasonably practicable to minimise the risk of a problem arising at all. On this basis, should a problem still arise in spite of the precautions you have taken, you will be in a far stronger position to defend any claim.

The impact of the English cases may well be reflected in developments in the law here; in changes in the rules or practice regarding separate representation in security transactions and in changes in the terms of lenders' instructions. It is in the interests of practitioners to consider now what implications these developments and changes will have and to consider how the conduct of security work can be made as free of risk from the practitioner's point of view.

What does this mean in practice?

There are many issues that need to be considered routinely when instructions from a lender involve arranging signature of security deeds. A checklist which prompts you to consider relevant issues may be helpful. This might include the following points:

- Are you quite clear which party/parties is/are your client(s)? Lender, borrower, borrower's spouse? Are your instructions such that you could have a duty of care to more than one of these parties?
- Should you act for/advise more than one party?
- Is there an actual conflict of interest? If so, have you made it clear to the other parties that they should seek separate legal advice?
- Has the borrower's spouse been advised to take independent legal advice and, if so, has such advice been given?

If you are acting for the spouse

- Have you ensured that the spouse knows and understands who has instructed you and the basis on which advice has been given?
- Are you satisfied that the spouse was not subject to undue influence on the part of the borrower or the lender?
- Have you considered the implications of Rule 7 of the Conflict of Interest Rules (issuing deeds, etc., for signature by a party who has chosen not to instruct a solicitor)?
- Have you ascertained whether the spouse will receive direct financial benefit from the loan to which the security relates?
- Have you ascertained whether the spouse is involved in any way in the business to which the loan relates?
- Have you made other enquiries with a view to establishing whether the spouse might be advised not to sign the security deed? (Note: it may be only by examining the finances/accounts of the borrower's business that meaningful advice could be given in this regard)
- Has the spouse been advised of the implications of securing business borrowings over the matrimonial house/other matrimonial property?
- Has the spouse been advised that the security is an all sums security/a security for a fixed amount?
- Have you ensured that there are letters/attendance notes recording advice given?

When acting for the lender

- Have you considered whether it may be appropriate to qualify your report on title (to note, for instance, concerns in respect of potential conflict of interest)?
- If your instructions require you to warrant that the security deeds are properly executed, how have you satisfied yourself before reporting to the lender that the signatures are genuine? If you cannot warrant that signatures are genuine (*e.g.* by seeing the spouse sign and seeing evidence of identity), do not do so.

Remember, if a claim a rises and the cause of the claim is or is attributable to breach of the Conflict of Interest Practice Rules, the self-insured amount will be double the standard amount.

The information in this note is (a) intended to provide guidance on matters of practical risk management and not on issues of law and (b) is necessarily of a generalised nature. It is not specific to any practice or to any individual and should not be relied on as stating the correct legal position.

Alistair Sim is *Associate Director of Marsh U.K. Ltd*

[1] Law Society Guidance Notes on Exhibition of Title Deeds

In a conveyancing transaction, the seller/landlord's solicitor should, other than in exceptional circumstances, forward the title deeds for examination by the purchaser/tenant's solicitor at the latter's office.

If a title is likely to be in heavy demand, the seller/landlord's solicitor should make up sufficient sets of extracts and/or copies to ensure that the progress of transactions is not impeded by the unavailability of deeds. In such a case, it is acceptable to send copies of deeds, provided the originals or extracts are available for examination at the offices of the seller/landlord's solicitor if so desired.

Exceptional circumstances would include, for example, the situation where an extract did not contain the plan annexed to the original deed, which was in particularly heavy demand, or in fragile condition; or where the number of relevant deeds involved would render compliance with the guideline impracticable.

NOTES

[1] Reproduced with kind permission of the Law Society of Scotland, Conveyancing Committee. The Guidance note first appeared in J.L.S.S., vol. 41, No. 5, May 1996.

Guidelines on Letters of Obligation in Land Registration Cases 1997

An Edinburgh firm asked whether, in a land registration case, it was appropriate on delivery of the land certificate to return the letter of obligation marked as fully implemented. The firm on the other side of a particular transaction had declined to do so, on the basis that the Keeper might require to rectify the land certificate at a later stage. The Committee agreed that, where a land certificate had been issued without exclusion of indemnity, the proper practice was for the purchaser's solicitor to return the letter of obligation marked as implemented.

Law Society Guidelines on Retention of Funds

The Professional Practice Department at the Society receives a substantial number of inquiries about solicitors' obligations in relation to funds retained at settlement of conveyancing transactions. Solicitors frequently find that they are unable to get instructions from clients who either decline to reply to letters or who have disappeared. Some general guidance may be of assistance in these situations.

Where a sum of money is to be retained at settlement of a conveyancing transaction, the conditions upon which it is retained should be set out in writing at settlement. The agreement should specify the time-limit for implementation. Matters should not be left to recollection of telephone conversations which may become vague with the passage of time.

If funds were retained pending fulfilment of certain conditions by the seller, they should be released when those conditions have been fulfilled in terms of the written agreement. The purchaser's solicitor does not need to seek instructions from his or her client at that stage.

Solicitors are entitled to rely upon agreements reached with other solicitors at settlement which set out conditions on which funds will be released. If the client instructs the solicitor not to release funds there could be a conflict of interest between solicitor and client requiring the solicitor to withdraw from acting.

It may be that the conditions for release of the funds have not been fulfilled by the seller. In these circumstances if the purchaser's solicitor produces vouching for the actual or estimated expenditure required to fulfil the conditions, the seller's agent does not require the seller's instructions to agree to the release of the funds as so vouched. Again solicitors are entitled to rely on the reciprocity of such agreements.

Law Society Guidelines on Faxed and E-Mail Documents

The Professional Practice Committee and the Council have looked again at a solicitor's duty in relation to a fax of a contractual document such as a Missive. The Committee re-affirmed its previously published view (Council Report—December 1991) that there is a duty on a solicitor to follow up a fax of a contractual document with the original as soon as possible. If the solicitor is instructed by the client not to send the hard copy that fact must be communicated to the other solicitor immediately and the solicitor must withdraw from acting if the client cannot be persuaded to withdraw such instructions. Furthermore, if a solicitor is not sure if a contractual document can be sent, a fax should not be sent of it. It has been held in the sheriff court that a bargain was concluded where the final Missive was communicated by fax.

The Committee also considered the question of E-Mails. They observed that normally an E-Mail is more akin to a phone call than to a fax and that solicitors should ensure they have an appropriate security level to deal with the question of confidentiality. If a solicitor is dealing by E-Mail with a matter in which instructions need to be recorded, written confirmation should be sent of the instructions received by E-Mail putting the onus on the client to correct the instruction if it has been wrongly noted. The E-Mail should be printed out and put on the file if it contains instructions.

E-Mails which carry attachments containing facsimile signatures should be treated as faxes.

Law Society Guidelines on Property Schedules and Mortgage Advice Service

The Professional Practice Committee has issued the following Guideline on Property Schedules and the promotion of a firm's Mortgage Advice Service:

Rule 5 of the Solicitors (Scotland) Practice Rules 1986—commonly known as the Conflict of Interest Rules—prohibits the same firm from acting for buyer and seller of heritable property "at any stage". The Professional Practice Committee have decided that giving advice about a mortgage or finance to a prospective purchaser of a property is acting at a stage. The firm selling the property can therefore only give such advice when the prospective purchaser is an established client or a client otherwise exempt from the general prohibition on acting for buyer and seller in the Rules.

The Committee has therefore decided that solicitors should take care about the wording of Property Particulars. If the firm's own Mortgage Advice Service is promoted to prospective purchasers in the Schedule, the Schedule must include a warning advising that the firm may not be able to act for the would be purchasers in giving mortgage advice or in any other matter connected with the purchase.

Law Society Guidelines on Avoidance of Delay in Concluding Missives

It is increasingly common for Missives to be in an unconcluded state until shortly before—or even at—the date of entry. While solicitors require to have regard to the interests of their clients and to take their clients' instructions, they must have regard to the principles of good professional conduct and may not accept an improper instruction. They should not knowingly mislead professional colleagues and must act with fellow solicitors in a spirit of trust and co-operation (Code of Conduct for Scottish Solicitors articles 2, 5(a) and 9).

In residential property transactions solicitors acting on behalf of both purchasers and sellers have a professional duty to conclude Missives without undue delay. Clients should be advised at the outset of this duty and of the consequences.

Where a solicitor for a purchaser is instructed to submit an offer but to delay concluding a bargain until some matter outwith the selling agent's control has been resolved—*e.g.* the purchaser's own house has not been sold; a survey or specialist's report is required; or funding arrangements are to be confirmed—these circumstances should be disclosed to the selling solicitor. If the purchaser instructs the solicitor not to disclose such matters to the selling solicitor, the purchaser's solicitor should withdraw from acting. To continue acting could amount to a breach of article 9 of the Code of Conduct by knowingly misleading a fellow solicitor. Where a purchaser instructs his solicitor to delay concluding a bargain without giving any reason the solicitor should similarly withdraw from acting.

Where a selling client instructs a solicitor to delay concluding a bargain having given an indication that an offer is to be accepted, the reason for that delay should be disclosed to the purchaser's solicitor. If the seller instructs the solicitor not to disclose the reason, or does not give a reason for such an instruction, the solicitor should also withdraw from acting.

If a solicitor—whether for seller or purchaser—withdraws from acting in terms of this Guideline, the confidentiality of the client should not be breached without the client's authority but when intimating withdrawal that should be done by stating that it is in terms of this Guideline.

Law Society Guidelines on Fixed Price Offers

The Professional Practice Committee published Guidelines on Closing Dates in 1991. At that time the Committee decided not to issue a Guideline in relation to fixed price offers, but after reviewing the matter in the light of more recent developments, they have now issued the following Guideline:

The use of fixed price offers should be considered carefully. Problems can arise when two or three prospective purchasers attempt to express interest simultaneously or when offers are submitted subject to conditions.

A sale advertised at a fixed price is an invitation to prospective purchasers to submit offers at that price. In the Committee's view it does not imply an undertaking on the part of the solicitor that the first such offer will be accepted.

If a solicitor is instructed to advertise a property at a fixed price, the Property Particulars should state if the date of entry is material and whether offers subject to survey, subject to finance being obtained, subject to the purchaser's own house being sold or subject to some other suspensive condition will be considered. Other matters material to the seller should also be clearly stated.

Law Society's Guidelines on Acting for Separated Spouses

[(July 1998)]

Separation Agreement

Sale of jointly owned property

1. In 1994, the Committee published a Guideline in relation to the sale of the matrimonial home where the spouses are separated. That has now been reviewed in the light of experience. The Committee have re-affirmed the basic principle that unless the parties have agreed in writing—i.e. an agreement signed by the parties themselves—how the sale proceeds will be distributed, neither of the solicitors' firms acting for the individual spouses in their matrimonial affairs should act in the sale. A separate firm should be instructed. The agreement to be signed does not have to be a full separation agreement. It may be an agreement about the free proceeds alone.

2. The guidance applies where the property is in joint names. Where the property is in the name of only one entitled spouse, there is a clear conflict of interest between the spouses and the same firm should not act for both of them. The firm acting for the entitled spouse may accept instructions in the sale of the property, but must not act for the non-entitled spouse.

3. Where a firm are acting in the sale of jointly owned property and in the course of the transaction it transpires that the spouses have separated or are about to separate, the firm can continue to act in the sale, but cannot act for either of them in relation to their matrimonial affairs. The clients must be referred to other agents for such advice. The firm acting in the sale should distribute the free proceeds in accordance with the title, or in accordance with the spouses subsequent written agreement. The firm cannot advise either of the spouses on such an agreement as there is a clear conflict of interest between them in relation to that.

4. The same firm of solicitors should not act for both spouses in relation to a separation agreement. Again there is a clear conflict of interest and even if the spouses have agreed on matters, a firm of solicitors should act for only one of them in preparing an actual agreement. If the other refuses to seek separate advice, the firm can deal with that spouse as an unrepresented party. In that case—whether or not the agreement deals with heritable property—the solicitor sending any document for signature by the unrepresented spouse must advise that spouse in writing that signature of the document will have legal consequences and he or she should seek independent legal advice before signing it.

5. Where solicitors are acting for one of two separated spouses and the jointly owned property is to be sold, unless the parties have signed an agreement dealing with the free proceeds of sale, the parties must be referred to a separate firm of solicitors to deal with the conveyancing. It would not be improper for the firm acting for one of the spouses to accept instructions to market the property, but unless there is a signed agreement by the time an offer is received, they should not act in the conveyancing.

6. If the parties have signed an agreement dealing with the free proceeds, the solicitors acting for one of the spouses may act in the sale but must account to the parties in accordance with the signed agreement. They cannot accept unilateral instructions from one of the parties to alter that. There is a clear conflict of interest between the parties in that event. Where solicitors are not acting for both parties in the sale, they are able to accept instructions from their own client to do diligence on the dependence of an action or in execution of an agreement.

Law Society Guidelines on Settlement Cheques Sent to be Held as Undelivered

[(October 1998)]

As part of their Review of Practice Guidelines, the Professional Practice Committee have considered Guidelines which were issued in 1992 and 1994, and have agreed that there should be no change to the most recent Guideline, which was published in 1994. The Committee reaffirmed that such matters should be agreed in advance if at all possible, and that it is improper professional practice to impose unilaterally a condition that a cheque in settlement of a transaction be held as undelivered pending confirmation that the sender is in funds. The Committee accepted, however, that while as a matter of law the seller's solicitor may be entitled to encash the cheque and ignore the condition, such action would not be good professional practice as it would destroy the professional trust between agents. The text of the Guideline is as follows:

In the 1992 journal at page 323 a note was published after a purchaser's agent, without prior agreement or discussion, sent the selling agent a cheque for the purchase price "to be held as undelivered" until the purchaser's agent telephoned to say it could be cashed. The Chief Accountant's advice as contained in the note was that the selling agent should have ignored the unilaterally imposed condition relating to delivery of the cheque and should have cashed it.

Exception was taken to this view and the matter was extensively debated within the Society's Conveyancing Committee, the Professional Practice Committee and the Council. The considered view of the majority, approved by Council, contradicted important elements in the Chief Accountant's note.

It is not competent unilaterally to impose a condition, whether made verbally or in writing, in a contract such as for the sale of heritable property. In the absence of subsequent agreement, the missives prevail. It is professionally wrong for an agent to impose a unilateral condition, the first intimation of which to the other side is in a letter on the morning of settlement. Prior discussion and agreement is necessary. Professors Cusine and Rennie touch on this at para. 6.15 of their recent book, Missives, where they state: "It is not open to the purchasing solicitor, at the time of dispatch of the cheque, to require the cheque to be held as undelivered where the seller's obligations under the contract are unimplemented, unless of course that has been agreed with the seller's solicitor".

It is acknowledged that a practice has developed of sending cheques to be held as undelivered with both sides being agreeable to this. This practice avoids alternative courses of action such as bridging or effecting settlement in person, all of which can be viewed as adding expense, though agents should be aware of the benefits of electronic transfer of funds. Assuming trust between practitioners, arrangements which rely on mutual acceptance of an undertaking nor to cash the cheque can be made. It is analogous to the customary sending of the settlement cheque to be held as undelivered pending dispatch of a duly executed disposition, etc.

It is also important to bear in mind that the question of conditional delivery of a cheque is dealt with in s.21 of the Bills of Exchange Act 1882.

The Society's view is that it was wrong and improper professional practice for the purchasing agent to impose the unilateral condition which he did. However, that did not entitle the selling agent to cash the cheque, given that it was sent subject to the words "to be held as undelivered". The Professional Practice Committee and the Council have confirmed that where money or deeds are sent to be held as undelivered pending purification of a condition, they should be so held if the condition is not purified. Settlement will not take place until they can be treated as delivered, with consequent penalty interest if provided in the missives. The matter is one of practice between agents rather than of law.

Gazumping, Gazundering And Closing Dates

[February 2005]

In the light of increasing concern both within and outwith the profession about the integrity of the system of offer and acceptance for houses in Scotland, the Professional Practice Committee have reviewed the existing Practice Guideline on Closing Dates and Notes of Interest. The Committee were particularly concerned about the increasing frequency of both gazumping and gazundering. The following Practice Guidelines have been approved by the Council of the Society:

Gazumping

Where a solicitor for a seller has intimated verbally or in writing to the solicitors for a prospective purchaser that their client's offer is acceptable – whether after a closing date or otherwise – the seller's solicitor should not accept subsequent instructions from the seller to accept an offer from another party unless and until negotiations with the original offeror have fallen through. The solicitor should advise the seller to instruct another solicitor if he wishes to accept the later offer.

This Guideline extends the guideline on Closing Dates to a situation where no closing date has been fixed.

Gazundering

Solicitors acting for prospective purchasers of residential property whose offer is accepted – either verbally or in writing – should withdraw from acting if the client subsequently wishes to re-negotiate the price downwards without having made the offer subject to a satisfactory valuation or obtaining satisfactory finance. If there is a valid issue arising out of an unforeseen problem with the title that would not require the agents to withdraw. Where an offer has been submitted subject to survey, and the survey discloses a problem – e.g. unauthorised alterations; new windows; damp or rot requiring specialist treatment – the solicitors would be entitled to accept instructions to seek to adjust the price in the light of that problem. However if the offer is only subject to survey and the survey discloses no such problem but the valuation is regarded as too low by the offeror, solicitors should not accept instructions to withdraw the original offer and re-submit a lower offer but should refer the client to other solicitors if the client insists on doing so.

Purchasers solicitors should advise the clients in advance of submitting an offer that if the client subsequently wishes to re-negotiate the price downwards without good reason, the solicitor will require to withdraw from acting.

There is no difficulty where a seller initiates renegotiation at a lower price if the prospective purchaser has withdrawn an offer due to an unsatisfactory survey, whether or not valuation was the sole issue.

Closing Dates

Selling Solicitor

1. There is no legal requirement on a selling solicitor to fix a Closing Date when more than one interest is noted. Selling solicitors are entitled to accept their client's instructions to accept an incoming offer without having a Closing Date and without giving other parties who may have noted an interest an opportunity to offer although every effort should be made to give them such an opportunity if at all possible. Where a client has instructed a solicitor to intimate a closing date to other solicitors who have noted

interest, that solicitor should withdraw from acting if the selling client wishes to cancel the closing date and accept an offer submitted in advance of it unless the Closing Date is brought forward giving those who have noted an interest a reasonable opportunity to offer. Sellers solicitors should therefore advise their clients of this in advance of fixing a closing date.

2. Where possible when fixing a Closing Date, the client should be advised to make him/herself available to consider the offers received. If this is not possible (e.g. Executries, Trusts, Companies etc.) prospective offerers should be told this when being advised of the Closing Date.

3. In taking instructions from the selling client to fix a Closing Date, solicitors should advise the client that, although not bound to accept the highest—or indeed any—offer, if the client instructs the solicitor to enter negotiations with a view to concluding a bargain with a party who has submitted an offer at the Closing Date, the solicitor will not be able to accept any subsequent instructions to enter negotiations with or accept an offer from another party unless and until negotiations with the original offerer have fallen through. Unsuccessful offerers should, of course be advised as soon as possible after the Closing Date of the situation.

4. In the event of the selling client subsequently attempting to instruct the solicitor to discontinue such negotiations in order solely to enter into negotiations with or accept an offer from another party the solicitor should decline to act further in the sale unless the client reconsiders and adheres to the original instructions.

5. Where, at a Closing Date, two or more offers are received in terms that are such that they cannot be distinguished by the selling client, the solicitor may revert to those offerers and give them equal opportunity to revise their offer.

6. These Guidelines apply equally to solicitors acting as estate agents as well as solicitors acting in the conveyancing. Different considerations may apply however to sales of commercial property and to sellers owing statutory or fiduciary duties to others.

Solicitors Acting for Prospective Purchasers

7. Where a prospective purchaser instructs the solicitor to submit an offer at a Closing Date, the solicitor should advise the client that if the offer is unsuccessful the solicitor will not be able to accept subsequent instructions to submit a revised offer or formal amendment unless expressly invited to do so by the seller's agent.

8. In the event of an unsuccessful prospective purchaser subsequently attempting to instruct the solicitor to submit a revised offer or formal amendment after a Closing Date has passed and without an express invitation by the seller's agent, the solicitor should decline to implement those instructions. The solicitor may accept instructions to intimate to the seller's agent that in the event of negotiations with the successful party falling through, the prospective purchaser would be willing to enter negotiations, but no indication of any increased bid should be given.

9. Solicitors acting for purchasers who have received a verbal or qualified acceptance—whether following a Closing Date or not—should advise clients that although an initial acceptance may have been given by the seller, the contract will not be binding until Missives are concluded.

Notes of Interest

Solicitors acting for prospective purchasers should advise their clients that noting an interest may not guarantee the clients an opportunity to offer, and if the clients are not in a position to put in an early offer they may not be allowed an opportunity to submit an offer at all.

Guidelines on the Electronic Transfer of Funds 1999

The Professional Practice Committee have been in correspondence with the Committee of Scottish Clearing Bankers regarding electronic transfer of funds in which the following information has been given. The Committee felt that this information should be published for the benefit of the profession as a whole.

CHAPS is a Real Time Gross Settlement (RTGS) system. This means that every payment is settled immediately at the Bank of England by passing a debit against the remitter bank's Sterling Settlement account and crediting the beneficiary bank's settlement account. This gives finality for the payment and removes credit risk for the receiving bank and enables funds to be credited same day to customer accounts.

To enable the funding and flow of funds member banks have to ensure their Bank of England Account has enough liquidity. This is not as straightforward as it sounds. The CHAPS system processes about twice the UK's GDP every week. In effect, therefore, money is "washing" round the system as people pay each other for goods and services. The country overall simply does not have a limitless supply of "cash" and payments in high value same day systems have to be scheduled. Member banks can find themselves in the position of having to wait for incoming funds before any further payments can settle at the Bank of England.

Most settlement member banks have electronic banking packages that enable customers to key and authorise their own CHAPS payments. This will nearly always be quicker than instructing the payment via a branch or call centre. Problems with systems, accuracy of keying, or the funding issues noted above are the only reasons such payments would not reach their destination within several minutes of being released in the customer premises. Traditionally, solicitors have tended not to use such packages.

The CHAPS Clearing Company has 17 settlement members. This means that if you are a customer of a financial institution that is not one of these 17 members then issues arise which are outwith the sphere of CHAPS. How payments are handled and the timing of passing payment instructions between a participating bank/building society and a settlement member is a matter solely for the two institutions involved.

With regard to the suggestion that "Scottish" transactions be routed through Edinburgh, the view is that, with today's technology, there is no need for such a system as there would be no benefit. A possible exception might be a slightly later cut-off time than the present 1530 hours deadline but the benefit would be marginal and the costs prohibitive.

The banks advise that what some members of the profession perceive as delays are in fact simply part of the processing system. The Professional Practice Committee reaffirmed the view that settlement of transactions with a cheque drawn on the clients' account should remain the norm in Scotland, unless the parties agree otherwise.

Guidelines on Common Repairs 1999

The Scottish Consumer Council has recently published a report on the views and experiences of owner occupiers in Scotland who share common property with their council. Its recommendations include the following:

"Solicitors should always make sure prospective purchasers are aware of the conditions contained in their title deeds about the management of repairs."

"The Law Society of Scotland should take steps to improve pre-purchase information given by solicitors about common repair responsibilities."

The Society's Conveyancing Committee is of the view that current best practice already covers this but feels it appropriate to bring practitioners' notice to the recommendations.

The report makes further recommendations to the Scottish Parliament, national bodies and local authorities.

Guidelines on Deed of Conditions for Housing Estates 1999

The Society has received further representations from the Associations of Proprietors on Housing Estates, Solicitors are reminded that they should draw to the attention of prospective purchasers the existence of a Deed of Conditions and to highlight any difficulties which may arise in such Deed and to comply with the conditions therein, including notification to the secretary of the Proprietors Association of change of ownership.

Guidelines on Postal Settlement 2001

In the settlement of conveyancing transactions, should the practice be discouraged whereby the seller's solicitor only sends the Disposition and other titles to the purchaser's solicitor on or after the day of settlement, whereby the purchaser's can only be sure that a validly executed Disposition has been placed in his hands after his settlement cheque has been encashed, by which point he has lost of his clients and/or his clients' lender's money? Is the former practice of exchanging cheque and Disposition and titles on the day of settlement itself not safer, and better risk management?

The Conveyancing Committee agrees. Although the mechanics of settlement are something which ought to be the matter of agreement between the solicitors, the Committee feels that, where postal settlement is envisaged, the preferable course of action, wherever possible, is that the seller's Solicitor should send the executed deed and deliverable title deeds contemporaneously with the purchaser's solicitor sending the settlement cheque, each to be held by the receiving party as undelivered pending performance by the other side, to be confirmed by an exchange of communications (telephone, fax or e-mail) on the settlement date itself. The Committee would encourage all practitioners to adopt this practice.

[NEXT TEXT PAGE IS F 1229]

Law Society's Guidance Notes on Capital Adequacy

Introduction—Why issue guidance on this subject?

Following a period of consultation and discussion the Guarantee Fund Committee Working Party has recommended the production of Guidance Notes on the subject of Capital Adequacy in legal practices. The Guidance Notes are thought to be a valuable and confidential method of allowing solicitors to measure their own firm's financial standing. The problem of not having any standard to apply to the firm's balance sheet and profitability means that each firm is forced to make a personal decision about its level of reserves. This healthy independence has drawbacks in dealing with banks and other financial institutions because there are no opportunities for solicitors to make comparisons with other equivalent businesses.

The Law Society is increasingly aware of market pressures and tighter lending policies combining to give real problems to practices where these questions have never been faced before. The Guidance Notes are intended to help the independent firm to check on its financial health. Help and advice is also available if the standard is not being met by the practice. Telephone 0131 226 7411 and ask for Leslie Cumming or one of his team on the subject of Capital Adequacy.

The Guidance Notes are intended to help solicitors to assess their financial position by fixing realistic values in areas where business optimism can traditionally over-rule prudence. It is also recognised that many solicitors have adopted conservative accounting policies in dealing with debtors and work in progress. If the test check produces a negative or poor Balance Sheet result because of these accounting policies *e.g.*, cash based accounts or nominal work in progress values, it is recommended that a realistic value be included in the adjusted figures in order to produce the most accurate result.

The trend of the business measured consistently and regularly can be a powerful management tool. In addition to testing earlier years accounts, the ratios can be done quarterly or half-yearly to measure the rate of improvement and decline. The more regularly this check is carried out the better judgment can be made on the state of the practice's financial health.

The Basic Standards

The standard measures are intended to look at balance sheet ratios and profitability. The results of the tests should be considered in three stages, action being taken or advice being sought depending on the results of your firm's own calculations.

1. *Is the practice solvent?*

If the method of calculating the value of your Balance Sheet as set out in Schedule I is applied to your firm's balance sheet, does the result show a negative value? If the answer is yes, get some advice on how to deal with the situation. The position is serious and must not be ignored.

2. *Are the capital reserves inadequate?*

The standard measures should be applied to the balance sheet figures. If the firm is solvent but the partner's capital does not achieve 20% of the value of total assets then the balance sheet needs some action to be taken in order to strengthen the position. Again, advice should be sought if the remedial action to be taken is not obvious.

3. *Profitability*

The net profit before tax should be at least 20% of income.

If equity partners charge salaries to the Profit and Loss account these should be added back to the profit.

If the results of the calculations do not achieve the 20% level on both balance sheet and profitability calculations the practice is considered to be in a marginal position. If this is the case, then action must be taken to improve the ratios without delay. Again, advice should be sought if the remedial action is not obvious.

The Benchmark Tests

The two key tests are defined as follows:—

(1) *Partnership Solvency Test/Capital Adequacy Test*

$$\frac{\text{Total partners capital reserves} \times 100}{\text{Total gross partnership assets}} = X\%$$

where X% is less than 0% the partnership is deemed to be insolvent and advice must be sought at once. Where X% is a positive figure, this measures the extent of capital cover in the practice. A target of over 20% is thought to be prudent.

(2) *Profitability of the practice*

$$\frac{\text{Total annual profits before tax} \times 100}{\text{Total annual income}} = Y\%$$

where Y% is targeted to be more than 20% of income.

The higher the assets and profitability ratio are, the stronger the firm's position is. Results in the 0%–20% range are a cause for concern and indicate a lack of financial stability. Well run partnerships may be targeting annual profit ratios in excess of 30%

Strong balance sheets will include a 50% partnership funding of working capital and at least a 30% stake in any properties owned by the partnership.

It will be helpful to check the equivalent figures in the previous 2 years in order to measure whether the position is stable, improving or declining. Any reduction in performance even in a strong set of accounts should be treated as an early warning.

Conclusion: If you are unable to meet the basic minimal standards as set out above you must take advice from another experienced solicitor, accountant or the Law Society. The smaller the ratios, the more urgent is the need for advice. Firms with losses or negative capital reserves must act at once.

Schedule II shows three examples where the original profit and partnership reserves range from adequate to strong. The tests show up inherent weaknesses in the figures. Complacency is dangerous in these circumstances.

SCHEDULE I

Benchmark Tests

Definitions and calculations to be used

Step 1. *Valuing assets*

—*Fixed assets.* Using written down values per your balance sheet is generally acceptable and will include properties, office equipment and cars.
—*goodwill.* This asset is ignored for the purposes of the test.
—*work-in-progress.* This must be prudently valued. Any estimate of work-in-progress must be capable of being confirmed by reference to time records or files and should not exceed 3 months average fee income (excluding any element of profit).
—*debtors.* The value must exclude any bad or doubtful debts. The total for this asset must be linked to the annual fee income. The test value should be the lesser of the actual total or 3 months fee income.
—*cash.* Actual value on deposits.

—*listed investments.* Cost or market value. If market value is the lesser figure this should be used.

The total assets value which has resulted from these calculations are used for the balance sheet ratio calculation.

Step 2. *Calculating liabilities*

This will include any bank overdrafts, loans or business mortgages or personal loans by third parties to the partnership or the sole practitioner in his business.

Also to be included are creditors of the business hire purchase liabilities on the firms assets and income tax and VAT liabilities on the profit and income figures included in the accounts.

Step 3. *Adjusted Balance sheet Partnership reserves*

The partnership capital reserves which form the balancing figure to the revised balance sheet calculations will reflect the balance sheet adjustments for the value of any assets which require to be written down or excluded as set out under Section 1 above. The gross balance sheet value of assets including current assets and the net partnership capital figures devised from the adjusted balance sheet are used in the calculation of the balance sheet ratios required under Test No. 1 and 2. The resulting figure is used for the balance sheet ratio calculation.

Step 4. *Calculating the ratio*

The revised capital reserves figures (Step 3) should be divided by the adjusted gross assets (Step 1) and expressed as a percentage.

Step 5. *Total income and net profit*

The figures for total income should be as per the annual accounts and may include fees, commissions, interest earned or other income generated by the practice.

The figure of annual profit after all overheads and operating charges including finance and depreciation charges but before tax and partners drawings is used for this calculation.

Step 6. *Profitability in the Practice*

The calculation of the annual figure of profitability as a percentage is done by using the values set out in Step 5.

SCHEDULE II

Sample Calculations—Example I

(a) Balance sheet adjustments

	Actual	*Test*
Goodwill	£100,000	£NIL
Property at valuation	120,000	120,000
Other fixed assets	60,000	60,000
	280,000	180,000
Current assets		
W.I.P.	140,000	61,000
Debtors	45,000	45,000
Clients account surplus (net)	1,000	1,000
	186,000	107,000
Total assets	£466,000	£287,000
Liabilities	*Actual*	Test
Trade creditors	£ 15,000	£ 15,000
Bank overdraft	50,000	50,000
Term loan	100,000	100,000
Total liabilities	165,000	165,000
Partner capital	301,000	122,000
	£466,000	£287,000
Comparative ratios		
—capital/assets	65%	43%

(b) Profit and loss statement

	Actual	*Actual*
Income—fees		£280,000
—commissions		20,000
		300,000
Expenses		
Salaries	£160,000	
Office expenses	30,000	
Car expenses	15,000	
Professional fees	7,500	
Miscellaneous	12,000	
Interest	6,000	
Depreciation	15,000	245,500
Net profit before tax		£ 54,500
Profit ratio		18%

(c) Benchmark ratios

Balance sheet

$$\frac{\text{Capital} \times 100}{\text{Total Assets}} = X\%$$

$$\frac{£122{,}000 \times 100}{287{,}000} = 42.5\%$$

Profitability

$$\frac{\text{Net Profit} \times 100}{\text{Total income}} = Y\%$$

$$\frac{£54{,}500 \times 100}{300{,}000} = 18.2\%$$

WIP figure is replaced by 3 months' costs as a reduced valuation. The strong balance sheet is being threatened by a weak profit position. If this three partner firm can't live on the profits a slow decline in the balance sheet position will result in a problem.

SAMPLE CALCULATIONS—EXAMPLE II

(a) Balance sheet adjustments

	Actual	Test
Goodwill	£100,000	£NIL
Fixed assets	60,000	60,000
	160,000	60,000
Current assets		
WIP	140,000	43,000
Debtors	45,000	45,000
Client account surplus (net)	1,000	1,000
	186,000	89,000
Total Assets	£346,000	£149,000
Liabilities		
Trade creditors	£ 25,000	£ 25,000
Bank overdraft	100,000	100,000
	125,000	125,000
Partners capital	221,000	24,000
	£346,000	£149,000
Comparative ratios		
—capital/assets	64%	16%

(b) Profit and loss statement

		Actual	Actual
Income—fees			£280,000
Income—commissions			20,000
			300,000
	Salaries	£160,000	
	Office expenses	42,000	
	Car expenses	15,000	
	Professional fees	7,500	
	Miscellaneous	12,000	
	Interest	5,000	
	Depreciation	15,000	256,500
	Net profit		£ 43,500
	Profit ratio		14.5%

(c) Benchmark ratios

Balance sheet $\frac{24{,}000 \times 100}{149{,}000} = 16.1\%$

Profitability $\frac{43{,}500 \times 100}{300{,}000} = 14.5\%$

Note: Balance Sheet. The strong position shown per the original Balance Sheet is undermined by the lack of property assets, the high goodwill and work in progress figures. Revalued WIP is included in the revised Balance Sheet at an actual valuation of files.

Note: Profit and Loss statement. Below average results. The problems have to be addressed before they get worse. Profits must be improved and the balance sheet strengthened. There is very little leeway.

SAMPLE CALCULATIONS—EXAMPLE III

(a) Balance Sheet adjustments

	Actual	*Test*
Goodwill	£50,000	£NIL
Fixed assets	15,000	15,000
	65,000	15,000
Current assets		
WIP	25,000	13,000
Debtors	15,000	15,000
Client account surplus	1,000	1,000
	41,000	29,000
	£106,000	£44,000
Liabilities		
Trade creditors	10,000	10,000
Overdraft	35,000	35,000
	45,000	45,000
Partners capital	61,000	(1,000)
	£106,000	£44,000
Comparative ratios		
—capital assets	58%	Negative

Note: WIP is revised to actual values from the original estimate used. The reduction in asset value has produced a negative capital value—insolvency on this benchmark test.

(b) Profit and loss statement

Total Income	£85,000
Total expenses (not set out in detail)	65,000
Net profit	£20,000

(c) Benchmarks ratios

Balance sheet **Insolvent**

Profitability $\frac{20,000 \times 100}{85,000} = 23.5\%$

The sole practitioner's profitability is acceptable but modest. Take advice on the apparent insolvency. How can the weak balance sheet be improved. Action to reduce borrowings and improve profit should be taken now.

Guide To The Solicitors' (Scotland) Accounts, Accounts Certificate, Professional Practice and Guarantee Fund Rules 2001 and Solicitors' (Scotland) Accounts Etc (Amendments) Rules 2004

[March 2005]

The Rules incorporate all of the Rules for which the Guarantee Fund Committee have the responsibility to report on to Council.

They are referred to as the Solicitors' (Scotland) Accounts etc. Rules 2001, and have been organised into separate sections for ease of reference.

The Rules are arranged in six sections, with three supporting schedules and full index, as follows:

Part I	**General**
Part II	**Accounts Rules**
Part III	**Accounts Certificate Rules**
Part IV	**Inspection and Investigations**
Part V – I	**Professional Practice—Loans**
Part V—II	**Professional Practice—Secured loans to Solicitors etc.**
Part V—III	**Professional Practice—Powers of Attorney**
Part V—IV	**Professional Practice—Money Laundering**
Part VI	**Guarantee Fund and Other Questions**
Schedule I	**Form of Certificate**
Schedule 2a	**Form of Certificate (no client monies)**
Schedule 2b	**Form of Certificate (acting as agent)**
Schedule III	**Application Form for Grant from Guarantee Fund**

The 2004 (Amendment) Rules amend, by specific changes, the 2001 Rules Nos 2(1), 6(2), 22 and 24. They also amend the form of Accounts Certificate contained in Schedule I.

The following Guide takes the format of question and answer. Wherever a question relates to a specific Rule or Rules a cross reference is given to the Rule number. Both the Rules and the Guide are also available on the Society's web-site—*www.lawscot.org.uk*, under "Commonly Used Rules".

Part I General

This section includes a section containing definitions as used in the Rules, covering basic concepts such as "client monies", "Banks" etc, and is a useful starting point to understanding the Rules.

The Rules are known as the Solicitors' (Scotland) Accounts etc. Rules 2001. They consist of six sections for which the Guarantee Fund Committee have the responsibility to report to Council. The six sections in these Rules are:

I. General (including helpful definitions),
II. Accounts Rules (book-keeping section),
III. Accounts Certificate,
IV. Inspections and Investigations,
V. Professional Practice (non-accounting rules covering Bridging loans, Secured loans to Solicitors, Powers of Attorney and Money Laundering).
VI. Guarantee Fund Rules (including how to make a claim on the Fund).

When do the Rules apply?

The 2001 Rules were effective from 1st February 2002, and the Amendments are effective from 1 September 2004.

PART II ACCOUNTS RULES

This section deals with the book-keeping systems and accounting procedures. Non-accounting Rules linked to the work of the monitoring team are now dealt with later in Parts V-I to V-IV.

(Rule 4(1))

When do the Accounts Rules require me to pay money into a client account?

When a solicitor receives more than £50 from a client, and the money does not belong to the solicitor, it must be lodged in a client bank account without delay. This normally means on the same day.

(Rules 4 and 12)

Do I have to keep all my client funds in the client bank account and can I off-set sums due by clients to me?

Yes—you must keep client money in a client bank account at all times. Off-setting sums due to you is only allowed where you have a legal right to off-set for sums due to/by the same client.

(Rules 4(3) and 20)

Can I arrange bridging or other loan accounts on behalf of clients?

Yes—provided you have written authority from the client and made disclosure of the client details to the lender.

(Rule 5)

Can I pay my own money into the client bank account?

Yes—many solicitors hold a float or surplus money in the client bank account. These funds are usually held to take care of minor mistakes on the solicitors' part i.e. paying outlays for clients who have not yet put them in funds. Using a small surplus funds as a routine source of funding for clients' outlays has led to unintended shortages and should not be done routinely.

(Rule 6(1))

What monies can be paid from the client bank account without the clients' specific written authority?

Any sums due to be paid on behalf of the client where an account has been submitted to the solicitor for work instructed on behalf of a client <u>or</u> for a debt due to the solicitor <u>or</u> to transfer money into a named client bank account to be held for the client <u>or</u> money paid in by the solicitor including sums paid into the account in error.

(Rule 6(1)(d))

Does this include payment for fees?

Yes—provided the solicitor has carried out the work and raised a note of fees due and sent it to the client. The amount of the fee should be charged to the client ledger and then an equivalent sum of money can be transferred to the firm's account.

(Rule 6(1)(c))

I see the Rule refers to money drawn on a client's authority. Does this have to be in writing?

Although the authority can be oral, written confirmation should be obtained to vouch that authority has been obtained. If questions are raised by the client at a later date, you will need this written authority to rely on.

(Rule 6(1))

Do I have any other important matters to keep in mind about payments made from the client bank account?

Always remember the prohibition on using one client's money for the benefit of another client. This is only allowed if it is authorised in writing.

The fact that the Accounts Rules allow such payments if authorised in writing should not result in you overlooking the potential conflict of interest in such a transaction.

(Rule 6(2))

How should a cheque to a bank or building society be designated?

Rule 6(2) covers this. You should ensure that the payee's name is shown as part of the payee information on the face of the cheque. The account number may be shown but is not recognised as part of the payee description unlike the payee name.

(Rule 7)

What should I do if I find that I have received funds which are not to be lodged in the general client account but are to be paid onwards to the client or a third party on the same day?

It is important to record the receipt and payment of the funds as a cross-entry on the client's ledger account. This discloses the whole sequence of the financial dealings on behalf of the client on the ledger card. It is no longer necessary to disclose the whole price on the face of the ledger where the solicitor will not be in receipt of the balance of the sale/purchase price.

(Rule 7(b))

Are there any other changes to this Rule?

No—but Rule 7(b) now clarifies the position of monies paid on account of a professional fee incurred by a client to a solicitor or as an agreed fee for business done by the solicitor, which do not need to be treated as client monies and do not therefore need to be paid into a client account.

(Rule 8)

Do the Rules tell me what type of accounting records should be made and how much detail is needed?

Rule 8 is helpful on this point—it explains the importance of separate records for firm and client business, separate records for each client and the need to keep cash books and ledger accounts fully up to date.

(Rule 8(4))

How often do I have to write up my accounting records?

The books should be kept up to date at all times, so work should be done every day. It is not helpful to write books up in arrears and if for reasons of illness or holidays the records are not written up each day, cover must be arranged.

(Rule 8(4))

When do I have to balance my books?

The books must be balanced every month. This requires a trial balance to be prepared from both firm's and client's daybooks and ledgers.

(Rule 8(6))

Does the Society provide advice as to suitable computer systems?

Solicitors can use any system, manual or computerised, provided the Rules are complied with. Unfortunately, given the wide range of possibilities, the Society is not in a position to monitor and assess them. The best advice we can offer is to speak to other firms where there are parallels in terms of size, location and type of business. In addition to finding out whether they would recommend the system they can also advise you on the quality of support provided.

A list of known providers of legal software is available on the Society's website, *www.lawscot.org.uk* , Select Links from the left hand list and scroll down the alphabetical list to H for Hardware and Software suppliers.

(Rule 8(7))

How long must I keep the accounting records?

In general 10 years but further guidance, covering vouchers as well as accounting records, is given under Rule 19.

(Rule 9(2))

Once I have set up a daily routine for dealing with my accounting entries, are there any other regular tasks which need to be organised?

You must reconcile your general client bank ledger with the bank statements every month. If the practice is very busy, getting this check done daily or weekly is a big help in reducing the month end work to manageable levels. You should keep all reconciliations and associated documents for at least three years.

(Rule 9(1))

Is there any other monthly check which I must do?

Prepare a list of monies due to clients and compare it to the reconciled bank figures. A written statement of surplus/deficit must also be prepared. If a deficit is disclosed take action to correct it and refer to it in your next Accounts Certificate.

(Rule 10)

What about monies held in specific accounts for named clients—are they included in the check?

They are also to be reconciled but the Rules only need this to be done quarterly. Tackling this work more regularly—say monthly—can cut down on the amount of checking and adjusting which is needed at the end of the quarter.

(Rule 11)

When should I invest monies in an individual bank account for a specific client?

The Rules refer to sums of £500 or more, likely to be held for more than two months as an example. You should be aware of larger sums held for shorter periods which would earn the equivalent amount of interest. Keep a sliding scale in mind when thinking about this aspect of the Rules.

Are there any other changes to this Rule?

Rule 11(5)(a) now clarifies that monies held on behalf of a client for the purpose of paying all outlays, including stamp duty and recording and registration dues, do not require to be invested to earn interest.

(Rule 12)

Can you explain the role of the Designated Cashroom Partner and how it interacts with other partners and their responsibilities?

All partners are responsible for ensuring compliance with the Accounts Rules. The Designated Cashroom Partner is required to sign the Accounts Certificate and normally accepts a supervisory role on behalf of the partnership or incorporated practice. More than one Cashroom Partner can be appointed at any one time but there should be clear definition of their individual roles. Sharing or rotating of the checking tasks can be arranged if suitable to the firm and the partners.

Do all the Rules and Regulations apply to Incorporated Practices.

Yes.

Part III Accounts Certificate Rules

The obligations of the 1997 Accounts Certificate Rules are continued through into the new Rules and are explained in this section. It has been set up so that the transition can be managed without separate Certificates being needed for the period which includes 1st February 2002.

(Rule 14)

Does the Accounts Certificate apply to my firm?

Yes—even if you do not operate a client bank account. There is a special style of Certificate for that situation. You have to keep the firm records up to date and confirm that you do not continue to hold client monies. See Schedules I, 2a and 2b of the Rules for the format. They are also included at the end of these guidance notes.

(Rule 14(1))

When should I provide an Accounts Certificate?

You should set up an accounting period of no more than six months from the start of a new practice and report in the approved style within one month of the accounting period end. Certificates should be for consecutive periods of time, without gaps or overlaps, and not cover more than six months.

(Rule 15)

Who should sign the Certificate?

Two partners—one being the current Designated Cashroom Partner.

(Rule 16)

What happens when the firm operates separate accounting systems at every branch or has more than one set of accounting records?

You must provide an Accounts Certificate for each set of accounting records. Take care to have the same accounting period ends for all the systems under your control.

What information is needed for the Certificate?

The Certificate should be prepared on the firm's own headed notepaper and disclose the following details:

(a) The start and finish dates of the accounting periods.
(b) The identity of the Designated Cashroom Partner or Partners.
(c) The list of Powers of Attorney should be included. A separate list can be attached to the Certificate if the firm holds a large number of Powers.

On the reverse of the Certificate, information taken from the accounting records each quarter should be included as follows:

(a) Total sums due to clients in the general client accounts.
(b) Total monies held in general client bank accounts.
(c) Surplus or deficit which results.
(d) Total sums due to named clients as per your reconciled records.
(e) Total monies held for named clients reconciled to the passbooks, statements etc.
(f) Total sums borrowed as bridging loans for named clients.
(g) Total liabilities due to lenders for bridging loans for named clients.
(h) The firm's financial position shown as a total. Monies held in the practice balance sheet for the firm should be shown in total. If the firm has term loans, practice loans, overdrafts or other borrowings then these must be disclosed. Hire purchase liabilities which fund partnership assets are included but unexpired leases are not. Personal loans arranged outwith the firm are excluded.

If an Accountant is instructed to help with the work of preparing the Certificate, information should be included as to the level of assistance given. This is best done by attaching a copy of the Letter of Engagement between accountant and solicitor.

What happens if I have breached the terms of the Accounts Rules or the Accounts Certificate Rules?

You should take steps to correct the breach or breaches and write to the Society explaining the position. If you are unable to correct the problem immediately, contact the Chief Accountant or a member of his team for advice. The Society appreciates that breaches of Rules do happen from time to time and the Chief Accountant and his team will be happy to give appropriate advice and assistance when asked.

PART IV INSPECTIONS AND INVESTIGATIONS

This section covers the arrangements for inspections and investigations.

(Rule 19)

The monitoring team employed by the Society aims to visit all firms on a two year cycle.

New firms are also visited to see how their accounting system has been set up.

All of these visits are covered in the annual subscription to the Guarantee Fund.

Notice in writing is given for all inspections. Although the Rules only require 48 hours' notice, normally seven to ten days' notice is given. Sometimes, because of circumstances, there is less notice. Wherever possible the solicitor will be contacted by telephone when visits on shorter notice are being arranged.

The Society constantly strives to achieve a balance between the organisation required in scheduling the work of a monitoring team covering the whole of Scotland and the convenience factor for each firm.

Sometimes a non-routine inspection or investigation is the appropriate course.

Do the documents and vouchers produced have to be originals or are scanned representations sufficient?

Originals will be required for certain documents, in particular bank statements, passbooks, client account paid cheques etc.

Where the document serves as a voucher in relation to intromissions with client funds, the original is likely to be required.

Many firms scan incoming documentation such as letters, redemption statements etc. Provided the scanned document is clearly legible it may be relied upon, however, in certain circumstances confirmation of the information contained within the scanned document may have to be obtained to verify the position. You should keep in mind that such information may have to be available for up to 10 years.

Provided the scanned document is legible and it would be possible to obtain independent confirmation of the information provided in the document, the original would not have to be retained.

It is important to ensure that the scanning process is authorised and checked by a suitable person.

How long do I have to keep records and vouchers for?

Guidance on Retention/Destruction of Records

Specific obligations regarding the retention of financial records are noted in the Solicitors (Scotland) Accounts etc. Rules. The client ledger records, including invested funds ledger, daybook records, inter-client transfer record, such books and records necessary to show the true financial position of the practice and trial balances must be retained for a period of ten years, from the date of the last entry. The Society therefore recommends that any document, which may be required to be produced to vouch payments or receipts within the client ledger account, should be retained for a period of ten years.

Client files which deal with conveyancing, executry or trust accounting matters will contain within the general correspondence files matters of importance, which will require to be kept for the full ten year period. Bank statements, cashed cheques, VAT fee notes or any passbooks or print-outs which relate to funds invested or borrowed on behalf of clients will fall directly into this category.

Those solicitors who use a system of debit/credit posting slips to instruct the cashroom in its work should also ensure that these documents are retained safely for the ten year period. Previous advice from the Society had suggested that these posting slips might not require to be retained for the full ten year period. Police enquiries into matters of solicitor or employee fraud have now indicated that these documents are of vital significance since the handwriting will give significant evidence as regards the source of instruction in respect of any misleading or false entries. You may wish to take account of this advice.

The only financial records which are not covered by the ten year rule are the documents which comprise lists of client balances, bank reconciliation workings, invested funds reconciliation workings and statements of surplus/deficit. These working papers are required to be retained for a period of three years.

The Society is aware that a convention has grown up, amongst solicitors who carry out a significant amount of criminal legal aid work, whereby files which relate to completed cases are routinely destroyed twelve months after the matter has been concluded. The Society has no concerns regarding this procedure, subject to the guidance detailed below, provided there are no client account funds involved in the transaction. In the event that the solicitor is dealing with client funds any relevant vouchers would require to be separated and stored for the full ten year period, prior to the remaining contents of the file being destroyed.

If you are in any doubt with regard to the destruction of specific client files or papers then every effort should be made to retain all documents for the minimum ten years.

Guidance specific to the retention/destruction of files can be found at in the Code of Conduct for Criminal Work, Article 12 (Parliament House Book F1008) and Solicitors: Practice Guidelines—Guidelines on the Ownership and Destruction of Files 2001 (Parliament House Book F1312)

Consideration should also be given to the requirements of the Inland Revenue and Customs and Excise in relation to the retention of records.

Part V–I Professional Practice—Loans

(Rule 20)

How do I deal with bridging loans?

You must not enter into a bridging loan agreement on behalf of a client in circumstances which may impose on you personal liability for repayment in the event of default by the client. Bridging loans must always be in writing and you must give the lender full details of the client and what the arrangements are for repayment.

Can I lend money to a client?

Yes—but you should consider whether a conflict of interest might arise.

(Rule 21)

Can I borrow money from a client?

No—unless the client has been independently advised about the loan or is in the business of lending money. (*N.B.* Personal and business loans are not covered by the Guarantee Fund).

Part V–II Professional Practice—Secured Loans to Solicitors etc.

These notes have been prepared with the help of the Director of Professional Practice. If you are unsure how your specific case is affected by the Rule, enquiries are welcomed before you begin to act.

LOANS AFFECTED

(Rule 22)

(a) CREATION, VARIATION AND ASSIGNATION OF SECURITIES

What loans are affected?
Secured loans to any of the principals in the practice or their spouse or any partnership of which they or their spouse are a partner or any company in which they or their spouse are shareholders (except holdings of less than 5% of quoted companies).

Can I act for the partner or their spouse?
Yes—the Rule only prohibits acting for the lender.

Can I act for the lender if the borrower is a consultant, associate or employee of the practice?
Yes—provided the consultant, associate or employee is not married to a partner in the practice (or member if it is an incorporated practice) and provided no partner or spouse of a partner is guaranteeing the loan.

Can I act for the lender where the borrower is the parent, brother, sister, son or daughter of a partner?
Yes—provided that no partner or spouse of a partner will be guaranteeing the loan.

Why are guarantors included?
Rule 22 (3) defines loan as including any obligation to pay money. That includes a guarantee of a loan to somebody else, even though it is only a contingent obligation.

Can I act in a variation or assignation of an existing standard security?
Again the firm can act for the borrower, but not for the lender as the Rule applies equally to variations and assignations as it does to the constitution of a standard security.

(b) DISCHARGING SECURED LOANS

What about discharges?
The Rule has changed. The firm may not act for the lender.

At what stage in relation to a discharge does a solicitor act for a lender?
Only at the stage where the discharge has been drafted and is sent to the lender for execution. Drafting the discharge is done on behalf of the borrower, not the lender.

Can I send the discharge direct to the lender for execution?
Yes—but you must advise them not to return it to you but to either retain it until the loan has been redeemed or to send it to their own agents for onward delivery to you only after the loan has been redeemed.

(c) OTHER QUERIES

If I am buying a property with the aid of a secured loan, can the seller's solicitors act for the lender?

No—the Society's Professional Practice Committee take the view that there is a conflict of interest between the seller and the lender to a purchaser.

If I am buying property and another firm are acting for the lender, can the lenders forward the loan funds direct to my firm or do they have to go through their own solicitors first?

The loan funds can be remitted direct to your firm if another firm are acting for the lender. Receipt of the loan funds does not of itself constitute acting for the lender.

(d) WAIVERS

In what circumstances would the granting of a waiver from the Rules be considered?

Waivers will only be granted in relation to particular circumstances. They may be subject to conditions and will not be granted routinely. A waiver will not be granted solely because the solicitor concerned is a partner in any particular firm. There would need to be something particular about the circumstances of the transaction to justify granting a waiver. Under the previous Rules the waiver provision was restricted to partnerships (apart from the firm of solicitors itself) or companies in which the solicitor had an interest. Few requests for waivers were received.

An example of a case where a waiver was granted included a company where the solicitor or solicitor's spouse was a nominal shareholder and the principal shareholders were clients or other members of the family.

Another example where a waiver could be considered is where a small piece of ground is being sold to a neighbour or a utility company for a nominal consideration and a deed of restriction is required.

Who should I contact at the Society if I am still in doubt about Rule22?

You should contact Bruce Ritchie (Direct Line 0131 476 8124).

PART V–III PROFESSIONAL PRACTICE—POWERS OF ATTORNEY

Please note that the book-keeping entries are dealt with under Rule 8(2) in Part II of these Rules.

(Rule 23)

Do I need to keep a list of Powers of Attorney?

Yes—the Designated Cashroom Partner must keep an up to date list of active and dormant Powers of Attorney in the name of any Solicitor for submission with the Accounts Certificate.

(Rules 8(2) and 23)

What records do I have to keep to operate a Power of Attorney?

A clear record of money paid in or out of the client's own bank account should be kept in a client ledger and cash book. Where you have exclusive control of the client's bank account then that bank balance should be treated as client funds which should be included in invested funds held for named clients.

What effect does the Adults with Incapacity (Scotland) Act 2000 have?

If you are dealing with a continuing Power of Attorney, you must ensure that client funds are treated as client monies and are recorded in the invested funds records and reconciled.

What about the Money Laundering Regulations?

The simplification of this Rule, dealing with money laundering, is intended to make it easier to manage for practising solicitors.

The Money Laundering Regulations, which came into force on 1st April 1994, apply to all aspects of a solicitor's work, whenever clients' money is being handled, and the Rules now include the Money Laundering Regulations 2003 and the Proceeds of Crime Act 2002 where it applies to money laundering.

The Regulations are intended to prevent the proceeds of unlawful activities, such as Inland Revenue and Customs & Excise frauds, drug trafficking and terrorism, being legitimised by being applied to carry out legitimate transactions.

The scope of the Regulations is such that almost every aspect of a solicitor's normal workload may be affected by the need to introduce anti-money laundering procedures within the firm.

(Rule 24)

To what do the Regulations apply?

- to transactions which involve the payment by or to or on behalf of the client of an amount of €15,000 (currently approximately £9,000) or more, and to any amounts which appear to be linked with others where the aggregate of the amounts involved is in excess of €15,000;
- if you suspect that your client is engaged in money laundering, or that a transaction is being carried out on behalf of someone else who is engaged in money laundering;
- to every case where the firm forms or resolves to form a business relationship.

The terms "relevant financial business", "business relationship" and "one-off transaction" are defined in the Regulations. The definitions are wide and any transaction which involves the handling/handing over of money of €15,000 or more, is likely to be subject to the Money Laundering Regulations.

Can you give any help regarding the categories of work where Money Laundering Regulations will apply?

Solicitors are potentially at risk of carrying out money laundering on behalf of clients in many common areas of work. Great care therefore needs to be taken when accepting and following instructions, particularly when these cover both the receipt and disbursement of client monies. The following general comments may be helpful:

a. **Conveyancing.** In both purchase and sale property transactions, consideration needs to be given to the proper identification of clients and source of incoming funds. This is particularly important when a purchase of property is being contemplated. If funds are being received from the identified client's own bank account, then no further checks are necessary.

   Any changes to this arrangement, particularly when carried out without reasonable explanation and close to the settlement date, require to be considered, particularly if funds are being introduced from a third party.

   Purchasing a property in nominee name for the benefit of an undisclosed principal also requires to be considered carefully to ensure you have an official owner is properly identified.

   Ownership of heritable property and land is a very desirable target for money launderers. Setting up a number of unnecessary steps in creating final ownership or holding the title in a corporate vehicle is a popular device employed by money launderers.

The simple step of providing funds as a deposit for a substantial conveyancing transaction, then cancelling the project and seeking recovery of the funds to a third party's nominated account is another a popular device to use the solicitor to achieve the money launderer's ends.

b. **Trusts and Offshore Investment Vehicles**. The creation of specialist trusts or other corporate structures, sometimes in an offshore jurisdiction, in such a way as to obscure the true beneficial ownership of funds or assets, is also a popular target for money launderers. Particular care should be taken in dealing with monies which are being placed offshore as part of a tax planning regime. Tax avoidance is legitimate but tax evasion constitutes a crime and would fall foul of the Money Laundering Regulations.

c. **Executries**. This is much less likely to be an area of concern. Unusual instructions from beneficiaries or legatees regarding the payment of funds to their order should be reviewed, particularly if the sums are in any way substantial.

d. **Investment Business**. This is specifically caught under the Money Laundering Regulations and must always be handled with particular care.

e. **Matrimonial and Family Work.** The placing of funds in the name of a spouse or children is common place. First stage enquiry regarding such arrangements should always be made and a proper note of any explanation given should be included in the file.

Why am I a target for money launderers?

Solicitors should always be conscious of the real benefits to money launderers of having funds passed through a solicitors' client bank account on the way to the next level, since solicitors' funds are deemed to have been thoroughly vetted on receipt. Particular care should be paid to any last minute change of instructions, unusual or unnecessary arrangements or the use of third party names in connection with normal commercial arrangements.

How can I minimise these risks?

In all circumstances you should make a full note of your enquiry and answers in connection with client identification and source of funds. Remember this involves a two-stage check—of both clients and their money. You should also make a note of any concerns which you may have raised at the time and fully record the client's response. This record is important to you and may in fact become very significant at a much later date in circumstances where investigations are being carried out under the proceeds of crime legislation.

What else do I have to do under the Regulations?

- You should be familiar with the relevant legislation and regulations.
- You should review carefully all existing systems to ensure they comply with the new standards.

Further guidance is available at *www.lawscot.org.uk/mlg* or in printed format from the Publications Department, Law Society of Scotland, Tel: 0131 476 8165.

Part VI Guarantee Fund

Only a relatively small number of solicitors ever need to know about or deal with a claim on behalf of a client of a former solicitor. This section helps by setting out the Rules and the Form of Application for each reference.

The Rules have a section headed Guarantee Fund. What does this cover?

You will see that this part covers the operation of the Scottish Solicitors Guarantee Fund, including how to make a claim against the Fund. Schedule III of the Rules has the Form of Application which must be completed if a claim is to be considered. It is also included at the end of these notes.

Are there time limits to making a claim on the Fund?

Anyone who wishes to make a claim for a grant from the Fund should do so as soon as practicable and within twelve months of the date when the loss first came to their knowledge.

What else must be done to lodge a claim?

The person who suffered loss through dishonesty on the part of the solicitor or an employee in the conduct of their practice must have the application form notorised in the presence of a suitable person.

What happens then?

The claim is considered. Further enquiries may require to be made and more evidence may be requested before the Council consider the matter. The Council's decision is intimated to the claimant and arrangements are made to pay the amount of any grant admitted by the Council.

FURTHER QUESTIONS

What if I have any questions about the Accounts etc Rules 2001 and Amendment Rules 2004. Who should I contact?

Speak to the Chief Accountant, Leslie Cumming or a member of his team or write to him with your enquiry at 26 Drumsheugh Gardens, Edinburgh EH3 7YR.

Legal Post LP 1
Edinburgh 1
Direct telephone No: 0131 476 8172
Direct Fax No: 0131 476 8103
E-mail: lawscot@lawscot.org.uk
www.lawscot.org.uk

SCHEDULE I

FORM OF CERTIFICATE

(In respect of an accounting period ending on or after 1st September 2004).

The Secretary
The Law Society of Scotland
26 Drumsheugh Gardens
Edinburgh EH3 7YR

Dear Sir

I/We confirm that, within the premises at (Note (a)), ...

....

being the address at which I/we carry on practice as solicitor(s) that I/we have maintained the necessary books of account, bank passbooks, bank statements, deposit receipts including building society or local authority deposits, statements, deposit receipts and other accounting records required by the Solicitors (Scotland) Accounts etc. Rules 2001 for the accounting period from .... to .... and I/we certify subject to the points referred to under item 4 of additional matters noted overleaf:—

Note (b)

1) That the accounting records are up to date and balanced as at the last day of the accounting period, and
2) That the accounting records, to the best of my/our knowledge and belief, are in accordance with the terms of the Solicitors (Scotland) Accounts etc. Rules 2001, and
3) That all outstanding reconciling entries noted as at the balance dates disclosed overleaf under Rules 9 and 10 have been entered in the records or confirmed as correct, and
4) That the following Powers of Attorney were held by the undernoted or granted in favour of the undernoted during the accounting period:

GRANTER	ATTORNEY	DATE GRANTED

and

5) That during the said accounting period the Designated Cashroom Partner(s) in terms of Rule 12 of the Solicitors (Scotland) Accounts etc. Rules 2001 was/were as follows:

NAME	DATE DESIGNATED	DATE DESIGNATION CEASED

I solemnly and sincerely declare that the information given by me in this Certificate is true to the best of my knowledge and belief.

CURRENT DESIGNATED CASHROOM PARTNER

(FULL NAME) ....

SIGNATURE .... DATE ....

SECOND SIGNATORY

(FULL NAME) ....

SIGNATURE .... DATE ....

ADDITIONAL MATTERS

1. Client account reconciliations as at	....	....
Note (c)		
(i) (a) Monies held on general client account	£	£ ....
(b) Monies due to clients	£	£ ....
(c) Surplus or deficit	£	£ ....
(ii) (a) Funds held for named clients	£	£ ....
(b) Monies due to named clients	£	£ ....
[1] (iii) (a) Loans for named clients	£	£ ....
(b) Balances due by named clients	£	£ ....
Note (d)		
2. Firm's account balances		
Due to the firm	£	£ ....
Due by the firm	£	£ ....

3. If the assistance of an external accountant was needed to prepare this Certificate, please indicate the scope of the assistance here. (If none, state NONE):—

Note (e)

4. Other matters which require to be reported:— (If no other matters, state NONE)

NOTES

(a) State addresses of all places of business of the solicitor or firm of solicitors in respect of whom the Certificate is granted.

(b) This balance is to be a balance of the whole books covering client and non-client accounts.

(c) These dates are those quarterly dates required to be reconciled under the terms of Rule 10.

(d) These balances should disclose bridging loans taken on behalf of named clients under Rule 20.

(e) It is anticipated that many solicitors will instruct an external accountant to assist them in the checking of the accounting records and/or the preparation of the Certificate in respect of investment business. If the services of an external accountant are required you should indicate the extent of the help offered. The following tasks are examples of the assistance which may be obtained from the accountant:—

1) The preparation of day books, ledgers and other records for client's or firm's accounting records; or
2) Reconciling the funds' position under Rules 9 and 10; or
3) Testing for compliance with aspects of the Accounts Rules as agreed per a letter of engagement; or
4) Balancing the client's or firm's accounting records; or
5) Conducting a review of compliance with all aspects of the Accounts Rules in support of the solicitor's certification of compliance with the Rules.

SCHEDULE 2a

FORM OF CERTIFICATE

Solicitors (Scotland) Accounts etc Rules 2001

(In respect of an Accounting Period for which **no client monies have been held**)

NAME: ....

BUSINESS ADDRESS:

....

....

Tel No: .... **Fax No**: ....

I hereby confirm to the Council of the Law Society of Scotland that:

(Note 1) (a) I/We have contributed to the Guarantee Fund in respect of the practice year;

(b) I/We submit accounts to the Scottish Legal Aid Board for payment to my/our own account;

(c) I/We make any payments due to third parties from my/our bank account in advance or not later than the date on which the matching remittance is lodged in the firm bank account.

(Note 2) (d) I/We have not handled client monies during the accounting period from: ....
to: ....

(e) If circumstances change with the result that I/we require to hold or intromit with client monies, I/we shall immediately advise the Council.

I solemnly and sincerely declare that the information given by me in this Certificate is true to the best of my knowledge and belief.

CURRENT DESIGNATED CASHROOM PARTNER

(FULL NAME) ....

SIGNATURE .... DATE ....

SECOND SIGNATORY

(FULL NAME) ....

SIGNATURE .... DATE ....

Note 1. The current practice year for this figure commences on 1st November within the accounting year which includes the six-month period shown at item (d);

Note 2. The accounting period must be six months or less and follow immediately on from the previous accounting period without a gap or overlap in the dates concerned.

SCHEDULE 2b

FORM OF CERTIFICATE

Solicitors (Scotland) Accounts etc Rules 2001

(In respect of an Accounting Period for which **no client monies have been held**)

NAME: ....

ADDRESS:

....

....

Tel No: ....

Fax No: ....

E-mail: ....

I hereby confirm to the Council of the Law Society of Scotland:

(a) I have contributed to the Guarantee Fund in respect of the practice year; (*Note 1)
(b) I act solely as an agent for other solicitors.
(c) I do not submit accounts to the Scottish Legal Aid Board and have not received any fee directly from them.
(d) I have not handled client monies during the accounting period and have not operated a client bank account.
(e) If circumstances change with the result that I require to hold or intromit with client monies, I shall immediately advise the Council.
(f) Accounting Period: (*Note 2)
From...To..

I solemnly and sincerely declare that the information given by me in this Certificate is true to the best of my knowledge and belief. FULL NAME .... SIGNATURE .... DATE ....

*Note 1. The current practice year for this figure commences on 1st November within the accounting year which includes the six-month period shown at item (e).
*Note 2. The accounting period must be six months or less and follow immediately on from the previous accounting period without a gap or overlap in the dates concerned.

SCHEDULE III

THE LAW SOCIETY OF SCOTLAND
THE SCOTTISH SOLICITORS' GUARANTEE FUND

APPLICATION FORM FOR A GRANT OUT OF THE SCOTTISH SOLICITORS' GUARANTEE FUND

To: The Law Society of Scotland
The Law Society's Hall
26 Drumsheugh Gardens
Edinburgh EH3 7YR

I, (Full name of applicant) ....
Designation ....
Address ....
....
Post Code ....
Telephone Number ....

hereby apply to the Council of The Law Society of Scotland that in the exercise of the absolute discretion conferred upon them by the Solicitors (Scotland) Act 1980, they make to me a grant of £ ....
or such other sum as they may think proper out of the Scottish Solicitors' Guarantee Fund by way of compensation for a pecuniary loss sustained by me by reason of the dishonesty of

Name ....
Designation ....
Address ....
Firm ....
Status in firm if known ....
Date the original notice of claim was sent to the Secretary ....

Schedule of Particulars

Please state as clearly and concisely as you can the answers to the following questions:—

1. Please give the date or dates upon which the money or other property in respect of which your loss has been sustained came into the possession of the solicitor, or his or her employee.
   ....

2. Please give full particulars of such money or property.
   ....
   ....
   ....

3. Please explain why you allege dishonesty.
   ....
   ....
   ....

4. State the date which your loss first came to your attention

5. Explain briefly how this happened.
   ....
   ....
   ....
   ....

6. If you have any documents which you think would help your claim, please list them here and enclose a copy of each.
   ....
   ....
   ....
   ....

7. Are you aware of any other application that may be made in respect of this loss?
   Yes/no* *Please delete as appropriate.

   If yes, please give name and address of other applicant.

   ....
   ....
   ....
   ....

8. Are you aware of any civil, criminal or disciplinary hearings arising out of this matter?
   Yes/no* *Please delete as appropriate.

   If yes, please give details including the result if known.

   ....
   ....
   ....
   ....

9. Have you taken court or other proceedings in respect of your loss?
   Yes/no* *Please delete as appropriate.
   (a) If yes, please give brief details.

   ....
   ....
   ....
   ....

   (b) If no, are you considering taking court or other proceedings in respect of your loss?
   Yes/no* *Please delete as appropriate.

   If yes, please give his name, firm, address and telephone number

   Name ....
   Firm ....
   Address ....
   ....
   Post Code ....
   Telephone Number ....

10. Is there any other relevant information which you think would be of assistance to the Guarantee Fund Committee in considering your application?
    If so, please detail.

    ....
    ....
    ....
    ....

I solemnly and sincerely declare that the information given by me in this application is true to the best of my knowledge and belief, and I make this solemn declaration conscientiously believing the same to be true, and by virtue of the Statutory Declarations Act 1835.

.... Claimant

Declared at ....
on (date) ....
before me ....

(This application should be signed in the presence of a Notary Public, Commissioner for Oaths, Justice of the Peace or other person authorised to administer oaths.)

[NEXT TEXT PAGE IS **F** 1267]

Suggested List of Items that Should be Special Areas of Concern to Designated Cashroom Partners

Consider:—

1. The methods used to record incoming funds and make sure that all funds are lodged in the bank on the day of receipt.

2. Your arrangements to handle cash handed in by clients.

e.g. Do you have special arrangements to cope with larger cash sums brought to you by clients?

Do you see the detailed workings of the client account balances each month?

How much checking do you do each month on:—

(a) List of client balances
(b) Bank reconciliation working papers
(c) Statements of surplus/deficit?

Do you have an automatic reporting and investigation procedure set up if your accounting system discloses a temporary shortage?

Can you confirm at least quarterly that all client funds including funds invested for named clients are properly accounted for? What checks are done to verify the position?

Are all large fees reviewed to confirm they are fully charged but not excessively or prematurely charged?

Do you have any controls over the level of interim fees being charged during an ongoing piece of business?

Guidelines on Reporting on Dishonest Employees 2001

At a meeting of the Council of the Law Society of Scotland held on May 25, 2001, the members reviewed the current policy regarding the reporting of non-solicitor employees of a legal practice who were accused of stealing funds from either the client bank account or the firm's own account. The current policy is to report all instances of dishonest employees to the Crown Office where the firm has declined to do so.

The Council confirmed that this is still their policy and it was appropriate to publicise this policy in order to ensure that all members of the profession and their employees would be aware of the position in relation to dishonesty. The Council were satisfied that in cases where client funds have been stolen there was a clear responsibility on the Council to report such matters directly to the Crown Office for further investigation. The Council were also satisfied that where funds were stolen only from the firms' account that allegations of this type require to also be reported to the Crown Office so that a formal investigation could be carried out. The decision regarding subsequent prosecution of the individual would thereafter be a matter for Crown Office and the Procurator Fiscal Service.

Guide to Professional Conduct and Ethics in Insolvency

[July 1995]

The Council has resolved that the Society of Practitioners of Insolvency Ethical Guidelines (the SPI Guidelines), shall, with effect from 1st September 1995, apply to all work carried out by an Insolvency Practitioner authorised by the Law Society of Scotland.

The SPI Guidelines are in addition to the obligations incumbent upon solicitors arising out of the Code of Conduct for Scottish solicitors and, in the event of any conflict between the two, the Law Society of Scotland Code of Conduct shall have precedence.

The SPI Guidelines may be varied from time to time and all variations must be observed by Insolvency Practitioners.

(In the event of any conflict between the SPI Guidelines and the Code of Conduct, the Insolvency Practitioner should consult the Law Society of Scotland).

GUIDE TO PROFESSIONAL ETHICS IN INSOLVENCY

Introductory note

1. [This paragraph refers to the revision of the Guide and its adoption by the Society of Practitioners of Insolvency with effect from 1st July 1993.]

2. The fundamental principles direct the attention of each member to the overriding importance in his or her professional life of integrity and objectivity. These elements are as important in the acceptance and conduct of insolvency work as in any other area of professional life. In certain insolvency roles the preservation of objectivity needs to be protected and demonstrated by the maintenance of a member's independence from influences which could affect his or her objectivity. Before a member accepts or carries out those roles, which are detailed in the guidance which follows, the member must not only be satisfied as to the actual objectivity which he can bring to his judgment and decisions but must also be mindful of how his or her acceptance and conduct will be perceived by others.

3. For the purposes of this Guide, "principal" means a sole practitioner, a partner in a firm or a director of a corporate practice.

Obtaining Insolvency Work

4. The special nature of insolvency appointments makes the payment or offer of any commission for, or the furnishing of any valuable consideration towards, the introduction of insolvency appointments inappropriate.

5. The attention of members is also drawn to section 164 of the Insolvency Act 1986, which creates an offence punishable by a fine of offering to a member or creditor of a company any valuable consideration with a view to securing nomination as a liquidator, and to the Insolvency Rules 1986, which provide for remuneration to be disallowed to a liquidator (rule 4.150) or trustee (rule 6.148) whose appointment has been procured by improper solicitation.

Solicitation for proxies

6. In addition to any statutory consequences which it may incur, solicitation for insolvency work in any way amounting to that which a reasonable person would regard as harassment, renders a member liable to reference to the Investigation Committee.

Professional Independence and the Acceptance of Insolvency Appointments

General

7. The following paragraphs refer to specific situations in which a member may not properly accept appointment. In situations other than those dealt with, a member should only accept office in any insolvency role sequential to one in which the member or his or her practice or a current employee of the practice has previously acted after giving careful consideration to the implications of acceptance in all the circumstances of the case and satisfying him- or herself that objectivity is unlikely to be compromised by a prospective conflict of interest or otherwise. If he or she remains in doubt as to his or her position, the member should seek advice from the Ethics Committee via the Secretariat.

8. The attention of members is drawn to the statutory disqualification on acting as an insolvency practitioner in section 390 of the Insolvency Act 1986.

Joint appointments

9. A member who is invited to accept an insolvency appointment jointly with another practitioner should be guided by similar principles to those set out in relation to sole appointments. Where a member is specifically precluded by the guidance which follows from accepting an insolvency appointment as an individual, a joint appointment will not render the appointment acceptable.

Appointment as supervisor of a company voluntary arrangement, administrator, administrative or other receiver

10. Where there has been a material professional relationship (as to which see paragraphs 13 to 16 (below)) with a company, no principal or employee of the practice should accept appointment as supervisor of a voluntary arrangement, administrator or administrative or other receiver in relation to that company. (See also paragraphs 17, 18, 30 and 31 (below).)

Appointment as supervisor of an individual voluntary arrangement, trustee in bankruptcy or trustee under a deed of arrangement

11. Where there has been a material professional relationship (as to which see paragraphs 13 to 16 (below)) with a client, no principal or employee of the practice should accept appointment as supervisor of a voluntary arrangement or as trustee in bankruptcy or as a trustee under a deed registered under the Deeds of Arrangement Act 1914 in relation to that client. (See also paragraphs 30 and 31 (below).)

Appointment as liquidator

12. Where there has been a material professional relationship (as to which see paragraphs 13 to 16 (below)) with a company, no principal or employee of the practice should accept appointment as liquidator of the company if the company is insolvent. Where the company is solvent, such appointment should not be accepted without careful consideration being given to all the implications of acceptance in the particular case and a member should satisfy him- or herself that the directors' declaration of solvency is likely to be substantiated by events. (See also paragraphs 30 and 31 (below).)

Material professional relationship

13. A material professional relationship with a client, such as is referred to in paragraphs 10, 11 and 12 (above) arises where a practice or, subject to the provisions of paragraphs 30 and 31 (below), a principal or employee of a practice is carrying out, or has during the previous three years carried out, material professional work for that client. Material professional work would include the following:

(i) where a practice or person has carried out, or has been appointed to carry out, audit work for a company or individual to which the appointment is being considered; or

(ii) where a practice or person has carried out one or more assignments, whether or a continuing nature or not, of such overall significance or in such circumstances that a member's objectivity in carrying out a subsequent insolvency appointment could be or could reasonably be seen to be prejudiced.

14. A material professional relationship with a company or individual (as referred to in paragraphs 10, 11 and 12 (above)) includes any material professional relationship with companies or entities controlled by that company or individual or under common control where the relationship is material in the context of the company or individual to whom appointment is being sought or considered. A material professional relationship could also arise where a practice or person has carried out professional work for any director or shadow director of a company of such a nature that a member's objectivity in carrying out a subsequent insolvency appointment in relation to that company could be or could reasonably be seen to be prejudiced.

15. In forming views as to whether a material professional relationship exists, members should have regard to existing or previous relationships with firms with which they are, or have been, associated which might affect or appear to affect their objectivity, including relationships whereby they or their firm are held out by name association or other public statements as being part of a national or international association.

16. A member should take reasonable steps prior to his or her acceptance of any insolvency appointment to ascertain whether any of the above work has been performed.

Appointment as investigating accountant at the instigation of a creditor

17. A material professional relationship would not normally arise where the relationship is one which springs from the appointment of the practice by, or at the instigation of, a creditor or other party having an actual or potential financial interest in a company or business to investigate, monitor or advise on its affairs, provided that:

(*a*) there has not been a direct involvement by a principal or employee of the practice in the management of the company or business; and

(*b*) the practice has its principal client relationship with the creditor or other party, rather than with the company or proprietor of the business, and the company or the proprietor of the business is aware of this.

18. If the circumstances of the initial appointment are such as to prevent the open discussion of the financial affairs of the company with the directors, an investigating member or other principal in the practice may be called upon to justify the propriety of their acceptance of the subsequent appointment.

Conversion of members' voluntary winding up into creditors' voluntary winding up

19. Where a member has accepted appointment as liquidator in a members' voluntary winding up and is obliged to summon a creditors' meeting under section 95 of the Insolvency Act 1986, because it appears that the company will be unable to pay its debts in full within the period stated in the directors' declaration of solvency, the member's continuance as liquidator will depend on whether he or she believes that the company will eventually be able to pay it debts in full or not.

(*a*) If the company will not be able to pay its debts in full and the member has previously had a material professional relationship with the company such as is set out in paragraphs 13 to 16 (above), he or she should not accept nomination under the creditors' winding up.

(*b*) If the company will not be able to pay its debts in full but the member has had no such material professional relationship, he or she may accept nomination by the creditors and continue as liquidator with the creditors' approval, subject to giving the careful consideration as to the implications, etc., referred to in paragraph 7 (above).

(*c*) If the member believes that the company will eventually be able to pay its debts in full he or she may accept nomination by the creditors and continue as liquidator. However, if it should subsequently appear that this belief was mistaken the member must then offer his or her resignation and may not accept re-appointment if he or she has previously had a material professional relationship with the company.

Insolvent liquidation following appointment as administrative or other receiver

20. Where a principal or employee of a practice (subject to the provisions of paragraphs 30 and 31 (below)) is, or in the previous three years has been, administrative receiver of a company or a receiver, under the Law of Property Act 1925 or otherwise, of any of its assets, no principal or employee of the practice should accept appointment as liquidator of the company in an insolvent liquidation. This restriction does not apply where the previous appointment was made by the court. However, before a court-appointed receiver accepts subsequent appointment as liquidator, he or she should give careful consideration as to whether his or her objectivity could be open to question and, if so, the appointment should be refused.

Liquidation following appointment as supervisor of a voluntary arrangement or administrator

21. Where a member, or any principal or employee of his or her practice, has been supervisor of a voluntary arrangement or administrator of a company, the member may, if the considerations indicated in paragraph 7 (above) are satisfied, accept appointment as liquidator if so nominated by the creditors or appointed by the Secretary of State under section 137 of the Insolvency Act 1986.

22. However, where the relevant previous role is that of administrator, the member should not accept nomination or appointment as liquidator unless either:

(*a*) the member has the support of a creditors' committee appointed under section 26 of the Insolvency Act 1986; or

(*b*) he or she has the support of a meeting of creditors called either under the Act or informally, of which all known creditors have been given notice.

Bankruptcy following appointment as supervisor of individual voluntary arrangement

23. Where a member, or any principal or employee of his or her practice, has been supervisor of a voluntary arrangement in relation to a debtor, the member may, provided the considerations indicated in paragraph 7 (above) are satisfied, accept appointment as trustee in bankruptcy of that debtor provided that it is effected by a general meeting of the creditors under the provisions of section 292(1)(*a*) of the Insolvency Act 1986 or if the member has been appointed by the court under section 297(5) of the Act or by the Secretary of State under section 296 of the Act.

Administration following appointment as administrative receiver or LPA or other receiver

24. Where a principal or employee of a practice (subject to the provisions of paragraphs 30 and 31 (below)) is, or in the previous three years has been, an administrative receiver of a company or a receiver, under the Law of Property Act 1925 or otherwise, of any of its assets, no principal or employee of the practice should accept appointment as administrator of the company, unless the previous appointment was made by the court.

Supervision of a voluntary arrangement following appointment as administrative receiver

25. Where a principal or employee of a practice (subject to the provisions of paragraphs 30 and 31 (below)) is, or in the previous three years has been, an administrative receiver of a company, no principal or employee of the practice should accept appointment as supervisor of a voluntary arrangement in relation to that company.

Audit following appointment as supervisor of a voluntary arrangement, administrator or administrative or other receiver

26. Where a principal or employee of a practice (subject to the provisions of paragraphs 30 and 31 (below)) has acted as supervisor of a voluntary arrangement, administrator or administrative receiver of a company or receiver of any of its assets, no principal or employee of the practice should accept appointment as auditor of the company for any accounting period during which the supervisor, administrator or receiver acted.

Pension schemes of companies in liquidation, administration or receivership—appointment of "Independent Trustee"

27. A member should not appoint a principal or employee of his practice, or any close connection of any of the above or of himself, as "Independent Trustee" of the pension scheme of a company of which he is the liquidator, administrator or administrative or other receiver. A member should be aware of the threat to objectivity if he were to engage in regular or reciprocal arrangements in relation to such appointments with another practice or organisation.

Other potential conflicts of interest

(i) Group, associated and family-connected companies

28. Members should be particularly aware of the difficulties likely to arise from the existence of inter-company transactions or guarantees in group, associated or "family-connected" company situations. Acceptance of an insolvency appointment in relation to more than one company in the group or association may raise issues of conflict of interest. Nevertheless, it may be impracticable for a series of different insolvency practitioners to act. A member should not accept multiple appointments in such situations unless he or she is satisfied that he or she is able to take steps to minimise problems of conflict and that his or her overall integrity and objectivity are, and are seen to be, maintained.

(ii) Relationships between insolvent individuals and insolvent companies

29. A member who, or a principal or employee of whose practice, is acting as insolvency practitioner in relation to an individual may be asked to accept an insolvency appointment in relation to a company of which the debtor is a major shareholder or creditor or where the company is a creditor of the debtor. It is essential, if the member is to accept the new appointment, that he or she should be able to show that the steps indicated in paragraph 28 (above) have been taken. Similar considerations apply if it is the company appointment which precedes the individual appointment.

Transfer of principals and employees including practice merger

30. When two or more practices merge, principals and employees of the merged practice become subject to common ethical constraints in relation to accepting new insolvency appointments to clients of either of the former practices. However, existing appointments which are rendered in apparent breach of the guidance by such merger need not be determined automatically, provided that a considered review of the situation by the practice discloses no obvious and immediate conflict, such as a potential need to sue a new colleague.

31. Where a principal or an employee of a practice has, in any former practice, undertaken work upon the affairs of the company or debtor in a capacity which is incompatible with an insolvency assignment of his or her new practice, he or she should not personally work or be employed on that assignment, save in the case of an employee of such junior status that his or her duties in the former practice did not involve the exercise of any material professional judgement or discretion.

Personal relationships

32. The current legislation includes specific duties to report on the conduct of directors or shadow directors of an insolvent company. (See for example the requirement under section 7(a) of the Company Directors Disqualification Act 1986 to report "unfit" conduct to the Secretary of State and sections 213 and 214 of the Insolvency Act 1986 on fraudulent trading and wrongful trading.) A member should have regard at all times to the spirit of the guidance on independence set out in paragraph 2 (above) and should not accept an insolvency appointment in relation to an individual or a company where any personal connection with the individual or with a director, former director or shadow director is such as to impair or reasonably appear to impair the member's objectivity. The attention of members is also drawn to the definitions relating to the persons "connected" with a company in sections 249 and 435 of the Insolvency Act 1986.

Relationship with a debenture holder

33. A member should, in general, decline to accept an insolvency appointment in relation to a company if he or she or a principal or employee of the practice has such a personal or close and distinct business connection with the debenture holder as might impair or appear to impair the member's objectivity. It is not considered likely that a "close and distinct business connection" would normally exist between an insolvency practitioner and, for example, a clearing bank or major financial institution. However, such a close and distinct business connection would exist where a member, or a principal or employee of the practice, holds an insolvency appointment in relation to such a bank or financial institution.

Purchase of the assets of an insolvent company or debtor

34. The Insolvency Rules 1986 contain prohibitions on members of a liquidation or creditors' committee acquiring any asset in the estate of an insolvent company or debtor (save with leave of the court or the committee). Save in circumstances which clearly do not impair his or her objectivity, a member appointed to any insolvency appointment in relation to a company or debtor should not him- or herself acquire directly or indirectly any of the assets of the company or debtor nor knowingly permit any principal or employee of his or her practice, or any close relative of the member or of a principal or employee, directly or indirectly to do so.

35. Where a contract is already in existence between the insolvent company or debtor and a principal or an employee of the member's practice, the member should seek guidance from the Ethics Committee via the Secretariat as to the propriety of accepting the appointment.

Guidance to the Incidental Financial Business Regime Under The Financial Services and Markets Act 2000 and The Solicitors (Scotland) (Incidental Financial Business) Practice Rules 2004

1. Regulatory Framework

The Financial Services Authority (FSA) is the principal regulator for investment business in the United Kingdom. The FSA became fully operational on 1st December 2001 and its powers are set out in the Financial Services and Markets Act 2000.

The Act provides that no individual or firm may carry on a regulated activity unless that individual/firm is authorised by the FSA. From 1st December 2001 to 31st October 2004 the FSA's regulatory regime was confined to the conduct of investment business. However, with effect from 31st October 2004, the FSA's regulatory regime is extended to incorporate mortgage business and with effect from 14th January 2005, the regime is extended to include general insurance business.

Regulated activities are defined in the Financial Services and Markets Act 2000 (Regulated Activities) Order 2001 which has been amended by the Financial Services and Markets Act 2000 (Regulated Activities) (Amendment No.1) Order 2003 to include mortgage business and by the Financial Services & Markets Act 2000 (Regulated Activities) (Amendment No.2) Order 2003 to include insurance business.

An individual solicitor or firm of solicitors can undertake certain regulated activities and thereby be exempt from the requirement to be authorised by the FSA if that solicitor/firm is licensed by the Society under Part XX of the Financial Services and Markets Act 2000. The Part XX regime allows the establishment of exempt professional firms (exempt from the FSA's regime) to undertake exempt regulated activities provided such activities are an integral part of a solicitor's professional services. For the purposes of the Part XX regime, the Society is a Designated Professional Body and licenses firms to conduct exempt regulated activities.

The Society's regime is known as the "*Incidental Financial Business (IFB) Regime*" effective from 31st October 2004 and this regime replaces the Incidental Investment Business Regime which has been in operation since 1st December 2001. The IFB regime allows firms to conduct certain activities which would otherwise require FSA authorisation. The essence of these incidental financial business activities is that they are integral to the professional services provided to clients and are not conducted on a stand-alone basis. Furthermore, such activities must not be marketed on a stand-alone basis.

As the FSA's regime has been expanded to include mortgage and insurance business, there has been a similar expansion to the Society's IFB regime so that it incorporates investment, mortgage and general insurance business.

There are four options open to firms of Scottish solicitors under the UK's investment business regulatory regime and these are—

- FSA authorisation.
- An IFB Licence from the Society.
- Acting as an introducer to an independent financial adviser—this option can be undertaken in connection with either of the first two options.
- None of the above.

It is important to recognise the wide definition of a regulated activity which includes—

- advising on investments, mortgages and general insurance.
- making arrangements in investment, mortgages and general insurance.
- selling investments, mortgages and general insurance.

The definition of regulated activities is therefore very wide and is not confined only to the giving of advice but includes making arrangements in the following product areas—

Insurance products includes after the event legal expenses insurance, Bonds of Caution, building insurance, defective title indemnity insurance, household contents insurance, missing beneficial indemnity insurance, term assurance, unoccupied property insurance and warranty in insurance.

Investment products includes shares, fixed interest stock, individual savings accounts, pension and collective investment schemes, unit trusts and open-ended investment companies, home reversion plans, home purchase plans and personal pension products.

Regulated mortgage contract is one which is secured by a first legal mortgage on land which is in the United Kingdom and where at least 40% of the land is, or is to be used, as a dwelling by the borrower.

2. Direct Authorisation by the FSA

There are currently just over 60 firms of Scottish solicitors authorised for investment business by the FSA. The FSA has its own rules and procedures for those firms which it authorises.

An application for authorisation should be made direct to the FSA whose contact details arc:

The Financial Services Authority,
25 The North Colonnade,
Canary Wharf,
London E14 5HS

FSA switchboard number—020 7066 1000
Website address—*www.fsa.gov.uk*

A firm which is authorised by the FSA will be able to give its own specific advice on individual investment products and investment companies. Furthermore an FSA authorised firm will also be able to give specific advice on mortgage lenders and mortgage products.

A firm which is authorised by the FSA for investment business cannot also be authorised for incidental financial business by the Society. A firm's FSA authorisation also covers such a firm for incidental financial business as the Society's "incidental regime" does not cover any incidental financial business conducted by FSA authorised firms. The relevant FSA rules cover the incidental financial business of FSA authorised firms.

3. Incidental Financial Business Regime

The Society's Incidental Financial Business (IFB) regime came into operation on 31st October 2004. The IFB regime is much wider than the previous incidental investment business regime which was restricted as its name implies, to investment work arising from legal work.

The IFB regime incorporates four types of incidental business as follows—

- Incidental insurance business
- Incidental investment business
- Incidental long-term care insurance business
- Incidental mortgage business

The Society's Client Relations Office will have responsibility for handling any complaints arising from any of the above four types of incidental financial business.

Before looking at the specific types of business which may be conducted under this regime it is necessary to highlight the conditions which must be followed if a firm is to be licensed for IFB.

Conditions for conducting Incidental Financial Business

(a) A firm's incidental financial business services must be an integral part of its professional services. A firm cannot have stand-alone incidental financial business.
(b) The incidental financial business conducted must be linked to the provision of a particular professional service to a particular client.
(c) A firm licensed for incidental financial business cannot also be authorised by the FSA and must not hold itself out as being so authorised.
(d) Any commission, financial or other pecuniary benefit received from third parties due to the conduct of incidental financial business belongs to the client. This means that any commission arising from the incidental financial business must either be given to the client or the client can agree to the commission being offset against his/her fees. However, the client must agree to this offsetting in writing in advance. Typically, this can be arranged by a pro forma letter signed by the client agreeing to this offsetting. Such a letter can be sent to the client for signing along with the terms of business letter.
(e) The firm's income from incidental financial business cannot account for more than 50% of the firm's total income.

The above conditions must be met in relation to the four types of incidental financial business which may be conducted. Each of these four categories of incidental financial business are explained below—

Incidental Insurance Business

The regulation of insurance business as a category of incidental financial business will bring more firms into this regulatory regime than under the previous regime. This is because of the wide definition of insurance business within the legislation. The incorporation of insurance business into the regulatory regime has been taken on a staged basis as follows—

- with effect from 31st October 2004 long-term care insurance is a regulated activity under the Society's IFB regime and the FSA regime.
- with effect from 14th January 2005, all other insurance business (principally general insurance) is a regulated activity under the Society's IFB regime and the FSA's regime.

The legislation refers to insurance business as "insurance mediation". The insurance business which falls into the incidental financial business regime consists of the following activities—

- introducing, proposing or carrying out other work preparatory to the conclusion of contracts of insurance.
- concluding contracts of insurance.
- assisting in the administration and performance of contracts of insurance, in particular in the event of a claim.

A firm will be conducting insurance business under the IFB Licence when, in connection with its professional services it introduces, sells, arranges and advises on general insurance, such as after the event legal expenses insurance, buildings insurance, contaminated land insurance, defective title indemnity insurance, household contents insurance, missing beneficiary indemnity insurance, trustees indemnity insurance and unoccupied property insurance. Significantly, as the definition of insurance mediation includes "*assisting in the administration and performance of contracts of insurance, in particular in the event of a claim"* where a firm acts for an insured in bringing a claim against his/her own insurer, this activity when undertaken in conjunction with professional services will fall into the new regime. Where a firm acts for an insurance company in the defence of a claim, this activity will not fall under the new regime if the activity is covered by the exemption in Article 39B of the Regulated Activities Order 2001. This Article provides an exemption where a firm "manages claims on behalf of an insurer" as part of the firm's professional services. It should be noted that where a firm acts for a third party in an insurance claim such an activity will not fall under the definition of insurance mediation as the third party is not making a claim under his/her own insurance policy. An example of such a third party claim is where a pedestrian is injured in a road traffic accident and then he/she wishes to bring a personal injury claim against the car driver who caused the accident.

The insurance element of the incidental financial business regime does allow a firm to give its own advice and recommendations to a client on a specific contract of insurance. A firm therefore can give its own advice on insurance contracts or insurance companies under the IFB regime.

Incidental Investment Business

The following activities are examples of what may constitute investment incidental financial business—

(a) arranging for the purchase or sale of shares on the instructions of clients without providing advice on those shares. Such arrangements may arise within an executry or trust work.

(b) discussing with a client investment advice which has been provided by an independent financial adviser. The firm may comment upon such advice and, acting on the client's instructions, carry out investment arrangements based on the advice.

(c) a firm undertaking matrimonial work can obtain the advice of an independent financial adviser regarding the matrimonial investment assets. The firm can comment upon the advice in negotiating a financial settlement in the matrimonial work on the client's instruction.

(d) a firm at its own initiative can advise a client that the investment advice or investment arrangements provided by another person do not appear to be in the client's best interest and that the client should seek further independent financial advice.

A firm under this section of the IFB regime may not give its own specific advice on investment products or investment companies. A firm may, however, give generic advice on the range of investment products and investment companies.

Incidental Long-Term Care Insurance Financial Business

This section of the IFB regime allows a firm to introduce, arrange or advise on long-term care insurance polices, products and providers.

Incidental Mortgage Financial Business

The IFB regime for incidental mortgage financial business comes into force on 31st October 2004.

A firm which wishes to arrange a mortgage on the instructions of a client will be able to undertake such arrangements through this element of the IFB regime. However, a firm will not be able to give its own advice on a specific mortgage product, or mortgage lenders to a client and such specific advice will have to come from an independent mortgage adviser. On receipt of such third-party advice a firm will be able to discuss the advice with a client and acting on the client's instructions arrange a mortgage.

4. Introductions

A firm either with or without an IFB Licence may undertake introductory business where a client is referred to an independent financial adviser. There are different rules depending on the type of financial business which is introduced. The types of financial business which may be introduced can be categorised as follows—

Introductory Insurance Business—either general insurance or long-term care insurance—if a firm wishes to introduce clients to an independent insurance broker for any contract of insurance a firm will require an IFB Licence. This is because the general statutory provisions on introductions under Article 33 of the Regulated Activities Order are disapplied for insurance mediation.

Introductory Investment Business—a firm may introduce a client to an independent financial adviser. The firm making the introduction must do no more than bring together the client and the independent financial adviser to whom the introduction is made. Any commission arising from the introduction can be retained by the firm.

Introductory Mortgage Business—a firm may introduce a client to an independent mortgage broker. There are two principal conditions which apply to such introductions which are—

- a firm must not receive any money paid by the borrower in connection with the introduction; and
- before making the introduction the firm must disclose to the borrower details of any payment or any other reward which may arise out of the introduction.

5. *Incidental Financial Business Practice Rules 2004*

(a) *Commencement date of IFB Practice Rules*

The new Practice Rules come into operation on 31st October 2004 for incidental investment business, incidental long-term care insurance and incidental mortgage business. The Rules for incidental insurance business come into force on 14th January 2005.

(b) *Application for an Incidental Financial Business Licence*

An application for an IFB Licence must be made by a firm to the Society by submitting the application form contained in Schedule 1 to the Rules. The deadline for submission of a firm's application form before the commencement of the new Rules was 31st August 2004. Firms can apply for an IFB Licence at anytime after the commencement of the Rules if an application form was not submitted ahead of the 31st August 2004 deadline.

The application form requires details of the principal within the firm who will have overall responsibility for the conduct of insurance mediation where a firm wishes to undertake incidental insurance or incidental long-term care insurance. No person having a criminal record disclosing a serious criminal conviction, involving any crime against property or related to financial services can fulfil this role. No person who is subject to bankruptcy proceedings can fulfil this role. These prohibitions are requirements of the Insurance Mediation Directive from which the Society's IFB Rules are derived.

The application form also seeks notification to the Society of those solicitors who are to be individually licensed for each incidental financial business activity. Each solicitor identified must indicate which incidental financial business activities will be undertaken by ticking one or more of the appropriate boxes. The options are—incidental investment business (IB); incidental insurance business (IM); incidental long-term care insurance (LTC) and incidental mortgage business (MMA).

No solicitor who wishes to conduct incidental insurance or long-term care insurance work can undertake such work where they have a criminal record (as defined above) or where they have been subject to bankruptcy proceedings.

The application form then asks as firm to identify those non-solicitors who will conduct any form of incidental financial business. The same information is requested for non-solicitors as for solicitors. The same prohibitions also apply to those persons as they do to a solicitor.

The application form asks the firm to provide the date from which the new Incidental Financial Business Licence is required.

(c) *Duration of an Incidental Financial Business Licence*

The Licence runs for the normal twelve month term of the Society's practice year, from 1st November to 31st October.

(d) *Renewal of an Incidental Financial Business Licence*

A firm's IFB Licence will be renewed annually through the Practising Certificate renewal forms which are sent out by the Society's Records Department in October. If a firm does not wish to renew its IFB Licence, notice of this intention and the date from when the Licence is to be revoked must be sent to the Records Department.

(e) *Annual fee for an Incidental Financial Business Licence*

The annual fee for an IFB Licence will be set at the Society's Special General Meeting in September each year. Notification of these fees will be included in the Practising Certificate renewal application form which is sent to each firm. Fees for the practice year 2007/2008 are £65 per licensed firm and £55 per licensed person.

(f) *Display of the Incidental Financial Business Certificate*

A firm must display at its placc of business its Incidental Financial Business Certificate (or a copy). This requirement is contained in Rule 23(2). A firm will be issued with an Incidental Financial Business Certificate after it first applies to be licensed for such work from the Society.

(g) *Notification to the Society in changes of personnel who undertake Incidental Financial Business*

A firm must notify the Director of Financial Services in writing of any changes to the list of personnel originally provided to the Society of those who conduct incidental financial business within a firm. This notification must be made to the Society within one month of any change to the original list of licensed individuals (Rule 10(1) and 10(2)).

(h) *Specific Rule requirements for insurance mediation activity (general insurance and long-term care insurance)*

- every firm which undertakes incidental general insurance or incidental long-term care insurance must appoint a principal who has overall responsibility for the conduct of such work within the firm. This person will be referred to as the Insurance Mediation Officer. (Rule 11(1)). It is this person who will be identified on the FSA's website as being responsible for insurance mediation within a firm.
- A firm will not be able to undertake any form of insurance mediation work (general insurance or long-term care insurance) until that firm is registered on the FSA's Register for this work. It is the Society which has responsibility for transmitting this information on firms and their insurance mediation officer to the FSA. The Society will update the information on the FSA's Register on a weekly basis.
- Provision of information—certain information requires to be provided to a client where a firm concludes a contract of insurance for a client. The information which requires to be provided is set out in pro forma style in Schedule 1 to this guide. The information can be provided orally if the client requests this or if the client requires immediate cover. Furthermore, where the contract is concluded by telephone and the client agrees to receiving limited information after the conclusion of the contract, the general information to be provided in writing need not be given.

- Scope of services—where a firm acts as an insurance intermediary providing advice on particular types of insurance a firm must have undertaken an appropriate analysis of the insurance market to show that the advice given on a particular contact of insurance is adequate to meet a client's needs. A record should be made of how a firm has undertaken an appropriate analysis of the insurance market.
- Statement of demands and needs—where a firm makes a personal recommendation to a client of a specific contract of insurance or arranges for a client to enter into a specific contract of insurance, before the conclusion of that contract the client must be provided with a statement of his demands and needs in respect of that insurance contract. This statement is in essence a "reason why letter" explaining to the client why a particular contract of insurance has been recommended by the firm. The letter should also clearly state the demands and needs of the client. A pro forma style of this statement is provided in Schedule 2 to this guide.

(i) *Incidental Financial Business Compliance Certificate*

A firm is required to submit an Incidental Financial Business Compliance Certificate for each six-month period within a firm's financial year. The form of Compliance Certificate which must be submitted to the Society is set out in Schedule 3 to the Rules. The Compliance Certificate requires the following information—

- The accounting period to which the Certificate relates.
- Confirmation that the six statements set out in the Certificate do apply to the firm.
- Date and signing of the Certificate by a partner, sole practitioner/director/controller/member.

The Society's team of inspecting accountants will monitor a firm's compliance with the new Rules as part of the Society's two-yearly cycle of Accounts Rules inspection.

(j) *Terms of business*

Whenever a firm undertakes incidental financial business a terms of business letter must be issued to a client. A pro forma style of terms of business letter form incidental financial business is provided in Schedule 3 to the guidance.

(k) *Disclosure on a firm's notepaper*

A firm is not required to state on its notepaper that it is licensed by the Society for incidental financial business—Rule 23(1). No such disclosure on a firm's notepaper is required due to the requirement to issue terms of business letters.

(l) *Training*

There is no requirement to undertake an investment business exam or any specified level of investment business CPD for those individuals who are licensed to conduct incidental financial business. The training obligations for individuals who undertake incidental financial business are set out in general terms in Rule 24. The responsibility is on firms and those licensed individuals to ensure that they keep themselves up to date on incidental financial business matters.

(m) *Record keeping requirements*

The record keeping requirements are set out in Rule 25. The general obligations under Rule 25 are as follows—

- Best execution—instructions from clients to carry out specific incidental financial business should be arranged with due timeliness.
- Records of statements of demands and needs—these must be kept for

a minimum of three years from the date on which a firm's personal recommendation on a specific contract of insurance or the arrangements to enter into a specific contract of insurance have been made.

- Records of a client's instructions—a firm must retain records of instructions from clients to carry out specific incidental financial business and instructions from the firm to any third party to effect or arrange such incidental financial business. These records must be retained for at least ten years from the date of the instruction.
- Records of accounting to clients for commission etc.—a firm must retain records of how it has accounted to its clients for any IFB commission or other pecuniary reward from third parties. Such records must be kept for at least ten years from the date of accounting. This record keeping can be achieved by retaining copies of the letter and payment details where commission is paid direct to the client. Alternatively, where the commission is deducted from a firm's fee note, a copy of the fee note detailing this deduction is sufficient.
- Safe-keeping of assets—where a firm holds for safe-keeping purposes documents of title i.e. share certificates, a firm should ensure that at all times such documents are readily accessible and are separately identifiable form any of the firm's own investments. A firm should also ensure that storage facilities are appropriate to the value and risk of loss of the investments to be safe-guarded and provide protection from damage, misappropriation or other losses. Where a firm uses a third party custodian to safe-keep such documents a firm must be satisfied that such a third party is suitable to act as a custodian.

SCHEDULE 1

Style of information letter to be used before or immediately after the conclusion of a contract of insurance with a client.

1. The firm of AB has its principal place of business at ....
2. The firm of AB is not authorised by the Financial Services Authority. However, the firm is included on the Register maintained by the Financial Services Authority so that this firm can carry on insurance mediation activities, which is broadly the advising on, selling and administration of insurance contracts. This part of our business, including arrangements for complaints or redress if something goes wrong, is regulated by the Law Society of Scotland. The Register can be accessed via the Financial Services Authority website at *www.fsa.gov.uk/register*.
3. The information provided in parts 1 and 2 above may be checked on the FSA's Register by visiting the FSA's website at *www.fsa.gov.uk/register* or by contacting the FSA on 0845 606 1234.
4. The firm of AB does not have any holding, direct or indirect, representing more than 10% of the voting rights of, or the capital in, an insurance undertaking.
5. No insurance undertaking or parent of an insurance undertaking has a holding, direct or indirect, representing more than 10% of the voting rights of or capital in this firm.
6. The contract of insurance on which this firm has provided advice or arranged has been selected on the basis of a fair analysis of the insurance market. This analysis was undertaken by reviewing the range of insurance products on the market.
7. The firm of AB has Professional Indemnity Insurance under the Law Society of Scotland of Scotland's Master Policy. The current level of indemnity on the Master Policy is £1.5m per claim. The firm of AB is also covered by the Scottish Solicitors Guarantee Fund which is a fund established by Section 43 of the Solicitors (Scotland) Act 1980 for the purpose of making grants in order to compensate persons who, in the opinion of the Council of the Law Society of Scotland suffer pecuniary loss by reason of dishonesty on the part of a Scottish solicitor in connection with the practice of the solicitor.
8. Any complaint which you may have about any service provided by the firm should be directed to the partner within AB. Furthermore, you have a right to complain to the Law Society of Scotland, 26 Drumsheugh Gardens, Edinburgh EH3 7YR (website address:

www.lawscot.org.uk and telephone 0131 226 7411) and thereafter to complain against any finding of the Society to the Scottish Legal Services Ombudsman, 17 Waterloo Place, Edinburgh EH1 3QL (telephone number 0131 244 3044).

SCHEDULE 2

Style of Statement of Demands & Needs when advising on or arranging a specific contract of insurance.

1. The firm of AB has recommended that you [*name of client*] take out a contract of insurance for household contents with CD insurance company of [*insert address of insurance company*].
2. The demands and needs of [*client's name*] in respect of this insurance contract are that insurance cover is required for your household contents for your newly purchased property.
3. The firm has recommended the household insurance contract of CD insurance company because [*insert reasons for recommendation which should relate to the insurance contract meeting the client's insurance needs*].

SCHEDULE 3

Style of Terms of Business letter for incidental financial business

1. The specific incidental financial business undertaken by this firm will be the sale of a ABC shares in DE through stockbrokers FG on your instructions. The firm has limited its incidental financial business activities to arranging the sale of these shares given the limited scope of activities allowed under the incidental financial business regime.
2. The firm of AB is licensed by the Law Society of Scotland to carry on incidental financial business under the Solicitors (Scotland) (Incidental Financial Business) Practice Rules 2004.
3. The firm of AB is not authorised by the Financial Services Authority under the Financial Services and Markets Act 2000.
4. The firm of AB has Professional Indemnity Insurance under the Law Society of Scotland of Scotland's Master Policy. The current level of indemnity on the Master Policy is £1.5m per claim. The firm of AB is also covered by the Scottish Solicitors' Guarantee Fund which is a fund established by Section 43 of the Solicitors (Scotland) Act 1980 for the purpose of making grants in order to compensate persons who, in the opinion of the Council of the Law Society of Scotland suffer pecuniary loss by reason of dishonesty on the part of a Scottish solicitor in connection with the practice of the solicitor.
5. Any complaint which you may have about any service provided by the firm should be directed to the partner within AB. Furthermore, you have a right to complain to the Law Society of Scotland, 26 Drumsheugh Gardens, Edinburgh EH3 7YR (website address *www.lawscot.org.uk* and telephone 0131 226 7411) and thereafter to complain against any finding of the Society to the Scottish Legal Services Ombudsman, 17 Waterloo Place, Edinburgh EH1 3QL (telephone number 0131 244 3044).

Guidance on the end of the Polarisation Regime in the Financial Services Market.

[April 2005]

Introduction

1. The existing polarisation system in the financial services market will come to an end on 1st June 2005. Under the old polarisation regime, financial advisers were said to be polarised between those who were independent financial advisers (IFAs) and those who were tied advisers. Following the removal of the polarisation restrictions with effect from 1st June 2005 it will be possible for financial advisers to offer advice from—

(a) the whole of the market;
(b) from a limited number of providers (multi-tied); or
(c) from a single provider.

An individual or firm will only be able to designate itself as an independent financial adviser if advice is offered across the whole market and clients are given the option of being charged on a fee basis.

Principles for referring business to independent financial advisers

2. In the light of the end of the polarisation regime the Society has agreed that the following principles should apply for the referral of business to an IFA—

(a) A solicitor who is not licensed for any form of investment business or who is licensed for incidental financial business by the Society may only make a referral to a truly independent IFA—one where a client is given the option to be charged on a fee basis.
(b) A solicitor or firm may not become an appointed representative of any firm of financial advisers.
(c) A firm which is authorised for financial business by the Financial Services Authority may not become an appointed representative or become a multi-tied firm. An FSA authorised solicitor or firm must, under the FSA regime, be a truly independent financial adviser.

If you require any further advice on the above please contact David Cullen at the Society on davidcullen@lawscot.org.uk.

Guidelines on Precognoscing Untried Prisoners 1993

It is frequently the case that in preparing defence precognitions a statement will have to be taken from a witness who is an untried prisoner. Almost without exception an untried prisoner will have a solicitor representing him. The Professional Practice and Development Committee has been considering the practice issues from an allegation that representatives of a solicitor's firm, while precognoscing a prisoner who was to be a Crown witness against their client, queried the prisoner's satisfaction with his own solicitor. Thereafter a representative of another firm called to see the prisoner, ostensibly to take a precognition, but raising the matter of satisfaction with his own solicitor and leaving a business card.

In considering the issue of proper practice which arises in precognoscing prisoners, the Committee was mindful of art. 9 of the Code of Conduct and of rule 5 of the Solicitors (Scotland) (Advertising and Promotion) Practice Rules 1995 (both reprinted in section F of the *Parliament House Book*). The former states: "It is not permissible for a solicitor to communicate about any item of business with a person whom the solicitor knows to represented by another solicitor. A solicitor in such circumstances must always communicate with the solicitor acting for that person." Rule 5 states: "A solicitor shall not make a direct or indirect approach whether verbal or written to any person whom he knows or ought reasonably to know to be the client of another solicitor with the intention to solicit business from that person."

The Committee's views, as approved by the Society's Council, are that an untried prisoner on remand must be known to be represented by a solicitor and that another solicitor seeking to take a statement from such a person in connection with another case should not communicate directly with the untried prisoner but should request permission to precognosce him through his own solicitor. The precognoscing solicitor should only discuss the case in which he is involved and should not attempt to discuss the case in which the witness is himself or herself awaiting trial.

Law Society Guidelines on Duty to Lodge a Joint Minute and move for decree

The Professional Practice Committee has reaffirmed a Guideline originally published in December 1996. The Committee was asked for guidance about a divorce action where the wife defender had agreed terms with her husband in a Joint Minute which was signed by her solicitors. The action was allowed to proceed as undefended, but when the affidavits and Minute for Decree were lodged by the husband's solicitors, decree was not sought in terms of the Joint Minute, which had included a payment of periodical allowance.

The Committee agreed that a solicitor acting for a pursuer has a duty not only to lodge the Joint Minute, but also to seek decree in the terms of the Joint Minute. The solicitor for the defender is entitled to rely on that being done without requiring to check the Court Process.

Guidelines on Pension Sharing on Divorce 2001

Under the Welfare Reform and Pensions Act 1999 the following guidance in relation to the requirements of the financial services legislation has been given to the Judicial Procedure Committee of the Society. There are three stages to be considered separately in this area.

The first stage is the gathering of information about the value of the assets including the pension. This stage is not of itself Investment Business and can be done by a solicitor. Valuation methods used should be in accordance with the pension regulations, such as the cash equivalent method.

The second stage is the important decision on whether to opt for ear marking, sharing, or offsetting the pension entitlement. This stage is Investment Business under the Society's current Investment Business Rules. After the new legislation on Investment Business comes into force November 2001 this will probably be an incidental activity which firms which do not need FSA authorisation can undertake under Law Society rules where it is connected with legal work. Until the new regime is brought into force, which is expected later this year, such financial advice can only be given by a firm authorised to conduct investment business or an independent financial adviser.

The third stage only applies if the client wishes to opt to share the pension. Advice on how to deal with that, and in particular whether leave it in the existing pension scheme or take it out to put into a separate scheme, is specialist pension advice and would only be available from those with that particular authorisation. Currently there are only about six solicitors firms in Scotland with that authorisation but other Independent Financial Advisers with specialist pension authorisation could also provide this advice.

It should be borne in mind in all cases that, even where pension sharing is not used, clients may require pensions and other investment advice in their changed marital and financial status.

Guidelines on Correspondence between Prisoners and Solicitors 2002

In 1988 the Scottish Prisons Service and the Law Society of Scotland reached an informal agreement about how correspondence to prisoners from their solicitors should be dealt with on receipt at Scottish prisons. Guidance was produced in the Journal at that time setting out the procedure to ensure that the confidentiality of correspondence between solicitors and prisoner clients is secured in the most effective way possible. To ensure that the confidentiality of these communications is preserved, the Society has reproduced below the original guidance which remains good today.

When writing to a prisoner client the letter should be sealed in a plain envelope addressed to the prisoner. That envelope should also bear the name, address and telephone number of the firm and a reference number, the words "legal correspondence" and the signature of the legal adviser or his/her assistant. Alternatively, this information could be contained in a covering letter to the prison authorities. In either case, the correspondence should be addressed to the Governor of the establishment concerned and on receipt at the prison the outer envelope would be opened and the inner envelope passed unopened to the prisoner.

This will ensure that legal correspondence between solicitors and their clients remain confidential.

[1] Guidance Notes on Confidentiality

NOTE
[1] As amended in January 2000.

Confidentiality

General

Confidentiality is related to conflict of interest but is also a separate and distinct question. There are no Practice Rules dealing with this but the position is set out in Article 4 of the Code of Conduct which states, "The observance of client confidentiality is a fundamental duty of solicitors. This duty applies not only to the solicitors but also to their partners and staff and the obligation is not terminated by the passage of time."

Confidentiality is a privilege which is exercisable by the client and which can therefore be waived by the client. It covers matters which are actually confidential and not in the public domain. For example, the contents of a document which has been registered in a public register can never be confidential, although the circumstances in which it was entered into, the advice given to the client and the instructions which were received from the client will be confidential so far as not set out in the document.

Specific situations:

1. *Party in dispute with former client:*

Where a solicitor's firm used to act for one party and is now instructed by another party with whom the original client is in dispute, if the original client has instructed a new solicitor there will be no breach of the Conflict of Interest Rules but you may not be able to act for the new client. If you are in possession of confidential information about your original client which would be of benefit to the new one, you must make certain that this is not disclosed and not made use of. The best way to achieve this is to decline to act for the new client.

You should always remember the client's perception of the matter which will be different from your own. He may make a complaint to the Society anyway. While it will be a matter for your own judgment, you would not be criticised for declining to act. If the former client has not yet instructed a new solicitor, you should exercise even more caution before accepting new instructions as the original client may wish to instruct you in the matter anyway.

2. *Solicitor moving firm:*

A solicitor who had moved from one firm to another was the subject of a case in England which was reported in the Law Society Gazette in June 1995. He had had been a partner in one of the foremost firms specialising in the field of intellectual property and a firm which at all times had acted for the plaintiff in a patent case. The solicitor was not in any way involved in those proceedings and was engaged on work for different clients. He left the firm to join a different firm who were acting for the defendant in the patent case.

The plaintiff sought an injunction to prevent the individual solicitor—but not his new firm—being involved in any part of the patent case on the grounds that he might be in possession of confidential information. The High Court in London did not grant the injunction and set out the test relating to solicitors who move firms. A solicitor will only be disqualified from acting in a contentious matter against his previous firm's clients if he or she has (or there is a real risk that he or she has) relevant confidential information; that is, information which was confidential at the time of communication and which remains both confidential and relevant. The onus of proof is on the solicitor. While the matter has not been tested in the courts in Scotland the test set down in England is a valid one.

Chinese Walls—the Prince Jefri Case

The question of Chinese Walls was considered at length by the House of Lords in the case of Bolkiah (Prince Jefri) v KPMG [1999]2WLR 215—also [1999] 1ALL ER 517. Lord Hope (at page 217) stated that the solicitor's duty to preserve confidentiality "extends well beyond that of refraining from deliberate disclosure" and encompasses a duty to ensure "that the former client is not put at risk that confidential information which the solicitor has obtained from that relationship may be used against him in any circumstances". If the Court is satisfied that there is no risk of disclosure, it will not intervene.

Lord Millett (pages 226–227) stated "it is in any case difficult to discern any justification in principle for a rule which exposes a former client without his consent to any avoidable risk, however slight, that information which he has imparted in confidence in the course of a fiduciary relationship may come into the possession of a third party and be used to his disadvantage. Where in addition the information in question is not only confidential but also privileged, the case for the strict approach is unanswerable. Anything less fails to give effect to the policy on which legal professional privilege is based. It is of over-riding importance for the proper administration of justice that a client should be able to have complete confidence that what he tells his lawyer will remain secret. This is a matter of perception as well as substance. It is of the highest importance to the administration of justice that a solicitor or other person in possession of confidential and privileged information should not act in anyway that might appear to put that information at risk of coming into the hands of someone with an adverse interest . . . The Court should intervene unless it is satisfied that there is no risk of disclosure. It goes without saying that the risk must be a real one and not merely fanciful or theoretical, but it need not be substantial."

He also said that the Court should restrain the firm from acting for the second client unless satisfied on the basis of clear and convincing evidence that effective measures have been taken to ensure that no disclosure would occur. Although there is no rule of law that Chinese Walls or other arrangements of a similar kind are insufficient to eliminate the risk, the starting point must be that unless special measures are taken information moves within a firm. He approved of the terms of a consultation paper prepared by the Law Commission in England in 1992 which described Chinese Walls as normally involving some combination of the following:

(a) "The physical separation of the various departments in order to insulate them from each other—this often extends to such matters of detail as dining arrangements;
(b) An education programme, normally recurring, to emphasise the importance of not improperly or inadvertently divulging confidential information;
(c) Strict and carefully defined procedures for dealing with a situation where it is felt that the Walls should be crossed and the maintaining of proper records where this occurs;
(d) Monitoring by compliance officers of the effectiveness of the Walls;
(e) Disciplinary sanctions where there has been a breach of the Wall."

In a subsequent case, also in England, the High Court held that where cases were being handled by two separate departments and all documentation was in hard copy only there was clear departmental and physical separation of the matters and that the information barrier was entrenched within the firms organisation structure (Current Law March 2000 page 147 item 460). In another case the Court of Appeal held that where a solicitor had no recollection of ever representing a party and checks on records held at her firm revealed no potential conflict of interest or risk of injustice, the solicitor should not be prevented from acting for the other party (Current Law February 2000 page 73 item 226). In both these cases, Prince Jefri was followed.

Although Prince Jefri was an English case dealing with a firm of Chartered Accountants, there can be no doubt that the same approach would be taken to a firm of solicitors in Scotland. It follows therefore that if there is a risk of inadvertent disclosure of confidential information, that is an unacceptable risk. The only way in which it could be avoided with certainty is for the firm declining to act for clients in circumstances where the clients themselves may perceive there to be a risk of a breach of confidentiality.

3. *Statement to the police:*

The Professional Practice Department regularly receive calls from solicitors who have been asked to give a statement either to the police or to the solicitors acting for the former client's opponent. The authorities on confidentiality were reviewed in the reported case of Micosta v. Shetland Islands Council 1983 SLT 483 where Lord President Emslie giving the opinion of the court stated the general rule, "that communications passing between a party and his law agent are confidential." He then went on to say, "So far as we can discover from the authorities the only circumstances in which the general rule will be superseded are where fraud or some other illegal act is alleged against a party and where his law agent has been directly concerned in the carrying out of the very transaction which is the subject matter of enquiry." In the particular case the court refused a motion to open up a confidential envelope which had been recovered by specification in a civil action.

The principle was taken slightly further by Lord Macfadyen in the case of Conoco v. The Commercial Law Practice in 1996. In that case the Commercial Law Practice had been consulted by a client who had asked them to write to Conoco without mentioning his name but advising them that he was aware of circumstances in which they had made substantial overpayments on a contract which he would be willing to provide further information about in return for a proportion of what was recovered.

Instead of responding positively to this invitation, Conoco brought a Petition under the Administration of Justice Act to require the solicitors to disclose their clients' name and address, which was granted. Lord Macfadyen stated, "The public policy consideration which underlies the fraud exception may be capable of extension to a situation in which a party and his solicitor, not themselves either guilty of fraud or involved in carrying out a fraudulent transaction, are involved in a transaction the purpose of which is to derive for the client benefit from his knowledge of a fraud committed by another party."

If you are asked to give a statement to the Police or the Procurator Fiscal, the Professional Practice Committee view is that you should offer to be precognosced on oath before the sheriff. If you answer a question on the direction of the court you would not be subject to a complaint of breach of confidentiality, as the matter is fundamentally one of law not of practice. The High Court in 1999 refused a Bill of Suspension in the case of Kelly and Sarwar where the solicitor appealed against a citation to give a precognition on oath.

You should not hand over your file or papers to the Police or the Fiscal unless they have obtained a warrant. You should pay close attention to what is called for in such a warrant and only deliver that. If you feel the material is confidential you should put it in a sealed envelope and mark it as such. If the authorities complain about the difficulty in obtaining a warrant, then *a fortiori* you should not hand over your papers voluntarily.

If you are cited to give evidence at a trial you must appear but again should follow the judge's directions. If you are required to answer a question you should do so. Whether the evidence is admissible is a matter for the courts to determine and might form grounds of appeal.

4. *Crime about to be committed:*

You may receive information from your client about a crime which he is threatening to commit. In those circumstances the client is *not* entitled to the privilege of confidentiality and you would be quite entitled, and some would say obliged, to draw the circumstances to the attention of the authorities. For example, if Thomas Hamilton—who had consulted a number of different solicitors about different matters—had advised any of them of his intentions at Dunblane primary school, those solicitors would have been duty bound to alert the authorities so as to prevent the tragic events from happening.

5. *Insolvent client:*

Finally, you may find yourself asked to produce information to a trustee in sequestration or a liquidator. If you acted for the bankrupt or the company which has gone into liquidation, the trustee or the liquidator steps into the client's shoes and is entitled to all the papers which you hold for the client—although in a sequestration only so far as relating to the bankrupt's financial affairs. You do not need to take your client's instructions on whether such information should be given.

You should however be careful to separate out papers in relation to individual directors or shareholders where you were acting for a company and only deliver those papers in relation to your acting for the company—unless of course the same person has been appointed trustee to the individual directors or shareholders.

Law Society Guidelines on Comments to the Media by Solicitors

[(September 1998)]

The media continue to show great interest in legal matters, particularly cases of a sensational nature. The media is increasingly seeking the views of solicitors involved in court proceedings and also those representing special interest groups or with recognised experience in a particular field. While it is quite proper for solicitors to assist the media in conveying accurate information to the public, there should be no infringement of solicitors' obligations to their clients, the courts, the profession or the administration of justice. The Professional Practice Committee have therefore approved the following Guideline:

(1) Solicitors presenting information to the media in relation to their clients' affairs are acting in a professional capacity. Solicitors should conduct themselves in their public appearances and public statements in the same manner as they would with their fellow practitioners and with the courts.

(2) Before making a public statement concerning a client's affairs, a solicitor must first have the client's authority to do so and must also be satisfied that any communication is in the client's best interests. Solicitors should nor permit their personal interests or those of other causes to conflict with their client's interests.

Law Society Guidelines on Mandates in Executries

In 1986 the Council published a Guideline on a solicitor's duty to implement a mandate where the solicitor is one of the executors and also acting as agent in the executry. Two partners of a firm were executors along with the deceased's widow. The widow consulted other agents and a mandate from her was sent to the solicitor executor's firm. They declined to implement it which led to a finding of professional misconduct.

As part of their recent Review of Practice Guidelines the Committee considered this matter and re-affirmed the Council's view as follows:

1. Where there is a combination of solicitor and non-solicitor executors, a solicitor executor should not use his power as executor to secure the continuity of his acting as solicitor in the winding up of the estate. In such circumstances the solicitor may either cease acting or resign as executor.
2. If the solicitor ceases to act but remains as executor, he should bow to the wishes of the other executors on which firm should take over the administration of the estate. Failure to do so gives rise to a conflict between the interests of the executors and the interests of the solicitor's practice.
3. If the solicitor decides to resign, he should seek a discharge and obtemper any mandate if the remaining executors resolve that another firm should act.

Law Society Guidelines on Mandates

The Professional Practice Committee has recently reviewed the current guidance to the profession on the subjects of Mandates. This is contained in several sources and the purposes of this article is to update the guidance. The main guidance at the present time may be seen as being Scott Galt's article in the Journal in 1989 (see n. 1 at end) and an article on behalf of the Professional Practice Committee in 1995 (see n. 2 at end).

Times have changed since 1989. Clients now shop around more than they did and at times it may be difficult to draw lines between a response to advertising, competitive quoting and touting.

It remains the case, however that a Solicitor should not directly approach someone else's client (see n. 3 at end). We therefore have to look at both sides of the Mandate situation, the obtaining of a Mandate and the response to a Mandate.

Obtaining Mandates:

Since a Solicitor cannot approach another Solicitor's client other than as part of a general circulation, mail-shot or advert, the initial approach must come from the client. The exception to this, the situation of Partnerships breaking up, is considered below. There may be a variety of reasons why a client may wish to change Solicitors.

(a) **Client Moving:**

The simplest situation which will seldom cause any difficulties is the obvious one of the client moving from one part of the country to another and wanting to instruct a local Solicitor, *e.g.* in an ongoing matrimonial case.

(b) **Client Dissatisfied:**

The client may or may not be moving but wants a new Solicitor. This should be straightforward enough but points to note include:—

(i) Ensuring that the instruction to the new Solicitor is from the **client** as opposed to a relative or friend who has suggested the change of Solicitor; and

(ii) The client should be asked if the dissatisfaction should be communicated to the previous Solicitor and, if so, whether in general or detailed terms.

(c) **New Cases:**

For a variety of reasons, (moving, dissatisfaction, lower quote, personal connection or recommendation) a client may give instructions to a new Solicitor at the beginning of a new piece of business although that client was represented by a different Solicitor in previous matters. Most commonly this would be the situation where a property has been bought using one Solicitor and a few years later is to be sold through another who then has to obtain the titles. Obviously if the titles are with a Bank or Building Society the new Solicitor just requests them and gets on with it and no Mandate is needed. If the titles are with the previous Solicitor a Mandate will be required.

The situations outlined at (a), (b) and (c) above are relatively straightforward. For whatever reason the client has instructed a new Solicitor. Things are much less straightforward, however, in the situation where the Solicitor's Partnership is breaking up. There are two slightly different situations here. One is the Partner leaving the continuing firm and the other is the firm itself dissolving.

Partner Leaving:

The Partners of the firm involved should agree on the procedure to be adopted in advising clients of the change in the firm. In some cases it may be agreed amongst the partners that the departing Solicitor should carry on with certain cases. In others it may be desired to leave it to their clients to decide whether to stay or go with the departing Partner. It makes sense to agree the approach in advance. An unseemly squabble may well alienate the client from all of the Partners. The terms of a joint communication should be agreed and sent to the client who should be invited to indicate a preference to stay with the established firm or go with the departing Partner. In an age of ever increasing competitiveness, however, it may be that the established firm and the departing Partner wish to set out their respective stalls in their own distinct ways. It is to be hoped that they can at least agree to send their letters in the same envelope.

Particular difficulties arise where there is no co-operation between the departing and remaining Partners. Some Solicitors take the view that all clients are clients of the firm rather than individual Solicitors and maintain that a departing Partner has no right to try to take clients away from the continuing firm. If that were the case then the departing Partner would not be allowed to seek Mandates from the clients. The Committee has re-affirmed its view however that subject to what the Partners may themselves have agreed a departing Partner is entitled to contact clients for whom he or she has acted personally as the responsible Partner and invite them to continue to be clients at the new firm.

The right to contact clients applies both while the departing Partner is still a Partner of the firm whose clients are being contacted; and also for a reasonable time after the Partner has left. What is a reasonable time will depend on the circumstances but in a case in the early 1990's the Committee decided that 3 months was still within a reasonable time.

Associates and Assistants Leaving:

All of the above applies only to Partners, (*i.e.* Partners in the previous firm). Unless there is a specific agreement which allows it, a departing Assistant/Associate is not entitled to contact clients of his or her employers to seek Mandates with the sole exception of those who are Nominated Solicitors on a Legal Aid Certificate. The Professional Practice Committee accepts that an Assistant may very well attract business to a firm. However it is the firm, and the Partners thereof, who have the authority to deal with the clients. An Associate/Assistant does not act for the client. It is anticipated, however, that where there is a significant element of *delectus personae* the clients may wish to follow the Assistant elsewhere. The approach has to be from the client however.

Nominated Solicitors:

In terms of the Legal Aid Act, legal aid is available through individual Solicitors not firms. The Court of Session has held that "so long as a nominated Solicitor remains in that position he is under a clear professional duty to render all normal services provided by a Solicitor" (see n. 4 at end). It follows that an employed Solicitor who is a nominated Solicitor is obliged to advise the client of a move and if the client wishes, is entitled to continue as nominated Solicitor.

Dissolution of Partnerships:

Occasionally a firm may be dissolved completely with various Partners going in various directions. If the firm ceases to exist then it can only be the personal relationship between an individual Solicitor and the client which is important. In most cases arrangements would be made for each Partner to take certain files etc. and the client would be advised of this and given an opportunity to instruct otherwise.

In the odd situation where there is no agreement between the Partners the proper course is for the client to be advised of the position, told the new business addresses of all the relevant Partners and asked to choose which, if any, to instruct to hold files etc. All of the Partners of the dissolving firm have a duty to ensure proper arrangements are made for the retention of all necessary files and documents.

Receiving Mandates:

The simple rule (except that there is no specific practice rule on the matter) is, and always has been, that when you receive a Mandate you must respond to it "timeously" either by sending the items requested to the new Solicitor or stating that you are exercising a lien pending settlement of fees and outlays. A delay in doing so will normally be misconduct. You cannot retain papers, even if you have a right of lien, if to do so would prejudice the client (*e.g.* in a continuing Court case or transaction) but you can deliver the papers reserving your right of lien and requesting the papers to be returned when the case is concluded. Prejudice is more than inconvenience and will depend on the particular circumstances of the matter.

Any Solicitor receiving a Mandate will usually want to know why. Sometimes the reason is obvious but various questions and problems can arise.

1. **Did the new Solicitor tout for the business?**—It is not for the established Solicitor to judge. You may suspect and if you have evidence you may report but you must, in any event, take the Mandate at face value and hand over the papers.

2. **There is an outstanding fee note.**—You can exercise your lien but you must still respond to the Mandate by writing to the new Solicitor immediately to say you are doing so.

3. **Work has been done for which a fee will be payable but no fee note has been sent out.**—One sometimes gets the response when sending a Mandate that the file has been sent to the Law Accountants and will be forwarded in due course once the fee has been advised and paid. Whether this is acceptable depends on the case in question. If a few weeks without the file will make no great difference then it may be acceptable for the established Solicitor to do this but if the new Solicitor needs the file quickly it is not. The file etc. can be delivered reserving the right of lien. A reasonable time to render an account is in order but it should not exceed four weeks unless the circumstances are truly exceptional. It may be that having extracted such information as required the new Solicitor does not need the actual file in which case it should be returned. This imposes a duty on the new Solicitor to say whether the file is needed urgently and to return the file for feeing as soon as reasonably practicable. If the new Solicitor gives an undertaking (not the clients undertaking) that the account will be paid out of the proceeds of the matter in hand, that should normally be accepted by the original Solicitor and the file and papers delivered.

4. **To whom should a fee note be sent when a Mandate is received.**—Views differ but the Professional Practice Committee decided in March 1997 that it is not a breach of Article 9 of the Code of Conduct for a Solicitor to send a fee direct to the former client. This followed the view that the debt was due by and would require to be enforced directly against the client. If a lien is being exercised the new Solicitor should be informed anyway. If a lien is not being exercised it might be wondered whether there is a duty on the established Solicitor to tell the new Solicitor that a fee note has been/is being sent. One doubts if it could be categorised as misconduct not to tell the new Solicitor this was being done but it might be seen as a matter of professional

courtesy. It should be emphasised, however, that if anything at all is to be sent directly to a client who has instructed a new Solicitor then there should be nothing in that communication which invites the former client to resume the original connection. If fee notes can be sent direct to the client after a Mandate it seems to follow that reminders can also be sent direct but these should be just that, reminders and nothing more. Any invitation to discuss or the like would be a breach of Article 9 of the Code of Conduct and any such matters should be raised through the new Solicitor.

5. **Can the established Solicitor ask why the Mandate has been sent?**—Yes, but only after the mandate has been implemented. Implementation means delivery of the papers and not simply telling the new Solicitor that a lien is being exercised. The idea behind this is that no undue pressure should be brought to bear on the client and the danger of that happening clearly still exists while the established Solicitor still holds the papers.

6. **To whom should the request for reasons be made?**—In his article Scott Galt considered that a request for reasons for a Mandate should be addressed to the new Solicitor. The May 1995 Journal article states, however, that a Solicitor having implemented a Mandate "may write to the former client making a reasonable enquiry as to why the client has instructed a new Solicitor". The Solicitor can ask for information but must not in any way invite the former client to resume the original connection. Many Solicitors may disagree with the view that the Solicitor can write directly to the former client at all. On the other hand it may be one of the few ways in which touting might come to light. The current position is, therefore, that the established Solicitor can write directly to the client once the Mandate has been implemented but must be extremely careful in the wording of any such communication.

7. **Criminal legal aid cases.**—Specific rules apply and are set out at Article 7 of the Code of Conduct for criminal work. (See Schedule attached.)

8. **Civil legal aid cases.**—Again specific rules apply relating to SLAB's approval of the transfer of Legal Aid Certificates.

In both criminal and civil cases the guidance on request for reasons would apply. With regard to the payment of fees, it can be a source of great frustration in Advice and Assistance cases that SLAB will not consider an account until the whole matter is completed. The original Solicitor may have no way of knowing the matter has been completed unless this information is received from the new Solicitor and is therefore entitled to exercise a lien until a satisfactory undertaking from the original Solicitor is received. There is a clear duty on the new Solicitor to tell the original Solicitor when the account can be submitted or to pay the account out of the proceeds recovered or preserved.

9. **Assistants leaving.**—As noted above, the general rule here is that the client is a client the firm and not the individual and so the Assistant should not approach the client. A Mandate received in these circumstances however still has to be treated at face value and still has to be implemented, although the Solicitor's conduct could be brought to the attention of the Law Society.

10. **Partial Mandated and General Mandates.**—A difficulty which may occasionally arise is the situation where the client wants a particular firm to do a particular transaction without in any way intending to shift allegiance in general. Sometimes this has not been reflected in the Mandate which followed which might request "all title deeds and documents" leading to misunderstandings and quite possibly a falling out between Solicitors, none

of which tends to impress the client very greatly. It is not uncommon these days for clients to use different Solicitors for different types of business or even for the same type and a new Solicitor should not simply assume that he or she is going to be acting for a new client in all matters. This difficulty could be addressed by producing a *pro forma* Mandate along the following lines:

I hereby authorise and instruct you to send:—
* *All title deeds and documents and files*
* *The title deeds of (specify property)*
* *The documents and papers relating to (specify matter concerned) held by you to (new Solicitors)*
* **Delete where applicable.**

NOTES

[1] Journal February 1989 p. 54—Article by Scott Galt.

[2] Journal May 1995 p. 207—Article—"The Departing Assistant and Mandates".

[3] Code of Conduct—Rule 9. (Also Rule 5 of the Advertising and Promotion Practice Rules 1995)

[4] *per* Lord Osborne in *McKinstry v. Law Society of Scotland*, 1995 S.L.T. 191.

SCHEDULE

Mandates in Criminal Work (Article 7 of the Code of Conduct for Criminal Work)

All Mandates requesting the transfer of papers and legal aid relating to a criminal matter shall be completed and executed by the assisted person in the form agreed by the Scottish Legal Aid Board and the Law Society of Scotland. The Mandate should include the place and date of signing and a full explanation as to why the Mandate has been issued.

Guidance Note

The matter is governed by the Criminal Legal Aid (Scotland) Regulations 1987, paragraph 17(3), which states "where an assisted person desires that a solicitor, other than the solicitor presently nominated by him shall act for him, he shall apply to the Board for authority to nominate another specified solicitor to act for him and shall inform the Board of the reason for his application; and the Board, if it is satisfied that there is good reason for the application and, in the case of Legal Aid made available under Sections 24 or 25 of the Act that it is in the interests of justice or, as the case may be, is reasonable, for him to receive or continue to receive Criminal Legal Aid, may grant the application".

It seems clear from a plain construction of this Regulation that changes of agency where the client is legally aided in a criminal case can only take place if the Board gives the client authority to nominate another specified solicitor. Until the Board gives its authority the client cannot instruct another solicitor unless he wishes to do so without the benefit of Legal Aid, which fact should be notified to the Board.

Therefore the chronology of transfers of agency in criminal cases should be (1) the client approaches his proposed new solicitor to ascertain if he is willing to act; (2) client applies to Board for authority to transfer the agency; (3) Board grants authority; (4) client instructs new solicitor; (5) new solicitor serves Mandate on previous solicitor.

The Board's authority to transfer must ante-date any Mandate.

This Statement would solve many issues including inducements to transfer agency and "Mandate wars". Adoption of this interpretation would of course mean that legally aided clients and fee paying clients will not be treated precisely equally. However, that objection has to be seen in the light of the need to comply with the Regulations which effectively impose a statutory suspensive condition on any Mandate and the requirement that solicitors will require to inform a transferring client that instructions cannot be accepted until the Regulations are complied with.

Form of Mandate approved by the Council

Dear Sir,

I write to inform you that the Scottish Legal Aid Board has transferred Legal Aid Certificate No.   from you to my new nominated solicitor who is   I authorise and instruct you to transfer to   all papers, documents and files which you hold on my behalf in relation to this matter.

Yours faithfully,

Law Society's Risk Management Flowchart and Procedures

(March 27, 1999)

Starting a Piece of Work

Common Failures	Good Service	How to Ensure Excellence	Model Procedures
Not finding out what the client wants us to do for him/her	**Ensure** that you always listen and ask questions when taking instructions	**Use** a questionnaire, checklist/aide-memoire	**See** examples in the Client Care Manual and Ensuring Excellence
Not telling the client what we will do—and not do	**Ensure** that the client knows what you will (not) do for him/her	**Issue** Letters of Engagement/Terms of Business	**Model** Procedure 1 **See** examples in the Client Care Manual and Ensuring Excellence
Not telling the client the fee or basis of feeing and not being paid/complaint about fee	**Ensure** the client understands the basis of charges and why/how that may vary	**Explain** basis of fees in Letter of Engagement/Terms of Business	**Model** procedure 1 **See** examples in the Client Care Manual and Ensuring Excellence
Not avoiding conflicts of interest [complying with the Conflict of Interest Rules]	**Ensuring** that conflicts of interest are identified as soon as they arise and are avoided	**Establish** a file opening procedure. Maintain a full and accurate record on any database	**Model** procedure 2
Not complying with Money Laundering Regulations	**Ensure** consistent observance of the Regulations	**Establish** a set procedure and use standard forms/ checklists	**See** procedures in Client Care Manual

Doing the Work

Common Failures	Good Service	How to Ensure Excellence	Model Procedures
Not communicating	**Ensure** that the client is kept informed at all times	**Establish** a policy regarding reporting	
Not recording a discussion	**Ensure** that proper notes are made of all conversations	**Use** a standard format of attendance note	
Not recording/acting on a time limit	**Ensure** that critical dates are verified at the outset and a system of reminders set up	**Use** a critical date diary	**Model** procedure 3
Not being able to locate a file/papers/ titles/Wills etc.	**Ensure** that there are good safe procedures	**Establish** a formal office procedure	**Model** procedure 4
	Ensure that there is a system for tracking files, papers etc. outside the safe	**Use** a system of borrowing cards	**Model** procedure 5

Common Failures	Good Service	How to Ensure Excellence	Model Procedures
Not following instructions	**Ensure** that proper notes are made of all conversations	**Use** a standard format of attendance note	
	Ensure that work is planned from the start and reviewed at intervals	**Use** a checklist/case plan	**See** sample case plans and commentary on planning of work in Client Care Manual
	Confirm oral instructions in writing immediately		
Not doing the job properly	**Ensure** that an absent fee-earner's work is dealt with promptly	**Establish** a set procedure/ contingency plan	**Model** procedure 6
	Ensure that work is planned from the start and reviewed at intervals	**Use** a checklist/case plan	**See** sample case plans and commentary on planning of work in Client Care Manual
	Ensure that the styles and pro formas you/ your colleagues use are up-to-date styles and pro formas	**Monitor** and review all styles and pro formas **Create** a record of all styles and pro formas	**Model** procedure 7
	Ensure that partners supervise incoming and outoing mail	**Establish** a formal office procedure and stick to it	**Model** procedure 8
	Ensure that good instructions are give to third parties	**Follow** proper procedures when engaging and instructing third parties	**See** commentary in Client Care Manual
Not avoiding unreasonable obligations	**Ensure** that partners supervise incoming and outgoing mail	**Establish** a formal office procedure and stick to it	**Model** procedure 8
	Ensure that only standard formats of undertaking are ever granted by the firm, ideally undertakings which will be treated as "classic"	**Establish** an approved office style and ensure that this is only deviated from with partner approval	**Model** procedure 9
Not reviewing work regularly	**Ensure** that files are reviewed regularly	**Follow** a standard format of audit checklist/audit record	**Model** procedure 10
Not recording securities/charges timeously	**Ensure** that work is planned from the start and reviewed at intervals	**use** a checklist/case plan	**See** sample case plans and commentary on planning of work in Client Care Manual

Common Failures	Good Service	How to Ensure Excellence	Model Procedures
	Ensure that critical dates are verified at the outset and a system of reminders set up	**Use** a critical date diary	**Model** procedure 3
Not following accounts Rules and other Regulations	**Ensure** that work is planned from the start and reviewed at intervals	**Use** a checklist/case plan	**See** sample case plans and commentary on planning of work in Client Care Manual
	Ensure that files are reviewed regularly	**Follow** a standard format of audit checklist/audit record	**Model** procedure 10

Finishing a Piece of Work

Common Failures	Good Service	How to Ensure Excellence	Model Procedures
Not storing and recording papers	**Ensure** that there are procedures for concluding a piece of work and closing a file	**Establish** and follow a set office procedure	**Model** procedure 11
Not advising client of conclusion	**Ensure** that there are procedures for concluding a piece of work and closing a file	**Establish** and follow a set office procedure	**Model** procedure 11
	Ensure that an accounting is provided		
Not rendering fee	**Ensure** that there are procedures for concluding a piece of work and closing a file	**Establish** and follow a set office procedure	**Model** procedure 11
	Ensure that files are never closed unless fee rendered and client account balance is Nil	**Use** a simple checklist and auditing procedure to ensure files are not closed without account being clear	
Not closing the file	**Ensure** that files are never closed unless fee rendered and client account balance is Nil	**Use** a simple checklist and auditing procedure to ensure files are not closed without account being clear	**Model** procedure 11
Not dealing adequately with complaints	**Ensure** that complaints are handled in a consistent, prompt and clear manner	**Establish** and enforce a documented complaints procedure to be handled by a nominated Complaints Partner	**See** guidelines in Client Care Manual

RISK MANAGEMENT PROCEDURES

Model Procedures

1. Letters of Engagement/Terms of Business
2. File Opening
3. Critical Date Diaries
4. Safe Custody of Document Procedures
5. File Tracking
6. Fee Earner's Absence
7. Control of Styles/Pro Formas
8. Supervision of Incoming Mail
9. Undertakings
10. File Review
11. Concluding a Piece of Work & Closing a File

Model Procedure 1

Letters of Engagement/Terms of Business

Ensure that the client knows what you will (not) do for him/her.
Issue Letters of Engagement/Terms of Business

- Give the client the terms under which you work
- Advise a client when the terms of business change
- A Letter of Engagement allows a firm to tell a client what it will and will not do, what the cost will be and so on. It gives the terms of business. It may also deal with things which appear mundane but are actually important to the client, such as opening hours. The Letter of Engagement allows the firm to manage the expectations of a client as well as reduce risk of misunderstandings.
- A Letter of Engagement should therefore ALWAYS be issued to a new client.
- A Letter should IDEALLY be issued at the start of a new matter/transaction/case. For the work that has been done for the client before may be different, the fee structure not the same and so on.
- Where acting for a client with similar, multiple cases, *e.g.* debt collection, then issue a Letter of Engagement periodically. This might be once a year or when the fee structure changes.
- Refer to the Law Society's Guideline on Letters of Engagement (page F970, *supra*) when making up your style. The Society could provide suggested wording but there would never be agreement about exact wording, layout etc. Your version is best for you!

Model Procedure 2

File Opening

Ensure that conflicts of interest are identified as soon as they arise and are avoided.
Establish a file opening procedure.

- Establish that you can do the work
- Obtain basic information from client and record (see below).
- check that there is no conflict of interest with any other client. Consider what the client objective is and whether the process of attaining that objective could affect any other Firm client. Normally, when the conflict has arisen it is too late.
- Check that you or the firm are able to carry out the agreed action

- Verify client's identity for Money Laundering Purposes and to be sure as to whom you take instructions from
- Enter basic information on a database and allocate a client account/new matter number
- Issue a file bearing name, type of work, account number and name of fee earner (except where cash transactions only)
- Create a plan for the work

New Client Record

Full Name:				
Address incl Postcode:				
Phone Nos:	Home:		Work:	
Fax No:			E-Mail:	
Client Type:	Single/Joint/Married:			
Fee Earner Name:				
Conflict of Interest Check carried out (Tick)				
Work can be done by me/us (Tick)				
Money Laundering form completed (Tick or N/A)				

Model Procedure 3

Critical Date Diaries

Ensure that critical dates are verified at the outset and a system of reminders set up.
Use a critical date diary.

- A Critical Date is a date on which or by which an action should be taken or specified so as to ensure that the client is not seriously prejudiced. This may be a date some days or week before the last date on which it is possible to take time-barred action.
- Examples are given in the appendix. These are not exclusive.
- Critical Date diaries may take several forms. Those described below are examples:—
- The simplest system is a desk diary kept by the fee-earner. This is easy to administer but can be lost and is not necessarily reviewed by another fee-earner. Therefore, it should be supplemented by another system.
- An enhancement of the individual diary system is one to be kept by department or

firm. Each fee earner is responsible for entering their own critical dates in to it. One person is given the responsibility to monitor the diary and to remind the fee-earner of an action to be taken.

- A wall chart is also simple but has the advantage that other fee-earners can easily refer to it. Coded stickers enable different types of Critical Dates to be identified. Someone must be given the responsibility to monitor each day/week so as to remind a fee-earner that some action must be taken.
- A computerised system is within reach of any office having straightforward software. Many office systems have a diary. Each fee earner notifies a person of a Critical Date which that person enters on to the diary system. When the diary for that day is consulted in due course. The Critical Date appears and is notified to the fee earners. Some fee earners will wish to operate the system themselves but, in any event, anyone may consult the diary.
- It is good practice to have the fee earner confirm that a necessary action has been taken Failing that, a person must be responsible for reminding them. In the event of no response, someone else in the organisation should be told.

Appendix

Personal Injury Triennia
Defamation Triennia
Quinquennia
Proofs/Jury Trials/Tribunals Hearings
Appeals
Debates/Procedure Roll Hearings
Criminal Pleading Diets
Criminal Trial
Criminal Appeals
Inhibitions
Industrial Tribunal Applications
Options Hearings
Procedural Hearings

COMMERCIAL
Notice to Quit—all types of Leases
Notices of Rent Reviews—all types of Leases
Registering changes at Companies House
Annual Returns and Accounts—Companies
Resiling Notices—Missives
Dates by which Disposition and/or Standard securities must be recorded in order to keep "live" the seller's and/or debtor's letter of obligation
Liquor Licensing Applications

AGRICULTURAL
Notice to Quit
Notices to Rent Reviews
Intimations of bequests of Tenancies
Applications to transfer agricultural quotas

PRIVATE CLIENT
Executries: Inheritance Tax Interest Charge
Executries: Deed of Variations and a Disclaimer of Legal Rights
Discretionary Trusts; charge to tax
Trusts: Vesting Dates

RESIDENTIAL PROPERTY
Closing dates for offers
Dates of entry

Model Procedure 4

Safe Custody of Document Procedures

Ensure that there are good safes procedures.
Establish a formal office procedure.

- Good practice dictates that there should be in place a simple and workable procedure for storing, locating and tracking Title Deeds, Wills, Securities and other documents held for client and Third Parties. The following is an example of a good-practice system.
- Safeguard all papers relevant to a matter
- The movement of Titles within and outwith the Office should be recorded on a database or register.
- All Title Deeds coming into the Office either from a Lender, client or Third Party

(other than Titles received for examination in connection with a purchase transaction) should be recorded on this database/register.

- Titles should be stored within a "Title" envelope. The envelope should be marked on the outside with the identity of the client, the client file reference, and the address of the property.
- Each envelope should be allocated a number.
- Envelopes should be held in safe storage in numerical order.
- All movements in relation to Titles should be recorded on the database including lending of the Titles to Third Parties, delivery of the Titles to Lenders and other institutions, and delivery of the Titles to clients.
- The envelope retains its allocated number until Titles finally leaves the custody of the firm's offices.
- The number allocated is then freed for use in respect of other Titles.
- The data relating to the outgoing Titles is still however retained on the database/register.
- Date is recorded both in relation to identity of client and location of property.
- To prevent loss of data, a hard copy is printed on a regular basis. A disk back-up should be made regularly and stored in an appropriate safe or off-site.

Model Procedure 5

File Tracking

Ensure that there is a system for tracking files, papers etc. outside the safe.
Use a system of borrowing cards.

- Prevent loss of papers and files outside the safe
- Create a file for each matter and keep all papers with it or note in the file where they are
- Create a borrowing card (see sample below) and place one in each file as it is opened
- Whenever a files is taken by someone other than the fee earner or his/her secretary, the person so borrowing fill in the card and puts it where the file was

---

Style Borrowing Card

Clients Name:

A/C Number:

Case Title:

Fee Earner:

IF YOU REMOVE THIS FILE FROM THE CABINET AND YOU ARE NEITHER THE FEE EARNER NOR HIS/HER SECRETARY PLEASE COMPLETE BELOW

Name	Date Removed	Name	Date Removed

Model Procedure 6

Fee Earner's Absence

Ensure that an absent fee earner's work is dealt with promptly.
Establish a set procedure/contingency plan.

- It is important that progress is made on client's work despite the absence of the fee earner.
- A fee earner should, if possible, make a temporary or permanent arrangement for some other person(s) to look after his/her work or in the case of illness or holiday.
- Someone in the firm/department should always know what that arrangement is. In an emergency and failing allocation of responsibility, that person should do so.
- Arrangements should be made to divert phone calls.
- An absent partner's mail should be seen by another partner.
- The fee earner's mail should be checked by say 9.30 in the morning of absence by either another fee earner or preferably a partner.
- A fee-earner leaving the building temporarily should advise his/her Secretary and the receptionist. They should divert their phone to their secretary.
- A notice board in *e.g.* a secretary's room noting the whereabouts of fee earners/ meetings is valuable.
- Advise the client that someone else is looking after his/her work.
- A basic checklist/case plan inside the front cover of the file to be filled in with the most up-to-date information could prove to be beneficial.

Model Procedure 7

Control of Styles/Pro Formas

Ensure that the styles and pro formas you/your colleagues use are up-to-date.
Monitor and review all styles and pro formas.
Create a record of all styles and pro formas.

- Introduce and enforce an office rule discouraging the use of styles and pro formas other than those which have been approved by [ ]
- Ensure that all styles and pro formas used throughout the firm are reviewed on a regular basis and whenever there is a change in law. Changes should be approved by a partner.
- To assist in the control and review of styles and pro formas, maintain a record of all styles and pro formas [for each area of work] **See sample below**
- Use the record of styles and pro formas to ensure that regular reviews of all styles and pro formas are carried out and logged
- On each style and each pro forma the author and the date of the latest review/update should be noted. These particulars should also be noted in the record of styles and pro formas
- Responsibility for maintaining the record of all styles and pro formas; checking that it is kept updated and ensuring that regular reviews of styles and pro formas are actually carried out should be allocated to a nominated fee earner

Record of Styles & Pro Formas

Style/ Pro Forma	**Author/ Drafted**	**F/E resp. for review**	**Review Frequency**	**Review Date/ Review Done**	**Review Date/ Review Done**	**Review Date/ Review Done**	**Etc, Etc.**
Offer to purchase (residential)	AJS 1/11/96	BKT	6 monthly 4/5/97 (BKT)	5/97 9/11/97 (BKT)	11/97 7/5/98 (BKT)	5/98	11/98
Lease—furnished residential	BKT 10/1/98	BKT	6 monthly	7/98 2/7/98 (BKT)	1/99	7/99	1/2000
Will (simple form)	CGD 9/2/97	CGD	Yearly	2/98 19/2/98 (CGD)	2/99	2/2000	2/2001
Power of Attorney	BKT 10/1/98	CGD	Yearly	1/99 17/1/98 (CGD)	1/2000	1/2001	2/2002
Etc							
Etc							

Model Procedure 8

Supervision of Incoming Mail

Ensure that partners supervise incoming and outgoing mail
Establish a formal office procedure and stick to it

- It is important that a partner sees all items of mail. They own the business and they take the risk.
- Mail should be opened in the presence of a partner (on a rota basis if more than one partner!)
- All mail should then go to the relevant partner (if there is more than one) before going to any other fee earner
- Any complaint should be immediately referred to the [Complaints Partner] and any letter indicating a claim to the [Senior Partner]
- If the partner cannot be identified from the letter/mail then the person dealing with it should refer to the firm's client listing. Any unidentified mail should be left in the mail area for identification.

Model Procedure 9

Undertakings

Ensure that only standard formats of undertaking are ever granted by the firm, ideally undertakings which will be treated as "classic"
Establish an approved office style and ensure that this is only deviated from with partner approval

The provisions of the Master Policy Certificate of Insurance relating to "classic" letters of obligation are as at March 1999 as follows:

- "Classic Letter of Obligation" shall mean an undertaking given by a solicitor in connection with the settlement of any transaction for the disposal for onerous consideration of any interest in property or the granting of security over any such property by a client of that solicitor in terms of which the solicitor personally undertakes any one or more of the following
  - (i) to deliver a clear Search in the Property and Personal Registers or a Letter of Obligation in or substantially in the styles of Letter of Obligation set out in the Registration of Title Practice Book (HMSO Edinburgh) paragraphs G 2 20 to G 2 25 with reference to the later of (a) the date of settlement of the transaction or (b) where the disponee, feuar, tenant, assignee or lender as the case may be requires to complete title by recording in the Register of Sasines or registration in the Land Register the date of recording of that title or the Land or Charge Certificate (as the case may be) provided that in the case of (b) such undertaking is effective for no more than a reasonable period after settlement of the transaction (which in the case of an undertaking granted on or after 1st November 1994 shall be a period not exceeding fourteen days)
  - (ii) to deliver a duly executed (and recorded if appropriate) discharge to be registered in the Land Register provided that the solicitor granting the undertaking has or will on settlement of the transaction to which it relates have control of sufficient funds to discharge in full the Obligations to which that security relates or
  - (iii) to deliver a redemption receipt in respect of ground burdens in circumstances where the solicitor granting the undertaking is aware of the identity and whereabouts of the party entitled to the redemption monies and has available sufficient funds with which to redeem the ground burden in question

- The Self-Insured Amount shall not apply to any claim which arises (or to the extent that it arises) from having granted a Classic Letter of Obligation provided that
  - (i) such claim is intimated to the practice after 31st October 1991 and
  - (ii) in so far as the claim relates to an undertaking as described in (i) or (ii) above the practice provides evidence to the reasonable satisfaction of the Insurers that proper enquiry as to outstanding securities was made of the client and that immediately prior to settlement of the transaction to which the undertaking

relates an up to date Search in the Computerised Presentment Book (after 6th April 1992 only) and an Interim Report on Search in the Property and Personal Registers or equivalent Form 10 11 12 or 13 Land Register Report (as the circumstances may require) was obtained which were clear except only as regards any security to which on or before settlement the provisions of (ii) above applied

- The foregoing shall not apply in the event that the solicitor granting a Classic Letter of Obligation
  - (i) is aware of any outstanding security and
  - (ii) has control of sufficient funds with which to discharge the obligations to which the security relates but fails to procure that a discharge of such security is recorded or registered as the case may be

Model Procedure 10

File Review

Ensure that files are reviewed regularly.
Follow a standard format of audit checks/audit record

- The purpose of the procedure is to set out the system for monitoring progress and quality of work by means of regular file reviews.
- Each fee earner must
  - Keep the file in order
  - Make sure that other relevant papers are kept together and are easily identifiable
  - Ensure that the file can be easily located (See Model Procedure 5)
  - Keep the checklist up-to-date
  - Complete a Critical Date Diary, where appropriate (see Model Procedure 3)
- Fee Earners are responsible for their own file reviews.
- At least once every three months, the fee earner will be issued with a list of current files for which he/she is responsible. The fee earner reviews all these files, marks the list to show the review has taken place and returns the list to [the Senior Partner]. Any action required should be carried out immediately.
- Each fee earner must review the files of another fee earner in order to ensure that work is being carried out properly. That should be done on a sampling basis and at least once every three months. The reviewer marks each file and makes a separate report to [the Senior Partner]
- The fee earner should review each file before closing it/completing the matter, Ideally, a partner should always see a file before it is closed.

Model Procedure 11

Concluding a Piece of Work & Closing a File

Ensure that there are procedures for concluding a piece of work and closing a file
Establish and follow a set office procedure

- Ensure that work has been completed properly, that the client knows the position and that the firm has received all monies due to it.
- A firm should have a common method of closing and archiving files, dealing with cash balances etc.
- Fee earners should close files regularly so as to ensure that dead files are not littering up their room. They will be encouraged to do so if there is a secure system of storage and speedy means of retrieval of a file in storage.
- The fee earner must carry out a review:

A checking that the work has been fully completed
B ensuring that the clients' requirements have been met
C making sure that the client has been advised of the outcome and any further action required
D dealing properly with documents and other material
E checking that the clients' details in the database are correct

- To close a file the fee earner shall first ensure:
  A that the work has been feed
  B that the cash balance is Nil
  C that the time record, if any, is Nil

- The fee earner then sends the file and any papers to storage, indicating how long they are to be kept

- The method of storage is one for the firm to determine. Usually, it will be on-site, in which case there must be:
  A a database or list of all files closed, with classification as to *e.g.* Name of Client; Client Account Number; Fee Earner; Date of Destruction
  B a secure method of storing the files
  C an efficient means of retrieving them
  D a borrowing index

- A good method of on-site storage is in boxes. These have a list of contents on the top. There should also be kept a separate, central list by box number and some other classification such as client or account number.

- At the end of each calendar year, the firm will list all files whose destruction date fell during that year. That list is reviewed and either a file destroyed or a new destruction date attached to it.

Law Society Guidelines on Closing of Files

The matter of a solicitor's duty on closing a file was discussed in 1992 and a brief note on the subject appeared in the summer "Council Report" of that year. The Professional Practice Committee agreed:—

"That there is a professional duty upon a solicitor to advise a client in writing that the file will be closed in the absence of his instructions within a specific period of time."

This is clearly sound common sense in the situation where the solicitor is sitting waiting for further instructions. There must be some way of bringing the matter to a close so that the filing cabinet can be cleared of dormant files, accounts can be rendered either to the client or SLAB and both solicitor and client know the matter has come to an end. However there are cases such as old conveyancing transactions after the delivery of the Search and other cases where the matter is obviously concluded where the duty is not the same.

The matter has now been reviewed and the Committee have agreed that:

In cases where the matter in which the solicitor was instructed has not come to an obvious and natural conclusion there is a duty upon a solicitor to advise the client in writing that the file will be closed in the absence of his instructions within a specific period of time.

Law Society Guidelines on Terms of Business

As soon as instructions are received from a client or when tendering for business, a Solicitor should issue a terms of business letter of engagement. The content of the letter will vary depending on the status of the recipient and the type of work which may be undertaken. The letter should be clear and unambiguous using straightforward language thus ensuring that the recipient will be in no doubt as to the meaning of the content.

On all occasions, the following matters should be addressed in the letter of engagement:

1. The Source of authorisation of the Solicitor—Law Society of Scotland.
2. Method by which instructions should be given and received.
3. Authority of the client to instruct (*e.g.* who is the authorised person if the client is a company or a partnership; husband/wife or other multiple clients).
4. Supervision of client business. (*i.e.* name and status of person responsible for day-to-day conduct of matter and principal responsible for overall supervision if different).
5. Conflict of interest.
6. Requirement of confidentiality.
7. Procedures for resolving problems.

The following matters would normally be included in addition to those listed.

1. Holding client money.
2. Fee estimate (except in legal aid cases) to include VAT and prospective outlays.
3. Timing of payment of fees.
4. Outlays.
5. Timescale in general.

In addition, it is good practice for the following matters also to be included:

1. Indemnity/liability for loss.
2. Client's right to taxation.
3. Separate agent and client account in court matters (including legal aid).
4. Lien over titles and papers.
5. Level of service to be provided.

Clients who provide a regular flow of instruction of the same type of business and subject matter may not require a separate letter of engagement each time they instruct the Solicitor. In these cases, clients should receive a letter of engagement at least once a year and every time the terms of the letter of engagement are amended by the Solicitor.

Guidelines on the Ownership and Destruction of Files 2001

The following information is based on an Opinion from the Dean of Faculty provided to the Society in June 2000. This follows on from an earlier opinion from C.K. Davidson (now Lord Davidson) given in 1982. A fresh opinion was sought to ensure that the Society's guidance in this matter reflected the current legal position.

Who Owns What in Files?

The answer is not entirely straightforward and drawing on the opinion of Counsel the Society has produced this note which we hope will deal with the main queries which arise:

Finished Documents or Drafts/Notes

- Material Ordinarily Owned by Client

  Documents produced by the client or produced by the solicitor for the client.

  Written Opinions (whether principals or copies) but not preparatory personal notes prepared for the solicitor's benefit.

  Draft formal documents and deeds. (These may be of evidential importance to the client in the event of the loss or destruction of the principals.)

  Written submissions tendered in Court, but not detailed research notes and other documents generated for the solicitor's own personal use.

  Precognitions taken by the solicitor or obtained from other parties but see No. 11 of the Code of Conduct for Criminal Work where they may contain sensitive material and where it might be inappropriate to pass this information to clients. See *Swift v. Bannigan* 1991 S.C.L.R. 604, although the Dean had reservations about this case.

  Original letters received from and copy letters to third parties.

  Copies of letters written to the client, although if these have been retained by the solicitor as part of a private record or if the contents relate exclusively to the contractual relationship between the solicitor and the client, the solicitor may own them.

  Notes of meetings and telephone calls, which constitute the solicitor's work on behalf of the client.

  Files and documents received under a mandate.
- Material Ordinarily Owned by Solicitor:

  Original letters received by the solicitor from the client.

  Notes of meetings and telephone calls, which form part of the solicitor's preparatory work.

  Inter-office memoranda.

  Sensitive material and precognitions in criminal cases should be dealt with in accordance with No. 11 of the Code of Conduct for Criminal Work.
- Mandates:

  It is matter of judgment whether a file should be copied, but copying is prudent. The costs should be borne by the solicitor.

  If a mandate is received from one of two or more clients and the consent of the other cannot be obtained the file can be exhibited or copies offered at the client's expense, provided that nothing is disclosed or copied which is confidential to the other party.—see also the next paragraph "Multiple Clients".

Multiple Clients

Issues of confidentiality, duties of disclosure and informed consent of multiple clients must be borne in mind.

- Where a matter develops to the extent that a solicitor cannot continue acting for multiple clients due to a conflict of interest arising or developing, care must be taken with the nature of the material copied or delivered.

- Any release of correspondence or documents must either be with the consent of all or the file should be divided into parts relevant to each client, *e.g.* in the lender/borrower situation the file should be divided into those parts belonging to the lender and borrower respectively.
- Where there are common documents they can be copied to all clients.
- If a lien is to be exercised, the solicitor cannot prejudice one client, *e.g.* a lender if that client has no liability for fees. If one client requests a file where fees are due by the other, the file should be forwarded under reservation of the lien so that it cannot be passed on to new agents.
- A file can be delivered subject to an undertaking to produce it to "the other side" if called upon.
- Each client has the right to inspect documents in which he or she has a proprietary interest and also to receive copies at his or her own expense.

Destruction of Files

Following the previous Opinion obtained by the Society regarding ownership and destruction of files the Society issued guidance in the Journal and subsequently in the Better Client Care Manual (page 9.2). The Terms of Business letter should include information about the intention to destroy files and/or papers after conclusion of a transaction after a certain period to provide evidence of consent to destruction.

The following points should be noted:

(1) The client's informed consent should be obtained before the files and papers may be safely destroyed. The client's documents may be returned, by agreement. However, it may be prudent to retain copies.

(2) Documents that may be relevant to a claim should *prima facie* be kept for at least the period of long negative prescription if the claim has not previously been disposed of.

(3) Documents containing client's tax or VAT affairs must be retained for at least the relevant statutory subscribed period.

(4) There is no specific date beyond which the obligation to hold a client's own documents can be said to expire. Deeds or other documents constituting or evidencing rights should be preserved indefinitely but it is virtually impossible to predict when they might turn out to be of value. There is therefore a risk attached to destroying them.

(5) In storing and insuring files and papers, solicitors are providing clients with a continuing service for which they can properly charge.

(6) The client might be advised in writing again prior to the file being destroyed, that this is about to happen in accordance with the agreed Terms of Business letter. This is a matter of judgment.

(7) At the end of each transaction a letter might be sent to the client to advise as to the location of title deeds and/or other important documents or confirmation of what is to happen to these.

(8) The Master Policy Insurers have clarified that destruction of the file will not affect the insurance position but clients could take issue with the fact that the file had been destroyed if their position was prejudiced.

(9) Destruction of the client's property without consent could expose the solicitor to liability and damages.

(10) Solicitors must ensure that sensitive or privileged documents and files are not disposed of in any way which might compromise them.

(11) Document shredding within the office or by a reliable specialist contractor would appear to be the safest option.

Electronic Storage of Files

Electronic storage of files on CD or on a server may be a practical way of dealing with storage. Commercial firms provide these services and give the option of destroying paper files after calculating and assessing the risk. Alistair Sim from Marsh has written an article about the scanning of files and the paperless office, see *Journal* March 2001, p.42.

Where it is not possible to store files electronically without time limit the Society has issued the following guidance for solicitors:

These are guidelines only. The onus rests with the solicitor as to whether or not it is safe to dispose of a file in any particular case and, in considering that, the solicitor should always have regard to the nature of the transaction and the circumstances.

- Files should only be destroyed under the direct instructions of the principal of the firm.
- Consent of the clients should be obtained before files are destroyed.
- Information on this should be contained in a Terms of Business letter.
- Care must be taken to ensure that no important papers such as confirmations, decrees, etc., which should normally be kept separate from other correspondence are in any file being destroyed.
- So far as financial records are concerned regard should be had to the terms of Rules 8(7) and 9 of the Solicitors (Scotland) Accounts etc. Rules 2001.

Suggested Timing in Different Categories

Simple Debt Collection

On completion—*i.e.* after the time for appeal has elapsed.

Divorce and Consistorial Matters

Five years after final completion, *e.g.* after maintenance, residence and contact orders, etc., have ceased to have effect, or children have reached majority.

Civil Court Cases

Ten years after completion.

Criminal Cases

- Murder and other cases involving life imprisonment—the papers should be retained indefinitely.
- Solemn cases—files should be kept for the duration of the sentence if more than three years.
- Summary cases—the papers should be retained for three years.

A copy of the complaint or indictment and a copy of the legal aid certificate should be kept indefinitely.

Executries

Ten years after completion although an executry may never be complete. Relevant documents and papers might be sent to the Executor for safekeeping since unclaimed legal rights never prescribe.

Conveyancing Transactions

Purchase:

Ten years after completion—although the file may be of use until the property is subsequently disposed of.

Sale:

One year later after completion (*i.e.* after implementing Letter of Obligation; dealing with any funds retained; and after Missives have ceased to have effect).

Continuing Trusts

Ten years after the termination of the Trust.

Company Work

Ten years after completion.

Other Correspondence Files

Five years after completion of the business.

IMPORTANT NOTES

- In all cases, important papers such as confirmations, decrees, etc., should be retained indefinitely and should be kept separately from the correspondence.

The whereabouts of these documents should be set out in a closing letter once the transaction has been completed so that there is no dubiety about who holds them. Documents containing client's tax and VAT affairs must be retained for at least the relevant statutory periods.

Guidelines on Improving Client Relations 2001

A good client relation policy makes good business sense. Businesses from the public to the private sector know that relations and client care are often as important as the goods or services provided. With this in mind, the Society has run a series of initiatives over the past few years to encourage and assist solicitors with their client relations procedures.

The Society's work includes the recommendation for all firms to have a Client Relation Partner and encouragement to provide training on dealing with a dissatisfied client. The Client Relations Video, "Improving Client Relations," which was sent to all firms in 1999, and the Risk Management Video, produced in 2000, aimed to give some helpful suggestions to firms. (Copies are still available.) The Society has also recommended and promoted the use of Terms of Business letters, giving clients information about getting the best from their solicitor. It has also placed information for solicitors and their clients on the Society's website. The Society has also run client relations road-shows throughout Scotland which give training on how to recognise and deal with client concern or dissatisfaction. Some firms have contacted the Society for advice about the best way to improve their client relations and the Client Relations Office has now developed an internal complaints model which practices can adapt to meet their own needs.

The basic elements of handling complaints successfully are straightforward. Always:

- respond quickly and positively
- listen carefully to the client's concerns
- be open and objective
- avoid assumptions
- look for a practical solution
- act quickly on an agreed solution and stick to it
- take advice if necessary

The importance of appointing the right person as Client Relations Partner is the key to successful client relations. The appointment need not be according to seniority in a partnership but should be a person who has empathy, is open in their communications and is a good listener. Ensure that the person chosen has the authority of the practice to resolve complaints and some training to assist in that process. A badly handled complaint can become a conduct complaint in itself, so it is important to have the skills as well as the time to deal with client relations.

- The Legal Defence Union Ltd.—publish a Duty Rota of solicitors available for defence work which is printed in: The Blue Book 2001—divider "C Law Firms". See also page C2. The Scottish Law Directory—contact information on page A68.
- The Director or Deputy Director of the Society's Client Relations Office (Tel: 0131 476 8131/8152). Enquiries will be treated in the strictest confidence and may be anonymous if desired.
- The Better Client Care and Practice Management Guidance manual—published on the Solicitors' pages of the Society's Web site at www.lawscot.org.uk
- Council Members—your Council member can help you with information on dealing with a complaint and client relation.

The following model of an internal complaints system can be adapted to meet the needs of individual firms. In simple flow chart form it could be given to a client at the point where dissatisfaction or concern is expressed.

Flow chart

A Client Relations Partner is appointed to whose job it is to assess any complaints and to act on them. He or she will have control of the situation from the point at which a complaint is expressed until the matter is resolved. There is no fee charged by the Client Relations Partner for handling complaints.

↓

All complaints, whether made by telephone or in writing are passed immediately to the Client Relations Partner or substitute.

↓

The Client Relations Partner acknowledges the letter or telephone call and arranges a meeting to discuss your concerns.

← It is not possible to arrange a meeting, the Client Relations Partner will make other arrangements to discuss the concerns e.g. by telephone, e-mail or letter.

↓

If the Client Relations Partner cannot find a solution which satisfies the concerns, he will write setting out a note of the concerns and the firm's response.

↓

If a solution cannot be found which satisfies the concerns the client is entitled to take these up with the Client Relations Office of the Law Society of Scotland (Helpline tel no.0845 113 0018).

↓

If a practical solution can be found, the Client Relations Partner will write setting out what has been agreed and will be responsible for seeing that the firm sticks to the agreement.

Guidelines on Terms of Business Letters and Pension Trustees 2001

The Society's Professional Practice Committee and Pensions Law Committee recently considered the implications of the Pensions Act 1995 and the requirements it imposes on the legal profession.

Section 47 of the Pensions Act 1995 together with the relevant regulations, requires trustees of occupational pension schemes to have a written agreement in place with their advisers. If there is no such agreement, trustees cannot rely on the terms of the Pensions Act 1995 for protection.

Following a recommendation by the Pensions Law Working Party and the Professional Practice Committee, the Council of the Law Society of Scotland agreed that solicitors should enter into a written agreement with trustees as required by the Act. Consequently, there is a duty on solicitors to advise pensions trustee clients of the terms of the Pensions Act 1995, including the requirement to enter into written agreement with their legal advisers.

Those solicitors carrying out work in terms of the Pensions Act 1995 are reminded of this obligation and advised to incorporate reference to this professional obligation in terms of business letters.

Guidelines on Information Provided by Solicitors for Company Audit 2001

An article dealing with, amongst other things, requests for information from auditors, appeared in the "Risk Management" section of the Journal in July 2000 ("Reminder of routine risk issues", JLSS Volume 45 No 7 Page 41). The Society's Company Law Committee would reiterate the advice contained in that article regarding the importance of keeping accurate records, and of ensuring that Directors of the client company are kept informed of all requests from auditors for information.

However, the Committee would, in addition, like to stress that some requests for information may go beyond those to which it is appropriate for the company's legal advisor to reply. Information which has traditionally been requested of solicitors as legal advisors to companies has included information as to titles, outstanding fees and any consultation with the solicitor with regard to litigation involving the company. It is appropriate to respond to these types of question. It must be stressed, however, that requests for information falling outwith these areas such as whether the solicitor is aware of any matter where the company may have failed to comply with the law or regulatory standards, or whether the solicitor is aware of any contingent liability other than litigation matters which he or she has been consulted on, should always be referred to the company's directors and no response should be made other than on the specific instructions of directors. Failure to do so could potentially open a company's legal advisor to risk.

Provision of an auditor's letter or certificate is an important step in the audit process which has to be handled with care, takes time and carries significant risk for the solicitor giving it. For all these reasons, he or she is entitled to make an appropriate charge.

Companies House Direct

Companies House Direct has recently introduced revised contractual terms and conditions. Clause 11.1 of the revised terms and conditions purports to restrict the liability of Companies House Direct to the extent of the outlay for the information and clause 11.4 purports to exclude liability for inaccurate information, including errors which are not the result of inaccurate information supplied to Companies House. For this reason, the Committee would recommend that solicitors treat information emanating from Companies House Direct with caution as its accuracy cannot be guaranteed and any remedy may be of limited value.

It should also be noted that under Condition 21 contracts with Companies House Direct are governed by English law and parties submit to the jurisdiction of the English Court.

Law Society of Scotland Guidelines for Compliance with Continuing Professional Development Regulations

The Regulations came into full effect on 1st November 1996. They apply to solicitors holding a Practising Certificate. The Guidelines will be reviewed periodically and may be amended in the light of experience.

Annual Requirement

Solicitors to whom the Regulations and Guidelines apply will require to undertake 20 hours Continuing Professional Development in each practice year. For solicitors practising in Scotland, England or Wales, a minimum of 15 hours will require to be in Group Study and up to five hours can be by Private Study, except for authors of published books or articles (see below). Solicitors practising outwith Scotland, England or Wales may comply with the Regulations by undertaking 20 hours Private Study.

Where a solicitor has achieved the required number of hours of group study by the end of September in any year, time spent during the month of October at any further event which qualifies as group study may be counted towards the requirement for the following practice year which commences on 1st November of that year. Also, where a solicitor has failed to achieve the required number of hours of group study by the end of October in any one year time spent during the month of November at any event which qualifies as group study may be counted towards the requirement for the year ended on 31 October of that year.

***Note**: If you fall into the category of carrying forward attendances please do not record them in cards for both years. They should be recorded only in the card for the year in which they are being claimed. The Society will not make any attempt to reallocate hours incorrectly recorded.*

Trainees

Trainee solicitors in their second year who have a restricted practising certificate are admitted solicitors and will require to undertake C.P.D. in accordance with these Guidelines.

Definition

In the Regulations Continuing Professional Development is defined as "relevant education and study by a solicitor to develop his or her professional knowledge, skills and abilities".

This means education and training in:

1. Specific legal areas and topics.
2. Management and organisation.
3. Communication and client care skills.
4. Other areas relevant to the solicitor's practice.
5. Any area designed to improve an individual's ability to operate properly and effectively as a solicitor.

Method

The Society wishes solicitors to have as much control and responsibility for their own development as possible. The parameters are therefore expressed in broad outline.

Private Study

Private Study means study undertaken by less than three persons together. No more than five hours private study per annum will count towards fulfilling the C.P.D. requirement.

Private study includes:

1. Distance learning by audio/visual/correspondence courses, television and radio courses, and computer-based learning.
2. The reading of relevant periodicals and books.
3. Writing relevant books or articles in periodicals or text books which are published (in which case the time occupied may be up to ten hours of the total C.P.D. requirement for the particular practice year).

Note: This list is not exhaustive but merely illustrative.

Group Study

Group study means study in a group of three or more people which lasts for a minimum of half an hour. For solicitors in Scotland, England or Wales, with the sole exception of authors of books or articles as stated above, it must occupy a minimum of 15 of the required hours per annum and must be in a form which can be verified.

Group study includes the following: discussion groups; tutorials; study meetings of special interest groups; workshops; seminars; or courses.

These may feature in house training or training by outsiders and may be run by firms; departments of organisations and/or firms; local faculties and societies; groups of firms; the Society's UPDATE Department; or other providers.

Group study may take place within or outwith Scotland and does not require to be in groups which only comprise solicitors. It does require to be relevant to the solicitor's practice.

The Law Society does not intend to award accreditation to any courses or course providers nor will it guide solicitors on what is relevant to them. Solicitors should exercise their own judgment on what training is relevant to their particular practice requirements. Such judgment will require to be exercised reasonably.

The preparation and delivery of training for others is a very effective means of learning. Solicitors involved as lecturers, tutors or leaders in any form of relevant group study may count preparation time up to a maximum of four hours towards the C.P.D. group study requirement, in addition to actual presentation time.

Some group study will involve workshops and role play. Courses requiring delegates' active participation in these ways are more effective than traditional lecture-based courses. Solicitors undertaking such participation may count an additional one-quarter of the actual time of the course towards their C.P.D. requirement.

Management and Professional Development Skills

A frequent cause of difficulty for solicitors arises out of lapses in management either of the office or the case and/or poor communication with clients, rather than simple ignorance of law or procedure. For this reason at least five hours of the total annual requirement (of which a minimum of three hours must be in group study) shall be spent on training in management (including self-management), organisation, client care and communication skills. These include Professional Ethics, Financial and Business Management, Budget Control, Computer Skills, Foreign Languages, Interview Techniques, Setting Priorities and Time Management. This list is only illustrative not exhaustive.

Double Training Relief

Solicitors who require to undertake compulsory training other than by reason of the Continuing Professional Development Regulations may count such training as part of the requirement for C.P.D. in that particular practice year. The following are some examples. They are not an exhaustive list:

Practice Management Course: Solicitors who require to attend a Practice Management Course by virtue of the Solicitors (Scotland) (Practice Management Courses) Practice Rules 1989.

Extended Rights of Audience: Solicitors who require to attend a Training Course in terms of the Solicitors (Scotland) (Admission with Extended Rights of Audience) Rules 1995.

England and Wales: Solicitors practising in England and Wales who require to undertake continuing training in that jurisdiction will not require to undertake further C.P.D. to comply with these Rules. Solicitors who do not require to undertake such continuing training shall undertake C.P.D. in accordance with the above requirements.

Monitoring and Enforcement

Solicitors will be expected to complete the record card honestly and truthfully, and will be required to produce their record card at the end of the practice year.

The Society will study in detail a random sample of 5 per cent of returned record cards to check that the required hours of C.P.D. have been properly completed and will take steps to verify that the solicitors in the sample have undertaken the group study part of C.P.D. Group study may be verified by for example an Attendance Register.

If a solicitor has not complied with the requirement and is not entitled to exemption, further time will be given for compliance as a first sanction and independent evidence of group study will require to be produced to show that compliance has been achieved. Continued failure to comply may be referred to the Society's Client Relations Office for consideration as professional misconduct. Records of compliance will be maintained by the Society.

Solicitors Not Working Full Time Throughout The Year

Solicitors who do not work full time throughout the year will be exempt from the requirement to undertake 20 hours C.P.D. per annum as follows:

1. Solicitors, other than locums, working *150 hours or less* during the practice year—total exemption. However, members in this category are required to complete and return a CPD record card to the Society at the appropriate time claiming the exemption in the space provided on page 6 of the card.
2. *Part-time* solicitors who work for more than 150 hours in the practice year will undertake one hour's C.P.D. per annum for every two hours per week worked with a minimum of ten hours C.P.D. per annum.
3. *Locums and Solicitors who only work part of the year* will undertake 1½ hours C.P.D. for every four weeks worked in aggregate with a minimum of ten hours C.P.D. per annum.
4. Solicitors who are *unemployed* for part of the year will undertake 1½ hours C.P.D. for every four weeks worked in aggregate.
5. Solicitors suffering *long-term* illness for ten weeks or more in respect of the same illness in any practice year may reduce their C.P.D. requirement in proportion to the number of weeks worked during the practice year rounded up to the nearest complete hour. To calculate the required number of hours divide the number of weeks worked by 2.6 and round up to the nearest whole number. (*e.g.* solicitors who work between 37 and 39 weeks in a practice year will require to undertake 15 hours C.P.D. in that year).

6. Solicitors taking *maternity leave* may reduce their C.P.D. requirement in proportion to the number of weeks worked in the practice year rounded up to the nearest complete hour in accordance with the formula in No. 5 hereof.
7. Solicitors who take *sabbatical* leave of six weeks or more in the practice year may reduce their C.P.D. requirement in proportion to the number of weeks worked in the practice year but with a minimum of ten hours C.P.D. per annum.
8. Solicitors *admitted during the practice year* (1st November to 31st October) will be exempt in the course of that practice year, but will require to undertake full C.P.D. in the following practice year.
9. Solicitors *retiring during the practice year and not renewing their practicing certificate* will be exempt in the course of that practice year.

Note: In all of the above the proportions of group study, management and professional development skills and private study will be reduced pro-rata.

Monitoring of CPD takes place throughout the whole of the following practice year. Members are requested to ensure that relevant papers are retained to be available, during the monitoring process.

Law Society Guidelines on Powers of Attorney

[(July 1998)]

In 1995 the Society's Professional Practice Committee considered a complaint from a consultant psychiatrist that a solicitor, in setting up a Deed of Power of Attorney, did not satisfy himself that the grantor had the capacity to grant such a power. It was alleged that prepared paperwork was passed to the family, who obtained the signature from their elderly relative in hospital. There were no discussions with those in charge of her treatment. In this particular case the Mental Welfare Commission was satisfied after inquiry that the patient had not suffered and decided not to challenge the extant Power of Attorney.

The Professional Practice Committee reminds solicitors (a) that a solicitor must have instructions from his or her client (b) that the client is the granter of the Power of Attorney and (c) that solicitors are not the judges of mental capacity. That is for the medical profession from whom advice should be sought if there is any doubt as to a client's capacity.

Law Society Guidelines on Sending Document to Unrepresented Party for Signature

[(October 1998)]

In April 1998 the Committee published a Guideline on the question of documents being signed by unrepresented parties. In response to views expressed by the profession, the Committee have amended that Guideline so that it now matches more exactly the wording of the Practice Rule. An additional paragraph has been added at the end advising that notice may be given in a separate letter or contained within the document to be signed. The full text of the amended Guideline is as follows:

Rule 7 of the Solicitors (Scotland) Practice Rules 1986—the Conflict of Interest Rules — requires a solicitor dealing with an unrepresented party in a transaction involving heritable property to advise the unrepresented party in writing when issuing any deed, missive or other document for signature that signature will have legal consequences and the party should take independent legal advice before signing it. There is no equivalent Rule for other types of transaction.

The Professional Practice Committee have agreed that there is no justification for distinguishing between transactions involving heritable property and other types of transaction, and have decided that as a matter of proper practice solicitors dealing with unrepresented parties in any kind of transaction on behalf of a client should not issue any document for signature by the unrepresented party without advising that party in writing that signature may have legal consequences and to take independent legal advice before signing it.

Such a notice may be in a separate letter or may be contained within the document to be signed. It does not require to be acknowledged.

Law Society Guidelines for Immigration Practitioners

[(August 2004)]

The following guidelines, approved by the Professional Practice Committee of the Law Society of Scotland in 2004, constitute an amplification of the standard of practice that the Society considers essential for compliance with the rules of professional conduct when undertaking immigration, nationality and asylum work and contain best practice guidance. The guidelines may be taken into account by the Society in its investigation and determination of complaints (including those made by third parties) alleging inadequate professional service and/or professional misconduct arising from immigration, nationality and asylum work.

The following guidelines apply to solicitors and registered European lawyers (RELs) and to registered foreign lawyers when in practice with solicitors/RELs, and to anyone, including non-solicitors, supervised by solicitors or RELs. References to solicitors in the guidelines includes RELs.

General Duties

1. Solicitors are expected to maintain the standards of the profession in the conduct of activities as advisers and representatives in the field of immigration, nationality and asylum and practice related matters. In particular:

(a) They should give sound advice having familiarised themselves with the relevant law, the immigration rules, and details of any published concessions outside the rules.

(b) They should at all times show sensitivity to the particularly vulnerable position of those seeking immigration advice. Practitioners should pay due regard to the related difficulties faced by such a client, and should ensure that the client fully understands the implications of any decision or proposed course of action, making full use of an interpreter for translation purposes only as necessary.

(c) They must not deceive or deliberately mislead the immigration authorities or the courts or knowingly allow themselves to be used in any such way.

(d) They should consider whether, by virtue of their knowledge, skills and experience, they are competent to act in the particular case, and must not take on cases outside their area of competence or beyond their caseload capacity.

(e) They must maintain proper records of their professional dealings, including records of the matters set out below.

Fees

2. Solicitors must give advance information about fees and outlays.

3. The question of whether the client is eligible for Advice and Assistance under the "pink form scheme" should be explored and discussed with the client at the outset. If eligible for Advice and Assistance the client should be advised accordingly. If eligible for Advice and Assistance but the client does not wish to obtain Advice and Assistance then the solicitor should ensure that the client signs a written statement to the effect that the client understands the client's entitled to legal Advice and Assistance but does not wish to apply for it.

4. Where a charge is to be made to a client for the provision of legal services, a written estimate of the costs should be supplied to the client at the outset of the matter to which the charge relates, with a description of the work to be done to a specified stage and the method of calculation of such fee (unless the fee is fixed) and the likely overall cost including outlays and VAT. Where the fee is likely to exceed the estimate given or requires variation, a written revision of the estimate and mode of calculation should

be given as soon as it becomes apparent that the original estimate is likely to be exceeded or requires revision, and in any event before it is in fact exceeded.

Appeals

5. In the conduct of appeals a solicitor must take all reasonable steps to comply with the rules of procedure and with Practice Notes both to protect the interest of the client and to meet obligations to the court. "Court" includes tribunal.

6. A solicitor must not withdraw from acting except for good reason and upon reasonable notice, recording the reasons for withdrawing from acting in the file. Where, for good reason, whether the client has been granted Advice and Assistance by the Scottish Legal Aid Board or otherwise the solicitor decides to withdraw from acting for the client, it must be with as much notice to the client as possible in all the circumstances. Issues of merits, funding and arrangements to provide advocacy must be addressed as soon as reasonably practicable so as to avoid damage either to the client's interests or to the effective operation of the court. Such advice as may be appropriate should be given to the client for alternative representation. Notice of withdrawal from representation must be promptly given to the court in such manner as to minimise prejudice to the client.

7. If a practitioner is without funds to cover a hearing it is unacceptable for the solicitor to withdraw from acting so close to the date of the hearing as to prevent the client having any opportunity of seeking to find alternative representation, or to hinder the court in adequately disposing of matters pending.

Lien (Privately Funded)

8. If the client withdraws instructions just before a hearing date and a successor solicitor is appointed, the Society recommends the papers be released to the successor solicitor, subject to a satisfactory undertaking as to costs being given in lieu of the exercise of a lien.

Standard of Work

9. A solicitor should not normally agree to represent a client where adequate preparation of a case is not possible, but in cases of urgency the solicitor may agree to act or continue to act for the purpose of applying for an adjournment. Where an adjournment is refused, the solicitor must consider whether continuing to act compromises effective standards of representation. If so, the solicitor should then not participate further in the hearing.

Supervision

10. Solicitors must ensure that all staff are properly supervised. There is a general duty to ensure that a practice is properly supervised, managed, and compliant with any Quality Assurance criteria in force. Every office must have at least one solicitor qualified to supervise with that office being that solicitor's usual place of work. When the solicitor qualified to supervise at an office is away for any reason suitable arrangements must be in place to ensure that duties to clients and others are met.

11. Solicitors must be confident that non-solicitor staff providing Immigration, Nationality or Asylum advice to clients are of good standing and repute and have proper knowledge and experience of the work for which they are being recruited. Non-solicitor staff must also be properly supervised under a supervising solicitor's direction.

12. Solicitors must exercise great care in the recruitment of non-solicitor staff whom it is intended will undertake immigration work so as to avoid employing unsuitable staff. Before employing non-solicitor staff thorough enquiries should be made as a matter of course about the prospective

employee's background including whether the prospective employee has been the subject of any disciplinary charge upheld by the Immigration Services Tribunal; and references should be sought.

13. Non-solicitor staff include paralegals; legal executives; clerks from time to time working away from the office, for example, attending with clients at Home Office interviews, attending clients at detention centres or at court; persons working out of solicitors' offices even if only in the office for a few hours each week; and any person paid by a solicitor to undertake immigration work or where there is any arrangement, however vague, between a practice and a non-solicitor, for the purposes of gain. Even if it could be argued that there is not strictly an employer/employee relationship, for example if a person is an independent self-employed contractor working in the name of the firm, that person is the responsibility of the principal/s when engaged to carry out work on behalf of the firm and proper supervision must be exercised. The term "non-solicitor staff" should not be taken to include members of the Faculty of Advocates or trainee solicitors under a Training Contract registered with the Law Society of Scotland.

14. Solicitors instructing firms of solicitors in another part of the United Kingdom are not responsible for supervision of the staff of such other firm or any person instructed by such other firm to carry out any part of such instructions. Paragraphs 10-13 of these guidelines do not apply when a solicitor in another part of the United Kingdom is instructed.

15. Persons qualified to provide immigration advice or immigration services under Part V of the Immigration and Asylum Act 1999 include those authorised to practice as solicitors in Scotland by the Law Society of Scotland or those working under the supervision of such persons. The Society may treat failure to supervise properly as professional misconduct. In considering any complaint received by the Office of the Immigration Services Commissioner in connection with an alleged failure of a solicitor to properly supervise, the Commissioner may also apply these guidelines.

Application of the Guidelines

16. Solicitors are subject to all the rules of professional conduct and any contractual terms.

Duties Of Solicitors Acting For Clients In Money Claims For Children

[March 2004]

This guidance is issued to solicitors taking instructions from a child's legal representative or guardian in relation to a money claim on behalf of the child.

The claim may be made under any rule of law. The money, for example, may be due to a child under a contract, a lease, or a trust: under the laws relating to intestate succession to a relative's estate, or under a will; by way of damages for delictual liability or breach of contract; by virtue of a claim for unjustified enrichment; or under an obligation of accounting to the child.

Taking Instructions from the Child's Legal Representative

The concept of parental guardianship ceased to exist with the coming into force of the Children (Scotland) Act 1995 ("the Act").

A child's mother exercises parental responsibilities and rights in respect of her children by virtue of her relationship to them. A father has parental responsibilities and rights only if he is, or has been married, to the child's mother, has entered into a parental responsibilities and rights agreement with the mother under section 4 of the Act, or has had parental responsibilities and rights conferred on him by order of the court.

Other persons, such as grandparents or step-parents, may have had parental responsibilities and rights conferred on them by order of court, or through an adoption order.

In rare cases, a parent may have been deprived of his or her parental responsibilities and rights by order of the court.

It is both a parental responsibility and a parental right "to act as the child's legal representative".

It is this responsibility/right which allows a parent or other person to administer a child's property, raise and defend actions on behalf of the child, and compromise court proceedings raised on the child's behalf.

Some persons may have been granted the limited parental responsibility/ right to act as the child's legal representative for the purpose of certain specified court proceedings.

Before taking instructions from a parent or other person to make a financial claim on behalf of a child, a solicitor:

- Must ensure that that person has parental responsibilities and rights for the child, or the specific parental responsibility/right to act as the child's legal representative in relation to a particular claim. It should be particularly borne in mind that fathers do not have parental responsibilities and rights unless through marriage to the child's mother, agreement with her under section 4 of the Act, or order of court.

Taking Instructions from Guardians and Persons with Residence Orders

A guardian is now a person appointed by a parent with parental responsibilities and rights for the child (or another guardian of the child) to act as the child's guardian after her death, or appointed to that office by order of the court.

Guardians have all the parental responsibilities and rights that parents with parental responsibilities and rights have, and thus may act as the child's legal representative.

Persons in whose favour a residence order for a child has been granted have the right to act as the child's legal representative while the residence order remains in force.

Legal Capacity

A child has legal capacity to raise a court action, or make a financial claim, and to instruct a solicitor for those purposes, if he or she "has a general understanding of what it means to do so".

The child is presumed to have such an understanding if he or she has attained the age of twelve; the presumption may be rebutted if for any reason it is evident that child does not have such an understanding. A solicitor may exceptionally be satisfied a child under twelve has legal capacity to raise proceedings. There is no presumption that a child under that age does not have capacity.

A person who attains the age of sixteen has complete legal capacity in relation to his or her affairs and is regarded in law as an adult. Accordingly, a solicitor:

- May take instructions from a person entitled to act as a child's legal representative, or the child him or herself if satisfied the child has capacity to give instruction. The solicitor may only take instructions from the minor him or herself when the minor has attained the age of sixteen.

If there is any question that the child is under a mental or physical incapacity such that the child does not have a general understanding of what it means to instruct the solicitor, then the solicitor may only take instruction from those having the right to act as the child's legal representative.

Where the minor attains the age of sixteen, and remains under mental or physical incapacity, the solicitor must treat the minor as an incapacity adult under the Adults with Incapacity (Scotland) Act 2000, and act accordingly under that Act. Proceedings under that Act are beyond the scope of this guidance note.

Duties in Relation to Administration of Child's Property or Money

Section 5(1) of the Age of Legal Capacity (Scotland) Act 1991 ("the 1991 Act") "in relation to any rule of law" provides that guardians of persons under the age of sixteen have in relation to the child and his estate "the powers and duties which...a tutor had in relation to his pupil [at common law]".

The 1991 Act repealed the Tutors and Curators Acts 1672 and 1969, which had required tutors, on entering office, to lodge an inventory of the child's estate with the court, upon pain of removal from office. Tutors were liable to the child, in attaining majority for any wrongful dealings with the child's property, and had to find caution on entering office.

The law has now been reformulated in the Children (Scotland) Act 1995 ("the Act").

Section 10 of the Act requires a person acting as a child's legal representative administering a child's property: "to act as a reasonable and prudent person would act on his own behalf".

He or she is fully entitled to do whatever the child, if of full legal capacity, could do in relation to the child's property, subject:

1. to any limitations imposed by an order of the court; and
2. to a liability account to the child for his or her intromissons with the child's property.

He or she is not liable in respect of funds properly used in discharge of his or her responsibility to safeguard and promote the child's health, development and welfare.

Safeguarding the Child's Property

Where a solicitor has taken instructions from a person entitled to act as the child's representative, or the child's guardian, and has recovered money which he must transfer to that person for administration on behalf of the child he or she has a professional responsibility:

- To inform the person to whom the money is to be transferred of his or her duties and liabilities under section 10 of the Act; and
- Of that person's duties to administer the money prudently on

behalf of the child, and in discharge of his of her duties to safeguard and promote the child's health, development and welfare.

The solicitor must in all cases comply with sections 9 or 13 of the Act.

Settlements where no court proceedings (Section 9)

If the solicitor is *not* acting as executor or trustee then he *may* apply to the Accountant of Court for a direction as to the administration of the property *unless* the person to whom the money is to be transferred has been appointed trustee under a trust deed to administer the property. This requirement does not apply if the sum recovered is less than £5,000.

Accordingly, the solicitor may:

- Transfer sums less than £5,000 to the legal representative/guardian on informing him or her *in writing* as to his or her duties and liabilities under section 10 of the Act and of his or her duties to administer the money prudently on behalf of the child, and in discharge of his or her duties to safeguard and promote the child's health, development and welfare;
- Transfer sums of any amount to the legal representative/guardian acting as trustee under a trust deed set up to administer the child's property; or
- In cases where the sum recovered is or exceeds £5,000 apply to the Accountant of Court for directions.

In cases where the solicitor is acting as executor or trustee, he **must** apply to the Accountant of Court for directions if the sum recovered exceeds £20,000 *unless* the money is to be transferred to the legal representative/guardian acting as trustee under a trust deed set up to administer the child's property.

Where a solicitor applies to the Accountant of Court for directions, the Accountant of Court may apply to the court for appointment of a judicial factor, or direct that all or part of the money be transferred to himself or to the legal representative/guardian for administration on the child's behalf. He may direct that the legal representative/guardian does not incur capital expenditure, and/or make an annual report to him, if he directs the transfer of the property to that person.

Solicitors holding funds, or cheques, for legal representatives/guardians may only transfer the funds, or cheque, on taking the measures to safeguard the child's property set out in this guidance note.

In those cases where they have a discretion to ask the Accountant of Court for directions, they must consider whether or not to do so and record the reasons for their decision in their file.

Appropriate cases for seeking a direction include those:

- Where the legal representative/guardian has indicated he or she has no intention of complying with his or her duties in respect of administering the child's property.
- Where there is a reasonable cause to believe that the legal representative/guardian will not comply with his or her duties, or may indeed dissipate the property, such as where the legal representative/guardian:
  - — is insolvent, or bankrupt;
  - — is financially irresponsible;
  - — has substantial debts of his or her own;
  - — is an alcoholic, or drug addict;
  - — does not have the capacity or understanding to comply with his or her duties.

Solicitors may wish to obtain a written undertaking from the legal representative/guardian as to compliance with his or her duties, and, if thought necessary, an indication of how it is intended the money will be invested/applied for the child's benefit. If these undertakings or assurances are not forthcoming, then the solicitor would have reasonable cause to ask the Accountant of Court for directions.

It is entirely within a solicitor's discretion (except if acting as executor/trustee where the sum exceeds £20,000 when he or she must do so) to ask the Accountant of Court for directions. If in any doubt, it would be prudent for the solicitor to do so. He or she should not be pressurised or influenced by the legal representative/guardian as to how he or she is to exercise this discretion. The solicitor should bear in mind his or her duty of reasonable care to the child, and that the money concerned is not the legal representative/guardian's, but the child's whose interests are paramount. A solicitor should never hand over money or a cheque without at least considering whether it is appropriate to ask the Accountant of Court for directions, and reminding the legal representative/guardian of his or her duties in regard to administration of the child's property. A solicitor who does not do these things may find him or herself incurring liability to the child for loss suffered by dissipation of his or her estate by the legal representative/guardian, together with being the subject of a complaint by the child for inadequate professional service and/or professional misconduct. There are cases in which it would clearly be negligent for a solicitor *not* to ask for directions, for example, where he or she knows the legal representative/guardian is bankrupt, or a drug addict.

Settlements or Awards Where There Have Been Court Proceedings (Section 13)

Where, in any Court proceedings, a sum of money becomes payable to a child under sixteen the Court may but is not obliged to make an Order relating to the payment and management of the funds. Section 13 applies equally to awards made by the Court and to extra judicial settlements.

Accordingly, the Solicitor must always consider whether it is necessary to make application to the Court to consider the most appropriate method for administration of the money for the child. (It is also open to the defenders in Court proceedings also to make such an application.)

Under Section 13(2) of the Act, the Court may:

- appoint a Judicial Factor;
- order the money to be paid to the Sheriff Court (Sheriff Court);
- order the money to be paid to the Accountant of Court;
- order the money to be paid to the legal representative/guardian to be invested, applied or otherwise dealt with, under directions of the Court for the benefit of the child;
- order the money to be paid direct to the child.

In normal course, an application to the Court by the Solicitor is only likely if there is reason to be concerned that funds will be dissipated or not applied in the child's best interests. If the legal representative/guardian wishes to be appointed to administer the funds under the direction of the Court, it will be necessary to satisfy the Court that he or she will do so prudently and broad details will be required as to how the legal representative/guardian intends to discharge his or her responsibilities. The Court may, for example, wish to know the extent to which the legal representative/guardian will seek professional advice in relation to the administration of the funds.

Most families will wish to avoid the appointment of a Judicial Factor because of the rigidity that imposes upon administration of the funds. It should be remembered that the cost of a Judicial Factor may form a legitimate head of the claim in the proceedings.

It is only in very unusual cases that money would be paid directly to the child.

Applications to the Court for administration of a child's property under Section 13 of the Act can be made by Motion in the process of the action for damages or payment.

Section 13(2) of the Act does not lay down particular sums which would more appropriately be administered by the legal representative/guardian or the court/judicial factor.

This is a matter for the court to be determined in the light of all the circumstances of the case, the needs of the child, and the circumstances of the legal representatives/parents.

Applications to the court as to administration of a child's property under section 13 of the Act are made by minute in the process of the action for damages or payment in accordance with the relevant rules of court.

Cases in which Two or More Persons Act as the Child's Legal Representative

The general rule is that where two or more persons act as a child's legal representative (including guardians), any one of them may give instructions without consent of the other.

- A solicitor need not therefore enquire if any other person has the right to act as the child's legal representative/guardian, or to obtain that person's consent.

However, the general rule is subject to any "decree or deed" making the appointment.

- Accordingly if a person is acting as legal representative by order of the court, or as guardian by virtue of a court order or deed of appointment by a parent, the solicitor must obtain a copy of the decree or deed to ensure there are no restrictions on the powers of the person purporting to give instructions on behalf of the child.

A separation agreement registered in the books of council and session or sheriff court books should be treated as a "decree" of the court and consulted to see if it contains limitations on the rights of married parents, or unmarried parents sharing parental responsibilities and rights by virtue of an agreement under section 4 of the Children (Scotland) Act 1995 ("the Act"), to act as the child's legal representative.

Those who draft separation agreement should consider whether only one or two persons with parental responsibilities and rights, and the other on that person's death, should exercise the right to act as the child's sole legal representative.

If separating parents, or other persons, have a dispute about the administration of a child's property, then this may be referred to the court for determination under sections 11(1)(d), 14(1) and 14(2) of the Act if the child is habitually resident, or his or her property is situated, in Scotland.

Applications to the Court by the Solicitor

There is no reason why in unusual cases the solicitor him or herself cannot apply to the court for an order for the administration of the child's under sections 11(1)(d), 14(1) and 14(2) of the Act.

The solicitor need only establish that he or she has an "interest" in making the application.

Applications to the court would be needed if the sum involved is less than £5,000 as in these cases there is no power for the solicitor to apply to the Accountant of Court for a direction as to the application of the funds.

Where the sum involved is or exceeds £5,000 the solicitor should always make an application to the Accountant of Court for a direction if he or she is concerned that the funds will be dissipated or not applied in the child's best interests. An application to the court would only be necessary if the solicitor's concerns arose after the transfer of the funds to the legal representative/guardian, or the legal representative/guardian refused authority to have the cheque issued in the solicitor's name for the transfer to the Accountant of Court, a trustee, or a judicial factor, to be administered for the child's benefit.

Applications by a solicitor under section 11(1)(d) of the Act are made by ordinary action in the sheriff court, or by family action in the Court of

Session, in accordance with the relevant rules of court.

The solicitor should claim his expenses from the defender, or the child's estate if necessary.

Because of the expenses implications, which are ultimately in the discretion of the court, the solicitor is advised in all but the most urgent cases to seek agreement from the legal representative/guardian or any other interested party, before making an application to the court under section 11(1)(d) of the Act.

The solicitor has no duty to make an application under section 11(1)(d) of the Act. Whether he or she does so depends on all the circumstances. The solicitor will no doubt be guided by his or her conscience and by any perceived need to limit the risk of liability to the solicitor's firm, and damage to the interests of the child or the child's property, where the solicitor has paid money to the legal representative / guardian in circumstances where he or she considers, on reflection, that he or she should not have done so.

Confidentiality

The solicitor taking instructions from a child who has capacity to instruct the solicitor owes a duty of confidentiality to the child and must not disclose any information to the child's legal representative/guardian about the conduct of the claim without the child's express and informed consent, in writing, to do so.

If the solicitor is taking instructions from the legal representative/guardian, he owes a duty of confidentiality both to that person, and the child. Where the child has legal capacity to instruct a separate solicitor, or attains sixteen years of age, he has the right to have disclosed to his or her new solicitors the contents of the original solicitors file, so far as relating to his claim and the transfer of any funds to the child's legal representative/guardian, whether or not the legal representative/guardian who gave instructions to the original solicitor consents to this.

MIB and CICA claims

At page 8 of the Guidance Notes, page 8 paragraph 2, line 2 delete the words "The Solicitor has a duty in these cases apply" and substitute therefor "The Solicitor may, in these cases, apply to".

Guidance in relation to the Solicitors (Scotland) (Client Relations Partner) Practice Rules 2005

[June 2005]

Records to be kept (Rule 6)

1. It is not intended that the record keeping exercise should simply be an administrative one. Experience shows that keeping records of complaints received can assist a practice in identifying areas which need to be improved in the service to clients and often point up either problems with systems or the way in which a member of staff may be dealing with matters.

It is considered that the Client Relations Partner of a firm should hold a record of all written complaints received even if the firm itself splits into various different departments for business. That way the Client Relations Partner can get an overview of the work being carried out and where difficulties may be arising.

The central record itself could take various forms. It is accepted that the central record might simply be a file retained by the Client Relations Partner with the correspondence received in connection with complaints showing what has happened and how they have been dealt with.

However, either instead of or in addition to that a number of firms keep a central summary record of complaints which they have received.

That record could show the following information—

1. The name of the client.
2. The type of business giving rise to the concern.
3. The name of the solicitor involved.
4. The concerns expressed by the client.
5. The action taken to deal with the complaint.
6. Any other issues arising.

This type of record does help a Client Relations Partner see at a glance if there is a common theme to complaints being made, or common issues that might need to be tackled.

It is recommended that records of individual written complaints should be retained for five years from the date the matter is resolved or closed.

Written procedure (Rule 7)

2. In September 2001 a protocol was published in the Journal (page 8) for handling complaints within firms. The principles set out in that protocol have not altered in the intervening years.

It is believed that where a client wants to make a complaint they should be given clear written information about what to do, who to contact, and how to set out the complaint.

It is suggested that the written procedure should be kept as simple as possible and can be contained either in a leaflet or on a single A4 sheet of paper which can be handed to a client who indicates they wish to make a complaint.

The essentials of the procedure are considered to be as follows—

1. Who should the client contact in the first instance if they have a concern ?
   It could be the solicitor they are instructing, the departmental head or the Client Relations Partner.
2. What should they do if they are dissatisfied with the answer they receive?
   At that stage should they contact the Client Relations Partner or if they have been to the Client Relations Partner they can be advised to contact the Client Relations Office.
3. What information does the firm need from them to enable them to investigate the complaint?
4. What timescales will be involved in dealing with the complaint?
5. Will the matter be dealt with in writing or will the complainer be offered a meeting to discuss matters?
6. How will the matter be finalised ?
   Will a letter be sent confirming the outcome of any attempt to resolve matters or set out, if matters are not resolved, why they have not been resolved?

The Practice Rule refers to a "written complaint" but there is a need to be aware of the Disability Discrimination Act and to vary the procedure if the client seeking to express concern either has difficulty in writing, or has language or other difficulties which would make insisting on a written complaint a barrier to them.

Guidance Notes On The Solicitors (Scotland) (Client Communication) Practice Rules 2005

[August 2005]

The above Practice Rules will come into force on 1st August 2005. They have been made under Section 34 of the Solicitors (Scotland) Act 1980. The Rules have been approved by the Lord President. They require solicitors to provide information in writing to clients about certain specific matters namely

(a) Details of the work to be done;
(b) An estimate of the total fee including VAT and outlays or the basis upon which the fee will be charged, including VAT and outlays;
(c) Details of any contribution towards Legal Advice & Assistance or Legal Aid and details of the effect of preservation or recovery of any property if relevant;
(d) Who will do the work;
(e) Who the client(s) should contact if they wish to express concern about the manner in which the work is being carried out.

With certain exceptions (see below) this information must be provided at the earliest practicable opportunity upon receiving instructions. It does not have to be contained in a single letter to comply with the Rule, but unless there is a particular reason why it cannot be done in a single letter, there is a risk of omitting certain of the information if it is done in different stages.

If a firm is tendering for new business, either from an established client or a new client, the information can be given when tendering. If it is, and the tender is accepted, there is no need to repeat the information subsequently.

It is quite in order to give the client more information than is necessary to comply with the Rule, but the Rule sets out the minimum requirement.

Exceptions

There are only 3 automatic exceptions to the Rule:

First where a client regularly instructs a solicitor in the same type of work, the information does not have to be provided repeatedly but it will have to be provided on at least the first occasion, and it will have to be updated if there is a change in the information previously provided. Client means any person who instructs a solicitor, which includes lenders as well as individual purchasers or borrowers. If the fee for the lenders work is included in the fee to be charged to the individual purchaser or borrower, that is all that need be said about fees in the information given to the lender.

The second exception is where there is no practical opportunity for the information to be provided before the conclusion of the work. That means where the work is completed at a single meeting. For example a client who may be about to go on holiday and wishes to make a will may have instructions implemented immediately and sign the will at the first meeting. It will not be necessary for solicitors receiving instructions on an agency basis to provide information to the principle solicitor acting, although it is prudent to have an agreed basis of charging for agency work.

The third exception is children under the age of 12. If the client is the child's parent or guardian (for example in a personal injury case) the information will still need to be provided.

Fees

With the withdrawal of the Society's Table of Fees, it will not be appropriate to refer to fees recommended by the Society. If, for example in executries, the file is to be feed by an external fee charger such as an Auditor or Law Accountant, the basis on which the external fee charger will be asked to fee up the file needs to be stated to the client needs to be included. If hourly rates are reviewed during the course of the work, the clients will need to be told about any increase or there is a risk that firms will be unable to charge the higher rate.

As well as the hourly rate any commission which will be charged on capital transactions or on the sale of a house would need to be included. In any matter where the account is being rendered on a detailed basis, the charges for letters, drafting papers, etc will need to be expressed as well as the hourly rate. They can be in a separate schedule referred to in the basic letter.

In terms of Section 61A of the Solicitors (Scotland) Act 1980, where a solicitor and client enter into a written fee charging agreement it is not competent for the Court to refer any dispute in the matter to the Auditor for taxation. Where an hourly rate is specified, and that is accepted in writing, the client would still be entitled to seek a taxation, but would not be able to challenge the agreed hourly rate at such a taxation.

It should be made clear at the outset whether the fee quoted is the fee to be charged or only an estimate. If it is not stated as an estimate and the client accepts it in writing, that could be regarded as a written fee charging agreement under Section 61A of the 1980 Act. If a client has been given an estimate, they should be advised in writing when it becomes known that the cost of work will materially exceed such an estimate. It is good practice to advise the client when the limit of the original estimate is being approached.

Information should be clear, and terms with which the client may not be familiar such as "outlays" may need to be briefly explained. If a payment to account is required, that should be clearly stated, as well as the consequences of failing to pay it on time. For example in a Court matter if the client is advised that failure to make a payment to account will lead to the solicitor withdrawing from acting, there is unlikely to be a professional difficulty about withdrawing from acting in compliance with that. However if the consequence is not stated, and the proof is approaching, solicitors could be vulnerable to a complaint if they withdraw at a late stage to the potential prejudice of the client.

If the clients costs are to be paid by a third party such as a Trade Union or Legal Expenses Insurer, specific details of the basis of charging do not need to be set out when writing to the individual client but any part of the fee which that client may be asked to pay should be included—such as a success fee in a speculative action.

While it is not strictly necessary to comply with the Practice Rule, it is also strongly recommended that any potential liability for other people's costs should be explained. This would include a tenant's liability to meet a landlord's fees as well as the potential liability for expenses in a Court action.

Executries and Trusts

In executries where the only executors are solicitors in the firm, the information should be provided to the residuary beneficiaries, as they will be meeting the fees out of there shares of the residue. In other executries the information should be provided to the non solicitor executors.

Legal Aid

It is not necessary to comply with the Rule for solicitors to explain the Statutory payment Scheme to Legal Aid clients in relation to Legal Advice & Assistance or Legal Aid. Solicitors may wish to forward copies of leaflets provided by SLAB to clients in receipt of Advice & Assistance or Legal Aid. If solicitors do wish to communicate detailed advice to clients about Advice & Assistance or Legal Aid, including for example the clients requirement to report changes in circumstances, that is optional and may be done in a separate letter.

Waivers

The Rules give the Council power to grant a waiver which may be subject to conditions. In practice this power will be delegated to the Professional Practice Committee, which meets monthly except in August. A specific reason should be given for seeking the waiver, and the request is likely to be continued for such information if it is not provided initially.

Failing to Comply with the Rules

The Rules state in terms that a breach may be treated as professional misconduct. For the avoidance of doubt, an occasional failure to send the information required, or sending information which does not fully comply with the Rule, is likely to be dealt with in the first instance as a matter for professional practice guidance. However regular failure to provide the information required may lead to a formal complaint about the solicitor's conduct, which may be categorised as professional misconduct.

Guidelines on Form of Accounts and Taxation 2005

[November 2005]

1. Accounts—preparation and presentation

(a) The form in which a Solicitor presents an account is a matter for the Solicitor's personal preference but if the person liable to pay requires details, the Solicitor must give a narrative or summary sufficient to indicate the nature and the extent of the work done. If a breakdown is requested the Solicitor should give such information as can readily be derived from the records, such as the total recorded time spent, the number and length of meetings, the number of letters and of telephone calls. No charge may be made for preparing the note of fee or for the provision of such information. However if having been given such information the party paying insists on a fully itemised account the cost of preparing that may be charged to them.

(b) If the paying party is still dissatisfied the Solicitor must inform them of the availability of taxation by an Auditor and the procedure. If the payer requests a taxation without a fully itemised account the Solicitor may have such an account prepared at his own expense. That full account may be submitted for taxation even if it is for a greater amount than the original note of fee.

(c) A Solicitor may submit the file to an Auditor of Court or a Law Accountant for assessment of the fee, but it is stressed that a unilateral reference of this kind does not constitute a taxation. Such an assessment of a fee must never be represented as a taxation or as having any official status. The fee for such a reference is not chargeable to the party paying unless that has been included in the terms of business intimated to the client at the outset. If the note of fee is disputed, the Solicitor must advise of the right to taxation as above, although the fee note should be taxed by a different Auditor from the one who prepared it.

2. Taxation

(a) Remit

The essence of taxation is that it proceeds upon either a remit by the Court or a joint reference by both the Solicitor and the party paying, including non contentious cases in (c) below.

(b) Disputed Accounts

When the party paying, whether client or third party, requires that the

Solicitor's account be taxed, the Solicitor cannot refuse to concur in the reference unless the Solicitor and client have entered into a written fee charging agreement in which the actual fee has been agreed as opposed to the basis on which the fee is to be charged. The Solicitor must forthwith submit the file and all relevant information including a note of fee or detailed account to the Auditor. It is for the Auditor to determine the procedure to be followed. In normal cases this will be a diet of taxation which should be intimated to the client by the Solicitor. Evidence of such intimation, which may be by ordinary first class post, may be required if the client does not appear at the diet. If either of the parties wishes to make written submissions, the Auditor will ensure that each party is fully aware of the other's representations.

(c) Non Contentious Cases

Taxation is necessary by law and in practice in certain circumstances. The accounts of a Solicitor acting for:

- an administrator of a company under the Insolvency Acts;
- a liquidator appointed by the Court;
- a creditor's voluntary liquidator;
- a trustee in bankruptcy;
- a judicial factor;
- curators of all kinds

must be taxed.

A Solicitor who acts:

- as an administrator of a client's funds under a Power of Attorney where the granter is incapable;
- in a representative capacity e.g. a sole executor

should have a fee note prepared or taxed by an Auditor of Court. A certificate by an Auditor is appropriate in these cases.

A Solicitor who is a co-executor with an unqualified person must not make a unilateral reference to the Auditor for taxation. Such a reference needs the concurrence of the other executor. The Auditor may require intimation of the taxation to any other party with an interest in the residue of the estate.

(d) Style of Remit

A formal remit may be in the following form—

(place) (date). 1, AB as Executor of the late CD and we, Messrs E & F. Solicitors to the -Executor, hereby request the Auditor of the (Sheriff Court of .... /Court of Session) to tax the remuneration due and payable to the Solicitors for their whole work and responsibility in connection with (matter).

Signed: AB, E & F

This, however, is not essential; all the Auditor requires is to be satisfied that the client is concurring in the request for taxation and accepting that it will be binding. It is often in practice a matter of agreement reached at an early meeting between Solicitor and client. Any reasonable record of such an agreement having been reached will be sufficient for the Auditor.

3. Expenses of taxation

The auditor will usually charge a fee for the taxation. It may be 3% or 4% of the amount of the account after taxation and may attract VAT. Any award of expenses of the taxation—not only the auditor's fee but also the time and expenses of parties attending—is wholly within the discretion of the auditor. If the matter is settled within the seven days preceding the diet of taxation the auditor may still charge a proportion of his fee, not exceeding 50%, at his discretion.

Voluntary Pre-Action Protocol in Scotland for Personal Injury Claims

[January 2006]

1. Purpose Of Voluntary Protocol

1.1 The Voluntary Protocol has been kept deliberately simple to promote ease of use and general acceptability.

1.2 The aims of the Voluntary Protocol are:

- To put parties in a position where they may be able to settle cases fairly and early without litigation;
- To ensure the early provision of reliable information reasonably required to enter into meaningful discussions re liability and quantum;
- To enable appropriate offers to be made either before or after litigation commences.

1.3 It also sets out good practice making it easier for the parties to obtain and rely upon information required.

1.4 The Voluntary Protocol encourages the joint exploration of rehabilitation at an early stage, in appropriate cases, without prejudice to liability.

1.5 The standards within the Voluntary Protocol are to be regarded as the normal, reasonable approach to pre-action conduct in relation to Voluntary Protocol cases.

2. Introduction

A Voluntary Pre-Action Protocol in Scotland

2.1 Unlike England, there is no statutory basis for a pre-action protocol. The Protocol will therefore require to be entered into voluntarily on an individual case by case basis by mutual agreement. It will be for the pursuer's agent to intimate the claim in the general format of specimen letter A1 or A2 which will invite the defender or insurer to agree on a case by case basis that conduct of the pre-action negotiations is to be undertaken in terms of the Voluntary Protocol. When a defender or Insurer accepts, a letter in the general format of specimen letter B will be sent within 21 days of receipt of the letter of claim. Thereafter the claim will proceed in terms of the Voluntary Protocol in respect of the negotiations, disclosure, repudiation of liability, settlement and calculation of fees.

2.2 The agent may wish to notify the insurer as soon as they know a claim is likely to be made but before they are able to send a detailed letter of claim, particularly for instance, when the insurer has no or limited knowledge of the incident giving rise to the claim or where the claimant is incurring significant expenditure as a result of the accident which he/she hopes the insurer might pay for, in whole or in part. If the pursuer's agent chooses to do this, it will not start the timetable for responding.

2.3 The Voluntary Protocol if entered into will apply in all cases which include a claim for personal injury (excepting clinical negligence and disease and illness cases) and will apply not merely to the personal injury element of a claim but also to other heads of loss and damage. It is primarily designed for road traffic, tripping and slipping and accident at work cases where the value of the claim is up to £10,000. The Protocol is voluntary and there is nothing to prevent parties by mutual agreement dealing with any claim of a higher value under the Protocol.

2.4 Where proceedings are raised in a Voluntary Protocol case, whether for the payment of damages or for the recovery of evidence and other orders under the Administration of Justice (Scotland) Act 1972, without prejudice to any existing rule of law, it shall be open to any party to lodge Voluntary Protocol communications for the sole purpose of assisting the court in any determination of expenses.

3. Letter Of Claim

3.1 The agent shall send to the proposed defender (or to his insurer if known) a letter of claim as soon as sufficient information is available to substantiate a claim and before issues of quantum are addressed in detail. The letter should ask for details of the insurer if not known and the letter should request that a copy should be sent by the proposed defender to the insurer where appropriate. If the insurer is known, a copy shall be sent directly to the insurer.

3.2 The letter shall contain a clear summary of the facts on which the claim is based, including allegations of negligence, breaches of common law or statutory duty, together with an indication of the nature of any injuries suffered and of any financial loss incurred, so far as known. In all cases the letter should provide the name and address of the hospital where treatment has been obtained and where appropriate, the name and address of the claimant's own motor insurer.

3.3 Agents are recommended to use a standard format for such a letter, specimen letter A1 or A2: this can be amended to suit the particular case.

3.4 Sufficient information should be given in order to enable the insurer to commence investigations and at least put a broad valuation on the "risk".

3.5 The insurer should acknowledge the letter of claim within 21 days of the date of receipt of the letter. The insurer should advise in a letter in the terms of specimen B whether it is agreed that the case is suitable for the Voluntary Protocol. If there has been no reply by the defender or insurer within 21 days, the claimant will be entitled to issue proceedings.

3.6 Where liability is admitted, the insurer will be bound by this admission for all Protocol claims with a personal injury value, as laid down in 2.3, of less than £10,000.The exception to this will be when, subsequently, there is evidence that the claim is fraudulent.

3.7 The insurer will have a maximum of three months from the date of specimen letter B to investigate the merits of the claim. Not later than the end of that period, the insurer shall reply, stating whether liability is admitted or denied and giving reasons for their denial of liability, including any alternative version of events relied upon and all available documents supporting their position.

Documents

3.8 The aim of early disclosure of documents by the insurer is to promote an early exchange of relevant information to help in clarifying or resolving the issues in dispute. If the insurer denies liability, in whole or in part, they will at the same time as giving their decision on liability, disclose any documents which are relevant and proportionate to the issues in question, with reference to those identified in the letter of claim.

3.9 Attached at Appendix A are specimen, but not exhaustive, lists of documents likely to be material in different types of claim. Where the pursuer's agent's investigation of the case is well advanced, the letter of claim should indicate which classes of documents are considered relevant for early disclosure. Where this is not practical, these should be identified as soon as practical but disclosure will not affect the timetable.

3.10 Where the insurer admits primary liability but alleges contributory negligence by the pursuer, the insurer should give reasons supporting these allegations and disclose those documents from Appendix A which are relevant and proportionate to the issues in dispute. The pursuer's agent should respond to the allegation of contributory negligence before proceedings are issued.

Medical reports

3.11 A medical report will be instructed at the earliest opportunity but no later than five weeks from the date the insurer admits, in whole or part, liability unless there is a valid reason for not obtaining a report at this stage. In those circumstances, the pursuer's agent will advise accordingly and agree an amended timetable with the insurers or withdraw the case from the Protocol. Any medical report obtained and on which the pursuer intends to rely will be disclosed to the other party within five weeks from the date of its receipt. By mutual consent, the insurers may ask the examiner, via the pursuer's agent, supplementary questions.

3.12 The pursuer's agent will normally instruct a medical report, will organise access to all relevant medical records, and will send a letter of instruction to a medical expert in general terms of specimen letter C. Where it has been agreed that the insurer will obtain the medical report, the pursuer's agent will agree to disclosure of all medical records relevant to the accident. Pre-accident medical records will be disclosed only with the specific agreement of the pursuer's agent and if relevant to the claim. Any medical report on which the insurer intends to rely will be disclosed to the pursuer's agent within five weeks of receipt.

Damages

3.13 The pursuer's agents will send to the insurer a Statement of Valuation of Claim ("the Statement of Valuation") with supporting documents, where the insurer has admitted liability. The pursuer's agents are recommended to use a standard format for the Statement of Valuation. An example is at Appendix D. This can be amended to suit the particular case.

4. Settlement

4.1 Where the insurer admits liability, in whole or in part, before proceedings are issued, any medical reports, supporting Valuation obtained under this Voluntary Protocol on which a party relies, should be disclosed to the other party. The pursuer's agent should delay issuing proceedings for five weeks from the date the insurer receives the statement of valuation to enable the parties to consider whether the claim is capable of settlement.

4.2 Where a Statement of Valuation with supporting documents has been disclosed under 3.12, the insurer shall offer to settle the claim based on their reasonable valuation of it within five weeks of receipt of such disclosure, serving a counter-schedule of valuation if they dispute the pursuer's agent's valuation.

4.3 The pursuer's agent will advise insurers whether or not their offer is to be accepted or rejected, prior to the raising of proceedings and in any event within five weeks of receipt.

4.4 Where a Voluntary Protocol case settles, cheques for both damages and agreed expenses must be paid within five weeks of receipt of the settlement. The date of settlement will be the date when the insurer receives notification of settlement. Thereafter, interest will be payable on both damages and expenses due and payable in accordance with the agreed settlement terms at the prevailing judicial rate from the date of settlement until payment is made in full.

SPECIMEN LETTERS

SPECIMEN LETTER A1

Letter of Claim—Where Insurers Known

Dear Sirs *[insurance company]*

Re: *[Claimant's full name*
Claimant's full address
Claimant's date of birth
Claimant's payroll or reference number
Claimant's employer (name and address)
Claimant's national insurance number]

We are instructed by the above named to claim damages in connection with *an [accident at work/road traffic accident/tripping accident]* on *[date]* of *[year]* at *[place of accident—which must be sufficiently detailed to establish location]*.

The circumstances of the accident are: *[brief outline and simple explanation e.g. defective machine, vicarious liability]*

Your insured failed to: [brief details of the common law and/or statutory breaches]

Our client's injuries are as follows: *[brief outline]*

i Our client received treatment for the injuries at
[name and address of GP/treating hospital].

[in cases of road traffic accident]
ii Our client's motor insurers are: *[name of insurers]*

Our client is still suffering from the effects of his/her injury. We invite you to participate with us in addressing his/her immediate needs by use of rehabilitation.

He is employed as *[occupation]* and has had the following time off work *[dates of absence]*. His approximate weekly income is *[insert if known]*.

We are obtaining a police report and will let you have a copy of same upon your undertaking to meet half the fee.

At this stage of our enquiries we would expect the undernoted documents to be relevant to this claim.

This is a claim which we propose should be negotiated in terms of the Voluntary Pre-Action Protocol as agreed between the Law Society of Scotland and the Forum of Scottish Claims Managers.

Yours faithfully

Documents referred to:

SPECIMEN LETTER A2

Letter of Claim—Where Insurers Not Known

Dear Sirs

Re*: [Claimant's full name*

Claimant's full address

Claimant's payroll or reference number

Claimant's employer (name and address)]

We are instructed by the above named to claim damages in connection with an *[accident at work/road traffic accident/tripping accident]* on *[day]* of *[year]* at *[place of accident—which must be sufficiently detailed to establish location]*.

The circumstances of the accident are*: [brief outline and simple explanation e.g. defective machine, vicarious liability]*

You failed to: *[brief details of the common law and/or statutory breaches]*

Our client's injuries are as follows: *[brief outline]*

i Our client received treatment for the injuries at
[name and address of GP/treating hospital].

[in cases of road traffic accident]
ii Our client's motor insurers are: *[name of insurers]*

Our client is still suffering from the effects of his/her injury. We invite you to participate with us in addressing his/her immediate needs by use of rehabilitation.

He is employed as *[occupation]* and has had the following time off work *[dates of absence]*. His approximate weekly income is *[insert if known]*.

We are obtaining a police report and will let you have a copy of same upon your undertaking to meet half the fee.

At this stage of our enquiries we would expect the undernoted documents to be relevant to this claim.

You should acknowledge receipt of this letter, forward it to your insurers and ask them to advise us within 21 days of the date of this letter whether the case is to proceed as a Voluntary Pre-Action Protocol Claim.

Yours faithfully

Documents referred to:

SPECIMEN LETTER B

Response to Letter of Claim

[Claimant's solicitor]

Dear Sirs,

Re*: [Claimant's full name*
Claimant's full address
Claimant's payroll or reference number
Employer (name and address)]

We are the insurers of ____ and acknowledge your letter of ____.We confirm that this claim is to be/is not to be handled under the Voluntary Pre-Action Protocol and the Forum of Scottish Claims Managers.

We will notify you of our decision on liability within three months of this date. If liability is denied, in whole or in part, we will write to you further in respect of documents requested by you as soon as is practicable.

Yours faithfully

SPECIMEN LETTER C

Letter of Instruction of Medical Expert

Dear Sir,

Re: *[Name and address*
Date of birth
Telephone no
Date of accident]

We act on behalf of the above named in connection with a claim for damages arising out of an accident which occurred on ____. On that date our client was involved *in [a road accident/an industrial accident]* and sustained *[brief description of injuries]*. Our client was unfit for work until ____/remains unfit for work.

We should be obliged if you would examine our client and provide a full and detailed report dealing with the injuries sustained, treatment received and present condition, dealing in particular with the capacity for work, if relevant and giving a prognosis.

Please send our client an appointment direct for this purpose. Should you be able to offer a cancellation appointment, please contact us direct. We confirm we will be responsible for your reasonable fee.

We are obtaining the GP and hospital records and will forward them to you when they are to hand/or please request the GP and hospital records direct and advise that any invoice for the provision of these records should be forwarded to us. (Please provide details of GP and hospitals attended.)

We look forward to receiving your report as soon as possible. If there is likely to be any unusual delay in providing the report, please telephone us on receipt of these instructions.

When acknowledging these instructions, it would assist if you could give an estimate as to the likely timescale for the provision of your report and also an indication as to your fee.

Yours faithfully

Appendix A: Standard Disclosure Lists

RTA CASES

SECTION A
In all cases where liability is at issue—
- (i) Documents identifying nature, extent and location of damage to defender's vehicle where there is any dispute about point of impact
- (ii) MOT certificate where relevant
- (iii) Maintenance records where vehicle defect is alleged or it is alleged by defender that there was an unforeseen defect which caused or contributed to the accident

SECTION B
Accident involving commercial vehicle as potential defender—
- (i) Tachograph charts or entry from individual control book, where relevant
- (ii) Maintenance and repair records required for operators' licence where vehicle defect is alleged or it is alleged by defendants that there was an unforeseen defect which caused or contributed to the accident

SECTION C
Cases against local authorities where highway design defect is alleged—
- (i) Documents produced to comply with section 39 of the Road Traffic Act 1988 in respect of the duty designed to promote road safety, to include studies into road accidents in the relevant area and documents relating to measures recommended to prevent accidents in the relevant area

ROAD/FOOTWAY TRIPPING CLAIMS

Documents from the highway authority or local authority for a period of 12 months prior to the accident—
- (i) Records of inspection for the relevant stretch of road/footway
- (ii) Maintenance records including records of independent contractors working in relevant area
- (iii) Statement of the roads authority's policy under the Code of Practice for Delivering Best Value in Highway Maintenance 2001 or alternatively records of the minutes of Highway Authority or Local Authority meetings where maintenance or repair policy has been discussed or decided
- (iv) Records of complaints about the state of roads/footway at the accident locus for a 12 month period prior to the accident
- (v) Records of other accidents which have occurred on the relevant stretch of road/footway within 12 months of the accident

WORKPLACE CLAIMS

- (i) Accident book entry
- (ii) First aider report
- (iii) Surgery record
- (iv) Foreman/supervisor accident report
- (v) Safety representatives accident report
- (vi) RIDDOR report to HSE
- (vii) Other communications between defenders and HSE
- (viii) Minutes of Health and Safety Committee meeting(s) where accident/matter considered
- (ix) Report to DSS
- (x) Documents listed above relative to any previous accident/matter identified by the claimant and relied upon as proof of negligence
- (xi) Earnings information where defender is employer

Documents produced to comply with requirements of the Management of Health and Safety at Work Regulations 1999—
- (i) Pre-accident risk assessment required by regulation 3
- (ii) Post-accident re-assessment required by regulation 3
- (iii) Accident investigation report prepared in implementing the requirements of regulation 5
- (iv) Health surveillance records in appropriate cases required by regulation 6

(v) Information provided to employees under regulation 10
(vi) Documents relating to the employee's health and safety training required by regulation 13

WORKPLACE CLAIMS—DISCLOSURE WHERE SPECIFIC REGULATIONS APPLY

SECTION A
WORKPLACE (HEALTH SAFETY AND WELFARE) REGULATIONS 1992

(i) Repair and maintenance records required by regulation 5
(ii) Housekeeping records to comply with the requirements of regulation 9
(iii) Hazard warning signs or notices to comply with regulation 17 (traffic routes)

SECTION B
PROVISION AND USE OF WORK EQUIPMENT REGULATIONS 1998

(i) Manufacturers' specifications and instructions in respect of relevant work equipment establishing its suitability to comply with regulation 4
(ii) Maintenance log/maintenance records required to comply with regulation 5
(iii) Documents providing information and instructions to employees to comply with regulation 8
(iv) Documents provided to the employee in respect of training for use to comply with regulation 9
(v) Any notice, sign or document relied upon as a defence to alleged breaches of regulations 14 to 18 dealing with controls and control systems
(vi) Instruction/training documents issued to comply with the requirements of regulation 22 insofar as it deals with maintenance operations where the machinery is not shut down.
(vii) Copies of markings required to comply with regulation 23
(viii) Copies of warnings required to comply with regulation 24

SECTION C
PERSONAL PROTECTIVE EQUIPMENT AT WORK REGULATIONS 1992

(i) Documents relating to the assessment of the personal protective equipment to comply with regulation 6
(ii) Documents relating to the maintenance and replacement of personal protective equipment to comply with regulation 7
(iii) Record of maintenance procedures for personal protective equipment to comply with regulation 7
(iv) Records of tests and examinations of personal protective equipment to comply with regulation 7
(v) Documents providing information, instruction and training in relation to the personal protective equipment to comply with regulation 9
(vi) Instructions for use of personal protective equipment to include the manufacturers' instructions to comply with regulation 10

SECTION D
MANUAL HANDLING OPERATIONS REGULATIONS 1992

(i) Manual handling risk assessment carried out to comply with the requirements of regulation 4(1)(b)(i)
(ii) Re-assessment carried out post-accident to comply with requirements of regulation 4(1)(b)(i)
(iii) Documents showing the information provided to the employee to give general indications related to the load and precise indications on the weight of the load and the heaviest side of the load if the centre of gravity was not positioned centrally to comply with regulation 4(1)(b)(iii)
(iv) Documents relating to training in respect of manual handling operations and training records
(v) All documents showing or tending to show the weight of the load at the material time

SECTION E
HEALTH AND SAFETY (DISPLAY SCREEN EQUIPMENT) REGULATIONS 1992

(i) Analysis of work stations to assess and reduce risks carried out to comply with the requirements of regulation 2
(ii) Re-assessment of analysis of work stations to assess and reduce risks following development of symptoms by the claimant

(iii) Documents detailing the provision of training including training records to comply with the requirements of regulation 6
(iv) Documents providing information to employees to comply with the requirements of regulation 7

SECTION F
CONTROL OF SUBSTANCES HAZARDOUS TO HEALTH REGULATIONS 2002
(i) Risk assessment carried out to comply with the requirements of regulation 6
(ii) Reviewed risk assessment carried out to comply with the requirements of regulation 6
(iii) Copy labels from containers used for storage handling and disposal of carcinogenics to comply with the requirements of regulation 7(2A)(h)
(iv) Warning signs identifying designation of areas and installations which may be contaminated by carcinogenics to comply with the requirements of regulation 7
(v) Documents relating to the assessment of the personal protective equipment to comply with regulation 7
(vi) Documents relating to the maintenance and replacement of personal protective equipment to comply with regulation 7
(vii) Record of maintenance procedures for personal protective equipment to comply with regulation 7
(viii) Records of tests and examinations of personal protective equipment to comply with regulation 7
(ix) Documents providing information, instruction and training in relation to the personal protective equipment to comply with regulation 7
(x) Instructions for use of personal protective equipment to include the manufacturers' instructions to comply with regulation 7
(xi) Air monitoring records for substances assigned a maximum exposure limit or occupational exposure standard to comply with the requirements of regulation 7
(xii) Maintenance examination and test of control measures records to comply with regulation 9
(xiii) Monitoring records to comply with the requirements of regulation 10
(xiv) Health surveillance records to comply with the requirements of regulation 11
(xv) Documents detailing information, instruction and training including training records for employees to comply with the requirements of regulation 12
(xvi) Labels and health and safety data sheets supplied to the employers to comply with the CHIP Regulations.

SECTION G
CONSTRUCTION (DESIGN AND MANAGEMENT) (AMENDMENT) (REGULATIONS 2000
(i) Notification of a project form (HSE Fl 0) to comply with the requirements of regulation 7
(ii) Health and safety plan to comply with requirements of regulation 15
(iii) Health and safety file to comply with the requirements of regulations 12 and 14
(iv) Information and training records provided to comply with the requirements of regulation 17
(v) Records of advice from and views of persons at work to comply with the requirements of regulation 18

SECTION H
PRESSURE SYSTEMS AND TRANSPORTABLE GAS CONTAINERS REGULATIONS 1989
(i) Information and specimen markings provided to comply with the requirements of regulation 5
(ii) Written statements specifying the safe operating limits of a system to comply with the requirements of regulation 7
(iii) Copy of the written scheme of examination required to comply with the requirements of regulation 8
(iv) Examination records required to comply with the requirements of regulation 9
(v) Instructions provided for the use of operator to comply with regulation 11
(vi) Records kept to comply with the requirements of regulation 13
(vii) Records kept to comply with the requirements of regulation 22

SECTION I
LIFTING OPERATIONS AND LIFTING EQUIPMENT REGULATIONS 1998

(i) All documents showing the weight of any load to establish lifting equipment of adequate strength and stability to comply with regulation 4
(ii) All notices and markings showing the safe working load of machinery and accessories to comply with regulation 7
(iii) All documents showing lifting operations have been planned by a competent person, appropriately supervised and carried out in a safe manner to comply with regulation 8
(iv) All defect reports to comply with regulation 10

SECTION J
THE NOISE AT WORK REGULATIONS 1989

(i) Any risk assessment records required to comply with the requirements of Regulations 4 and 5.
(ii) Manufacturers' literature in respect of all ear protection made available to claimant to comply with the requirements of Regulation 8.
(iii) All documents provided to the employee for the provision of information to comply with Regulation 11.

SECTION K
CONSTRUCTION (HEAD PROTECTION) REGULATIONS 1989

(i) Pre-accident assessment of head protection required to comply with regulation 3(4)
(ii) Post-accident re-assessment required to comply with regulation 3(5)

SECTION L
GAS CONTAINERS REGULATIONS 1989

(i) Information and specimen markings provided to comply with the requirements of regulation 5
(ii) Written statements specifying the safe operating limits of a system to comply with the requirements of regulation 7
(iii) Copy of the written scheme of examination required to comply with the requirements of regulation 8
(iv) Examination records required to comply with the requirements of regulation 9
(v) Instructions provided for the use of operator to comply with regulation 11
(vi) Records kept to comply with the requirements of regulation 13
(vii) Records kept to comply with the requirements of regulation 22

SECTION M
CONSTRUCTION (HEALTH, SAFETY AND WELFARE) REGULATIONS 1996

(i) All documents showing the identity of the principal contractor, or a person who controls the way in which construction work is carried out by a person at work, to comply with the terms of regulation 4
(ii) All documents and inspection reports to comply with the terms of sections 29 and 30

Appendix B Personal Injury Cases—Protocol Fees From 1 January 2006

The fees for claims intimated after 1 January 2006 and dealt with entirely under the Protocol comprise the following elements:

1. INVESTIGATION FEE

On settlements up to and including £1,500	£ 300
On settlements over £1,500	£ 660

2. NEGOTIATION AND COMPLETION FEE

On settlements up to £2,500	25%
On the excess over £2,500 up to £5,000	15%
On the excess over £5,000 up to £10,000	7.5%
On the excess over £10,000 up to £20,000	5%
On the excess over £20,000	2.5%

NOTES
(1) In addition, VAT (on all elements) and outlays will be payable.

(2) In cases including payment to CRU the Protocol fee will be calculated in accordance with the following examples:

(i) Solatium £5,000
Wage loss £5,000
CRU repayment £2,000
Sum paid to pursuer £8,000
In these circumstances the Protocol fee will be based on £10,000 being the total value of the pursuer's claim.

(ii) Settlement as above but repayment to the CRU is £6,000 and only £5,000 can be offset. Payment to the pursuer is £5,000 and £6,000 to the CRU. The protocol fee will be on £10,000 being the value of the pursuer's claim, as opposed to the total sum paid by the insurer—£11,000.

(3) In cases involving refundable sick pay the Protocol fee will be calculated by including any refundable element.

Appendix C Membership Of The FSCM

The following insurers are currently members of the FSCM:

* NFU
* E-sure
* Halifax
* Sainsbury's Bank
* First Alternative
* Zurich Municipal
* Zurich Commercial
* Eagle Star Direct
* Zurich London
* Zurich Personal Lines Insurance
* Norwich Union
* Norwich Union Direct
* Ford Insure
* AIG Europe (UK) Ltd on behalf of New Hampshire Insurance Co
* Landmark Insurance Co
* Allianz Cornhill
* RSA
* More Than
* Direct Line
* Churchill
* Prudential
* Tesco
* Privilege
* Devitt
* UKI Insurance—(Peugeot, Citroen,Barclay, NatWest, BMW Fleet, Vauxhall, Egg and Renault)
* Pearl
* NIG
* Nationwide
* Lloyds TSB
* AXA
* QBE
* Marsh (on behalf of self insured clients)
* AON (on behalf of self insured clients)
* CIS General Insurance Society Limited

Appendix D

Form of Statement of Value of Claim

Head of Claim	**Components**	**Valuation**
Solatium	Past Future	£x £x
Interest on past *solatium*	Percentage applied to past *solatium* (State percentage rate)	£x
Past wage loss	Date from which wage loss claimed (..................) Date to which wage loss claimed (..................) Rate of net wage loss (per week, per month or per annum)	£x
Interest on past wage loss	Percentage applied to past wage loss (State percentage rate)	£x
Future wage loss	Multiplier (..................) Multiplicand (showing how calculated) Discount factor applied (if appropriate) Or specify any other method of calculation	£x
Past services	Date from which services claimed (..................) Date to which services claimed (..................) Nature of services (..................) Person by whom services provided (..................) Hours per week services provided (..................) Net hourly rate claimed (..................) Total amount claimed (..................) Interest	£x
Future loss of capacity to provide personal services	Multiplier (..................) Multiplicand (showing how calculated)	£x
Needs and other expenses	One of Multiplier (..................) Multiplicand Interest	£x £x
Any other heads as appropriate (specify)		

Professional Practice—Where Can I Find It?

Index to practice rules, journal articles etc. on aspects of professional practice. Compiled by Bruce A. Ritchie, Director (Professional Practice), The Law Society of Scotland, who will be pleased to receive users' suggestions for further items for inclusion.

Note—Includes items not printed in PH Book or this Handbook

OFFICE: 26 Drumsheugh Gardens, Edinburgh EH3 7YR. Tel. 0131 226 7411; fax. 0131 225 2934; LPI Edinburgh-1; email: lawscot@lawscot.org.uk

Website: *www.lawscot.org.uk*

Brussels Office Address—The Law Society of Scotland, 141/142 Avenue de Tervuren, 1150 Brussels Tel. 00 322 743 8585; fax 00 322 743 8586; email: brussels@lawsociety.org.uk

Note—the Practice Rules and Guidelines can be found on the Society's website at *www.lawscot.org.uk* (Members Information).

ADVERTISING

Solicitors (Scotland) (Advertising and Promotion) Practice Rules 2006 with Guideline on Advertising Fees—P.H. Book, Vol. 3, F 248

Consumer Credit (Advertisements) Regulations 1989 (SI 1989/1125).

A NON DOMINO

Law Society Journal, February 1997, page 72. (also on website)

BANKRUPTCY

Register of Undischarged Bankrupts, *Journal*, October 1990.

BUILDER/DEVELOPER

1986 Practice Rules—Rule 5 (P.H. Book, Vol. 3, F 270).

Article—*Journal*, November 1994, page 423. (See also Guidelines on Conflict of Interest—P.H. Book, Vol. 3, F 270).

BUILDING SOCIETY FLOTATIONS/MERGERS

Journal, May 1997, page 206. (also an website)

BOOKS

Profession Ethics and Practice for Scottish Solicitors by Janice Webster (Butterworths).

Professional Conduct for Scottish Solicitors by Jane Ryder (Butterworths).

CERTIFICATE OF TITLE

See Commercial Securities.

CLIENT CARE

See Terms of Business

CLOSING A FILE

Journal, April 1998, Page 44 and P.H. Book, Vol. 3, F 1310 (also on website)

CLOSING DATE GUIDELINES

P.H. Book, Vol. 3, F 1222.

See also *Journal* February 1999, page 42.

CODE OF CONDUCT (See also Code for Criminal Work)

P.H. Book, Vol. 3, F 1001. Also on *www.lawscot.org.uk* (Public Information | Using a Solicitor | Codes of Conduct)

CODE OF CONDUCT FOR CRIMINAL WORK

P.H. Book, Vol. 3, F 1008. Also on *www.lawscot.org.uk* (Public Information | Using a Solicitor | Codes of Conduct)

COMMENTS TO THE MEDIA

Journal, September 1998, page 8. (Also P.H.Book, Vol. 3, F 1291). (also on website)

COMMERCIAL SECURITY TRANSACTIONS

Guidance Note—March 15, 1994 (P.H. Book, Vol. 3, F 1201). (also on website)

Articles—*Journal*, April 1994 ("Lenders' Need to Know"); February 1995 ("Expanding Duty of Care") and October 1995 ("Certificate of Title").

President's letter of July 25, 1995—Copies available from Professional Practice Department.

COMMON REPAIRS

Journal, October 1999, page 10. (P.H. Book, Vol. 3, F 1225). (also an website)

COMPANY AUDIT ENQUIRIES

P.H. Book, Vol. 3, F 1319. (also on website)

CONFIDENTIALITY

Code of Conduct, paragraph 4 (P.H. Book, Vol. 3, F 1001).

Micosta v Shetland Islands Council, 1983 S.L.T. 483.

Conoco v Commercial Law Practice—Journal, April 1996, page 132 also 1996 G.W.D. 12–731.

Bolkiah (The Prince Jefri Case) v KPMG [1999] 1 ALL E.R. 517

Guidance Notes—P.H. Book, Vol. 3, F 1287.

CONFLICT OF INTEREST

Solicitors (Scotland) Practice Rules 1986 (P.H. Book, Vol. 3, F 270).

Code of Conduct, Paragraph 3 (P.H. Book, Vol. 3, F 1001).

Greens Property Law Bulletin, December 1994, page 7.

Guidance Notes—P.H. Book, Vol. 3, F 1204.

Journal, March 1999, page 40.

Marks & Spencer v Freshfields [2004] EWCA Civ. 741.

CONSUMER CREDIT LICENCE COVER

Journal, October 1999, page 8.

CONVEYANCING COMMITTEE SNIPPETS

Journal, May 1997, page 193. (Also see Members Information | Conveyancing Essentials on *www.lawscot.org.uk*)

COURT WORK—DUTY TO LODGE JOINT MINUTE

Journal, June 1998, page 43. (Also P.H. Book, Vol. 3, F 1284) (also on website)

CRIMINAL WORK

See Code of Conduct for Criminal Work

DEED OF CONDITIONS FOR HOUSING ESTATES

Journal, October 1999, page 8. (Also P.H. Book, Vol. 3, F 1226) (also on website)

DESTRUCTION OF FILES

Journal, November 2001, page 46. (Also P.H. Book, Vol. 3, F 1312) (also on website)

See also Code of Conduct for Criminal Work (P.H. Book, Vol. 3, F 1008—Article 12).

DEVELOPERS

Journal, November 1994, page 423. (Also P.H. Book, Vol. 3, F 270).

DISCOUNT STANDARD SECURITIES—DISCHARGES

Journal, January 1987, Page 4 and July 1998, page 8.

INVESTMENT BUSINESS
Guidance Note—P.H. Book, Vol. 3, F 1275

JOINT MINUTE
See Court Work.

LEGACIES TO SOLICITORS
Code of Conduct, Article 2 (PH Book page F 1003)
Drafting Wills in Scotland, paragraph 6.150, page 347 *et. seq.*
Webster on Professional Ethics, paragraph 2.11, page 20.

LENDER—DUTY TO WHERE ALSO ACTING FOR BORROWER
See Commercial Securities. (The articles and cases are also applicable to domestic securities).

LETTERS OF ENGAGEMENT
See Terms of Business.

LETTERS OF OBLIGATION
Journal, articles April 1973, page 121 (Professor Henry); May 1991, page 171; November 1993, page 431 (Professor Rennie).
P.H. Book, Vol. 3, F 1214

LIMITED LIABILITY PARTNERSHIPS
See Incorporated Practices

LIVING WILL
Style available from Professional Practice Department.

MANDATES
From client—*Journal*, May 1998, page 46. (Also P.H. Book, Vol. 3, F 1293). (also on website)
In executries—*see* Executries
From banks, creditors etc.—*Journal*, May 1993, page 185.

MEDIA
See Comments to the Media

MISSIVES—AVOIDANCE OF DELAY
Journal, June 1998, page 42. (Also P.H. Book, Vol. 3, F 1218). (also on website)

MONEY LAUNDERING
Journal, May 1998, page 40. (Also P.H. Book, Vol. 3, F 116/1) (also on website)

MORTGAGE ADVICE
See Property Schedules.

MULTI DISCIPLINARY PRACTICES PROHIBITED
Solicitors (Scotland) (Multi Disciplinary Practices) Practice Rules 1991—P.H. Book, F 330/5.

MULTI NATIONAL PRACTICES RULES
P.H. Book, Vol. 3, page F 358/1–F 358/27

NOTARY PUBLIC
Article—*Journal*, February 1997, page 50.

NOTES OF INTEREST
See Closing Dates.

NURSING HOME COMMISSION
Journal, October 1999, page 10.

OWNERSHIP OF FILES
Article—*Journal*, November 2001, page 46. (Also P.H. Book, Vol. 3, F 1312) (also on website)

PERSONAL INJURY CASES
Pre Action Protocol & Fees Journal December 2005 and P H Book Page F 1340.

POSTAL SETTLEMENT
P.H. Book, Vol. 3, F 1227. (also on website)

POWERS OF ATTORNEY—TAKING INSTRUCTIONS FROM GRANTER
Journal, July 1998, page 43. (Also P.H. Book, Vol. 3, F 1324). (also on website)

PRECOGNITIONS IN CRIMINAL CASES NOT DELIVERABLE TO CLIENT
Code of Conduct for Criminal Work, Article 11 (P.H. Book, Vol. 3, F 1008).
Swift v Bannigan, 1991 S.C.L.R. 604.

PRECOGNOSCING UNTRIED PRISONERS
Article—*Journal*, March 1993, page 115. (Also P.H. Book, Vol. 3, F 1283).

PROPERTY SCHEDULES AND MORTGAGE ADVICE
Journal, April 1998, page 44. (Also P.H. Book, Vol. 3, F 1217). (also on website)

RANKING AGREEMENTS—CONFLICT OF INTEREST
Journal, April 1998, page 44. (Also P.H. Book, Vol. 3, F 1210). (also on website)

REDEMPTION STATEMENTS
Guidelines issued by Council of Mortgage Lenders May 1994. (Copies available from Professional Practice Department).

RESTRICTION ON PRACTISING AS A PRINCIPAL
Practice Rules, P.H. Book, Vol. 3, F 337.
Article—*Journal*, June 1997, page 214.

RETENTIONS OF FUNDS
Journal, July 1998, page 42. (Also P.H. Book, Vol. 3, F 1215). (also on website)

SECURED LOANS TO SOLICITORS—PROHIBITION ON ACTING FOR LENDER
Rule 22 of Solicitors (Scotland) Accounts etc Rules 2001 (P.H. Book, Vol. 3, F 253).
Guidance Notes—P.H. Book, Vol. 3, F 1235.

SEPARATED SPOUSES—SALE OF MARIMONIAL HOME
Guidance Note—*Journal*, July 1998, page 43. (Also P.H. Book, Vol. 3, F 1220).
Dawson v R. Gordon Marshall & Co., 1996 G.W.D. 21–1243

SETTLEMENT CHEQUES SENT TO BE HELD AS UNDELIVERED
Article—*Journal*, October 1998, page 47. (Also P.H. Book, Vol. 3, F 1221). (also on website)
Greens Property Law Bulletin—August 1994, page 6.

SHARING FEES WITH NON SOLICITORS
Solicitors (Scotland) Practice Rules 1991 (P.H. Book, Vol. 3, F 339) with Guidance Note attached.

SIGNATURE OF MISSIVES ETC.
Article—*Journal*, February 1991, page 73—"Who signs for the firm?" (signature by assistant).
Article—*Journal*, April 1996, page 158 "Requirements of Writing (Scotland) Act 1995".

SIGNATURE OF DOCUMENTS BY UNREPRESENTED PARTY
Journal, October 1998, page 47. (Also P.H. Book, Vol. 3, F 1325). (also on website)

SMALL CLAIMS—EXTRA JUDICIAL FEES
See Personal Injury Cases.

SPECULATIVE ACTIONS
Solicitors (Scotland) Act 1980, section 61A (P.H. Book, Vol. 3, F 48/2).
Court of Session, Rule 42.17 Scottish Law Directory Fees Supplement, page 44.
Sheriff Court—Act of Sederunt (Fees of Solicitors in Speculative Actions) 1992. (Scottish Law Directory Fees Supplement, page 63).
Article by Walter Semple—*Journal*, February 1994, page 57.

STAMPING DEEDS
P.H. Book, Vol. 3, F 1228. (also on website)

TERMS OF BUSINESS LETTERS
Solicitors (Scotland) (Client Communication) Practice Rules PH Book page F 336/2
Code of Conduct, Article 5 (e)
Also *Journal*, April 1998, page 44 and P.H. Book, Vol. 3, F 1318.
Better Client Care Guidance Manual, pages 1.3 and 25.1.

TITLE DEEDS—EXHIBITING TO OTHER AGENTS
Journal, May 1996, page 195. (Also P.H. Book, Vol. 3, F 1213) (also on website)

WRITING DIRECT TO ANOTHER SOLICITOR'S CLIENT IMPROPER
Code of Conduct 2002, Article 9 (P.H. Book, Vol. 3, F 1001).

WRITTEN FEE CHARGING AGREEMENTS
Solicitors (Scotland) Act 1980, section 61A (P.H. Book, Vol. 3, F 482).
Solicitors (Scotland) (Written Fee Charging Agreements) Practice Rules 1993—P.H. Book, Vol. 3, F 305.
Article by Walter Semple—*Journal* October 1993, page 395.